THE CAMBRIDGE HISTORY OF
THE SECOND WORLD WAR

The military events of the Second World War have been the
subject of historical debate from 1945 to the present. It mattered
greatly who won, and fighting was the essential determinant of
victory or defeat. In Volume 1 of *The Cambridge History of the
Second World War*, a team of twenty-five leading historians offers
a comprehensive and authoritative new account of the war's
military and strategic history. Part 1 examines the military cultures and strategic objectives of the eight major powers involved.
Part 11 surveys the course of the war in its key theatres across the
world, and assesses why one side or the other prevailed there
Part 111 considers, in a comparative way, key aspects of military
activity, including planning, intelligence, and organization of
troops and matériel, as well as guerrilla fighting and treatment
of prisoners of war.

JOHN FERRIS is Professor of History at the University of Calgary,
Honorary Professor in the Department of International Politics,
University of Wales, Aberystwyth, and Adjunct Professor in the
Department of War Studies, Royal Military College of Canada.

EVAN MAWDSLEY is Honorary Professorial Research Fellow and
formerly Professor of International History at the University of
Glasgow.

THE CAMBRIDGE HISTORY OF
THE SECOND WORLD WAR

GENERAL EDITOR

EVAN MAWDSLEY, *Honorary Professorial Research Fellow and formerly Professor of International History at the University of Glasgow.*

The Cambridge History of the Second World War is an authoritative new account of the conflict that unfolded between 1939 and 1945. With contributions from a team of leading historians, the three volumes adopt a transnational approach, to offer a comprehensive, global analysis of the military, political, social, economic and cultural aspects of the war. Volume I provides an operational perspective on the course of the war, examining strategies, military cultures and organisation, and the key campaigns, whilst Volume II reviews the 'politics' of war, the global aspirations of the rival alliances, and the role of diplomacy. Volume III considers the war as an economic, social and cultural event, exploring how entire nations mobilized their economies and populations, and dealt with the catastrophic losses that followed. The volumes conclude by considering the lasting impact of the Second World War and the memory of war across different cultures of commemoration.

VOLUME I
Fighting the War
EDITED BY JOHN FERRIS AND EVAN MAWDSLEY

VOLUME II
Politics and Ideology
EDITED BY RICHARD J. B. BOSWORTH AND JOSEPH A. MAIOLO

VOLUME III
Total War: Economy, Society and Culture
EDITED BY MICHAEL GEYER AND ADAM TOOZE

THE CAMBRIDGE
HISTORY OF
THE SECOND WORLD WAR

*

VOLUME I
Fighting the War

*

Edited by
JOHN FERRIS
and
EVAN MAWDSLEY

CAMBRIDGE
UNIVERSITY PRESS

CAMBRIDGE
UNIVERSITY PRESS

University Printing House, Cambridge CB2 8BS, United Kingdom

Cambridge University Press is part of the University of Cambridge.

It furthers the University's mission by disseminating knowledge in the pursuit of
education, learning and research at the highest international levels of excellence.

www.cambridge.org
Information on this title: www.cambridge.org/9781107038929

First published 2015

Printing in the United Kingdom by TJ International Ltd. Padstow Cornwall

A catalogue record for this publication is available from the British Library

ISBN 978-1-107-03892-9 Hardback

Contents

Contents

Illustrations

The colour plates can be found between pages 466 and 467

Every effort has been made to contact the relevant copyright-holders for the images reproduced in this book. In the event of any error, the publisher will be pleased to make corrections in any reprints or future editions.

Figures

Maps

Tables

Contributors to Volume I

MARTIN S. ALEXANDER is Emeritus Professor of International Relations at Aberystwyth University.

SIMON BALL is Professor of International History and Politics at the University of Leeds.

MARY KATHRYN BARBIER is Associate Professor of History at Mississippi State University.

TAMI DAVIS BIDDLE is Professor of National Security Strategy and Military History at the US Army War College.

ELIOT A. COHEN is Robert E. Osgood Professor of Strategic Studies at Johns Hopkins University's School of Advanced International Studies.

JOHN FERRIS is Professor of History at the University of Calgary, Honorary Professor in the Department of International Politics, University of Wales, Aberystwyth, and Adjunct Professor in the Department of War Studies, Royal Military College of Canada.

DAVID FRENCH is Professor Emeritus at University College London.

COLONEL (RTD) DR KARL-HEINZ FRIESER is former Chief of the Department 'Age of World Wars' in the Militärgeschichtliches Forschungsamt at Potsdam.

JOHN GOOCH is Emeritus Professor of International History at the University of Leeds, and a Cavaliere dell'Ordine della Stella della Solidarietà Italiana.

JONATHAN HOUSE is Professor of Military History at the US Army Command and General Staff College.

JOHN T. KUEHN is the General William Stofft Chair for Historical Research at the US Army Command and General Staff College. He retired from the US Navy in 2004 at the rank of Commander, after 23 years' service as a naval flight officer.

THOMAS G. MAHNKEN is the Jerome E. Levy Chair of Economic Geography and National Security at the US Naval War College, and a Senior Research Professor of Strategic Studies at Johns Hopkins University's School of Advanced International Studies.

SANDERS MARBLE is Senior Historian at the US Army Office of Medical History.

EVAN MAWDSLEY is Honorary Professorial Research Fellow and formerly Professor of International History at the University of Glasgow.

BRUCE W. MENNING is a private scholar, affiliated with the University of Kansas as Adjunct Professor of History and Russian and East European Studies. Before retirement in 2011, he was Professor of Strategy at the US Army Command and General Staff College.

MARC MILNER is Professor of History and Director of the Gregg Centre for the Study of War and Society at the University of New Brunswick, Canada.

BOB MOORE is Professor of Twentieth-Century European History at the University of Sheffield.

PHILLIPS PAYSON O'BRIEN is a Reader in History and Director of the Scottish Centre for War Studies at the University of Glasgow.

ALESSIO PATALANO is a Lecturer in War Studies at the Department of War Studies, King's College London.

BEN H. SHEPHERD is a Reader in History in the Department of Social Sciences, Media and Journalism at Glasgow Caledonian University.

DENNIS SHOWALTER is Professor of History at Colorado College.

DAVID R. STONE is Pickett Professor of History at Kansas State University.

JAY TAYLOR is Associate in Research at the Fairbank Center for Chinese Studies, Harvard University.

HANS VAN DE VEN is Professor of Modern Chinese History in the Department of East Asian Studies at the University of Cambridge.

GERHARD L. WEINBERG is retired Professor of History at the University of North Carolina at Chapel Hill.

General introduction

EVAN MAWDSLEY

The Second World War, terrible in its course and far-reaching in its consequences, was the most complex event of the twentieth century. This three-volume history of the global conflict brings together the work of an international team of nearly eighty experts, men and women at different stages in their careers, but with a level of scholarship that is consistently first-class. A collection of substantial article-length chapters, the *Cambridge History of the Second World War* (*CHSWW*) provides a comprehensive and authoritative treatment of the war and its context.

As a large-scale collective history of the Second World War, the project is ambitious and innovative, taking a comprehensive view of all aspects of the conflict. The very broad scope of the *CHSWW* means that military operations and diplomatic interaction can be considered alongside political, economic, social and cultural developments. The historical context and legacy of the war, up to the present day, are also fully considered. The *CHSWW* has been written in the second decade of the twenty-first century and takes into account changes in the configuration of world power and in the nature of warfare. This vantage point also allows an approach to the history of the Second World War which is less complicated by Nationalist or Cold War polemics. Although the majority of the contributors are historians working in Europe and North America, the perspective of the project is genuinely global, in particular giving appropriate weight to the Asian participants in the war.

There is no single self-evident way to package the vast subject of the Second World War, and the arrangement of three volumes is inevitably arbitrary. Nevertheless, the *CHSWW* has a broadly logical structure. Volume I, *Fighting the War*, deals with the directly 'military' aspects of war. It includes chapters discussing the national wartime strategies of the major states, which resulted from geographical, political, economic and historical factors, and the specific military instruments available. Other chapters lay out, in broad-brush terms, what happened in the war's major campaigns, both in Europe and Asia, and consider why one side prevailed over the other. The final part of this volume looks in transnational terms at aspects of the armed forces of the era, covering themes from war planning to the treatment of prisoners of war.

Volume II, *Politics and Ideology*, goes beyond military strategy, operations and instruments, and the work of military elites. On the one hand, this volume covers broader national (and international) 'policy' and ideology, in an attempt to clarify what it was that the leaders of various states were attempting to achieve before and during the war, and how political elites tried to rally or compel support from their populations, or were themselves subject to the pressure of public opinion. Diplomacy was also an extremely important aspect of the war, despite the evident failure of statesmen to head off aggression by Japan, Italy and Germany in the 1930s; despite the Allied concept of 'unconditional surrender'; and despite the fact that the fighting was ended in the summer of 1945 only by the most extreme military means. The building and maintenance of alliances was, in fact, a crucial part of grand strategy on both sides. Meanwhile, one basic dynamic of the Second World War, examined in depth in this volume, was the attempt by individual states to extend their control into neighbouring states, or into regions controlled before the war by other states. This was done for economic, strategic or ethnocentric reasons, and it was done on a much greater scale than in any previous war. Expansion and annexation raise the related and extremely significant themes of occupation and resistance. Perhaps the most important single consequence of the Second World War was national liberation, not only in the obvious sense of delivering populations from Axis occupiers, but also ending, immediately or within a few years of 1945, the direct colonialist systems of the European powers and Japan.

The scope of Volume III, *Total War: Economy, Society and Culture*, is also broad and ambitious. Economic factors, especially pressure to obtain natural resources, were undoubtedly one of the basic causes of the conflict. At the same time – paradoxically or consequentially – the effective mobilization by the Allies of their greater national economic and technological potential was also one of the reasons why they eventually prevailed. (The Axis Powers, starting from a position of perceived inferiority, were trying to 'catch up'; they failed to do so, fought the war from their weaker position, and lost.) The pressure for economic mobilization in 'total war' also had profound social consequences, which are discussed in several chapters. Part III of Volume III considers other implications of total war in the realm of morality and culture. The final part of the volume looks at the consequences of the Second World War, both in the immediate post-war years, where it had a decisive impact on 'the new world order', and in the decades to 2015, still reached by its long shadow.

The *CHSWW* trilogy is a collective work, and the sum of its parts. Each volume was put together by a team of co-editors, who tried to ensure adequate, but non-overlapping coverage, and who played the larger part in organizing their volume and commissioning contributions. Near eighty contributors, specialists in a very broad range of subjects, have given their interpretations. Despite a certain amount of discussion at conferences connected with the *CHSWW* project, and directly with editors, the content remains, first of all, the view of the individual contributors.

Not many people will read the *CHSWW* trilogy like a novel or a textbook, from beginning to end. Nevertheless, there was discussion at an early stage about the order of the volumes. It was tempting to begin with the various political, social, economic and cultural underpinnings or causes of the conflict – race, imperial rivalry, ethology, personal ambition, historical context and so on (in effect, what is currently in Volume ɪɪ and parts of Volume ɪɪɪ) – and only *after that* to look at the details of the resulting war, with its military forces and campaigns. There was also a chronological case for this, to begin with the pre-war diplomacy and international crises in order to establish causes of the Second World War, and only then to move forward to the actual fighting. Instead, the series jumps off with the military aspects and campaigns, and moves into the political and diplomatic in Volume ɪɪ, and the economic and social in Volume ɪɪɪ. Moreover, although the approach of the whole series is broadly transnational, Volume ɪ also starts by using the individual nation states (or, rather, eight major nation states) as the units of conflict.

The justification for all this is that the *CHSWW* is the history of a *war*, a particular event, although one that lasted an agonizingly long time and took in vast – nearly global – territory. It is not an account of all aspects of world history in the middle decade of the twentieth century. This was a war that was fought between states with particular interests and ideologies. It also greatly mattered who won, although it was not simply a struggle of good versus evil. In addition, because we are so interested in the transformative political, social and economic effects of war, we need to look first at the military events and pressures that caused those effects. It makes sense, for example, to consider occupation, resistance and liberation *after* the military campaigns that enabled the military forces of one state to occupy the territory of another. We need not worry too much about start and end dates for the *CHSWW* (or for the Second World War), as they differed for each of the states involved. The war began in 1937 in China, and the notion of the Second World War as essentially a component of a thirty-year-long 'German wars' is too Eurocentric, although elements of continuity and patterns of development certainly existed.

Why write a large-scale history of the Second World War now? It is the seventieth anniversary of the end of the war in 2015, but is that in itself sufficient justification? There is an abiding interest in the history of various aspects of the war by the general reading public – or, at least, by those who still frequent bookshops – judging by the books on sale about the Second World War. University students, too, find the history of the war a compelling subject, and new books are important for each new generation of readers. The *CHSWW* is not a textbook, handbook or encyclopaedia,[1] but it does provide bibliographical essays about the most recent research upon which the various chapters are based.

Is there anything new to be said about the Second World War? On the military side there was an important development in the 1970s and 1980s, when information about special intelligence (ULTRA) became available, but even that development is now twenty to twenty-five years old.[2] After that, however, with the loosening of censorship in Moscow in the late 1980s and 1990s, much better information became available about Stalinism and the conduct of Russia's 'Great Patriotic War'; and the Russian archives also provided access to important captured German documents. Understanding Nazi Germany is of great importance. In the 1990s there was a greater sense of Wehrmacht complicity in war crimes, and overall a very much clearer awareness of the German side of things, thanks to the appearance – and translation into English – of the numerous volumes of the outstanding semi-official history *Germany and the Second World War*.[3] In the last two decades there has been a better sense of the role of China in the war; for a long time

---

1 For an excellent multi-author survey of the historiography, see Thomas W. Zeiler and Daniel M. DuBois (eds.), *A Companion to World War II* (2 vols., Malden, Mass.: Wiley-Blackwell, 2013). As a short specialised encyclopaedia, I. C. B. Dear and M. R. D. Foot (eds.), *The Oxford Companion to the Second World War* (Oxford University Press, 1995), remains valuable.

2 The most important publication dealing with this was F. H. Hinsley et al. (eds.), *British Intelligence in the Second World War: Its Influence on Strategy and Operations* (4 vols., London: HMSO, 1979–90)

3 *Germany and the Second World War* (10 vols., Oxford: Clarendon Press, 1990–), originally published in German as *Das deutsche Reich und der Zweite Weltkrieg* (10 vols., Stuttgart: Deutsche Verlags-Anstalt, 1979–2008). Two volumes remain to be translated.

the role of that huge country in the Second World War had been ignored, discounted or misunderstood in the West. At the same time, Chinese-Japanese disputes about the history of a war which began nearly eighty years ago remain politically sensitive.

Changing generations live in a changing world, and every change shifts our perspective. We no longer live in the heroic age of the early 1940s. The Cold War and the European Community rebooted the orientation of alliances. The Suez crisis in 1956 displayed the weakness of the old imperial European states. The Vietnam War demonstrated both limits to American staying power and the potential of wars of national liberation (the features of asymmetrical warfare were also evident in Iraq in 2003–10). In the last twenty years we have seen the end of Communism in the Soviet Union and the emergence of a genuinely independent Eastern Europe, a region over whose fate the Second World War was notionally fought; Yugoslavia has been shattered. China has enjoyed an astonishing economic rise, matched to some extent by its military power. American and Japanese power had been in relative decline. The nature of warfare has changed profoundly, developing from the thermonuclear arsenals of the high Cold War, through the high-tech operational weaponry of the 'revolution in military affairs' and on to global terrorism. Yet so much of the world, even as we know it today, can be traced back to the Second World War.

In his introduction to the 2014 *Cambridge History of the First World War*, Jay Winter discussed the development of war historiography in generational terms and identified a new (fourth) generation of historians working on the 1914–18 conflict, whom he referred to as the 'transnational generation'. They differed from their predecessors, he argued, in their global outlook, which he contrasted with an older 'international' approach.[4] It is difficult to accept that history has never been written on a comparative basis before, or that historians have not thought about levels of historical experience below and above the national level. However, it is certainly right to urge that historians should aspire to this, within the limitations of language skills and access to archives. It is better not to become too fascinated with historical fashion. The 'new military history', the 'new social history', the 'new cultural history', the 'new international history' – even 'contemporary history' – are none of them all that 'new' or 'contemporary' any more. With the passage of time, their definition becomes looser and looser.

4 Jay Winter (ed.), *The Cambridge History of the First World War* (3 vols., Cambridge University Press, 2014), vol. III, p. 6.

Transnational history, moreover, has been aptly described as 'the latest incarnation of an approach that has successively been characterized as comparative, international, world, and global history',[5] and the *Cambridge History of the Second World War* is certainly all of these. I would share David Reynolds's judgement that 'the traditional agenda of international history – life-and-death governmental decisions for peace or war' is and will remain of vital importance.[6] But making such decisions is only part of the story. What historians have to do, especially for a topic as broad, rich and challenging as the Second World War, is to combine every approach in the historical arsenal. This has been achieved by the contributors to the current Cambridge History.

---

5 'On Transnational History', *American Historical Review* 101 (2006), 1441.
6 David Reynolds, 'International History, the Cultural Turn and the Diplomatic Twitch', *Cultural and Social History* 3 (2005), 75–91.

Introduction to Volume I

JOHN FERRIS AND EVAN MAWDSLEY

The three-volume *Cambridge History of the Second World War* (*CHSWW*) is not exclusively or even fundamentally a work of military history. However, Volume I is indeed about the 'war-fighting' or 'operational' aspects of that conflict, as opposed to the politics and diplomacy of the war, or its economic, social or cultural properties. The volume approaches nations, institutions and topics from a comparative and transnational perspective. It is subdivided into three related parts. Part I assesses the 'grand strategies' and 'strategic cultures' of the eight major states involved. It questions what those states attempted to do militarily during the war, how they expected to achieve those objectives, and how these matters related to national traditions and organizations. The second part of the volume discusses the fighting across the years of the Second World War, what might be called a 'campaign narrative', although the treatment is more analytical than that term suggests. Broadly speaking, this part assesses the war at both the strategic and 'operational' levels, which, of course, are related to grand strategic issues, and from comparative and competitive perspectives. Part III examines, thematically, the military institutions and instruments that featured in the war, from the planning of campaigns to the treatment of prisoners. Inevitably, the chapters, and the three parts, overlap, but repetition has been kept to a minimum.

The military events of the Second World War have been the subject of historical inquiry for six decades.[1] This body of work might be divided into three broad chronological phases: early, intermediate and recent. Each phase has been influenced in different ways by factors such as the availability

---

[1] For a detailed historiography of the topic, we suggest the excellent collection in Thomas W. Zeiler and Daniel M. DuBois (eds.), *A Companion to World War II* (2 vols., Malden, Mass.: Wiley-Blackwell, 2013).

of sources, personal perspectives and contemporary events, and by changing approaches to history.

The early phase – the 'post-war' period – took in the years from the late 1940s to the mid-1960s. This older literature on the military history of the Second World War was conditioned by the immediate impact of experience (first-person accounts, memoirs), by nationalism, and by limited access – at least by 'non-official' historians – to the archives.

The governments of the victor powers, and various military institutions, produced official histories written by teams of specialists, many of whom had participated in the planning or fighting; some of these histories were published, others were secret and reserved for in-house use. They sought, among other things, to assess and defend their commanders, forces and strategies before national and international publics, and to accumulate information useful for future conflicts, not only from their own experience but from that of former enemies. Among the series intended for publication, the British official history was the most impressive, opening debates with power and sophistication, and incorporating – in a more or less standard layout – the military, diplomatic and economic aspects of state policy. The British 'theatre of war' histories told the story from the viewpoint of all three armed services, and attempted to combine operational and strategic issues, breadth and depth. The American and Dominion histories, conversely, focused on single services and offered great detail about narrow issues, about which they remain important today. Historians of the victorious countries had the benefit of captured enemy sources, including documents which had been physically transferred to London, Washington or Moscow. Some documents related to war planning and operations (as well as war crimes) became widely available through the Nuremberg and Tokyo trials, but most remained closed to the public.

There was also, especially in the victor countries, but in Germany and Italy too, a flood of memoirs and unofficial histories of battles and campaigns intended for a broad public. In Western countries, this flood was driven by commercial publishing decisions, in the Soviet Union by the state, but in all cases the initiative reflected high levels of popular interest. These accounts were characterized by traditional approaches to military history, which focused on campaigns, commanders and weaponry, combined with descriptions of military genius and clashes of personality. This has been called the 'traditional "drum and trumpet" or "good general–bad general" approach'.[2]

2 Robert Citino, 'Military Histories Old and New: A Reintroduction', *American Historical Review* 112 (2007), 1070.

Memoirs were of particular interest, as retired generals and admirals gathered in their masses to defend their records in victory and defeat; especially influential were the rise of personality cults around the commanders in Africa and southern and western Europe during 1942–45, and efforts by former German generals to lay the blame for defeat on Hitler's incompetence, to sidestep responsibility for the crimes of his regime, and to suggest that the Eastern Front was really the first campaign of the Cold War, where the Western Allies fought on the wrong side. Personality cults dominated and disfigured debates within the USSR. Over the first post-war decade, Joseph Stalin was given credit for the successes of the Red Army, and wartime victory served to legitimize Communist rule. After Stalin's death in 1953, he was blamed for the catastrophes of 1941–42. Soviet treatment of the war history evolved further in the period after the fall of Nikita Khrushchev in 1964; Stalin was more ignored than criticized, and Marshal Zhukov – sacked by Khrushchev in 1957 – was allowed to publish his memoirs. The Red Army increasingly used memoirs to bolster its position in the Soviet state.

These 'early' years were also those of the high Cold War. David Reynolds has written a splendid volume demonstrating the influence of the Cold War on Winston Churchill's *The Second World War*.[3] Churchill, unique in his freedom of access to the documents and ability to state his mind, set the agenda for future Western histories of the conflict. The Cold War affected the military history of the Second World War in several ways. On one side of the ideological divide were the United States, Britain and France (and from the late 1950s, their newly rearmed German, Italian and Japanese partners). On the other side were previous wartime allies in the form of the Russians and the Chinese, who soon fell out with one another. Each victor power tended to stress its own role, downplay that of its allies, and read the Cold War back into the events of 1939–45.

The Cold War also affected notions of warfare. By the middle 1950s, the advent of thermonuclear weapons meant that any great future war would be technically different from the Second World War. Mass armies, navies and air forces, and long-term industrial mobilization seemed decreasingly central to conflict, though until 1991 both sides maintained large conventional forces, shaped by the experiences of the Second World War, for purposes of power politics. Indeed, at this time, the original meaning of war-fighting came into use, which described a mutually destructive thermonuclear exchange as a

---

3 David Reynolds, *In Command of History* (London: Penguin, 2005).

disastrous alternative to deterrence. At the same time, contemporary 'strategy' came to focus on *deterring* war, rather than conducting it ('war-fighting').[4] In the 1950s and 1960s, again, more and more was written about 'people's war' and 'counter-insurgency'. Guerrillas or partisans had not been a leading feature of the Second World War (regular forces could contain them), but in the first decades after the war, Communist or Nationalist insurgents won victories in China, in former European colonies and in other parts of the newly conceptualized 'Third World'. These achievements made guerrillas seem more formidable than they later proved to be, once removed from the context of 'wars of national liberation'. Nonetheless, although the First and Second World Wars had been very different from previous conflicts, they now themselves seemed irrelevant from a contemporary military point of view. Between nuclear war and guerrilla war, the experience of large-scale 'conventional' war seemed a matter more of history and commemoration than of practical interest.

The intermediate phase includes the period from the late 1960s to the 1990s. The wartime leaders largely left the scene. Memories of the war, and to some extent even Nationalist passions, faded. Germany, Japan and Italy were full allies (albeit successful economic rivals) of the United States, Britain and France. Cold War tensions continued. The Soviet government continued to use memories of victory – history and myth – as a means of self-legitimization. It also used memories of liberation from Nazi Germany to garner support in the Eastern European satellites. Far more than in Western countries, officials who had held important wartime posts remained in the Kremlin gerontocracy until the 1980s. During this period, other conflicts engaged public attention, including that of historians. In particular, the war in Indochina tested the American military and the staying power of its population, and seemingly validated the Leninist concept of 'wars of national liberation'. The Communist government in China, however, took less interest in the military history of the war against Japan led by their old rival Chiang Kai-shek (who died in 1975), than in their own struggle against his forces.

New developments with evidence and analysis challenged the older literature, which had been Nationalist and operational in focus, and dominated by official writing, with little public access to primary documents. Large quantities of captured Axis records now entered the public domain. In some countries, accelerated public access to the official records produced new

---

4 Herman Kahn, *On Escalation* (Westport, Conn.: Greenwood, 1986 [1965]), p. 294; Hew Strachan, *The Direction of War: Contemporary Strategy in Historical Perspective* (Cambridge University Press, 2013), pp. 36–42.

insights about the conduct of the war, and enabled the production of the first unofficial histories, based on primary documents, opening the key trend in the historiography to follow. The British government's change in 1967 from a 'fifty-year rule' to a 'thirty-year rule' for public records foreshadowed developments elsewhere. The early 1970s also saw revelations about Special Intelligence ('ULTRA' and the activities of Bletchley Park), and then a new series of the British official history incorporating this information.[5] The Russians matched the efforts of their erstwhile allies by publishing two ambitious multi-volume official histories (in 1960–64 and 1973–82). They were valuable on operational matters, though less good and influential than the topic merited, because of the tone, mendacities, exaggerations and omissions necessitated by the party line. Official histories of other belligerents also proved useful on operational matters, but had limited impact for various reasons – the Italians due to an overly defensive tone, and the Japanese because the works (reconstructing a documentary record that had been destroyed deliberately) were not translated into Western languages. None of these series addressed the internal political and administrative matters that were central to the war, and to earlier series of official histories among the Western Allies. Conversely, the Germans began publication of their own official histories in 1979, having repatriated captured military and other archives held in the United States or Britain. *Germany and the Second World War (Das Deutsche Reich und der Zweite Weltkrieg)* proved to be the most successful of all the official histories. The volumes are regularly cited on broad and narrow matters, because of Germany's centrality to the European war and because of the quality of the individual authors. The depth of research and analysis was outstanding, as was the integration of operational, diplomatic, strategic, economic and administrative matters; the authors also built effectively on the international literature written before 1990.

This intermediate period also saw the beginning of what was called the 'new military history'. Although the term has been understood in different ways, we agree with Peter Paret, writing in 1991, that it referred to 'a partial turning away from the great captains, and from weapons, tactics, and operations as the main concerns of the historical study of war', instead paying 'greater attention to the interaction of war with society, economics, politics and culture': 'The New Military History stands for an effort to integrate the study of military institutions and their actions more closely with other kinds

---

5 Frederick Winterbotham, *The Ultra Secret* (London: Weidenfeld & Nicolson, 1974), started the stampede.

of history.'[6] Most chapters in the three-volume *CHSWW* do address society, economics, politics and culture, and the project strives to integrate military and non-military aspects.

The third, recent phase of historical work on the military events of the Second World War covers the period from 1990 to the present, beginning fifty years from its start. During 1990, even in Western countries, the public record had important gaps. By 2014, access had expanded dramatically, even in Russia. Most records that have survived are available in archives, including material on topics previously concealed, like intelligence and the war on the Eastern Front. The events of the war generally have moved beyond personal memory. Most new historians of the conflict – academic and popular – had no direct adult memories of it, and even less so their readers. Interest in the conflict, however, remains as high as ever.

During this phase, the Cold War ended and political revolutions or transformation occurred in some of the major participant countries of the Second World War. Russia experienced a degree of liberalization under Gorbachev in the late 1980s, and then the consecutive break-up of the satellite system in Eastern Europe and of the USSR itself. Military history (and the military archives) remained under the control of the Russian armed forces, and to some extent Russian nationalism replaced Marxist-Leninism as a state ideology, with the Second World War remaining a great source of legitimization. Doors opened to a flood of popular histories, however, often strikingly revisionist in nature.[7] The ending of the Cold War eased challenges to myths among both sets of victor powers: Western writers more fully appreciated the significance and nature of Soviet successes over Germany, while Soviet ones recognized the importance of Lend-Lease and Western operations.

The end of Soviet Communism, the loss of Russian influence in Eastern Europe and the rise of successor states across the region was accompanied by the equally dramatic reunification of Germany. This process saw the development of more open debate in the enlarged Federal Republic. Nowhere more than Germany has history defeated lies and myths about the Second World War. There was no fundamental re-evaluation of the military campaigns of the Third Reich, but much discussion of related issues. These

---

6 Peter Paret, 'The New Military History', *Parameters* 21 (1991), 10.
7 The best-known example of revisionism was *Icebreaker*, written under the pseudonym Viktor Suvorov, by the émigré author V. B. Rezun; this book argued that Stalin and the USSR had offensive war plans in 1941. Although *Icebreaker* was first published abroad (in Germany and Britain) in 1989/90, the book and various sequels have enjoyed long print runs in the post-Soviet Russian Federation.

included the complicity of the German armed forces in the perpetration of the Holocaust and other war crimes, the relative criminality of the Hitler's Third Reich and Stalin's Soviet Union, and the victimhood of German people during and after the war. Part of this debate developed in the late 1980s within what was called the *Historikerstreit* ('quarrel of the historians'); in the late 1990s there was another furore about a travelling exhibition on Wehrmacht war crimes, with Germans divided over whether the armed forces in which their grandfathers had fought were complicit in criminality.[8]

Developments in East Asia pushed historians away from an excessively Eurocentric (or 'Europe-Pacific') view of the Second World War. They followed from the emergence of China as a major economic power in the 1990s, and revived conflict between the People's Republic and Japan over the history of what the Chinese now called the 'War of Resistance against Japan (1937–1945)'. Although the conflict primarily was about larger political / territorial issues and occupation policy, it did raise questions concerning the conduct of the campaign. The sanitized treatment of the war in secondary-school textbooks, an issue within Japan since the 1960s, was now attacked in China and other states that had been subject to Japanese aggression. Another issue was the Yasukuni temple in central Tokyo, where, among the millions of 'enshrined' Japanese soldiers and civilians from every war fought since 1861, were General Tojo Hideki and thirteen other leaders (mostly generals) who were classified as 'Class A' war criminals in the post-war Tokyo trials. Visits to the temple by Japanese politicians caused repeated conflicts with neighbouring Asian states. The leaders of China, Japan and South Korea all exploited wartime history to current political advantage, more than they ever had done before. Chinese works on the war became increasingly common, not to mention Nationalist and politicized. Some Japanese academic works shared this characteristic, especially on issues relating to atrocities, prisoners, comfort women and the use of the atomic bomb, but most were fairly objective. The readiness of Japanese historians to discuss the conduct of the war was influenced by the death of the Showa Emperor in 1989, who had ruled Japan in the period of aggression. However, the topic has a small popular presence in Japan, where the Second World War draws less attention than among any other of its major belligerents.

Meanwhile, the character of war advanced to a globalized world with precision-guided munitions, drones, insurgency, terrorism, international

---

8 www.verbrechen-der-wehrmacht.de / docs / home.htm (accessed 18 September 2014).

humanitarian intervention and small conventional forces – although the meaning of these developments remained controversial. These matters seemed even further removed than the Cold War from the 'classical' conflict of 1941–45. Some writers argued that not only were the mass forces of the two world wars obsolete, but even any kind of inter-state armed conflict.[9] Conversely, after a long period of reduction, from 2010 major powers began to rearm with conventional forces that shared key points with those of the Cold War.

Military history continued to develop as a discipline – indeed, it entered a golden age. In 1945, the discipline had strength in official agencies and the popular market, but stood in an academic ghetto. Soon, it became even less fashionable. Many academics still view the topic and its practitioners as suspect. These experiences left military historians defensive and afraid of marginalization, yet in fact their status has risen sharply. They retain their professional audience and have bolstered their academic base, and the discipline ranks among the largest components of popular history. The field is as multi-archival, multi-linguistic and comparative as any other form of history. There are more military historians today than ever before, and more good ones. Their works are mature in theory and practice. The discipline is a loose coalition of sub-disciplines, primarily national (e.g. German) and thematic (e.g. war and society) in nature, all bound by a focus on power, strategy, armed forces and war, on ideas about these matters and the human experience of them. In 2007, Robert Citino – a major historian of the Wehrmacht – made a distinction between three trends in 'scholarly military history': '"war and society" scholars'; 'operational historians'; and those who seek to apply 'the newest trends in historical inquiry – especially the history of memory and culture'.[10] This is a useful division, but in order to describe the 'history of war', the categories of strategic and diplomatic/international history must be added. Historians in Citino's second group, in his words, 'remain unabashed in their attempts to analyse the how and whys of actual warfare, strategy, and battle'. Although this group occasionally sees itself as intellectually or organizationally embattled, this has not affected the flow of innovative and solidly researched work, or the appearance of specialist journals.

---

9 Two works which develop the notion of fundamental change are Martin van Creveld, *Future War* (London: Brassey's, 1991), and Mary Kaldor, *New and Old War: Organized Violence in a Global Era* (3rd edn., Cambridge: Polity, 2013). See also Hew Strachan and Sibylle Scheipers (eds.), *The Changing Character of War* (Oxford University Press, 2011).
10 Citino, 'Military Histories', 1070–1.

What Citino describes as the 'big tent' of scholarly military history – British historians might think of it as a 'broad church' – characterizes recent work on the Second World War. Men and women who would describe themselves in a variety of ways – as cultural, economic, intellectual, military or social historians – address issues new and important to all of them; three examples would be the memory of war, medicine or atrocities as matters linking the military and social spheres, and militarization as a political and economic phenomenon. Recent work treats military institutions as human and social organizations; takes discipline, training and morale as topics for analysis; considers how civilians are made into soldiers, sailors or aviators; and ponders how and why armies and military personnel act as they do. The study of strategy, meanwhile, has been transformed by the academic analysis of grand strategy, which embraces all categories of decision-makers, and of the inputs to power and strategy. Modern students follow the methods of masters ranging from Thucydides to Julian Corbett; and apply formal lessons derived from the theory of strategy to the practice of strategists.[11]

Only by studying where we have been and where we stand, can we see where we are going. Most obviously, these sixty years of writing about the Second World War have produced an expansion and improvement of knowledge, in the positivistic sense. However unfashionable a doctrine, positivism does describe a pillar of the historical enterprise. Facts have been found, mysteries solved and errors eliminated, including misconceptions driven by politicization and nationalism, and lies and myths encouraged by leading states and elites. Hidden issues, once most secret, have been integrated into the events and interactions they shaped. Facts are easy to disparage, until you need them – they are essential to defeat errors, lies and myth. Admittedly, answers to one set of questions open the door to another, and errors emerge whenever cases are made, but this solid foundation of knowledge eases future work, and guides it. Mysteries and problems have been marked for further attack. The quality of historical work has risen. Poor or mediocre books about the Second World War abound, but so too serious studies – whether narrowly focused and thoroughly researched, conceptually sophisticated, or multi-archival, multilingual and multidisciplinary. Perhaps more than in any field of study, good works about this war combine

---

11 See, for example, Beatrice Heuser, *The Evolution of Strategy: Thinking War from Antiquity to the Present* (Cambridge University Press, 2010). For an argument attempting to distinguish 'strategic history' from traditional military history, see Colin S. Gray, *War, Peace and International Relations: An Introduction to Strategic History* (2nd edn., London: Routledge, 2012).

academic and popular history. The quality of operational history, the core concern for the first generation of scholars and significant ever since, has risen, as personality cults are replaced by examination of how armies train and fight, and how commanders think and act. A new study, strategic history, assesses how states mobilize resources and combine diplomacy and war, and why they act as they do. Works of the new military history, older than it once was, and comparative and transnational studies, enrich the field. New trends in assessment emerge.

Historical interpretation is driven by changes not just in evidence and scholarship, but also in contemporary concerns. The greatest drivers in the memory and historiography of the Second World War have been the breadth and depth of its impact, and its role as myth. The First World War, arguably, is the greatest event in modern history. The Second World War, however, runs it at least a close second, looms larger in popular culture, and remains the greatest recent event. Great events, especially wars, shape memory, as both myth and history. Thucydides justified his account of a thirty-year struggle between Greeks, the first work of history entirely distinct from myth, and the founding study for the disciplines of war and society, strategic history and international relations, on the grounds that it was 'a great war, and more worthy of relation than any that had preceded it'; 'nothing on a greater scale, either in war or in other matters ever had happened before'. That war could be understood only by treating it as history.[12]

Both myth and history are appropriate responses to great events, but they must be distinguished from each other. Myths about the Second World War, an ideological and existential struggle for survival, have taken many forms since it was fought. Their most consistent role has been to legitimize states, which remains true today. Governments in Russia and China continue to exploit myths and memories about the war so as to bolster their position, and to demonize anyone they wish. Myth also moves in mysterious ways, beyond the power of states. In popular culture, the events of 1940 are a founding myth for modern France and Britain, as 1941 is for Australia and the United States. Both in myth and reality, Israel was founded on the Holocaust. The date for the foundation myth of modern Germany, 1945, is scarcely conducive to celebration. One source of difference between the populations of Germany (and, to a lesser degree, Italy) and those of other belligerents of that conflict is their inability to celebrate, mourn or recognize those events,

12 Thucydides, *The Peloponnesian War* (New York: Simon & Schuster, 1996), p. 3.

or to harness the myth for political or cultural purposes, in a simple fashion. Any attempt to do so in Japan becomes politicized, at home and abroad. In France, the myth is fragile, stretching over painful memories. In recent decades, within the English-speaking world and its powerful cultural exports, sentimentalized concepts of good defeating evil and of the 'greatest generation', embodied by images of the last veterans taking their final bow, have driven popular interest in the Second World War. It is remembered increasingly as a matter of morality, almost as moral theatre, with mass murder taking centre stage. The war is represented through that modern genre of mythology, comic books. In a cyclical fashion, myth fuels interest in the war, which bolsters the power of myth about it. We seem unable to stop talking about the war. Where myths about the war once were driven by states and individuals, however, now the roots are social and cultural. As ever, the place of history can be found only by putting myth in its own place.

PART I

*

GRAND STRATEGIES

Introduction to Part I

JOHN FERRIS AND EVAN MAWDSLEY

Part I has no ideal title, but 'Grand strategies' conveys the general intention. 'Grand strategy' is a conceptual level of war – and object of theoretical discussion – which conventionally is situated above 'strategy', 'operations' and 'tactics'. It describes what, in the broadest terms, a state at war wishes to achieve, and how. The term was used by the influential British military thinker J. F. C. Fuller in 1923, in the aftermath of the First World War, although his definition was rather different: something concerned not just with the 'movement of armed masses' – which was simple 'strategy' – but with the material and psychological 'motive forces' behind such movement.[1]

In 2001, Michael Howard argued that Nazi Germany had a 'coherent Grand Strategy for attaining [its objectives]': to use its limited resources 'to conquer her neighbours in Western Europe and use their resources to undertake the conquest of the East [i.e. Russia]'.[2] This strategy failed because it attempted too much. In the present volume, Jay Taylor outlines a Chinese Nationalist grand strategy of attrition, which combined stalemate against Japan and obtaining support from the Allies, especially the United States. This strategy was bold and calculated, but failed due to the weakness of the regime, the strength of its enemies and interference from its allies. Martin Alexander outlines something similar in the form of General Gamelin's 'long-term' grand strategy of holding firm and gradually building up the strength of France and its empire against Germany, in the hope that 'time would work for us'.

---

1 J. F. C. Fuller, *The Reformation of War* (London: Hutchinson, 1923), pp. 211–28. Fuller, as he was prone to do, took the idea too far and spoke of states' necessity, even in peacetime, for a 'grand strategist', a leader who had the characteristics of a military dictator.
2 Michael Howard, 'Grand Strategy in the Twentieth Century', *Defence Studies* 1 (2010), 5–6.

The term grand strategy is *not* used here to mean just non-military inputs into warfare, which is one way to understand Michael Howard's much-cited 1972 definition that it is 'the mobilisation and deployment of national resources of wealth, manpower and industrial capacity, together with the enlistment of those allied and, when feasible, of neutral powers, for the purpose of achieving the goals of national policy in wartime.'[3] Instead, we include economic mobilization and diplomacy *alongside* national military strategy and resources for war-fighting, following Howard's later definition that grand strategy means using armed force, 'wealth', allies and 'public opinion' to achieve national objectives.[4]

This volume discusses the use of these tools to achieve such objectives *in wartime*.[5] In particular, it addresses eight 'powers' – China, Britain, France, the Soviet Union and the United States among the Allies, and Germany, Italy and Japan among the Axis states – which had grand strategies in the Second World War. These are the states which public opinion in 1940 would have identified as the most important on earth, although since that year their status has ebbed and flowed.[6] Grand strategy is linked to the grandest states in any system, those with the strength to achieve visions, and the ambition to use power. As Williamson Murray writes: 'Yes, grand strategy is a matter involving great states and great states alone. No small states and few medium-size states possess the possibility of crafting a grand strategy'.[7]

The grandest strategy open to weak states in great wars is survival. During the Second World War, some medium-sized European states – Finland, Romania and Hungary – fought for years, but in subsidiary roles within alliances. When Poland, a stronger state, fought a great power by itself, its armed forces were crushed in a month. Greece did rather better in 1940–41

---

3 Michael Howard, *Grand Strategy*, vol. IV: *August 1942–September 1943* (6 vols., London: HMSO, 1972), p. 1.

4 Howard, 'Grand Strategy', pp. 2–3. Howard argued that public opinion became a factor only after the French Revolution.

5 Paul Kennedy, following Liddell Hart, used the term in a broader sense and argued that a 'true' grand strategy was concerned 'with peace as much as (perhaps even more than) with war. It was about the evolution and integration of policies that could operate for decades, or even for centuries.' See his edited collection, *Grand Strategies in War and Peace* (New Haven, Conn.: Yale University Press, 1991), p. 5. Hew Strachan criticizes such a view of grand strategy in *The Direction of War: Contemporary Strategy in Historical Perspective* (Cambridge University Press, 2013), pp. 235–52.

6 For example, China did not merit its own chapter in vols. II and III of the important series edited by Allan R. Millett and Williamson Murray, *Military Effectiveness* (Boston, Mass.: Allan & Unwin, 1988); the other seven powers of the Second World War did.

7 Williamson Murray et al. (eds.), *The Shaping of Grand Strategy: Policy, Diplomacy, and War* (Cambridge University Press, 2011), p. 1.

because of Italian weaknesses and mistakes. The conventional campaigns against Germany by the armed forces of Norway, Belgium, the Netherlands, Greece and Yugoslavia were short-lived. Within the British Empire, the 'Dominions' – Australia, Canada, New Zealand and South Africa – were independent, and like the colonies, especially India, made large military contributions to the war for six years. But they did not have a grand strategy of their own, beyond supporting and influencing Britain and, increasingly, the United States. Their role is incorporated here within discussions of the 'British' armed forces, although chapters on the British (and French) overseas territories may be found in Volume II, and the Canadians receive hard-earned credit in Marc Milner's chapter on the Battle of the Atlantic in Part II of the present volume.

Grand strategy is the highest form in which strategy is applied. It can be understood only by a comparative, competitive and transnational approach. Strategy, in turn, is a universal way to use force so as to achieve aims, but ends and means are human constructs. It is a competition between wills with power and freedom, whose weapons and ambitions clash in a realm of uncertainty. Strategy defines many ways to achieve ends, sometimes mutually exclusive, any one of which may defeat another, depending on circumstances, the competition, your choices and those of the enemy. There are principles of strategy – the trick is knowing how and when to apply them. Its basic aims are to play to your strengths and not to your weaknesses; higher ones are to shelter your weaknesses behind your strengths and to attack the enemy's weaknesses with your strengths; the highest are to turn your weaknesses to strengths, and the enemy's strengths to weaknesses. If you are strong and the enemy weak, you may press it to decisive battle, which it will seek to evade; if you wish to manage risk and uncertainty, you may prefer a strategy of attrition; if you feel yourself at a peak of strength which must over time decrease, you may prefer a high-risk/high-gains approach; perhaps you can do what you want to do, possibly the enemy may impose its will on you. The point of strategy is not just how to fight a war; but when and how *not* to do so. At its highest levels – as grand strategy – it links military and diplomatic matters, where it takes new forms, like how to borrow resources from third parties, or divert your enemy against them.

The logic of power and war is timeless, not culture-bound, yet states apply strategy in different ways, with varying emphasis on aggression, uncertainty, cost, risk and war. Grand strategies can be localized or long-term policies – 'ways of war', stemming from the 'strategic culture' of countries, which are determined by matters like history, geography, society, economy, regime and ideology. These issues, which have been assessed by writers like Liddell Hart, Russell Weigley and Robert Citino, are complex.[8] The term 'strategic culture' came later and was original defined as 'the sum total of ideas, conditioned emotional responses, and patterns of habitual behavior that members of a national strategic community have acquired through instruction or imitation and share with each other'.[9] The term 'culture' is vague, while strategic traditions are easy to oversimplify. Concepts of 'Eastern' and 'Western' ways of war stretching over 2,500 years are vague, overgeneralized, ethnocentric and largely useless. Carefully defined, however, the ideas of 'strategic culture' or 'ways of war' can illuminate how states use power. If a group maintains the same body of ideas about force and interests, and the same conditions of power and enemies, for long periods of time, it may define the same range of options and make similar choices among them, create institutions of specific character and quality, use them in distinct ways and follow a strategic style – playing for a long game of attrition, for example, as against immediate knockout. In his chapter in this volume, David French argues that Britain developed a 'grand strategy' in the eighteenth century, from when '[t]he British expected their European allies to raise large armies to defeat their common enemies on the Continent, while the British employed their powerful navy and small army to protect and enlarge their overseas empire'. Gerhard Weinberg sees a similar long-term German 'grand strategy' – conditioned by Germany's location in the middle of Europe – which was 'to concentrate in war against one enemy at a time while deferring trouble elsewhere'. The concept of strategic culture does take in continuities after profound political change – for example, between the armies of Prussia and the Third Reich, or those of Imperial Russia and the Soviet Union. Even so, these national 'ways of war' have variants, and they end when the circumstances do. Between 1700 and 1945, neither Britain nor

8 Basil Liddell Hart, *The British Way in Warfare* (London: Faber & Faber, 1932); Russell Weigley, *The American Way of War: A History of United States Military Strategy and Policy* (New York: Macmillan, 1973); Robert M. Citino, *The German Way of War: From the Thirty Years' War to the Third Reich* (Lawrence: University Press of Kansas, 2005).

9 Jack L. Snyder, 'The Soviet Strategic Culture: Implications for Limited Nuclear Operations' (RAND Paper R-2154-AF, 1977), p. 8 (www.rand.org/content/dam/rand/pubs/reports/2005/R2154.pdf – accessed 19 September 2014). A dozen years later, as the USSR seemed to be democratizing, Snyder qualified his view in 'The Concept of Strategic Culture: Caveat Emptor', in *Strategic Power: USA/USSR*, ed. Carl G. Jacobsen (Basingstoke: Macmillan, 1990). For a current view of strategic culture, see Antulio J. Echevarria, 'American Strategic Culture: Problems and Prospects', in Hew Strachan and Sibylle Scheipers, eds., *The Changing Character of War* (Oxford University Press, 2011), pp. 431–45, and, more critically, Strachan, *Direction*, pp. 136–50.

Prussia-Germany always used their stereotypical 'ways of war', and in any event, those things died when the strategic positions of the two states were transformed after 1945.

Grand strategy rests on a comparison of your own strengths and weaknesses with those of your rivals, and the exploitation of comparative advantage in competitions against them. It involves making decisions, mobilizing and using forms of power, and applying strategic principles. Major states pursued several species of grand strategy before and during the Second World War, with different strengths and weaknesses. The clash between them involved states and the strategies they embodied, the rationality of decision-making (and intelligence-interpreting) structures, the connections between civilian and military leaderships, and the ways that inter-service rivalries were handled and armed services coordinated with war production (a special feature of 'grand' strategy). The conventional view, that the liberal powers did better at grand strategy than the Axis, is true, but requires nuance.

Before the war, the Axis Powers sought to mobilize their resources for maximum immediate power, with the aim of overthrowing the international system and eating up their neighbours. Their pursuit of these aims revealed problems which proved costly in war, especially an inability to calibrate aims and means, to overcome interdepartmental rivalries, and to understand the limits to their economic and strategic power. Still, rearmament aided all the Axis states in power politics between 1931 and 1941. Germany and Japan entered the war when they seemed to be close to their peak strength, relative to the states they were confronting; they were certainly better placed than anyone could have expected in 1931. During 1939–41, their high-risk/high-gains gambles to escape an attritional struggle, which they must lose, had some success and further weakened their foes. Yet even these successes involved fluke, perhaps best demonstrated by Martin Alexander in his chapter on France, and by Karl-Heinz Frieser in his description of the battles of May 1940 in Part II. Despite these flukes, the Axis lost the war. Once war began, Axis decision strategies became poor. All had to make complex choices, like how to conduct a single-handed fight against three great powers across Europe, or eastern Asia and the western Pacific. None handled these problems well.

All the Axis Powers had dysfunctional high commands. In Germany and Italy, autocrats worked badly with bureaucrats, who did the same between themselves. Gerhard Weinberg sees Hitler's dominance as the flaw in German grand strategy, while John Gooch sees the Italian problem as an incompetent dictator and a lack of coordination. In Japan, Alessio Patalano argues, military leaders 'feigned' a grand strategy – rather, two grand strategies – in a policy marked by spectacular failure to assess power or to use it well. The Axis, the weaker coalition, mobilized and used their resources worse than did their foes.

Britain, the United States and the USSR proved better at grand strategy than their Axis opponents, although whether this was the cause of victory or the product of greater power is debatable. As Jonathan House and Bruce Menning show, before the war the USSR militarized its demographic and economic resources for maximum power more effectively than any other state. In 1941, Stalin lost many of these advantages by falling victim to fool's mate. During wartime, however, his regime confronted a simple grand-strategic problem – how to fight on one front against an enemy dividing its efforts between five of them. The Soviets eventually handled the problem well, despite operational failures, stemming partly from Stalin's efforts at micromanagement, though over time the Soviet dictator became better at the task and gave more autonomy to his generals. The USSR mobilized and used its resources ruthlessly. It survived greater losses than any other state in history, but much of the cost was unnecessary.

The three great liberal powers, Britain, France and the United States, had similar grand strategies. Before the war, their decision-making processes were slow, cumbersome and factionalized, but still more coordinated than those of the anti-liberal states. Their grand strategies, constrained by public opinion and liberal ideologies of internationalism and political economics, focusing on defence, deterrence, avoidance of war or rearmament, and the husbanding of strength for war, were flawed. They let weaker enemies become stronger and fight at their chosen moment. The initially slow but hastening pace of rearmament encouraged Axis pre-emption, and gambling, to which the liberal powers proved vulnerable. France collapsed quickly. As Martin Alexander's chapter argues, this was not because it was weak or had a poor grand strategy – the focus on building strength, finding friends and making time work as a kind of ally was good. France collapsed precisely because its success drove Germany into a gamble, where French forces were out-thought rather than out-fought in battle, and defeat triggered political chaos. During 1942, Japan shattered the grand strategy of Britain and the United States in the Pacific Ocean, and almost across the world. That fate was avoided only when President Roosevelt refused pressure from his top advisors either to make Britain launch a premature assault in Europe, or else to abandon the focus on Germany. In wartime, however, the Western

Allies gained from open systems of decision-making, which combined charismatic leadership with rational bureaucracy, and blended the best of all approaches through highest-common-denominator decisions. They efficiently turned resources into power and took bold but calculated actions across oceans, which overturned Axis strategy, like invading Guadalcanal in the South Pacific in August 1942, or North Africa three months later. Granted, in 1939–40, key Anglo-French strategic decisions were foolish, and many Anglo-American ones were debatable; any judgement on this issue will turn on what one thinks about the returns for the extraordinary resources poured into the strategic bombing offensive (CBO). As David French and Thomas Mahnken demonstrate, even the rational, technocratic and successful British and American decision-making system suffered from infighting and error. Nonetheless, the Western Allies made better wartime decisions than the Axis, despite confronting more complex choices. This subject is addressed further in illuminating chapters in Part III of this volume by Eliot Cohen and Dennis Showalter.

British military strategy

DAVID FRENCH

Introduction: 'the British way in warfare'

In the course of the long eighteenth century, the British developed a grand
strategy that was designed to minimize their weaknesses and play to their
strengths. Labelled in the 1930s by the journalist and strategist Sir Basil
Liddell Hart as 'the British way in warfare', it has been dismissed as a strategy
of avoidance. The British expected their European allies to raise large armies
to defeat their common enemies on the Continent, while the British
employed their powerful navy and small army to protect and enlarge their
overseas empire. But in reality, the strategic culture that the British
developed after 1688, as they emerged as one of the European great powers,
was more complex. In the eighteenth century, the British did pour millions of
pounds into maintaining a large and technologically sophisticated navy. But
the navy did not just exist to enlarge the empire. It also served to deter
continental powers from invading Britain, and prevented the nation from
starving. Unable to feed their population from their own resources, the
British developed a worldwide system of maritime trade, which had to be
protected in wartime if the British were to be able to continue fighting.

But confronted by a power with ambitions to fasten its hegemony over
Western Europe, such as France under Louis XIV or Napoleon, or the
Kaiser's Reich, the British knew that they could not avoid becoming
involved in European affairs. However, their own relatively small population meant that they could not hope to prevail unless they fought alongside
continental allies, who could make good their own deficiencies in manpower, and binding such allies into a secure relationship required the British
to take on a share of their common burden. Maritime power alone would
not suffice. Their allies also insisted that they commit soldiers to the

Continent to fight alongside them, and that they divert some of the wealth generated by their burgeoning overseas trade and industrial might to subsidize them.

The final defeat of Napoleon in 1815 represented the triumphant vindication of this policy. A stable preponderance of power had been established on the European continent that was to last until the 1870s, while outside Europe, Britain had eliminated the empires of its European rivals. Coupled with their naval deterrent, the British discovered that carefully calculated political concessions – a policy that was later labelled appeasement – could buy off threats from most potential enemies. It was a policy that worked around the turn of the twentieth century to eliminate threats from two great power rivals, France and Tsarist Russia. But it did not work against the Kaiser's Germany. The result was that between 1914 and 1918, the British had no option other than to resort to their strategy of burden-sharing and commit a huge army to the Western Front.

The human and financial cost of doing so was horrendous. It was, therefore, unsurprising that when the post-war settlement began to crumble in the 1930s, as Japan, Germany and Italy emerged as revisionist powers, that many British policy-makers were reluctant to repeat the exercise. In 1934–35, the General Staff, contemplating the possibility that they might again have to dispatch an expeditionary force to fight alongside France to contain Germany, prepared a programme to modernize and expand their small army. But their political masters first scaled back their plans and then, in early 1938, the Prime Minister, Neville Chamberlain, quashed them. There was to be no British continental commitment. Chamberlain hoped that a combination of appeasement and deterrence would enable Britain to avoid another bloody continental commitment and prevent hostilities elsewhere. The RAF was to be built up to deter Germany, while most of the fleet was to be stationed in the Mediterranean. Its immediate task was to deter Mussolini, but it might also be required to sail to the Far East to give teeth to Britain's Far Eastern deterrent, the naval base and fortress at Singapore. What might happen if Italy and Japan acted in concert and the fleet was required to be in two places at once was a question left unanswered until 1941. The army's roles were to contribute to the air defence of Great Britain by manning anti-aircraft guns, and to garrison the ports and coaling stations that the fleet depended on for its worldwide mobility.[1]

---

1 N. Gibbs, *Grand Strategy. Vol. 1: Rearmament Policy* (London: HMSO, 1976).

The long-haul strategy, 1939–1940

Following the Munich crisis and the German occupation of Prague in March 1939, Britain's strategy of avoiding a continental commitment began to unravel with alarming speed. British governments in the Edwardian period had been able to appease France and Russia because, thanks to Britain's relative economic power, they could maintain a credible level of armaments to deter their rivals. Further, neither France nor Russia before 1914 had tried to create a new world order, so political compromises over secondary issues were possible. But by the late 1930s that had changed. The Axis Powers sought to rearrange the global balance of power in ways that would leave little room for Britain to remain a major power.

Faced by so many threats, the British once again looked for allies with whom to share their burdens. They were hard to find. The Russians had succumbed to Communism in 1917 and were not to be trusted, and the USA had withdrawn into isolation after 1919. That only left France. When the Chamberlain government had abandoned a continental role for the British Army, it had ignored the possibility that French morale might collapse unless the British gave them significant support on land. But now the Foreign Office reported the spread of defeatism in France, and in February 1939 the Chiefs of Staff warned the Cabinet that Britain would have to play a role in the land defence of France, for if they did not, some French politicians might opt for a rapprochement with Germany.

This was the background against which, in the spring of 1939, the Chiefs of Staff Committee prepared plans for a war against Italy and Germany. They were based on two assumptions: the French army was strong enough to forestall a German advance in the west with, initially, only minimal British support on land, and that time was on the side of the Allies. They planned for a long war that would fall into three stages. The Treasury believed that if Germany continued to borrow to finance its rearmament programme, it would soon face bankruptcy. Hence it was bound to try to win quickly by mounting a massive offensive in the west against France. The British would do what they could to help the French, which, given the size of the British Army, would amount to very little, while retaining control of Egypt, from where they hoped to mount an eventual counter-offensive against Italy. In the meantime, it would be essential to maintain peace in the Far East, because the fleet would be tied down in the Mediterranean and could not be dispatched to Singapore until after Italy's defeat. If matters went according to plan, the initial German offensive would be checked in a matter of a couple of months, and the war

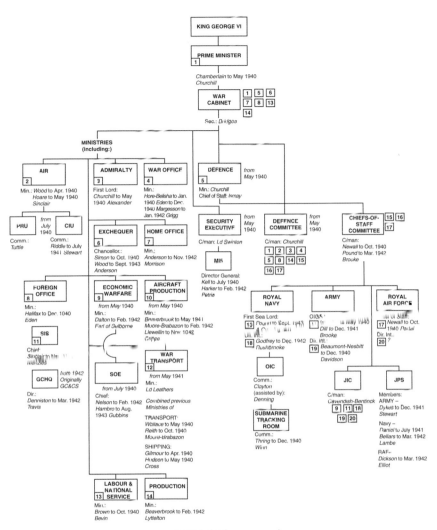

1.1 British high command

would then enter its second phase. The Allies would mobilize their own resources and, thanks to the Royal Navy's command of the seas, draw upon those of their colonies and neutral trading partners, while simultaneously weakening Italy and Germany by a combination of propaganda and economic blockade. The third phase would begin about two years after the start of hostilities, when, with their own forces fully mobilized, the Allies would mount a counter-offensive into Germany and crush their main enemy.

The French were opposed to mining the Rhine because it might provoke the Germans into taking reprisals against their own industries. But they originally welcomed operations in Scandinavia. Not only would they hurt the German war economy, but they would keep the fighting at a safe distance from France. Chamberlain eventually acquiesced because of reports that there were limits to French readiness to maintain mobilization unaccompanied by military operations, and because they blamed the British for the inactivity of the Phoney War. Fortunately for long-term British interests, Finnish resistance collapsed before Allied troops could reach them, so they did not add Russia to their enemies. But in all other respects, the dispatch of Anglo-French forces to Norway in April 1940 was a disaster. The Germans landed just ahead of them, and although the German navy suffered crippling losses, they established enough troops on the ground to force the British and French into a series of humiliating and costly evacuations.

War without major allies, June 1940–December 1941

The evacuation of Norway marked the start of a political and strategic revolution in Britain. On 10 May 1940, the same day that the Germans invaded Holland, Belgium and France, Chamberlain resigned, and Churchill became Prime Minister of a coalition government. By the end of May, British and French troops, who had rushed to the assistance of Belgium and Holland, had been driven into a pocket and were being evacuated from Dunkirk. Less than a month later, France signed an armistice, with the result that the foundation of British military strategy, the assumption that the French army would at least be strong enough to hold the Germans in the west, had collapsed. After briefly considering and rejecting the possibility of a negotiated peace, Churchill's government decided that there could be no peace short of total victory.[3] But how they were to secure that, bereft as they were of continental allies, was problematic. They found themselves with no options other than to do what an earlier British government had done when faced by a similar crisis. The defence of the home islands had to be their first priority, and in the summer of 1940, RAF Fighter Command and the superiority enjoyed by the Royal Navy in home waters sufficed to deter a German invasion. This was Hitler's first major strategic setback since the start of the

---

3 C. Hill, *Cabinet Decisions and Foreign Policy: The British Experience October 1938–June 1941* (Cambridge University Press, 1991), pp. 146–87.

war. But the British could not win the war merely by defending themselves. The army had left most of its heavy equipment behind in France, and it would be many years before it would be possible for it to return to the Continent. In the meantime, they had to find ways of carrying the war to Germany, and they hoped they could do this by a combination of economic blockade, air attacks, propaganda and subversion.[4]

British intelligence continued to assume that the German war economy was already fully mobilized, and that consequently Germany would be vulnerable to a combination of air attacks on its industrial cities and economic blockade. However, like so many of the ideas that underpinned British military strategy in the early part of the war, this was based on wishful thinking. The German economy was only partially mobilized in 1940, and German war production did not peak until 1944. Furthermore, the Germans could avoid some of the most threatening consequences of the blockade by drawing upon the resources of the countries they had conquered in 1940–41. The efforts of the blockade and the bomber were to be supplemented by the work of the Special Operations Executive (SOE). Churchill had been deeply impressed by the success of the Irish Republican Army between 1919 and 1921 in loosening Britain's grip on Southern Ireland, and in July 1940 he created SOE to organize guerrilla resistance in occupied Europe.[5] In September 1940, the Chiefs of Staff optimistically predicted that the Wehrmacht, paralysed by guerrilla attacks and shortages of essential supplies, would collapse under its own weight by 1942. The British Army would then be able to return to the Continent, not to fight expensive battles of attrition, but to accept the Germans' surrender. Faith in the bomber, the blockade and subversion had thus expanded to fill the vacuum at the heart of British military strategy left by the collapse of the French army. Despite their uncertain foundations in reality, these beliefs became deeply ingrained in the minds of British military strategists, and help to explain their opposition to American proposals for a cross-Channel invasion between 1942 and 1944. And underpinning all these calculations was the hope that either the USA or the USSR would conclude that they could not allow Britain to go under, or that the Germans would make the egregious mistake of dragging one or both of them into the war.

Italy declared war on Britain in June 1940, and posed an immediate threat to the British Empire in the Mediterranean and Middle East, a threat that was

---

4 Chiefs of Staff, British strategy in a certain eventuality, 25 May 1940. TNA CAB 66/7/48.
5 David Stafford, 'The Detonator Concept: British Strategy, SOE and European Resistance after the Fall of France', *Journal of Contemporary History* 10, 2 (1975), pp. 185–217.

doubly dangerous because the French fleet could no longer contain Mussolini's navy. Indeed, there was a possibility that the Germans might seize it, and to prevent that from happening, Churchill exhibited a streak of ruthlessness. When part of the French fleet at anchor in the Algerian port of Mers-el-Kébir refused to intern itself, he ordered that it be sunk.[6] It was a measure of how vital they regarded their hold on their Mediterranean and Middle Eastern possessions that in August 1940, with an invasion of Britain still possible, the War Cabinet risked sending 150 precious tanks to Egypt. Between December 1940 and February 1941, they enabled the greatly outnumbered but more mobile Western Desert Force to drive the Italians from Cyrenaica, and for a short time it seemed that the British would be able to eliminate the Italian Empire in North Africa. However, in March 1941, Hitler invaded the Balkans. The British feared that by doing so he would be able to break the blockade, spread discontent among the Arab populations of Britain's client states in the Middle East, and cut Britain's communications between the Mediterranean and its Far Eastern empire. Consequently, they diverted the troops that might have been able to conquer the Italian Empire in Tripolitania to the Balkans, in a vain attempt to buttress Greek resistance against the Axis Powers. By April 1941, what was left of their forces were evacuated from mainland Greece, while in the meantime, the arrival of a small German expeditionary force, under the command of Erwin Rommel, enabled the Axis to reoccupy Cyrenaica.

To write of the *British* war effort in the Middle East between 1940 and 1943 is a misnomer, for the land war was, in reality, a British imperial, rather than a purely British undertaking. Before 1939, the Chiefs of Staff had calculated that in a long war the empire would represent a major military asset, not because the colonies and Dominions could manufacture weapons and munitions in large quantities, but because they could provide large numbers of soldiers, and they were right in this. Between 1940 and 1942, the British concentrated most of their own army in the United Kingdom, where they prepared to meet a German invasion. Elsewhere they relied heavily on manpower from their overseas possessions to do the fighting. Thus, for example, in October 1941, nearly three-quarters of the combat divisions allocated to the Eighth Army in North Africa were drawn from the empire. It was the forces of the colonies and Dominions that allowed the British to safeguard their interests in the Middle East in the first half of the war.

6 C. Smith, *England's Last War Against France. Fighting Vichy 1940–1942* (London: Phoenix, 2009), pp. 73–82.

By the middle of 1941 it was becoming implausible to believe that bombers, the blockade and subversion would together cause the collapse of Hitler's empire. It was, therefore, extraordinarily fortunate for the British that in the second half of the year they gained two allies whose combined military strength, when it was fully mobilized, meant that the defeat of the Axis Powers would only be a matter of time. Initially, however, the British were almost blind to their good luck. When Hitler invaded Russia in June 1941, few policy-makers thought that the Russians would be able to resist for long. Initially, they saw Russia's entry into the war not as an opportunity to rethink their own strategy from first principles, but as a short-term opportunity to be grasped. Consequently, when the Soviets asked them to mount an invasion, or at least a large-scale raid on the coast of Western Europe to divert German divisions westward, they hardly considered it, contenting themselves merely with intensifying their air attacks on Germany. Meanwhile, Churchill encouraged his commanders in North Africa to take the opportunity of Germany's preoccupation in Russia to mount a counter-offensive in Libya, while simultaneously the British worked with the Russians to eliminate German influence from Persia and Iraq. It was only in September 1941 that Churchill had sufficient confidence in the Soviets' ability to resist the Wehrmacht that he inaugurated a large-scale Lend-Lease programme to assist Russia.[7] Henceforth the British recognized that a new and permanent factor had entered into their military calculations; they now had an ally with an army that was sufficiently powerful to match the Germans on the Continent.

By then, the British had acquired a second major ally. In 1935, Chamberlain had tried to appease Japan by negotiating a Far Eastern Non-Aggression Pact. When he failed, the British were thrown back on deterrence. At the May 1937 Imperial Conference, the Admiralty explained that the Singapore naval base was the cornerstone of imperial defence in the Far East, and that in an emergency it hoped to send between eight and ten capital ships to Far Eastern waters. But what the British carefully avoided promising was that those ships would be dispatched even if a war had already broken out in Europe, and in mid-1940, the collapse of France and the belligerence of Italy made that a pressing issue. Churchill opted to concentrate British and imperial resources in the Mediterranean and Middle East, and to avoid war with the Japanese for as long as possible. Staff talks that began in October

---

7 J. Beaumont, *Comrades in Arms. British Aid to Russia 1941–45* (London: David-Poynter, 1980), pp. 23–60.

1940 with the Dutch, Americans and the Dominions only highlighted the deficiencies in all of their Far Eastern war preparations. What the British most wanted was for the Americans to send their fleet to Singapore, something that might have given the Singapore deterrent strategy real teeth, but they refused. Once it was apparent that the Japanese would not be appeased, Churchill could only opt for a weak deterrent. Rather than send between eight and ten capital ships, he could only scrape together two, the *Prince of Wales* and the *Repulse*. They arrived in December 1941, and were promptly sunk by Japanese aircraft.[8] The land defences of Malaya were in no better shape. Troops that might have been able to block a Japanese advance had been retained in the Middle East, and those that were available were either badly trained or were road-bound because they had been prepared for mobile operations in the Middle East which required masses of motor transport. Consequently, they repeatedly found themselves outflanked by more lightly equipped, but more agile Japanese forces. Singapore fell to the Japanese in February 1942, and by May they had conquered not only Malaya but also Burma, and arrived at the northeastern frontier of India. From the British point of view, the only good thing to come out of these calamities was that the Japanese had begun this new phase of their war of an expansion in the Far East by attacking the American fleet at Pearl Harbor, thus precipitating the entry of the USA into the war on Britain's side.

Burden-sharing, 1942–1944

Even before Pearl Harbor, the British and Americans had reached a major decision about their future strategy. In February 1941, they agreed that if the USA entered the war, it would follow the British lead and accord priority to the war against Germany, deploying only sufficient forces in the Far East to contain Japan. This decision was quickly reaffirmed at the ARCADIA conference in December 1941, when Churchill and Roosevelt met as allies for the first time. It was entirely consistent with the Churchill government's larger strategic objectives. Between Dunkirk and Pearl Harbor, their overriding aim had been to ensure national survival. But after the entry of the USA into the war, and once they were convinced that the Soviet Union would not collapse, they realized that the combined human and economic resources of the Allies meant that they would eventually wear down their enemies.

---

8 C. Bell, 'The "Singapore Strategy" and the Deterrence of Japan: Winston Churchill, the Admiralty and the Dispatch of Force Z', *English Historical Review* 116 (2001), 604–34.

Henceforth, therefore, Britain's main goal was to ensure that Allied military strategy evolved in ways that were consistent with Britain's own strategic and political interests. The war against Germany had to have priority because, unlike Japan, Germany posed a direct and immediate threat to the security of the British home islands.

The British also recognized that the USA's entry into the war would enable them to revert to the kind of attritional strategy they had agreed with France in 1939. At ARCADIA, Churchill and Roosevelt agreed that the Germans could be worn down by the Russian army, supplied with Western war materiel, combined with large-scale air and amphibious raids mounted from Britain. They would isolate the European Axis Powers and tighten the blockade by occupying North Africa and by persuading Turkey to join the alliance. That, in turn, would both reduce the strain on Allied shipping by reopening the Mediterranean, and, Churchill hoped, culminate in the surrender of Italy. Only then would a final assault be launched against Germany, with simultaneous land operations mounted by the Russians, the Americans and the British.[9]

The British and Americans took one other important decision at ARCADIA, which was to establish the Combined Chiefs of Staff. It consisted of the American and British Joint Chiefs of Staff, although the British Chiefs remained based in London, and were represented in Washington by a former Chief of the Imperial General Staff, Sir John Dill. A dynamic tension emerged between policy-makers and, until the middle of 1943, the Combined Chiefs of Staff gave the British the opportunity to foist many of their own strategic priorities onto the Americans. Even in 1944–45, when the balance of military power in the Anglo-American alliance had shifted in favour of the Americans, it did at least give them a platform from which they could make their voices heard.

But it would be wrong to think that harmony now reigned within the Anglo-American alliance. The British had won most of the strategic arguments in 1941 because they had come to the conference table carefully briefed, and because they had far more forces in contact with the enemy than did the Americans. But some American policy-makers were reluctant to accept all of the British proposals, suspecting that the emphasis the British placed on the Mediterranean was an attempt to divert American resources to defending British imperial interests. The US Navy, smarting from the Pearl

9 J. M. A. Gwyer, *Grand Strategy. Vol.* III (London: HMSO, 1964), Part 1, pp. 325–65.

Harbor debacle, wanted to give priority to the Pacific War, and the army was sceptical of Churchill's preference for a peripheral strategy, and his apparent insistence that it would be possible to defeat Germany without also beating its army in the field. General George C. Marshall, the Army Chief of Staff, opted for a more direct approach. He wanted to raise an army of as many as 200 divisions, deploy it on the plains of Northwest Europe, and smash a way by the shortest route into the Reich.

The British thought that Marshall was being naive in failing to recognize the formidable practical problems involved in fighting the Germans in Northwest Europe. The defeats that the British had suffered in Norway, France, Greece and Crete, not to mention memories of the horrific casualties their armies had endured in France between 1914 and 1918, had left them deeply impressed with the fighting power of the German army. Further- more, the apparent willingness with which so many British soldiers had surrendered in France, North Africa and Singapore led Churchill, and some field commanders, to wonder if the army's morale was sufficiently robust to sustain a long period of costly fighting. The destruction of the amphibious expedition they had sent to Norway, the heavy losses suffered by the Mediterranean fleet in evacuating troops from Crete in May 1941, and the sinking of the *Prince of Wales* and *Repulse* by the Japanese, had demonstrated to them that the strategic flexibility which sea power had once conferred was a thing of the past.[10] Those benefits could only be reaped if the marshalling of large fleets of surface warships, troop transports and specialized landing craft took place under the secure umbrella of friendly aircraft. If it was to be effective, sea power now had to be combined with air power, and bringing together the necessary components for successful amphibious operations was a time-consuming business. Unless the attacker achieved complete surprise, and by the use of his own air power could paralyse the movement of the enemy's reserves from their inland concentration areas to the landing site, it was likely that the attacker might find himself pinned to the beaches. The failure of the British raid on the French port of Dieppe in August 1942 pointed to the pitfalls of mounting an invasion without adequate preparations.

Tensions between British and American military strategists about the future course of the war first emerged in April 1942, when the Americans tried to persuade the British to agree to an invasion of Northwest Europe in the spring of 1943. The British initially accepted the suggestion, although with

---

10 T. Ben-Moshe, *Churchill, Strategy and History* (Hemel Hempstead: Harvester Wheatsheaf, 1992), pp. 121–200.

the proviso that enough forces had to be maintained to protect the Middle East and Indian Ocean, which were then threatened by the appearance of Japanese warships in the Bay of Bengal. But when the proposals were subject to closer scrutiny, they showed that the forces that the Allies could muster for a cross-Channel invasion were totally inadequate. On paper, the British Army in the UK was a formidable force. But since 1940 it had been organized and equipped for one role – the defence of Britain against an invasion. It was an unbalanced organization, in which priority had been given to creating front-line fighting units, on the assumption that it would be able to draw upon civilian resources to meet many of its logistics needs. The British did not deliberately over-insure themselves to safeguard the home islands, but British industry could not provide the equipment needed by the supply, transport, communications, repair and medical units that the Home Forces would need if they were to throw off an expeditionary force to operate in an overseas theatre.[11] By May 1942, the British Army could have sent no more than six properly supported divisions overseas, and as the Americans could commit even fewer troops, Churchill was able to veto the plan.

But the Western Allies could not afford to do nothing in 1942. President Roosevelt had promised Stalin that he would mount a second front in 1942 to take some of the pressure off the Red Army, and he also wanted to focus American public opinion on the European theatre at a time when Pearl Harbor had riveted their attention on the Pacific. In July 1942, therefore, he was willing to fall in with Churchill's suggestion that an Anglo-American expeditionary force should land in northwest Africa to implement their strategy of tightening the ring around Germany. The American Chiefs of Staff were uncomfortable with what they believed was Churchill's opportunistic strategy, and they were correct to argue that mounting Operation TORCH would divert so many resources from the build-up of forces in Britain that a cross-Channel invasion in 1943 would be impossible. But despite their misgivings, British and US forces began to land in French Morocco and Algeria on 8 November 1942. The difficulties they experienced in bringing that campaign to a successful conclusion suggested that the British had been right to reject a cross-Channel invasion in 1942.

Four days earlier, the British and Commonwealth forces of General Sir Bernard Montgomery's Eighth Army had finally broken through the Axis positions at El Alamein, thus ending a period of nearly two years of fighting

---

11 D. French, 'Invading Europe: The British Army and its Preparations for the Normandy Campaign, 1942–44', *Diplomacy and Statecraft* 14 (2003), 272–6.

along the North African littoral that had seen the front line seesaw from the western frontier of Cyrenaica to a line only sixty miles from Alexandria. By March 1941, less than two months after his arrival, Rommel had advanced to the frontier of Egypt and besieged the British garrison in Tobruk. In November 1941, the British mounted a successful counter-offensive, relieved Tobruk, and themselves advanced to the frontier of Cyrenaica. Rommel then mounted a brief counter-offensive that drove the Eighth Army eastward, and the two sides then settled down to prepare for their next offensive. The Axis struck first, and in June and July 1942 routed the Commonwealth forces and drove them back to the El Alamein position. Both sides were then exhausted, but Rommel's supply lines were now dangerously overextended, and Allied submarines and aircraft based on Malta prevented more than a trickle of supplies and reinforcements from reaching him. At the same time, the El Alamein position offered the British a unique advantage. It was only sixty miles long and was one of the few defensive positions in North Africa that could not be outflanked to the south. The most important lesson that the British military had learned from the casualty lists of the Somme and Passchendaele was that never again would their countrymen allow them to be so prodigal with the lives of their men.[12] Henceforth, if they had to fight on land, they would have to do so by using the maximum of machinery and firepower, and the minimum of manpower. El Alamein represented the first occasion during the Second World War when the British were able successfully to practise that doctrine. Reinforced by fresh troops and weapons, including 300 new US medium tanks, Montgomery used his superiority in manpower and machinery to wear down the Axis forces in what proved to be the decisive battle in the defence of Egypt.[13] He then advanced westward along the North African coast, linked up with the Anglo-American forces in Tunisia, and together they accepted the surrender of the Axis armies in North Africa in May 1943.

The Casablanca Conference, which took place in January 1943, is best remembered as the moment when the Western Allies declared their intention of imposing unconditional surrender on the Axis Powers. But Churchill and Roosevelt also took three important strategic decisions. Defeating the U-boat offensive in the Atlantic had to be a top priority, to ensure both that Britain did not starve, and that American troops could reach Britain in safety.

---

12 D. French, *Raising Churchill's Army: The British Army and the War Against Germany, 1919–1945* (Oxford University Press, 2000), pp. 12–47.
13 N. Barr, *Pendulum of War: The Three Battles of El Alamein* (London: Jonathan Cape, 2004).

They agreed to mount a combined bomber offensive from bases in Britain to weaken Germany's war-making capability to the point at which an invasion of the Continent by the Allies would become possible. But when the Americans pressed once more for an early cross-Channel attack, Churchill again insisted that such an operation would be premature. The British and Americans had committed considerable land forces to the Mediterranean. They lacked the shipping and landing craft to mount a cross-Channel invasion in 1943, and they could not afford to do nothing after the collapse of the Axis position in North Africa, while the Russians continued to tie down the bulk of the Wehrmacht. So they opted to exploit their North African successes by invading Sicily, an operation that they hoped, when combined with naval and air attacks, would persuade Italy to surrender. If it worked, this 'Mediterranean strategy' would assist the Russians, and pave the way for a cross-Channel invasion in 1944, by forcing the Germans to assume heavy extra troop commitments, not only in Italy, but also in Italy's Balkan empire.[14]

Casablanca was also significant because it was almost the last such occasion when the British were able to persuade the Americans to accept their strategic priorities. American military mobilization was gathering pace, and soon the military balance of power within the Anglo-American alliance would swing decisively toward Washington. The implications of that for Britain's military strategy started to become apparent at the TRIDENT conference in Washington in May 1943. The British succeeded in persuading their allies that the invasion of Sicily should be followed by landings on the Italian mainland. Not only would that tie down still more German divisions which might otherwise be sent to the eastern front or northern France, but it would also allow the British and Americans the use of Italian airfields, from which they could bomb targets in Southeast and Central Europe, and give encouragement to resistance movements in the Balkans. But in return, the Americans were able to insist that a firm date, 1 May 1944, should be fixed for the cross-Channel invasion, codenamed OVERLORD. The Mediterranean would become a subsidiary theatre, a fact signified by the withdrawal of four American and three British divisions from there to Britain, in preparation for OVERLORD.[15]

British and American forces landed in Sicily in July 1943 and had occupied the whole island by mid-August. The operation did lead to Mussolini's

14 Michael Howard, *Grand Strategy*, vol. IV: *August 1942–September 1943* (6 vols., London: HMSO, 1972), pp. 225–85.
15 Howard, *Grand Strategy*, pp. 409–34.

overthrow, and in September Italy surrendered when Allied troops landed in the south of the country. The Germans proved to be unwilling as the British had hoped to give up the territory of their erstwhile ally, and by December 1943 they had dispatched twenty-five divisions to Italy itself, and another twenty divisions to retain control of the Balkans. The Mediterranean strategy, therefore, fulfilled its promise of diverting German forces from other theatres. But that should not hide the reality that OVERLORD would not have been possible in 1944, but for the fact that the Red Army tied down about two-thirds of the German army on the Eastern Front.

It is more difficult to assess the record of the British air offensive against Germany.[16] At the start of the war, they had hoped to mount daylight precision bombing raids, but they quickly discovered that German fighter defences made such operations prohibitively expensive. Consequently, in the winter of 1940–41, they switched to night attacks against precision targets such as factories and railway marshalling yards. Their strategy failed for three reasons. They had too few aircraft, for by mid-1941, Bomber Command could only commit about 400 bombers to operations. Secondly, the Air Staff wrongly believed that the interdependence of a modern industrial economy would work in their favour. In fact, it worked against them, for although the German economy did have numerous bottlenecks, it also had alternative sources of power and supplies. Finally, the bombers could not hit precision targets. A study concluded in August 1941 that navigation errors meant that only 20 per cent of aircraft came to within even five miles of their targets.

In February 1942, Bomber Command received a new commander, Sir Arthur Harris. In the knowledge that the smallest target they could be sure of hitting at night was a medium-sized town, the Air Ministry told him that henceforth his bombers' main mission was to destroy the morale of the enemy civilian population, and in particular of the industrial workers. This policy of area bombing was assisted by the introduction of new navigation and bomb-aiming aids, and the creation of an elite Pathfinder Force, whose mission was to fly in advance of the main bomber stream to find and mark targets for them. The availability of larger numbers of heavier bombers did enable Bomber Command to increase the tonnage of bombs dropped on Germany. They did compel the Germans to divert fighter aircraft, anti-aircraft guns and manpower from the fighting fronts to defend their cities and to clear up the damage. But they could not wreck the German economy nor win air

---

16 R. Overy, *The Bombing War: Europe 1939–1945* (London: Allen Lane, 2013), pp. 237–409.

superiority over Western Europe. Between March 1943 and March 1944, Bomber Command mounted a series of campaigns against the Ruhr, Hamburg and Berlin, which inflicted massive casualties on the German civilian population and checked the expansion of German war production. But in the winter of 1943–44, the German defences were able to impose unacceptably heavy losses on the British bomber forces, and Harris had no option but to halt his attacks. His aircraft were then switched to interdicting German communications in France, in support of the Allied landing in Normandy, and by the time they resumed night attacks on Germany, in the autumn of 1944, the situation in the air had been transformed. In the spring and early summer of 1944, the long-range fighters of the US Eighth Air Force had destroyed the Luftwaffe's fighter arm in a series of daylight raids over Germany. Air superiority had passed to the Allies, and in the final months of the war, Bomber Command, operating in conjunction with the US Eighth Air Force, flattened most of Germany's cities, produced an oil famine and destroyed its transport system.

Winning air superiority over Western Europe was one essential precondition for OVERLORD. Winning the Battle of the Atlantic was another. It was all very well for Britain to have an ally, in the shape of the USA, with enormous economic potential that could, in time, be transformed into huge armies, navies and air forces. But the USA was 3,000 miles away, across the Atlantic, and it would avail the British nothing if they starved before American assistance arrived. By December 1941, the Allies had lost nearly 8 million tons of merchant shipping, and only one-third of it had been replaced by new launchings. The Allies finally prevailed because the Germans made mistakes – underestimating, for example, the tonnage they would have to sink to force Britain to surrender – and because Britain and its allies showed they could adjust better than their enemies to the changing demands of the U-boat war. Some factors that brought about the Allies' victory had little to do with the British. They included the ability of US shipyards to replace merchant ships sunk by U-boats, and the ability of the US aircraft industry to produce the very long-range aircraft needed to provide Allied convoys with air cover over the mid-Atlantic. At sea, the Royal Navy, which included a large contingent drawn from the Royal Canadian Navy, employed convoys to protect its merchant ships, as it had done in 1917–18. The British also built large numbers of specialist anti-submarine escorts, and progressively equipped them with an array of scientific devices, including sonar to detect submerged U-boats, radar to detect them on the surface, and high-frequency radio detection equipment, to pinpoint their position at a distance. Scientific operational research indicated the best ways to engage the enemy; and new weapons, such as the forward-firing hedgehog mortar, provided better ways of destroying U-boats once they had been detected. Finally, in June 1941, British code-breakers succeeded in cracking the German naval Enigma codes, and, although they lost access to German messages between February 1942 and early 1943, for as long as they could read them, they were able to plot the position of waiting wolf packs, and try to divert convoys away from danger areas.[17]

The Battle of the Atlantic convoys reached its climax in the spring of 1943. The Kriegsmarine now had so many U-boats at sea that the British could not route their convoys around them. But the convoy escorts knew their location, and at last they had the aircraft, ships, detection devices and weapons to destroy them. The U-boats were fought to a standstill in a battle of attrition they could not win. Between January and May 1943, the Germans lost nearly a hundred U-boats in the Atlantic. Such a loss rate was unsustainable, and at the end of the month, the German naval command admitted defeat and withdrew its forces.

The Second Front

In 1944–45, British air and naval power could not have liberated Western Europe. That could only be done if the Western Allies landed troops on the Continent and defeated the German army in the west in a ground war, something that Churchill was reluctant to accept until a surprisingly late stage in the war. When he went to Quebec for the QUADRANT conference in August 1943, he was not only intoxicated by the possible implications of Italy's collapse, he was also still haunted by memories of the Western Front, and impressed by the ability the Germans had demonstrated in Sicily and Italy to wage a stubborn defensive war. Instead of OVERLORD, he wanted a major amphibious landing in northern Italy, so that in 1944 the Allies could advance either west into southern France or northeast into Austria. But his advocacy was in vain. The balance of power within the Grand Alliance was now tilted decisively against the British. When the Americans, British and Soviets met at Tehran in November 1943, the British were told that whether they liked it or not, OVERLORD would have priority and would take place in the spring of 1944.

---

17 P. Kennedy, *Engineers of Victory: The Problem Solvers Who Turned the Tide in the Second World War* (London: Allen Lane, 2013), pp. 5–74.

But once the decision had been taken, Churchill did not shy away from its implications. If the British were to have a significant voice in the conduct of the operation, they had to be seen to be making a major contribution in terms of the resources they committed to it. But doing so was increasingly problematic, for Britain had passed the limits of its manpower reserves. Within days of his victory at El Alamein, Montgomery had been compelled to disband two divisions in order to maintain the rest at something near to their proper strength. In November 1943, the War Office had earmarked a dozen divisions for OVERLORD. Churchill did not think that was enough. The Americans were committing fifteen divisions in the first part of the campaign, and he insisted that the British had to match them. 'We have carried the recent trouble entirely by mentioning that we had preponderance on the battlefront', he wrote, and 'We ought to have at least equality in this other critical task.'[18] The British also dominated much of the detailed planning and preparations for the initial landing, so that the eventual operation came about through a combination of American will, British brains and Anglo-American-Canadian muscle.[19]

The Allied armies landed in Normandy in June 1944. Given America's growing military preponderance, there was never really any doubt that their Supreme Commander would be an American. The man chosen was General Eisenhower, who had previously been the Supreme Allied Commander in Italy. But Britain's contribution at sea, in the air and on land enabled them to claim the three subordinate posts of the naval, air and land forces commanders. After nearly two months of bitter fighting, the Anglo-American forces broke out from their beachheads in late July, and by the end of August had liberated Paris. Brussels fell in early September, but the Allies, beset by logistical problems, could not maintain the momentum of their advance. Montgomery was not a commander renowned for taking risks, but in September 1944 he belied his reputation for caution. He laid a carpet of three airborne divisions (two American and one British) across Holland in an attempt to secure a crossing over the Rhine. By doing so, he hoped that he could bring the war to a rapid end by advancing swiftly into the heart of Germany. Underpinning the operation was his knowledge that the British Army was now a wasting asset. Britain was now so short of men that he had already been forced to disband two of the divisions that had landed in Normandy. If the British were plausibly to claim to be a major military power

18 Churchill to Grigg, 6 November 1943. TNA WO 259/77.
19 I am grateful to John Ferris for this point.

at the end of the war, the fighting had to be finished quickly, preferably by a knockout blow delivered by British forces, and while the British could still maintain an army of some size in the field.[20] But tactical errors, poor weather which delayed the arrival of reinforcements to the Arnhem bridgehead, and unexpectedly strong German resistance meant that the operation ended in failure, and the Allies were exposed to a further winter of war. It was only in March 1945 that Montgomery's forces crossed the Rhine in a carefully planned operation, and then advanced westward until all German forces in northern Germany, Holland and Denmark surrendered on 4 May.

The war in the Far East

After the fall of Singapore, the 'Europe first' strategy meant that the main weight of the burden of containing and then defeating Japan fell on the USA and China. The Americans were responsible for the conduct of the Pacific War, and Britain abdicated her responsibility for the defence of Australia and New Zealand in favour of the USA. The British effort in the war against Japan focused largely on the Burma front and the defence of India. Churchill was intent on reconquering Britain's lost empire in Southeast Asia, but he wanted to avoid a costly land campaign in Burma, by outflanking the Japanese through mounting amphibious operations against either Singapore or northern Sumatra. However, the British did not have the shipping or landing craft for such operations, and the Americans would not provide them. The Americans were not interested in supporting a campaign they thought was designed to re-establish British imperial power. Burma was only important to them in as much as its reconquest would pave the way for reopening land communications between India and China via the 'Burma road'. That, in turn, would enable them to send supplies to Chinese Nationalist forces tying down a large part of the Japanese army in the interior of China.

That the British and Commonwealth forces did succeed in reopening a land route to China and reconquering Burma overland owed at least as much to Japanese miscalculations as it did to their own foresight. In the spring of 1943, a brigade under Brigadier Orde Wingate crossed the Chindwin River and entered northern Burma. Wingate's troops operated in small, independent

---

20 S. A. Hart, *Montgomery and 'Colossal Cracks': The 21st Army Group in Northwest Europe, 1944–45* (London and Westport, Conn.: Praeger, 2000); J. Buckley, *Montgomery's Men: The British Army and the Liberation of Europe, 1944–45* (New Haven, Conn. and London: Yale University Press, 2013).

columns, supplied entirely by air-drops. Their objective was to attack Japanese lines of communication, and although their material impact was slight, they not only proved to the British themselves that ordinary soldiers, with the appropriate training, could master the problems of jungle warfare, they also undermined the myth that the Japanese were military supermen. But most important of all, they provoked the Japanese into invading Assam, where they played into the hands of the Anglo-Indian Fourteenth Army and its commander, Sir William Slim. Slim had three advantages over his enemy. They were operating at the end of lengthy and inadequate lines of communication. He was operating near to his base. Even when the Japanese surrounded his formations, they could sit tight and fight because the existence of US transport aircraft meant they could be supplied by air. And fight they did, because since 1942, the British and Indian army formations he commanded had been transformed. Rigorous training in the demands of jungle warfare had given his soldiers the confidence that they had lacked in 1941–42. The result was that when the Japanese clashed with Slim's forces in the twin battles of Imphal and Kohima in March and April 1944, they found it impossible to overcome their stubborn resistance. British artillery, air power and small arms killed large numbers of the attackers, and even more died from disease and starvation as their logistics collapsed during their retreat. That enabled Slim to encircle the remaining Japanese forces in Burma at Meiktilia in central Burma, and to retake Rangoon in May 1945.[21]

The reconquest of Burma was a military triumph for the Fourteenth Army, but it played almost no part in bringing about the final defeat of Japan. By early 1945, the American air and naval blockade had crippled the Japanese economy, and American amphibious forces had broken through the Japanese defensive perimeter in the Pacific and enabled the Americans to establish airbases within range of the Japanese home islands. The British sent a fleet to assist the Americans in the Pacific, partly to demonstrate to the 'anti-imperialist' Americans that they were not just concerned to reconquer their empire, but were also willing to fight the Japanese on their homeland, and partly to ensure they could claim a voice at the peace conference. But it gave them little influence over US strategy. In August 1945, without consulting his allies, Roosevelt's successor, President Truman, obviated the need for an invasion of Japan and forced the Japanese government to surrender by dropping atomic bombs on Hiroshima and Nagasaki.

21 R. Miller, *Uncle Bill: The Authorised Biography of Field Marshal Viscount Slim* (London: Weidenfeld & Nicolson, 2013), chapters 15–17.

Conclusion

British military strategy during the Second World War reflected the strategic culture that its policy-makers had developed since the eighteenth century. In 1940, the Navy and RAF combined to deter a German invasion of the home islands, and the Navy was able to safeguard Britain's maritime lines of communication. The two services also worked together to apply pressure on the German Empire in Western Europe at a time when British land forces had been expelled from the Continent. Together with the army, they combined to protect many of Britain's overseas possessions in the Mediterranean and Middle East, although not in the Far East. The British also showed that they could overcome two of the most difficult problems that confronted the belligerents. They created a successful working relationship between military planners and civilian leaders, both at the national and, with the Americans, at the inter-allied levels. Once again with the Americans, they also overcame the manifold practical problems inherent in conducting joint operations involving all three services. But the British alone could not have hoped to defeat the Axis Powers. Paradoxically, it was during the Second World War, when their control over their empire was loosening, that the British came to rely more heavily than ever before on imperial manpower to fight their wars. Of the 103 divisions that the British mobilized, no fewer than 54 were raised in the Dominions, colonies or India. The empire also provided nearly 40 per cent of the RAF's aircrews. But the single most important factor in ensuring that Britain ended the war among the victors was that in 1941 it entered into successful burden-sharing arrangements with the USA and USSR. To the extent that the human price the British paid between 1939 and 1945 was a great deal lighter than that of some of their allies, this policy was a success. The British suffered 325,000 fatalities during the war, a figure that included more than 60,000 civilians killed by German bombing. This was a good deal higher than the 274,000 combat deaths suffered by the USA, but it was only a minute fraction of the roughly 27 million Soviet citizens who were killed during the war.

2

China's long war with Japan

JAY TAYLOR

Strategic, diplomatic, political, economic and idiosyncratic factors

When Chiang Kai-shek was born in 1887 and Mao Zedong in 1893, two geopolitical realities had dominated Asia for about four decades and would do so for the next fifty-eight years – a virtual century. These conditions were the awesome weakness of the long-time Asian hegemon, China, and the astonishing rise of the small nation of Japan. China was 35 times larger geographically than Japan and in 1937 had seven times the population, but it was far weaker in current and potential military strength.[1] The firepower gap was starkly evident in the 1927 'Jinan Incident' in China, when several thousand Chinese soldiers and civilians died, as compared to thirty-eight Japanese soldiers.

The real difference between the two forces was Japan's advanced civilian industry and its ability quickly to switch to and expand arms production. The industrial revolution in Japan, beginning only in the latter half of the nine-teenth century, was also able continually to enhance the relative quality and effectiveness of the complex weapons and fighting machines it designed, such as the A6M Zero fighter. For example, from 1937 to 1945, Japanese factories conceived and turned out about 76,000 war planes.[2] Before 1937, China assembled a few American and European fighters, but before and during the eight-year war it never itself produced a single operational, military aircraft.[3]

---

1 Population figures based on total Chinese population in 1937, including Manchuria and subsequently Japanese-occupied areas, which were about one-third of the total.
2 See United States Statistical Abstract 1957, p. 213. Of these, 50,000 were combat planes. Walter J. Boyne (ed.), *Air Warfare: An International Encyclopedia* (e-book, Santa Barbara, Calif.: ABC-CLIO Inc., 2002 [1966]), p. 433.
3 www.world-war-2-planes.com/japanese-aircraft.htm

In 1895, Japan's rise in industrial and military power first found its imperial destiny in its war on decadent China, with its seizure of Taiwan and effective hegemony over Korea. Next followed its 1914 assertion of a sphere of influence over China's Shandong Province, its humiliating 1915 'Twenty-one Demands' on China, its invasion and occupation of Manchuria in 1931, its bloody attack on Shanghai in 1932, and its subsequent creeping assertion of military authority over increasing parts of north China. Japan's long tradition of a military caste and the example of Western imperialism and racism shaped this triumph of ultra-nationalism and imperialism. After a short liberal period, by the early 1930s the model in Japan became the ultra-Nationalist, militarist and racist ideology of European fascism.

China was in good part to blame for its obscurantist failure to modernize as the West and Japan had. After the fall of the tottering Qing or Manchu dynasty in 1911, in addition to the sporadic but devastating aggression of Japan, China turned on itself – suffering almost twenty-five years of chaos, warlord rebellions, a persistent insurgency by the Chinese Communist Party (CCP; headed by Mao Zedong and backed by the Soviet Union) and a backwardness in almost every economic and technological field. Sun Yatsen died in 1925 and Chiang Kai-shek, a Sun loyalist and long-time officer in the National Revolutionary Army and Nationalist Party (the Guomindang or GMD), eventually succeeded him as both military and political leader of the Republic of China.

Chiang defeated the warlords one way or another and persuaded them to swear allegiance to the GMD and its new Chinese government. Having lived on and off in Japan for almost five years, he understood the great power and the potential for arrogance of the Japanese nation. His strategy was to gain time by appeasing Japan, but never officially to sign away Chinese sovereignty. Meanwhile, with German assistance – paid for with strategic minerals – he would try to build a modern army and an industrial economy, hoping to duplicate Japan's achievements.

Chiang's appeasement policy was not popular, but by 1936 critical papers and journals began to praise his management of the powerful threat. By then, geopolitical developments in Russia, Germany and Japan were dramatically reshaping international relations. In October that year, Germany, Italy and Japan signed the Anti-Comintern Pact, an accord that made clear that their primary enemy was the Soviet Union. The Pact further goaded the already strong interest of the Soviet dictator in boosting China against Japan, and thereby directing the latter's military efforts further into the vast swamp of the former. Pushed by Stalin, who had called for a global united front against fascism, Mao Zedong urged a united front with the GMD against Japan and, in effect, endorsed Chiang's leadership. The GMD and the CCP began secret negotiations on a united front in the autumn of 1936.

By that time, the Chinese army and the Nationalist Party seemed to have finally defeated the last post-1927 rebellious warlords and chased the Communists into an enclave in a remote northwest province. With the extensive German support provided during this period, Chiang had also created a small, elite force in the army and the beginning of a heavy industrial base. Despite high military expenses, the government even expected a balanced budget. Chiang's popularity was at an unaccustomed high. Then he was kidnapped by two warlords demanding an immediate united front with the Communists, to be led by Chiang. With Stalin again working behind the scenes, an oral agreement to this effect was reached and Chiang was released, to wild public acclaim.

The domestic political situation for Chiang, however, remained highly complex, and would continue to be so during the great war that was soon to come. For example, none of his future 'Big Four' Allies, while fighting the war, had to handle the likes of Chiang's warlord generals. As indicated above, Chiang also had a unique uneasy truce and nominal alliance with a foreign-armed and growing Communist party – the CCP. Chiang believed his new, superficial war partner constituted a 'disease of the heart', but the Japanese threatened Chinese civilization and posed the most immediate threat.[4] It was, he thought, a potentially lethal 'disease of the skin'.

To complicate matters further, once the war broke out, China would depend for key military support on the same foreign power that was the inspiration and patron of the CCP. Except for the threat of collapse, Chiang would have no leverage with the Soviet Union – nor, after 7 December 1941, with his new ally the United States. Despite all these problems, Chiang's military, political and diplomatic strategies were central to China's actions before and during the coming eight-year war. His influence on implementation would be considerably less strong and less successful. Nevertheless, his interaction with his own generals – including the warlords – and with Mao Zedong, Zhou Enlai, Joseph Stalin, Franklin Delano Roosevelt, the American General Joseph Stilwell, his own wife, Soong Mei-ling, and her brother, T. V. Soong, would form the central, human dynamic of China's life-or-death struggle, which would begin on 7 July 1937.

---

4 During the war, over a million Japanese civilians would move to China to oversee administration, education and other civilian fields in occupied areas. Already, Japanization was advanced in Korea and Taiwan.

Chiang and General Alexander Falkenhausen, his chief German advisor, both calculated that China needed two or more years to prepare for war with Japan. But they agreed that it might not be possible or advisable to appease Japan further. In either a time-limited or a long, drawn-out conflict, Chiang believed, China in 1937, for the first time in modern history, enjoyed two basic strategic assets essential to success. The first was the new spirit of patriotism among the Chinese people. This was a key condition for Chiang, who believed that Japan's most important source of power was not its weapons or its industry, but the 'do- or die' spirit of the Japanese people. For ten years, his diaries had continually underscored this grand, strategic assumption. His own unaccustomed popularity, beginning in 1936, and the united front with the CCP contributed to the country's sense of unity and the surge of nationalism. To most Chinese, the country seemed finally of one mind on the need for resistance. From experience, however, Chiang knew it was uncertain how long this national fervour and formal unity would last. Thus, in this respect, a moment of truth existed that might be gone in two years or less.

Chiang also believed that a second essential requirement for success in an all-out conflict with Japan was an alliance with a major power that could and would give the Chinese army modern arms and equipment. The only such power available was the Soviet Union. Informal Sino-Soviet talks had proceeded for some time on the possibility of Soviet aid and Moscow's quid pro quo – a Nationalist-Chinese united front with the CCP.

Chiang would have been pleased if Japan had sought its imperial adventures in Russia rather than China, but not to the extent of becoming partners with Japan (i.e. joining the Anti-Comintern Pact). Tokyo and Berlin had tried to interest the Nanjing government in this option, which Chiang's main internal GMD rival, Wang Jingwei, supported. Instead, Chiang wished to exploit the dynamic of Soviet fears to win not just a large programme of military aid, but even – if necessary – the direct involvement of the Red Army in the war with Japan.

Chiang knew that any direct – necessarily massive – intervention by the powerful Communist motherland would give the CCP enormous, very possibly decisive advantages in its post-war competition and likely civil war with Chiang's government. In reality, just such a dynamic would emerge in August 1945, when the Red Army would attack the Japanese in Manchuria with fatal consequences for the Nationalists. But that event would be eight years later. After the war began in 1937, Chiang, in vain, would several times urge Stalin to send the Red Army into China.

Almost all Chinese, except a small minority of collaborators, wanted to defeat the Japanese as soon as possible. But Chiang had a special reason to risk a Soviet invasion in order to cut short the war. His long suppression wars against the CCP had brought him to admire the courage and dedication of the Communist soldiers and political cadre compared to their GMD counterparts. He wanted to curtail the opportunity for the CCP – with its cult like organization and new legal status – to grow ever stronger as the war dragged on.

As with the welcome rise of patriotism in China, Chiang also calculated that while in 1937 Stalin seemed ready to provide serious military aid to China, he or a new Soviet leader might well abandon such an ideologically difficult and diplomatically risky gambit. This uncertainty was another key factor in Chiang's decision that it was time to stand up to Japan. Only two years later, this calculation proved prescient. Following the astounding Nazi-Soviet Pact of August 1939, Stalin would lose much of his interest in aiding Nationalist China against Japan.

But in 1937, Hitler was itching to attack the USSR, and in the caves of Yan'an, Mao understood that Stalin wanted the CCP seriously to aid the nationalist resistance against Japan. From the beginning, however Mao had no intention of living up to his commitment to follow the orders of the National Defence Council headed by Chiang. Mao aimed to avoid costly military action and to exploit the party's new legitimacy, building up the Communist armed forces, and expanding the area and population under their control.[5]

For the next eight years, Mao stuck to this strategy, with the exception of his 'Hundred Regiments offensive' against Japan in 1940, which was a costly defeat. Stalin may initially have expected Mao actually to cooperate with Chiang and take a significant part in the war fighting, as the Chinese Military Council directed. But after the first two critical years, the Soviet leader likely came to approve of Mao's priorities. Even in the desperate week after Germany attacked the USSR in June 1941, Stalin sent US$ 1 million to the CCP, but he would not urge Mao to take offensive action or even launch guerrilla attacks against the Japanese – unless Japan first attacked the USSR.[6]

Chiang accepted the GMD/CCP united front, despite knowing it was a sham, as the price to be paid to gain critical, large-scale aid from the Soviet

5 Zhang Guotao, *Rise of the Chinese Communist Party* (2 vols., Lawrence, University Press of Kansas, 1972), vol. II, pp. 533–9.
6 Alexander Pantsov with Steven I. Levine, *Mao: The Real Story* (New York: Simon & Schuster, 2007), p. 334.

Union. In 1937, he agreed with Falkenhausen that the Chinese army might win a defensive campaign against Japan in Shanghai, particularly if the Western powers early on pressured Japan to desist. The objective would not be to solidly defeat the Japanese army in Shanghai, but to fight them to a draw and compel Tokyo to make concessions in a temporary political settlement, giving China more time to close the still horrendous gap in military and economic power. But if this all-out initial fight with limited goals did not succeed and Shanghai was lost, Chiang was prepared to continue maximum resistance in a war of many years. For a decade, plans had been made and initial steps taken to evacuate key factories and skilled workers to the interior.

That war began in earnest on 14 August in Shanghai, when half a million soldiers and marines – Chinese and Japanese – engaged in fierce hand-to-hand slaughter, blowing each other apart with mortars, naval cannon and bombers. The battles in Shanghai in August–November 1937, Nanjing in December 1937 and, finally, Wuhan in October 1938 were gigantic and costly defeats for the Chinese army. They cost Chiang most of his remaining elite forces and 30,000 young officers in both the elite and regular forces. As Chiang anticipated, however, these heroic stands provided a powerful rallying cry for the Chinese people. The horrible atrocities that the Japanese committed on civilians – particularly in Nanjing – added immensely to national and international outrage.

Stalin also followed through on his commitment. As the Chinese fought fanatically in the streets of Shanghai, Soviet freighters and trucks began delivering what today (2013) would total several billion US dollars' worth of war planes, artillery, and other weapons and ammunition – equipment and supplies delivered at exceptionally low prices.[7] Soon, hundreds of Soviet war planes, many with Soviet pilots, would take part in the war. Meanwhile, in the autumn of 1938, the Soviet Union won a serious border conflict with Japan; but the real determinant of Tokyo's intentions toward the USSR were the actions of Germany. During that year, Hitler would cow England and France into rank appeasement. If the democracies remained neutral, a German-Japanese attack on the USSR might well succeed. Before some of the democratic leaders of the West fully discerned that this outcome would

---

7 *Chiang Kai-shek, Diaries* (Stanford University, Hoover Institution Archives, Chiang Kai-shek Collection, 2007), 2 and 11 November 1939, box 40, folder 1. Hereafter, *Chiang, Diaries*, Hoover. Zhang Baijia, 'China's Quest for Foreign Military Aid', in Mark Peattie, Edward J. Drea and Hans van de Ven (eds.), *The Battle for China* (Stanford University Press, 2001), pp. 288–93.

be the ultimate worst scenario for Russia, but also for China and the world, Chiang fully understood.

In October 1938, after the fall of Wuhan, Chiang told senior commanders that his initial strategy of aggressive defence had been successfully concluded. It was a blueprint aimed at inflicting high costs on the Japanese, while accepting many times the casualties of the enemy. In the next stage, he said, China's strategy would be 'to slow everything down...fighting a long war of attrition', and eventually turning 'defense into offense'.[8] In practice, this approach differed little from the concept he had followed from the start. Positional defence of key cities and areas continued to dominate Chinese strategy, including, where possible, ambushes, counter-attacks and flanking movements – many or most involving costly human wave assaults. Underscoring the profound gap between the capabilities of the weapons employed by the two sides, Chiang also decreed that in any large engagement with the Japanese, the Chinese side should normally possess a phenomenal six or nine times the number of divisions as the enemy.[9] One thinks of the Zulus against the British in the nineteenth century.

The great sacrifice required in Chiang's strategy and temperament was most tragically manifested in his decision in the spring of 1938 to destroy the dikes of the Yellow River, despite the hundreds of thousands and perhaps a million Chinese who could and would drown or die in the famine that followed. This action has been rightly condemned as a surpassingly inhuman act, but justified by some current mainland scholars on military grounds. It may also be explained in part as another example of Chiang's willingness to take the most extreme and brutal measures if he thought they might defeat the Japanese, save the nation, and protect his leadership and place in Chinese history. His bloody purge of the CCP in 1927 and his atrocities against the people of Taiwan in 1947, and again in 1949–50, were other illustrations of this temperament.

In 1939, the aggressive defence policy entailed another major 'stand and fight' loss in the defence of Nanchang, capital of Jiangxi Province, and the following year of Yichang, a key river port below the Yangzi gorges. By this time, Chiang and his generals were touting guerrilla warfare as a major part of China's strategy, but its success is difficult to measure. CCP guerrillas

---

8 Qin Xiaoyi (ed.), *Zong tong Jiang gong da shi chang pian chu gao* (Preliminary Draft of President Chiang's Chronological Biography), (12 vols., Taipei Chung Chang Cultural and Educational Foundation, various years), vol. IV, p. 1311. Hereafter, Qin Xiaoyi, *Zong tong*.

9 Chiang, *Diaries*, Hoover, 2 and 11 November 1938, box 40, folder 1.

and their commanding unit – the New 4th Army – however, were clearly controlling increasingly large areas behind Japanese lines, but avoiding casualties.

Only a major role in the two Allied campaigns – in Burma from 1942 to 1945, and a Chinese winter offensive in 1939–40 – would interrupt the purely defensive posture by the Chinese army before 1945. In the latter case, 450,000 Chinese troops gained ground in various areas, but soon were back to their starting points. At this time, with its heavy losses in men and weapons, the Chinese army, despite supplies and arms from the Soviets, was very likely weaker in equipment and training than before the war began, but its soldiers were still fighting and dying in large numbers.[10]

Chiang's strategy – including destruction of the dikes – reflected his recognition that China's continental size and its huge population gave it extraordinary strength and a high threshold of national pain. Through most of the war, the Japanese occupied only a quarter of the vast country.[11] Outside of Manchuria, many if not most of the occupied areas in the countryside were infested with anti-Japanese guerrillas – Nationalists and Communists. Because China's population was seven times that of Japan, per-capita military losses before Pearl Harbor may not have been very different, but after 1941 were likely lower than in Japan. Thus, the losses suffered by the Japanese people were probably felt as a whole more extensively than was the case in China. Conscription rates were also lower in China, and high school as well as college students and most graduates at these levels were exempt. Thus the well-to-do and the intellectual class in China were mostly not in danger unless they volunteered.[12]

The basic assumption of Chiang's sacrificial defence strategy was that the Japanese high command would eventually understand the prevailing geographic and demographic dynamic and settle for a stalemate. And they did until 1944, but even then, after launching a great, final offensive – Ichi-Go – they did not expect Chinese surrender. Shortly after the June 1941 German

---

10 Ma Chendu, 'Analysis of the Strategy of the Chinese Troops during the Sino-Japanese War', paper presented at the Harvard University Conference on Wartime China, Maui, January 2004, pp. 46–9.

11 Werner Gruhl, *Imperial Japan's World War II, 1931–1945* (Edison, NJ: Transaction, 2007), p. 35.

12 The Chinese population is taken as including the occupied areas. Ho Ping-ti, *Studies on the Population of China, 1368–1953* (Cambridge: Harvard University Press, 1959). Zhang Ruide, 'The Central Army from Whampoa to 1949', in David A. Graff and Robin Higham (eds.), *A Military History of China* (Boulder, Colo., and Oxford: Westview, 2002), pp. 200–1.

invasion of the USSR, Chiang predicted that Russia would ultimately defeat Hitler as it had Napoleon.[13] No doubt for the same reason he expected a Chinese victory.

But the Soviet Union at its worst moments in the war retained a large war industry and access to its allies. China had neither. Soon after the war began, however, Chiang concluded that China would achieve victory from an eventual full alliance with America. There was nothing craven about this strategy. Churchill and then Stalin, after they separately endured the Nazi onslaught, also understood that alliance with the United States was critical to their country's survival and, like Chiang, they did everything possible to bring America into the war.

In early 1939, Chiang learned – probably through the Soviet spy, Richard Sorge – that Moscow and Berlin were holding secret talks that could lead to an even more shocking alternative to the feared Western deal with Berlin – a German-Soviet alliance.[14] Thus in March 1939, Chiang urged London to conclude a defence pact with the USSR. Or else, he warned, Stalin would negotiate such a treaty with Hitler, who would then turn his Panzers to the West.[15] No doubt he notified FDR of this assessment as well. By now, he and his ambassador in Washington, Dr Hu Shi, had established a good relationship with the President and his key advisor, Harry Hopkins.

Since boyhood, President Franklin Delano Roosevelt had always had a sentimental attachment to China, and as a statesman he had long seen China as the future great and benevolent peacekeeper in Asia. Politically and philosophically, Roosevelt sympathized with the giant task that Chiang faced. FDR's personal and temperamentally based sympathy for Chiang as well as China would literally prevent the alliance from falling apart. Shortly after the 1937 Battle of Shanghai, Roosevelt made his 'quarantine the aggressors' speech. Chiang could see that the American President was not only sympathetic to China, but also recognized that Japanese conquests threatened US global interests and were symbiotically related to the German menace in Europe.

13 Owen Lattimore, *China Memoirs* (Tokyo University Press, 1990), pp. 135, 149, 155.
14 Important to Chiang's diplomacy was his indirect access to the extraordinary intelligence reporting to Moscow from Tokyo by the famous Soviet spy, Richard Sorge, that foresaw the extraordinary events in Europe in 1933–41. Jerrold Schecter and Leona Schecter, *Sacred Secrets* (Washington DC: Brassey's, 2002), pp. 15–16. Sorge, as a German correspondent in Tokyo, travelled to Chongqing, where he had meetings with Walter Stennes, the leader of Chiang Kai-shek's bodyguard, who was also a KGB agent.
15 *Chiang, Diaries*, Hoover, 29 May 1939, box 40, folder 8.

Chiang viewed the American President as the leader of a grand moral as well as political coalition, and he would adopt at times an almost reverential attitude toward him. When tough messages came from the White House, he assumed the words did not originate from Roosevelt. The dour Chiang was not good at personal relations; nevertheless, he and the gregarious, extrovert President clearly hit it off, not as friends, but as respected colleagues in the same tough business. Chiang's view of the temperament and behaviour of Americans, including Roosevelt, was shaped by the Generalissimo's close, pro-American relatives, including his wealthy wife, Soong Mei-ling, her brother, and brother-in-law.

In early 1938, Chiang explained his and no doubt his family's analysis of the American character. Great Britain, he wrote, was 'experienced and astute', 'a hard-nosed practitioner of *real politic*', and thus it was 'hard [for China] to lobby the British for help'. But the United States, he thought, was a 'democratic country...public opinion matters, and [thus] it is relatively easy to activate her chivalrous spirit'.[16] But during his often painful alliance with the United States, Chiang also came to believe that America's mercurial democratic system and the naivety that sprang from its 'idealistic approach to foreign affairs' also made it a frustrating, unpredictable and thus potentially undependable partner.

Chiang and his generals

The devastating losses of loyalist divisions at Shanghai weakened Chiang's control over the mixed bag of military units and commanders that, as Commander-in-Chief, he officially led. Most warlords, and some central army generals trained at China's early modern military academy, Baoding, did not like the aloof Chiang and his micromanagement of the battlefield. An exception among this group was his favourite, the soft-spoken, honest and competent general, Chen Cheng. The commanders who disliked Chiang or his strategy, however, still followed him throughout the war. No general officer defected. This was mostly because they were patriotic and did not want to upset the war effort by divisive scheming.

Probably most of the non-central as well as central army commanders also admired Chiang's steel determination, austere living in his several comfortable but bland quarters and, not least, his strong anti-communism. But most

---

16 Zhang Qiyun, *Dang Shi Gaiyao* (Outline of Party History) (Taipei: Zhonghua Wenwu Gong Ying she, 1979), vol. III, p. 973. *Chiang, Diaries*, Hoover, 25 June 1939, box 40, folder 9.

importantly, seemingly against all odds, he had gained critical assistance from a normally hostile great power and – ruling over a truncated and blockaded, but somehow working economy–fought the Japanese to a stalemate. Moreover, by the end of 1941, with his sharp card playing – as he must have reported it to his senior brass – he had manoeuvred the USA into virtually forcing the Japanese to attack America. All this seemed not a bad outcome. This leadership dynamic persisted until the Japanese Ichi-Go offensive in the spring of 1944, when there were two serious if short rumbles of plotting.[17] Finally, the generals and the Chinese people very likely admired Chiang's fortitude during the great defeats from 1937 to 1938 – usually staying in the battle zones until near the very end. The leading commanders would also stick with him until near the end of the post-VJ Day civil war, which after mid-1947 would be one debacle after another.

The history-shattering geopolitical developments in Europe beginning in 1939 were out of reach of Chiang or China's influence. He could, however, play some of these turns of history to China's advantage. Thanks again, indirectly, to Richard Sorge, Chiang often had good insight into the most secret of German and Japanese secrets, most especially – on the German side – the paradoxical, previously mentioned, German-Soviet Non-Aggression Pact of 23 August 1939. This accord did not surprise Chiang; nor did the German invasion of Poland on 1 September. But the massive Soviet sweep into western Poland on 17 September may have. Immediately after his deal with Hitler, Stalin quickly sent Chiang a message indicating that Soviet aid to China would continue, but in fact the Kremlin leader began to cut back on materiel and other assistance. Meanwhile, via the Comintern, he informed Mao that he could henceforth exercise more autonomy in major decisions. Articles critical of Chiang began to appear in the Moscow press. Stalin clearly felt the grave threat to the USSR had diminished for some time, thanks to his accord with Hitler.

The shock of the Bolsheviks joining with the Nazis cracked the isolationist wall in the United States. Chiang believed it was time to push Roosevelt a little harder. In a message to the President, he asked for 500–1000 military aircraft.[18] Then playing his 'collapse card' with the Americans for the first

---

17 For an insightful portrayal of Chiang's relations with his generals, see Steven Mackennon, 'The Defense of the Central Yangtze', in Peattie et al. (eds.), *Battle*, pp. 205–6.
18 Zhang Baijia, 'China's Experience in Seeking Foreign Military Aid and Cooperation for Resisting Japanese Aggression', paper presented at Harvard University Conference on Wartime China, Maui, January 2004, pp. 13–14. See also Qin Xiaoyi, *Zong tong*, vol. IV, pp. 1636–7; and Baijia, 'China's Quest', pp. 295–6.

time, he warned the US ambassador that China's continued resistance would depend upon 'substantial aid from the United States'. He asked again for a special force of US warplanes and volunteer pilots from the US Army Air Forces (USAAF). Roosevelt soon announced a new $100 million US loan to China, and told the American people that the Nazi-Bolshevik axis posed the gravest danger to America in its history. The next year he agreed to the organization and funding of the American-led and-staffed volunteer air group in the Chinese air force – the Flying Tigers. An informal Sino-American alliance had now emerged. Although the CCP continued to grow rapidly, defeat of the invaders remained Chiang's immediate, overriding preoccupation. The same month (January 1941) that he ordered the destruction of the CCP's New 4th Army – which had disobeyed his orders to move north of the old Yellow River course – he deployed 200,000 central troops from their position blocking the Communists in the northwest to oppose a Japanese offensive in Henan. In the operation, the Chinese lost 16,000 men. Mao Zedong reported this development to Moscow as evidence that three years after the war began, Chiang still gave precedence to fighting the Japanese, not the Communists.[19]

The fact that the Nationalists were carrying the greatest burden of the fighting was also made clear by Zhou Enlai in the autumn of 1939. Zhou reported to the Politburo and the Comintern that Nationalist and Communist Chinese military forces together had suffered 1.3 million casualties since July 1937. Of these losses, Zhou indicated, the CCP military accounted for less than 3 per cent of the total.[20] Another CCP document of December 1944 indicated a similar proportion of casualties since that time.

BARBAROSSA to Pearl Harbor

In February and then in April 1941 – once again, apparently based indirectly on Richard Sorge's reporting – Chiang informed the Americans about Operation BARBAROSSA – the German army's operational plan for the invasion of its soon-to-be-former ally, the USSR. Chiang wanted the attack to go ahead – as no doubt did Roosevelt and Churchill – but none of them wanted Germany to triumph over the giant state of Russia. Japan almost certainly would join in the attack when and if that appeared likely. So, the

19 Alexander Dallin and F. I. Firsov, *Dimitrov and Stalin, 1934–1943, Letters from the Soviet Archives* (New Haven, Conn.: Yale University Press, 2000), pp. 130–40.
20 Ibid., pp. 115–17, 120.

day before the 22 June invasion, Chiang asked Zhou Enlai – Mao's man in Chongqing during the war – to warn Stalin, who, when the message was passed on – as he had with Sorge's own direct reports to Moscow – did not listen.[21]

Before BARBAROSSA began, Roosevelt sent a personal representative to Chongqing, Laughlin Currie, to inform Chiang that the USA would soon provide China with another $45 million of arms and military equipment. Chiang expressed deep thanks, but then again asked for 1,000 warplanes and – in a new request – arms for three army divisions. The American government's continued benign view of the CCP also came up during this visit, indicating for Chiang a worrisome, fundamental difference with the USA.[22]

Soon, BARBAROSSA gave the Soviet Communists and Communists in general a renewed acceptability among democratic countries. The erstwhile Communist ally of Nazi Germany suddenly became a de facto and, after 7 December, an official ally of the democratic West and authoritarian China in the great history-shaking war against the Fascist totalitarians in Europe. At this time, Chiang still hoped the USSR would also end up as an all out ally in the Pacific War.

On the day of the German invasion of Russia, 22 June 1941, Chiang immediately aligned China with the Soviet Union, warned Stalin of a possible Japanese attack, proposed a Sino-Soviet treaty of alliance, and urged Roosevelt to support the USSR. That fateful day, Stalin was no doubt more worried than ever about the possibility that Tokyo would let the dogs of war loose into Siberia. Hitler was urging his tripartite partner in Tokyo to do just that.[23] But Tokyo no longer trusted the Germans and it ignored the invitation. Instead, it continued strategically to deploy southward into Indochina and likely conflict with the United States and the UK. In response, Roosevelt instituted – along with the British – a serious blow: an embargo of oil sales to Japan.

The next month, in a formal diplomatic note, the United States called on Japan to withdraw completely from China as well as Indochina, and to abandon its puppet governments in China.[24] No conceivable Japanese

21 *Chiang, Diaries*, Hoover, 13 April 1941, box 41, folder 10.
22 Baijia, 'China's Experience', pp. 43–4.
23 John W. Garver, *Chinese-Soviet Relations, 1937–1945* (New York: Oxford University Press, 1988), pp. 184–5.
24 United States note to Japan, 26 November 1941 (*Department of State Bulletin*, 5:129, 13 Dec. 1941).

government at the time could accept the total surrender of its enormous and costly gains in China over almost fifty years. Tokyo proposed a 'cooling-off' period with the USA, and Hitler jumped in, offering – as he had early in the war – to broker a Sino-Japanese peace treaty.[25] Chiang quickly told Roosevelt and Churchill that if the USA accepted Tokyo's proposal, China would have to accept the German offer. In response, Churchill cabled FDR urging no softening of the American stand. The President had learned of the major Japanese military deployments for war in Southeast Asia and he stuck to the original demands.[26] Chiang believed that he himself had 'saved the situation at the last moment'.[27] So it was that on 7 December 1941, at Pearl Harbor, Japan struck the famous first blow.

After hearing the news from Hawaii, Chiang immediately moved to formalize the alliance and demonstrate that China would be an active and effective partner. He immediately proposed to Roosevelt that China, the United States, Britain and the USSR declare war on all the Axis Powers and pledge no separate peace. He stressed with his colleagues and Roosevelt that an objective 'of special importance' was to bring the Soviet Union into the Pacific conflict.[28] He suggested that this colossal move be made a condition of US aid to the USSR. Nothing came of the effort, but it underscored once more Chiang's priority of defeating the Japanese as quickly as possible, even if it took Soviet intervention in China. But this grand idea was, in Chiang's mind, also linked to a new objective: ending or limiting the Anglo-American global war strategy baldly stated as 'Europe first'.

In practice, the catchphrase initially meant 'Russia first'. This priority made sense, as Germany appeared to be the strongest enemy and it was at the gates of Moscow, on the verge of an earth-shattering victory in the USSR. In contrast, the war in China seemed stalemated, and the only critical threat was a Japanese advance into Burma – and possibly India. Thus, among the non-Anglo-American Allies, the Soviet Union would by far be the largest recipient of US and British aid.

The Combined Chiefs of Staff (CCS) of the American and British armed forces would also henceforth determine worldwide war strategy, except in the Soviet Union and Eastern Europe, but also, in effect, in China. It set priorities subject to the British and American leaders' approval. Then, Chiang

---

25 *New York Times*, 4 December 1941.
26 See Henry Stimson diary entry for 26 November 1941, Yale University Library, Manuscripts and Archives, MS 465.
27 *Chiang, Diaries,* Hoover, 25 December 1941, folder 17.
28 Owen Lattimore, *China Memoirs* (University of Tokyo Press, 1990), p. 161.

would be notified. The CCS established a Munitions Assignment Board for dividing *all* Anglo-American war production among themselves and all their Allies, including the USSR and China.

For Chiang Kai-shek, the threat to China's interests posed by the strategy of 'Europe first' confirmed the value of a Soviet Red Army attack on Japanese forces in China. Such dramatic action would put the war on the Asian mainland on the same scale and level of urgency as that in Europe. Chiang was right to worry about the implications of the 'Europe first' policy. Until the last twelve months or so of the war, few American land force arms or other Lend-Lease aid would go to Chinese ground forces actually fighting the Japanese inside China. The great bulk went to those in combat in Burma or training for that campaign.[29] Likewise, the only American air unit fighting in China – the US Fourteenth Air Force, successor to the Flying Tigers – received far fewer warplanes than USAAF commands flying in the European and Pacific theatres. Of the $50 billion of US Lend-Lease deliveries to all the Allies during the war, less than US $2 billion went to China.[30]

A common explanation for the small delivery of war planes and supplies to the Fourteenth and of Lend-Lease items to China (compared to the UK and the USSR) is that for more than half the war little tonnage could be flown to China over the great 'Hump' of the Himalayan foothills. Except for this route, China was, in effect, blockaded. But for more than three years, the low volume of Hump traffic, according to US Army Air Transport Service commanders of that operation, was due 'above all, to insufficient multi-engine transport aircraft suited to the difficult flight conditions'. By the spring of 1943, US war production of military planes of all sorts was skyrocketing. More than 300,000 aircraft, including 22,000 transports, were turned out by VJ Day. Meanwhile, by August 1943, the German army was in general retreat in the Soviet Union, mitigating the urgent need to send huge numbers of US war planes to the Soviets above all other priorities.

The day after Pearl Harbor, Chiang showed his dedication to the Allied cause, sending his remaining, best-armed 80,000 troops to Burma. The Flying Tigers, with seventy-five serviceable P-40s, were the most effective combat

---

29 He Yingqin interview with Central News Agency reporters, Chongqing, 20 September 1944. 'News of the Central News Agency', 7 October 1944, in Qin Xiaoyi (ed.), *Zhonghua Minkguo Zhongyao shiliao chubian dui er Kanzhan shichi* (Preliminary Compilation of Important Historical Material of the ROC), Resist Japan Period, pt. 3: *Zhanshi Waijiao* (Wartime Diplomacy) (Taipei: KMT Historical Archives, 1981), vol. 1, pp. 512–14.

30 Approximately another $700 million of Lend-Lease arrived in China after VJ Day.

squadrons that Chiang possessed. He assigned all of them to the Burma campaign.[31] These early moves reflected Chiang's understanding that the more China helped to defeat the Japanese, the more influence it would have in achieving international political, diplomatic, economic and military support during and after the war.

The Japanese move into Burma would not only shut down the Burma Road, but would also threaten India and the soon-to-be built US military transport airfields in Assam, a state in the northeast region of India. Chiang worried about India. In February, he rushed to Calcutta and won Gandhi's promise that the Indian National Congress would do nothing to help Japan's war of aggression against China.[32]

The Allies named Chiang Supreme Commander of the China theatre and Roosevelt publicly proclaimed China as one of the 'Big Four'. FDR also quickly approved an unconditional US $500 million loan to the Chinese government. In his first military order after 7 December, Chiang instructed troops under General Xue Yue to move a large force toward Guangzhou to relieve pressure on the British defending Hong Kong. But the colony fell quickly. A follow-up battle over the wasted city of Changsha was a rare victory for the Chinese – and, at that point, for the Allies as well.

Claire Chennault – a retired USAAF colonel and a favourite of the Chiangs – commanded the US Fourteenth Army Air Force. Chennault devised a naively simple strategy for winning the war principally by air power. With the support of only 150 or so war planes (later raised to 255) and 30–40 per cent replacements per month, Chennault believed, the Allies could not only defeat the Japanese in China, but also disrupt its key supply lane through the East China Sea. Chiang accepted Chennault's assumptions and enthusiastically backed the concentration on air power as the quickest way to defeat the Japanese. Chennault's plan was remarkably unsophisticated, not only in the small number of war planes it required, but also in his and Chiang's belief that the Chinese army could defeat a concerted Japanese offensive to capture and destroy the necessary new airfields.

After the collapse of the first Burma campaign (see below), Chiang correctly assumed that almost all US Lend-Lease assigned to the Chinese army would for some time be devoted to the second campaign in Burma. This situation lasted for more than two and a half years. This was another

---

31 Claire Chennault, *Way of a Fighter* (Tucson, Ariz.: James Thorvardson & Sons, 1949), pp. 126–7.
32 Qin Xiaoyi, *Zong tong*, vol. v, p. 1857.

reason that Chiang accepted the emphasis on air power. By also accepting Chennault's impossible numbers, however, Chiang weakened future efforts to obtain many more aircraft than called for in the American general's plan. Likewise, the air strategy weakened efforts to get the War Department to even propose possible strategies for the arming and training of ninety Chinese army divisions, a total Roosevelt accepted at the 1943 Cairo Conference.

By the spring of 1944, the Sino-American air units had achieved air superiority over China. This was due largely to Tokyo's transfer of most of its China-based combat planes to the Pacific. But until late in the war, the still very small number of Chinese air force and American war planes available for operations inside the vast theatres of Burma and China mitigated the effect of superiority.

Even with their increased numbers in 1944, the combat planes of the Sino-American air units in China could not stop the steady advance of the enormous Ichi-Go ground offensive beginning at that time. Shortage of fuel supplies flown over the Hump, which reflected the shortage of transport aircraft, contributed to the problem. Consequently, until the summer of 1945 – except for the important, but still limited gain in air support – the Chinese army was no better prepared than four years before to launch offensive operations against the Japanese army in China. Still, after seven years, China was fundamentally unconquered.

Domestic issues

The survival of the domestic economy in the free areas of the nation, including a small-calibre ordinance industry, was as much the core reason for China's survival as was Soviet aid and the sacrifices of the Chinese army. The civilian economy of Nationalist China was under near-blockade even before the Japanese took Rangoon. With the loss of that port, except for small-scale border trade, civilian imports and exports virtually ended. But thanks to Chinese ingenuity, farmers, households, small industries and local shops made do. Thirty million refugees added to the Herculean task of maintaining stability and avoiding mass hunger or starvation. Nature for a time cooperated. There was not a great famine until the 1942 drought in Henan Province, in which 1 to 5 million died and the limited efforts of the government to provide relief were overwhelmed.

Monumental budget deficits were also unavoidable. Beginning in 1942, spending by the American military added to the flow of yuan, which by

1944 were flooding free China. Inflation rose twenty times in the first four years of war and higher in the last four, but at neither period was it as astronomical as it would be during the future civil war. The grain tax collected in kind fed millions of urban dwellers, refugees and soldiers. There was ample corruption, but the system still worked.

Through all eight years of war, however, three domestic demons remained largely untreated – inflation, the land tenure problem and corruption. Chiang believed that serious measures to deal with these maladies would be highly destabilizing politically and could safely be put off until the end of the war. With a largely subsistence and barter rural economy, the great majority of Chinese in the free areas were little affected by the fiscal problem. Thus China survived huge budget deficits, sky-high but not prodigious inflation, an increasing level of graft in the military and the bureaucracy – particularly after the Americans arrived – and no substantial effort to reform land-ownership. During the eight years of war, the CCP also largely avoided a confiscatory land reform programme.

Stilwell

In March of 1942, General Stilwell took up his often conflicting positions in East Asia, including as Chief of Staff to Chiang Kai-shek in the latter's role as Supreme Allied Commander for the China theatre. Chiang and Stilwell immediately disagreed on military strategy in Burma. Stilwell pressed hard to launch an all-out counter-offensive to retake Rangoon, but Chiang thought the Japanese too strong and preferred to retreat to north Burma. In fact, the Japanese forces were even larger than Chiang believed. Chiang soon distrusted his new Chief of Staff and in the coming battles undercut Stilwell's authority. Soon, the Allied force, commanded overall by the British, was overwhelmed and retreated in confusion. Stilwell – separated from the Chinese armies he commanded – made no effort to join large, retreating, but cohesive segments. Instead, he and his staff 'walked out' through western Burma to India. Chiang believed Stilwell had deserted his troops, but not wanting to embarrass FDR, he did not ask for Stilwell's recall.[33]

The Chiang–Stilwell mutual animosity, however, was soon apparent. Roosevelt understood that whatever the merits of the quarrel, the situation was unacceptable in the middle of a fierce world war. Yet it dragged on for

---

33 Qin Xiaoyi, *Zong tong*, 14 May 1942, p. 1922.

almost three years, poisoning Sino-American relations, seriously complicating the conduct of the war, and ending China's chance to play a key role in the endgame of the Pacific War.

At the Cairo Conference in November 1943, Chiang and FDR had several hours of conversation. They agreed that the future Japanese government should be left to the Japanese people and that Western colonialism must be dismantled after the war. Chiang promised a government of national unity with the Communists, while Roosevelt endorsed the return of Taiwan and Manchuria to China and – as noted – promised that America would arm and train ninety Chinese divisions.[34] Then the President gave Chiang the big news. With Chongqing's approval, the USA would build four large airfields in Sichuan Province, to support B-29 bombing missions against Japan originating in India.[35]

But a few weeks later (December 1943), Chiang reacted foolishly when Roosevelt reneged on his firm pledge in Cairo that he would support Chiang's insistence that a British amphibious landing be part of the coming second Burma campaign. Seeking to leverage the matter to gain American concessions, Chiang warned Roosevelt that China was on the brink of military and financial disaster. He also refused to send a US-armed and-trained Chinese multi-divisional 'Y Force' into Burma as part of the second Burma campaign, until the amphibious landing was agreed to. All this seemed to confirm Stilwell's portrayal of Chiang as a poor, unpredictable ally. Even worse were Chiang's threatened measures to squeeze more earnings from American military spending within China. The game did not work. This episode gave Stilwell the upper hand in Washington over how to deal with Chiang. As a result, Stilwell abandoned the plans to kill Chiang that he had separately asked two subordinates to devise.[36]

In mid-1944, things went badly again in Burma, although Chiang had finally sent in the Y Force. Meanwhile, also uncertain was the outcome of a savage battle between British-led colonial troops and a large Japanese force that had invaded India and attacked Imphal. At this time, the Japanese Ichi-Go

34 *Chiang, Diaries,* Hoover, 17, 23, 24 November 1943, box 43, folder 10.
35 'The Superfortress Takes to the Skies', in Daniel L. Haulman, *The US Army Air Forces in World War II. Hitting Home: The Air Offensive Against Japan* (Washington DC: Air Force History and Museums Program, 1999) (http://permanent.access.gpo.gov/lps51153/air-forcehistory/usaaf/ww2/hittinghome/hittinghomepg4.htm – accessed 12 October 2014).
36 Frank Dorn, *Walkout with Stilwell* (New York: Thomas W. Crowell, 1971), pp 75–9. And for the second incident, Thomas H. Moon and Carl F. Eifler, *The Deadliest Colonel* (New York: Vantage Press, 1975), pp. 145–6.

offensive of almost half a million soldiers, having cleared out Henan Province, rolled into Hunan, and were set to attack Changsha for the third time. This was the biggest Japanese offensive of the whole Pacific War – one that Stilwell had insisted would not happen. In a pessimistic message to Marshall on 22 May 1944, Stilwell reported that the whole Burma campaign was stalled. Opening a land route to China, he prophesied, would require an American army corps.[37] None of these calamities could be avoided, he added, without a 'shakeup of the British and the Chinese high command' – that is, his two Supreme Command superiors, Louis Mountbatten and Chiang Kai-shek, had to go. But by mid-June, Imphal would become the biggest defeat for the Japanese army in its entire history up to that point, and Stilwell himself would declare a major victory in north Burma – without a US Army corps. The principal exception to this good news was the Ichi-Go offensive in China itself, which continued to roll over defending Chinese forces.

In July, the President signed a message orchestrated by Stilwell asking Chiang to give Stilwell 'real military authority' over all Chinese forces in the field. Chiang was stunned, but played for time. He now insisted that China was 'not on the brink of collapse', and convinced Roosevelt to appoint a mediator between himself and Stilwell. Meanwhile, during the May to August battles for Changsha and Hengyang, Chiang grew suspicious that the two respected generals who commanded the defence of the two cities were plotting against him. He refused to send them supplies. Instead, he sent large relief forces, which could not break through. Meanwhile, Stilwell intended to do as little as possible to help defend these cities. He made clear to his staff that he wanted to avoid a military success for Chiang as long as his own appointment to head the Chinese army was pending. Changsha and Hengyang fell that summer. In October, Stilwell rashly pushed his contest with Chiang to a head. Chiang finally demanded his recall. Roosevelt agreed and appointed General Albert C. Wedemeyer to replace him.

Grand strategy

Long-term thinking about the China theatre by Anglo-Americans command-ers early in the war was superficial. At first, Washington and London seemed to think of China's role as focused simply on doing what they had been doing

37 Charles F. Romanus and Riley Sunderland, *Stilwell's Command Problem* (Washington DC: U.S. Army Center of Military History, 1978), pp. 362–4.

for years – tying down a million Japanese troops in China proper and Manchuria, while fighting to recover Burma and open a land route to China. At the Casablanca Conference in January 1943, Roosevelt and Churchill envisioned a more critical role for China. The two leaders informed Chiang that after the Burma operation reopened the port of Rangoon, supplies and equipment could be sent to US airfields in China for offensive air operations against Japanese shipping and, ultimately, Japan proper. This fitted in with Chiang and Chennault's strategic thinking.

The possibility of an even more fundamental shift resulting in a truly key role for China soon became apparent. The heavy losses of young Americans in the island-hopping campaign increasingly disturbed the President. In a February 1943 speech, he explained that the United States did not expect to continue just advancing 'island to island across the vast expanse of the Pacific'. Instead, he said, 'great and decisive' actions against the Japanese would be taken 'to expel the invaders from the soil of China'. Harry Hopkins, Roosevelt's principal advisor, told T. V. Soong that 'The best minds among American strategists had come to believe that China should be the principal base of operations (against Japan)'.[38]

Stimulated by these reports, Chiang asked Roosevelt to concentrate resources over the next few months on launching Chennault's air offensive by building more airfields and delivering more American war planes and related supplies to China.[39] Inexplicably, he did not specifically call for more arms and training for the Chinese army. A few months later (August 1943), at the Quebec Conference, FDR and Churchill officially reaffirmed that China could provide the best bases for attacking Japanese shipping, bombing Japan with B-29 bombers, and eventually invading the Japanese home islands. Allied troops would land on the coast of China, while retrained and rearmed Chinese armies would advance from the west. The epic invasion of Japan would in part, or even largely, be staged from China, with large numbers of Chinese as well as American troops. This was a fundamental reconceptualization of the grand scenario for the second half of the war. Chiang was highly pleased.[40]

A few months later, however, the grand strategy shrunk into oblivion. Chiang's anguished but contrived reports in December 1943 that China was

---

38 T. V. Soong, 'Note on Conversation with Harry Hopkins on August 16, 1943', T. V. Soong Papers, Hoover Institution Archives, Stanford University, box 61, folder 6.
39 Romanus and Sunderland, *Stilwell's Mission to China* (Washington, US Army Center of Military History, 2002), pp. 318–320.
40 Ibid.

on the brink of collapse seemed to confirm Stilwell's portrayal of the near-total disaster the war effort faced in China and Burma. At the same time, the successes of the Japanese Ichi-Go offensive suggested that the US airbases in China – even the B-29 staging fields in far Sichuan – were at risk. This caused the Anglo-American Combined Chiefs of Staff to decide that the final defeat of Japan would, after all, be sought without a major land campaign on the mainland of China or the use of Chinese troops in an invasion of Japan.

In his 27 May message, Marshall informed Stilwell of this decision. Hereafter, he wrote, the highest priority for the Allies in China and Burma would be to build on the air effort and increase the Hump tonnage for this purpose, but with no mention of a high priority for this limited mission or even its goal, and nothing about the Chinese army. The Anglo-American strategists had decided that building up the Chinese army to fight the Japanese in China and Japan was not a priority. Thus China would not be a major player in the Allied invasion of the imperial home islands.

The B-29s in China dropped a small tonnage of bombs on southern Japan, and in January 1945 moved to the Marianas, ending China's last finger-hold on a strategic mission striking directly at Japan. In February 1945, a State Department policy paper stated that 'to make (China) a strong power' did not appear 'practical'. Implicitly reflecting the still benign, official view of the CCP, the paper explained that US interest in a democratic China did not mean necessarily that 'China should be united under the Generalissimo'.[41] Mao's 'New Democracy' was clearly the unspoken alternative. Washington made clear to Wedemeyer that no US divisions would be available for combat operations in China against the Japanese.[42] Thus the prospect of a giant Sino-American army advancing up the coast of China and eventually landing on a Japanese beach was rejected for good.

Wedemeyer's command position was streamlined and more manageable than Stilwell's conflicting assignments. Most importantly, he was freed from commanding Chinese operations in Burma. Shortly after Wedemeyer's arrival, the Japanese achieved their main mission – control of a rail line from Southeast Asia to Korea, and from there, by sea, to Japan. Once obtained, however, the railway would prove of limited use, as American and Chinese war planes blew up tracks, bridges and tunnels at will. Moreover, in the countryside, Communist guerrillas were increasingly in control behind

---

41 Herbert Feis, *The China Tangle: The American Effort in China from Pearl Harbor to the Marshall Mission* (Princeton University Press, 1953), p. 277.
42 Ibid., p. 342.

Japanese lines. Yet in 1945, Ichi-Go pushed on, although behind the advance, the Japanese mostly occupied only rail lines and railheads.

The last year

After winning the Combined Chiefs' approval, Wedemeyer brought in as reinforcements against Ichi-Go two Chinese Y Force divisions from Burma. He also shifted increasing Hump supply tonnage to the divisions in China fighting the Japanese, and by July 1945 had withdrawn all Chinese troops from Burma to fight in China. After Wedemeyer's arrival, relations between the American and Chinese military and between the American ground and air generals themselves became much more collegial. Wedemeyer had shown that in the assignment he now had, diplomacy was as vital as military skills.

The Ledo or Stilwell Road – as Chiang named it – linking up India with the old Burma Road, opened on 12 January 1945. In the last month of the war, the tonnage carried from India to China by this road would be only about 7 per cent of that delivered by the hundreds of US Air Transport Service transports by then flying from Assam. The port of Rangoon fell to the British on 1 May 1945, and it and the rail line to Lasio were soon again shipping boxcars of supplies to China. Churchill and Chennault were right. By the time the road was finished, it was out of date.

In early 1945, at the Yalta Conference in Russia's war-devastated province of the Crimea, Roosevelt and Churchill suffered from the ill-advised belief that they must offer concessions to bring the USSR into the war with Japan. Thus they agreed to recognize Mongolian independence and certain Soviet rights in Manchuria – territories historically recognized as Chinese. When Chiang learned of the matter he was incensed at the offence to the sovereign rights of an ally, but also because he had intended to offer some of the same concessions in negotiating a future friendship treaty with the USSR. In return, Chiang hoped to obtain some meaningful commitments from Stalin of no interference in Chinese internal affairs. But, once again, Chiang had absolutely no leverage. The Sino-Soviet Treaty of Friendship and Alliance – signed on 14 August 1945 – gave only a perfunctory pledge that the Soviet government would not interfere in China's internal affairs – nothing about non-interference from the Communist Party of the Soviet Union.

The last wartime summit was in Potsdam, Germany, from 17 July to 2 August 1945. Chiang was back home in Chongqing. He was only notified *ex post facto* of the Potsdam Declaration on the terms of surrender sent to

Tokyo. This was another insult to the ally that had been fighting the Japanese for eight years and had lost more soldiers and civilians in this struggle than all the other Allies in the Pacific War combined. But Chiang was busy writing a long analysis of the post-war dynamics as he saw them. He perceived that the coming Cold War between the Soviet Union and the United States would dominate world affairs. But he did not suggest how this dynamic might play out in regard to his main post-war concern – dealing with the USSR and the CCP. He simply assumed that if the national government tried to 'suppress' the CCP, Stalin would support Mao and 'the outlook [for nationalist China] would then be bleak'.[43] This was another prescient judgment.

Nevertheless, Chiang concluded that China should focus on trying to establish friendly and cooperative relations with the USSR, while emphasizing economic ties with America. He observed, however, that he would also have to show that – if necessary – the Chinese National Army was prepared to take on the CCP militarily in Manchuria and elsewhere. The USA, he knew, would not want to see China become a Communist country, much less half of a prospective Sino-Soviet bloc. But Chiang's brief reference to America in his analysis suggests he understood that the highest post-war priority regarding China for the already rapidly routinizing American Republic would be to avoid getting involved in a Chinese civil war.

The Ichi-Go offensive was finally turned back in a Chinese counter-offensive in the spring of 1945. This was the long-awaited turning of the tide. Wedemeyer and the Chinese generals then began planning a historic counter-offensive, which, according to plans, would begin by capturing a port on the China coast. On 8 August, the first A-bomb fell on Japan. The next day, 750,000 Soviet Red Army soldiers stormed into Manchuria. One hundred thousand of Mao's men were not far behind. Japan's official surrender came seven days later.

Chiang was not in a celebratory mood. He knew he would have to lead a vast, complex, difficult resumption of central authority in the huge Japanese-occupied areas. Economic and fiscal stability in the newly reunited giant economy would be a high, but difficult priority. Tens of millions of refugees and evacuees would have to be helped home. Two million Japanese soldiers and civilians would need to be repatriated. But in Chiang's mind, looming above everything, was the Chinese Communist Party and its now 1.5 million soldiers, reinforced with a 2 million-man militia spread over 310 counties in

43 *Chiang, Diaries*, Hoover, 28 July 1945, box 44, folders 8, 13.

north and northwest China, plus large areas behind Japanese, now Nationalist lines. As Chiang had feared, the CCP and its army had in four years grown at a phenomenal rate.

Eight years before, after the bloody defeats at Shanghai, Nanjing and elsewhere, Chiang had been confident that China would persevere and win a long, protracted war against mighty Japan. But now he was pessimistic about the chances of keeping the Soviet Union from interfering in the twentieth century's second great struggle over the future of China, and about the results of such a failure. Within a year, the possibility of a retreat to Taiwan was on his mind. But still, he would try both negotiation and war with the CCP. He immediately invited Mao to Chongqing. 'Talk, talk–fight, fight' (*tan, tan, da, da*) was a favourite slogan of both Mao and Chiang.

Wartime corruption in China would be compounded when, after VJ Day, hundreds of thousands of senior GMD, government and military officials and officers ended eight years of sacrifice and personal hardships with a powerful sense of entitlement. Chiang appointed many technocrats to key central government posts, but handed out governorships and other provincial posts with the scrutiny of a drunk sailor. After VJ Day, the long, contained effect during the war of corruption and the other two major domestic evils – the land issue and inflation – convinced Chiang that he probably had another three or four years before they would cripple his efforts to defeat the Communists. Misgovernment in general, however, would further feed the three afflictions and eat away at the morale of the people. Together with critical covert aid to the CCP from the USSR, these failures would bring about Chiang Kai-shek's final defeat on the mainland.

Commentary

That China prevailed in the long war of attrition and atrocities inflicted by Japan was testimony not only to its new patriotism and the sacrifices of its soldiers, but also to the organizational and innovative talents of the Chinese people, as well as their social cohesion and discipline. This was a culture that thirty-odd years later – once freed of war and doctrinaire Marxism – would ignite the miracle take-off of China in the era of Deng Xiaoping. But it almost certainly would have blossomed much earlier if either Japan's aggression or the Soviet Union's interference had not happened. Chiang Kai-shek would show on Taiwan that he was a political authoritarian – at times, extremely brutal – but also a pragmatic and effective modernizer. On the mainland, however, the great war had clearly given Mao the opportunity to challenge the Nationalists, who, unlike the Communists, were weakened, not strengthened by the eight-year struggle.

It seems incomprehensible that China was receiving less than 2 per cent of America's Lend-Lease programme of US $50 billion while it was tying down a million Japanese troops and fighting bigger land battles in Asia than the Americans and British. If China, beginning in 1943, had received more or less 8 per cent of US war production of fighters, bombers and air transports, and Chiang had emphasized modernizing his ground forces as well as the air war against Japan, by the spring of 1944, the Chinese army could have possessed many more air squadrons and modern army divisions than in fact it had at that time. Conceivably, Ichi-Go would have failed early on and the Chinese could have marched to the sea. This is highly uncertain, but China, in any event would have ended the war with a significantly stronger army, and probably closer ties with the Americans and a better image in the United States. This could have impacted the post-war political dynamic, including Soviet and American positions on the looming prospect of a Chinese civil war.

On the other hand, if there had been no atom bombs with which to quickly end the war with Japan, the Combined Chiefs would have actually faced the daunting task of invading Japan. If, in the meanwhile, the Chinese army fighting in China itself had been given enough resources to capture a major Chinese port, as Wedemeyer, Chiang and, earlier, Stilwell intended, the idea of sharing the casualties with China could again have become powerfully appealing to the Americans. The Allied landing could have equalled or possibly overshadowed Normandy, and among the soldiers streaming ashore, a large number – perhaps a majority – could have been troops trained by Stilwell and Wedemeyer. Such a scenario obviously could have had far-reaching and positive consequences for post-war China – and Chiang Kai-shek.

Chiang and his supporters had many grievances against the treatment they received at the hands of their US ally. Chiang never knew who would be the source of his next crisis: the Japanese, the CCP, the Soviet Union, internal foes in his own regime or his American ally. Washington and London treated China as a third- not a second-rate ally. But the Sino-American alliance was likely the only realistic circumstance within decades or longer in which China could have defeated Japan and fully recovered its lost sovereignty.

The US alliance would also provide the context and leverage with which (1) Chiang would successfully press all the Western democracies to end their unequal treaties with China and their outlandish 'rights', such as extraterritoriality; (2) the Western powers would recognize China's sovereignty over Tibet and Xinjiang, as well as Taiwan and Manchuria; and (3) China would formally – although hardly in terms of relative military and economic strength – assume its position among the most eminent great powers as a permanent member of the United Nations Security Council.

The Sino-American alliance in the Second World War should have sealed Chinese-American friendship for generations. But it was not to be. Beginning in the period of Deng Xiaoping, however, this relationship began to change in fundamental ways. Despite many disputes and political/philosophical differences on matters such as human rights, as well as the existence of hawkish elements on both sides, extraordinary economic integration, as well as other strong geopolitical common interests, provided the framework for an increasingly competitive, but still basically positive relationship. A failure to find a peaceful path to China's long-term rise to military parity with America may eventually lead to a collapse in this critical détente of virtually half a century. But it is China's rise itself that has led to a Sino-American relationship that seems increasingly marked by a more equal, and thus perhaps lasting status than Chiang Kai-shek ever enjoyed

Despite his Aryan racism, Hitler dreamed of allying with China's teeming masses. As we have seen, in 1936, Chiang Kai-shek could have opted to join the Anti-Comintern Pact instead of continuing his ten-year preparation for a prolonged and devastating war with Japan. If Japan had been willing militarily to pull out completely from China, but with China's position on Manchuria left unsettled, Chiang might have considered this path. If so, history very likely would have been changed in a powerfully and dramatically unpleasant way. The Axis could have destroyed and divided up the Soviet Union, and the new superpower of Germany possibly could have been the first to develop an atom bomb. Perhaps such a Nazi regime would still be around today. But Chiang, in fact, gave this option no serious consideration, and instead began the bloody and, for years, mostly lonely struggle to save China, thereby conceivably also rescuing the USSR and perhaps the world.

3

French grand strategy and defence preparations

MARTIN S. ALEXANDER

Introduction

This chapter explores the components of French strategic analysis and decision-making down to the defeat of June 1940. Almost twenty years after France's capitulation that summer, General Maurice Gamelin, Chief of French National Defence Staff since January 1938 and Commander-in-Chief in 1939–40, a man highly respected in France and abroad until May 1940, defined the essence of the grand strategy adopted against the Axis. 'We could hope', he reflected, 'that time would work for us, if we could use it to full advantage, the British and ourselves. I have not changed my mind.'[1] The strategy, and how it unravelled in May and June 1940, are the focus of this chapter. It proposes that the leaders of France, those wearing suits as much as those wearing uniforms, had no choice from the mid-1920s onward but to adopt the grand strategy, though not all the operational campaign plans, that they utilized in 1939–40.

French security policy in the 1920s

A European power – one conscious of its relative decline compared with a generation before – France was both blessed and cursed with a global strategic footprint. The legacies of French grandeur from the eras of Louis XIV and Louis XV, and of Napoleon Bonaparte, challenged early twentieth-century French leaders to match past glories and contemporary expectations. The attrition resulting from France's central part in the fighting of 1914–18 further complicated the strategic calculations required of those who aspired

---

1 France: Service Historique de la Défense-Terre (hereafter: SHD-Terre): Fonds Maurice Gamelin, 1K224 (Carton 7), 'Les causes de nos revers en 1940' (undated c.1956–7).

to lead the Republic. If Britain was a 'weary Titan' after 1918, France was an exsanguinated neighbour.[2] Over thirty of metropolitan France's *départements* had smaller populations in 1919 than at the census of 1913. Around 1,358,000 Frenchmen under the age of thirty-five were killed in the war, with another 4,266,000 wounded (many so gravely that they were permanently unemployable). Massive damage was done to industrial facilities, farmland and French homes.[3]

In 1919, France stood among the victorious Allies. Yet France was not much better than a 'survivor of a kind' (to adapt the title of the autobiography of Guy Chapman, an eminent historian of the French Third Republic).[4] Moreover, France was a territorially satisfied power, one whose grand strategy focused on upholding the new status quo. French thinking about the relationships between diplomatic commitments and military structures was driven by defensive and even idealistic motivations. In his book about Louis Barthou, Foreign Minister from February to October 1934, Robert J. Young notes the French outlook:

> in the face of a Nazi regime already rearming, what made sense was to postpone disarmament discussions until collective security pacts obviated the need for large standing armies. That had been France's position all along, and Barthou never departed from it. So 'security first', not constructed around potentially destructive alliance systems but rather, ideally, around collective security through the League [of Nations].[5]

French policy sought peace and security, not war or revenge. Consequently, planning staffs and political elites strove to assure their nation's strategic interests by a twin-track approach. They utilized instruments of soft power – but also sharper tools, represented by military force, concrete and conscript soldiers. As Peter Jackson has emphasized, French grand strategy assigned a crucial role, especially in the 1920s, to legalistic and treaty-based statecraft.[6] That brand of statecraft significantly downgraded security through hard military power and traditional alliances. France sought to assure a peaceful

2 A. Friedberg, *The Weary Titan: Britain and the Experience of Relative Decline, 1895–1905* (Princeton, NJ and Oxford: Princeton University Press, 1988).
3 H. Clout, *After the Ruins: Restoring the Countryside of Northern France after the Great War* (University of Exeter Press, 1996).
4 G. Chapman, *A Kind of Survivor* (London: Gollancz, 1975).
5 R. J. Young, *Power and Pleasure: Louis Barthou and the Third French Republic* (Montreal and Kingston: McGill-Queen's University Press, 1991), p. 220.
6 P. Jackson, *Beyond the Balance of Power: France and the Politics of National Security in the Era of the First World War* (Cambridge University Press, 2013).

Europe by constructing an elaborate mesh of instruments, such as arbitration, conventions, arms control and arms reduction agreements, and with provision via the League of Nations at Geneva to impose sanctions on parties that broke international undertakings.[7] The Geneva Protocol of 1925 prohibited the use of gas and chemical weapons. The Locarno accords of October 1925 gave France (along with Belgium and Germany) solemn assurances, underwritten by Britain and Italy, against any forcible revisions of the 1919 frontiers in Western Europe. The London Naval Conference of 1930 completed some of the unfinished business on naval armaments from the Washington Treaty of 1922.[8]

French policy in the late 1930s: a return to 'national means'

By the later 1930s, the international climate had turned much colder. The arrival in Europe of the global economic collapse triggered by the 1929 Wall Street Crash, along with the rise of political extremes, especially the coming to power of Adolf Hitler in Germany in January 1933, threatened French strategic aims for peace and security. Germany, in October 1933, abandoned the world disarmament conference that had opened at Geneva in February 1932. Soon afterwards, Germany also left the League, followed in 1937 by Mussolini's Italy. On 17 April 1934, Barthou announced that France would take the steps it judged necessary to ensure its security by national means. This, in practice, called for French rearmament – a call that at first privileged air and naval programmes.[9]

Barthou's 'Note of 17 April' also spurred efforts to revive old alliances and secure new ones. On the former count, General Maxime Weygand, then the French Army Chief, visited Britain in June 1934, with military conversations

---

7   E. M. Spiers, *Chemical Warfare* (Basingstoke: Macmillan, 1986), ch. 3; G. Johnson (ed.), *Locarno Revisited* (London: Routledge, 2001); L. S. Gibson, 'The Role of International Sanctions in British and French Strategy and Diplomacy: A Comparative Perspective, 1919–1935' (unpublished PhD thesis, Aberystwyth University, 2007).

8   J. Blatt, 'The Parity that Meant Superiority: French Naval Policy towards Italy at the Washington Conference, 1921–22, and Interwar French Foreign Policy', *French Historical Studies* 12:2 (Fall 1981), pp. 223–48; W. G. Perett, *French Naval Policy and Foreign Affairs, 1930–1939* (Ann Arbor, Mich.: University Microfilms International, 1977); C. M. Bell, *At the Crossroads of Peace and War: The London Naval Conference of 1930* (Annapolis, Md.: Naval Institute Press, 2014).

9   Young, *Power and Pleasure*, pp. 208–22; A. Webster, 'An Argument without End: Britain, France and the Disarmament Process, 1925–34', in M. S. Alexander and W. J. Philpott (eds.), *Anglo-French Defence Relations between the Wars* (Basingstoke: Palgrave Macmillan, 2002), pp. 49–71.

beginning in December 1935, after Italy's aggression in Ethiopia, and resuming in 1936 with a focus on Germany – though remaining so sporadic and their remit so restricted that the senior French officer likened them to 'a football match', in which he 'constantly expected the referee to blow his whistle for off side'.[10] On the latter count, Pierre Laval, who became Foreign Minister after Barthou's assassination in October 1934, travelled to Moscow in summer 1935 and concluded a mutual assistance pact with the USSR.[11] These diplomatic initiatives, however, were vehemently contested. Some French politicians and press bemoaned a partnership with 'perfidious Albion'; others decried any overture to the regicidal and debt-reneging regime of the Soviet Union. In any case, French leaders did not reckon that a diplomatic revival alone would guarantee French security. 'No diplomatic error is so serious', ventured Bertrand de Jouvenel, a conservative commentator who became a Vichyite after French defeat in 1940, 'that it isn't retrievable at the decisive moment by energetic use of a large military force. But no amount of diplomatic cleverness can fashion a system sure to withstand military disaster.'[12]

The defence of metropolitan France

Therefore, France needed to hone its military muscles, as well as strap on diplomatic protection. The best-known expression of the military revival at the heart of French grand strategy was the eastern frontier fortifications named after André Maginot, the War Minister who piloted their funding through parliament. Built between 1929 and 1937, the system rested on ninety miles of strong, deep and sophisticated subterranean fortresses. Bréhain had a garrison of 800 troops, while the largest forts, such as Hackenberg and Hochwald, were underground cities. They housed narrow-gauge railways, electricity generators and barracks for their soldiers. Linking them was a chain of lighter works: concrete bunkers, pillboxes and blockhouses, observation turrets, anti-tank rails and minefields.[13]

10 M. L. Dockrill, *British Establishment Perspectives on France, 1936–40* (Basingstoke: Macmillan, 1999), p. 134.

11 M. Baumont, *The Origins of the Second World War*, trans. Simone de Couvreur Ferguson (New Haven, Conn., and London: Yale University Press, 1978), chs. 2, 5, 8, 9, 10, 12.; R. J. Young, *In Command of France: French Foreign Policy and Military Planning, 1933–1940* (Cambridge, Mass.: Harvard University Press, 1978), pp. 76–98, 142–50.

12 B. de Jouvenel, *Après la défaite* (Paris: Plon, 1941), p. 99; J.-B. Duroselle, *Politique Etrangère de la France, 1871–1969. La décadence, 1932–1939* (Paris: Imprimerie Nationale, 1979), pp. 88–112, 139–42, 156–7.

These fixed defences were intended as a 'force multiplier' for the French field armies. The latter, however, faced straitened circumstances after 1919. 'There can be no good policy', wrote de Jouvenel, 'with a bad army'.[14] Another prominent French conservative, Paul Reynaud, who strove mightily to uphold the Republic when he became Prime Minister during the great crisis of 1940, spoke on this issue in the Chamber of Deputies in January 1937. Reynaud implored French politicians to give the nation either a foreign policy commensurate with its army – or an army commensurate with its foreign policy. France should not overextend its commitments by treaties that obligated it to render difficult assistance to distant allies, unless it equipped the army with well-trained armoured and motorized divisions, able to strike far and strike fast.[15]

Unavoidably, however, French military forces reflected the financial constraints and public mood after 1919. France had contracted enormous war debts to Britain and the USA. These, along with the even greater cost of reconstructing the devastated northeastern *départements*, location of the 1914–18 Western Front, required public spending cuts. The armed forces were not spared. Procurement of innovative defence technologies, including new tanks, aircraft and warships, was cancelled or curtailed. The French navy was restricted to parity with the ambitious Italians by the Washington Treaty of 1922. The French air force did not become independent until 1928; and it took until 1933, when the energetic Pierre Cot was Air Minister, to establish an Air Force Staff and Air War College.[16]

The army, meanwhile, not only saw its equipment programmes slashed; its strategic plans had to cope with fewer well-trained soldiers after conscript service was shortened. In 1923, the draft was reduced to 18 months (beyond which troops were supposedly updated on tactics and weapons via annual

---

13 J. M. Hughes, *To the Maginot Line: The Politics of French Military Preparation in the 1920s* (Cambridge, Mass.: Harvard University Press, 1971); M. S. Alexander, 'In Defence of the Maginot Line: Politics, Economics and War Preparation', in R. Boyce (ed.), *French Foreign and Defence Policy 1918–1940: The Rise and Decline of a Great Power* (London: Routledge, 1998), pp. 159–91.
14 Jouvenel, *Après la défaite*, p. 99; R. A. Doughty, *The Seeds of Disaster: The Evolution of French Military Doctrine, 1919–1939* (Hamden, Conn.: Archon Books, 1985), pp. 41–65.
15 S. Grüner, *Paul Reynaud (1878–1966). Biographische Studien zum Liberalismus in Frankreich* (Munich: Oldenbourg, 2001); M. S. Alexander, *The Republic in Danger: General Maurice Gamelin and the Politics of French Defence, 1933–1940* (Cambridge University Press, 1993), pp. 37–44, 124–5.
16 S. Janssen, *Pierre Cot: Les Pièges de l'antifascisme (1895–1977)* (Paris: Fayard, 2002); R. Higham, *Two Roads to War: The French and British Air Arms from Versailles to Dunkirk* (Annapolis, Md.: Naval Institute Press, 2012), pp. 2–6, 32–5, 51–71.

refresher training in the Series-A reserve). Another category, the Series-B reserve (for men who had reached their thirties), received the lowest priority for new rifles, radio sets, vehicles and mortars – and even for boots, greatcoats and waterproofs.[17]

The hardening of the concrete that constructed the Maginot Line led to further cuts in French military service. The duration fell to 12 months from 1927–28, and dipped again to just 10.5 months in 1933. The army was also hit hard by the advent of the 'hollow years', *les années creuses* (when the military demographic began a five-year decline caused twenty years before, when men of family-starting age were on the battlefields, not in their bedrooms).[18] Only once fears of German remilitarization crystallized, after Adolf Hitler's speech of 15 March 1935 – which restored conscription in the Third Reich and tripled the German army's size – was French military service restored to 24 months from October 1935.[19]

Air defence requirements

Meanwhile, technological leaps in aircraft speed, range and armament in the 1930s brought an alarming new threat – attack from above. The re-forming of a German air force from 1935, and the deterioration of French relations with Italy when Benito Mussolini's troops invaded Ethiopia, exposed metropolitan France to the risk of a knockout 'bolt from the blue'. French planners agreed with the notorious warning in November 1932 by Stanley Baldwin, the British Conservative Party leader, that the bomber would always get through.[20] Reynaud alerted the Chamber of Deputies in 1937 that the soaring capabilities of aircraft menaced France because 'our capital, alas, is not at Bourges nor Clermont-Ferrand' – cities much further than Paris from airbases in Germany. The vulnerability of France's urban populations was addressed from

---

17 E. C. Kiesling, *Arming Against Hitler: France and the Limits of Military Planning* (Lawrence: University Press of Kansas, 1996), pp. 63–71, 75–6, 85–8, 98–115; Doughty, *Seeds of Disaster*, ch. 2.

18 P. C. F. Bankwitz, *Maxime Weygand and Civil-Military Relations in Modern France* (Cambridge, Mass.: Harvard University Press, 1967), pp. 83–97, 107–14; C. Dyer, *Population and Society in Twentieth-Century France* (London: Hodder & Stoughton, 1978).

19 H. Dutailly, *Les Problèmes de l'Armée de terre française, 1935–1939* (Paris: Imprimerie Nationale, 1980).

20 D. MacIsaac, 'Voices from the Central Blue: The Air Power Theorists', in P. Paret (ed.), *Makers of Modern Strategy: From Machiavelli to the Nuclear Age* (Princeton, NJ: Princeton University Press, 1986), pp. 624–47; U. Bialer, *The Shadow of the Bomber: The Fear of Air Attack and British Politics, 1932–1939* (Woodbridge: The Royal Historical Society, 1980).

1931 by forming a new air defence command, the DAT (*Défense Anti-Aérienne du Territoire*). The appointment as its first Director General of Marshal Philippe Pétain, venerated since he had 'saved' Verdun from German capture in 1916, proved the issue's importance.[21]

In the mid-1930s, Paris and other cities hosting big munitions factories, such as Nancy, received telephone-networked observation posts to furnish early warning of air raids, along with searchlight batteries and anti-aircraft guns to engage them. Other provisions were expedited by the war scare during the September/October 1938 Munich crisis. A secret 'General Instruction' was issued to French local government and regional military authorities that prepared evacuations and traffic regulation by the army, and worked up plans to withdraw civilians from northern cities such as Strasbourg and Reims. Against this, France was slower than Britain or Germany in developing radar, and its air defence system remained weak right into 1940 – Paris suffering a destructive bombing raid on 3 June.[22]

Imperial defence obligations

French strategic and foreign security concerns properly focused upon the gathering threats on the European continent. Yet planners could not escape other defence obligations. France was also an imperial power, second only to Great Britain in the size, population and global territorial dispersion of its empire. This meant worldwide colonial interests and dangerously far-flung defence responsibilities.[23] Paul M. Kennedy's famous phrase about 'imperial overstretch' was coined to describe British dilemmas in the 1900s. But it perfectly encapsulated French interwar geostrategic problems.[24]

Looking beyond mainland France, it fell primarily to the French navy – fourth largest in the world until 1940 – and to the French imperial armies

---

21 France: Assemblée Nationale – Journal Officiel de la Chambre des Députés. Débats (27 January 1937), pp. 169–70; General H. Niessel, General R.-A. Chabord and G. de Guilhermy, *D.A.T. Défense Aérienne du Territoire* (Paris: Editions Cosmopolites, 1934); L. Simon and M. Arnoux, *Défense Passive contre les Attaques aériennes: Premières réalisations françaises* (Paris: Charles-Lavauzelle, 1936).
22 N. Dombrowski Risser, *France under Fire: German Invasion, Civilian Flight and Family Survival During World War II* (Cambridge University Press, 2012); O. H. Bullitt (ed.), *For the President: Personal and Secret. Correspondence between Franklin D. Roosevelt and William C. Bullitt* (London: André Deutsch, 1973), pp. 187–8, 372–3, 448–51.
23 M. Thomas, 'European Crisis, Colonial Crisis? Signs of Fracture in the French Empire from Munich to the Outbreak of War', *International History Review* 32 (2010), 389–413.
24 P. M. Kennedy, *The Rise and Fall of the Great Powers* (London: Allen & Unwin, 1988).

raised and stationed in the colonies and North African settler territories, to meet overseas strategic obligations.[25] The problem of the global distribution of French possessions was complicated by metropolitan demographic and industrial inferiority to Germany. Thus the empire's resources, chiefly its reservoir of military manpower (the *Force noire*, as General Charles Mangin had termed it in 1910), were conceived as assets to be rushed to France under naval protection in the event of war.[26]

More sketchy were arrangements to defend the empire itself. The likelihood, especially after Germany's army and air force expansion became rapid and ambitious from 1935, was that no significant relief operations would be dispatched from the *métropole* to a beleaguered corner of overseas France. There was no French equivalent to British planning to dispatch a powerful Royal Navy squadron to reinforce threatened British imperial dependencies or deter distant powers that demonstrated hostile intent. The capacity to do so did not exist.[27]

French strategists who analysed the global issues facing them, such as the admiral and naval theoretician, Raoul Castex, concluded that the empire was indefensible.[28] Its territories were distributed from St Pierre and Miquelon to Guadeloupe, Martinique and Guyana, from Morocco, Algeria and Tunisia to Syria and Lebanon; from Senegal, Ivory Coast, Cameroun and the Congo to Djibouti on the Red Sea; and via Madagascar and Réunion in the Indian Ocean to Indochina, New Caledonia and Polynesia. They were linked by long and vulnerable maritime lines of communication.[29]

The strongest cog in the global machine of French power was North Africa. Algeria was its crown-wheel, French since 1830, its coastal cities and their hinterlands a constitutional part of France since 1848. Tunisia had been a French colony since 1881, Morocco a French protectorate since 1912. Yet even North Africa was imperfectly integrated into broader political, economic

---

25 A. Clayton, 'Growing Respect: The Royal Navy and the *Marine Nationale*, 1918–39', in Alexander and Philpott (eds.), *Anglo-French Defence Relations*, pp. 26–48; Philippe Masson, *La Marine française et la guerre, 1939–1945* (Paris: Tallandier, 2000), pp. 9–34.

26 M. Michel, *Les Africains et la Grande Guerre: L'appel à l'Afrique (1914–1918)* (Paris: Karthala, 2003); M. J. Echenberg, *Colonial Conscripts: The Tirailleurs Sénégalais in French West Africa, 1857–1960* (Portsmouth, NH: Heinemann, 1991); G. Pedroncini and C. Carlier (eds.), *Les Troupes coloniales dans la Grande Guerre* (Paris: Economica, 1999).

27 See C. M. Bell, *The Royal Navy: Seapower and Strategy between the Wars* (Stanford, Calif.: Stanford University Press, 2000); S. W. Roskill, *Naval Policy between the Wars, 1919–1939* (2 vols., London: Collins, 1968, 1976), vol. II.

28 R. Castex, *Strategic Theories*, selections trans., ed. and introd. Eugenia C. Kiesling (Annapolis, Md.: Naval Institute Press, 1994), pp. 290–305.

29 M. Thomas, *The French Empire at War, 1940–1945* (Manchester University Press, 1998).

and strategic concepts of a 'Greater France'. In 1938, improvements to the deep-water harbours and fuel-oil storage tanks at Sfax, Sousse and Bizerte in Tunisia made possible the swift shipment of troops to Marseilles and Toulon if war came. But the lateral railway across Morocco, Algeria and Tunisia, a logistical umbilical cord, had not been multi-tracked. Nor had aircraft, artillery or tank factories been developed to supplement more vulnerable metropolitan manufacturers. By 1940, North Africa remained unready to act as the arsenal for a war economy, were invasion or aerial bombardment to knock out the war-making base in mainland France.[30]

Imperial defence preparations and infrastructure

With 14 billion francs of rearmament money committed in September 1936 by the Popular Front government of Léon Blum and its Minister for Defence and War Edouard Daladier, and the Maginot Line essentially complete by 1937, priority rose in French strategic planning for colonial defence and security preparations.[31] 'North Africa possesses extensive [natural] wealth: phosphates, cobalt, manganese', stressed Senator Albert Chaumié in 1938; 'with North Africa, France is a great power, without it she sinks to the level of Portugal.'[32] A document issued after inter-ministerial consultations on 21 October 1937 offered a blueprint to safeguard imperial communications and bases in time of war. The paper, the handiwork of the naval staff's Operations Branch, was issued on 5 January 1938 to every French diplomatic post overseas and every colonial Governor General.[33]

Ports and airbases in North Africa were enlarged and refurbished, as possible platforms for offensive action against Italy. French parliamentary visitors assessed the relationship between North African resources and French war preparations. In June 1938, the Senate expressed concerns over whether North Africa could function as a base of large-scale operations.[34]

30 C. Levisse-Touzé, *L'Afrique du Nord dans la guerre, 1939–1945* (Paris: Albin Michel, 1998); M. Thomas, 'Resource War, Civil War, Rights War: Factoring Empire into French North Africa's Second World War', *War in History* 18 (2011), 225–48.

31 M. Thomas, 'At the Heart of Things? French Imperial Defense Planning in the Late 1930s', *French Historical Studies* 21:2 (Spring 1998), 325–61.

32 France (Palais du Luxembourg, Paris): Archives du Sénat (hereafter AS) – Commission de l'Armée (1938: vol. II): 'Séance du 14 décembre 1938', p. 69.

33 France (Chateau de Vincennes): Service Historique de la Défense–Marine (hereafter SHD-Marine): TT. A.16, Ministère de la Marine – C.M. 956 EMG/3, 'Instruction sur la défense des communications maritimes en temps de guerre' (21 October 1937); and ibid.: Etat-Major Général (Marine) 3ᵉ Bureau – No. 6 EMG/3 (5 January 1938).

34 France: AS – Commission de l'Armée (1938: vol. II): 'Séance du 14 décembre 1938', p. 72.

Senator Jean Fabry warned of a deficit in troops and NCO cadres, the essential bedrock for an expanded army. 'We must not', said Senator Jean Rambaud with a rhetorical flourish, 'be preparing the war of 1948 or 1950, but the war of tomorrow!'[35] Despite such anxieties, progress was made – if not rapidly enough.[36] By December 1938, Senator Chaumié could declare that North Africa's infrastructure was becoming less constrained by what 'one could say [were] "barbed wire barriers" between Morocco, Algeria and Tunisia', and that a 'major effort' was occurring in Tunisia, with 'extensive works in hand to construct railways and roads'.[37]

Sections of the rail network from Morocco to Tunisia were double-tracked in 1938–39, and an inventory of the potential reservoir of labour and soldiers represented by North Africa was established. As Senator Chaumié noted in 1938, 'the majority population are warrior types who can in time furnish a supplement of 1 million troops to our military contingent.'[38] Britain's military attaché in Paris, Colonel William Fraser, wrote in December 1938 that 'the manpower of her African Empire...inspires General Weygand in his public utterances to refer to France and French Africa as one country with a population of 110 million, and to urge his countrymen to realise and make use of this fact.'[39] As hostilities with Germany – and perhaps Italy – grew more likely, French mobilization plans in 1939 emphasized North African reinforcements as a crucial counter-weight to Germany's demographic superiority in Europe.

After Munich: North Africa as a defence resource

As historians have observed, the autumn crisis of 1938 elevated the attention paid to the imperial dimensions of French strategy. Closer focus was now devoted to ways in which – defensively and offensively – 'Greater France' might feature.[40] Edouard Daladier, Prime Minister after April 1938 and still the Minister for Defence, made a highly publicized tour of Morocco, Tunisia

35 Ibid., pp. 51, 53.
36 SHD-Marine: TT. A16, Le Directeur des Travaux Publics au Vice-Amiral, Préfet Maritime de la 4ᵉ Région, 'Objet: Ports de Sousse et de Sfax', no. 753 (Tunis: 19 November 1938).
37 France: AS – Commission de l'Armée (1938: vol. II): 'Séance du 14 décembre 1938', pp. 71–2.
38 Ibid., p. 69.
39 Great Britain: The National Archives – Public Record Office, Kew, London (hereafter: TNA-PRO): FO371, 22915, C1608/36/17 – Appreciation of the French strategic position after Munich (22 December 1938), p. 5.
40 M. Michel, 'La puissance par l'Empire: note sur la perception du facteur impérial dans l'élaboration de la Défense nationale (1936–1938)', *Revue française d'histoire d'Outre-mer*

and Algeria in February 1939.[41] The visit rallied the French public. Newsreels reminded French cinema-goers that their country was a front-rank power, possessing the military potential not just of 39 million metropolitans, but of a great empire too.[42]

In early 1939, reports of an imminent German *coup de main* against the Netherlands and Belgium led to much closer Anglo-French strategic coordination.[43] On 3 February, the British government proposed to widen staff talks with France. 'Conversations should proceed on the basis of a war against Germany and Italy in combination. . . scope to include all likely fields of operations especially the Mediterranean and the Middle East'.[44] On 24 February 1939, Daladier granted General Gamelin, the Commander-in-Chief designate, the authority to coordinate the inter-Allied negotiation of land, sea, air and colonial plans.[45] By 7 March, directives were drafted for planning with Britain's armed forces. In a conflict pitting France and Britain against Germany and Italy, it was noted that Germany was 'a great deal more materially and morally solid than its ally'. Thus it was agreed that 'the first Franco-British offensive endeavours will have to be directed' against territory controlled by Mussolini's regime, major operations against Germany following only 'after decisive, or at least significant, results are obtained against Italy'.[46] The Italian contingents helping the Nationalist cause in Spain had become bogged down in the protracted civil war there. Consequently, in 1937–38, French intelligence analysts felt that the Mediterranean was becoming less of a vulnerability and more of a potential opportunity to hurt Germany's Axis partner.

Meanwhile, French and British intelligence services knew that 200,000 Italian troops were mired in a counter-insurgency fight in Ethiopia. Italy now appeared less a dynamic 'fascist man', and more a bombastic pretender

69:254 (1982), 35–46; M. Thomas, *The French Empire between the Wars: Imperialism, Politics and Society* (Manchester University Press, 2005).

41 E. du Réau, *Edouard Daladier* (Paris: Fayard, 1993).

42 E. Daladier, *Défense du Pays* (Paris: Flammarion, 1939), pp. 110–32; A. Werth, *The Last Days of Paris: A Journalist's Diary* (London: Hamish Hamilton, 1940), p. 245.

43 See M. S. Alexander, 'Les réactions occidentales à la menace stratégique allemande en Europe occidentale', *Cahiers d'Histoire de la Seconde Guerre Mondiale* 5 (1982), 5–38.

44 *Documents on British Foreign Policy* (London: HMSO), 3rd ser., vol. IV, no. 81: Halifax to Phipps, 3 February 1939.

45 SHD-Terre: 5N579, dossier 1, folder 14: Cabinet du Ministre (10 February 1939); General M.-G. Gamelin, *Servir* (3 vols., Paris: Plon, 1946–7), vol. II, p. 401.

46 SHD-Terre: CSDN Dossier 135/1, no. 443/DN3 (7 March 1939), 'Note sur les accords d'Etat-Majors Franco-Anglais (Directives pour la délégation envoyée à Londres)', p. 1.

with military feet of clay. Mussolini's reach had exceeded his grasp.[47] Of the situation a few months later, MacGregor Knox has commented: 'Italy's dependence on seaborne coal, oil and food; its exposed strategic position facing the combined naval might of Britain and France; the desperate unpreparedness of its armed forces; the anguish with which Italian opinion regarded war; and – last but decidedly not least – the king's veto forced the Duce to declare Italy's "nonbelligerence" on 1 September [1939]'.[48] In short, in the spring and summer of 1939, opportunities beckoned for France, with British help and by means of a more offensively framed grand strategy, to land a heavy blow, perhaps even a knockout punch, on the weaker Italian end of the Rome–Berlin Axis.[49]

Staff talks conducted 'in a real spirit of cooperation' between the French and British agreed the 'Broad Strategic Policy for the Allied Conduct of the War'. Germany and Italy could 'not hope to increase their resources appreciably in the course of the war' and would 'therefore stake their chances of success on a short war.' France and Britain, on the other hand, could expect accruing strength from their empires and perhaps from allies. Thus Anglo-French strategy was to 'be adapted to a long war implying, i) a defensive strategy at the outset, at least on the Continent, while executing the greatest possible measure of economic pressure, ii) the building up of our military strength to a point at which we can adopt an offensive strategy.'[50]

Franco-British strategists contemplating options in the Mediterranean felt that Germany should be contained while Italy was humbled. But the scale of a Mediterranean offensive, agreed the planners, would be determined by how many divisions might be spared from the French front with Germany,

---

47 J. Gooch, *Mussolini and his Generals: The Armed Forces and Fascist Foreign Policy, 1922–1940* (Cambridge University Press, 2007); M. Knox, *Hitler's Italian Allies: Royal Armed Forces, Fascist Regime, and the War of 1940–43* (Cambridge University Press, 2000); M. Knox, *Mussolini Unleashed, 1939–1941: Politics and Strategy in Fascist Italy's Last War* (Cambridge University Press, 1982).

48 Knox, *Hitler's Italian Allies*, p. 16; R. M. Salerno, *Vital Crossroads: Mediterranean Origins of the Second World War, 1935–1940* (Ithaca, NY, and London: Cornell University Press, 2002).

49 R. L. DiNardo, *Germany and the Axis Powers: From Coalition to Collapse* (Lawrence: University Press of Kansas, 2005), pp. 30–48; R. M. Salerno, 'The French Navy and the Appeasement of Italy, 1937–9', *English Historical Review* 112:445 (February 1997), 66–104; R. Mallett, *The Italian Navy and Fascist Expansionism 1935–1940* (London: Cass, 1998).

50 TNA-PRO: Cabinet Office, CAB 53/47: COS 877, Anglo-French staff conversations – UK delegation. Report on Stage 1 (11 April 1939). The 'broad strategic policy for the Allied conduct of the war' was embodied in a joint paper from the newly established Anglo-French Liaison Committee, paper AFC (J) 29, co-written by the French and British delegations, consultable in TNA-PRO, CAB.85.

and how much Britain contributed.[51] The 'French general staff', concluded Britain's military attaché in Paris, 'have a low opinion of the fighting qualities of the Italians and they believe...the Italian morale would not be very high'.[52]

Daladier and Gamelin, however, lacked the enthusiasm of colonial army commanders for action against the Italians; moreover, French senior naval officers had little input to strategy-making. Under Admiral Georges Durand-Viel, Chief of French Naval Staff, a rapprochement had been cultivated with the Italian fleet in the mid-1930s, before a wave of resentment washed through the French naval officer corps at being cut out of the 18 June 1935 bilateral Anglo-German naval agreement. Under the stern and secretive Admiral François Darlan, who succeeded Durand-Viel in 1937, the French navy's relationships with the British remained, right into the war of 1939–40, no better than cool, if correct.[53]

By April 1939, the military officials doubted that Mussolini's forces would risk an attack on metropolitan France across the Provence or Alpine frontiers. Yet around the Mediterranean littoral, military operations might commence straightaway. Italy's armed forces were deemed potent enough to strike at Tunisia and Djibouti, and the British protectorates and colonies of Egypt and East Africa, with the *Regia Aeronautica* attacking the Royal Navy's dockyards at Valletta in Malta.[54] As talks continued, however, the chief French representative, General Albert Lelong, notified Gamelin of progress toward agreement that openings might be exploited for action against Italy.[55] As regards the general conduct of a war, however, the French team had 'in the first instance, found our interlocutors almost

51 SHD-Terre: 7N2816: EMA/2 Grande-Bretagne (Correspondance: janvier–juin 1939): Lelong to Gamelin: 'Rapport sur les conversations franco-britanniques d'Etat-Major (1ère Phase: Londres, 29 mars au 4 avril 1939)', Section I: 'Politique de guerre – 2ᵉ Phase'.

52 TNA-PRO: FO371, 22915, C1608/36/17 – Appreciation of the French strategic position after Munich (Col. W. Fraser to Sir E. Phipps, ambassador at Paris, 22 December 1938), pp. 5–6.

53 E. Daladier, *Prison Journal, 1940–1945*, comp. and ed. Jean Daladier with Jean Daridan (Boulder, Colo., and London: Westview, 1995), p. 107; R. C. Hood III, *Royal Republicans: The French Naval Dynasties between the World Wars* (Baton Rouge: Louisiana State University Press, 1985), pp. 153–63, 170–9; G. E. Melton, *Darlan: Admiral and Statesman of France, 1881–1942* (Westport, Conn.: Praeger, 1998).

54 TNA-PRO: CAB 53/47: COS 877, 'Anglo-French staff conversations – UK delegation. Report on Stage 1' (11 April 1939).

55 SHD-Terre: 7N2816: EMA/2 Grande-Bretagne (Correspondance: janvier–juin 1939): Lelong to Gamelin: 'Rapport sur les conversations franco-britanniques d'Etat-Major (2ᵉ Phase: Londres, 24 avril – 4 mai 1939)', Annex III: 'Mesures d'exécution immédiate'.

obsessed with the defensive in every theatre...; it is only little by little that they have admitted that the opportunity to take the offensive should not be abandoned a priori' – such as, potentially, 'in Tunisia, in Ethiopia, in mainland Italy.'[56]

Further Anglo-French staff talks and the overall Allied approach

Though the uncertainty surrounding Mussolini's likely decisions still clouded the Allied sense of how a war would look, the second stage of the Anglo-French staff talks (24 April – 4 May 1939) saw offensive plans against Italy assume a more distinct shape. The French air generals developed contingency plans to switch a number of bomber groups to airbases in southern France, much nearer to industrial targets at Milan and Turin, and the Italian dockyards and oil storage facilities at Genoa, La Spezia and Livorno. It was agreed that an RAF officer would visit Tunisia to discuss air coordination with the *Armée de l'Air* command in North Africa.[57]

This all reflected broad confidence in achieving a stalemate in a general war, before bringing blockade and attrition to grind the Axis to defeat in a war of long duration. Hostilities would unfold in successive stages, the first being 'directed towards maintaining as far as possible the integrity of the territory of the two Empires and defending those of their vital interests that are attacked'. The second phase 'should be directed to holding Germany and to dealing decisively with Italy. At the same time we should be building up our military strength until we can adopt an offensive major strategy'. In the third and final phase, the Allies would concentrate on defeating Germany. However the timetable and the 'lines of action' remained ill-defined. The Allies 'must be prepared to face a major offensive directed against either France or the UK or against both. To defeat such an offensive we should have to concentrate all our initial efforts and during this time our major strategy [against Germany] would be defensive.'[58]

Between 4 and 6 May 1939, in Rabat, Morocco, French and British military chiefs more closely coordinated their planning for the Mediterranean.

---

56 SHD-Terre: 7N2816: EMA/2 Grande-Bretagne (Correspondance: janvier–juin 1939): Lelong to Gamelin: 'Rapport sur les conversations franco-britanniques d'Etat-Major (1ère Phase: Londres, 29 mars au 4 avril 1939)', Section I: 'Politique de guerre – 2ᵉ Phase'.

57 SHD-Terre: 7N2816: Lelong: 'Rapport... (2e phase: Londres, 24 avril – 4 mai 1939)'.

58 TNA-PRO: CAB 53/47: COS 877, 'Anglo-French staff conversations – UK delegation. Report on Stage 1' (11 April 1939).

So if the Royal Navy's size meant that Britain got its way at sea, on land the French army led and regarded their opposite numbers 'as learners in the military arts', in the words of a senior British liaison officer in 1939–40.[67] Operational hypotheses were the province of the 3rd Bureau or plans department of the French General Staff. In the early and mid-1920s, French plans had a punitive and retaliatory character. They aimed for swift French armed intervention eastward, into Belgium and beyond, so as to enforce the 1919 settlement on Germany. A military convention with Belgium's General Staff in September 1920 enabled coordination of the rapid transit of French units from their peacetime quarters to the Belgo-German border or beyond. However, the changing political and diplomatic landscape forced a climbdown from this forward strategy. From 1923, financial cutbacks necessitated by government deficits shaped the structure of the French army, shortening conscription and seeing the Maginot Line constructed.

French strategy and planning adjusted to a new equilibrium. The plans of the early and mid-1930s assumed a defensive and non-provocative complexion. The manning of the military was perhaps closer to a home defence militia than at any other time in modern French history. Although service in the French army was extended to 24 months in 1936, in response to Hitler's rearmament, French war plans remained defensive. 'Why, having built our fortifications of the Maginot Line', asked General Louis Maurin, the French War Minister in 1935, 'would we leave them to embark on who knows what adventure?'[68]

The Maginot Line, however, extended only from the Rhine to the southwestern corner of Luxembourg. France's long northern border lacked fixed defences between Givet and Dunkirk, for technical reasons (the high water table of Flanders hampering deep-set underground fortifications) and political ones (fortifications would cast Belgium adrift on the far side, adjacent to a fast remilitarizing Reich). French strategy hence faced a conundrum when, in October 1936, King Leopold III of the Belgians ended

Recherche Scientifique (CNRS), 1979), pp. 461–87; M. Gowing, 'Anglo-French Economic Collaboration up to the Outbreak of the Second World War', and 'Anglo-French Economic Collaboration before the Second World War: Oil and Coal', in *Les Relations Franco-Britanniques, 1935–1939* (Paris: Editions du CNRS, 1975), pp. 179–88 and 263–75.

67 Brig. G. M. O. Davy (1898–1983), unpublished typescript memoirs, p. 1209 (consultable on microfilm GMOD/1, Department of Documents, Imperial War Museum, London) (www.nationalarchives.gov.uk/a2a/records.aspx?cat=062-gmod&cid=-1#-1 – accessed 30 September 2014).

68 Quoted in Hughes, *To the Maginot Line*, p. 248.

the military coordination of the previous sixteen years, declaring that Belgium would pursue a policy of 'independence'.[69]

Intensive work ensued thereafter in the French army's plans department to meet the challenges of the all-but-undefended northern frontier. In 1936–37, the first new disposition was codenamed Plan Dbis, followed in 1938 by Plan E. The results were never satisfactory. Through the Belgian military attachés in Paris, the French Commander-in-Chief, General Gamelin, was able to maintain confidential communications. In 1937, a visit was contrived for General Victor Schweisguth, Deputy French Chief of Staff – disguised as a holidaymaker – to inspect half-built Belgian fortifications and anti-tank obstacles. But these informal channels were no substitute for regular consultations with Belgian generals.[70] Since a fog of uncertainty shrouded Belgium's intended deployments and troop strength, French strategists wavered between a 'minimal' plan for a forward defence by an advance to positions on the Escaut (the Scheldt), and a riskier 'maximal' one that would see the best-equipped French armies make a dash to the Dyle River. The latter approach carried the danger of meeting westward-rushing German forces in an encounter battle (anathema to the French army's doctrine of methodical battle). But it also offered the alluring prospect of stalemating the Germans east of Brussels and rallying the Belgians and their army of twenty-two fielded divisions as a full partner of the Allies.[71]

On 22 December 1938, the Chief of French Military Intelligence, the 2nd Bureau, General Maurice Gauché, advised General Alphonse Georges, Commander-designate of forces facing Germany, that in a conflict: 'The initial action will be reserved for Italy. Germany will support her at the decisive moment by applying the greater part of its forces upon Belgium and Holland.'[72] Equivocation as to which operation would be implemented sowed the seeds for the fateful Dyle-Breda manoeuvre of May 1940 on which Gamelin insisted, and which was unavailingly opposed by his senior deputy,

69 J. A. Gunsburg, '*La Grande Illusion*: Belgian and Dutch Strategy Facing Germany, 1919–May 1940 (Part 1)', *Journal of Military History* 78 (2014), 101–58; Young, *In Command of France*, pp. 151–4; D. O. Kieft, *Belgium's Return to Neutrality: An Essay in the Frustration of Small Power Diplomacy* (Oxford: Clarendon Press, 1972).

70 M. S. Alexander, 'In Lieu of Alliance: The French General Staff's Secret Co-operation with Neutral Belgium, 1936–1940', *Journal of Strategic Studies* 14:4 (December 1991), 413–27.

71 Kiesling, *Arming Against Hitler*, pp. 140–3; Doughty, *Seeds of Disaster*, pp. 89–90, 101–8, 179–82; B. Chaix, *En Mai 1940, fallait-il entrer en Belgique? Décisions stratégiques et plans opérationnels de la campagne de France* (Paris: Economica, 2005).

72 SHD-Terre: 1N47 – Etat-Major du général Georges. Etat-Major de l'Armée. 2e Bureau – compte-rendu de renseignement, le 22 Décembre 1938, pp. 4, 5–6.

General Georges. That operation fatally diverted over twenty of the strongest French and British divisions (from General Gaston Billotte's First Army Group: French First Army, French Seventh Army and the BEF). These advanced fast into central and northern Belgium and the southern Netherlands, too far from the German assault through the Ardennes – unhinging Allied defensive integrity and wrecking Allied political unity.[73]

Phoney War, September 1939 to 9 May 1940: strategy, armaments and anarchic politics

Meanwhile rearmament progressed, manifesting long-evident structural shortcomings in the political culture of the Third Republic and the French economy, but also displaying impressive improvisation, and the capacity to adapt and knuckle down, to produce a surge, in some sectors, of French armaments production.[74]

One success of French mobilization came in strengthening the army. In November 1939, Gamelin began a five-month plan that delivered significant results by the time Germany invaded in May 1940. Italian non-belligerence, though frustrating to admirals and colonial officers, permitted the move to metropolitan France of many divisions from North Africa. These fresh arrivals on the new Western Front were reinforced when Gamelin raised four additional regiments of volunteer Foreign Legionnaires, from the Spanish Republic's fighters who crossed the Pyrenees in 1939 when the Nationalists won the Spanish Civil War, anti-Fascist Italians and Jewish refugees from Central Europe.[75]

When fighting began in the West in 1940, the French had therefore boosted their order of battle. As an officer of Gamelin's staff wrote: 'in the...first nine months of war the French army underwent important modifications in the disposition, composition and armament of its forces'. Another reinforcement

---

73 D. W. Alexander, 'Repercussions of the Breda Variant', *French Historical Studies* 8:3 (Spring 1974), 459–88; Gunsburg, *'La Grande Illusion'*, 605–71; K.-H. Frieser with J. T. Greenwood, *The Blitzkrieg Legend: The 1940 Campaign in the West* (Annapolis, Md.: Naval Institute Press, 2005), pp. 90–3; T. J. Knight, 'Belgium Leaves the War, 1940', *Journal of Modern History* 41 (1969), 46–67.

74 Deficiencies that persisted in French planning are exposed in T. Imlay, 'Preparing for Total War: The *Conseil Supérieur de la Défense Nationale* and France's Industrial and Economic Preparations for War after 1918', *War in History* 15 (2008), 43–71.

75 SHD-Terre: 34N319 – 'Historique du 22e RMVE'; V. Caron, 'The Missed Opportunity: French Refugee Policy in Wartime, 1939–1940', in J. Blatt (ed.), *The French Defeat of 1940: Reassessments* (New York and Oxford: Berghahn, 1998), pp. 126–70.

was the ten BEF divisions deployed on the northeast French frontier by 10 May 1940.[76] The Allies were not appreciably inferior by May 1940 in numbers of soldiers, and enjoyed some superiority in quantity and quality of armoured fighting vehicles, artillery and motorized transport (though, aside from the motorized BEF, it was still largely horse-powered French armies that were defeated by largely horse-powered Germans).[77]

Unfortunately, expansion and modernization of the Allied armies was not matched by air rearmament. The skies remained a realm of German superiority, especially in the autumn of 1939, accounting for the rarity of Allied air operations in that period. On 26 August, the French Chief of Air Staff, General Joseph Vuillemin, warned that the Luftwaffe could not be brought to battle for another six months. Such sorties over German territory as were flown dropped propaganda leaflets, not bombs, for fear of German reprisal attacks. Both Gamelin and Colonel Fraser, the British military attaché, made their wives leave Paris at the start of September 1939, convinced that heavy bombing raids would begin immediately.[78] Allied weakness in the air arose because French aviation had been a political plaything. At the Air Ministry in 1936–38, under Pierre Cot, dispersal of aero engine and airframe manufacture had been effected, leveraged by nationalizations under the 1936–37 Popular Front government of left-centre parties. That itself was far-sighted. But in the short- and medium-term, the reduction of manufacturing in the Paris suburbs, in favour of new factories further south and almost beyond German reach, notably at Toulouse, caused a slowdown in re-equipping the *Armée de l'Air*. Productivity plumbed the depths in early 1938, before steadily recovering under a new Aviation Minister from the Radical Party, Guy La Chambre, a man politically close to the Minister for National Defence and War, Edouard Daladier (who was also Prime Minister from April 1938 to March 1940).[79]

If output of aircraft stuttered until March 1940 (it did surge impressively in April, May and June, just as the Allies crashed to defeat), the French government was no well-oiled machine either. It was not that the French public was

---

76 Minart, *P.C. Vincennes*, vol. II, p. 67.

77 J. A. Gunsburg, *Divided and Conquered: The French High Command and the Defeat of the West, 1940* (Westport, Conn.: Greenwood, 1979); R. L. DiNardo, *Mechanized Juggernaut or Military Anachronism? Horses and the German Army of World War II* (Mechanicsburg, Pa.: Stackpole, 2008).

78 Alexander, *The Republic in Danger*, pp. 314–22.

79 Bullitt (ed.), *For the President*, pp. 298–9; H. Chapman, *State Capitalism and Working-Class Radicalism in the French Aircraft Industry* (Berkeley: University of California Press, 1991).

beaten before fighting began. Daniel Hucker's study of opinion shows that the French populace entered the conflict calmly – suffering anxieties, but by no means defeatist. Yet without subscribing to dated, largely discredited writing that ascribed 1940 to 'decadent' Third Republic institutions and individuals, one nonetheless notes persistent weaknesses in administrative structures and the political culture.[80] Daladier reshaped his government on 13 September 1939, taking over foreign affairs from the architect of French appeasement, Georges Bonnet. He also created a new Ministry for Armaments under Raoul Dautry, a businessman who had modernized the French railways. And headed by the playwright Jean Giraudoux, Daladier established a Commissariat for Information to match Britain's Ministry of Information – agencies to counteract the 'munitions of the mind' fired by the Reich Propaganda Chief, Dr Josef Goebbels.[81]

No transformation resulted from the new apparatus, however, nor from the new men running the war effort. Bonnet was merely shuffled to the Ministry of Justice. He could not be ditched: he led too strong a faction in Daladier's own Radical Party, the parliamentary keystone to the government. Dautry got mixed reviews at the Armaments Ministry: a superb motivator, but unable to delegate, he 'lost sight of the forest for the trees', wrote the journalist André Géraud. But the US military attaché was told he was 'the Right Man in the Right Place'. At the very least, Dautry brought a more managerialist approach to French industrial mobilization, a clearer allocation of the female and male workforce and an acceleration of munitions manufacture.[82] Undeniably, however, Giraudoux's Information Commissariat and its radio broadcasts to woo neutral powers such as the

---

80 D. Hucker, *Public Opinion and the End of Appeasement in Britain and France* (Farnham: Ashgate, 2011).

81 A.-J. Tudesq, 'L'utilisation gouvernementale de la radio', in R. Rémond and J. Bourdin (eds.), *Edouard Daladier, chef de gouvernement: Avril 1938 – Septembre 1939* (Paris: Presses de la Fondation Nationale des Sciences Politiques, 1977), pp. 255–64; G. Marceau, 'Jean Giraudoux, un écrivain-diplomate à la tête d'une propagande d'Etat (1939–1940)', in J. Massicotte, M. Neagu and S. Savard (eds.), *Actes du 7ᵉ colloque étudiant du Département d'histoire de l'Université Laval* (Quebec: 2007), pp. 95–110 (www.erudit.org/livre/artefact/2007/index.htm – accessed 30 September 2014)

82 Pertinax, *The Gravediggers of France: Gamelin, Daladier, Reynaud, Pétain, and Laval. Military Defeat, Armistice, Counter-Revolution* (New York: Doubleday, Doran, 1944), pp. 125–6; US National Archives and Record Administration (College Park, Md.): record group 165, box 1793, file 2724-C-37/41 (Col. H. H. Fuller to War Department, 29 September 1939); J.-L. Crémieux-Brilhac, *Les Français de l'An 40* (2 vols., Paris: Gallimard, 1990), vol. II, pp. 105–14, 132–64; R. Baudouï, *Raoul Dautry, 1880–1951: Le technocrate de la République* (Paris: Balland, 1992), pp. 183–231.

USA, along with the War Ministry unit of Colonel Edouard Thomas for press censorship, proved disappointing.[83]

Arguably most damaging was that France's toxic party politics were not suspended 'for the duration'. It was a politics characterized by back-biting, short-lived coalition governments and precarious majorities. In the winter of 1939–40, individuals able to damage Daladier roamed the corridors of the Chamber of Deputies and Senate. When not making speeches or demanding votes, they plotted over long lunches at their favourite neighbourhood restaurants. Among them was Jean Montigny, the pro-Munich Chairman of the Chamber's Foreign Affairs Committee, Pierre-Etienne Flandin and Pierre Laval (former and future Prime Ministers). Though his two-year government from 1938 to 1940 was durable by the Third Republic's standards, Daladier was never secure in the saddle. His ambitious Finance Minister, Paul Reynaud, constantly jockeyed for the leadership, finally becoming Prime Minister on 21 March 1940, when the deputies who voted for Daladier were matched by the number who abstained in a confidence motion on non-provision of military aid to Finland in its 'winter war' with the USSR.[84]

And the question of aiding Finland exemplified the fissures, false trails and fantasies that bedevilled plans in the Phoney War. Some French leaders grew emboldened by the sight of Italian military embarrassment in Albania (invaded by Mussolini in April 1939). Others were outraged that Vyacheslav Molotov, Soviet Foreign Affairs Commissar, signed the German-Soviet Non-Aggression Pact on 23 August 1939, making the USSR almost a German ally. A fixation followed about largely imaginary Communist saboteurs in the French armaments factories in 1939–40. Calls also grew to exploit Soviet military discomfiture in Finland (Stalin's purges having previously eliminated the best Red Army commanders).[85]

Cries went up for Allied intervention in the Balkans – urged by General Maxime Weygand, who came out of retirement to take over the French Near East command at Beirut, showing alarming amnesia about the French and

83 J.-B. Duroselle, *Politique Etrangère de la France, 1871–1969. L'Abîme, 1939–1945* (Paris: Imprimerie Nationale, 1983), pp. 67–70; R. Cardinne-Petit, *Les soirées du Continental: ce que j'ai vu à la censure, 1939–1940* (Paris: Jean-Renard, 1942).

84 J. Nevakivi, *The Appeal that Was Never Made: The Allies, Scandinavia and the Finnish Winter War* (London: Hurst, 1976); J. C. Cairns, 'Reflections on France, Britain and the Winter War Prodrome, 1939–1940', in Blatt (ed.), *The French Defeat of 1940*, pp. 269–95.

85 T. C. Imlay, 'Mind the Gap: The Perception and Reality of Communist Sabotage of French War Production during the Phoney War, 1939–1940', *Past & Present* 189 (November 2005), 179–224; G. Roberts, *Unholy Alliance: Stalin's Pact with Hitler* (London: I. B. Tauris, 1989); M. J. Carley, *1939: The Alliance That Never Was* (Chicago: Ivan J. Dee, 1999).

British military stalemate in Greece after the 1915 Salonika landing.[86] And study plans or *projets* were worked up to assemble a Franco-British air force in Lebanon and Syria, to bomb Soviet oil wells in the Caucasus that were, from the autumn of 1939, helping Reich war industries to circumvent the Allied blockade. Historians remain undecided about how serious the likelihood was of returning to Salonika or bombing Baku – and estimating the consequences, if they had, would entail speculation bordering on guesswork.[87] The third area considered by planners, and much favoured by Reynaud, was Northern Europe. From that perspective, the Franco-British air forces drafted Operation 'Royal Marine', to drop fluvial mines into the Rhine and disrupt German river traffic and, much more developed, the movement of a French Alpine infantry division under General Antoine Béthouart to Scotland, to join an Anglo-French expedition to sail for Norway and seek to disrupt the Third Reich's iron ore imports from Sweden.[88]

Epilogue: six weeks of disaster, 10 May to 25 June 1940

When the shooting started on 10 May 1940, French plans unravelled as fast as the German Panzers slashed to the Channel, reached on 19 May, and Paris, captured on 14 June. In the popular mind, the French conduct of operations was an unmitigated disaster. The Maginot Line appeared to be in the wrong place, a 'useless bastion'; the French tanks (though more numerous and better gunned and armoured than any Panzer except the not-numerous Pz Kpfw IVs) dispersed in penny packets. French troops were thought to be demotivated, if not downright defeatist. France suffered from absent or inadequate allies – Belgium capitulating on 28 May, Britain cutting and running at Dunkirk, and the USA selling Curtiss and Glenn Martin aircraft

86 M. Thomas, 'Imperial Defence or Diversionary Attack? Anglo-French Strategic Planning in the Near East, 1936–40', in Alexander and Philpott (eds.), *Anglo-French Defence Relations*, pp. 157–85; F. G. Weber, *The Evasive Neutral: Germany, Britain and the Quest for a Turkish Alliance in the Second World War* (Columbia and London: University of Missouri Press, 1979); Duroselle, *L'Abîme*, pp. 72–7.

87 T. C. Imlay, *Facing the Second World War: Strategy, Politics and Economics in Britain and France, 1938–1940* (Oxford University Press, 2003); C. O. Richardson, 'French Plans for Allied Attacks on the Caucasus Oil Fields, January–April 1940', *French Historical Studies* 8:1 (spring 1973), 130–56.

88 R. A. C. Parker, 'Britain, France and Scandinavia, 1939–40', *History* 61:20 (October 1976), 369–87; Duroselle, *L'Abîme*, pp. 87–94, 108–16; E. R. May, *Strange Victory: Hitler's Conquest of France* (New York: Hill and Wang, 2000), pp. 343–6; F. Kersaudy, *Norway 1940* (London: Harper Collins, 1990); N. Smart, *British Strategy and Politics During the Phony War: Before the Balloon Went Up* (Westport, Conn., and London: Praeger, 2003), pp. 191–235.

to France, but failing to ride to the rescue and enter the war, despite Prime Minister Reynaud's pleas in the June 1940 crisis.[89]

Yet the French military performance was more impressive than older accounts acknowledge. The Maginot Line did its job well – perhaps too well. It economized on French manpower, enabling fielded forces to be concentrated elsewhere, chiefly on the border with Belgium, but also in manoeuvre groups and with some divisions in the Pyrenees and Provence, mounting guard over Fascist Spain and Italy.[90] The Maginot fortifications made Wehrmacht planners scratch their heads. This directly accounts for the original 1939 German strategy to advance through central Belgium, essentially retracing the route of the Kaiser's soldiers in 1914; it also accounts for Case Yellow (*Fall Gelb*), adopted by Hitler in February 1940. The revised German line of march, brainchild of General Erich von Manstein, delivered its heaviest blow through the Belgian and Luxembourg Ardennes and across the lightly defended crossings of the Meuse River at Sedan, Monthermé and Dinant.[91]

Because Belgium had remained obdurately neutral, and with its twenty-two divisions and ten more Dutch ones a tempting reinforcement for Allied theatre forces, Gamelin had insisted on positioning the French First and Seventh Armies far to the northwest of the Maginot Line. There, incorporating most of the French armoured, mechanized cavalry and motorized infantry divisions, these armies plunged forward, the moment they were let out of the traps on 10 May 1940, to Breda, Tilburg and the Dyle River. They sought to stop the German advance in central Belgium and the southern Netherlands. And had Hitler not embraced Manstein's different plan, a stalemate to suit the Allied grand strategy – exemplified by the Phoney War poster proclaiming 'We shall win because we are stronger' – would probably have resulted.[92]

The dash to the Dyle and Breda, however, left insufficiently strong, insufficiently manoeuvrable French formations behind the Meuse breakthrough

---

89 C. Armand-Masson, *Ligne Maginot, bastion inutile* (Paris: Fasquelle Editeurs, 1942); J. McV. Haight Jr, *American Aid to France, 1938–1940* (New York: Atheneum, 1970); Bullitt (ed.), *For the President*, pp. 313–26, 428–77; G. Wright, 'Ambassador Bullitt and the Fall of France', *World Politics* 10 (1957), 63–90.

90 Smart, *British Strategy and Politics*, pp. 92–8.

91 Frieser, *The Blitzkrieg Legend*, pp. 60–89; M. Melvin, *Hitler's Greatest General – Erich von Manstein* (London: Weidenfeld & Nicolson, 2010).

92 Poster at http://mapage.noos.fr/moulinhg01/Histoire/2.guerre.mondiale/affiches. strat.frse.html (accessed 30 September 2014); cf. the gloomier view of Allied prospects in Imlay, *Facing the Second World War*.

points in May 1940. There was nothing to block the German punch into open country toward Charleroi, Maubeuge, Amiens and the English Channel. This punch split, and then fatally shattered, the Franco-Belgian-British defences.[93]

Yet it was not the building, nor the placement of the Maginot Line that made a German breakthrough possible, and so devastating. There was, too, much excellent equipment in France in 1940 (including slightly more Allied tanks than German). Some French tanks were scattered in separate companies for close infantry support, unable to manoeuvre. But not all. Six French armoured divisions took the field. A further incomplete division, Charles de Gaulle's 4th DCR (*Division Cuirassée de Réserve*), formed quickly and was soon in the thick of the fight. The mechanized cavalry corps of General Jules Prioux, with fast and well-gunned Somua S.35 and Hotchkiss H.39 tanks, stopped the xv Panzer Corps of General Hermann Hoth literally in its tracks in central Belgium, in the war's first big armoured battles.[94] At Montcornet and Laon, the boldly led 4th DCR blunted the westward charge by the xix Panzer Corps of General Heinz Guderian before counter-attacking fiercely, if ultimately to no avail, at Abbeville.[95]

What of the French infantry? Gamelin, dismissed by nightfall on 19 May, shamefully wrote in a valedictory report to the government that many 'had no taste for the fight'. And some infantry certainly did collapse around Sedan. But those troops were mostly from the Series-B reserve, the third-line 55th and 71st Divisions, men in their middle and late thirties, with just two regular officers per battalion and a smattering of experienced cadres. They had to fight with serious shortages of anti-aircraft guns, anti-tank artillery, anti-tank mines, mortars and motor transport. That some units like these succumbed to the blows of Panzers, Ju 87 Stuka dive-bombers and low-flying Me 110 fighter bombers should be no surprise, nor a reason to excoriate them.[96] The German

---

93 R. A. Doughty, *The Breaking Point: Sedan and the Fall of France, 1940* (Hamden, Conn.: Archon Books, 1990).

94 R. H. S. Stolfi, 'Equipment for Victory in France, 1940', *History* 55 (February 1970), 1–20; J. A. Gunsburg, 'The Battle of the Belgian Plain, 12–14 May 1940: The First Great Tank Battle', *Journal of Military History* 56:2 (April 1992), 207–44; J. A. Gunsburg, 'The Battle of Gembloux, 14–15 May 1940: The "Blitzkrieg" Checked', *Journal of Military History* 64:1 (January 2000), 97–140.

95 F. K. Rothbrust, *Guderian's XIXth Panzer Corps and the Battle of France: Breakthrough in the Ardennes, May 1940* (Westport, Conn., and London: Praeger, 1990); H. de Wailly, *De Gaulle sous le casque: Abbeville, 1940* (Paris: Perrin, 1990).

96 J. T. Jackson, *The Fall of France: The Nazi Invasion of 1940* (Oxford University Press, 2003), pp. 163–73; Frieser, *The Blitzkrieg Legend*, pp. 145–78; M. S. Alexander, ' "No taste for the fight"? French Combat Performance in 1940 and the Politics of the Fall of France', in P. Addison and A. Calder (eds.), *Time to Kill: The Soldiers' Experience of War in the West, 1939–1945* (London: Pimlico, 2007), pp. 161–76.

air force was superior, by perhaps two-to-one across the total spectrum of air forces in the operational theatre. The effects of this, however, were not clear-cut. The Allied shortage of fast, long-range photo-reconnaissance squadrons denied ground commanders vital warning intelligence about impending German assaults. The Allied reliance on poorly armed light bombers such as the Fairey Battles of the British Advanced Air Striking Force (AASF) meant that courageous missions in mid-May 1940 against German army choke-points at the Maastricht bridges and Meuse crossings failed, and at terrible cost. But once the air battles over Dunkirk had worn down Luftwaffe machines and crews (27 May – 4 June), German aviation was not decisive and the legendary Panzer–Stuka combination all but disappeared. German infantry had to expend much blood and many thousands of artillery rounds to cross the well-defended Oise, Seine, Marne and Loire rivers in June 1940.[97]

Elsewhere along the battlefront, the French regular army and the Series-A reserves fought well. The tenacity of 3rd North African Division turned the wooded hills at Inor, above the Meuse, into a 'green hell' for their shocked German assailants.[98] The 2nd North African Division at Dunkirk formed a valiant rearguard, crucial to the evacuation of 338,000 British, French and Belgian troops. During *Fall Rot* (Case Red), the second-stage German attack launched on 5 June to end the war in the West, the French 13th Infantry Division stoutly defended strongpoints southwest of Amiens. Meanwhile, below the Somme, in barricaded villages nicknamed 'fighting hedgehogs', the 23rd Infantry and 29th Alpine Divisions fought well, as did the 10th, 14th and 44th Infantry Divisions on the Aisne and Vesle, and the 1st Colonial Division on the upper Meuse.[99]

This defiance and the rallying of morale stemmed not from training exercises, but from lessons absorbed under fire. French troops and their commanders, especially divisional generals and regimental officers, ascended their own battlefield learning curve – exactly as the men on the Western Front had done in 1917–18. It was too late to save mainland France from defeat in June 1940. But with greater initiative and delegated authority now granted to junior and mid-level officers, and improved tactics being applied,

---

97 R. J. Overy, *The Bombing War: Europe 1939–1945* (London: Allen Lane, 2013), pp. 41–3, 60–6; R. Jackson, *Before the Storm: The Story of Bomber Command, 1939–42* (London: Arthur Barker, 1972), chs. 3–6; Frieser, *The Blitzkrieg Legend*, pp. 342–3.

98 E. Gehring, *Die Grüne Hölle von Inor* (Munich: Zentral Verlag der NSDAP, 1941).

99 M. S. Alexander, 'Colonial Minds Confounded: French Colonial Troops in the Battle of France, 1940', in M. Thomas (ed.), *The French Colonial Mind* (2 vols., Lincoln: University of Nebraska Press, 2011), vol. II, pp. 248–82; R. McNab, *For Honour Alone: The Cadets of Saumur in Defence of the Cavalry School. France, June 1940* (London: Robert Hale, 1988).

the French rearguards punished the German spearheads right down to the armistice on 25 June.[100]

Furthermore, high above the battle, the fight in the air was relentless and the attrition heavy. Contrary to some complaints from troops who got strafed, the skies were not empty of Allied aircraft.[101] Sometimes the action was simply elsewhere. 'Our fighters must be some miles ahead at the front', supposed one 2nd North African Division officer, bombed on 15 May, 'for we do not see a single machine in the sky.'[102] The RAF vigorously contested the airspace above Dunkirk to protect the evacuation from 27 May till 4 June.

The French air force then engaged Luftwaffe bomber fleets and their escorts over northern France when the Germans brought up artillery and infantry to assault General Weygand's 'hedgehog' villages. Between 5 and 13 June 1940 occurred, according to the aviation historian Patrick Facon, 'the French fighter arm's finest hour'. By 16 June, the Luftwaffe had lost, through combat, crashes and irreparable battle damage, a quarter of its machines operational on 10 May. Among some aircraft types, the attrition rate touched 30 per cent. Casualties among trained and combat-experienced aircrews were also heavy – and harder to replace. One consequence was the need for a pause before Reichsmarschall Herman Göring could launch the campaign for air supremacy over southern England now known as the Battle of Britain.[103]

French tactical doctrine and combat techniques improved rapidly in the cauldron of battle. In six weeks during May and June 1940, the French went a long way toward working out the successful fighting methods of the major belligerents later in the war. A clear line of authority, starting at the top, was the first thing needed. True enough, an Anglo-French Supreme War Council (SWC) was constituted from the outset in 1939 (something not done until 1917 in the previous war).[104] But the British military attaché in Paris found

100 M. S. Alexander, 'After Dunkirk: The French Army's Performance against "Case Red", 25 May to 25 June 1940', *War in History* 14 (2007), 219–64.

101 F. d'Astier de la Vigerie, *Le Ciel n'était pas vide: L'Armée de l'Air française dans la campagne de 1940* (Paris: Julliard, 1952).

102 D. Barlone, *A French Officer's Diary, 23 August 1939 to 1 October 1940* (Cambridge University Press, 1942), p. 48.

103 P. Facon, *L'Armée de l'Air dans la Tourmente: La bataille de France, 1939–40* (Paris: Economica, 1997), pp. 210–27; *Germany and the Second World War*, vol. II: *Germany's Initial Conquests in Europe* (10 vols., Oxford: Clarendon Press, 1991), pp. 252–3, 278–9; H. Boog, 'The Luftwaffe's Assault', in P. Addison and J. A. Crang (eds.), *The Burning Blue: A New History of the Battle of Britain* (London: Pimlico, 2000), pp. 39–54.

104 W. J. Philpott, 'The Benefit of Experience? The Supreme War Council and the Higher Management of Coalition War, 1939–40', in Alexander and Philpott (eds.), *Anglo-French Defence Relations*, pp. 209–26; F. Bédarida, *La Stratégie secrète de la drôle de guerre: Le Conseil suprême interallié, septembre 1939–avril 1940* (Paris: Presses de la FNSP, 1979).

after hostilities had begun that the War Office in London was 'fundamentally incapable of understanding the French organisation', while the diffused command structures of 1940 left Gamelin directing French land forces, with a coordinating remit over the BEF, but no control over Allied aviation.[105] A second thing required was accurate and timely intelligence – strategic, operational and tactical. A third necessity was robust and rapid communications, to permit flexible command and control, both horizontally between the air and ground forces, and vertically, up and down the chain of command. A fourth essential was what came to be seen as a 'modern' style for conducting operations – 'mission command' or *Auftragstaktik,* which the Germans used so devastatingly in 1940 to consign the French 1914–18 heritage of a phased and always centrally 'directed battle' (*la bataille conduite*) to history's proverbial dustbin.[106] After 20 May 1940, albeit too late, the French had re-established a Supreme Joint Services Commander in Weygand (Chief of Staff to Marshal Foch when the latter held the role in 1918). And at lower levels, the French army was rapidly acquiring operational and tactical effectiveness in this 'age of machine warfare'. With new methods came new men, a rising generation of talented French officers, eager to put the lessons into practice, and who, from 1941 to 1945, in Africa, Italy and then France, re-joined the fight to overthrow the Axis.

Conclusion

The collapse in the West in 1940 remains something of a 'strange defeat', in the famous description by the Sorbonne medieval historian, Resister and Gestapo victim, Marc Bloch. It is still easier to explain why France should *not* have lost than it is to account for why the Germans won. The campaign was, in the words of Ernest R. May, a 'strange victory' – one that very few had foreseen in Berlin, Paris or London, or for that matter in Washington DC.[107] At the shocking moment of French capitulation, many contemporaries veered from thinking this an impossible eventuality to viewing it as one of

105 Col. W. Fraser, letter to his wife, 22 September 1939 (correspondence shown to the author, by courtesy of Gen. Sir David Fraser).

106 Doughty, *Seeds of Disaster*, pp. 74–86, 91–111; Frieser, *The Blitzkrieg Legend*, pp. 325–6, 329–41; M. S. Alexander, 'Radio-Intercepts, Reconnaissance and Raids: French Operational Intelligence and Communications in 1940', *Intelligence and National Security* 28:3 (June 2013), 337–76.

107 M. Bloch, *Strange Defeat: A Statement of Evidence Written in 1940*, trans. Gerard Hopkins (New York and London: W. W. Norton, 1968); May, *Strange Victory*, pp. 388–90, 449–84.

the most decisive battles ever known. In reality, it was neither. Pessimistic Frenchmen since 1919 – 'hauntingly obsessed by decline', in Robert Frank's phrase – had always feared another fight with Germany in conditions where France had too few allies and, in the case of Britain, an ally insufficiently mobilized when the test of battle occurred. There were echoes of the dictum of Field Marshal Lord Kitchener, British Secretary of State for War in the autumn of 1914, that one had to make war as one must, not as one would like. General Weygand, who succeeded Gamelin and belatedly gained the authority of a Supreme Commander, bitterly fulminated that France was reduced to playing sacrificial advance guard for the slumbering British Empire and United States.[108]

However, those who thought Germany's victory a decisive triumph missed the bigger picture. What had occurred was best discerned by de Gaulle, a junior general, but an authentic emergent statesman. He understood that France and her small band of partners had lost a battle of shocking magnitude, but had not lost the war. 'In the long run', writes Richard Vinen of Franco-British defence planning and strategy in the run-in to the Second World War, 'their analysis was right. . . .Unfortunately the attention with which France prepared for the long-term world war contributed to her defeat in the short-term battle for France.'[109] French failure and German success in 1940 indeed had strong elements of strangeness about them; but decisive or war-terminating they assuredly were not. The British and some of the French fought on; the Germans, fatally and inevitably, turned east. Ultimately, 1940 was not just an unexpected victory but an unfinished one; and it was a frightening but not fatal defeat.

---

108 R. Frank, *La hantise du déclin. La France 1920–1960: finances, défense et identité nationale* (Paris: Belin, 1994); M. Weygand, *Memoirs: Recalled to Service* (London: Heinemann, 1952), pp. v–vi.

109 Vinen, *France 1934–1970*, p. 32.

4

German strategy, 1939–1945

GERHARD L. WEINBERG

Plans and preparations

All German strategies before and during the Second World War were conditioned by the position of Germany, like its predecessor Prussia, in the middle of Europe. There was, therefore, in the eyes of its leaders, always the hope that it would be possible to concentrate in war against one enemy at a time, while deferring trouble elsewhere. If there were problems on more than one front at a time, interior communications or if necessary, territorial sacrifices on one front would be utilized to allow concentration on the one thought to be most critical. The way that Adolf Hitler hoped to cope with this issue as he launched the Second World War will be engaged next, but he continued to hold to this grand strategy, even when that war turned into one in which Germany fought enemies simultaneously on several fronts. A good example of that was his decision in the late autumn of 1943 to shift emphasis from the Eastern Front, where, in his opinion, land could be yielded without catastrophic implications, to the West, to ward off an expected Anglo-American invasion that could relatively quickly threaten Germany's most important industrial area.

Since the 1920s, Hitler expected and intended for Germany to take over the whole globe. How could this be accomplished by a country in the middle of Europe, a continent that he, like most Europeans of the time, saw as the centre of the earth? This would be accomplished by a sequence of wars, each concentrated on one front, each thereby facilitating the next as Germany's territory and resources grew with the conquests that each victory brought with it. That along the way compromises, and even alliances, might prove necessary would in no way eliminate the ultimate goal. Instead, by careful manipulation, compromises and alliances would facilitate the current and future steps toward the ultimate goal. In this regard also, an example from the war may serve as an illustration of a consistently held strategy, even as a temporary compromise appeared to be expedient. After entering the wider war in December 1941, as Hitler had urged, the Japanese proposed a division of Asia with the Germans at the seventieth degree longitude. Key figures in the German high command of the armed forces (*Oberkommando der Wehrmacht* – OKW) wanted Germany to have more of the Siberian industrial area and proposed an alternative line, which left Afghanistan and what is today Pakistan to Japan, instead of a substantial part of Siberia. Hitler disregarded that proposal and accepted the Japanese one.[1] He had no interest in discouraging the Japanese when they had finally taken the plunge he had been urging, but that concession in no way affected his long-term plans for a very wide-track German railway system that would extend to the Pacific Ocean at the Russian Far Eastern port of Vladivostok.[2]

Once Hitler had become Chancellor of Germany at the end of January 1933, he immediately accelerated the secret rearmament that had already been initiated, gave it the highest priority of the regime, and explained to his generals that this was for the conquest and ruthless Germanization of land in the east. Two aspects of this programme as Hitler faced it in and after 1933 need brief explication: the personal and the geographic. Since Hitler was always in a hurry, fearful that he might not live long and that no one else would have the courage to implement the programme he wanted fulfilled, he realized that he would have to work with the military officers he had inherited, whether he liked them and they liked him or not. His recognition of this reality led to several procedures and policies. In the first place, he quashed the effort of his own comrades in the Nazi Party's storm trooper organization to shift military command from the old professionals to a new group of party activists, by having a large number of the latter killed on 30 June 1934. That not only removed an alternative military hierarchy, but bound the existing one more closely to him by asserting their monopoly and involving them in the murder operation. A second procedure to assure their loyalty and obedience was rapid and very public promotions. A third one, begun on a substantial scale in 1938, and extended in wartime to all higher-level army, navy and air force leaders,

1 See the text with a map in Johanna Menzel Meskill, *Hitler and Japan: The Hollow Alliance* (New York: Atherton Press, 1966), pp. 108–13. Germany's relations with its European allies are covered in Richard DiNardo, *Germany and the Axis Powers: From Coalition to Collapse* (Lawrence: University Press of Kansas, 2005).
2 Anton Joachimsthaler, *Hitlers Breitspurbahn* (Freiburg: Eisenbahn-Kurier Verlag, 1981), pp. 81, 170, 295–6. The German Ministry of Propaganda's magazine *Signal* of March 1943 carried a big map and mentions the 9,932 km track from Berlin to Vladivostok.

was a massive system of secret, regular and tax-free bribes.[3] The effect of this can be seen in what happened on 20 July 1944, when the higher commanders inside Germany and in the then still German-occupied portions of Europe received over their teletype machines two sets of orders: one from Hitler, then in East Prussia, and one from General Ludwig Beck, the former Army Chief of Staff who headed the opposition to Hitler, from Berlin. With the exception of the commander in Paris, every single one of those who had accepted bribes voted for Hitler in Nazi Germany's last 'election'.

There was one further development in the field of personnel. During the course of the war, the armed units of the black-shirted SS, the Waffen-SS, grew in size and importance. The officers rising in that service could be considered absolutely loyal to Hitler and could be expected in the future to become replacements for the more traditional higher military officers. Since victory, not defeat, was the anticipated outcome of the fighting, here was the long-term solution to the problem of military personnel.

Now to the geographic aspect of the situation Hitler faced. It was Hitler's view that the first war had to be against Czechoslovakia, a war that would strengthen Germany's position in Central Europe, make possible the recruitment of several additional divisions for the German army out of the 3 million people of German cultural background in that country, and enlarge Germany's industrial base. That war would be followed by one against France and England, thereby removing any possible threat to Germany's main industrial region, while its army headed for the Ural mountains. That campaign, in turn, would not only provide settlement space for German farmers, but also the resources, especially the oil, needed for the subsequent war against the United States. Thereafter, all would be easy.[4]

German rearmament was carried out in the direction Hitler and his military advisors thought necessary for this sequence of wars. The accelerated general rearmament under way would be adequate for the attack on Czechoslovakia. For the war against France, the tank models under construction, together with masses of Ju 87 dive-bombers, the famous Stuka, should suffice. For England, a longer-range bomber also capable of diving, the Ju 88, was considered

---

3 Gerd R. Ueberschär and Winfried Vogel, *Dienen und Verdienen: Hitlers Geschenke an seine Eliten* (Frankfurt am Main: S. Fischer Verlag, 1999); Norman J. W. Goda, 'Black Marks: Hitler's Bribery of His Senior Officers in World War II', *Journal of Modern History* 72 (2000), 413–52.

4 See Gerhard L. Weinberg, 'Hitler's Image of the United States', in Weinberg, *World in the Balance: Behind the Scenes of World War II* (Hanover, NH: University Press of New England, 1981), pp. 53–74.

DAF: *Deutsche Arbeitsfront* or German Labour Front
RSHA: *Reichssicherheitshauptamt* or Chief Office for Reich Security
SD: *Sicherheitsdienst* or Security Service
SS: *Schutzstaffel* or Protection Department
WVHA: *Wirtschaftsverwaltungshauptamt* or Chief Office for Economic Policy

FÜHRER

REICH CHANCELLOR

MINISTER OF WAR

C-in-C WEHRMACHT

Hitler•

• Because of uncertainty and jealousy over the relative status of the Wehrmacht high command and those of the three services, individual theatres of war were placed under the command of either the OKW or the OKH. The division of authority was as follows:

OKW:
Denmark
Norway
Finland
Africa
Balkans (from July 1941)
Italy

OKH:
Poland
W. Europe (to Mar. 1941)
Balkans (to July 1941)
E. Front

OKW

• Chief of Staff: Keitel
• Chief of Operations Staff: Jodl
• Deputy Chief of Operations Staff:
  v. Butlar to Dec. 1944
  Winter
Chief of Plans: Warlimont
Chief of Foreign and Counter-Intelligence:
  Canaris (absorbed by RSHA Feb. 1944)
Chief of Military Economy and Armaments:
  Thomas to July 1944†

OKH

C-in-C: v. Brauchitsch to Dec. 1941
  Hitler
• C. of S.: Halder to Sept. 1942
  Zeitzler to July 1944
  Guderian to Mar. 1945
  Krebs
‡ O.Qu. 1: Stülpnagel to May 1940
  Mieth to Sept. 1940
  Paulus to Jan. 1942
  Blumentritt to Sept. 1942
  Heusinger to July 1944
‡ C. of Ops: v. Greiffenberg to Oct. 1940
  Heusinger to Sept. 1942
  ? to July 1944
  v. Bonin

OKL

• C-in-C: Göring to Apr. 1945
  v. Greim
• C. of S.: Jeschonnek to Aug. 1943
  Korten to June 1941
  Kreipe to Oct. 1944
  Koller
• C. of Ops: v. Waldau to Apr. 1942
  Jeschonnek to Mar. 1943
  Meister to Oct. 1943
  Koller to Oct. 1944
  Christian to Apr. 1945
C. of Supply and Procurement:
  Udet to Nov. 1941
  Milch to Mar. 1944
  Milch/Saur to Aug. 1944**
  Saur**

OKM

• C-in-C: Raeder to Jan. 1943
  Dönitz to May 1945
C. of S.: v. Friedeburg
  Schniewind to June 1941
  Fricke to Feb. 1943
  Meisel
C-in-C: U-Boats: Dönitz to Jan. 1943
  v. Friedeburg
C-in-C: High Seas Fleet: Boehm to Nov. 1939
  Marschall to May 1941
  Lütjens to May 1941
  Schniewind to July 1944
  Meendsen-Bohlken

REICH MINISTRIES including:

STATE FUNCTIONARIES including:

PARTY OFFICES including:

FOREIGN
von Ribbentrop to May 1945

MUNITIONS
from Mar. 1940
Todt to Feb. 1942
Speer

AVIATION
Göring
State Secretary:
Milch to May 1944
(post abolished)

INTERIOR
Frick to Aug. 1943
Himmler

TRANSPORT
Dorpmüller

PROPAGANDA
Goebbels to May 1945
Naumann

EASTERN OCCUPIED TERRITORIES
from July 1941
Rosenberg

CHANCELLERY
Hess to May 1941
Bormann

ORGANISATION
Ley

PRESS
Dietrich to Mar. 1945

TREASURER
Schwarz

YOUTH
von Schirach to Aug. 1940
Axmann

FOREIGN
Rosenberg

SS
Himmler
including:

RSHA
Heydrich to June 1942
Kaltenbrunner

GESTAPO
Müller

SD
Heydrich to Oct. 1939
then split into:

WVHA
Pohl

FOREIGN
Göring Schellenberg

HOME
Ohlendorf

DAF
Ley

INSPECTORATE ROAD SYSTEM
Todt

LABOUR MOBILISATION
from Mar. 1942
Sauckel

FOUR-YEAR PLAN
from Oct. 1936
Göring

† In May 1942, many of the responsibilities of Thomas's department (the Wehrwirtschafts and Rüstungsamt) were handled over to Speer's Ministry of Arms and Munitions. After Thomas's departure, the OKW remnant was renamed the Field Economic Department (Feldwirtschaftsamt), responsible largely for the collation of economic information on occupied and foreign territories.

‡ The O.Qu. 1 and the Chief of the Operations Department are often indiscriminately referred to as the Army Chief of Operations. In fact, the former (Oberquartiermeister I) was the Chief of Staff's deputy and closest advisor also responsible for all matters pertaining to training, organisation and operations. The Chief of the Operations Department was just one of his deputies, up until Sept. 1940, when that department was made directly subordinate to the Chief of Staff.

** From March to Aug. 1944 Milch retained some responsibility for aircraft procurement as joint chairman (with Speer) of the Fighter Staff (Jägerstab) of which Saur was the Director. In August, however, all responsibility was handed over the Speer's Ministry.

• All officials and officers marked thus were normally present at Hitler's daily briefing discussions (Lagebesprechungen). Also present though not named in Table 5 were the Service Liaison Officers, a representative of the Navy Chief-of-Staff and a permanent Navy representative on the OKW.

4.1 German high command

appropriate; and to cope with Britain's powerful navy, Germany would build submarines and battleships in sizes and numbers in violation of a 1935 treaty, designed to fool the London government into imagining that their naval superiority was assured. Since Hitler and his top generals shared the view that conquering the Soviet Union would be fast and simple, no new weapons systems were thought necessary for that campaign. Even when a Soviet mission of tank specialists visited a factory where the German Mark IV tanks were produced and asked where the Germans made their big tanks, and the Germans truthfully responded that these were the big ones, no one understood the obvious implication that the Soviets had bigger ones. The Germans would learn the hard way in 1941 that this was so, and began to take delivery of the new models that appeared necessary in early 1943.

While it was assumed that no special preparations were needed for the war against the Soviet Union, and it was similarly assumed that the United States could be defeated easily, that country was far away and had a large navy. Accordingly, in 1937, as soon as the weapons systems for the war against France and Britain were in the production stage, the systems needed for war with the United States were initiated. This was done as early as possible because it was correctly believed that it would take years to design and build the new weapons systems. An intercontinental bomber would be needed to bomb the United States and return to Germany without refuelling. This is the origin of the Me 264, of which only preliminary models ever flew. As for coping with the American navy, the Germans independently came to the same conclusion as the Japanese: since the Americans could always build more battleships, Germany would build bigger ones that could carry larger-calibre guns and destroy the American warships before coming within the range of them. In practice, this meant eighteen-inch guns rather than sixteen-inch ones on super-battleships of about 56,000 tons (at a time when the Japanese were going for 70,000 tons). The designs of the new ships were initiated in 1937, and keels for the first two super-battleships were laid down early in 1939. None was ever completed, but that issue will be reviewed subsequently.[5]

Starting war: Poland, Norway, France

The broad strategy for the first war, the one against Czechoslovakia, was worked out in the spring of 1938, but never implemented. At the last moment,

---

5 Ibid.

Hitler drew back from launching war in 1938 at the Munich Conference, a step he immediately regretted. No one could cheat him of war in 1939, as he believed British Prime Minister Neville Chamberlain had done in 1938. The war against France and Britain would most certainly come, and when it became clear in the winter of 1938–39 that Poland, unlike Hungary and Lithuania, would not subordinate herself to Germany as she launched her offensives in the West, that country would be attacked, whether or not the Western powers came to its defence. Both to speed the crushing of Poland and to preclude any effective blockade of Germany by the Western powers, an agreement was made with the Soviet Union. Since that country was to be conquered quite easily after the defeat of France and England, it made little difference from the German perspective just how much of Eastern Europe was yielded to the Soviets, and the German Foreign Minister flew to Moscow authorized to sign away more than the Soviet dictator, Josef Stalin, asked for.

The strategic plan for defeating Poland involved rapid advances to break the Polish defences at several points from the German provinces of East Prussia and Silesia. Bombing of Polish cities was designed to terrorize the Polish population, as the Germans called on the Soviets to invade Poland from the east. The latter did so once they had arranged a settlement with Japan over the fighting between them on the border of Manchuria and Mongolia. Thereafter it was a matter of the two invading armies meeting and then moving to the agreed demarcation line. The latter was changed somewhat at a second meeting in Moscow, but all was implemented with appropriate formalities.

Since England and France had declared war on Germany but done little during the weeks that Poland was crushed, Hitler very much hoped to strike in the West still in 1939. The basic strategy for this had been announced by him in May 1938, when it looked as if the two countries might go to war with Germany if the latter invaded Czechoslovakia. In anticipation of a relatively quick victory in the West, Hitler had made it clear to his commanders that German forces would sweep through all three Low Countries into northern France, not sparing the Netherlands as had happened in the prior war. The details of such an operation were worked out in the autumn of 1939, but to Hitler's very great regret, that operation could not be launched in 1939. A central issue that affected repeated postponements, eventually until May 10 1940, was the weather. This point requires clarification.

The campaign in the West, like its predecessor in Poland, and also the subsequent one against the Soviet Union, was to be short and quick. The German air force was designed primarily for ground support operations.

It would provide a kind of long-range artillery in support of advancing motorized forces accompanied or followed by infantry. In view of the technology of the time, this meant that there had to be a substantial number of days of anticipated good, clear weather for the German air force to play its designated role. While the timing of the Polish campaign was for the last good weather in Eastern Europe, so that the French and British would not have time to launch a major offensive before winter set in, the reality turned out to be that this also restricted the Germans. It may be noted in this connection that the German offensive of December 1944 known as the Battle of the Bulge would be launched deliberately in the poorest possible weather, because by that time command of the air had shifted to the Allies, and this looked like the best time for Germany to move because Allied air forces would be hindered from supporting their troops by the weather.

During the winter of 1939–40, as the planned strike in the West was repeatedly postponed, there were other strategic decisions that Germany had to make. Two major strategic initiatives were suggested to Hitler by the Commander-in-Chief of the German navy, Admiral Raeder, on 10 October. One was that Germany acquire bases in Norway, either by diplomatic pressure or by occupation. This issue had long been a subject of discussion within German naval circles as a means of facilitating the naval war against Britain.[6] It should be noted that the subject was raised with Hitler six weeks before the Soviet invasion of Finland at the end of November that has sometimes been alleged to have provoked German moves into Scandinavia, because of British and French discussion of ways to assist Finland and simultaneously cut off German iron supplies from Sweden. Over several months, Hitler considered this possibility, decided to adopt it, and sent the German navy and air force, both carrying troops, to occupy Denmark and Norway in April 1940. While these measures achieved surprise and, after some serious fighting in Norway, complete success, they also led to very heavy German naval losses that would impact German strategy toward England in the summer of 1940, as reviewed below.

The other initiative recommended by Admiral Raeder in early October, and periodically thereafter, was to direct Germany's submarines to sink American ships instead of trying to spare them. On this point, Hitler refused Raeder's proposal. He saw no sense in awakening the United States to mobilization at a time when neither the intercontinental bomber nor the

---

6 Carl-Axel Gemzell, *Raeder, Hitler und Skandinavien: Der Kampf für einen maritimen Operationsplan* (Lund: Gleerup, 1965).

super-battleships were ready. Germany would go to war with the United States at a time of Germany's choosing and when, hopefully, the Americans had done little to prepare.[7]

One other question in the strategic field came before the German government in the winter of 1939–40, through an initiative of the Soviet Union. Its invasion of Finland raised the obvious question of whether and how Germany should adhere to its agreement with Moscow that turned Finland, like the three Baltic States, over to the Soviets. Hitler decided that Germany would adhere to its agreement and at one point agreed to provide minimal assistance to the Soviet blockade of Finland.[8] What was critical from the German perspective was the willingness of the Soviet Union to allow Germany use of a naval base on Soviet territory west of Murmansk. This would be critical in the German strike at Norway, because German warships sent to Narvik, the port through which Germany obtained Swedish iron in winter, could be resupplied only from such a base. While Stalin was quite willing to assist the Germans in this regard, he also returned to Finland, in the March 1940 peace treaty, almost all the Finnish territory the Red Army had occupied in the north on the Arctic Ocean, thereby precluding another border with Germany once the latter occupied Norway.

A further aspect of the Russo-Finnish war in its impact on German grand strategy must be noted: the inability of the Red Army to overrun the Finnish defences in short order, instead suffering substantial losses, reinforced the existing German view of the Soviet Union's military weakness. No attention was paid either to the frequent willingness of Red Army men to continue fighting under the most desperate conditions, or to the nature of the final Soviet push that forced the Finns to sign a peace treaty yielding important territory. Hitler and his military advisors looked only for confirmation of their prior views, as they had done when they ignored the Red Army's defeat of Japanese forces in border clashes in East Asia in 1938 and 1939.[9]

When the Germans struck in the West in May 1940, they had substantially changed the original strategic plan for this offensive. The original plan had been for a move through the Low Countries, with major emphasis on the

---

7 H. L. Trefousse, *Germany and American Neutrality 1939–1941* (New York: Bookman, 1951), remains very useful.

8 Gerhard L. Weinberg, *Germany and the Soviet Union 1939–1941* (Leiden: Brill, 1972), pp. 85–91.

9 There are good brief accounts of the Changkuofeng (1938) and Nomonhan (1939) fighting in Edward J. Drea, *Japan's Imperial Army: Its Rise and Fall, 1853–1945* (Lawrence: University Press of Kansas, 2009), pp. 101–2, 203–5.

right (or northern) wing of the advancing German forces. This way of attacking was especially designed to assure German seizure of French ports on both the Channel and the Atlantic. The new plan reduced emphasis on the Atlantic ports, probably in view of the occupation of Norway, and instead placed the emphasis on the left or southern thrust through the Ardennes to the Channel, on the correct assumption that the British and French would send troops to assist the invaded countries.[10] Such a thrust could reach the Channel and cut off both the Dutch and Belgian armies and all Allied units that had come to their assistance. It is not clear whether the Germans knew this at the time that they changed plans, but the decision of the French commander, General Maurice Gamelin, to send the French reserve army into Holland at the northern end of the Allied advance would play into this German strategy, by both increasing the force that would be cut off and eliminating any possible major French counter-offensive into the German thrust from the south. The German advance was to be supported by the German air force operating in two ways, as it had in Poland. It would provide immediate support to advancing German columns of tanks and soldiers on the one hand, and by terror attacks on cities and refugees, it would disorgan ize resistance on the other.

This German strategy worked very well, assisted by the refusal of the Belgians and Dutch to coordinate their preparations with the Allies for fear of provoking the Germans; the disorganization of the French and the Allied command structure; Gamelin's misallocation of French army units; and some demoralization within a few of the French units. Once the Germans had reached the Channel coast, a new strategic decision had to be reached. It was a choice between concentrating on the Allied forces cut off by this thrust or preparing for the attack south, to prevent any new French front from being formed as an effective barrier. Between these possibilities, both Hitler and the relevant German field commander, Gerd von Rundstedt, favoured the second alternative. A critical factor in their thinking as they made this decision was that German units that had broken through needed a pause to reorganize and repair vehicles, so that a thrust south could prevent what had happened after the first great advances of the Germans in 1914: a stalemated front across France. Hitler's decision for the priority of the push south was reinforced by the assurance of Hermann Göring, head of the German air force, that it could destroy the cut-off Allied forces.

10 Ernest R. May, *Strange Victory: Hitler's Conquest of France* (New York: Hill and Wang, 2000).

The effects of the German choice to give priority to the thrust south were, on the one hand, that over 200,000 British and 100,000 French soldiers escaped to England, although without their equipment, and on the other hand, that the early June German attack against the new defence line the French were trying to create was relatively quickly and overwhelmingly successful. The German air force could not accomplish its mission, in spite of inflicting heavy losses, in part because it was now operating in an area where British planes could fight from home bases in southern England. The successful evacuation of the bulk of the British Expeditionary Force would have a significant impact on government deliberations in London and public morale in Britain, both important for the subsequent development of the war. The rapid collapse of French forces in June had major military and political effects on German strategy.

On the basis of the mistaken impression that the war was about over, Benito Mussolini, the dictator of Italy, decided that this was the time to join Germany in hostilities against the Western powers, so that Italy could share in the spoils of victory. This decision had major effects on German strategy beginning in the autumn of 1940, and these will be reviewed subsequently. Meanwhile, the clear signs that the French military was disintegrating had immediate strategic results for Hitler. In June and July, Hitler made important decisions about the next two wars: those against the Soviet Union and the United States (while agreeing to an armistice with France and planning an invasion of Britain if it did not follow the French example of suing for an armistice). Even before the French government of Marshall Pétain asked for an armistice, both Hitler and Army Chief of Staff General Franz Halder began making plans for an attack on the Soviet Union, preferably still in 1940. Originally thinking of an invasion in early September of that year, a number of practical considerations had persuaded Hitler by the end of July that this invasion would have to be postponed into the spring or early summer of 1941. The decision about war with the United States was the early July secret order for the resumption of construction on the blue-water navy, including aircraft carriers and super-battleships.

The expectation of invading the Soviet Union, preferably still in 1940, and the need for a big navy to fight the United States contributed to Hitler's decision to grant France an armistice, if its terms assured Germany of complete control of the French Channel and Atlantic coasts, and precluded any domestic French military revival. With the French government agreeable to such terms, Hitler restrained Mussolini from insisting already at this time on far-reaching colonial and territorial demands. A partition of Africa between Germany, Italy and an allied Nationalist regime in South Africa could come later; the main current issues of preparing the invasion of the Soviet Union and crushing Britain had to come first.[11]

New decisions: June 1940 – June 1941

Several studies of how best to crush the Soviet Union quickly were drafted by German generals in the summer of 1940, and Hitler reviewed these and developed the plan that would be finalized in December. While practical preparations were made to improve transportation and supply arrangements in East Prussia, Silesia and German-occupied Poland, there also began troop movements into those areas. The plans that were developed looked to rapid German thrusts toward Leningrad, Moscow and Kiev, with assistance from Finland in the north and Romania in the south. It was assumed that these offensives would collapse the Soviet state so that after a few months the main fighting would be over and only mopping-up operations might have to follow. The defeat of the Soviet Union would encourage Japan to move in East Asia and keep the United States preoccupied there until Germany was ready to fight and defeat that country. If Britain had not succumbed by the time the Soviet Union was crushed, it would surely sue for peace then.

Since the London government made it clear in late June and early July of 1940 that they would fight on, the country would have to be invaded. It was in this context that the heavy German naval losses in the Norwegian campaign were a major handicap. It was not only that several cruisers and many destroyers had been lost, but that the two battlecruisers *Scharnhorst* and *Gneisenau* had been damaged and would not be repaired until after the time for a 1940 invasion had passed. Under these circumstances, complete control of the air would be absolutely essential. The effort to attain that control was made in June, July, August and the first part of September, but failed in the face of a British resistance that combined radar, spotters, fighter planes, anti-aircraft guns and a population willing to endure all manner of deprivations, damages and losses. The last factor, the attitude of the British public, also made the heavy bombing of British cities a blunted weapon.[12] A variety of invasion preparations had been made by the Germans, from

---

11 Klaus Hildebrand, *Vom Reich zum Weltreich: Hitler, NSDAP und koloniale Frage 1919–1945* (Munich: Fink Verlag, 1969); Gerhard L. Weinberg, 'German Colonial Plans and Policies, 1938–1942', in Weinberg, *World in the Balance*, pp. 96–136.

12 There is a new take on this in Richard North, *The Many not the Few: The Stolen History of the Battle of Britain* (London: Continuum, 2012).

designating a police chief for London and printing an arrest list, to training horses to ride on barges so that they could be included in the first invasion wave.[13] All had to be postponed as the weather in the Channel ended the 1940 season during which an attempt might have been made. Here was the first significant check to German grand strategy in the war.

The decision to invade the Soviet Union with the assistance of Romania presented the Germans, as a by-product, with a new strategic problem. Since Hitler did not in 1940 explain the intent to invade the Soviet Union to Mussolini, the latter worried that the movement of German troops into Romania, beginning in September 1940, signalled German plans to dominate the Balkans. In order to mark Italy's interest in that area, he ordered an invasion of Greece in October 1940. That invasion was first stalled and then reversed by the Greeks, who pushed the invading force back into Albania (occupied by Italy in 1939). This opened two possibilities from the perspective of Berlin: from airfields in Greece, the British air force might bomb the Romanian oilfields that were of critical importance for the Germans, and there might be an overthrow of the Mussolini regime in Italy. This latter possibility also looked like a conceivable result of simultaneous Italian defeats in Africa.

From Germany's perspective, the British conquest of Italian colonies in northeast Africa in the winter of 1940–41 was unfortunate, but hardly critical. The possibility that the British Army in North Africa might not only defend Egypt successfully, but conquer the whole Italian colony of Libya, looked far more dangerous. The loss by Italy of the main colony it had acquired in 1912 by war with the Ottoman Empire looked to the German government like another danger to Mussolini's rule. Whatever others in the German government and military thought about the Italians in general and Mussolini in particular, there was never any doubt in Hitler's mind about the importance of Italy as an ally, and about Mussolini as a key figure in keeping Italy on Germany's side in this war – as opposed to its role on the other side in the last war. One should also note Hitler's great admiration for Mussolini as a person.

These concerns about Italy led to two closely related decisions in Berlin. The German army would rescue Italy's Greek adventure by invading that country from Bulgaria, hopefully with assistance from Yugoslavia. Also a German force would be sent to North Africa to rescue Libya for Italy, with that force commanded by one of Hitler's favourite generals, Erwin Rommel.

---

13 In 1983, a former German soldier explained to the author that his assignment in the summer of 1940 had been to take batches of horse onto a barge on the Rhine River to accustom them to standing on something that wiggled.

Preparations to implement these two decisions went forward in January, February and March of 1941 and were successfully implemented in April of that year. While Bulgaria cooperated with Germany's plans for attacking Greece in anticipation of acquiring a piece of that country, Yugoslavia moved away from cooperation at the last moment and thus became the victim of a combined German-Italian invasion and occupation, which started with a peacetime Sunday bombing of its capital of Belgrade. The German invasion of Greece succeeded both in occupying the whole country and in driving out British forces that had been sent there. The subsequent costly but successful conquest of the island of Crete, at a time when the German-Italian force in Libya was driving the British back into Egypt, raised new strategic questions for the Germans.

The heavy losses of the German parachute unit in the fighting on Crete led to the decision never to try an airborne landing operation again, and that decision would preclude any operation to seize the island of Malta, which long looked and really was critical for the whole campaign in North Africa. The success of the fighting in Crete, however, appeared to open a strategic possibility in the Middle East, as anti-British Nationalists rose in Iraq, and the Vichy French authorities in Syria allowed the Germans to assist them. With a possible thrust also from Libya into and through Egypt, and massive rather than nominal German intervention in Syria and Iraq, was this Germany's opportunity to take over the area, deprive the Allies of their oil resources, and cut the imperial route to India all at one blow? While some in the German military and diplomatic services argued for this strategy, Hitler turned it down. The invasion of the Soviet Union that was being prepared had an absolute prior claim on Germany's military resources. While it was assumed that victory could be attained quickly, that presupposed a concentration of German effort. Units sent into Yugoslavia and Greece would be needed in the East, and only minimal army and air resources could at that time be spared for the Middle East. It would be conquered from the north once German forces had occupied the Caucasus as part of the campaign in the East. Those Arab Nationalist leaders looking forward to the arrival of German troops in Egypt, Iraq and Palestine would have to wait their turn, which would come after the invasion of the Soviet Union had succeeded.

Invading the Soviet Union and war with the United States

A number of factors had led to a postponement of the invasion of the Soviet Union for several weeks, to 22 June 1941. The delay also benefited the

Germans, as Stalin provided additional supplies of critical materials to them and ran extra trains to transfer rubber and soybeans from East Asia. Although, as anticipated, Finland and Romania joined in on Germany's side, and Mussolini insisted on sending some divisions to help, the operation did not go as expected. Because Stalin refused to believe the information about German plans that he had received from his own intelligence services and from the British and American governments, the initial German attack surprised the Soviet forces. Vast numbers of Red Air Force planes were destroyed on the ground and there was much confusion. German forces advanced rapidly, cutting off much of the Red Army that had been moved from the prior fortified border line into the newly annexed territory. As the recent work by David Stahel shows, however, by the end of July, early August, it was clear that the basic German concept had failed.[14] The Soviet Union did not collapse at the first blow as the Germans anticipated. There were counter-attacks at some places, like at Yelnya on the central part of the front, which either pushed back or at least temporarily held the Germans. Unlike either the Tsarist regime in 1917 or the provisional government in 1918, the Soviet regime maintained effective control of the unoccupied portions of the country, and mobilized its human and material resources to continue the fight.

When it was all over, German military leaders would blame the winter and every other factor they could think of for the failure of the offensive. It was, however, invariably as cold and the snow as deep for the Soviets as for the Germans, and both German planning and operational procedures contributed heavily to the success of the Red Army. German intelligence had grossly underestimated Soviet capacity, and hence what might be needed to overcome it. No one in the German high command understood the relationship between great distances and the maintenance problems of tanks and trucks. The assumptions about the racially inferior Slavic population and the incompetence of their leaders – the factors that had made victory certain in Hitler's thinking and had contributed to his view that the Bolshevik revolution was a most fortunate event for Germany – turned out to be false. The purges of 1937–39 had indeed weakened the Soviet Union, but not nearly enough to offset both the German mistaken assessment and the effects of their conduct. It was, in large part, the latter that converted Stalin from being

---

14 David Stahel, *Operation Barbarossa and Germany's Defeat in the East* (New York: Cambridge University Press, 2009).

seen by the Soviet population as a feared and hated dictator into the benign saviour of his people from a fate too horrible to contemplate.

Before launching the invasion, the Germans had decided to slaughter much of the local population and starve or enslave the rest, to kill certain categories of prisoners of war and let the rest mostly starve or die of disease, and to kill all Jews in the newly occupied Soviet territory.[15] While the details of this behaviour would not be known for years, the general thrust of German policy became obvious from the start, and could easily be compared by those in the occupied area of middle age and older with their experience of the German army in the preceding war. There had been some bad incidents then, but this was obviously a different army, and word quickly spread throughout the Soviet Union.

The operational details of the 1941 campaign cannot be reviewed here, but German local defeats at both the southern and the northern end of the front preceded and accompanied the defeat in November–December before Moscow. The Soviet government had made extensive preparations for continuing the fighting if Moscow were captured; but, except for the transfer of foreign diplomats to Kuibyshev, these did not have to be implemented. In the far north, the Finnish army made some progress, but the Germans were unable to advance as far as the Soviet port of Murmansk that was their objective. Similarly, in the south, the Romanian forces and an Italian contingent helped, but the Germans were halted long before the approaches to the Caucasus. Already in the autumn it was increasingly clear to Hitler and most of his top military commanders that the campaign in the Soviet Union would continue into 1942. Under these circumstances, what would be German strategy for the coming year?

In one field of high priority there would be no change. As the systematic killing of Jews had gone forward in June and July without any serious objection from the military, and instead substantial cooperation, the appearance of imminent victory had led to Hitler's decision in July to extend the killing programme to whatever portions of Europe Germany controlled.[16] There would be no change in this general policy as the campaign in the East faltered. High-ranking German military leaders commented in their diaries and correspondence that there were no trains to ship winter clothing to their

---

15 Gerhard L. Weinberg, 'Another Look at Hitler and the Beginning of the Holocaust', in Sara R. Horowitz (ed.), *Lessons and Legacies X* (Evanston, Ill.: Northwestern University Press, 2012), pp. 5–12.
16 Ibid.

freezing soldiers, but there were plenty of trains to run on the same tracks in the same direction to carry Jews from elsewhere in Europe to their deaths in the East.[17]

But what about the continued fighting? Obviously not only had the Soviet Union not been crushed, but Britain was also still fighting. Bombing British cities in the winter of 1940–41 caused casualties and damage, but was not having the effect the Germans hoped for. In this context, they urged Japan to move against Britain's possessions in East Asia, and in particular to seize Singapore when the British had to concentrate on defence of the home islands. Tokyo answered that they saw the realities and expected to take advantage of the situation in Europe, beginning with the occupation of northern French Indochina in September 1940, thereby cutting the supply route to Nationalist China over the Hanoi–Haiphong railway. They also pressured the British into a temporary closure of the Burma Road, with its similar role. As for seizing Singapore and other British possessions, that would come, but in 1946.

The Germans understood that this year had been selected by Tokyo because, under the existing American legislation, it was the year that the United States would evacuate its bases in the Philippines that were to become independent in 1944. From the German perspective, 1946 was far too late, but the Japanese had chosen it from concern about American forces threatening the left flank of any move south. Since the Germans planned to fight the United States anyway, they would relieve this Japanese worry by promising to go to war with that country the moment Japan did. This commitment also fitted with the projected development of Germany's armaments programme. In the summer of 1941, it increasingly favoured the navy and air force because of the assumption that victory over the Soviet Union required less emphasis on the army. The course of the campaign in the East forced a revision of these priorities. Construction on super-battleships and other warships was again halted, as the emphasis on armaments shifted back to the army. Just one example: new, bigger tanks had to be designed and

---

17 See, for example, the letter of General Helmuth Stieff to his wife of 19 November 1941, commenting on the difficult railroad situation and contrasting this with the availability of a train every second day for the transportation of Jews from Germany to Mink and their fate, in Hans Rothfels (ed.), 'Ausgewählte Briefe von Generalmajor Helmuth Stieff', *Vierteljahrshefte für Zeitgeschichte* 2 (1954), 302–3. The impact of the Holocaust on German military operations is covered in Yaron Pasher, *Holocaust versus Wehrmacht: How Hitler's 'Final Solution' Undermined the German War Effort* (Lawrence: University Press of Kansas, 2014, 1).

then developed; and those of the current models held back in desert camouflage for the anticipated strike into the Middle East from the Caucasus area were sent to the Russian front in October and November 1941, where soldiers had to cover them with white paint. If Japan attacked the United States, along with its descent on the British, Dutch and French colonies in East Asia and the Pacific, Germany would have on its side the big navy there had not been time to build itself, and the Americans would be kept busy elsewhere while the Germans finished off the Soviets.

Hitler personally promised Japanese Foreign Minister Matsuoka Yosuke, when he was in Berlin in March 1941, that Germany would declare war on the United States when Japan did, and the Japanese received similar assurances from Mussolini. This promise, and the German attack on the Soviet Union in June 1941, which removed Japanese concerns about an attack by the Soviets when Japan headed south, produced the Japanese decision of July 1941 to begin the move south by occupying southern French Indochina, a move clearly away from their war with China. The continued negotiations of the Japanese with the United States greatly worried the Germans; and as the campaign against the Soviets did not go as easily as Hitler had expected, he became increasingly worried that the Japanese might balk at expanding their war.[18] He drove the German army forward and made and authorized optimistic announcements about the military situation to encourage the Japanese, ironically at the very time that President Roosevelt hoped that continued negotiations would delay any Japanese strike until they could see for themselves that German victory in the war was not as certain as they thought. Hitler won this race by about ten days. He and Mussolini reassured Tokyo that their promise held a few days before the Japanese struck, at a time when the Germans were being beaten before Moscow and the British were about to launch an offensive in North Africa.

As soon as he learned at his East Prussian headquarters that the Japanese had attacked the United States and Great Britain, Hitler instructed the German navy to initiate hostilities against the United States and eight other countries in the western hemisphere. He had been holding back the German navy that had been urging war with the United States since October 1939; now he did not want to wait the three or four days needed to gather the German Reichstag in Berlin to give them the good news and to carry out the

---

18 On this, see the document included in Marianne Feuersenger, *Im Vorzimmer der Macht: Aufzeichnungen aus dem Wehrmachtführungsstab und Führerhauptquartier 1940–1945* (Munich: Herbig, 1999), p. 110.

necessary diplomatic procedures. There was great enthusiasm in German military headquarters, and German submarines mounted a substantial campaign against shipping off the fully lighted American Atlantic coast. Cooperation and coordination with Japan did not ever really take place, but Hitler was at least temporarily enthused by an ally who had repeated his recent act of striking in peacetime on a Sunday.

If Japan was expected to keep the United States busy and threaten Britain and its colonies and Dominions with disaster, what about the Soviet Union? Stalin's major error in the winter of insisting on offensives on the whole front, instead of concentrating all efforts on the central front where the German army group was reeling from its defeat before Moscow and might have been completely shattered, facilitated German stabilization of the front in March–April 1942. The strategic concept for the Eastern Front for 1942 was fairly simple. Unable to replace all the losses incurred in the preceding fighting, Germany could not repeat the 1941 strategy of three major thrusts: in the north, the centre and the south. Minimal local offensives would improve the situation at selected segments of the front, but there would be only one major offensive in the south, having the Caucasus oilfields as its objective. Such a single thrust deep into the Soviet Union would produce lengthening flanks as it succeeded, and hence a major part of German preparation was directed at getting their Romanian, Italian and Hungarian allies to increase their troop commitments. While this effort proved successful, the Germans failed to provide their allies with the equipment, especially the armour and anti-tank artillery, that they would need. The Germans later blamed their allies when Red Army forces broke through the extended fronts the Germans had asked them to hold, but in reality the fault was their own.

The German offensive, codenamed Operation BLUE, was launched on 28 June and at first appeared to be succeeding. This time, however, the Red Army not only fought more skilfully, but Stalin allowed withdrawals when these appeared necessary, so that the German encirclements did not produce the huge numbers of prisoners that had characterized 1941 battles. As the two German army groups conducting the campaign headed southeast toward the Caucasus, and east toward Stalingrad to protect the northern flank of the expected conquest of the oilfields, both were slowed by Soviet resistance. The street fighting inside the city of Stalingrad made for a concentration of German forces there. This contributed to the success of the planned Soviet enveloping offensive, which broke through the Romanian and German units protecting the flanks of the German army grinding its way through the city. This success of the Red Army was also assisted by developments in Africa reviewed below, but it had two further significant effects on German strategy. The German offensive to break through the encirclement of Stalingrad failed, and the Red Army launched a further offensive that crushed the Italian army at the front northwest of Stalingrad. The German army group that had been fighting toward the Caucasus had to be withdrawn, lest it be cut off if the Red Army retook the city of Rostov, as it had in the preceding winter. The Germans were able to strike a hard blow at the advancing Red Army by retaking the important city of Kharkov in a counter-offensive in March 1943. The main strategic result of the German 1942 offensive, however, was not only that the oilfields of the Caucasus remained in Soviet hands (the one at Maikop was recovered when the Germans retreated), but also that the defeat at Stalingrad had a major impact on how people in Germany and the rest of the world saw the course of the war. Hitler had ordered the holding of a portion of the northern Caucasus area, generally referred to as the Kuban bridgehead, as a base for a renewed effort to seize the Caucasus oilfields in 1943, but the failure of the 1943 German summer offensive ended that hope, and the area was evacuated in October 1943.

The changing tide of war, 1942–1943

In 1942, the Germans found themselves in a multi-front war – precisely what they most wanted to avoid. While the British could land only Commandos on the coast of German-controlled Europe, with some failures and some successes, the main British effort that had some effect on German strategy was their bombing campaign. Under the impact of German terror bombing, the British had substituted bombs for leaflets. Their raids increased in number and weight as well as changed in nature during 1941 and 1942. As the leadership in London realized that daytime raids led to heavy losses of aeroplanes and those that actually bombed generally missed their targets, the shift was made to night-time bombing of cities.[19] For the German leadership, this meant a major diversion of resources. Parts of the German air force had to stay at home to defend industries and cities, and an increasing proportion of guns and ammunition was directed at the sky rather than used at the front. This also required a diversion of human resources, to service the anti-aircraft defences and contain or repair the increasingly substantial damage in Germany itself and parts of

---

19 The report by Mr Butt which set off the bombing policy change is printed in Sir Charles Webster and Noble Frankland, *The Strategic Air Offensive against Germany 1939–1945*, vol. IV: *Annexes and Appendices* (4 vols., London: HMSO, 1961), pp. 205–13.

German-occupied Europe. Already in the winter of 1941–42, the Germans had been forced to transfer a whole air fleet from the Eastern Front to the Mediterranean – just as the crisis there developed – but in November 1942, this diversion of air power from the Eastern Front was increased by the landing of American and British forces in French northwest Africa.

Operation TORCH, as the Allies called it, came as a complete surprise to the Germans. In May and June of 1942, the German-Italian force in Libya had won a series of victories and had again driven into Egypt. It had looked for a moment that this thrust might conquer Egypt, take the Suez Canal, and move into Palestine to meet the German army that was to seize the Caucasus oilfields and then move into the Middle East from the north. Since Hitler did not trust the Italians to participate effectively in the policy of killing all Jews on earth, the Jews of Egypt, Palestine and the rest of the Middle East were to be killed by a murder commando attached to Rommel's headquarters before the area was turned over to Italy.[20] In July 1942, however, the British Army stopped the German advance with the help of American tanks. The German-Italian army tried to break through in July and August, but failed. At the end of October and in the first days of November, the British launched a major offensive that defeated Rommel's force. The latter, in violation of Hitler's order to stand and die at El Alamein, pulled his troops back across Libya. A few days after the battle in Egypt, on 8 November, the Allies landed in French northwest Africa to attack Rommel's army from the west and clear the Mediterranean coast of North Africa.

The Germans had discouraged Pétain from going to North Africa to raise the enthusiasm of his troops there for fighting the Allies, but Hitler was very interested in driving the Allies out of the area. He directed Rommel to accomplish this, and together with Mussolini sent a large force from Sicily to Tunisia. While that army prevented the Allies from quickly capturing the key ports of Tunis and Bizerte, the Soviet offensive at Stalingrad prevented the Germans from sending more troops to North Africa, just as the army sent to Tunisia could not assist the effort to break the encirclement of the German army in Stalingrad. The fighting in North Africa had already obliged the Germans to divert air force units from the Eastern Front to the Mediterranean theatre; now German transport planes could not simultaneously fly to

---

20 Klaus-Michael Mallmann and Martin Cüppers, *Nazi Palestine: The Plans for the Extermination of the Jews in Palestine*, trans. Krista Smith (New York: Enigma Books, 2010). Since Erwin Rommel had moved his family into a house stolen from the Jewish community of Stuttgart and given to him by Hitler, there is no reason to believe that he had any objections.

Stalingrad from Ukraine and to Tunisia from Sicily. Total disaster followed in both when Hitler prohibited the German army from breaking out of the Stalingrad encirclement and ordered no effort to rescue German soldiers in Tunisia.

As the remainder of Italy's colonial empire was lost and an Italian army was crushed on the Eastern Front, Hitler became increasingly concerned about the situation in Italy. The country might be invaded by the Allies, Mussolini might be overthrown, and the Italian military was likely to become less and less willing to fight. The German leadership faced a strategic choice. They could initiate the movement of German troops into Italy against any of these possibilities. Alternatively, they could let the whole country go, and defend Germany and its Austrian, French and Yugoslav possessions from positions in the Alps. Hitler decided to defend Italy and began to shift troops into the country. These would fight whatever Allied troops might try to land anywhere in Italy or on the islands of Sicily and Sardinia, and, if necessary, fight the Italians themselves if they switched sides. The results of this strategic decision became evident in the summer of 1943.

German strategy for the Eastern Front in 1943 looked to an offensive in the south that would crush the Soviet forces in the Kursk area and thereby regain the initiative on the front, with the further hope, as already mentioned, of another attempt to seize the Caucasus oilfields, as well as an operation in the north to take Leningrad. What looks like hopelessly unrealistic planning should be seen in the combination of continued German underestimation of the Soviet Union and excessive expectations of the new model tanks beginning to be produced (and for the delivery of which the date of the offensive was repeatedly postponed). With Stalin persuaded by his generals to await a German offensive and then strike, the Germans launched Operation CITADEL on 5 July 1943. German forces ground forward on both the northern and southern portions of CITADEL, but failed to break the determined Soviet resistance in their very extensively developed defences. The offensive was called off after a week, because the Allied landing in Sicily led Hitler to send more forces into Italy, and a massive Soviet offensive into the rear of the German northern part of CITADEL in the Orel area dramatically drove back German troops. The last German summer offensive was now followed by the first major Soviet summer offensive, and thereafter German strategy on the Eastern Front was primarily one of trying – usually unsuccessfully – to hold what they had conquered in 1941. Their strategy in this was affected by the turn in the war at sea that also occurred in the summer of 1943.

German naval strategy in 1942–43 concentrated on the campaign against Allied shipping. Submarines, long-range aeroplanes and some surface raiders were fairly successful, as the Allies lost more tonnage almost every month than they built. This put a stranglehold on their strategy, as England could be kept in the war, the Soviet Union supplied with aid, and the Americans project their growing power across the Atlantic and Pacific only by coping with the German effort in this field. When the Allies turned the tide in this campaign in May–June 1943,[21] and the new Commander of the German navy, Admiral Karl Dönitz, therefore withdrew submarines from the key battle zone in the North Atlantic, Hitler had to make a major strategic decision. Germany could accept defeat in the war at sea and concentrate on the production of tanks and other weapons for land warfare, or follow the advice of Dönitz to continue emphasis on the war at sea by investing resources into the development and construction of large numbers of new types of submarines, which could stay under water longer and move far more rapidly. Hitler decided in favour of the new submarines and a hoped-for reversal of the war at sea in Germany's favour.

The decision in favour of building the new types of submarines and training crews for them had major implications for German strategy at the northern portion of the Eastern Front for the rest of the war. If the new submarines were to be run in and their crews trained, that would necessarily be in the Baltic Sea. Hitler therefore ordered territory along the south shore of the Baltic to be held by German forces, even when cut off by the Red Army. The new submarines did not become available for operations until April 1945, but this is the context for the strange appearance of that portion of the Eastern Front from late 1943 until the surrender of May 1945.[22]

Another massive allocation of German material and manpower resources in the latter part of the war was Hitler's decision for the new weapons systems that were designed to level London and other English cities, perhaps a sign of the love for the English that some have invented for him. These weapons, the V-1 pilotless aeroplane, the V-2 ballistic missile, the V-3 ultra-long-range cannon and the V-4 multi-stage rocket all absorbed vast resources for development, production and, in the case of V-1 and V-3, launching sites. The first two were employed in 1944, but although they caused some

---

21 Weinberg, *A World at Arms: A Global History of World War II* (2nd edn, New York: Cambridge University Press, 2005), p. 382 and nn. 65–6.
22 Howard D. Grier, *Hitler, Dönitz and the Baltic Sea: The Third Reich's Last Hope, 1944–1945* (Annapolis, Md.: Naval Institute Press, 2007).

casualties and damage in England and Belgium, they never had a significant impact on the course of hostilities. Although Germany had made some scientific advances in the nuclear field, there was never a major resource allocation to that area.[23]

The 10 July 1943 landing of American and British troops on Sicily succeeded in a hard campaign, but events confirmed Hitler's concerns about the decline in the willingness of Italian troops to fight and the stability of Mussolini's position. The Italian dictator was dismissed by his own associates, arrested by the Italian king, and had to be rescued and installed in a puppet government in northern Italy by the Germans. The bulk of the German soldiers on Sicily were evacuated and could be integrated into the very substantial German forces being ordered by Hitler into Italy in pursuit of his earlier strategic decision. The new Italian government botched the exit from the war about as badly as Mussolini had its entrance, and the country became the scene of bitter and destructive fighting as German forces faced the Allies. Two whole German armies were assigned to the fight there, and other German units had to replace Italian occupation forces in France, Yugoslavia and Greece. Large numbers of Italian soldiers were murdered, and those surviving became slave labourers.

Two strategic developments of the autumn of 1943 must be noted. The massive allocation of German resources to air defence began to turn the air war against the Allies. Ever higher losses faced the British and Americans, who knew that absolute control of the air over France and Belgium would be essential for an invasion in the West planned for 1944. Unlike the Germans, who were unable to recover from the summer 1943 reversal of the war at sea, the Western Allies turned the air war around in the first months of 1944. The other strategic shift was that Hitler ordered that priority be given to the defence of the West in Directive No. 51 of 3 November 1943. As he phrased it, territory could be given up in the East if necessary, but a successful Allied invasion in the West would have most serious repercussions.[24] He had ordered the unoccupied portion of France invaded when the Allies landed in northwest Africa, and the Vichy army had not fired a shot. Hitler retained his hatred for the French, but their coast had to be defended.

---

23 Geoffrey Brooks, *Hitler's Nuclear Weapons* (London: Leo Cooper, 1993); Mark Walker, 'Legenden um die deutsche Atombombe', *Vierteljahrshefte für Zeitgeschichte* 38 (1990), 45–74.
24 Alan F. Wilt, *The Atlantic Wall 1941–1944: Hitler's Defenses for D-Day* (New York: Enigma Books, 2004).

Defeat

Beyond defending as effectively as possible, there were few strategic choices to be made by Germany in 1944. As its leaders saw the possibility of satellites jumping off the sinking German ship, plans were developed to occupy Hungary and Romania. That for Hungary was implemented in March 1944, but that for Romania could not be as that country switched sides in late August. Finland signed an armistice with the Soviet Union in September, in spite of German efforts to keep it in the war. By the end of the year, German and Finnish troops were fighting each other at the very northern tip of the front.

Both in the East and in the West, the Germans launched local counter-offensives after the Allied invasion in Normandy and the Soviet BAGRA-TION offensive on the central part of the Eastern Front succeeded. Neither advance could be stopped. As Soviet forces threatened to cut off the German units in Greece, Albania and southern-occupied Yugoslavia, Hitler author-ized the army group there to retreat. Similarly, as the Western Allied forces from the landing in Normandy and the subsequent landing on the French Mediterranean coast threatened to meet and cut off the army group in southwest France, he authorized its withdrawal. The German units cut off at the northern part of the Eastern Front, including an army group in western Latvia, however, were not allowed to withdraw, because of the Baltic strategy previously mentioned.

The final strategic decision of the war was to launch the country's last reserves into a major offensive against the US Army in the West in Decem-ber. This Ardennes offensive, or Battle of the Bulge, had double strategic aims. On the strictly military side, the offensive was to split the American and British armies and seize the key port of Antwerp. The strategic side was the assumption that a major defeat would shatter the American home front and its support for the war, and drive the United States out of the European war. Such a German victory would enable them to move substantial masses of soldiers and equipment to the Eastern Front, to halt and then drive back a Red Army which had suffered very great losses in the preceding fighting. The offensive failed and, simultaneously, a Soviet winter offensive drove into the eastern parts of Germany. In February 1945, the Western Allies resumed their offensives and drove into Germany to meet the Red Army. At the end, German forces still controlled most of Norway, which had been kept reinforced for fear of an Allied landing there, all of Denmark, some parts of Germany and Austria, but little else. The German commanders in Italy had surrendered a few days before Dönitz, as Hitler's successor, authorized unconditional surrender.

Conclusion

The grand strategy that Germany followed in the Second World War was essentially one developed and ordered by Adolf Hitler. The country's military leaders were generally supporters of Hitler and his strategy, only occasionally offering alternatives or minor criticisms. Hitler generally listened to these, sometimes adopting their ideas, as in the case of Admiral Raeder's advocacy of an occupation of Norway, while rejecting others, such as that admiral's advocacy of war with the United States in 1939 and a Mediterranean strategy in 1940. Neither Göring as head of the air force, nor Walter Brauchitsch as head of the army until December 1941, ever pushed for substantial alternative strategies. Admiral Dönitz, Raeder's successor as naval chief, certainly influenced Hitler's strategic decisions about the navy and about the Eastern Front in the latter years of the war, as already mentioned, and would be selected by Hitler as his own successor. The field marshals accepted their secret tax-free bribes and generally did as they were told.

The basic concept of Germany conquering the globe and instituting a demographic revolution was surely a fantastic one, but German strategy was adapted to what were assumed to be the requirements for its realization. Defeats in the Battle of Britain in 1940 and on the Eastern Front in 1941 placed Germany in a position from which it neither could nor wanted to find an exit; at the same time, the coalition it had created against itself insisted on total victory. Hitler's repeated insistence that there would be no repeat of 1918 ironically proved to be correct, as the fighting moved into Germany itself and ended in unconditional surrender.

5

Mussolini's strategy, 1939–1943

JOHN GOOCH

'One man and one man alone has ranged the Italian people in deadly struggle against the British Empire,' Winston Churchill told a radio audience on 23 December 1940.[1] Since then, the view that the war of 1940–43 was 'a fascist war, willed, conducted and lost by Mussolini', has gained widespread currency – its drivers a prestige-driven foreign policy and a colonial war that could deliver easy successes, and so distract the populace from mounting economic and social stresses.[2] With it has gone the view that Mussolini progressively emasculated the General Staffs of the Italian armed forces, shrinking their professional autonomy to the point of extinction, and creating a docile instrument to carry out his directions and fight his war.[3] While true in essentials, this is not the whole story. Mussolini's hands were on the levers of power and he frequently imposed his own strategic ideas – such as they were. However, his military played an important supporting role in devising and executing Italian strategy, developing the plans that underpinned Italian operations in all theatres of war, converting the Duce's often wild strategic ideas into organizational designs without ever seriously questioning them, and loyally following orders.[4]

---

1 Winston S. Churchill, *The Second World War,* vol. II: *Their Finest Hour* (6 vols., London: Cassell, 1950), p. 548.
2 Giorgio Rochat, 'La Guerra di Grecia', in Mario Isnenghi (ed.), *I luoghi della memoria: Strutture ed eventi dell'Italia unità* (Bari: Laterza, 1997), vol. II, p. 347; Giorgio Rochat, 'Mussolini, chef de guerre (1940–1943)', *Révue d'histoire de la deuxième guerre mondiale* 100 (October 1975), 44, 46, 47.
3 Renzo De Felice, *Mussolini l'alleato,* vol. I: *Italia in guerra 1940–1943,* tomo I: *Dalla guerra "breve" alla guerra lunga* (4 vols., Turin: Einaudi, 1990), p. 40; Denis Mack Smith, *Mussolini* (London: Penguin, 1981), p. 237.
4 The structures of command at the top of the Italian armed forces were complex and overlapping – deliberately so, as this reinforced Mussolini's powers of control. The post of Chief of the Armed Forces General Staff was created in 1925, supposedly to coordinate the planning of the Chiefs of Staff of the three armed services; but with vague and limited powers, and a staff of only half a dozen officers, Marshal Badoglio (who held the post until December 1940) could do little – which was all he seems to have been

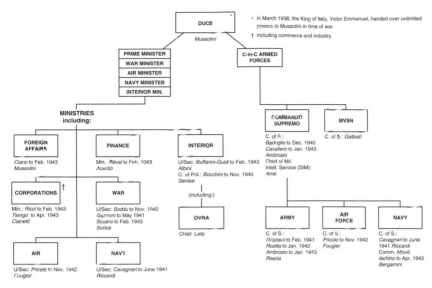

5.1 Italian high command

A past master at the arts of political manipulation, Mussolini had no real understanding of military strategy. His time in the trenches during the First World War simply strengthened his belief in the overarching importance of morale. Mostly he paid little attention to questions of materiel. Other than from experience and a priori reasoning, his military ideas – such as they were – came from reading, from which he took the lessons he wanted and those which matched his predilections. However, too much reading, or reading of the wrong sort, was to be avoided: Garibaldi, Mussolini told his son-in-law Galeazzo Ciano in 1938, was lucky to have been illiterate: 'Had he been literate

inclined to do. The *Comando Supremo* (Italian high command) was created on 29 May 1940; Mussolini, as its head, directed the overall conduct of the war, determined the military objectives and assigned them to the respective armed services, with Badoglio as his assistant. The king was persuaded to derogate his constitutional powers as head of the armed forces to Mussolini for the duration of the war. Mussolini also held the post of War Minister and worked mostly through his Under-Secretaries; two of them, Admiral Cavagnari (navy) and General Pricolo (air force), were also Chiefs of their respective General Staffs, which gave them direct access to the Duce, while the third, General Soddu (army), was Badoglio's deputy. General Ugo Cavallero, who succeeded Badoglio, extended and reinforced the *Comando Supremo's* control over the three service chiefs and secured full control of the army; but the navy and air force Chiefs of Staff, in their capacity as Under-Secretaries, continued to enjoy direct access to Mussolini. Cavallero and his successor, General Vittorio Ambrosio, had primacy in operational and strategic questions – but only so far as Mussolini allowed.

he would have read Clausewitz and he would have lost the battles.'[5] On the whole, he cared little for generals, and after the war they eagerly highlighted his shortcomings: General Mario Roatta, Army Chief of Staff twice over during the war, coolly observed that 'The substance, the true essence of military questions. . .escaped him.'[6] At the time, though, loyal Fascist generals were ready to accommodate his idiosyncrasies. General Ubaldo Soddu, Under-Secretary of State for War in 1939, served a leader who was always improvising 'on the basis of the inspiration of the moment', and was therefore incapable of giving his generals the precise directives they needed. Not 'mad', Mussolini just reasoned in a different way.[7] General Alberto Pariani, the army's last pre-war Chief of the General Staff, had no difficulty in accepting that Mussolini, 'being a genius, is a very intuitive man, and he sees certain things according to his inner feelings, and not the tangible facts.'[8]

Mussolini's approach to strategy was shaped by geopolitics and National-istic prejudice. Building on both pre-First World War and wartime goals, many of which Italy had been forced to abandon at the time, his ambitions encompassed large swathes of the Balkans, Anatolian Turkey, parts of the Arabian Middle East, and an African Dominion stretching from Tunisia in the east to Ethiopia in the west and extending below the Sahara desert. In September 1922, he enfolded the whole opportunistic design in one of his characteristically bombastic slogans – 'Mediterranean Italy will be imperial or it will not exist'.[9] Along with geopolitics went a crude racialism. The published diaries of Galeazzo Ciano and the unpublished diaries of Dino Grandi (Minister of Foreign Affairs and then ambassador to Britain) are laden with disparaging remarks about alien Slavs, syphilitic Frenchmen and, be it said, mandolin-playing Italians. By the eve of the Second World War, the chief targets of his angry appetite were Great Britain and France, threats to his control of the Mediterranean, along with Yugoslavia and Greece, the latter a potential British cat's paw, whose inhabitants he despised.

It is easy – and by no means incorrect – to see Mussolini's international programme as a crude expression of braggadocio. However, behind it lay

---

5 Galeazzo Ciano, *Diario 1937–1943* (Milan: Rizzoli, 1980), p. 84 (6 January 1938).
6 Mario Roatta, *Otto milioni di baionette* (Milan: Mondadori, 1946), p. 21.
7 Ubaldo Soddu, 'Memorie e riflessioni di un Generale (1933–1941)', unpublished ms (1948), pp. 11, 35.
8 Hungarian National Archives (hereafter HNA), Foreign Ministry Archives K.100: N.277/178, Szabo to Chief of Staff, 12 May 1938.
9 Giorgio Rumi, *Alle origini della politica estera fascista (1918–1923)* (Bari: Laterza, 1968), pp. 40, 196; Paul O'Brien, *Mussolini in the First World War: The Journalist, the Soldier, the Fascist* (Oxford: Berg, 2004), pp. 42–3.

real strategic concerns, which make sense of at least parts of his strategy. Italy's long coastlines made the country difficult to defend, and the Slavs were no more than a short step away across the Adriatic. A 'forward' policy toward the Balkans thus made sense of a kind, and the admirals favoured it almost to a man.[10] It was no less important that Italy dominate the central Mediterranean, in order to maintain communications with her colony in Libya and prevent her potential enemies, the Western democracies, from joining hands. At the same time, she had to deny those same enemies control of the Eastern Mediterranean, so that in wartime, much-needed supplies could get through from Russia and Romania. Vulnerable to sea power, Italy was no less vulnerable to air power. Strategically, Italy was difficult to defend against France: the French air force could launch attacks from Corsica and the Côte d'Azur, and French bombers could hit Italy's northern industrial triangle, but targets of comparable significance were beyond the range of Italian aircraft. Such considerations helped restrain Mussolini during the 1930s, when he wanted to fight a war with France, but also made him more determined to eradicate the danger as soon as he could. As far as Yugoslavia was concerned, the lack of major industrial and population centres made it difficult for the *Regia Aeronautica* to inflict Douhetian-type destruction on her and bring her to her knees. The Yugoslav army could seriously impede an Italian land attack across the frontier, particularly if it teamed up with the French. Military calculations of this kind reinforced Mussolini's inclination to gain control of the Balkans and the Mediterranean as and when he could. In 1940, the opportunity seemed to have arrived.

Non-belligerence, 1939–1940

When Italy signed the Pact of Steel in May 1939, Mussolini was ready for war – but not yet. A clash between the 'plutocratic and egoistically conserva-tive' nations and their 'populous and poor' counterparts was inevitable, he told Hitler, but Italy needed a 'period of preparation' and would not be ready until 1943.[11] Shelving for the moment the idea of attacking Egypt and taking the Suez Canal, he hoped for German support in a war against France. Conversations were held in Rome, and Italian delegations were sent

---

10 Naval matters have been excluded from this chapter for reasons of space; for reading suggestions, see bibliographical essay.
11 Mussolini to Hitler, 30 May 1939: *Opera Omnia di Benito Mussolini* (hereafter O.O.) (36 vols., Florence and Rome: La Fenice, 1951), vol. xxxv, pp. 135–7.

to Berlin to concert strategic, military and economic preparations for war; but due to diffidence and mistrust on both sides, they did not amount to much.[12]

In the first months of the war, Mussolini had a crude political strategy to match his rough-and-ready assumptions about how international affairs were going to develop. The war, he thought, might last for three years. This would suit Italy: the two sides would destroy one another and then Italy would step in to finish them both off. As the war moved into its third month, he began to wonder whether Hitler had not made a mistake: the French were getting stronger and time was working against Germany. Like his generals, he believed the Maginot Line to be insuperable: overcoming it might cost Hitler a million lives. After learning that the armed forces were in a parlous state, he began to worry that he was in danger of being thrown into the war too soon, or too late: 'What could be done before with little now costs double and is very difficult to do'.[13]

On 31 March 1940, in the middle of the Phoney War, Mussolini laid out his strategic conspectus. France and Germany would not attack one another. The French were defensive-minded, and Germany, having already achieved her war objectives, would only unleash a land offensive 'with the mathematical certainty of a crushing victory or as a desperate gamble'. All this gave Italy the opportunity to fight what he termed 'the parallel war'. His goal was the creation of a great and independent imperial power, and to attain that status, Italy must take Corsica, Biserta, Malta, Gibraltar and Suez. 'If Italy wants to be a truly world power', he told his military minions, 'she must resolve the problem of her maritime frontiers.' His war plan amounted to nothing more than 'wait and see': no offensives on any land frontiers and no initiatives, 'except in the case, which is to my mind improbable, of a complete French collapse under German attack.' As far as the Balkans were concerned, Yugoslavia should be watched carefully, but only attacked in the event of an internal collapse, and Greece was only important in relation to whatever happened regarding Yugoslavia. Given French military strength in North Africa and Syria, the idea of an offensive against Egypt was to be discarded.[14]

---

12 John Gooch, *Mussolini and his Generals: The Armed Forces and Fascist Foreign Policy, 1922–1940* (Cambridge University Press, 2007), pp. 459–61, 475–9, 483, 501–2.

13 Claretta Petacci, *Verso il disastro. Mussolini in guerra: Diari 1939–1940* (Milan: Rizzoli, 2011), pp. 190, 224–5, 231, 267, 275 (11 September, 22 October, 3 November, 14 December 1939, 16 January 1940).

14 Memoriale, 31 March 1940: *O.O.*, vol. XXIX, pp. 364–7.

On the eve of Germany's attack on France, Mussolini's eyes were not on France or North Africa, but on the Balkans. Aware of German-Hungarian talks about the possibility of attacking Romania, he was prepared to take military action against Yugoslavia within months: 'In the West I will assume a defensive posture, on the seas I will attack, in the Balkans I will defend my Lebensraum,' he told the Hungarian military attaché, Colonel Szabo.[15]

The 'parallel war', 1940–1941

Mussolini's intention in launching the 'parallel war' was simple: to take advantage of Germany's military virtuosity in order to carve out a substantial territorial sphere of control in North Africa and the Balkans, and in so doing, to put Italy on a more or less equal footing with her Axis partner. However, the speed of German successes after 10 May 1940 confounded Hitler's ally almost as much as his enemy. As always, Mussolini's calculations were rooted in the politics of prestige: 'neutrality would shame us for centuries', he moaned to his mistress Clara (Claretta) Petacci.[16] Afraid of being left behind, he was furious when the French asked for peace terms on 16 June. Military action was necessary – and quickly. The soldiers' preference was to send units to operate north of the Alps on the left flank of the German advance into southern France, much as they had planned to do before the First World War, but Mussolini would have none of it. Over the objections of Marshal Badoglio, head of the Armed Forces General Staff, General Roatta, Deputy Chief of the Army General Staff, and the local commander, General Pintor, the army was ordered to activate pre-war plans for a direct attack across the Alps. 'The decision to attack France is essentially a political question which I alone must decide and bear the responsibility,' Mussolini declared.[17] For the first time – but not the last – professional strategic advice was disregarded. The result was a shambles: in five days' fighting (21–25 June), during which the army made next to no progress at all, 600 men died, 2,500 were wounded and 2,500 got frostbite.

The brief Alpine campaign and the French armistice left a legacy of bitterness and unfinished business. The generals felt cheated by the French armistice terms: Giovanni Messe, a corps commander who later commanded

---

15 HNA, Foreign Ministry Archives K.100: N.815, Szabo to Chief of Staff, 9 May 1940; [unnumbered] Szabo to Chief of Staff, 19 April 1940.
16 Petacci, *Verso il disastro*, p. 326 (2 June 1940).
17 H. James Burgwyn, *Mussolini Warlord: Failed Dreams of Empire, 1940–1943* (New York: Enigma, 2012), p. 15.

in Russia and Tunisia, bemoaned a lost opportunity to secure Italian mastery of the Mediterranean; Badoglio felt the French should be punished for refusing to demobilize forces in North Africa; and Roatta thought it was time to act 'with the mentality of victors' and teach the arrogant French a lesson.[18] For the time being, though, Mussolini looked elsewhere, as he attempted to lever territorial gains on the back of Germany's victories.

A North African campaign had been among the General Staff's portfolio of contingency plans before the war, but Mussolini had lost interest in it at the beginning of 1939. His interest was reignited when the war began in September 1939, and Suez became one of the five goals of the 'parallel war'. Hitler's attack on France made the matter an urgent one, and on 10 May 1940, Mussolini told Italo Balbo, formerly the party ras (leader) of Ferrara and now governor of Libya, to be ready to move by the end of the month. Balbo's pleas for more resources came to an abrupt halt when he was shot down and killed over Tobruk by his own anti-aircraft guns in June. Marshal Rodolfo Graziani replaced him, while retaining his position as Chief of the Army General Staff, thus adding to the complexity of command arrangements that helped to maintain the Duce's dominance.

The French armistice on 25 June 1940 left Mussolini with only one front on which he could act – Cyrenaica. Learning the next day, incorrectly, that the Germans planned to invade England within a week, Mussolini demanded an attack on Egypt. Graziani's task was now 'of fundamental strategic and political importance.'[19] North Africa got German endorsement when, on 14 July, Mussolini received a letter from Hitler, indicating that the attack on England was going to take a little time and advising him to concentrate on Egypt and the Suez Canal. Mussolini and Badoglio wanted Graziani to attack quickly, and believed he had enough mobility to aim beyond the frontier and strike for strategic targets. Graziani seemed inclined to agree and to want to drive first on Mersa Matruh and then on Alexandria, which was some 370 miles from the frontier. Hitler's advice chimed with the views of the man on the spot, but Rome characteristically combined two separate strategies into one. Graziani was given permission to unleash a strategic attack in depth when he was ready, but had Mussolini's approval to undertake a preliminary action against Halfaya–Sollum 'on the day you will

---

18 Ibid., pp. 24–5.
19 Direttive, 11 July 1940: In Africa settentrionale. La preparazione al conflitto. L'avanzata su Sidi el Barrani (ottobre 1935–settembre 1940) (Rome: Ufficio Storico dello Stato Maggiore dell'Esercito, 1955), pp. 205–6.

select'.[20] 'I hope', Mussolini told Hitler, 'to unleash the offensive at the same time as your attack on England.'[21] The offer of German armoured and motorized divisions was turned down – unwisely, as with their aid the Italians might have been able to roll up then fragile British positions – because for different reasons neither Mussolini nor Badoglio wanted to share the laurels with their ally.

While the North African campaign was gestating, Italian distrust of Greece mounted, reinforced by suspicions that she was allowing Great Britain to compromise her neutrality and sheltering vessels of the Royal Navy. Greek denials, and offers to let the Italians see for themselves, were ignored, as was ambassador Emanuele Grazzi's report that the four torpedo boats in question were Greek 'beyond a shadow of a doubt'. Encouraged by Hitler, who was 'decidedly in favour' of any action to prevent the British making use of the Ionian Islands, and ready to welcome immediate Italian intervention in Yugoslavia if anti-Axis outbreaks arose elsewhere in the Balkans, Ciano piled on the pressure. The Greeks were told that it was up to them to dispel the suspicion and distrust with which they were regarded in Rome; and almost at the last, Grazzi portrayed Greece in terms sufficiently ambiguous as to encourage Rome.[22]

Mussolini also nursed a desire to fight Yugoslavia and Hitler initially encouraged this, telling the Italian ambassador on 1 July, on the basis of the collection of Allied documents found in a railway waggon at La Charité-sur-Saône, that Belgrade had pursued a 'hostile' policy toward Rome and that Italy would have to settle the account 'at the opportune moment'. Six days later, however, talking to Count Ciano, he warned Rome off action against Yugoslavia, which would be dangerous unless a general Balkan war had already broken out. As far as Greece was concerned he was much less forthright, thereby allowing Ciano to exaggerate German support for an action that would forestall any British move against the islands of Crete or Cyprus.[23] Mussolini was warned not to take military action against Yugoslavia, but to wait for her to cede without recourse to arms.

20 Badoglio to Graziani, 15 July 1940: Emilio Faldella, *L'Italia e la seconda guerra mondiale: Revisione di giudizi* (Bologna: Capelli, 1960), p. 212.
21 Mussolini to Hitler, 17 July 1940: *I Documenti Diplomatici Italiani* (hereafter *D.D.I.*) 9th ser., vol. v, no. 264, p. 248.
22 Ciano to Grazzi, 4 July 1914; Ciano to Mussolini, 7 July 1940; Grazzi to Ciano, 13 August 1940; Grazzi to Ciano, 23 September 1940: *D.D.I.*, 9th ser., vol. v, nos. 177, 200, 409, 634, pp. 167, 186–90, 392–4, 613–14.
23 MacGregor Knox, *Mussolini Unleashed, 1939–1941* (Cambridge University Press, 1982), pp. 140–2.

On 12 July 1940, the Army General Staff, very much 'up in the air' as far as operational intentions went, began studying action in the east, and four days later, General Carlo Geloso was tasked by its Deputy Chief, Mario Roatta, with drawing up plans for 'Contingency G' (an incursion into Epirus in northwestern Greece – as far as Missolonghi – and the occupation of the Ionian Islands), as well as plans for an attack on Yugoslavia from Albania ('Contingency E'). Next day, smarting perhaps at the rejection of his offer of troops for the invasion of England, Mussolini added to the expanding strategic list with his commitment to begin a North African offensive at the moment that the Germans attacked England. At this point, the shaping of Italian strategy sank into total disarray.

The army began drawing up transport plans for the Yugoslav operation, and early in August it made contact with the German Army General Staff to explore the possibility of collaboration in opening a second northern front against Yugoslavia from Carynthia and Styria. Then, on 12 August, Mussolini called together his selected military and political advisors to go over the Greek option. Ciano and the Viceroy of Albania, Francesco Jacomoni, pressed for action, claiming that it would be a walkover, given Albanian enthusiasm and disaffection within Greece itself, and General Visconti Prasca, slated to command the venture, thought a 'large-scale *coup de main*' could be carried out within a fortnight if extra battalions were drafted into Albania. As they left the meeting, no one agreed on exactly what the Duce intended and what action was therefore necessary. Visconti Prasca thought he was tasked with a two-stage action: first, to threaten Greece, and then to occupy the part demanded by Albania (Ciamuria, the northern part of Epirus), for which he needed two divisions and a regiment of cavalry. Badoglio, apparently not yet aware of Mussolini's aggressive intentions, believed that once 'the other matters' had been sorted out, Italy could get what she wanted from Greece without deploying a single soldier there, and reversed the decision to send out the two divisions. Soddu, now Deputy Chief of the new *Comando Supremo*, believed that Italy could act against Greece, but that this did not rule out a potential or actual action against Yugoslavia.[24]

The timing of Italian strategic action against Egypt, initially tied to Germany's invasion of England, was now affected by the sudden decision to prioritize Greece. A compromise was in order, and Badoglio was just the

---

24 De Felice, *Mussolini l'alleato*, pp. 192–5.

man to find one: the Italian offensive would occupy the Halfaya–Sollum Line and, if it developed favourably, would push forward to Sidi-el-Barani, fifty miles inside the border. Graziani now began a lengthy game of procrastination, first telling Rome that he was ready to set up as wide-ranging an operation as possible, and then, that the heat, lack of water and shortage of transport made an advance on Sollum impossible until the end of October. A high-level conference in Rome early in August ended cordially, but only because of misunderstanding: Rome thought Graziani had agreed to strike at Sidi-el-Barani, whereas he thought the objective should be Mersa Matruh, both of which were in any case presently out of the question. Backed by his local commanders, Graziani reported on 18 August 1940 that only small local actions were possible, chiefly because of 'the persistent insufficiency of the means of transport at our disposal', and offered to resign.[25] Believing Operation SEALION to be imminent, Mussolini told Graziani the next day to be prepared to act within a week or a month: 'The day the first German platoon touches British soil you will attack'. After twelve months of waiting, it was time to act. The loss of Egypt would be 'the coup de grâce for Great Britain'.[26] Graziani caved in. Orders would be carried out, he told Rome, though his generals were gloomy about their chances, since they lacked parity in the air and their transport was very inadequate.

The rickety strategic edifice being cobbled together by Mussolini now threatened to come apart. The German military made it clear that they would only collaborate in action against Yugoslavia on the basis of pre-existing and appropriate political accords – which Mussolini was not inclined to make. The obvious conclusion, reached by both Badoglio and Mussolini, was that the Germans did not want an 'adventure' in the Balkans until they had settled matters with Great Britain. Ciano, meanwhile, had taken things into his own hands, telling Visconti Prasca to be ready to act within a fortnight, and arranging for the Army General Staff to send more troops to Albania without Badoglio's knowledge. When confronted with this, Mussolini declared it 'an error' and returned authority to the Army General Staff.[27] But by now Berlin was growing concerned about Italian intentions vis-à-vis Greece too. Ciano sought to put his ally off the scent, claiming that Italy was taking measures to prevent a British *coup de main*, but Ribbentrop made it

25 Graziani to Badoglio, 18 August 1940: *In Africa settentrionale*, pp. 104–5, 221–2.
26 Mussolini to Graziani (via Badoglio), 19 August 1940: *In Africa settentrionale*, pp. 105–6.
27 Archivio Centrale di Stato (hereafter ACS): Roatta to Graziani, 27 August 1940. Carte Graziani scatola 58/47/9.

clear that defeating England – a 'life or death question' – was the absolute priority. While he had no objections to 'precautionary measures' against Yugoslavia, they might precipitate an unwelcome intervention in Balkan affairs by Russia. Italy must not allow itself to be distracted from the principal task: 'Every activity or effort directed against other ends represents a dangerous dispersion of energies which should absolutely be avoided.' It was, as Ciano said, a 'complete order to halt all along the line'.[28] The planning cycle for both operations was slowed down (Badoglio thought that in view of the Germans' attitude, the planned operation against Greece would not now be carried out at all), the Army General Staff began to consider deploying Italian troops in metropolitan France or Tunisia, and Mussolini sent a directive to the Chiefs of Staff announcing that Libya was now 'the pre-eminent sector'.

Political calculation was always the inspiration – if such a word can be used – for Mussolini's strategy, and it now came to the fore. Learning that the Germans needed three weeks of good weather to destroy the RAF's defences, Mussolini decided to start his North African war even if the Germans did not launch their invasion of England. His fear was that 'if there is an accord between the Germans and the English, we shall remain outside any discussions unless we have at least fought against the English.'[29] The news that the invasion of England had been postponed, which reached him at the end of the month, when ambassador Alfieri finally summoned up the courage to tell him, probably simply confirmed for Mussolini the wisdom of his strategic decision. Graziani was warned to be ready to start operations within the next ten to twelve days, and on 7 September 1940, Mussolini ordered that action begin two days later. Over the next week, Italian units trudged forward into Egypt at a rate of just over seven miles a day before reaching Sidi-el-Barani, where they came to rest on 16 September. Graziani told Rome that he did not know how long the pause was going to be, and Badoglio told him not to worry – Rome was not impatient.

September was a wicked month for Italian strategy – and not just in North Africa. Reversing direction yet again, Mussolini ordered the army to be ready to launch a limited attack on Greece at the end of the month, and to be prepared for war with Yugoslavia by the end of October. It was also to be prepared to act against Corsica and should start reinforcing Tripolitania

28 Alfieri to Ciano, 14 August 1940; Ciano to Alfieri, 15 August 1940; Alfieri to Ciano, 17 August 1940: *D.D.I.*, 9th ser., vol. v, nos. 413, 420, 431, pp. 396, 402, 414–15. Ciano, *Diario 1937–1943*, p. 458 (17 August 1940).
29 Badoglio to Graziani, 29 August 1940: *In Africa settentrionale*, p. 230.

(western Libya) at the end of the month, so as to be able to act against Tunisia too. He was now convinced that the war could finish quickly following the collapse of England, and for this reason pressure was also put on Graziani in Libya to hurry up in order not to 'repeat the case of France and kill a dead man'. At this point, the Germans attempted to put a spoke in Mussolini's strategic wheel. Visiting Rome between 19 and 22 September, Ribbentrop advised his ally to concentrate on defeating England before tackling the problem of Greece and Yugoslavia. Three days after the German Foreign Minister left, Badoglio relayed the Duce's latest change of mind: Greece was a problem that would be resolved at the peace table.[30] With five separate strategic hypotheses now 'on the boil' – operations against Yugoslavia, the occupation of France as far as the Rhône, the occupation of Corsica, operations against Greece and the occupation of Tunisia – and no clear strategic orientation whatever, Roatta, presently acting head of the Army General Staff in Graziani's absence, was in a state of considerable perturbation. Italy needed to concentrate its meagre resources on a single theatre and mobilize her resources more completely: 'So far we have gone ahead in the belief that everything will gradually resolve itself'.[31]

As September drew to a close, Mussolini laid out his thinking on how the war would develop. The Greek and Yugoslav problems would be resolved at the peace table; the landing in England would not occur; and the 'barycentre' of operations would shift to the Mediterranean. His strategic design now required Graziani to march on Mersa Matruh no later than mid-October, putting Alexandria within range of Axis air power, whereupon Italian and German aviation would render the port untenable, the British fleet would leave, and Italy would have mastery of the Mediterranean. Badoglio said it was impossible, and Graziani, after initially declining to give a firm opinion, reported that the necessary logistics could not be completed before the end of 1940. Once again, political calculation trumped military reality. At the Brenner meeting on 4 October, Mussolini told Hitler that the second phase of his offensive, operations against Mersa Matruh, would begin shortly and would then be followed by the third phase, which would lead to the Nile Delta and occupation of Alexandria. Wanting to ensure that success was his alone, Mussolini twice turned down the offer of German troops. Convinced that Graziani had means enough to do what was

---

30 Quirino Armellini, *Diario di guerra: nove mesi al Comando Supremo* (Milan: Garzanti, 1946), pp. 79, 83, 94–5 (11, 12, 25 September 1940).
31 ACS: Roatta to Graziani, 27 September 1917. Carte Graziani scatola 58/47/9.

required of him and that the English would only fight a delaying action while disengaging their troops, he ordered that the operation begin between 10 and 15 October. Once in Mersa Matruh, 'we shall see which of the two pillars of England's Mediterranean defence[s] is to be demolished – the Egyptian [one] or the Greek.'[32] Shortly afterwards, Mussolini decided to try both gambits at once.

With the army apparently about to march on several fronts, the War Ministry took the extraordinary decision to begin demobilizing 600,000 of its 1,100,000 men on 10 October, a task that was to be completed by mid-November. Soddu, as Under-Secretary of State for War, supinely effected the task and subsequently blamed the Treasury. Another version had it that the Agricultural Ministry bowed to the pressure of the agrarian lobby, which needed labour for the autumn sowing. Roatta protested vigorously, but to no avail. Badoglio did not protest. Then, on 12 October, German units entered Romania. The move, advanced notice of which had been given to the Italians, but not passed up to Mussolini, catapulted the Duce into action. Next day, General Mario Roatta was given twenty-four hours' notice of a meeting which would discuss a future campaign to occupy the whole of Greece. 'This was the first time that I and the general staff had heard of this matter', Roatta said afterwards. At the meeting on 14 October, Mussolini told Badoglio and Roatta that war with Greece was now inevitable, given her overly favourable attitude toward the Allies. Asked about the military requisites, Roatta calculated that twenty divisions would have to be deployed from the start, which meant devising a transport plan for at least twelve divisions, which in turn would take three months from the executive order to the start of hostilities – as long as the army was re-mobilized.[33]

Next day, called urgently to another meeting at Palazzo Venezia, the military learned that their strategic advice counted for nothing. The attack on Greece was now to go ahead, not in three months' time, but in eleven days – on 26 October. After first taking Epirus, the Ionian Islands and Salonika, the army would then occupy the whole of Greece. It was, Mussolini declared, 'a campaign that has been maturing in my mind for months, since before we entered the war, even before the war was declared'.[34] Ciano,

32 Mario Montanari, *Politica e strategia in cento anni di guerre italiane,* vol. II: *Il periodo fascista,* tomo 2: *La seconda guerra mondiale* (Rome: Ufficio Storico dello Stato Maggiore dell'Esercito, 2007), p. 262.
33 Roatta, *Otto milioni di baionette,* pp. 120–22.
34 Riunione presso il Capo del Governo..., 15 October 1940: *D.D.I.,* 9th ser., vol. v, no. 728, p. 699.

Visconti Prasca and Soddu all encouraged Mussolini to take a strategic gamble on the basis of meretricious claims about Albanian enthusiasm and internal Greek disaffection, which, they argued, made a swift success certain. Convinced that the meeting was a put-up job, Roatta could not imagine why Mussolini had changed his mind in twenty-four hours. He heard afterwards 'in the corridors' that highly placed Greek political and military personalities averse to Metaxas and the Allies would force his government, or another if it was replaced, to accept the demands Italy would have made before starting the operations.[35] Ciano thought the Greeks easy meat – 'two hundred aeroplanes over Athens would be enough to make the Greeks capitulate' – and so did his master. 'If we weren't able to beat the Greeks, I would resign as an Italian', Mussolini told the Council of Ministers.[36]

Naval and air force leaders had not been invited to the meeting on 15 October. When the Chiefs of Staff met two days later, Admiral Cavagnari and General Pricolo (the Chiefs of Staff of the navy and the air force) pointed out that the Albanian ports were too shallow to handle the necessary traffic and there was no time to build additional airfields. In their view, this made Mussolini's two-phase strategy unfeasible. In Mussolini's absence, Badoglio took their objections to Ciano, who assuaged his doubts by unveiling the 'favourable political circumstances' that were going to ensure an easy passage for the army. With that, Badoglio climbed aboard the bandwagon. In a last-minute attempt to bring some economic realism to bear on strategy, General Carlo Favagrossa, Head of War Production, by his own not entirely reliable account, advised Mussolini not to increase the number of theatres of operations. Mussolini replied that war was only a matter of days, after which Greece could be a useful source of supplies, especially minerals.[37]

Although overall direction was in Mussolini's hands, Badoglio now contributed to what would become a strategic fiasco by steering Mussolini away from accepting a German helping hand in Egypt. Given the grave deficiencies in shipping, ports and escorts, he advised, the involvement of German ground forces could not help Italy in any way; the best help she could give was dive-bombers. At the same time, however, he also advised that attacking the British in the Nile Delta was 'an irresolvable problem'. Italy should aim to advance only as far as Mersa Matruh. Moving any deeper into Egypt would require the careful building up of forward magazines and depots

35 Roatta, *Otto milioni di baionette*, pp. 122–7.
36 Giuseppe Bottai, *Diario 1935–1944* (Milan: Rizzoli, 2001), p. 228 (24 October 1940).
37 Carlo Favagrossa, *Perchè perdemmo la guerra* (Milan: Rizzoli, 1946), pp. 146–7, 151, 153–5.

capable of supporting a force of at least 300,000 men.[38] With Greece now the strategic priority and things in that theatre not yet spiralling downward, Badoglio sent Graziani instructions in early November to take Mersa Matruh. A month later, on 7 December, Wavell's Operation COMPASS struck the forward Italian positions around Sidi-el-Barani. As the Italian armies were driven backward, Graziani announced that he was heading back to Tripoli. Having just sacked one marshal – Badoglio (see below) – Mussolini was in no mood to be undermined by another. Graziani was ordered to defend Bardia and Tobruk to the last, to which he replied that only more land forces and air power could save eastern Libya.

Meanwhile the attack on Greece, postponed for forty-eight hours because of the weather, began at 6 a.m. on 28 October 1940. The Italians, initially 174,000 men, 4,000 motor vehicles and 686 guns, faced 35,000 Greek defenders. Bad weather, bad roads and a lack of transport soon bogged them down. First, they were stopped by the fortified line of Gianina; then the Greeks drove them back into Albania. After a week, realizing that the war needed a new commander and more troops, Mussolini demoted Visconti Prasca. Soddu, who replaced him, was quickly out of his depth. Mussolini called Badoglio and the heads of the three armed services to Palazzo Venezia, and after remarking that things had not gone as they had thought, laid out his own somewhat simplistic ideas on how to proceed. When he had finished, Badoglio took a most unusual step. Having hitherto gone along with everything, he now pointed out that professional advice about how to organize and prepare for the Greek campaign had been consistently ignored. The whole logistics issue should at once be handed over to the armed services, who could produce a full report on what was necessary and what was possible in two days. 'When I think of the Greek affair', he concluded, 'I blush'. Mussolini agreed without demur – and permitted the official account to include what was a scarcely veiled criticism of himself – but Badoglio's days as Chief of the Armed Forces General Staff were numbered.[39] Shortly afterwards he resigned, after an article in the Fascist paper *Regime Fascista* indirectly blamed him for the Greek debacle. A belated attempt to withdraw his resignation failed.

38 Promemoria di Badoglio per il Duce, 27 October 1940: *Diario Storico del Comando Supremo* (Rome: Ufficio Storico dello Stato Maggiore dell'Esercito, 1988), vol. II, tomo 2, no. 56, pp. 114–15.

39 Verbale della riunione tenuta nella sala di lavoro del Duce a Palazzo Venezia il 10 novembre 1940-XIX: Faldella, *L'Italia e la seconda guerra mondiale*, pp. 760–7.

The enemy would give the Italians no time to mend the gaping holes in their strategy. Stripping units from the Bulgarian border, the Greeks launched a counter-offensive on 13 November, pitting 192,000 men against 115,000 Italians. With his forces in retreat, General Soddu telephoned Rome on 4 December: with a complete collapse looming, it was impossible to continue operations and there must now be a diplomatic intervention. Very shortly, he too would be replaced. In retirement, he shrugged off all responsibility for anything, putting down the reversals that cost him his job to the fierceness with which the Greek army, stiffened by English officers, defended their *patria*, 'while our detachments, put together as best as possible and badly armed, fought a war for interests they did not understand.'[40]

On 13 December 1940, with Italian armies bogged down in Albania and retreating in North Africa, General Mario Roatta produced what has been adjudged the only strategic appreciation of any depth and seriousness to come from the military throughout the war. England was the enemy number one. It now looked unlikely that a German landing would knock the British Isles out of the war, but even if it did, the empire would go on fighting. Italy could not fight her alone. It was time to replace 'parallel action' with 'collective action in the war theatre where its effects would be most rewarding for the common aims'. This collective action should focus on the Balkans, where the possibility of another 'Salonika front' like that of the First World War could not be ruled out; on North Africa, where Italy needed armour equal to British armour and lots of anti-tank weapons, 'which – for now – we don't possess'; and on combined sea and air action to hit the enemy's fleet and bases. Vichy France should also be occupied at a suitable moment, to prevent her from raising her head again. For all this to work, three prerequisites had to be met. First, there must be a close, clear and lasting politico-military understanding between Italy and Germany. Second, there must be 'virtually unique [*sic*] direction of the war', so that the individual actions of each of the three armed forces fitted into a collective design. Third, materiel must be shared in common, 'it being inadmissible that one party fights with inadequate means while the other gives arms to third parties who cannot be trusted.'[41] Roatta's design was a political pipe dream.

Badoglio had consistently opposed any kind of collaboration with the Germans, encouraging Mussolini to fight his own war. His replacement as

40 Soddu, 'Memorie e riflessioni di un Generale', pp. 194–5.
41 Roatta to Guzzoni, 13 December 1940: Lucio Ceva, *La condotta italiana della guerra. Cavallero e il Comando supremo 1941/1942* (Milan: Feltrinelli, 1975), pp. 139–41.

Chief of the Armed Forces General Staff, General Ugo Cavallero, who took office on 8 December 1940, was much more open to a strategic partnership, and so was his deputy, General Alfredo Guzzoni. Two factors, above all, forced Italy out of her entrenched position of strategic independence: the military position and the armaments situation. With the army hanging on by its fingernails in Albania and retreating in Cyrenaica, the operational balance was anything but favourable. Nor did Italy have the wherewithal – other than manpower, always fetishized by Mussolini – to put matters right. To have some hope of victory, she needed German aid, and lots of it – 7,850 trucks, 800 tanks, artillery of all sorts, including 2,640 anti-aircraft guns, and more besides.[42] Cavallero saw the German military attaché, Enno von Rintelen, and asked urgently for a Panzer division, and on 22 December Guzzoni requested immediate German intervention in view of the situation in Albania and Libya. The 'parallel war' was over.

The 'subaltern war', 1941–1943

Cavallero was delighted to take on both Badoglio's job and theatre command in Albania. 'It's Caporetto all over again', he told his son, 'and just like then I've got to put right Badoglio's errors'.[43] Although he tried on occasions to focus Italian strategy more clearly, his powers were limited as it became increasingly shaped by or responsive to German intentions. Mussolini became less and less able to direct Italian strategy – a blessing in disguise – though he could still make decisions that went against all strategic logic. He also continued to make the bombastic speeches that were his true forte. On 23 February 1941, he told Fascist leaders that in strictly logical terms, England could not win the war and that the cooperation now offered by Hitler represented 'proof that all the fronts are common fronts and the effort is a common effort'. Germany was getting stronger, the Axis was 'the arbiter of the continent', and there was nothing to fear from the United States, 'a politico-financial oligarchy dominated by Jews'.[44]

The Greek campaign did not go well for Cavallero. Early in January 1941, the Army General Staff learned that the German Armed Forces high command planned to intervene in Greece. At the same time, the spectre of

---

42 Roatta to Cavallero, 17 December 1940: *Diario Storico*, vol. II, tomo 2, no. 108, pp. 291–4.
43 Carlo Cavallero, *Il dramma del Maresciallo Cavallero* (Milan: Mondadori, 1952), p. 89.
44 Il discorso al teatro Adriano di Roma, 23 February 1941: *O.O.*, vol. XXX, pp. 55, 57.

Greece requesting German arbitration suddenly appeared. The last thing the Italians wanted was to see German troops occupy Greece peacefully. 'Make [them] understand that Italy intends to defeat Greece', Guzzoni told the Italian military attaché in Berlin, Colonel Marras, at the end of February; 'it is a question of prestige and nobody should understand this better than the German military'.[45] News that Hitler intended to march his troops into Greece sometime after the end of March, Rommel's arrival in North Africa on 12 February and a Greek attack in the middle of the month prompted Cavallero to launch an offensive of his own on 9 March 1941. It quickly failed, and his proposal to try again was turned down. German troops marched into Yugoslavia and Greece on 6 April, and a week later the Greeks began to retreat from the Albanian front, fighting a strong rearguard action. By 23 April, the war was over. The Epirus army surrendered twice – first to the Germans and then, after some agitated toing and froing, to the Italians. By then, there were 491,700 officers and men in Greece. Italian casualties totalled 154,172 and included 13,755 dead and 25,067 missing.

As the year began, Italy's hold on North Africa also seemed about to dissolve. Tobruk fell on 22 January 1941, Beda Fomm was lost on 7 February and with it Cyrenaica. Eight thousand three hundred men of Tenth Army made it back to Tripolitania; 20,000 were captured, along with an embarrassing number of generals. All that remained to defend Italian North Africa were 80,000 men of Fifth Army, along with 160 guns and 209 light tanks. On 8 February, Graziani resigned as theatre commander, and two days later he also gave up the post of Chief of the Army General Staff. He was succeeded in Rome by Roatta and in North Africa, first by General Italo Gariboldi and then, in July, by General Ettore Bastico, who was, in name at least, Rommel's superior commander.

At the beginning of January 1941, Guzzoni, Deputy Chief of the Armed Forces General Staff, warned Mussolini that, with only three months' supplies and a crippling lack of fuel, Italy was going to lose East Africa – which she duly did four months later.[46] On 19 January, Mussolini, accompanied by

---

45 Burgwyn, *Mussolini Warlord*, p. 70.
46 All pre-war plans had acknowledged that Italian East Africa could not defend itself without outside help – and so it proved. Local Italian offensives took Kassala in Sudan and British Somaliland (3 July – 19 August 1940). A two-pronged British counter-offensive from Sudan and Kenya began in January 1941, and by the end of March the Italians had lost Eritrea and Somaliland, and with them all their main logistical bases and supply dumps. Addis Ababa, the capital, was abandoned on 7 April for a central defensive redoubt around Amba Alagi, in the heart of the country, which fell on 17 May. The last embers of Italian resistance in East Africa were extinguished on 28 November 1941.

Guzzoni, met Hitler – the first time the Duce had had a responsible military advisor at his side. Guzzoni asked for a light division and tanks for North Africa. The *Comando Supremo* estimated that it would take at least six months to ship over the men and trucks needed to attempt the reconquest of Cyrenaica, but Rommel's arrival changed everything. Aided by German air attacks on Malta and by a six-month period in which convoying losses were negligible, Rommel reconquered Cyrenaica in thirty days and then fought off the British BREVITY and BATTLEAXE offensives in May and June. Although the Afrikakorps commander was now either disregarding his Italian superior or treating him with what the South African official history terms 'studied insolence', Cavallero was ready to accept more German armoured units in Libya, and at the Brenner meeting on 2 June 1941, the Germans did agree to reinforce North Africa. However, General Wilhelm Keitel, Head of the German Armed Forces high command, was unwilling to make any firm operational plans until he knew what the supply situation was. Cavallero's strategic objectives were now Egypt and then the recovery of Italian East Africa. After the Brenner meeting, Hitler sent Mussolini detailed advice on how to continue the North African campaign, its only strategic recommendation the need to retake Tobruk as the necessary premise for 'the continuation of the offensive against Alexandria'. Cavallero's response was to press for the use of the French port of Bizerta as a supply base, a will-o'-the-wisp that he pursued for months to no avail.[47] At this point, Mussolini once again exerted his political authority and Italian strategy took another ill-considered lurch deeper into the mire.

Mussolini's decision to volunteer his unfortunate soldiery for the Russian war, perhaps the most foolish of his many ill-advised strategic ventures, has seemed, in retrospect, devoid of any comprehensible motive. In fact, it was the culmination of a path along which Italo-Russian relations had travelled during the preceding couple of years. Mussolini had wished to avoid Moscow falling into line with the Allies and also needed Russian fuel oil. Rome followed Berlin's line as it swung from amity (under the 1939 German-Soviet Non-Aggression Pact) to hostility, concerned too to avoid being manoeuvred into diplomatic agreements on the Danube-Baltic region or the Dardanelles, which is what Moscow wanted. The chimera of a commercial agreement with Russia disappeared in the early months of 1941, as Ribbentrop's tone

---

47 Appunto [von Rintelen to Cavallero], 10 June 1941; Appunto [Cavallero to von Rintelen], 12 June 1941: Emilio Canevari, *La guerra italiana: Retroscena della disfatta* (2 vols., Rome: Tosi, 1949), vol. II, pp. 448–9.

grew more violently hostile. As between an alliance with the Soviet Union and war, Mussolini preferred the former, as he told Hitler at the Brenner meeting on 2 June 1941.[48] By then, though, Rome knew that a German attack on Russia was probably imminent. At the beginning of May, there was talk in Berlin of action against Russia in the summer; in mid-May, Italian military intelligence warned Ciano that an attack was a month away; and at the end of that month, Colonel Efisio Marras, the well-informed Italian military attaché in Berlin, reported that the Germans were moving toward solving their problems with Russia by force, in order permanently to liquidate 'communism and the bolshevik armed forces'. On 5 June, Marras estimated that 75 per cent of Germany's armed forces were more or less ready to take part in operations against the Soviet Union, and eight days later, his deputy telegraphed that the German military authorities had for the first time admitted that action against Russia was 'very close', and would take place at some time between 20 June and the first days of July.[49]

By the time of the Brenner meeting, Mussolini's mind was made up. On 30 May, he told Cavallero that he foresaw the possibility of war between Germany and Russia. If that happened, Italy could not stand aside 'because it is a matter of the fight against communism'. Cavallero was warned to ready an armoured and a motorized division, as well as a grenadier division.[50] Attempts to warn him off Russia by the industrialist Alberto Pirelli, among others, failed completely. The Army General Staff, when it learned of his intentions, apparently opposed them strongly, basing its argument on the necessity not to weaken the defences of the *Madrepatria* (homeland), against which the enemy would make a decisive effort sooner or later.[51] If this was indeed what the soldiers said, it is perhaps not surprising that Mussolini took no notice of them. With Great Britain's only potential continental partner apparently about to be shredded by the all-conquering Wehrmacht, an enemy invasion of Italy could pardonably have been the last thing on Mussolini's mind.

Mussolini received Hitler's explanation for his attack on Russia as the first German units tore into Russia. He accepted without question Hitler's argument that delaying would be 'fatal to our cause', and found ideological

48 Manfredi Martelli, *Mussolini e la Russia: Le relazioni italo-sovietiche dal 1922 al 1941* (Milan: Mursia, 2007), pp. 311, 313, 345, 348, 350–1, 355.

49 Sergio Pelagalli, *Il generale Efisio Marras addetto militare a Berlino (1936–1943)* (Rome: Ufficio Storico dello Stato Maggiore dell'Esercito, 1994), pp. 136–7.

50 Ugo Cavallero, *Diario 1940–1943* (Rome: Ciarrapico, 1984), p. 188 (30 May 1941).

51 Roatta, *Otto milioni di baionette*, pp. 186–7.

and diplomatic reasons to applaud it. It corresponded to their joint 'doctrinal conceptions', temporarily abandoned for tactical reasons, and it would draw to the side of the Axis all the anti-Bolshevik currents around the world, especially the Anglo-Saxons. Far from considering whether Italy might be militarily overextending herself, Mussolini reassured Hitler that he intended simultaneously to consolidate the Axis position in North Africa against the French on the west and the British on the east.[52] Once decided on war, the size of Italy's military contribution became for Mussolini a question of prestige. Italy must be present in a strength at least equal to that of Romania and Hungary, which meant two army corps. Italy had to 'pay our debts to our ally', he told King Vittorio Emanuele III a month after the invasion had begun. In practical terms, this meant the dispatch of the Italian Expeditionary Corps (CSIR) – three divisions comprising 61,000 men, along with 145 guns, 5,500 motor vehicles (badly needed in North Africa) and 83 aircraft.

A month after the invasion of Russia had begun, Mussolini put his thoughts on the politico-military situation down on paper. Italy had two active fronts and two potential fronts in which to operate. To take the initiative in Cyrenaica would require twelve divisions, two of them armoured, two motorized and two German, while status demanded that a second army corps be sent to Russia, 'more or less motorized according to what the possibilities allow'. The attitude of ambiguity and hostility displayed by France – another potential front comprising the Alps, Corsica and Tunisia – was such that Italy had to be prepared to take the measures needed to meet any eventuality. In total, this added up to another seventeen divisions, one of them armoured and two motorized. In Croatia too, Italy had to be ready for anything, which meant another ten divisions, two of them armoured and two motorized. Then there was another potential front – missing from the Duce's initial list: the islands of Sicily and Sardinia. They required seven more divisions. Finally, Mussolini threw in the absence of domestic reserves. At least twenty divisions were needed to fill the gap. With not enough resources to handle two fronts, Mussolini had identified seven theatres where military force was required. His generals were told that by the following spring the army must have at least eighty divisions, five of them armoured divisions and six motorized.[53] None of them baulked at this absurd calculation.

---

52 Mussolini to Hitler, 23 June 1941: *O.O.*, vol. xxx, pp. 197–202.
53 Relazione per lo stato maggiore generale sulla situazione politico-militare, 24 July 1941: *O.O.*, vol. xxx, pp. 112–13.

With the German attack on Russia, North Africa sank down the German order of priorities, and so did Italy. 'It is not timely to develop the common Axis war plan against the English positions in the Mediterranean before the Russian campaign is concluded', Keitel told Cavallero on 28 July.[54] The aim should be to take Tobruk, presently under siege; but if the British attacked first, it would be necessary to pull Axis forces back west, rather than risk a defeat on the Egyptian frontier. In the event, the British did not move until November. At the end of October, with the campaign in the East seemingly won, and the war 'in substance, definitely decided', Hitler's chief concern was protecting the transports to Africa. A delighted Mussolini expected that with Russia beaten, the war would assume its 'Mediterranean-eastern character', but German help was needed in the shape of a million tons of coal a month and over 200,000 tons of fuel oil for the navy. Over the next two months, Italian dreams collapsed. On 9 November 1941, Force K, the British cruiser squadron based at Malta, destroyed the Italian 'Beta' convoy that was on its way to North Africa. Nine days later, the British launched Operation CRUSADER and Rommel, who with other German generals had been dissembling about the likelihood of an enemy offensive, swiftly retired, ignoring Italian wishes to stay put and fight. On 13 December, the Italian navy suffered a major defeat at the Battle of Cape Bon, and on 29 December, faced with an unexpected Russian offensive, Hitler gratefully accepted the offer of six more Italian divisions on the Eastern Front. Mussolini now foresaw the war lasting at least another four or five years, but assured the Council of Ministers that as far as the final outcome was concerned, 'my certainty is unshakeable'.[55]

As the 1942 campaigning season began, the Army General Staff proposed repatriating the CSIR in its entirety. For one thing, the Germans were clearly not going to provide the transport and replenishments it needed, and for another, the new British offensive in Cyrenaica sharpened the dangers in the Mediterranean theatre. Mussolini's response was to expand the CSIR into an army (Eighth Armata or ARMIR – *Armata Italiana in Russia*), on the grounds that 'a great country such as Italy could not decently be represented in Russia by a contingent smaller than that of Hungary'.[56] Six divisions went to Russia, with next to no transport or anti-tank guns and most of Italy's few modern anti-aircraft guns, stripped from Italian cities. Supply was now becoming

---

54 Montanari, *La seconda guerra mondiale*, p. 500.
55 Ibid., p. 543.
56 Roatta, *Otto milioni di baionette*, p. 188.

even more critical. Cavallero had calculated that the CSIR needed 700 trucks a month and North Africa 600 simply to cover wastage, an amount equal to the total monthly production. Ever optimistic about his German ally, he believed that if Italy gave ARMIR some vehicles, then the Germans would provide the rest. The Germans did not come to his rescue. In 1942, Italy raised her presence in Russia to 227,000 men, 16,700 vehicles, 588 guns (including most of the modern heavy guns) and fifty-two 75 mm anti-aircraft guns (one-quarter of the available stock of modern weapons). The materiel that went to Russia could, in all probability, have been shipped to North Africa via Benghazi and Tripoli, despite their limited capacity, and might have made a considerable difference there. It made none in Russia, where the Italian force was destroyed in the Stalingrad offensive.

During the first six months of 1942, North African strategy was determined by factors that neither Mussolini nor Cavallero could do anything about. Disregarding directives from both Hitler and Mussolini to launch only limited attacks and under no circumstances to undertake a major drive to the Nile Delta, Rommel began an offensive on 21 January 1942 which led, six months later, to the surrender of Tobruk. A delighted Mussolini, who always thought his own generals too defensive-minded, declared that the battle for the Delta was next. Cavallero, who had more strategic vision than anyone else in the Italian high command, saw the Mediterranean as the key theatre, but his ideas about strategy made no impression on Mussolini or on the German high command, as three examples show. In spring 1942, with a victorious Rommel bounding toward Tobruk and beyond, he proposed halting the advance along the Ain-el-Gazala line west of Tobruk: 'Tobruk [to the] Nile is only imagination', he confided to his diary.[57] That advice was doomed to fail. Four months later, in July 1942, he tried to stop Mussolini sending three *Alpini* divisions into the Russian meat-grinder and failed again. But perhaps his most significant strategic failure came over Malta.

By the autumn of 1941, Malta's role in disrupting the supply line to North Africa could scarcely be overlooked, and in October Cavallero ordered plans for an assault on the island (Operation C3) to be updated. Admiral Raeder shared his views about the island's importance, but was unable to convince Hitler and the German high command, preoccupied with the upcoming summer offensive in Russia, Operation BLUE. Cavallero pushed hard for Malta, arguing that possessing it meant possession of Alexandria too, but in

---

57 Ugo Cavallero, *Comando Supremo: Diario 1940–43 del Capo di S.M.G.* (Bologna: Capelli, 1948), p. 233 (7 March 1942).

March 1942 he was forced to accept prioritizing ground operations in North Africa, partly out of strategic logic (preventing the British Eighth Army from interrupting the assault on the island) and partly out of economic and material necessity (the Germans were unable, or unwilling, to provide the requisite parachute division, ships and 40,000 tons of fuel oil before mid-June). When the Axis military leaders met at Klessheim in April 1942, they agreed to get plans ready by late June.

With Tobruk about to fall to Rommel, Cavallero again pressed the case for Malta. The positive grounds were that taking it would solve the Libyan supply problem and free the air force; the argument against was that the Italian navy, having prevented two convoys from reaching Malta, was now completely out of fuel, and without German resupply it could neither attack Malta nor defend the convoys.[58] On 21 June, as Tobruk surrendered, Mussolini put Cavallero's strategy to Hitler – 'Malta is at the centre of our strategic picture' – and at the same time detailed Italy's crippling shortage of fuel. In reply, Hitler told him that they must take advantage of the opportunities that beckoned in Egypt to finish off the English.[59] General Bastico, the nominal Axis Commander-in-Chief in North Africa, believed that if the Germans were likely to conquer Egypt, then the Italians must be alongside them, and with intelligence suggesting that the enemy was short of tanks and artillery, and morale was low, and enough fuel in Tobruk for Rommel to continue his advance, Cavallero was fighting a lost cause. On 27 June 1942, the *Comando Supremo* issued a directive completely adhering to Rommel's design: the objective was now the Suez Canal; Italian and German forces were to be equally represented in the advance; and the problems of Malta and fuel were left entirely to one side.

With the failure of Rommel's attack on Alam Halfa in September 1942, Axis forces in North Africa started down an ever steeper slope, which would end with the surrenders in Tunisia in May 1943. On the eve of the Allied invasion of Morocco and Algeria, Mussolini thought that Libya would probably be lost. Once the invasion had occurred, Bastico was ordered to defend Tripolitania to the last. As Rommel retreated across Tripolitania, Hitler and Mussolini exhorted their armies to resist to the last, as they would continue to do until the bitter end. On 26 December 1942, the king was

---

58 Cavallero, *Diario 1940–1943*, pp. 410–11 (20 June 1942).

59 Mussolini to Hitler, 21 June 1942; Hitler to Mussolini, 23 June 1942: Ministero della Difesa, *Seconda controffensiva italo-tedesca in Africa settentrionale da el Agheila a El Alamein (gennaio–settembre 1942)* (Rome: Ufficio Storico dello Stato Maggiore dell'Esercito, 1951), pp. 375–7, 377–8.

warned that the army was preparing to evacuate Tripolitania and make a final stand in Tunisia. A month later, Tripoli fell, and on the same day (23 January 1943), General Giovanni Messe was appointed overall field commander in Rommel's place. Mussolini's orders to Messe were stupefyingly unrealistic: 'During the summer you will resume the initiative with a great offensive towards Algeria and Morocco and the reconquest of Libya.'[60] Behind them was a somewhat more intelligible intention. Messe's task was to delay an Allied attack on Italy itself until 1944, to win time to prepare her defences.

As the year turned, Mussolini pursued ever wilder strategic and political chimeras. Attempts to persuade Hitler to consider a compromise peace with Russia came to nought when Hitler told him that he intended to 'fight in the East until this colossus falls, with or without allies'.[61] So did the idea of persuading Franco to allow Axis troops to transit Spain, cross the Straits of Gibraltar, and fall on the Anglo-American armies from the rear. With things beginning to fall apart, Mussolini faced 1943 with blind optimism. In a strategic *tour d'horizon* delivered to his commanders on 29 January, he acknowledged that the enemy had taken the initiative in ground operations, had 'set foot' in North Africa and had the initiative in the air, but believed that strategically nothing fundamental had changed. The situation in North Africa would be contained and overcome, and the Germans would stabilize the situation on the Russian front because they had not yet used the bulk of their reserves. There were fleeting moments of realism. When Cavallero pointed out that Italy could not meet all her other requirements, including an ambitious armaments programme for 1943, and reconstitute her II Corps in Russia, Mussolini admitted that rebuilding it would depend on Germany supplying the guns and motor vehicles. But in general, the soldiers, sailors and airmen were encouragingly upbeat. Only General Vittorio Ambrosio had the courage to point out that the rearmament programme could not be done and that Italy now had to prioritize her own defences.[62]

On 31 January 1943, Mussolini fired Cavallero and appointed Ambrosio, Army Chief of Staff, as his replacement. Like many Italian generals, Ambrosio thought that the Axis could not hold on to North Africa very much longer and that it was time to pull out, while troops and equipment could

60 Burgwyn, *Mussolini Warlord*, p. 278.
61 Hitler to Mussolini, 16 February 1943: *D.D.I.*, 9th ser., vol. x, no. 31, p. 45.
62 Verbale della riunione tenuta il giorno 29 gennaio 1943: Favagrossa, *Perchè perdemmo la guerra*, pp. 278–97.

yet be saved. Unlike Cavallero, he did not trust the Germans to fulfil their promises of help to hold on there. During April, he tried to persuade Mussolini to put the defence of Sicily and Italy first and to reconsider the German alliance. Mussolini ignored him. Very shortly, Ambrosio was proved right: on 13 May, the Italian First Army in Tunisia surrendered, two days after the Germans. With Geloso's Eleventh Army in Greece unravelling in the face of uprisings and partisan actions, Albania starting to dissolve, and the Balkans disintegrating, the Allied landings in Sicily on 10 July finally brought down Mussolini's house of cards. He failed abysmally to squeeze more military help out of Hitler when they met at Feltre on 19 July. This finally triggered a move against him, in which the army was an active participant, that had been brewing since the start of the year. At 10.45 p.m. on Sunday 25 July 1943, the Italian radio announced that Mussolini had been removed from office.[63]

Conclusion

The key to understanding Mussolini, A. J. P. Taylor liked to say, was always to remember that he was a journalist. In terms of his war record, it is more helpful to see him as a politician of the *piazza*, used to getting his way by force, not reason. His conception of the inter-relationship between military force, strategy and politics was simplistic in the extreme. The rank and file, Mussolini believed, wanted to fight, but the generals, socially conservative and professionally cautious, did not. The generals' job was simply to realize his ambitions. 'We do the politics, they fight the war', he told the Fascist Council of Ministers shortly before the Greek campaign began – 'we' meaning himself, and not the ministers.[64] At root, his was not a military strategy at all, but a political one. Every one of his military decisions was designed to get Fascist Italy – and himself – into the most favourable position possible for the peace that was to come.

In 1940, Mussolini was Hitler's confederate; between 1941 and 1943, he was increasingly Hitler's pensioner. The German-Italian coalition was, as Giorgio Rochat has written, more a sum of its collective weaknesses than of the forces it had available to it. Both parties had vast and indeterminate

---

63 John Gooch, '"Neither Defeat nor Surrender": Italy's Change of Alliances in 1943', in Holger Afflerbach and Hew Strachan (eds.), *How Fighting Ends: A History of Surrender* (Oxford University Press, 2012), pp. 351–65.
64 Bottai, *Diario 1935–1944*, p. 228 (19 October 1940).

expansionist objectives, and both preferred to keep their freedom of action rather than surrender anything to a common strategy.[65] Shaping coalition strategy was beyond both men. Bringing influence to bear on Hitler, as an ever weaker Mussolini found out, was an equally hopeless task. Imprisoned in an increasingly dysfunctional alliance, Mussolini was not helped by Badoglio, by the Chiefs of Staff of the three armed services or by the under-secretaries who ran the service ministries, none of whom gave him real strategic alternatives.[66] Strategic arguments were in any case unlikely to sway a leader who thought in quite different terms. 'The decisions have been taken by Mussolini on the basis of political considerations', Marshal Cavallero told General Messe at the start of 1942, 'and it is useless to discuss them'.[67]

Questions can be asked about Mussolini's mental capacity. His preoccupation with sexual conquests certainly intruded on his work and worried some of his subordinates. In December 1940, General Quirino Armellino, attached to Badoglio's staff, thought the country was in the hands of 'a man who is perhaps softening into an erotic senility'.[68] Potentially more serious is the possibility that Mussolini suffered from the effects of syphilis, caught some time before or during the First World War, though on that the jury is still out.[69] At the moment, there are no mitigating circumstances to take into account. Mussolini took his country into the war without a clear objective, without any strategic consideration of ends and means, and without a plan. For that, his countrymen would pay a heavy price.

65 Giorgio Rochat, 'Lo sforzo bellico 1940–43: Analisi di una sconfitta', *Italia contemporanea* 160 (September 1985), 8–9.
66 Ceva, *La condotta italiana della guerra*, p. 47.
67 Cavallero, *Diario 1940–1943*, p. xxxvi.
68 Armellini, *Diario di guerra*, p. 182 (2 December 1940).
69 See Paul O'Brien, 'Al capezzale di Mussolini: Ferite e malattia 1917–1945', *Italia Contemporanea* 226 (March 2002), pp. 5–29.

6

Feigning grand strategy

Japan, 1937–1945

ALESSIO PATALANO

Now we are in the very day to which we have been looking forward so cagerly. That is, the long-cherished 'X' day for the outbreak of war now offers itself.[1]

As Lt Commander Sadao Chigusa committed these thoughts to the pages of his diary in the early hours of 7 December 1941, the destroyer *Akigumo*, on which he served as executive officer, was steaming in formation with the carrier force ready to unleash the full strength of its air wing over Pearl Harbor. Three hours later, the first laconic battle report reached the fleet: 'Succeeded in our surprise attack. , , Attacked the main force. Had a great effect'.[2] Indeed, the Japanese air raid over Pearl Harbor had a 'great' effect. What followed - in the words of John Dower – was a 'war without mercy', a forty-four-month-long conflict, stretching from the high seas of the Pacific to the jungles of Southeast Asia and the plains of China. Japanese authorities had locked themselves in an all-out fight against a coalition of nations. The great effect was something they did not anticipate: the destruction of the Imperial Navy, the demise of the Japanese Empire, and the moral and physical collapse of the Japanese people.

Yet for Japanese commanders deployed in the battlefields in China, and for army planners in Tokyo, the navy's long cherished 'X' day did not mark the outbreak of war. The navy, too, had seen action off the coasts of Shanghai and in the skies of eastern China in 1937 and 1938. These experiences were instrumental in the development of naval air doctrine.[3] For the

---

1 Rear Admiral Sadao Chigusa, JMSDF (Ret.), 'Conquer the Pacific Ocean Aboard Destroyer Akigumo: War Diary of the Hawaiian Battle', in Donald M. Goldstein and Katherine V. Dillon (eds.), *The Pearl Harbor Papers: Inside the Japanese Plans* (Washington DC: Brassey's, 1993), p. 192.
2 Ibid., p. 193.
3 Mark R. Peattie, *Sunburst: The Rise of Japanese Naval Air Power, 1909–1941* (London: Chatham, 2001), pp. 102–28.

army, however, major battles and proxy war across China and along the Mongolian border, most notably the 1939 Japanese-Soviet conflict at Nomon-han that saw the engagement of some 100,000 troops, had been taking place since 1937.[4] These differences in perception among soldiers and sailors revealed bureaucratic fragmentation over the aims of national strategy, and the means to achieve them. In Japan, grand strategy resembled a compromise masking the inability to reconcile diverging organizational positions and the visions embedded within them. Was this really the case? If so, what were these visions about? Why were national authorities unable to reconcile them? What factors drove the debate over grand strategy and the mobilization of national resources to implement it? Why and how did this approach fail?

This chapter addresses these questions by examining the evolution of Japan's grand strategy from 1937 to 1945. In 1972, Michael Howard defined grand strategy as 'the mobilisation and deployment of national resources and wealth, manpower and industrial capacity, together with the enlistment of those allies and, when feasible, of neutral powers, for the purpose of achieving the goals of national policy in wartime'.[5] This definition focuses on the decision-making process designed to channel national power toward the use or the threat of use of force as a tool to achieve a set of political objectives.[6] War-fighting is as central to grand strategy as the avoidance of war is in peacetime. These are the two faces of the same coin.[7] Following that focus, this chapter explores the factors that informed the grand strategy-making process in Japan from 1937 to 1945. In particular, it examines the organizations that shaped that process and the dynamics of their interaction, and the notions and material factors informing their actions.

After the war, numerous scholars of Japanese foreign and security policy questioned whether the country ever had a coherent grand strategy between 1854 and 1945 – with one of them indicating the decade from 1895 to 1905 as

---

4 Stuart D. Goldman, *Nomonhan, 1939: The Red Army's Victory that Shaped World War II* (Annapolis, Md.: Naval Institute Press, 2012), p. 3; Edward J. Drea and Hans van de Ven, 'An Overview of Major Military Campaigns during the Sino-Japanese War, 1937–1945', in Mark R. Peattie, Edward J. Drea and Hans van de Ven (eds.), *The Battle for China: Essays on the Military History of the Sino-Japanese War of 1937–1945* (Stanford University Press, 2011), pp. 27–47.

5 Michael Howard, *Grand Strategy,* vol. IV: *August 1942–September 1943* (6 vols., London: HMSO, 1972), p. 1.

6 Hew Strachan, *The Direction of War: Contemporary Strategy in Historical Perspective* (Cambridge University Press, 2013), pp. 30–6.

7 Michael Howard, 'Grand Strategy in the Twentieth Century', *Defence Studies* 1 (2001), 1, 2.

the single exception to the rule.[8] Indeed, if one took at face value General Tojo Hideki's argument to Prime Minister Prince Konoe Fumimaro for war in 1941, that 'sometimes a man has to jump, with his eyes closed, from the veranda of the Kiyomizu Temple', these doubts would seem appropriate.[9] Yet between 1919 and 1941, in Japan, an interactive decision-making process centred on the army–navy bureaucratic confrontation addressed how best to mobilize national resources for war. Competing visions about what a war was meant to achieve drove the crafting of national strategy. This chapter draws upon the intellectual frameworks set by two other British thinkers, Julian Corbett and J. F. C. Fuller to offer a first comprehensive review of the impact of bureaucratic competition over grand strategy.[10] Whereas previous scholarship on Japan at war focused on single-service strategies in the conflicts in China and in the Pacific, this chapter represents a first attempt to bring the different narratives together to shed light on the logic behind Japanese strategic choices. In so doing, the chapter offers an original contribution to the wider debate on strategy, by adopting the Japanese notions of 'line of sovereignty' and 'line of interest' as core explanatory variables to comprehend the tension underpinning the country's competing grand strategic visions.

Corbett argued that the mobilization of military resources required a careful assessment of the balance between maritime and military operations, and their subordination to the wider objectives of war. The 'paramount concern' of maritime strategy was 'to determine the mutual relations of your army and navy in a plan of war'. Only then, 'naval strategy can begin to work out the manner in which the fleet can best discharge the function assigned to it'.[11] The key question to address was '(w)hat will the war be about?' The formulation of grand strategy rested on the answer. For Corbett, military plans were 'minor' parts of a 'major' or grand strategy, according to which land and maritime operations must be coordinated.[12] So too, decades later, Colin S. Gray noted

---

8 Hisahiko Okazaki, *A Grand Strategy for Japanese Defense* (Lanham, Md.: University Press of America, 1986), pp. 129–31; Saburo Ienaga, *The Pacific War, 1931–1945* (New York: Pantheon Books, 1978), pp. 33–54.
9 The Kiyomizu Temple is a Buddhist temple positioned on the hills east of Kyoto, with a veranda overlooking the city. Quoted in Richard J. Samuels, *Securing Japan: Tokyo's Grand Strategy and the Future of East Asia* (Ithaca, NY: Cornell University Press, 2007), p. 1.
10 On the contributions by Corbett and Fuller on grand strategy, cf. Strachan, *The Direction of War*, pp. 31–3.
11 Julian S. Corbett, *Some Principles of Maritime Strategy* (London: Longmans, Green & Co., 1911), p. 14.
12 Ibid., p. 15.

that 'because the human race occupies and can live only on the land, sea power derives its strategic meaning strictly from its influence over events on land'.[13] One theme for this chapter concerns operational coordination between the imperial armed services and its effect on decision-making.

A second theme concerns the relationship linking military and non-military means to wage war. Fuller emphasized that a core function of grand strategy was to understand and nurture 'the moral of the civil population and the commercial and industrial resources at their disposal'.[14] The duties of the 'grand strategist' were 'to appreciate the commercial and financial position of his country; to discover what its resources and liabilities are', and to 'understand the moral characteristics of his countrymen, their history, peculiarities, social customs and system of government'. In Fuller's view, 'all these quantities and qualities form the military arch which it is his duty to construct'.[15] Grand strategy, therefore, centred on the assessment and development of the material and human resources needed to generate military power, and also connecting peacetime preparations to wartime conduct.[16] In this respect, the chapter explores how Japanese authorities understood the resources at their disposal and so shaped grand strategy as they moved from a quasi-peacetime state involving a number of 'incidents', to wartime mobilization.

Geography, the nature of the Japanese government structure and the character of military leadership, all shaped how grand strategy was formulated. Since the mid-nineteenth century, Japan's insular geography drove the development of a 'maritime' and a 'continental' vision of 'grand strategy'. The former stemmed from the writings of late Tokugawa samurai Sakamoto Ryoma and Meiji intellectual Yukichi Fukuzawa; the latter was first articulated by the leading oligarch of the Meiji era, Field Marshal Yamagata Aritomo.[17] The chapter investigates the changing perceptions of the strategic function of geography between 1854 and 1945.[18] Similarly, it explains the

---

13 Colin S. Gray, *The Navy in the Post-Cold War World: The Uses and Value of Strategic Sea Power* (University Park: Pennsylvania State University Press, 1994), pp. 3–4.

14 J. F. C. Fuller, *The Reformation of War* (London: Hutchinson & Co., 1923), p. 214.

15 Ibid., p. 218.

16 Strachan, *The Direction of War*, p. 16.

17 Makoto Iokibe, 'Introduction: Japanese Diplomacy from Prewar to Postwar', in M. Iokibe (ed.), *The Diplomatic History of Postwar Japan*, trans. and annotated by R. D. Eldridge (Abingdon: Routledge, 2010), pp. 7–9; Kitaoka Shin'ichi, 'The Strategy of the Maritime Nation Japan: From Yukichi Fukuzawa to Shigeru Yoshida', in Williamson Murray and Tomoyuki Ishizu (eds.), *Conflicting Currents: Japan and the United States in the Pacific* (Santa Barbara, Calif.: Praeger Security International, 2010), pp. 39–44.

18 Williamson Murray, Richard Hart Sinnreich and James Lacey (eds.), *The Shaping of Grand Strategy: Policy, Diplomacy, and War* (Cambridge University Press, 2011), pp. 11–14.

rise to dominance of military leaders and how this affected the formation of grand strategy.[19] The chapter further addresses the impact of military leadership on Japan's ability to define and, as the war progressed, to adjust grand strategy.[20] All told, the Japanese never really developed a 'grand strategy'; rather, 'grand strategy' simply aggregated different service driven 'minor' strategies – as Corbett had it – that initially maximized tactical advantages, but eventually failed to grasp the limits of national means and resources.

The chapter has four sections. The first assesses the literature, focusing on how the difficulty to 'name' Japan's war has limited analyses of Japanese grand strategy. The second part engages with the mechanics overseeing the development of grand strategy, exploring who were the 'makers of strategy' and what drove their interactions. The third part investigates the 'visions of strategy' articulated by Japanese military elites as the war evolved, until the end of 1942. The fourth part looks at how, from 1943, unresolved issues among the army and navy and the inability to adjust grand strategy led to defeat, examining the 'failures of strategy'. The chapter is organized themat-ically, though its sections follow a historical narrative, each carrying the analysis from the mid-1930s until the end of the war in 1945.

The 'names' of grand strategy

In the English language, except for a small number of studies exploring Japanese strategy in specific phases of the war, the lion's share of the literature tends to separate analyses of the maritime theatres of the Pacific from the war in China.[21] Narratives on the former focus on the Imperial Navy during 1941–45, while those on the latter emphasize the imperial army, often stretching the timeline from 1937, or 1931.[22] In recent times, multi-

---

19 Ibid., pp. 14–21.
20 Ibid., pp. 21–5.
21 Michael A. Barnhart, *Japan Prepares for Total War: The Search for Economic Security, 1919–1941* (Ithaca, NY: Cornell University Press, 1987); Richard B. Frank, *Downfall: The End of the Japanese Empire* (New York: Penguin, 2001); Haruo Tohmatsu and H. P. Willmott, *A Gathering Darkness: The Coming of War to the Far East and the Pacific, 1921–1942* (Lanham, Md.: SR Books, 2004); Richard B. Frank, 'Ketsu Gō: Japanese Political and Military Strategy in 1945', in Tsuyoshi Hasegawa (ed.), *The End of the Pacific War: Reappraisals* (Stanford University Press, 2007), pp. 65–94.
22 Paul S. Dull, *A Battle History of the Imperial Japanese Navy, 1941–1945* (Annapolis, Md.: Naval Institute Press, 1978); David C. Evans (ed.), *The Japanese Navy in World War II: In the Words of Former Japanese Naval Officers* (Annapolis, Md.: Naval Institute Press, 1986); Dan Van der Vat, *The Pacific Campaign* (Edinburgh: Birlinn, 2001 [1991]).

archival interdisciplinary research has done much to further articulate specific aspects of Japanese pre- and wartime strategic designs, political ambitions, economic achievements and structural limitations.[23] The publication of translations of Japanese documents complements these works, enabling a wider audience to comprehend the country's decision-making process.[24] Nonetheless, Sarah Paine's recently published *The Wars for Asia* is the first monograph to address Japanese grand strategy from the 1930s until 1945 in its regional and global dimensions, against the background of the wider conflicts that shaped the region for the first half of the twentieth century.[25] This chapter complements Paine's work by looking at how Japanese domestic politics and bureaucratic tensions helped to shape how military elites approached the nature of these regional and global conflicts.

This separation between a 'Pacific' and a 'China' war marked a similar intellectual divide in Japan, where scholars debated the 'names' of the war in relation not to matters of grand strategy, but to the political affiliation that a particular name implied. According to a recent Japanese study on the subject, occupation authorities fired the opening salvos of the controversy when, in December 1945, they prohibited the Japanese official name 'Greater East Asian War' as part of the move to dismantle imperial wartime institutions and vocabulary.[26] The use of the name 'Pacific War' emerged instead, a name quickly seen as less controversial, though more limited in geographic scope. In March 1946, the GHQ Civil Information and Education Section consolidated this choice, publishing 'The Pacific War History: From the Mukden Incident to the Unconditional Surrender'; this work went on to sell

23 David C. Evans and Mark R. Peattie, *Kaigun: Strategy, Tactics, and Technology in the Imperial Japanese Navy, 1887–1941* (Annapolis, Md.: Naval Institute Press, 1997); Herbert P. Bix, *Hirohito and the Making of Modern Japan* (New York: Perennial, 2001); Brian Bond and Kyoichi Tachikawa (eds.), *British and Japanese Military Leadership in the Far Eastern War, 1941–1945* (Abingdon: Frank Cass, 2004); Sadao Asada, *From Mahan to Pearl Harbor: The Imperial Japanese Navy and the United States* (Annapolis, Md.: Naval Institute Press, 2006).

24 Akira Iriye, *Pearl Harbor and the Coming of the Pacific War: A Brief History with Documents and Essays* (Boston, New York: Bedford/St. Martin's, 1999); Donald M. Goldstein and Katherine V. Dillon (eds.), *The Pacific War Papers: Japanese Documents of World War II* (Washington DC: Potomac Books, 2006). One significant source that remains available only to specialists with Japanese language skills is Sanbo Honbu (ed.), *Sugiyama Memo: Daihon'ei Seifu Renraku Kaigi nado Hikki* (Sugiyama Memo: Matters related to Record of Imperial Headquarters–Government Liaison Conferences) (Tokyo: Hara Shobo, 1967).

25 Sarah C. M. Paine, *The Wars for Asia, 1911–1949* (New York: Cambridge University Press, 2012). Also, Haruo Tohmatsu, 'The Strategic Correlations between the Sino-Japanese and the Pacific Wars', in Peattie et al., *Battle for China*, pp. 423–45.

26 Jun'ichiro Shoji, 'What Should the "Pacific War" Be Named? A Study of the Debate in Japan', *NIDS Journal of Defense and Security* 12 (2011), 48.

some 100,000 copies and quickly entered school curricula.[27] From 1950 to 1954, a series of multi-volume histories of the *Pacific War*, published by the authoritative Japanese Society for Historical Studies, further consolidated this trend.[28] In the foreword of a later edition, the decision to use this name was explained as follows:

> The title of the History of the *Pacific War* that gives too much weight to the war between Japan and the United States is not necessarily appropriate, and the History of World War II or the History of 15-Year War focusing on Japan more closely correspond to the contents of the book, but these names of the war are not yet used commonly. And we cannot use the History of *Greater East Asian War* that glorifies Japan's invasion. Therefore, we settled with the more widely used name of the History of the *Pacific War* for reasons of convenience.[29]

By the end of the 1950s, the name Pacific War was favoured in academic and general history writing, though Japanese academics debated the reinstatement of the names Great East Asian War and 15-Year War. Conservative novelist Hayashi Fusao and Kyoto school philosopher Ueyama Shumpei championed the use of the former to challenge the vision of history promoted by occupation authorities, presenting the war as necessary to self-preservation and to the promise to liberate Asia.[30] Motivated by a similar dissatisfaction with the conceptual and geographic boundaries imposed by the name Pacific War, liberal philosopher Tsurumi Shunsuke and left-wing historian Ienaga Saburo argued in favour of 15-Year War as a name that better connected wartime Japan to its responsibilities for the military campaigns conducted in China since 1931. As Ienaga wrote, the events from the Manchurian Incident to the surrender were all 'inseparable, all part of the same war', for which the wartime nomenclature was 'utterly unacceptable'.[31]

---

27 Ibid., 49.
28 The main exception being the work by Takushiro Hattori, *Daitoa Senso Zenshi – A Complete History of the Greater East Asian War* (4 vols., Tokyo: Masu Shobo, 1953). A former colonel in the imperial army, during the occupation, Hattori worked for the G-II's 'Historical Section' under General Willoughby, and later plotted to become the first Chief of Staff of the National Police Reserve and to assassinate the Japanese Prime Minister Yoshida Shigeru. John L. Weste, 'Staging a Comeback: Rearmament Planning and Kyūgunjin in Occupied Japan, 1945–1952', *Japan Forum* 11:2 (1999), 165–78; Joseph Coleman, 'Papers Tie US to 1950s Japan Coup Plot', *The Washington Post* (28 February 2007).
29 Quoted in Shoji, 'What Should the "Pacific War" Be Named?', 50–1.
30 Sebastian Conrad, *The Quest for the Lost Nation: Writing History in Germany and Japan in the American Century* (Berkeley: University of California Press, 2010), pp. 116–17.
31 Ienaga, *The Pacific War*, p. xiii.

In following decades, the use of Pacific War remained undisputed, especially in newspapers and magazines, though academics increasingly came to consider Greater East Asian War as a more appropriate name, given its use at the time of the events and for its ability to convey the geographic area of the war.[32]

The political nature of this debate overlooked a key feature of grand strategy: the connection between peacetime preparations and wartime conduct. Indeed, for most of these publications, the investigation of national strategy mattered less than the exploration of the political causes of the war. On matters of strategy, the Japanese post-war debate resembled that of official wartime authorities. Japan entered the war at 1.30 a.m. on 8 December 1941. Before then, the country had been involved in a series of 'incidents' in China, Manchuria and along the Mongolian border.[33] On 10 December 1941, the Imperial General Headquarters–Government Liaison Conference decided that 'the latest war against the United States and Britain and the war that may arise depending on the future developments of the situation, including the China Incident' would be named the Greater East Asian War.[34] Two principles guided Japanese discussions on the selection of a name, the geography and purpose of the war. Against naval proposals emphasizing the nature of the main operational theatre (i.e. Pacific War), or the main countries that Japan would fight (i.e. War against the United States and Britain), other members proposed names that stressed the war's wider ends (i.e. War for the Development of Asia). In the end, the name Greater East Asian War seemed a good compromise, conveying both the purpose and the geographic scope of the war. The tension over how to prioritize these principles was never fully resolved. As of February 1942, one senior officer wrote in his memoirs:

> There were those who emphasised the purpose of the war is self-existence and self-defence, those who argued for the dual purpose of self-defence and construction of the 'Greater East Asian new order' and those who regarded the construction of the 'Greater East Asian new order' as the primary war purpose, there was complete lack of unity in ideas.[35]

This diversity in ideas strengthened the argument that from 1937 to 1945, the Japanese fought different types of war, some simultaneously, others in a

---

32 Shoji, 'What Should the "Pacific War" Be Named?', 77–8.
33 Paine, *The Wars for Asia*, 7–9.
34 Bix, *Hirohito and the Making of Modern Japan*, p. 443.
35 Quoted in Shoji, 'What Should the "Pacific War" Be Named?', 48.

close sequence, and also conceptualized them as separated in strategic terms. In turn, that conclusion favoured a post-war analysis that looked at strategy in its specific naval and military dimensions, and with different names for the war. For the Japanese, the expansion of military operations in East Asia from 1937 to 1945 had multiple dimensions; they were regional and global; they fashioned ambitions of colonial expansion and imperial defence. The debates concerning the right name for the conflict were rooted in the political implications of a conflict with multiple dimensions. This leads to a crucial question. How did Japanese strategy-makers envisage strategy, and what mechanisms regulated the interaction among them?

Makers of strategy

In reviewing the Japanese imperial policy-making system, Samuel Huntington argued that civil-military relations were governed by 'sustained disorder'.[36] The problem, he held, was the autonomy granted by the 1889 Constitution to the armed forces. During the Meiji era, the national ideology combining the religious precepts of Shinto and the moral code of the medieval military class, *bushido*, contributed to make Japan 'authoritarian, ethnocentric, Nationalistic, imperially oriented (in the sense of the Emperor-worship and glorification of the Japanese Empire), expansionist, and bellicose with high value assigned to warrior and warrior virtues'.[37] The Emperor was the Supreme Military Commander. The Chiefs of Staff responded only to him on military matters, while the Army and Navy Ministers could exert pressure on budget allocations by means of their access to the Emperor.[38] The independence of the Supreme Command from civilian oversight, known as *Tosuiken no Dokuritsu*, allowed the military significant influence on government policy and national strategy.[39]

In fact, the Japanese military was subject to a form of civilian oversight. When the Meiji reformers developed political institutions, influence on national security depended on regional affiliation and personal connections. In particular, the Dominions of Choshu (Yamaguchi prefecture) and Satsuma (Kagoshima prefecture) dominated the political landscape, the former

---

36 Samuel P. Huntington, *The Soldier and the State* (Cambridge, Mass.: Harvard University Press, 1954), p. 99.
37 Ibid., p. 125.
38 Bix, *Hirohito and the Making of Modern Japan*, p. 154.
39 Huntington, *The Soldier and the State*, p. 130.

maintaining close affiliation with the army, and the latter with the navy.[40] As one Japanese scholar remarked, domestic debates over strategy and the allocation of resources tended to be prompted by pro-army and/or pro-navy positions, rather than by divisions between civilian and military leaders. In times of crisis, on the other hand, the common samurai lineage and a shared 'sense of pride and responsibility' allowed civilian and military leaders to place military power within a wider national agenda.[41] Nine of this first generation of leaders, including four members from each of the two main regional clans, went on to form a group of influential elder statesmen known as *genro*. They strove to balance civilian and military powers, and army–navy competition, until the end of the Taisho era.[42] Their existence helps to explain how the Japanese approach to the wars against China and Russia and the First World War differed from the wars of the Showa era: why the actions of 1894, 1904 and 1914 had different natures to those of 1931, 1937 and 1941.

Within this context, the establishment in 1878 of the Army General Staff as an independent body from the War Ministry planted the seeds for the *Tosuiken no Dokuritsu* system.[43] The War and Navy Ministries emerged in 1872, with the army upholding overall responsibility for national defence, or *kokubo*, and the navy more narrowly handling maritime security. Naval planning and command were placed under the authority of the Army General Staff, which had direct access to the Emperor and remained independent of the War Ministry.[44] In 1893, however, Admiral Yamamoto Gonnohyoe – the main architect of the Meiji navy – secured an independent chain of command through the creation of a Navy General Staff.[45] Control over naval operations did not alter the navy's overall subordination to the army, as defined in the regulations for the wartime command structure, the Imperial General Headquarters (IGHQ).[46] Eventually, on 28 December 1903, weeks

40 Captain Malcolm D. Kennedy, *The Military Side of Japanese Life* (Westport, Conn.: Greenwood Press, 1973 [1924]), pp. 316–17; Leonard A. Humphreys, *The Way of the Heavenly Sword: The Japanese Army in the 1920s* (Stanford University Press, 1995), pp. 2–14; Evans and Peattie, *Kaigun*, pp. 8–11.

41 Shin'ichi Kitaoka, 'The Army as a Bureaucracy: Japanese Militarism Revisited', in Anthony Best (ed.), *Imperial Japan and the World, 1931–1945: Critical Concepts in Asian Studies* (4 vols., Abingdon: Routledge, 2011), vol. I, p. 36.

42 Tatsuji Takeuchi, *War and Diplomacy in the Japanese Empire* (University of Chicago Press, 1935), pp. 20, 467–8.

43 Ibid., p. 453.

44 Kennedy, *The Military Side of Japanese Life*, pp. 319–20.

45 Evans and Peattie, *Kaigun*, pp. 22–3.

46 Goldstein and Dillon (eds.), *The Pacific War Papers*, 27.

before the outbreak of the Russo-Japanese War, Admiral Yamamoto succeeded in revising IGHQ regulations, to place the army and the navy on equal terms (Figure 6.1).[47]

The establishment of two independent commands did much to drive military involvement in national politics and exacerbate inter-service relations in the 1930s, prompting both services to pursue ever-growing political influence. Indeed, one well-informed contemporary observer noted that the army did 'exercise a decided influence over the country for good'.[48] The deterioration of civil-military relations, by contrast, depended on the changing relationship between the two General Staffs and their respective ministries. In the army, the General Staff enjoyed considerable independence from, and in times of crisis predominance over, its ministry. By the end of the First World War, the General Staff had proven to be difficult to control, notably in 1918, when it decided to deploy 70,000 men in Siberia, some ten times the number of troops the government had agreed.[49] By 1937, this behaviour – exacerbated by the initiatives of individual commands and garrisons across the empire – took the form of insubordination, especially from groups of younger dissatisfied officers.[50] From 1930 to 1935, army officers were involved in 'twenty major domestic terrorist incidents, four political assassinations, five planned assassinations, and four attempted coups, the March and October incidents of 1931, the May 15 Incident of 1932, and the great mutiny of February 1936'.[51] After this last incident, the political power of the Army General Staff grew further, as the Chief of Staff, Prince Kan'in Kotohito, reinstated the provision that only active-duty officers could serve as War Ministers, in part justifying this choice as a necessity to restore control within the ranks.[52]

By contrast, in the navy, the Chief of the General Staff was placed initially under the authority of the Navy Minister.[53] This difference stemmed from the army's adoption of the Prussian model, and the navy's of that of the Royal Navy.[54] Until 1 October 1933, this structure remained unchallenged.

47 Evans and Peattie, *Kaigun*, p. 95.
48 Kennedy, *The Military Side of Japanese Life*, p. 321.
49 Humphreys, *The Way of the Heavenly Sword*, pp. 25–9; Takeuchi, *War and Diplomacy in the Japanese Empire*, p. 458.
50 Takafusa Nakamura, *A History of Showa Japan, 1926–1989* (University of Tokyo Press, 1998), pp. 60–5; Humphreys, *The Way of the Heavenly Sword*, pp. 116–25.
51 Edward J. Drea, *Japan's Imperial Army: Its Rise and Fall, 1853–1945* (Lawrence: University Press of Kansas, 2009), p. 181.
52 Goldstein and Dillon (eds.), *The Pacific War Papers*, p. 30; Kitaoka, 'The Army as a Bureaucracy', pp. 254–6.
53 Evans and Peattie, *Kaigun*, pp. 26–7.
54 Goldstein and Dillon (eds.), *The Pacific War Papers*, p. 26.

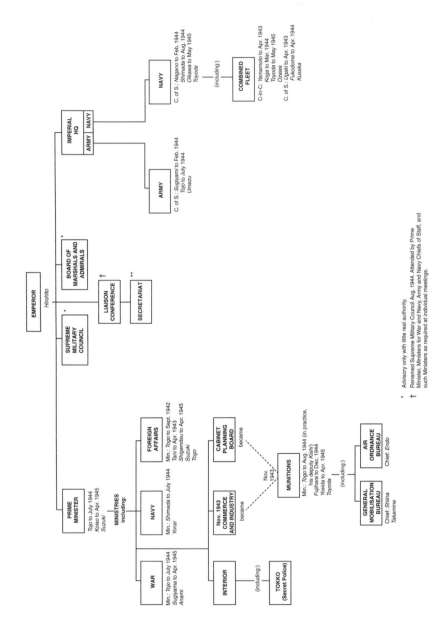

6.1 Japanese high command

The chart shows the Japanese high command structure:

EMPEROR
Hirohito

Connected to SUPREME MILITARY COUNCIL *, BOARD OF MARSHALS AND ADMIRALS *, PRIME MINISTER, and IMPERIAL HQ.

SUPREME MILITARY COUNCIL *
LIAISON CONFERENCE †
SECRETARIAT **

BOARD OF MARSHALS AND ADMIRALS *

PRIME MINISTER
Tojo to July 1944
Koiso to Apr. 1945
Suzuki

MINISTRIES
including:

WAR
Min.: Tojo to July 1944
Sugiyama to Apr. 1945
Anami

NAVY
Min.: Shimada to July 1944
Yonai

FOREIGN AFFAIRS
Min.: Togo to Sept. 1942
Tani to Apr. 1943
Shigemitsu to Apr. 1945
Suzuki
Togo

INTERIOR
(including:)
TOKKO (Secret Police)

Nov. 1943 COMMERCE AND INDUSTRY
became

CABINET PLANNING BOARD
became

Nov. 1943 —

MUNITIONS
Min.: Togo to Aug. 1944 (in practice, his deputy Kishi)
Fujihara to Dec. 1944
Yosida to Apr. 1945
Toyoda

(including:)
GENERAL MOBILISATION BUREAU
Chief: *Shiina*
Takamine

AIR ORDNANCE BUREAU
Chief: *Endo*

IMPERIAL HQ
| ARMY | NAVY |

ARMY
C. of S.: Sugiyama to Feb. 1944
Tojo to July 1944
Umezu

NAVY
C. of S.: Nagano to Feb. 1944
Shimada to Aug. 1944
Oikawa to May 1945
Toyoda

(including:)
COMBINED FLEET
C-in-C: Yamamoto to Apr. 1943
Koga to Mar. 1944
Toyoda to May 1945
Ozawa
C. of S.: Ugaki to Apr. 1943
Fukudome to Apr. 1944
Kusaka

Notes:

*   Advisory only with little real authority.

†   Renamed Supreme Military Council Aug. 1944. Attended by Prime Minister, Ministers for War and Navy, Army and Navy Chiefs of Staff, and such Ministers as required at individual meetings.

** Comprising Cabinet Secretary (*Hoshino* to late 1944), and Chiefs of Army and Navy Military Affairs Bureaux at the respective Ministries.

Subsequently, however, peacetime control of the fleet was removed from the ministry to the Navy General Staff, like in the army. By 1936, the army provisions for the selection of serving officers were applied for the appointment of the Navy Minister too. In the words of Prince Fushimi Hiroyasu, the Chief of the Navy General Staff, this was 'a great reform for the regeneration of the Imperial Navy'.[55]

Thus, as of 1937, the operational branches of the army and the navy had acquired crucial independent influence on national policy. Leverage was exercised in two ways, through unrestrained access to the Emperor and political coercion. After the 1936 reforms, the Chiefs of General Staff and ministers, all serving officers, could present their views on armament, defence and foreign policy directly to the Emperor, without having to consult with the government. Concurrently, by threatening to not let flag officers serve as ministers, the military de facto controlled the fate of a cabinet.[56] The first effects of this new domestic political balance were felt in August 1936, when the government announced that a little over 69 per cent of its budget would go to the military, and in November 1936, as the army budget was granted a 31 per cent increase from the previous year.[57] Until 1944, consecutive Army Ministers, including Field Marshal Sugiyama Hajime, General Itagaki Seishiro, Field Marshal Hata Shunroku and General Tojo Hideki all came from the ranks of the General Staff. Their concerns rested more on implementing army policies than on interactions with political parties or the coordination of civilian and military relations.

In the navy, these structural revisions did not generate an immediate ousting of all officers with views different from those of the General Staff. The Navy Ministers from February 1937 to September 1940, Yonai Mitsumasa and Yoshida Zengo, were the 'last fortresses' to resist mounting pressures from the Navy General Staff to join the army on the warpath. Pressure from the General Staff increased incessantly, to the point that Admiral Yoshida noted 'there is nobody reliable to assist me, yet the situation is momentous, and if we make one false step, it can very well lead to war'.[58] When Admiral Oikawa Koshiro replaced Yoshida at the helm of the ministry, the two General Staffs' control over policy was complete.[59]

55 Asada, *From Mahan to Pearl Harbor*, p. 172.
56 Chitoshi Yanaga, 'The Military and the Government in Japan', in Best (ed.), *Imperial Japan and the World*, p. 150.
57 Drea, *Japan's Imperial Army*, p. 186; Barnhart, *Japan Prepares for Total War*, p. 95.
58 Asada, *From Mahan to Pearl Harbor*, p. 222.
59 Yanaga, 'The Military and the Government in Japan', pp. 151–2.

The military rise to power explains the implosion of civil-military relations in Japan and the military takeover, but not their motivations. Within their junior and middle ranks, the quest for more power and control was nurtured by a combination of frustration for the slow modernization imposed by budgetary restrictions, and anxiety over the growing gap between the requirements of national security in the 1930s, and the reality of military capabilities.[60] The army, led by Army Minister Ugaki Kazunari (also read as Kazushige), pursued modernization to accommodate doctrinal, operational and tactical changes in land warfare, against the Japanese financial retrenchment of the 1920s.[61] In a similar fashion, the international regimes of the Washington and London naval treaties of 1922 and 1930 restricted naval rearmament. By the mid-1930s, limitations to military spending caused bitter fights between the Army and Navy General Staffs and their respective ministries. Younger hawks in both services thought these limitations strangled Japanese ambitions, power and status. After 1936, internal disagreements within the armed services were coupled by rivalry among them, a situation that was partly resolved in September 1940, when Admiral Oikawa became Navy Minister precisely to smooth interactions with the army.[62]

In the army, a strong 'imperial' faction, or *Kodo-ha*, emerged in the 1930s to question a modernization process that was undermining the élan of the 'magnificent tradition of Japanese arms'.[63] Manuals published from 1928 to 1930 played to this view, stressing the centrality of the spirit of Japanese soldiers over material capabilities. The divisions between 'traditionalists' and 'modernizers', whose members were known as the 'control' faction or *Tosei-ha*, reflected also a different understanding of the evolving character of war. The control faction saw the Soviet Union as Japan's main threat, whereas the imperial faction focused on Japan's interests in China. Modernizers too assigned a crucial role to Japan's interests in China, but since they feared the next war would be a protracted affair, they considered full 'control' of national resources, including those in north China, Mongolia and Manchuria, as essential to support the army in the ultimate fight against the Soviet threat.[64]

---

60 Tohmatsu and Willmott, *A Gathering Darkness*, pp. 14–15; Asada, *From Mahan to Pearl Harbor*, pp. 169–72.
61 Humphreys, *The Way of the Heavenly Sword*, pp. 75–95; Drea, *Japan's Imperial Army*, pp. 151–4.
62 Asada, *From Mahan to Pearl Harbor*, p. 222.
63 Drea, *Japan's Imperial Army*, p. 158.
64 Ibid., pp. 176–7; Tohmatsu and Willmott, *A Gathering Darkness*, p. 55.

The army reached a breaking point with the mutiny of 26 February 1936. It was ignited by the media coverage of the court martial of Lieutenant Colonel Aizawa Saburo – an imperial faction member who sought to resolve differences of opinion at the point of a sword by hacking to death the leader of the modernizers, Major General Nagata Tetsuzan.[65] By 1937, the army had implemented a series of purges and forced retirements, and reconciled internal divisions by expanding operations in China in the quest for resources to power the Japanese military machine. The army optimistically planned for a three-month, short, decisive war. War Minister Sugiyama Gen told the Emperor that all would be resolved in a month.[66] Initial victories in Inner Mongolia, north China and the Yangzi River valley seemed to prove them right; yet three years after these aims had not been achieved, operations in China were imposing heavy economic costs.[67] Active duty personnel increased from 950,000 in 1937 to 1,350,000 in 1940, with 150,000 new troops deployed in the battlefields across China between 1937 and 1939, and plans to field some 65 divisions and 200 air squadrons by 1942.[68] By 1940, the war on the continent had solved the army's internal crisis, at the cost of tying the country's resources to a conflict with no end in sight.

Since the abrogation of the naval treaties in 1934, the navy too was divided by similar quarrels, but the expansion of land operations in China added an extra layer of concerns over its budgetary allocations. To the navy, the main potential enemy since 1907 was the United States, but senior officers from the ministry and the General Staff were divided over how to approach naval defence.[69] By February 1937, the senior officers of moderate views who had not been purged in 1934 by Navy Minister Osumi Mineo were led by Admiral Yonai Mitsumasa, a long-time member of the 'administrative' group, also known as 'treaty' group, or *Joyaku-ha*. Nominated Navy Minister in February of that year, Yonai considered that a diplomatic posture avoiding war with the Anglo-Saxon powers, backed by capabilities sufficient to deter Japan's competitors, was the best option to maintain naval prominence in East Asia.[70] Officers like Admirals Yamamoto Isoroku and Inoue Shigeyoshi complemented this view by calling for a revision of existing naval doctrine, which should be focused on the pursuit of a surface fleet decisive engagement, by

65 Drea, *Japan's Imperial Army*, p. 181.
66 Paine, *The Wars for Asia*, p. 129.
67 Ibid., pp. 138–50; Barnhart, *Japan Prepares for Total War*, pp. 106–9.
68 Drea, *Japan's Imperial Army*, p. 207.
69 Asada, *From Mahan to Pearl Harbor*, pp. 164–6.
70 Asada, *From Mahan to Pearl Harbor*, pp. 214–19.

strengthening carrier and land-based air power.[71] Until September 1940, Admiral Yonai and his successor, Admiral Yoshida, rejected plans for open war. They opposed pressure from officers of the 'command' group, or *Kantai-ha*, who championed an alliance with Nazi Germany and Fascist Italy and war with Britain and the United States. The 'command' group could count on influential senior and mid-ranking officers in key posts, like Admiral Suetsugu Nobumasa and Captain Ishikawa Shingo, and on the 'imperial' bestowing of Prince Fushimi, the Chief of the General Naval Staff.[72]

For the command faction, a policy of diplomacy and deterrence endangered the navy's place in national strategy, especially with the army in China requesting increasing funding. Instead, its members emphasized preparations for a short, decisive surface clash to overwhelm numerically stronger peer competitors (i.e. the United States) at the outset of hostilities. This strategy was both key to the command of the Pacific, and to contain the army's expanding resource allocations.[73] In mid-1940, the evolution of the war in Europe favoured new army plans to expand operations in south China, French Indochina, Burma and Hong Kong – especially as an offensive in the south could cut off supplies to Chinese forces and bring victory on the continent. Such an action would prompt an American intervention that would catch the Imperial Navy unprepared; yet, unwilling to accept that the navy could not secure the resources needed to defeat that threat, fleet faction officers pressed for war preparations and a deal with the army to secure materiel requirements.[74] This argument also prevented plans that favoured a southern advance ignoring hostilities with the United States.[75] As 1940 drew to a close, the operation section of the Navy General Staff told its army counterparts that by April 1941 the navy would be ready to strike United States assets in the Pacific.[76] In so doing, the navy, conscious of the shortfall in materiel, took a risk, but one that paid off – so far as politics were concerned. On 30 October 1941, the new Navy Minister Admiral Shimada Shigetaro concluded months of negotiations with the army, giving his

---

71 Evans and Peattie, *Kaigun*, pp. 471–9; Peattie, *Sunburst*, pp. 159–61; Seno Sadao, Commander JMSDF, 'A Chess Game with no Checkmate: Admiral Inoue and the Pacific War', *Naval War College Review* 26 (January–February 1974), 31–5.
72 Asada, *From Mahan to Pearl Harbor*, pp. 174–82.
73 Sadao Asada, *Culture Shock and Japanese-American Relations: Historical Essays* (Columbia: University of Missouri Press, 2007), p. 157.
74 Ibid., pp. 157–9. On the navy's tonnage problems, cf. Tohmatsu and Willmott, *A Gathering Darkness*, pp. 83–7.
75 Barnhart, *Japan Prepares for Total War*, pp. 162–3.
76 Asada, *Culture Shock and Japanese-American Relations*, p. 159.

Table 6.1 *Steel allocations for FY 1942 (000 metric tons)*

Recipient	FY 1941 plan	FY 1942 plan	Revised FY 1942
Army	900	810	790
Navy	950	850	1,100
Civilian	2,910	2,640	2,610
Total	4,760	4,300	4,500

Table 6.2 *Imperial conferences at IGHQ, 1937–43*

Date	Event
24 Nov. 1937	Army/Navy report on operational plans to Emperor
16 Feb. 1938	Outline of China operations for summer/autumn 1938
15 June 1938	Wuhan Operation approved
13 Jan. 1939	Hainan Island occupation approved
31 Dec. 1942	Guadalcanal withdrawal approved
5 March 1943	1943 operational policy approved
26 March 1943	Eight Area Army (Rabaul) established
20 May 1943	Aleutians withdrawal approved

approval to the army's proposed strategy in exchange for additional steel. In the mobilization plans for 1942, the navy was to receive 1.1 million tons of steel and the army 790,000 tons (Table 6.1).[77] The navy resolved its internal quarrels by agreeing to wage war, by signing a pact of steel with the army.

In formal terms, the main forum where the army and navy sought to reconcile their views was the IGHQ, reactivated on 27 November 1937. The Prime Minister and other civilian Cabinet members were excluded from its deliberations. Instead, matters of military policy were first agreed by the two services before seeking the Emperor's authorization during special conferences held at the IGHQ. From November 1937 to May 1943, eight sessions were convened. Land operations dominated the debate on national strategy, with the navy constantly seeking to 'counter-argue' its case (Table 6.2). Coordination with civilian bodies was reached in special Liaison Conferences that included the two Chiefs of the General Staffs, the War and Navy Ministers, the Prime Minister and the Minister of Foreign Affairs (Figure 6.2). The Liaison Conference met in the presence of the Emperor to ratify major

77 Ibid., p. 166; Barnhart, *Japan Prepares for Total War*, pp. 256–7.

national policies. From January 1938 to August 1945, fifteen of these meetings, known as Imperial Conferences, took place. The IGHQ retained a central role in shaping strategy and policy, and enabled the army and the navy to contain each other while controlling civilian authorities. Because of its nature and the dominance of the military in it, war-making decisions were examined through the prism of complex institutional rivalries and service requirements, while operational autonomy dictated the terms of national strategy.

Visions of strategy

Inter-service rivalry in Japan occurred not merely over political influence and budgets. Its foundations had deeper roots in a fundamental intellectual divide between two ways to understand the relationship between geography and national strategy in Japan. As early as 1867, samurai leader Sakamoto Ryoma presented an eight-point plan outlining a national strategy of a strong maritime flavour, using the sea as a source of trade and economic security, and as a shield against invasion. Sakamoto's beliefs stood in sharp contrast with those of Meiji oligarch Yamagata Aritomo, who, as Prime Minister, presented in the 1890 inaugural speech at the Diet a strategic vision that was continental at heart. He articulated two geographic notions, a 'line of sovereignty' (*shukensen*), corresponding to the geographic boundaries of a country, and a 'line of interest' (*riekisen*), including regions that could have a direct impact on the *shukensen*.[78] At the time of Yamagata's speech, the Japanese commitment to the security of the *riekisen* implied an involvement to maintain the Korean peninsula outside the influence of the Russian and Chinese Empires. By 1937, Korea and Manchuria were part of the *shukensen*, while China was included in the *riekisen*. Emerging ideas in Japan about Pan-Asianism indirectly changed this notion, and, by 1945, China had become part of the *shukensen*.[79] In terms of grand strategy, until 1943, the debate on Japanese grand strategy was over where the nation's *shukensen* and *riekisen* fell and how to defend them.

Over previous decades, the army and the navy had articulated two opposite visions to meet the security of the *riekisen*, known as the northern and southern advances (*hokushin-ron* and *nanshin-ron*). Until the 1930s,

78 Pia Moberg, 'Lines of Argument in the First Inauguration Speech Held in the Japanese Diet: The Case of Yamagato Aritomo in 1890', *Asia & Africa* 2 (2002), 83–7.
79 Masataka Matsuura, 'Japan and Pan-Asianism', in Anthony Best (ed.), *The International History of East Asia, 1900–1968: Trade, Ideology and the Quest for Order* (Abingdon: Routledge, 2010), pp. 84–6; Tohmatsu and Willmott, *A Gathering Darkness*, p. 17.

Japanese national authorities never had to reconcile the two doctrines. The imperial defence policy documents of 1907, 1918 and 1926 indicated Russia, and subsequently the Soviet Union, as the army's primary threat, and the United States as the navy's. In practice, however, the army's progressive expansion in Manchuria after 1931 paved the way for control faction officers from the Kwantung Army, like Colonel Ishiwara Kanji, to give new purpose to the *hokushin-ron*. Since 1929, Ishiwara had envisaged placing Manchuria at the heart of a project of economic self-sufficiency to harvest the resources to tackle the Soviet Union.[80] The economic interests of large corporations like *Mantetsu* (South Manchuria Railway Company, founded in 1906) offered both the opportunity and the motivation to plan firm Japanese control over the region.[81] In 1936, Ishiwara adamantly emphasized that 'over the next decade we must not expand our national effort on anything outside Manchuria'.[82] The operations following the Marco Polo Bridge Incident, set on two parallel axes following the Tianjin–Pukou and Peking–Wuhan rail lines, secured operational success but not definitive victory, with Chiang Kai-shek able to secure in 1939 foreign support to fight another day.[83] By mid-1940, combat operations in China had reached a stalemate, the defeat at Nomonhan had exposed the limits of Japanese logistics, and heading 'south' to cut off the remaining supply lines from French Indochina and southern China looked the only appealing alternative. Offensives against the Soviet Union had to be postponed. The army turned south before heading north again.

Whereas Yamagata authored the intellectual blueprints of the northern advance in the Japanese Diet, the navy developed the southern advance in the 1870s to counter the army's arguments, and to instil among the Japanese a 'sense of destiny' in expansion toward the South Seas.[84] During the First World War, the navy's initiative to occupy German possessions in the Pacific – including the Mariana, Caroline and Marshall island groups – embodied this vision. When the navy withdrew from the naval treaties, its development entered a new stage.[85] As relations with the United States

80 Mark R. Peattie, *Ishiwara Kanji and Japan's Confrontation with the West* (Princeton University Press, 1975), pp. 203–5.
81 Ibid., pp. 107–10.
82 Ibid., p. 204.
83 Paine, *The Wars for Asia*, p. 145.
84 Charles Schencking, 'The Imperial Japanese Navy and the Constructed Consciousness of a South Seas Destiny, 1872–1921', *Modern Asian Studies* 33:4 (1999), 769–96.
85 Charles J. Schencking, 'Bureaucratic Politics, Military Budgets and Japan's Southern Advance: The Imperial Navy's Seizure of German Micronesia in the First World War', *War in History* 5:5 (1998), 308–26.

deteriorated and concerns about the shortage of petroleum increased, the navy instructed the Committee to Investigate Southern Policy – chaired by the Vice Chief of the General Staff Admiral Shimada Shigetaro – to prepare the first full investigation of the oil resources in Southeast Asia.[86] Captain Nakahara Yoshimasa – known also as 'the King of the South Seas' – drafted the principles that informed the debate and the decisions taken about imperial defence policy in 1936. They stressed the importance of harvesting the resources of the Dutch East Indies, which strengthened the claim for funds for a fleet that must confront the United States and Britain. In September 1936, the killing of a Japanese national in Pakhoi (Beihai), on the Chinese shore of the Gulf of Tonkin, enabled the General Staff to prepare a draft plan to invade Hainan, for use as a springboard for operations in the South China Sea. Nakahara oversaw the project and Rear Admiral Kondo Nobutake approved it. As the war in China expanded, the navy operational-ized its plans. By March 1939, it occupied Hainan and the Spratly Islands.[87]

Against this context, in July 1940, the army gave the navy a policy draft, penning its own strategy for a 'southern advance' into French possessions. Economic self-sufficiency animated the creation of a Japanese *Lebensraum* under the banner of the Greater East Asian Co-Prosperity Sphere, presenting Japan, Manchuria and China as its new *shukensen*, and Southeast Asia as its primary *riekisen*. The navy noted that the plan underestimated the signifi-cance of the American naval threat to this policy, which it reinforced at the Liaison Conference of 27 July 1940, when the new principles for Japan's future strategy were adopted.[88] Given American approval of the third Vinson Act and the Stark Plan – massively increasing the tonnage of the US Navy – Japanese naval planners faced danger. In the July negotiations for the new national strategy, Kondo insisted on securing the army's share of war materiel so that the navy could meet the American challenge. As the United States prepared to create a navy twice the size of Japan's within three years, pressure increased within the Navy General Staff to exploit its existing numerical advantage. In September, with Japan joining the Tripartite Pact, the navy was given a guarantee of larger shares of steel, making it impossible for the service to show any doubt in its ability to defeat the United States. The navy was now at the forefront of the southern advance, but the margins of success seemed small.

---

86 Asada, *From Mahan to Pearl Harbor*, p. 207.
87 Ibid., pp. 208–10.
88 Asada, *Culture Shock and Japanese-American Relations*, pp. 157–8.

As Japanese troops entered Indochina on 22 September, the Operation Section of the General Staff advocated naval plans for further advance in Southern Indochina. American initiatives to deter Japan by limiting its access to primary resources, especially iron and scrap metal, obtained opposite results, inflaming middle-echelon naval officers who pressured superiors for war.[89] In December 1940, the capture of secret documents revealing British strategy in case of war in East Asia further emboldened the navy to seize the initiative.[90] By April 1941, Captains Nakahara and Ishikawa finalized an internal paper that outlined the necessity to advance south to secure bases for operations in the region, and to destroy the Anglo-American threat to the empire. The doctrine of the southern advance was now the navy hardliners' solution to Japan's strategic impasse. Admiral Nagano made this position clear at the Liaison Conference of 21 July 1941, and 40,000 troops were sent to Indochina on 28 and 29 July. British, American and Dutch reactions were immediate and trade to Japan came to a halt.[91] The navy's worst fears were now a reality and a total embargo of Japan was in place.

'Battleships without oil cannot move'. In August, this self-explanatory assessment fully captured the concerns of the Navy Ministry.[92] Without access to resources in the Dutch East Indies, oil stockpiles would be depleted within eighteen months. With the US Navy bound for a massive build-up, Admiral Nagano told the Imperial Conference on 6 September that a 'quick encounter, quick showdown' represented the navy's best option for securing command of the Pacific. This strategy would minimize the impact of material deficiencies by establishing an impregnable maritime fortress in the southern area.[93] Among the senior officers, Vice Admiral Inoue expressed doubts on the feasibility of this plan. As he transferred to the Fourth Fleet in August, he discovered that only minimum fortifications had been built in Micronesia. In the summer of 1941, Admiral Yamamoto too expressed deep reservations, but realized that, against American military build-up, time would quickly run out.[94] As the Commander-in-Chief of the Combined Fleet, he had to offer its fleet the best chances of victory. As of January 1941, he had instructed Admiral Onishi Takijiro to prepare plans for an air attack on the American

---

89 Asada, *From Mahan to Pearl Harbor*, p. 243.
90 Ken Kotani, 'Pearl Harbor: Japanese Planning and Command Structure', in Daniel Marston (ed.), *The Pacific War Companion: From Pearl Harbor to Hiroshima* (Oxford: Osprey, 2005), pp. 33–4; Tohmatsu and Willmott, *A Gathering Darkness*, p. 90.
91 Asada, *From Mahan to Pearl Harbor*, pp. 252–4.
92 Ibid., p. 261.
93 Ibid., pp. 265–6.
94 Paine, *The Wars for Asia*, p. 183.

fleet in Hawaii, in case a decision was taken to secure the Dutch East Indies. For this reason, until October 1941, he challenged the Navy General Staff seeking approval to change the navy's long-rehearsed strategy of intercepting the American fleet as it steamed across the Pacific to defend assets in the Philippines.[95]

At the Imperial Liaison Conference of 5 November, the stage was set for global war, but a grand strategy seemed missing. The Imperial Army had few 'American' experts, little intelligence on the United States and its military, and had never really contemplated large-scale operations in the maritime theatres of the Southwest Pacific.[96] Indeed, until late 1940, it had no plans for campaigns in Malaya or against Singapore, nor accurate maps of the area.[97] Yet the Army Chief of Staff General Sugiyama argued that, provided sea lanes could be maintained to support logistics, the army could establish a firm position in the southern areas. By the end of the conference, the army and the navy had an almost diametrically opposite understanding of the operational meaning of the southern advance. For army planners, the aim was to set a defensive perimeter around the nation's *shukensen*, where attrition and exhaustion were core operational assumptions. For the navy, the conquest of territories across Southeast Asia served to lure enemy fleets into battle to secure a quick victory. To that end, advanced airbases in the South China Sea and Micronesia extended the radius of the 'decisive engagement', from the pre-war Marianas line to the Marshalls and the Bismarck Archipelago.[98] Neither had clearly identified what would constitute victory in the southern advance, nor how to achieve it. The army had joined the navy's version of a southern advance to better secure Japan's *shukensen* in Manchuria and China. Yet from a naval perspective, the southern advance could not be a grand strategy because it did not address the security of the *riekisen* and the *shukensen*.

On 7 December 1941, the Japanese launched one of the most ambitious campaigns in modern military history. The first landings in Thailand and on the Malay peninsula preceded the air raid on Pearl Harbor, followed shortly after by bombing raids over Singapore, Hong Kong, Shanghai and Wake Island, and further landings on Guam. By mid-December 1941, Japanese

95 Kotani, 'Pearl Harbor', p. 34.
96 Edward J. Drea, *In the Service of the Emperor: Essays on the Imperial Japanese Army* (Lincoln: University of Nebraska Press, 1998), p. 32.
97 Tomoyuki Ishizu and Raymond Callahan, 'The Rising Sun Strikes: The Japanese Invasions', in Marston (ed.), *The Pacific War Companion*, p. 47.
98 Drea, *In the Service of the Emperor*, pp. 33–4.

forces had occupied vital Dutch oilfields in Borneo, and by 8 March 1942, Manila, Rabaul, Singapore, Malaya and Burma had all fallen. In 'the first five months of 1942, Japan took more territory over a greater area than any country in history and did not lose one single ship'.[99] Operationally, a combination of luck, effective executions and Allied weaknesses enabled the Japanese to secure their strategic objectives in Southeast Asia.[100] In December, consistent with its main war objectives on the continent, a confident Japanese army also launched the Go-Go campaign, a massive operation conducted south of the Yangzi River to crush Nationalist forces and secure central China.[101] In March, the navy – stunned by the magnitude of its successes and still anxious to complete the task of destroying the American fleet – sought to extend Japan's defensive perimeter to include Port Moresby, Papua New Guinea, Midway and the Aleutian Islands, all by the end of June.[102] The German spring offensive of 1942 seemed to ease the limits of Japanese strategy: driving the Soviet Union out of the war, Japan could focus on neutralizing Britain by cutting the support of its colonies, creating the conditions for the United States to remain isolated in the war effort. The disaster at Midway in May 1942, and the enormous amount of resources, especially air capabilities, spent in the Guadalcanal and Solomon campaigns, however, soon stripped the initiative from Japan and ended the southern advance. Indeed, by September 1943, the new IGHQ policy was to hold the 'absolute zone of national defence'.[103] Japanese strategy was showing the first cracks in the wings.

Failures of strategy

As a process of interaction, any grand strategy requires a degree of adaptability to meet the evolving circumstances of war. By mid-1943 and for the reminder of the conflict, two fundamental problems affected Japan. First, no agreed objective emerged as an alternative to the northern and southern advances. Second, the Japanese failed to grasp Allied strategy in order to adapt to it. Japan's advances 'became a function of both operational success

---

99 Paine, *The Wars for Asia*, p. 188.

100 Ishizu and Callahan, 'The Rising Sun Strikes', pp. 52–7; Tohmatsu and Willmott, *A Gathering Darkness*, pp. 124–38.

101 Paine, *The Wars for Asia*, 192–193.

102 Jonathan Parshall and Anthony Tully, *Shattered Sword: The Untold Story of the Battle of Midway* (Washington DC: Potomac Books, 2005), pp. 33–4.

103 Drea, *In the Service of the Emperor*, p. 38.

and strategic failure'.[104] This is particularly true of the navy's relentless pursuit of a decisive engagement with its American opponent, failing to detect the implications of the US Navy's focus to destroy the economic foundations of the Japanese war machine. Japan spent the conflict seeking ways to defend the *sukensen* as resources were becoming too overextended to safeguard the *riekisen*. The Doolittle raid over Tokyo's skies in April 1942 proved the weaknesses of the Japanese Empire by hitting its beating heart, convincing the Japanese navy to extend further operations to prevent that from happening again.[105]

In the second half of 1943, pressure from the Allied counter-offensive in the Pacific constrained the ability of the army to reorganize its defensive perimeter and restore the capabilities to defend it. By February 1943, the defence of Guadalcanal showed the first signs of the limits of Japanese air power. In the months up to the fall of Guadalcanal, Japanese pilots from land-based air assets suffered an 87 per cent casualty rate, while carrier-based pilots had a 98 per cent casualty rate. These numbers dropped to lower figures, 60 and 80 per cent respectively, during the second half of 1943, but the loss of highly trained veterans, together with that of skilled carrier naval technicians, crippled Japanese air power.[106] Losses in manpower were coupled by drastic reductions in industrial output and innovation. In 1944 alone, Japan lost some 7,000 front-line aircraft in combat, its total losses approximately 12,000 aircraft. Its production of roughly 18,000 aircraft could replace losses, but was a far cry from the 55,000 aircraft the army and navy had demanded for the prosecution of the conflict. While the Allies produced new and better aircraft, Japanese equipment stagnated.[107]

Thus, as resources grew thinner on the ground, the army strategy in the Pacific changed from attrition to one of inflicting a decisive defeat on the advancing foe. After the fall of Saipan in 1944, Japanese army planning aimed to erect defences on islands of strategic significance, where manpower could counter the technologically superior and logistically better-equipped Allied forces, no matter the costs. The army envisaged four possible areas where the final engagements might happen: the Philippine Islands (Sho 1), Taiwan and the Ryukyu Islands (Sho 2), the Japanese home islands (Sho 3) and Hokkaido (Sho 4). Notwithstanding the efforts of General Yamashita Tomoyuki at Leyte

---

104 Paine, *The Wars for Asia*, p. 196.
105 Tohmatsu, 'The Strategic Correlations between the Sino-Japanese and the Pacific Wars', p. 427.
106 Paine, *The Wars for Asia*, p. 194.
107 Drea, *In the Service of the Emperor*, p. 39.

and Luzon to win the decisive battle against the Allied forces, it became apparent once the Philippines were lost that the army's best option was to inflict the highest possible casualties to the enemy, so as to force a negotiated peace. The battles for Iwo Jima and Okinawa sought to achieve this goal. The southern perimeter had crumbled; it was no longer part of the *riekisen*. It was an ever-receding front line to stop the invasion of the Japanese islands.[108]

In December 1942, the Japanese redeployed forces from China along the southern defensive perimeter, slowing the Go-Go offensive. Until June 1943, while the army retained 30 per cent of its overall strength in China, operational gains were limited. The army did not possess enough capabilities and manpower to conduct major operations in two areas. In 1943, the costs of southern operations doubled from the previous year, while those in China saw similar major increases.[109] One year later, with the southern *riekisen* in disarray, the Japanese army regrouped to launch the two last major offensives of the war, aimed to secure the *shukensen* on the continent. In March, Japanese forces initiated the U-Go campaign against India, and in April, the Ichi-Go campaign – the army's largest land operation, deplaying twenty divisions, including 510,000 men supported by almost 800 tanks, 15,500 vehicles and 240 aircraft, to fight 700,000 Nationalist troops.[110] Ichi Go aimed to connect the *shukensen*, including Japan, Korea and Manchuria, and the occupied territories in China by land, and to forestall allied air raids from Nationalist bases in China to Japan. Until December 1944, the Japanese made considerable gains in Henan, Hunan, Guangxi and Guangdong, capturing large key cities like Changsha, Guilin and Nanning. By early 1945, Nationalist causalities mounted to more than 100,000 soldiers, and some ten bases and thirty-six airports had been captured. The Japanese army crippled Chiang Kai-shek and many bases, but the campaign did little to improve Japan's overall situation. The U-Go campaign was a disaster, on the other hand, one of the most severe defeats in Japanese military history. More importantly, the capture of airfields in the Marianas meant that as of 24 November 1944, the air bombing campaign against Japan commenced, keeping the Japanese islands under tremendous pressure.[111] By April 1945, Japan could be defended only by a decisive victory on the main islands of the archipelago.

---

108 Ibid., pp. 39–40.
109 Tohmatsu, 'The Strategic Correlations between the Sino-Japanese and the Pacific Wars', p. 433.
110 Drea, *Japan's Imperial Army*, p. 244.
111 Tohmatsu, 'The Strategic Correlations between the Sino-Japanese and the Pacific Wars', pp. 437–8.

When the Japanese navy entered the war in 1941, it fielded a fleet of 'superb night fighters' that in ship-to-ship engagements won ten out of the thirteen surface battles that occurred until October 1943. Then, however, attrition took its toll, and this situation was reversed in subsequent months. The Japanese were unable to win any battle against the American navy, which won eight instead.[112] One study explained that this was the case because the fleet was 'ill-suited to the kind of extended naval conflict that Japan was obliged to wage'.[113] Crucially, assets to cover other vital wartime functions, like tankers for fleet logistics and escort vessels for convoys, were never built in sufficient numbers, nor fully integrated in the navy's operational grammar. In the words of a retired Japanese admiral, the wartime fleet was the intellectual child of a 'shock and awe' naval doctrine.[114] In this respect, the Japanese navy differed from some of its peer competitors, notably the Royal Navy. Throughout the 1930s, the British Admiralty developed escort vessels integrating combat systems, like the anti-submarine detection system ASDIC and the high-angle/low-angle (HA/LA) anti-aircraft guns to reflect submarine and air threats.[115] In the Imperial Navy before 1943, no major asset was destined to the protection of shipping. Only coastal defence vessels were designated for these tasks, and these were poorly suited to anti-submarine warfare (ASW).

Yet the real issue rested on the adaptability of Japanese naval strategy. The doctrinal grammar the Japanese developed to implement this strategy focused so much on fleet-to-fleet engagements that little room was left for force and command structures to adapt to other operations, if the enemy fleet was not sunk in one blow. The Grand Escort Command Headquarters, the command dedicated to convoy activities, was established only in November 1943. On paper, it included four escort carriers (CVEs) and the 901st Air Group; in reality, no carrier was able to conduct operations until July 1944, due to refit, and the air group had no crews trained for anti-submarine duties.[116] Radar, sonar and communication systems were also either lacking

112 Dull, A Battle History, pp. 353–4.
113 Mark R. Peattie, 'Japanese Naval Construction, 1919–1941', in Phillips Payson O'Brien, Technology and Naval Combat in the Twentieth Century and Beyond (London: Frank Cass, 2001), p. 103.
114 Vice Admiral Yoji Koda, JMSDF (Ret.), 'Introduction', in Jim Bresnaham (ed.), Refighting the Pacific War: An Alternative History of World War II (Annapolis, Md.: Naval Institute Press, 2011), p. 3.
115 Andrew Lambert, 'Seapower 1939–1940: Churchill and the Strategic Origins of the Battle of the Atlantic', Journal of Strategic Studies 17:1 (1994), 86–108.
116 Atsushi Oi, 'Why Japan's Antisubmarine Warfare Failed', in Evans (ed.), The Japanese Navy in World War II, pp. 402–3.

Table 6.3 *Japanese shipping losses in Southeast Asia, 1 November 1943 – 30 March 1945*

	Naval shipping	Military shipping	Civilian shipping
Southeast Asia	534,896.52 tons	764,748 tons	1,116,916 tons
Total losses	1,819,829 tons	1,394,888 tons	1,861,316 tons

or of limited use. Improvements in training and preparations for ASW continued until the end of the war, but by then these counted for too little, too late. As one senior escort officer noted, the 'Japanese ASW had irrevocably failed'.[117] Allied forces became more aware of that weakness, and they exploited it. By the end of 1943, Japan had already lost over 2 million tons of shipping, suffering a 3 million ton shortfall in bulk commodities compared to the previous year. The situation worsened dramatically in 1944 and 1945, when Japanese oil imports fell from a 1943 peak of 740,000 tons to a meagre 178,000 tons (third quarter of 1944). Just 9 per cent of oil shipments from Southeast Asia reached their final destination in Japan in 1945 (Table 3).[118] Japan's *riekisen* in the south had become the graveyard of the empire. The navy's greatest strategic failure was that it did not adapt, let alone anticipate, avoiding this dramatic turn of events.

In February 1945, Japan's situation was worsening, but military elites did not feel that all was yet lost. The defences of the *shukensen* in occupied China were shaky, but the country possessed sufficient manpower to mount a formidable defence – one that would make any invasion so costly to American manpower as to achieve peace on favourable terms. On 20 January 1945, the Emperor sanctioned the 'final decisive battle' of the war.[119] Within three weeks, the army and the navy agreed to a joint air defence of the Japanese islands, and to a massive 1.5 million-men mobilization plan, aimed at bringing homeland commands to 2,903,000 men, 292,000 horses and 27,500 motor vehicles.[120] On 8 April, hours after Operation HEAVEN ONE – the last major surface operation of the Imperial Navy – ended with the sinking of the battleship *Yamato*, plans were completed for the final battle on Japanese soil, known as Ketsu-Go. As these preparations started in earnest, in Okinawa the 62nd Division's defence of the city of Shuri proved just how costly every inch

---

117 Ibid., p. 414.
118 Mark P. Parillo, *The Japanese Merchant Marine in World War II* (Annapolis, Md.: Naval Institute Press, 1993), pp. 215, 247.
119 Frank, 'Ketsu Go', pp. 68–9.
120 Ibid., p. 71; Drea, *Japan's Imperial Army*, pp. 249–50.

of Japanese territory would be to conquer in human terms. Confidence on the defences was such that until 9 August, even after the first atom bomb struck Hiroshima, military authorities at the IGHQ, Prime Minister Suzuki Kantaro and Foreign Minister Togo Shigenori rejected an unconditional surrender. Then, the second atomic bomb of Nagasaki showed that the Allies possessed a weapon that did not require an invasion of Japan, negating the relevance of Ketsu-Go.[121] This situation, combined with the massive Soviet offensive in Manchuria, prompted the Emperor to intervene against a disaster that could not defend the Japanese home islands.[122] Continuation of war created two major risks. Domestically, the social fabric faced implosion, or as one of the Emperor's aides put it, the 'state of utter exhaustion and bewilderment' of the Japanese people.[123] Militarily, the chain of command might break. To prevent this, on 17 August, the Emperor issued a special rescript to ensure that the imperial armed forces fighting across East Asia would surrender. It explained that to continue the fight 'under present conditions at home and abroad would only recklessly incur even more damage to ourselves and result in endangering the very foundations of the empire's existence'.[124]

Conclusions: feigning grand strategy

On 12 August 1945, Navy Minister Admiral Yonai admitted to Rear Admiral Takagi Sokichi that:

> I think the term is perhaps inappropriate, but the atomic bombs and the Soviet entry into the war are, in a sense, gifts from the gods [tenyū, also 'heaven-sent blessing']. This way we don't have to say that we quit the war because of domestic circumstances. I've long been advocating control of our crisis, but neither from fear of an enemy attack nor because of the atomic bombs and the Soviet entry into the war. The main reason is my anxiety over the domestic situation. So, it is rather fortunate that we can now control matters without revealing the domestic situation.[125]

Even in the darkest hour, the Japanese military did not see external adversaries as its primary concerns – the centre of gravity for its strategy.

121 Frank, 'Ketsu Go', pp. 86, 90.
122 Ibid., pp. 87–8.
123 Bix, *Hirohito and the Making of Modern Japan*, p. 491.
124 Frank, 'Ketsu Go', p. 92.
125 Quoted in Bix, *Hirohito and the Making of Modern Japan*, pp. 509–10.

Instead, fears about 'the domestic situation', about Japan's internal vulnerabilities, drove grand strategy. Uncertainty over the ability to possess sufficient resources to protect the nations' *shukensen* prompted the revolts culminating with the army mutiny in February 1936, and the navy's internal upheavals in mid-1930s. In turn, military leaders took stronger, and often adventurist, actions to restore order within the ranks and secure more resources. In the army, modernizers and traditionalists fought to make Japan's small economy fit for the all-out war with the Soviet Union. Thus they started wars with China and the USSR, gaining heartache and humiliation. Overarching concerns over limited resources impaired the navy's vision, making it progressively impossible to envisage options other than war, yet to court it. This 'siege mentality' both caused and was exacerbated by international actions – from the US Navy shipbuilding programme of 1938 to the economic sanction of 1940 – which exposed military weakness. In turn, moves designed to deter Japan consistently obtained the opposite effect, which then drove escalation from foreign states. Japanese strategy gave its enemies no option between surrender, war or overwhelming superiority.

Two primary factors drove the military takeover of grand strategy. The first is the disappearance of the *genro*, whom, after 1922 declined to one less influential man, former Prime Minister Saionji Kinmochi. Their political function as mediators to reconcile civilian and military spheres of interest, army and navy agendas, domestic and foreign policy, was never replaced. With the *genro* passed Japan's only means to master the military. From the middle 1930s, the right of the military to access the Emperor directly offered them an exclusive channel of communication and power. They used this position to press their policies on and through Emperor Hirohito, and to exploit other forms of imperial intervention in policy. Through the enlistment of members of the imperial family as Chiefs of the General Staffs, Prince Kan'in from 1931 to 1940 in the army, and Prince Fushimi from 1932 to 1941 in the navy, the two services used the highest source of authority in Japan to consolidate their grip on the policy-making system. The second factor concerned the changing nature of the Japanese military elites themselves. In the 1930s, young and middle-echelon officers were no longer samurai brought up to experience war and politics, and to recognize the different functions each had to exercise for the nation. The professionalization of the Japanese military made officers more versed in narrow technical issues than in wider political and strategic matters. The debates over strategy in the Japanese army and navy were affected increasingly by an inability to connect considerations about operations and fleet configurations to the wider diplomatic and policy uses of force. Similarly, peacetime preparations were hostages of bureaucratic politics.

The army and navy offered competing visions of aims and means, and failed to generate a grand strategy. Inter-service rivalries and internal concerns about force structure and capabilities prevented the navy from understanding and applying Corbett's ideas on the coordination between maritime and grand strategy. Indeed, when the army proposed a 'southern strategy' in 1940, the navy made it include hostilities against the United States, for narrow bureaucratic reasons, even though many senior officers feared that prospect. By mid-1942, the staggering operational successes across Southeast Asia did not help the army and navy to reconcile their differences on how the southern advance would lead to victory. For the army, China was the primary theatre, even when forces were redeployed from mainland to Southeast Asia to prevent the fall of the defensive perimeter on Guadalcanal and the Solomon Islands. For the navy, Southeast Asia was the stage for the ultimate titanic clash with the United States. Neither vision came to fruition; China remained a quagmire; the decisive battle did not materialize; and the structural inability to reconcile operational plans hindered the services' understanding of the changing circumstances of the war. As of January 1945, the only grand strategy Japanese military leaders could agree upon envisaged a final battle on the shores of the archipelago, where victory was possible only by sacrificing millions of Japanese. Military leaders behaved like a wounded *ronin*, the master-less samurai of the feudal period. Alone, aware of their limits, they opted for an all-out fight they knew they could start, but did not know how to finish. That fight was risky, reckless, but consistent with their value system – that of warriors, not of strategists.

7

US grand strategy, 1939–1945

THOMAS G. MAHNKEN

Between 1939 and 1945, the US government faced the challenge of fighting and winning a multi-theatre coalition war. Roosevelt and his advisors worked with America's allies, principally Great Britain, to develop common aims and to formulate and implement a common strategy. Although these discussions frequently witnessed controversy and disagreement, President Franklin D. Roosevelt and his military advisors compromised and adapted when necessary in order to maintain Allied solidarity. The United States assisted its allies materially and supported them operationally. It mobilized US economic and technological resources to arm both the US Armed Forces and those of its allies. As a result, US troops played a decisive role in both the Atlantic and Pacific theatres, ultimately providing the United States with the opportunity to play a leading role in founding and leading the post-war world.

Introduction

When the Second World War began in 1939, the United States possessed neither the political will nor the military might to act as a major power on the world stage. In 1939, the US Army was only the world's eighteenth largest land force, with less than 200,000 men under arms. The US Navy, which possessed the world's second largest battle fleet, was in better shape. The US economy had yet to recover from the Great Depression. The Neutrality Acts of 1935–37 limited the ability of the United States to sell arms and war materiel or to provide loans and credits to belligerents. Public opinion polls showed a strong desire by a majority of the American population to stay out of the war.

By 1945, the United States had nearly 12 million personnel under arms. The US Army, which had swelled to a strength of 8.2 million, had become the largest ground force the United States had ever fielded. The US Navy, with a strength of 3.4 million (including 484,400 Marines), was the largest and most powerful naval force in history, with 1,200 warships, as well as 50,000 support and landing craft. The Army Air Corps, with a strength of 2.3 million personnel and 159,000 aircraft, represented the largest and most powerful air armada in the world. The US economy had recovered and its industrial base had been converted to war production. US industrial output had almost doubled and was producing more than twice the output of all the Axis Powers combined.[1] The American economy supplied the United States and its allies with an unprecedented quantity of materiel. By the end of the war, the United States had built 269,000 aircraft and 351 million metric tons of bombs; it had launched 147 aircraft carriers and 952 warships displacing 14 million tons, as well as 5,200 merchant ships totalling 39 million tons; and it had produced 86,333 tanks and 12.5 million rifles.[2] The United States had also fielded advanced technology, including radar and the atomic bomb.

The war was not without cost. More than 400,000 Americans died in the Second World War, including 292,000 in combat. Although the death toll was higher than that for any other conflict in American history except the Civil War, the United States suffered fewer deaths than any other major combatant. It was, in fact, the only major power to end the war stronger than when it entered it. As a result, the United States was in a position to play a decisive role in creating a new global order, one that included the United Nations as well as liberal international economic institutions.

Pre-war planning

The roots of US strategy in the Second World War can be traced back to the 'colour' plans that the army and navy developed in the years that separated the two world wars. A conflict with Japan was the US Navy's top planning contingency throughout the interwar period, because only the Japanese fleet was strong enough to threaten US interests in Asia. Beginning in 1897, the army and navy developed a series of plans for a war with Japan, known as War Plan ORANGE. In 1923, the Joint Army-Navy Board, composed of the

---

1 Mark A. Stoler, 'The United States: The Global Strategy', in David Reynolds, Warren F. Kimball and A. O. Chubarian (eds.), *Allies at War: The Soviet, American, and British Experience, 1939–1945* (New York: St. Martin's, 1994), p. 55.
2 Andrew Roberts, *The Storm of War: A New History of the Second World War* (New York: HarperCollins, 2011), p. 215.

Army Chief of Staff, the Chief of Naval Operations, their deputies, and their chief planners, identified a war with Japan as the most pressing contingency facing the United States, a judgement it reaffirmed five years later.[3]

War Plan ORANGE envisioned a clash between the United States and Japan; planners assessed that neither side would have allies and that the war would not escalate. It would be confined to the Pacific, with the decisive actions occurring in the waters of the western Pacific. In its original form, War Plan ORANGE envisioned a trans-Pacific naval thrust to defend US possessions, primarily the Philippines, against Japanese aggression. The plan made no provision for a landing on the Japanese home islands. Rather, Japan was to be defeated by 'isolation and harassment', the disruption of its sea lines of communication, and by 'offensive sea and air operations against her naval forces and economic life'. If these measures were insufficient, then it was envisioned that the United States would have to take 'such further actions as may be required to win the war'.[4]

As Japanese naval power grew, War Plan ORANGE shifted to a sequential campaign to recover the islands that, it was assumed, would fall to the Japanese before assistance could arrive. In one of the great ironies of history, the 1935 version of the plan, which consigned the Philippines to its fate, was prepared during the tenure of Douglas MacArthur as Army Chief of Staff. Six years later, MacArthur would live out the consequences of that shift.

The operational challenge posed by the need to cross the Pacific, establishing support bases along the way, in order to recover US territories in the western Pacific, served to promote innovation in the Navy and Marine Corps during the interwar period. It helped drive the Navy to develop carrier aviation and under-way replenishment, and it motivated the Marine Corps to develop amphibious warfare to seize and hold island bases.

As influential as it was, War Plan ORANGE, a contingency confined to two belligerents in a single theatre of operations, was a far cry from the strategic situation that the United States would face in the Second World War. Closer was Joint Plan RED-ORANGE, which envisioned a two-theatre war between the United States on the one hand and an alliance of Japan and

---

3 Edward S. Miller, *War Plan ORANGE: The US Strategy to Defeat Japan, 1897–1945* (Annapolis, Md.: Naval Institute Press, 1991); Louis Morton, 'War Plan ORANGE: Evolution of a Strategy', *World Politics* 11:2 (January 1959), 221–50. Joint Board to Secretary of War, 'Coordination of Army and Navy War Plans', 7 June 1923, JB325, Ser. 210, *Records of the Joint Board*, Roll 9, Record Group 225, National Archives, p. 1; Joint Planning Committee to Joint Board, 'Order of Priority in Preparation of War Plans', 21 April 1928, *Records of the Joint Board*, Roll 9, RG 225, p. 1.

4 Joint Army-Navy Basic War Plan ORANGE, 1924, Joint Board (JB) 325, Ser. 228.

Great Britain on the other. Planners viewed this contingency as presenting a grave threat to American security, one that would require a full-scale mobilization and total military effort. Whereas the central feature of a war with Japan would be a naval campaign in the Pacific, RED-ORANGE required planners to contemplate a two-ocean war against two great naval powers. The strategic options open to the United States in such circumstances were limited to either assuming a defensive posture on both fronts, or taking the offensive in one theatre while standing on the defensive in the other. Given these options, as well as the assumption that the enemy in the Atlantic posed the greater threat, planners recommended a focus on obtaining a favourable decision in the Atlantic while remaining on the defensive in the Pacific.

The idea that the United States would face an Anglo-Japanese alliance was politically unrealistic, a fact that planners at the time readily acknowledged. Yet as a strategic exercise, War Plan RED-ORANGE forced planners to confront the problems the United States would face in a two-ocean war, an experience that was useful in thinking through the strategic circumstances the United States would confront after the outbreak of the Second World War.

Not surprisingly, given the experience of the Great War, the War and Navy Departments also paid considerable attention to industrial mobilization. In 1924, the War Department established the Army Industrial College to focus on wartime procurement and mobilization procedures. These preparations had a considerable influence on America's ability to wage a multi-theatre industrial war.

As Fascist power grew in Europe, so too did concern over the possibility of a German or Italian incursion into the western hemisphere, in violation of the Monroe Doctrine. In the winter of 1938–39, army and navy planners studied the possibility that the European Axis Powers, having defeated France and Great Britain, would seek to establish bases in the western hemisphere. Although planners viewed this as a remote possibility, they did feel the need to begin exploring the possibility of a war against Germany.

In 1939, the Joint Army-Navy Board began drafting a new series of war plans, dubbed RAINBOW, for a multi-theatre coalition war. The most limited plan, RAINBOW 1, envisioned a defensive campaign to protect the United States and the western hemisphere north of ten degrees south latitude, in which the United States was assumed to be acting alone. RAINBOW 2 assumed that the United States would be allied with France and Britain and that it would focus its efforts on the Pacific. RAINBOW 3 was essentially a recapitulation of Plan ORANGE, with the addition of the need to protect the western hemisphere. RAINBOW 4 was similar to RAINBOW 1, but also assumed the United States would defend the entire western hemisphere.

German success against France and the Low Countries in May and June 1940 and Japanese aggression in Asia presented the United States with an increasingly dire situation, and US political and military decision-makers sought to understand the implications of events on the battlefield for the United States. In doing so, they produced a wide range of assessments of the situation. The most influential of these was a memorandum describing the major strategic decisions facing the United States, prepared by the Chief of Naval Operations, Admiral Harold R. Stark, in consultation with Admiral Richmond Kelly Turner and other assistants. Indeed, the Plan Dog Memorandum ranks as one of the most important essays on policy and strategy ever written by an American military leader.

Stark argued that American security was bound up with that of Great Britain. As he put it, 'if Britain wins decisively against Germany we could win everywhere; but...if she loses the problem confronting us would be very great; and, while we might not <u>lose everywhere</u>, we might, possibly, not <u>win anywhere</u>.' Stark examined various scenarios that might bring the United States into war: a war between the United States and Japan alone; a war between the United States, Britain and the Netherlands, on the one side, and Japan on the other; a war between the Axis and the United States, with or without allies; and a war between the United States and Britain, on the one hand, and Germany and Italy, on the other. Stark concluded that should Britain lose the war, the military consequences for the United States would be dire. Victory 'might, conceivably, be accomplished by bombing and by economic starvation through the agency of the blockade. It surely can be accomplished only by military successes on shore, facilitated possibly by overextension and by internal antagonisms developed by the Axis conquests.' He argued that Britain lacked the manpower and material resources to defeat Germany; as a result the British needed assistance from powerful allies such as the United States.

> Victory would probably depend upon her ability ultimately to make a land offensive against the Axis powers. For making a powerful land offensive, British manpower is insufficient. Offensive troops from other nations will be required. I believe that the United States, in addition to sending naval assistance, would also need to send large air and land forces to Europe or Africa, or both, and to participate strongly in this land offensive.

Stark concluded that the United States had to choose from four options:

A. Shall our principal military effort be directed toward hemispheric defense, and include chiefly those activities within the Western Hemisphere which contribute directly to security against attack in either or both oceans?. . .

B. Shall we prepare for a full offensive against Japan, premised on assistance from the British and Dutch forces in the Far East, and remain on the strict defensive in the Atlantic?. . .

C. Shall we plan for sending the strongest possible military assistance both to the British in Europe, and to the British, Dutch and Chinese in the Far East?. . .

D. Shall we direct our efforts toward an eventual strong offensive in the Atlantic as an ally of the British, and a defensive in the Pacific?

Stark believed that option D ('Dog' in the phonetic alphabet of the US military) offered the best chance of victory, 'particularly if we insist on equality [with the British] in the political and military direction of the war'.[5]

With the concurrence of the Army Chief of Staff, General George C. Marshall, Stark forwarded the plan to Secretary of the Navy Frank Knox, who in turn sent it to the White House. Although Roosevelt did not formally approve it, Stark and Marshall took the President's silence as approval, and Plan Dog provided the basic guidance for US strategy throughout the war.

Soon after, Roosevelt approved secret staff talks with the British and Canadian armed forces, and on 29 January 1941, planners from the three nations met secretly in Washington DC to outline a combined strategy for the war, with Stark's Plan Dog memo forming the basis of agreement. The British hoped to put off direct confrontation with Germany for as long as possible, relying instead upon economic pressure and extensive bombing to weaken Germany, while the Allies created a ring of bases around the Reich. American planners, by contrast, wanted to concentrate forces to launch decisive operations as soon as possible.

The result of the talks, ABC-1, became the fundamental statement of Anglo-American strategy. It established the principle that defeating Germany first should be the primary aim of the Allies. It did not, however, resolve Anglo-American disputes regarding strategy or the division of labour to implement it. The British believed that the US contribution to the alliance should

---

5 Harold R. Stark, 'Memorandum for the Secretary', 12 November 1940, Op-12-CTB, safe files, box 4, *Navy Department 'Plan Dog' Files*, FDR Presidential Library, pp. 1, 5, 17, 21–4, 24.

emphasize America's financial and industrial strength as well as its naval power. They also supported an indirect strategy based upon bombing, blockade and limited operations in North Africa and the Mediterranean. Their American counterparts, by contrast, favoured a more direct offensive strategy.

Following the conference, the US Joint Army-Navy Board recommended the development of a plan for war with Germany, Italy and Japan. The result was War Plan RAINBOW 5, which was completed in April 1941. Like ABC-1, it affirmed a Germany-first strategy. It envisioned the application of economic pressure, a sustained air offensive, and a series of raids and minor offensives to capture positions around the periphery of Europe in preparation for an offensive against Germany. It also reflected the American commitment to a single thrust against Germany, foreseeing the primary immediate effort of the US Army to be 'the building up of a large land and air force for major offensive operations against the Axis powers'. It called for the United States to 'project the armed forces of the United States to the Eastern Atlantic and to either or both of the African or European Continents, as rapidly as possible consistent with [hemispheric defence] in order to effect the decisive defeat of Germany, or Italy, or both'.[6] RAINBOW 5 became the basic US plan for the Second World War.

Formulating policy and strategy

The United States fought the Second World War to achieve the total defeat of the Axis Powers, which American leaders saw as both a physical threat to the security of the United States and an ideological threat to American values and interests. From 1940 on, American political and military leaders agreed that Nazi Germany posed a greater threat to the United States than Imperial Japan, and thus that defeating Germany should be accorded top priority. To achieve this aim, the United States undertook a massive mobilization of its economic, military and technological resources. It provided extensive assistance to its allies, while simultaneously creating a large force for expeditionary operations in the Atlantic and the Pacific.

Roosevelt was convinced earlier than many of his military advisors that Great Britain's survival was vital to US national security, and that the United

---

6 Quoted in Richard W. Steele, *The First Offensive, 1942: Roosevelt, Marshall and the Making of American Strategy* (Bloomington: Indiana University Press, 1973), p. 24; Maurice Matloff and Edwin M. Snell, *The War Department: Strategic Planning for Coalition War, 1941–1942* (Washington DC: US Army Center of Military History, 1999), p. 8.

States possessed the means to ensure that survival. When France fell and the British Expeditionary Force was driven off the Continent, assistance to Britain became essential to the Allied war effort. Roosevelt and his advisors believed, or at least hoped, that Hitler would become bogged down in a protracted conflict on the Continent, allowing Britain to bring its naval power to bear to quarantine Germany on the Continent. Speaking at the University of Virginia on 10 June 1940, Roosevelt pledged that the United States would supply the Allies with the material resources they needed to fight Germany. In August, he dispatched the Emmons-Strong Mission to Great Britain and appointed Rear Admiral Robert L. Ghormley as Special Naval Observer attached to the American Embassy in London. In September, the United States traded fifty old destroyers to London for a ninety-nine-year lease on British bases on islands in the western hemisphere.

Roosevelt ran for re-election in 1940, on a platform of aiding Great Britain while keeping the United States out of war. His Republican challenger, Wendell Wilkie, held a position not dramatically different from Roosevelt's. Roosevelt nonetheless realized that the American public was lukewarm to the idea of making great sacrifices on behalf of Britain. Roosevelt faced opposition from those who believed that there was no compelling reason for the United States to involve itself in war in Europe. Some believed that the United States should remain aloof from the war in Europe, out of dislike for Britain or admiration of Nazi Germany; others saw foreign entanglements as a distraction from more pressing matters, such as economic recovery at home.

Roosevelt faced resistance to his efforts to aid Britain from within his Cabinet as well. During the summer, fed up with opposition from his Secretary of War, Harry Hines Woodring, and his Secretary of the Navy, Charles Edison, to greater involvement in the war, he replaced them with two internationalist Republicans: Henry Stimson, a respected public servant who had served as President Taft's Secretary of War and Hoover's Secretary of State, and Frank Knox, the Republican vice-presidential candidate in 1936 and owner of the Chicago *Daily News*. Both men shared Roosevelt's view of the need for an active American international role, and both had spoken out forcefully in favour of American preparedness and aid to Britain.

Germany's bombing of Great Britain from September 1940 to spring 1941 built greater sympathy for Britain in the United States. The Blitz killed 43,000 civilians and injured another 139,000. Vivid reporting by the American radio commentator Edward R. Murrow brought home the danger posed by Nazi Germany. Moreover, Britain's ability to weather the Blitz demonstrated that backing London was a worthwhile endeavour.

As war raged in Europe, American political and military leaders became increasingly concerned about the widening conflict in Asia. In April 1940, the United States Fleet deployed to Hawaii to conduct its yearly exercises. On 27 May, Stark informed the Pacific Fleet Commander, Admiral James O. Richardson, that it would remain there for the foreseeable future in order to deter the Japanese from moving southward against British and Dutch colonies in Southeast Asia.

On 22 September 1940, Japan, with the acquiescence of the Vichy regime, occupied the northern part of French Indochina. Five days later, Germany, Japan and Italy signed the Tripartite Pact. Aimed at deterring the United States from intervening in either Europe or the Pacific by raising the prospect of a two-front war, the agreement among the Axis Powers in fact linked the two theatres and became the vehicle that brought the United States into the war in Europe after being attacked in the Pacific.

On 5 November 1940, Roosevelt was re-elected as President of the United States. Having pledged during the electoral campaign to keep the United States out of the war in Europe, following his inauguration he moved the United States closer to belligerency. On 29 December 1940, Roosevelt used one of his fireside chats to warn that the 'Nazi masters of Germany', who sought to 'enslave the whole of Europe', and their Axis partners could 'dominate the rest of the world' if Britain fell. Rather than 'live at the point of a gun', he asked Congress to make the United States an 'arsenal of democracy', by giving him the authority to lend or lease materiel to nations resisting aggression which he deemed essential to US security. When he followed up in his inaugural address calling for a post-war world governed by what he termed the Four Freedoms – freedom of speech, freedom to worship, freedom from want and freedom from fear – Congress and the American people gave him broad backing.[7]

The Lend-Lease Bill to provide war materiel to the Allies nonetheless proved contentious, linking the United States as it did even closer with those fighting the Axis. When it passed in March 1941, Roosevelt told his secretary, 'this is tantamount to a declaration of war by the United States'.[8]

Harnessing the economic strength of the United States to the common cause was crucial to Allied success. Great Britain (and, until June 1940, France)

7 Warren F. Kimball, *Forged in War: Roosevelt, Churchill and the Second World War* (Chicago, Ill.: Ivan R. Dee, 1997), p. 72.
8 Quoted in Richard J. Overy et al., 'Co-Operation: Trade, Aid, and Technology', in Reynolds et al. (eds.), *Allies at War*, p. 205.

purchased large orders of American armaments to support their war efforts. Before 7 December 1941, Great Britain had paid for literally billions of dollars' worth of American military materiel, very little of which had been delivered. Indeed, it was not until autumn 1942 that the United States began to provide equipment under Lend-Lease to Great Britain that it had not already paid for.

Throughout the war, Lend-Lease provided the Allies with between $42 and $50 billion in aid, without the disputes that would have attended the need for repayment. Much the larger share of Lend-Lease assistance went to Great Britain. In May 1941, Roosevelt declared the defence of China to be vital to the United States, extending Lend-Lease to it; in the autumn, American assistance began flowing to the Soviet Union as well.

The challenges of US military industrial mobilization were exacerbated by the fact that US firms and officials, and especially Roosevelt, overrated the ability of American industry to produce high-quality arms rapidly and in large numbers. As a result, Roosevelt found himself promising arms both to the US Armed Forces and Great Britain and being unable to fulfil his promises to either.

Even after Lend-Lease became law, the American public remained luke-warm to the thought of America assuming a more active role in the war. Peacetime conscription, implemented in 1940, became the venue for debating the extent of American involvement in the war. In July 1941, the adminis-tration introduced a bill to extend the services of draftees and eliminate a provision restricting them to service in the western hemisphere. The meas-ure met with strong and emotional opposition. Roosevelt avoided direct involvement in the matter, fearing it would further polarize the debate; instead, Marshall took the lead with Congress. When the extension of the draft passed on 12 August, it was by the narrowest of margins. Moreover, it represented only a partial victory for the administration, as draftees' terms of service were set at 18 months and the limitation of their service to the western hemisphere remained in law.

In July 1941, Japan followed its occupation of northern Indochina with the occupation of southern Indochina. On July 26, Roosevelt signed an Executive Order freezing Japanese assets in the United States and forbidding trade with Japan, including oil exports; Britain and the Netherlands joined the effort. In early August, Secretary of War Stimson approved the dispatch of first-line aircraft (including just over half of the United States' most modern B-17s) to deter Japan and defend the Philippines, should war come. In September, the Japanese leadership secretly decided to include the United States in its forthcoming attack on British and Dutch possessions in Southeast Asia.

Creating and sustaining a multinational coalition

The success of coalitions in war depends upon the existence of a common enemy, the development of common aims and a common strategy, and leadership. In the case of the Allies, Germany was the common enemy and the goal of defeating the Nazi regime the central aim. Although the United States was clearly the strongest member of the alliance, there nonetheless remained divisions over strategy. Although Plan Dog, ABC-1 and RAINBOW 5 all emphasized a Germany-first strategy, such an approach was not always followed in practice. In addition, there remained controversy over the pursuit of a peripheral or direct strategy, as well as the timing of the invasion of the European continent.

The centrepiece of the alliance was the Anglo-American partnership. Although the Soviet Union bore the brunt of fighting Nazi Germany, and China tied down the majority of the Japanese army throughout the war, neither played a central role in the development and implementation of the coalition's overall strategy.

The Anglo-American alliance was both personal and institutional. Certainly, the relationship between Roosevelt and Churchill was vital to its effectiveness, and each emphasized personal diplomacy. After Churchill became Prime Minister in May 1940, communication between the two proved to be an indispensable channel for strategy formulation and implementation. Beyond the personal relationships forged among American and British leaders lay an unprecedented level of institutional cooperation between the two powers. At its peak, the British Army had more than 400 officers and 500 enlisted members in the United States at any one time; during the war, more than 1,500 British Army officers and soldiers served at forty-five locations across North America.[9] The two countries also achieved unprecedented economic and technological collaboration, including on radar, intelligence and nuclear weapons, with an unrestricted flow of information in both directions.

From 9 to 12 August 1941, Roosevelt and Churchill met at Placentia Bay, off the village of Argentia in Newfoundland, one of the bases that the United States had just leased in the destroyer-for-bases deal. Churchill arrived aboard the *Prince of Wales*, while Roosevelt arrived aboard the *Augusta*. The meeting was secret: Roosevelt had boarded *Augusta* only after arranging for a double

9 Theodore A. Wilson et al., 'Coalition: Structure, Strategy and Statecraft', in Reynolds et al. (eds.), *Allies at War*, p. 89.

to sail on the presidential yacht *Sequoia* on Cape Cod, in full view of reporters. Their conversations during the four days built their personal rapport and set the broad parameters of Anglo-American cooperation, including agreement to the contours of a Germany-first strategy.

During the conference, Roosevelt suggested to Churchill that the United States and Great Britain would have to work together to keep the peace following the war. He envisioned an international security organization that would be composed of a General Assembly representing all nations, an Executive Committee (the Big Four) and an Advisory Council that would meet periodically to advise the Executive Committee. In Roosevelt's conception, the Big Four – the United States, Great Britain, the Soviet Union and China – would have responsibility for making the most consequential decisions, would serve as trustees for colonial areas, and would collectively keep the peace.

On 12 August, the two leaders announced the Atlantic Charter. The Charter represented Roosevelt's attempt to gain agreement to the main features of the post-war world at the outset of the conflict. In soaring prose, the charter held that the alliance fought to ensure basic freedoms and called for the establishment of a post-war international system. The charter's other goals – achieving self-determination and economic liberalism – annoyed both the British and the Soviets, but great power collaboration won out.

It is easy to dismiss the Atlantic Charter as mere rhetoric, but the value of political discourse in building and sustaining support for a long and costly war in modern democracies should not be underestimated. Nor should Roosevelt be slighted for thinking through the contours of the post-war world even before the United States became a formal belligerent.

Despite statements such as the Atlantic Charter, public opinion defined what was politically feasible in Washington, and Roosevelt was a keen observer of it. Although he and his military advisors discussed plans for US involvement in the war, Roosevelt realized, as he told Secretary of War Stimson on 25 September 1941, that any proposal 'that we must invade and crush Germany' would elicit 'a very bad reaction' from the American public.[10]

By autumn 1941, Roosevelt knew that Germany needed to be defeated, and that the United States should play a key role in that defeat in order to gain a strong voice in the post-war world. However, he was unable bring the United States fully into the war with Germany; nor did he want to have to

10 Quoted in Stoler, 'The United States', p. 61.

fight Japan. As a result, he pressed Germany to take actions that would give the United States the pretext to enter the war. For example, when, on 4 September, a German submarine attacked the destroyer *Greer*, Roosevelt moved the United States closer to belligerency by authorizing US warships to escort British vessels from the east coast of the United States to Iceland.

Pearl Harbor and its aftermath

The Japanese attack on Pearl Harbor on 7 December 1941 was a transformational event. Far more significant than the damage that the Japanese inflicted upon the US Navy and Army that Sunday morning was the galvanizing effect the surprise attack had on the American body politic. The following day, Congress voted 470 to 1 in favour of war, the lone 'no' vote coming from pacifist Jeanette Rankin of Montana. Almost overnight, isolationist sentiment in the US Congress evaporated. As Senator Arthur H. Vandenberg, Junior of Michigan wrote in his memoirs, 'In my own mind, my convictions regarding international cooperation and collective security for peace took firm form on the afternoon of the Pearl Harbor attack. That day ended isolationism for any realist.'[11] His colleague, Senator Gerald P. Nye of Nebraska, echoed the sentiment:

> [There is] but one thing an American can want to do – win the war and win it with the greatest possible dispatch and decisiveness. It is not time to quibble over what might have been done or how we got where we are. . . To give our commander in Chief unqualified and unprejudicial backing in his prosecution of the war is an obligation which I shall gladly fulfill.[12]

War with Japan represented both an opportunity and a challenge for Roosevelt. On the one hand, it resolved the question of American involvement in at least the Pacific War. On the other, the Japanese attack complicated efforts to implement a Germany-first strategy. Immediately after Pearl Harbor, Roosevelt concluded that the American public 'would insist that we make the war in the Pacific at least equally important with the war against Hitler'.[13] He nonetheless reaffirmed the importance of defeating Germany first, of assistance to the Allies and of collaboration with Britain.

11 Arthur H. Vandenberg, Jr (ed.), *The Private Papers of Senator Vandenberg* (Boston, Mass.: Houghton Mifflin, 1952), p. 1.
12 Wayne S. Cole, *Senator Gerald P. Nye and American Foreign Relations* (Minneapolis: University of Minnesota Press, 1962), p. 199.
13 Quoted in Steele, *The First Offensive*, p. 51.

The Japanese attack temporarily quieted criticism of the Roosevelt administration. The vast majority of the American public supported the war effort, but according to one poll taken in the aftermath of Pearl Harbor, only 59 per cent of Americans were willing to fight an all-out war with Japan that included bombing Japanese cities. In addition, such enthusiasm as did exist for war with Japan did not translate into eagerness for war with Germany. There was also widespread confusion about American aims in the war. A poll taken in early December showed that 45 per cent of those questioned did not know what the United States was fighting for.[14]

On the afternoon of 11 December, Hitler declared war on the United States, even though the Tripartite Pact with Japan and Italy did not require that he do so. Hitler had, however, promised the Japanese government that he would enter the war against the United States, and obviously thought it was a good thing to do. He likely believed that US entry into the war was both inevitable and imminent and wanted Japan to distract Washington. Hitler's declaration of war reflected a fundamental failure to understand just how much the United States was capable of contributing to the war against Germany. It was, as Andrew Roberts has put it, 'an unimaginably stupid thing to have done in retrospect, a suicidally hubristic act less than six months after attacking the Soviet Union.'[15]

Churchill decided to meet with Roosevelt as soon as he heard about Pearl Harbor, and he left London for Washington on 12 December. Their first wartime conference, which took place under the codename ARCADIA, was held in Washington DC from 22 December 1941 to 14 January 1942. Despite the Japanese attack on the United States, Roosevelt agreed that Europe remained the most important theatre and thus he accepted the continuation of a Germany-first strategy. The conference also led to an agreement to form an Anglo-American Combined Chiefs of Staff (CCS), headquartered in Washington, to develop and implement Allied military strategy for the war. As a result, Washington became the seat of decision for almost every aspect of the war, and Roosevelt became the de facto leader of the coalition.

The ARCADIA conference also led to a series of major decisions that shaped the war effort in 1942–43. The Allied leaders decided to plan a combined offensive in North Africa in 1942 (GYMNAST) and to send American bombers to bases in England. The conference also drafted the

14 Ibid., p. 49.
15 Roberts, *The Storm of War*, p. 193.

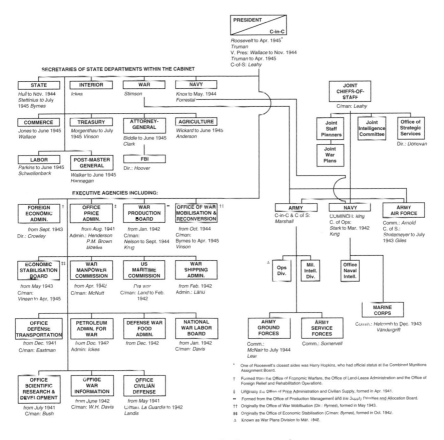

7.1 American high command

Declaration by the United Nations, in which the Allies pledged to employ total means until they achieved victory and not to seek a separate peace with the Axis.

In March 1942, Roosevelt and Churchill agreed to a global division of labour for the war effort. The Pacific theatre was to be 'predominantly American', so the chain of command for operations in the Pacific would run through the US Joint Chiefs of Staff. India and the Middle East were so 'predominantly British' that the chain of command would run through the British Chiefs of Staff. In the European and Atlantic theatres, the senior officers would report directly to the CCS. In practice, this arrangement ensured that both allies had substantial input into strategy decisions in each theatre of operations.

The depth and breadth of Anglo-American cooperation was remarkable. Never before in the history of warfare had two nations agreed to such close intertwining of their efforts. Beyond formal arrangements, an elaborate web of personal and professional communication linked American and British officials. Nothing comparable existed with either the Soviet Union or China. Military collaboration with the Soviet Union consisted of the procurement and delivery of Lend-Lease materiel, periodic communication of intelligence, and correspondence among the three leaders; cooperation with China largely consisted of advice and assistance.

These agreements nonetheless masked a number of Anglo-American, inter-service and civil–military disagreements over the strategic direction of the war. The British favoured a peripheral strategy, putting off as long as possible an Allied offensive against Germany. Roosevelt was sympathetic to such an approach, but his military advisors advocated a direct approach. They believed that the quickest and ultimately best and least costly way to defeat Germany was to attack it directly. George C. Marshall, for his part, feared that the American people would not long support a protracted war on foreign shores.

Concern over the extent of Axis gains in late 1941 and early 1942 created pressure for offensive action. Roosevelt sought an Anglo-American offensive for a mixture of domestic and coalition considerations, including the need to strengthen support for the war at home, silence criticism of Allied war leadership and take pressure off the Soviets. The proposal for a joint invasion of French North Africa (GYMNAST), discussed at ARCADIA, had been abandoned, partly due to a lack of shipping. In March, Marshall's chief planner, General Dwight D. Eisenhower, proposed that Allied forces assume the defensive in all theatres but the Atlantic, and prepare to concentrate American and British forces for a cross-Channel invasion of the European continent at the earliest possible opportunity. On 1 April, Eisenhower pre-sented the outline for BOLERO, the build-up of men and materiel in England in preparation for ROUNDUP, a forty-eight-division invasion of northern France in 1943. In the event of an imminent Soviet collapse, army planners believed that Allied forces should be prepared to execute SLEDGEHAM-MER, a five- to ten-division invasion slated for autumn 1942.

The British opposed both SLEDGEHAMMER and ROUNDUP. They noted that any cross-Channel attack in 1942 or 1943 would be composed primarily of British and Commonwealth troops and would be a dubious proposition without control of the air and the English Channel. They argued that such landings would be unsustainable and would fail to divert substantial German forces from the Eastern Front. As an alternative, they returned to the plan for an invasion of French North Africa in 1942, in conjunction with a renewed British offensive in Egypt. The Joint Chiefs opposed a North African invasion, arguing that it would lend little assistance to the Soviets and would only further disperse US forces. In their estimates, an invasion of North Africa would require postponing a cross-Channel invasion by two years.

Out of frustration with the British, Marshall responded by proposing that the United States turn away from Europe and toward the Pacific as the theatre of decisive action against the Axis. Such a move would have been highly popular with the US public, particularly on the West Coast. It was also a course of action favoured by commanders in the Pacific and by navy planners. He and Admiral Ernest J. King, the Chief of Naval Operations, also believed that, second only to BOLERO, a Pacific offensive would have the greatest effect on relieving pressure on Russia.[16] As a result, the Chiefs drafted a memo to Roosevelt that concluded, 'If the United States is to engage in any other operation than forceful, unswerving adherence to full BOLERO plans, we are definitely of the opinion that we should turn to the Pacific and strike decisively against Japan; in other words assume a defensive attitude against Germany, except for air operations, and use all available means in the Pacific'.[17]

In June 1942, Churchill met with Roosevelt at Hyde Park, New York. His main purpose was to argue against a 1942 cross-Channel invasion, and he enjoyed some success. On 8 July, the British chiefs sent a message to Roosevelt and the Joint Chiefs outlining the obstacles that made a 1942 invasion impossible and a 1943 one unlikely. They also asked that the Americans consider the invasion of North Africa instead.[18]

This disagreement marked the time when Roosevelt and his military advisors were the furthest apart, and when he exercised his leadership the most. Roosevelt intervened decisively, ruling against both BOLERO-ROUNDUP and a Japan-first strategy favoured by Marshall and King. The President was intent upon preserving the Germany-first strategy and launching offensive operations in 1942, to yield an incremental victory to boost morale at home and abroad. Roosevelt needed to arouse the American public's interest in the war against Germany and to indicate to US allies,

---

16 Stoler, 'The United States', p. 63.
17 Quoted in James Lacey, 'Toward a Strategy: Creating an American Strategy for Global War, 1940–1943', in Williamson Murray, Richard Hart Sinnreich and James Lacey (eds.), *The Shaping of Grand Strategy: Policy, Diplomacy, and War* (Cambridge University Press, 2011), p. 196.
18 Ibid., p. 195.

including the Soviet Union, that the United States was committed to the war in Europe. At the same time, he was sympathetic to British concerns over launching a direct assault on the European continent prematurely. As a result, Roosevelt directed his military chiefs to plan to launch the invasion of North Africa, with Operation GYMNAST now assigned the more inspiring codename TORCH.

Despite the United States' commitment to a Germany-first strategy, most of its deployments and battles in 1942 were waged in the Pacific, both to contain Japan's advance and, beginning in mid-1942, to launch limited counter-offensives. The US Navy checked the Japanese advance and crippled the Imperial Japanese Navy Air Force, during the Battle of the Coral Sea from 3 to 8 May and the Battle of Midway from 4 to 6 June. Six months after Pearl Harbor, the Japanese advance in the Pacific had been halted and the tide had begun to turn in America's favour. Naval commanders and General Douglas MacArthur sought to take advantage of this shift in momentum, supported by US public opinion as well as the governments of Australia, New Zealand and China. As a result, the United States launched the Guadalcanal campaign (WATCHTOWER), followed by the US-Australia Papua New Guinea campaign. Both became long-term campaigns of attrition against Japan.

For reasons of both personal and inter-service rivalry, Roosevelt decided to maintain two separate campaigns and theatres of operations in the Pacific: the Southwest Pacific Area under MacArthur and the Pacific Ocean Areas under Admiral Chester Nimitz. The two commanders pursued very different concepts of operations. Whereas Nimitz advocated a gradual trans-Pacific attack that had featured in War Plan ORANGE, MacArthur favoured an advance from Australia to New Guinea, New Britain and the Admiralty Islands. Such a dispersed effort resulted in a constant drain on resources.

China remained a weak, but vital member of the alliance. China's vast but disorganized army, which had a strength of 5.7 million men in 1941, tied down half a million or more Japanese soldiers throughout the war, and Chiang Kai-shek's membership in the alliance denied Tokyo the ability to portray their war in Asia as an anti-colonial struggle. At the same time, Washington faced repeated Chinese demands for supplies, as well as operations to open up the Burma Road to southwest China.

The economic dimension of war

Implementing the American strategy for the Second World War required that the United States aid the Allies, create massive ground and amphibious forces, inaugurate a huge shipbuilding effort, support two strategic bombing campaigns, and project military power across two oceans. To do this, the United States needed to mobilize its economy for war.

Industrial mobilization was a central pillar of American grand strategy in the Second World War. The United States converted its economy rapidly for war, and in an effort to share sacrifice for the prosecution of the war, it accepted a level of government control that previous generations of Americans would have found unthinkable. Congress implemented a freeze on commercial, farm and commodity prices, which were fixed under the Emergency Price Control Act by the Office of Price Administration. The government controlled wages and rents and introduced rationing.[19]

As John Morton Blum has written, 'In the emergency production of war materials, Franklin Roosevelt was said to believe, energy was more efficient than efficiency. Furthermore, speed was often as important as quality, and costs mattered less than results.'[20] In 1942, the US government established the War Production Board under Donald Nelson of Sears Roebuck, the mail order and department store chain, and gave it overall supervision of the war economy. During the war, the United States experienced a 17 per cent increase in agricultural production, doubled its production of non-ferrous metals, more than doubled its output of manufactured goods, experienced a 300 per cent increase in the production of machine tools, and a 600 per cent increase in heavy transportation.

In January 1942, Roosevelt approved yearly production goals for the United States of 20,000 anti-aircraft guns, 45,000 tanks and 60,000 aircraft. Most would be achieved by the war's end. At its peak, the United States was out-producing the Axis and generating 60 per cent of Allied war production. The United States produced 300,000 aircraft, 315,000 artillery pieces, 86,000 tanks, warships totalling 8.5 million tons and 51 million tons of merchant shipping.[21]

To supply the United States and its allies with war materiel, the Roosevelt administration developed a unique partnership with private industry. Although the US government played a central role in funding and regulating war production, it also left control of individual enterprises to industrialists and businessmen. Henry Ford's Willow Run plant outside Detroit turned out a B-24 bomber every sixty-three minutes, for a total of 8,685. Chrysler's tank

---

19 Roberts, *The Storm of War*, pp. 197–8.
20 John Morton Blum, *V was for Victory: Politics and American Culture During World War II* (New York: Harcourt Brace Jovanovich, 1976), pp. 111–12.
21 Theodore A. Wilson, 'The United States: Leviathan', in Reynolds et al. (eds.), *Allies at War*, pp. 173, 177, 187.

plant, built in late 1941, produced a hundred medium tanks per week. Henry J. Kaiser's application of mass production to shipbuilding yielded the Liberty Ship. By 1943, production time for the vessels had shrunk from thirty to seven weeks, and, ultimately, the United States launched more than 5,000 cargo vessels.[22] In 1944, while the Germans built 40,000 aircraft, the United States turned out 98,000.[23]

The American design philosophy emphasized reliability and mass production over the capabilities of a single unit. Perhaps the best example of this was the M4 Sherman tank. Although decidedly inferior to many of the German tanks that it faced, the Sherman was reliable, based on a stable design, and could be produced in large numbers.[24]

From peripheral to direct strategy

On 8 November 1942, Anglo-American forces under the command of Dwight D. Eisenhower landed in French North Africa, launching Operation TORCH. By the end of the first week of the operation, Morocco and Algiers were under Allied control. Still, the Allied advance proved too slow to reach Tunisia before German and Italian forces.

Marshall had decried TORCH as 'political', as if strategy could ever be divorced from its political context. He later complained that 'the politicians must do something every year during a war'.[25] He was correct, in that it is important in a protracted war to provide incremental victories, to convince both domestic and foreign audiences of the effectiveness of a strategy. Far from being 'merely' political, such incremental victories are integral to strategic success in protracted wars.

By the end of 1942, the tide of war had begun to shift. In Russia, North Africa and the Pacific, Axis offensives had been halted and the Allies had begun launching counter-attacks. Still, the need to reconcile different Allied theories of victory remained. Stalin was insistent that the United States and Britain open a second front on the European continent as soon as possible, just as the British remained intent on pursuing a peripheral strategy.

---

22 Ibid., p. 189.
23 Roberts, *The Storm of War*, p. 194.
24 Constance McLaughlin Green, Harry C. Thomson and Peter C. Roots, *The Ordnance Department: Planning Munitions for War* (Washington DC: Office of the Chief of Military History, 1955), pp. 275–301.
25 Kimball, *Forged in* War, p. 153.

When Allied leaders met in January 1943 at Casablanca, the survival of the alliance appeared assured and victory seemed increasingly likely. Stalin absented himself from the conference by his own choice. Events on the Russian front meant that he no longer had to worry about Soviet collapse, but rather could focus on offensive operations.

At Casablanca, the United States acceded to a peripheral strategy for 1943, one focused on defeating the German U-boat threat in the Atlantic and the Mediterranean, expanding control of North Africa, invading Sicily (Operation HUSKY) and launching the Combined Bomber Offensive against the German aircraft industry (Operation POINTBLANK).[26] At the same time, the Combined Chiefs of Staff committed to a substantial landing on the European continent (ROUNDUP) in 1944.

This agreement was made possible by Marshall's increasing doubts about the feasibility of a cross-Channel invasion in 1943. After TORCH, American officers realized just how difficult an opposed amphibious landing in Europe would be. They were also aware that American industrial production was lagging, so the materiel needed to launch a large scale invasion would not be available in 1943.[27]

During a news conference toward the end of the Casablanca Conference, Roosevelt announced:

> The elimination of German, Japanese, and Italian war power means the unconditional surrender of Germany, Italy, and Japan. It means a reasonable assurance of future world peace. It does not mean the destruction of the population of Germany, Italy, or Japan, but it does mean the destruction of the philosophies in those countries, which are based on conquest and the subjugation of other peoples.[28]

The decision to announce an aim of unconditional surrender, which had been discussed both in Washington and among American and British leaders and diplomats, has remained controversial, with some arguing that the failure to negotiate prolonged the war. Given the repugnant nature of Nazi Germany and Imperial Japan and the bloodshed they had brought on, it is difficult to imagine the Allies being either willing or able to reach a negotiated settlement with either. Moreover, an effort to do so could easily have split the Allies: agreement on unconditional surrender was part of the glue that held the alliance together.

---

26 Stoler, 'The United States', p. 65.
27 Lacey, 'Toward a Strategy', p. 206.
28 Quoted in Jean Edward Smith, *FDR* (New York: Random House, 2008), p. 567.

By the middle of 1943, due to the British advantage in signals intelligence and sea power, and the American advantage in shipbuilding capacity, the Allies had largely won the Battle of the Atlantic. On 9 September, American and British troops landed at Salerno, launching Operation AVALANCHE. The Red Army, for its part, checked the Wehrmacht at Kursk during Operation CITADEL.

As the war progressed, the Anglo-American strategic bombing campaign played an increasingly vital role. Great Britain had launched its strategic bombing offensive against Germany in May 1940. The United States joined the effort on 17 August 1942, when US B-17s made their first high-altitude daylight raid against the railway yard in Rouen, France. In March 1943, the bomber offensive escalated during the Battle of the Ruhr. Over five months, the Allies dropped 34,000 tons of bombs. Following the raids, steel production fell by 200,000 tons; between July 1943 and March 1944 there were no further increases in the output of German aircraft.[29] However, these effects came at a heavy price for the Allies. In response, the British had shifted to night-time area bombing in order to reduce losses, whereas the United States continued to fly daylight raids against specific targets and sought ways to improve the precision of their bombing effort.

The American public continued to demand that greater attention be paid to the Pacific. As Secretary of War, Stimson told Churchill in mid-1943 that it was 'only by intellectual effort' that the American people had 'been convinced that Germany was their most dangerous enemy and should be disposed of before Japan; ...the enemy whom the American people really hated, if they hated anyone, was Japan which had dealt them a foul blow'.[30]

For the US Army, the operations of 1943 were a diversion from the all-important cross-Channel invasion. In August, at Quebec (QUADRANT), the Combined Chiefs of Staff agreed to a compromise whereby the Allies would allocate forces to invade Italy and knock it out of the war, and also retain the initiative in the Pacific while planning for a twenty-nine-division cross-Channel attack in May 1944, codenamed OVERLORD.

At the Cairo Conference (SEXTANT), Churchill tried to delay OVERLORD in favour of operations in the Aegean and the allocation of more troops to Italy. However, at the Tehran Conference (EUREKA), both

29 Adam Tooze, *The Wages of Destruction: The Making and Breaking of the Nazi Economy* (London: Allen Lane, 2006), pp. 597–8.
30 Henry L. Stimson and McGeorge Bundy, *On Active Service in Peace and War* (New York: Harper, 1948), pp. 429–30.

Roosevelt and Stalin insisted on launching a cross-Channel invasion as planned. For the first time in the war, the British had been outvoted.

Tehran was the first time the Soviets played a direct role in overall Allied strategy. Stalin insisted on the timetable for OVERLORD, urged an operation to support OVERLORD through an invasion of southern France (ANVIL), and spoke out against giving priority to operations in the Mediterranean. In exchange, Stalin pledged to launch a simultaneous offensive against the Germans in the East. He also agreed to enter the war against Japan once Germany had been defeated.

Throughout the first five months of 1944, American, British and Canadian forces concentrated in England, and an integrated multinational staff at the Supreme Headquarters Allied Expeditionary Force in London planned the campaign. On 6 June, the Allies conducted a successful cross-Channel invasion. OVERLORD took place under the overall command of Eisenhower, with Field Marshal Bernard Law Montgomery in charge of Allied ground forces

Following the breakout from Normandy, British and American commanders proposed various courses of action to cross the Rhine and end the war in 1944. Montgomery tried and failed to do so during Operation MARKET GARDEN at Arnhem. After the failure of the operation, Eisenhower decided to pursue a more conservative, broad-front approach as a compromise.

By the autumn of 1944, success in Europe had begun to breed a sense that the war was all but won. At home, there was growing frustration with wartime restrictions and mounting calls for higher wages. When Hitler launched a counter-offensive through the Ardennes in December 1944, a development that had seemed nearly impossible to Allied planners, it demoralized the Allies. It appeared likely that the European war would drag on into late 1945, or even 1946, followed by the need to win the Pacific War.

By the middle of 1944, the British were essentially out of men, and the United States faced a growing manpower shortage as well. As a result, in late January 1945, the Allies began to escalate their bombing campaign against Germany, instituting a new directive that called for attacks on cities where westward German refugee flows were creating bottlenecks, making it difficult for German troops and supplies to reach the Eastern Front. The Allied bombing offensive aided the Russian winter offensive that would, it was hoped, lead to a German surrender in the summer of 1945.

As the end of the war neared, operational interactions among the Allied armies intensified, including increasing exchanges between Eisenhower, Montgomery and Zhukov. In March 1945, US forces captured the intact bridge over the Rhine at Remagen. Eisenhower altered his plans to shift the Allied offensive further south to exploit the avenue. Meanwhile, Montgomery crossed the Rhine in the north two weeks later. Despite growing political tensions among the Allies, there was considerable operational cooperation. After another heated Anglo-American debate, Eisenhower emphasized a limited US offensive southeast to the Elbe, rather than a British-led move on Berlin, leaving Berlin to the Soviets. His reasoning was both political and military: he sought to preclude a collision with the Soviets; moreover, both Britain and the United States had already obtained occupation zones in Berlin.

In the Pacific, the US island-hopping campaign was nearing the Japanese home islands, and Japanese army and navy's defence became tenacious. The commander of the US Twentieth Air Force, Major General Curtis LeMay, began to fly his B-29s on low-level incendiary raids against Japanese cities. When Tokyo was attacked on the night of 9 March, more than 100,000 civilians died. Incendiary attacks on more than 60 Japanese cities followed in a campaign that was designed to bring Japan to its knees without the need to launch an amphibious attack (OLYMPIC and CORONET) on the home islands, a contingency that held the prospect of massive casualties. When atomic bombs became available in summer 1945, they were integrated into the campaign.

Conclusion

Developing and implementing a coherent grand strategy against a competent opponent is difficult. Doing so as part of a coalition across multiple theatres is even more so. Despite considerable challenges, Roosevelt and his military advisors developed a strategy to achieve their goal of defeating Nazi Germany and Imperial Japan, one that emphasized defeating Germany first. The United States implemented that overall strategy consistently but flexibly, allowing it to respond to opportunities on the battlefield as well as the demands of allies and the American public. Roosevelt compromised where he needed to in order to maintain coalition unity, and adjusted where necessary to maintain public support for a protracted war. He husbanded US forces in both the Pacific and the Atlantic until American industrial and technological power could be brought to bear, and then projected American power in both theatres in time to claim victory and shape the post-war order.

8

Soviet strategy

BRUCE W. MENNING AND JONATHAN HOUSE

The strategist A. A. Svechin wrote in 1926 that any strategic decision was in essence 'extraordinarily simple'. It answered three basic questions: 'Who, Where, and When?' Accordingly, Svechin held that strategy admitted only three standards of measure: 'Mass, Space, and Time'.[1] However, during the Great Patriotic War of 1941–45, even Svechin's simple questions defied easy answers. Worse, means and methods evolved only haltingly in service of metrics. During the first two periods of the conflict, June 1941 to December 1943, the result was improvisation that gradually gave way to imperfect orchestration. It was only during the last eighteen months of the war that the Soviets fashioned a reasonably coherent military strategy to resolve mass-space-time dilemmas.

Legacy of the 1920s and 1930s

As a former tsarist officer in the service of the Bolsheviks, Svechin's cryptic formula only implied the myriad politics, policies, assessments and allocations, all of which figured in the complexities of strategy formulation.[2] During

---

1 A. A. Svechin (ed.), *Strategiia v trudakh voennykh klassikov* (2 vols., Moscow: VVRS/ Gosvoenizdat, 1924, 1926), vol. II, p. 7.
2 A gifted military theorist and historian, Alexander Andreevich Svechin (1878–1938) was a field artillerist and General Staff Officer in the Imperial Russian Army. He served on staff and held combat command in both the Russo-Japanese War and the Great War. He entered the Red Army in March 1918, shortly after his brother, Mikhail, had gone over to the Whites. In Bolshevik service, Svechin first headed the Commission on the Study and Utilization of War Experience (1914–18) and then taught at the Red Army Military Academy. He wrote prodigiously throughout the 1920s, and even after his arrest for alleged counter-revolutionary activities in 1931 – followed by release in 1932 – he edited a Russian edition of Clausewitz's *On War* and finished a book on strategy in the Russo-Japanese War. After re-arrest, he was shot on 28 July 1938.

the 1920s, he treated these issues at length in his classic, *Strategiia* (Strategy), and participated in a wide-ranging series of debates that shaped both the political outlook and the intellectual foundations of the Soviet armed forces.[3] Discussions ranged from military doctrine and force generation to the nature of future war, and from the characteristics of the initial period of war (*nachal'nyi period voiny*) to offensive-defensive correlations in modern war.[4] Because Svechin was a disciple of Clausewitz, his views on the subordination of war to politics resonated well with a new order dedicated to Marxism-Leninism. Moreover, Svechin defended military doctrine as the formal enunciation of state views on the nature of war and of the means and methods required to prepare for and fight it. This understanding put him squarely in the company of M. V. Frunze, a founding father of the Red Army (RKKA).[5]

It was adapting these concepts to domestic realities and international perils that triggered Svechin's fall from grace. Although his views were prophetic, they were also often out of step with orthodoxy because they went either too far or not far enough. For example, he was a premature exponent of the militarization of the state economy to contend with the material backwardness of Soviet society.[6] Mass mobilization – the antidote that Svechin prescribed to the challenge of military backwardness and numerous external foes – would one day stand Stalin's Soviet Union in good stead. In the mid-1920s, however, Soviet leaders still favoured revolutionary internationalism. Only by the decade's end would Stalin's doctrine of 'socialism in one country' emerge to justify forced economic and military development as a defence against 'capitalist encirclement'.

Although Svechin never denied the class contradictions inherent in modern conflict, he held that large-scale future war would resemble a more technologically intensive version of the Great War. Because the young Soviet state was weak, he underscored the importance of Hans Delbrück's di-pole strategy in pursuit of either the offensive or the defensive as appropriate to

3 *Strategiia* (originally written in 1926) has been reprinted as A. A. Svechin, *Strategiia* (Moscow/St Petersburg: Kuchkovo pole, 2003). The second edition is also available in English translation as A. A. Svechin, *Strategy*, ed. Kent D. Lee (Minneapolis, Minn.: East View Publications, 1992).
4 V. O. Daines, 'Voennaia strategiia mezhdu grazhdanskoi i Velikoi Otechestvennoi voinami', in V. A. Zolotarev (ed.), *Istoriia voennoi strategii Rossii* (Moscow: Kuchkovo pole, 2000), pp. 191–202.
5 A. A. Kokoshin, *Soviet Strategic Thought, 1917–91* (Cambridge, Mass.: MIT Press, 1998), pp. 25, 29–30.
6 Svechin, *Strategiia*, pp. 164–5.

preparedness for future war.[7] For revolutionary zealots, defence equated with defeatism. Svechin was more in tune with his Red Army contemporaries in the 1920s when he advocated a small, mixed cadre/militia army until industrial development might support a modern mass force.

In early 1930, at a time when he was falling from political favour, Svechin did concede that a future war might prove to be one of attrition. In this case, the Soviet Union might expect European enemies to conduct primary offensive operations in the south, through the Kiev axis, rather than in the centre, over the high road to Moscow. His rationale was that such a conflict, by its very nature, would become protracted. In a war of attrition, opponents in quest of greater resources would require foodstuffs from Ukraine and oil from Transcaucasia.[8] A decade later, in 1941, the initial German assault, weighted to favour the central axis, would demonstrate the error in Adolf Hitler's expectation of a quick victory. The events of 1942, when the enemy concentrated his forces in the south, would prove Svechin correct in determining the 'where' in what had become an all-out war of attrition.

The Great Patriotic War also demonstrated the wisdom of Svechin's assertion that leadership in such a struggle required the attributes of an 'integrated great captain' whose politico-military prowess might weld disparate parts into a cohesive whole.[9] This term would later be identified more closely with the writings of B. M. Shaposhnikov, another serious strategist and a future Chief of the RKKA General Staff. However, neither Svechin nor Shaposhnikov anticipated that Stalin, and not the Chief of the General Staff, would assume this role.

During the late 1920s and early 1930s, as Soviet ideologists pondered whether contradictions within the imperialist system might pit the major capitalist powers against each other, RKKA planners gravitated to a scenario for war that was closer to Svechin than to Lenin or Trotsky. Because all-consuming revolutionary class conflict appeared less than imminent, the practical focus shifted to the threat emanating from a possible coalition of medium-sized neighbouring states backed by the major capitalist powers. From this calculus flowed the first recognizable war plans of the post-revolutionary era, the so-called 'PR' series (1927–34), featuring Poland and Romania as the primary adversaries. The Soviet strategic railroad network

---

7 A. A. Svechin, 'Sokrushenie i izmor', reprinted in A. E. Savinkin, A. G. Kavtaradze et al. (comps.), *Postizhenie voennogo iskusstva. Ideinoe nasledie A. Svechina* (Moscow: Voennyi Universitet/Russkii put'', 1999), pp. 316–24.
8 Kokoshin, *Soviet Strategic Thought*, 82–3.
9 Svechin, *Strategiia*, pp. 118–20.

was inadequate, so once determination was made against whom to deploy, the strategy adopted was defensive/counter-offensive. This decision, in turn, determined the when and where. Military weakness and initial enemy superiority dictated a prolonged defensive period (around forty days) against Poland and Romania, while Soviet forces simultaneously underwent general mobilization and overran the Baltic States to secure Leningrad and the RKKA's open right flank. Once these tasks had been fulfilled, at approximately M+45 (mobilization day plus forty-five days), the reinforced Soviet field armies, which would have withdrawn east as far as the Dneper, might shift to the counter-offensive.[10]

This approach made military common sense. After 1922, the ravages of war and post-war settlements had left Soviet state boundaries vulnerable and the strategic railroad network in a shambles. Meanwhile, the post-civil war demobilization of the Red Army and the military reforms of 1924–26 had left the Kremlin with a mixed cadre/militia army that was slow to mobilize and short of trained manpower, especially capable higher command and staff officers. Like Svechin, most theorists by 1927 had settled on the notion that future war would include massive infusions of aviation, armour and fire-power. In the short term, until further economic development provided such infusions, the objectives were to match the troop mobilizations of the tsarist army and to create sufficient trained manpower to match the aggregate numbers of potential front-line adversaries. Meanwhile, theorists scrutinized the lessons of the Great War to overcome the battlefield stalemate resulting from the ascendancy of defensive firepower over the offensive. As for the initial period of war, the greatest fear was a surprise attack with aerially delivered poison gas that might disrupt the slowly mobilizing RKKA.

During the first half of the 1930s, two developments prompted change in the Soviet calculus for future war. First, the advent of Stalin's Five-Year Plans for industrialization promised ultimately to open a cornucopia of advanced military technology. Second, the nature of the external threat changed: Fascist Germany and a militaristic Japan confronted the RKKA with potentially first-rate adversaries. Soviet military weakness in the Far East initially left few options but to surrender the initiative. Germany, meanwhile, bore watching, as Hitler's rise to power portended ominous changes. In 1934, when Germany concluded a Non-Aggression Pact with

---

10 Bruce W. Menning, 'Soviet Railroads and War Planning, 1927–1939', unpublished paper, Convention of the AAASS, 14 November 1996, pp. 7–9; additional detail comes from Daines, 'Voennaia strategiia', pp. 247–8.

Poland, the Soviet Union joined the League of Nations and concluded a mutual assistance pact with France. Also in 1934, the Soviet perception of threat, together with the modest attainments of industrialization, spurred changes in force structure. Like the tsarist army before it, the RKKA remained wedded to a territorial system of peacetime organization based on military districts, but now began the transition to a pure cadre-and-reserve system of recruitment. In September 1935, the RKKA Staff became the General Staff of the RKKA, thus acknowledging the increasing role of the 'brain of the army' in defence planning. The peacetime strength of the armed forces grew from 1.1 million in 1936 to more than 2 million in August 1939. Between 1930 and 1939, artillery increased sevenfold; while by 1935, the RKKA counted 10,000 tanks, many of which were deployed in four gigantic mechanized corps. Between 1929 and 1939, the number of aircraft grew by a factor of more than six, nearing 7,000.[11]

Further developments in military art marched in lock-step with enhancements to technology and force structure. By the mid-1930s, after extensive internal debate, the RKKA high command formally adopted 'deep operations' as the guiding principle for future offensives by armies and army groups. A combination of aviation and mechanized formations would enable Soviet commanders to penetrate fixed defences while striking simultaneously through their entire depths. Once defences were ruptured in depth, mobile and air-dropped formations would exploit the gap, both to unhinge resistance and to forestall resurrection of a coherent enemy defence. More comprehensive than the contemporaneous German notion of Blitzkrieg, the Soviet vision held out the prospect of either limiting or banishing protracted combat from the battlefields of future war.[12]

Differences in national vision notwithstanding, new methods and technologies threatened to wreak havoc on traditional views for the 'initial period of war'. During the 1930s, some Soviet theorists had concluded that the well-worn choreography – a period of heightened diplomatic tension followed by formal troop mobilization, war declaration and border battles – had become irrelevant. Now states might covertly build up troops opposite a potential enemy

---

11 R. A. Savushkin, *Razvitie sovetskikh vooruzhennykh sil i voennogo iskusstva v mezhvoennyi period (1921–1941 gg.)* (Moscow: Voenno-Politicheskaia Akademiia, 1989), pp. 37–41.

12 A comprehensive explanation of the concept appears in Georgii Samoilovich Isserson, *The Evolution of Operational Art*, trans. Bruce W. Menning (Fort Leavenworth, Kan.: Combat Studies Institute, 2013), pp. 43–76; see also Mary R. Habeck, *Storm of Steel: The Development of Armor Doctrine in Germany and the Soviet Union, 1919–1939* (Ithaca, NY: Cornell University Press, 2003), pp. 206–28.

frontier and launch an invasion without formal mobilization or war declaration. Unleashed by surprise, armoured spearheads and supporting aviation might strike deeply into enemy territory to disrupt defences and mobilization. As torrents rushed through the gaps, more slowly mobilizing reinforcements from the rear would complete deployments on enemy territory.[13]

These pointed observations appeared to produce little ostensible impact, in part because contemporary wars offered scant precedent, and in part because the theorists were swept away by the whirlwind of Stalin's military purges. The first to fall (in 1929–33) had been 'military specialist' survivors of the tsarist officer corps – later including even Svechin. As fear of the internal threat began to rival that of the external threat, the old guard was followed in 1937–38 by the new generation of Soviet commanders. Names like those of M. N. Tukhachevskii and I. P. Uborevich garnered the headlines, but just as damaging were losses among mid-career officers. Roughly 28,000 officers disappeared from the rolls, including leading theorists for deep operations and the initial period of war. Ideas associated with the victims were immediately suspect; thus, a kind of self-imposed amnesia set in. At the same time, Stalin forbade instruction in strategy at the newly created Academy of the General Staff, asserting that he alone was the source of Soviet strategy.

Still, before the purges began in earnest, the prophets and proselytizers left their mark on Soviet war planning. The marriage of mobile ground and air assets to the concept of deep operations opened new vistas. Novel ideas and hardware found immediate application in the 'GP' series of war plans between 1936 and 1939. As the designation indicated, Germany and Poland were now the primary foes, and the overarching concept differed in important ways from PR predecessors. A combination of covert mobilization, surprise and pre-emption suddenly figured prominently in the planning calculus. Broadly speaking, the operational concept provided for three army groups, Northwestern, Western and Southwestern, built respectively on the Leningrad, Belorussian and Kiev military districts. While the first kept watch on Finland and the Baltic States, forces evenly balanced between the latter two would attack north and south of the Pripiat Marshes. Objective depths were shallow to the north of the Pripiat; but below the marshes, the Southwestern Army Group's mission was to conduct deep operations as far west as the River San. At the very outset of conflict, mobile ground and air forces, which had already been secretly mobilized and concealed in fortified regions

---

13 Savushkin, *Razvitie*, 59–62.

along the border, were to cross the state frontier immediately and disrupt the enemy mobilization and strategic deployment in depth. Follow-on Soviet forces would complete their mobilization on enemy territory.[14]

As in the PR series, there were important logistical shortcomings, only some of which might be vitiated. Immediate engagement in offensive operations mandated a pre-hostilities troop and supply build-up in forward areas. Thus, the still inadequate strategic railroad network would not be over-taxed during the initial period of war. However, differing views arose within the Soviet high command over the axis of the main effort. In March 1938, after a close study of railroad throughput capacities, Shaposhnikov, Chief of the RKKA General Staff, argued strongly for prioritizing one or the other primary offensive efforts, in accordance with intelligence on enemy railroad movements. Then, beginning with the tenth day of mobilization, the Soviets might shift their primary offensive effort from one axis to another. He held that the characteristics of the railroad net in Poland would require up to sixteen more days for completion of enemy concentrations across the southern axis than north of the Pripiat. This comparison, plus Shaposhnikov's placement of the northern variant first in his written deliberations, left little doubt over which alternative he favoured.[15] Pre-emption would now lurk in the background of Soviet war planning until June 1941. The distance between Germany and the Soviet frontier imposed an immense re-deployment requirement on the Wehrmacht. One sure Soviet expedient for reducing the odds was to engage the Germans sequentially, via pre-emption, before they completed concentration and strategic deployment.

Meanwhile, contingencies of lesser significance than a potential European theatre of war fell under the purview of separate military districts. With little direct assistance from Moscow, in July–August 1938, the Far Eastern Red Banner Army dealt a severe reverse to Japanese forces contesting Soviet positions at Lake Khasan, opposite the border with Japanese-occupied Korea and uncomfortably close to Vladivostok. In the following year, the reinforced Japanese 23rd Division brazenly crossed the Manchurian frontier into Outer Mongolia, a Soviet protectorate. In response, a combined Soviet-Mongol 'group of forces' was built up over three months under G. M. Shtern and

---

14 Menning, 'Soviet Railroads and War Planning', pp. 29–31; Daines, 'Voennaia strategiia', p. 248; and Iu. A. Gorkov, 'Gotovil li Stalin uprezhdaiushchii udar protiv Gitlera v 1941 g.', *Novaia i noveishaia istoriia* 3 (1993), 30–1.
15 V. P. Naumov (ed.) and L. E. Reshin (comp.), *1941 god: V 2-kh knigakh*, in series *Rossiia XX vek. Dokumenty* (2 vols., Moscow: Mezdunarodnyi fond 'Demokratiia', 1998), vol. II, pp. 560, 562.

G. K. Zhukov, including 57,000 troops, 500 aircraft and 500 tanks. In August 1939, Zhukov executed a surprise encirclement operation, inflicting 61,000 Japanese casualties during a four-day battle. In this case, Soviet logistics met requirements: 4,000 trucks bridged the 400-mile gap from the nearest rail-head to support the first massive battlefield application of tanks and aircraft in Soviet history. Despite the dazzling victory, in April 1940, Stalin belittled the achievement at Khalkin-Gol and events at Lake Khasan before the assembled officers of the Soviet high command.[16]

For Stalin, developments in the West perhaps overshadowed the Far Eastern clashes. The most immediate requirement for Stalin was to buy time, and the result was a heretofore unthinkable Faustian bargain, the German-Soviet Non-Aggression Pact of 23 August 1939. The Soviet dictator apparently expected that Hitler would become involved in a prolonged stalemate in the West while the RKKA remedied its deficiencies.

Secret protocols provided not only for Soviet economic aid to Berlin, but also for a division of Eastern Europe into German and Soviet spheres of influence. Thus, in September 1939, when the German invasion of Poland ignited the Second World War, the Red Army overran eastern Poland. The following spring, Soviet troops occupied the Baltic States, and in the summer, Bessarabia and Northern Bukovina. With few natural obstacles to incursion from the west, perhaps the best insurance seemed to be to push the Soviet frontier westward. However, the occupation of these areas often revealed a hapless RKKA, a military force scarcely able to execute an orderly march against no organized opposition. Railroad and engineering troops came in numbers far too few to knit newly acquired infrastructure into the Soviet whole. Tracks were the wrong gauge, while road beds lacked adequate ballast for heavy military traffic, and debarkation platforms and signalling systems were inadequate. In a rush, Soviet troops abandoned fixed fortifications within the old Stalin Line for a new, so-called Molotov Line that would require months to complete. As a result, the western territories constituted what amounted to a wide 'strategic dead-space' of nearly 200 miles, with an infrastructure ill-suited to the requirements of either offence or defence.[17] Shaposhnikov allegedly recommended that no substantial military forces occupy this space, but that

---

16 E. N. Kulkov and O. A. Rzheshevskii (eds.), *Zimniaia voina 1939–1940*, bk. 2, *I. V. Stalin i finskaia kampaniia (Stenogramma soveshchaniia pri TsK VKP (b))* (Moscow: Nauka, 1999), p. 276.

17 James J. Schneider, 'The Cobra and the Mongoose: Soviet Defensive Doctrine during the Interwar Period and the Problem of Strategic Dislocation', *Journal of Slavic Military Studies* 19 (2006), 9–10.

it be held lightly as a kind of buffer zone, which any invading forces must cross before contending with primary Soviet defences.[18]

From 'white death' to crisis planning

The Soviet-Finnish War of 1939–40 demonstrated just how troublesome deep defensive belts could be for an invader. As in the case with Soviet incursions into the western territories and the Baltic States, the objective was breathing space – in this instance, along the Gulf of Finland and the distant approaches to Leningrad. On 30 November, after Finnish refusal to cede these territories, the Kremlin went to war. Partial mobilization yielded half a million troops, endowing the Soviets with two-to-one superiority. However, the Soviet high command had reckoned neither with terrain and weather, nor with Finnish resolve. The result was a stunning series of reverses. With no room either to manoeuvre heavy forces or to bring superior firepower and logistics to bear, entire Soviet divisions were cut to pieces or frozen to death. Meanwhile, on the Karelian Isthmus south of Lake Ladoga, Finnish defenders on the Mannerheim Line fought successive waves of attackers to a standstill. Only in February 1940, after substantial reorganization and reinforcement, were the Soviets able to pound the first two defensive belts into submission. Ironically, for a military system that had trumpeted the merits of mobile warfare and deep operations, the situation more resembled Verdun in 1916 than Khalkin-Gol a few months previously. Fortunately for the Kremlin, the exhausted Finns came to terms in early March 1940.[19]

Now was the time for introspection to rectify deficiencies. Although the Soviet Union was now an international pariah, Stalin might take comfort from the fact that his pact with Hitler had held – no German assistance had gone to the Finns. Meanwhile, the Soviet dictator had clearly miscalculated the debilitating impact of an unsuccessful war on his troops and the Soviet populace. There were few heroes of stature and more than a few executions for incompetence and cowardice. Peace terms had brought more territory than Stalin had originally demanded, or, as one Soviet general purportedly remarked, 'enough ground to bury our dead', numbering about 53,500. The Soviet casualty rate had been roughly five times that of the Finns. Even as Stalin's commanders scrutinized the conflict for lessons learned, on 9 April

---

18 M. V. Zakharov, *General'nyi shtab v predvoennye gody* (Moscow: Voenizdat, 1989), pp. 224–5.
19 H. M. Tillotson, *Finland at Peace and War* (Norwich: Michael Russell, 1993), chs. 9–12.

1940, Hitler seized Denmark and invaded Norway. The seemingly unstoppable Wehrmacht next overran the Low Countries and France in six weeks; only Britain remained.

It was therefore with a sense of urgency that Stalin and a revamped Soviet high command reviewed lessons from the Finnish war. Senior leaders were removed, with S. K. Timoshenko replacing K. E. Voroshilov as head of the Defence Commissariat, and K. A. Meretskov replacing Shaposhnikov as Chief of the General Staff. For officers, traditional military ranks replaced revolutionary-style titles; service in the Russian Civil War was no longer a requisite for senior command. Headquarters underwent thorough reorganization, while field forces were restructured. The peacetime strength of the Red Army grew to 5.37 million by June 1941.

Renewed emphasis also fell on increasing industrial output to replace outmoded weapons. Between 1939 and June 1941, Soviet industry produced more than 80,000 guns and mortars, 17,000 aircraft and 7,500 tanks. During the summer of 1940, tank production shifted from older models to the KV-1 heavy tank and the T-34 medium tank, of which 1,851 were produced before June 1941. Similarly, 2,739 modern aircraft supplanted outmoded types.

Interestingly, the same decisiveness and impulse for speed failed to obtain in the realm of military planning. Between the summers of 1940 and 1941, neither Stalin nor the General Staff found satisfactory answers to Svechin's questions of where and when. Shaposhnikov, who remained Chief of the General Staff until August 1940, expected in an assessment prior to his reassignment to encounter as many as 233 enemy divisions in the western theatre (counting Germany and its allies, including Hungary, Romania, Italy, Finland and possibly Turkey). In the Far East, Japan remained a concern, although that country's continued commitment to a land war in China lessened Soviet apprehensions. In the more worrisome west, Shaposhnikov did not rule out a primary enemy axis of advance into Ukraine (south of the Pripiat River), but he judged that the more likely main effort would fall north of the Pripiat. This axis would permit rapid movement of German troops from East Prussia through the Baltic States to Leningrad, and from northeastern Poland through Minsk and Smolensk to Moscow. Therefore, of the 237 Soviet divisions allocated to the western theatre, he would assign some 70 per cent to the two potential army groups (Western and Northwestern) arrayed against the assumed Axis main effort.[20]

20 S. N. Mikhalev, *Voennaia strategiia: Podgotovka i vedenie voin novogo i noveishego vremeni* (Moscow: Kuchkovo pole, 2003), pp. 309–11.

Shaposhnikov was more ambiguous in his strategic overview about whether to pursue defensive or offensive action. On the one hand, he prescribed the primary mission of Soviet forces as 'inflicting defeat on German forces concentrating in East Prussia and in the region of Warsaw', together with a secondary strike to defeat enemy forces south of Warsaw. These German groupings he calculated capable of offensive operations on the tenth to fifteenth day after concentration. On the other hand, Soviet troops opposite the Germans would not complete mobilization until M+30. Left unwritten in his recommendations was the understanding that to pre-empt the Germans, the Soviets would require excellent intelligence and at least partial covert mobilization. Otherwise, the would-be pre-emptors (i.e. the Red Army) would find themselves pre-empted and engaged in defensive operations until completion of mobilization. Also left unwritten was the assumption that determination of the 'when' would lie with the political leadership (i.e. Stalin).

In September 1940, Meretskov, new Chief of the General Staff, forwarded a revised version of Shaposhnikov's recommendations. It was at this juncture that Stalin made the first of three fateful decisions that would heavily influence the opening months of the war. Meretskov's revisions included the proposal to alter the basis for planning the Red Army's strategic deployments. On 5 October, Stalin approved the revised assumption that the primary German effort would be directed south of the Pripiat into Ukraine, and not on the central axis north of the Pripiat.[21] This altered assumption led to a maldeployment of Soviet forces when the Germans indeed launched their main effort in the north. Already on 17 November, a draft version of the new war plan, formally adopted on 15 December, raised the number of divisions in the west to 182.5, and the number of air force regiments to 159. Of these numbers, the Southwestern Army Group (in Ukraine) was allocated 113 divisions and 140 air regiments, or 74.5 per cent of ground assets and 88 per cent of air assets.

There are several plausible explanations for this shift in emphasis from the central to the southern axis. The first was a mirror image of 1930 vintage Svechin. That is, whatever the Soviet posture, political-economic considerations mandated a major Soviet effort to cut off Germany from Romanian

21 Naumov (ed.) and Reshin (comp.), *1941 god*, vol. 1, p. 289; Zakharov, *General'nyi shtab*, p. 219, clearly implicates Meretskov's General Staff, and not Stalin, as the source of revisions to Shaposhnikov's concept. However, Stalin wholeheartedly agreed.

series.[25] Yet, by 1940–41, the larger geostrategic picture had changed, and under altered circumstances it was the Germans who, in July 1940, elected to engage in pre-emption. For the Soviets subsequently to entertain the possibility of pre-empting pre-emption was to engage in a dangerous game that required accurate perceptions, a realistic capacity to act and a delicate sense of timing. These requirements, in turn, relied on an intelligence apparatus that Stalin had decimated during the purges. The situation worsened over the first half of 1941, as a shift of German deployments eastward substantially reduced warning time and narrowed the window for pre-emption.

Losing the race to pre-emption

In light of these complexities, offensive / defensive strategies and correlations have figured prominently in debates among historians over Soviet preparations for war in the final run-up to 22 June 1941.[26] The collapse of the Soviet Union in 1991 facilitated only partial access to pertinent archives. Not all documents have become available, and the editors / compilers of documentary collections have sometimes chosen to publish only parts of key documents, thus increasing doubt over the exact nature of Soviet offensive / defensive intentions.[27] Against this background of a limited evidentiary base, but with an emphasis on continuities in planning, materials for 1941 seem to indicate that pre-emption remained a possible course of action. Until May, pre-emption via a surprise offensive may have been the preferred option, but this assertion rests on scattered evidence. By mid-May, however, the terms had changed. Pre-emption probably remained the preferred course of action, but of necessity – thanks to the German military build-up in Poland – under conditions of engagement in counter-offensive / offensive operations, rather than an offensive *á outrance*. By mid-June, neither option was viable.

During the first half of 1941, Soviet preparation for war progressed through three overlapping phases, each with its own concerns.[28] The first phase, in

---

25 The continuity is noted in M. I. Mel'tiukhov, *Upushchennyi shans Stalina* (Moscow: Veche, 2000), pp. 386–7.

26 The issues are as old as Second World War vintage propaganda, but debates during the 1990s owed much of their impulse to Victor Suvorov, *Icebreaker: Who Started the Second World War?* (London: Hamish Hamilton, 1990).

27 One of the more obvious examples appears in Naumov (ed.) and Reshin (comp.), *1941 god*, vol. I, pp. 741–6, in which refinements of 11 March 1941 to the war plan inexplicably exclude force allocations and mission statements for army groups and armies.

28 The following treatment owes much to P. N. Bobylev, 'Tochky v diskussii stavit' rano: K voprosu o planirovanii v General'nom shtabe RKKA vozmozhnoi voiny s Germaniei

February–March, witnessed an emphasis on measures initiated the previous year for reorganizing, rearming and re-equipping the armed forces. The General Staff mandated completion of a new mobilization plan, MP-41, that would not be finished until July. A new set of adjustments to the war plan was approved on 11 March, and, with altered figures to reflect additional mobilized manpower and units, the concept refined and extended the Meretskov variant of late 1940. In this document, Chief of the General Staff Zhukov affirmed the decision against a Soviet main effort north of the Pripiat, holding that 'combat on this front can lead to protracted battles'. More advantageous was 'the deployment of main forces south of the Pripiat with the primary strategic goal by means of a powerful blow against Liublin–Radom–Kraków to crush enemy main forces and to cut off Germany from Balkan lands'.[29]

The fundamental idea was to hold defensively on the flanks (opposite the Baltic and Odessa military districts) and to launch punishing offensive operations from the Kiev district, supplemented by forces from the south flank of the Western district. The immediate objectives were to defeat the Liublin–Radom–Sandomierz enemy grouping, to seize Kraków and Warsaw, and to emerge on the line Warsaw–Łódź–Opole. Subsequent objectives were to develop offensive operations either to Poznan–Berlin or to Prague and Vienna. These methods and objectives owed much to conclusions drawn from the outcome of the second operational-strategic war game of the previous month. In addition, the notation of Lieutenant General N. F. Vatutin (Chief of the Operations Directorate, General Staff) on the reverse side of page 27 of the plan was highly significant. He wrote, 'The offensive is to be initiated on 12.6' (12 June). This notation clearly indicates that a pre-emptive surprise attack was at least among the options considered by the Red Army General Staff. In the words of the military scholar S. M. Mikhalev, 'to negate this fact is senseless'.[30] Mikhalev also rightly noted that any decision for pre-emption lay with Stalin, and not with the Soviet high command.

At the same time, it is worth bearing in mind that pre-emption might find application under various circumstances. It could take the form of a surprise

v 1940–1941 godakh', *Otechestvennaia istoriia* 1 (2000), 47–54; periodization and useful detail come from E. V. Zhukunov (ed.), *1941 g. – Uroki i vyvody* (Moscow: Voennoe Izdatelstvo, 1992), a formerly closed publication, now available on the internet.

29 Ten pages of materials excluded from this plan in the documentary collection, Naumov (ed.) and Reshin (comp.),*1941 god*, are cited by Mikhalev, *Voennaia strategiia*, pp. 312–13.

30 Mikhalev, *Voennaia strategiia*, p. 313.

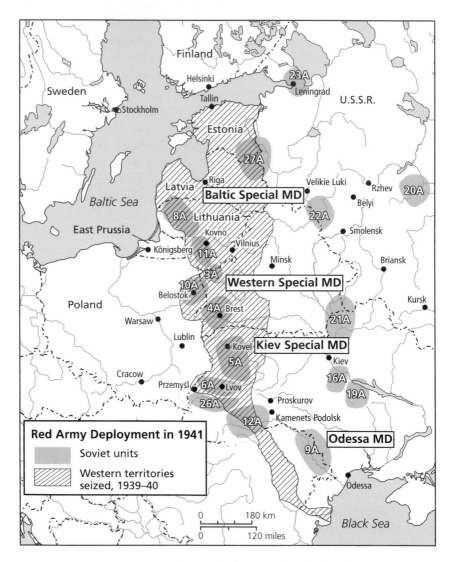

8.1 Red Army deployment in 1941

attack, *before* the formal initiation of hostilities, as Zhukov and the General Staff perhaps intended in early March 1941. Or it could occur soon *after* the initiation of hostilities, on the heels of border battles, but before completion of enemy concentration and strategic deployments (with the egregious assumption, contra Isserson, that perceptible gaps existed over the course of this process). The threat was imminent, but its contours remained indistinct, so planning continuities from the previous autumn and winter evidently governed. Moreover, pre-emption might plausibly have been viewed as a means for palliating deficiencies in Soviet preparation for war. Whatever the case, emphasis for a time seemed to be on pre-emption by surprise. This understanding would explain, for example, why there was no provision for the construction of concrete fortifications on the shoulders of the salient formed by the Western Special Military District. They invited penetrations for encirclement, but until early May, the command emphasis was on offensive operations, not on hardened defences.[31]

As the threat grew more ominous, the second phase of Soviet preparations for war, April to early June 1941, witnessed the beginnings of covert mobilization, and, too late, an increased emphasis on defensive measures to supplement pre-emption. It was during this phase that Stalin made the second fateful decision that would affect the coming campaign. On 13 May, he approved a General Staff recommendation for the covert mobilization of seven armies from interior military districts to create a second strategic echelon.[32] The *first* strategic echelon, already deployed within the boundaries of the frontier military districts, comprised three *operational* echelons: the first not far from the border trace; the second at depths of perhaps forty miles from the border; and the third, largely an operational reserve of mechanized corps, some sixty to ninety miles from the frontier. Deployment of the second strategic echelon would gradually commence along the Dnepr and the Western Dvina, where the assembling armies were located beyond the range of German aerial reconnaissance. Troop transit was to occur at night, without disruption of peacetime railroad timetables. This measure corresponded with requirements for pre-emption and added to a steady increase in the peacetime strength of the Red Army. Meanwhile, in early May, the frontier military districts received orders to complete their covering plans and to redouble construction in the fortified regions.

At the same time, there was a renewed emphasis on pre-emption in a fresh set of 'considerations' (*soobrazheniia*) for war planning submitted to Stalin by Timoshenko and Zhukov on 15 May. Although this document has received much scrutiny, its contents varied little from the refinements of 11 March, with the exception of a greater sense of urgency and an explicit call for pre-emption. The May variant held that Germany was maintaining

---

31 Denisova and Tumash (eds.), *Nakanune*, 391.
32 S. P. Ivanov (ed.), *Nachal'nyi period voiny* (Moscow: Voenizdat, 1974), pp. 211 and note.

its army in a state of mobilization, with rear services in place. As a result, 'it [Germany] has the capacity of beating us to the punch and launching a surprise attack'. Therefore, it was essential 'not to leave the initiative to the German command, but to forestall the enemy in deployment and to attack the German army while it is still in the deployment stage and has not yet had the time to organize the front and coordination among the service branches'.[33] Meanwhile, other documents suggest a concomitant emphasis on defensive measures along the frontier that would seem to indicate, in the event that surprise proved impossible, the necessity to prepare for a modified version of pre-emption inherent in a defensive/counter-offensive strategy.

The third phase embraced the last three weeks before the onset of hostilities, during which further Soviet precautions took effect. These included the forward redeployment of troops within the second operational echelon and the elevation of the overall readiness level within the first operational echelon. However, on 14 June, Stalin took the last of his three fateful decisions: against recommendations from Timoshenko and Zhukov, he forbade commanders to elevate the front-line troops to the highest possible readiness. Zhukov had already forbidden them to occupy their forward fighting positions. Stalin's decision corresponded with earlier prohibitions against responses to enemy over-flights and ground reconnaissance.

Stalin stubbornly refused to engage in any provocation that might justify a German onslaught. He entertained only best-case intelligence estimates and dismissed friendly warnings as 'disinformation'. The situation in the Far East remained unsettled, and there was the assumption that Germany would not turn east until after having dealt decisively with Britain. Although by April–May it was clear that German forces were concentrating in East Central Europe, Hitler's spring offensive into the Balkans sowed confusion over the scale, pace and location of the German build-up. Perhaps in Stalin's mind, a German build-up opposite the Soviet Union presaged, at worst, an ultimatum, at which time he might strike another temporizing bargain. Moreover, Germany's home front had not yet assumed full mobilization, and there was no anti-Soviet war hysteria in Berlin to signify preparation of the German populace for a gargantuan effort in the east.[34] Finally, even if the situation at the Soviet frontier invited

---

33 Naumov (ed.) and Reshin (comp.), *1941 god*, vol. II, p. 216.
34 Gabriel Gorodetsky, *Grand Delusion: Stalin and the German Invasion of Russia* (New Haven, Conn.: Yale University Press, 1999), pp. 188–90, 231–6, 243–5, 275–9.

pre-emption, had not the operational-strategic war game of early 1941 indicated that a first blow might be accepted, thus preparing the ground for a decisive strategic riposte?

However, there were readiness measures beyond troop alert levels, and herein lay much of the explanation for what occurred on 22 June. The complement of the Red Army was more than 5 million troops, but only 2.7 million were located in the western border regions. Meanwhile, the Germans and their allies counted 5.5 million. The Soviets had nearly 13,000 tanks in the west, but only 469 and 832, respectively, were of the new KV-1 and T-34 types. The Soviets counted a two-to-one edge in combat aircraft, but few were dispersed among forward combat airfields.[35] Newly mobilized divisions had not requisitioned horses and other mechanized means for transport. Such requisitions would serve as intelligence indicators of mobilization and would also deprive the economy of means to bring in the winter wheat harvest. Meanwhile, of thirty two divisions moving forward from the second operational echelon to the first, only four or five would arrive at their new positions by 22 June. The various armies of the second strategic echelon would not complete redeployment until mid-July. Readiness reports indicated shortages almost everywhere. Even along the border trace, the majority of troops were in peacetime quarters, not in their defensive positions.[36] Fortified regions were critically undermanned, and railroad throughput capacity in the newly occupied western territories dropped to one-half of that available to the Wehrmacht on the other side of the frontier. The Red Army's primary armoured formations, the mechanized corps, were too large to command and control effectively, and they were maldeployed. Those with the best readiness rates were located in the Kiev Special Military District, not within the Western Special District that would in reality face the brunt of the German mechanized onslaught. Insufficient resources went to communications assets, with the result that civilian landlines were the primary means of communication between Moscow and the frontier military districts. There were simply not enough means to match ends; the Soviet Union was unprepared either for offensive or defensive war at the outset of the fourth week of June 1941.

---

35 Iu. N. Morukov (ed.), *Velikaia Otechestvennaia voina 1941–1945 gg. Kampanii i strategicheskie operatsii v tsifrakh* (2 vols., Moscow: Obedinennaia redaktsiia MVD Rossii, 2010), vol. 1, p. 6.

36 Among the more comprehensive catalogues of deficiencies is David M. Glantz, *Stumbling Colossus: The Red Army on the Eve of World War* (Lawrence: University Press of Kansas, 1998), esp. ch. 5–8.

War of annihilation vs people's war

The result for the Red Army was surprise, destruction and dislocation on every level. Attacking on 22 June 1941, the armoured fists of three Wehrmacht army groups (North, Centre and South) pounded their way through unprepared and often inept defences. Local defensive measures and counter-attacks proved ineffective. With two armoured corps in the lead, Army Group Centre drove deeply into the Western Special Military District.

Meanwhile, confusion reigned in Moscow, thanks to the shock of surprise and the failure of communications. When Stalin and his generals sought to regain the initiative, they ordered counter-attacks that were hopelessly discordant with the situation at the front.[37] For the next seventeen months, the defenders often possessed sufficient mass and space to satisfy Svechin's imperatives, but rarely got the timing right. The frantic pressure from Moscow to regain the strategic initiative resulted in the premature launch of many offensives, before inexperienced commanders and staffs had properly supplied and coordinated their forces.

As the Soviets blindly flailed at and missed opportunities, the German advance gained momentum. Army Group North overran Lithuania within a few days, and by the end of the first week of July had occupied much of Latvia. During the same time span, Army Group Centre reached the pre-war border of Belorussia, while Army Group South was poised to break into Ukraine. Gigantic encirclement operations, especially in the centre, netted huge numbers of prisoners, and with little pause, the seemingly relentless armoured spearheads plunged ahead. The governing German intent, which had worked well against Poland and France, was to destroy Soviet military power with a series of well-orchestrated initial blows. In effect staking everything on an opening gambit, the German high command left few troops in reserve.

The initial results appeared to justify the risk. On 3 July, General Franz Halder, Chief of the Army General Staff, recorded in his diary, 'on the whole, one can say that the assignment of smashing the mass of the Russian Army before the Dvina and Dnepr has been fulfilled... It is probably not too much to say when I assert that the campaign against Russia has been won within two weeks'.[38] What Halder ignored was that objective depths were greater in

---

37 Geoffrey Roberts, *Stalin's Wars: From World War to Cold War, 1939–1953* (New Haven, Conn.: Yale University Press, 2006), pp. 93–5.
38 Franz Halder, *The Halder War Diary, 1939–1942*, ed. C. Burdick and H.-A. Jacobsen (Novato, Calif.: Presidio, 1988), p. 446.

the vast Soviet expanses, just as was the Kremlin's capacity to field additional military manpower, and that there was no geographical barrier against which to pin the adversary. As a German study of August 1940 had indicated, even occupation of European Russia might not induce a Soviet collapse.[39] Meanwhile, logistical dilemmas lay not in the far approaches to the Urals, but on the immediate horizon. Still, the Panzers forged ahead, leaving in their wake infantry, artillery and supply columns bound to movement by mare and shank's mare. However, the next cycle of encirclements, reaching east to Smolensk in the centre and north to the outskirts of Leningrad, seemed to portend nothing but more German victories and more losses for the Red Army.

In turn, official Moscow recovered from its initial shock to fashion a strategy, not for victory, but for simple survival. Higher organs were reorganized to afford improved means for overall direction and command and control. On 10 July, the newly minted Headquarters of the Supreme Command (*Stavka*) created three theatre-strategic headquarters, known as Main Commands or Directions (*napravlenii*), to consolidate the disparate headquarters of military districts transformed into army groups. Initially, these strategic Directions were entrusted to Stalin's pre-war Red Army cronies, but the dictator soon perceived the wisdom of relying on a new generation of professional commanders.[40]

These measures helped to restore some semblance of order to the Soviet war effort. The emphasis was on stabilizing the front, plugging gaps, rushing deep reserves into the fight and, wherever possible, wresting back the initiative. On 3 July, Stalin made a historic radio address in which he exhorted his 'brothers and sisters' to come to the defence of their homeland. The intent was to summon popular resolve to wage a 'people's war'. Hitler obligingly pursued a 'war of annihilation' in the east. Soon, mass murders and reprisals reinforced popular Soviet sentiment for a kind of protracted war for which the Wehrmacht was ill-suited. Many Soviet soldiers stood firm, while Soviet institutions, especially the Communist Party, refused to fold under stress, in contrast with tsarist institutions during the Great War.[41]

---

39 Rolf-Dieter Müller, 'From Economic Alliance to a War of Colonial Exploitation', in *Germany and the Second World War*, vol. iv: *The Attack on the Soviet Union* (10 vols., Oxford: Clarendon Press, 1998), pp. 136–7.
40 Dmitri Volkogonov, *Stalin: Triumph and Tragedy*, trans. and ed. Harold Shukman (Rocklin, Calif.: Prima Publishing, 1992), pp. 419–20.
41 Roger Reese, *Why Stalin's Soldiers Fought: The Red Army's Military Effectiveness in World War II* (Lawrence: University Press of Kansas, 2011), p. 75.

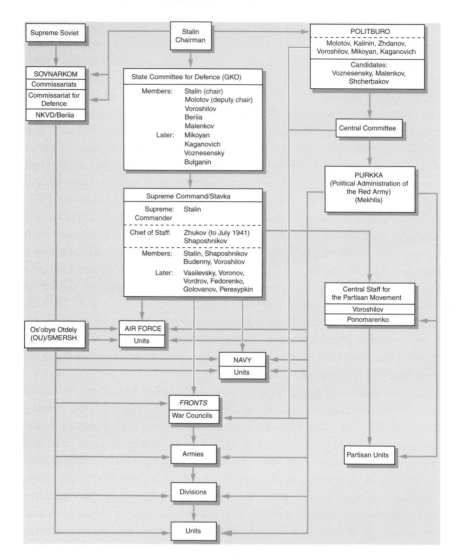

8.1 Soviet high command
From I. C. B. Dear (ed.), *The Oxford Companion to the Second World War*
(Oxford University Press, 1995), p. 1211.

Meanwhile, orders went out to evacuate industry to the east, beyond the
reach of the German army and air force.[42]

42 Mark Harrison, 'Industry and the Economy', in David R. Stone (ed.), *The Soviet Union
at War, 1941–1945* (Barnsley: Pen & Sword, 2010), pp. 21–30.

Even in late July, Soviet resilience and reserves were beginning to exact their toll. After the victories within the frontier military districts, German military commanders expected to break into the open, but instead they encountered the still-assembling armies of the second strategic echelon. Stalin had hoped to retain these as the nucleus for a massive strategic counter-stroke, but in the event they were committed piecemeal in response to threatening German advances. This sudden stiffening of resistance, plus the fact that Army Group Centre's armoured spearheads were now more than 400 miles from their original railheads, brought movement of these leading elements to a halt. A combination of troop losses, physical exhaustion and materiel shortages imposed the necessity for an operational pause.[43] This hard lesson was not lost on General Halder, who reflected in his war diary: 'The whole situation makes it increasingly plain that we have underestimated the Russian colossus... if we smash a dozen [divisions], the Russians simply put up another dozen'.[44] From this time, the Germans could no longer rely on the surprise and concentration of forces that had made possible the initial phase of Operation BARBAROSSA.

Engagement in successive strategic operations now forced the Germans to improvise, but as Halder acknowledged, 'they [the Soviets] are near their own resources, while we are moving farther and farther away from ours'. A renewed German offensive across an 800-mile-wide front was now impossible, so Hitler and his high command elected to halt Army Group Centre's advance. Limited reinforcements went to Army Group North, while Army Group Centre's armoured spearheads turned to Army Group South. When the redeployed armoured formations of Hoth and Guderian came into play, the result was another gigantic victory of encirclement at Kiev. Meanwhile, Zhukov had left Moscow to instil resolve into the defence of Leningrad. By the time that Hoth and Guderian returned to Army Group Centre and the road to Moscow, German offensive assets were pale shadows of their former selves. Still, the Germans mounted a last-gasp effort, codenamed Operation TYPHOON, to take Moscow. As they drove fitfully onward, each step brought them closer to the mirage of victory – but also further from their logistical support. The time was now ripe for a counter-stroke.[45]

43 David M. Glantz, *Barbarossa Derailed: The Battle for Smolensk, 10 July–10 September 1941* (2 vols., Solihill: Helion Publishers, 2010), vol. I.
44 Halder, *War Diary*, p. 506.
45 Evan Mawdsley, *December, 1941: Twelve Days That Began a World War* (London: Yale University Press, 2012).

Flow and ebb

The Soviet counter-attack before Moscow in December 1941 achieved both surprise and a local superiority of combat power, knocking the Germans back on their heels and resulting in a shakeup of their command structure. This success, however, caused both Stalin and his subordinates to dream that the Germans could be expelled as quickly as they had invaded. Once again, the belief in a short offensive war obscured the fact that much of the Soviet accomplishment in December was due to the attritional defence and German logistical problems of the previous five months. In January 1942, Stalin directed, and most *Stavka* officers eagerly agreed, that the victory at Moscow should be followed by a general offensive along the entire front. In many portions of that front, however, the Soviets had no numerical advantage over their enemies. Moreover, Soviet operations were as much subject to the weather as were those of the Germans, albeit with shorter supply lines. As a result, the counter-offensive sputtered in some places. By the time the fighting ground to a halt in March 1942, the front-line units of the two sides were hopelessly intermingled in some areas. Still, the belief that they had come close to strategic victory distorted the Soviet viewpoint throughout the spring of 1942.

Soviet relations with the Western Allies were seriously strained during this period. For the Soviet leaders, this was as much a matter of status and prestige as it was of actual aid to war-fighting. Clearly, Stalin believed that his state was bearing the brunt of the conflict against the Germans, while his allies failed to treat him as an equal partner. For the remainder of the war, Soviet diplomacy exhibited this sense that the Western Allies would not accord equal military or political consideration to Soviet interests. Viewed in this light, the Combined Bomber Offensive and the invasion of North Africa seemed to be mere gestures, representing far fewer sacrifices than those of the Soviet peoples.

Given the geographic difficulties involved, Lend-Lease aid could not begin to satisfy Soviet needs during the first winter of the war. Moscow believed that the United States had fallen behind its promised shipments of tanks and aircraft, even before Pearl Harbor complicated American logistical priorities. By the end of June 1942, British-supplied aircraft represented only 8 per cent of total Soviet production during the previous six months, while American and British tanks together made up 16 per cent of the Red Army's total numbers.[46]

---

46 Alexander Hill, *The Great Patriotic War of the Soviet Union, 1941–45: A Documentary Reader* (London and New York: Routledge, 2010), pp. 170–3.

Moreover, for reasons of propaganda and diplomacy, the Moscow government minimized the scale and value of Lend-Lease aid. In reality, Lend-Lease raw materials and finished products undoubtedly shortened the Soviet-German war by months, if not years. To cite but one example, 409,000 American-supplied trucks eventually became the mainstay of Soviet logistics, allowing each operation to begin more quickly and last longer than would otherwise have been possible.[47]

Within the *Stavka*, the spring 1942 debate was about whether the Soviets should absorb a renewed offensive before they launched their own counter-offensive, or whether they should instead pre-empt the Germans and attack first.[48] The ailing Shaposhnikov, his deputy A. M. Vasilevsky and (with some ambiguity) Zhukov argued in favour of the former course of action, sometimes referred to as fighting 'on the backhand', as opposed to a pre-emptive offensive 'on the forehand'. Remembering the incredible successes of December–January, however, Stalin could not rid himself of the belief that the Germans were on the verge of defeat. Reluctantly acceding to his advisors' recommendations, in early March 1942, he nonetheless ordered the three Direction headquarters to prepare staff estimates concerning the coming campaign, including opportunities for local offensives. Eager to satisfy the dictator, these headquarters produced proposals to exploit perceived opportunities along the front. These plans led to several failed offensives, including the destruction of A. A. Vlasov's Second Shock Army south of Leningrad. The most serious case of strategic overextension was in Timoshenko's Southwestern Direction. Despite critical shortages of weapons, Timoshenko produced an optimistic proposal to encircle German forces east of Kharkov. Although this attack caught the enemy off guard, it did not seriously disrupt their plans for the summer. The resulting second Battle of Kharkov cost the Red Army 267,000 casualties, as well as many of its newly manufactured weapons.

The Soviet leadership also misjudged the intentions of its opponents. Despite Marxist convictions about the primacy of economic factors and Svechin's earlier admonitions, Stalin and his generals were convinced that the new German offensive would aim at the political capital in Moscow,

---

47 For figures on Lend-Lease supplies, see ibid., pp. 174–91.
48 For the strategic debate in the spring of 1942, see David M. Glantz, *Kharkov, 1942: Anatomy of a Military Disaster* (Rockville Center, NY: Sarpedon, 1998), pp. 22–30; and David M. Glantz and Jonathan M. House, *To the Gates of Stalingrad: Soviet-German Combat Operations, April–August 1942* (Lawrence: University Press of Kansas, 2009), pp. 37–46, 77–83.

rather than at the economic resources, especially oil, of the Caucasus. They persisted in this view, even after a breach of security by German staff officers allowed the Red Army to capture a summary of the initial phase of Germany's plan for the summer offensive. Stalin understandably dismissed this captured document as a deception, since it seemed incredible that a German officer would take such a vital plan on an aerial reconnaissance over enemy positions.

Once this renewed German offensive, Operation BLAU, began, the Soviets again launched relentless counter-attacks against the ever-lengthening Axis left flank. The 1942 German campaign is often represented as an example of the Soviets steadily learning about mechanized warfare, while withdrawing skilfully to avoid encirclements. This was certainly true of the tactical performance of the Red Army, and its hard-won experience and renewed equipment allowed it to delay and wear down the German advance, while suffering fewer casualties than in 1941. At the strategic level, however, the Soviet leadership remained dedicated to rigid defence and constant counter-attack. This attitude was epitomized by the famous Order 227 of 28 July 1942, usually referred to as 'Not one step back!' (*Ni shagu nazad!*).

By this point in the war, both Stalin and his senior leaders were increasingly confident in themselves and their conduct of the war. Less than a month later, when Churchill visited Moscow in August 1942, Stalin expressed his strong belief in the Soviet ability to defeat the Axis.[49] By the time the German spearheads approached Stalingrad and the Caucasus oilfields in the late summer of 1942, the combination of overextended logistics and constant Soviet counter-attacks meant that those spearheads could barely defend themselves, let alone secure their ultimate objectives.

Turning point on the Volga

There remains the question of Soviet intentions during the Battle of Stalingrad. Neither side had planned for a battle there, but once joined, the city's name almost guaranteed a fight. The natural tendency is to focus on the tactical drama of thousands of soldiers struggling for control of a few square miles of urban terrain. Viewed in this light, the defenders appeared to be holding on by their fingertips, barely denying the Germans their prize. At the operational and strategic levels, however, one must consider the hypothesis

---

49 Roberts, *Stalin's Wars*, pp. 131–40.

that this situation was a deliberate decision, that the Soviet leadership fed Lieutenant General V. I. Chuikov just enough troops and munitions to keep the attackers ensnared in street fighting, while saving most of their military resources for the counter-offensives outside the city. There, the ever-lengthening Axis left flank depended on the ill-equipped forces of Germany's Romanian, Italian and Hungarian allies. This hypothesis, however, may give Stalin and his generals too much credit.

Still, the net result of urban combat was to gain the time and skills necessary for the Red Army to launch Operation URANUS on 19 November 1942. For the first time, the Soviets satisfied all three of Svechin's requirements, with sufficient mass at the correct place and time. They mounted a well-prepared counter-offensive, focused not on the German troops around Stalingrad, but rather on the poorly equipped troops of the flanking Third and Fourth Romanian Armies. Thus, whether it was a deliberate economy of force measure or a fortunate coincidence, Chuikov's desperate defence of Stalingrad paved the way for a major victory.

Yet, just as in the Moscow counter-offensive of the previous winter, Soviet over-optimism combined with German operational skill to limit the fruits of victory. This time, unlike the previous winter, the concept of a general offensive was embedded in the original Soviet plans to encircle Stalingrad. *Stavka* officers had projected a series of operations, each named for a different planet, against the Axis forces. Unfortunately, despite their success in November, the Soviets still had much to learn about coordinating complex operations against prepared German defences. In Operation MARS, a November–December 1942 offensive against the Rzhev salient of Army Group Centre, Zhukov blundered badly, losing four mechanized and tank corps. Because the encirclement at Stalingrad trapped more Axis troops than anticipated, the Soviets had to truncate Saturn, the follow-on operation that they had intended should cut off German Army Group A in the Caucasus. Field Marshal Erich von Manstein could not save the encircled German forces, but his skill at manoeuvre contained and eventually drove back the Soviet spearheads, permitting the withdrawal of Army Group A.

Toward victory, 1943–1945

When the two armies again came to an exhausted halt in March 1943, the Soviet leaders reprised their planning debate of the previous spring: should they launch another offensive as soon as they were ready, or wait until they had first absorbed the third German offensive? Both the Germans and the

Soviets tended to assume that, while they had recovered strength during the spring thaw, their opponent remained as weak as he had been at the end of the previous campaign. Fortunately for the Soviets, this time caution prevailed. Having watched the planetary series of offensive plans fail during the winter, Zhukov and Vasilevsky urged the dictator to remain on the defensive until the Germans had again expended their combat power. Moreover, the intended German objective was obvious: the huge westward bulge of the Kursk salient was the natural focus for the next encirclement. For the first time in the Second World War, the defender was able to predict the exact location of a major German offensive, thereby concentrating forces to block any penetration. In this instance, the Soviets not only constructed six successive defensive belts, but also created a strategic reserve, the Steppe Army Group, east of the bulge, blocking exploitation even if the initial attacks had succeeded.[50]

Although the defenders of Kursk outnumbered the attackers by a ratio of 5:2, the Soviet advantage also lay in the balance of resources, especially munitions. To cite but one example, the Luftwaffe pilots at Kursk received only two-thirds of their required supplies of aviation fuel.[51] More generally, the German economy was still not fully converted to wartime production in 1943. This incomplete mobilization, together with the German penchant for building a small number of high-quality tanks and other weapons, meant that the combination of Soviet manufacturing and Lend-Lease gave the defenders huge numerical advantages in war materiel.

Of course, the true significance of Kursk lay in the fact that the Red Army not only contained the German offensive, but immediately launched two of its own: Operation KUTUZOV against the Orel bulge north of Kursk, and Operation RUMIANTSEV to the south, around Kharkov. This time, the Red Army retained the strategic initiative it had gained at Kursk, pushing the Germans back to the Dnepr River by September 1943.

With Zhukov, Vasilevsky and most senior leaders increasingly involved in field operations, the *Stavka* operations chief, A. I. Antonov, frequently acted as Chief of the General Staff, a post to which he was formally elevated in early 1945. By the mid-point of the war, Stalin had not only learned a great deal himself, but had also come to trust Antonov and selected field

---

50 David M. Glantz and Jonathan M. House, *The Battle of Kursk* (Lawrence: University Press of Kansas, 1999), pp. 27–33, 63–77.
51 Herman Plocher, *The German Air Force Versus Russia, 1943* (New York: Arno Press, 1967), pp. 78, 81.

commanders to implement his desires. The dictator's March 1943 self-promotion to Marshal of the Soviet Union was quite justified.[52]

In April 1944, Stalin and his high command began planning a new series of offensive operations that was to ripple across the entire front, from north to south. The intent was to keep Hitler and his generals off balance, to wrest the remaining Soviet territory from German hands, and to position the Soviet Union favourably in Central Europe for the closing stages of the Second World War. With the opening of a second front in the West now imminent, Stalin pressed the advance not only for political purposes, but also to prevent the Germans from shifting troops to counter an Allied assault on France. The German salient in Belorussia represented a significant strategic objective. In a brilliant operational deception, the Soviets misled their opponents to expect the main blow to fall further south, prompting Germany to reposition its counter-attack forces away from the Belorussian bulge. Operation BAGRATION (June–August 1944) tore such a huge hole in Army Group Centre that it denied Hitler any hope of a long-term defensive stalemate and cleared the way for subsequent advances into the Balkans.[53]

As victory appeared increasingly certain, Stalin focused on the strategic goals of the war. Self-evidently, the Soviet leadership wanted to destroy Germany and ensure that the USSR was never again threatened by invasion. At the same time, Stalin and his henchmen, acutely conscious of the devastation of their country, intended to exploit the resources of Germany and Central Europe to rebuild. This, in turn, meant Soviet dominance of the region, which had the added benefit of spreading Soviet control to those states.

Beyond this, Soviet goals suggest a continued sense of having been treated as less than an equal partner. This eventually led to a desire in Moscow for the trappings of the other powers, including forward bases in the Baltic and the Adriatic. When Stalin could achieve both his security goals and equal treatment, he was willing to make cynical deals with his allies. The most famous was the 'percentages agreement' with Churchill in October 1944, an expression of British and Soviet relative interests in East European countries.

---

52 Volkogonov, *Stalin*, pp. 469–72; Roberts, *Stalin's Wars*, pp. 159–62.
53 Evan Mawdsley, *Thunder in the East: The Nazi-Soviet War, 1941–1945* (London: Hodder Arnold, 2005), pp. 292–309; see also *Belorussia 1944: The Soviet General Staff Study*, trans. and ed. David M. Glantz and Harold S. Orenstein (London: Frank Cass, 2001), pp. 43–4, 56–77; and David M. Glantz, *Soviet Military Deception in the Second World War* (London: Frank Cass, 1989), pp. 362–74.

Although one should not overemphasize this agreement, it does suggest Stalin's willingness to work with his allies, both during and after the conflict.[54]

By contrast, the Polish exile government of Stanislaw Mikolajczyk and its conservative-led resistance movement, the Home Army, strongly opposed Soviet domination over their country. To pre-empt an imminent Soviet conquest, the poorly armed Home Army rose up against the German occupiers on 1 August 1944. The resulting struggle for Warsaw, an epic battle than ran for sixty-three days, is sometimes regarded as the first round in the Cold War. The Soviets not only failed to aid the revolt, but delayed authorization for the US Army Air Forces to parachute weapons to Warsaw. Stalin appeared quite willing to permit his German and Polish opponents to kill each other off, facilitating the subsequent Soviet occupation. There is considerable truth to this interpretation, and diplomatic arguments over this uprising certainly reinforced Soviet antipathy for the London exile government. Yet there were also practical considerations that argued against Soviet support to the Home Army. The Red spearheads that appeared so close to the Warsaw at the end of July were at the end of a long campaign, leaving them weak when the German defenders counter-attacked outside the Polish capital.[55] Moreover, it was far easier, in a military sense, for the Red Army to bypass Warsaw than it would have been to clear it house by house. Politically, Moscow was determined to regain the Ukrainian and Belorussian territories that it had seized in 1939. That does not mean, however, that the Soviets tried to emasculate Poland. Quite the contrary, they wanted a strong, friendly Poland as a buffer against future German adventures. To achieve this, the final occupation of the region reimbursed Poland for its territorial losses in the east by giving it German lands up to the Oder–Neisse line, expelling millions of Germans in the process.

Soviet strategy during the final year of the war continued to reflect a combination of military necessity and realpolitik. Moscow successfully separated Finland and Romania from Germany and showed flexibility in compromising about the post-war status of Finland, rather than expending resources to completely crush that country. Yet Stalin was not satisfied with simply having these states withdraw from the war. He insisted that the Finnish army actively pursue its former German allies during their withdrawal from the country, while the devastated Romanian state found itself

54 Roberts, *Stalin's Wars*, pp. 217–19.
55 Ibid., pp. 204–7; and Mawdsley, *Thunder in the East*, pp. 330–3.

locked in yet another struggle against its traditional Hungarian adversary. Such battles not only contributed to Soviet victory, but ensured that the former Axis members would be too weak to make trouble after the conflict.

The Soviet government conducted its final campaigns with full regard for inter-Allied relations. In January 1945, the *Stavka* accelerated by eight days the Vistula-Oder campaign (the conquest of Poland and eastern Germany), in response to Western requests to distract German attackers in the Ardennes. Then, despite wartime diplomatic agreements that allocated eastern Germany (surrounding Berlin) to the Soviet Union as its zone of occupation, Stalin again rushed preparations for the final conquest of the capital of the Reich, encouraging a race between his subordinates to pre-empt any possible British or American occupation. Finally, the dictator fulfilled his promise to attack Japanese Manchuria exactly ninety days after the German surrender. Of course, part of the Soviet objective was to regain territory lost in 1905, such as the Kuril Islands and southern Sakhalin. Still, once again, Soviet casualties mounted higher than necessary in order to establish and maintain Stalin's desired post-war relations with his allies.

Conclusion

Despite the offensive operational doctrine and Marxist-Leninist liberation rhetoric of the 1930s, Soviet strategic planning was largely defensive in nature, albeit tinged with pre-emption, throughout the interwar period. The result was a disconnect, in which advocates of rapid offensive warfare seemed to dominate, neglecting defensive preparations, even though Soviet strategy, industrial development and reserve manpower seemed designed to prepare for prolonged attritional warfare.

In 1940–41, Stalin began belatedly to mobilize and repair the damage of the purges. His strategic policy was aimed at gaining time for such repairs. However, once the invasion began, the dictator and his advisors were slow to recognize just how weak the Red forces were in comparison with the Wehrmacht. This led to numerous ill-prepared counter-strokes against the German 1941 and 1942 offensives, wasting resources that might have been more effective, given more preparation time. During the first two winters of the war, not just Stalin, but the senior Soviet commanders, repeatedly tried, prematurely, to expand local successes into general counter-offensives, again wasting lives and resources.

Gradually, however, the growing capacity of Soviet logistics and staff work allowed the Red Army to conduct multiple offensives on different strategic directions, outclassing the Germans even when the Soviets did not necessarily have overwhelming numerical superiority. Indeed, Svechin's 1919 critique of the Great War German high command seemed just as appropriate to the latter stages of the Great Patriotic War. He asserted that the German military leadership was 'talented'. However, 'it was probably only one inch shorter than the height needed for victory, but it is precisely that missing inch which differentiates genius from an ordinary mortal'.[56] Meanwhile, the maturation of the Soviet war machine encouraged Stalin to place more trust in his subordinates, although he continued to exercise centralized control throughout the conflict.

Soviet strategic goals remained relatively consistent throughout the war. Despite mutual suspicions, the Soviets actually cooperated more often and more effectively with their Western allies than is usually recognized.

56 Quoted in Kokoshin, *Soviet Strategic Thought*, p. 31.

PART II

*

CAMPAIGNS

Thu, Dec 12, 2019
Standard
Marc
Bibb Sells

Introduction to Part II

JOHN FERRIS AND EVAN MAWDSLEY

Part II breaks the military operations of the Second World War into nine 'campaigns'. The breakdown is controversial, because no two historians would divide the war into the same episodes. Even the meaning of the word 'campaign' is loose, while alternatives like 'front' or 'theatre' are not an improvement. We accept the definition of a campaign as being 'a sustained operation designed to defeat enemy forces in a specified space and time with simultaneous and sequential battles'.[1]

The section starts with a chapter by Hans van de Ven on the fighting in China from 1937 to 1945. It then moves to a chapter by Karl-Heinz Frieser on the early German successes in Poland and Northwest Europe (in 1939–40), and another by John Ferris and Evan Mawdsley on the second half of 1940. The concentration on Western Europe in 1940 might seem disproportionate, but the events of that year are of singular importance. They saw the unexpected establishment of German domination over Central, Northern, Western and – with Italian help – Southern Europe. Another outcome, however, was the survival of the British Empire as an uncompromising opponent of the Third Reich, around which the anti-Axis alliance would coalesce. In the following two chapters, David Stone covers the Russian-German campaign (1941–45), and Simon Ball, the less bloody, but strategically and politically more complex fighting in the Mediterranean (1940–45). In the sixth chapter, Mary Kathryn Barbier covers the long-awaited Anglo-American counter-attack in Northwest Europe in 1944–45; and then John Kuehn deals with the Pacific campaign (from December 1941). The final two chapters

---

1 Allan R. Millett and Williamson Murray (eds.), *Military Effectiveness* (Boston, Mass.: Allen & Unwin, 1988), vol. 1, p. 7. The US Army used the term 'campaign' more narrowly, identifying thirty-six of them; see Wayne M. Dzwonchyk, *A Brief History of the US Army in World War II: The US Army Campaigns of World War II* (Washington DC: Center of Military History, 1992).

provide an account of two different 'campaigns'; from the Allied point of view, one was defensive, the other offensive, and both were critical. The Battle of the Atlantic is discussed by Marc Milner and the strategic air campaign (the Combined Bomber Offensive or CBO) by Tami Davis Biddle. (Other aspects of the war at sea are treated in Michael Miller's chapter, 'Sea transport', in Volume III.)

Some significant and distinct events are difficult to fit into the nine-campaign summary, where authors – who were given free rein to deal with 'their' campaigns – have chosen to concentrate on the decisive areas in a theatre. Examples are Poland in September 1939, Norway in April–June 1940, Burma, New Guinea and northeast India in 1942–44, and Manchuria in August 1945. Meanwhile, omitting the actions of the big-ship surface navies in European waters seems justified by the numerical weakness of the German battle fleet and poor fighting quality of the Italian one; it was the war of the U-boats and convoys that was ultimately most important.

The authors of these chapters combine mastery of the sources and arguments with conceptual power. They speak for themselves, but more might be said about the spaces that they share. Nationalism, myth and experience influence ideas about the campaigns of the Second World War. Thus, compared to other belligerents, the English-speaking countries avoided high levels of military casualties, while their forces were capital-intensive, focused on machines above manpower. Their publics still tend to believe that this war was fundamentally unlike the First World War, characterized by low casualties and high manoeuvre. In fact, attrition characterized the campaigns of the forces of the British Empire and the United States, especially their greatest one, the strategic air attacks of the CBO. Meanwhile, other major belligerents, the Germans, Russians, Italians, Chinese and Japanese suffered military casualties which, in absolute and percentage terms, were like those of the First World War, or greater. (The details of those losses are outlined in Richard Bessel's chapter, 'Death and survival', in Volume III.)

Campaign studies tend to be national histories, written primarily by historians from the countries involved. This has consequences; Nationalist historiography, for example, marks the accounts of every campaign where American, British and Commonwealth forces fought side by side. Judgement of the relative importance of various campaigns was, until fairly recently, reinforced by the impact of the Cold War. The Russians overrated their contribution to victory and downplayed that of the Western Allies, and vice versa, distorting the synergistic way that they defeated Germany, or the impact of issues like Lend-Lease. Sometimes these Nationalist accounts interact with a tendency to overrate German performance (as an excuse for Allied setbacks, or a bonus for eventual Allied victory); the performance of the Wehrmacht was more spotty than is generally realized. Institutional loyalties – to particular units or branches of service – have the same effect. Advocates and analysts of air power assess campaigns differently than do those with other views, whereas accounts of army and naval combat characteristically underplay the role of aviation.

Campaigns varied in breadth, accounting for territorial scale, force size and range and time duration. They varied in depth, considering the demographic and economic strength of competitors, the mobilization of societies and their will power for war, the strength, quality, training and learning curves of military institutions. And they varied in their effect on the war. Only by viewing campaigns as a whole and in a comparative fashion can one judge key strategic decisions, such as whether the United States correctly allocated its resources between the Pacific and European theatres, or what was the relative contribution of Soviet and Western forces to the struggle against Germany. So too, any judgement of the strategic air offensive must consider the outcome of a hypothetical reallocation of the large resources applied to it, so as to create larger and better British-American armies (with stronger tactical air support) or a more rapid victory over the U-boats – compared to what Germany might have done with the aircraft, artillery and manpower freed from the exigencies of strategic air defence.

Campaigns were competitions, between competitors prepared to fight in similar or different ways. To use a sporting metaphor, each sought to make its 'game' dominant. This issue was settled by the interaction between them and their environment. Campaigns usually involved cooperation between two services – air forces and an army or navy – and often between all three.

A short, victorious war, or an apparently decisive victory, was possible the first time any type of forces engaged in a campaign, and that was indeed the aim of some belligerents. Surprise and confusion enabled knockouts, as with the fall of France or the capture of Singapore. These outcomes happened because the loser could not recover from the losses produced by several revolutionary military developments as the war began, ranging from armoured warfare to air support for armies, amphibious techniques (Japanese, in Thailand and Malaya) and carrier aviation. The paradoxical exception was the 'knockout-blow' – incapacitating bomber raids on big cities, which several governments expected at the very outbreak of war and which did not occur; expectations here were complicated by an overestimation of the capability of the bomber, and an underestimation of air-defence systems. In all of these instances, many different things changed at once. Decision-makers, intellectually unprepared for such revolutions, were unable to anticipate accurately the individual changes, or the interactions between them. Military institutions could not easily or effectively prepare war plans or force structures (especially given the problem of long lead-times) suited to these circumstances. In making these mistakes, no nationality was better than the rest, though some were worse than most; conversely, some specific forces proved to be better at adapting than others.

Soon, however, the effect of surprise waned and enemies adapted, forcing campaigns into a competition of endurance, learning and attrition, which took many forms. The key issues were the relationships between the resources that each side could throw into the fight, their learning curve and improvement, sometimes against a better enemy who punished their forces as they learned; again, some institutions proved better at the task than others. Learning curves and qualitative superiority were institutionalized through doctrine, continuity of commanders and training – military culture. Military success occurred through varying combinations of attrition, strike and manoeuvre.

Attrition was part of all these campaigns, even those ostensibly involving high levels of manoeuvre or strike, though the differences between its forms were fundamental. Sometimes attrition involved a clash between intangible matters, like willpower and morale, or else the coercive power of states over societies, as between Germany and the USSR. Attrition turned on relative losses and the ability to replace forces, whether small numbers of pilots, or masses of infantrymen. One side's ability to impose its game on the enemy or to shelter its weaknesses (the power of machines versus masses, for example, perhaps most clearly exemplified between American and Japanese forces during 1944–45) might determine victory or defeat. After a period of varying length – short against a force without resources and resilience, as with Japanese forces in New Guinea and Italian ones everywhere, or long – as on the Eastern Front – one side could not ratchet up to a new level or replace losses forced by its enemy; it then suddenly collapsed. Some navies and air forces broke simply because they could not overcome one technical development by an enemy, as with the Japanese inability to replace the Mitsubishi Zero with a better fighter, or the U-boats' inability to cope with Allied sensors.

Attrition affected forces in different ways. In 1939, no army matched those of 1914 in the basic issue of numbers of trained personnel. Thus the elementary improvement of personnel was systematically harder to achieve in

1940 than in 1915. The German army acquired and held an advantage until 1943 because it began better than its enemies – despite many weaknesses. By 1941, the armies of Germany's enemies were untrained masses, attempting to improve in quality while being hammered by a large and better foe. Attrition drove all armies in the same direction, toward massive human losses. No army was ready for the casualties forced by circumstances and the enemy; all eventually reacted by throwing poorly trained masses into the meat-grinder.

Several air forces and navies on both sides, conversely, began as good machines of war. However, some were better able than others to absorb attrition of equipment and well trained combat personnel, and to maintain the required quantity and quality. Weakness in these spheres was fundamental to the decline of German and Japanese air and sea power. The RAF and the American air forces (including the huge 'air force' of US Navy) were the best on earth, because they emphasized the production of good aircraft and aircrew in great numbers. (The race for technological innovation and superiority is discussed by Cathryn Carson in Volume III.) Failure with combat personnel, as with German and Japanese air forces and navies, meant the waste of millions of high-quality support personnel, who, when eventually thrown into ground combat in 1944–45, made low-quality infantry. The impact of attrition spilt across services.

There were further patterns to these campaigns. Most featured an Axis offensive, followed by an Allied counter-offensive. The May 1940 campaign was the only complete German victory against a great power – and Karl-Heinz Frieser makes clear how much of a gamble on Hitler's part that was. Even that did not mean success for the war effort of the Third Reich as a whole; while France was knocked out of the war, the British Empire was not. The ground war in Western Europe (excluding the Mediterranean) is treated in two separate chapters – by Frieser and Barbier – because the German victory in 1940 was followed by a period of near inactivity of four years, from June 1940 (the exception was the 1942 Dieppe raid). When battle resumed in June 1944, its essence was the Allied attack. While the scale of fighting on the Russian front in 1941–45 was overall much greater, it can at least be treated as one huge event – and David Stone achieves a remarkable feat of compression in his chapter. In the Eastern Front, as in other theatres, the winter of 1942/43 was crucial. With the Battles of Guadalcanal and El Alamein, the amphibious invasions of Morocco and Algeria (Operation TORCH) and the titanic struggle at Stalingrad, the Allies gained the initiative in, respectively, the Pacific, the Mediterranean and Russia. This period also witnessed an intensification of the air attacks on Germany and Italy, and the defeat of the U-boats in the Atlantic. By the autumn of 1943, the Allies were able to mount vigorous offensives, while Axis forces sagged toward collapse – in the South and Central Pacific, Italy and across Ukraine. The exceptions were in Southeast Asia and China, where the Japanese army was able to hold its position and even mount offensives in the spring and summer of 1944 – from Burma into India (the Imphal-Kohima campaign) and deep into south China (the Ichi-Go campaign).

How did all the campaigns fit together in the Second World War as a whole, to produce Axis defeat and Allied victory? Hans van de Ven (and Jay Taylor in Part 1 of this volume) describe a war in China that was largely isolated, but the war effort of Chiang Kai-shek was always sustained by hopes of finding allies to help defeat Japan. The latter, in turn, was torn between the north Asian mainland and a campaign in the Pacific and Southeast Asia; the Japanese onslaught in the Pacific during December 1941 was motivated partly by a desire to isolate China and resolve the military stalemate there. The Allies never achieved strategic synergy against Japan, but then they did not need it either – a portion of American power alone did the trick.

Despite Hitler's strategic premonitions about a two-front war (discussed by Gerhard Weinberg in Part 1), his Wehrmacht ended up fighting on not two, but three land fronts (Western, Eastern, Mediterranean) – five fronts in all, if air defence and the U-boat war are included. This stemmed, in the end, from the crucial inability of the Wehrmacht to overcome Britain by air-bombing or invasion in 1940. Hitler later claimed that he struck east in June 1941 in order to convince the British government to come to the peace table – by showing it had no possible ally on the continent, not even Stalin's Russia. That claim is probably partly true, and there was even a certain logic in declaring war on the United States in December 1941, after the Japanese attack (an event over which Hitler had had no control). But within a year, or at most eighteen months, the military position of the Third Reich would be untenable.

Britain's war effort was also overextended, and it was indeed ultimately dependent on allies, as David French demonstrated in Part 1. John Ferris and Evan Mawdsley make clear that Britain possessed powerful air and naval strength, even in the embattled second half of 1940. However, in the early part of the war (through 1942), when the revisionist Axis states were driving ahead for a 'new order', the British Empire was their main common object-ive. Britain's forces and economy were hard-pressed, on their own, to hold off two European great powers, prepare to defend the empire in Asia, protect the vital sea lanes, and mount a massive strategic air attack on Germany;

there could be no thought of a return to the Continent. The unsuccessful German attack on the Soviet Union in June 1941 thus represented a fundamental change in Britain's fortunes, not least by ending the possibility of invasion (or even serious German air attack). Churchill's delight on hearing the news of the attack on Pearl Harbor is also understandable. Even with Russian and American help, however, the war effort would prove a fatal strain on British resources; the task included sending a large army to Europe in 1944–45.

As David Stone shows, the campaign in Russia, like that in China, was essentially self-contained until 1943. From September 1939 to June 1941, Stalin hoped that mutual destruction in the West would wreck the capitalist world. This stance unexpectedly enabled Germany to crush France cheaply, and then to turn against the USSR. During 1941–42, Britain and the USSR both stood on the defensive against Germany, while they and the United States mustered their power for the counter-attack. Although material aid from Britain and the United States mattered to Russia during 1941–45, the 'Second Front' came late.

Even so, the Allies stumbled into synergy, a virtuous circle in their struggle against the European Axis powers. Soviet forces engaged and destroyed the bulk of German military manpower, inflicting 80 per cent of its military casualties. This let Anglo-American forces fight a capital-intensive war against a fraction of the foe, using firepower and high technology to smash a numerically smaller army at the minimum possible cost, and also, along with the strategic bomber offensive, to engage and destroy the Luftwaffe and half of the firepower available to the German army. This forced Germany to fight a labour-intensive and low-technology war in the East, where the Western Allies divided German firepower and multiplied Soviet strength for strike. That helped the Red Army, superior in both numbers and technology, to engage and destroy most German military manpower, the point where the equation began.

Meanwhile, as Simon Ball makes evident in an elegant argument, the Mediterranean campaign and that in Northwest Europe were linked in complex ways. In 1940–42, the southern flank served as a surrogate for both sides; the Germans were unable to invade the British Isles, and the Western Allies were unready to risk a cross-Channel invasion. Action in the Mediterranean was influenced by perception of Fascist Italy as the weaker opponent (by Britain) or an unreliable ally (by Germany). During 1943–45, however, the theatre sucked in substantial Allied and Axis resources, probably to the greater cost of Germany.

The most significant inter-theatre relationship was between the war in Europe (involving seven campaigns) and that in East Asia (involving two). Could Germany and Japan have done more to help one another in 1941–42? The idea of Axis expeditionary forces somehow joining hands in the Indian Ocean or the Ural mountains is fantasy. Germany and Japan never established physical air communications, or gave one another significant economic or technical support. But the Axis could have pursued some forms of synergy. They did so only once, against the British Empire between December 1941 and June 1942, inflicting its greatest disasters of the war, which broke its world power. Alternatively, Japan, too, could have attacked the Soviet Union in 1941, the biggest 'what if?' of the war, though that is unlikely to have saved the Axis from annihilation.

Hitler welcomed the Pacific War in December 1941 (and President Roosevelt did not), because he thought it would draw limited American forces away from involvement in Europe. The leaders of Britain, China and the USSR all worried that a campaign against Japan might distract the United States, but on balance they thought it more likely that full-scale American involvement in the war would make greater resources available for their own campaigns, and that American operations would keep Japan from further mischief against themselves. Ultimately, the United States, the country with the greatest exploitable resources and freedom to deploy them as it chose, devoted the largest part of its resources to Europe, with the Pacific a close second. It also aided the USSR substantially, so as to kill Germans, and gave China just enough help to distract Japanese forces. Synergy was fundamental to the war, through the Allied ability to achieve it, and the Axis failure to do so.

The *CHSWW* does not address a final military aspect of the Second World War. This was the first war where weapons of mass destruction affected strategic issues, though in complex ways. During 1941–45, Germany and Britain deterred each other from using their stockpiles of chemical and bacteriological weapons; Britain also publicly threatened Germany with massive retaliation if it used those weapons against the USSR. All major belligerents investigated the prospect of developing atomic bombs. Driven by British and American fears of German physics and engineering and of Nazi ruthlessness, the Western Allies embarked on one of the greatest scientific and industrial efforts of the war. The first atomic bombs became available only after the Third Reich had been crushed. Instead, the two nuclear strikes – on Hiroshima and Nagasaki – affected like a *deus ex machina* what was now, effectively, an East Asian War. The Allies had expected to defeat Japan only after a full-scale invasion campaign, costing the lives of hundreds of thousands of their men transferred from Europe, and millions of Japanese. Events in China (for both the Nationalists and the Communists) and in Southeast Asia (for the people of the Japanese-occupied European colonies) were also greatly affected by the sudden and unexpected surrender of the Emperor's forces. Most importantly, however, the abrupt surrender of the Japanese government showed that a new age of power and war had begun.

and computing. All these were based on the belief that technological innovation can deliver decisive advantages on the battlefield. Less studied, but equally significant, was the demonstration by the Second World War of the limits of conventional warfare, and the emergence of guerrilla warfare linked with a disciplined national liberation movement. This chapter on military campaigning in China during the Second World War uses the China theatre to examine this development. In the vast spaces of China, a large agricultural and politically fragmented country confronted the invasion of a modern industrialized army backed by strong bureaucracies. While the Nationalists were able to force the Japanese into a stalemate, the social, political and economic disruption that followed enabled the Chinese Communists to develop people's war. Their success inspired followers in East and Southeast Asia, the Middle East, South America and Africa.[6] Michael Ryan, a senior executive the US Departments of State and Defense, has argued that Abu Ubayd al-Qurashi, a leading Al Qaeda strategist, drew on the Chinese Communist example to devise a strategy to defeat the USA.[7] In the context of the Second World War as a whole, the China theatre was a marginal one, but it would have lasting consequences for the post-war world.

The beginning

Late in the evening of 7 July 1937, Shimizo Setsuro's Eighth Company of Japan's North China Garrison Army began live-fire night exercises near the Marco Polo Bridge just south of Beijing.[8] This army was stationed between Tianjin at the sea and Beiping, as Beijing was then called. The 1901 Boxer Protocol permitted Japan, and other countries, to station troops along the Beiping–Tianjin corridor in the name of protecting their diplomatic missions, which had come under attack during the Boxer Rebellion. When a Japanese soldier went missing at the nearby town of Wanping, the Japanese demanded

---

6 For the general point, see Dennis Showalter, 'Introduction to Part III', in Roger Chickering, Dennis Showalter and Hans van de Ven, The Cambridge History of War, vol. iv: War and the Modern World (Cambridge University Press, 2012), p. 415. See also Anthony Clayton, 'Wars of Decolonization', in ibid., pp. 515–41.

7 Michael Ryan, Decoding Al-Qaeda's Strategy: The Deep Battle against America (New York: Columbia University Press, 2013), pp. 84–96.

8 Edward Drea, 'The Japanese Army on the Eve of the War', in Peattie et al. (eds.), Battle, pp. 105–6.

entrance into the city, declining a Chinese offer of a search by Chinese troops accompanied by a Japanese liaison officer. While it is unclear who fired the first shot, in the early morning of 8 July, Japanese forces were fighting their way into Wanping, beginning a war that neither side wanted, at least not at this time, and which would last for eight years.

Japan was hesitant about fighting China because it had only just begun a large effort to upgrade and restructure its army and navy. For Japan, the Soviet Union was enemy number one: Manchukuo, the Manchu monarchy Japan had fostered in Manchuria after it detached the area from China and where its Kuantung Army was stationed, shared a long border with the Soviet Union. The region's agricultural resources, mining deposits, railroads and industries were considered critical assets for the Japanese Empire to survive in a world of isolationist trade blocks rapidly moving toward a new world war. In case of a war with an increasingly anti-Japanese China, it would wage a short war of no longer than three months to seize areas south of the Great Wall, including Beiping and Tianjin.

What was true for Japan was even more so for China. The military reforms the Nationalists had begun in 1932 still remained at an early stage. A conscription system had only been instituted in a small part of the country in 1936. The air force was embryonic, there was no navy, there was a dearth of staff officers, and military industries had been planned but were far from being operational. Qing dynasty military manuals continued to be used at the Central Military Academy. China remained deeply divided politically and militarily. north China accepted Nationalist rule more in name than in reality, and the military forces there had little loyalty to Nanjing and were of even lower quality than the main Nationalist forces. In contrast to the Japanese, though, the Chinese leadership did realize that any war was unlikely to be over soon: they may have hoped for an early success or for a sharp battle followed by negotiations, but a long war of attrition seemed likely, and would offer China's best bet.

For weeks after the Marco Polo Bridge Incident, Chiang Kai-shek convened meeting after meeting at the summer resort, high up in the Lushan Mountains, China's natural 'air cooler', where the Nationalist elite and foreigners escaped the summer heat of the Yangzi Valley. Statements were issued about resistance, but none which made retreat impossible. However, Japanese troops were in control of Beiping and Tianjin by the end of July; Japan's Imperial General Headquarters had issued mobilization orders to divisions in Japan; reinforcements from the Kuantung Army had been deployed to north China; and the 3rd Fleet was on its way to the China coast.[9] Uncertain about Japan's intentions, which in truth remained limited, and learning from German military advisors that Chinese armies in north China were failing to stand up to the Japanese, on 12 August, Chiang Kai-shek decided to open up a second front in Shanghai, so to seize the strategic initiative and to push the few Japanese forces there into the Huangpu River before Japanese reinforcements could arrive.[10] They nearly succeeded. Had that been the case, negotiations might then have begun, but they failed. Japan and the Nationalists then poured ever more forces into the Shanghai cauldron, until some 700,000 Chinese troops were fighting over 200,000 Japanese soldiers. The die was cast.

Conventional failures

In the first sixteen months of the war, Chinese and Japanese armies waged three enormous battles. The Battle of Shanghai, from 13 August to 8 November 1937, left much of Chinese Shanghai, although not its Western enclaves, devastated. Next spring, at Xuzhou in north China, Japan's Central China Army from the Yangzi Valley and the North China Area Army struck toward Xuzhou, in the hope of encircling and wiping out some 600,000 Chinese troops concentrated there in the Fifth War Zone. They would win, but Chinese troops were able to escape through the many wide gaps in the encirclement. The Battle for Wuhan, located in Hubei Province in central China at the confluence of major rivers, and also an important railroad junction, began in early June 1938 and would last until 27 October. It involved around 800,000 Chinese and 350,000 Japanese troops, and ended with the withdrawal of Nationalist forces, who then continued the war from Chongqing, the capital of Sichuan Province in western China, surrounded by high mountain ranges.

Little is to be gained from reprising these battles in detail. Some general points are worth making, though. The first is the importance of railroads, on which the Japanese logistical system depended and which caused the first year of the Second World War in China to resemble the European wars of the middle of the nineteenth century.[11] North China had three trunk lines. One ran from Tianjin to Nanjing, and another from Beiping to Wuhan. These north–south running railroads were intersected by the Long-Hai

---

9 Hatori Satoshi with Edward Drea, 'Japanese Operations from July to December 1937', in Peattie et al. (eds.), *Battle*, pp. 159–63; Hans van de Ven, *War and Nationalism in China, 1925–1945* (London: Routledge, 2003), pp. 196–7.

10 Van de Ven, *War and Chinese Nationalism*, pp. 189–99.

11 Drea, 'The Japanese Army on the Eve of the War', pp. 122–3.

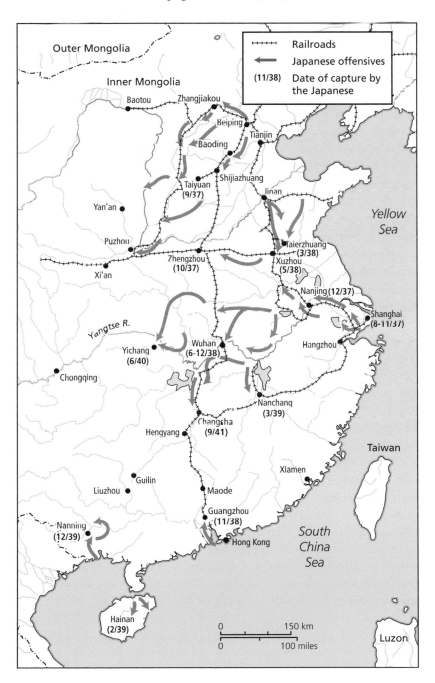

9.1 War in China, 1937–41

railroad from the east of Xian to a port city on the China coast west of Xuzhou. The Battle of Xuzhou was important because here the Long-Hai and Tianjin–Nanjing railroads intersected. The capture of this junction allowed the Japanese to deploy troops at will across north China, and so to begin an immediate assault on Wuhan, which, after the fall of Shanghai, the Nationalists hoped to make into their centre of resistance. The decision to break the Yellow River dikes at Huayuankou delayed this offensive, but only temporarily: during the summer of 1938, the Japanese advanced along both shores of the Yangzi River to Wuhan, which they occupied in October.

Air power played a role even in this early phase of the war. On 14 August, Japanese Mitsubishi G3M2 bombers attempted to attack targets in Shanghai and Nanjing, but were thwarted by bad weather and the Nationalist air force flying Northrop and Curtiss Hawk aeroplanes. Cities such as Nanjing and Guangzhou were also defended by modern anti-aircraft defences. However, largely because of their numerical superiority, the Japanese were able to degrade the Nationalist air force, and they established air supremacy within a month of the beginning of the Battle of Shanghai. The bombing raids they then conducted on Shanghai, Nanjing, Xuzhou, Wuxi, Guangzhou and other cities and towns restricted Chinese operational manoeuvrability and forced Chinese commanders to move troops and supplies at night. If the destruction was limited, the photographs and the accounts by journalists of cities reduced to rubble and bodies lying mangled in the streets, published around the world, ensured that Japan became seen as a brutal aggressor. Playing into deep fears about the indiscriminate destructiveness of aerial bombardment, few continued to accept Japan's claim to be fighting to restore Asia to a new period of glory.[12]

On the Chinese side, suspicions between Nationalist and local leaders, and the lack of coordination between central and local armies, repeatedly undermined military operations. General Han Fuju was the military governor of Shandong Province. After the beginning of the fighting, he was made Deputy Commander of the Fifth War Zone and Commander of the 3rd Army. Han offered no resistance when the Japanese landed at Qingdao, a port on the south side of the Shandong Peninsula. Hoping to preserve his forces, on which his wealth and political position depended, he withdrew

---

12 On the development of Japanese air power, see Mark Peattie, *Sunburst: The Rise of Japanese Naval Power* (Annapolis, Md.: Naval Institute Press, 2007); on the negative international reaction, see Hans van de Ven, 'Bombing, Japanese Pan-Asianism, and Chinese Nationalism', in Antony Best (ed.), *The International Relations of East Asia, 1900–1968* (London: Routledge, 2009), pp. 99–117.

from the provincial capital of Jinan and declined to give battle to Japanese units moving south along the Tianjin–Nanjing railroad, thus opening a road of advance toward Xuzhou for Japanese forces.

His execution following a court martial had only limited effect on instilling unity among China's defenders. Before the Battle of Wuhan, the Nationalists had constructed three barriers over the Yangzi River to stem the Japanese naval advance. One of these was the Madang Barrier, near Jiujiang and just down river from Bohai Lake. It consisted of thick iron chains, some twenty coastal and river steamers sunk into the river bed, artillery batteries scattered through the hills north of Jiujiang, machine gun nests sited all over the area, and four Nationalist divisions. German advisors who assisted the Nationalists in constructing the barrier claimed that it would be able to hold out for six months. The Japanese began the assault of the barrier on 14 June, with twenty naval vessels and thirty planes. The barrier fell on 26 June, after 167th Division Commander Xue Weiying declined to deploy his forces to repulse a Japanese landing party, despite urgent orders from the very top of the Nationalist chain of command. Xue faced the same fate as Han Fuju,[13] but the lack of military unity and the desire of commanders to preserve their forces again and again crippled China's efforts to resist Japan. The Nationalists were never able to overcome this problem.

Nationalist tactics dated from the First World War and even before. Given Japanese superiority in weapons, the Nationalists had little option but to opt for the defensive. However, although infantry manuals called for the dispersal of troops and defence in depth, few commanders had read them and few units had been trained in these tactics. Nationalist forces usually formed single front lines, with the consequence that a Japanese breakthrough threatened the collapse of the entire front.[14] They also dug trenches and fought from fortified positions prepared in advance, allowing the Japanese simply to overwhelm them with superior artillery or to bypass them. New units were brought to the front in closely packed formations, with the result that many fell to Japanese fire even before arrival.

Despite the excellence of Japanese troops, highly skilled in combined arms operations and amphibious warfare, Japanese forces too had significant weaknesses, of which logistics was an important one.[15] Infantry soldiers

---

13 Van de Ven, *War and Chinese Nationalism*, pp. 195–6.
14 Ibid., pp. 228–9.
15 Drea, 'The Japanese Army on the Eve of the War', p. 123.

looked down on those in supply services, while logistics officers were openly scorned as second-rate.[16] A British military report noted that during the 1937 battle for Shanghai, 'the fighting troops have been compelled to live on biscuits, bully beef, and tinned plums for weeks at a stretch', and that 'blankets have not been carried'.[17] When winter came, Japanese forces were ill-equipped to deal with the cold. Even the resupply of ammunition became a problem, compelling many units to reduce their rate of fire. Japanese medical services were rudimentary at best. During the Japanese advance on Wuhan, many soldiers succumbed to malaria and dysentery.

By the end of this year of ferocious fighting, both sides had to recognize that pitched battles by large army concentrations would not deliver a decisive result. Both had ended up in a situation far worse than they had anticipated. The Nationalists had been unable to stem the Japanese advance at Wuhan. Their options were limited: they could surrender or try to keep going. Those of Japan were to push on into Sichuan to attempt to defeat the Nationalists there; to swallow their pride and pull out of a war that damaged the country's general strategic position and cost vast amounts of money; or to try to consolidate the areas it had occupied.

The search for solutions

Neither Japan nor China simply kept going mindlessly. Each attempted to develop new approaches to war to gain a critical advantage. However, their innovations consisted of doing on a larger scale some of what they had been doing from the beginning. For the Japanese, this included a large terror bombing campaign, as well as efforts to bring about a new political reality in China favourable to Japan. The Nationalists expanded guerrilla campaigns, kept up their scorched-earth policy, and tried to internationalize the war. None of these efforts delivered the advantages that their promoters predicted; neither side gained enough of an edge to break the stalemate.

The Nationalists

The Chinese phrase, 'strengthen the walls and clear the fields', referred to the concentration of people, grain, livestock and other resources in well-fortified

16 Ibid., pp. 123–4.
17 'Report by Major G. T. Wards on a visit to Shanghai', 15 December 1937, in 'Sino-Japanese War: Reports on Japanese Operations in North China', The National Archives, Kew, WO 106/5576.

towns to deny them to the enemy. When they opted for a scorched-earth policy, the Nationalists were thinking of this strategy, but also of Russia's response to Napoleon's invasion. Following the outbreak of the Battle of Shanghai, the Nationalists ordered industries, mines, banks, shipping companies, bureaucracies and universities to Nationalist rear areas. In the following years, the Nationalists organized the move inland of around 1,500 companies, tens of thousands of technical experts, and 250,000 tons of equipment.[18] Even railroads were lifted, packed up and sent away when the Nationalists evacuated the lower Yangzi region.

The breaking of the Yellow River dikes was an extreme instance of this policy. It succeeded in its objective, but only at the cost of the inundation of a large swathe of the Henan countryside, causing perhaps some 500,000 deaths and making 3 to 5 million residents refugees.[19] The devastation likely contributed to the horrendous famine that gripped the area during the last two years of the war. This atrocity came back to bite the Nationalists: during the 1944 Ichi-Go offensive, the local population turned on Chinese defenders.

If this was the worst case, it was not the only one. After the fall of Wuhan, the Nationalists feared an immediate Japanese assault on Changsha, the capital of Hunan Province, to the south of Wuhan, in one of the most fertile regions of China. The Japanese would drive south, but stop short of Changsha. However, when news came that the Japanese had breached the last defensive line before Changsha, which in fact was not true, orders went out to torch the city. Numerous people died in their beds, as no warnings had been issued. General Xue Yue would use scorched-earth policies habitually in subsequent years.

Urban terror campaigns fitted the same strategy. Trained, funded and directed by Dai Li's Military Intelligence Organization, assassination squads set to work in cities such as Shanghai, Tianjin, Guangzhou and Nanjing, to kill traitors and destabilize local bureaucracies cooperating with the Japanese. They exploded bombs in public places on symbolically important days, such as anniversaries of the Marco Polo Bridge Incident. These campaigns developed into low-grade urban warfare between Dai Li's units and Japanese and collaborationist police forces.[20]

---

18 Zhang, *Kang Ri de Zhengmian Zhanchang*, vol. III, p. 434.
19 Mitter, *China's War with Japan*, p. 161.
20 On urban terrorism, see Frederic Wakeman, *The Shanghai Badlands: Wartime Terrorism and Urban Crime, 1937–1941* (Cambridge University Press, 1996).

Contrary to the idea that the Nationalists fought positional warfare and that only the Communists conducted guerrilla operations, the Nationalists embraced guerrilla warfare to prevent the Japanese from consolidating the areas they had occupied.[21] After the Battle of Wuhan, Chiang declared that 'guerrilla warfare is more important than conventional warfare. Turn the enemy's rear into the front. Use one third of our troops in the enemy's rear'.[22] By the end of 1938, the Nationalists had 600,000 to 700,000 troops assigned to guerrilla warfare, or about a third of their total.[23] They were concentrated in the Taihang mountain range in Shanxi Province, the Dabie mountain range between the Huai and Yangzi Rivers, the Zhongtiao Mountains of southern Shaanxi, the Lüliang Mountains in Shanxi and the Wutai Mountains in southern Anhui Province. Besides mounting attacks on isolated Japanese units, their main strategic assignment was to disrupt Japanese transport lines, such as the Tianjin–Nanjing railroad and the Yangzi River. They stepped up their activities at times of major main force operations, as they did during the 1939 Battle of Nanchang, the winter offensive of December 1939 to January 1940, the Zaoyang-Yichang campaign of 1940, and the four battles for Changsha.[24]

By 1943, though, the Nationalists were compelled to end their guerrilla effort. Their guerrilla units fought in large concentrations and defended territory, with the result that the Japanese could destroy them, as they did when they invaded the Zhongtiao Mountains in May 1941. Worsening economic conditions after 1940 meant that the Nationalists were unable to continue to provide financial and material support. Some units therefore switched sides, offering their services to the Japanese or collaborationist governments. Relations with the local population, with whom Nationalist guerrillas competed for resources, deteriorated not only because of this, but also because Nationalist guerrilla units soaked up the dross of society: hoodlums, toughs, rowdy youths, criminals, the destitute and deserters.[25] Morale also weakened because victory seemed ever more elusive. Already in May 1941, a Military Affairs Committee meeting noted that the 470,000 guerrillas of that time had in many cases deteriorated into bandit gangs. Their reputation was so low that villagers often fled as soon as they heard mention of the word 'guerrilla'.[26]

---

21 Yang Kuisong, 'Nationalist and Communist Guerrilla Warfare in North China', in Peattie et al. (eds.), *Battle*, pp. 313–14.
22 Quoted in ibid., p. 314.
23 Yang, 'Guerrilla Warfare', pp. 313–14.
24 Ibid.
25 Ibid., pp. 313–19.
26 Van de Ven, *War and Chinese Nationalism*, pp. 283–4.

The Nationalists' best hope of outlasting the Japanese was by bringing in a third powerful country. In pursuing this policy, it had more success, but not to the extent of securing the active participation of a third country in the fighting in China. Stalin was the object of Chiang Kai-shek's most strenuous overtures during the first years of the war. The Soviet Union did much to help the Nationalists, forcing the Chinese Communists to accept them as China's wartime leadership, and sending aeroplanes, tanks, heavy artillery, advisors and no fewer than 2,000 Soviet pilots to China, where they gained valuable experience. However, fearing a war on two fronts and merely aiming to draw the Japanese into a Chinese morass, Stalin declined repeated requests by Chiang to deploy armies in China. Soviet aid stopped altogether after the Battle of Nomonhan in the summer of 1939, when, with three tank brigades, General Georgy Zhukov destroyed General Michitaro Komatsabura's 23rd Division of the Kuantung Army. This led first to a Soviet-Japanese armistice, and then to a neutrality pact. Having secured his eastern flank, from then on Stalin focused on greater dangers to the west.

From Nomonhan until Pearl Harbor, China faced the Japanese alone. Japan's invasion of Southeast Asia provided the Nationalists with new opportunities to internationalize their war with Japan. While the inclusion of China as one of the Allies was useful to the USA and Britain, in order to demonstrate that the Second World War was not a race war and that the Allies were not fighting for imperialist motives (although Britain actually was doing so), both powers were determined to avoid involvement in the fighting in China. The only place where the Nationalists would fight together with their allies was Burma. However, while the Nationalists deployed their best divisions there, neither Britain nor the USA was convinced of Burma's strategic value. During the defence of Burma in 1942, the British used Chinese divisions largely to protect their flank, while for the USA, Burma was important to suggest to US audiences that it was taking on Japanese troops somewhere. In truth, China was a bargain-basement ally of whom much was demanded, but to whom little was granted. The Nationalists would never receive more than a minimum amount of US Lend-Lease supplies.[27]

However, China profited from the alliance in two ways. The first was the deployment into China of what was initially a US volunteer air force, which then became the Fourteenth US Air Force. The USA thought for a while of

---

27 Ibid., pp. 53–61.

in Nanjing.[31] Liang, like Wang Kemin, had close connections with northern warlord governments. He had been protected by the Japanese after the Nationalists rose to power and issued a warrant for his arrest. Wang formally ran north China, while Liang's government was supposed to rule Jiangsu, Zhejiang and Anhui.

Wang Jingwei's defection from the Nationalists in December 1938 provided Japan with a huge opportunity, but also a problem. Wang had a long revolutionary career and he had been close to Sun Yatsen. His belief that he, rather than Chiang Kai-shek, was Sun Yatsen's rightful successor, combined with his own and his wife's ambitions, caused deep tensions between Wang and Chiang. Wang joined any rebellion going against Chiang during the first five years of the national government's existence. However, in 1932, after the Japanese occupation of northeast China, the two had come to an accommodation. Wang was put in charge of the civil bureaucracy, while Chiang controlled the military. The defection of Wang, the Nationalists' number two, one year into the war, was a shock. Besides his rivalry with Chiang Kai-shek, Wang was motivated by his horror at the damage the Japanese inflicted, the destruction wreaked by the Nationalists' scorched-earth policy, and his conviction that the Nationalists could not win. After his defection, he began what he called a peace movement, stating that opposition to communism, economic cooperation and good neighbourliness could form a basis for peace. This followed Japanese Prime Minister Konoe's declaration that Japan would cooperate even with the Nationalist government, as long as it changed its policies and its personnel.[32]

The negotiations between Wang and the Japanese revealed a chasm. The Japanese wanted Wang to become the Wang Kemin or Liang Hongzhi of several south China provinces, including Guangxi, Yunnan and Guangdong. They hoped that generals and politicians in this region with a limited commitment to Chiang Kai-shek would join Wang. Had that happened, the Chongqing government might well have collapsed. This was not unlikely, because General Li Zongren, the leader of the Guangxi clique who commanded China's second-best force, had repeatedly fought Chiang Kai-shek. Yunnan Province's Long Yun was also no friend of Chiang Kai-shek. However, Wang insisted that any government of which he was to be the head had

31 Cai Dejin, *Lishi de Guaitai: Wang Jingwei Guomin Zhengfu* (History's Monster: The Wang Jingwei National Government) (Guilin: Guangxi Shifan Daxue Chubanshe, 1993), pp. 14–21.
32 Cai, *Lishi de Guaitai*, pp. 42–4.

to be a central government, to which Li Hongzhi and Wang Kemin had to subordinate themselves. Wang demanded that Japan agree to a definite schedule for the withdrawal of its forces from China, that his government should have its own military forces, and that it would continue Nationalist laws, institutions, nomenclatures and symbols, including its flag.[33] He declared that he would never fight Chongqing's armies. Wang's vision of the future did not mesh with Japan's preference for a China organized along federal lines.

A drawn-out process of negotiation did not end until 30 March 1940, when Wang Jingwei was inaugurated as President of a reorganized national government in Nanjing, which declared to be committed to 'Peace, Anti-Communism, and National Reconstruction'. Besides Liang and Wang's governments, it also incorporated Inner Mongolia in its territory. That long delay, the reluctance of Liang Hongzhi and Wang Kemin to embrace Wang Jingwei, the beginning of war in Europe, and especially the fact that no other significant political or military leader joined Wang's peace movement, meant that his government was stillborn. Had Japan jumped wholeheartedly and immediately on Wang's offer, Wang's peace movement might have had a different outcome.

Japan's attempt to use force to create the conditions for a new political reality in China was an early illustration of a key problem faced by militaries in the age of nationalism and total warfare. Its commanders had been trained at military academies which taught them to think about issues as military problems, to be solved by the use of force on the battlefield. They were not pushed to analyse the post-battle impact of their actions. Moreover, warfare had become absolutist, ending in total defeat or total victory. A settlement on the bases of a political compromise, an indemnity or the cession of a smaller or larger piece of territory could no longer bring the fighting to an end. Warfare, too, had become a broad concern for large sections of the Chinese population, even if not for all. The Japanese did not realize that this made it difficult to shoot a new political arrangement into existence, nor that the fact that many people in significant parts of China disliked the Nationalists did not mean that they would welcome a Japanese takeover.

The mainland campaigns after Wuhan

After the Battle of Wuhan, the Japanese divided the territories they had occupied into zones of 'peace and order', where no more military activity

---

33 Ibid., p. 53.

was to be conducted than was necessary to maintain stability, and 'areas of operation', where there would be serious campaigning. Only Wuhan and Guangzhou were defined as the latter, with Wuhan, where the 11th Army, with its seven divisions, was stationed, being the most important by far. Unsurprisingly, most battles after Wuhan and before the beginning of Japan's southern advance took place in the regions surrounding Wuhan.

The first operation of the Japanese 11th Army was to seize Nanchang, a major transhipment point from which the Nationalists supplied forces in south China, and a possible jumping-off place for a counter-offensive. During the Battle of Wuhan, Japanese forces had bypassed the city. On 20 March 1939, the 101st and 106th Divisions began their assault on the city, defended by the Nationalist 1st, 19th, 30th and 32nd Armies, with a total strength of 170,000 troops. While the fighting was fierce, Nanchang was in Japanese hands a week later.

In the same month, General Li Zongren moved thirty divisions of the Fifth War Zone into the Hongshan mountain range of north Wuhan, to interdict the Beiping–Wuhan railroad. Fearing an attack on Wuhan, the Japanese decided on a pre-emptive operation. The 3rd Division opened this battle with a feint toward Xinyang, while the 16th and 30th Divisions attacked Li Zongren's main forces east of Zaoyang. They drove Nationalist forces away from the railway line, but they did not pursue them, returning to their bases after two weeks. Li's armies had retreated to an area well beyond the sphere of operations set for the 11th Army.[34] Dependent on supply by rail, Japanese forces could not move far away from railheads. These realities determined the pattern of most of the land battles in this period of the war: a massive, but short, Japanese offensive, followed by retreat to their jumping-off point.

The first Battle of Changsha of September 1939 played out according to this scenario. The Japanese advanced toward their goal in two columns. The 106th Division moved west from near Nanchang, while the main attacking column, made up of the 6th, 33rd and 13th Divisions, descended south from west of Wuhan, following rivers and railroads in this area. General Xue Yue, Commander of the Ninth War Zone, fell back gradually as the Japanese advanced, clearing the countryside and attacking the Japanese flank. At the limit of their supply lines, facing very determined opposition and running out of ammunition, the Japanese stalled before Changsha and returned to their

---

34 Tobe Ryoichi, 'The Eleventh Army in Central China, 1938–1941', in Peattie et al. (eds.), *Battle*, pp. 216–17.

starting lines. Whether Japan had intended to take Changsha this time, which they denied, remains a moot point; it would seem strange had they not. Regardless, the Nationalists celebrated the failure of the Japanese to do so as a great victory.[35]

The Nationalists took the Japanese by surprise in December 1939, when they attacked the 11th Army with no fewer than seventy-one divisions. This determined counter-offensive aimed to throw the 11th Army out of Wuhan. The Nationalists mobilized their forces in the Third, Fifth and Ninth War Zones, while guerrilla units went into action along the north China trunk lines and the Yangzi River. Chinese forces attacked simultaneously, preventing the Japanese from countering with single thrusts. The winter offensive, lasting two months, had the Japanese genuinely worried, as it demonstrated that Chinese forces had recovered some combat worthiness and because the attacks came simultaneously from all directions, indicating an unanticipated level of central control. General Okamura Yasuji, the 11th Army Commander, wrote, 'We have never seen the Chinese army undertake such a large-scale and determined attack'.[36] A Japanese campaign history noted that a new offensive spirit animated Chinese forces and that troops had made good use of night-fighting to get close to Japanese forces.[37] A secondary, but important objective behind the winter offensive was the Nationalists' need to demonstrate that they continued to have the will and the capacity to challenge the Japanese. The offensive came just after the defection of Wang Jingwei and the Soviet Union's withdrawal of support.[38]

The winter offensive prompted a Japanese troop surge. Anticipating the outbreak of a new world war in about two years, the Japanese strengthened their forces and stepped up operations in China, hoping to be able to reduce them subsequently. One result was the Battle of Zaoyang-Yichang of May 1940. The 11th Army was to occupy the fertile plains of central and north Hubei, drive Li Zongren's forces out of the area, and occupy Yichang in west Hubei, near the entrance to Sichuan Province. Yichang was strategically important, as a transhipment and communications point between Sichuan and the various Nationalist war zones to the east. Its capture would facilitate Japanese bombing campaigns of the Chinese rear.

---

35 Ibid., pp. 218–19.
36 Ibid., pp. 220–1.
37 Van de Ven, *War and Chinese Nationalism*, p. 243.
38 Ibid., p. 243.

In the first stage of the campaign, the Japanese 3rd, 13th and 39th Divisions thrust north to surround the 31st Army of General Tang Enbo, one of Chiang Kai-shek's most trusted generals, who had been assigned to Li Zongren's command. When the 13th and 39th Divisions began what Tang believed to be the usual Japanese withdrawal after an offensive, he surrounded and inflicted serious damage on the Japanese 3rd Division.[39] While some Japanese leaders then began to doubt the wisdom of trying to take Yichang during the summer season, that operation went ahead. Advancing along different lines, Japanese forces swept toward Yichang and captured it on 12 June.

Nationalist forces under General Chen Cheng nearly succeeded in dislodging the Japanese from Yichang in September 1941, during the second Battle of Changsha. In April 1941, Lieutenant General Anami Korechika was placed in command of the 11th Army. Believing that a knockout blow would force Chiang Kai-shek to surrender, and tired of the back-and-forth campaigning until then, he decided to try to wipe out Nationalist forces in the Ninth War Zone and seize Changsha. Were he to succeed, the Japanese would control the fertile plains of Hubei and Hunan, crippling Nationalist resistance. In mid-September, when the weather had begun to cool, the Japanese 3rd, 4th, 6th and 40th Divisions thrust south toward Changsha, taking the city on 28 September.

For the Changsha campaign, the 11th Army had withdrawn forces from Yichang. Fifteen Chinese divisions commanded by Chen Cheng used this opportunity to attempt to throw the Japanese out of the city. They made rapid progress and were near the city before 10 October, the anniversary of the 1911 Revolution. The Japanese in Yichang believed the city would fall and had begun to burn archives and prepare to commit suicide. However, their forces were narrowly able to hold out. Faced with these difficulties, Imperial General Headquarters decided that holding Changsha would impose too heavy a burden. Under its orders, Japanese troops withdrew from that city on 1 October.

After the Japanese launched the southern offensive, Chinese and Japanese forces would face each other more in Burma than in China, but even in China, military operations did not cease altogether. The Japanese began yet another campaign to take Changsha shortly after Pearl Harbor, in an effort to prevent Ninth War Zone forces from offering support to the British in Hong Kong. They failed once more. In the spring and summer of 1942, the Japanese

---

39 Tobe, 'The Eleventh Army', p. 223.

planned to invade Sichuan, but battles with US forces in the Pacific, including at Guadalcanal and the Solomon Islands, led the Imperial General Head-quarters to withdraw troops from China, putting paid to this operation. The Japanese did drive Nationalist guerrilla forces from the Taihang Moun-tains. Another major campaign was the Battle of Changde of November to December 1943, when six Japanese divisions converged on this town, 125 miles southwest of Wuhan. They would take Changde, but the Nationalists retook the city with the support of US air units. The Japanese had become hugely overextended, with commitments elsewhere precluding the deployment of sufficient numbers of troops to reach their objectives.

After the Battle of Wuhan, the Nationalists and the Japanese did not mindlessly keep going as before, nor can the period be described adequately as a stalemate, not only because there was too much campaigning for that, but also because the Japanese essentially aimed at bringing about a new political reality behind a military screen rather than seeking the destruction of the Nationalists. Both sides searched for ways to solve the problem that large-scale operations by conventional forces would not decide the outcome of this war. However, each remained wedded to approaches which their commanders had learned in military academies – frequently the same ones, as many Chinese officers had learned their trade in Japan. They did learn from their experiences, but neither side gained the critical edge to achieve victory.

People's war

If, for a long time, it was thought that the Nationalists had done little to fight Japan, it is now common to argue that this was more the case for the Communists. It is true that the Communists only in one instance – during the Battle of the Hundred Regiments of autumn 1940 – took on the Japanese in a major operation. Nonetheless, their activities made a genuine difference to China's ability to outlast Japan. Their guerrilla operations behind Japanese lines in north China and in the lower Yangzi region harassed Japanese supply lines. Their actions served as a constant reminder that the Japanese were unable to consolidate control over the areas they had occupied. In addition, their rapid growth compelled Japan to allocate large numbers of troops to mopping-up campaigns and to guard duty, thus relieving pressure on the Nationalists.

The main form of war that the Communists used during the Second World War in China was guerrilla warfare, in which they proved far more competent than the Nationalists. While it remains open to discussion whether Communist people's warfare was truly different from traditional guerrilla warfare, it is the case that it appeared in a different context, namely when conventional armies attempted to fight total wars and when national liberation ideologies were powerful. The Communists demonstrated that guerrilla warfare was useful even in dealing with modern industrialized forces and that it could be used to further their political mission.[40]

People's war was not simple. It did not merely involve the arming of the local population to harass and exhaust Japan. It involved developing a set of tactics that took into account the huge disparity in weapons and training, the creation of base areas in which forces could be stationed and from which resources could be drawn, developing sophisticated intelligence networks, conducting covert operations to unnerve the enemy, and taking the war into areas where the enemy did not have the same advantages as on the battlefield – that is, into schools, the media, social and religious organizations, and political institutions. People's war closely connected the fighting with broader political and social aims – that is, with revolution – which suggested that sacrifices today would lead to a better future for large numbers of people. This kind of warfare was brought into being not by military men trained in military academies, but by Mao Zedong, who had no formal military education and never held a commission in a conventional army, although he had led troops and directed campaigns when he began to construct rural bases in the late 1920s and early 1930s. Through his experiences and his careful studies of the Chinese countryside, Mao had gained rich insight into organizing mass warfare in an agricultural society.

If Communist warfare was totalizing and revolutionary in intent, the actual mobilization of the population was strictly limited, and Maoist policies during the War of Resistance were remarkably cautious. In 1942, when the Communists came under sustained Japanese pressure, the Chinese Communist Party (CCP) Central Committee issued a directive that the ratio between central and local forces in mountainous areas should not be more than two to one, and that it should not even exceed one to one in low-lying regions, while the 'the total number of those not actively engaged in production (including those serving in the party, the government, mass organizations, and schools) should constitute no more than

---

40 Lyman Van Slyke, 'The Chinese Communist Movement during the Sino-Japanese War, 1937–1945', in John Fairbank and Albert Feuerwerker (eds.), *The Cambridge History of China*, vol. XIII: *Republican China, 1912–1942, Part 2* (Cambridge University Press, 1986), pp. 609–722, provides an excellent overview.

3 percent of the total population'.[41] The Communist approach ensured that the local population did not turn against them, something that the Nationalists were unable to avoid. Limited mobilization eased logistical and control issues, and had the further advantage that the Communists could be highly selective, which the Nationalists had not been.

The construction of territorial bases, called 'the buttocks of the revolution' by Mao Zedong,[42] was paramount in Communist strategy. As soon as the united front was agreed, the newly legitimized forces of the Communists immediately left Yanan in search of new bases behind enemy lines. Two thousand troops of General Nie Rongzhen's 115th Division marched to the border area between Shanxi, Chahar and Hebei Provinces, where they established the Jin-Cha-Ji Border Region. Units of General Liu Bocheng's 129th Division moved into the Taihang Mountains in south Shanxi, and then expanded into Hebei, Henan and Shandong, where they created the Ji-Lu-Yu Border Region. General He Long's 129th formed a base area between Shanxi and Suiyuan Provinces. These areas were selected so as to minimize possible conflict with the Nationalists, while also making it possible for the Communists to suggest that they were confronting the Japanese. These bases enabled the rapid expansion of the CCP and its armed forces during the first three years of the war. Party membership grew from 40,000 to 800,000 members. By 1940, its armed forces had grown from 30,000 to 500,000 troops.

The Communist approach to base area construction consisted, first, of moving in troops. When they had established a foothold, party cadres made contact with local elites, usually through connections of local supporters, often students and teachers. Avoiding immediate radical social policies, they built up new government structures, recruited youths, women, poor peasants and workers into mass organizations, and created a three-tiered military structure. At the lowest level were militia, in which, theoretically, all able-bodied adult men up to the age of forty-five had to serve. They had little training and no weapons other than farm tools and fowling pieces, but provided logistical support, intelligence, shelter and food. Local forces served permanently, but never left their local area, where they carried out harassing operations, such as sniping at Japanese soldiers, attacking Japanese outposts and small convoys, and destroying roads. The CCP's main forces were stationed in base areas, living off them, but they would move away when

---

41 Quoted in Yang, 'Guerrilla Warfare', p. 321.
42 Van Slyke, 'The Chinese Communist Movement'. For the point about Mao's determination to seize ground, see p. 614.

the Japanese moved in with overwhelming force. An important Maoist principle, surely going against all the instincts of the professionally trained soldier, was to avoid battle and fight only when success was virtually guaranteed. Mao did not want generals out for battlefield glory. Mao's approach gained Communist forces a reputation for always being victorious, the best form of propaganda. As one Communist cadre observed: 'after a victory in battle, the masses fall all over themselves to send us flour, steamed bread, meat, and vegetables. . .and new soldiers swarm in'.[43]

The creation of a positive reputation for the CCP and its forces was critical to its success.[44] It worked hard to overcome the traditional prejudices against soldiering, not only by enforcing strict military discipline, but also by having young men first serve in militia to defend their family's home and fields, and then recruiting them into higher-level units. The CCP's forces undertook policing duties, enforced social policies and, famously, assisted with farm work, including the collection of the harvest. Short-term training courses, schools and universities provided a huge range of new opportunities, including for acquiring literacy. Base area newspapers and magazines, cartoons, posters, bulletins chalked on walls, theatre perform-ances and lectures by leading cadres provided information on international, national and local affairs, in which the achievements and goals of the CCP were central. Life under communism was full of meetings, creating a new sense of political involvement for all those traditionally excluded from participation in public life.

It would be a mistake to believe that the Communists only appealed to the peasantry. Urban youths flocked to Yanan, dismayed at Nationalist corruption, oppression and weakness, and hopeful about the possibilities of a new era under communism. They learned about this in their schools and universities from CCP members and sympathizers, and by reading authors such as Lu Xun, Guo Moruo, Tian Han and Mao Dun, as well as Edgar Snow's *Red Star over China*, translated into Chinese in 1938. The united front allowed the Communists to operate across China, and hence to distribute party newspapers and journals such as the *New China Daily*. Liaison offices of the 8th Route Army in Chongqing and Xian became important hubs of activity, maintaining contacts with local sympa-thizers, while also directing covert operations and gathering intelligence. Wartime conditions also provided the CCP with political opportunities.

43 Ibid., p. 673.
44 Ibid., pp. 624–6.

It participated in the Political Consultative Conference, using it as a platform from which to criticize the Nationalists, demand political reform and gain allies among national elites.

'Mountaintop-ism' – that is, the splintering of the organization – was a constant danger. During the Long March, this tendency had even led to the emergence of two competing Central Committees. Mao Zedong did not want a series of base areas, each following its own policies, led by party secretaries concerned with their own area and merely aiming at survival. While that was a natural tendency at this time of war, it ran the risk of the CCP degenerating into an alliance of local warlords.

Mao used his vision of rural revolution to discipline the party and its armed forces, instil a shared ideology and centralize power. Taking his cue from Stalin's approach to unifying the Soviet Communist Party, including his determination to instil a common understanding of its history, in 1942 Mao launched the Rectification campaign. It began at the top of the CCP, with the leadership required to study texts by Mao and Stalin, as well as CCP documents illustrating the Maoist vision of its past, including the erroneous ideological line and political errors of all previous CCP leaders. In meetings, participants were required to maintain diaries and write self-criticisms, which were discussed and analysed collectively. At the end of the process, the participants wrote confessions and indicated their embrace of the Maoist vision. This process was replicated throughout the CCP, from the top downward. Although torture and executions occurred, the Rectification Movement was much less brutal than its predecessor of the early 1930s and its post-1949 successors. Mao used the Rectification campaign to ruthlessly humiliate his enemies among the CCP leadership. It left the CCP with one clear leader, a unified senior leadership, and a tightly organized and disciplined party, which controlled the armed forces through its system of military commissars, who were subject to party discipline. That system went down to platoon level, and thus penetrated further down the military hierarchy than was the case in the Soviet Union.

The rapid expansion of the CCP and its armed forces inevitably created clashes with Nationalist forces. Communist units clashed with Nationalist guerrillas in Shandong and Hebei as early as 1939. Similar conflicts also took place in the Zhongtiao Mountains in south Shanxi. The rapid expansion of the New 4th Army in the lower Yangzi region was especially provocative, as it came at the expense of Nationalist main forces in what had been the Nationalist heartland. The result was the famous New 4th Army Incident of

January 1941. The Nationalists destroyed a part of it after it declined orders to limit its size and move to a designated area.[45]

Communist expansion also prompted the Japanese to take action. In the 'Hundred Regiments offensive' of 1940, Communist units attacked Japanese transportation networks and blockhouses by mobilizing about 40,000 men, and eventually virtually the entire 8th Route Army. The offensive was triggered by Japanese attacks on Communist areas. The disparity in firepower, logistical capacity and available troop numbers meant that the offensive badly misfired: the Communists lost 20 per cent of their forces. The Communists halted expansion and limited operations. 'Our line', the CCP declared afterwards, 'is to wait for improvements in the situation. In the meantime, we preserve our strength while carrying out guerrilla operations employing every sort of tactic, from fierce skirmishing and nonviolent revolutionary duplicity to manoeuvres against the enemy'.[46] As was true for the Nationalists, the middle years of the war were extremely difficult for the Communists. Only the Ichi-Go offensive allowed them once again to step up their activities.

The Ichi-Go offensive

For the Ichi-Go offensive, lasting from April 1944 to February 1945, the Japanese deployed 500,000 troops, 100,000 horses, 15,000 vehicles and 1,500 artillery pieces.[47] Fighting took place along a 900-mile stretch of land from the Yellow River in Henan Province all the way to China's border with Indochina. Its objective, as approved by General Tojo Hideki, Japan's Chief of General Staff, was to seize US airbases in China. However, discussions between the Operations Section of the Imperial General Headquarters and the China Expeditionary Army during the planning for the campaign, which had begun in 1943, reveals that some had broader aims in mind. At Imperial General Headquarters, Ichi-Go originated as part of a long-range strategic plan to deal with the loss of control by Japan over the Pacific. Ichi-Go, in this concept, would clear out Chinese forces from the Chinese mainland and

---

45 Note that much remains obscure about this incident, including Mao's role. For a summary discussion, see Van Slyke, 'The Chinese Communist Movement', pp. 664–9. For an extensive discussion of the New 4th Army, see Gregor Benton, *New Fourth Army: Communist Resistance along the Yangtse and Huai, 1938–1941* (Richmond: Curzon Press, 1999).
46 Yang, 'Guerrilla Warfare', p. 321.
47 Hara Takeshi, 'The Ichigo Offensive', in Peattie et al. (eds.), *Battle*, p. 392.

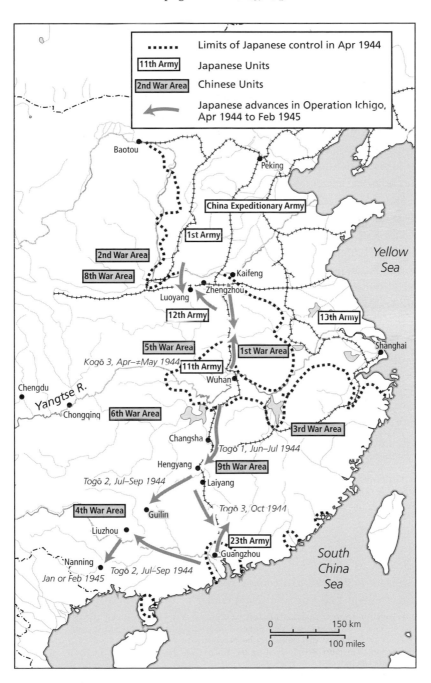

Limits of Japanese control in Apr 1944

11th Army — Japanese Units

2nd War Area — Chinese Units

Japanese advances in Operation Ichigo, Apr 1944 to Feb 1945

Baotou

Peking

China Expeditionary Army

1st Army

2nd War Area

8th War Area

Kaifeng

Zhengzhou

Luoyang

12th Army

13th Army

Yellow Sea

Shanghai

5th War Area

1st War Area

Kogō 3, Apr–≠May 1944

11th Army

Wuhan

Chengdu

Yangtse R.

Chongqing

6th War Area

3rd War Area

Changsha

Togō 1, Jun–Jul 1944

Hengyang

9th War Area

Togō 2, Jul–Sep 1944

Laiyang

Togō 3, Oct 1944

4th War Area

Guilin

Liuzhou

23rd Army

Guangzhou

South China Sea

Nanning

Togō 2, Jul–Sep 1944

Jan or Feb 1945

0   150 km

0   100 miles

9.2 War in China, 1944–45

construct an overland route to Southeast Asia. Japan would then not depend on sea lanes to move troops and ship-critical resources such as oil and rubber from Southeast Asia.[48] The China Expeditionary Army had continued to toy with the idea of taking the war to Chongqing after all; some hoped that Ichi-Go would provide an opportunity to do so. Bolstering morale at a time that the news from all fronts was bad was no doubt an important consideration, while it is possible that the Japanese hoped that the campaign would induce the Allies to accept a negotiated settlement. The Japanese could not know that the Allies meant it when they had declared that only an unconditional surrender could lead to the restoration of peace.

The Ichi-Go offensive proceeded in three stages. In mid-April, four divisions of the North China Area Army, supported by a tank division and air units, crossed the Yellow River near Zhengzhou. They drove south along the Beiping–Wuhan railroad toward Luoyang, a strategic town where this and the Long-Hai railroad intersected. After securing their flanks, the Japanese assaulted Luoyang and seized it on 25 May, thus clearing the Beiping–Wuhan railroad. The offensive led to the destruction of the forces of General Tang Enbo, Commander-in-Chief of the First War Zone. They lived off the land when the Henan famine was wracking the province, ensuring that the local population often welcomed the Japanese. The poor showing of the Nationalists and their inability to relieve famine sufferers was widely reported by US journalists, with consequences for Nationalist prestige.

The Nationalists only developed an accurate understanding of Japanese aims in early May, when the Battle of Henan was already nearly over.[49] Even then, the Nationalist high command failed to reach agreement about an appropriate response. General Xu Yongchang, in charge of the Department of Military Operations of the Military Affairs Council, favoured a counter-offensive in north China and holding firm in Hunan. General Bai Chongxi, the Vice Chief of the General Staff, advocated a retreat all the way south to the Hunan–Guangxi railway, believing that Chinese forces were too weak to offer effective resistance. General Xu opposed this suggestion because it might lead to a general collapse and would cause the USA to lose faith. General Xue Yue, the Commander of the Ninth War Zone in which Hunan Province was located, and General Yu Hanmou of the Seventh War

---

48 Ibid., pp. 395–9.
49 Wang Qisheng, 'The Battle of Hunan and the Chinese Military's Response to Operation Ichigo', in Peattie et al. (eds.), *Battle*, pp. 404–7.

Zone near Guangzhou, were slow to make preparations, even when ordered to do so, because they underestimated the continuing combat capability of the Japanese. Such indecision did little to help the Nationalist cause.

The second stage of Ichi-Go began on 26 May, when 150,000 troops of the Japanese 11th Army advanced into Hunan toward Changsha in three columns, along a seventy five-mile front.[50] General Xue Yue followed his usual strategy of clearing the countryside and conducting a fighting withdrawal to wear out the Japanese, in preparation for counter-attacks on Japanese flanks. However, this time, the Japanese placed their strongest forces on their flanks. The defence of the city descended into chaos when General Zhang Deneng attempted to ferry troops from the city across the Xiang River to Yuelu Mountain, to the west of Changsha, where Chinese artillery had been concentrated. The Japanese captured the city on 18 June, and this time they would hold it.

The Japanese had failed to destroy General Xue Yue's main forces. They therefore decided to attempt to bring them to battle by attacking southward to Hengyang, anticipating that General Xue would continue to follow his usual strategy. They were right. The Nationalists used only one army to defend Hengyang, but deployed thirteen armies near the Japanese flanks. The Japanese reached Hengyang on 23 June. They once again used just two divisions to besiege the city, while three divisions moved into eastern Hunan and one into western Hunan. The Battle of Hengyang was very hard fought indeed, lasting for forty-seven days. Outnumbered, outgunned and without adequate air cover, the city was doomed and fell on 8 August. Even then, the Nationalists did not give up, launching counter-offensives during the rest of August. These were, however, unsuccessful.

Following the capture of Hengyang and the effective annihilation of the Ninth War Zone's forces, the road lay open for the Japanese to advance further south to the Indochina border and clear the Wuhan–Guangzhou railroad. They did so in a three-pronged attack: 100,000 troops were concentrated near Hengyang, to strike south along the Hunan–Guangxi railroad; two divisions of the 23rd Army, stationed in the Leizhou Peninsula in the far south of Guangxi Province, struck north; while another two divisions moved west from the Guangzhou area along the West River toward Guangxi. The strategy of General Zhang Fakui, Commander of the Fourth War Zone, was to concentrate troops along the shores of the West River where it enters

---

50 Ibid., p. 409.

Guangxi Province and resist the Japanese there. This plan failed and the Japanese were in control of Guilin on 7 November, and of Liuzhou three days later.

While the Japanese concluded Operation Ichi-Go successfully, developments elsewhere nullified its strategic value. Following the US capture of Saipan in the Mariana Islands, essentially secured by July 1944, the USA gained another locale from which to launch B-29 strikes on Japan, thus rendering US airbases in China superfluous. The overland route to Southeast Asia never functioned properly. By late 1944, Germany's defeat was assured, meaning that all Allied might would soon be deployed against Japan. The Nationalists had suffered a terrible defeat, but the prospect of ultimate victory ensured that there was no collapse or *coup d'état*.

For the Nationalists, Ichi-Go proved an unmitigated disaster. The failure of their defensive efforts demonstrated that their forces had lost much of their fighting capacity. Relations with the USA deteriorated badly. US President Franklin Roosevelt insisted that Chiang Kai-shek hand over control of his forces to General Joseph Stilwell, Commander of US forces in China and of the Chinese Expeditionary Army in Burma, and in charge of US Lend-Lease supplies to China. Although he was winning in Burma, Stilwell was uninformed about the situation in China and unwilling to release resources for deployment there. Having lost all confidence in Stilwell, a deeply humiliated Chiang Kai-shek nonetheless agreed to Roosevelt's request, on the condition that Stilwell was recalled and someone else appointed. The fallout of the Stilwell Incident was so severe that relations between the Nationalists and the Americans would never recover.

The territories under Nationalist control were cut in half and they lost key resource areas such as Hunan Province. Essentially, they were thrown back on Sichuan Province, where resistance had grown widespread and in places had erupted into open rebellion. Because under US pressure the best forces of the Nationalists were deployed in Burma, and because they lacked the necessary transport capacity, at the time of Japan's surrender the Nationalists could not deploy troops rapidly back to coastal China. Embarrassingly, they had to depend on the Japanese to maintain order and prevent an immediate Communist takeover in north China.

For the Communists, Ichi-Go was everything that it was not for the Nationalists. Because of the shortage of Japanese troops in China, Ichi-Go involved 80 per cent of Japanese forces in China. The Communists could swarm out over areas in north and central China vacated by the Japanese. By late 1944, large swathes of the provinces of Shaanxi, Shanxi, Suiyuan,

Rehe, Hebei, Shandong and Jiangsu were in Communist hands, as were parts of Hubei. And so, Japan's surrender meant not the outbreak of peace, but the beginning of civil war.

An argument implicit in this discussion, which now should be made explicit, is that it is only of limited value to think about the China theatre as part of a coherent world war. The China theatre certainly had linkages with other theatres in the Second World War. By 1941, the Japanese abandoned their earlier stance that the war in China should be wound up before stronger powers should be taken on, instead arguing that a broader Pacific War was necessary to end the fighting in China. It is possible that Japan would have joined Germany in its attack on the Soviet Union had they been able to consolidate control over China. Similarly, China figured for a while in US strategic thinking as a possible base from which to attack Japan. That drew the Americans, despite doubts, into China on the side of the Nationalists, with consequences that have lasted through the Cold War until today. Similarly, facing defeat in the Pacific War, the Japanese turned toward China and Burma in the hope that they could turn the tide of war there, or, perhaps, draw the Americans into a blood-letting to bring them to the negotiation table and so avoid total defeat.

Nonetheless, such connections were limited. The Second World War began in China in 1937, two years before the Phoney War in Europe. From 1939 until 1941, China faced Japan alone. By 1945, China's stock had declined to such an extent that Roosevelt and Churchill did not consult Chiang Kai-shek about the contents of the Potsdam Declaration and merely asked him to sign it. Chiang had to plead for China to be included in the main text as one of the Allies demanding Japan's surrender.

If China's allies regarded China as a sideshow, for China, its survival as a nation lay in the balance. However, even more than this was at stake. The Nationalists thought of the war as an opportunity to bloody the nation they wanted to call into being. That meant ending European imperialism, returning China to its historically central role in Asian and world affairs, and unifying and modernizing the country. They would secure China's independence and end the war on the side of the victors, but they were driven to Taiwan shortly afterwards. The reasons for this lay largely in the Second World War. Repeated heavy defeats caused the Nationalists the loss of their best forces. They sustained their war of attrition by beating recruits and food out of the starving countryside, thus alienating the population. The dismal showing of their forces during the Ichi-Go offensive cost them much international and domestic prestige. After Japan's surrender, the Nationalists had to rely on Japanese forces to keep order, and on US aeroplanes to fly them back to coastal China, where they were then unable to bring an inflationary spiral under control.

As to the Communists, they had been fighting the Nationalists for a decade before the war broke out and had nearly been defeated. They would use the war to regroup, to grow their party and their armed forces, and to extend their territorial reach. They did so, first, during the first three years of the war, and then again after Operation Ichi-Go. Given the history of hostility and the deep distrust between the Nationalists and the Communists, it is unsurprising that fighting, often on a substantial scale, erupted between them again and again. By the end of the Second World War, the civil war between them had resumed in all but name. The Second World War in China was also about which vision of China's future would prevail – that of the Nationalists or the Communists.

When the Second World War came to an end, it was clear that Japan's gambit to establish a Great East Asia Co-Prosperity sphere had failed for good, but many other issues remained undecided. There was therefore no sharp break between the Second World War and the Chinese Civil War, or even between the Second World War and the Cold War. These concepts are only of limited use in analysing the fighting that took place in China between 1937 and 1951, when the Korean front lines settled down into a stalemate. In other words, the fighting in China must be studied not from a perspective originating in Washington, London, Berlin or Moscow, but on its own terms.

As much as the USA, the USSR and Britain avoided becoming entangled in the China theatre during the Second World War, they would not escape its consequences afterwards, politically, of course, but also militarily. Even during the Chinese Civil War, but especially after the communist victory, the people's war of the communists became a model that inspired national liberation movements around the globe. This would change the world just as much as the technologies that originated in the Second World War.

10

The war in the West, 1939–1940

An unplanned Blitzkrieg

KARL-HEINZ FRIESER

TRANSLATED BY HARVEY L. MENDELSOHN

In May 1940, there occurred 'the most mystifying event in the history of modern war'.[1] In the First World War, during four long years, the German army had tried in vain to break through the French lines. Yet in the 1940 campaign in the West, they broke through at Sedan in just four days. The tanks then rolled unstoppably behind the Allied front in the direction of the Channel coast and encircled a total of 1.7 million Allied soldiers in a giant pocket. After six weeks, the campaign came to an end. The world initially reacted with bewilderment, but soon a plausible explanation was found. It was called Blitzkrieg.[2] Nazi propaganda exploited the situation to create the legend that the German victory derived from a concept established long before, by none other than Adolf Hitler, 'the greatest field commander of all time'. But the real 'Blitzkrieg legend' was first created after the war by a number of historians endowed with rich powers of fantasy. They sketched out the fictional story of a brilliant Blitzkrieg strategy, which aimed at nothing less than world domination.

Hitler's failed *vabanque-politik*

Politically, Germany had already lost the Second World War even before it had really begun militarily. Paul Schmidt, Hitler's chief translator, reports on

---

1 Golo Mann, *Deutsche Geschichte des 19. und 20. Jahrhunderts* (Stuttgart and Hamburg: Deutscher Bücherbund, 1958), p. 922. English-language version, *The History of Germany since 1789*, trans. Marian Jackson (New York: Frederick A. Praeger, 1968), p. 470.
2 Karl-Heinz Frieser, *Blitzkrieg-Legende. Der Westfeldzug 1940* (4th edn, Munich: Oldenbourg-Verlag, 2012). English-language version: Karl-Heinz Frieser with John Greenwood, *The Blitzkrieg Legend: The 1940 Campaign in the West* (Annapolis, Md.: Naval Institute Press, 2005).

a somewhat ghostly scene at the Reich Chancellery, where, on 3 September 1939, he had to translate the British declaration of war:

> After I finished, there was total silence. . . Hitler sat there as if petrified and stared straight ahead. . . After a while, which seemed like eternity for me, he turned to Ribbentrop who kept standing at the window as if frozen. 'What now?' Hitler asked his Foreign Minister with a furious gaze in his eyes as if he wanted to indicate that Ribbentrop had misinformed him about the reaction of the British. Softly, Ribbentrop replied: 'I assume that the French will shortly give us an identical ultimatum'. . . Göring turned to me and said: 'If we lose this war, may Heaven have mercy on us!'[3]

Hitler's determination to launch the Polish campaign constitutes one of the most catastrophic wrong decisions in German history. Once again, like a *va banque* gambler, he placed everything on one card – and, of course, this time he lost.[4] Great Britain and France declared war on him. Now there emerged the scenario that had always been the nightmare of German military strategists: a war on two fronts. Hitler had summoned up the ghost of the defeat of the First World War. There can be no doubt that – from a long-term perspective – Hitler wanted war, but September 1939 was much too early. Hitler had explained to his generals that 1944 was the earliest date at which the German Reich could catch up with its future adversaries. The Wehrmacht, which later became so feared, was still in a somewhat embryonic state. The Treaty of Versailles had at first allowed Germany to form only a derisively small army of 100,000 men. True, at the start of the war, Hitler had called 4.5 million men to arms – though only 1.7 million were fully trained. The French armed forces numbered over 6 million men. Even Poland could mobilize an army of 3.6 million men, counting the reserves. The Polish army, however, was equipped and trained in outmoded ways, and was also led in an outmoded manner. After four days, the Polish campaign was decided, and in eighteen days it was essentially over.

It is important to emphasize that the Polish campaign cannot really be considered a Blitzkrieg, but only the preliminary version of one. Neither at the strategic nor at the operational level was the planning based on a novel conception. Once again, the military leadership, faced with a two-front war on account of Germany's geographically unfavourable middle position,

---

3 Paul Schmidt, *Statist auf diplomatischer Bühne 1923–45. Erlebnisse des Chefdolmetschers im Auswärtigen Amt mit den Staatsmännern Europas* (Bonn: Athenäum, 1954), pp. 437f.
4 *Va banque* is a term originally used in the baccarat card game, in which a player stakes everything on one card. It implies here an 'all or nothing' gamble.

sought to bring about an immediate decision. Yet the encirclement of the enemy did not require complicated manoeuvring along the lines of the operational plans of Moltke and Schlieffen; that outcome was actually preordained by geography. Simply from the initial disposition of the respective troops, the German divisions, which had already been deployed in East Prussia and Slovakia, had the Polish army surrounded from three sides. Moreover, in the East, the assault troops of the Red Army were standing ready. The initial position was entirely different on the Western Front, where the Wehrmacht confronted the Franco-Belgian fortified defensive line. And precisely in the case of the tanks, the action in Poland differed in an essential way from the campaign in the West. Unlike Panzer Group Kleist in May 1940, in the Polish campaign they were not yet operating independently. Instead, the tank formations generally fought on the tactical level as divisions (brigades in today's terms), incorporated within infantry armies. Several 'trump cards', which later became well-known elements in the German Blitzkrieg (for example, the airborne troops), were intentionally kept in the background to preserve the effect of surprise. Although the German General Staff thoroughly analysed the Polish campaign, it did not consider it a useful point of comparison in assessing a conflict with the Western powers. Interestingly, the military leadership of the latter came to the same conclusion. Thus the French Minister-President Reynaud characterized the attack on Poland as simply an 'Expedition'.

In reality, the success of the 'triumphant' Polish campaign hung by a thread. General Halder, the Chief of the Army General Staff, later explained: 'The success against Poland was only possible by almost completely baring our western border'.[5] The Western powers could have just walked into the Ruhr, the heartland of German industry, and occupied it. Yet they let slip this unique opportunity. Thus there arose that strange state of suspended animation known as the *drôle de guerre*, which the Germans termed the *Sitzkrieg* and the British, the Phoney War or Twilight War.

Even today, it is almost unknown that at the end of the Polish campaign the German forces stood at the edge of a debacle and were judged by their military leadership as 'no longer capable of operations' (*nicht mehr operationsfähig*). That is to say, they were no longer logistically in a position to pursue the war. Only the sudden end of the Polish campaign saved the army and the air force from collapse, especially in the munitions sector. For example,

---

5 William L. Shirer, *The Rise and Fall of the Third Reich: A History of Nazi Germany* (New York: Simon & Schuster, 1960), p. 634.

General Milch, the Inspector General of the Luftwaffe, warned that his pilots had sufficient bombs for only fourteen more days of fighting and then they 'could play skat'. When Hitler received these ill tidings he was at first bewildered and then flew into a rage. A high point of the ensuing 'crisis of nerves' was the suicide of General Becker, the head of the army ordnance branch, who felt forced – unjustifiably – into the role of the scapegoat. Hitler had pushed the still unprepared Wehrmacht into the adventure of a war, even though its strength was just enough to last for a short campaign. Later, however, some historians imagined that behind it all lay a carefully crafted plan.

The legend of the 'Blitzkrieg strategy'

One of the most fascinating theories of the history of the Second World War is that of Hitler's 'Blitzkrieg strategy'. In the First World War, the so-called 'grab for world power' (*Griff nach der Weltmacht*) had failed. It had been shown that the German Reich was economically not in a position to carry out a long-running war against the Western naval powers, with their virtually inexhaustible reserves of raw materials. According to this theory, that is why, in the 1930s, Hitler developed a new, supposedly brilliant strategy for victory, the 'Blitzkrieg strategy'. Now, the same exalted goal was no longer to be reached in a single global war, but rather stage by stage, via a strategy of small steps – that is, via a series of Blitzkriegs. The opponents would be overthrown, one by one, in individual campaigns with limited aims and of limited duration, requiring only limited mobilization of the war economy. In the pauses between the individual Blitzkriegs, Germany's strength would grow stepwise through the exploitation of the recently conquered lands.

The fantasy of the historians was particularly stimulated by the notion of the so-called 'Blitzkrieg economy'. By means of a quickly accomplished, broad preparation – and accepting the risk of giving up a deeper preparedness, spread out in time over several stages – in a very short period one could supposedly achieve a first-strike capacity sufficient to overpower in a short campaign the next opponent on the list. In this way, one could square the circle, and bridge the chasm between Hitler's worldwide expansion plans and the – otherwise insufficient – supply of raw materials needed to execute them.

This theory was expounded in the United States as early as 1945 by Burton S. Klein, and later in Great Britain, mainly by Alan S. Milward. Eventually, this thesis of the 'Blitzkrieg strategy' also gained some acceptance in German historical writing.[6] This is true above all of the 'intentionalist' school, whose proponents believe Hitler's political actions were determined by a long-established programme. Particular attention was accorded to Andreas Hillgruber's two-stage (*Stufenplan*) model, with its notion of a *Weltblitzkrieg*. According to this model, in the first stage, Hitler wanted to conquer the European continent from his base in *Mitteleuropa,* and in a second stage bring the bulk of Asia under his control. Only then would the economy be organized for total war, in order to challenge the United States for world dominance.

Yet, as with many other fascinating theories, here, too, the question arises of whether the politicians of that time really planned future developments with such specific goals in mind, or whether it is not rather the historians who have devised, from hindsight, systems and strategies to explain events whose occurrence was more a matter of chance. An investigation of the German sources yields a wholly different result: the Blitzkrieg, from its very beginning, was not a political-strategic but rather a military-tactical phenomenon. This idea developed completely independently of Hitler's plans for conquest, and its earliest stage is already recognizable in the First World War. At that time, the Germans were looking for new methods to overcome the rigidity of positional warfare and get back to a war of movement. Toward this end, they developed special assault-troop tactics for breaking through a line and for a deeper thrust. The attacks of these assault troops were meant to be lightning fast, in order to exploit the effects of surprise. General Guderian adopted this assault troop tactic and incorporated into it the elements of modern technology, such as the tank, the aeroplane and the radio. The result was a breathtaking increase in the tempo of attack, which produced a great psychological shock. Never again was the shock of surprise to be as complete as it was in the 1940 campaign in the West, which may be considered the Blitzkrieg par excellence. In what follows, however, it will be shown that this Blitzkrieg was not in any way planned to take the form it actually did.

Hitler's 'Blitzkrieg economy' proves to be, upon closer examination, a fiction. At the beginning of the Second World War, the leaders of Germany faced a dilemma: should they carry out armament 'in breadth' for a short war, or armament 'in depth' for a long one. In this situation, it was the spectre of the First World War that had the most influence. Hitler and his

---

6 Examples from both American and German historiography can be found in Frieser, *The Blitzkrieg Legend*, pp. 8f., 360–2.

generals were clearly aware of the traumatic experiences of positional warfare, with its endless battles of attrition. Accordingly, Germany's economic potential should be designed not to burn out in a lightning-fast manner, like fireworks, but rather to be kept at a low flame and thus be able to last for a long time. In planning the Western campaign, Hitler did not work on the assumption that it would take six weeks (which is all it actually lasted), but rather that it would go on for five or six years. Armament production was planned in such a way that a significant increase would be perceptible only after a year. The high point, however, was not supposed to be reached until the autumn of 1941. Yet at that moment in time, the Wehrmacht stood not before Paris, but before Moscow.

The priority scheme for weapons procurement established before the Western campaign likewise provides no evidence of any expectation of a quick decision following on a Blitzkrieg. In *first* position are requirements which clearly point toward preparation for a long, stationary war, like the First World War: munitions and gunpowder factories, machines and machine tools. The *second* level of priority is the production of new U-boats, as well as Ju 88 aeroplanes. These were weapons that would be used in the long run as part of the war strategy against Great Britain. Only in the *third* (and penultimate) position do tanks appear. An especially revealing figure is the distribution of steel within the armaments slated for the army. From the 445,000 tons allocated for the second quarter of 1940, only 25,000 tons in total, or barely 5 per cent, remained for armoured vehicles. This was less than the 26,000 tons foreseen for barbed wire, obstacles, and so forth, to be used in fighting a positional war. About twice as much steel was allotted simply to preparing the factories to produce future munitions than was made available for the production of armoured vehicles.

Even more revealing are the organization and structure of the German army. The military planners confronted the following opposing choices regarding the right goal to pursue: Should they create a small, elite army with motorized divisions, which would be suited to an operational war of movement – that is, a Blitzkrieg? Or should they form a large number of second- and third-class infantry divisions, which would be suited for positional warfare? Here, too, the image of the First World War prevailed. In May 1940, only 10 per cent of all the German divisions, in other words, the spearheads, were fully motorized and could be employed in a war of movement. The great mass of the army moved at the pace of an infantryman or the trot of a horse-drawn cart. The notion of the armoured German military moving like an avalanche of steel was only a propaganda fantasy.

In the First World War, the Germans had used 1,400,000 horses, and in the Second World War as many as 2,700,000. Following the campaign in the West, the Allied secret services were accused of total failure, because in spite of abundant information, they supposedly had not grasped the structure of the German 'Blitzkrieg army'. This criticism seems unjustified, because the German army, in terms of its structure, actually was *not* a Blitzkrieg army.

After the failure of the Schlieffen Plan in the First World War, the German generals were totally opposed to any military adventurism. This attitude is expressed in a remark made in July 1938 by the General of the Artillery Ludwig Beck, at the time the Army Chief of Staff: 'The idea of a Blitzkrieg. . .is an illusion. One should really have learned from the modern history of warfare that surprise attacks have hardly ever led to lasting success.'[7]

The struggle over the 'Sickle Cut' Plan

According to the calculations of the General Staff, the French campaign was not really winnable. France had taken shelter behind its Maginot Line and, together with its allies, was clearly superior to the German attacker. In May 1940, the Allies had at their disposal twice as many artillery pieces as the Germans (14,000 to 7,000). In terms of armoured vehicles, they were also clearly superior, with 4,204 tanks against the Germans' 2,439. Moreover, their tanks were of better quality. They were technologically a generation ahead, since for a long period the Germans had been forbidden to produce tanks and aircraft by the Treaty of Versailles. Thus the French Char B and the British Matilda tanks proved to be nearly invulnerable to German tank cannon and anti-tank weapons. Almost two-thirds of German tanks were unusable in combat against enemy tanks because of their inferior weaponry. Despite a widely held view to the contrary, the Western powers also enjoyed superior air power. Specifically, if one counts, in addition to the few planes that were operational at the front on 10 May, those that had been pushed back to the rear areas out of concern about a surprise German attack, then the Allies' total comes to 4,469 planes, as compared to Germany's 3,578.

The German generals were rarely as united in their views as they were in their opposition to the campaign in the West. Hitler's plans for the attack were dismissed internally as 'insane' (*wahnsinnig*) and 'criminal'

---

7 Wolfgang Foerster, *Generaloberst Ludwig Beck. Sein Kampf gegen den Krieg* (Munich: Isar Verlag, 1952), p. 123.

(*verbrecherisch*).[8] Even Göring spoke out against a Western offensive. But the dictator was obsessed by the notion of waging an offensive war in the near future. In response, a conspiracy formed, led by the Chief of the Army General Staff, General of the Artillery Halder. He planned a *coup d'état* and the assassination of Hitler in order to protect Germany from a catastrophe. For a time, he even carried a pistol in his briefcase, 'in order possibly to gun down "Emil"' (his codename for Hitler).[9] In the end, however, he lost his nerve. At some point, Hitler flew into a rage against General von Brauchitsch, Commander-in-Chief of the army. The dictator accused him of defeatism, roaring at him as if he were a recruit. And an expression used by Hitler in the heat of emotion led Halder to believe – falsely – that the plans for the coup had been betrayed. He panicked and ordered all the relevant documents to be destroyed. The resistance of the generals thus collapsed from within. Now there was nothing left for Halder to do but to carry on and turn to the planning of the inevitable campaign.

Immediately following the Polish campaign, the army's Supreme Command had elaborated an operational plan for an offensive against the Western powers. According to this first deployment order, the troops would push forward toward the Belgian Channel coast on each side of Brussels, with the point of main effort falling to the right wing. But this uninspiring proposal seemed only at first glance a copy of the failed Schlieffen Plan of 1914. As Chief of the General Staff, Schlieffen had planned an oversized new edition of Hannibal's battle of encirclement at Cannae (216 BCE). He wanted to envelop all the enemy armies stationed in northeastern France in a huge pincer movement and decide the outcome of the war with lightning speed. His successors in 1939, however, planned precisely what he had fervently rejected, namely an 'ordinary' victory without a strategic decision. Other proposals continued to be developed for the disposition of the troops, but none of them showed any trace of brilliance.

Then an outsider developed a plan which could make the seemingly impossible possible. This was Major General von Manstein, Chief of Staff of Army Group A. He characterized the operational plan proposed by the army high command (*Oberkommando des Heeres* – OKH), with its centre of gravity in the north with Army Group B, as too transparent. This was exactly

8 Wilhelm Ritter von Leeb, *Tagebuchaufzeichnungen und Lagebeurteilungen aus zwei Weltkriegen*, ed. Georg Meyer (Stuttgart: Deutsche Verlagsanstalt, 1976), pp. 184–5.
9 Helmuth Groscurth, *Tagebücher eines Abwehroffiziers 1938–1940*, ed. Helmut Krausnick and Harold C. Deutsch (Stuttgart: Deutsche Verlags-Anstalt, 1970), p. 167.

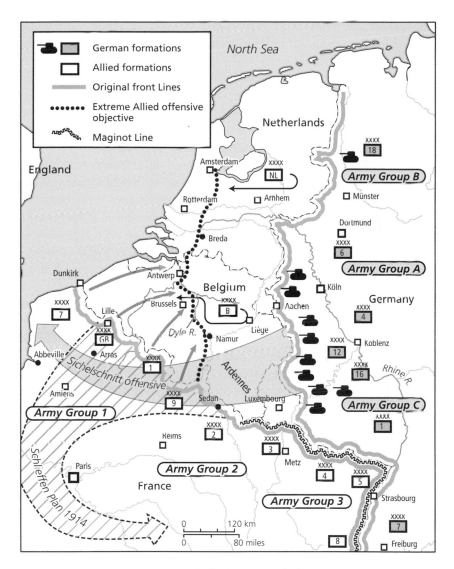

Legend:
- 🪖 ▨ German formations
- ▢ Allied formations
- ▬ Original front Lines
- ••••••• Extreme Allied offensive objective
- ∿∿∿ Maginot Line

North Sea

England

Netherlands

Amsterdam
XXXX NL

Rotterdam
Arnhem

XXXX 18

Army Group B

Münster

Dortmund
XXXX 6

Breda

Dunkirk
Antwerp
Belgium

Köln

Army Group A

Germany

Lille
Brussels
XXXX B
Aachen
XXXX 4

XXXX 7

XXXX GR
Dyle R.
Namur
Liège

Koblenz
XXXX 12

Abbeville
Arras
Sichelschnitt offensive
XXXX 1

XXXX 16
Rhine R.

Amiens
XXXX 9
Sedan
Luxembourg
Army Group C
XXXX 1

Army Group 1

Reims
XXXX 2

XXXX 3

Metz
XXXX 4
XXXX 5

Schlieffen Plan 1914

Paris

Army Group 2

France

Army Group 3
Strasbourg

XXXX 7

0   120 km
0   80 miles

XXXX 8
Freiburg

10.1 German and Allied operational plans, 1940

where the French would expect a German offensive. The consequence would be a frontal clash with the enemy's main forces. The greatest concentration of power on one side would confront its match on the other. The result would be, at best, a partial operational success. What was needed, however, was not a frontal push designed to drive the enemy back behind the Somme, but rather to get behind him, cut him off at the Somme and surround him. Only in this way could a decisive victory of strategic importance be achieved.

Thus Manstein proposed that the point of main effort be transferred from Army Group B on the right wing to Army Group A in the middle. Strong tank forces would attack there, where the Allies least expected it, through the wooded hills of the Ardennes. If the surprise attack worked and the Meuse River was crossed at Sedan, the German tank divisions could next push through the French rear areas to the coast, behind Allied front lines. Then, all of the Allied troops in northern France and Belgium would be surrounded in a giant pocket. This plan was later called the 'Sickle Cut' (*Sichelschnitt*).

Manstein's proposal was based on the following assessment of the enemy's position. The Allies assumed that the Germans would once again follow the overall schema of the Schlieffen Plan, and thus expected that the enemy's forces would be concentrated in Flanders. France was protected along the front line's right sector by the Maginot Line. In the centre, the Meuse River and Ardennes formed a double geographical barrier. Thus the Allies could concentrate their best units along the left wing. Yet, not wanting to let all of Belgium fall unprotected to the aggressors, they planned, in case of a German attack, to allow British and French intervention troops to move north as far as the Dyle Line between Antwerp and Dinant. Mobile units would even push forward as far as Holland. However, precisely through this forward movement, the Allies would fall into the trap, for they would unwittingly set in motion a 'revolving-door mechanism'. The further to the north they pressed, the easier it would be for the German tank divisions to push in behind them from the south.

Liddell Hart compared this situation to a bullfight. In this analogy, Army Group B attacking from the north represented the toreador's red cape. It was supposed to attract the Allied intervention forces, like a raging bull, to storm toward Belgium – right into the trap. For then tank divisions concentrated in Army Group A could thrust like a dagger into the bared right flank.

Yet the first victim of the 'Manstein Plan' was Major General Manstein himself. On account of this 'adventurous' idea of an Ardennes offensive, which in some ways recalled Hannibal's crossing of the Alps with war elephants, he was sent off to an unimportant post. Previously, however, he had succeeded in convincing Hitler of the feasibility of his plan. In the meantime, the Chief of the Army General Staff, General Halder, had also changed from a bitter opponent to a strong defender of the idea, having been favourably impressed by the results of several map exercises. Now he, too, advocated transferring the point of main effort to Army Group A and wanted the majority of the tanks to attack through the Ardennes in the direction of Sedan. On 24 February 1940, he presented the fourth, and definitive, operational plan for the deployment of the troops.

Alistair Horne described 'Sickle Cut' as 'one of the most inspired blueprints for victory that the military mind has ever conceived'.[10] But the plan was condemned by higher-ranking generals as 'crazy and foolhardy'. After Halder had adopted Manstein's basic idea, he suddenly found himself being named the 'gravedigger of the Panzer forces'. The new plan of operations was stigmatized by the trauma of the failed Schlieffen Plan. Once again, everything was to be wagered on one card, and a campaign to be decided by a single turning manoeuvre. The most vehement criticism came from General von Bock, Commander-in-Chief of Army Group B, who reproached Halder for playing *va banque* with Germany's fate:

> You will be creeping by 10 miles from the Maginot Line with the flank of your breakthrough and hope the French will watch inertly! You are cramming the mass of the tank units together into the sparse roads of the Ardennes mountain country, as if there were no such thing as air power! And you then hope to be able to lead an operation as far as the coast with an open southern flank 200 miles long, where stands the mass of the French Army!

This, Bock declared, was 'transcending the frontiers of reason'.[11]

General Halder had replaced Manstein with the outspokenly conservative Major General von Sodenstern, but this should have backfired on him, since the new Chief of Staff of Army Group A proved to be unwilling to go along with Halder's sudden change of mind. Yet Sodenstern would hold a key post in the upcoming offensive, and when the tank divisions foreseen for the 'Sickle Cut' drive to the Channel coast were finally concentrated in Army Group A, he devoted all of his energy to wrecking the plan, which he considered to be unworkable, or at least to weakening it decisively.

The breakthrough at Sedan

The 'Sickle Cut' operation was a leap into the unknown, a gamble, for which there were no precedents in the history of warfare. Added to this was the

---

10 Alistair Horne, *To Lose a Battle: France 1940* (London: Macmillan, 1969), p. 141.
11 Ibid., p. 140.

enormous time pressure. The feint in the north could succeed only if, by the fourth day, at the latest, the invaders had traversed the Ardennes and had crossed the Meuse. Otherwise, the Allies would realize in time that the German forces were concentrated not in Flanders, but near Sedan, and could call up sufficient reserves. Panzerkorps Guderian, which was to spearhead the attack, had to cover a stretch of 110 miles – through woods and defiles. Finally, it was necessary to get over the Meuse River, which was protected by the bunkers of the extended Maginot Line. Accordingly, Guderian, with his feel for catchy slogans, hammered home to his soldiers the line: 'In three days at the Meuse, on the fourth day over the Meuse!'

The precondition for all this was to stake everything on one card, namely the tank. This was to be the first-ever autonomous employment of the Panzer force on the operational level. Panzer Group Kleist included five tank divisions and three motorized infantry divisions. The novelty here was that this Panzer group – which would be far in advance of the infantry armies marching on foot – was supposed to carry out an operational attack all on its own. With a total of 1,222 tanks, General von Kleist disposed of half of the German Panzer force. Yet this Panzer group suffered under the burden of being viewed as provisional. If the surprise attack failed already at the Meuse, the formation would disintegrate within a few days.

General von Rundstedt, the Commander-in-Chief of Army Group A, suddenly came to doubt that the attack could succeed. Now the consequences of Manstein's transfer became very evident. Rundstedt, influenced by Sodenstern, decided on a bifurcated solution. Actually, the original intention was to have the Panzer divisions lead the attack in an initial echelon, which would have required the existence of a large network of roads. But Army Group A wanted, instead, to proceed along two tracks. The infantry divisions were to attack in parallel with the Panzer divisions, in order to achieve what the latter were not trusted to do, namely, get across the Meuse. The road system in the Ardennes, however, was not sufficient for such simultaneous activity. Consequently, this ambivalent decision provoked an immensely chaotic transport situation and – even without any action on the part of the enemy – might have almost completely ruined the *Sichelschnitt* Plan already in the Ardennes. Panzer Group Kleist disposed of over 41,140 motor vehicles, which makes it hard to understand for what reason this giant armada of vehicles was constrained to travel within a ravine-like corridor with only four routes of advance. The result was the biggest traffic jam ever seen in Europe, right up to the present time. On 12 May, the third day of the offensive, the columns were stalled for as much as 160 miles from the

Meuse, as far back as the Rhine River, spread out over French, Belgian, Luxembourg and German territory. This offered the Allied air forces a unique opportunity to destroy the German tank forces already in the Ardennes, where they sat trapped. Yet the German tanks remained almost completely undisturbed.

But now something occurred that even to Guderian – as he wrote in his memoirs – seemed 'almost a miracle'[12]: the breakthrough at Sedan. The attacker's inferiority to the defender in terms of artillery was very pronounced: as low as one to three. Moreover, a considerable portion of the German marching units remained stuck along the overcrowded roads in the Ardennes. This included even the munitions columns, so that only twelve rounds were available for each artillery piece. In this situation, Guderian was entirely dependent on the air force, 'the vertical artillery' of the Blitzkrieg. The most violent event in the campaign in the West was the massive bombardment carried out by the Luftwaffe on 13 May at Sedan. It was one of the biggest surprises of the entire war. The effect of the psychological shock surpassed even that of the use of poison gas or tanks in the First World War. Never again did the German air force carry out such a massive attack against such a narrow stretch of the front line. The bulk of three tank divisions attacked at a bend, two and a half miles wide, in the Meuse River at Sedan. Here, at the focal point, the Luftwaffe carried out 1,215 bomber and Stuka missions. What was decisive, however, was the first use of the 'rolling raid' (*rollender Einsatz*) method. The air attacks continued throughout the entire day, and the continuous bombardment had a devastating effect on the defenders' nerves.

While the tanks were still standing in the Ardennes forest, the infantry was able to get across the Meuse in the first assault. French resistance collapsed like a house of cards. The cause was one of the key events of the campaign in the West, the 'panic of Bulson'. It began when the report of a French artillery observer was falsely transmitted. Suddenly, the rumour arose that German tanks had crossed the Meuse and already stood in Bulson, right in front of the division command post. The rumour spread like wildfire, and in a few hours, the French units dissolved in a tumult of panic. When, later, a parliamentary commission investigated the causes of this mass psychosis, soldiers of every rank asserted that they had seen German tanks with their own eyes. In reality, however, the first German tanks did not cross the

---

12 Heinz Guderian, *Panzer Leader* (Cambridge, Mass.: Da Capo Press, 1996), p. 106.

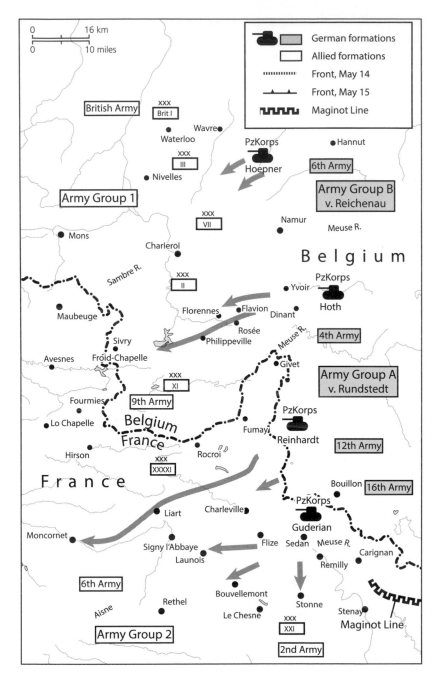

10.2 Collapse of the French front on the Meuse, May 1940

Meuse until twelve hours later. The French investigative report consequently spoke of *un phénomène d'hallucination collective*. Sedan was thus the site of one of the most curious tank victories of the Second World War. It happened again and again during the war that tanks caused the enemy to flee without firing a single shot – just through their appearance. Here, however, tanks caused the enemy to flee without having appeared at all!

Yet, carefully considered, this was not a one-time curiosity, but rather a model case which lays bare particularly clearly the secret of the Blitzkrieg's success. It caused a revolution in the image of war in comparison to the battles of attrition of the First World War. The principle of physical annihilation was replaced by the principle of psychological confusion. The indirect effect became more important than the direct one. Already in the First World War, German assault troops had been employed to sow panic and confusion. This shock effect was now intensified to a monstrous degree with the appearance of the tank and the aeroplane. The most penetrating psychological effect was achieved by the Stuka: during its dive-bombing missions it activated a siren, the so-called Trumpet of Jericho. The horrible screeching of that siren became the terror fanfare of the Blitzkrieg. Never again would the surprise effect of the new attack methods be as powerful as it was at Sedan, where, for the first time in military history, tanks and planes were employed in huge numbers on the operational level. Even the German leadership was surprised. Thus the breakthrough of Panzerkorps Guderian led to the breakthrough of Guderian's ideas.

Remarkable, too, were the minimal losses. During the Battle of Sedan on 13–14 May, Panzerkorps Guderian suffered 120 deaths and 400 injuries. These figures are nothing short of astonishing, when compared to the losses suffered in the – overall unsuccessful – breakthrough battles of the First World War. In 1916, the British lost 60,000 of the 140,000 attacking soldiers on the very first day of the Battle of the Somme; altogether, the Allies sacrificed 660,000 men in that battle and the Germans 500,000 men.

What was decisive at the Battle of Sedan, however, was not so much the breakthrough as the breaking *out* from the bridgehead. The army high command's operational plan was only a half-hearted imitation of Manstein's bold 'Sickle Cut' Plan. The logical breach point was at Sedan. Manstein and Guderian, who had advised Manstein as his tank expert, planned an operation 'at one stroke'. The Panzers should thrust forward from the Luxembourg border at the highest speed, going non-stop to the Channel coast. Otherwise, the Allied armies on the north wing would have sufficient time to withdraw southward from the Belgian trap and get behind the

Somme. The potential danger was that after the breakthrough at Sedan, the German Panzer divisions would be completely isolated, with their flanks exposed, as they pushed forward through the enemy's rear areas.

This breathtaking idea frightened Hitler and the higher-ranking generals. They planned, instead, a 'slow-motion Blitzkrieg'. Not daring to make the great leap – in one go – to the Channel coast, they wanted instead to remain for a time, literally, at the halfway point at Sedan. The armoured divisions should wait several days at the bridgehead, until the infantry divisions marching behind them had also crossed the Meuse and could secure the flanks. Guderian had always objected to this approach, since it would allow the Allies enough time to form a new defensive line at Sedan.

But then came the decisive moment of the campaign in the West. On 14 May, one day after the breakthrough at Sedan, General Guderian, in the euphoria of the success, tossed aside all the commands of Hitler and his superiors. On his own authority, he pushed forward with his Panzers from the bridgehead toward the west – in the direction of the Channel coast. He thereby caused an avalanche effect, for he drew the remaining armoured divisions along with him. The generals at the high command level temporarily lost control of the situation, so that the operation increasingly took on a dynamic of its own. Ultimately, it developed exactly in accord with Manstein's visionary prediction. Now the German armoured thrust, lacking the flanking protection of the infantry divisions, took on the shape of a narrow sickle. This is why, after the fact, it became known as the 'Sickle Cut' (*Sichelschnitt*), an expression first used by Winston Churchill.[13]

At the time, Sedan was linked in the thinking of German officers with another high point of the art of operational command. It was there that, in 1870, Moltke won the famous battle of encirclement which became known as the 'Cannae of the nineteenth century'. Here, of all places, was resurrected in May 1940 an idea that had perished in the fires of the First World War. The pendulum of military technology swung back again from an emphasis on firepower to an emphasis on movement. The British General J. F. C. Fuller, who may be considered one of the pioneers of Guderian's ideas, later characterized Operation 'Sickle Cut' as the Second Battle of Sedan. He drew a parallel between Moltke's encircling movement and Manstein's even bolder idea of encirclement. Whereas, in 1870, the meeting point of the two

---

13 Churchill spoke about a 'sickle cut' and an 'armoured scythe stroke'. Winston S. Churchill, *His Complete Speeches, 1897–1963*, vol. VI: 1935–1942, ed. Robert Rhodes James (New York and London: Bowker, 1974), p. 6226.

pincer armies was six miles away from Moltke's hilltop command post near Illy, the 1940 operation was a gigantic encircling movement, nearly 250 miles long, stretched out in the form of a sickle, from the Luxembourg border to the Channel coast. In 1870, the Germans managed to encircle an army of 120,000 men; in 1940, about 1.7 million Allied soldiers fell into the 'sickle cut' trap. Today, military historians all agree that the breakthrough at Sedan spelled certain defeat for the French. It was already evident by 14 May that the Allied troops were outmanoeuvred on account of their poor position and that they had lost the campaign. Yet even more significant is the turning point which the battle represents in modern military history. The positional warfare which derived from 1918 was abruptly replaced by the modern operational war of movement. And it was just this concept which stood behind the suggestive slogan 'Blitzkrieg'.

The advance to the Channel coast and the danger of the exposed flanks

From the very beginning, Major General Manstein had taken into account the weak spot in the 'Sickle Cut' Plan. After crossing the Meuse at Sedan, the German Panzer divisions were to turn westward toward the Channel coast. It was precisely at this moment, however, when the tanks had left the bridgehead, and the infantry divisions, marching on foot, had not yet caught up with them, that the French troops could launch a counter-attack against the Panzerkorps Guderian along its unprotected flanks. Accordingly, in addition to the main thrust to the west, Manstein had also ordered a secondary thrust toward the south, in order, by means of an 'aggressive defence', to push into the area where the French would be preparing their expected counter-attack and prevent them from carrying it out. Lying nine miles south of Sedan, near the village of Stonne, the heavily wooded hills of Mont-Dieu (*massif de Stonne*) rise up steeply and threateningly – an ideal springboard for a counter-attack. It was at Stonne that the battle culminated. The most fiercely contested location of the campaign in the West, the village changed hands seventeen times within a period of three days. Here, on 14 May, the French made their sole attempt at a counter-attack on the operational scale. It was to be carried out by two army corps moving from the south toward Sedan. They included Group Flavigny, with its total of 300 tanks, among which there were about seventy Type Char B 'monster tanks', which were virtually invulnerable to German anti-tank guns. If these 300 tanks had begun to roll, the German units would have had no chance to stop the avalanche of steel. It therefore had to be their goal to attack the avalanche before it started to move.

The failure of this potentially dangerous French counter-attack was already foreseeable, however, in the formulation of the attack orders. In conformity with a schema deriving from the First World War, the general in charge, Jean Flavigny, was supposed to: (1) seal off the enemy attack frontally via a defensive line along the *massif de Stonne*, and (2) attack in the direction of Sedan as soon as possible. But this was – in the case of a tank offensive – self-contradictory, since the defensive and offensive portions of the order excluded each other. Defence meant spreading the French units out in a linear pattern along a front line, while an attack required a narrow organization in depth and concentration at a single point.

On 14 May, at 6 a.m. – an hour before the first German tank crossed over the Meuse bridge – the French tank units had reached the southern edge of the *massif de Stonne*. Yet instead of immediately attacking the weak German bridgehead, they used up another ten hours for a maintenance halt in the assembly area. It was not until 5.30 p.m. that Group Flavigny was ready to attack.

Now came one of the most decisive moments of the campaign in the West. If there was ever a chance to stop the German tanks, it was in the late afternoon of 14 May. From the perspective of the Panzerkorps Guderian, this was the worst possible moment. The 1st and 2nd Panzer Divisions had already pushed on toward the west. They were no longer available to defend the bridgehead; and the 10th Panzer Division, which was still lagging behind, was not yet ready for deployment. Yet General Flavigny, one of the leading French experts on tanks, lost his nerve. He was completely frustrated by constant delays as his tank units tried to take up positions on the start line of the attack. Above all, however, the 'panic of Bulson' made itself felt indirectly: throughout the entire day, Flavigny had again and again witnessed catastrophic scenes of terrified French soldiers streaming to the rear, with tales of hundreds, even thousands, of attacking German tanks. Thus, at the last minute, he rescinded the attack order.

Now he began to consider the defensive portion of his task and divided his tanks linearly along a twelve-mile stretch, in the course of which all the roads and passages were closed by so-called 'corks'. Each cork consisted of one heavy and two light tanks. When, on the following day, he wanted to carry out his attack, it proved to have been easier to spread the tanks out than to bring them back together. Furthermore, in the meantime, German units had penetrated the French assembly area. Since the newly arrived

10th Panzer Division was too weak to be employed for defence, General Guderian decided to let it attack. Most importantly, the French forces were unable to gain permanent control of Stonne. General Flavigny now definitively cancelled his attack order. Thus the only French attempt at a counter-attack on the operational level had failed before it had begun.

During the push toward the Channel coast, two conflicts were playing out simultaneously: one on the battlefield and the other among the German generals. The traditionalists still showed themselves to be caught up in linear thinking. Their instinctive anxiety concerning gaps or exposed flanks derived from a time when there were no tanks. They found dizzying the idea of allowing the armoured divisions to push fully unprotected through the enemy's rear areas. Added to this was the breathtaking tempo of the attack. For the progressives, on the other hand, above all Guderian, it could not go fast enough. The latter explained that any delay meant strengthening the opponent. He had no anxiety concerning exposed flanks, seeing their best protection as lying in the enemy's confusion.

The conflict within the German high command culminated in the temporary replacement of Guderian by Kleist on 17 May at Montcornet (forty miles west of Sedan). Guderian's belief in the rightness of his ideas led him consistently to disregard the orders of his conservative-minded superiors. This time, however, he had gone too far, for he dared at Montcornet to attack beyond the line where the army group had ordered a halt. Yet on the same day he was restored to his command by a directive from higher up.

At just this moment, another German tank general undertook a forward thrust, one which brought his division the French nickname *la division phantôme* (the ghost division). This was Brigadier General Rommel, the commander of the 7th Panzer Division. The degree to which he took matters into his own hands on the night of 16–17 May far exceeded anything that other tank generals had allowed themselves during this campaign. By evening, his division had reached the extended Maginot Line at the French-Belgian border. Now he dared to do something no one had ever attempted: a frontal attack with tanks, off the march, against a fortified defensive line – and at night! The defenders were so surprised that the breakthrough succeeded with the very first assault. Rommel decided to exploit the enemy's confusion and pushed on further. In this case, a chance event came to his aid. The French 5th (motorized) Infantry Division had bivouacked for the night on the road to Avesnes, with their vehicles lined up along the road. Rommel's tanks drove right through their midst, cannon blazing on both sides. In the shortest imaginable time, the French division dissolved in a wave of fleeing soldiers. They were literally rolled over in their sleep. Yet Rommel's forward thrust that night was not to be stopped. He did not halt until Le Cateau, where his fuel finally ran out. The success of this night-time tank attack over a distance of thirty miles was overwhelming. Right at the start, two of the enemies' operative lines had been penetrated within a period of a few hours: the extended Maginot Line and the Sambre–Oise Line. On that night, the French II Army Corps was largely destroyed or, in certain instances, simply melted away.

Yet in the grey light of dawn, Rommel saw that during his impetuous attack he was followed only by the advance detachment, a strengthened tank regiment. The bulk of the division still stood on Belgian territory and had given itself a night's rest. Radio contact had been lost; no one knew where General Rommel was. Thus his Panzer division had become the 'ghost division' not just for the enemy, but for his own headquarters. That night, Rommel and his tanks disappeared without a trace. The army high command was in a state of complete agitation. Even Hitler spent a sleepless night. Still, it was impossible to bring such a successful general before a court martial. Instead, Rommel received the Knight's Cross of the Iron Cross (*Ritterkreuz*) award.

Only a few generals realized as quickly as Rommel what unexpected possibilities were presented by this new weapon, the tank, if only one employed it decisively enough. To the contrary, the dizzying success of the Panzer divisions felt eerie to some of the higher-ranking generals. They did not encourage the efforts of these divisions; they even hindered them. Hitler himself now gave way to panic. General Halder noted in his diary for 17 May: 'An unpleasant day. The Führer is terribly nervous. Frightened by his own success, he is afraid to take any chances and so he would rather pull the reins on us. Puts forward the excuse that it is all because of his concern for the left flank!'[14] On the following day, Halder wrote: 'The Führer unaccountably keeps worrying about the south flank. He rages and screams that we are on the best way to ruin the whole campaign and that we are leading up to a defeat.'[15] Although German reconnaissance revealed no evidence at all of an Allied counter-attack, Hitler was a captive of the clearly deluded belief in an imaginary 'danger from the south'. He wanted to avoid a 'second miracle at the Marne'.

This phase of activity was thus marked by a complete reversal in the respective attitudes of these two utterly opposed personalities. Hitler, who,

---

14 Franz Halder, *The Halder War Diary, 1939–1942*, ed. Charles Burdick and Hans-Adolf Jacobsen (Novato, Calif.: Presidio Press, 1988), p. 302.
15 Ibid.

being a gambler by nature, had taken nearly criminal risks in his adventurous foreign policy, was suddenly filled with such anxiety by his own daring that he came close to suffering a nervous breakdown. In contrast, Halder, who before the campaign was derided for being timid, was suddenly bursting with self-assurance and confidence in victory. On 16 May, he wrote in his diary, 'Our breakthrough wedge is developing in a positively classical manner'.[16]

The danger on the south flank which held Hitler so transfixed did not exist at all. This is also clear from Winston Churchill's memoirs. Alarmed by the breakthrough of the German tanks at Sedan, the British Prime Minister flew to Paris. There, on 16 May, the French Supreme Commander, General Gamelin, presented him with a very sombre report on the situation, after which Churchill asked him where the operational reserve was. General Gamelin's answer was shattering, consisting of a single word: *Aucune* – it no longer existed. The Allied General Staffs were beginning to be gripped by an end-of-the-world feeling. General Ironside, the British Chief of the Army General Staff, wrote in his diary on 17 May: 'Right now, it looks like the biggest military catastrophe in history.'[17]

The Allies, in conceiving of the tempo of events, were still thinking in terms of their experience in the First World War, and they could not manage to gather their forces for an operational counter-attack. Once it was clear that the French army high command was not going to undertake any serious counter-measures, Ironside seized the initiative. The German tanks, meanwhile, had pushed ahead so quickly that a gap had opened between them and the infantry armies marching behind them. This was the right moment for an Allied pincer movement at Arras against the corridor, which was only twenty-five miles wide. The French army, however, was not in a position to concentrate its forces quickly enough at the south flank of the corridor. Thus, on 21 May, the British attacked from the north, essentially alone. But the whole action amounted to no more than an uncoordinated attack employing eighty-eight tanks, and after an advance of only a few miles, it was stopped by the guns of Rommel's 7th Panzer Division. On that same day, Panzerkorps Guderian reached the Channel coast and then turned northward along the coast in order to cut the Allies off from the Channel ports.

16 Ibid., p. 297.
17 Sir Edmund Ironside, *The Ironside Diaries, 1937–1940*, ed. Roderick Macleod and Denis Kelly (London: Constable, 1962), p. 317.

The halt order at Dunkirk

On 24 May, the German troops were within nine miles of Dunkirk, the sole Channel port east of the Somme that was still in Allied hands. No significant forces remained any longer between the German tanks and Dunkirk. It would only be a matter of a few hours and then the last escape route would be closed, and about one million British, French and Belgian soldiers would be trapped. The Allied forces were still locked in battle – at least sixty miles from Dunkirk – with the divisions of Army Group B, and they had no chance at all of reacting to the deadly threat behind them. Rather, they were in danger of being pulverized, of falling victim to the hammer-and-anvil principle. In accordance with General Halder's plan, Army Group B advancing from the northeast formed the anvil. It was to tie down the Allies frontally, while the Panzer divisions of Army Group A coming from the south would swing the hammer from behind them. At this point there occurred one of the strangest episodes in modern military history, 'the miracle of Dunkirk'. The Allied soldiers looked on in astonished disbelief as the German tanks suddenly stopped, seemingly halted by a magician's hand.

The moment of salvation for the Allies was, once again, owing to a controversy between the German 'progressives' and 'traditionalists'. On 23 May, the cautious Commander-in-Chief of Army Group A, General Rundstedt, issued a halt order (limited to twenty-four hours) for the tanks for the following day, in order to allow the infantry divisions to close ranks. General Brauchitsch, Commander-in-Chief of the Army, and Chief of the Army General Staff Halder, however, wanted to push forward to Dunkirk immediately. Worn down by Rundstedt's continual attempts to slow the tempo of the operation, the two senior generals removed him from command of the tank divisions – against Hitler's wishes and without his knowledge. When the latter arrived at the headquarters of Army Group A on 24 May, he found Rundstedt, his trusted man, virtually disempowered. Hitler flew into a rage and removed control of the Panzer divisions from Brauchitsch and Halder. At the same time, he confirmed Rundstedt's halt order. It was now Rundstedt who would decide when the tank divisions should continue their advance. On the afternoon of 24 May, General von Brauchitsch was summoned to meet with Hitler. Since his arguments appeared to be overwhelming, he was fully convinced that he could persuade the Führer to immediately rescind the halt order. But Hitler was completely uninterested in his arguments, and instead accused him vehemently of having acted without authority. As for the halt order, he

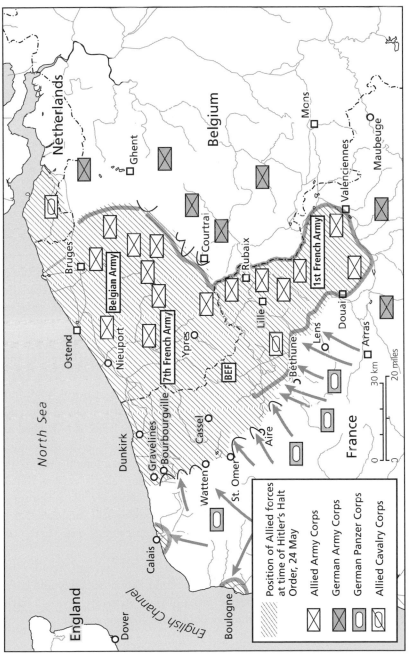

10.3 Dunkirk

mockingly told him to see Rundstedt. A greater humiliation of the top leadership of the German army can scarcely be imagined. Generals Brauchitsch and Halder now had to come before their subordinate Rundstedt as suppliants in order to get him to continue the attack. But Rundstedt was deeply insulted and rejected their request.

During the Second World War, no other order provoked such passionate protest in the German army as Hitler's halt order at Dunkirk. Reporting on the reactions of some of the leading generals, Colonel Schmundt, Hitler's Chief Adjutant wrote: 'They resembled a pack of hunting dogs that are halted at a dead stop, directly in front of the game, and that see their quarry escape.'[18] Even the simple recruits were bewildered. From Gravelines on the coast as far as Arras, the German tanks stood lined up in rows as in a parade, and their crews had to look on powerlessly as, all day long, Allied units marched by them in the direction of Dunkirk.

Not until the morning of 26 May did Rundsted give in to the heavy pressure from his subordinate generals and turn to Hitler. The latter lifted the halt order at 1.30 p.m., but it was not until 27 May at 8 a.m. that the troops had taken up their previous attack formation and were able to continue the offensive. This meant that the armoured divisions had been forced to remain stuck in place for three days and eight hours. During this time, however, the situation had changed fundamentally in favour of the Allies. On 24 May, a few German Panzer companies would have been sufficient to take the virtually undefended Dunkirk in a surprise raid, but by now the Allies had massed several divisions before this Channel port and formed a thin defensive position. Moreover, numerous units had marched in from their inland positions to the safety of the coast, where, in the meantime, an evacuation fleet had been assembled. It was not until 4 June that Dunkirk fell to the Germans. As a result of the halt order, about 370,000 Allied soldiers, including almost the entire British Expeditionary Force, escaped the trap and were evacuated by sea. In short, Hitler had diminished the strategic victory Manstein had sought to a merely operational one. There was no 'Cannae' at the Channel coast.

Hitler's halt order was one of the most fateful wrong decisions of the Second World War. Without his intervention, Great Britain would have experienced the greatest catastrophe in its history. Actually, it would have been a double catastrophe. Britain would have lost almost the whole of

---

18 Jacques Benoist-Méchin, *Der Himmel stürzt ein: Frankreichs Tragödie 1940* (Düsseldorf: Droste Verlag, 1958), p. 146.

its professional army. Beyond that, universal military service had only very recently been introduced. Who could have trained the recruits if nearly all the army's experienced soldiers and officers had been taken prisoner at Dunkirk? In the estimation of British historians, this would surely have meant the end of Churchill's government, and a new government could hardly have spurned political negotiations. The Anglophile Hitler had always dreamed of an alliance with the 'Germanic' naval power England, and would have been ready to offer it a ceasefire on generous terms. What the course of world history would have been if Germany could have concentrated all its power against the Soviet Union is a dreadful question to contemplate.

Ever since that time, historians have tried to explain what Hitler's motive was for the halt order, but all of the proposed answers fail to stand up to close examination. For example, the supposed softening of the terrain around Dunkirk can hardly have been the reason, since the rain which softened the ground did not begin to fall until after the halt order. The most absurd motive, however, is the one that Hitler himself gave. At that moment, compelled to justify himself, he sought to anticipate the expected criticism by asserting that he intentionally let the English escape: 'He simply could not have allowed himself to wipe out an army of the "good consanguineous English race"'.[19] Here he was referring to their common Germanic roots; for ultimately the Anglo-Saxons came from Germany. The halt order was thus supposedly a generous gesture to spare the English a shameful defeat and to make them willing to negotiate. Actually, this response was a way of glossing over his mistake. Indeed, during the evacuation he wanted to make use of specially fused anti-aircraft shells to bring about a bloodbath of the (consanguineous) Englishmen who were jammed together on the beach. Moreover, no German politician could have been so stupid as to intentionally allow the British Army to escape, since it represented a priceless bargaining chip for peace negotiations.

The real motive for Hitler's brutal intervention was a power struggle between himself and the army high command, since he suddenly found himself marginalized as military leader. The question at issue was who should have the final say regarding operational decisions: the civilian Hitler or the generals of the army high command? Thus, for the dictator, it was not a matter of tactical, strategic or political arguments, but rather a purely personal claim to power, namely the Führer principle (*Führer-Prinzip*). That is

---

19 Otto Abetz, *Das offene Problem* (Cologne: Greven Verlag, 1951), p. 129.

why he so vigorously asserted his authority over Generals Brauchitsch and Halder. Hitler's army military aide, Major Engel, was witness to this confrontation. He later revealed that Hitler's decision 'had nothing whatsoever to do with objective arguments but [was] merely intended to let the Commander-in-Chief of the Army know that he [Hitler] was in command and nobody else.'[20] To this extent, Hitler was in fact the 'victor of Dunkirk' – but at what cost! The strategic collateral damage he caused with respect to his own war plans was considerable. As a result of his intervention, the potential effects of the 'miracle of Sedan' were nullified by the 'miracle of Dunkirk'.

In fact, Dunkirk was a decisive turning point in the Second World War, not only because of Britain's successful evacuation operation, which enabled it to pursue the war, but also because of the power shift within Germany's military leadership. The German General Staff constituted a superb military brain. Had Hitler made proper use of this instrument of the art of operational leadership, it would have been a dangerous weapon as he pursued his plans for further conquest. Since he considered himself a military genius, however, he basically viewed the generals who surrounded him as merely setting the stage for decisions he made on his own. When the French request for a ceasefire arrived at Hitler's command post on 17 June, General Keitel called the Führer 'the greatest warlord [*Feldherr*] of all time'. At that moment, Hitler definitively succumbed to the delusion that he was a new Caesar. A frightful dilettante draped himself in a field commander's mantel far too large for him, and ultimately led his still victorious army into catastrophe.

Case Red: only an epilogue

In accord with Manstein's conception, the campaign was divided into two successive major operations. First, Case Yellow (*Fall Gelb*) aimed at the encirclement of the Allied northern wing along the Channel coast. Then, in Case Red (*Fall Rot*), the Allied southern wing, which was spread out along the Maginot Line, was to be encircled. Yet, after Dunkirk, the campaign was already decided, and thus Case Red turned out to be only an epilogue. The French soldiers displayed more fighting spirit than they did during May at the Meuse, where many had succumbed to a kind of shock, and the French army had changed its tactics in the meantime. Instead of a linear defence, they adopted an echeloned defence in depth. Yet the French troops still

---

20 Hans Meier-Welcker, 'Der Entschluss zum Anhalten der deutschen Panzertruppen in Flandern 1940', *Vierteljahrshefte für Zeitgeschichte* 2 (1954), 289.

remaining had no chance of changing the outcome; for the Allies, superiority in forces at the beginning of the campaign had turned into its opposite.

Now, after a twenty-six-year delay, came the successful execution of the Schlieffen Plan. Guderian, whose Panzer corps had meanwhile been enlarged to a Panzer group, pushed out of the Sedan area behind the Maginot Line and up the Swiss border. In the meantime, the Seventh Army had crossed the Rhine at Breisach and broken through the Maginot Line. Attacking through southern Alsace, on 19 June it joined up with Panzer Group Guderian at Belfort. This move created a gigantic pocket, in which three French armies were trapped. Unlike at Dunkirk, this time there was a complete 'Cannae', in which about 500,000 French soldiers were taken prisoner. Moreover, the Maginot Line had been outmanoeuvred within a few days.

Simultaneously, the newly formed Panzer Group Kleist pushed far south into the French rear areas. On this occasion, Rommel's 7th Panzer Division set a record when, on the single day of 17 June, it advanced 150 miles without any contact on either side. Three days earlier, on 14 June, German troops had marched into Paris. The loss of the capital, which was undefended, was a major psychological blow to the French. On 22 June, the armistice was signed in the Forest of Compiègne. Hitler had very deliberately chosen the site of the armistice agreement of 11 November 1918. The signing ceremony took place in the same railway salon car in which the German negotiators of that time had been obliged to affix their signatures. This spelled the end of the French Third Republic, which had been created in 1870 as a consequence of the defeat at Sedan. Soon afterwards, Marshall Pétain established an authoritarian regime at Vichy, which was effectively under German control.

Conclusion

Upon closer examination, the Polish campaign of 1939 turns out not to have been a Blitzkrieg. Instead, it conformed to the model of classic German military strategy. In contrast, the 1940 campaign in the West may be considered the Blitzkrieg par excellence. In reality, however, it was not at all planned as such. Hitler was counting, instead, on a years-long struggle, as in the First World War. Above all, the Blitzkrieg of 1940 had no connection whatsoever with the 'Blitzkrieg strategy' that has been ascribed to Hitler. According to that notion, the goal of world domination was no longer to be reached by making a single, all-out effort, as in the First World War, but rather stepwise, through a number of short Blitzkriegs. Yet up to this point, Hitler had planned no war against the Western powers – and certainly no

Blitzkrieg; as a result of the Treaty of Versailles, the Wehrmacht was still at the stage of rebuilding itself. Instead, it was Great Britain and France who declared war on Hitler, following Germany's march into Poland. Thus, through his failed *va banque* politics, he had manoeuvred the German Reich into a total impasse. Since, in the long run, time worked against Germany, the only real chance it had to escape was by pushing forward, to wager everything on one card and to catch the enemy off-guard via a surprise attack.

It was precisely this risky undertaking, however, that frightened the German leadership, which was still traumatized by the failure of the Schlieffen Plan in the First World War. As Clausewitz explains, men do 'not [act] reasonably during big crises, since, driven to utter despair, they see no salvation other than risking a daring leap'.[21] This 'daring leap' over the Meuse River straight to the Channel coast was Manstein's 'Sickle Cut'. A desperate move of this kind was not something the Allied generals had reckoned with. They observed this breathtaking development with the same bewilderment as the irresolute Hitler, who was beginning to lose control over an operation that was becoming increasingly independent. Moreover, he felt relegated to the status of an extra by the generals, whose self-confidence was becoming more and more evident. In response, he allowed himself to be drawn into making an error through his intervention at Dunkirk, which ultimately nullified the strategic success they had all been seeking.

The campaign in the West was thus not a planned campaign of conquest. Instead, it was an operational act of despair to get out of a desperate strategic situation. The so-called 'Blitzkrieg concept' (*Blitzkrieg-Denken*) developed only *after* the campaign in the West. It was not the cause, but the consequence of the victory. What was successful in May 1940, to the surprise of everyone, was then made to serve as the 'secret of victory' for the realization of Hitler's visions of conquest.

---

21 Carl von Clausewitz, 'Aufzeichnungen aus den Jahren 1803 bis 1809', in Hans Rothfels, *Carl von Clausewitz, Politik und Krieg. Eine ideengeschichtliche Studie* (Berlin: F. Dümmler, 1920), p. 212.

11

The war in the West, 1939–1940

The Battle of Britain?

JOHN FERRIS AND EVAN MAWDSLEY

The victories of the Wehrmacht in May–June 1940 transformed the Second World War. France fell, Germany mastered Western Europe, and Italy entered the war. The British Empire fought on.

The summer of 1940 is hallowed in the memory of the English-speaking peoples. The BEF returned, alive but beaten, leaving its kit behind. On 4 June, Winston Churchill, a month in office as Prime Minister, promised resistance, 'if necessary for years, if necessary alone': '[W]e shall defend our island, whatever the cost may be, we shall fight on the beaches, we shall fight on the landing grounds, we shall fight in the fields and in the streets, we shall fight in the hills; we shall never surrender'. After Paris surrendered on 14 June, Churchill declared the end of the 'Battle of France' and the start of a 'Battle of Britain', which would decide the fate of civilization. He ended with an admonition: Britons should act so that if their empire lasted a thousand years, men still would say, 'This was their finest hour'.[1] On 22 August, as the air assault began, Churchill made his third great speech of that summer, emphasizing how British airmen were 'turning the tide of the world war': 'Never in the field of human conflict was so much owed by so many to so few'.[2] His rhetoric shaped history, and misshapes our view of what it was.

The fall of France started a cascade. The clash between British and German forces and strategies determined its direction. These events are associated with the 'Battle of Britain', but that matter is less simple than is often

---

1 http://hansard.millbanksystems.com/commons/1940/jun/04/war-situation; http://hansard.millbanksystems.com/commons/1940/jun/18/war-situation – accessed 6 October 2014.

2 http://hansard.millbanksystems.com/commons/1940/aug/20/war-situation – accessed 6 October 2014.

assumed.[3] It is surrounded by myths stemming from wartime propaganda, aimed to boost morale at home and to gain support abroad, and also from post-war ideas about British inefficiency, and a tendency to explain success by stereotype. The Battle of Britain is portrayed as a near-run thing, won by character and brains, wizard boffins, top kit, upper-class pilots, loyal lower ranks and a stubborn people trusting their superiors, inspired by charismatic leadership. Victory had more boring causes. Germany fought from its weaknesses at sea and in the air. Britain fought to its strengths, the power and system of Fighter Command and the Royal Navy. Both forces were prepared for the threat. Only one was tested; neither failed. Nor did German leaders intend to annihilate England, and lose. The Luftwaffe's commanders believed they could crush Britain, but generals and admirals were less optimistic. No German leader thought that amphibious assault could beat Britain. Many doubted that air power could do so. Hitler ordered attack simply to ensure that he did not miss an easy chance to coerce Britain into making peace overtures and accepting his diplomatic terms, becoming dependent on the Reich, and ultimately a satellite. He stopped once he realized that such an aim was impossible.

SEALION, sea power and German strategy

Hitler plunged into war with little planning. When it began, he declared Britain the 'leading enemy power', which must be beaten for Germany to win. Initially, German leaders gave little thought to how to do so, beyond destroying Britain's economy and alliances. In November 1939, for example, Hitler ordered the German armed forces high command (*Oberkommando der Wehrmacht* – OKW) to prepare 'extensive operations against the economic foundations upon which England rests', industry, utilities and ports. Only during their triumph in France, as unexpected for Germans as anyone else, did they consider this problem. Hitler increasingly wanted to punish Britain, for past transgressions and future considerations. In late May, he demanded a 'full-scale' and rapid air offensive against Britain. A 'devastating retaliatory attack' should avenge its attacks on the Ruhr. The Luftwaffe must smash a

---

3 For the classic views, cf. Derek Wood and Derek Dempster, *The Narrow Margin: The Battle of Britain and the Rise of Airpower, 1930–1940* (London: Hutchinson, 1961), which was a main source for the film, *The Battle of Britain* (1969); and Robert Wright, *Dowding and the Battle of Britain* (London: Macdonald, 1969).

British evacuation from Dunkirk, and prepare 'to attack the English home-land in the fullest manner'.[4]

On 30 June, when victory over France was sure, Hitler received a proposal about how to beat Britain, from his chief advisor in the OKW, General Jodl. Although Jodl combined the efforts of the three Wehrmacht services, his emphasis was on shattering Britain's air force and economy. The purpose of a landing (*Landung*) by the army was not to defeat Britain militarily. Instead, in September 1940, thirty German divisions would deliver the *coup de grâce* (*Todesstoss*) to a Britain that the Luftwaffe and the Kriegsmarine had already rendered economically paralysed and defenceless by air and sea attack. Tentative preparations on these lines were ordered by the OKW on 2 July, and in Hitler's Directive No. 16 of 16 July. The latter document used the codename SEELÖWE (SEALION) and set an end-date for preparations of mid-August.[5]

The half-baked preparations that followed, with army and navy planners pursuing rival concepts and the Luftwaffe supporting neither, demonstrate that these services, intellectually and materially, could not conduct combined operations on the scale required. None of them supported amphibious assault as the primary means to defeat Britain. (A German division had been trapped for two months in Narvik during the Norwegian campaign, showing the risks of such operations.) Above all, the Kriegsmarine opposed the idea, because British superiority was overwhelming. 'As far as the Navy is concerned', Admiral Raeder wrote in September 1939, 'obviously it is in no way very adequately equipped for the great struggle with Great Britain'. Its 'surface forces...are so inferior in number and strength to those of the British Fleet that...they can do no more than show that they know how to die gallantly'.[6] So they did off Norway in April 1940, when most German surface warships were sunk or crippled. When the German navy considered SEALION, it had one heavy cruiser, two light cruisers and four destroyers ready for war. In home waters, Britain had five capital ships, an aircraft

4 Klaus A. Maier, 'The Operational Air War until the Battle of Britain', in *Germany and the Second World War*, vol. II: *Germany's Initial Conquests in Europe* (10 vols., Oxford: Clarendon Press, 1991), pp. 338–9.

5 Karl Klee (ed.), *Dokumente zum Unternehmen Seelöwe: Die geplante deutche Landung in England 1940* (Göttingen: Musterschmidt, 1959), pp. 298–9, 301–2; Walter Warlimont, *Inside Hitler's Headquarters 1939–45* (London: Weidenfeld & Nicolson, 1962), p. 107; W. Hubatsch (ed.), *Hitlers Weisungen für die Kriegführung 1939–1945: Dokumente des Oberkommandos der Wehrmacht* (Frankfurt: Bernard and Graefe, 1962), pp. 61–5.

6 *Kriegstagebuch der Seekriegsleitung 1939–1945*, Teil A, Bd. 1 (Bonn: E. S. Mittler, 1988), pp. 15-E to 17-E.

carrier, eleven cruisers and eighty destroyers; and in the Mediterranean, another seven capital ships, two carriers, seven cruisers and thirty destroyers.[7] Raeder made this disparity of strength plain to Hitler, as well as his professional reservations about the feasibility of SEALION.

Jodl's operational outline of 12 July stressed that *'England is in possession of command of the sea'* (his emphasis). Thus the only possible landing area was the eastern part of the Channel coast (Kent, Sussex and Hampshire), where the Luftwaffe could strike British warships and the approach route was shortest. Flanking positions would block the Royal Navy: minefields and guns at the Dover Strait in the east, and minefields in the Cherbourg–Portland narrows in the west. Since a fleet of invasion barges had to be assembled in the French Channel ports, operational surprise was impossible – unlike the invasion of Norway; a bad portent.[8]

Although SEALION is often discussed as a great 'might have been', and linked to the German air assault, it existed fitfully for just a few weeks in the heads of German generals and admirals, and possibly in that of the Führer. The idea was abandoned long before the German air campaign began in August; invasion and air assault were distinct matters, linked only by ideas about and preparations for *Todesstoss*. On 31 July, in a conference at the Berghof, Hitler rehearsed the technical factors against invasion which Raeder had emphasized, regarding preparations for the landing and the weather. 'Our small navy is 15 per cent [the size] of the enemy, the number of destroyers is 8 per cent that of the enemy, the number of motor torpedo boat equally is 10–12 per cent that of the enemy'. Interestingly, he did not emphasize the RAF as an impediment. SEALION was impossible, Hitler said, but Britain was in a hopeless situation – 'the outcome of the war had already been decided', but England was 'not aware of it' yet – and must soon follow France to the peace table. He told his military advisors that he had decided to attack the USSR, which indirectly would also force Britain out of the war, by depriving it of any hope for allies. Hitler's decision to attack the Soviet Union had several long-term

---

7 Bernard Stegemann, 'Operation Weserübung', in *Germany and the Second World War*, vol. ii, p. 218; Basil Collier, *The Defence of the United Kingdom* (London: HMSO, 1957), p. 440; Correlli Barnett, *Engage the Enemy More Closely: The Royal Navy in the Second World War* (London: Hodder & Stoughton, 1991), pp. 214, 228–9; I. S. O. Playfair, *The Mediterranean and Middle East, vol. i: Early Successes against Italy* (London: HMSO, 1954), p. 156.

8 Klee (ed.), *Dokumente*, pp. 305–9.

causes, ideological and geopolitical, but an immediate factor was the impracticability of a cross-Channel invasion.[9]

Physical preparations for SEALION progressed, especially the assembly of a fleet of improvised landing craft. By the middle of September, sufficient barges were assembled to physically transport ten divisions across the English Channel,[10] but there were no combined exercises or interest from senior commanders. Not unnaturally, British authorities took this threat seriously until October 1940 – indeed, until 1942 – but their fears proved overstated.[11] This German effort built a cheap and useful bluff against Britain, which paid strategic dividends for eighteen months, and also an immediate means to deliver a *Todesstoss*, if the Luftwaffe was able to bleed the beast.

Hitler abandoned SEALION and turned to Operation BARBAROSSA against Russia once he saw the difficulties of an amphibious assault, and considered its consequences. He thought that Britons were dangerous, especially with their backs to the wall; but the Soviets, in contrast, could be crushed easily – one kick and the rotten structure would collapse. Ideology, racism and victory disease – dangerous traits shared with his generals – distorted these views. Hitler, however, correctly calculated that defeat in SEALION would wreck his power and prestige; to beat Britain would cost much time and resources, while everyone else picked up the pieces of its empire, and the USSR and the United States continued to sabotage his strategy. Hitler did not want to destroy Britain, nor even to gamble against it, if he could avoid the need. He had mastered Western Europe by placing all his chips, *va banque*, because no lesser gamble could wreck French power on the Continent. That done, destroying Britain seemed a luxury, or an error. As the Italian

---

9 Franz Halder, *Kriegstagebuch: Tägliche Aufzeichnungen des Chefs des Generalstabes des Heeres, 1939–1942* (3 vols., Stuttgart: Kohlhammer, 1965), vol. II, pp. 48–9; Gerhard Wagner (ed.), *Lagevorträge der Oberbefehlshabers der Kriegsmarine vor Hitler, 1939–1945* (Munich: Lehman, 1972), pp. 126–8. This important meeting is discussed in Walter Ansel, *Hitler Confronts England* (Durham, NC: Duke University Press, 1960), pp. 164, 182–9.

10 Ronald Wheatley, *Operation Sea Lion: German Plans Made by the German High Command under Adolf Hitler for the Invasion of England, 1939–1942* (Oxford University Press, 1958), the earliest thorough study of German preparations, is based on work for the British official histories. Wheatley's suggestion that this effort shows that Hitler was 'serious' (p. vii) cannot be sustained. For later studies of low-level preparations, see Egbert Kieser, *Hitler on the Doorstep: Operation 'Sea Lion': The German Plan to Invade Britain, 1940* (London: Arms and Armour, 1997), and Peter Schenk, *The Invasion of England 1940: The Planning of Operation Sealion* (London: Conway, 1990), both translations of German works.

11 On British fears, see Lord Alanbrooke, *War Diaries, 1939–1945* (London: Weidenfeld & Nicolson, 2001), pp. 105–13.

Foreign Minister, Count Ciano, said, 'Hitler is now like the gambler who, having made a big win, would like to leave the table, risking nothing more'.[12] Hitler turned toward what he thought was a sure bet – BARBAROSSA. He did not understand the odds.

In the meantime, he could not ignore Britain, nor the chance to make it surrender or negotiate on the cheap: he was willing to place one large but limited bet that air power could achieve that end. He saw bombing as a powerful tool against Britain, distinct from the novel idea of invasion. Right after cancelling SEALION, on 1 August Hitler's Directive No. 17 ordered an air assault on Britain, to crush the RAF.[13] That objective was more ambitious than he knew.

Strategic air defence

During the interwar years, Britain built on the strategic air defence system, characterized by advanced command, control, communications and intelligence (C3I), which it had erected against German bombers between 1915 and 1918. Britain worked harder at strategic air defence than any other country, because it thought the task vital, yet difficult. The field was the second largest part of the RAF, including 20 per cent of its squadrons, steadily expanding in aircraft and pilots. They aimed to direct concentrations of aircraft at lightning speed, in real time, against fast, high-flying formations. Uniquely close links between scientists, engineers and officers produced the first integrated C3I system on earth. Fighter Command, the earliest force to adopt radio-telephones, teletypes, radar and operational research, led the world in the application of science to warfare. When radar was first tested in 1935, RAF officers immediately knew how to integrate it into air defence at a national level. No other military institution between the wars handled any matter of equal complexity better, or more consistently.[14] Between 1937 and 1940, the system was upgraded to incorporate the latest developments in aviation, communication and intelligence, led by a commander experienced in organization and technology, Hugh Dowding. Like the architect of Panzer divisions, Heinz Guderian, Dowding's background in commanding radio units

12 Galeazzo Ciano, *Diary, 1937–1943* (London: Phoenix, 2002), p. 363.
13 Hubatsch (ed.), *Weisungen*, pp. 65–7.
14 John Ferris, 'Achieving Air Ascendancy: Challenge and Response in British Air Defence, 1915–1940', in Sebastian Cox and Peter Grey (eds.), *Air Power History, Turning Points from Kitty Hawk to Kosovo* (Portland, Oreg.: Frank Cass, 2002), pp. 21–50.

helped him to create a command system that was cybernetic and net-centric, long before these terms were coined.

Many technical matters were changing at one time, and each had to be tested in isolation rather than in context. The whole picture remained unclear, while opportunities to prove the system and to acquire accurate data were rare. The process was slowed by delays in procuring and integrating Spitfires and radar. This recalibration was not complete until 1941, and the system had flaws in 1940. It was designed to handle a bad case, but not the worst one – against an enemy 300 per cent larger than Fighter Command across the North Sea, rather than one 400 per cent greater across the Channel. Even worse, the latter figures included escort fighters, which the system was not designed to handle at all; and worst of all, these escorts, Messerschmitt Bf 109s and 110s, were high in quantity and quality. Though British aircraft production soared past German, the RAF could not yet train large numbers of good pilots regularly, though neither could the Luftwaffe. Fighter Command's tactics were flawed, because they were designed to smash bomber formations (and did so well), rather than engage fighters in air superiority battles. Friction between senior officers over tactics, such as whether to intercept attackers with one squadron or several, and about information processing within its C3I system, complicated its performance. Key components – overhead telephone lines, unhardened sector controls and radar stations – were vulnerable to air attack.

Had the Germans understood how the system worked, they might have wrecked it by assaulting these weaknesses. Nonetheless, in 1940, Fighter Command was effective and efficient, supported by redundancy (two types of first-line fighters and an overlap in intelligence sources between ULTRA, low-grade signals intelligence, high- and low-level radar sets, and observers using their eyeballs). Intelligence located German attackers and displayed the data to commanders within seconds, in time for immediate response. Powerful and flexible signals linked units, commanders and pilots, enabling concentration and efficiency of force for the biggest decisions and the smallest – which squadrons to deploy, and when and how to guide fighters to visual range of their victims.[15] RAF pilots used these edges well, against an able enemy.

15 Ibid.; David Zimmerman, *Britain's Shield: Radar and the Defeat of the Luftwaffe* (Stroud: Sutton Publishing, 2001). This judgement survives a hostile analysis of Fighter Command in 1940; Anthony J. Cumming, *The Royal Navy and the Battle of Britain* (Annapolis, Md.: Naval Institute Press, 2010).

The Luftwaffe was excellent at ground support and air superiority. Its fighter aircraft matched British ones, its pilots initially were better, and their tactics remained so.[16] Yet the Luftwaffe was too weak to defeat Britain, and suffered from fundamental problems in strategy and intelligence. Britons prepared for the worst, which Germans could not deliver, because victory disease caused laziness in thought and action. Fighter Command was beyond the comprehension of its enemy; they did not understand its strengths and weaknesses. The Germans had no strategic air defence system and had never prepared to attack one.[17] They could not understand what the RAF did with radar, and what that might do to them. Germans had better radar sets, but used them only to provide tactical warning for individual airbases; they could not understand that integrated air defence let Britain concentrate its aircraft at a national level. Luftwaffe intelligence ignored radar in its assessments of the RAF. It underrated British aircraft and airmen, despite bitter experiences over Dunkirk. When they intercepted directions from ground control for aircraft, Britain's means to guide the hunters, Germans thought it meant that British pilots could not hunt at all.[18] The Luftwaffe expected to crush Fighter Command rapidly, and then cow Britain. Its head, Herman Göring, said, 'our first aim is to destroy his fighters. If they avoid combat in the air, we shall attack them on the ground or force them up to accept a fight by using bombers to attack targets within the range of our fighters'.[19] Yet the Luftwaffe had no means to make Fighter Command stand and die, rather than fall behind London, and wait. The payload of German bombers was inadequate to wreck any of the targets they selected. The Luftwaffe had no idea which targets to attack, or why, and overestimated its ability to damage them. German leaders believed that strategic bombing was powerful, and civilian morale fragile. Influenced by pre-war ideas on that matter, seemingly proven by Luftwaffe strikes on Guernica, Warsaw and Rotterdam, and the sight of refugees streaming down the roads of France, German leaders assumed that attacks on London would crack British morale and win the

---

16 Horst Boog, *Die deutsche Luftwaffenführung, 1935–1945: Führungsprobleme; Spitzengliederung; Generalstabsausbildung* (Stuttgart: Deutsche Verlags-Anstalt, 1982); James Corum, *The Luftwaffe: Creating the Operational Air War, 1918–1940* (Lawrence: University Press of Kansas, 1997).

17 Donald Caldwell and Richard Muller, *The Luftwaffe over Germany: The Defence of the Reich* (Barnsley: Greenhill Books, 2007), offers the best account of this topic.

18 Sebastian Cox, 'A Comparative Analysis of RAF and Luftwaffe Intelligence in the Battle of Britain, 1940', in Michael Handel (ed.), *Intelligence and Military Operations* (Portland, Oreg.: Frank Cass, 1990), pp. 436–7.

19 Klaus A. Maier, 'The Battle of Britain', in *Germany and the Second World War*, vol. II, p 385.

war. Thus Fighter Command would have to fight to stop it. British leaders, however, always assumed that the bomber must get through, and that London would be bombed in war: civilians must learn to take it, and would do so. Hitler unleashed precisely the sort of attack that Fighter Command was built to beat.

The air attack on England

Both air forces were mauled in the battle for France, losing 30 per cent of their aircraft. Each rebuilt during July, though Fighter Command did so better. When the Luftwaffe attacked, its hopes for quick annihilation collapsed, and a battle of attrition at medium intensity ensued. The Luftwaffe could win only by forcing an absolute level of losses, especially in pilots, that Fighter Command could not stand, at a relative level the Luftwaffe could abide. It failed in both aims. Between 10 July and 31 October, 915 British aircraft (half of them bombers striking at SEALION targets, tribute to the success of the invasion bluff) were destroyed, for 1,733 Germans.[20] The Luftwaffe could not continually attack, but had to stop every few days, because of the impact of losses and weather. When that happened, Fighter Command restored its number of aircraft and aircrew. This the Luftwaffe could not do.

Göring's directive for the Eagle Attack (*Adlerangriff*) was issued on 2 August, but due to bad flying weather mass bombing began only on 13 August (*Adlertag*), mainly against RAF airfields in southeast England. On most days of combat, and across the board, German losses were far higher. In the core competition during 1–31 August 1940, Fighter Command lost 164 Hurricane and Spitfire pilots, killed and missing, to 144 pilots in Messerschmitt Bf 109s and 96 in Bf 110s, not to mention 251 in medium and dive-bombers, excluding other German aircrew.[21] Numbers of experienced British fighter pilots fell. Between 10 July and 31 October, 544 fighter pilots died in combat from an initial pool of 1,300 and another 1,700 replacements (some excellent, most raw). Hurricane and Spitfire pilots suffered over 50 per

---

20 The best account of relative losses during the air campaign remains Winston Ramsey (ed.), *The Battle of Britain Then and Now* (London: Battle of Britain Prints International, 1996).

21 German figures from Williamson Murray, *Strategy for Defeat: The Luftwaffe, 1933–45* (Maxwell Air Force Base, Ala.: Air University Press, 1983), p. 50; British figures from Fighter Command Operational Diaries, entries 1–31 August 1940 (www.raf.mod.uk/history/campaign_diaries.cfm – accessed 7 October 2014).

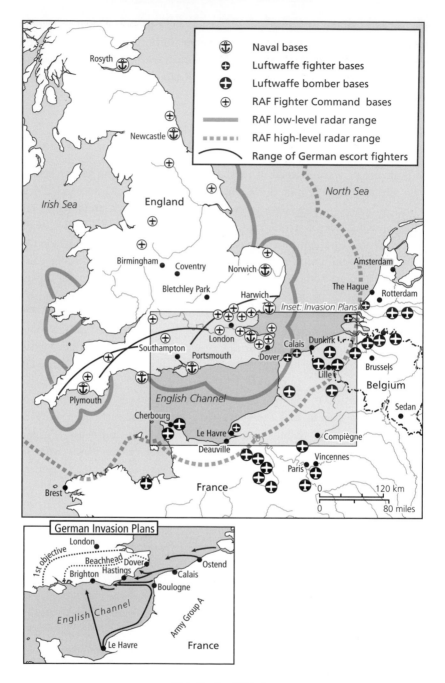

11.1 Battle of Britain

cent losses by 18 September, compared to their initial establishment.[22] Yet all categories of Luftwaffe aircrew suffered heavier relative and absolute losses. Fighter Command always had just enough good pilots to sustain the battle despite the damage, and especially the forces in its first line of defence, those most requiring skill, the 300 Hurricanes and Spitfires of No. 11 Group in southeast England. They remained ready and able to fight during the final quarter of an hour, when their rivals ran.

The Luftwaffe was most effective between 24 August and 5 September 1940, when it attacked forward RAF airbases and their C3I systems. Even then, it caused too little damage to approach victory, and could not sustain its losses. Fighter Command, battered but unbroken, steadily achieved operational victories which unravelled its rival. A triumph over the North Sea on 15 August smashed all threats to Scotland and northern England, turning that area into a safe training ground for new pilots and enabling the transfer of fifty trained ones south. By 18 August, Ju 87 Stukas had to leave the battle, after they had lost 50 per cent of their pilots, taking with them the capability for pinpoint bombing that most threatened C3I on the ground. Meanwhile, the twin-engined Bf 110s ceased to serve as fighters and thus became irrelevant to operations, leaving Bf 109s, agile but short-ranged, alone against greater numbers of Spitfires and Hurricanes. Then the value of Bf 109s fell as they had to serve as close escorts for bombers, whose crews were increasingly skittish. German morale eroded, maintained only by erroneous assessments that Fighter Command was near death, one of the most significant intelligence failures of the war. That idea rested on the politicization of Luftwaffe intelligence, geared to please Göring, on massive underestimates of British aircraft strength and production, and on overestimates of its losses, which were placed at 300 per cent above the true levels.[23] Just before the major attack on 18 August, Luftwaffe intelligence claimed that Fighter Command had lost 770 fighters in combat or accident and gained 300 new ones between 1 July and 15 August, leaving 430 machines, of which but 300 were combat-effective. In fact, during that period, Fighter Command lost 318 fighters and gained 720 new ones. On 18 August, it had 1,438 modern fighters in units, reserves and training establishments, with 706 effective.[24]

---

22 Fighter Command Operational Diaries, entries 10 July – 31 October 1940 (www.raf. mod.uk/history/campaign_diaries.cfm – accessed 7 October 2014).

23 Cox, 'Comparative Analysis'; and Horst Boog, 'German Air Intelligence in the Second World War', in Handel (ed.), *Intelligence and Military Operations*, pp. 355–73.

24 Alfred Price, *The Hardest Day: 18 August 1940* (London: Phoenix, 1998), Appendix D, pp. 192–3.

By 16 September, the day of the last great attack, Germans believed they had driven Fighter Command down to 177 effective fighters. The true number was 300 per cent higher, 216 Spitfires and 356 Hurricanes.[25]

These assumptions shaped the Luftwaffe's turn from attacking airfields and C3I to London – an error, but less significant than is often claimed.[26] Those early attacks inflicted little damage. Had Germans continued them, they still would have lost, just less quickly or badly. This margin was too narrow to matter. The aim was retaliation against RAF raids on Germany – as Hitler shouted in the Sportspalast on 4 September, 'We will put these night pirates out of business, God help us! The hour will come when one of us will crack, and it will not be National Socialist Germany!'[27] Even more, Hitler hoped either to crush Britain or force it to offer peace. Bombing cities would shatter British morale, or air defence, by driving all fighters up over targets that must be defended, to die in their defence.

Attacks on London, imposing sensational but superficial damage, boosted German hopes. By 14 September, Hitler remained unclear about the outcome. Britain might not negotiate or fall in 1940. The RAF's losses were uncertain, yet it must have 'suffered badly', while the Luftwaffe's attacks had been 'enormously successful'. Continued bombing might break Britain. 'If eight million people go mad, it might very well turn into a catastrophe. If we get the fine weather, and we can eliminate the enemy's air force, then even a small invasion might go a long way', backed by terror attacks. Hitler reserved 'deliberate attacks on residential areas as a final means of pressure and as a reprisal for British attacks of this nature'.[28] In the best case, perhaps the most optimistic that Hitler ever conceived, the *Todesstoss* from SEALION might place the British Empire at his command. Intelligence raised his hopes. Spitfires shot them down, in an equal but opposite reaction. These misconceptions spurred the great German daylight raids of 15–16 September. When they cracked, and Fighter Command showed its power, Hitler abandoned any idea of beating Britain in 1940, dispersing the landing craft needed to

---

25 Klaus A. Maier, 'The Battle of Britain', in *Germany and the Second World War*, vol. II, p. 396; Fighter Command Operational Diaries, entry for 16 September 1940 (www.raf. mod.uk/history/campaign_diaries.cfm – accessed 7 October 2014).
26 Wood and Dempster, *The Narrow Margin*; Wright, *Dowding*.
27 For an English-language version of Hitler's 4 September speech, see Max Domarus (ed.), *Hitler: Speeches and Proclamations 1932–1945. The Chronicle of a Dictatorship* (4 vols., Mundelein, Ill.: Bolchazy-Carducci Publishers, 1996), vol. III, pp. 2081–90.
28 Wagner (ed.), *Lagevorträge*, p. 142; Maier, 'The Battle of Britain', pp. 386–97; David Irving, *The Rise and Fall of the Luftwaffe: The Life of Field Marshal Erhard Milch* (Boston, Mass.: Little Brown and Co., 1973). pp. 104–5.

mount the *Todesstoss*, and turned single-mindedly to the campaign against Russia.[29] The Luftwaffe still pursued victory on its own, through occasional daylight raids, but increasingly by night bombing against industrial targets and cities. Over several months, these night raids killed 10,000 civilians, and caught Fighter Command in operations for which initially it was unprepared, but they produced no strategic gains for Germany. German air power stagnated in quantity and quality, while British air power surged.

In June 1940, Churchill predicted a battle that never happened. Instead, Germans launched a spasmodic air campaign, *Die Luftschlacht um England*,[30] which extended to 1945, and failed. Britain did not have to fight on the beaches, nor in the hills. Ink still spills over whether the Royal Navy or the RAF won the Battle of Britain. In fact, that battle never happened, because both services won their own.[31] The Royal Navy deterred a seaborne invasion of Britain, driving the Germans to rely on air power. The RAF smashed the enterprise over England. Britain had prepared air and naval forces fit for war; Germany had not. The turning point in the battle was the day it started, when Germany lost. Only if the Germans had possessed far greater nerve, resources and intelligence could they have beaten Fighter Command – and never the Royal Navy. The Germans did not know their enemy. Britons knew themselves, their enemy and the battlefield. They scored a stalemate in battle and triumph in strategy.

Toward the Second World War

After France fell, the cascade could have swept in many directions. Hitler and Churchill turned it toward world war. Had Hitler offered a compromise peace, he might have consolidated French disaster, British defeat and a German victory in Europe to surpass Bismarck, but still a limited one. Hitler never considered this option, nor that of attacking the British Empire alone. His speech to the Reichstag on 19 July merely taunted and threatened Britain,

---

29 The 'run-up' (*Anlauf*) to SEALION, involving preliminary minelaying, depended on air successes against London. It was postponed on 11 September, and abandoned on 17 September (Klee (ed.), *Dokumente*, pp. 373–7, 436; Hans Umbreit, 'Plans and Preparations for Landing in England', in *Germany and the Second World War*, vol. II, p. 371).
30 *Die Luftschlacht um England* (The air battle over England) is the name given to the air campaign of 1940 in *Das deutche Reich und der zweite Weltkrieg* (10 vols., Stuttgart: Deutsche Verlags-Anstalt, 1979), vol. II, p. 375.
31 Brian James, 'Pie in the Sky', *History Today* 56 (2006), 38–40; Christina Goulter, Andrew Gordon and Gary Sheffield, 'The Royal Navy did not win the "Battle of Britain"', *RUSI Journal* 151 (2006), 66–7; Cumming, *Royal Navy*.

Churchill prepared a campaign against Italy, by sending scarce resources – 150 tanks, 48 anti-tank guns, an aircraft carrier, a battleship and two anti-aircraft cruisers – from Britain to Egypt and the Eastern Mediterranean. Churchill did not think that Britain could win by bombing Germany or promoting resistance in occupied countries ('setting Europe ablaze'); what he thought was that if Britain fought on, other powers would be dragged onto its side. He understood the risks, but misconstrued the percentages, overestimating the ease of getting American help, and hoping to achieve these ends without destroying the British Empire. Even here, his ambitions were more modest than is often supposed. In 1938, he told a friend, 'my ideal is narrow and limited. I want to see the British Empire preserved for a few more generations in its strength and splendour. Only the most prodigious exertions of British genius will achieve this result'.[35] Instead, it achieved the finest hour: from hindsight, a fair substitute.

Churchill's strategy would have been disastrous against another enemy, but he knew his man. He forced Hitler back to roulette, and onto the Führer's worst traits – ignorance of the odds, reliance on bluff and luck. Churchill's strategy was heaven-sent to exploit Hitler. His actions drove Germany to attack the USSR and shaped the American entry into the war. His rhetoric transformed air attacks on Britain into a battle for civilization, where each must make his stand. Churchill spurred the industrial capacity available against Germany. He maximized war production at home and spent all Britain's hard currency on arms purchases in the United States. That action primed the pump of American industry, advancing its mobilization by twelve months, and paved the road to Lend-Lease. Hitler, meanwhile, made the fatal decision to slacken mobilization for war, precisely as he began one with two fronts. Hitler and Churchill gambled for the highest of stakes. Only one could win. Each pushed or pulled the rest of the world into war. As the cascade swelled, driven by strategy, perception, force and fluke, the intentions and effects of all states become entangled. Statesmen improvised amidst a revolution which no one had gamed in advance. Everyone made errors. Miscalculation mattered as much as calculation. Two of the greatest surprise attacks in history punctuated events. When the world settled, the outcome of the war was decided.

---

35 John Ferris, '"The Greatest Power on Earth": Great Britain in the 1920s', *International History Review* 13:4 (November 1991), p. 749; cf. David Edgerton, *Britain's War Machine: Weapons, Resources, and Experts in the Second World War* (London: Allen Lane, 2011), esp. ch. 3.

12

Operations on the Eastern Front, 1941–1945

DAVID R. STONE

In a conflict as massive as the Second World War, no theatre can claim absolute centrality to the war's outcome. If any campaign comes close, however, it is the Soviet-German struggle on the Eastern Front. From the time German troops crossed the Soviet border on 22 June 1941 in Operation BARBAROSSA, until Adolf Hitler's suicide in his Berlin bunker, the Eastern Front consumed the bulk of German manpower and resources. More German soldiers died on the Eastern Front than on all other fronts combined – though precise figures are still in dispute and will never be satisfactorily reconciled, a figure of 3 million German soldiers killed, missing or dying in captivity on the Eastern Front seems approximately correct. Soviet military losses were far greater: 9 million soldiers killed, missing or dead in prisoner-of-war camps.[1] These figures, in turn, are dwarfed by Soviet civilian dead: an additional 20 million. In addition to its incalculable impact on human lives, the outcome of the Soviet-German war shaped the destinies of the eastern half of Europe for fifty years to come, and was fundamental to Soviet politics and society until and beyond the end of the Soviet Union itself.

Preparing for Armageddon

When the Wehrmacht attacked in June 1941, Joseph Stalin's Red Army was peculiarly unprepared for its onslaught. While many factors were involved, a small but vocal group of scholars have argued that Soviet defences were inadequate because the Red Army was in fact preparing an offensive, echoing

---

1 These figures are, at best, approximate. For the most thorough discussion, see G. F. Krivosheev, *Soviet Casualties and Combat Losses in the Twentieth Century* (London: Greenhill, 1997).

a charge made by Nazi propaganda to justify war with the Soviet Union.[2] Most historians have been unconvinced, seeing less insidious reasons for this lack of preparedness and the resultant Soviet military disasters in 1941. Soviet doctrine was fundamentally offensive, lacking serious consideration of defence, so Soviet deployments were well forward, eschewing defence-in-depth. The Red Army expected to fight on the border with forces-in-being until mobilization enabled a move decisively to the offensive. Fixed fortifications which had protected the old Soviet-Polish border had been abandoned in 1939, but replacements on the Soviet-German border had not yet been completed. More generally, the Great Purges of 1937–38, which had removed some 40,000 officers from the Red Army, had a terrible impact on military effectiveness.[3]

Nonetheless, Stalin showed a critical failure of leadership in the earliest days of the war. The Soviets protested German reconnaissance overflights, but took no action to stop them. Soviet deliveries of vital raw materials to Germany under the terms of the Molotov–Ribbentrop Pact continued unabated. Repeated warnings of Hitler's intent, from the United States, the United Kingdom and Stalin's own agents went unheeded. Stalin seems to have engaged in a fateful combination of denial and wishful thinking. Real indicators of German preparations to attack were accompanied by a coordinated disinformation campaign, intended to convince Stalin to expect an ultimatum and German demands before any attack. It would be folly, this campaign suggested, for Germany to open a new front against the Soviet Union while Britain remained in the war, particularly given Germany's shortages of vital raw materials. This disinformation had the virtue of truth: it was indeed folly for Hitler to attack, but Hitler was not bound by conventional notions of prudence. Signs of an imminent German attack were so clear that in May 1941, the Red Army's Chief of Staff Georgii Zhukov presented Stalin with a plan for a spoiling attack against German forces massing in Poland, a plan Stalin rejected contemptuously. The German

---

2 Viktor Suvorov has argued this extensively. For a recent summary, see Suvorov, *The Chief Culprit: Stalin's Grand Design to Start World War II* (Annapolis, Md.: Naval Institute Press, 2008). See also R. C. Raack, *Stalin's Drive to the West, 1938–1945* (Stanford University Press, 1995). For a counter-argument, focusing more on diplomacy than military history, see Gabriel Gorodetsky, *Grand Delusion: Stalin and the German Invasion of Russia* (New Haven, Conn.: Yale University Press, 1999).

3 David M. Glantz, *Stumbling Colossus: The Red Army on the Eve of World War* (Lawrence: University Press of Kansas, 1998). Roger R. Reese, *Stalin's Reluctant Soldiers: A Social History of the Red Army, 1925–1941* (Lawrence: University Press of Kansas, 1996) downplays the impact of the purges, suggesting instead that the Red Army's excessively rapid expansion was responsible.

invasion, when it came, thus destroyed Stalin's illusions that he could manage and contain the German threat. While old stories of Stalin's emotional collapse immediately on word of Soviet invasion are clearly false, evidence does suggest that Stalin lost his nerve a week into the war when Minsk fell, bringing home just how disastrous Soviet performance in the first days of the war had been. His inner circle had to venture to Stalin's dacha outside Moscow to persuade him to return and direct the war effort.[4]

The German plan, envisaging three separate attacks by three Army Groups, was a direct violation of the principle of unity of effort. The geography of Russia, which meant that the front widened like a fan as the Germans moved from west to east, necessarily forced some dispersion, but the problem was worsened by Hitler's refusal and the German high command's acquiescence in a fateful division of effort. The four vital Panzer groups were split – one each to Army Group North and Army Group South, and two to Army Group Centre. Army Group North was assigned the mission of hooking northeast to take the industrial city of Leningrad. Army Group Centre attacked east through Minsk and Smolensk toward Moscow. Army Group South drove through the grain fields of Ukraine toward the coal of the Donets River basin. Though the post-war memoirs of Germany's generals stress their disquiet with Hitler's cavalier overconfidence, this was not evident in 1941. Easy successes in Poland and France combined with a sense of racial superiority over the Soviet Union's Slavs and Jews to convince Hitler and the German high command alike that standard notions of military prudence did not apply. Rather than a true plan to defeat Soviet forces in the field and occupy enough Soviet territory to win the war, German planning and its division of effort was instead based on the idea that the bulk of Soviet forces could be encircled and destroyed at the border, at which point the regime would collapse.[5]

The primary striking force of Hitler's 3-million-man invasion army consisted of seventeen Panzer divisions, averaging about 200 tanks each.

---

4 Compare Cynthia Roberts, "Planning for War: the Red Army and the Catastrophe of 1941," *Europe-Asia Studies* 47.8 (December 1995), 1293–1326 and Steven J. Main, "Stalin in June 1941: A Comment on Cynthia Roberts," *Europe-Asia Studies* 48.5 (July 1996), 837–839.
5 There is an extensive literature on the prevarications of the German generals. See Johannes Hürter, *Hitlers Heerführer. Die deutschen Oberbefehlshaber im Krieg gegen die Sowjetunion 1941/42* (Munich: Oldenbourg Verlag, 2006); Geoffrey P. Megargee, *War of Annihilation: Combat and Genocide on the Eastern Front, 1941* (Lanham, Md.: Rowman and Littlefield, 2006); Wolfram Wette, *The Wehrmacht: History, Myth, Reality* (Cambridge, Mass.: Harvard University Press, 2006); David Stahel, *Operation Barbarossa and Germany's Defeat in the East* (Cambridge University Press, 2009).

12.1 German invasion of Russia, 1941–42

These were concentrated into four Panzer groups, soon renamed Panzer armies. The bulk of the German divisions, however, were infantry, creating an immediate problem of coordination between the mechanized German spearheads moving deep into Soviet territory and the supporting infantry necessary to complete the destruction of encircled and bypassed Soviet formations. Their advance was limited to the speed at which a man could walk, with artillery and supplies pulled by horses. In addition, the Germans were supported in their initial attack by over a dozen good Finnish divisions and a similar number of under-equipped Romanian divisions. Hungarian and Italian troops, and even a token Spanish force, would also join the campaign. The quality of these forces varied markedly; the Finns were by far the best, but their aims in the war were self-consciously limited to regaining territory lost in the Russo-Finnish War of 1939–40. The rest of Hitler's minor allies lacked the equipment to cope with Soviet troops, a problem that would become increasingly serious over the course of the war. Hitler never trusted their leaders or took them into his confidence, a problem evident all the way down the German chain of command.[6]

Soviet strategy, as suggested above, was to meet the enemy at the border and shift quickly to a counter-offensive into German territory. Stalin misjudged the likely axis of German advance, anticipating that the main German effort would attack Ukraine, south of the Pripiat Marshes, not north of the marshes toward Moscow and Leningrad. The October 1940 Soviet war plan responded accordingly, shifting the weight of Soviet dispositions to the south. Still, measured in strictly numerical terms, the Soviets seemed to have an unbeatable edge over the forces of the Axis. Germany's 3,000 tanks were vastly outnumbered by the Soviet tank park, and the best Soviet tanks were among the best in the world. Though some Red Army tanks were obsolete and of dubious military worth, and others stationed on the long eastern frontier with Japan, the Soviets had at least 15,000 tanks at their disposal. The T-34 medium tank and the KV-1 heavy tank, of which the Soviets possessed at least 1,500, were better than anything the Germans

6 For numerous accounts of problematic German relations with allies, see Richard DiNardo, *Germany and the Axis Powers: From Coalition to Collapse* (Lawrence: University Press of Kansas, 2005); Jonathan R. Adelman, *Hitler and His Allies in World War II* (London: Routledge, 2007); Hope Hamilton, *Sacrifice on the Steppe: The Italian Alpine Corps in the Stalingrad Campaign, 1942–1943* (Philadelphia, Pa.: Casemate, 2011); Henrik O. Lunde, *Finland's War of Choice: The Troubled German-Finnish Coalition In World War II* (Newbury: Casemate, 2011).

fielded. The Soviet Union also possessed an immense peacetime army of 5 million men, which by itself outnumbered the invading Germans, to say nothing of the additional 5 million men whom the extensive Soviet mobilization system called to arms during the first weeks of war.

Initial German victories

As a result of German tactical and operational superiority, combined with surprise, the first days and weeks of the invasion were a Soviet disaster. Germany fell far short of the human, industrial and raw material resources of the Soviet Union and the British Empire, to say nothing of the United States. This strategic weakness, however, was almost overcome by the Wehrmacht's operational and tactical expertise. Put another way, Hitler's foolhardy grand strategy was nearly salvaged by his soldiers' victories on the battlefield. The bulk of the Soviet air force along the western frontier was destroyed on the ground, giving the Germans a vital advantage in reconnaissance and air support. The problem was worst in the central part of the front, where Fedor von Bock's Army Group Centre employed two of the four German Panzer groups against the Soviet Western Army Group. Ivan Kopets, Commander of the Western Army Group's aviation, shot himself on the first day of the war (saving Stalin the trouble). Dmitrii Pavlov, commanding the Western Army Group, completely lost control of his troops and could not coordinate a defence, a performance so disastrous that Stalin had him shot a month into the war. Hitler's Army Chief of Staff Franz Halder noted in his diary on 3 July that the Soviet army had been essentially destroyed.

The general pattern of fighting in the first weeks, particularly north of the Pripiat Marshes, was that German Panzer and mechanized divisions knifed through uncoordinated defences, wrecking the links that maintained command and supply to Soviet units, and seizing road and rail nodes. German mobile units left behind them confused, demoralized and leaderless masses of Soviet troops, to be pocketed and destroyed wholesale by slower-moving German infantry. The Soviet instinct for the offensive made matters worse, particularly in western Ukraine, as units that might have withdrawn to fight more effectively instead remained in place or even advanced, making German encirclement operations easier. In the first few months of the campaign, Soviet troops were repeatedly trapped in giant pockets. Hundreds of thousands were killed or captured on the road to Moscow: 400,000 at Minsk, 300,000 at Smolensk, 600,000 at Viazma and Briansk.

The Wehrmacht did little to keep their Soviet prisoners fed, and most starved to death before later German difficulties convinced the Nazi regime that prisoners should be kept alive for slave labour.[7]

At Smolensk, guarding the road from Belorussia to Moscow, the Soviets engaged in a desperate struggle to stop Army Group Centre's advance in July and August. Semen Timoshenko, commanding the defence of Smolensk, repeatedly threw divisions and corps against the Germans in desperate counter-attacks, to seemingly little effect. In Ukraine, where the *Stavka*, the Soviet high command, had expected the main enemy blow, the weaker German Army Group South under Gerd von Rundstedt, with only a single Panzer group, had made slower progress against large Soviet formations bolstered by a series of natural defensive river lines. By July, though, Soviet positions in Ukraine west of the Dnepr had begun to crumble.[8] On the road to Leningrad through the former Baltic states, Wilhelm von Leeb's weaker Army Group North had made similarly slow progress relative to Army Group Centre. The Soviets withdrew toward Leningrad in reasonably good order, avoiding the major encirclements that devastated whole armies in more open terrain to the south. Zhukov, no longer Chief of Staff, kept the Germans out of Leningrad itself in September and October. Nonetheless, by early September, Army Group North had cut land links from Leningrad to the rest of Soviet territory with the assistance of the Finns. Hitler deliberately chose not to take the city by storm, preferring instead to preserve his tanks and manpower and starve the city into submission. In bitter fighting in November and December, the Soviets managed to restore their control over a rail line at Tikhvin, just close enough to Leningrad to allow some supplies into the city over the frozen waters of Lake Ladoga. This lifeline was enough

---

7 In discussions of operations, I have avoided unnecessary repetition of references to Earl F. Ziemke, *Stalingrad to Berlin: The German Defeat in the East* (Washington DC: Center of Military History, 1968); John Erickson, *The Road to Stalingrad* (London: Weidenfeld & Nicolson, 1975); John Erickson, *The Road to Berlin* (London: Weidenfeld & Nicolson, 1983); Earl F. Ziemke and Magna E. Bauer, *Moscow to Stalingrad: Decision in the East* (Washington DC: Center of Military History, 1987); and David M. Glantz and Jonathan M. House, *When Titans Clashed: How the Red Army Stopped Hitler* (Lawrence: University Press of Kansas, 1995). For detailed operational accounts of all campaigns, readers should consult these sources.

8 David M. Glantz, *Barbarossa Derailed: The Battle for Smolensk, 10 July–10 September 1941* (2 vols., Solihull: Helion, 2010), vol. I, argues that the repeated Soviet counter-attacks, despite their enormous cost, were important for reducing German strength and disrupting German offensive plans. On early battles in western Russia, see also David Stahel, *Operation Barbarossa and Germany's Defeat in the East* (Cambridge University Press, 2011).

to keep the city functioning, but insufficient to prevent the starvation of hundreds of thousands of its citizens.[9]

Confidently assuming that Soviet resistance before Moscow was broken beyond repair, Hitler made a fateful decision in late July to slow the drive on Moscow and allow German infantry to catch up, and then in early August turned Army Group Centre's vital Panzers south. Substantial Soviet forces still held the Dnepr River line and the city of Kiev. Army Group Centre's rapid advance had taken German armour far enough east that it could now move south *behind* the Pripiat Marshes to cut off Kiev and its defenders. Stalin had entrusted Kiev's defences to Semyon Budennyi, an old crony of his and a thoroughgoing incompetent. At the end of August and beginning of September, German Panzers broke into Soviet rear areas north and south of Kiev, and Stalin stubbornly insisted on holding Kiev rather than withdrawing men and equipment to safety further east. By the middle of September, German pincers met east of Kiev, trapping some 600,000 Soviet troops in the largest single defeat of the war. Soviet defences were shattered, and Army Group South now ranged free, quickly clearing Ukraine east of the Dnepr, reaching all the way to the mouth of the Don River and briefly seizing Rostov in November. The city of Odessa, which had held out valiantly against a siege by Hitler's Romanian allies, was evacuated in mid-October. The Crimea was cleared of Soviet defenders, with the exception of the major naval base at Sevastopol, which remained in Soviet hands until the summer of 1942.[10]

After the liquidation of the Kiev pocket secured the German southern flank, Hitler prepared to renew his drive on Moscow. At the end of September, Army Group Centre, now with three Panzer groups, launched Operation TYPHOON against the hastily assembled Soviet defences intended to keep the Germans out of the capital. Again the Germans employed tanks for deep penetrations, which isolated huge masses of Soviet troops for wholesale destruction. The Soviets threw up yet another desperate defence at the Mozhaisk Line west of Moscow, employing hastily mobilized reservists and almost entirely untrained factory militia to slow the German advance at terrible cost. Stalin was beginning to learn who his effective generals were. His pre-war cronies had been manifest disasters as high-level theatre commanders: Budennyi at Kiev and Kliment Voroshilov at Leningrad. Finding

9 David M. Glantz, *The Battle for Leningrad, 1941–1944* (Lawrence: University Press of Kansas, 2002), pp. 3–118.
10 David Stahel, *Kiev 1941* (Cambridge University Press, 2013).

Zhukov to be one of his few effective generals, Stalin brought him south from Leningrad on 10 October to take over the defence of Moscow. Much of the Soviet government and many foreign embassies were evacuated east to Kuibyshev on the Volga. With the road to Moscow essentially blasted open, only the autumn rains and the disintegration of Soviet roads into mud halted the German advance. When the temperature dropped enough to freeze the ground, German advances resumed in November. Two great wings of the German advance, representing the last drive of Army Group Centre's Panzer groups, approached Moscow from the north and south.[11]

The first Soviet counter-offensive

The pace of the German advance was already slowing, worn down by attrition and extended supply lines, when Zhukov launched a massive counter-attack on 5 December. Improvised Soviet formations were supplemented by experienced Siberian divisions, freed by Soviet intelligence suggesting that Japan intended to move into the Pacific, not the Soviet Far East. The German troops were forced into rapid withdrawal under horrific weather conditions. The strategy that had served Hitler so well since the beginning of the war – short campaigns that used operational skill to overcome strategic shortcomings – had failed. The Germans lost vital stocks of equipment that they could not withdraw, and the myth of German invulnerability was shattered: Moscow marked the first major defeat of the Wehrmacht on land. As a result of the failure of the German drive on Moscow, Hitler dismissed Walther von Brauchitsch as head of *Oberkommando des Heeres* (OKH – army high command), tasked with command of the war in the east, taking the office for himself. Since Hitler had, in 1938, taken over *Oberkommando der Wehrmacht* (OKW – armed forces high command), responsible for overall command and theatres other than the Eastern Front, leaving its day-to-day management in the hands of his subservient lackey Wilhelm Keitel, Hitler now had full responsibility for operational control of the war in all theatres.[12]

---

11 Niklas Zetterling and Anders Frankson, *The Drive on Moscow: Operation Taifun and Germany's First Great Crisis in World War II* (Oxford: Casemate, 2012); David Stahel, *Operation Typhoon: Hitler's March on Moscow, October 1941* (Cambridge University Press, 2013).

12 Michael Parrish, *Battle for Moscow: The 1942 Soviet General Staff Study* (London: Brassey's, 1989); Klaus Reinhardt, *Moscow: The Turning Point. Failure of Hitler's Strategy in the Winter of 1941–42* (Oxford: Berg, 1992).

Success at Moscow bred terrible overconfidence in Stalin. Rejecting the advice of his generals for a limited but still potent offensive at Moscow to further the Soviet initial successes, Stalin instead ordered counter-attacks along the whole length of the front. These lasted until the spring thaw halted operations in April 1942. Given the unexpected reverse before Moscow, the German generals wished to engage in a limited withdrawal west. Hitler refused such a retreat in the dead of winter, arguing that it would be impossible to stop once it started, and would require the abandonment of too many supplies and heavy equipment. He issued a stand-fast order on 18 December, requiring his troops to maintain their positions at any cost. As a result, Stalin's efforts at a vast encirclement of Army Group Centre west of Moscow, aided by massive paratrooper drops and cavalry raids behind German lines, failed to dislodge the Germans from their strongpoints – towns and villages hastily fortified to hold back the Soviet advance until better weather and reinforcements restored German fortunes. West of Moscow, Soviet forces made deep penetrations between enemy strongpoints, only to be trapped when the Germans were able to restore the integrity of their front. The abortive and overly broad Soviet offensives cost hundreds of thousands of lives in clumsy attacks which lacked real mass. German discipline and cohesion were still far superior to Soviet at this point in the war, so few German units were entirely cut off. Those that were surrounded maintained their integrity and fought on in the Soviet rear, unlike the millions of Soviet soldiers in the autumn of 1941, who ceased resistance and marched into German captivity when the chain of command disintegrated. While the German momentum was broken, the huge disparity of casualties in favour of Germany would provide the Wehrmacht with a renewed opportunity in late spring.

Soviet offensives around Leningrad did little better. After the December 1941 Tikhvin offensive, a further Soviet push in January on the Volkhov River toward Liuban failed to break through. The abortive attack led to the encirclement and annihilation of the 2nd Shock Army and the capture of its commander Andrei Vlasov, later to become the collaborationist figurehead of the German-sponsored Russian Liberation Army. Though the Soviet advances were not enough to keep the population from mass starvation in the winter of 1941–42, the tenuous link across Lake Ladoga provided just enough to keep the city's garrison fighting and its factories working, while enabling the evacuation of just enough surplus mouths to keep Leningrad from complete starvation. A million people died during the siege, most in the first year of the war, before the city's reduced population and improved Soviet supply efforts succeeded in stabilizing food provisions in the city.[13]

Exhaustion on both sides produced a brief pause in major operations in spring 1942. Much of the pattern of subsequent developments was already becoming clear. On the German side, the material constraints on Hitler's war were increasingly evident. The vaunted German Panzer divisions only averaged a dozen operational tanks each at their low point in early 1942. While repairs and new production would correct that deficit, Germany was already losing the production war. By the end of 1941, German manpower reserves were already under strain as well, a situation only partly relieved by additional divisions from Hitler's allies. Two months into the war, the Germans had lost more men than they had in the battle for France, and by the end of 1941 they had suffered a million killed and wounded. Conquest of Ukraine had brought large agricultural resources, as well as important coal reserves under Hitler's control, though exploiting those would prove problematic. More serious was the ongoing shortage of oil. War in the open spaces of the Soviet Union consumed large amounts of fuel, to say nothing of the air war over Western Europe and the demands of naval war and the campaigns in North Africa. Germany's thirst for oil drove Hitler's strategy for 1942, leaving him no choice to but to push hundreds of miles still further in hopes of reaching Soviet oil in the North Caucasus and Azerbaijan.

The Soviet Union, by contrast, was adapting with remarkable speed to the new strategic circumstances. Much of Soviet industry had been evacuated east and resumed production of the arms and equipment needed to equip a new Red Army. The Soviet manpower system never broke down under the strains of war, continuing to conscript and train the Soviet male population, while women, young people and the elderly poured into Soviet factories. The Soviets replaced the 4 million men lost in 1941 and built still larger formations, drafting some 30 million men into the Red Army during the war. The Soviet army restructured itself to accommodate its inexperienced officers and men. Its organizational structure was simplified, temporarily eliminating corps as intermediate links between divisions and armies. Artillery and aviation were stripped away from lower units to make commanders' tasks simpler and concentrate their power at higher levels. Soviet doctrine slowly became more realistic, enabling retreat from hopeless positions and encouraging manoeuvres other than frontal assault. Rather than dividing the

---

13 Glantz, *Leningrad*, pp. 119–88.

front line into three to four army groups, as the Germans typically did, the Soviets reduced the responsibility of any individual commander by dividing the front line into a dozen sectors, each the responsibility of a particular army group, each made up of several armies. While nominally equivalent to a German army group, each Soviet army group was much smaller. To coordinate the actions of multiple army groups, the Soviets created ad hoc command structures for particular campaigns to maximize the use of their limited pool of capable strategic commanders. Zhukov, in particular, played this role repeatedly during the war.

Despite massive losses of men and officers, Soviet military performance slowly but surely began to improve, and continued to do so throughout the war. Man-for-man, the Germans maintained a qualitative edge over the Soviets, as the Red Army was always playing catch-up in training effective soldiers. Still, the gap in performance, terrible in June 1941, had been largely erased by 1945. Furthermore, contrary to a popular perception of German technological superiority, Soviet military industry outproduced German by a wide margin. While individual pieces of German equipment were superbly designed in an abstract sense, simpler and more crude systems were cheaper and quicker to construct, and more reliable under Eastern Front conditions. The Soviet T-34 tank produced panic among German soldiers who encountered it in 1941 and found that they had no anti-tank weapons capable of dealing with it. The German Panther, by contrast, broke down in large numbers during the 1943 Kursk offensive, critically weakening German attacks.[14]

Hitler's pathological domination of the high command and his generals' acquiescence in his strategic leadership increased over time. Hitler and Stalin moved in opposite directions in their relations with their commanders. As victory remained elusive, Hitler grew increasingly frustrated with his generals, dismissing them for failure, replacing them with more subservient officers, and taking more of the command burden upon himself. In September 1942, he took over for Wilhelm List as Commander of Army Group A, thus serving simultaneously as Führer of the German state, Head of the Wehrmacht, Commander-in-Chief of the German army, and commander of an army group. Stalin, by contrast, over time grew to trust his professional

---

14 On the rebuilding of Soviet capacity, see Von Hardesty and Ilya Grinberg, *Red Phoenix Rising: The Soviet Air Force in World War II* (Lawrence: University Press of Kansas, 2012); David M. Glantz, *Colossus Reborn: The Red Army at War, 1941–1943* (Lawrence: University Press of Kansas, 2005).

military leadership, though always questioning them sharply over any points of disagreement. The inner circle of commanders he had in place by 1942, purged of the party hacks and old cronies devoid of military talent, was consummately professional. Zhukov acted as a fireman, shifting to key theatres as needed, to coordinate the actions of multiple Soviet army groups. Aleksandr Vasilevskii, Chief of the General Staff, handled planning at Soviet high command in Moscow. Aleksei Antonov, Vasilevskii's deputy, managed the all-important task of liaison with Stalin and replaced Vasilevskii at the General Staff late in the war.[15]

Once the spring 1942 thaw had ended and Russian mud had become solid ground again, both sides entertained thoughts of new offensives, and both fatefully planned to attack in the southern part of the front. By this point, the resource constraints on the German war effort were becoming clear, and the German need for Soviet oil demanded that Hitler push his already overextended armies southeast, between the Black Sea and the Volga, in order to keep his tanks and planes running. On 5 April, Hitler declared his intent to make the southern sector his point of main effort. Skilful German deception operations, however, convinced the Soviet leadership that the main effort in spring 1942, as in late 1941, would be directed against Moscow, and most Soviet reserves were stationed there. Nonetheless, the Soviets planned a limited offensive using a salient around the town of Izium on the west bank of the Donets River as a jumping-off point. This would serve as the basis for one pincer of a two-pronged attack, totalling four armies, toward the industrial city of Kharkov. The Germans, however, had prepared offensives of their own. At the same time, and with more pernicious consequences, the Soviet attack on the Donets River on 12 May 1942 moved directly into the teeth of the best German mobile formations. The Izium salient became a trap, and Soviet divisions were encircled and destroyed on a scale reminiscent of autumn 1941. In early May, the Germans also cleared a Soviet foothold from the Kerch Peninsula on the eastern shore of the Crimea, and then spent two more months digging stubborn Soviet defenders out of the surrounded Soviet naval base of Sevastopol on the Crimea's western shore.[16]

---

15 Cf. Corelli Barnett (ed.), *Hitler's Generals* (London: Weidenfeld & Nicolson, 1989) with Harold Shukman (ed.), *Stalin's Generals* (London: Weidenfeld & Nicolson, 1993). Geoffrey Megargee, *Inside Hitler's High Command* (Lawrence: University Press of Kansas, 2000) has the most detailed account of the particular pathologies of Hitler's command style. Ian Kershaw's biography, *Hitler 1936–45: Nemesis* (London: Allen Lane, 2000), also vividly portrays the chaos at the heart of the Third Reich.

16 David M. Glantz with Jonathan M. House, *To The Gates of Stalingrad: Soviet-German Combat Operations, April–August 1942* (Lawrence: University Press of Kansas, 2009),

After a month to reorganize and resupply, the Germans began their own offensive into the breach in Soviet lines created by the failure of the Kharkov offensive. The plan was to clear the right (western) bank of the Don River, using its giant bend east as protection for the northwestern flank of a further drive south to the Caucasus and its oil. On 28 June 1942, Bock's Army Group South began Operation BLUE. The German attack first broke through in the north, toward Voronezh, then turned southeast down the western bank of the Don, systematically rolling up Soviet defences as it progressed. The Wehrmacht covered enormous ground in its advances, first to the Don and then beyond it. Soviet losses in the battle for the Don bend were particularly heavy, even though increasingly effective Soviet resistance and willingness to make tactical withdrawals rather than be annihilated in place meant that German loss ratios worsened; even space itself drained German manpower, as supply lines stretched and the long flanks of the German drive on the Caucasus grew increasingly attenuated. Stalin did not quite see things this way; on 29 July 1942, he issued his Order 227, mandating 'not one step back', a strategy so at odds with reality that it had little appreciable effect on developments at the front. The Germans spent late July and early August clearing the Soviets from the western bank of the Don River in its bend eastward, in preparation for further offensives.

Hitler took a fateful step in late July, ordering a continued advance east and south simultaneously. The Don's great swing east brought it close to the Volga's great swing west. Hitler now saw the need to push beyond the Don in order to prevent Soviet troops on the southern Volga – from Stalingrad downstream to Astrakhan – from attacking the eastern flank of the drive south to the Caucasus. As the Germans cleared the western bank of the Don, Army Group South split in two, with Army Group B under Bock moving east toward Stalingrad and Army Group A under List attacking southeast toward the Caucasus and Baku. This put overstretched German supply lines and scanty manpower reserves under still further strain.[17]

German high tide at Stalingrad

On 21 August, Friedrich Paulus's Sixth Army began its renewed offensive east and advanced quickly. The foremost German spearheads reached the Volga

pp. 1–121; Joel S. A. Hayward, *Stopped at Stalingrad: The Luftwaffe and Hitler's Defeat in the East* (Lawrence: University Press of Kansas, 1998), pp. 1–94.

17 Glantz, *To the Gates*, pp. 122–320; Hayward, *Stopped at Stalingrad*, pp. 120–221.

just north of Stalingrad on 23 August, and south of the city a few days later. Stalingrad was then isolated, connected to the rest of the Soviet Union only by ferry boats and pontoon bridges that shuttled men and ammunition across the Volga into the city. Stalingrad itself was reduced to rubble, first by a massive Luftwaffe raid and then by bitter street fighting, as Germans clawed their way toward the Volga to eliminate the last Soviet toeholds on the western bank. The German advantage in operational manoeuvre in open terrain was now useless, so Hitler's troops paid in blood for every yard they gained. Vasilii Chuikov's 62nd Army suffered terribly in weeks of struggle for the city, while additional Soviet armies fought to the north and south to maintain pressure on German flanks. Even German air superiority was of limited utility. While the Germans pounded the Soviet river crossings, in the city itself Soviet troops deliberately stayed as close to enemy lines as possible, to minimize the effect of German bombing and artillery fire.[18]

Stalingrad is often glibly portrayed in popular accounts of the war as a battle dictated by propaganda: Hitler desperately wanted the city named for Stalin, and Stalin could not afford to give it up. In reality, the city had real strategic importance. The broad lower Volga could serve as an excellent protection for the left flank of the German push toward the Caucasus; leaving the city in Soviet hands would provide an excellent staging area for a flank attack to cut off the German spearheads moving south to the Caucasus. In addition, the river itself served as a vital north–south transportation link for the Soviets. Cutting the Volga would in turn prevent much of the Soviet oil supply at Baku from getting to the rest of the Soviet Union further north.

The terrible manpower losses the Germans suffered in the streets of Stalingrad and their extended front lines forced them to rely on their allies to hold the ostensibly quiet sectors to the north and south of the city, where the front lines arced back toward the west. As the desperate struggle in the city continued, Vasilevskii spent two months massing an enormous strike force to break the sectors held by the Romanian Third (north) and Fourth (south) Armies. On 19 November, the Soviet Operation URANUS used the Southwest and Don Army Groups to shatter the Romanian defences northwest of Stalingrad, which were poorly equipped with tanks and anti-tank guns. Soviet tanks and cavalry sped into the space behind Paulus's Sixth Army. The southern pincer of the encirclement, the Stalingrad Army Group,

---

18 Glantz, *To the Gates*, pp. 321–486; David M. Glantz with Jonathan M. House, *Armageddon in Stalingrad: September–November 1942* (Lawrence: University Press of Kansas, 2009).

attacked the next day. By 23 November, Soviet advance formations met thirty-seven miles behind Stalingrad, trapping the Sixth Army and its 300,000 men in the city. The Soviets rapidly built up a ring, facing inward and outward, to contain the Sixth Army and prevent relief by the rest of Army Group B. Paulus asked for permission to break out of the trap; Hitler refused and Paulus lacked the moral courage to disobey, dooming his army. Hitler promised but could never deliver sufficient supplies to sustain the Sixth Army by air.

The Germans tried to break through the Soviet ring around Stalingrad, while the Soviets strove to force them to withdraw further. Erich von Manstein, now commanding a new Army Group Don, attacked toward Stalingrad on 12 December but could not reach the city; in the meantime, the Soviets began a second breakthrough and encirclement, Operation LITTLE SATURN, this time targeting the Germans' Italian allies. This attack seized the airfields supplying Paulus, further isolating the Sixth Army. Soviet armies sped toward the Black Sea, hoping to seize Rostov at the mouth of the Don River and cut off the retreat of the entire German Army Group A. Though Ewald von Kleist was forced into precipitous withdrawal north to avoid being trapped in the Caucasus, he managed to extricate his forces essentially intact. The last frozen, starving survivors of Paulus's Sixth Army finally surrendered on 2 February. Rostov fell on 14 February 1943, compelling the Germans to build a new defensive line on the Donets and Mius Rivers. At the same time as the Soviets made gains on the lower Don at Rostov, they likewise advanced on the upper Don. In mid-January, the Soviet Voronezh Army Group broke through the Hungarian Second Army south of Voronezh, then followed with an offensive against Voronezh itself, liberating the city on 25 January. The German Second Army, faced with possible encirclement, had no choice but to withdraw further west toward Kursk.[19]

Soviet momentum could not continue forever. The relentless pace of advance against fierce German resistance drained men and supplies from the Red Army, leaving it vulnerable to sharp local counter-attacks. Particularly in central Russia, a series of ambitious Soviet offensives in February were spoiled by an aggressive German defence. In the open territory of eastern Ukraine, Manstein used a masterful mobile defence to bloody several Soviet armies and succeeded in recapturing substantial amounts of lost

---

19 David M. Glantz, *From the Don to the Dnepr: Soviet Offensive Operations, December 1942– August 1943* (London: Frank Cass, 1991); Frank Ellis, *The Stalingrad Cauldron: Inside the Encirclement and Destruction of the 6th Army* (Lawrence: University Press of Kansas, 2013).

ground, including the industrial city of Kharkov. The after-effect of German defeats not only shook German morale, but made Hitler's allies increasing fearful of their fate in what increasingly seemed like a lost war. Hungary, Romania and Italy began to consider abandoning the Axis.[20]

Stalingrad and its consequences – the destruction of an entire German army and the resulting precipitate retreat of Axis forces in southern Russia – are well known. At the same time, however, an operation of similar scale was taking place west of Moscow, but without matching results. Operation MARS was an attack against the large German salient around Rzhev, left by the end of the Soviet counter-offensive around Moscow in late 1941 and early 1942. Far more Soviet troops were deployed here, west of Moscow, than around Stalingrad. Zhukov, coordinating the efforts of the Kalinin and Western Army Groups, attacked the Rzhev salient at the end of November 1942. Skilful German defence, bolstered by the timely addition of Panzer divisions, soon blunted the Soviet offensive. The battle for Rzhev lacked the drama of the clash at Stalingrad, and, because of its failure, was ignored in subsequent Soviet historiography. Zhukov's signal lack of success and the Red Army's massive casualties were obscured by the much greater victory at Stalingrad. Despite the failure of Operation MARS, the collapsing German position in the south made Germany's defences west of Moscow untenable as well, and Army Group Centre's commander Günther von Kluge carried out a planned withdrawal in March 1943.[21]

The last major battle of the winter of 1942/43 took place in the north. In late August 1942, a Soviet offensive outside Leningrad at Siniavino had succeeded in spoiling a German attack against the city, but fell far short of opening a land corridor into the city. By the end of 1942, as German attention and resources were drawn south to cope with the crisis around Stalingrad, the Soviets prepared a final breakthrough of the German blockade of Leningrad. Beginning on 12 January 1943, the Leningrad and Volkhov Army Groups managed to smash through well-fortified and long-established German positions. While the siege of Leningrad was not completely lifted, the Soviets did open a narrow path along the southern shore of Lake Ladoga, along which a light railway was quickly constructed to improve the flow of supplies into the city. A much more ambitious

20 Dana V. Sadarananda, *Beyond Stalingrad: Manstein and the Operations of Army Group Don* (Mechanicsburg, Pa.: Stackpole Books, 2009).
21 David M. Glantz, *Zhukov's Greatest Defeat: The Red Army's Epic Disaster in Operation Mars, 1942* (Lawrence: University Press of Kansas, 1999).

follow-up offensive, Operational POLAR STAR, failed to achieve the vast encirclements that Stalin hoped for.[22]

Kursk: the last major German offensive

As the Soviet offensives of early 1943 slowly ended, they left a front line dominated by an enormous salient around the city of Kursk, ninety miles north to south and sixty miles in depth. By spring 1943, Hitler was clearly losing the strategic initiative: the German position in North Africa was evaporating; the Allied bombing campaign was taking an increasing toll and pulling men and resources into anti-aircraft defence; and German losses of territory, manpower and equipment on the Eastern Front were deeply alarming. Hitler chose to deploy his scarce reserves in a summer offensive against the Kursk salient. Though in operational terms the Kursk salient made an obvious target – a giant bulge west into German lines invited attack from north and south to destroy it – it is difficult to find strategic sense in Hitler's thinking. Liquidating the Kursk salient would destroy Soviet formations and shorten the front line, but at a cost in scarce German lives and materiel; and shorter front lines for the Germans meant shorter lines for the Soviets as well. Breaking the Soviet front line at Kursk would offer the Germans no subsequent lucrative targets for a further offensive. It is difficult to avoid the impression that Operation CITADEL, the German attack on Kursk, was an offensive for its own sake: no conceivable outcome of the offensive could correct Germany's fundamental strategic shortcomings. Even hopes of more limited gains were lost by delay after delay in assembling men and equipment.[23]

The German offensive against Kursk finally began on 5 July 1943, with the Ninth Army attacking south from Orël and the Fourth Panzer Army north from Belgorod. The Soviets had spent the early summer preparing defensive works of impressive depth and complexity, defended by 1.3 million soldiers. Increasing Soviet advantages in production provided Konstantin Rokossovskii, commanding the northern flank, and Nikolai Vatutin, commanding the southern, parity in the air that deprived the Germans of one of their key previous advantages. Extensive Soviet obstacles, minefields and

---

22 Glantz, *Leningrad*, pp. 119–304.

23 Robert M. Citino, *The Wehrmacht Retreats: Fighting a Lost War, 1943* (Lawrence: University Press of Kansas, 2012), is particularly critical of Manstein's failures of imagination and leadership in the planning of Kursk.

12.2 Soviet-German front, 1943–44

trenches compelled the Germans into a positional battle of attrition, not the war of movement at which they still routinely bested the Soviets. Attrition did the Germans no good, as their 900,000 troops were decidedly outnumbered. The paired German offensives were slowed and finally halted, first the northern wing, and then the southern. A week after the German offensive began, the Soviets began their own carefully prepared counter-offensives into the Orël salient north of Kursk. The German southern offensive took longer to halt, culminating in an enormous tank clash at Prokhorovka. Losses were great on both sides, but the outnumbered Germans could ill-afford the burden. Mounting casualties compelled Hitler to call a halt to CITADEL on 13 July, and the Soviets followed on 3 August with a counter-offensive south of Kursk. The Southwestern and Southern Army Groups pushed toward Kharkov, which the Soviets finally took on 28 August. The Soviets now possessed clear materiel superiority as measured by tanks and artillery pieces, and German defences were simply overwhelmed by the massive application of force. The Germans still possessed operational superiority, though, avoiding wholesale encirclements and the resulting destruction of increasingly scarce divisions. Nonetheless, losses of irreplaceable manpower were increasingly serious, and the Wehrmacht would never again be able to amass a striking force akin to that at Kursk.[24]

In what had become the typical Soviet pattern, success in one sector was then followed by offensives at other points along the front. This time, however, resources were concentrated in a particularly important sector: against German positions in economically vital eastern Ukraine. In August and September, an attack in the Donbass cleared the region of Germans and then raced west toward the Dnepr River. The Soviet threat to the Dnepr crossings and thus to German escape forced the rapid evacuation of all of eastern Ukraine. The Germans then attempted to rebuild their defences using the Dnepr itself as a barrier, which meant that the front lines in the south had swung back to what they had been two years before, when the Germans destroyed the Soviet pocket at Kiev. By the end of the Soviet offensive in late summer and autumn, the Red Army had seized isolated bridgeheads on the Dnepr's western bank, including a large salient at Dnepropetrovsk. On 3 November, Nikolai Vatutin's Voronezh Front broke

24 David M. Glantz and Jonathan M. House, *The Battle of Kursk* (Lawrence: University Press of Kansas, 1999); Niklas Zetterling and Anders Frankson, *Kursk 1943: A Statistical Analysis* (London: Frank Cass, 2000); Dennis E. Showalter, *Armor and Blood: The Battle of Kursk: The Turning Point of World War II* (New York: Random House, 2013).

out of a small bridgehead north of Kiev, unhinging German defences along the Dnepr, forcing still further retreat, and liberating Kiev a few days later.

The momentum of the remarkable and essentially uninterrupted Soviet advance continued through western Ukraine, despite repeated local counterattacks, giving Hitler's generals little chance to set up coherent defensive positions. The effects of years of attrition, combined with the Soviet Union's decisive victory in the production war, meant that German forces were stretched too thin to sustain any halt or reverse they imposed on the Soviets. In December, the Soviet pursuit through western Ukraine trapped a half-dozen German divisions at Korsun, south of Kiev. In bitter fighting, the majority of the German troops managed to break out, but at least a third of their number and much of their equipment were left behind. The Soviet advance through western Ukraine crossed the region's numerous north–south rivers without serious delay. By April 1944, the Soviet pursuit, which had begun the previous August, finally stopped at the Dnestr River and the Carpathian Mountains.[25]

Northern Russia had been a comparatively quiet theatre once the Soviets had established a narrow lifeline to Leningrad. In January 1944, though, the Soviets removed all remaining danger to Leningrad by a daring offensive launched, in part, from an enclave on the Gulf of Finland, just west of the city. Though German losses were not catastrophic, front lines were pushed well back from the city. By summer 1944, the Soviets followed up by attacking Vyborg, first seized by the Soviets as a result of the Russo-Finnish War of 1939–40, then retaken by the Finns in 1941. Accepting that further fighting was pointless, the Finns in September made a peace deal with the Soviets. They escaped occupation, but sacrificed territory and had to eject German troops from northern Finland with their own forces.

The destruction of Army Group Centre

By spring 1944, Soviet advances in Ukraine and around Leningrad left the German Army Group Centre holding an enormous salient stretching toward Smolensk, and bordered on the south by the Pripiat Marshes. Just as the Kursk bulge had been an obvious German target in summer 1943, Army Group Centre was clearly vulnerable to Soviet attack in summer 1944. To the credit of Soviet deception and the chagrin of German intelligence, the Soviets

25 Niklas Zetterling and Anders Frankson, *The Korsun Pocket: The Encirclement and Breakout of a German Army in the East, 1944* (London: Casemate, 2008).

managed to conceal their plans for Operation BAGRATION, an enterprise stunning in its scope and ambition. Mistakenly preparing for a further Soviet attack in western Ukraine, the Germans were utterly unready for the attack that came. Zhukov and Vasilevskii assembled the forces of four separate army groups, including 4,000 tanks and 5,000 aircraft, to break through Army Group Centre's defences at multiple points, in order to carry out mechanized exploitation deep into German rear areas and prevent retreat. Army Group Centre, by contrast, had been stripped of most of its armour and a good portion of its infantry divisions to deal with crises north and south, as well as to prepare for the expected Anglo-American invasion of Western Europe.

Beginning on 22 June, Operation BAGRATION annihilated the German front lines at multiple points. German static defences, lacking sufficient reserves, were deployed far forward. Soviet partisan units, strongest behind German lines in Belorussia, finally came into their own by systematically attacking the German transportation network, preventing the dispatch of reinforcements or the withdrawal of men and materiel. The Germans recorded tens of thousands of separate acts of sabotage or attack on their rail network in the days before the offensive. Unable to retreat or effectively resist, dozens of German divisions were annihilated in place. Most of the German Ninth Army was encircled at Bobriusk and the Fourth Army at Minsk. On 17 July, 57,000 German prisoners were paraded through Moscow, in tribute to the scope of the Soviet victory. In just over a month, the Soviets advanced through all of Belorussia and eastern Poland to the suburbs of Warsaw, before exhaustion of men and supplies halted the advance.[26] In conjunction with the Soviet advance to the Vistula, the Polish Home Army launched an uprising in Warsaw against the German garrison. The Germans systematically crushed the Polish resistance and levelled the city, while the Soviets waited on the far bank. Historians have disputed ever since the degree of Stalin's responsibility for encouraging and then abandoning the Warsaw uprising. Soviet troops were certainly exhausted by their lengthy advance, but the destruction of the Home Army also eased Stalin's task of managing post-war Poland.[27]

Advances in Belorussia enabled further Soviet offensives elsewhere. In the north, the Soviets temporarily broke through to the Baltic coast, briefly

---

26 Gerb Neipold, *Battle for White Russia: The Destruction of Army Group Center, June 1944* (London: Brassey's, 1987).

27 Norman Davies, *Rising '44: The Battle for Warsaw* (New York: Viking, 2003), argues for Stalin's deliberate decision to withhold the Red Army.

isolating Army Group North in Estonia and Latvia. Though the Germans re-established contact, a Soviet offensive in September 1944 began collapsing the German pocket in the Baltic from the north. By October, a renewed Soviet offensive on the corridor south to Germany broke through to the Baltic again, trapping two German armies in Latvia. Though some units were evacuated from the pocket by sea, Hitler kept substantial forces in Latvia until the very end of the war, perhaps in hopes of using continued occupation of some sliver of what Stalin considered Soviet territory as leverage in a separate peace.

In the south, Soviet offensives began again in Ukraine in mid-July and advanced to the Carpathians and the Hungarian border. The Soviets had attempted an improvised invasion of Romania in the spring of 1944, but failed.[28] In August, the Soviets renewed their efforts in full strength and with much greater success. While German divisions continued to fight, exhausted and demoralized Romanian troops ceased effective resistance. With Romanian collapse, the Soviets encircled and destroyed the German Sixth Army (repeating the fate of its namesake at Stalingrad). On 23 August, an unexpected royal coup overthrew Romania's Marshal Ion Antonescu, and the country joined the Allies. This did not prevent Soviet occupation of the country. Romania's about-face subtracted hundreds of thousands of men from the Axis and added them to the Allies, while also depriving Germany of access to the oilfields at Ploieşti. Romania then joined the Soviets in a bitter campaign in Hungary. Bulgaria, which had joined the Axis but had not participated in the invasion of the Soviet Union, likewise abandoned Germany as soon as Soviet troops entered the country at the beginning of September. The collapse of the German position in the Balkans mandated the withdrawal of German occupying forces in Greece. By October, Hitler had removed Admiral Miklós Horthy from power in Hungary and replaced him with compliant Hungarian Fascists, not wishing to lose another ally. A Soviet offensive moved through the Hungarian plain to the outskirts of Budapest, starting a three-month struggle for the city. By the end of December, Soviet troops had completely encircled Budapest, though German and Hungarian troops fought on for another six weeks, and Hitler expended much of his precious remaining armour in futile attempts to break through to the city.

The headlong Soviet offensives over the summer and autumn of 1944 had made remarkable gains, but could not be sustained without lengthy pauses.

---

28 David M. Glantz, *Red Storm over the Balkans: The Failed Soviet Invasion of Romania, Spring 1944* (Lawrence: University Press of Kansas, 2007).

Soviet supply lines grew longer, and passed through transportation networks devastated by the fighting and, at least on Soviet territory, only a short time previously systematically sabotaged by partisans. Soviet troops were exhausted, while at the same time, German supply lines grew shorter, as did the length of front to be defended. German soldiers were now fighting not to hold on to Soviet territory, but instead to keep the Red Army off German soil. The way forward would be much more difficult. The long pause in Poland from September 1944 to the beginning of 1945 only signalled still greater carnage to come.

On the Soviet approach to East Prussia in summer 1944, anxiety, but not yet panic, gripped the German population. The region had been central to the German war effort as site of the Wolf's Lair, holding training grounds for soldiers headed to the Eastern Front, and hospitals for wounded soldiers returning the other way. After the destruction of Army Group Centre, the region organized for defence and the interception of deserters and refugees. Those who had been evacuated east to escape Allied bombing were now evacuated back west, while the local population was compelled to stay and bombarded with propaganda. In general, the Nazi leadership turned its population to building defensive barriers, not because of their actual usefulness – many were completely useless, intended only to maintain morale and distract popular discontent. The construction of the trenches served instead as a useful model of total mobilization for the rest of Germany to emulate. German civilians, though perhaps not fully aware of the extent of crimes in the occupied Soviet Union, nonetheless feared what life under Soviet occupation might mean. The death throes of Nazism, combining conscription of old men and teenaged boys, widespread application of the death penalty against cowardice or desertion, and resistance long past the point of rationality, did much to discredit Hitler's regime in the eyes of at least some Germans.[29]

Endgame

The Soviets planned a renewed offensive in central Poland for January 1945. The mass of men and materiel accumulated on a shrinking front left

29 David K. Yelton, *Hitler's Volkssturm: The Nazi Militia and the Fall of Germany, 1944–1945* (Lawrence: University Press of Kansas, 2002); Stephen G. Fritz, *Endkampf: Soldiers, Civilians, and the Death of the Third Reich* (Lexington: University Press of Kentucky, 2004); Alistair Noble, *Nazi Rule and the Soviet Offensive in Eastern Germany 1944–45: The Darkest Hour* (Eastbourne: Sussex Academic Press, 2009); Ian Kershaw, *The End: The Defiance and Destruction of Hitler's Germany, 1944–1945* (New York: Penguin, 2011).

less room for operational flexibility. The Red Army abandoned its system of *Stavka* representatives coordinating multiple army groups in a single operation. Instead, Stalin took direct control of the final campaigns and played his army group commanders against one another: Zhukov abandoned his previous role coordinating multiple army groups to take command of the First Belorussian Army Group at Warsaw. Ivan Konev, now Zhukov's chief rival for martial glory, commanded the First Ukrainian Army Group to its south. Soviet industry provided them both with tanks, artillery and aircraft on a massive scale. At the same time, the British and American bombing campaign, combined with the Allied advance through Western Europe, had finally begun to bite. Men and materiel were drawn into the fight in the West, and persistent fuel shortages limited the effectiveness of the tanks and planes that Germany could still muster in the East.

In mid-January, Konev and Zhukov exploded out of the Soviet bridgeheads on the western bank of the Vistula and raced toward Berlin, moving into the vital industrial region of Silesia and pocketing additional German divisions on the Baltic's southern coast. Within a month, Soviet advance units had reached the Oder, tantalizingly close to Berlin; but the persistent problem of maintaining supply lines, combined with substantial German forces still remaining in northern and southern Poland and the Baltic coast threatening the flanks of the Soviet advance, halted the offensive. Having failed to take Berlin off the march, the Soviets had to assemble once again the men and materiel for a full-scale assault on the city. For two months, Soviet troops systematically cleared German holdouts on their flanks to enable the final attack on Berlin itself.

By mid-April, the Soviet offensive, mustering 2.5 million men, was ready. Konev and Zhukov, now joined by Rokossovskii's 2nd Belorussian Army Group, ground slowly and at great cost through a desperate German defence. Soviet troops worked their way into Berlin's eastern suburbs, and Konev and Zhukov's forces linked up behind Berlin on 25 April. As fighting still raged in the streets of the city, Hitler killed himself on 30 April, and the remaining defenders of Berlin surrendered soon after. In a messy and chaotic finish, two separate surrenders of all German forces took place soon after, on 7 May in the west and 9 May in the east.[30]

---

30 Tony Le Tissier, *The Battle of Berlin 1945* (London: Jonathan Cape, 1988); Christopher Duffy, *Red Storm on the Reich : The Russian March on Germany, 1945* (London: Routledge, 1991).

13

The Mediterranean and North Africa, 1940–1944

SIMON BALL

Between 1940 and 1944, there was a series of significant Mediterranean land, sea and air campaigns. An analysis of these campaigns reveals that there were four parallel Mediterranean wars: the campaigns fought *in* the Mediterranean; the war *for* the Mediterranean littoral; the war for passage *through* the Mediterranean; and the war fought *to escape* the Mediterranean.

The distinctive character of the war in the Mediterranean was shaped by the existence of four strategic dispositions. Fighting for territory around the Mediterranean was the preserve of those we might call *dominators*, fighting to get through the Mediterranean, *voyagers*, and fighting to get out of the Mediterranean, *escapers*. A fourth disposition developed during the war that could be characterized as that of *fighters*. Fighters were waging war *in* the Mediterranean, but the Mediterranean held no particular strategic interest for them: its unique geographical and spatial features, however, did seem to offer specific opportunities for causing the enemy casualties, almost devoid of strategic and political context. Depending on disposition, a policy-maker would be willing to allocate a different level of resources to the Mediterranean. Perhaps as importantly, they would regard the same level of allocation with a different degree of enthusiasm: this shaped how they recorded the decisions that were made, and thus the subsequent historical record. Thus escapers endorsed a resource-intensive war in the Mediterranean, while often expressing scepticism about its importance.

No disposition was the sole property of any one belligerent, although they were present in different proportions in each. Even the Italians, the power fighting most straightforwardly for conquests around the Mediterranean, had a mixed disposition. One could fight, Mussolini had said in the 1930s, for the 'natural space' of the Mediterranean. Yet, Il Duce feared, the Mediterranean would become a prison. The proper 'historical objectives' of his empire were Asia, Africa and 'the Oceans', not the Mediterranean itself.[1]

Strategic debate operated at two levels. The first tier of policy-makers did not explain themselves clearly in public. 'I have announced in Parliament', Churchill said of the September 1943 Salerno landings, 'that the Italian campaign is "The Third Front"'. 'This form of statement should be adhered to', he instructed, 'as it...avoids arguing...as to whether the Italian campaign is the second front or not'.[2] Nevertheless, there was a 'strategic public sphere' in which politicians and journalists tried to work out what the Allies were fighting for. This public sphere persisted throughout the post-war period, and also shaped the memory of the Mediterranean war. The question of belligerents' goals remained a puzzle in the 'strategic public sphere'. John North, one of the first historians of the war, noticed in 1944 that 'the war in the Mediterranean was...only superficially a struggle between land armies for victory or defeat on the field of battle'.[3] As a result, North wrote in 1945, there would be 'the attempt to resolve [the] as yet unresolved question of grand strategy' in the Mediterranean. He also warned, in vain, that 'today, after victory, these are but arid topics'.[4]

Voyagers

The British described the Mediterranean as an 'artery'.[5] Armies and navies made the passage to the East through the artery; raw materials, tin, rubber, tea and, above all, oil, made their way West. The Mediterranean was not, however, Britain's only arterial route. Many of the same destinations could be reached by sailing the Atlantic–Indian Ocean route around Africa via the Cape of Good Hope. The Mediterranean's chief attraction was speed. A ship steaming from the Port of London to Bombay would take a full fortnight longer, and travel nearly 4,500 miles more to reach its destination, if it did not pass through the Mediterranean. For the British, Mussolini charged, the

1 Reynolds Salerno, *Vital Crossroads: Mediterranean Origins of the Second World War, 1935–1940* (Ithaca, NY: Cornell University Press, 2002), p. 106.
2 Churchill to General Sir Harold Alexander, 25 September 1943, CHAR 20/119, Churchill Papers, Churchill College Archives Centre (hereafter CHAR).
3 John North, 'Lessons of the North African Campaign', *Military Affairs* 8 (fall 1944), 161–9, quotation at 161.
4 John North, 'Two Armies', *Military Affairs* 9 (fall 1945), 270–4.
5 Elizabeth Monroe, *The Mediterranean in Politics* (Oxford University Press, 1938), p. 11.

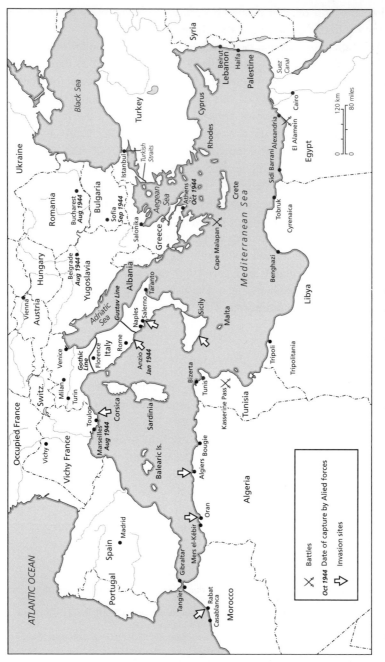

13.1 Mediterranean and North Africa, 1940–44

Mediterranean was no more than 'a short cut whereby the British empire reaches more rapidly its outlying territories'.[6]

A hostile Italy made it hard to imagine 'the artery' as a centrepiece of strategy. As early as 1925, the iconoclastic British military thinker Basil Liddell Hart had written that, 'when to the proved menace of submarine power is added the potential effect of aircraft attack against shipping in the narrow seas, it is time the British people awoke to the fact that, in the case of such a war, the Mediterranean would be impassable, and that this important artery would have to be abandoned'. The Suez Canal was really of little use, since shipping would have to sail instead round the Cape. Returning to the subject in the wake of the Italian conquest of Ethiopia and the outbreak of the Spanish Civil War in 1936, Liddell Hart was satisfied that his predictions had proved accurate.[7]

In public, navalists rejected new thinking on Mediterranean strategy.[8] Yet for all their protestations about the sanctity of their battleships, the Admirals were, in reality, far from sanguine. Dudley Pound, the wartime British First Sea Lord, then commanding the Royal Navy's Mediterranean Fleet, believed that the movement of a convoy through the Mediterranean, if opposed by Italian submarines and aeroplanes, would become a major fleet operation. As a result, 'the Central and Eastern Mediterranean, though seemingly one of the nearest of the foreign stations, becomes...the most distant of all'.[9] In 1938, General 'Tiny' Ironside, subsequently Chief of the Imperial General Staff, was sent to inspect British military preparations in the Mediterranean. He confided to his diary 'that it would be far too dangerous for our ships to think of going into the Mediterranean until we have cleared the air properly'. Ironside concluded that 'the Mediterranean was now much more vulnerable than the Navy will ever admit'.[10]

The Royal Navy used a friendly defence correspondent, Hector Bywater, subsequently famous as 'the man who predicted Pearl Harbor', to put its doubts into the public domain. Bywater challenged 'myths' about the Mediterranean. 'In my experience four people out of five are convinced that denial

---

6 'Italian Role in Europe; Mediterranean Interests', *The Times*, 2 November 1936, p. 14.

7 Basil Liddell Hart, 'The Strategic Future of the Mediterranean', *Yale Review* 26:2 (1937), 232–45.

8 Admiral Sir Herbert Richmond, 'The Strategy of the Mediterranean', *Foreign Affairs* 14 (1935/36), 274–82.

9 Lawrence Pratt, *East of Malta, West of Suez: Britain's Mediterranean Crisis, 1936–1939* (Cambridge University Press, 1975), p. 119.

10 Sir Edmund Ironside, *The Ironside Diaries, 1937–1940*, ed. Roderick Macleod and Denis Kelly (London: Constable, 1962), 26 June 1937 and 2 October 1938.

of the Mediterranean route would lead to grave shortage of foodstuffs and raw materials in Britain, if not to famine conditions', he wrote. 'And yet', Bywater warned, 'that belief is unfounded'. Britons should know 'what an appalling liability the Mediterranean was to us during the last war'. 'It is', Bywater concluded, 'quite probable that a compromise policy would be adopted, the effect of which would be that we should retain...our strategic grip on the Mediterranean route between Gibraltar and the Suez Canal by the conjoint use of naval, military and air power, while declaring that route out of bounds for all non-combatant traffic'. Bywater's account was an accurate description of the strategy Britain adopted when it went to war with Italy in the summer of 1940.[11] Within days of becoming Prime Minister, Winston Churchill declared: 'I regard the Mediterranean as closed'.[12]

The 'compromise policy' narrowed the bounds of debate about the artery from grand strategy to operations. It set up a persistent discord between Churchill and his admirals as to whether military convoys could, or should, sail through the Mediterranean. In July 1940, Churchill said that he was 'going to insist that convoys should come through the Mediterranean'.[13] The admirals, on the whole, took a cautious line. The result was that between 1940 and 1942, each convoy sent through the Mediterranean, beginning with HATS in August 1940, was the subject of detailed and pressured debate. The convoys were infrequent, carefully planned and resource-intensive. Their purpose was threefold: to transfer naval forces into the Eastern Mediterranean, to reinforce Middle East Command in Egypt and, latterly, to resupply Malta.

Sea power thus became the servant of land and air power. This subordination was costly. In February 1942, the Kriegsmarine were able to report to Hitler that 'the most significant factor at this time is that not a single heavy British ship in the Mediterranean is fully seaworthy. The Axis rules both the sea and the air in the Central Mediterranean... the Mediterranean situation is definitely favourable at the moment'.[14] And it was seaworthiness that presented the British with their main challenge. Sixteen major surface units were sunk in the Mediterranean in 1941 and 1942, including two aircraft

---

11 Hector Bywater, 'The Changing Balance of Forces in the Mediterranean', *International Affairs* 16 (1937), 361–87.
12 Churchill to Major General 'Pug' Ismay, 29 May 1940, in Martin Gilbert (ed.), *The Churchill War Papers*, vol. II: *Never Surrender* (3 vols., New York: W. W. Norton, 1995).
13 Bernard Freyberg, 'Diary', 8 July 1940, in ibid.
14 Report by the Commander-in-Chief of the German navy to the Führer, 13 February 1942, *Fuehrer Conferences on Naval Affairs* (London: Admiralty, 1947).

carriers and a battleship. This amounted to about 20 per cent of the front-line strength of the Royal Navy.[15] The operational losses to the fleet were magnified, however, because of battle damage that required months in repair. When two battleships were seriously damaged in December 1941, one of them only returned to service in the summer of 1943. The British naval Commander-in-Chief in the Mediterranean, Andrew Cunningham, admitted in March 1942 that although he had the largest command in the Royal Navy, 'there is now no fleet to go to sea in'.[16]

In his valedictory report, Cunningham charged that Britain had lost sight of why it was fighting in North Africa. 'The strategic reason for our presence in Gibraltar, Malta and the Middle East', he wrote in June 1942,

> is in order that we may have control of the Mediterranean Sea. At the moment that control has lapsed to an alarming extent owing to our weakened sea power which is due in part to war losses and weakness in the air and in part to the enemy success on land in capturing the important air and sea bases which we need... Until our strategical direction is fully alive to the implications of sea power we shall fail to achieve our objects. Within the Mediterranean the problem is principally that of application of sea power and our fighting ashore should be directed to assist in that application.[17]

The Chief of the Imperial General Staff, Alan Brooke, believed that Churchill did not understand the true import of Cunningham's argument: 'the situation as regards shipping [without the Mediterranean route] is most disturbing and one that the PM will not face', he wrote in February 1942, 'and yet it is the one situation that will affect our whole strategy during the coming year'.[18]

When he returned to the Mediterranean in November 1942, however, as naval commander for the TORCH landings in Morocco and Algeria, Cunningham discomfited Brooke by pointing out that the arterial Mediterranean strategy was different from 'the Mediterranean strategy'. He told the Combined Chiefs of Staff at Casablanca that he could command the Mediterranean without the possession of Sicily. He openly doubted whether

15 S. W. Roskill, *The War at Sea, 1939–1945* (5 vols., London: HMSO, 1953–61), vol. I, pp. 50, 586–7; vol. III, pt. 1, p. 376; vol. III, pt. 2, pp. 436, 448.

16 Michael Simpson (ed.), *The Cunningham Papers*, vol. I: *The Mediterranean Fleet, 1939–1942* (2 vols., Aldershot: Ashgate, 1999), 15 March 1942.

17 Cunningham, 'Memorandum on Command in the Middle East', in Simpson (ed.), *Cunningham Papers*, vol. I, 10 June 1942.

18 Alex Danchev and Dan Todman (eds.), *War Diaries, 1939–1945: Field Marshal Lord Alanbrooke* (London: Weidenfeld & Nicolson, 2001), 4 February 1942.

possession of the island 'would add very greatly to the security of the sea route through the Mediterranean'. 'If we were in Sicily', Cunningham observed, 'he would estimate the route as being 90% or more secure, without Sicily it would be 85% secure once we held the whole of the North African coast'.[19] Nevertheless, when General George Marshall, the Chief of Staff of the US Army, came to justify the American Joint Chiefs of Staff's eventual support for an invasion of Sicily in July 1943, he said it was because the capture of Sicily would make the Mediterranean more secure for Allied shipping and save merchant vessels from the long haul around South Africa.[20] Admiral Doenitz, Commander of the German navy, identified the opening of the Mediterranean, achieved without the conquest of Sicily, as a major Allied strategic victory: 'the Anglo-Saxon powers have gained two million tons in shipping space since the Mediterranean was cleared'.[21]

The 'arterial strategy' made the most sense of the North African campaigns. There was never a 'Desert War'. The British, Italians and Germans fought for a coast road, a series of port settlements and aerodromes in North Africa. Marshal Balbo had built a 1,300-mile highway from the Tunisian border to the Egyptian frontier – the 'Balbia' – in 1937. British ambition was defined by how far west they intended to travel along the Balbia. When the British recaptured the town of Sollum in Egypt in December 1940, the Commander-in-Chief, Middle East, Sir Archibald Wavell, agreed with his air and sea counterparts that their target should be the Mediterranean ports of Italian Cyrenaica, first Bardia and ultimately Tobruk.[22] In the spring of 1941, 'the Chiefs of Staff were of the opinion that we should make certain of our hold of the Eastern Mediterranean... to carry out this policy, we must first of all clear out Cyrenaica, and secure Benghazi'.[23] Following the fall of Crete in May 1941, Andrew Cunningham defined strategy as 'to try and close [the] southern flank'. 'If', he said, 'the army can advance sufficiently to reach, say, Derna, a good deal will have been done... the whole object of thus clearing

19 Ibid., 18 January 1943.
20 Meeting of the Combined Chiefs of Staff with Churchill and Roosevelt, 18 January 1943, US Department of State, *Foreign Relations of the United States: The Conferences at Washington, 1941–1942, and Casablanca, 1943* (Washington DC: US Government Printing Office, 1968), p. 631.
21 Report to the Führer at HQ Wolfsschanze, 14 May 1943, *Fuehrer Conferences on Naval Affairs*.
22 I. S. O. Playfair, The Mediterranean and Middle East, *vol.* i: *The Early Successes Against Italy* (6 vols., amended edn, London: HMSO, 1974), pp. 257–75.
23 Minutes of Defence Committee (Operations), 20 January 1941, in Martin Gilbert (ed.), *The Churchill War Papers*, vol. iii: *The Ever-widening War, 1941* (3 vols., New York: W. W. Norton, 2001).

the Southern flank is to provide a series of airfields'.[24] Derna was located on the bulge of the Libyan plateau, which pushed out into the Mediterranean: not only was it a short flight from the Sicilian Narrows, but it was in range of Greece and the Aegean. One excuse made for the slow advance of the Eighth Army in November 1942, after El Alamein, was the pivotal importance of Derna. Montgomery claimed that his goal was to establish the RAF in the 'Derna triangle' of aerodromes, from whence it could 'dominate the Mediterranean'.[25]

In retrospect, the land campaigns in Libya and Tunisia could be reconfigured to be the handmaidens of a naval strategy. Indeed, that strategy was portrayed as a specifically British triumph. On Trinity Sunday, 20 June 1943, King George VI sailed in triumph from Tripoli to Valletta. 'I thought', Cunningham wrote, 'a visit to Malta would have a great effect all over the British Empire'.[26] The visit had an effect on His Majesty. He subsequently advocated welching on agreements to invade Northwest Europe. Since things had 'turned out even better than we could ever have hoped for...would it not be possible to carry on there'? he asked Churchill. 'Look', he urged his Prime Minister, 'at the present position in the Mediterranean. The whole of North Africa is ours, we command the Mediterranean Sea itself'.[27]

'The Mediterranean route to the East', the British declared in June 1943, 'was again open'. By this, they meant that 'super convoys' of over a hundred ships at a time could sail east through the Sicilian Narrows, passing beyond Malta to points in the Eastern Mediterranean. Due to their size, these super convoys had a relatively low proportion of escorts to merchant ships. Their composition was thus in stark contrast to the 'compromise policy', in which a few merchant ships were fought through the Mediterranean by a much larger flotilla of warships. A ship sailing from Liverpool to Egypt now had its journey time shortened by forty-five days, as a result of cutting through the Mediterranean instead of having to sail round South Africa. The 'opening' of the Mediterranean actually increased Allied ship casualties in the short term: there were now many

24 Cunningham to Pound, in Simpson (ed.), *Cunningham Papers*, vol. i, 28 May 1941.
25 Nigel Hamilton, *Monty: Master of the Battlefield, 1942–44* (Sevenoaks: Sceptre, 1987), pp. 56–7.
26 Cunningham to Aunt Doodles, in Michael Simpson (ed.), *The Cunningham Papers*, vol. ii: *The Triumph of Allied Sea Power, 1942–1946* (2 vols., Aldershot: Ashgate, 2006), 24 June 1943.
27 King George VI to Churchill, 14 October 1943, CHAR 20/92.

more merchant ships to sink. As a proportion of the whole, however, such losses were annoying rather than serious.[28]

By the summer of 1944, well over 800 convoys, comprising 12,000 ships, had passed through the Mediterranean.[29] In his immediate retrospect of the North African campaign, John North argued that 'the clearing of the North African coastline, as a preliminary to the re-opening of the Mediterranean route to Allied shipping, was a major strategic objective from the transportation angle alone'.[30] He went on to acknowledge that a belief in the primacy of the arterial strategy, 'the safety of the Mediterranean route – the first priority of the whole Allied strategy of the war', posed difficult questions for the later conduct of the war.[31]

Escapers

In the 1930s, Mussolini had predicted that the Mediterranean would become a prison. The Italian navy did not, however, get very far in providing a detailed escape plan. As an existing global empire, the British had historically been less concerned about becoming trapped in the Mediterranean. As a result, thinking about 'the escape from the Mediterranean' was much less developed than the 'arterial strategy'.

In March 1940, Winston Churchill, then still First Lord of the Admiralty, wrote that 'the question that stares us in the face is "How are we going to win the war?"'[32] Churchill argued that the 'supreme strategic operation' should be an escape from the Mediterranean. The argument about the form and direction of this escape is what came to be known as 'the Mediterranean strategy' in Michael Howard's classic use of the phrase. The argument formed the centrepiece of Anglo-American debates in the middle years of the war. By that time, the British and the Americans had a complex system of strategic decision-making: large staffs produced endless papers on the subject. They indulged in what became known as a 'transatlantic essay contest'.

---

28 'The Story of the North African Coastal Convoys', AIR 23/7511, The National Archives, Kew, London (hereafter TNA).

29 *Mare Nostrum*, 14 September 1944, AIR 23/920, TNA; 'British, Allied and Neutral Merchant Ship Losses in the Mediterranean and the Indian Ocean due to Enemy Action', AIR 41/54, TNA.

30 North, 'Lessons of the North African Campaign', 161.

31 North, 'Two Armies', 270–4.

32 Churchill to Admiral Dudley Pound, 23 March 1940, in Martin Gilbert (ed.), *The Churchill War Papers*, vol. 1: *At the Admiralty, September 1939–May 1940* (New York: W. W. Norton, 1993).

At root, however, Allied strategy rested on British assumptions held over from the early years of the war. These assumptions boiled down to two beliefs. First, the Axis could be 'bottled up' in the Mediterranean. Second, a *coup de main* in the Mediterranean would provide a 'quick fix' that would unravel the Axis.[33]

Contemporaries made great claims for 'bottling up'. *The Spectator* argued in April 1941 that 'the importance of [the Mediterranean] is beyond exaggeration... it is the scene today of a strategy vast in its conceptions... [the] German pincers movement is...directed from the north and south of that sea, with the remainder of the Balkans, Turkey, Syria, Palestine, Iraq and Egypt as its destined prey...[and] geographically still more ambitious, aiming at securing Spain, Morocco, Tunis, Algeria and Libya'.[34] The press carried interviews with German POWs who made much the same point. 'We are not going to attempt to conquer all Russia', boasted a captured Luftwaffe flyer in perfect English, but 'come through the Caucasus and take Iraq, Iran, and probably Egypt. Then we will offer you peace'.[35] After the war, on the basis of his interviews with the former commander of the Afrikakorps, von Thoma, Basil Liddell Hart became sceptical of 'bottling up'. He quoted von Thoma as saying that 'the great pincer movement against the Middle East, which your people imagined to be in progress, was never a serious plan. It was vaguely discussed in Hitler's entourage, but our General Staff never agreed with it, nor regarded it as practicable'.[36] Against von Thoma, however, Hitler himself could be quoted. The British geopolitical writer, Gordon East, wrote in 1952 of 'the grandiose strategy of the enemy, which would have outflanked the Allied position in the Mediterranean by a gigantic pincer movement directed toward the Middle East from the Caucasus and from Libya'.[37] Norman Angell 'put again and again to American anti-imperialists the question: "Would not Germany and Japan have won their war against the West and its institutions if there had been no British Empire in 1940 – no Gibraltar, Malta, a base in Egypt to prevent the junction of the totalitarian powers?"'[38]

---

33 Churchill to Pound and Vice Admiral Tom Phillips, 1 May 1940, in Gilbert (ed.), *Churchill War Papers*, vol. 1, pp. 1181–2.
34 'The Mediterranean War', *The Spectator*, 25 April 1941, pp. 440–1.
35 'When Rommel Failed', *The Times*, 1 August 1942, p. 4.
36 B. H. Liddell Hart, *The German Generals Talk* (London: Harper Perennial, 2002 [1948]), p. 162.
37 Gordon East, 'The Mediterranean: Pivot of Peace and War', *Foreign Affairs* 31 (1952/53), 619–33.
38 Sir Norman Angell, 'America-Britain', *The Spectator*, 20 September 1946, pp. 281–2.

The actual importance of Egypt, as the stopper in the bottle, remained a moot point. Churchill himself had been heard to say that Egypt was not vital, although that was not his settled position.[39] Sir Arthur Longmore, the commander of the RAF in the Middle East, said 'it really didn't matter whether we held Egypt or not. All we had to do was to fall South and let the Mediterranean look after itself'.[40] Military doubts about 'bottling up' culminated in a confrontation between Churchill and Sir John Dill, the Chief of the Imperial General Staff, which resulted in an irreparable breach between the two men. Dill told Churchill that 'the loss of Egypt...would not end the War'. Churchill replied contemptuously that, 'I gather you would be prepared to face the loss of Egypt and the Nile Valley, together with the surrender or ruining of the Army of half a million we have concentrated there... I do not take that view'.[41]

If 'bottling up' remained in place from 1940 to 1942, the 'quick fix' had been abandoned as a strategy before the outbreak of the war. Mediterranean war planning reached a crescendo in the spring and early summer of 1939. Then the bubble of expectations burst. In May 1939, Sir Roger Backhouse, the most outspoken British champion of the 'quick fix', died in office. His successor as First Sea Lord, Dudley Pound, who would hold the post until his own premature death in 1943, arrived at the Admiralty fresh from commanding the Mediterranean Fleet. From his headquarters in Malta, Pound had regarded the stream of scenarios for a knockout blow against Italy that had flowed from London with contempt. The Royal Navy performed a volte-face. 'Britain', it now stated, 'could not, as hitherto contemplated...undertake offensive naval action' in the Mediterranean.[42]

Although Pound killed off the specific naval war plans, the belief in the 'quick fix' proved too strong to shake for long. It was publicly resuscitated by Churchill's Christmas 1940 'Appeal to the Italian People'. 'One man and one man alone has ranged the Italian people in deadly struggle against the British Empire', Churchill claimed, 'to stand up to the battery of the whole British Empire on sea, in the air, and in Africa'. The response should be clear: 'the Italian nation will once more take a hand in shaping its own fortunes; surely

---

39 Anthony Eden, 'Diary', 12 August 1940, in Gilbert (ed.), *Churchill War Papers*, vol. II.
40 Trefor Evans (ed.), *The Killearn Diaries, 1934–1946* (London: Sidgwick and Jackson, 1972), 14 April 1941.
41 Alex Danchev, 'Dilly-Dally, or Having the Last Word: FM Sir John Dill and PM Winston Churchill', *Journal of Contemporary History* 22 (1987), 21–44.
42 Salerno, *Vital Crossroads*, p. 131.

the Italian army...[which] evidently has no heart for the job, should take some care of the life and future of Italy'.[43]

Experience of the 'quick fix' proved disappointing, but was frequently explained away as a failure to put enough effort into the blow. Pre-war naval 'quick fixers' had identified Genoa as an exposed target for naval bombardment. In February 1941, Force H was ordered to shell Genoa, overruling the objections of its commander, Admiral James Somerville. Nevertheless, Somerville's unseen approach on Genoa was a masterpiece of the naval operational art. The bombardment of the city was claimed as a triumph of political daring in London.[44] The impression was similar in Rome and Berlin.[45] But there could be no sustained follow-up to the operation once the Italians established proper air and sea patrols.[46] A mission of thirty-five parachutists was inserted into southern Italy to attack an aqueduct, but was lost. This failure effectively halted special force operations in Italy until after the Allied invasion in 1943. In the same month, an attempt to establish a base on the small Italian Aegean island of Castelrizzo turned into a farce.[47] Churchill claimed that the problem was lack of ambition: 'all that the Commanders-in-Chief had so far wished to attempt was the landing of small forces on unimportant islands'.[48]

With regard to both 'bottling up' and the 'quick fix', it could be argued that others' assumptions about what the British could do were as important as actual British plans. In December 1940, it was Hitler who believed that it was 'important to frustrate English efforts to establish...an air base that would threaten Italy in the first place and, incidentally, the Rumanian oilfields'.[49] His answer was a plan for the seizure of important points on the north Mediterranean littoral, particularly Salonika, and the immediate deployment of significant air forces in the Mediterranean. In January 1941,

43 'Mr. Churchill Speaks to the Italian People', *The Times*, 24 December 1940; Lord Hood to No. 10, 24 December 1940, enclosing Ministry of Information, Censorship Division, Intelligence Unit report on Churchill's Speech to the Italian People, CHAR 9/176A-B.

44 Michael Simpson (ed.), *The Somerville Papers: Selections from the Private and Official Correspondence of Admiral of the Fleet Sir James Somerville* (Aldershot: Scolar Press, 1995), 6 February 1941.

45 Fred Taylor (ed.), *The Goebbels Diaries, 1939–1941* (New York: Putnam's, 1983), 13 February 1941.

46 Simpson (ed.), *Somerville Papers*, 10 February 1941.

47 Simpson (ed.), *Cunningham Papers*, vol. 1, 24 February 1941.

48 Minutes of Defence Committee (Operations), 20 January 1941, in Gilbert (ed.), *Churchill War Papers*, vol. III, pp. 101–4.

49 Hugh Trevor-Roper (ed.), *Hitler's War Directives, 1939–1945* (Edinburgh: Birlinn, 2004), Directive 20, 20 December 1940.

Hitler directed that 'the situation in the Mediterranean area, where England is employing superior forces against our allies, requires that Germany should assist for reasons of strategy, politics and psychology'.[50] In February 1941, Hitler decided to intervene with land forces in North Africa. His reasoning was based on the fear of a British escape from the Mediterranean. The loss of Libya in itself was bearable, but it might cause Italy to drop out of the war. Germany would then be 'bottled up' in the south coast of France.[51]

After the war, Kesselring argued that Germany had played into Britain's hands by taking a half-hearted approach to the threat of itself being 'bottled up', while the British escaped from the Mediterranean. The 'main error', he claimed,

> lay in a total misunderstanding of the importance of the African and Mediterranean theatre. I never understood the ideas of Hitler and the Wehrmacht operations staff. Their fundamental mistake was completely to misjudge the importance of the Mediterranean theatre. They would not or could not see that from the end of 1941 the colonial war had taken on a different aspect, that Africa had become a theatre in which decisions vital to Europe were maturing.[52]

There were attempts by those gathered around Hitler to persuade him that the Mediterranean was the key to victory. The Führer never accepted their arguments. His eyes were cast ever eastward. His judgement took lapidary form in June 1941, when he issued his directive on the future of the *Mittelmeer*. The key to the removal of the Mediterranean bottle-stopper lay on the Steppes. The conquest of Russia would change everything. Turkey would have its twin fears – the Soviets and the Germans – unified into one terror. It would not resist as the forces of the Reich moved through the Straits by sea and Anatolia by land. The Spanish were timid: Franco had squirmed his way out of an attack on Gibraltar. With further proof of the Reich's invincibility, his courage would improve and the British would be swept off the Rock. The French would see that full collaboration was their only chance of survival: North Africa would be open to German forces. Then the British Mediterranean would be choked to death, squeezed from East and West by what Hitler called a 'concentric' attack. The Mediterranean could wait months before the final reckoning. It was the three gates to the

---

50 Hitler, in ibid., Directive 22, 11 January 1941.
51 Franz Halder, *The Halder War Diary, 1939–1942*, ed. Charles Burdick and Hans-Adolf Jacobsen (London: Greenhill, 1988), 3 February 1941.
52 Albert Kesselring, *Memoirs* (London: William Kimber, 1953), p. 157.

sea – Gibraltar, Suez and the Straits – which were the important blocks, not the central Mediterranean.[53]

If Mussolini's regime collapsed before Germany had finished with Russia, then the completion of the concentric attack on the Mediterranean would be complicated. Hitler was prepared, therefore, to commit some resources to the Mediterranean, not least to fuel the efforts of his most photogenic general, Erwin Rommel.[54] A naval force was added to the land and air forces.[55]

The strategy of 'bottling up' always ran, in British minds, in parallel with the 'quick fix'. Even before any significant victory had been won in North Africa, Churchill was confident that the deployment of American military power in French North Africa would make escape a genuine political and military possibility. He proposed a spacious definition of the 'Second Front' as comprising 'both the Atlantic and Mediterranean coasts of Europe', along with the idea that 'we can push either right-handed [in the Mediterranean], left-handed [across the English Channel], or both-handed as our resources and circumstances permit'.[56] When Churchill attempted to sell this version of 'escape' to a sceptical Stalin in August 1942, he drew a sketch of a crocodile. Northern France, he said, constituted the 'hard snout' of Hitler's Europe; it was better, therefore, first to strike at the enemy's 'soft belly' in the Mediterranean.[57]

The concept of the 'soft underbelly' was, to some extent, a political convenience for Churchill and Roosevelt. 'We believe', they jointly assured Stalin after Casablanca, 'that these operations [in the Mediterranean]...may well bring Germany to its knees in 1943'. The US Joint Chiefs of Staff were enduringly sceptical: 'Italy is not a vital Axis area', they declared. The 'chances' of a successful conquest of Italy were 'acceptable', 'but further exploitation toward France doubtful'.[58] There were, however, genuine military adherents of the Mediterranean 'quick fix'. Alan Brooke said to his staff officer, John Kennedy, before they set off for the Casablanca Conference in

---

53 Hitler, in Trevor-Roper (ed.), *Hitler's War Directives*, Directive 32, 11 June 1941.

54 Taylor (ed.), *Goebbels Diaries*, 21 March 1941.

55 Conference of the Commander-in-Chief of the navy with the Führer at HQ Wolfsschanze in the afternoon of 22 August 1941, *Fuehrer Conferences on Naval Affairs*.

56 Churchill to Ismay for Chiefs of Staff, 23 July 1942, CHAR 20/67.

57 David Reynolds, *In Command of History: Churchill Fighting and Writing the Second World War* (London: Penguin, 2005), p. 316.

58 'Invasion of the European Continent from Bases in the Mediterranean in 1943–44', 8 May 1943, JCS 288/1, President's Secretary's File, Current Strategic Studies, book II, box 2.

January 1943, that he was 'quite determined to go flat out in the Mediterranean: if we can get near enough to bomb the Rumanian oil fields and cut the Aegean and Turkish traffic there is a real probability that the Germans may collapse within a year'.[59]

When Brooke had taken office in December 1941, he wrote, 'I am positive that our policy for the conduct of the war should be to direct both our military and political efforts towards the early conquest of North Africa. From there we shall be able to re-open the Mediterranean and to stage offensive operations against Italy'.[60] On the first day of the Alamein offensive, he confirmed that 'just after taking on CIGS I had planned my policy for running the war. I wanted to clear North Africa, open the Mediterranean, threaten Southern Europe and at some later date liberate France'.[61] Under Brooke's chairmanship, the British Chiefs of Staff in London continued to talk of dramatic advances that could be made in the Mediterranean, in Sicily, Sardinia, Italy or even Turkey, at relatively little cost.

According to the version Churchill put to Stalin,

> it is my earnest and sober hope that we can knock Italy out of the war this year, and by doing so we shall draw far more Germans off your Front than by any other means open... After Italy has been forced out of the war, the Germans will have to occupy the Riviera, make a new Front either on the Alps or the Po, and above all provide for the replacement of the thirty-two Italian divisions now in the Balkans. The moment for inviting Turkish participation in the war, active or passive, will then arrive. The bombing of the Roumanian oilfields can then be carried through on a decisive scale.[62]

In private, Churchill admitted that 'the fall of Italy, the effect upon the other German satellites and the subsequent utter loneliness of Germany *may conceivably* produce decisive results in Europe'. He concluded that 'no objective can compete with the capture of Rome... there is no use in looking farther ahead'.[63]

Actual experience in North Africa led some to doubt the validity of the 'quick fix'. The Allied Commander in North Africa, Dwight Eisenhower, was horrified when, within days of landing in Morocco and Algeria, his generals

---

59 Kennedy Diary, 8 December 1942, quoted in Nicholas Tamkin, 'Britain's Relations with Turkey during the Second World War' (unpublished PhD thesis, Cambridge University, 2006), p. 142.
60 Danchev and Todman (eds.), *War Diaries: Alanbrooke*, 3 December 1942.
61 Ibid., 23 October 1942.
62 Churchill to Stalin, 20 June 1943, CHAR 20/113.
63 Churchill to Alexander, 22 July 1943, CHAR 20/115.

began politicking to use a supposedly quick and painless victory to enhance their own careers. 'For God's sake', he expostulated to his Chief of Staff, 'let's get one job done at a time. . . It would take only five minutes actually on the ground to convince anyone that nothing could be further from the truth'.[64] He repeated this complaint toward the end of the Tunisian campaign. Eisenhower emphasized 'the toughness and skill of the Germans, both in offensive and defensive battle'.[65] He added that 'the fighting. . .has had a definite influence on our thinking and calculations. Even the Italian, defending mountainous country is very difficult to drive out and the German is a real problem'.[66] Despite the easy victories of American forces in western Sicily, he remained of this opinion.[67]

Eisenhower's inability to deliver the 'quick fix' earned him accusations of military incompetence.[68] But on the same theme, Harold Macmillan, the British Resident Cabinet Minister Churchill sent to the Mediterranean in January 1943, observed that 'the trouble is that no one really has any idea as to the future course of the war. . .and the experts cannot give them any guidance. The better they are, the less willing I find them to express a view. Certainly there is no sign of any break in German morale on this front. They are fighting fiercely and valiantly'.[69] Count Ciano, the Italian Foreign Minister, General Amè, the head of Italian military intelligence, and Admiral Canaris, the head of the German armed forces intelligence, all of whom believed in the inevitable defeat of the Axis, recovered from their initial shock at the North African landings to conclude that 'the fight will be a long one'.[70]

From July 1943 onward, the Germans were further committed to 'bottling up' in the Mediterranean. This decision was taken first by operational fiat, and then confirmed by Hitler. The German Commander in the South, Field Marshal Kesselring, was determined to avoid another Tunisia, where German forces had been trapped: he decided to fight to lose rather than fight to win. Within days of the invasion of Sicily, the Germans concluded

---

64 Eisenhower to Bedell Smith, 9 November 1942, in Alfred Chandler (ed.), *The Papers of Dwight David Eisenhower: The War Years* (Baltimore, Md.: Johns Hopkins University Press, 1970).

65 Eisenhower to Marshall, 5 April 1943, in ibid.

66 Eisenhower to Marshall, 5 May 1943, in ibid.

67 Eisenhower to Combined Chiefs of Staff, 19 August 1943, in ibid.

68 Eisenhower to Combined Chiefs of Staff, 26 December 1942, in ibid.; Danchev and Todman (eds.), *War Diaries: Alanbrooke*, 28 and 31 December 1942.

69 Harold Macmillan, *War Diaries: The War in the Mediterranean, 1943–1945* (London; Macmillan, 1984), 1 April 1943.

70 Galeazzo Ciano, *Diary, 1937–1943* (London: Phoenix Press, 2002), 9 December 1942.

that 'the counter-attack against enemy landings has failed'.[71] The Germans rapidly improvised an operational plan that they described as the 'swinging door'. They sent two more divisions into Sicily – one Panzer grenadier, one parachute – to create a bloc of forces capable of fighting its own battle. They abandoned southern and western Sicily and the Italian troops stationed there, in order to defend northern and eastern Sicily. The 'hinge' of the door was the port city of Catania on the east coast. Inland, the 'door' of German troops made a fighting retreat, 'swinging' north and east using the 'favourable terrain' of the mountains of northeastern Sicily and, in particular, the huge volcanic mass of Mount Etna. The asset that they were defending was the port of Messina in the far northeast of the island. The two-mile-wide Strait of Messina was all that separated Sicily from the mainland. As long as Messina was safe, it would be possible to escape from Sicily. 'During the night of 15–16 July', Kesselring recalled, 'I flew to Milazzo, in north Sicily...and gave General Hube detailed instructions on the spot. His mission was to dig in on a solid line even at the cost of initially giving ground... I also told him that I was reckoning with the evacuation of Sicily, which it was his job to postpone for as long as possible'.[72] Kesselring won the argument for bottling up the Allies as far south as possible not least because Hitler was determined to keep the Allies away from the Balkans, as well as from Germany and Austria.[73]

In planning the invasion of Italy, Eisenhower advised that 'either we shall have to fight all the way to Rome or at some point there may be an Italian surrender or collapse. No one can tell which of these will take place'.[74] As planning progressed, he reported that 'there are many indications of German intentions to reinforce Italy'. This would initiate an arms race in which the Allied reinforcement 'rate is contingent upon landing craft and shipping availability and the German rate is contingent upon Italian co-operation and the availability of German divisions'. Once both sides were 'committed to operations on the Continent', he doubted whether it would be 'practicable to...contemplate an Allied Army in central Italy and a German force in

---

71 Quoted in Carlo D'Este, *Bitter Victory: The Battle for Sicily, 1943* (London: Collins, 1988), pp. 295–6.
72 Kesselring, *Memoirs*, p. 164.
73 Hitler, in Trevor-Roper (ed.), *Hitler's War Directives*, Directive 48, 26 July 1943; Ralph Mavrogordato, 'Hitler's Decision on the Defense of Italy', in Kent Roberts Greenfield (ed.), *Command Decisions* (Washington DC: US Government Printing Office, 1960), pp. 303–22.
74 Eisenhower to Combined Chiefs of Staff, 19 July 1943, in Chandler (ed.), *Papers of Dwight David Eisenhower*.

northern Italy with a no man's land between them. There would be constant and hard-fought military operations. There was not even a guarantee that the Allies could 'hold a position in the Naples-Rome area'.[75] Visiting the Salerno beachhead, Eisenhower merely re-stated his observation that a quick fix was unlikely: 'there was every indication that the Germans had expended their energy and were battle-weary: signs of withdrawal were evident all along the front; but it was a certainty that this withdrawal would be planned to impede our advance and to inflict the greatest number of battle casualties on us'.[76] Eisenhower, and his British operational commander, Harold Alexander, explained that the reality of combat was the polar opposite to the 'quick fix': 'we are committed to a long and costly advance to Rome, a "Slugging Match" with our present slight superiority in formations on the battlefront offset by the enemy opportunity for relief'.[77]

The 'quick fix', however, remained at the heart of Allied strategy. In a presentation to his fellow Allied commanders, at the beginning of June 1943, in Marshall, Brooke and Churchill's presence, General Alexander argued that 'in war the incredible often occurred. A few months ago it would have been impossible for him to believe what has happened to Rommel and his Afrikakorps. A few weeks ago he would have found it difficult to believe that 300,000 Germans [sic] would collapse in a week'.[78] In July 1943, Eisenhower and his three chief subordinates, all British, agreed that caution needed to be thrown aside. The Italian collapse on Sicily made an ambitious assault on the Italian mainland a viable prospect. 'I recommend carrying the war to the mainland of Italy immediately Sicily has been captured', Eisenhower wrote to his reluctant bosses in Washington. Ike's conversion to the operation long advocated by his British colleagues was a vital coup.[79] 'There might occur', Eisenhower advised Marshall, 'a vast but possibly fleeting opportunity to accomplish all we are seeking in the Italian peninsula'.[80] As late as December 1943, Eisenhower argued that 'the most important land objective in the Mediterranean, from a strategic standpoint, is the Po Valley

75 Eisenhower to Marshall, 12 August 1943, in ibid.
76 Quoted in C. J. C. Molony, *The Mediterranean and the Middle East*, vol. v: *The Campaign in Sicily, 1943, and the Campaign in Italy, 3rd September 1943 to 31st March 1944* (6 vols., London: HMSO, 1973), pp. 323–4.
77 Churchill to Anthony Eden (Moscow), forwarding a telegram from Eisenhower, 26 October 1943, CHAR 20/122.
78 Eisenhower to Patton, 4 June 1943, in Chandler (ed.), *Papers of Dwight David Eisenhower*.
79 Eisenhower to JCS, 18 July 1943, in ibid.; Churchill to Smuts, 16 July 1943, CHAR 20/115.
80 Eisenhower to Marshall, 29 July 1943, in Chandler (ed.), *Papers of Dwight David Eisenhower*; Danchev and Todman (eds.), *War Diaries: Alanbrooke*, 15 August 1943.

because of the fact that land forces based there are extremely threatening to the German structure in the Balkans, France and in the Reich itself.[81]

The specifically British addiction to the 'quick fix' was manifested in an additional operation in the Eastern Mediterranean, the 'shoe-string' British attempt to seize the Aegean islands in the autumn of 1943. The British 'quick fix' thus ran directly into German 'bottling up'. In July 1943, Hitler had ruled that 'it is as important to reinforce the Balkans as it is to hold Italy'.[82] 'At times', Ciano wrote, 'I have the impression that the Axis is like a man who is trying to cover himself with a bedspread that is too small. His head is cold if he warms his feet, and his feet freeze if he wants to keep his head warm'.[83] Faced with resolute American refusal to become involved with an operation in the Dodecanese, Cairo scraped together troops from the Malta garrison, some destroyers and an array of special forces. The great potential prize was the island of Rhodes, on which the Italians had developed sophisticated air and submarine bases since the 1930s. It housed the headquarters of the Italian commander for the entire Aegean, who had made independent contact with Cairo to negotiate his own surrender. Many who looked seriously at the plan were sceptical about its chances, not least because signals intelligence had charted the steady stream of German reinforcements who had arrived to 'aid' the Italians in the defence of Rhodes.

Military logic suggested that an operation launched against an enemy with a powerful air force, operating from well-appointed bases close to the action, without air support, would fail. The Italian wild card was the factor that overrode this logic. When a joint special forces team parachuted onto Rhodes, they discovered that they were already too late. The German commander on the island had arrested his treacherous opposite number. The senior Italian commander in the Aegean rapidly surrendered his forces. British special forces did succeed in occupying seventeen islands where there no German troops.

Just as in Italy itself, albeit on a much smaller scale, the 'quick fix' proved nothing of the sort. In early October 1943, the Germans began rounding up the British garrisons that had been deployed on the Aegean islands. Their first target, Cos, was caught by surprise. The British commander in the Middle East, Henry Maitland-Wilson, flew to Tunisia to appeal for help from

81 Robert Ferrell (ed.), *The Eisenhower Diaries* (New York: W. W. Norton, 1981), 6 December 1943.
82 Mavrogordato, 'Hitler's Decision on the Defense of Italy', pp. 303–22.
83 Ciano, *Diary*, 6 January 1943.

Eisenhower. Attempts to use the Aegean crisis to mobilize American support failed. 'I believe', Churchill wrote in impassioned terms to Roosevelt, 'it will be found that the Italian and the Balkan peninsulas are militarily and politically united and that really it is one theatre which we have to deal with. It may not be possible to conduct a successful Italian campaign ignoring what happens in the Aegean. The Germans evidently attach the utmost importance to this Eastern sphere'.[84]

Eisenhower rebuffed Wilson's request for aid.[85] At first sight, Eisenhower's refusal to help appeared to be an exercise in American muscle-flexing: but Eisenhower was supported by most British Mediterranean commanders, all of whom were sceptical of the 'quick fix' in the Eastern Mediterranean. Harold Macmillan, on a flying visit to London, lamented that he simply could not get Churchill to focus on the Mediterranean as whole: 'he was only interested in Cos, Leros, Rhodes'.[86] 'Another day of Rhodes madness', snarled Alan Brooke; 'he is in a very dangerous condition, most unbalanced, and God knows how we shall finish this war if this goes on'.[87]

At the time of the Aegean crisis, Churchill, Eisenhower and the British commanders were in full agreement that a crucial breakthrough in the Mediterranean was imminent.[88] Eisenhower's own stance changed almost as soon as he was told that he was to be transferred from the Mediterranean to Northwest Europe. The loss of Eisenhower from the Mediterranean ended the 'quick fix' as a credible strategic option. When the British made a final attempt to persuade their allies that one more push would create war-changing possibilities, Eisenhower was playing for the opposition team. He delivered the damning verdict that 'our forces in Italy do not directly threaten any area vital to the enemy who, therefore, has the initiative'.[89] The British bid was unveiled at a grand dinner held at Caserta in June 1944 in honour of George C. Marshall.[90] General Alexander disavowed the invasion of southern France in favour of a major offensive launched from within the

---

84 Churchill to Roosevelt, 7 October 1943, in Warren Kimball (ed.), *Churchill and Roosevelt: The Complete Correspondence*, vol. II: *Alliance Forged, November 1942 – February 1944* (3 vols., London: Collins, 1984).

85 Eisenhower to CCS, 9 October 1943, in Chandler (ed.), *Papers of Dwight David Eisenhower*; Churchill to Roosevelt, 10 October 1943, in Kimball (ed.), *Complete Correspondence*, vol. II.

86 Macmillan, *War Diaries*, 7 October 1943.

87 Danchev and Todman (eds.), *War Diaries: Alanbrooke*, 7 October 1943.

88 Eisenhower to Marshall, 1 October 1943, and Eisenhower to Marshall, 7 November 1943, in Chandler (ed.), *Papers of Dwight David Eisenhower*.

89 Eisenhower to Combined Chiefs of Staff, 23 June 1944, in ibid.

90 Macmillan, *War Diaries*, 19 June 1944.

Mediterranean. His forces would move up the eastern coast of Italy and around the head of the Adriatic. From there, they would invade Yugoslavia, striking across Slovenia for the Ljubljana Gap. Their eventual target would be Vienna and a direct attack on the 'soft underbelly' of the Reich.

The most remarkable thing about the Ljubljana Gap plan was that its authors thought that it had any chance of serious consideration. Immediately after the dinner, a delegation took off from Naples, picking up express aeroplane relays in Algiers and Casablanca, so that they might rush to London, striking while the iron seemed hot. Their journey was so quick that they arrived, as planned, 'unheralded'.[91] Eisenhower signalled Marshall, while the delegation was still in the air, however, that 'to contemplate wandering off overland via Trieste and Ljubljana' was little more than a fool's errand.[92]

Thus when Harold Macmillan called upon Churchill, he was 'able to get the PM to see the picture as we saw it in the Mediterranean'; but when a British staff officer had a similar exploratory interview with Eisenhower, the latter 'said he wanted [the invasion of southern France] and he wanted it quick'.[93] This disconnection between Caserta and the outside world was not, at least in its origins, purely an Anglo-American affair. The reaction of many in London to the Mediterranean entrepreneurs was equally lukewarm. Alan Brooke described 'Alexander's wild hopes of an advance on Vienna' as 'not based on any real study of the problem, but rather the result of elated spirits after a rapid advance'. The Mediterranean was producing little more than 'strategic ravings'.[94] The Mediterranean balloon, however, was pricked finally by a 'rude', 'brusque' and 'offensive' retort from Washington. The Caserta enthusiasts provoked the Americans into a series of straightforward statements about the Mediterranean. The invasion of southern France would go ahead as part of the European campaign; American ships and troops would move toward their embarkation ports, whatever the orders British commanders in the Mediterranean might choose to issue. The Caserta dinner turned out to be the last supper for the 'quick fix'.[95] After June 1944,

91 Ibid.
92 Eisenhower to Marshall, 20 June 1944, in Chandler (ed.), *Papers of Dwight David Eisenhower*.
93 Macmillan, *War Diaries*, 22 June 1944.
94 Danchev and Todman (eds.), *War Diaries: Alanbrooke*, 22 and 23 June 1944.
95 Ibid., 28 and 30 June 1944; Macmillan, *War Diaries*, 28 June 1944; Roosevelt to Churchill, 29 June 1944, in Warren Kimball (ed.), *Churchill and Roosevelt: The Complete Correspondence*, vol. III: *Alliance Declining, February 1944 – April 1945* (3 vols., London: Collins, 1984); Churchill to Roosevelt, 1 July 1944, CHAR 20/167.

the British and the Americans both argued, in a mirror image of each another, that they were wasting lives fighting in the Mediterranean. The Americans believed that the waste took place in Italy; the British that it occurred in southern France. Churchill described the campaign in France as an 'abortion'.[96]

Fighters

In a forlorn attempt to avert Italian belligerency, Churchill wrote to Mussolini in May 1940 that 'we can no doubt inflict grievous injuries upon one another and maul each other cruelly, and darken the Mediterranean with our strife'.[97] On the other hand, he remarked to the Foreign Secretary, Lord Halifax, that 'nations which went down fighting rose again, but those which surrendered tamely were finished'.[98] Churchill acknowledged that with defeat in Northern and Western Europe, 'we must now look to the Mediterranean for action'.[99] Churchill and Mussolini had much the same thought. 'What can you say', Mussolini stated, justifying his declaration of war in June 1940, 'to someone who doesn't dare risk a single soldier while his ally is winning a crushing victory'.[100] Strategy was driven by the fear of failing to fight.

In 1941, during an argument with the senior US Army officer in the UK, Vice Chief of the Imperial General Staff, Sir Henry Pownall, concluded that 'we can't beat Germany in the Middle East...but we can fight Germans there'.[101] General Eisenhower came to believe that American officers needed extensive 'blooding' in the Mediterranean: seemingly five months of combat in North Africa was not sufficient.[102] In 1943, General Marshall said that he supported the decision to invade Sicily from Tunisia 'because we will have in North Africa a large number of troops available'.[103]

The act of fighting in the Mediterranean, it sometimes seemed, had a metaphysical rather than a strategic value. 'Far more important than the loss

---

96 Churchill to Smuts, 25 August 1944, CHAR 20/170.
97 Churchill to Mussolini, 16 May 1940, in Gilbert (ed.), *Churchill War Papers*, vol. II.
98 War Cabinet Minutes, Confidential Annex, 28 May 1940, in Gilbert (ed.), *Churchill War Papers*, vol. II.
99 Churchill to Alexander and Pound, 12 July 1940, in ibid.
100 Quoted in MacGregor Knox, *Mussolini Unleashed, 1939–1941: Politics and Strategy in Fascist Italy's Last War* (Cambridge University Press, 1982), p. 87.
101 Brian Bond (ed.), *Chief of Staff: The Diaries of Lieutenant-General Sir Henry Pownall*, vol. II: *1940–1944* (London: Leo Cooper, 1974), 20 September 1941.
102 Eisenhower to Bradley, 16 April 1943, in Chandler (ed.), *Papers of Dwight David Eisenhower*.
103 *Foreign Relations of the United States*, p. 631.

of ground is the idea that we cannot face the Germans and their appearance is enough to drive us back many scores of miles', Churchill wrote in April 1941. 'Sooner or later we shall have to fight Huns'.[104] Churchill 'was anxious to give the war a more active scope in the Mediterranean. . .by aggressive action at some point'.[105] The Permanent Under-Secretary at the Foreign Office noted of the 1941 Greek expedition that 'it *must*, in the end, be a failure. . .[but] better to have failed in a decent project than never to have tried at all'.[106] Churchill agreed that it was 'difficult. . .to believe that we have any power to avert [the] fate of Greece', but to fight and lose was better than to submit.[107] He warned Sir Claude Auchinleck in March 1942 that 'it will be thought intolerable that the 635,000 men. . .on your ration strength should remain unengaged preparing for another set-piece battle'.[108]

Churchill came close to suggesting that not only the British Army but the Royal Navy needed to deliver a 'blood sacrifice' to prove it could face the Germans.[109] There is some evidence that the Germans encouraged such thinking in order to lure the British into a fight.[110] Both the Kriegsmarine and the Royal Navy characterized the Mediterranean as a 'killing zone' for the other side. Admiral Cunningham wrote that 'the key. . .and the one which will decide the issue of our success or otherwise in holding the Mediterranean lies in air power'.[111] In response to the German invasion of Crete in May 1941, he re-stated his view even more strongly. 'The operations of the last four days have been nothing short of a trial of strength between Mediterranean Fleet and German Air Force. . . I am afraid that. . .we have to admit defeat', the British Mediterranean Commander-in-Chief told the First Sea Lord.[112] The head of the German navy predicted, accurately, that although U-boats could enter the Mediterranean, they could never leave, and would, eventually, be sunk. By the end of 1941, twenty-three German

104 Churchill to Eden, 3 April 1941, in Gilbert (ed.), *Churchill War Papers*, vol. III.
105 Minutes of Defence Committee (Operations), 20 January 1941, in ibid.
106 David Dilks (ed.), *The Diaries of Sir Alexander Cadogan 1938–45* (London: Cassell, 1971), 24 February 1941.
107 Churchill to Eden, 5 March 1941, in Gilbert (ed.), *Churchill War Papers*, vol. III.
108 Churchill to Auchinleck, 15 March 1942, CHAR 20/71B.
109 Pound to Cunningham, 11 April 1941, in Simpson (ed.), *Cunningham Papers*, vol. I; Churchill to Alexander and Pound, 12 April 1941, in Gilbert (ed.), *Churchill War Papers*, vol. III, p. 483.
110 Taylor (ed.), *Goebbels Diaries*, 17 April 1941.
111 Cunningham to Pound, 25 April 1941, in Simpson (ed.), *Cunningham Papers*, vol. I.
112 Cunningham to Pound, 23 May 1941, in ibid.

submarines were operating in the Mediterranean; the last vessel was destroyed in September 1944.[113]

There is some evidence that certain Axis leaders fantasized about making Tunisia, or even Sicily, places of conflict where a stunning operational defeat could be inflicted on the Allies. An analysis of intelligence intercepts led the Allies to conclude that the *Oberkommando der Wehrmacht* (OKW – the German armed forces high command) was 'slow to realise that Rommel and Arnim were in effect the rearguard and not the centre of the defence of the central Mediterranean'.[114] Experienced Axis commanders had moments of hope that the nature of sea-land warfare in the Mediterranean might generate an unexpected victory. An exemplary statement by a former commander of the Afrikakorps, Crüwell, was picked up by a British microphone: 'so far they have never succeeded in making a landing where there was any resistance'.[115] The German commander at Salerno, von Victinghoff, believed he had defeated the landings, signalling Kesselring, 'after a defensive battle lasting four days enemy resistance is collapsing'.[116] Such moments of optimism were fleeting.

Following defeat in Tunisia, where aircraft losses had already been debilitating, the Luftwaffe made command changes with a view to winning an air battle over Sicily. Kesselring was removed from the command of Luftflotte II. His replacement, Wolfram von Richthofen, arrived from Russia and sacked those with 'Mediterranean experience' of defeat in order them to replace them with 'Easterners'. Declaring that 'the centre of gravity for the Luftwaffe in 1943 is the Mediterranean', Germany's most famous fighter leader, Adolf Galland, personally took charge of fighter forces in the western Mediterranean. The exceptionally good intelligence that the Allies had on the Luftwaffe demonstrated that its attempts to reinforce, and fight, over Tunisia, Sicily and Italy were highly damaging. Air intelligence concluded that 'not less than 850 operational aircraft were totally destroyed in the

---

113 Report of the Commander-in-Chief of the German navy to the Führer, 20 April 1941; Conference of the Commander-in-Chief of the German navy with the Führer at HQ Wolfsschanze in the afternoon of 25 July 1941; Report by the Commander-in-Chief of the German navy to the Führer in Berlin, 12 December 1941, *Fuehrer Conferences on Naval Affairs*; *Germany and the Second World War*, vol. VI: *Global War* (10 vols., Oxford: Clarendon Press, 2001), p. 348.
114 'Kesselring's Abwehr Arm', 18 May 1943, KV3/74, TNA.
115 Recording of the Conversation of General der Panzertruppe Crüwell and General der Panzertruppe Thoma, 23 November 1942, WO 208/4136, TNA.
116 Vietinghoff to Kesselring, 13 September 1943, quoted in Martin Blumenson, *The United States Army in World War II: Mediterranean Theater of Operations – Salerno to Cassino* (Washington DC: Center of Military History, 1969), p. 117.

central Mediterranean area alone during July, 1943, of which approximately 600 were single-engined fighter types'.[117]

There was thus a strong case to be made on the Allied side that the Mediterranean was a 'killing zone', where Axis air power could, and should, be destroyed: but this argument was only ever put in semi-apologetic terms, and for political convenience.[118] Churchill's apologia to Stalin for not invading Atlantic France included the statement that 'already we are holding in the West and South of Europe the larger part of the German air forces and our superiority will increase continually. Out of a first-line operational strength of between 4,800 and 4,900 aircraft Germany according to our information has today on the Russian Front some 2,000 compared with 2,500 this time last year'.[119] The official history written by the RAF at the end of the war was similarly defensive: 'although the Allies never succeeded in turning their Mediterranean victories into a major strategic success, the strain imposed on the German Air Force...had important results which were felt on all battle-fronts'.[120]

Churchill, Roosevelt and Stalin were obsessed with the number of troops engaged on land. Counting land forces produced very different results from counting air forces. In the summer of 1943, less than 5 per cent of the German armoured divisions, but nearly 40 per cent of the bomber units were in the Mediterranean. 'I will in no circumstances allow the powerful British and British-controlled armies in the Mediterranean to stand idle', Churchill declared to his confidant Jan Christian Smuts.[121] Smuts's own view was that 'our comparative performance on land is insignificant... Our Air Force is magnificent. But almost all the honours on land go to the Russians and deservedly so... to the ordinary man it must appear that it is Russia who is winning the war'.[122] Churchill was at pains to point out that if the Russians were carrying the burden of the land war, then the British Empire was in second place on land. The Chairman of the US Joint Chiefs of Staff was reminded that 'we have been fighting and sustaining casualties in Tunis, Sicily, and Italy on something like a 2½ to 1 basis, although we are serving

117 Air Ministry, *The Rise and Fall of the German Air Force, 1933 to 1945* (London: Air Ministry, 1948), p. 270.
118 Williamson Murray, *Luftwaffe: Strategy for Defeat, 1933–1945* (London: Grafton, 1988), pp. 211, 230.
119 Churchill to Stalin, 20 June 1943, CHAR 20/113.
120 Air Ministry, *Rise and Fall of the German Air Force*, p. 270.
121 Churchill to Smuts, 16 July 1943, CHAR 20/115.
122 Smuts to Churchill, 31 August 1943, CHAR 20/117.

loyally under a US General'.[123] These figures were regarded as particularly sensitive by Churchill because the fight for Northwest Europe would have a different complexion: 'we shall', he admitted, 'be able to match the American expedition with nearly equal force of British divisions, but after the initial assault the build-up must be entirely American as I am completely at the end of manpower resources'.[124] As late as 1948, Churchill was still trying to prove that, thanks to the Mediterranean theatre, Britain had 'outfought' the United States on land up to the conquest of Rome and the invasion of Northwest Europe in June 1944.[125]

Dominators

Domination shows up relatively little in wartime strategic debates. It was, however, ever present in the political discussions that ran alongside strategy. Nazi Germany and Fascist Italy were, at their atavistic core, dominators rather than strategists. Their drive was the seizure of land and the exploitation of peoples and raw materials. Despite Hitler's claims that his goal was to aid Italy in containing British power in the Mediterranean, his true practice was predation. 'Our people', Goebbels observed, 'feel something close to hatred for the Italians'.[126] Franz Halder said of the Führer that 'he hoped to double-cross his "friend"'.[127]

Starvation stalked the Axis Mediterranean. The rural populations of the littoral had no say in strategy. That did not mean they were passive. Peasants and merchants hoarded food. The merchants knew that the Mediterranean was closed to the bulk containers that, until 1940, had shipped grain from the Western to the Eastern Mediterranean. The peasants could see that the 1941 harvest was one of the poorest on record. Hot winds in May were partly to blame. The war played its part as well; in the 1930s, the Eastern Mediterranean lands had benefited from German mass-produced nitrate fertilizers for the first time. With the failure of supply, consumers scrambled for what there was. But there were now more, and more rapacious, consumers. Armies competed with civilians for food supplies and always won. The 'food situation' was characterized by 'too many heavy-eating and

---

123 Churchill to Dill, 8 November 1943, CHAR 20/123.
124 Churchill to Smuts, 5 September 1943, CHAR 20/117.
125 Pownall to Churchill [comments on draft of *Their Finest Hour*, 1948], CHUR 4/196.
126 Taylor (ed.), *Goebbels Diaries*, 29 April 1941.
127 Halder, *War Diary*, 22 April 1941.

faced the jockeying of interests between colonial authorities, national governments, military commanders and private profiteers. Perversely, however, the more severe the food crisis, the more dominating the control of food made the British. The original plan had been to include Greece in the arrangements for Mediterranean relief; without the British, Greece starved. Thereafter, the threat of famine was worst in Syria and Lebanon. Control of food became a crucial weapon in ensuring British domination in the Levant over the competing claims of France.[136]

The United States joined the MESC in 1942. Some Americans sent to Cairo came to believe that domination was at the core of wartime strategy. James Landis, the senior US official attached to the MESC, was particularly vocal on this score. Landis argued that the MESC was such an effective method of dominating the Mediterranean and Middle East that it was imperative that the USA should destroy it. On the surface, the British gave the Americans a fair crack of the whip. In reality, they were so deeply embedded in the political life of the Middle East that it was almost second nature for them to thwart American interests. This was particularly galling since the supply that kept local economies in reasonable health was largely American, much of it supplied 'free' through the Lend-Lease scheme. Landis wished to reinvent the MESC as a purely American body, working for American interests. Officials in Washington chose to hear only half of his message, about dismantling the organization. It is hard to conclude that the bickering of lower-tier officials was the primary driver for strategy in the Mediterranean. The American observation that the British manifested an unconscious belief in their own right to rule is probably more revealing.[137]

Conclusion

The ambiguities of the parallel Mediterranean wars were apparent to contemporary commentators. In 1952, the British geopolitical writer Gordon East, a champion of the 'pivotal' importance of the Mediterranean, returned to a subject that he had first tackled in 1937. Then he had been sure that the Mediterranean 'should be regarded in its entirety. . .as part of the continent of Europe, with which its relationships, physical and human, have been

---

136 Mrs Warner, 'Preliminary Brief on the Early History of the Middle East Supply Centre', CAB 102/432, TNA.
137 J. M. Landis, 'Anglo-American Co-operation in the Middle East', *Annals of the American Academy of Political and Social Science*, 240 (1945), 64–72.

closest'.[138] Fifteen years later, he still maintained that the Mediterranean had been vital to victory in Europe. 'Allied sea power', East argued, 'taking advantage of the peninsular character of Europe, thus made practicable the invasion of Italy... the "Mediterranean" school of strategists had justified its views'. The Allies had thus fought a rational and successful war that contrasted favourably 'with the failure of the Mediterranean strategists' of the First World War. But, East admitted, the war *to escape* the Mediterranean had, in fact, become a war *for* the littoral, and had had entirely unpredicted consequences: 'the revolutionary advent of the state of Israel and the creation of an independent Libya in place of Italian North Africa'.[139]

The North African campaigns made perfect sense if the Allies had been pursuing the arterial strategy, the war *through* the Mediterranean. It is the Italian campaign that can be challenged on that score. But from the beginning, Britain, the weather-maker for strategy, was playing a bigger, if ill-defined, game in the Mediterranean. The game comprised wars *for*, *in* and *to escape* the Mediterranean. Even at the highest levels of policy-making, the relative balance between them remained unclear. In the post-war words of Sir Alan Brooke, 'we worked from day to day, a hand-to-mouth existence with a policy based on opportunism. Every wind that blew swung us like a weathercock'.[140]

What John North feared in 1945 came to pass: the special character of the war in the Mediterranean became obscured by 'arid' counter-factual about who won the Second World War. In contrast to its position in the actual strategic debates of 1940–44, the Mediterranean was relegated to the status of a 'secondary' theatre. As Churchill's writings reveal, the British elite was engaged in apologetics for fighting in the Mediterranean, aimed at the Americans, the Soviets and its own population, even before the war ended. By the end of the war, the escapers had established the benchmark for success: this measure occluded and diminished what voyagers, fighters and dominators had sought to achieve.

The Mediterranean had its own grammar of war. The sophistication and intensity of operational warfare in the Mediterranean was unmatched. As John North observed in 1944, it was 'superficial' to give too much attention to battles on land. The Mediterranean was the one theatre that produced a true 'war in three dimensions', land, sea and air, as early as 1942.

---

138 Gordon East, 'The Mediterranean Problem', *Geographical Review* 28 (January 1938), 83–101.
139 East, 'The Mediterranean: Pivot of Peace and War', 619–33.
140 Danchev and Todman (eds.), *War Diaries: Alanbrooke*, 3 December 1941.

The intensity of war in the Mediterranean is striking. In early 1943, for instance, a modest proportion of the German armoured divisions – a little over 10 per cent – were deployed in the Mediterranean. The same proportion of the U-boat force was active in the sea. Yet nearly half the bomber forces were to be found in the theatre. At the height of the battles for Stalingrad, the Luftwaffe shifted its offensive air forces to the Mediterranean. Less apparent, but just as striking, is the fact that the intensity of the British air effort was less than that of the Germans. The Mediterranean power par excellence had a lower ratio of bomber squadrons to armoured divisions. These ratios were obscured, at the time and since, by the superiority in absolute numbers enjoyed by the Imperial-US forces, and by the assumption that the British were making more effort in their 'main theatre'.[141]

Even British commentators spoke of the eye-popping air-power efforts made by the Germans in the Mediterranean in the context of diverting forces away from their main theatre in the East. It was argued but rarely that the Russians were diverting resources from the main theatre in the Mediterranean. In order to survive, however, the Axis had to defeat Britain and give the Americans such a bloody nose that they would withdraw their forces to the West. The failure to concentrate resources in the Mediterranean was the 'fundamental mistake' identified by Kesselring. As it was, the Axis was dismantled in the summer of 1943 in the Mediterranean. Even Hitler – at the height of his success in the spring of 1941 – had feared such an eventuality. Mussolini's ouster and Italy's defection deprived German of any half-credible ally, reducing it to, in Churchill's phrase, 'utter loneliness'. Even worse – and at the same time – Germany itself was reduced to the operational status of a second-class power – unable to fight a sophisticated war in three dimensions – also in the Mediterranean.

---

141 Denis Richards and Hilary Saunders, *Royal Air Force 1939–1945*, vol. II: *The Fight Avails* (3 vols., London: HMSO, 1954), pp. 380–402; H. F. Joslen, *Orders of Battle: Second World War, 1939–1945* (London: HMSO, 1990 [1960]).

14

The war in the West, 1943–1945

MARY KATHRYN BARBIER

In discussing 'The War in the West, 1943–1945', historians frequently choose specific events as foci of their analyses: the Allies' decision to invade Italy in 1943; Allied and German preparations before Normandy; the debates among Allied commanders about how to achieve and then how to exploit victory in Normandy; the shortcomings and abilities of senior generals; and Eisenhower's final decision not to attack Berlin.[1] The key points around which this narrative is shaped, however, are the underlying factors that shaped the individual decisions made by the participants: timing, location, exploitation and completion.

In the Pacific theatre, 1943 was a year of Allied victories in New Guinea, at Guadalcanal and in the Battle of the Bismarck Sea. In Europe, however, 1943 was the year of decision. By May, German and Italian troops in North Africa had surrendered in numbers greater than the total loss suffered at Stalingrad. Allied forces captured Sicily and landed in Italy, prompting the Italians to change sides. Above all, 1943 marked the beginning of the end for German forces on the Eastern Front.[2] After the Battle of Kursk in July, a coordinated series of Soviet offensives began a process of driving the Germans back to the Reich that ended in Berlin and on the Elbe River.[3]

---

1 Recent examples of these shopping lists include Philip Bell, *Twelve Turning Points of the Second World War* (New Haven, Conn.: Yale University Press, 2012); and Paul Kennedy, *Engineers of Victory: The Problem Solvers Who Turned the Tide in the Second World War* (New York: Random House, 2013).

2 See Williamson Murray and Allan R. Millett, *A War to Be Won: Fighting the Second World War* (Cambridge, Mass.: Belknap Press of Harvard University Press, 2000), pp. 196–233, 273–303; Gerhard L. Weinberg, *A World At Arms: A Global History of World War II* (Cambridge University Press, 1994), pp. 408–70, 587–666.

3 See David M. Glantz and Jonathan M. House, *The Battle of Kursk* (Lawrence: University Press of Kansas, 1999); Dennis Showalter, *Armor and Blood. The Battle of Kursk: The Turning Point of World War II* (New York: Random House, 2013).

Three factors dominate any narrative of the war in the West during this period. First, up to this point, the German military was strong on all fronts. Timing, location, exploitation and completion had come together as if the stars were aligned in Germany's favour, and the Wehrmacht had reaped the benefits. Second, the battlefields reflected fluidity – the give and take of the opposing forces, the fog and friction that is at the heart of war. Finally, the initiatives of both sides dictated the ways in which the battles/campaigns played out.[4] The chapter will focus on the Anglo-American preparation for a return to the Continent in the West, on D-Day and the campaigns that began in France and drove into Germany; on the Soviet steamroller's simultaneous advance from the East; and on the final defeat of Nazi Germany in May 1945. But the context is key to understanding those developments. It is correspondingly important to examine the Second Front debate. This controversy affected the Allies' relationships during and after the war; it influenced Allied operations in North Africa, Sicily and Italy before the Western Allies established what Stalin considered to be a true second front.

Since the German invasion of the Soviet Union, Josef Stalin had called upon his Western Allies to create a 'second front'. Though what he meant by a second front has been debated, the consensus is that Stalin called for an immediate invasion across the English Channel into France. Both the British and the Americans temporized. When British Prime Minister Winston Churchill and US President Franklin D. Roosevelt met at the ARCADIA conference in December 1941, they agreed that a cross-Channel invasion in 1942 was not yet feasible. In June 1942, at the Second Washington Conference, the 'Second Front' debate continued. While the Americans advocated a cross-Channel invasion before the end of the year, the British did not think it was feasible and argued instead for an invasion of North Africa. American agreement to launch Operation TORCH – the North African campaign – solidified the postponement of the cross-Channel invasion until 1943.[5]

On 8 November 1942, Operation TORCH began with an Allied landing in Morocco and Algeria, in conjunction with a British offensive near El Alamein in Egypt. As British forces pushed westward from Egypt, Anglo-American troops pushed German and Italian forces eastward into Tunisia. As the Allied offensive in North Africa reversed the balance in the Mediterranean, the

---

4 See Robert M. Citino, *The Wehrmacht Retreats: Fighting a Lost War* (Lawrence: University Press of Kansas, 2012).

5 Mary Kathryn Barbier, 'SECOND FRONT: Should the Second Front Have Been Opened Earlier than June 1944?' in Dennis Showalter (ed.), *History in Dispute*, vol. IV: *World War II* (New York: St. James Press, 2000), pp. 208–11.

Soviets succeeded in crippling the Germans' strategic position on the Eastern Front by a series of major offensives, culminating at Stalingrad.[6]

The victories of 1942 nevertheless presented the Allies with a paradox – a paradox that dominated the conversation when Churchill, Roosevelt and the Combined Chiefs of Staff met in Casablanca, 14–24 January 1943. While the next logical step seemed obvious, the successes in North Africa supported an alternative path. Although the Americans, in particular General George Marshall, pushed for an invasion of France in 1943, the British made a different argument.[7] According to the British, the Allies would be better served taking advantage of the North African victories and of the presence of Allied troops in the Mediterranean. Consequently, they advocated additional offensives in the region – in Sicily first and then in Italy – to knock the Italians out of the war, even though such action would delay the establishment of the 'Second Front' in Northwest Europe. German U-boat activity in the Atlantic was delaying the movement of American troops and materiel to Britain, to a degree guaranteeing that an operation across the English Channel in the spring of 1943 would be a small-scale one – too small to draw German troops from the Eastern Front during the upcoming Soviet summer offensive.[8]

The plan advocated by the British did not sit well with the Soviets. In addition to citing Soviet victories against the Germans, Stalin suggested that his allies were not fulfilling their agreement. He went a step further and intimated that the Soviets were 'virtually fighting alone'. Stalin's suggestion gave Roosevelt and the Americans pause. The failure of the Western Allies to launch the cross-Channel assault in a timely fashion would lend credence to a possible post-war scenario that would favour the Soviet Union. The Soviet Union could also claim all of the credit for the defeat of Germany and be in a correspondingly strong position to determine the state of the post-war world. These factors weighed heavily on the Americans. Marshall opposed the British proposal and argued for a cross-Channel offensive in 1943. The Casablanca Conference ended in compromise. The Americans agreed to the implementation of the British plan, and the British agreed to

---

6 Rick Atkinson, *An Army at Dawn: The War in North Africa, 1942–1943* (New York: Henry Holt and Company, 2002), pp. 69–115, 301–38; Peter Calvocoressi, Guy Wint and John Pritchard, *The Penguin History of the Second World War* (New York: Penguin Books, 1989), pp. 347–95.

7 Murray and Millett, *A War to Be Won*, pp. 299–300.

8 Mary Kathryn Barbier, *D-Day Deception: Operation Fortitude and the Normandy Invasion* (Westport, Conn.: Praeger Security International, 2007), pp. 2–3.

determine a firm date for opening a second front in Europe – in other words, in France. The decision to continue operations in the Mediterranean meant two things. First, the 'Second Front' would not occur before 1944. Second, Sicily would be the site of the next Allied offensive.[9]

In May 1943, prior to the invasion of Sicily, British and American military and political leaders met in Washington at the TRIDENT conference. The British reiterated their advocacy for operations in the Mediterranean theatre; the Americans ultimately recognized the validity of their ally's argument that building on their momentum enabled taking advantage of both timing and location. Once they accepted that premise, the Americans agreed that, following a successful operation in Sicily, the next logical step was to take the war to Italy. Their acceptance of the British plan did not come without a price. The British were forced to agree that the invasion of France would occur in May 1944.[10]

'The invasion of Sicily was the largest amphibious operation of the war, at least on the first day'.[11] As such, it was a dress rehearsal for the amphibious operation against France now slated for May 1944. The invasion caused the overthrow of Benito Mussolini, the first step toward Italy switching sides in the conflict. Operation HUSKY was also the first Allied offensive that had a direct impact on the Eastern Front.[12] Following the invasion of Sicily, the Germans ended Operation ZITADELLE (CITADEL), the Reich's last major offensive in Russia. Concerned that Allied successes would have an adverse effect on Italy's commitment to the Axis cause, the Germans transferred troops from Austria to Italy. Even as the Germans prepared to shore up the defence of Italy, King Vittorio Emanuel III ordered Marshal Bodoglio, who replaced Mussolini, to explore avenues to extricate the country from the conflict. In fact, an Italian envoy conducted talks with Allied officials in Portugal beginning in August 1943.

Meanwhile, the Allies continued their preparations for the invasion of Italy – Operation AVALANCHE – with landings at Salerno and Taranto.[13] September 1943 began with a bang. On 3 September, the Allies landed a small force at Reggio, on the toe of the Italian boot, and Italy surrendered.

---

9 Ibid.; Barbier, 'SECOND FRONT', pp. 210–11; Mark A. Stoler, *Allies in War: Britain and America Against the Axis Powers* (London: Hodder Arnold, 2005), pp. 86–96.

10 Stoler, *Allies in War*, pp. 117–21; Weinberg, *A World At Arms*, pp. 439–41, 591, 611–12.

11 Murray and Millett, *A War to Be Won*, p. 302.

12 Barbier, *D-Day Deception*, p. 13. See Rick Atkinson, *The Day of Battle: The War in Sicily and Italy, 1943–1944* (New York: Henry Holt and Company, 2007).

13 Atkinson, *The Day of Battle*, pp. 180, 184, 197–203, 206; Murray and Millett, *A War to Be Won*, pp. 377–81; Calvocoressi et al., *History of the Second World War*, pp. 401–3.

Avalanche proper commenced on 9 September 1943, with Allied landings at Salerno. Thus began the contest for control of Italy, a contest that was long and hard. For the Germans, if British and American troops were engaged in battle in Italy, they could not initiate a campaign elsewhere. For the British and Americans, if the Germans were tied down in Italy, they could not send more troops to the Eastern Front. In fact, they might withdraw even more troops from Russia to enter the fray in Italy, which would help the Soviets, in particular, and the Allied cause in general. Both the terrain and the staunch German resistance made it difficult for the Allies to exploit their successful landings. The Germans established a series of defensive lines so effective that the Allies did not succeed in entering Rome until 4 June 1944, two days before the first Allied soldiers stormed the beaches at Normandy. The commencement of the Normandy invasion demanded a commitment of resources that subsequently became unavailable for the Italian campaign. As a result, this further delayed the successful completion of the battle to wrestle the Italian boot from the Germans. (For a more detailed discussion of campaigns in North Africa and the Mediterranean theatre, see Chapter 12.)[14]

As Allied forces struggled to advance north on the Italian peninsula, German troops impeded that advance. The campaign demanded more and more resources and made Stalin's vision of a second front in 1943 increasingly unlikely. Stalin fumed about the delay, and his Western Allies knew it. For many reasons, and not just to satisfy Stalin, Churchill, Roosevelt and their military advisors remained committed to the invasion of France. Above all, they recognized that the invasion of France would be a way to bring the war to Germany and defeat to Adolf Hitler.

The Second Front was a major topic discussed by the Big Three – Churchill, Roosevelt and Stalin – and their military and political advisors at the Tehran Conference, 28 November to 1 December 1943. During the meetings in Tehran, the Allied leaders reached crucial agreements about the invasion of France and the Soviet spring offensive. Two factors influenced the decisions made by the Big Three. First, was the way that the war was progressing; post-war planning, however, also affected the decisions.[15]

The situation really began looking up for the Allies in 1943. The Soviets stopped the Germans at Stalingrad in February and at Kursk in July. After

---

14 Murray and Millett, *A War to Be Won*, pp. 375–87; Atkinson, *The Day of Battle*, pp. 565–79, 583–4; Calvocoressi et al., *History of the Second World War*, pp. 406, 533, 536. See also Lloyd Clark, *Anzio: Italy and the Battle for Rome – 1944* (New York: Atlantic Monthly Press, 2006).
15 Barbier, *D-Day Deception*, pp. 3, 12, 18–19, 63.

halting the German operations, the Soviets were able to go on the offensive all along the front. That eliminated the immediate Soviet need for a 'second front'. According to Marshal Georgii K. Zhukov, 'By the end of 1943, we had finally overcome our grave situation and means of war, firmly held the strategic initiative and, generally speaking, no longer needed a second front in Europe so much as we had during the earlier two grim years. However, desirous of seeing the speediest possible defeat of Nazi Germany and the earliest possible termination of the war we all looked forward to the Second Front being opened in the immediate future'.[16]

What the Soviets viewed as good alarmed their Western Allies. Anglo-American strategists feared that the Soviets would be able to expand westward unhindered when Germany collapsed. The British and American perspectives, however, were not the same. While Churchill and the British did not want to see an expansion of Soviet influence in Europe, Roosevelt took a different position. The establishment of a second front would open the door to better East–West relations. In addition, the United States would be firmly rooted in Europe and in a position to prevent post-war Soviet domination of the continent. In effect, Roosevelt viewed this as a compromise in establishing a post-war balance of power in Europe.

The bulk of the decisions that the Big Three reached at Tehran involved the Allied invasion of France: Operation OVERLORD. From the first day of the meetings, Stalin insisted that the primary operation in 1944 should be OVERLORD, even if the Allies had to shift to a defensive position in Italy and delay the liberation of Rome. British and American military leaders simultaneously continued their ongoing conversation about planning for OVERLORD and their concerns about its possible success. To demonstrate their commitment, Churchill and Roosevelt announced the selection of General Dwight D. Eisenhower as Supreme Allied Commander for the invasion. Allied intelligence correctly indicated that the Germans had concluded that their enemy would land a large number of troops in northwest France in the summer of 1944. In addition, they acknowledged that weather conditions would limit exactly when the amphibious assault could occur. The only real question for the Germans was where on the coast of France the enemy would land.

---

16 Marshal Georgii K. Zhukov, quoted in Olivier Wieviorka, *Normandy: The Landings to the Liberation of Paris*, trans. M. B. DeBevoise (Cambridge, Mass.: Belknap Press of Harvard University Press, 2008), p. 33.

The location of the invasion was the subject of much discussion by the Allied planners, as was the exact date for the landings. A shortage of landing craft forced a delay until June. The importance of the landing craft was indelibly etched in the plans. As Winston Churchill noted: 'The letters "L.S.T." (Landing Ship, Tanks) are burnt in upon the minds of all those who dealt with military affairs in this period'.[17] The need for low-tide conditions and a full moon dictated the Allies' narrow invasion windows. Equally important was location. Several factors influenced this decision. Crucial to the plan was air cover. Consequently, the invasion site had to be in range of Allied air forces. It had to be easily accessible to naval forces. Finally, the planners understood that they had to have access to established port facilities in order to support the invasion effectively.

The Dieppe raid in August 1942 demonstrated the difficulty in landing an amphibious force near a fortified, well-defended port. The establishment of beachheads anywhere along the French coast would be correspondingly difficult, if not impossible. Enemy forces would greatly outnumber the invading troops and could prevent Allied forces from gaining a foothold in Normandy. Therefore, Allied planners, particularly the British, concluded that Operation OVERLORD needed an insurance policy, a cover plan that would mask the invasion and possibly persuade the Germans to fortify the wrong place. They had to keep the Germans from moving reinforcements into Normandy for as long as possible, both before and after the commencement of the invasion. Even before the meeting in Tehran, efforts to design such a cover plan, eventually called Operation FORTITUDE, had commenced. Not until the Tehran Conference, however, did Allied leaders agree on an overall policy of strategic deception. Only one aspect of the ultimate strategic deception plan specifically provided cover for OVERLORD. That was Operation FORTITUDE. The rest of the strategic deception plan was designed to tie down German forces elsewhere in Europe.

Following the meeting of the Big Three in Tehran, the real work began – finalizing OVERLORD's plans, the massing of sufficient troops, equipment and landing craft, and launching the amphibious assault that would return Allied forces to France – over four years after the evacuation of British and French troops from Dunkirk. The Western Allies were not the only ones making preparations. The Germans, in an effort to thwart their enemy, made plans of their own. In the spring of 1942, Hitler had given orders for the

---

17 Winston Churchill, *The Second World War*, vol. v, *Closing the Ring* (6 vols., New York: Houghton Mifflin Company, 1951), p. 226.

erection of an Atlantic Wall extending from Norway to the Bay of Biscay. He believed that once it was completed, only a small number of troops would be needed to man the fortifications. After the Dieppe Raid, Hitler ordered the construction of 15,000 additional fortified positions along the Channel coast by the summer of 1943. Allied victories in the Mediterranean led Hitler in November 1943 to accelerate construction further.

As *Oberbefehlshaber* West (Supreme Commander of German armies stationed in the West), Field Marshal Gerd von Rundstedt had major reservations about the capabilities of the Atlantic Wall, particularly in light of its state of completeness and the number of troops available for its defence. Because he believed both were insufficient to stop an Allied invasion, Rundstedt requested that an operational reserve of nine armoured and motorized divisions be placed under his command. Both Rundstedt and Hitler recognized the need to defeat the landing as soon as possible. In March 1944, Hitler informed his generals about the need for a quick, decisive victory in the West:

> The destruction of the enemy's landing attempt means more than a purely local decision on the Western front. It is the sole decisive factor in the whole conduct of the war and hence in its final result. The 45 divisions which we now have in Europe, excluding the Eastern front, are needed in the East, and will and must be transferred there so as to effect a fundamental change in that situation as soon as the decision in the West has been reached.[18]

After another alarming assessment of the Atlantic Wall by Rundstedt in October 1943, Hitler assigned the task of strengthening the Atlantic Wall to Field Marshal Erwin Rommel. In addition to overseeing construction of the Wall, Rommel received command of Army Group B. His evaluation of German defences and Allied intentions led him to disagree fundamentally with Rundstedt regarding the disposition of German front-line and reserve forces. While Rundstedt argued that the Allies would land in Pas de Calais and try to seize the Calais port, Rommel expected the Allies to do the unexpected, which they had done so many times before. Therefore, he believed that the Allies would land anywhere on the coast between Dunkirk and Cherbourg. Both the Pas de Calais and the Normandy beaches fell between these parameters. In addition, recognizing the importance of Cherbourg, he stressed that the defence of that port city was vital.

---

18 Adolf Hitler, quoted in Wieviorka, *Normandy*, p. 152.

The generals also disagreed over the placement of the German central armoured reserve. Arguing that the reserves should be centrally located, Rundstedt advocated that they be based near Paris. This would allow the rapid deployment of the forces to any endangered location along the French coast. Rommel, on the other hand, contended that the reserves should be located closer to the coast in order to prevent the Allies from gaining a foothold. The Germans would be able to push the Allies back into the English Channel and, consequently, stop the invasion before it had actually started. Hitler therefore made the final decision, which ultimately proved disastrous because it rendered both strategies ineffective. Hitler placed three Panzer divisions – the 2nd, 21st and 116th – under Rommel's direct command. He also assumed direct control of three other divisions – 1st and 2nd SS Panzer and Panzer Lehr, the best of the armour. Only Hitler could order them into battle. On the one hand, Hitler eliminated Rundstedt from the equation; on the other, he also tied Rommel's hands because only Hitler could order these divisions into battle.

While the Germans tried to guess the exact location of the looming Allied invasion, strengthen their defences and eventually thwart their enemy, Allied preparations for Operation OVERLORD continued. General Sir Frederick Morgan, Chief of Staff to the Supreme Allied Commander, and his staff had spent a year working on the OVERLORD plan. Drawing upon lessons learned from the 1942 Dieppe raid and intelligence that indicated an enemy focus on Pas de Calais, Morgan chose the Normandy beaches as the invasion site, even though Allied forces would not have immediate access to port facilities. Although the invasion forces would be tasked with the immediate capture of Cherbourg and Le Havre, the Allies would need to land additional troops and supplies in the meantime. Consequently, they would construct two artificial floating harbours, or MULBERRIES, that would be towed to the beaches after the landing. According to Morgan's plan, three divisions would make the initial landing. Air and naval bombardment would cover their disembarkation from landing craft. Prior to the infantry assault, airborne troops would be dropped and would secure key exits from the beaches. Once the beaches were secure and reinforcements had landed, the troops would break out of the beachhead and move into Brittany and the western part of France. Securing key cities, including Caen, Cherbourg and Le Havre was paramount.

With his appointment as commander of the landing force in early January 1944, General Bernard Montgomery immediately – and predictably – argued that certain amendments be adopted. According to Montgomery, the

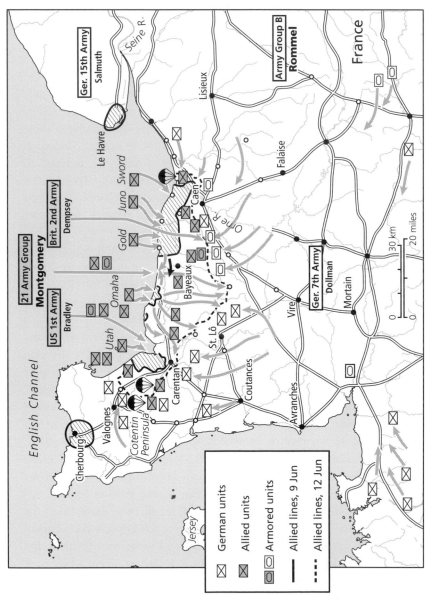

14.1 Battle of Normandy

landings of British and American forces should be separate. In addition, he contended that the landing force should be increased to five divisions – two Americans, two British and one Canadian. Each division would land on separate, but connected beaches. From west to east, the beaches were UTAH (American), OMAHA (American), GOLD (British), JUNO (Canadian) and SWORD (British). Montgomery also recommended that the airborne forces be increased from two brigades to three divisions. Two American airborne divisions would drop along the Vire River at the base of the Cotentin Peninsula, while one British airborne division would land along the Orne River, to prevent the Germans from driving the invading forces off the beaches. Allied navies would transport the ground troops.[19]

Once the revised plan received approval, Great Britain became the site of a great deal of activity. Training commenced. The Allies amassed the troops, equipment, ships, landing craft, aircraft, ammunition and other supplies needed for the largest amphibious landing ever attempted. Another aspect to the planning must be acknowledged – the cover plan. The Allies recognized that the Germans expected and were preparing for the invasion. In an effort to focus German attention away from Normandy, they implemented Operation FORTITUDE. FORTITUDE had two parts. FORTITUDE NORTH, which was the smaller of the two plans, suggested an assault against Norway, with landings at Narvik and Stavanger. FORTITUDE SOUTH was not only much larger, but was also much more ambitious than its northern counterpart. The goal of FORTITUDE SOUTH was to keep German attention focused on Pas de Calais, which the Germans thought was the most likely site of the Allied invasion. In fact, FORTITUDE NORTH eventually merged with FORTITUDE SOUTH. (For more on this topic, see Chapter 22 – Intelligence.)[20]

In many respects, the same resources were utilized for both OVERLORD and FORTITUDE. For example, troops training for OVERLORD in south-east England also participated in the FORTITUDE deception. Prior to D-Day, Eisenhower authorized implementation of the Transportation Plan, which accomplished two goals. First, the bombing of railways and bridges hindered enemy reinforcement of the Normandy area. Second, because

---

19 Both the air forces and the navies would play crucial roles in the invasion. For a more detailed assessment of Allied strategic air operations, see Chapter 17. See also Chapter 19 – Armies, navies, air forces: the instruments of war.

20 Barbier, *D-Day Deception*, pp. 1–40; Mary Kathryn Barbier, 'Deception and the planning of D-Day', in John Buckley (ed.), *The Normandy Campaign 1944: Sixty Years On* (London: Routledge, 2006), pp. 170–84.

some of the targets were in the Pas de Calais region, bombing them also supported the deception plan. In fact, in the months before D-Day, the Allies dropped approximately twice as many bombs in the Pas de Calais area than in Normandy.[21]

Originally slated to occur in May 1944, Operation OVERLORD was delayed a month because of a shortage of landing craft. As D-Day neared, however, the pieces came together nicely, or so both sides thought. Under Operation NEPTUNE, Allied navies amassed almost 6,500 vessels, 4,000 of which were landing craft, for the cross-Channel assault. Tasked with destroying the Atlantic Wall's coastal batteries, the battleships and destroyers would provide a pre-dawn bombardment to prepare the way for the landing force. British and American air forces, numbering 12,000 planes, would support the landings from the air. Almost half of the aircraft were fighters. The Allies' overwhelming air superiority gave them a major edge on D-Day.[22]

The Allies were not the only ones who were preparing for the big assault. The Germans constantly constructed appreciations of Allied troop strength and of where they expected the assault to land, and adjusted their defences and troop deployments accordingly. By early June 1944, they had sixty-two divisions for the defence of the Channel coast. The Germans recognized the importance of Brittany, Normandy and the Cotentin Peninsula, but, because of its proximity to the Ruhr, they thought that Pas de Calais was the most likely site for an enemy landing. Although they concentrated fifteen divisions in northeast France, the Germans placed seventeen west of the Seine River. Apparently, 'this division of German forces reflected an indecision within the German high command that recognized that north of the Loire only Normandy and the Pas de Calais offered themselves as possible landing areas'.[23]

Although for months, German officers, especially Rundstedt, thought that the most likely landing site was Pas de Calais, as D-Day neared, the Germans acquired an increasing amount of intelligence that suggested another target

21 The Transportation Plan was a component of the British-American strategic air campaigns. For an in-depth assessment of the Allies' strategic air operations, see Chapter 17.
22 Barbier, *D-Day Deception*, pp. 144, 177–9, 181, 190–1. See also Arthur William Tedder, *With Prejudice: The War Memoirs of Marshal of the Royal Air Force* (Boston, Mass.: Little, Brown & Company, 1966); Max Hastings, *Bomber Command* (New York: Dial Press, 1979); W. W. Rostow, *Pre-Invasion Bombing Strategy: General Eisenhower's Decision of March 25, 1944* (Austin: University of Texas Press, 1983); and Vincent Orange, 'Arthur Tedder and the transportation plans', in Buckley (ed.), *The Normandy Campaign*, pp. 147–57. See also Chapter 17 – Anglo-American strategic bombing, and Chapter 19 – Armies, navies, air forces: the instruments of war.
23 Chester Willmott, *The Struggle for Europe* (New York: Harper and Brothers, 1952), p. 357.

area – Normandy. In early May, several German commanders, including Commander-in-Chief West, assessed intelligence reports and concluded that the Allies would land between Cherbourg and Le Havre – in other words, in Normandy. As late as 1 June 1944, General Erich Marcks predicted an enemy landing in Normandy within a few days. His prediction, however, did not receive support. After the war, Major Anton Staubwasser acknowledged that the movement of landing craft in English southwestern coastal ports had been observed by German reconnaissance planes a few days before the invasion commenced. Unfortunately for the Germans, the prevailing appreciation did not agree with these assessments or with the intelligence. In fact, because the Germans overestimated Allied troop strength and because they believed that the Allies might launch more than one invasion, the Germans anticipated a second landing in Pas de Calais after the enemy forces invaded the Normandy beaches.[24]

While the Germans tried to guess the enemy's invasion plans, the Allies were finalizing their preparations. In early May, Eisenhower set the new target date – 5 June – but the weather would not cooperate. By 3 June, the landing forces were loaded on ships. By 4 June, weather conditions threatened to cause another delay. Eisenhower met with his staff and they discussed options. That evening, Group Captain James Martin Stagg, the chief meteorologist, suggested that there might be a window of opportunity – a thirty-six-hour break in the weather. On the morning of 5 June, Eisenhower received confirmation of Stagg's prediction, and he ordered the invasion to start the next day. Timing was everything. The invasion had to begin before the Germans got wind of it.

Ships put to sea. The Eastern Naval Task Force carried British Second Army troops (including the 3rd Canadian Division) slated to land on SWORD, GOLD and JUNO beaches, while the Western Naval Task Force headed for UTAH and OMAHA beaches with the US First Army. Vessels loaded with 130,000 men and 20,000 vehicles would disembark in three waves. Sailing with the Task Forces were fifteen hospital ships that carried 8,000 doctors, 450,000 litres of plasma, and 600,000 doses of penicillin. Paratroopers completed their final checks in preparation for departure. Aircraft, transporting paratroopers and towing gliders, would release their loads in the early morning hours of 6 June.

As the invasion troops headed for their targets, the Germans evaluated current weather and forecasts. They determined that conditions would force

---

24 Barbier, *D-Day Deception*, pp. 152, 158–9, 163–4.

the Allies to postpone their invasion. Therefore, several commanders, including Rommel, were not at their posts when the invasion began. This affected the Germans' ability to react in the early morning hours, as advance Allied forces landed on the beaches of Normandy. In addition, General Alfred Jodl's unwillingness to wake Hitler, when the first reports and requests for assistance arrived, further delayed the Germans' commitment of key forces to the battle for over twelve hours.[25]

Before dawn on 6 June 1944, hundreds of Allied aircraft crossed the Channel and flew toward their target areas. Paratroopers of the British 6th Airborne Division and the 82nd and 101st American Airborne Divisions leaped from the aircraft and slowly descended to the ground. Many did not land in their designated areas. Confusion reigned, but the men linked up and proceeded to carry out their tasks. In the pre-dawn hours, the guns from the Naval Task Forces opened fire in an effort to neutralize the beaches and facilitate the landing. Landing craft headed for the beaches. The battle was on. Allied troops landed on five different beaches. While not walkovers, the attacks on four of the five beaches – UTAH, JUNO, GOLD and SWORD – went well. The invaders established secure positions relatively quickly and with relatively light casualties. On OMAHA beach, a number of problems plagued the landing. The navy launched the landing craft too far from shore. Rough seas swamped many of the landing craft and caused heavy casualties in men, tanks and artillery. Once ashore, soldiers of the US 1st and 29th Infantry Divisions faced fierce resistance when they encountered the German 352nd Division, an experienced unit that had recently arrived in the area. The Germans pinned down the Americans on the beaches for hours. Late in the day, however, the Americans succeeded in establishing a secure position.

Despite this early success, none of the Allied forces succeeded in achieving their first-day goals. That ultimately contributed to a much slower progress in Normandy than had been anticipated. In particular, the British were unable to seize Caen, where a key communications centre was located. German resistance prevented liberation of Caen until early July. The Allies continued to land forces. During the first two days of the battle, approximately 100,000 Allied soldiers came ashore. Ten days later, five times that number were in Normandy. Almost a million Allied soldiers were inside the

---

25 Carlo D'Este, *Decision in Normandy* (New York: Harper Perennial, 1991), pp. 107–19; Wieviorka, *Normandy*, pp. 185–90.

beachhead by 1 July. During that same period, German troop strength increased to fourteen divisions. Nine of them were Panzer divisions.[26]

Two distinct battles emerged in Normandy. In both, the German defenders faced overwhelming firepower, air power and armoured resources. The British and Canadians fought in the eastern sector, while the Americans engaged the enemy in the West. As the struggle for Caen raged, American forces tried to achieve their first objective – pinching off the Cotentin Peninsula and capturing Cherbourg intact. German resistance stymied the American efforts just long enough. Cherbourg finally fell to the Americans on 27 June, but not before the Germans had blocked the harbour, which was not cleared completely until late September.

Across the front, the fighting was brutal. It was made extremely difficult by three factors. First, the experience and determination of the soldiers involved – German, British, Canadian and American – defined the nature of the fighting. The Allies were determined to land, establish a beachhead and break out into France. The Germans were equally determined to throw the invaders back into the sea. Second, the terrain made the fighting more difficult. The thick shrubs and sunken lanes of the bocage country gave the defender the advantage. The mechanized Allied forces found that the soft ground limited their mobility. The hedgerows divided Normandy into a series of rectangular boxes. With limited entrances and exits through the hedgerows, the Germans established strong defensive positions and utilized snipers to increase the number of enemy casualties. Allied ingenuity levelled the playing field, but not before both sides paid a heavy cost in terms of casualties. Finally, the weather had an impact on the battlefield. July 1944 was one of the wettest and windiest in fifty years. These conditions limited both air support and mobility on the ground. In spite of these factors, the growing Allied strength in Normandy by the end of July resulted in the establishment of two army groups – the Twenty-First Army Group commanded by Montgomery, and the Twelfth Army Group commanded by General Omar Bradley.[27]

Several factors hindered the German ability to reinforce the battlefield quickly enough to achieve their primary goal – the defeat of the enemy.

---

26 D'Este, *Decision in Normandy*, pp. 107–19; Wieviorka, *Normandy*, pp. 190–200; Stephen Badsey, 'Culture, Controversy, Caen and Cherbourg: The First Week of Battle', in Buckley (ed.), *The Normandy Campaign*, pp. 48–65.

27 Badsey, 'Culture, Controversy', pp. 48–65; Peter R. Mansoor, *The GI Offensive in Europe: The Triumph of American Infantry Divisions, 1941–1945* (Lawrence: University Press of Kansas, 1999), pp. 133–59; Michael D. Doubler, *Closing with the Enemy: How GIs Fought the War in Europe, 1944–1945* (Lawrence: University Press of Kansas, 1994), pp. 31–62.

Before the first Allied troops had landed on the beaches at Normandy, Allied aircraft had destroyed or heavily damaged all rail and road bridges across the Seine River north of Paris, which limited German reinforcement from the east. As soon as the invasion commenced, Allied bombers had another task – destroy the rail and road bridges across the Loire River south of the battlefield. In addition, the Germans immediately encountered difficulty in moving mechanized forces during daylight hours. When weather permitted, Allied aircraft attacked enemy forces as they advanced toward Normandy. Because of these obstacles, the Germans committed their forces as advance units arrived. They did not have time to mass their forces for a counter-attack in force, which ultimately limited their ability to defeat their enemies. Furthermore, Allied aircraft destroyed Panzer Group West's headquarters, which hindered the coordinated movement of Panzer forces.

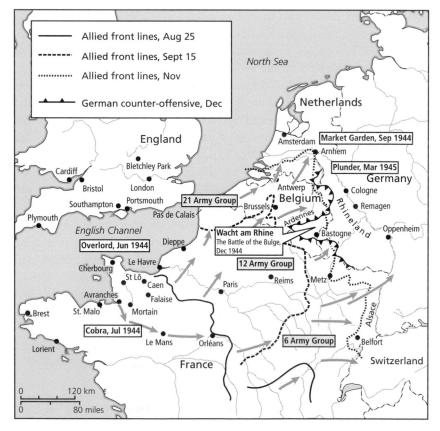

14.2 The campaign in Northwest Europe, 1944

As the Allies' position in Normandy strengthened, they prepared for the breakout phase. Timing and location aligned, and the Allies were ready to exploit their success in Normandy. On 25 July, the Americans launched Operation COBRA – a thrust west of Saint-Lô to break out of the bocage country and to cut off the Cotentin Peninsula; while the British, a few days earlier, had unleashed Operations GOODWOOD and ATLANTIC – to complete the liberation of Caen and tie down seven of the nine German Panzer divisions in Normandy. Two days later, the Germans began to retreat under pressure from the Americans. The Americans drove the Germans to the south and then east, and the British advanced south from Caen. As the American First Army moved eastward around the German southern flank and the British pressured them from the north, the Germans realized that they were in danger of being surrounded. In an effort to entrap the Germans, Bradley sent elements of the First and Third Armies north through Argentan, to link with the Canadian First Army that was advancing south toward Falaise. As the noose tightened, the Germans counter-attacked, but in vain. By the evening of 15 August, with Canadian forces only a couple of miles from Falaise, German troops fled eastward – a gap the Allies just failed to close. Although cadres succeeded in escaping, the Germans lost over 60,000 troops killed or captured, and large quantities of irreplaceable equipment.[28]

While opposing forces fought in the Falaise pocket, the Allies launched other operations, in particular the invasion of southern France. Although originally slated to coincide with Operation OVERLORD, the shortage of landing craft forced a two-month delay. Originally called ANVIL, the operation received a new name – DRAGOON – by the time it commenced on 15 August. Elements of US Seventh Army forces, commanded by General Alexander Patch, and General Jean de Lattre de Tassigny's First French Army, mostly African troops, landed between Toulon and Cannes. German opposition was weak. German defenders in France were stretched thin by the Allies' push to exploit their successful return to France. As combined American-French assaults led to the liberation of Toulon and Marseille, ULTRA intercepts indicated that German forces in southern France had received orders to retreat northward. The Allies pursued rapidly; the so-called (and miscalled) Champagne campaign linked up with the US Third Army north of Dijon on 12 September. Although critics suggest that ANVIL/

---

28 Doubler, *Closing with the Enemy*, pp. 57–8, 79–84, 229; Mansoor, *The GI Offensive in Europe*, pp. 158–70, 180, 263, 270; D'Este, *Decision in Normandy*, pp. 337–46, 358, 364, 384, 390, 400–6, 507.

DRAGOON prevented the Allies from fully exploiting the situation in Italy, the capture of Marseille more than made up for it. During the period September 1944 to January 1945, the Allies unloaded more supplies for the war effort at the port of Marseille than at any other port.[29]

The German situation in the West continued to deteriorate. The closing of the Falaise pocket signalled the complete collapse of the German defence in France. Allied armies – tanks and mechanized troops – rushed east against little opposition. Although the US First Army advanced toward Paris, Eisenhower did not initially plan to liberate the French capital. Because he did not think that the Germans would relinquish the city easily, Eisenhower envisioned intense street fighting. Liberation of Paris could result in destruction of the city and heavy casualties. Furthermore, Eisenhower understood another reality of liberation: the Allies would become responsible for feeding the French residents of Paris, which would be a logistical nightmare.

The French – both Parisians and non-Parisians – forced Eisenhower to alter his plans to bypass the capital. When French Forces of the Interior revolted against the Paris garrison, General Charles de Gaulle demanded that the Allies provide military support for the Resistance units because they were insufficiently armed to liberate Paris from the Germans. While Eisenhower pondered his response, General Jacques Philippe Leclerc, Commander of the Free French 2nd Armoured Division, took matters into his own hands. Disobeying orders, he ordered troops to Paris. Giving in to the apparently inevitable, Eisenhower approved Leclerc's orders. When the French advance was delayed by their celebrating countrymen, Bradley diverted American units to aid in the liberation of Paris. French and American forces liberated Paris on 25 August.

The liberation of Paris only briefly slowed the Allies' rush to the east. The steamroller unleashed by the breakout forced the Germans to retreat. Exploitation of the Allies' success in Normandy continued. Three armies – the British Second, the Canadian First and the US First – pushed through Belgium. Patton's Third Army advanced into northeastern France. By 15 September, most of Belgium and Luxembourg were in Allied hands. Advance forces rapidly approached the German border. As the Allies surged forward, however, cracks in their partnership emerged. The Allies had outrun their supply lines. Shortages, particularly of fuel, began to cause problems of prioritization.[30]

---

29 Mansoor, *The GI Offensive in Europe*, pp. 174–5, 269, 271.
30 Murray and Millett, *A War to Be Won*, pp. 432–3, 450; Mansoor, *The GI Offensive in Europe*, pp. 160, 170–2, 180, 256; Calvocoressi et al., *History of the Second World War*, pp. 542–5; John Buckley, *Monty's Men: The British Army and the Liberation of Europe* (New Haven, Conn.: Yale University Press, 2013), pp. 169, 177, 181–3. See D'Este, *Decision in Normandy*.

These issues, along with differing visions regarding the nature of post-war Europe, coloured the debate as Eisenhower and his staff discussed the next step. Montgomery advocated a 'single thrust' approach. He argued that the British Second and US First Armies should push toward the Rhine River and the Ruhr industrial region. In order to conserve supplies, however, this would require that Patton's Third Army, which was running wild across France, stop its advance eastward. Arguing that both army groups advance simultaneously along a 'broad front', Eisenhower and his American subordinates disagreed. Rejecting Montgomery's argument for a single thrust, Eisenhower compromised by agreeing to the English general's ambitious plan to cross the Rhine River in several locations in the Netherlands – Operation MARKET GARDEN. In advocating this operation, Montgomery emphasized two points. The Rhine River provided a formidable border for Germany. Crossing it would result in a breach of the German defences beyond repair. Allied forces were poised to exploit a breach. MARKET GARDEN would allow the Allies to get round the northern part of the West Wall that lined the German-Dutch border. Furthermore, the Allies could put the German V-2 rocket-launching sites located in the Netherlands in jeopardy.

Montgomery's plan was both complicated and ambitious. Four other rivers and three canals had to be crossed before advancing to Arnhem and the Lower Rhine – a distance of over sixty miles. MARKET GARDEN was a high-risk plan, but sufficiently promising that, despite ULTRA intelligence reports indicating that two SS Panzer divisions were refitting near Arnhem, neither Eisenhower nor Montgomery favoured cancelling it. First in was the US 101st Airborne Division, whose most important objective was the bridge across the Maas/Meuse/Mass River. The target of the US 82nd Airborne Division, next in line, was the bridge spanning the Waal River, a branch of the Rhine near Nijmegen. The British 1st Airborne Division, the Red Devils, received the most important – and difficult – assignment: the bridge across the Lower Rhine at Arnhem. The British xxx Corps had orders to advance through the resulting corridor to link up with the airborne troops in Arnhem and open the way to the North German Plain.

MARKET GARDEN commenced on 17 September and, from the beginning, faced obstacles that adversely affected its chances. Some were beyond the Allies' control. Bad weather delayed the arrival of some of the paratroopers, and it prevented timely air reinforcements and supply during the battle. Fog and friction contributed as well. The Germans succeeded in retrieving a complete battle plan from a glider that had crashed, killing all on board, including the officer who had broken the rules by having the plans with him. Other contretemps reflected the ignoring of intelligence warnings. The British 1st Airborne Division, in particular, faced two major threats. The first was posed by the 9th and 10th SS Panzer Divisions that were indeed situated near Arnhem. The second was caused by the distance between their drop zone and their target. The Germans prevented them from achieving their objective – the capture of the Rhine bridge at Arnhem. The Germans succeeded in sealing off the drop zone and prevented all but one battalion from reaching the Arnhem bridge. Although Lieutenant Colonel John Frost and his 500 men captured the northern approach, they could not cross the bridge without help from XXX Corps. Its advance through the Netherlands was not swift enough to strengthen the precarious position in which Frost and his men found themselves. Both the German Fifteenth Army and the terrain – characterized by mud and water – prevented rapid advance by the XXX Corps and restricted the movement of its armoured vehicles to one road. German anti-tank guns had a field day.

But the British did not entirely gridlock themselves. The US 82nd Airborne Division focused on seizing the high ground around Nijmegen before proceeding to the lightly guarded bridge over the Waal. The Germans had time to reinforce their position by the time the Americans arrived and held the bridge for three days. It was long enough. The XXX Corps reached all the American paratroopers except those at Arnhem. That bridge, as the movie *A Bridge Too Far* aptly demonstrated, was one too far. The British Red Devils defended their position for nine days. Only 2,400 of the original 9,000 escaped. MARKET GARDEN's failure dashed the Allies' hope of forging across the Rhine River and perhaps ending the war before Christmas 1944.[31]

On 22 September, Eisenhower, in an effort to support the British offensive, ordered Bradley to advance toward Cologne. Bradley tasked the First Army with fighting through the West Wall at Aachen. Some of the campaign's fiercest street fighting occurred in bombed city of Aachen between 13 and 21 October. And the Allied advance toward Germany slowed. The Germans had achieved what seemed unimaginable a few weeks earlier. They had stopped the Allied offensive, blunted their exploitation and threatened the Allies' completion of the offensive and final victory.

Other factors contributed as well. The Allies continued to outdistance a supply system drastically hindered by the lack of railroads and undamaged roads. Much of the French transportation network had been damaged or

---

31 Buckley, *Monty's Men*, pp. 7, 12, 21–2, 208–31, 233.

destroyed by Allied bombers, either in preparation for the invasion or in an effort to isolate the Normandy battlefield once the invasion had begun. To alleviate the problem, the Allies needed access to ports, especially Antwerp, and rivers, particularly the Scheldt. Although the battle for the Scheldt began in early September, Canadian forces did not succeed in wrestling the area from the Germans until mid-November. The first Allied supply ships docked in the Antwerp harbour on 28 November.

In the late autumn of 1944, British movement in the Netherlands had virtually stopped in the wake of Operation MARKET GARDEN. The Americans also encountered difficulties. After the intense battle against the West Wall and the struggle for Aachen, Lieutenant General Courtney Hodges and the US First Army faced a greater challenge – the Hürtgen Forest.[32] Some of the bloodiest fighting of the war occurred there over several vital months. American units advancing directly east and through southern France also encountered difficulties. The hilly Lorraine country slowed the Third Army's push to the West Wall in the Saar's coal-mining region. The Vosges mountains of Alsace thwarted the Franco-American Army Group coming from the Loire Valley. Had exploitation come to an end? As hopes of a quick end to the war vanished, Eisenhower and his commanders prepared to continue the push across the Rhine River and into Germany, but the Germans had one more ace up their sleeve.

As 1944 drew to a close, the Germans found themselves pressed on all sides. The Soviets were rolling back the Eastern Front. Allied forces tied them down in Italy. In the West, although the Allies' advance toward Germany had been halted temporarily, the situation did not seem promising in the long term. Needing to regain the strategic initiative from the Allies, Hitler had begun contemplating a counter-attack in the West as early as September 1944, despite the fact that his troops were retreating headlong toward the German frontier. For Hitler, a decisive German victory on the battlefield might well sow fatal discord between the British and Americans. The timing was right for a counter-attack, and Hitler had the perfect location. The objective was logistical: the key port of Antwerp. The main German attack would surge through the Ardennes Forest, as it had in 1940. Unfortunately, the mechanized forces lacked the fuel to advance beyond the Meuse

---

32 See Robert Sterling Rush, *Hell in Hürtgen Forest: The Ordeal and Triumph of an American Infantry Regiment* (Lawrence: University Press of Kansas, 2001); Edward G. Miller, *A Dark and Bloody Ground: The Hürtgen Forest and the Roer River Dams, 1944–1945* (College Station: Texas A&M University Press, 2003); and Gerald Astor, *The Bloody Forest: Battle for the Hürtgen, September 1944–January 1945* (Novato, Calif.: Presidio Press, 2000).

River. Therefore, the plan also directed the capture of Allied fuel dumps. Gamblers call this 'betting on the come'. It seldom works out well.

The scope of the proposed counter-attack horrified Rundstedt and Field Marshal Walter Model, both of whom thought that it was too ambitious. To carry out the planned counter-attack, however, Hitler needed more than fuel resources. He needed more troops, and he decided to get them from the Eastern Front. Powerful primarily on paper, the striking force consisted of three armies – the Sixth SS Panzer Army commanded by General Josef Sepp Dietrich in the north; in the centre, the Fifth Panzer Army under General Hasso von Manteuffel; and in the south, General Erich Brandenberger's Seventh Army, which had been rebuilt after Normandy.

While the Germans massed their forces for a counter-attack, the Allies assessed the situation and contemplated their own plans. Basically optimistic, despite German frontier resistance, the Allied commanders failed to take seriously the possibility of an enemy counter-attack. They did not believe that the Germans had the resources necessary for such an audacious move. Consequently, their defences, particularly in the Ardennes Forest, were lacking. Manpower shortages impeded rapid replacement in battle-ravaged units. The British, in particular, lacked the manpower resources to ensure that their units remained at full strength. In early December 1944, Eisenhower, Montgomery and Bradley conferred and sketched out plans for an offensive in early January 1945. Although Eisenhower was still wedded to a 'broad front' strategy, the strongest thrust would occur in the north. Thus, both sides spent early December planning for the next attack. While the Allies prepared to drive across the Rhine and into Germany, the Germans put the finishing touches on the ambitious counter-attack that they were about to launch.

The Allies were so focused on their own preparations that they did not pay attention to signs indicating that the enemy was doing the same. Wedded to the idea that the Germans lacked the resources necessary for an attack, the Allied commanders did not put much stock in ULTRA intercepts that suggested otherwise – that the Germans were massing ammunition and fuel dumps in the Ardennes. Moreover, because that sector was believed to be quiet, the divisions stationed there included many inexperienced troops. The only reserves in the region were the 82nd and 101st Airborne Divisions – both recovering from MARKET GARDEN.[33]

---

33 Dwight D. Eisenhower, *Crusade in Europe* (Norwalk, Conn.: The Easton Press, 1948), pp. 321–42. See also Rick Atkinson, *The Guns at Last Light: The War in Western Europe, 1944–1945* (New York: Henry Holt and Company, 2013).

German actions fed Allied underestimation of their enemy. Following Hitler's orders, the Germans involved in the counter-attack maintained complete radio silence, which in and of itself should perhaps have raised some red flags. Because the Germans did not communicate their intentions over radio waves, ULTRA intelligence did not have any enemy communications indicating the impending offensive that would spring out of the Ardennes Forest. Numerous intelligence sources, including ULTRA, did indicate, however, the relocation of Panzer divisions and aircraft from the Eastern to the Western Front.

In response, Eisenhower, Hodges and their staffs concluded, erroneously, that the Germans were planning a small offensive near Aachen, which was north of the Ardennes. Furthermore, they discounted ULTRA intelligence that indicated increasing German activity behind the forest. The Allies, in short, made the same mistake that the Germans did before the Normandy invasion. They were so focused on their own offensive that they ignored intelligence that the Germans were going to strike first.

In the predawn hours of 16 December, the German counter-offensive – Operation AUTUMN FOG – commenced with a massive unexpected artillery barrage. German tanks and troops poured out of the Ardennes and assaulted the American-held line between Monschau and Echternach along a fifty-mile front. Although the Americans requested air support, the weather intervened. Clouds obscured the battlefield. Along the northern part of the line, the Sixth SS Panzer Army met its match when it tangled with the US 99th and 2nd Divisions. Despite a fierce assault, the American line held. That was not the case to the south, where the Fifth Panzer Army assaulted the 106th and 28th Divisions. There, the line, which was thinly defended, gave way, and the Germans quickly moved forward to exploit the breach. Caught off guard, the Americans were slow to react, and the Germans benefited as a result.

Across the front, English-speaking German soldiers, dressed in American army uniforms, crossed into US-held territory and created confusion and fear behind the lines. They severed telephone lines, altered road signs and eliminated military policemen tasked with directing advancing Allied convoys. Soon, front-line troops did not know whom to trust. Consequently, they used informal questioning to ferret out the imposters. The subject matter of the questions varied – major league baseball teams, state capitals, Hollywood celebrities and their spouses. This strategy, however, proved problematic, because not everyone knew the answers to the questions. In some cases, those asking the questions did not know the correct answers either. General Bradley was stopped on more than one occasion. In the first instance, he was allowed to advance, even though he did not know the name of Betty Grable's husband. On another occasion, he was briefly detained when the sentry disputed his identification of the capital of Illinois, even though his answer subsequently proved to be correct. The Germans did more than impersonate American soldiers. In the early days of the offensive, First SS Panzer Division murdered captured Americans. The most significant event occurred near Malmédy, where the Germans executed eighty-six American servicemen.

In the north, the 99th and 2nd Divisions held the high ground – the Monschau and Eisenhorn Ridge area – which enabled them to maintain control of critical roads and funnelled the German advance along secondary routes. Once they grasped the seriousness of the situation, American commanders rushed to defend key road junctions, particularly at St Vith and Bastogne. For six critical days, the American defenders held on to the road junction at St Vith, which fell to the Germans on 22 December. More importantly, a small force denied the Germans access to the junction in Bastogne long enough for reinforcements – the 101st Airborne Division – to arrive. The Germans completely surrounded the Bastogne defenders, but they refused to surrender. When the Germans contacted General Anthony McAuliffe and requested his surrender, his response – 'Nuts!' – indicated the American determination to continue their defence of Bastogne and the critical road junction.

When the weather finally cleared on 23 December, Allied air forces went to work. Tactical and strategic air forces pounded the German attackers throughout the Ardennes. They targeted the enemy's armoured spearheads. The air assault forced the Germans, who were low on fuel, to abandon their offensive a day later. Manteuffel's Fifth Panzer Army came the closest to reaching the Meuse River. He was stopped a few miles away on 24 December. General George S. Patton had turned elements of the Third Army north, and the 4th Armoured Division reached the Bastogne defenders on 26 December. North of the bulge, Montgomery's Twenty-First Army Group, which now included the US First and Ninth Armies, attacked southward on 3 January 1945. With Patton's forces pushing northward, the Germans were in danger of being trapped. Both Manteuffel and Rundstedt wanted to order a retreat. Hitler initially refused, but by the end of January, American forces had succeeded in pushing the Germans back and eliminating the bulge in their front line.

On 31 December, as the Allies were threatening to close off the bulge, Germans forces – seven infantry and three Panzer divisions – attacked from the Colmar pocket to engage the Sixth Army Group – Patch's US Seventh Army and de Lattre's French First Army – commanded by General Jacob Devers. The Germans had two objectives. They hoped to convince Eisenhower to redirect the Third Army to meet this new threat, thereby removing its divisions from their attack against the southern part of the bulge. Hitler also wanted to retain a strong forward position in Alsace. Allied intelligence sources, including ULTRA, however, revealed the German intentions. Because the Allied line was stretched and thinly defended, the German attack caused Eisenhower to consider a withdrawal from Alsace. Staunch French opposition caused Eisenhower to reconsider this option.

After making only a moderate advance, the Germans called off the offensive on 25 January and began to move units back to the Eastern Front. Five days earlier, American and French forces had counter-attacked along the southern flank of the Colmar pocket. Although progress was initially slower than expected, French forces liberated Colmar on 2 February. Within a week, the Allies had eliminated the pocket. The Germans had expended crucial resources for no tangible gain. The Allies' overwhelming response to the enemy counter-offensive thwarted the German effort at completion – liberation of Antwerp.

The Battle of the Bulge had several consequences. It was the last major German offensive in the West. The cost was great in terms of mobile reserves and 100,000 lost men. From this point on, retreat back to Germany defined the Germans' war. Second, it opened the Allies' path to Germany. Although the Allies' final offensive had been delayed, the Germans would have far fewer resources to meet it once it began. In addition, German morale on the Western Front declined. Finally, by withdrawing forces from the Eastern Front to mount Operation AUTUMN FOG, the Germans weakened their own situation and placed the Soviets in a much better position for their final push toward Vienna and Berlin.

The failure of the Ardennes offensive left the Germans unable to establish and hold defensive positions on the west bank of the Rhine River. The Allies planned to launch three separate operations to capture the Rhineland. In the north, two armies – the British Second and Canadian First – would push south, while the US Ninth Army would advance north to link up with them. In the centre, the US First Army would advance toward Cologne and Bonn

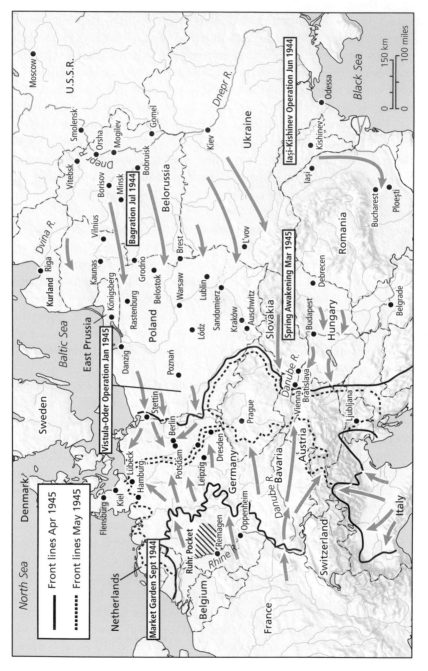

14.3 Defeat of Germany, 1945

before moving south on the west bank of the Rhine. The Third Army would move up the Moselle River to join them. The Seventh Army would also advance north to meet Patton near Koblenz.[34]

Although their defences were crumbling, the Germans did not give up the fight easily. On 8 February, the British and Canadians began their operation with a huge artillery bombardment. The terrain and German resistance hindered their advance. On 21 February, they finally reached the Rhine River. The US Ninth Army, advancing to link up with them, had an even harder time. To get into position for their attack, the Ninth Army had to cross the Roer River. Opening dam gates upstream, the Germans succeeded in flooding the area. The slowly subsiding water held up the Americans for two weeks. They did not make contact with the Canadians until 4 March.

The US First Army offensive got under way on 26 February. While the VII Corps' assault on Cologne ended in the capture of the city on 5 March, the III Corps headed for Bonn and Remagen, fifteen miles to the south. On 7 March, a platoon of the Ninth Armoured Division stormed the Hohenzollern railroad bridge across the Rhine at Remagen. Not only did the Germans staunchly resist, but they also tried twice to blow up the bridge. After the main charge failed to detonate, the Americans were able to seize their objective and establish a bridgehead on the west bank of the river. Over the next 24 hours, 8,000 crossed the river. The Ninth Armoured Division had the distinction of accomplishing what no other unit achieved. They captured an intact bridge across the Rhine River. Although they had not intended the Remagen Bridge to be a major crossing point, the Allies quickly exploited the situation and expanded their bridgehead.

Patton's Third Army was on the move as well. Advancing along the Moselle River's north bank, it travelled sixty-five miles in three days to reach the Rhine. Then Patton did not do what the Germans expected. Instead of sending the XII Corps north to reinforce the bridgehead at Remagen, the Corps turned south along the river on 15 March. With the US Seventh Army advancing north through the Saar toward Patton, the Allies ended all organized German resistance west of the Rhine by 25 March. The German struggle to hold onto this sector was costly: over 200,000 irreplaceable casualties and an irreparable blow to German morale.

---

34 Eisenhower, *Crusade in Europe*, pp. 342–65; Buckley, *Monty's Men*, pp. 260–1; Doubler, *Closing with the Enemy*, pp. 198–226; Mansoor, *The GI Offensive in Europe*, pp. 190, 217–18, 220, 228–9, 231, 234, 236. See also Charles B. MacDonald, *A Time for Trumpets: The Untold Story of the Battle of the Bulge* (New York: William Morrow and Company, 1985).

The last Allied operation to get under way was that of the British. Montgomery was a proponent of thorough preparation, and his troops underwent two weeks of intense training before getting started. Facing five poorly equipped and manned German divisions, defending a thirty-mile front, the British, using 3,300 artillery guns, strategic and tactical air forces, and two airborne divisions, crossed the Rhine on 23–24 March. Although the ground forces got off to a slow start, they soon gained momentum. Once the breakout began, it proceeded at a much faster pace than that in Normandy. Along the front, the Allied steamroller pushed the Germans back. All seven Allied armies had crossed the Rhine River barrier by 27 March. The doorway to the German heartland was open, ready for exploitation. By 1 April, Allied forces had encircled the Ruhr region – Germany's industrial heart. Allied forces greatly outnumbered their enemy both in manpower and materiel. Allied aircraft bombed German cities and troops at will. Fuel shortages greatly limited the Germans' use of tanks and aircraft. Equipment failures and supply shortages contributed to the demoralization. German soldiers – German defences – had reached their breaking point.[35]

For the first two weeks of April, the Ruhr defenders fought on as the noose tightened around them. By 14 April, the Allies succeeded in splitting the Germans and achieving their capitulation five days later. Over 300,000 German soldiers surrendered. Some, like Model, chose suicide over capture. Even as the battle in the Ruhr pocket raged, other Allied forces advanced deep into Germany. Elements of the Ninth and First Armies reached the Elbe River on 11 April. Within two days, they had established a bridgehead on the east bank and were only fifty miles from Berlin. The way to Berlin appeared to be open. Simpson was poised to race for the capital when Eisenhower stopped him. Eisenhower wanted to mop up Germans forces both north and south of Simpson's position on the Elbe. The American advance shifted focus to Leipzig, Chemnitz and Dresden to the southeast, and to Bavaria and Austria.

Although not all of his commanders agreed with his decision, Eisenhower stood firm. Shortages of fuel had again become an issue. While Simpson had reached the Elbe River, most Allied forces were much further west. The American spearhead had little artillery and fewer than 50,000 men. The Soviet Army was in a much stronger position. Thirty-three miles from the

---

35 Atkinson, *The Guns at Last Light*, pp. 512, 542–7, 552, 567, 571, 580–4; Mansoor, *The GI Offensive in Europe*, pp. 237–48.

capital, the Soviet command was ready to unleash 1,250,000 men with approximately 22,000 artillery pieces.

Eisenhower also understood the ramifications that would result if Western Allied forces accidently clashed with their Soviet allies in Berlin. Furthermore, he was aware of decisions made by the Big Three – Roosevelt, Churchill and Stalin – at the Yalta Conference in February 1945 regarding the dissolution of Germany and the establishment of occupation zones after the war. Consequently, Eisenhower decided to let the Soviets capture Berlin, while his forces mopped up German resistance elsewhere.[36]

On 16 April, the Soviets launched their final thrust against Berlin. They reached the suburbs less than a week later. Soviet forces completely encircled the city by 26 April and were only a mile from Hitler's bunker. On 25 April, while the battle for Berlin raged, advancing American and Soviet units met on the Elbe River. They effectively cut Germany in two. Berlin was on the verge of collapse. Soviet forces savagely wrestled control of the capital from its defenders. Unable to cope with the collapse of the armies of the Reich throughout Germany, and accepting the inevitable end, Hitler weighed his options and made a decision. On 29 April, he and Eva Braun, his long time mistress, married. Then he wrote his last political statement and issued his final decrees. Naming them traitors to the Reich, Hitler expelled from the party two of his staunchest supporters – Herman Göring and Heinrich Himmler. He also designated his successor. Admiral Karl Dönitz became the new President and Commander-in-Chief of Germany's armed forces. On 30 April, Hitler and Braun committed suicide. After poisoning their children, Goebbels and his wife also committed suicide. The end was near.

Fighting in Berlin ended on 2 May, but it continued elsewhere. American forces mopped up resistance in southern Germany and Austria, and they crossed the Brenner Pass into northern Italy. Allied forces captured numerous German officers. Bowing to the inevitable, German forces in Italy put down their weapons. Dönitz, fearful of Soviet retribution against his countrymen, sought a separate peace with the Western Allies. He also indicated that Germany would continue the fight against the Soviets. Because the Big Three had announced their determination to achieve unconditional surrender, the British and Americans refused the admiral's request. On 7 May, the Germans signed the surrender in a schoolhouse in Reims, France. On 8 May, a second surrender signing ceremony occurred. Both Allied and

36 See Stephen E. Ambrose, *Eisenhower and Berlin, 1945: The Decision to Halt at the Elbe* (New York: W. W. Norton, 1967).

German military leaders formally agreed to the surrender terms. The war in Europe was finally over.[37]

The tide, which began to shift in 1942, flowed against the Germans on all fronts in 1943. What caused the shift, the flood that overwhelmed the Germans by May 1945? To say that the Soviet steamroller, combined with the Western Allies' industrial and military might, overwhelmed the Axis Powers is too simplistic an answer. A deeper evaluation reveals that, by 1943, the Allied war effort had coalesced. The British and Americans had figured out how to work together. Their combined arms operations clicked and allowed them to achieve success on the battlefield. Their timing in launching offensives worked. As the Normandy invasion demonstrated, the British and Americans got location right. Once they gained a beachhead in Normandy, the Allies successfully exploited their foothold. Although their advance was not as rapid as planned, the Allies were able, slowly and steadily, to force the Germans to retreat. Pressed in the East by the Soviets and in the West by the Allies, the Wehrmacht collapsed. As their momentum built, the Allies increased the pressure on their enemy and brought the offensive that began in Normandy to completion. While the Germans had the advantage in timing, location, exploitation and completion at the beginning of the war, the pendulum had swung in the other direction by 1943. With one exception, the Germans were no longer on the offensive on any front – Mediterranean, Eastern or Western. That one exception was the Battle of the Bulge. Here, the Germans got the timing and location right. They succeeded in catching their enemy off-guard and in gaining ground at the beginning of the offensive. The Germans failed, however, in exploiting their early success and in completing the offensive with a victory.

The Allies achieved victory in the West by becoming better than their opponents in timing, location, exploitation and completion. Historians agree that the first critical step was the Normandy invasion, which was a close-run offensive. Maintaining secrecy prior to commencement was crucial. Eisenhower agonized over postponement. Should the delay be a day, two weeks, a month? The longer the delay, the less certainty there was that the Germans could be caught off-guard. Despite extensive planning, the massing of personnel, materiel, armaments and munitions, ships and aircraft, the outcome

---

37 Evan Mawdsley, *Thunder in the East: The Nazi-Soviet War, 1941–1945* (London: Hodder Arnold, 2005), pp. 361–96; Chris Bellamy, *Absolute War: Soviet Russia in the Second World War* (New York: Vintage Books, 2008), pp. 630–69; Buckley, *Monty's Men*, pp. 265–95; Mansoor, *The GI Offensive in Europe*, pp. 246–8; Eisenhower, *Crusade in Europe*, pp. 387–426.

of the landing was not a certainty. Evidence of this concern was the speech that Eisenhower prepared to deliver in the event that the amphibious assault failed. In it, he assumed full responsibility for the failure. The success of the invasion forestalled Eisenhower's delivery of the speech – permanently. Because the Normandy invasion, which has been romanticized and perceived as easy, was a success, there is a tendency not to acknowledge that it was the culmination of intense planning, training and orchestration. It was an amazingly successful solution to an extraordinarily hard problem and reflected the excellence of Allied strategy and decision-making. The Allies found a game-winning plan at the very time that the Germans, who were pressed on all fronts, no longer had the resources – personnel, materiel, aircraft – needed to achieve victory. When the Allies gained a foothold on the Normandy beaches, it marked the beginning of the end for the Germans on the Western Front. Russian forces exerted pressure on the Germans in the East and prevented the high command from transferring sufficient units to meet the larger than anticipated threat in the West. Although it took longer than expected or planned, from this point on, the Allies assaulted the Germans on multiple fronts. They exploited the foothold that they had gained in Normandy and brought the offensive to a successful completion on the Elbe River, where they linked up with their Russian allies, who had assaulted and captured Berlin. During the Battle of the Bulge, materiel and personnel shortages impeded their counter-attack. By the spring of 1945, the German war effort was in a state of collapse. Historians frequently contend that Hitler's interference hampered the German war effort. Equally, the Germans had not entertained the possibility of defeat, and when defeat stared them in the face, they were unable to recover and to return to the strategy and decision-making that had brought them success in the early years of the war. The strategy and decision-making of the Allies, however, improved during the same period as the German decline, and culminated in ultimate victory.

15

The war in the Pacific, 1941–1945

JOHN T. KUEHN

The road to war

The outbreak of war in the Pacific between Japan, the United States and the British Commonwealth nations can be attributed to two primary causes – as fallout from the war in Europe and as a result of a clash in Japanese-American policies in China. As to the first cause, relations between the United States and the Empire of Japan had been strained for some time over the issue of Japan's encroachments in China. The Washington Naval Conference of 1921–22 resulted in a Nine-Power Pact meant to protect China; however, it proved of little value. Additionally, the Naval Arms Limitation Treaty, signed after the same conference, assigned the Imperial Japanese Navy (IJN) an 'inferior' position in numbers of capital ships relative to the United States, which caused considerable resentment inside the officer corps of the IJN. As the prosperous 1920s gave way to worldwide depression, militant elements inside Japan began to undermine the basis for peace in the Far East. In 1930, insubordinate Imperial Japanese Army (IJA) officers stationed in southern Manchuria invaded that region and then established a Japanese puppet state (Manchukuo). Condemned by the League of Nations, Japan withdrew from that international body in 1933. After another army-engineered 'incident' in 1937, Japan became involved in open conflict in China against Chiang Kai-shek's Nationalists and Communist forces under Mao Zedong. Although victorious on the battlefield, Japan found China simply too big to conquer. Incidents such as the 'Rape of Nanjing' further alienated Japan in world opinion. The USA instituted a policy of material support for the Nationalists via the 'Burma Road' through the Himalayas and the 'loan' of officers like Claire Chennault to help establish a Chinese air force.[1]

---

1 John T. Kuehn, *Agents of Innovation* (Annapolis, Md.: Naval Institute Press, 2008), chs. 3, 4 and 8; Ronald H. Spector, *Eagle Against the Sun: The American War with Japan* (New York: Vintage Books, 1985), chs. 1–3.

American and Japanese interests also clashed as a result of the war in Europe (and beyond) and were tightly linked to events in China. The USA saw China as a means to tie down Japan and keep her out of the camp of the Axis. Generalissmo Chiang Kai-shek and the Nationalists' engagement of Japan also allowed the USA to rearm while providing Great Britain, and eventually the Soviet Union, with Lend-Lease material. With the US Navy and US Army Air Forces as deterrents in the Pacific, aided by China, the USA might avoid commitment of ground troops and serve only as the 'arsenal of democracy'. For Japan, the success of Germany seemed to offer an opportunity out of her dilemma in China. If Germany could be used to open a second front against the USA (especially her navy), Japan might finally get the freedom of action she needed to resolve the China incident. A quick stroke to the south might solve her dependence on US oil and raw materials by conquering the rich East Indies colonies of the collapsing European colonial powers. As US sanctions over China bit deep into Japan's financial and economic means, Hitler seemed unstoppable in the West. Japan might miss her opportunity. Accordingly, Japan formally joined the Axis Powers of Europe in the Tripartite Pact in 1940, soon after France had fallen. Japan's economic situation worsened with new US sanctions, and she bullied the Vichy French into accepting 50,000 Japanese troops in southern Indochina. Instead of cowing the USA, relations worsened. The USA, Great Britain and the Netherlands cut off Japan's access to oil. This event forced Japan's hand; not only did the timing for war seem ripe, with Germany advancing deep into the Soviet Union, but Japan's situation would now only grow worse with the passage of time unless she acted. Accordingly, she decided for war against all three Western powers in the late summer of 1941, under her new Prime Minister, Tojo Hideki.[2]

Admiral Yamamoto Isoroku, who had opposed the alliance with Germany, reluctantly planned for war against the United States, and conceived the brilliant but risky idea of a surprise air and mini-submarine attack on the US Fleet – an attack only possible because the Americans had left the Pacific Fleet in Hawaii after manoeuvres the previous year. After working through technical problems with launching aerial torpedo attacks in shallow Pearl Harbor, the six big aircraft carriers of *Dai Ichi Kido Butai* (The First Mobile Strike Force) departed from their forward anchorage in the Kurile Islands in late November, for a stealthy North Pacific transit. *Kido Butai* was something

2 H. P. Willmott, *Empires in the Balance: Japanese and Allied Pacific Strategies to April 1942* (Annapolis, Md.: Naval Institute Press, 1982), pp. 72–4.

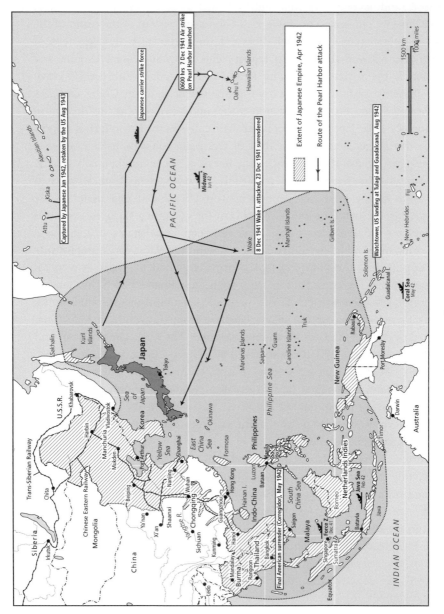

Captured by Japanese Jun 1942, retaken by the US Aug 1943

Aleutian Islands

Attu

Kiska

Japanese carrier strike force

0600 hrs 7 Dec 1941 Air strike on Pearl Harbor launched

Oahu I.

Hawaiian Islands

PACIFIC OCEAN

Midway
Jun 42

8 Dec 1941 Wake I. attacked, 23 Dec 1941 surrendered

Wake

Marshall Islands

Gilbert Is.

Watchtower, US landing at Tulagi and Guadalcanal, Aug 1942

New Hebrides

Fiji

Solomon Is.

Guadalcanal I.

Coral Sea
May 42

Rabaul

Truk

Caroline Islands

Guam

Saipan

Marianas Islands

Philippine Sea

New Guinea

Port Moresby

Darwin

Australia

Kuril Islands

Sakhalin

Japan

Tokyo

Sea of Japan

Korea

Okinawa

East China Sea

Formosa

Yellow Sea

Shanghai

U.S.S.R.

Khabarovsk

Harbin

Vladivostok

Port Arthur

Mukden

Manchuria

Beijing

Nanjing

Wuhan

Hong Kong

Hainan I.

Luzon

Manila

Philippines

Bataan

Final American surrender (Corregidor), May 1942

South China Sea

Saigon

Indo-China

Borneo

Netherlands Indies

Java Sea
Feb 42

Batavia

Java

Timor

INDIAN OCEAN

Equator

Sumatra

Singapore

Force Z
Dec 41

Malaya

Bangkok

Thailand

Rangoon

Burma

Mandalay

Ledo

Kunming

Sichuan

Chongqing

Guangzhou

Yangtze R.

Xi'an

Shaanxi

Ya'nan

China

Mongolia

Siberia

Irkutsk

Chita

Trans-Siberian Railway

Chinese Eastern Railway

Extent of Japanese Empire, Apr 1942

Route of the Pearl Harbor attack

1500 km

1000 miles

15.1 The Asia-Pacific war, 1941–42

422

new in warfare – a mobile naval air striking force with an operational capability not seen before in naval history. The closest thing to it in terms of firepower and innovation was the Germans' *Panzergruppe* Kleist, which had spearheaded the German Blitzkrieg against France in 1940. *Kido Butai*'s air groups were almost entirely veterans of combat in China since 1937, and its deck crews at a peak of perfection in getting their planes airborne. It was this key innovation that would give the Japanese the tactical surprise they achieved over the American naval and air forces at Pearl Harbor.[3] While the Japanese prepared for war, they used their diplomatic mission, headed by a moderate diplomat-admiral, to distract the Americans from their bellicose purposes.

However, the Americans were on their guard. On 27 November, Admiral Husband Kimmel, Commander-in-Chief of the US Pacific Fleet (CINC-PACFLT), received a 'war warning', which was in part based on decryption of the Japanese secret diplomatic code (MAGIC). Kimmel convened a meeting of his major commanders to discuss reinforcement of both Wake and Midway Islands with additional aircraft, in anticipation of a blow that might soon fall. This reinforcement constituted part of a larger effort, ongoing for over a year, to beef up US defences throughout the Pacific. The outcome was a heightened alert status for the forces in Pearl Harbor and a decision to send the two aircraft carriers present out to ferry aircraft to the islands. The third Pacific Fleet carrier, *Saratoga*, was already en route to the West Coast of the United States for a scheduled yard period. Neither of the two carriers took the slower battleships with them, since speed was of the essence.[4]

From mid-November to 5 December, the Navy Office tasked with the decryption of vital diplomatic signal intelligence with Japan had performed magnificently. It intercepted, decrypted signals and rapidly delivered them to strategic intelligence consumers at the highest levels of American government. On 6 December, this performance suffered its first real setback. Because of a series of failures and compromises, most of the key decision-makers in Washington DC went to bed that night without having been informed that the Japanese were sending their diplomatic entourage instructions that masked a declaration of war, prior to a final section that had yet to

---

3 Jonathan Parshall and J. Michael Wenger, 'Pearl Harbor's Overlooked Answer', *Naval History* 25:6 (December 2011), 16–21.
4 Glen M. Williford, *Racing the Sunrise: Reinforcing America's Pacific Outposts, 1941–1942* (Annapolis, Md.: Naval Institute Press, 2010).
5 Ladislas Farago, *The Broken Seal: Operation Magic and the Secret Road to Pearl Harbor* (New York: Random House, 1976 [1967]), pp. 329–53.

be decrypted.[5] Roosevelt was aware that the situation was tense, but had decided to leave the initiative for peace or war with the Japanese. At the end of a midday budget meeting, Roosevelt remarked to his budget director that 'we might be at war with Japan although no one knew'. However, he had little idea of where the first attack would occur; after all, the war warnings had been sent and everyone had acknowledged them.[6]

On the other side of the 180th meridian – the international dateline – 7 December 1941 had arrived. In Malaysia, the British military commanders were fighting a losing battle, trying to prepare for the storm they knew would break upon them. Up until 5 December, the British ground commander, Lieutenant General Arthur E. Percival, had been trying to get the colonial government to agree on a redeployment of troops, to try to pre-empt any Japanese invasion by occupying the excellent harbour of Singora (which the Japanese planned to seize). However, the strategy of not provoking the Japanese prevailed, and the British were unready in any case to launch a pre-emptive strike. That day, a Catalina flying-boat took off from Kota Bahru, in British Malaysia, to search for reported Japanese convoys, which had last been sighted steaming west from Thailand toward the Kra Peninsula, which connects Thailand with Malaysia to the south. At 1.30 p.m., Japanese aircraft providing cover to the invasion convoys shot this aircraft down, just after it had detected one of the Japanese invasion flotillas.[7]

Before sunrise on 8 December, Tokyo time, the IJN and IJA launched their coordinated attacks at Singora and Kota Bharu in Malaysia. About an hour later, the first wave of *Kido Butai*'s striking air groups arrived over Pearl Harbor, Hawaii. Several hours later, Japanese aircraft from Formosa, Mitsubishi 'Betty' medium bombers, struck at Clark Field and Cavite Naval Base in the Philippines. Never before in the history of warfare had a state launched such a finely synchronized attack on the land, air and sea, over such a broad geographic area, and in so short a period of time. Japan's Asian war now became a wider Pacific War.

Running wild

The United States has been criticized for not being ready for the war that came, yet in most details the US strategic planners got it right. They expected attacks on the Philippines, Guam and Wake, as well as the resource-rich

---

6 Farago, *The Broken Seal*, pp. 343–53.
7 Willmott, *Empires in the Balance*, pp. 104–6, 164–9, 220–32.

British and Dutch colonial possessions. All of these occurred on 7–8 December or shortly thereafter, but not foreseen was Admiral Yamamoto's bold attack on Hawaii, far across the Pacific from Japan. Militarily, the Pearl Harbor attack was nothing more than a spectacular and highly successful operational raid. However, had it never occurred, the United States would still have gone to war because of all the other assaults against America's possessions in the Pacific. However, the great resolve with which the US went to war was determined in great part by the perception of most Americans that it was an immoral, surprise attack, conducted without a declaration of war.[8]

Admiral Nagumo Chuichi's hundreds of naval aircraft caught the Pacific Fleet completely unaware on 7 December 1941. In addition to sinking or damaging all eight of the battleships present, the Japanese – perhaps more importantly – crippled the US Air Force as well. Over 3,200 military and civilian casualties were incurred. However, once sober minds evaluated the damage, it was realized that the critical repair facilities and fuel depots surrounding Pearl Harbor were virtually untouched. Even so, the results of Pearl Harbor were materially insignificant as far as the Japanese conquest of the 'Southern Resource Area' was concerned, because the US Fleet had little chance of reaching American possessions in the Western Pacific in time to prevent the loss of these key support bases once hostilities broke out.[9] Once the reality of war set in, the Navy did what it had planned to do all along – methodically island-hop across the Pacific. Pearl Harbor served not as a morale-destroying defeat, but rather as a rallying cry that motivated Americans to greater efforts and hardened their hearts. This hardness, when opposed by a manufactured Japanese warrior code modelled on bushido, would be one factor that made the Pacific War one of the most merciless, brutal and intense conflicts in history – a 'war without mercy'.[10] At the strategic level, Winston Churchill celebrated the attack along with the Japanese, realizing that the United States was now in the fight with all her resources and dedicated to a programme of complete victory. From the first day, the very nature of the conflict became asymmetric – Japan aiming at a short, decisive war, and the United States grimly implementing an approach that can only be characterized as a war of exhaustion and attrition.

---

8 Jonathan Parshall, 'A Grim December', *Naval History* 25:6 (December 2011), 22–28; Willmott, *Empires in the Balance*, pp. 142–3.

9 Parshall, 'A Grim December', 23.

10 John Dower, *War Without Mercy: Race and Power in the Pacific War* (New York: Pantheon Books, 1986).

Comparisons can sometimes be helpful. For the Pacific War, a doppel-ganger might come from consideration of the Eastern Front in the Second World War. Parallels emerge most readily at the theatre strategic and operational levels of war (the two overlap). Both theatres involved vast distances; indeed, the operational distances involved in the Pacific War dwarfed those of any previous conflict. In both theatres, the aggressor (Germany/Japan) launched a Blitzkrieg-type campaign, intended to secure a victory cheaply through means of modern combined arms warfare, cul-minating in 'decisive battle'. Air power was integral to the hoped-for success of both campaigns. Initially, both campaigns were wildly successful – in the Japanese case, at a relatively low cost in casualties. But the main avenues of advance in both theatres diverged, and soon both became fatally under-mined by this divergence of effort. Neither campaign achieved the quick victory it sought, and at the end of two incendiary ripostes by the sup-posedly defeated foe – primarily before Moscow by the Soviets and at Midway for the Americans – both conflicts settled into an attritional charac-ter that prevailed for the rest of the war, and that brought disaster and annihilation to those who had provoked them.

Returning to the opening days of the war, the Philippines campaign in 1941–42 was not among the brighter moments of General Douglas MacArthur's military career. Air power was a daytime weapon at this stage of the Second World War, and most of the Japanese aircraft waiting to strike the Philippine naval and airbases had to wait both for sunrise and for the fog to clear. While they waited, MacArthur's air commander, General Lewis Brereton, sent his bombers into the air to avoid the fate that occurred to land-based aircraft at Pearl Harbor. Unable to get permission to attack Formosa, they simply loitered, and when Brereton received the go-ahead, he recalled the aircraft to refuel. It was through this series of miscues, as well as a classic underestimation of the enemy, that Japanese bombers and fighters found Brereton's B-17 bombers on the ground. At one stroke, the Japanese elimin-ated half of MacArthur's air force and the majority of his bombers. There were over 250 casualties, including 80 killed, many of them valuable pilots. With air superiority achieved by their initial strike, the Japanese returned on 9 December to pound Cavite naval yard. The small US Asiatic Fleet suffered few losses, but that was because its commander, Admiral Thomas Hart, had already moved most of his major units to the south. This attack caused extensive damage to the shore facilities, destroying the Asiatic Fleet's reserve of torpedoes. The defence of the northern Philippines was now the responsi-bility of the US Army and indigenous Filipino forces. They would be virtually without naval or air support in their quixotic mission against an enemy that had command of both the air and the sea.[11]

Japanese strikes continued relentlessly at other locations throughout Southeast Asia and Micronesia. Poorly defended Guam in the Marianas fell easily on 10 December. Only at the tiny Wake Island did the Navy and Marine Corps defenders give the Japanese their first temporary setback. Here, the Japanese were guilty of underestimating their enemy and of overconfidence. Despite being softened up by bombers flying out of the Marshall Islands, a Japanese amphibious assault on 11 December was bloodily repulsed by Wake's defenders, with the loss of several Japanese warships. The news of the successful repulse was a ray of sunshine in an otherwise stormy sky. It served to bolster morale and had the impact of hastening an attempt to reinforce the island with additional resources. Unfortunately, the relief force under Rear Admiral F. Jack Fletcher was fatally delayed in its departure from Pearl Harbor, and was over 425 miles away from Wake when the gallant defenders surrendered. Over 1,600 Americans became prisoners.[12]

Meanwhile, events in the Philippines had gone from bad to worse. Without the ability to interdict Japanese invasion forces, by either land or sea, it was only a matter of time before the Japanese successfully established themselves on the main island of Luzon in late December. With his air force destroyed, and most of the small naval forces being evacuated to the south, MacArthur was holding a poor hand of cards. Accordingly, he scuttled his original plan to defend Luzon on a broad front. Instead of opposing the Japanese landings in the Lingayen Gulf, which is where MacArthur's intelligence predicted they would land, MacArthur decided to challenge the Japanese in the broad plain south of Lingayen.[13]

In the largest of their amphibious operations to date, the Japanese landed over 50,000 troops of General Homma Masaharu's Fourteenth Army at Lingayen Gulf on the northwestern side of the main Philippine island of Luzon, on 22 December 1941. After the first contact with the well-coordinated Japanese air-sea-ground assault, MacArthur decided to pull back into a fortified line of defences on the peninsula of Bataan, located between Subic and Manila Bays. Here, he would defend until relieved by the Navy's Pacific Fleet; yet any hope of executing this course of action had gone up in the pall

11 Louis Morton, *The Fall of the Philippines* (Washington DC: Center of Military History, 1952), pp. 79–85.
12 John B. Lundstrom, *Black Shoe Carrier Admiral: Frank Jack Fletcher at Coral Sea, Midway and Guadalcanal* (Annapolis, Md.: Naval Institute Press, 2006) pp. 28–47.
13 Morton, *The Fall of the Philippines*, pp. 156–7.

of smoke rising over Pearl Harbor on 7 December. Nevertheless, MacArthur had little choice other than to try to hold out, or at the very least tie down Japanese forces and prevent their use elsewhere. Fortunately, Homma was more interested in capturing Manila than destroying his opponent, and Major General Jonathan Wainwright's withdrawal into the Bataan Peninsula was accomplished relatively smoothly. Bataan was not prepared for the 80,000 troops (including 20,000 Americans) who retreated into it. Large stockpiles of food did exist, but they were scattered across Luzon to support MacArthur's original defence scheme, and MacArthur's prevarications prevented any realistic chance that most of these stores could be transhipped to Bataan. In the confusion of the retreat, most of these supplies fell into the hands of the Japanese. After only one week in their new defences, the 'battling bastards of Bataan' were already on half rations.[14]

In the meantime, the rapid advance of the Japanese armed forces, combined with clear thinking in Washington DC, resulted in the diversions of scheduled reinforcements, such as the convoy escorted by cruiser *Pensacola*, with valuable war materiel, troops and aircraft to the south, and the ongoing development of bases in the South Pacific and, especially, Australia. Most of these forces and logistics routes became the basis for a new defensive scheme in the south, although some would be lost as they were fed into the losing effort of defending the Dutch East Indies.[15] Despite all these misfortunes, MacArthur's troops partially accomplished their 'new' mission of wrecking the Japanese timetable. The fight settled into a siege, with disease and hunger afflicting both the Japanese and the Filipino-American forces. Meanwhile, Roosevelt and General George C. Marshall, the Army Chief of Staff, realized that it might be a catastrophe for American morale to have MacArthur captured, and perhaps executed. They ordered MacArthur to escape through the loose Japanese blockade to Australia. Upon MacArthur's arrival in Australia he announced, 'I shall return'. In the meantime, the horrors in Bataan continued, and in April, General Edward P. King ordered his famished and disease-ridden troops – some 78,000 Americans and Filipinos – to surrender with Wainwright's concurrence. The Japanese had expected to capture supplies along with these troops, and in a horror of logistics and maltreatment, marched their emaciated prisoners some sixty miles to a processing

---

14 Edward Drea, *Japan's Imperial Army: Its Rise and Fall, 1853–1945* (Lawrence: University Press of Kansas, 2009), pp. 223–4; Morton, *The Fall of the Philippines*, pp. 127–8, 150, 155–7.
15 Willmott, *Empires in the Balance*, p. 189.

camp, with over 10,000 dying en route, in an event now known as 'the Bataan Death March'. The majority of the dead were Filipino. Wainwright and a forlorn hope of 14,000 held on into May on Corregidor Island at the mouth of Manila Bay. In the final analysis, these heroic sacrifices achieved little – the stubborn defence of Bataan and Corregidor did not prevent, nor even slow, the Japanese conquest of Malaysia, Burma and the Dutch Indies.[16]

As all this was unfolding, the Allies agreed to establish an American, British, Dutch and Australian (ABDA) command under British Field Marshall Sir Archibald Wavell, to try to halt the Japanese advance to the south. Wavell's naval commander was Admiral Hart, which caused considerable resentment on the part of the Dutch. The principal weapons in Hart's inventory were his three cruisers, twenty-nine submarines and fourteen destroyers. However, they were woefully inadequate for the task at hand. Hart's force included warships from all four nations, including several heavy and light cruisers, as well as additional destroyers. They received their baptism of fire when the Japanese invaded the island of Borneo in late January. US destroyers slipped in among Japanese transports at Balikpapan at night, sinking four of them. They would probably have sunk even more were it not for their defective torpedoes.[17]

The event that doomed the Dutch East Indies was the fall of Britain's 'Gibraltar of the Far East', Singapore. Hong Kong, the other pillar of imperial defence, had fallen in December, after an unexpectedly tough defence. General Tomoyuki Yamashita was assured command of the air and sea after Japanese land-based naval aviators sank the battleship *Prince of Wales* and the battlecruiser *Repulse* on 10 December 1941, in a shocking defeat for the Royal Navy.[18] In a brilliant campaign, Yamashita's Twenty-Fifth Army conducted a Blitzkrieg against the British in Malaya under Sir Arthur Percival, advancing almost twelve miles a day. In perhaps the greatest defeat for the Allies in the Pacific War, Percival was pushed out of the Malay peninsula into Singapore. Worse, he was unable to repel an assault against the vulnerable rear by the Japanese assaulting across the Strait of Johore. Percival surrendered over 130,000 soldiers and other personnel on 15 February 1942. Referring again to the analogy with the Eastern Front in Russia, Singapore's fall was the Pacific

16 Morton, *The Fall of the Philippines*, parts IV and V, passim.
17 Steven B. Shepard, 'American, British, Dutch, and Australian Coalition: Unsuccessful Band of Brothers' (unpublished master's thesis, US Army Command and General Staff College, Fort Leavenworth, Kan., 2003), pp. 5, 59; Spector, *Eagle Against the Sun*, p. 132.
18 Mark Peattie, *Sunburst: The Rise of Japanese Naval Air Power, 1909–1941* (Annapolis, Md.: Naval Institute Press, 2001), pp. 168–70.

equivalent of the Kiev pocket. Many of the captured, both civilians and troops, would die of disease, famine and neglect, while building the infamous Thailand–Burma railroad for the Japanese, along with thousands of other slave labourers from captured colonies.[19]

Shortly after the fall of Singapore, Wavell advised the Combined Chiefs of Staff (CCS) that protecting the remaining Indies was hopeless and that the Allies needed to focus all their resources on the defence of Australia and Burma. He subsequently turned over their defence to the Dutch. The forces that remained were also put under the command of the Dutch Admiral C. E. L. Helfrich.[20] In late February, in the Java Sea, the Japanese smashed what little Allied sea power remained. The cruisers *Houston* and HMAS *Perth* perished in the Sunda Strait as they withdrew to the south. On 9 March, the Dutch East Indies surrendered. The Japanese now had nothing to impede their advance to the very shores of Australia.[21]

Meanwhile, Japanese operations reflected the poverty of Japanese strategic options. Even though victorious everywhere, Japan – like Germany – found itself torn as to which way to go. They could go east, west or southwest – but they could not go in all three directions at once. Their chief problem resided in the fact that they had provoked a limited naval war with the two greatest naval powers in the world. As Stalin tied down the main forces of their German ally in Russia, and as the Chinese tied down the bulk of the Japanese army in China, the Japanese navy desperately sought the means for what it saw as essential to achieve victory – the destruction of the US Fleet. All the subsequent misfortunes of Imperial Japan can be traced to the dilemma resulting from this unaccomplished task. Japan's unique style of consensus and compromise decision-making resulted in a series of diverging operations that diluted Japan's most powerful tool to hand – *Kido Butai*.[22]

Reflecting this divergence, Yamamoto's carriers, along with land-based bombers flying from bases in the Indies, conducted a punishing air attack on Darwin in northern Australia on 17 February.[23] That March, the bulk of *Kido Butai* proceeded into the Indian Ocean, and in late March and April ravaged the British naval forces and merchant traffic there. They pounded British

19 Drea, *Japan's Imperial Army*, p. 223; Willmott, *Empires in the Balance*, pp. 218–20.
20 Shepard, 'Unsuccessful Band of Brothers', pp. 59–62.
21 Ibid., pp. 65–8; Spector, *Eagle Against the Sun*, p. 134.
22 Jonathan Parshall and Anthony Tully, *Shattered Sword: The Untold Story of the Battle of Midway* (Washington DC: Potomac Books, 2005), pp. 33–8.
23 Shepard, 'Unsuccessful Band of Brothers', pp. 16, 62; Willmott, *Empires in the Balance*, pp. 303–4.

bases in India and Ceylon, sank a small British carrier and two cruisers, and sank over 100,000 tons of merchant shipping. Japanese submarines added to these totals during Japan's only major assault on Allied sea lines of communication. However, despite forcing the Royal Navy out of the area for the first time in 150 years, Japan's carriers accomplished no major strategic task. The Americans remained a powerful and dangerous presence in the Pacific.[24] Meanwhile, moving south from their bases in the Marianas and from Truk in the Carolines, Japanese naval, air and ground forces had captured the excellent harbour at Rabaul in the Bismarck Archipelago, and had begun to turn it into an impregnable fortress. Elsewhere, they occupied the British Gilbert Islands (including Tarawa), parts of the northern Solomon Islands, and established themselves along the northern shores of New Guinea. These operations paid far more handsome dividends, at much less cost, than those further west.[25]

Japan's efforts in the China-Burma-India (CBI) theatre were no less successful. After the fall of Singapore and the dissolution of ABDA command, the defence of Burma fell back to the India command. Burma served one strategic purpose – to protect India. To lose India was to lose the war in British eyes. In Burma, more than in any other theatre of the war, the Pacific War and the Japanese war in mainland Asia came together. The Americans wanted to defend Burma in order to protect the Burma Road to southern China, through which Lend-Lease aid flowed to the Chinese. However, before Singapore had even fallen, the Japanese Fifteenth Army under General Iida Shojiro began its offensive into Burma, on 20 January 1941. Iida captured Rangoon, the port terminus of Chiang's lifeline, in March. Roosevelt had sent General Joseph Stillwell as his personal representative to Chiang's government and to coordinate with the British for combined operations against the Japanese. The British resisted Chinese offers of military support, but the pace of Japanese operations caused them to relent. Chiang sent his best divisions to help protect his lines of communication through Burma. However, the combination of a divided command structure, the inferiority of the British, Burmese and Chinese troops, and Japanese air and sea domination resulted in catastrophe. Although Stillwell had been placed nominally in charge by Chiang, he found it very difficult to control his Chinese subordinates.

24 David Hobbs, *The British Pacific Fleet: The Royal Navy's Most Powerful Strike Force* (Barnsley: Seaforth Publishing, 2011), pp. 14–15.
25 Spector, *Eagle Against the Sun*, p. 150; John Miller, Jr, *Cartwheel: The Reduction of Rabaul* (Washington DC: Center of Military History, 1959), pp. 1–3.

By May 1942, the British, Stillwell and the Chinese had been run out of Burma – withdrawing on three different axes. In Stillwell's words, 'we got a hell of a beating'. However, the Japanese, just like the Germans later that year, had strategically culminated – they could neither retreat nor advance. General William Slim, the British commander, noted that, despite defeat, his army was still 'recognizable as fighting units'.[26]

On the other side of the world, at Pearl Harbor, a new US commander had arrived – Admiral Chester Nimitz. Nimitz was a 'team player'. His first actions were to retain the staff of Admiral Kimmel and leave existing command structures in place. Nimitz decided to conduct an active defence. His biggest limitation was in the number of escorts and oilers that he had available for his remaining ships. Because his aircraft carriers were ten knots faster than his battleships, he decided to make them the centrepiece for his strategy. He formed these into carrier task forces, usually built around a single carrier instead of the multi-carrier formations favoured by the Japanese. It was Nimitz, a non-aviator, who adopted the carrier-centric strategy that would defeat the Japanese navy.[27]

At the end of their wild run, the Japanese had indeed achieved incredible results. But these results were strategically empty. Their geographic objectives had been accomplished, but their larger objectives – the destruction of the US Fleet and initiation of diplomatic negotiations to end the war – had not been attained. Even worse, if they had cut the US Navy down to size, it remained large, with massive quantities of new construction poised to enter the fray. Unless the IJN could repeat its one-sided and rapid victories of the first months of the war, it would be forced into an attritional campaign, battered by superior forces as it was stretched thin to cover the largest front in history.

The defensive offensive[28]

Not long after the fall of the Dutch East Indies, the CCS oversaw the implementation of a new – and divided – command structure for the Pacific. This decision was driven as much by service rivalries as it was by logic.

26 Drea, *Japan's Imperial Army*, p. 225; Field Marshal Viscount Slim, *Defeat into Victory* (London: Cassell and Co. Ltd, 1956), pp. 109–10.
27 Lundstrom, pp. 48–9; Parshall and Tully, *Shattered Sword*, pp. 40–2; Spector, *Eagle Against the Sun*, pp. 145–7.
28 Fleet Admiral Ernest J. King, *US Navy at War, 1941–1945: Official Reports to the Secretary of the Navy* (Washington DC: United States Navy Department, 1946), p. 39.

MacArthur was put in charge of a Southwest Pacific Area (SWPA), Nimitz the Pacific theatre (CINCPOA), and the same messy arrangements remained in place in the CBI. The dividing line between the two Pacific theatres ran right along the line of the next axis for Japanese offensive operations, through New Guinea and down the Solomon Island chain. Nimitz had already begun to conduct limited strikes against the Japanese in this region. In this, he was very much aided by his cryptography unit (HYPO) at Pearl Harbor, led by Lieutenant Commander Joe Rochefort. These raids had little real physical impact, and their principal value lay in boosting the morale and confidence of the Pacific Fleet, as well as giving Nimitz's inexperienced carrier aviators much-needed combat flying without undue risk. They also put the Japanese on notice that the US Navy was still very much 'a fleet in being'. Nimitz was guided by the principle of 'calculated risk' that both he and his boss, Admiral Ernest King, Chief of Naval Operations (CNO) and Commander-in-Chief of the Navy (COMINCH), practised. Nimitz was only to risk his aircraft carriers (and battleships) if the probabilities were high that the enemy would sustain more damage than him and that the operational objective was achievable - a classic fleet-in-being strategy.[29]

This principle was emphasized in dramatic fashion in mid-April, when the Americans launched a carrier raid on Tokyo. The idea was to place B-25 medium bombers aboard the carrier *Hornet*, escorted by the *Enterprise* and under the overall command of Admiral Halsey. These forces would then steam stealthily across the Pacific, to a launch point about 500 miles from Tokyo. Lieutenant Colonel 'Jimmy' Doolittle was selected to command the bombers. After being detected short of the launch point by Japanese picket ships, Doolittle's force launched early, on 18 April, about 650 miles from Tokyo. Doolittle's bombers achieved tactical surprise and completed their bombing runs with no casualties. Most ended up crash-landing short of friendly Chinese airfields due to lack of fuel. Although the raid caused little physical damage, it provided a huge boost to US morale – both civilian and military. For the Japanese military leadership, the dishonour associated with the bombing led to the assignment of hundreds of veteran Japanese aviators back to Japan for defence of the homeland. These pilots would be sorely missed in the year to come.[30]

29 King, *US Navy at War*, pp. 34, 44–5; Elliot Carlson, *Joe Rochefort's War: The Odyssey of the Codebreaker Who Outwitted Yamamoto at Midway* (Annapolis, Md.: Naval Institute Press, 2011), pp. 239–43.
30 Parshall and Tully, *Shattered Sword*, pp. 42–3; Willmott, *Empires in the Balance*, pp. 447–9; King, *US Navy at War*, p. 45.

The Imperial Naval General Staff had proposed that the next step in the Pacific War should be to sever Australia's lines of communications with the United States. Some officers proposed that Australia itself be invaded, but the army leadership vetoed this plan, claiming that they simply did not have enough troops to secure an area so large – again reflecting the influence of the war in China. Alternatively, Yamamoto was convinced that the Americans could only be brought to negotiate by destroying their fleet. He advocated an invasion of Hawaii as a suitable objective that would bring about this result, but both the Army and the Navy General Staffs opposed this plan. He counter-proposed a seizure of the American base at Midway, at the western end of the Hawaiian chain. This proposal, too, was tabled. When Doolittle's aircraft dropped bombs near sacred Edo Palace in Tokyo, all resistance to the Yamamoto's plan to seize Midway evaporated. Approval of this course of action did not cancel *existing* plans to advance in the southwest along the Solomons chain and in New Guinea. Instead of focusing on one offensive axis, the Japanese advanced down three. Naval planners also saddled the Combined Fleet with the mission of seizing the westernmost islands in the Aleutians chain (Operation AL), in part because Doolittle's raid had exposed the open flank through the northern Pacific. All this led to a fatal watering-down of the striking forces Yamamoto would have available for what he saw as the main effort at Midway (Operation MI).[31]

The opening phase involved a two-pronged assault, codenamed Operation MO, which had two objectives: the seizure of the island of Tulagi in the southern Solomons and the capture of Port Moresby on the southeastern tip of New Guinea on the Coral Sea. With New Guinea and the Solomons in their possession, the Japanese would be poised to push into the Coral Sea and sever Australia's lifeline to the United States across the South Pacific. Unfortunately for the Japanese, Nimitz's code-breakers informed him of the outline and objectives of MO. Nimitz recognized the opportunity to strike a blow that might seriously damage the Japanese. He already had Admiral Fletcher's *Yorktown* Task Force (TF) operating in the area and immediately dispatched *Lexington* to join it.[32]

In a confused series of engagements during the first week of May, elements of the American, Australian and Japanese navies clashed in the Coral Sea. It was the first naval battle where neither side's ships saw each other, the first carrier-versus-carrier battle in history, and, finally, it was

31 Parshall and Tully, *Shattered Sword*, pp. 37, 43–4.
32 Carlson, *Joe Rochefort's War*, pp. 270–3, 286–8; Lundstrom, pp. 126–9.

Japan's first operational defeat in the war. The Americans lost the large carrier *Lexington*, as well as suffering damage to the carrier *Yorktown*. The Japanese lost the light carrier *Shoho* and sustained damage to the veteran Pearl Harbor carrier *Shokaku*. Large numbers of Japanese aircrew were shot down and the air group aboard the *Zuikaku* was effectively *hors de combat*. Admiral Inoue Shigeyoshi, the commander in Rabaul, made the critical decision to turn the Port Moresby invasion force around and try another day. The Japanese believed they had sunk two, if not three, of the American carriers. In reality, the Americans, due to the incredible efforts of the sailors aboard *Yorktown* and the dockworkers at Pearl Harbor, had three large aircraft carriers available to oppose Yamamoto's fleet when it came to attack Midway. Coral Sea had reduced the forces available for Yamamoto's main effort. The carriers *Zuikaku* and *Shokaku* and their air groups, battered at Coral Sea, were unavailable for the Midway operation. Yamamoto had also diluted his available naval air striking power by agreeing to the Aleutian operation, which subtracted the air groups of two medium carriers (*Ryujo* and *Junyo*). Thus the results of the Coral Sea were twofold: it stopped the Japanese advance in the south and compromised the chances of success for the operation at Midway.[33]

Yamamoto and Admiral Nagano Osami of the Naval General Staff both believed that the weight of the Combined Fleet must prevail at Midway. US cryptographers had broken enough of the Japanese JN-25 code to know that Yamamoto's objective for Operation MI was the American garrison and airbase at Midway. Nimitz acted decisively on this intelligence. He deployed all of his remaining carriers to a position northeast of Midway to ambush the Japanese. The American task forces were geographically separated into two groups – the *Yorktown* TF under Admiral Fletcher, and a second carrier force composed of *Enterprise* and *Hornet* (of Doolittle raid fame), under Rear Admiral Raymond Spruance. Spruance, a surface officer, replaced Halsey, who had been hospitalized due to a severe attack of dermatitis. Fletcher, the victor at Coral Sea, was the overall commander, but gave Spruance considerable latitude in conducting his own operations. Fletcher also had the 'unsinkable aircraft carrier' of Midway, with its Marine, Navy and Army aircraft available to attack the Japanese once they were located. Even though the Japanese aviators and aircraft were still superior at this point in the war to their improving American counterparts, it would be an even fight. Yamamoto's

---

33 Parshall and Tully, *Shattered Sword*, pp. 63–4; Lundstrom, *Black Shoe Carrier Admiral*, pp. 133, 141–83, 222.

forces, on the other hand, were divided into six different groups, none in immediate supporting distance of the other should things go awry. Of these forces, the Aleutians group was too far to the north to be of any use whatsoever until after the expected date of Midway's capture. If ever a force was organized to favour failure operationally, it was Yamamoto's steaming for Midway during the late spring of 1942.[34]

On the morning of 3 June 1942, a Navy flying-boat sighted the main Japanese armada (but not the main Japanese carrier force) 700 miles west of Midway. Despite this, Yamamoto pressed on with not a single change to his plans. Air power from the 'unsinkable aircraft carrier' based on Midway Island struck at the Japanese first on the afternoon of 3 June, by launching B-17s to attack a group of enemy transports; later that night, radar-equipped PBY Catalinas attacked the same group of transports, damaging one with the only successful torpedo attack by the Americans during the battle. Nagumo, in command of *Kido Butai*, had no idea that the American carriers were present and decided to pummel Midway with carrier air power at first light on 4 June. The day turned into a disaster when all three of Fletcher's carriers launched strikes at Nagumo's carriers. Nagumo had been fighting off attacks from Midway and the carriers (most recently VT-8) most of the morning, and had just recovered his Midway strike group when dive-bombers and fighters from both the *Yorktown* and *Enterprise* groups arrived almost simultaneously overhead the Japanese force. What few fighters the Japanese had airborne fruitlessly chased the American F4F Wildcats under Lieutenant Commander Jimmie Thach, who was successfully executing a new 'weave' tactic. In quick succession, the dive-bombers mortally wounded the carriers *Akagi*, *Kaga* and *Soryu*. Japanese damage control systems, inferior to those on the US ships, were quickly overwhelmed by the blazing infernos that the American bombs created in the hangar bays. Eventually, all three carriers would sink or be torpedoed by their own escorts to prevent their capture by the Americans.[35]

The battle was not over. The American dive-bombers had missed one Japanese carrier, the *Hiryu*. She soon launched a strike which crippled the *Yorktown*. Fletcher passed tactical command to Spruance while he evacuated *Yorktown*. Spruance's aviators located *Hiryu* and set her ablaze in the same manner as her three sisters. By early morning on 5 June, Yamamoto made the

---

34 Parshall and Tully, *Shattered Sword*, pp. 51–9, 90, 95–6, 296–8; Lundstrom, pp. 218–29, 235–6.

35 Parshall and Tully, *Shattered Sword*, pp. 106, 113, 114–282; John S. 'Jimmie' Thach, 'Flying into a Beehive: "Fighting Three" at Midway', *Naval History* 21:3 (June 2007), 24–31.

decision, much as had happened at Coral Sea, to abandon the invasion and return to Japan, despite having a preponderance of naval surface power at his disposal. As he withdrew, the Americans savaged two of his heavy cruisers, sinking one. As for the *Yorktown*, two days after she was first damaged, the Japanese submarine *I-168* sank the veteran carrier and an escorting destroyer as she was being towed back to Pearl Harbor. As for the northern forces attacking the Aleutians, they had accomplished their mission and captured the desolate islands of Attu and Kiska. Yet even this minor victory was pyrrhic, since they soon found that these islands were virtually useless as bases.[36]

Upon their return to Japan, the IJN's leaders decided not to tell the Japanese people of the disaster, and even withheld its extent from the Japanese army. This deception exacerbated the defeat, because the loss of over a hundred experienced naval aviators, as well as the veteran carrier deck crews of half the Japanese fleet, struck the Japanese potent weapon where it was most vulnerable. When these losses are added to those at the Coral Sea, Midway can be seen as the critical, almost mortal wounding, of the Japanese carrier force. The Japanese training pipeline for pilots was rigorous and slow, and did not cycle its front-line pilots out of the line to train the others as the USA did. Defeat did not lead to reformed programmes to replace them for the war of attrition that now ensued. As Yamamoto sailed grimly back to Japan, he must have realized that his task had just become infinitely harder. The opportunity now existed for the USA to seize the initiative and launch a strategic counter-stroke.[37] It was for this reason that Midway was the turning point of the Pacific War.

The offensive defensive

The disaster off Midway opened up new opportunities for two commanders itching to go over to the offensive – MacArthur and King, Nimitz's boss in Washington. King, alarmed by the Japanese seizure of Rabaul, broached the idea of a counter-offensive through the Solomons to capture it before Midway. MacArthur made a counter-proposal to use his command to seize Rabaul in a three-week operation. The final outcome was a compromise that established the offensive, attritional pattern of the war for the rest of 1942 and most of 1943. Nimitz would execute 'task one' by seizing the Japanese bases at Tulagi and, in a last-minute decision, an airfield on Guadalcanal. MacArthur

36 Parshall and Tully, *Shattered Sword*, pp. 238–9; Lundstrom, pp. 263–95.
37 Jonathan Parshall, 'Ignoring the Lessons of Defeat', *Naval History* 21:3 (June 2007), 32–7.

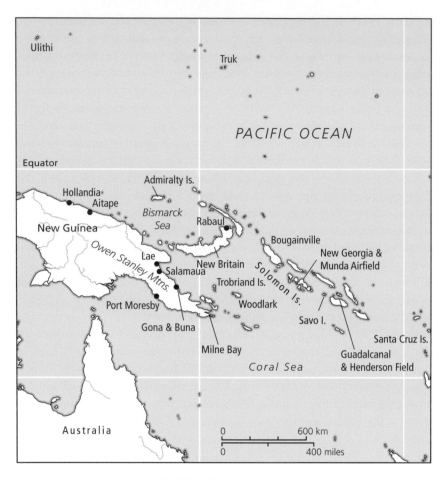

15.2 South Pacific operations, 1942–4   4

was to perform the second task, advancing along the northern coast of New Guinea at the same time as Navy and Marine forces advanced in the Solomons. The final phase, under MacArthur's overall command, would involve the capture of Rabaul.[38]

The Japanese struck first.[39] After capturing Buna on 21 July – an event US code-breakers had predicted, but MacArthur's staff discounted – the Japanese

38 Lundstrom, pp. 308–14.
39 Samuel Milner, *Victory in Papua* (Washington DC: Center of Military History, 1957), pp. 53–4.

advanced over rugged Owen-Stanley Range in New Guinea against Port Moresby. They pushed along the Kokoda Trail, which was believed to be unable to support major offensive operations. MacArthur found himself on the defensive. At the same time, Australians and a small contingent of US combat engineers defeated a supporting Japanese amphibious assault at Milne Bay, at the tip of New Guinea, on 25 July. King, exercising his command prerogative, launched Navy and Marine forces against Japanese positions at Tulagi and Guadalcanal on 7 August 1942. It was one of the most momentous decisions of the Pacific War.[40]

Guadalcanal proved to be a microcosm for the entire Pacific War – a campaign of amphibious assaults and fierce naval, air and jungle battles. The Marines seized Tulagi after a short, stiff fight. On Guadalcanal, they simply waded ashore as the Japanese construction workers ran off into the jungle. Upon landing, they found a pestilential, monsoon-swept hell-hole. The airfield, with bonus Japanese bulldozers and earth rollers, was secured easily, and the Marines began to establish security perimeters, finish the airfield and prepare for a Japanese counter-attack. The Eleventh (Navy) Air Fleet in Rabaul had just the range to get its bombers to the southern Solomons. But once there, they had little time to deliver their attacks, and did so without land-based fighter coverage. What was worse, Japanese carrier aviation, so reduced after the Battles of Midway and Coral Sea, could only provide temporary air coverage before it had to withdraw to refuel its few carriers in safer waters. The American carriers, as Admiral Fletcher had already pointed out, were under the same constraints, and were particularly vulnerable to Japanese submarines and land-based aircraft. The Japanese counter-attacked savagely from air and sea, winning the lopsided night surface action off Savo Island on 8–9 August. However, the Japanese commander missed a golden opportunity after Savo to sink US transports and supply ships, which slipped away and left the Marines to their own devices.[41]

The Japanese continued to make critical errors. Underestimating both the size and fighting prowess of the Marines, they landed the Ichiki Detachment

---

40 John T. Kuehn with D. M. Giangreco, *Eyewitness Pacific Theater* (New York: Sterling Press, 2008), pp. 95–6.
41 Lundstrom, pp. 333–403; Captain Toshikazu Omhae, 'The Battle of Savo Island', ed. Roger Pineau, *United States Naval Institute* Proceedings 83:12 (December 1956), 1263–78. Although not apparent in the comments about the article, it is implied by Pineau in his brief editorial comments that Omhae wrote the original manuscript in English, not Japanese, and that Pineau edited it for style, since no translator is listed either for Omhae's article or for the brief addenda at its end authored by Rear Admiral Gunichi Mikawa.

(one battalion) in an attempt to quickly recapture the airstrip, now named Henderson Field. On 21 August, these troops were wiped out at the Battle of the Ilu River. Additional Japanese reinforcements were turned back on 24 August, thanks to the timely return of the US Navy. Over the course of the next six months, there were six more major naval battles and at least nine more land battles – with attritional air combat occurring daily. The inspiring Halsey replaced the overwhelmed and sick Admiral Robert Ghormley in overall command that October. After a series of critical naval battles in November, American Army and Marine forces resumed the offensive to push the Japanese off the island for good. By the time the campaign ended in early 1943, Japanese land-based aviation was as decimated as its carrier counterparts. The IJA losses exceeded 24,000 men; however, it salvaged some of its troops from the defeat with a seaborne evacuation – these types of retrograde action soon become a rarity. American losses were no less severe, including, for a short time, the lack of any aircraft carrier presence at all in Halsey's theatre. The Americans, however, could afford these losses, while the Japanese could not.[42]

Similar attritional jungle battles occurred in New Guinea. Another benefit of Guadalcanal had been to divert resources from New Guinea in the critical period after the Japanese culminated along the crest of the Owen Stanleys.[43] The Allied counter-offensive operated here under the same harsh conditions that plagued their antagonists. By November, the Australians, with American support, had captured Kokoda. MacArthur next focused his efforts on the capture of the two key towns on the northern coast – Buna and Gona. While fierce fighting raged on Guadalcanal, MacArthur's Aussies and Yanks met stiff opposition, especially at Buna. MacArthur, unhappy with the progress of the 32nd Division, fired its commander and told the new commander, Lieutenant General Bob Eichelberger, to 'take Buna, or not come back alive'. Fortunately, the Australians captured Gona on 9 December 1942 and were able to assist the American effort. Buna fell in early January 1943, with its Japanese garrison dying almost to the last man. One bastion remained, at Sanananda, but the Japanese logistics situation had become intolerable and, on 13 January 1943, the troops who could still move withdrew further north to Lae and Salamaua. After six months, MacArthur was back to where his forces had been in July 1942, and over half of his men were *hors de combat* due to disease.[44]

---

42 Richard Frank, *Guadalcanal* (New York: Random House, 1990), pp. 598–618.

43 Drea, *Japan's Imperial Army*, p. 229.

44 Milner, *Victory in Papua*, pp. 72–100, 125–202, 324–5, 369–77.

The net impact of operations from May 1942 to February 1943 was a decisive shift in the momentum to the Allies in the Pacific. It was during this period that the Japanese can be identified as having lost the war, although the chimera of operations in mainland Asia seemed to offer them some hope of salvaging an honourable peace.

The offensive: island hopping

In the far north, a deadly sideshow played itself out. Nimitz tried to cut off Japanese supply lines to the Japanese-occupied islands of Kiska and Attu with naval forces. In March 1943, a cruiser force under Rear Admiral Charles H. McMorris fought an indecisive engagement near the Komandorskii Islands in the North Pacific, with a superior force of Japanese warships under Vice Admiral Hosagaya. In early May 1943, the Americans landed on Attu. It was a freezing, bloody slog for both sides, amidst ice, snow and fog. Another American division commander was relieved and the island was not secured for two weeks. The Japanese defenders had pulled into the interior and died fighting to the last man – a chilling preview of things to come. Meanwhile, the Japanese quietly withdrew their garrison from Kiska under the Americans' very noses.[45]

As the battles on Guadalcanal and Papua New Guinea ran down, Allied leaders met in Casablanca to discuss the next steps in the global war. Through a very complicated series of negotiations, the CCS agreed to underwrite offensives for both MacArthur and Nimitz – from this arrangement was born what has become known as 'the dual advance'. Nimitz retained command of any Navy forces not specifically assigned to MacArthur, and so began to prepare for an offensive in the Central Pacific based on the pre-war ORANGE Plan. MacArthur retained overall strategic direction over the forces under his command, as well as the nominally independent South Pacific forces of Admiral Halsey. However, his subordinate operational leaders, such as Sir Thomas Blamey with his Australians, and Americans like Generals Bob Eichelberger and Walter Krueger, and Admiral Dan Barbey, should get much more praise than historians have assigned for giving the SWPA generalissimo many of his 'victories'. Broad pressure would be applied against the Japanese defences, preventing them from massing against any single offensive. The first phase of this dual advance became more generally known as 'island hopping',

45 Spector, *Eagle Against the Sun*, pp. 178–82.

because once Americans realized that they need not take every island, they began 'hopping' over many of Japan's most formidable strongholds.

Fortunately, Halsey and MacArthur got along with each other, although MacArthur and his staff would often direct publicity their own way as much as possible. They came up with a new plan of mutually supporting offensives to take Rabaul, while the Australians fixed large numbers of Japanese in New Guinea. Halsey advanced up the Solomons, while MacArthur advanced with American-Australian forces along the north shore of New Guinea. Eventually, the two offensives would converge on the island of New Britain, where Rabaul was located.[46] MacArthur's air force was commanded by General George Kenney. Kenney's efforts, and those of the air-minded Halsey, would go a long way toward establishing permanent air dominance in both Halsey's and MacArthur's theatres. The Americans learned that once an airfield or anchorage was seized and a secure perimeter established, they could fight from a superior defensive posture against the ill-supplied Japanese ground forces. The Japanese, anticipating another round of US offensives, began moving divisions from Asia to New Guinea. In early March 1943, Kenney's air forces, including B-25 medium bombers, located and annihilated a convoy carrying a Japanese division in the Bismarck Sea. Japanese General Head-quarters reacted to this catastrophe by never attempting another major convoy again, and routing most of their reinforcements through western New Guinea. This placed even more strain on the inadequate and lengthy Japanese supply lines.[47]

That spring (1943), Admiral Yamamoto launched an air counter-offensive (I-Go) against Allied bases and shipping, in an attempt to recapture the initiative. Using precious carrier pilots, he gained little as a result and lost as many planes and pilots as the Allies. Worse, Yamamoto lost his own life, when US code-breakers detected his movement plans and ambushed the bombers transporting him and his staff with a squadron of P-38s. Although Yamamoto's strategic and operational acumen have been overstated, his loss was a real blow to morale.[48]

That summer, MacArthur moved against the Trobriand Islands and along the coast of New Guinea to Nassau Bay. Almost simultaneously, Halsey

---

46 David Rigby, *Allied Master Strategists: The Combined Chiefs of Staff* (Annapolis, Md.: Naval Institute Press, 2012), ch. 3; Miller, *Cartwheel*, pp. 3–8.

47 Miller, *Cartwheel*, pp. 39–41; see also Drea, *Japan's Imperial Army*, p. 230.

48 John Prados, *Combined Fleet Decoded: The Secret History of American Intelligence and the Japanese Navy in World War II* (Annapolis, Md.: Naval Institute Press, 1995), pp. 448–86; Spector, *Eagle Against the Sun*, pp. 227–30.

moved against the Japanese airfield at Munda on New Georgia Island. MacArthur's attack relieved the pressure of a Japanese offensive against the Australian airfield at Wau, bypassing many of their defences. Halsey's force, on the other hand, came under fierce attack by Japanese land, air and naval forces. The ground battles were bogged down in the face of fierce resistance, and another division commander was relieved. However, by the end of August, the US Army had secured Munda. Throughout Halsey's operations, a number of fierce surface ship battles occurred, but the Japanese navy found itself faced by improving American warships, which gave as good as they got and began to use their radars skilfully in night actions. Halsey's next step was to bypass Kolombangara Island and land on lightly defended Vella Lavella further north, which had a better airfield. Once this field was operational, the threat from the air diminished rapidly. Fighters from Vella Lavella also provided escort for bombers flying raids against Rabaul.[49]

MacArthur's offensive continued, pushing on to the Huon Peninsula, which poked like a finger toward Rabaul from New Guinea. Using a secretly built airstrip, he first neutralized Japanese air power in the area. MacArthur's forces then landed near the key villages of Lae and Salamaua, conducting the first operational airborne assault of the campaign in seizing a nearby airbase. By mid-September 1943, both towns were in Allied hands. MacArthur, advancing his timetable, then pre-empted a Japanese move to reinforce their garrison at Finschafen by landing an Australian brigade first. After some very hard fighting, the town was captured and all Japanese attempts to recapture it were defeated.[50]

With Vella Lavella secured, Halsey bypassed the strong Japanese garrison on Kolombangara and planned for the seizure of the key island of Bougainville, as a precursor to MacArthur's operations against New Britain. He would not only distract the Japanese from MacArthur's upcoming thrust across the strait to Cape Gloucester, but fighters from the captured bases on Bougainville could escort both Halsey's and MacArthur's bombers in attacks against Rabaul. Nimitz also lent Halsey several of his precious aircraft carriers to contest the still potent Japanese air forces based at Rabaul and in the northern Solomons. The Japanese sent the bulk of their carrier-based air from Truk to help contest these operations and defend Rabaul. The Japanese also tried to repeat their Savo Island victory, but the US code-breakers again provided

49 Trent Hone, '"Give Them Hell!": The US Navy's Night Combat Doctrine and the Campaign for Guadalcanal', *War and History* 13:1 (2009), 197–8.
50 Spector, *Eagle Against the Sun*, pp. 240–2; Miller, *Cartwheel*, pp. 189–217.

warning. The result was a punishing series of air and sea battles that erupted around Rabaul and the northern Solomons. These battles established American command of the seas and air around Bougainville and gave them air superiority over Rabaul. In late October, the Marines and New Zealanders conducted a series of diversionary attacks. The main landings at Bougainville, on 1 November, achieved surprise and went smoothly. The Americans learned that they need not capture the entire island, just the airfields and enough defensive terrain.[51]

With the Japanese fully distracted at Bougainville, MacArthur launched his assaults on western New Britain (Arawe and Cape Gloucester), with the veteran First Marine Division landing unopposed the day after Christmas. Despite horrendous weather conditions, Marines and GIs moved inland to secure defensive perimeters and airfields. By March 1944, fighters were flying missions from airfields on New Britain; however, Rabaul had already been neutralized. Allied aircraft had punished Rabaul throughout these operations, and in late February, Japan's Imperial General Headquarters decided to leave only ground forces to defend it. By April 1944, Rabaul's airfields were no longer usable. The Allies, secure in their defensive positions, simply left the considerable Japanese ground forces to their own devices. Rabaul was no longer of any importance. On the other side of the Vitiaz Strait, MacArthur attempted to cut off retreating Japanese forces by landing at Saidor, north of the Huon Peninsula, and linking up with the Australians advancing from the interior in January 1944. This occurred, but the Japanese managed to escape. If Guadalcanal can be seen as a microcosm of the Pacific War and its 'Stalingrad', the reduction and bypassing of Rabaul can viewed as its 'Kursk', the point at which the Japanese were clearly losing and her leadership recognized it as such.[52]

The offensive on the Central Pacific front, really a third axis of advance, got under way in late 1943. Situated on the flank of the advance were the Japanese-occupied Gilbert Islands. Nimitz and his staff felt it imperative to neutralize them prior to driving against the Marshall Islands, where strong Japanese forces were based. The campaign opened with the seizure of heavily defended islands in the Tarawa atoll, especially Betio, on 20

51 David C. Fuquea, 'Bougainville: The Amphibious Assault Enters Maturity', *Naval War College Review* 50:1 (winter 1997), 104–21; Spector, *Eagle Against the Sun*, pp. 239–45, 283–4.

52 Douglas T. Kane and Henry I. Shaw, Jr, *History of US Marine Corps Operations in World War II: Isolation of Rabaul* (Washington DC: US Government Printing Office, 1989), pp. 297–306, 453–4.

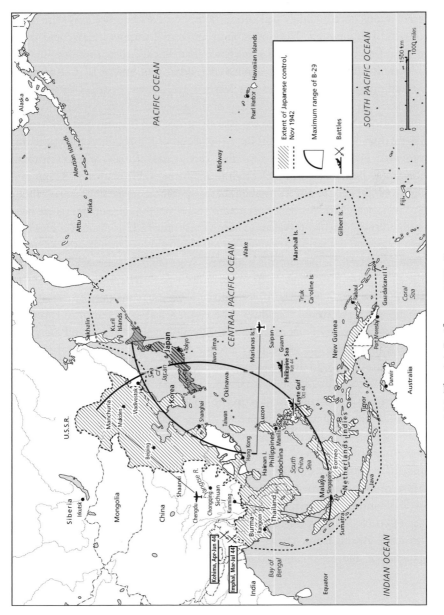

15.3 The Asia-Pacific war, 1943–45

November. It was a bloody opening to the campaign, with almost 3,000 Marine casualties on Betio alone. Although Nimitz's Marines had sound amphibious doctrine, they had very little practical experience and were short of critical equipment, like amphibious tractors (Amtracs) that could cross reefs at low tide. Tarawa was a slaughter that shocked the American public.[53]

Nimitz and his planners, against the advice of many of his admirals (including Spruance), used lessons learned at Tarawa to strike Kwajalein in the Marshall Islands for the next step of the advance. In late January 1944, the 4th Marine Division landed on the islands of Roi and Namur, and the Army's 7th Infantry Division landed on the main island of Kwajalein. Air support was provided principally by the new fast carrier task forces of Vice Admiral Raymond Spruance's Fifth Fleet. The Japanese navy, with no meaningful naval air power, barely contested these operations. For the cost of about 800 American lives, Spruance secured a major anchorage and operating base in the Central Pacific. It was now Nimitz who moved his timetable forward. In a follow-on operation, Spruance seized the important, but lightly defended Eniwetok Atoll, some 300 miles further west, later in February. This time, the air support came entirely from Spruance's fast carriers. In order to cover the Eniwetok landings, Spruance pushed his carriers west to attack the Japanese at Truk in the Carolines. The result was Pearl Harbor in reverse – especially on 30–31 March 1944. Almost 200,000 tons of warship and merchant tonnage was sunk and 270 enemy aircraft destroyed. Truk, like Rabaul, had been neutralized, and the Americans decided there was no need to capture it. Air power, including carrier air power, had made possible the bypassing of the Japanese 'pillars of Hercules' in the Pacific – Rabaul and Truk.[54]

Meanwhile, problems continued in the 'neglected' CBI theatre. The Allies flew supplies for Chiang's forces 'over the Hump' of the Himalayas, while at the same time they began construction on a new road from Ledo in British Assam, to connect with portions of the Burma Road not interdicted by Japan. Most of 1943 was spent conducting raids, building roads and in fruitless recriminations. Meanwhile, the Japanese surprised everyone by going on the offensive in the spring of 1944. Their goal was to cut the Ledo road and drive the British from Assam. By now, Allied superiority in men, materiel, experience and air power had reached decisive levels. General Slim, in a

53 Jerold E. Brown, 'Amphibious Operations: Tarawa: The Testing of an Amphibious Doctrine', in Roger J. Spiller (ed.), *Combined Arms in Battle Since 1939* (Fort Leavenworth, Kan.: US Army Command and General Staff College Press, 1992), pp. 19–26.
54 King, *US Navy at War*, pp. 72–4; Prados, *Combined Fleet Decoded*, pp. 531–9; Spector, *Eagle Against the Sun*, pp. 267–73; Drea, *Japan's Imperial Army*, pp. 233–5.

masterful campaign, defeated General Mutaguchi Renya's forces at Aykab, Imphal and Kohima. On the Japanese flank in north Burma, Stillwell's Sino-American forces threatened Mitkyina in late May and took it on 3 August 1944. Mutaguchi's army literally fell apart as it retreated in defeat, many of them starving and resorting to cannibalism.[55]

By early 1944, Japan was on the horns of a strategic dilemma. Only in China and Burma (temporarily) were her military operations successful. Meanwhile her island empire, seized at little cost, was now being reclaimed at great cost – to Japan more than to the Allies. By mid-1943, the Americans had fixed the problems with their torpedoes, and the Pacific Submarine Command, under Vice Admiral Charles Lockwood, conducted history's first successful unrestricted submarine campaign. By early 1944, more than 3 million tons of Japanese shipping had been sunk. By the end of the war, US submarines had sunk over 5 million tons of enemy shipping. The Japanese were now without a merchant marine to supply their far-flung empire.[56]

With the neutralization of Rabaul, MacArthur continued his audacious campaign, bypassing or outflanking Japanese strong points. MacArthur was driven by the knowledge that his theatre had become secondary to Nimitz's. This was because the Marianas Islands, Nimitz's next objective, could provide bases for the new B-29 bomber to attack Japan. MacArthur hoped to invade the Philippines by early 1945, but Nimitz might get there first. In early 1944, MacArthur began his most celebrated campaign – greatly aided by his own code-breakers – along the northeastern coast of New Guinea. In March, the Admiralty Islands fell, especially the critical island of Manus; and in late April, MacArthur's forces seized Aitape airfield, deep in the rear of the Japanese main army. The operations climaxed with General Bob Eichelberger's seizure of lightly defended Hollandia, with its airbases and anchorages. By late May, MacArthur had seized terrain on which to build bomber bases at Biak that could reach the southern Philippines. While Spruance distracted the Japanese in the Central Pacific, MacArthur seized the remainder of his objectives at the western end of New Guinea. MacArthur's seizure of the island of Morotai in September put his forces just 300 miles south of Mindanao in the Philippines.[57]

55 Slim, *Defeat into Victory*, pp. 275–81; Drea, *Japan's Imperial Army*, pp. 237–9.
56 King, *US Navy at War*, pp. 76–7, 201–3; Joel Ira Holwitt, *'Execute Against Japan': The US Decision to Conduct Unrestricted Submarine Warfare* (College Station: Texas A&M University Press, 2009), pp. 181–4; Spector, *Eagle Against the Sun*, pp. 483–6.

While MacArthur conducted his 'triphibious' Blitzkrieg up New Guinea, disaster again visited the Japanese navy in the Philippine Sea. Spruance and the Fifth Fleet arrived with a sea-borne juggernaut to take the critical Mariana Islands, which would put the new B-29 American bombers within range of the Japanese home islands. The Japanese had been slowly rebuilding their carrier force to challenge Spruance. Operation A-GO, the defence of the Marianas, was to provide the opportunity to turn the tables on the overconfident Americans. Over two days of aerial combat known as the 'Marianas Turkey Shoot', US carrier pilots and anti-aircraft guns destroyed Japanese carrier aviation. Additionally, American submarines and aviators sank three more Japanese carriers. Ashore, the fighting was fierce, especially at Saipan, where 30,000 Japanese inflicted 14,000 American casualties. The Japanese garrison and civilians died virtually to the last man, woman and child. Nonetheless, the disasters visited upon Japanese arms in the Marianas were so severe that Tojo resigned in disgrace.[58]

The Japanese army and navy had no intention of quitting the fight.[59] In fact, that summer, the Japanese continued their efforts to achieve decision in the Pacific War by operations in China. They conducted a punishing series of offensives against the Nationalists in China – the Ichi-Go offensive. Stillwell was removed, and replaced by General Daniel Sultan in Burma and General Albert Wedemeyer in China. The Japanese goal was to capture airbases in China from which the new B-29s of the Fourteenth Air Force began a strategic bombing campaign (MATTERHORN) against Japan. Rapid movement of Chinese and American troops from Burma managed to save Chiang from complete collapse, but the airbases were lost. Japan simply did not have enough troops to complete the conquest. The Americans, however, simply moved the Fourteenth Air Force to the newly captured Marianas, a much better location from which to continue the strategic bombardment of Japan.[60]

57 Edward Drea, *Defending the Driniumor: Covering Force Operations in New Guinea, 1944*, Leavenworth Paper no. 9 (Fort Leavenworth, KS: Combat Studies Institute Press, 1984), pp. ix–31, 135–42; Spector, *Eagle Against the Sun*, pp. 279–83, 285–94.

58 Gary J. Bjorge, 'Hard Fighting in Saipan's Death Valley: The 27th Infantry Division's Experience in a Harsh Environment of Combat', unpublished monograph, pp. 12–35, used in John T. Kuehn, Jonathan M. House, James M. Willbanks and Susan Rosell (eds.), *H200: Military Innovation in Peace and War* (Fort Leavenworth, Kan: US Army Command and General Staff College, 2008), pp. 393–421.

59 Edward Drea, 'Chasing a Decisive Victory: Emperor Hirohito and Japan's War with the West', in Drea, *In the Service of the Emperor: Essays on the Imperial Japanese Army* (Lincoln: University of Nebraska Press, 1998), pp. 208–10.

Throughout the spring and summer of 1944, the strategic councils were divided on which step to take next. King wanted to bypass the Philippines and seize Formosa, as a stepping stone on the way to invade the home islands. MacArthur was adamant in favour of an invasion of the Philippines, arguing it was the United States' sacred duty to keep *his* promise to return. After meeting with Nimitz and Roosevelt at Pearl Harbor, MacArthur prevailed. The decision was made to land in the central Philippines on the island of Leyte, with a follow-on invasion of the main island of Luzon. MacArthur made claims for a quick campaign that turned out to be grossly over-optimistic. However, the invasion of the Philippines might, itself, end the war, since their capture by the Americans would sever the Japanese home islands from critical oil and other strategic resources in the Indies.

As a precursor to the invasion, Nimitz assigned the mission of seizing key islands in the Palaus and the huge atoll and anchorage at Ulithi. In early September, Halsey sailed with fifteen aircraft carriers and their escorts for a series of pre-invasion raids. The Americans had gone beyond the original *Kido Butai* construct almost by a factor of three. Halsey's carriers savaged the airfields in the Philippines and the Western Carolines (including the Palau Islands). He reported light air defences and recommended to the Joint Chiefs of Staff that the timetable for the Philippine invasion be moved up to October. He also recommended cancellation of several other invasions, such as at Peleliu. Invasions of Mindanao and Yap were cancelled, but Morotai and Peleliu went in mid September. Peleliu (appropriately named STALEMATE) turned out to be a charnel house, and one of Nimitz's rare missteps during the war. The new Japanese strategy was to bleed the Americans and it worked, with a nearly one-to-one ratio of American to Japanese casualties during a two-month nightmare battle.[61]

Halsey sortied from the newly seized base at Ulithi in early October, to pound Formosa and the Ryukyus prior to the Philippine invasion. The Japanese mistakenly believed that an invasion of Formosa was under way. During a series of air battles, the recently trained Japanese pilots managed to damage two cruisers and shoot down some planes. However, they exaggerated their success so much that the leadership concluded that they had won a great victory. Subsequently, they were stunned when a US invasion armada

60 John D. Plating, *The Hump: America's Strategy for Keeping China in World War II* (College Station: Texas A&M University Press, 2011), pp. 183–201; Spector, *Eagle Against the Sun*, pp. 365–79.

61 Bobby C. Blair and John Peter DeCioccio, *Victory at Peleliu: The 81st Infantry Division's Pacific Campaign* (Norman: University of Oklahoma Press, 2011).

15.4 The defeat of Japan

appeared two weeks later in the Philippines. The American forces that sailed toward the Leyte Gulf were the most powerful assemblage of ships and men in history. Lieutenant General Walter Krueger commanded the Sixth Army (200,000 troops), embarked on 738 ships of Vice Admiral Thomas Kinkaid's Seventh Fleet. Kinkaid was supported by Halsey's Third Fleet, which included seventeen aircraft carriers, six new battleships and over eighty cruisers and destroyers. Only Kinkaid and Krueger were directly under MacArthur's command. Halsey, under Nimitz, had orders to destroy the Japanese Fleet if it appeared – but which fleet? Halsey thought it should be the carrier fleet, not realizing that Japan's carrier aviation was a spent force after the air battles in the Philippine Sea and off Formosa. On 20 October, Krueger's forces landed on Leyte.[62]

Despite the operational surprise that the Americans achieved, the Japanese believed a decisive victory in the Philippines might be possible. The Emperor cancelled the plan to make the main effort in Luzon and ordered the army and the navy to concentrate on Leyte – to make it the great decisive action for both the army and the navy. It was, but they lost. The IJN's Sho (victory) plan involved three forces that would converge on the US transports and amphibious ships in the Leyte Gulf. The Southern and Centre Forces were composed of Japan's intact surface fleet, while the Northern Force consisted of the pitiful remains of Japan's carriers and served as a decoy to lure Halsey to the north. On 23 October, Halsey's carriers decimated Japanese land-based air, while submarines and aircraft slowly whittled down the strength of the Centre Force under Vice Admiral Kurita Takeo. Kurita turned his Centre Force away after carrier aircraft sank the super-battleship *Musashi*. On the night of 24–25 October, PT boats, destroyers, cruisers and the old battleships raised from Pearl Harbor destroyed the Southern Force in the Surigao Strait. Meanwhile, Halsey detected the carriers and took the bait, leaving the San Bernardino Strait unguarded.[63]

Kurita pushed undetected through the San Bernardino Strait at night and collided, on the morning of 25 October, with Kinkaid's covering force of destroyers and escort carriers. Then the real 'miracle' of the Pacific War occurred. The Navy's 'third string' light forces aggressively attacked Kurita's potent force. Kurita, baffled by suicidal destroyer torpedo attacks and harassment by fighters and anti-submarine planes, came to believe he was actually up against Halsey. The Japanese admiral broke off the action and turned away within sight of Leyte Gulf. Sprague lost three of his gallant escorts and one of his small carriers. Ironically, a small kamikaze squadron also attacked Kinkaid's escort carriers and managed to sink as much as Kurita had. Meanwhile, Halsey savaged the decoy force, sinking several of the empty carriers, but had missed his chance to destroy the rest of Kurita's surface ships. It mattered little; there was no mistaking Leyte's decisiveness – Japan lost, and her connection with the Indies resources needed to continue the war would be cut in short order.[64]

On land, General Yamashita, of Singapore fame, moved more troops in to reinforce those already defending Leyte. Mother Nature seemed to aid the

62 Drea, *Japan's Imperial Army*, pp. 242–3.
63 H. P. Willmott, *The Battle of Leyte Gulf: The Last Fleet Action* (Bloomington: Indiana University Press, 2005), pp. 74–135.
64 Ibid., ch. 6; Drea, *In the Service of the Emperor*, pp. 196–7; see also Spector, *Eagle Against the Sun*, pp. 426–42.

451

Japanese, too, with three typhoons, constant rain and an earthquake making American operations more difficult, especially air support. The Japanese fought on, despite being cut off, and on 15 December, MacArthur declared victory, despite continued Japanese resistance. General Krueger and the Sixth Army invaded Luzon on 9 January 1945, at the same location where the Japanese had landed three years earlier. Manila was destroyed in a fierce urban battle, and Yamashita retired to the interior of the island. MacArthur spent the rest of the war liberating the Philippines. Yamashita held out until after the atomic bombs had been dropped. Nonetheless, the successful invasion of the Philippines sent the signal loud and clear to Japan's leaders that, no matter how successful the operations of her army (i.e. Ichi-Go) in China, it did not derail the US juggernaut in the Pacific and, with the movement of the B-29s to the Marianas, probably accelerated the end of the war.[65]

Armageddon

With the effective destruction of the Japanese Fleet and the fall of the Philippines imminent, America and her allies were now poised to begin the final destruction of Japan. The debates about how to do this varied. The Navy thought a blockade would starve the Japanese into surrender. The Army Air Forces was just as convinced that the strategic bombing campaign would end the war. Finally, the Army believed that an invasion of Japan would be necessary in order to bring about a Japanese capitulation. Roosevelt, and later Truman, believed the participation of the Soviet Union was also essential to end the war. The Japanese strategy was to bleed the Americans until public opinion in the United States forced an end to hostilities, leaving the Emperor in place, with Japan-proper unoccupied. To this end, the final great battles of the Pacific War reflected this sanguine strategy – Iwo Jima and Okinawa. The capture of these islands was considered absolutely essential. Iwo Jima, a sulphurous, volcanic rock some 600 miles south of Japan, had several airfields from which Japanese fighters could attack the B-29s flying from the Marianas, as well as warn of impending raids. Okinawa, on the other hand, would serve as the principal staging base for the invasion of Japan.[66]

---

65 Spector, *Eagle Against the Sun*, pp. 511–30; Willmott, *The Battle of Leyte Gulf*, ch. 7.
66 D. M. Giangreco, *Hell To Pay: Operation Downfall and the Invasion of Japan, 1945–1947* (Annapolis, Md.: Naval Institute Press, 2009), chs. 5–8, 14; Drea, *In the Service of the Emperor*, pp. 198–215.

Spruance's Fifth Fleet was given the task of capturing Iwo. The Marines landed on 16 February 1945. Despite an extensive air assault and a powerful naval bombardment, General Kuribayashi Tadamichi's 21,000 soldiers sold their lives dearly, burrowing into caves and then emerging from their subterranean sanctuaries to kill Marines. In a repeat of Peleliu, the Japanese died to the last man and inflicted over 28,000 casualties on the Americans in the bloodiest month in Marine Corps history.[67] Okinawa was Iwo Jima-Peleliu on a larger scale, with the added new weapon of kamikazes flying from Japan and Formosa. General Simon Buckner, Jr had the Tenth Army, with over half a million men, for the task. During the course of the two-month campaign, twenty-one ships were lost, sixty-six seriously damaged, and more than 10,000 sailors killed and wounded – the highest naval losses of the Pacific War after Guadalcanal. Ashore, the campaign was a reflection of the horrors of total war. In addition to the annihilation of the 100,000-man Japanese garrison, the civilian population lost at least 80,000 killed. American casualties numbered almost 70,000 killed, wounded and missing, including General Buckner, who was killed during the last days of the campaign.[68]

Okinawa was another strategic defeat for the Japanese, but the generals were not yet inclined to surrender, despite fire bombings that had destroyed many of Japan's major cities. Surely another bloodbath would convince the Americans to back down from their harsh surrender terms announced at the Potsdam Conference? American casualty estimates for the Kyushu operation and subsequent invasion of the Tokyo area on the island of Honshu amounted to of 720,000 'dead and evacuated wounded' for the Army and Army Air Forces alone. Two other factors came into play to end the war. As preparations for the invasion of Japan proceeded apace, two atomic weapons produced by the secret Manhattan Project were shipped to a special B-29 unit located on Tinian. The other factor was the entry of the USSR into the contest.[69]

On 6 August 1945, a B-29 piloted by Colonel Paul Tibbets dropped the first atomic bomb on the port city of Hiroshima, killing tens of thousands instantly, with the toll climbing to 80,000 from subsequent blast wounds and radiation sickness. On 9 August, the Soviets invaded Manchuria. Over the next few weeks, mechanized Soviet armies overran the Japanese puppet

---

67 Donald L. Miller, *D-Days in the Pacific* (New York: Simon & Schuster, 2005), chs. 7, 8.
68 Thomas Huber, *Japan's Battle of Okinawa: April–June 1945*, Leavenworth Paper no. 18 (Fort Leavenworth, Kan.: Combat Studies Institute Press, 1990).
69 Giangreco, *Hell To Pay*, chs. 1, 15–17, and Appendix A; Drea, *In the Service of the Emperor*, chs. 10, 11; Spector, *Eagle Against the Sun*, pp. 503–6.

state there. Hours after the Soviets attacked, a plutonium bomb obliterated Nagasaki and 35,000 more Japanese were incinerated. With the second bomb, the leaders of the Japanese army realized that if the Americans had more than one atomic weapon, their strategy for defending Kyushu was hopeless. The Americans could vaporize their defences. At the last moment, radical elements of the Japanese Guards Division in Tokyo attempted to prevent the Emperor from broadcasting the surrender over the radio. Loyal troops suppressed this coup and, on 15 August, Hirohito asked his people to 'endure the unendurable'. On 2 September 1945, General MacArthur received the surrender of the Japanese dignitaries on behalf of the Allied Powers, aboard the battleship *Missouri* in Tokyo Bay.

This sudden end to the war probably saved millions throughout Asia from starvation, to say nothing of those Japanese already starving due to the blockade. Japan's still substantial military forces throughout Asia were at first unsure, and the war might have continued. But when forces began to surrender in Manchuria, and with the dispatch of members of the imperial family to convey the Emperor's personal plea for his generals to lay down their arms, a sort of domino effect took place. Ironically, many Japanese troops found themselves as policing units in the devastated lands they had once conquered, as they waited for Allied forces to come to relieve them, from Thailand to north China. Others simply melted into the jungles and mountains, only surrendering many years after the war had ended. The final bill in lives and property damage will never be known, but the deaths due to the war probably exceeded 25 million (more than two-thirds civilians) if one starts counting from 1937. One account implies that the larger Asia-Pacific war lasted through the Vietnam War. As for the United States, it became a permanent feature of the East Asian security landscape as a result of the war, a posture that was codified in 1952 at San Francisco and is still in place today.[70]

---

70 Giangreco, *Hell To Pay*, pp. 194–204; Williamson Murray and Allan Millett, *A War to be Won: Fighting the Second World War* (Cambridge: Harvard University Press, 2001), pp. 554–8; Ronald Spector, *In the Ruins of Empire: The Japanese Surrender and the Battle for Postwar Asia* (New York: Random House, 2007), pp. xi–xiii, 1; Hara Kimie, '50 Years from San Francisco: Re-examining the Peace Treaty and Japan's Territorial Problems', *Pacific Affairs* 74:3 (fall 2001), 361–82.

16

The Atlantic war, 1939–1945

MARC MILNER

The 'Battle of the Atlantic' was the term coined by Winston Churchill in the spring of 1941 for a distinct phase of the war in the Atlantic. The title stuck, and it is now used for the whole Atlantic war, from September 1939 to May 1945. However, it was not a battle in the traditional sense of the word, but rather a series of discrete campaigns, with varying objectives for either side. Although much of the action was concentrated along the key shipping routes into and out of Britain, the Atlantic war reached virtually every corner of the ocean, from the Arctic and the Labrador Seas to the South Atlantic, into the Caribbean and the Gulf of Mexico, and hundreds of miles up the St Lawrence River.

Allied objectives in the Atlantic reflected those of great maritime powers: moving people and resources, blockading Europe, sustaining Britain, France and, later, Russia, and projecting military power overseas. All were obtainable without direct attack on Germany's vital maritime interests. Since Allied victory was predicated on free use of the sea, the Atlantic war was therefore shaped largely – although by no means exclusively – by German initiatives. Solid organization of merchant shipping and naval intelligence, the establishment of escorted mercantile convoys, and the cover of powerful fleets and air forces formed the foundation of Allied success in the North Atlantic.

The initiative in the Atlantic war fell to the Germans, whose Kriegsmarine and Luftwaffe were woefully unprepared for a major naval war. In hindsight, the Allies, too, were unprepared to defend North Atlantic shipping in 1939, but their efforts were probably appropriate to the threat level. Grand Admiral Erik Raeder, Commander of the Kriegsmarine, had been promised by Hitler that a major war with Britain would not start until 1944. All his small fleet could do in 1939, he confessed in his memoirs, was to 'die gallantly'.[1]

---

1 Quoted in Timothy J. Runyan and Jan M. Copes (eds.), *To Die Gallantly: The Battle of the Atlantic* (Boulder, Colo.: Westview Press, 1994), p. xiii.

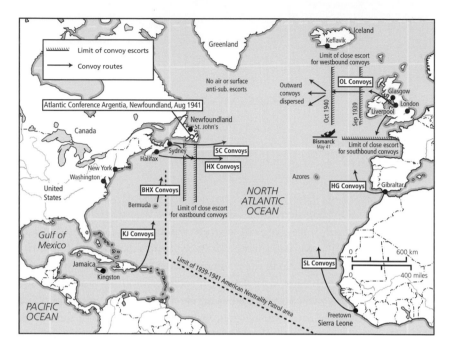

16.1 Battle of the Atlantic, 1940–41

German naval strategy during the Phoney War of 1939–40 was therefore one of harassment and containment of Allied naval forces. A war on shipping was conducted by surface raiders, routes off the British coast were mined, and British coastal shipping was attacked by aircraft, submarines and small warships. This produced some dramatic history. In December 1939, a force of British cruisers brought the pocket battleship raider *Graf Spee* to battle off the River Plate in South America. The damaged German raider escaped to Montevideo, and garnered intense international media attention. Fearing destruction at sea, the *Graf Spee* was scuttled and burned. In February 1940, the British breached neutral Norwegian waters in a dramatic rescue of merchant seamen held on board the replenishment tanker *Altmark*, which had supported German raiders. None of this had any appreciable impact on the war.

The Atlantic war began in earnest in the spring of 1940, with the fall of Norway and France to the Germans. For the first time in two great wars, Germany had bases on the open Atlantic. The isolation of Great Britain as the only major European enemy also provided Germany with a clear and simple objective: defeat Britain. Germany lacked the means to achieve this. The Luftwaffe failed to win air superiority in the Battle of Britain in August and September; the Wehrmacht had no serious amphibious capability; and the Kriegsmarine had suffered heavy losses in the Norwegian campaign. As the Luftwaffe slipped into a punitive campaign of aerial bombardment of British cities (the Blitz), including ports, the Kriegsmarine launched an assault on merchant shipping in and around the British Isles. The Germans estimated that if they destroyed some 750,000 tons of shipping per month for a year, Britain would sue for peace. The figure was a guess: even the British were uncertain about their shipping needs. By one pre-war estimate, they needed 47 million tons of imports per year: in 1942, Britain managed on about half of that.[2]

The Germans applied all their resources to this attack over the winter of 1940–41. The most serious inroads into British imports were made by the Luftwaffe. Their presence along the European littoral closed southern and east coast UK ports to overseas shipping. It took a year for the British to adjust their infrastructure and imports to west coast ports. Surface raiders caused the British their greatest anxiety in the second winter of the Atlantic war.[3] The pocket battleship *Scheer* roamed the Atlantic in the autumn and early winter, and also made some dramatic history. Her attack on convoy HX 84 in November began with destruction of the convoy's sole ocean escort, the armed merchant cruiser *Jervis Bay*. The former passenger liner's six-inch guns were no match for *Scheer*, but *Jervis Bay*'s ill-fated defence of the convoy allowed thirty-two of thirty-eight ships to escape. Meanwhile, the heavy cruiser *Admiral Hipper*, supported by very long-range aircraft and submarines, attacked several convoys west of Gibraltar in December, in the only instance of a coordinated surface, sub-surface and air assault on North Atlantic convoys. On Christmas Eve, *Hipper* approached troop convoy WS 5A: twenty ships bound for the Middle East. Three escorting cruisers and the aircraft carrier *Furious* drove *Hipper* off and forced her to seek shelter in France.[4]

In February and March 1941, the battlecruisers *Scharnhorst* and *Gneisenau*, cloaked by the sub-Arctic night and foul weather, broke into the North Atlantic and prowled the northern convoy routes – seemingly at will. Their primary task was to 'pull the lion's tail', and they did that superbly for two

2 C. B. A. Behrens, *Merchant Shipping and the Demands of War* (London: HMSO and Longmans, 1955), pp. 36–7 and Appendix x, p. 71.

3 Martin Doughty, *Merchant Shipping and War* (London: Royal Historical Society, 1982).

4 Captain S. W. Roskill, DSC, RN, *The War at Sea*, vol. 1: *The Defensive* (3 vols., London: HMSO, 1954), p. 291.

months. These two massive raiders did little more than disrupt shipping, but every effort by the British to bring them to battle failed. *Scharnhorst* and *Gneisenau* steamed into Brest (where *Hipper* lay) to a hero's welcome at the end of March 1941.

In the event, long-range Focke-Wulf Condor patrol aircraft and disguised merchant raiders, like *Atlantis*, *Kormoran* and *Pinguin* (operating in the Southern Ocean) sank more shipping than the cruisers and battlecruisers. *Pinguin* alone accounted for twenty-eight ships in 1941.[5] Large German warships accounted for only 6.1 per cent of Allied shipping destroyed during the war. By comparison, mines sank 6.5 per cent, aircraft 13.4 per cent, and unknown causes 4.8 per cent. By May 1941, with longer days, fairer weather and an increasing number of radar-equipped Allied aircraft, German raider operations in the North Atlantic were no longer possible. The last raider to try, *Bismarck*, was sunk on 26 May. Increasingly, Germany relied on its U-boat fleet, which eventually claimed roughly 70 per cent of Allied merchant ship losses by 1945.

The inability of large German raiders to find and destroy Allied convoys from the autumn of 1939 to the spring of 1941 speaks to the highly effective nature of the British Commonwealth's trade defence system. This was one of the lessons of the Great War. Naval Control of Shipping (NCS) operated like modern air traffic control: every movement, every route was planned, assigned and monitored. NCS ensured that shipping could be protected, either by routing it safely away from danger, or by assembling it into convoys so it could be escorted. It worked closely with shipping companies and agencies like the British Ministry of War Transport, and in close harmony with Naval Intelligence. In 1939, the British Empire and Commonwealth had a global NCS system, with regional centres such as Ottawa, Jamaica and Cape Town, all tied to London by wireless and submarine cables.[6]

The essence of British trade defence was avoidance of the enemy. Wartime propaganda described close escorts – like the *Jervis Bay* – as the first line of defence, but that was a necessary falsehood. The escort only fought if the intelligence, fleet operations and routing failed. Although this British Commonwealth system of trade defence was not foolproof, it worked fine against large merchant raiders in the North Atlantic. Its greatest test would come, however, from an unconventional oceanic threat to convoys: the U-boat.

---

5 Roskill, *The War at Sea*, vol. 1, p. 385.
6 Marc Milner, 'Naval Control of Shipping and the Atlantic War 1939–45', *The Mariner's Mirror* 83 (May 1997), 169–84.

The value of the U-boat as a commerce raider was understood from the Great War, during which Britain was brought to the brink of disaster by submarine attack in 1917. But the number of German submarines available at the start of the war was tiny. Admiral Karl Dönitz, commander of the U-boat fleet, had wanted 300 submarines for a war against Britain: in August 1940 he had twenty-seven, and by February 1941 only twenty-one. Only about a third could be on station at a time: thirteen were operational in the North Atlantic in August 1940, and only eight in January 1941, when the surface and air offensive against British shipping peaked. The number of U-boats increased dramatically in the spring of 1941, but by then Dönitz's chance to knock Britain out of the war had passed.

The British knew, in 1939, how small the U-boat fleet was, and they believed – not without reason – that the combination of convoys and air support would reduce them to the status of an inshore nuisance. So by 1940, anti-submarine (A/S) escort was provided only to twelve degrees west, and it focused on defence against submerged attack. It was understood that submarines would not operate in the broad ocean because finding and attacking escorted convoys in the vast expanse of the Atlantic was too difficult. Admiral Dönitz, however, had devised tactics to overcome the search and attack problems, and turned the U-boat into a mid-Atlantic weapon of enormous power.

Dönitz's solution was to deploy groups of U-boats, controlled from head-quarters ashore through high-frequency radio, in wide patrol lines perpendicular to the convoy route. These 'wolf packs' acted like a huge drift net, directed onto the target by the latest intelligence. The first U-boat to sight a convoy shadowed it, while transmitting routine reports to headquarters and a medium-frequency homing signal to other U-boats. When enough U-boats assembled around the convoy, the wolf pack was turned loose to attack. This usually happened at night, with U-boats operating independently on the surface like motor-torpedo boats, slipping inside the escort screen and often into the convoy at high speed, firing torpedoes, then escaping astern of the convoy or submerging in a quick dive. The 740-ton Type VIIc U-boat that formed the bulk of Dönitz's fleet was optimized for this kind of warfare.

The British were unprepared for these new tactics, and the autumn of 1940 and winter of 1940–41 became, for U-boat commanders, 'the happy time'. Targets were plentiful and easy, and there appeared to be nothing the British could do to stop the carnage. At the end of October 1940, the slow eastbound convoy SC 7 lost twenty-one of its thirty ships, and the fast westbound HX 79 lost twelve of forty-nine; other heavy losses followed. Not surprisingly, the Germans preferred to attack convoys outside the limits

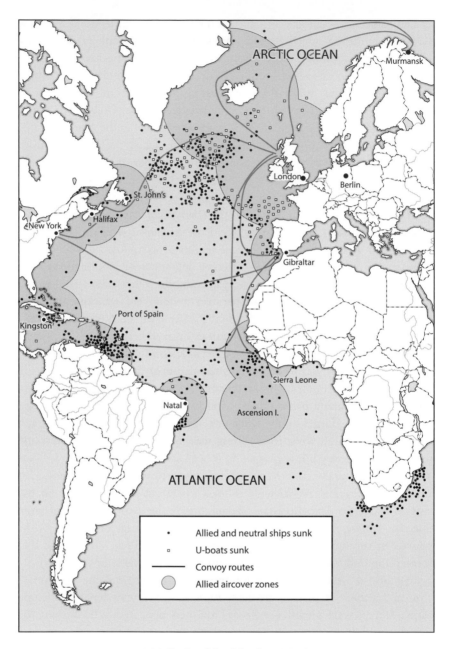

16.2 Battle of the Atlantic, 1942–43

of anti-submarine escort. When the dispersal/meeting point shifted westward to seventeen degrees, the U-boats shifted westward with it. In the autumn of 1940, the British had no clear solution to the problem of small submarines swarming convoys on the surface at night in the depths of the Atlantic. Hastily assembled escort groups, poorly trained and lacking essential equipment – like radio telephones and radar – found themselves groping for fleeting shadows in the inky darkness.

On 6 March 1941, Winston Churchill publicly declared British resolve to tackle the problem in the North Atlantic. 'The U-boat at sea must be hunted', he proclaimed; 'the U-boat in the building yard of the dock must be bombed'. And the Focke-Wulf Condor must be 'attacked in the air and in their nests'. As the Blitz drew to a close, Churchill declared that 'The Battle of the Atlantic has begun!' His Battle of the Atlantic Directive, prescribing measures to be taken to defeat the U-boats and conserve British shipping and imports, was issued that day.[7]

Things soon began to turn in Britain's favour. Shortly after Churchill's 6 March speech, the British killed two of Germany's leading U-boat aces – Schepke and Prien – and captured the third, Kretschmer. These events in the late winter of 1941 mark the end of the first U-boat happy time. Over the spring, the anti-submarine defence of North Atlantic convoys was sorted out. In April, the British occupied Iceland and established naval and airbases that pushed A/S escort of convoys to thirty-five degrees west. That same month, the Americans extended their self-declared Neutrality Zone eastward, from sixty degrees west to twenty-six degrees west, including all of Iceland. The expansion of America's patrolled space was intended to free the British to focus on the eastern Atlantic.

April also brought the establishment of Western Approaches Command in Liverpool to oversee A/S defence of convoys. Permanent escort groups and new tactics were developed, and new equipment was introduced. The doctrine of 'safe and timely arrival of the convoy' was enshrined in the new Western Approaches Convoy Instructions as the first duty of every escort. And Royal Air Force Coastal Command squadrons operating in trade defence in the Atlantic were placed under Western Approaches Command control. By the end of April, it simply remained to fill three gaps in convoy escort in the North Atlantic: one naval and two air.

---

7 Max Schoenfeld, 'Winston Churchill as War Manager: The Battle of Atlantic Committee 1941', *Military Affairs* 52 (July 1988), 122–7. For a copy of Churchill's Directive, see Roskill, *The War at Sea*, vol. 1, Appendix O, p. 609.

The naval gap was filled by the Royal Canadian Navy (RCN). It was on the verge of a massive expansion, with roughly 100 escort vessels – mostly 'Flower' class corvettes – under construction. In May 1941, the British asked the Canadians to base their burgeoning fleet in Newfoundland to close the final gap in the escort of Atlantic convoys, between the limits of Iceland-based forces and local RCN escort from the convoy assembly ports in Canada. The Canadian Naval Staff obliged, although it cautioned that its ships and men were still utterly unprepared for war. The Admiralty reminded the RCN that it was the convoy system that mattered more than the quality of the escorts. With the establishment of Newfoundland Escort Force (NEF) in June, A/S escort for transatlantic convoys was complete from Canada to the North Channel.[8]

The other gaps in the system were both in the air. The limits of land-based aircraft operating from Iceland and Newfoundland left a gap in the mid-ocean commonly known as the 'Black Pit'. Aircraft from British and Icelandic bases in 1941–42 typically reached 600 miles into the North Atlantic, while Canadian (and later American) aircraft operating from Newfoundland got only 400 miles from similar medium-range aircraft, because prevailing westerly winds reduced their return flights to a crawl. Newfoundland-based aircraft also had to contend with almost perpetual fog on the Grand Banks and towering icebergs. So the air coverage either side of the air gap was not symmetrical.

There was also a little known 'Azores air gap' on the Sierra Leone route in the eastern Atlantic. This crucial link to the South Atlantic and the Far East was, in many ways, the Royal Navy's primary operational commitment in the Battle of the Atlantic in 1941 and 1942. The escort groups were almost entirely British and were often the best and most powerful available. They received air support from Britain and Gibraltar. But the Luftwaffe bases in France often pushed their routing well to seaward, toward the Azores, and well beyond help from land-based aircraft. This air gap was therefore much less of a factor than the Black Pit to the north, but it too persisted until 1943.

Improvements in defence of the North Atlantic convoys, fairer weather and longer days curtailed U-boat success in the spring of 1941. They also frustrated the sortie into the Atlantic in May of the new 40,000-ton German battleship *Bismarck* and the cruiser *Prinz Eugen*. The destruction of *Bismarck*

---

8 W. A. B. Douglas, Roger Sarty, Michael Whitby et al., *No Higher Purpose: The Official History of the Royal Canadian Navy in the Second World War, 1939–1943* (St Catharines, Ont.: Vanwell Publishing Ltd, 2002), vol. II, pt. 1, ch. 3.

on 26 May by the Royal Navy is generally taken to mark the end of the surface threat to North Atlantic convoys. But the threat remained throughout 1941. *Prinz Eugen* remained on the loose in June, and *Scharnhorst*, *Gneisenau* and *Hipper* were still in Brest. Meanwhile, *Bismarck*'s sister, *Tirpitz*, was nearing completion.

The best that the British could claim in May 1941 was that the U-boat problem was being dealt with and that the German attempt to knock Britain out of the war had failed. Allied merchant shipping losses in 1941 averaged about 250,000 tons per month, well short of Dönitz's objective of 750,000 tons. Over the same period, the British saved some 3 million tons of shipping by cutting down on imports and reducing port congestion, and they launched some 1.2 million tons of new ships. In terms of needs and carrying capacity, Britain may have been better off in 1941 than a year earlier. In the meantime, it had ordered – through the new Lend-Lease arrangement with the Americans – over 7 million tons of new shipping from US yards. Only briefly, in 1942 and 1944, did Britain draw on her reserves of key commodities; in all other years – including 1941 – imports outpaced consumption.[9] The U-boat war in 1941 was therefore dramatic, but not decisive.

During 1941, German strategy in the North Atlantic, and indeed the war itself, underwent profound change, especially after the assault on Russia began at the end of June. The new German objective in the Atlantic was to support the war against the Soviet Union by disrupting the ability of the Allies to launch the Second Front. The Allies also struck back hard at the U-boats in 1941, inflicting a tactical defeat on wolf packs operating along the UK–Gibraltar route. As the year ended there were, once again, few U-boats in the North Atlantic.

The decline in German fortunes in the North Atlantic began in June, when the British captured *U 110* and its coding and cipher books and equipment. The British were well aware of the German naval Enigma cypher machine, and the Government Code and Cypher School at Bletchley Park was developing means of breaking it. Material from *U 110* provided the keys to the operational and tasking signals of North Atlantic U-boats for the first time. This, coupled with the British Commonwealth's sophisticated and highly efficient global direction finding network (so-called 'Y' information), allowed the positions of U-boats to be determined with great precision. As a

---

9 For a discussion of these figures, see Marc Milner, 'The Battle of the Atlantic', *Journal of Strategic Studies* 13 (March 1990), 45–66, special issue: *Decisive Campaigns of the Second World War*, ed. John Gooch.

result of the *U 110* capture, the British had the same information on U-boat positions that Dönitz possessed, and they tracked his intentions and movements. Regular and timely reading of this ULTRA intelligence allowed convoys to be routed safely for much of the period, and may have saved 300 Allied ships in late 1941.[10]

The penetration of the Enigma codes did not benefit all convoy routes equally. While a large group of U-boats patrolled unsuccessfully south of Iceland in July and August, a second concentration along the Sierra Leone convoy route gave the British serious trouble throughout the summer. Here, the U-boats' hunting was greatly assisted by long-range air patrols from France, agents in Spain watching Gibraltar, and excellent work by the German naval radio intelligence service, B-Dienst. From mid-July to the end of August, U-boats intercepted and attacked a series of convoys on the southern route. This success contrasted sharply with the total lack of interceptions in the mid-ocean. The Germans eventually put this failure in the north down to the existence of some new long-range surface warning device, like shipboard radar.

The German attack on Russia, which began on 22 June, profoundly changed the nature of the war. It was also good news for Britain. At a stroke, the pressure from Germany eased, although the demands on Britain's resources – especially in the Atlantic – increased. Russia, once a pariah state, immediately became a friend in the cause against Fascist aggression. Churchill broadcast to the Soviet Union on that fateful day, offering British support. The Russians, suspicious, and overwhelmed by the German offensive, took time to respond. Contact with Stalin was established by early July, as plans were made to push naval forces into the Norwegian Sea and, ultimately, to ship supplies to the Russian port of Murmansk. The first mercantile convoy for Russia sailed from Iceland on 21 August, and a regular series, the PQ convoys, started in September.

Meanwhile, the US involved itself in defence of Atlantic shipping. President F. D. Roosevelt had professed America's strict neutrality during the first years of the war, but he and most Americans knew whose side they were on. 'Neutrality Patrols' by the US Navy in the western Atlantic, in which they reported the positions of belligerent forces in clear, benefited the British: American forces, too, had searched for the *Bismarck*. The Lend-Lease

---

10 Jürgen Rohwer and Roger Sarty, 'Intelligence and the Air Force in the Battle of the Atlantic, 1939–45', paper presented at the XIIth International Colloquy on Military History, Helsinki, Finland, 31 May – 6 June 1988.

programme, announced in March 1941, perhaps more than any other act, signalled American commitment to an Allied victory.

Once this arrangement was signed, the Americans were drawn into the British Commonwealth's trade defence system. The network of British 'Consular Shipping Agents' throughout the USA, actually Royal Navy (RN) officers in civilian clothes, were authorized to work with their US Navy (USN) counterparts and to share information and experience. Meanwhile, NCS in Ottawa, which controlled trade in the western hemisphere north of the equator and ran the NCS network in the USA, issued confidential books and special publications to the USN and exchanged NCS liaison officers.

This American drift to war culminated in August 1941, when Roosevelt, Churchill and their senior staffs met at the new American naval base in Argentia, Newfoundland, to sort out war aims. They agreed to America taking strategic control of half of the world: from the mid-Atlantic right round to Indonesia. This meant that the North Atlantic west of thirty-five degrees (with a slant to the east to include Iceland) came under USN strategic and operational control. For its part, the USN agreed to deploy the necessary battle fleet units to control its new Atlantic zone, and fifty destroyers to escort convoys between the Grand Banks and Iceland. A pool of US-flagged shipping was established at the convoy assembly ports in Canada, to ensure that each HX and SC convoy had an American ship, making the convoy notionally American: others were free to join in if they wished. The first USN-escorted convoy, HX 150, was taken over from the Canadians on the Grand Banks on 16 September.

With the Arctic convoys now a reality and the Gibraltar convoys under siege, the surge of American naval power into the northwest Atlantic was an enormous boost to the Allies. It immediately freed British escorts for other duty, allowing the Arctic convoys to run and strengthening escorts on the Gibraltar route. That left the USN and the Canadians to handle convoy escort duty in the northwest Atlantic. Because USN escort forces were all destroyers, and the RCN's NEF was primarily much slower corvettes, a separation of tasks was worked out: the USN protected the fast convoys, while the RCN escorted the slow ones.

The agreements reached at Argentia divided control over defence of transatlantic convoys in the middle of their passage of the air gap, and disconnected the rapidly expanded RCN from British oversight. East of the 'Change of Operational Control' (CHOP) line (roughly thirty-five degrees west), the system remained in British hands, but west of it, escort forces came under American control. This resulted in the anomalous situation of

Canadian naval and air forces, which were officially at war with Germany, operating under an admiral whose country was still neutral. In August 1941, getting America into the shooting war was far too important to worry about what all this meant. In any event, the Anglo-Canadians still controlled the crucial matter of convoy routing.

But problems soon arose. In the late summer and autumn of 1941, the slow Canadian-escorted convoys came under attack in the American zone, and suffered serious losses. These demonstrated just how ill-prepared the RCN was for combat, and how difficult it was now going to be for the British to manage the Atlantic war west of the CHOP line. The perils of escorting slow convoys were revealed starkly in early September. Convoy SC 42, sixty-five ships escorted by just one Canadian destroyer and three RCN corvettes, was intercepted just south of Greenland on 9 September. It was routed almost due north, to avoid a very loose concentration of U-boats that Dönitz had set adrift in hopes of finding something – his response to the success of ULTRA-based routing in July and August. The Canadians sent reinforcements from St John's, and they sank a U-boat during their final approach to SC 42. But the escort was soon overwhelmed by a dozen U-boats: fifteen ships were sunk in two days of furious action. The British now insisted that NEF group size increase from four to six escorts: something the RCN could just manage.

After mid-September, the Canadians were able to get help from the USN, which kept losses to SC 44 low in late September. By then, the system seemed to be working well enough, so the British shifted the escort relay point south of Iceland five degrees further east, so more RN ships could be freed for other duty. In particular, the Gibraltar convoys were under attack again by October. This obliged RCN and USN escorts to stay at sea an extra day. Delays imposed on slow convoys by the onset of autumn storms lengthened the passage even further and drove the fledgling Canadian fleet to the verge of collapse in October. The Americans – who assumed no responsibility for the Canadians – looked on in amazement. The senior USN officer in Iceland warned that the Canadians were exhausted when they got there and their layover in wind-swept Hvalfijordhur was just a couple of days. American sailors watching the tiny corvettes corkscrew their way across the Atlantic thought that the Canadians should get submarine pay because they spent so much time submerged.

The British looked on in horror. Canadian radio discipline was poor, signalling appalling, ship handling dubious and knowledge of tactics virtually non-existent. Few RN officers knew that the Canadians lacked signal lamps, telescopes, binoculars, trained signallers, qualified officers, radio telephones,

1 The Chinese defenders of the Zhabei district of Shanghai are presented with supplies. The Battle for Shanghai in 1937 was one of first in the Sino-Japanese War. The best troops of the pre-war Chinese Army had been trained by German advisors and wore 'coal-scuttle' helmets; many were lost in the early fighting.

2 An air raid in progress on Chongqing during the Japanese invasion of China, October, 1938.

3 Horse-drawn vehicles of the German 213th Artillery Regiment in Poland, September, 1939. The German Army was large but not well supplied with motor vehicles; only a few of its divisions were motorised.

4 Leslie Illingworth cartoon in the London *Daily Mail* of 2 December, 1939. The British government believed an enhanced blockade was a key weapon against Germany. The winning goal here is kicked by Churchill, then First Lord of the Admiralty. The French ally, in the person of Premier Daladier (bottom), plays only a supporting role.

5 Gen. Heinz Guderian in his Sd. Kfz. 251/3 command vehicle, May/June, 1940. Guderian is discussing the military situation with a Panzer division commander. The dash to the Channel by Panzer Group Kleist, which included Guderian's XIX Corps, determined the campaign's outcome.

6 Guderian in his command vehicle; sequel to photograph above. Communications were crucial for the rapid successes of the Blitzkrieg. This shows an Enigma machine, which allowed rapid exchange of encrypted radio messages. Enigma was later compromised by British intelligence.

7 Knocked-out French Char B1 heavy tank, Belgium, 15 May, 1940. A myth of the 1940 campaign is that the invaders had superior equipment and manpower. The 28 ton Char B1 had thick armour and a heavy gun; French medium and light tanks were also as good – and numerous – as their German equivalents. Allied weakness lay in scattering of tank forces and faulty strategy.

8 German soldiers manoeuvring a small gun on the beach at Dunkirk, 4 June, 1940. In the background is the French destroyer *L'Adroit*, which was destroyed in a German air raid on 21 May, 1940.

9 A Chain Home Radar Station on the British east coast with standard steel transmitter towers in the foreground and wooden receiver towers in the background. Painting by Thomas William Rawlinson, 1946.

10 Operations room, RAF Duxford (near Cambridge), 1940. The integrated British air defence system, created in the 1930s, was crucial for defeating German air attacks. 'Ops. rooms' co-ordinated radar, ground observers, fighters and AA guns, and were linked to a national network.

11 The Germans experimenting with a converted submersible Panzerkampfwagen III tank in preparation for Operation SEALION (German invasion of England). Photograph from summer, 1940.

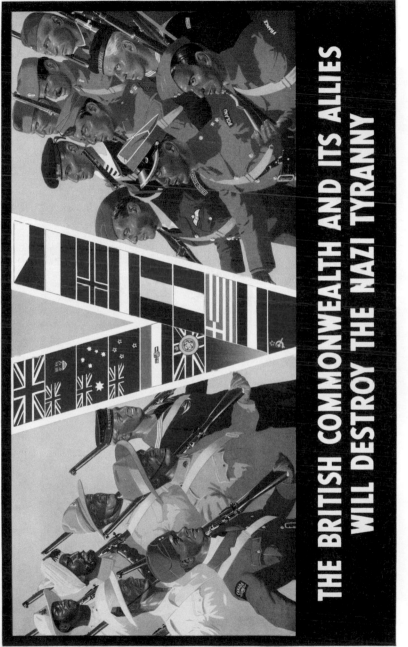

THE BRITISH COMMONWEALTH AND ITS ALLIES WILL DESTROY THE NAZI TYRANNY

12 British poster, late 1941. The stress is on the great human and material resources of the British Empire/Commonwealth. The 'V' (Victory) symbol was widely used in propaganda from early 1941.

13 HMS *Ark Royal*, painting by Eric Ravilious (1940). The big aircraft carrier was commissioned in 1938. She is depicted firing her AA guns off Norway in 1940, but her planes also crippled the battleship *Bismarck* in 1941. A U-boat sank *Ark Royal* in the Mediterranean in November, 1941.

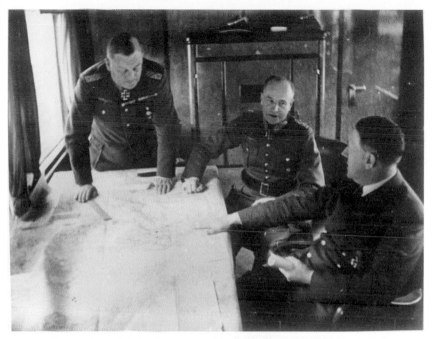

14 In April 1941, aboard his headquarters train, Hitler discusses the invasion of the Balkans. Seated next to him is Field Marshal Brauchitsch, the C-in-C of the German Army. Standing is Field Marshal Keitel, Hitler's subordinate at Wehrmacht headquarters.

15 German invasion of Russia, June/July, 1941. As in Poland and France, German forces available for war against the USSR were limited; the tank pictured here is a Czechoslovak vehicle pressed into service as a Panzer 38(t). Portraits of Stalin and Marshal Timoshenko, head of the Red Army, hang on either side of the gateway.

16 'We will defend Moscow!' Soviet poster, 1941. Hitler launched an attack toward the Soviet capital in October, 1941. The successful Red Army counter-attack, in December, showed that defeating the USSR in one campaigning season would be impossible.

17 Italian tankman in Tripoli, March, 1941. Taken at a parade honouring General Rommel, who had just arrived with the German Afrika Korps and Luftwaffe squadrons following serious Italian defeats. The tank is an Italian M 13/40; in the background stands a statue of Mussolini on horseback.

18 Japanese super-battleship *Yamato* fitting out, September, 1941. Built in conditions of extreme secrecy, *Yamato* displaced 70,000 tons, compared to the inter-war limit of 35,000. She mounted 18.1 in. guns, where the inter-war limit had been 16 in. Her size did not save *Yamato* from being sunk by American planes off Okinawa in 1945.

19 Wartime painting in oils on silk, by an unidentified Japanese artist, depicting the four officers and five crewmen who were lost with the five Japanese midget submarines that participated in the Pearl Harbour attack, 7 December, 1941.

20 'Farewell to Thee'. Following Hawaiian tradition, sailors honour men killed during the 7 December 1941 Japanese attack on Naval Air Station Kaneohe, Oahu.

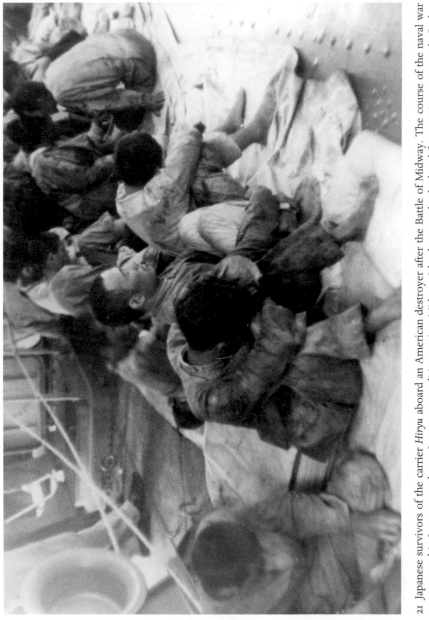

21 Japanese survivors of the carrier *Hiryu* aboard an American destroyer after the Battle of Midway. The course of the naval war was reversed in June, 1941 when a Japanese expedition against Midway Island was ambushed and four carriers were sunk. Such prisoners were unusual; in Japanese military culture capture by the enemy was regarded as shameful.

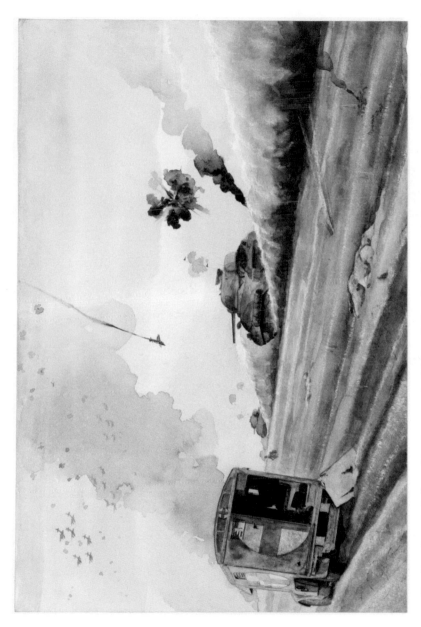

22 'Breaking through the last of the German minefields at El Alamein, 2 Nov. 1942'. A contemporary water-colour by war artist Alex J. Ingram. El Alamein was the turning point in the Desert War. The tanks are American-built Shermans; equipment for the USA was becoming more and more important.

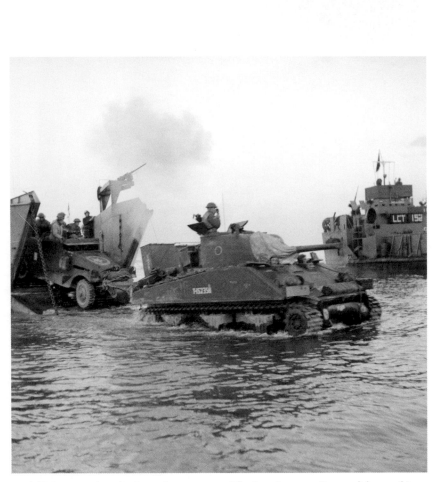

23 A Sherman tank at Anzio, 22 January, 1944. The invasion, near Rome, did not achieve the full results intended, but it followed successful landings in Morocco, Algeria, Sicily, and southern Italy. Inter-Allied co-operation was remarkable: here British troops drive ashore in American vehicles (a Sherman and an M3 armoured car) from British-built landing craft (LCTs).

24 A Rescue-ship in the Atlantic, March 1943. Painting by the war artist George Plante.

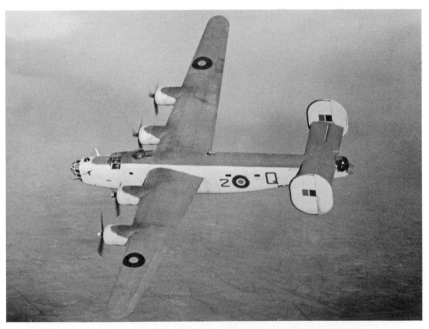

25 Liberator bomber on anti-submarine duty with the RAF. These aircraft were vital for closing the mid-Atlantic 'air gap'. Another example of inter-Allied co-operation, the American-built B-24 Liberator was flown here by an RAF Coastal Command squadron based in Northern Ireland. There was much debate about whether long range aircraft should be used for bombing Germany or patrolling the Atlantic.

26 David Low cartoon from the London *Evening Standard* of 23 September, 1943. There was pressure from the Americans and from the British Left for a 'second front' to relieve the USSR. Churchill and his advisors preferred a peripheral Mediterranean campaign to a premature cross-Channel assault.

27 Roosevelt, Churchill, Stalin at the Tehran Conference, November, 1943. The first meeting of the Big Three made a number of important political and military decisions, including an agreement to mount a British-American cross-Channel operation in May 1944.

28 US Marines seek cover among their dead and wounded behind the sea wall on Tarawa Atoll. The landing in the Gilbert Islands in November, 1943 was the first step in the advance across the Central Pacific. Inexperience with assault landings meant Marine losses in the four-day battle were very high. The Japanese defenders, some 2,500 men, fought nearly to the last man.

29 The anchorage at Ulithi Atoll in the Caroline Islands, December, 1944. By the middle of 1943 America began to develop an overwhelming naval superiority over Japan, as newly built ships entered service, including 'Essex' class carriers like these.

30 'The Tough Beach'. Watercolour by war artist Dwight Shepler. American troops and landing craft under heavy fire on OMAHA Beach, 6 June, 1944. Of the five D-Day beaches OMAHA proved the most difficult. In the foreground is a beached and damaged landing craft, an LCI(L.

31 Logistics 1941: German troops in Poland preparing for the attack on the USSR. The photograph gives a sense of the ramshackle nature of Wehrmacht motor transport, even in the minority of 'fast' units that were provided with trucks and other vehicles.

32 Logistics 1944: The speed and depth of the Red Army advance into Central Europe in 1944 was made possible by a huge fleet of Lend-Lease vehicles, mostly supplied by the US via Iran. Here a column of Studebaker US-6 trucks moves a Soviet artillery unit through Romania.

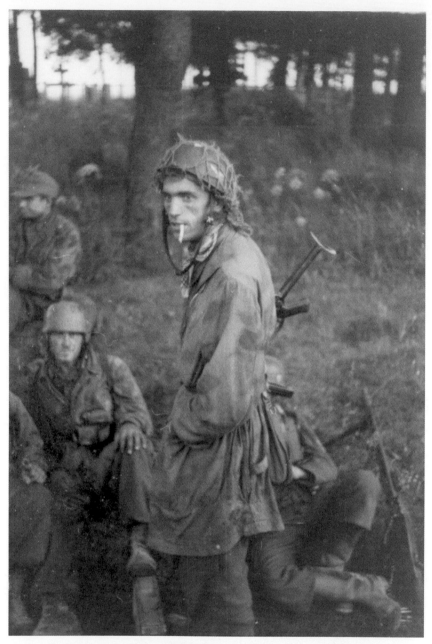

33 German paratrooper taking a break in Normandy, June/July, 1944. The quality, motivation and conduct of the Wehrmacht is still widely debated. The experience of individuals and the cohesiveness of small units were certainly factors in retaining fighting ability.

34 Goebbels and child soldier, 13 March, 1945. The 16 year old Willi Hübner is awarded the Iron Cross, 2nd Class, for his bravery. Many youngsters, radicalised by propaganda and the Hitler Youth, took part in the final battles. This photograph bears an uncanny resemblance to Illustration No.1.

35 British and Soviet troops meet in Germany, 1945. More handshakes; this time by the victors. The tank is a Soviet T-34-85, the most important armoured vehicle of the war.

36 The MANHATTAN Project. The Y-12 plant under construction, near Oak Ridge, Tennessee, 1943. The Americans pursued four different routes to enrich uranium; the electromagnetic separation process employed at Y-12 was crucial for developing the Hiroshima bomb.

37 Hiroshima, 6 August, 1945. This photograph, showing the early formation of the mushroom cloud, gives a sense of the devastation below; some 80,000 people, the great majority civilians, had been killed outright. It was taken from the B-29 bomber 'Enola Gay' which had dropped the 'Little Boy' uranium bomb. The next stage, photographed shortly afterward, is shown in the plate section of vol. III.

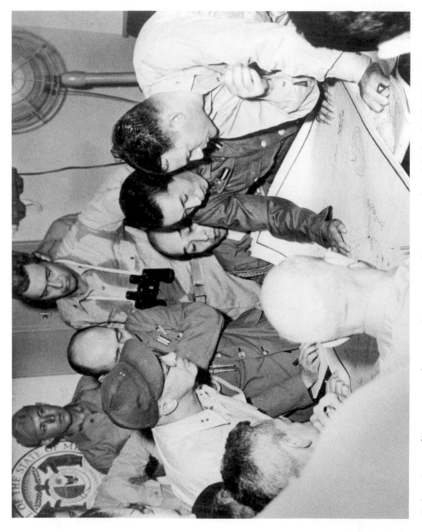

38 American and Japanese naval personnel meet on 27 August, 1945 aboard the battleship *Missouri* to prepare the movement of Allied ships into Tokyo Bay for the surrender ceremony. This was held on 2 September.

LES RAIDS DE LA ROYAL AIR FORCE ECRASENT L'INDUSTRIE ALLEMANDE

1942

1941

1940

BOMBES 225 KILOS

BOMBES 1.000 KILOS

BOMBES 4.000 KILOS

● Jusqu'à la fin de la troisième année de guerre, un total de 8.985 avions ennemis avaient été détruits. Dans ce chiffre sont compris les appareils détruits dans le Moyen Orient.

● De janvier à juin 1942, la R.A.F. et la R.A.A.F. ont pris part à plus de 400 raids effectués par les forces aériennes alliées contre les positions japonaises en Extrême Orient.

● Les appareils du Commandement de Bombardement ont couvert une distance de près de 50.000.000 de kilomètres et ceux du Commandement Côtier plus de 80.000.000 de kilomètres depuis le commencement de la guerre.

● Un groupe de Commandement de Chasse, seul, couvrit une distance de 3.200.000 kilomètres en mars et avril 1942, la majeure partie au-dessus de la Manche ou de la France occupée par l'ennemi.

● En 31 jours, entre le 12 juillet et le 11 août 1942, 26 jours furent marqués par des attaques et il n'y eut que trois périodes de 24 heures sans opérations des bombardiers de la R.A.F.

● Le Commandement de Bombardement a détruit d'un quart à un tiers de tout Cologne, la troisième ville d'Allemagne.

● Plus de 175.000 bombes incendiaires furent lancées sur Hambourg, en 35 minutes, durant la nuit du 26 au 27 juillet 1942.

● La Royal Air Force emploie maintenant des bombes de 4.000 kilos dans certains de ses raids sur les centres industriels allemands.

39 'Raids by the Royal Air Force are Destroying German Industry.' British poster, late 1942. This shows the growing size of RAF bombs, including some of 4,000 kg. The text gives details of RAF activities.

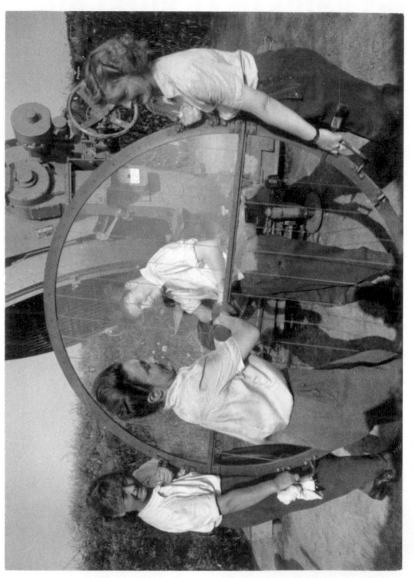

40 *Flakhelferinen* manhandle a searchlight, 1943/1944. As a result of the Allied bombing campaign and manpower shortages many high school pupils were called up to serve as auxiliary anti-aircraft personnel. Germans born in the late 1920s who experienced the war in this way are sometimes called the *Flakhelfer-Generation*.

41 Low-level RAF photograph of a German WÜRZBURG radar at Bruneval, France, December 1941. This was part of the enemy air defence system. Enigma decrypts and aerial photos provided information about this installation, and the key components were captured two months later in an airborne Commando raid.

42 A British Colossus computer. This was the world's first electronic computer with (limited) programmability; the first version became operational in early 1944 at Bletchley Park, and eventually ten were built. They were used to help decrypt German radio teleprinter messages.

43 Soviet POWs. Dated August 1942, this photograph was taken in southern Russia. Altogether some 5,700,000 Soviet prisoners were taken, of whom 3,300,000 (58%) died in the extremely harsh conditions of German camps and forced labour.

44 Captured Wehrmacht soldier, 1944. The young POW being registered here by an American officer, probably in Normandy, evidently comes from one of the Soviet non-Slav minorities. Many such men were recruited by the Germans from camps holding captured Red Army soldiers.

45 Hitler and Himmler stand before the gallows in this David Low cartoon from the London *Evening Standard* of 10 July, 1942. This appeared shortly after the announcement of massive repressions at the Czechoslovak village of Lidice; this followed the assassination on 27 May of Reinhard Heydrich, *Reichsprotektor* of the Czech lands.

46 American film poster, 1943. The Allies hoped to incite resistance in occupied Europe, and for some time the Serbian nationalist Chetniks under Draža Mihailović were supported in Yugoslavia. The propaganda film about Mihailović was released in February, 1943, but the Chetniks came to be seen as insufficiently active, and Allied support was shifted instead to Tito's Communist Partisans. Mihailović was tried and shot by the Tito government in 1946.

radar and – in most corvettes – even foul weather gear. British faith in Canadian ability reached its nadir on 1 November, when SC 52 was intercepted virtually off St John's, Newfoundland. Fearful of another SC 42, routing authorities ordered the convoy back to Sydney, Nova Scotia via the Straits of Belle Isle: the only North Atlantic convoy turned back by the U-boat action during the war. Otherwise the convoys moved, and in November the British apologized to the RCN for their carping criticism. The RCN, for its part, committed ever more of its growing resources to the mid-ocean campaign.

It helped that the U-boat presence in the North Atlantic dwindled as the autumn dragged on. U-boats were redeployed to the Mediterranean in response to British success in the naval war Mediterranean and the Western Desert. Meanwhile, Hitler's anxiety over Norway as a possible site for Allied landings in support of the Russians siphoned U-boats into the Norwegian Sea. Most clung firmly to positions along the Norwegian coast as part of a defensive scheme. Few ventured into the depths of the Arctic Ocean (and night) to find the convoys plodding between Iceland and the White Sea ports of Arkhangelsk and Murmansk. Six PQ convoys reached Russia between September and the end of the year: none was attacked.

By December, the only Atlantic convoy route under serious pressure was the one to Gibraltar and West Africa. There, in mid-month, the British fought a battle around convoy HG 76 that inflicted a stunning tactical defeat on the wolf packs, and provided the model for how Dönitz's 'Grey Wolves' would ultimately be beaten in 1943 The convoy was powerfully escorted by over a dozen RN sloops, destroyers, corvettes and a new auxiliary aircraft carrier, *Audacity*. Most of the escort had the new ten-centimetre surface warning radar (Type 271), and the operation was supported by new 'very long-range' (VLR) B-24 Liberators of 120 Squadron RAF and 'Martlet' fighters flying from *Audacity*.

Contact with HG 76 was firmly established on 16 December, and a week-long battle ensued. By the time it was over, four of Germany's precious Condors had been shot down and five U-boats sunk. Two merchant ships, a destroyer and *Audacity* herself were lost: an acceptable exchange from the British perspective. The escort maintained a tight radar barrier around the convoy at night, harassed and sank U-boats by day and shot down their reconnaissance aircraft. More importantly, the Germans concluded that these convoys were now very dangerous to attack.

It would be more than a year before the recipe worked out on the Gibraltar route in December 1941 was applied along the main transatlantic

Without a coastal blackout and with navigation lights still operating normally, U-boat captains ran amok. In March and April, they hunted off New York and the Virginia Capes. By May and June they were into the Gulf of Mexico, where few patrols operated. In those two months alone, German submariners sank over a million tons of shipping in US waters – half their total score for the whole year of 1941 in just nine weeks. Allied merchant shipping losses peaked in 1942: 8.3 million tons, of which 6.1 million fell to U-boats.[14]

American historians record the commencement of convoy operations in the US Eastern Sea Frontier (ESF) with the sailing of the first Key West–Hampton Roads convoy in mid-May, but that was simply the first American convoy in their own waters. The Canadians, who controlled routing and diversion of shipping in the western hemisphere north of the equator until July 1942 (when it finally passed to Washington), started the first convoys in the ESF in March, between Halifax and Boston. By May, the RCN was running Canadian oil tanker convoys through the ESF to Aruba.[15] They operated without loss until the end of the summer – despite at least one attempt by the Germans to mount a pack operation against them. But the Key West–Hampton Roads system was a crucial start. Gradually, the US coastal convoy system linked with those developed by the British and Canadians into the 'interlocking convoy system' of the western hemisphere: from Rio de Janeiro to Thule, Greenland.

As the western hemisphere convoy system expanded, it reduced Admiral Dönitz's basic measure of success: tonnage-sunk-per-U-boat-day-at-sea. That, in turn, forced U-boats to move to less well-protected areas, and much further afield in search of easy targets. So the 'front' of the U-boat assault swept steadily southward over the summer, into the Caribbean and down the coast of South America. But it could not be sustained. The small Type VIIc U-boat, the workhorse of the North Atlantic, was stretched to operate off the American and Caribbean coasts already, and could only be sustained by U-tankers – of which there were precious few. As the front moved south, the burden fell on a small number of larger, Type IX, U-boats. The law of diminishing returns began to force the bulk of the U-boat fleet back into the central North Atlantic by late summer.

---

14 Captain S. W. Roskill, DSC, RN, *The War at Sea*, vol. II: *The Period of Balance* (3 vols., London: HMSO, 1956), Appendix O, p. 485.
15 Rob Fisher, 'We'll Get Our Own: Canada and the Oil Shipping Crisis of 1942', *The Northern Mariner* 3 (April 1993), 33–40.

The expansion of the Atlantic convoy system in 1942 was made possible by the continued rapid growth of the Canadian navy. The RCN filled in for the Americans in the northwest Atlantic and drove its fleet hard. When the USN largely withdrew from transatlantic escort duty in the spring, the RCN and RN split the task. Iceland was abandoned as a relay point and the new Anglo-Canadian 'Mid-Ocean Escort Force' protected trade between the Grand Banks and northern Britain: the British got most of the fast convoys. When the western terminus for transatlantic convoys shifted from Nova Scotia to New York in September, the RCN created a new escort force to pick up the burden. And its oil tanker escorts to the Caribbean, some of the best, were absorbed into the US system south of New York. Finally, in August, the Canadians committed corvettes to the planned Allied assault on North Africa in the late autumn. To do this, the RCN gave up operational training, refits and modernization of the fleet. It also abandoned its convoy system in the St Lawrence Gulf and river system – Canada's main shipping artery – a decision which made operational sense, but exploded like a bomb in the Canadian press and parliament.

Few Allied naval officers needed convincing in 1942 that the Canadian decision to run the RCN hard was right. The Japanese onslaught on the Pacific was unstoppable in the six months after Pearl Harbor. Nothing that British, American, Dutch and Australian fleet units could do seemed to work. Meanwhile, in the summer, General Erwin Rommel and his Afrikakorps went on the offensive in Cyrenaica, and by late August were within eighty miles of the Suez Canal. And on the Eastern Front, German forces had crossed the Volga and reached the oilfields of the Caucasus along the Caspian Sea. Everywhere, the Axis was in full cry.

The situation was no better for the Russian convoys. During the winter of 1941–42, they had virtually a free pass through the Arctic night: only one of the first 158 ships travelling the route to Murmansk was sunk. Things changed dramatically in late February. Winter ice moved south to constrain the route just as daylight crept back into the sky, and the Germans moved to attack the Russian convoys with surface, U-boat and air forces. Convoys PQ 12 waiting in Iceland and QP 8 at Murmansk on 1 March were the first to be sailed as a joint operation and to receive the full support of the British Home Fleet. From then until January 1944, the movement of Arctic convoys became major naval operations, quite different from their cousins plodding the Great Circle route across the North Atlantic.

The passage of PQ 12 and QP 8 was supported by three battleships, the fleet aircraft carrier *Victorious*, a heavy cruiser and nine fleet class destroyers.

The convoy escorts themselves were either destroyers or cruisers. Six days after PQ 12 departed from Iceland, the new German battleship *Tirpitz* and three destroyers sortied from Trondheim. By 7 March, PQ 12, the British battle fleet and *Tirpitz* were playing cat and mouse in squalls and poor light. The RN staff history records that they were all within 100 miles of each other during the day, but failed to make contact. That day, PQ 12 and QP 8 passed within a mile of each other south of Bear Island in an Arctic fog, and the danger shifted to the southbound convoy – only fifty miles north of *Tirpitz*. A chance encounter between a German destroyer and a straggler from convoy QP 8 nearly brought the two forces together. The next day, *Tirpitz* swung north in search of PQ 12, which she was unable to find.

When the convoys cleared the area, the operation became a hunt for *Tirpitz*, which was finally located on 9 March by a strike force of eighteen Albacore torpedo bombers from *Victorious*. The aerial attack failed and *Tirpitz* eventually made harbour unscathed. So, too, did the convoys, but there were no more free passes.

As the days lengthened, the Arctic convoys came under aerial attack, the heaviest of the war. In fact, most of the losses to PQs 13, 15 and 16 through the spring fell to aerial bombing or torpedoes. Corvettes, trawlers and escort destroyers now provided the close escort for the convoys, while a system of close and distant fleet coverage developed as most of the German surface fleet moved north. As PQ 17 prepared to sail from Iceland, *Tirpitz*, *Lutzow*, *Scheer*, *Hipper* and nine fleet class destroyers, a score of U-boats and several squadrons of torpedo and bomber aircraft prepared to destroy it. The convoy's close and distant covering forces of British and American battleships and cruisers, the carrier *Victorious*, and their supporting destroyers were roughly equal in strength, but the Germans controlled the skies, and the sea was full of submarines – both Allied and German.

On 2 July, German aerial reconnaissance located PQ 17 north of Bear Island, and the next day, *Lutzow* and *Scheer* were ordered north to Altafjord to join *Tirpitz* and *Hipper* for the assault. While German surface forces awaited intelligence on the location of the British covering force, PQ 17 endured aerial and U-boat attacks throughout 3 and 4 July, losing four ships. Finally, late in the day on 4 July, anticipating an attack by the German fleet in confined waters between North Cape and the edge of summer ice, in an area dominated by German land-based aircraft with twenty-four hours of daylight, the First Sea Lord, Admiral Sir Dudley Pound, made one of the fateful decisions of the war. ULTRA decrypts of the movement of the German fleet were unclear at the time. British intelligence experts were convinced that *Tirpitz* had not put to sea on 4 July, but they could not produce conclusive proof.[16] Pound and the naval staff erred on the side of caution: the covering force was ordered to withdraw westward and PQ 17 to scatter. When German aerial reconnaissance reported the scattering of the convoy, *Tirpitz, Scheer* and *Hipper* left Altafjord the next day to help sweep up the refugees, but the damage was inflicted by aerial attacks and U-boats. Twenty-one of the convoy's thirty-six ships were lost after the convoy scattered. The abandonment of PQ 17 stands out as a singular error of judgement. In all, 3,350 vehicles, 410 tanks, 210 aircraft and nearly 10,000 tons of materiel were lost. Pound never interfered with the commander on the spot again: no more convoys were scattered.

PQ 18 sailed in September, carrying enough vehicles, tanks, aircraft, equipment and supplies to outfit an armoured division. Increasingly, the aid delivered through Persia (Iran) and across the Pacific to Vladivostok dwarfed what the Arctic convoys could carry.[17] It was therefore acceptable to suspend the Russian convoys after PQ 18 to allow the RN to concentrate resources on the landings in North Africa. The last of the PQ-QP convoy series, QP 14, cleared Allied merchant ships from White Sea ports in late November, coming home in horrific weather, with two losses to U-boats.

Meanwhile, Germany's U-boats drifted back into the mid-Atlantic air gap in the late summer and autumn of 1942, the only remaining theatre where they could operate on the surface with impunity and hope to achieve decisive results. By the winter of 1943, the number of operational U-boats ranged from 403 to 435, with an average of over 100 at sea each month, most in the Atlantic.[18] As the U-boat fleet concentrated for the final showdown, Dönitz shifted his guiding strategy. The critical link in the Allied shipping chain was now its merchant seamen. Dönitz surmised, rightly, that they were a finite and dwindling resource. He also assumed that they were war-weary, and that another round of high losses – in the depths of another stormy North Atlantic winter – would break their morale. Winston Churchill shared that belief. With losses in the Atlantic still high and a new series of Russian convoys about to start, he reminded the Admiralty in November that the Merchant Navy could not stand the strain for much longer.

16 See F. H. Hinsley et al. (eds.), *British Intelligence in the Second World War: Its Influence on Strategy and Operations* (4 vols., London: HMSO, 1981), vol. II, pp. 214–23.
17 Malcolm Llewellyn-Jones, preface to *The Royal Navy and the Arctic Convoys: A Naval Staff History* (London: Routledge, 2007).
18 Roskill, *The War at Sea*, vol. II, Appendix K, p. 475.

The British were therefore particularly sensitive to shipping losses in the autumn of 1942. It is true that new construction surged past losses in November 1942, so the Allies had won the tonnage war.[19] But the new construction was largely American, while much of the shipping lost in 1942 was British or under British charter. October was the worst month of the war in the South Atlantic, while November was the third worst month of the whole war: 128 ships lost. Most of these were independents sunk in the central and South Atlantic. The reason for these losses was only too clear; to find the escorts for Operation TORCH, the British closed down the Gibraltar–Sierra Leone convoy route. Trade off West Africa and in the South Atlantic now moved independently. It was a calculated risk, and the U-boats collected a rich harvest. Moreover, the abandonment of the east Atlantic convoy routes meant that all trade to and from the UK was now routed across the main transatlantic convoy routes and through the convoy system in the western hemisphere. As a result of TORCH, British imports were sharply down just as Britain became dependent on one embattled route in and out.

If that was not bad enough, TORCH consumed more resources and more shipping from British supplies than planners anticipated. The original estimate for ships operating between the UK and North Africa was sixty-six per month: the reality was 106, with a consequently higher draw on British resources and reserves – especially oil – than planned. By late 1942, the gap between what Britain needed to fight and what it needed simply to survive was dwindling fast.

So the North Atlantic convoy routes had to be made completely secure, just as Germany's rapidly expanding U-boat fleet surged into the mid-ocean. The new Commander-in-Chief of Western Approaches, Admiral Sir Max Horton, who took over in mid-November, had reason to believe that he could manage that task. Allied naval and air A/S and escort tactics, doctrine and equipment had improved steadily through 1942. Air patrols synchronized their efforts more effectively with convoys and escorts. Painting A/S aircraft white, flying higher patrol altitudes and more effective depth-charge fuses contributed to increasingly successful attacks on U-boats. What aircraft really needed, and what they got on a large scale in 1943, was ten-centimetre radar. They also needed to reach into the depths of the air gap, and that, too, was beginning to happen. In August, the VLR Liberator aircraft from 120 Squadron RAF began operating in the mid-ocean: a development noted with

---

19 Michael Salewski, *Die deutsche Seekreigslietung 1939–1945* (Frankfurt am Maine: Bernard & Grafe, 1970–75).

concern by the Germans. More were needed. RN escorts were also much better in late 1942. Effective barriers around convoys at night were possible with ten-centimetre radar, while the new shipborne high-frequency direction finders (HF/DF) allowed U-boats to be located, attacked and driven off as they made contact. The training and leadership of the seven notionally British escort groups in the mid-Atlantic (including many escorts of the European navies-in-exile) was good. It helped that most of their convoys were fast.

The great weakness in the mid-ocean in the latter half of 1942 remained the slow convoys, still largely escorted by Canadians. Slow convoys remained easy to catch and easy to hold onto. The RCN escorts in the mid-ocean were still less well trained than their British counterparts, and their equipment was also out of date. Their first-generation metric wavelength radars were incapable of providing a tight barrier around the convoy, and the U-boats' new metric wavelength radar detector 'Metox' could be used to find them – and their convoys. Canadian groups also lacked shipborne HF/DF and enough destroyers to provide a counter-attack force. This was all the legacy of running the fleet hard in 1942.

The Germans fed on them. The Admiralty's *Monthly Anti-Submarine Report* for January 1943 concluded that the Canadians bore the brunt of the U-boat offensive in the last half of 1942. Although only 35 per cent of mid-ocean escorts were RCN, their convoys suffered 80 per cent of mid-Atlantic losses from July to December 1942. Nonetheless, the British were convinced that the RCN remained a cup half empty, and that their convoys were intercepted more frequently because of undisciplined radio use. A study commissioned by Admiral Horton in late November claimed that poor leadership and training in the mid-Atlantic cost the Allies sixty ships in recent months. One of Admiral Horton's first tasks in mid-December was to ask that the Canadians be withdrawn from the North Atlantic for re-equipment, re-training and assignment of new group leaders. The RN, he said, could run the transatlantic convoys alone: he wanted the notional American group A.3 gone, too.

The Canadians protested that their real problems were lack of destroyers, outdated equipment and escorting slow convoys in the face of huge pack attacks, but their protests were undone by events at sea. The passage of HX 217 in mid-December was a lesson in how things ought to work. Modern radar, two destroyers, HF/DF and effective leadership allowed group B.6 (British destroyers and Norwegian corvettes) to push HX 217 through the air gap in the face of five U-boats. The convoy – a fast one – transited the narrowest portion of the gap in thirty-six hours, supported by a relay of VLR aircraft from Iceland. HF/DF allowed B.6 to track the build-up of the pack and make sensible dispositions to deal with it: radar kept them at bay at night. Two ships were lost in what was perhaps the best defence of a convoy in the mid-ocean during the war. Speed, modern equipment, destroyers and air support helped.

The Canadian-escorted ONS 154, travelling westward a week later, was a study in contrast. It took a week to transit the widest portion of the air: no VLR aircraft reached it. The escort group had only one destroyer, no functioning ten-centimetre radar, and the convoy – a slow one, travelling westward in ballast – steamed through the tail of a hurricane. It ran into a pack of twenty U-boats. On the night of 28 December, ONS 154 was attacked from all directions simultaneously. There were so many torpedoes that one Canadian watch officer commented laconically, '"There goes ours now, Sir!" as if the groceries were being delivered'.[20] Fifteen ships were lost. In early January 1943, the Canadian government acquiesced to the removal of its ships from the RCN's most prestigious operational commitment. As the Canadians drifted away, the convoys upon which Britain now utterly depended fell almost entirely into the Royal Navy's thinly stretched hands.

Apart from getting the escorts up to speed, the key to getting the trade through safely was still effective evasive routing. Since February 1942, the Allies had suffered a blackout of ULTRA intelligence from the German North Atlantic U-boat cipher. In mid-December, Allied code-breakers finally solved the problem of the fourth rotor in the German naval Engima machine. The results were immediate and profound. Despite the presence of forty U-boats in the air gap in mid-January, 'they swept and re-swept' the North Atlantic 'and found nothing'.[21] By early February, the Germans were growing suspicious that their inability to find convoys was due to more than dreadful weather.

As events in the mid-ocean moved inexorably toward a crisis, Karl Dönitz replaced Erik Raeder as the professional head of the Kriegsmarine. Dönitz managed to prevent Hitler from scuttling the whole surface fleet: it was too valuable an asset in tying down most of the British battle fleet to simply discard. Its role in future would be to haunt the Arctic convoy routes and keep the British busy trying to bring it to battle. The main effort, not

---

20 Quoted in Marc Milner, *North Atlantic Run: The Royal Canadian Navy and the Battle for the Convoys* (University of Toronto Press, 1985), p. 209.
21 Hinsley et al. (eds.), *British Intelligence in the Second World War*, vol. II, p. 557.

surprisingly, would now be the U-boat war in the Atlantic. Apart from trying to cripple the Allied merchant fleet by panicking its sailors into inaction, it was vital to forestall all attempts by the Western Allies to launch a second front in France. The main U-boat effort was therefore tied closely to larger German fortunes in the war.

While most U-boats, about sixty by mid-February, concentrated along the main convoy routes, others trolled the approaches to Gibraltar, trying to disrupt support to Allied forces ashore in French North Africa. One pack of these U-boats intercepted an attempt to bring fuel directly to the North African campaign in late January. Special convoy TM 1, of nine tankers, sailed direct from Trinidad to Gibraltar with a small escort of one destroyer and three corvettes. It was overwhelmed in the Azores air gap: only two tankers arrived. General von Arnim, holding on in Tunisia, sent Dönitz a personal telegram of thanks. The good news for the Allies coming out of January was that they finally decided to do something about winning the Atlantic war.

On the day that survivors from TM 1 arrived in Gibraltar, Roosevelt, Churchill and their senior staffs met in Casablanca to plan the next steps in the war. Their primary focus was the Second Front in France. All discussion quickly ran afoul of the unsettled situation in the North Atlantic. Barely enough trade was getting through to sustain Britain, let alone build up a massive army and its attendant resources to land in France. Nothing could be done – or even planned – until the Atlantic was sorted out.

The way forward was suggested by the operational research scientist P. M. S. Blackett, who prescribed three remedies: close the air gap, increase the size of escort groups and increase the size of convoys. Blackett demonstrated that 64 per cent of recent losses could have been avoided with continuous air support. Nearly 25 per cent could have been saved by increasing escort groups from six to nine ships. And the necessary escorts could be found by increasing the size of convoys from thirty or forty ships to eighty or more. Doubling the size of convoys only increased the perimeter of the convoy modestly. Moreover, since U-boats typically sank one ship for each attack, the rate of losses declined as the size of convoys increased: three U-boats might sink three ships from a thirty-ship convoy, but they would still only sink three ships if the convoy was ninety vessels. So fewer, much larger convoys, well escorted, were better than a steady stream of small, poorly escorted ones.

So at Casablanca the Allies resolved to commit resources to the North Atlantic until the problem was solved. This included shifting fleet class destroyers to A/S duty, finding enough VLR aircraft to close the gap, reassigning some of the new small auxiliary aircraft carriers to the main trade routes, and creating support groups to reinforce threatened convoys. Convoy size, too, would be allowed to creep up. Meanwhile, special US military convoys, the CU-UC series, would build-up American strength in the UK (Operation BOLERO) for the landings in France.

It took time for the decisions made at Casablanca to take effect. In the meantime, the situation in the North Atlantic deteriorated for the Allies. On 4 February, the sixty-one ships of SC 118 were intercepted on the western edge of the air gap, after intelligence failed to keep them clear: twenty U-boats were sent to attack. The escort, B.2, was normally one of the RN's best. On this occasion, it was powerful, but a scratch team under temporary leadership: five British and American destroyers, two US Coast Guard cutters and four corvettes (two of them Free French). The battle lasted three days, with VLR aircraft flying support in the middle of the air gap. By the time it was over, thirteen ships had been sunk, three U-boats destroyed and four seriously damaged. Brief and furious, the battle for SC 118 was regarded as one of the hardest fought of the Atlantic war.

In late February, with the air gap clogged by sixty U-boats, evasive routing failed dramatically again. The slow convoy ONS 166 was escorted by A.3: two US Coast Guard cutters and its five Canadian corvettes. Attempts to route it clear of two waiting wolf packs failed, while excellent work by the German naval intelligence service, B-Dienst, shifted the packs to intercept. Fifteen U-boats swarmed ONS 166 north of the Azores. Brief help came from a British VLR, which sank a U-boat, and both American cutters sank a U-boat, but the escort could not stop the waves of attackers. The timely intervention of Royal Canadian Air Force VLR Cansos – the Canadian-built version of the Catalina, stripped of all its unnecessary gear and weapons – 'blunted the U-boat onslaught'[22] on 24 February, 600 miles from their Newfoundland base. Three U-boats and eleven ships had gone down by the time the battle ended.

As ONS 166 reached New York, the situation for the Allies in the North Atlantic reached its nadir. In late February, code-breakers began experiencing serious delays in reading the U-boats' daily signal traffic; in the first ten days of March these delays became more pronounced. Finally, on 10 March, when the Germans changed the weather code for Atlantic U-boats, ULTRA failed completely. Easily identifiable by its short form, the weather signal had

---

22 W. A. B. Douglas et al., *The Official History of the Royal Canadian Air Force*, vol. II: *The Creation of a National Air Force* (University of Toronto Press, 1986).

provided a 'crib' for breaking the daily settings of the U-boats' Engima machines. Once that was obtained, the signal traffic could be run in virtual real time. It took nine days to solve the problem. In the meantime, Allied fortunes in the North Atlantic plummeted. In the first three weeks of March 1943, every transatlantic convoy was intercepted and half were attacked. Fully 22 per cent of shipping crossing the Atlantic during those three weeks was sunk. The scale of losses to North Atlantic convoys was unprecedented.

The crisis of the Atlantic war formed the backdrop of the Washington Convoy Conference, which convened in the first week of March. Called by Admiral Ernest King, the Commander-in-Chief of the USN, it was the result of months of lobbying and obstructionism by the Canadians. The essential problem was the muddled command structure of the Atlantic war. Operational command of transatlantic battles still switched between the British and Americans in mid-ocean, while in the northwest Atlantic no fewer than eight separate national and service commands controlled escort and A/S operations. The Canadians were also frustrated that their huge forces in the northwest Atlantic remained under American operational control. These problems had lingered since the end of 1941; now they needed to be fixed.

At Washington, the USN relinquished operational and tactical control of the main transatlantic trade routes to the British and Canadians (they retained strategic responsibility in the area), and withdrew A.3 from the mid-ocean. Western Approaches Command regained operational control of convoys to forty-seven degrees west, and a new 'Canadian Northwest Atlantic' emerged to control operations from there to the limits of the US Eastern Sea Frontier. The new command arrangements were set to take effect on 30 April 1943.

More importantly, in March, the resources promised at Casablanca began to appear. Some of these came from the closing down of the Russian convoys, again. These had only recommenced in mid-December and, apart from a sharp engagement between *Lutzow* and *Hipper* and British light cruisers in the Barents Sea in late December, they had proceeded without serious loss. When it became clear in early March that *Tirpitz* and *Scharnhorst* had moved north to Altafjord as well, the Commander-in-Chief of the Home Fleet recommended that the Russian convoys be stopped. The cruisers that supported convoys beyond fourteen degrees east were no match for what now lay at Altafjord. The urgent need for reinforcements in the mid-Atlantic sealed the case. The corvettes and destroyers of the Russian convoy force were reassigned to Western Approaches Command. The ships waiting in Iceland for convoy JW 54 to Russia sat idle until October before the convoy sailed.

The decisions taken at Washington were borne of urgency. As they met to sort out command issues, A.3 headed eastward with SC 121. It was a horrific passage. The convoy was beset by twenty-seven U-boats south of Greenland and lost thirteen ships: no U-boats were lost. A.3 now had the dubious distinction of having lost twenty-seven ships in two successive battles. Its senior officer complained bitterly that the promised escort carrier had failed to materialize. It was just to the south supporting HX 228, which was also helped by good weather and lost only four ships.

Allied fortunes reached rock-bottom with the next two eastbound convoys: SC 122 and HX 229. These, too, were sailed within supporting distance of each other – a pattern evident in 1943 and likely the fruit of Blackett's research. Their situation reports on 13 March were intercepted by B-Dienst, and forty U-boats were sent to intercept. It was, British intelligence observed at the time, 'the largest pack of U-boats that has ever been collected in one area for the same operation'.[23] Despite heavy air support, the naval escort was simply overwhelmed. Between 17 and 20 March, U-boats sank twenty-seven ships from SC 122 and HX 229 (which joined together to facilitate their defence). That brought total losses to transatlantic convoys for March to seventy-one. Only a storm of exceptional fury allowed the next series of convoys to slip through.

As the storm abated, so too did the fury of the German assault. In late March, ULTRA intelligence was restored and more support groups, some composed of destroyers drawn from the Russian convoys, began to reinforce the mid-ocean. ULTRA allowed these resources to be applied with devastating results. Moderating spring weather helped enormously, because U-boats could once again be detected on ten-centimetre radar. The return of the Canadian groups, banished from the mid-ocean for three months, allowed the British to shift more of their resources to offensive operations.

ULTRA also revealed the shaky morale in the U-boat fleet. A number of Dönitz's signals to his captains at sea chastised them for timidity and admonished them to press home attacks. The British took this as evidence that the U-boat fleet could be pushed to collapse. With resources pouring into the mid-ocean, fairer weather and ULTRA intelligence restored, it was time to shift to the offensive. The British understood that the U-boat fleet now had nowhere else to go. It would have to stand and fight around the Atlantic convoys.

---

23 Hinsley et al. (eds.), *British Intelligence in the Second World War*, vol. II, p. 563.

In April, the British began to target U-boat packs with reinforced convoys. Since not all the U-boats could be avoided, it made sense to steer most convoys clear, and then heavily reinforce a particular convoy and drive it into the waiting enemy. Support groups, land-based aircraft and often a small carrier concentrated around the threatened convoy about twenty-four hours before ULTRA suggested that first contact would be made. These forces then stayed with that convoy until the battle ended and shifted to the next 'bait' to be pushed through.

This pattern continued into May, when the command changes agreed at Washington came into effect and, for the first time since September 1941, the whole of the mid-ocean came under British control again. They did not waste their moment. The classic battle of this period is the passage of ONS 5 in early May, which finally broke the mystique of the wolf pack. The convoy was routed to the far north, to take advantage of air support from Iceland and some USN Catalinas based in Greenland (never a reliable operational base). The track then took ONS 5 just east of the new CHOP line, forty-seven degrees west, and therefore kept it nicely in the British zone.

The early phase of the battle was a grim see-saw affair, plagued by foul weather and intermittent air support from Iceland, Greenland and Canadian VLR Cansos from Newfoundland. Stormy weather prevented the larger escorts from refuelling and they departed on 4 May, leaving ONS 5 in the hands of only seven escorts. That night and the next day, nine ships were lost. The weather was so poor that a VLR Liberator from Iceland, operating 1,000 miles from its base, could not affect the gathering pack. Fifteen U-boats were in contact by dusk on 5 May. It seemed that ONS 5 was doomed.

Then the convoy steamed into fog on a glassy sea. All twenty-six attempts by the U-boats to attack that night were foiled by radar. Six U-boats were sunk by the escort – an unprecedented loss – and two U-boats collided in the murk and sank. By the time ONS 5 reached port, twelve ships had been lost, but nine U-boats were sunk.

The pace of German losses continued unabated through May. With more VLR aircraft now assigned to the North Atlantic, the air gap became a thing of the past. Liberators flew from bases in Newfoundland, Iceland and Northern Ireland in a steady relay. The British now switched from evasive routing to a fixed track along the Great Circle route. The Americans protested that this invited attacks: the British remonstrated that that was precisely the idea. So in May 1943, the U-boats were drawn into a battle they could not win. Between 10 and 24 May, ten convoys of 370 ships passed through U-boat concentrations in the mid-ocean. Only six were lost, and three of those were stragglers. Thirteen U-boats were sunk in the process. Of the hundred U-boats sunk in the Atlantic during the first five months of 1943, forty-seven went down in May. At the end of the month, Dönitz withdrew his battered packs: as far as the course of the war was concerned, the Battle of the Atlantic was over.

But the Allied offensive was not. American 'hunter-killer' groups, built around escort carriers, hunted U-boats and U-tankers across the central Atlantic through the summer and autumn. The Azores air gap finally disappeared in the autumn, when the Portuguese government allowed the British to base aircraft there. Meanwhile, radar-equipped Allied aircraft swarmed the U-boat transit routes in the Bay of Biscay. Dönitz's submariners led a fugitive existence: hunted, hounded and killed wherever they appeared. The fact that they remained dependent on surface manoeuvrability for strategic and operational purposes left them uniquely vulnerable to well-directed radar-equipped aircraft.

Dönitz knew that he had to get his subs back into the fight, so over the summer they were equipped with heavier anti-aircraft armament and new acoustic homing torpedoes. The U-boats would now blast their way through the naval and air escorts and get back into the convoys. The effort proved a dismal failure. No U-boat could withstand the fire from swarms of Allied aircraft. The acoustic homing torpedo was not unexpected. It was first used against convoys ONS 18/ON 202 in September, crippling the British frigate *Lagan* and sinking the RN corvette *Polyanthus*, and then virtually destroying the first RCN support group of the campaign by sinking its flagship *Itchen* and only destroyer *St Croix*. The British were uncertain if the problem was a torpedo or an acoustic mine. The Canadians knew it was a torpedo, and had fifty sets of anti-acoustic torpedo gear stacked on the wharf at St John's when the escorts from ONS 18/ON 202 arrived.

As a result of victory in the North Atlantic, Allied shipping losses plummeted. From January to May 1943, they averaged 450,000 tons per month. In the last half of the year they dropped to approximately 200,000 tons, with only about 40,000–60,000 tons accounted for by submarines. Meanwhile, the Mediterranean opened to shipping in the summer, saving tonnage on the Far Eastern routes; and an enormous volume of new construction flowed from Allied shipyards – 14 million tons in 1943 – outstripping losses by 11.5 million tons. By the autumn of 1943, the Allies began cancelling escort construction contracts by the hundreds. Much of the steel, the yards and the manpower were redirected to assault craft for the invasion of Europe and operations in the Pacific.

Two final acts remained to be played out in the Atlantic war by the autumn of 1943. The first came in the Arctic. By this time, the threat was much reduced. *Lutzow* had left for a long refit and *Tirpitz* had been severely damaged in a midget submarine attack in late September: only *Scharnhorst* and a few destroyers remained in northern Norway. So convoys to Russia resumed in late October. When *Scharnhorst* came out to attack JW 55A in late December off North Cape, the RN trapped her between a force of cruisers and the battleship *Duke of York*. A long chase through the Arctic night, punctuated by radar-directed gunnery, ended when British destroyers slowed *Scharnhorst* with torpedo hits. It took twenty minutes to beat the battlecruiser into a flaming wreck; then she was sunk by more torpedoes. For the first time since August 1941, the Arctic convoys were free of a surface threat, and future operations – dominated by A/S forces, including small aircraft carriers – concentrated on killing U-boats. The shift was confirmed in April 1944, when *Tirpitz* was sunk at her moorings in Trondheim by heavy bombers. In 1944–45, the Arctic convoys were more about fighting the remnants of the German navy than bringing cargo to the Russians.

Allied fortunes in the North Atlantic prospered in 1944 as well. In the face of repressive Allied naval and air power, the Germans adopted snorkels for their U-boats. Early trials were largely successful, although several of the first to use them at sea were targeted by ULTRA and sunk by the RN in February, and a couple appear to have been lost due to equipment or procedural failures. A few U-boats were fitted in time for the landings in France on 6 June 1944, but they had little impact on Allied use of the sea. What followed until the spring of 1945 was an inshore campaign by snorkel-equipped U-boats, primarily in British and Canadian waters.

Snorkel-equipped U-boats operating inshore did prove extremely difficult to locate and sink. As German submariners became adept with the new device and comfortable in confined waters, they operated very effectively by using the bottom and inshore tidal currents to outwit their hunters. In deep water, they fared less well. In either case, they could be pursued – weather permitting – until exhaustion of breathing air and batteries forced them to the surface.

The radically new submarines which Dönitz began to develop in 1943 finally made their appearance in April and May 1945: 100 of the new Type XXI ocean-going U-boats were operational in the spring. Two made successful cruises and the final two Allied shipping losses of the war fell to the inshore variant, the Type XXIII. Allied A/S systems – from the quality of the sonars, the nature of the weapons and even the speeds of the war-built hunters – were not up to the challenge of the new U-boats. But they came much too late. The best that the U-boat fleet could claim in 1945 was that they tied down enormous Allied forces: some 800 aircraft and 400 vessels alone were needed to contain the inshore U-boat threat in the British Isles by the end of the war.

There is no indication that the German attempt to disrupt Allied use of the Atlantic ever seriously impaired the development of Allied strategy. Certainly it was no more disruptive than Luftwaffe attacks on British ports in 1941 or – as the British complained – the American squandering of shipping through misuse.[24] The low point in Allied carrying capacity came in late 1942, just when there was little in the way of men, weapons and equipment ready to carry. It is true that the Allies were forced to build large escort fleets and replace a huge amount of lost merchant shipping as a result of Axis attacks at sea. But the war at sea cost the Germans a great deal as well, and from a very much smaller economy. The bottlenecks in Allied strategy were often those of simple logistics: availability and allocation of resources, mobilization and management – all problems compounded, it is true, by enemy action. The crisis winter of 1942–43 is a case in point, and probably the closest the Germans came to causing real grief in Britain. But the crisis was, to some extent, artificial, created by the demands of TORCH and the imbalance between American production and British need. Its greatest impact was probably on the Bengal famine, since the demands for shipping shut down cross-trades in the Indian Ocean. Only fifty B-24 Liberators were needed to permanently fix the problem of the mid-ocean air gap. The USN was flying nearly 300 on long-range reconnaissance in the Pacific at that time, and the numbers needed in the Atlantic amounted to the losses from one high-profile US air raid in Europe (on Ploesti). It would seem that Raeder was right in the end: all his fleet could do in aid of Germany's war effort was to die gallantly.

24 S. E. Morison, *History of United States Naval Operations in World War II*, vol. vx: *Supplement and General Index* (15 vols., Boston, Mass.: Little Brown, 1968), p. 164, agreed with the British criticism.

17

Anglo-American strategic bombing, 1940–1945

TAMI DAVIS BIDDLE

Both British and Americans decision-makers gave long range bombers a central role in their strategic plans for victory over their enemies in the Second World War. They did this even though they did not know how much the bombers might aid in defeating Axis forces and prompting Axis leaders to capitulate. In taking this gamble, they relied on a set of assumptions about aerial bombing that proved, in the event, to be overly optimistic. Once the commitment had been made, however, it was not easily reversed. Much of the narrative of Anglo-American bombing in the war, therefore, is about the way in which expectations crashed headlong into realities, and how the Anglo-American air forces attempted to recover and find a way forward that would make the long-range bomber an instrumental, or at least useful, contributor to victory.

The bomber campaigns would absorb a significant percentage of the total war effort of Britain (and her Dominions) and the United States.[1] And while

---

[1] The British Bombing Survey Unit argued that the Royal Air Force absorbed 28 per cent of the direct war effort of the British; Bomber Command, specifically, absorbed between 7 and 12 per cent – with the latter figure representing the last 2.5 years of the war. But the Bomber Command calculation must include significant contributions made by Canada and other Commonwealth nations and lands. In 1943, 37 per cent of the pilots of Bomber Command were from the Dominion air forces; by January 1945, the number reached 46 per cent. Canada also built bombers in the later stages of the war. In the USA, the cost of the overall air effort, from mid-1940 to mid-August 1945, was more than one-tenth 'of the total direct costs of the war to the United States'. British Bombing Survey Unit, 'The Strategic Air War Against Germany, 1939–1945', AIR 10/3866, pp. 33–9, The National Archives, Kew, London (hereafter TNA); B. Greenhous, S. J. Harris, W. C. Johnston and W. G. P. Rawling, *The Official History of the Royal Canadian Air Force*, vol. III: *The Crucible of War, 1939–1945* (3 vols., University of Toronto Press, 1994), pp. 13–15; Wesley Frank Craven and James Lea Cate (eds.), *The Army Air Forces in World War II*, vol. VI: *Men and Planes* (7 vols., Washington DC: Office of Air Force History, 1983 [1955]), pp. 32–3.

bombers would – eventually – make a notable contribution to Allied victory in the European and Far Eastern theatres, they would do so only after lengthy and costly struggles to overcome daunting operational challenges and unanticipated problems that would reveal themselves in the crucible of battle. Progress in the Allied bomber campaigns came to depend on a willingness to abandon or modify expectations that governed theories of victory, offence–defence relationships, and aircraft planning and production. This demanded constant, sometimes frantic, efforts to find new means and mechanisms to counter the unanticipated foes that lurked all around: at the enemy coast; in the relentlessly cloudy and smoggy skies over Northern Europe; and in the hearts and heads of aircrew themselves. Finding a way forward also came to rest upon a loosening, over time, of commitments to the moral obligation of discrimination (between combatants and non-combatants) inherent in the doctrine of just war. This meant a willingness to accept and embrace what was then considered wartime expediency, and what can be seen, now, as the brutalizing effect of total war.

This story is comprised of multiple themes, each one compelling and unsettling in its own way. Adaptation in the face of crisis is dependent upon human ingenuity and determination, scientific and technological agility, and the free flow of information across boundaries and potential barriers (institutional, cultural and social). It is dependent, too, on courage, the catalysing effect of urgency and fear, and, in this particular instance, the moral space that was pried open by crisis and emergency. Military service members realize, acutely, that a failure in the moment of truth will mean much more than a loss in profits or a bureaucratic reorganization; it will mean personal suffering, defeat in war and – in the worst case – the death of a society. They feel, therefore, an overpowering need to pass the tests that come in the crucible of war. For the air forces of Britain and the USA, this compulsion was felt even more keenly because they were largely untested institutions that had everything to prove.

In the end, Anglo-American long-range bombing enabled the British and the Americans to avoid a much-dreaded repeat of the grinding, protracted ground warfare of 1914–18. But in a sense, they traded one nightmare for another. The Anglo-American Combined Bomber Offensive (CBO), and the American air offensive against Japan were brutal campaigns for all involved – not just for the civilians of Europe and Asia, but also for the young aircrew who faced near-paralyzing casualty rates as they struggled to implement what had been intended as a more efficient, and therefore less costly, form of fighting than ground warfare.

Precisely what the bombers accomplished in the Second World War, and the degree to which they contributed to victory, has been a topic of intense, ongoing debate since 1945. Indeed, the Anglo-American strategic bombing campaign became one of the most controversial military campaigns in all of modern history, with advocates and critics locked in heated and divided post-war analyses that were frequently inflamed by moral arguments. Some have insisted that the vast investment in strategic bombing was misplaced – diverted into an enterprise that did not justify the time, effort and money it required. Others have argued that the effort made a meaningful contribution to victory, and – in light of the possible alternatives – may have spared at least as many lives (military and civilian) as it took. Due to the vast number of civilian deaths brought about by Anglo-American bombing, it has been impossible to debate the effectiveness of the campaigns in isolation from the ethical questions they posed.

Anyone wandering into this fraught terrain, however, must understand the political and economic realities of the interwar years, and the strategic culture of both Britain and the United States. Large armies are expensive, socially disruptive and politically worrisome. Nations with the geographical good fortune to believe they can survive without them will usually try to do so. This instinct, combined with the powerful revulsion felt toward the grinding, shocking ground combat of the Great War, made it nearly inevitable that the British and the Americans would grasp at an instrument that promised an alternative path to victory – or at least a means of reducing the burden that would fall upon ground armies in war. Indeed, at the height of Bomber Command's crisis of performance in 1941, the Chief of Air Staff Sir Charles Portal offered the prospect of a revised strategy to Prime Minister Winston Churchill. 'We could', he suggested, 'return to the conception of defeating Germany with the army as the primary offensive weapon'. He added, 'I must point out with the utmost emphasis that in that event we should require an air force composed quite differently from that which we are now creating'. Churchill, despite his immense frustration with Bomber Command's progress at that point, turned down the offer.[2]

This chapter will examine the Second World War history of Anglo-American strategic bombardment, explaining it as it was at the time: a crisis-driven effort to overcome battered assumptions and unanticipated problems that, on several occasions, nearly brought the entire enterprise to

---

2 Portal to Churchill, 2 October 1941, folder 2, The Papers of Lord Portal of Hungerford, Christ Church Library, Oxford (hereafter Portal Papers).

a crashing halt. Using chronology as a framework, I shall discuss several themes, including: pre-war expectations for bombing; urgent technological innovation; changing theories of victory; ongoing battles over resources and grand strategy; the vast burdens placed on the shoulders of those who fought in the air; the escalatory nature of the air war over time; and the moral freight burdening a campaign that weighed so heavily on civilians. Though the chapter will focus on the European theatre, it will also cover the American bomber campaign against Japan – a campaign that deserves to have a higher profile in public memory than it currently does.

Expectations for long-range bombing

The First World War had seen rudimentary tests of aircraft in nearly all the military roles they would play later in the twentieth century. While the air war of 1914–18 captured public imagination, it remained a sideshow in a conflict dominated by long-range artillery and machine guns. Many of the belligerent nations engaged in limited versions of what would come to be called 'strategic bombing' – the attack of enemy assets well behind the lines of battle. The Americans watched these efforts closely and designed a campaign that would have been implemented had the war lasted into 1919. By the war's conclusion, it was manifestly clear to all observers that aeroplanes would be an integral part of the landscape of future combat, even if the precise nature of their future roles was hotly disputed. Early advocates for air force independence and long-range bombing, including Guilio Douhet, Billy Mitchell and Sir Hugh Trenchard, warned that those nations failing to pay suitable attention to the future of air power – bombing, in particular – would do so at their own peril.

German long-range aerial attacks on Britain, made first by zeppelins and later by aircraft, had prompted a dramatic reorganization of the British defence structure in 1917–18, featuring the creation of an independent Royal Air Force (RAF). British policy-makers had felt themselves pressured by a domestic population that demanded better defences and retaliatory raids against German aerial invaders. This experience shaped the thinking of British elites; indeed, Trenchard, who would oversee those retaliatory attacks and later become post-war Chief of Air Staff, would argue that in a future war, the first goal would be to wage an immediate aerial offensive to push the enemy on to the defensive and into a downward spiral, leading to inevitable defeat. Needing to justify his under-resourced First World War bombing campaign, Trenchard emphasized the psychological impact of bombing. If this was an institutional survival tactic, it also reflected his Edwardian perspective, which prioritized offensive action and assumed that urban populations would do poorly under aerial attack. His rhetoric helped to give the RAF a rationale for independent existence, and articulated a deterrent threat (if a vague one) to Britain's potential enemies.[3]

When Hitler came to power in the early 1930s and dispensed with the constraints imposed by the Versailles Treaty, the young RAF was forced to design a hurried rearmament scheme, and to operationalize a largely untested body of assumptions about the nature and utility of strategic bombing. This meant deciding which aircraft to build (and for which purposes), and working out – in detail – the ways in which they would contribute to victory. This effort had to be undertaken in the exceedingly tense and conflicted environment of the late interwar years, while bombers were being employed by Italians in Ethiopia, Germans in Spain, and Japanese in China. Popular worries about aerial gas attack, and vivid newsreel images in the cinema, ensured that the late 1930s would be lived in 'the shadow of the bomber'.[4]

In 1936, the RAF's metropolitan command structure was reorganized around four divisions: Bomber Command, Fighter Command, Coastal Command and Training Command. As RAF planners began to envision ways that air power would contribute to a future war effort, the Air Ministry hastily developed the prototypes that would become the bulk of the long-range bomber force after 1942. Other types were in the works as well. De Havilland's fast and sleek Comet, built originally for the interwar Melbourne air race, would evolve in 1940 into the Mosquito – one of the most capable and versatile aeroplanes of the war.[5]

Through the late 1930s, the British played a nervous game of catch-up, trying to stay in step with the Luftwaffe in order to deter German aggression or manipulation.[6] But as RAF leaders began to take a hard look at their actual readiness for war, they found the situation disquieting indeed. Taking the helm of Bomber Command in 1937, Sir Edgar Ludlow-Hewitt found his organization to be 'entirely unprepared for war, unable to operate except

---

3 For more detail, see Tami Davis Biddle, *Rhetoric and Reality in Air Warfare: The Evolution of British and American Thinking about Strategic Bombing, 1914–1945* (Princeton, NJ: Princeton University Press, 2002), pp. 35–62, 69–94.

4 The phrase is drawn from Uri Bialer, *The Shadow of the Bomber* (London: Royal Historical Society, 1980).

5 Sir Charles Webster and Noble Frankland, *The Strategic Air Offensive Against Germany* (4 vols., London: HMSO, 1961), vol. I, p. 72.

6 For insights, see Wesley K. Wark, *The Ultimate Enemy: British Intelligence and Nazi Germany, 1933–1939* (Ithaca, NY: Cornell University Press, 1985).

in fair weather, and extremely vulnerable both in the air and on the ground'.[7] The RAF lacked adequate aircraft and had paid insufficient attention, in particular, to navigation and target acquisition methods. Indeed, in the two years prior to the outbreak of war, there were 478 forced landings due to pilots losing their way.[8] These unnerving revelations could hardly have stiffened the spine of Prime Minister Neville Chamberlain as he entered the Munich crisis in the late summer of 1938. But the stomach-churning anxiety that the crisis produced, including efforts to dig sheltering trenches in London's parks, at least put an end to the atmosphere of denial and political infighting that had hindered the British response to Hitler.

American political leaders watched from a wary distance, determined that they would not be drawn into another protracted and costly conflict. After the First World War, the US Army had been pared back dramatically. Despite the vigorous efforts of Billy Mitchell, American airmen did not win their independence. Over time, though, they managed to carve out some space for themselves. At the Air Corps Tactical School in Alabama (which thumbed its nose at the US Army with its motto, 'We Progress Unhindered by Tradition'), forward thinkers began to examine the possibilities for air warfare, envisioning ways in which long-range bombers might bring an enemy to its knees without attritional ground warfare.[9]

Distanced from the emotionally charged atmosphere of Europe, the Americans could afford to view long-range bombing through a rather more antiseptic lens. They were influenced by concepts that had, in fact, first been articulated by the RAF's Air Staff in 1918. These assessed an enemy in economic terms, seeking out 'bottleneck' targets that, when bombed, would unravel the enemy's war-making ability.[10] The 'Industrial Fabric' theory, as it later came to be called in the USA, was meant to be an economically efficient approach that eschewed the ugliness and moral reprehensibility of attacks on

---

7 Quoted material from John Terraine, *A Time for Courage* (New York: MacMillan, 1985), p. 82 (published in the UK as *The Right of the Line* (London: Hodder & Stoughton, 1985)). On interwar navigation, see Webster and Frankland, *Strategic Air Offensive*, vol. 1, esp. pp. 60–1, 110–14.

8 Terraine, *A Time for Courage*, pp. 83–4; also AIR 41/39, TNA; Webster and Frankland, *Strategic Air Offensive*, vol. 1, pp. 91, 101.

9 Biddle, *Rhetoric and Reality*, pp. 128–47; Peter Faber, 'Interwar US Army Aviation and the Air Corps Tactical School: Incubators of American Air Power', in Phillip Meilinger (ed.), *The Paths of Heaven: The Evolution of Airpower Theory* (Maxwell Air Force Base, Ala.: Air University Press, 1997), pp. 183–238; Stephen McFarland, *America's Pursuit of Precision Bombing, 1910–1945* (Washington DC: Smithsonian Institution Press, 1995).

10 George K. Williams, '"The Shank of the Drill": Americans and Strategic Aviation in the Great War', *Journal of Strategic Studies* 19:3 (September 1996), 381–431.

centres of population. The creation of a long-range bomber designed to intercept seaborne threats to US shores, the B-17 'Flying Fortress', and the development of a technically sophisticated bombsight, seemed to give the means of practical expression to this set of ideas. Long-range bombers flying in self-defending groups, in daylight, would seek out and attack vital 'key node' industries and resources.

When, after the Munich crisis, President Franklin Roosevelt began casting about for a deterrent threat that might protect US interests and reduce the need for direct US involvement in war, he was drawn to the long-range bomber. In 1938, he asked Congress for $300 million for national defence, with a priority for the Air Corps. In the first half of 1939, Congress approved a programme to procure 3,251 aircraft, and to increase the strength of the enlisted force by 150 per cent.[11] Like the British, however, the Americans devoted too little attention to the operational underpinnings of their theory, including the ability of crews to find their way to targets, and to bomb accurately once arriving there.

Inauspicious beginnings

When Hitler moved into Poland in the late summer of 1939, the RAF was still scrambling to prepare for war. As grim reality descended, the British Chiefs of Staff sought to leverage their limited assets for near-term survival, while seeking to build the means of future victory. During the first two years of the war, Bomber Command crews lacked the instruments and skills they needed to do what was asked of them. The very limited air campaign they carried out in the autumn and winter of 1939 exposed a daunting fact: they could not operate effectively in daylight due to the strength of German defences. This meant adopting the highly challenging expedient of flying to targets under cover of night.[12] When, in 1940, the German spring offensive extended the range of Hitler's control to the edge of Western Europe, the RAF faced another crisis: the English Channel was now the only buffer between Britain and the Luftwaffe. Germany had vastly extended its defensive perimeter, while Bomber Command, in order to reach German territory, had to fly for hours over decidedly unfriendly skies.

11 Wesley Frank Craven and James Lea Cate (eds.), *The Army Air Forces in World War II*, vol. 1: *Plans and Early Operations, January 1939 to August 1942* (7 vols., Washington DC: Office of Air Force History, 1983 [1948]), p. 104; Robert Dallek, *Franklin Roosevelt and American Foreign Policy, 1932–1945* (New York: Oxford University Press, 1979), pp. 171–5.
12 Webster and Frankland, *Strategic Air Offensive*, vol. 1, pp. 129–32.

In May 1940, in the midst of the crisis that brought him to power, Prime Minister Churchill argued that Britain should fight on rather than negotiate; he rested his case partly on the potential of the bomber. An aerial enthusiast and interwar advocate for air power, Churchill nonetheless harboured concerns, expressed eloquently back in 1917, about the ability of bombers to break civilian will.[13] In 1940, he hoped that bombers could be made into tools capable of undermining the enemy war economy, and that they could work synergistically with other instruments to coerce the Nazi regime. By embracing strategic air power, he was betting on an untried horse, but this seemed preferable to a repeat of the Western Front battles of the First World War, or to seeking terms with a man who had proven that he would not be bound by them. Churchill resolved to leverage Britain's strengths as well as he could while waiting for US help, and for Germany's internal weaknesses to work against her.[14]

Not wishing to draw an unrestricted air war upon themselves, the British sought to confine their air attacks to specific military targets.[15] But as the new head of Bomber Command, Sir Charles Portal, soon discovered, finding and hitting such targets at night was so difficult as to make the task a questionable use of limited resources; indeed, the bombing was so erratic that the Germans could rarely discern the intended targets. Bomber Command crews were wholly at the mercy of primitive navigation techniques and fickle north European weather. Crews were sent into the night with astro-sextants, maps and directional radio; they were expected, in essence, to find their way about by observation. As the British official historians would later point out, laconically, Bomber Command was, in the early years of the war, being defeated by 'the law that we cannot see in the dark'.[16]

In the summer and autumn of 1940, the Germans waged a pitched battle for control of British air space; but a determined and adaptive effort by

---

13 Churchill, 'Munitions Possibilities of 1918', reprinted in H. A. Jones, *The War in the Air* (Oxford University Press, 1937), Appendix IV, p. 19.

14 David Reynolds, 'Churchill and the British Decision to Fight On: Right Policy, Wrong Reasons', in R. Langhorne (ed.), *Diplomacy and Intelligence During the Second World War* (Cambridge University Press, 1985), pp. 156–7.

15 There is an ongoing debate over who started the escalatory ladder of attacks on cities; what is clear is that emotion and misperception shaped behaviour. German air attacks on Warsaw (1939) and Rotterdam (1940) were interpreted by the British as city bombing, even if the Germans intended them as integral parts of combined arms operations (not attacks on cities per se). Equally, the Germans perceived RAF attacks on the North Sea coast and Ruhr-Rhineland areas, beginning in May 1940, as provocative. See Richard Overy, *The Bombing War: Europe 1939–1945* (London: Allen Lane, 2013), pp. 83–9.

16 Webster and Frankland, *Strategic Air Offensive*, vol. I, p. 383. On 3 April 1940, Portal succeeded Sir Edgar Ludlow-Hewitt.

Fighter Command kept the Luftwaffe at bay.[17] Had the pivotal 'Battle of Britain' been lost, the island nation could not have played the central role it would play for the remainder of the war: the primary staging area for Anglo-Canadian-American air, sea and land campaigns. Interestingly, Germany's failure in the contest did not seem to give pause to those in Britain advocating a British bombing campaign against Germany. As one historian explained, '[T]he Air Staff, and indeed the government, were sustained by a faith wholly at variance with the known facts of the situation.'[18] But reality would continue to intrude on this grasping optimism.

While the Germans did not possess an integrated air defence system so sophisticated as the one protecting Britain, they nonetheless possessed the essential components: an observer network for reporting incursions; early warning radar (Freya); and an outstanding fighter, the Messerschmitt Bf 109. They also had substantial numbers of good flak guns, searchlights, sound detectors and visual ranging apparatus. Early in the war, they would also deploy a fire-control radar (Würzburg).[19] In response to Britain's night attacks in early 1940, Colonel (later General) Josef Kammhuber was tasked with creating a reliable night air defence system; the British came to call it 'the Kammhuber Line'. Sound detector crews and Freya radars provided early warning, while Würzburg radars controlled fighters and flak batteries. Searchlights were extended from Denmark to northern France. Making do with modifications to the Bf 110, and employing Dornier and Heinkel aeroplanes, the Luftwaffe built itself a night-fighting system that, subsequently, would be updated according to the challenges posed by British bombers.[20]

Acutely aware of the terrible limits on Bomber Command's capabilities at the time, Sir Charles Portal gradually began to argue for 'area raids', designed to erode German will and impose indirect costs on the German

17 The British were able to insert radar into a sophisticated air defence network that they had largely worked out during the First World War. See John Ferris, 'Airbandit: C3I and Strategic Air Defence during the First Battle of Britain, 1915–1918', in M. Dockrill and D. French (eds.), *Strategy and Intelligence: British Policy During the First World War* (London: Hambledon and London, 1996), pp. 23–66; and John Ferris, 'Fighter Defence before Fighter Command: The Rise of Strategic Air Defence in Great Britain', *Journal of Military History* 63:4 (October 1999), pp. 845–84.

18 Sebastian Cox, 'The Sources and Organization of RAF Intelligence', in Horst Boog (ed.), *The Conduct of the Air War in the Second World War* (New York: Berg, 1992), p. 577.

19 Flak is actually an acronym for *Fliegerabwehrkanone*, or air defence artillery.

20 For a concise survey of German defences, see W. A. Jacobs, 'The British Strategic Air Offensive Against Germany in World War II', in R. Cargill Hall (ed.), *Case Studies in Strategic Bombardment* (Washington DC: Air Force History and Museums Program, 1998), pp. 113–18. Also Donald Caldwell and Richard Muller, *The Luftwaffe over Germany* (London: Greenhill, 2007), pp. 42–7.

war effort. Although much less discriminate than attacks on specific industries or locations, these might at least be operationally feasible. If these raids could have a discernible impact on Germany, they might justify the blood and treasure they required, and give Britain more time to edge her way out of a supreme emergency. Elevated to Chief of Air Staff in October 1940, Portal would gain overall responsibility for the bombing campaign, and for its coordination with other instruments of military power.

Launched on the heels of the Battle of Britain, the Luftwaffe's aerial 'Blitz' of 1940–41 created more room for Portal to advocate a new approach. In London, the daily spectacle of bombed-out houses, displaced families, unexploded bombs crews and casualty service stretchers made it manifestly clear that Britain was in the throes of total war. Churchill believed that keeping national morale high would demand that Britain return the blows she was receiving.[21] On 16 December 1940, while London was being pummelled by the Luftwaffe, Bomber Command set off for the city of Mannheim.[22]

The German attack on the Soviet Union in June 1941, and its implications for a vast expansion of German resources, only increased the pressure on Portal and his crews. But more bad news was soon to follow. No fewer than 107 aircraft were lost in July and August. In the latter month, the British undertook a comprehensive photographic evaluation of their bombing accuracy. The jarring result, which Bomber Command leaders had trouble accepting, was that only about one in five bombers was getting within five miles of its target.[23] The Prime Minister, left despondent by the figures, lashed out at Portal in September; he suggested, sarcastically, that Bomber Command was fated to be little more than a 'heavy and. . .seriously increasing annoyance' to Germany. But since he declined to shift to an army-oriented strategy, the demands on Portal were clear: use the bombers as expediently as possible in the near term, while investing in the tools and techniques to support dramatic improvement.[24]

21 Referring to the British, historian Noble Frankland argued: 'The great immorality open to us. . .was to lose the war against Hitler's Germany. To have abandoned the only means of direct attack which we had at our disposal would have been a long step in that direction'. Frankland quoted by John Terraine in the latter's speech to the RAF Historical Society, 16 March 1987, reprinted in *Proceedings of the RAF Historical Society* 2 (1987), 24.

22 Webster and Frankland, *Strategic Air Offensive*, vol. 1, p. 215. This British raid, aimed at a city centre, came in the aftermath of the attack on Coventry.

23 The analysis was known as the 'Butt Report', after the civil servant who lead it. Ibid., p. 178.

24 Churchill to Portal, 27 September 1941, and Portal to Churchill, 2 October 1941, folder 2c, Portal Papers.

Assigned to attack Stuttgart and Karlsruhe on 1 October, Bomber Command aircraft were reported wandering over twenty-seven other cities, from Aachen to Chemnitz.[25] Navigation and target finding were, for obvious reasons, high on a list of urgent priorities. Portal accelerated the development of such new tools as marker bombs and powerful incendiaries; he developed crew skills (to include training 'expert fire-raising crews'); and he pushed forward with a vast expansion of capable heavy bombers. The Chief of Air Staff realized only too well that crews were struggling to guide inadequate machines on missions that were beyond their technical capacity to perform. The Chief of Air Staff also continued to modify targeting policy; a disastrous raid in early November 1941 prompted him to lean even more heavily toward area bombing, and to conclude that he would need a new head of Bomber Command.[26]

The gloves come off

During 1941, the British had endured serial setbacks on battlefields around the world. Entering 1942, they would face another daunting challenge to the homeland itself, as German U-boats threatened to cut the island off entirely from its overseas lifelines: staggering shipping losses seemed to be the hangman's noose around Britain's neck.[27] On 14 February 1942, Bomber Command came under a new directive authorizing attacks on area targets with the aim of undermining the 'morale of the enemy civil population and in particular of the industrial workers'. This approach was not devoid of an economic element: by 'de-housing' workers, the RAF would seek to erode German output and productivity.[28] But this dramatic decision, embraced at a

---

25 Webster and Frankland, *Strategic Air Offensive*, vol. i, pp. 185, 302.

26 Ibid., p. 399. Bomber Command lost thirty-seven aircraft on the night of 7 November. Portal feared that Bomber Command's chief, Sir Richard Peirse, had not respected the advice of his meteorologists. But one cannot easily accuse Peirse of naivety, since he had remarked, in February 1941, that 'A bomber commander has to be a meteorologist first and a strategist second'. Peirse's luck, a commodity hard to come by for any British commander in 1941, had run out.

27 As the number of U-boats available to Germany grew, their range was increased by the introduction of refuelling subs. Allied merchant fleets would lose 7.8 million tons to the submarine threat in 1942. Every element of the Allied war effort was imperilled by this fact. See Paul M. Kennedy, *Engineers of Victory* (New York: Random House, 2013), pp. 7, 21; R. J. Overy, *Why the Allies Won* (London: Jonathan Cape, 1995), p. 45.

28 The full text of the 14 February 1942 directive is in Sir Charles Webster and Noble Frankland, *The Strategic Air Offensive Against Germany*, vol. iv: *Annexes and Appendices* (4 vols., London: HMSO, 1961), pp. 143–7. The decision predated the arrival of Sir Arthur Harris. The bombing directives were the responsibility of the Chiefs of Staff (later the Combined Chiefs of Staff), overseen by the British and American governments.

dire moment, leaned toward a Trenchardian emphasis on the psychological impact of bombing, and pulled sharply away from the just war ideal of discrimination between combatants and non-combatants.

Since Portal genuinely believed that area bombing offered the best (indeed the only) prospect for achieving results at that point in time, he viewed the directive as a necessary expedient in a crisis. And he knew he needed the most capable field commander he could find. Neither he nor anyone else in the Air Ministry was under any illusions about Sir Arthur Harris. Brusque, opinionated and outspoken, Harris was nonetheless an able commander with a penchant for solving problems. He was technologically savvy, and had crucial experience as the head of Bomber Command's No. 5 Group. But Harris was also stubborn, and disinclined to work well with the other services. Portal judged that his strengths outweighed his weaknesses at that point in time, and so it fell to Harris to restore the morale of Bomber Command crews and make good on the nation's investment in bombing. When he took command, a week after the 14 February directive had been issued, the task on his plate was immense in both scope and intensity; he felt the weight upon his shoulders.[29]

Official questions swirled around Bomber Command in 1941 and 1942.[30] For his part, Harris had concluded that unceasing attacks on German cities – the hubs of German economic, political and military activity – offered the greatest opportunity for long-range bombing. To Harris, cities were the sinews of strength and communication that made modern warfare possible. His instinct found support in a March 1942 paper by Churchill's scientific advisor, Lord Cherwell, asserting that the aerial bombing of Germany's fifty-eight main cities would be decisive. The paper, which would later prove to be controversial and hotly criticized by other scientists, offered some good news to the Prime Minister at a particularly fraught moment in the war. Both Portal and Secretary of State for Air, Sir Archibald Sinclair, lent support to its conclusions. In early March, Sinclair had emphasized that Bomber Command was 'the only force upon which we can call in this year, 1942, to strike deadly blows at the heart of Germany'.[31]

Harris set to work immediately to silence the critics. On assumption of command, he had only fourteen heavy bomber squadrons; only two were

---

29 T. D. Biddle, 'Bombing by the Square Yard: Sir Arthur Harris at War, 1942–1945', *International History Review* 21:3 (September 1999), 626–64.
30 The Singleton Report, for instance, investigated Bomber Command in 1941–42. See Webster and Frankland, *Strategic Air Offensive*, vol. 1, pp. 338–9.
31 For the Cherwell Report and the Sinclair quote, see ibid., pp. 330–6.

Lancaster squadrons (neither one operational yet). Since he believed he could make headway only if he had mass and momentum, he argued for an expansion of his front-line strength.[32] Over the next three months, Harris would test the radio navigation aid GEE, marker aircraft techniques, and the possibilities inherent in heavy, concentrated raids. To swamp German defences, mitigate the losses among his crews and maximize the damage achieved per sortie, he sought to send a concentrated force through a narrow point. This approach, which the Prime Minister embraced, proved the basis for the development and implementation of the first 'thousand bomber' raids of 1942.[33]

Since Harris did not have the first-line resources needed to mount attacks of this scale, he used portions of his force that would not normally participate in such operations; by putting his training resources into the fight – including instructor pilots and students – he was jeopardizing the future of his force. The risks were immense, but Harris believed they were necessary, not only to work out the operational methods for a way forward, but also to determine if the bombers justified the resources being invested in them. If the strategists serving the Prime Minister were to have faith in long-range bombardment, then the bombers had to make their case.[34]

On 30 May, Harris ordered his force to Cologne. The route out would be stormy, and visibility would complicate the return journey; an interval of clear weather over the city, though, might offer the crews a chance for a first big victory. In the end, some 600 acres of Cologne, including 300 in the centre of the city, were completely destroyed. The losses, 3.8 per cent of the attacking force, were not unsustainable. Bomber Command had a triumph, and the press had a victory to celebrate.[35] The results quieted many of the critics, and, along with similar raids in June, were enough to convince Harris to make a strong case directly to the Prime Minister. Explaining that Britain was at a strategic crossroads, he held out the opportunity for 'victory, speedy and complete', if Churchill would commit to the 'proper' use of air power. In Harris's mind, this meant a rapid build-up of air assets, and a priority for

32 AIR 41/42, p. 8, TNA. Harris was aggrieved by the large number of aircraft that had been, in his mind, 'diverted' to supporting roles for the Navy and Army; but what he termed 'diversions' were, in the eyes of most others, crucial elements of the war effort.

33 Webster and Frankland, *Strategic Air Offensive*, vol. 1, pp. 382, 402. On the wartime accomplishments of British industry, science and production, see, generally, David Edgerton, *Britain's War Machine* (New York: Oxford University Press, 2011).

34 The British official historians wrote: 'The decision could only be taken by a commander endowed with exceptional courage and resolution'; Webster and Frankland, *Strategic Air Offensive*, vol. 1, p. 404.

35 Ibid., pp. 407–10.

long-range bombing over other wartime aerial tasks. When Churchill met Stalin in August 1942, he was able to temper the news of a delayed second front with reports of Bomber Command's progress.[36]

Bomber Command's progress also gave Portal ammunition for the important discussions on strategy held by the British military Chiefs of Staff in the autumn of 1942, in preparation for negotiations with the Americans at Casablanca early in 1943. The attack on Pearl Harbor, late in 1941, had finally drawn the Americans into the war (to Churchill's great relief). But in the summer of 1942, the Americans were just beginning a very limited air offensive in Europe; they would not strike German territory until January 1943. The usual problems of standing up a new force were exacerbated by production delays, the strategic commitment to the North Africa campaign, the demands of the Pacific War, and north European weather.[37] Despite this, the Americans were outspoken about the potential of their campaign, disparaging of British efforts, and inclined to draw comparisons between themselves and the British which placed the latter in an unflattering light. And they managed all this before they had done much more than venture, tentatively, over French airspace. Expressing unfettered optimism about the prospects for daylight 'precision' bombing against German targets, the first field commander of the American strategic air forces, Brigadier General Ira Eaker, head of the US Eighth Bomber Command, wrote: 'I believe it is clearly demonstrated that the efficiency of day bombardment over night bombardment is in the order of ten to one'.[38] If this was irksome to the British, it was also worrying.

Churchill felt the Americans had far too much faith in daylight bombing. In October, he warned Roosevelt's special assistant, Harry Hopkins, against committing too fully to producing bombers suited only to daylight work.[39] But the Americans, attached to their own theory – and certain they could

---

36 Overy, *Why the Allies Won*, pp. 101–3.

37 In the autumn of 1942, support for the North Africa invasion (TORCH) was made a first priority for the American long-range bombers. That invasion hinged on the safe passage of men and materiel across the Atlantic, which could be guaranteed only if German submarines were prevented from wreaking havoc at will. Thus submarine pens in western France were given targeting priority, but their concrete reinforcement made them largely impervious to Allied attacks. And while the bomber commanders understood this, the sub problem seemed so urgent that strategic priorities trumped tactical realities, leading to frustration all around. Craven and Cate (eds.), *Army Air Forces*, vol. I, pp. 237–9.

38 Letter, Eaker to Spaatz, 8 October 1942, Papers of Carl A. Spaatz, Diary, Library of Congress Manuscript Room, Washington DC.

39 Letter, Churchill to Hopkins, 16 October 1942, AIR 8/711, TNA. Churchill wrote: 'Whether the Fortresses and Liberators will be able to bomb far into Germany by day is one of the great tactical questions of the war and one that is at present unanswered'.

succeed where their allies had not – clung to their tactics. In the event, Churchill's worries were well-founded: the Americans would struggle throughout 1942–43.

During these early years, the British and American bombing campaigns rested heavily on the courage and fortitude of the crews, including their willingness to face – on a daily basis – the prospect of violent death or maiming. The early bombers, which were not pressurized, were cramped and uncomfortable; they were freezing cold and ear-splittingly loud. The tail-gunner on a Lancaster crammed himself into a space not much bigger than a garbage can, and the ball-turret gunner on a B-17 wedged himself into a sphere that hung precariously beneath the belly of the plane. The chest-high spar running through the Lancaster made moving around the aircraft difficult, especially in emergencies. The bumps, swerves, noise and havoc that were commonplace on bomber raids caused magnetic compasses to swing aimlessly and gyro-compasses to topple. And the available instruments did not give true readings: air speed indicators had to be corrected for position error, temperature and altitude; altimeters for barometric pressure; magnetic compasses for the magnetic field of the earth; and gyro-compasses for wander caused by the spin of the earth. Throughout the Second World War, no radar device was developed that served as a complete substitute for dead reckoning. But dead reckoning navigation was dependent on frequent calculation of the ground position of the aircraft, and this in turn depended on accurate assessments of the wind vector, which were notoriously difficult to obtain. Working with pencils and slide rules, navigators nonetheless had to make these calculations quickly and precisely, since planes could travel many miles off-course in minutes.[40]

Crews were drilled in the proper functioning of their oxygen systems, not least because those suffering anoxia have, ironically, a sense of well-being and even euphoria as death draws near. Tragically, many wounded aircraft that made it back to friendly airspace could not manage a safe landing, and many lives were lost on and around British airfields, despite the best efforts of ground crews to constantly improve emergency procedures. Many times, these crashes resulted from the thick soup of fog plus smoke (smog) from the coal fires that fuelled homes and power stations in wartime Britain. And take-offs could be as treacherous as landings, since aircraft operated right on the edge of their envelopes for fuel and ordnance weight; indeed, take-off crashes were

---

40 On navigation and technological aids to it, see Webster and Frankland, *Strategic Air Offensive*, vol. IV, Appendix I, 'The Principal Aids to Navigation and Bomb Aiming'.

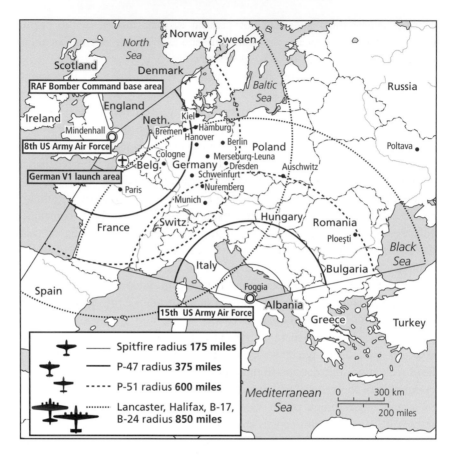

17.1 Allied strategic air campaign against Germany

notoriously fatal, due to the fireball produced by a plane packed full of aviation gas and explosives. Needless to say, burns were common injuries for flying crews.

A year of determination and despair

At the Casablanca Conference in January 1943, unresolved differences over how to prosecute the Anglo-American bombing campaign led to a 'round the clock' bombing strategy that allowed Britain and the USA to go their separate ways. A masterpiece of ambiguity and compromise, the 'Casablanca Directive' stated that 'the primary object will be the progressive destruction and dislocation of the German military, industrial, and economic system, and the undermining of the morale of the German people to a point where their capacity for armed resistance is fatally weakened'.[41] In the spring, the Anglo-American military chiefs made the German fighter industry the first priority of the bombing campaign. Defeat of the Luftwaffe would be a crucial step toward victory in that it would help to unravel Germany's ability to fight offensively, and to defend herself. The POINTBLANK Directive called for US Eighth Air Force daylight raids to be complemented by Bomber Command night attacks on nearby industrial areas.[42]

In 1943, Bomber Command would profoundly increase the destructiveness of its offensive. The Blenheim, Whitley and Hampden aircraft of the early years had been retired in 1942, after proving themselves remarkably unsuited to their task. The Manchester, which had a brief and disastrous operational career, was withdrawn in June 1942. Taking their place were Halifaxes, Stirlings and Lancasters – though only the latter would fully live up to the expectations held for it. In every regard (range, ease of flying, reliability and sturdiness), the Lancaster was a superior aircraft, and it quickly became the backbone of the force.

The focal point of Bomber Command's effort in early 1943 was the Ruhr region. Improved navigational and target-finding aids, including Oboe and H2S, and target indicator bombs, provided key tools for 'Pathfinder' aircraft – manned with particularly able crews – who would find and mark targets for follow-on forces.[43] Beginning in March, Harris's forces delivered pummelling raids on the Ruhr's cities. Ongoing advances in finding and attacking targets enabled Bomber Command to breach the Möhne and Eder dams in May. Indeed, in 1943, Bomber Command had worked out the essential choreography of what would be called the 'Newhaven' method of attack, wherein H2S illumination would facilitate visual ground marking of the target by target indicator bombs. This, in turn, would be reinforced by further marking and guiding for the benefit of the follow-on attackers. The continual refinement of this technique over time would lead, ultimately, to some of the most devastating bombing of the war.[44]

41 Webster and Frankland, *Strategic Air Offensive*, vol. I, pp. 378–9.
42 Biddle, *Rhetoric and Reality*, pp. 217–18.
43 For the debate over Pathfinders, see Sebastian Cox, 'Sir Arthur Harris and the Air Ministry', in Sebastian Cox and Peter Gray (eds.), *Air Power Leadership: Theory and Practice* (London: The Stationery Office, 2002), pp. 218–20.
44 Sir Charles Webster and Noble Frankland, *The Strategic Air Offensive Against Germany*, vol. II: *Endeavour* (4 vols., London: HMSO, 1961), pp. 108–37, 168–89.

Until recently, the contribution of the Ruhr campaign had been underestimated in the literature of the Second World War. It is now clear, however, that the campaign was crucial in keeping a lid on German industrial production at a pivotal moment in the war. The Ruhr valley was essential to Germany not only for the coking of coal and steel, but also for the production of intermediate components for the war economy. Bomber Command raids forced Germany's Supply Minister, Albert Speer, to travel to the region multiple times in an effort to stiffen worker morale. Indeed, the Ruhr region was given the status of a combat zone within the homeland: a special emergency staff had the authority to move and redeploy workers from factory to factory, like troops moving around a battlefield. The Ruhr campaign commenced just as Speer had launched an effort to bolster steel and ammunition production. But far from seeing increases in these realms, the German central planning office saw steel production face a shortfall of 400,000 tons. The ammunition programme had to be cut on the eve of crucial Russo-German battles on the Eastern Front, and the decline in subcomponents hampered the production of aircraft.[45]

In July 1943, during multiple raids over Hamburg, Bomber Command achieved unprecedented levels of destruction. This was facilitated not only by the effective use of H2S, but also by an innovation called 'Window', thin aluminium strips dropped from bombers to confuse German radar-based defences. RAF incendiary bombs produced fires far more extensive than anything previously seen in the history of warfare. Some 40,000 died in a campaign that destroyed 250,000 homes, and drove 900,000 souls to panic and flight.[46]

At Bomber Command headquarters, Harris kept oversized volumes, the 'Blue Books', which offered a direct insight into his theory of strategic bombardment. Each major town in Germany was assigned a 'key point rating', which was an index of its overall industrial importance. Each town was portrayed as a circle whose area varied with its key point rating, and each circle was divided into coloured segments, showing the proportion of various main groups of industry making up the whole. The diagrams,

---

45 Adam Tooze, *The Wages of Destruction: The Making and Breaking of the Nazi War Economy* (London: Allen Lane, 2006), p. 598: 'Bomber Command had stopped Speer's armaments miracle in its tracks'.

46 Ibid., pp. 601, 603. On the battle of Hamburg, see Webster and Frankland, *Strategic Air Offensive*, vol. II, pp. 138–67; *Germany and the Second World War*, vol. VII: *The Strategic Air War in Europe and the War in the West and East Asia, 1943–1944/5* (10 vols., Oxford: Clarendon Press, 2006), pp. 46–55, 203–4.

constantly updated, also indicated the proportion of a town's inhabitants directly engaged in or dependent on its industries, and the area of the town that Bomber Command had destroyed to date.[47]

The goal that drove Harris, night after night, was the devastation of enough of Germany's cities to force Hitler to sue for terms. He did not, however, have the luxury of concentrating fully on this objective. The Battle of the Atlantic and the ground campaign in Italy pulled bombers into other theatres. And British worries about German weapons development prompted a dramatic Bomber Command attack on the V ('vengeance') weapons site at Peenemünde in August 1943. Still, the progress that Bomber Command made through the year, in particular the results at Hamburg, convinced Harris that a concentrated attack on Berlin might be the masterstroke needed to finish the war in Europe. He said as much to Churchill in a letter of 3 November 1943.[48]

Had Harris realized at the time just how much his Ruhr attacks had put Germany on the ropes, he might not have been so seduced by the magnetism of Berlin. In any event, he might have been given pause by the indifferent results achieved against the heavily defended city in late August and early September. In one of these, on 23–24 August, the Germans shot down 8 per cent of the attacking force. The vast inland conurbation of Berlin presented the H2S operator with what the official historians have described as a 'blaze of incomprehensible light'.[49] This formidable problem was compounded by improvements in German defences, including new weapons, improved fighter tactics, and the dramatic expansion of flak defences. Of the new weapons, the most deadly was *Schrage Musik*, 20 mm twin cannon mounted on the cockpit or fuselage, and oriented upward, diagonally, at a seventy-degree angle. This cannon, which was later complemented by a radar gunsight, allowed German fighters to slip in under an enemy bomber unobserved and fire upward from a safe position. It was a frightening addition to the

47 Biddle, *Rhetoric and Reality*, pp. 217–18.
48 Webster and Frankland, *Strategic Air Offensive*, vol. II, p. 190; Max Hastings, *Bomber Command* (New York: Dial Press, 1979), pp. 245–6.
49 Webster and Frankland, *Strategic Air Offensive*, vol. II, p. 163. The weather, especially during the winter, when Bomber Command had the long nights it needed for deep penetrations into Germany, remained treacherous. Berlin – with its flak guns, search-lights, stone and plaster construction, and wide boulevards – had a natural impervious-ness to the toughest raids. In *Wages of Destruction*, Adam Tooze concludes: 'The Ruhr was the chokepoint and in 1943 it was within the RAF's grip. The failure to maintain that hold and to tighten it was a tragic operational error' (p. 602). See also Greenhous et al., *The Official History of the Royal Canadian Air Force*, vol. III, pp. 689–728; *Germany and the Second World War*, vol. VII, p. 206.

Luftwaffe's night-fighter repertoire, which also came to include a tactic known as *Wilde Sau* (wild boar), which allowed single-engined fighters to make independent attacks (uncontrolled by Kammhuber radar stations) on Allied bombers over German targets, using illumination from searchlights. It also allowed them to move quickly and rove from point to point, as needed. In a raid over Cologne and Mulheim on 3–4 July 1943, just twelve defenders using these tactics accounted for sixteen of the thirty bombers shot down. The tactic claimed another forty bombers over Berlin on 17–18 August.[50] But if the overall numbers were substantial, they might have been far worse if Hitler, fixated on Russia, had not denied the further intensification of German defences urgently sought by General Kammhuber.[51]

In any event, the great Berlin victory that Harris fought for, from November 1943 until March 1944, eluded him. While the Lancasters suffered, the Halifaxes and Stirlings – which were unable to reach similar altitudes – suffered even more. In January and February of 1944, the Halifax IIs and vs of No. 4 Group endured unsustainable casualty rates of 11 per cent missing against German targets. Historian John Terraine would later compare the Battle of Berlin to the disastrous First World War Battle of Passchendaele, fought in 1917.[52]

Back in the USA, the Navy had interpreted the North African campaign to mean that the pressure for a cross-Channel assault was now reduced; in turn, they argued that aircraft from the European theatre could be moved to the Pacific. Commander-in-Chief of the US Army Air Forces (USAAF), General Henry ('Hap') Arnold, fought fiercely against this interpretation, pointing out that any future invasion of the Reich would be successful only if air supremacy had been won, and Germany had been worn down through bombing. His argument largely won the day, but the first year of war must have seemed long and wearisome to Arnold – all the more so because US aircraft production had fallen badly behind schedule. In order to justify the resources devoted to them, US bomber crews had to produce results. But in January

---

50 *Germany and the Second World War*, vol. VII, pp. 188–9, 204–5. See, generally, Alfred Price, *Instruments of Darkness* (New York: Chas. Scribners, 1978); and R. V. Jones, *The Wizard War* (New York: Coward McCann, 1978).

51 The German official historians detail Hitler's behaviour in this period; see *Germany and the Second World War*, vol. VII, pp. 157–269. Göring was never willing to challenge Hitler.

52 Webster and Frankland, *Strategic Air Offensive*, vol. II, pp. 190–200, 208–9; Webster and Frankland, *Strategic Air Offensive*, vol. IV, Appendix 42, pp. 445–6. The British official historians argued that Berlin was more than a failure, 'it was a defeat'; Webster and Frankland, *Strategic Air Offensive*, vol. II, p. 193. Terraine, *The Right of the Line*, pp. 552–5; also *Germany and the Second World War*, vol. VII, pp. 88–102.

1943, when US crews finally began to fly over Germany, poor weather meant that they carried out only four of the fourteen missions planned for the month.[53]

Throughout 1943, the US campaign against the Luftwaffe fell to the flak guns increasingly assigned to the Western Front, and to German day fighters. The heavy flak forces of the Reich more than doubled during 1943 – as did the number of smokescreen companies and barrage balloon batteries. The Germans also greatly beefed up the number of searchlight batteries in support of *Wilde Sau* tactics; in addition, they invested substantially in creating decoy targets – and large fires – to draw Allied bombers away from real targets.[54] While Luftwaffe day-fighter forces did not increase as much or as rapidly as Fighter General Adolf Galland would have liked, they did increase overall in 1943. In August, Luftwaffe Commander Centre received the largest share of bombers and fighter destroyers coming from new production and repair. Heavily armoured and armed Focke-Wulf 190s were equipped to shoot down four-engined bombers at close range, and even to ram them. A particularly efficacious addition to daytime defence was the addition of two *Zerstorergeschwader*, 26 and 76.[55]

As the Americans searched for a 'bottleneck' target that would undermine the entire German war effort, their attention fell upon the factories around Schweinfurt, which manufactured about half of the total Axis supply of ball bearings.[56] On 17 August 1943, to celebrate the first anniversary of their operations in Europe, the Americans attacked the Schweinfurt anti-friction bearing plants and the Regensburg Messerschmitt factory. It was the largest and costliest mission US bomber crews had flown to date, with 16 per cent of the force shot down. During a second attack on Schweinfurt in October, the losses were even worse. Of the 288 bombers that reached Schweinfurt (of the 320 that set out), 60 were shot down, 5 crashed in England, 122 were damaged and 12 others had to be scrapped; 605 aircrew did not return and 43 came home injured.[57] Indeed, in four raids carried out over six days in October,

53 Craven and Cate (eds.), *Army Air Forces*, vol. I, pp. 274, 281, 288–9, 322.
54 'Target Priorities of the Eighth Air Force', Headquarters Eighth Air Force, 15 May 1945, dec. no. 520.317A, Air Force Historical Research Agency (hereafter AFHRA); Webster and Frankland, *Strategic Air Offensive*, vol. II, p. 27; *Germany and the Second World War*, vol. VII, pp. 217–18.
55 *Germany and the Second World War*, vol. VII, pp. 168–71.
56 Wesley Frank Craven and James Lea Cate (eds.), *The Army Air Forces in World War II*, vol. II: *Europe: Torch to Pointblank, August 1942 to December 1943* (7 vols., Washington DC: Office of Air Force History, 1983 [1949]), pp. 357–8.
57 *Germany and the Second World War*, vol. VII, p. 74.

148 American bombers had failed to return to their bases. And it is certain that these losses would have been even more devastating had Hitler not overruled Galland's pleas to move the dispersed fighters on the periphery to a more efficient centralization, deep inland.[58]

An American essay in the September 1943 *Royal Air Force Quarterly* proved to be especially poorly timed. Written to defend and promote the American bombing effort, the article argued triumphantly that the Americans had 'given the proof' that they could 'hit the target from the sub-stratosphere' and 'defend themselves against enemy fighters well enough to keep losses within reasonable bounds'.[59] While the Anglo-American offensive had forced the Germans to speed the redeployment of fighters and guns westward, providing relief to the Russian front, the American losses had become unsustainable: the autumn disasters finally brought an end to the theory of the self-defending bomber.[60]

In November, General Arnold officially pulled away from a strict reliance on 'precision' bombing, declaring that in bad weather American crews should be prepared to use radar aids to bomb area targets. In practice, this edging away from doctrine – which included an increase in the use of incendiary bombs – had been under way for a while; it took a notable step when the Muenster city centre was selected as a target on 10 October 1943.[61] Arnold's shift, an expedient designed to increase the tempo of the air campaign, closed the distance between the British and American efforts. And it meant the Americans were now novices, with a set of tactics they

---

58 Webster and Frankland, *Strategic Air Offensive*, vol. II, p. 39; Noble Frankland, *The Bombing Offensive Against Germany* (London: Faber and Faber, 1965), p. 77; Craven and Cate (eds.), *Army Air Forces*, vol. II, pp. 681–3, 704; *Germany and the Second World War*, vol. VII, pp. 165–6, 171–2.

59 'The American Bombing Effort', *Royal Air Force Quarterly* 14:4 (September 1943). A US wartime pictorial (written in 1943 and published in February 1944) told its British audience the 'official story' of the US Army Air Forces' first year of fighting. General Arnold wrote: 'In the past twelve months, the men and machines have proved themselves against the fiercest aerial opposition in the world. Thanks to their record, the American idea – high-altitude daylight precision bombing – has come through a period of doubt and experimentation to triumphant vindication'; *Target Germany: The US Army Air Forces' Official Story of the VIII Bomber Command's First Year Over Europe* (London, HMSO, 1944), p. v.

60 Craven and Cate (eds.), *Army Air Forces*, vol. II, p. 708.

61 Memo from the Commanding General, Army Air Forces, 'Combined Chiefs of Staff Air Plan for the Defeat of Germany', 1 November 1943, Papers of Henry H. Arnold, box 39, Library of Congress Manuscript Room, Washington DC. The Muenster city centre was selected – and approved in the tactical mission report – because it was believed that such an attack would kill Reichsbahn workers living there. See *Germany and the Second World War*, vol. VII, p. 73.

had previously avoided and aggressively denounced. During bad weather days in December 1943, the USAAF had accuracy rates no better than Bomber Command had had in the summer of 1941.[62]

With the build-up of the USAAF in Britain, German defences had to cope with round-the-clock operations; this strained their resources, since they were, by then, fully engaged in the Mediterranean, and on the brutal Russian front. The offence-defence battle was fierce, and the Luftwaffe maintained heavy pressure on the CBO throughout 1943 – consistently forcing the Anglo-Americans to pay a high price for their campaign. The stress of this pitched battle was felt very directly by General Arnold, who suffered the first of several heart attacks in May. But the expansion of the Allied bomber and fighter forces enabled the air war to continue forward, if haltingly at times. Between 1942 and 1943, Allied bomb tonnage dropped on Germany increased by 450 per cent, and civilian deaths rose dramatically, from 6,800 to more than 100,000.[63]

In the war at sea, the bombers proved themselves to be surprisingly effective. The tide had begun to turn against German submarines in 1942, and by the following year, no fewer than forty-one U-boats were sunk in the single month of May. Aircraft were responsible for over half of those kills. Particularly lethal was the very long-range four-engine Consolidated B-24 Liberator bomber.[64]

Rising like a phoenix

To make a cross-Channel invasion a viable prospect, the Anglo-Americans had to be in a position to gain a reasonable command of the air over the landing zone and the area around it. But time was running out. Facing disaster, the Americans made changes that would help their own circumstances as well as those of the British.[65] If the former had put their eggs in the

---

62 For further detail, see Biddle, *Rhetoric and Reality*, pp. 228–9. Also W. Hays Parks, 'Precision and Area Bombing: Who did Which, and When', *Journal of Strategic Studies* 18:1 (March 1995), pp. 145–74.

63 Dik Daso, *Hap Arnold and the Evolution of American Air Power* (Washington DC: Smithsonian Institution Press, 2000), pp. 198–9. For figures, see *Germany and the Second World War*, vol. VII, p. 159.

64 The Liberator could carry a 2,500-gallon fuel load, and could patrol for three hours at a distance of 1,100 miles from base. Terraine, *The Right of the Line*, pp. 244–5.

65 Both the British official historians and, more recently, Richard Overy (in *The Bombing War*), have given particular credit to the Americans for their commitment to defeating the Luftwaffe.

basket of the self-defending bomber, they had never entirely banished the idea that fighter escort might be necessary over enemy territory. During 1943, US Assistant Secretary of War for Air, Robert Lovett, had become an outspoken advocate of long-range fighters fitted with 'proper tanks' (auxiliary self-sealing fuel tanks that could be jettisoned when empty).[66] The subsequent flood of long-range fighters that followed – a turning point in the air war – was a tactical solution available to the Americans in part because the USA possessed a vast and still-growing industrial plant that was well out of enemy reach.

A bright spot for General Arnold in late 1943 had been the establishment of the US Fifteenth Air Force in Italy. The Allies had made enough progress to secure a site for the basing of a major air command that would be able to range over Southern and Eastern Europe, attacking resources – oil, in particular – that were sustaining the Wehrmacht's fight. The Fifteenth would join the Eighth Air Force to become the United States Strategic Air Forces (USSTAF) in Europe. The Fifteenth would also become part of the complex Allied structure known as the Mediterranean Allied Air Forces (MAAF). At the end of the year, General Arnold sent Eaker out of England (against his will) to take command of the MAAF; he named Lieutenant General Carl Spaatz head of USSTAF, and designated Major General James Doolittle to take field command of the Eighth.

Spaatz was expected to make rapid progress; despite the setbacks of 1943, he had several things working in his favour. Victory in the Battle of the Atlantic made it far easier to move materiel safely to Britain. With American industrial production in full stride, the number of heavy bombers increased from 461 to 1,655 between September 1943 and May 1944. By mid-February 1944, the Fifteenth Air Force was able to add twelve heavy bomber groups to the Allied effort in Europe.[67] The expanded pool of long-range fighter escorts meant that the Americans could now wage a direct counter-force campaign. By flying to key targets the Germans felt compelled to defend, American bombers drew German fighters into the skies, where American escort fighters would meet them in battle. The resulting duels strained the Luftwaffe, particularly its supply of pilots. An American push against the

---

66 He wished to see expanded production for P-47s, P-38s and P-51s. The latter came into its own when the British replaced its inadequate V-1710 engine with a far better Rolls-Royce Merlin 61. See Kennedy, *Engineers of Victory*, p. 125; Paul Ludwig, *P-51 Mustang: Development of the Long-Range Escort Fighter* (Hersham: Classic Publications, 2003).

67 Richard G. Davis, *Carl A. Spaatz and the Air War in Europe* (Washington DC: Center for Air Force History, 1993), pp. 289–90.

Table 17.1 *The bomber offensive, January 1942 to May 1945*[*]

Air Force	Aircraft attacking	Aircraft lost	High-explosive bombs (tons)	Incendiary bombs (tons)	Fragmentation bombs (tons)	Total tonnage
Eighth	273,841	4,182	570,293	96,775	19,984	687,052
Ninth	3,923	96	9,338	64	55	9,457
Twelfth	11,064	104	23,811	73	3,008	26,892
Fifteenth	128,496	2,189	280,131	7,011	16,192	303,334
Total AAF	*417,324*	*6,571*	*883,573*	*103,923*	*39,239*	*1,026,735*
Bomber Command	277,695	7,094	800,726	210,784		1,011,510
205 Group	23,953	352	45,989	1,245		47,234
Total RAF	*301,648*	*7,446*	*846,715*	*212,029*		*1,058,744*
Grand total	**718,972**	**14,017**	**1,730,288**	**315,952**	**39,239**	**2,085,479**

[*] This table includes all bombing, mining, leaflet, special operations, radar counter-measure and supply missions.

Source: Richard G. Davis, *Bombing the European Axis Powers: A Historical Digest of the Combined Bomber Offensive, 1939–1945* (Maxwell Air Force Base, Ala.: Air University Press, 2006), p. 568.

Luftwaffe, Operation ARGUMENT, commenced on 24 January 1944. General Arnold's order was brief: 'Destroy the enemy air forces wherever you find them, in the air, on the ground and in the factories'.[68] A spell of good weather in mid-February gave the Americans an opportunity they called 'Big Week'. Though not a fatal blow to the Luftwaffe, it allowed the Allies breathe more easily as the date for a cross-Channel invasion drew near.

Heavy fighting in the Mediterranean, and especially on the Russian front, thinned and dispersed German resources – and none of these was more vital than pilots. The failure to allot adequate attention to pilot training proved to be a fatal error for the Luftwaffe. As the Allies expanded their air campaign, the Germans increasingly sent inadequately trained pilots into the skies. But under-trained pilots are highly vulnerable to the fighting skills of a more seasoned enemy; thus the Luftwaffe was pushed into a downward spiral from which there was no recovery.[69]

68 Arnold to Doolittle, 27 December 1943, microfilm reel 168.491, vol. v, AFHRA.
69 On this attrition war generally, see Overy, *The Bombing War*, pp. 369–74.

Table 17.2 *The bomber offensive by target system*

Air Force	Target system	No. aircraft attacking	No. aircraft lost	Tons HE	Tons IB	Tons frag.	Total tons
Eighth	Airfields	32,925	367	68,495	7,084	5,410	80,989
	Air industry	15,520	617	27,379	10,600	843	38,822
	Armoured fighting vehicles	3,827	43	7,961	2,139	151	10,251
	Armaments	6,047	93	12,598	3,123	326	16,047
	Bearings	1,966	168	2,886	1,683	0	4,569
	City*	57,711	1,243	97,620	47,750	959	146,329
	Industrial areas	3,780	184	7,736	1,831	80	9,647
	Noball	11,498	76	32,636	226	0	32,862
	Oil	27,067	533	69,305	794	195	70,294
	Port areas	2,456	51	6,216	155	28	6,399
	Tactical targets	14,970	36	28,816	1,479	11,006	41,337
	Targets of opportunity (T/O)	5,606	81	11,207	2,562	228	13,997
	Transportation	70,440	459	176,284	14,438	450	191,172
	U-boats	5,782	185	13,991	1,113	164	15,268
Fifteenth	Airfields	12,530	195	16,047	609	10,835	27,491
	Air industry	5,966	268	13,299	674	505	14,478
	Armoured fighting vehicles	2,357	79	5,448	347	0	5,795
	Armaments	865	25	1,817	244	0	2,061
	Bearings	704	23	1,609	321	0	1,930
	City*	5,623	116	11,778	1,332	120	13,230
	Industrial areas	1,160	12	2,571	0	0	2,571
	Noball	132	4	329	0	0	329
	Oil	24,820	688	56,459	745	82	57,286
	Port areas	3,622	33	8,600	145	0	8,745
	Tactical targets	8,766	46	14,974	2	4,506	19,482
	T/O	279	0	554	104	10	668
	Transportation	60,281	657	143,244	2,488	141	145,873
	U-boats	1,151	15	3,179	0	0	3,179
Bomber Command	Airfields	4,593	68	18,574	321	0	18,895
	Air industry	1,215	39	4,039	556	0	4,595
	Armoured fighting vehicles	21	0	107	0	0	107
	Armaments	1,900	65	4,258	1,581	0	5,839

Table 17.2 (*cont.*)

Air Force	Target system	No. aircraft attacking	No. aircraft lost	Tons HE	Tons IB	Tons frag.	Total tons
	Bearings	77	0	216	15	0	231
	City	142,857	4,810	318,670	193,639	0	512,309
	Industrial areas	24	0	25	0	0	25
	Mining	13,189	359	0	0	0	0
	Noball	15,406	132	70,416	594	0	71,010
	Oil	22,370	358	99,936	1,598	0	101,534
	Port areas	3,238	70	10,400	125	0	10,525
	Tactical targets	17,055	122	91,488	1210	0	98,698
	T/O	17	0	26	8	0	34
	Transportation	29,406	639	134,156	3,400	0	137,556
	U-boats	6,370	100	19,342	4,568	0	23,910

[*] Includes command ordered and authorized city attacks, target of opportunity city attacks, and 'area-like' attacks.

'Noball' was an RAF code word for a target category that included V-1 launch sites and related facilities.

Source: Richard G. Davis, *Bombing the European Axis Powers: A Historical Digest of the Combined Bomber Offensive, 1939–1945* (Maxwell Air Force Base, Ala.: Air University Press, 2006), pp. 591–2.

The voracious demands of the war meant that Allied bomber commanders never had the luxury of focusing on one problem at a time. In early 1944, the Allies commenced their push for Rome, and in February the Combined Chiefs of Staff directed that the campaign in Italy would take priority over other operations (until further notice), and would receive first claim on all Allied resources – land, sea and air – in the Mediterranean.[70] At the same time, planning for a cross-Channel assault moved into a period of high intensity. Neither Harris nor Spaatz looked forward to what each one knew would be a long and massive claim on his resources. In January, Harris had argued that the best 'and indeed the only' efficient support which Bomber Command could give to OVERLORD was 'the intensification of attacks on suitable industrial centres in Germany as and when the opportunity offers'.[71]

70 Wesley Frank Craven and James Lea Cate (eds.), *The Army Air Forces in World War II*, vol. III: *Europe: Argument to V-E Day, January 1944 to May 1945* (7 vols., Washington DC: Office of Air Force History, 1983 [1951], pp. 28–9.
71 Harris, 'The Employment of the Night Bomber Force in Connection with the Invasion of the Continent from the U.K.', 13 January 1944, folder 10B, Portal Papers.

Portal held a different opinion: he directed Harris to carry out trial attacks against specific targets, including airfields, ammunition dumps and transport (including French railway marshalling yards). As the British official historians would later point out, the results, 'though not universally successful, were outstanding'.[72]

A veteran of the First World War, Harris was deeply wary of throwing ground troops directly against the Germans. But he did as he was told, sending crews on raids that were in support of the pre-invasion phase of OVERLORD, as directed by the Supreme Commander of Allied Forces, General Dwight Eisenhower, and his talented deputy, Air Marshal Sir Arthur Tedder. And from 6 June to 25 September, Harris and Spaatz remained under Eisenhower, supporting the advance of the ground forces. Because skilled Bomber Command crews were striking targets in Oboe range, and because the Lancaster could carry a heavy load of ordnance, these attacks made an important contribution to the overall success of the June landing. In the event, Harris worked dutifully and effectively under Eisenhower. In September, the Supreme Commander told General Marshall:

> In view of earlier expressed fears that Harris would not willingly devote his Command to the support of ground operations, he actually proved to be one of the most effective and co-operative members of this team. Not only did he meet every request I ever made upon him, but he actually took the lead in discovering new ways and means for his particular types of planes to be of use in the battlefield.[73]

Spaatz worried that Eisenhower and Tedder's preferred plan for an all-out, pre-invasion attack on French and Belgian transport targets would cause the bombers to miss a crucial opportunity for attacking Germany's oil supply. But Spaatz, too, came into line with the priorities of his new bosses – and was delighted to discover that they gave him latitude to attack oil, on occasion, in the spring and summer. Throughout the pre-OVERLORD campaign, both Bomber Command and the USSTAF forces sought to contain civilian casualties in occupied territory. But such casualties, which anguished Churchill, were inevitable if the preparatory air attacks were to go forward.[74]

---

72 Sir Charles Webster and Noble Frankland, *The Strategic Air Offensive Against Germany*, vol. III: *Victory* (4 vols., London: HMSO, 1961), p. 27.

73 Eisenhower, quoted in Henry Probert, *Bomber Harris: His Life and Times* (London: Greenhill, 2002), pp. 302–3.

74 About a hundred French civilians died in each of the attacks on French marshalling yards. See Richard Davis, 'German Railyards and Cities: US Bombing Policy, 1944–45', *Air Power History* 42:2 (summer 1995), 54.

To the relief of the air commanders, the hard battle against the German air force ensured that the aerial foe was hardly present on D-Day. Indeed, the Luftwaffe managed to send up only about 100 sorties on the first day of the invasion, and about 175 additional ones on the night of 6–7 June. It had re-positioned only 815 aircraft into France – of which only 75 were ground attack aircraft.[75] By seriously degrading the Luftwaffe, the Anglo-American bombers made the cross-Channel assault possible, and then helped to support a successful ground offensive thereafter. This was, perhaps, their greatest contribution to the war effort.

In addition to supporting the Italian front, the invasion of France and the post-Normandy breakout, the strategic bombers aided preparations for an Allied landing in southern France, and continued their attacks on Hitler's V-weapons sites (Operation CROSSBOW). Because of the incessant V-1 strikes against on England (over 300 V-1s were launched on 15–16 June alone), CROSSBOW was given high priority over the summer. Indeed, in July and August, the Allied air forces sent 16,566 total sorties against V-weapons targets – one-quarter of their total tonnage for those months.[76] In July, US strategic bombers had a major role in the opening act of Operation COBRA, laying down a withering bombardment against the German troops ahead of General Omar Bradley's men. But the risk of using heavy bombers in such operations was made painfully apparent, as friendly fire killed over 100 US soldiers and wounded over 400 more.[77] In August and early September, the Eighth and Fifteenth Air Forces continued to divide their resources between supporting the ground campaign, attacking V-weapons sites and attacking enemy oil facilities.[78] In July, a deciphered message from Luftwaffe chief Reichsmarschall Hermann Göring had argued: 'The deep inroads made into the supply of aircraft fuel demand the most stringent reduction in flying. Drastic economy is absolutely essential'. Indeed, the Germans were so concerned about their oil situation that they transferred large numbers of anti-aircraft guns from their cities to their synthetic oil plants.[79]

---

75 Davis, *Spaatz*, p. 414. Overy argues that missions for German pilots became 'all but suicidal' by D-day; Overy, *The Bombing War*, p. 372.
76 Davis, *Spaatz*, pp. 426–32.
77 Craven and Cate (eds.), *Army Air Forces*, vol. III, pp. 231–8, figures on p. 234. The deaths included Lieutenant General Lesley McNair, USA.
78 Davis, *Spaatz*, p. 440.
79 Göring, quoted in ibid., p. 442. See, generally, F. H. Hinsley et al. (eds.), *British Intelligence in the Second World War: Its Influence on Strategy and Operations* (4 vols., London: HMSO, 1979–90), vol. III, pt. 2 (New York: Cambridge University Press, 1988), pp. 497–532.

The last phases in Europe

The attempt on Hitler's life in July 1944, along with the German oil shortage and the rapid progress of troops immediately following the Normandy breakout, inspired the hope that victory in Europe might be near. Indeed, such optimism helped spur development of a joint venture, THUNDERCLAP, between the Air Staff, USSTAF, the Ministry of Economic Warfare and the Foreign Office. It envisioned a massive attack on German morale at a crucial moment – designed to hasten and consolidate the German surrender.[80] The plan worried some American airmen, who feared a further drift from 'precision' bombing. But Eisenhower imposed his own view, stating that while he too had 'always insisted that US Strategic Air Forces be directed against precision targets', he was nonetheless 'always prepared to take part in anything that gives real promise to ending the war quickly'.[81]

On September 25, executive responsibility for control of the Allied strategic bombing campaign reverted to Portal, who, under a new arrangement, would share authority with Arnold. A new bombing directive identified priority targets as the petroleum industry and the German rail and water-borne transportation systems. But the directive also specified that when 'weather or tactical conditions are unsuitable for operations against specific primary objectives, attacks should be delivered on important industrial areas, using blind bombing technique as necessary'.[82] In a new conception of air strategy, Tedder essentially integrated the oil plan into an overall transportation plan. He pointed out that strategic air operations could leverage the fact that German road, water and rail transport were interdependent, and that the oil plan would affect movement by road and air.[83]

In October, poor weather meant that US bombers were able to launch only three completely visual attacks on oil targets, allowing German production of aviation gasoline to triple. Even in the best conditions, oil plants were

---

80 Webster and Frankland, *Strategic Air Offensive*, vol. III, pp. 52–6, 98–103; Davis, *Spaatz*, pp. 432–9. A memorandum by the Chiefs of Staff stated: 'Rapid developments in the strategic situation are now taking place. It may become desirable in the immediate future, to apply the whole of the strategic bomber effort to the direct attack of German morale'; CCS 520/3 (Octagon), 12 September 1944, p. 4, copy in Papers of Carl A. Spaatz, box 18, Diary.

81 Spaatz to Eisenhower, 24 August 1944, and Eisenhower to Spaatz, 28 August 1944, Papers of Carl A. Spaatz, box 18, Diary.

82 Deputy Chief of the Air Staff to Air Officer Commanding-in-Chief, Bomber Command, 25 September 1944, with 'Directive for the Control of Strategic Bomber Forces in Europe' (attached), ibid. For more on command arrangements, see Davis, *Spaatz*, pp. 483–90.

83 Lord Tedder, *Air Power in War* (London: Hodder & Stoughton, 1948), pp. 118–19.

demanding targets. A post-war study by the United States Strategic Bombing Survey (USSBS), examining fifty-seven American strikes on three synthetic oil plants, revealed that only 2.2 per cent of bombs hit key buildings and equipment; no less than 87.1 per cent 'were spread over the surrounding countryside'.[84] In November, the Eighth put 39 per cent of its bombs on oil targets – although continuing bad weather ensured that none of it was purely visual; the Fifteenth was able to achieve 28.4 per cent on oil. Autumn weather greatly affected Bomber Command's campaign as well. The overall effect was to ease the fuel crisis that had been imposed on the Reich over the summer.[85]

Even as USSTAF committed itself to 'precision' in its public rhetoric, it continued the practice of area bombing through cloud cover. Between 1 September 1944 and 31 December 1944, weather forced the Eighth Air Force to rely heavily on H2X (a variant of Britain's H2S) bombing. Of 140,807 tons dropped on primary targets, 81,654 tons were H2X-guided. And of that total, only 674 tons got within 1,000 feet of the aiming point.[86] A March 1945 joint British-American conference on bombing accuracy revealed that in heavy cloud cover (the majority of missions over the winter of 1944–45), 42 per cent of Eighth Air Force bombs fell more than five miles from the target; of those inside five miles, the average circular error was 2.48 miles.[87]

US strategic bombers dedicated ever-increasing tonnage to marshalling yards in German cities. This had an important consequence: attacks on those yards (large, identifiable targets in urban areas) greatly inhibited the German transport of coal, which was the backbone of the German industrial economy. By January 1945, coal shortages in the Mannheim region were resulting in production declines of 80 per cent in some industries; Tedder had indeed

---

84 Of the 12.9 per cent of bombs that hit within the factory perimeter, 1.8 per cent of the total failed to explode, 7.6 per cent landed in empty spaces, and 1.3 per cent hit pipelines and other utilities. See United States Strategic Bombing Survey (USSBS), Oil Division Final Report (2nd edn, Washington DC: United States Government Printing Office, January 1947), p. 121.

85 Davis, *Spaatz*, p. 500.

86 The force bombed through 8/10ths to 10/10ths cloud cover fully 50 per cent of the time. See 'AAF Bombing Accuracy, Report No. 2' by the Operational Analysis Section of the Eighth Air Force, in RG 18, box 550, Air Adjutant General Files, 470, National Archives and Records Administration, Washington DC. Report No. 2 is also summarized in Charles W. McArthur, *Operations Analysis in the US Army Eighth Air Force in World War II* (Providence, RI: American Mathematical Society, 1990), pp. 287–98.

87 Spaatz to Arnold, 'H2X Pathfinders', 14 January 1944, Papers of Carl A. Spaatz, box 17; Conference on Bombing Accuracy, 22–23 March 1945, USSTAF Armament Memorandum No. 14–3 (1 April 1945), Spaatz Papers, box 76.

identified a crucial artery in the German war machine.[88] But such attacks were often done by blind bombing techniques and utilized high percentages of incendiary bombs. As historian Richard Davis has pointed out, 'a well-hit marshalling yard meant a well-hit city, with block upon block of residential areas gutted, families left homeless, small businesses smashed, and workers and others – including women and children – blown to bits or, more likely, burned or crushed by the hundreds if not thousands'.[89]

The fact that the Americans instinctively returned to 'precision' targets whenever weather permitted meant that they were motivated by a theory of air war distinct from that which animated Harris. And the USAAF never sought to develop or employ, in Europe, the specialized fire-raising methods used by the RAF. But while intent and motivation matter for *ex post facto* judgements, the fact remains that operational problems and the desire to prove the utility of bombers caused the Americans to stray very far indeed from their pre-war commitment to discrimination.

By the last months of 1944, Portal – who had led the RAF's transition to area targets early in the war – found himself arguing the opposite case to that which he had made four years earlier. Looking closely at ULTRA intelligence, he realized the Germans were in a bind: the advance of the Soviet front was closing off crucial resources. The Chief of Air Staff thus felt compelled to persuade his field commander of the potential for a sustained attack on oil. Over the autumn and winter of 1944–45, he and Harris wrestled over targeting, through the medium of an extraordinary exchange of letters. The core of the debate was about the close calls – the times when weather might or might not permit something more accurate than area bombing. Portal did not want Harris to opt for a city when there was *any reasonable chance* of successfully hitting an oil target. Both men felt strongly about their views, and both were highly articulate.[90] And Harris's good relationship with Eisenhower may have made him impatient, afterwards, with a stream of queries from his own Air Ministry.

Following the area bombing directive of 1942, Portal and others in the Air Ministry had seized upon any data which seemed to support it. But after the

---

88 Tooze, *The Wages of Destruction*, pp. 650–1.
89 Davis, *Spaatz*, pp. 508, 564–71; and Davis 'German Railyards and Cities', 46–63.
90 These ran to more than forty single-spaced pages. See Webster and Frankland, *Strategic Air Offensive*, vol. III, pp. 80–1. The correspondence itself can be found in folders 10b and 10c, Portal Papers. In January 1944, Portal argued, 'I can never feel entirely satisfied that the oil offensive is being conducted with maximum effectiveness by Bomber Command until I feel sure that you and your staff have really come to believe in it'. Portal to Harris, 8 January 1945, folder 10c, Portal Papers.

Battle of Berlin, many began to have doubts. In the absence of perfect information, all parties were guessing. But Portal and the Air Ministry felt that their guesses were now better informed than Harris's were. And they may have felt, too, an obligation to begin to consider Bomber Command's reputation in the post-war world, when wartime passions would ease and the area bombing policy would be scrutinized more carefully.

In the end, Harris responded to Air Ministry pressure: he went from placing 6 per cent of Bomber Command's total tonnage on oil targets in October to more than 24 per cent in November, despite appalling weather. Even if Harris believed this was a waste of bombs, he was not inclined to insubordination. Between January and April 1945, Bomber Command carried out seventy-four operations against forty-nine oil targets. The British official historians concluded that even if it was not a 'maximum effort', Bomber Command's part in the oil campaign of 1945 'was intensive and concentrated'.[91]

From the moment D-day had been launched, the Anglo-American ground campaign had been a roller-coaster ride of highs and lows. There was less German opposition to the amphibious landing than had been expected, but slow progress toward Caen and difficult hedgerow fighting caused a break in momentum. Restored movement in late July, followed by the capture of Paris and the routing of German troops in the Falaise gap, had led to a powerful sense of momentum and exuberant hopes that the war in Europe would be over by Christmas. But that optimism began to fade as Allied fortunes turned in the late summer and autumn. The V-1 'buzz bombs' that had been landing in Britain since June were joined, in September, by the far more ominous V-2 bombs – the world's first ballistic missiles.

The appearance of the unstoppable V-2s, along with Messerschmitt 262 jet fighters and Schnorkel submarines, reinforced deep fears that the Germans would produce a menacing array of secret weapons capable of prolonging the war and, perhaps, changing its direction yet again. The setback at Arnhem – Operation MARKET GARDEN – in September made it clear that the Germans were still determined to put up a bruising fight. The dreadful flying conditions in the autumn enabled the Wehrmacht to rebound, resupply and launch a counter-offensive. In December, the Battle of the Bulge left the Anglo-Americans in a scramble of shock and disbelief. Allied casualties soared; the US Army alone suffered 74,788 casualties on the Western Front in

---

91 Webster and Frankland, *Strategic Air Offensive*, vol. III, p. 200.

December, and would suffer a further 61,692 the following month. These setbacks were all the more troubling because the Americans had been facing manpower shortages in their army for much of 1944, and the British had no men to spare.[92]

The turn of events led to acute worry inside the Anglo-American camp, and much hand-wringing about how long the war might now last. The V-2 campaign had caused British decision-makers to anguish over war-weariness on the home front. American planners brooded over the prospect of a drawn-out European war overlapping with a costly US ground assault on the Japanese home islands. In January 1945, intelligence estimates began to signal that if the Soviets did not break through during their winter offensive, the war might last well into the summer and autumn.[93] This distasteful prospect prompted planners to investigate means for ensuring success on the Eastern Front. On 25 January, the Joint Intelligence Sub-Committee suggested an urgent review of the utilization of strategic bomber forces, insisting that: 'The degree of success achieved by the present Russian offensive is likely to have a decisive effect on the length of the war'. Well-timed attacks against Berlin would assist the Russians, especially if these could be coordinated with the isolation of East Prussia and the fall of Breslau.[94]

An intervention by Prime Minister Winston Churchill – made on the eve of the Yalta discussions – pushed the process along. Churchill enquired what plans the RAF had for 'basting the Germans in their retreat from Breslau'.[95] For some time, he had wanted to prove that the Anglo-American Combined Bomber Offensive had served as a kind of second front, aiding the Russians in their pitched battle with the Wehrmacht. Air attacks on cities in eastern

---

92 'US Toll is 425,007 on Western Front', *New York Times*, 16 March 1945, p. 3. On American manpower shortages, see Allan R. Millett, 'The United States Armed Forces in the Second World War', in Allan R. Millett and Williamson Murray (eds.), *Military Effectiveness*, vol. III: *The Second World War* (Boston, Mass.: Unwin Hyman, 1988), pp. 60–1. On British manpower, see Williamson Murray, 'British Military Effectiveness in the Second World War', in Millett and Murray (eds.), *Military Effectiveness*, vol. III, pp. 96–7.

93 War Cabinet Joint Intelligence Sub-Committee, Draft Report, 'German Will and Capacity to Resist as at Mid-April and Mid-August 1945', 16 January 1945, CAB 81/127, TNA.

94 Significantly, the report stated that 'a heavy flow of refugees from Berlin in the depth of winter coinciding with the trekking westwards of a population fleeing from Eastern Germany would be bound to *create great confusion, interfere with the orderly movement of troops to the front, and hamper the German military and administrative machine*'. Joint Intelligence Sub-Committee, 'Strategic Bombing in Relation to the Present Russian Offensive', 25 January 1945, pp. 1–2, CAB 81/127, TNA (emphasis added).

95 Churchill, quoted in Webster and Frankland, *Strategic Air Offensive*, vol. III, p. 101.

Germany would not only coordinate inter-Allied efforts and thus help the Red Army against the Germans, but would re-emphasize the contribution of strategic bombing to Allied victory, and help to impress the Soviets on the eve of a major conference (Yalta) to decide Europe's fate.

Harris was told to undertake attacks 'with the particular object of exploiting the confused conditions which are likely to exist in the above mentioned cities during the successful Russian advance'.[96] Portal discussed the plan with Spaatz, and on 1 February, the latter articulated the plan to the Allied Air Commanders' Conference at Supreme Headquarters, Allied Expeditionary Forces. Attacks on synthetic oil would remain the first priority, but the second priority would now be Berlin, Leipzig, Dresden 'and associated cities where heavy attack will cause great confusion in civilian evacuation from the East and hamper movement of reinforcements from other fronts'.[97]

Beginning in early February, the Anglo-Americans pummelled cities behind Wehrmacht lines in eastern Germany in order to cause chaos in the German rear and complicate the Wehrmacht's ability to move men and materiel to the front lines. The Americans launched a heavy raid on the city of Berlin on 3 February, and the British and Americans attacked the city of Dresden on 13–14 February, in what would become one of the most notorious raids of the war. Bomber Command waged two separate night-time attacks on the city; the Americans followed up the next day, and then hit the city a fourth time on 15 February, when bombers failing to reach their primary target bombed Dresden as a secondary. The tools and tactics used on these raids were the same as those that the British and Americans used on other targets in 1944–45. Indeed, the ratio of incendiary bombs to high explosive bombs that the British carried to Dresden was lower than on many of the other raids it carried out that month. What made Dresden different was that, operationally, *everything* fell into place for Bomber Command. A complex choreography of jamming and feints confused the Luftwaffe, enabling Mosquito target-marker bombers to sweep in low and mark in a particularly tight pattern. This, in turn, allowed the follow-on bombers to discern a clearly marked target-indicator 'bullseye' in the middle of the city. The concentrated bomb fall produced an inferno that led to a firestorm.[98]

---

96 Bottomley, quoted in ibid., p. 103.
97 Quoted in ibid., p. 104. See also the summary of the plan, included in 'Notes of the Allied Air Commanders' Conference held at S.H.A.E.F. on 1st February 1945, at 1130 Hours', decimal file K239.046-38 (Maxwell Air Force Base, Ala.: Air Force Historical Research Agency, 1945).
98 Tami Davis Biddle, 'Dresden 1945: Reality, History, and Memory', *Journal of Military History* 72:2 (April 2008), 413–49; Sebastian Cox, 'The Dresden Raids: Why and How',

Bomber Command's success at Dresden had depended on contingent elements; indeed, other raids taking place that same night – and on subsequent nights – did not produce similarly dramatic results. But the 13–14 February attack on Dresden proved to be a 'perfect storm' for the Germans: the city fell victim to the full brunt of Bomber Command at the very apex of that organization's strength and skill. The vast destruction in the architecturally distinguished city, and the high civilian death toll (among women, children and the elderly seeking to escape the fighting on the Eastern Front) provoked unusually close questioning of the raid in the USA and Britain in the last months of the European war.[99] Over time, Dresden became a symbol of the frighteningly ineluctable momentum of total war in its most destructive and chilling manifestation; today, one can hardly have a discussion about strategic bombing without the word 'Dresden' coming up right away.[100]

But this situation, which had seemed so dire in December and January, had eased considerably by March 1945; indeed, by then it was clear that the autumn crisis of 1944 had represented the last gasps of a desperate enemy. Even though Russian ground forces had to pound their way into Berlin, Germany was – in the spring of 1945 – on the brink of collapse. In April, the British chiefs argued that 'no great or immediate additional advantage can be expected from the attack of the remaining industrial centers of Germany'. In mid-April, the Combined Chiefs of Staff recommended that the main mission of the strategic bombers, henceforward, would be supplying any assistance that might be needed by the ground forces.[101]

in Paul Addison and Jeremy Crang (eds.), *Firestorm: The Bombing of Dresden, 1945* (London: Pimlico, 2006), pp. 29–48.

99 See Ronald Schaffer, *Wings of Judgment: American Bombing in World War II* (New York: Oxford University Press, 1985), pp. 95–103; Tami Davis Biddle, 'Wartime Reactions', in Addison and Crang (eds.), *Firestorm*, pp. 96–122. On the contested death toll at Dresden, see Richard Evans, *Telling Lies about Hitler* (London: Verso, 2002).

100 While the tactics and techniques used in the late war raids on eastern Germany's cities were no different than those used earlier by the Anglo-Americans, the bombing directive of January 1945, directing attacks designed to exploit the movement of refugees, placed these attacks in a different, more troubling moral category – one that spoke to the deep-seated fears, and fully brutalized atmosphere, of that moment in time.

101 Extract from Minutes of COS (45) 80th meeting, 29 March 1945; COS (45) 233 (0), Area Bombing, Note by the Air Staff, 4 April 1945, AIR 8/427; Note by COS (45) 263 (0) Revised Directive for Strategic Air Forces in Europe, 16 April 1945, AIR 8/427, TNA.

Air war in the Far East

As the war in Europe reached its endgame, the American strategic offensive in Japan moved into a climactic stage. Beginning in 1944, American bomber forces operated in the Japanese theatre under the direction of the US Joint Chiefs of Staff, with General Arnold in direct command of the newly formed Twentieth Air Force.[102] Just less than a year later, on the night of 9–10 March 1945, American B-29 bombers launched what proved to be the most deadly air raid of the war: sixteen square miles of Tokyo were burned out, and more than 100,000 residents were killed in a single night. The Tokyo raid marked a dramatic turn in the American air campaign in the Far East; following on the heels of many months of frustration, it loosed the full weight of American industrial might on the faltering Japanese.

On 18 April 1942, sixteen B-25 bombers had departed the carrier *Hornet* to wage an aerial assault on Tokyo. Led by then Lieutenant Colonel James Doolittle, the raid was intended to deliver a blow to Japanese morale, to give the Chinese a shot in the arm, and, more concretely, to persuade the Japanese to pull fighter squadrons out of combat theatres and back to the home islands. The brazen attack was heralded in the American press, and though it caused the Japanese to rethink some parts of their grand strategy, it also made clear the operational difficulties of operating over the very long distances in the Far Eastern theatre.

In the summer of 1944, the US Twentieth Bomber Command began operations in the China-Burma-India theatre. Commanded by Brigadier General Kenneth Wolfe, it faced a painfully slow build-up of fuel, ordnance and supplies, due to the formidable problem of bringing these in by air over 'the Hump' of the Himalayas. Crews had trouble reaching and finding targets, and then getting home again. Arnold fired Wolfe less than a month after the Twentieth's first combat mission, replacing him with Major General Curtis LeMay who, in Europe, had proven himself a determined and technically proficient combat commander – much like Harris.[103] LeMay did what he could to improve the combat performance of his organization, despite the problems posed by the theatre. In December, LeMay was persuaded by his immediate superiors to fly an incendiary attack on Hankow, a Chinese city

---

102 On the arrangements for the Twentieth Air Force, see Air Staff Meeting Minutes, 3 April 1944, in RG 18, AAG 42–44, 337, box 357, National Archives and Records Administration, Maryland.

103 Kenneth Werrell, *Blankets of Fire* (Washington DC: Smithsonian Institution Press, 1998), pp. 98, 112.

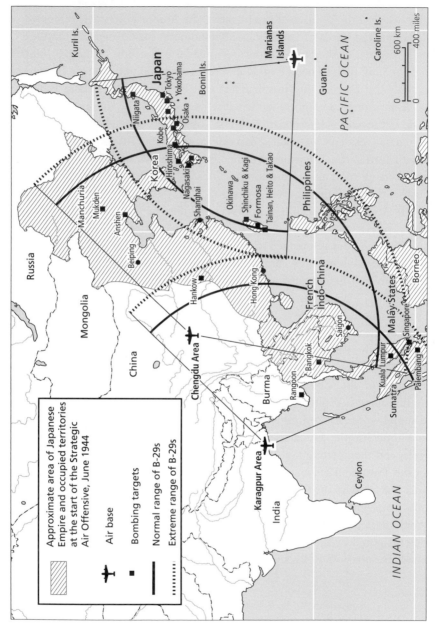

17.2 Allied strategic air campaign against Japan

being used as a base for Japanese operations. The raid was considered a great success by the Americans.[104]

By that time, the Twenty-First Bomber Command, under Brigadier General Haywood Hansell, had commenced its own bombing operations out of the Marianas Islands. But Hansell's early attempts against Japanese industry were disappointing. Arnold feared that if American bombers did not make headway, they would be parcelled out to army and navy theatre commanders. The large B-29 bomber, Arnold's 'three billion dollar gamble', was to be a war-winning aeroplane. After the second experimental B-29 had flown successfully on 27 June 1943, manufacturing sites were set up quickly around the USA, and B-29s were hurried off assembly lines for combat in Asia. But the rush had costs: the aircraft suffered engine failures, fires, dead power plants and jammed gear boxes. If these problems were a hurdle, a worse one was the weather over Japan. Constant cloud cover and the prevailing winds of the jet stream made it nearly impossible for bombers to keep and hold formation, and to bomb accurately. The vast distances also impeded progress, confining the bombers to predictable routes that defenders easily identified.[105]

As failures mounted, Arnold grew impatient; his fondest hope was that aerial bombing would play a conspicuous role in the final victory – vindicating expenditure on the B-29 and enhancing the USAAF's chances for full independence after the war. In mid-December, Arnold's deputy conveyed to Hansell an 'urgent requirement' for a full-scale fire raid on Nagoya. Hansell undertook it reluctantly, not wanting to be diverted from the priority mission of 'precision' bombing of industrial sites. He did not feel that events yet compelled such drastic measures. But Hansell's read of the situation was too complacent.[106]

In January 1945, Arnold opted for a reshuffling of command in the Far East. When he placed LeMay in charge of consolidated B-29 operations, he made it

---

104 Conrad Crane, *Bombs, Cities, and Civilians* (Lawrence: University Press of Kansas, 1993), pp. 127–8.

105 See 'Highlights of the Twentieth Air Force', Office of Information Services, Headquarters, Army Air Forces, [1945], decimal file no. 760.01, misc. 314.7 (Twentieth Air Force), 1942–45, AFHRA; 'Analysis of Incendiary Phase of Operations, 9–19 March 1945', Headquarters, Twenty-First Bomber Command, decimal file no. 760.01, 1 July – 2 September 1945, vol. vii, Narrative History, Headquarters Twentieth Air Force, AFHRA; Staff Presentation, 10 April 1945, binder xiii, Operations Div. Reports, docs. 103–109, decimal file no. 760.01, 1 July – 2 September 1945, vol. xiv, Narrative History, Twentieth Air Force, AFHRA.

106 Michael Sherry, *The Rise of American Air Power: The Creation of Armageddon* (New Haven, Conn.: Yale University Press, 1989), pp. 257–8.

clear that results were expected quickly.[107] The shift of command coincided with a strengthening of the B-29 force. Understanding the pressure he was under, LeMay acted to enhance the prospects of the campaign. He stripped his B-29s of their defensive armament, filled their bomb bays with incendiaries, and flew them over Japanese cities at low level. Arnold had made it clear that LeMay's tactical choices would not be questioned or sanctioned. Against the bloody backdrop of the Battle of Iwo Jima, LeMay said of the devastating 9–10 March raid, 'if the war is shortened by a single day the attack will have served its purpose'.[108] Over the course of the following months, LeMay waged an urban area bombing campaign of terrible fury, attacking more than sixty Japanese cities with incendiary weapons. In addition, he continued efforts to attack the aircraft industry and the Japanese oil supply. And though there was little enthusiasm for it in Arnold's headquarters, LeMay used the B-29s in a highly effective mine-sowing campaign advocated by the US Navy, and the British.

On 2 August, just days before the attack on Hiroshima, American bombers flew the largest single aerial strike in history, dropping 6,632 tons of bombs and burning out the cities of Hachioji, Toyama, Nagaoka and Mito.[109] In the Far Eastern theatre, the Americans followed a path similar to the one the British had followed in Europe: rationalizing their choices by reference to the psychology of the Japanese, and to the indirect effects of area bombing. Looking for a way to end the war quickly, and faced with operational problems even more daunting than those in Europe, Arnold further loosened whatever constraints remained on American bombing. In his final war dispatch (published after the conclusion of hostilities), he included a map of Japan, showing each of the sixty-six cities that had been firebombed. To help policy-makers and the American public appreciate the nature of the achievement, each Japanese city had listed next to it the name of an American city of roughly the same size.[110]

In Japan, the Americans did not wholly abandon their preferred theories of air warfare. As in Europe, American bombers typically returned to selective

---

107 See William W. Ralph, 'Improvised Destruction: Arnold, LeMay, and the Firebombing of Japan', *War in History* 13:4 (October 2006), 495–522.

108 Warren B. Moscow, 'Not a Building is Left in 15 Square Miles', *New York Times*, 11 March 1945, pp. 1, 13, quote on p. 13.

109 W. H. Lawrence, 'World Peak Blow', *New York Times*, 2 August 1945, pp. 1–2.

110 'Third Report of the Commanding General of the Army Air Forces to the Secretary of War', 12 November 1945, published in *The War Reports of General of the Army George C. Marshall, General of the Army H. H. Arnold, and Fleet Admiral Ernest J. King* (Philadelphia, Pa.: Lippincott, 1947). The graphic is on p. 441.

targeting whenever weather permitted. But the willingness of American planners and policy-makers to cross the line and prosecute mass fire raids on a repeated and systematic basis represented a descent to a new and terrifying level in the hell of total warfare. On 6 August, over Hiroshima, and on 9 August at Nagasaki, no moral threshold was crossed that had not been crossed earlier in the year. Those military planners who knew about the atomic bomb did not assume it would end the war. Planning for a ground invasion went on as usual, conventional air raids took place in between and after the two atomic attacks, and the Navy continued its stranglehold on enemy shipping and supply. The Japanese military, government and population were to be afforded no relief and no quarter until surrender was achieved under terms then being contested at the highest political levels. When that surrender came, on 14 August, it had been brought forth by a powerful combination of forces, including blockade and mining, bombing, the psychological impact of the atomic attacks, the shock of the Soviet entry into the war, and the realization of what an Allied ground assault would entail.

In many ways, the Anglo-American strategic bombing campaign had been born in the trenches of the First World War – amidst the mud, rats, lice and barbed wire – and against the backdrop of bloody, fruitless offensives on the Western Front. Air power visionaries proffered the restoration of offensive capability in an instrument that, they argued, would produce a quicker, more decisive victory. Some offered a silver bullet aimed at specific sinews in the enemy's economy. The lure of these ideas proved irresistible to politicians, who, despite their best efforts, could not head off another vast conflagration in the twentieth century, less than two decades after the first one. But the assumptions on which the bombing advocates had built their claims proved to be wildly optimistic, and the campaign they waged was one of unending adaptation in order, first, to stave off collapse, and then to make good on the sizeable investment that politicians had placed in their hands. They managed, despite vast operational problems, to place a ceiling (if a leaky one) on German munitions, to pave the way for the invasion into Normandy, and, late in the war, to erode and then strangle German battlefield manoeuvre and war production. In the Pacific, bombers helped to bring Japanese civilians – and eventually their reluctant leaders – to the brink of collapse. But the means were brutal.

No comprehensive counterfactual analysis has ever been undertaken to examine what might have happened if the Allies had created a campaign more fully oriented to ground–air cooperation, and tactical use of aircraft.

One can envision an outcome that would have been less deadly to enemy civilians, but more deadly to Allied combatants. The heavily freighted moral decisions made by the Second World War generation, taken under circumstances that none of us alive today would ever want to face, will be debated for decades and centuries to come.[111] And the Second World War strategic bombing campaign will, throughout history, be held up as an example of just what can happen once the lid on the Pandora's box of warfare has been lifted.

111 For insights into ongoing questions, see Yuki Tanaka and Marilyn B. Young (eds.), *Bombing Civilians* (New York: The New Press, 2009); and Matthew Evangelista and Henry Shue (eds.), *Changing Legal and Ethical Norms, from Flying Fortresses to Drones* (Ithaca, NY: Cornell University Press, 2014).

PART III

*

FIGHTING FORCES

Introduction to Part III

JOHN FERRIS AND EVAN MAWDSLEY

Part I of this volume addressed national strategies and military culture, and Part II the campaigns. Part III, on 'fighting forces', does not focus simply on 'fighting' or 'forces'. Instead, the chapters assess military institutions, functions and instruments taken broadly, including 'tail' and 'teeth'. Planning ('staff work'), supply, mobilization and organization of personnel, and intelligence shape the success of 'fighting forces' as much as do units deployed on the front line of the battlefield, although usually at less personal risk. (Richard Bessel tackles the issue of military and civilian casualties in Volume III: 'Death and survival'.) These seven chapters take the analysis of military forces above and beyond the traditional boundaries of strategy, operations and tactics, by defining some of the factors that give them depth. These are challenging chapters for the contributors, given the scale of the subjects, in some cases the limitations of source material, the comparative element, and the need not to duplicate coverage with contributors in other parts of the CHSWW.

Eliot Cohen and Dennis Showalter consider 'fighting forces' in the broadest sense. Cohen views them from above. His chapter on war planning returns to themes covered in Part I of this volume, assessed in a comparative way. He emphasizes relative success in the adaptation and integration of new instruments of war within this planning process, and the creation of civil-military institutions to control military establishments and collaborate with allies. The Allies (with a capital 'A') developed what Churchill called a 'design and theme' for coalition victory, which their opponents could not. Showalter's masterful overview considers how forces adapted to the conditions of the mid-twentieth century. He addresses themes arising throughout Volume I, and in the 'non-military' volumes: the nature and adaptability of armed forces based on energy rather than mass; the maintenance of popular support for the war effort; the relationship of armed forces to civilian leaders;

and the role of extraordinary military means, including attacks on civilians, in an era of total war.

The vital practicalities of the armed forces – the organization of personnel and supply – are often forgotten compared to more glamorous subjects, but as they say, 'amateurs study tactics, professionals study logistics'. Personnel and supply are central to the domination of the battlefield (or the sea and sky), especially when conflicts are prolonged. In an era of 'total' war, military and civilian spheres, both human and material, cannot easily be distinguished. What is the dividing line between mobilizing part of the population (misleadingly gendered as 'manpower') for military service, or the *whole* working population for combat and war production? Likewise, where best to break the long supply chain, stretching from extraction (or conquest) of raw materials, production in factories, through distribution of weapons to military depots and front-line units? The answers vary with time and nation. Military personnel policy and supply have been studied before, but usually within the context of national histories (dry works written by and for professionals). The two chapters on these topics in this volume are unusual in their international, comparative scope.[1]

Sanders Marble attacks the challenging and undeveloped subject of conscription and force generation. He takes the process from pre-war systems, through those used by both sides at the height of the Second World War as the 'manpower pool' began to drain away – or the stream was dammed to fill other waters. States managed this process in different ways – lowering standards or finding untapped sources of personnel. The process was especially challenging for democracies, where public opinion had to be taken more directly into account, especially as the Axis threat was not always immediate. Rüdiger Hachtman and others tackle the related subject of *general* mobilization of the wartime population – that is, deployment of (mostly) civilians to industry and other compulsory labour – in Volume III.

Likewise, Phillips O'Brien's chapter on supply achieves a remarkable overview. It covers integrated land and air supply, with a special stress on the rail system, which played the same vital role for the Germans and Russians as it did in 1914–18. He assesses the supply of aircraft to front-line squadrons, over enormous distances. The author handles the 'fighting forces' end of the supply chain, which goes from extraction of raw materials

---

1 Two notable – and lively – exceptions in the scholarly literature are Martin van Creveld, *Supplying War: Logistics from Wallenstein to Patton* (Cambridge University Press, 1977); and Richard Overy, *Why the Allies Won* (London: Pimlico, 1995).

to front-line units; the 'upstream' end is dealt with in Volume III by several contributors, notably Jeff Fear in his chapter on 'War of the factories', and Cathryn Carson on the management of technological innovation. In Volume III, Michal Miller handles the key issue of shipping; Marc Milner's chapter in Part II of the present volume also covers attack and defence on the most important shipping conduit, the Atlantic.

For both personnel and supplies, the Allies fought the war with a great advantage – on paper in 1942 (and 1939–40), and in action during 1943–45. The British Empire, the Soviet Union and the United States had a huge advantage over the Axis, even ignoring the enormous but less accessible resources of China. Allied propaganda emphasized this point, even in the dark spring of 1942. But it was not inevitable that they would also be superior in military intelligence. As John Ferris shows, however, the Allies did outperform the Axis in the second half of the war. The chapter on intelligence has the dubious advantage of addressing a sexier subject than conscription or logistics, but the disadvantage of limits (even now) to sources. It addresses the subject broadly, both in terms of national cases and the spectrum of intelligence-gathering and analysis, from radar to cryptology. What emerges here, and in other chapters, is the complex nature of what military and civilian leaders think they know about their enemy. This knowledge goes from simple 'bean-counting' of units to – incalculable – racist and cultural national stereotypes which shape strategy: nations of shopkeepers; myopic Japanese pilots; decadent, mongrel Americans; unimaginative Teutons; *slawische Untermenschen* (later transformed by Dr Goebbels' propaganda into more-worrying *Roboten*).

John Ferris argues that the role of intelligence is situationally determined, compared to enemies and circumstances. It is more important, for example, when the density of combat forces (on both sides) is low, than when it is high. He contends that intelligence (including even ULTRA) did not decide Allied victory, but certainly accelerated it. German intelligence started well, but stagnated. The British and Americans had greater faith in intelligence, and more imagination and technological advantages, which let them devise and mass-produce electronic equipment (including sensors and computers) and specialist platforms (long-range aircraft) on a greater scale than the Germans (let alone their less technologically developed partners). The Western Allies better harnessed the efforts of their intellectual and scientific communities. Compared to other states, the British and Americans also had more open and rational decision-making and suffered less from ideologically determined views, or reliance on the gut feeling of individual leaders. The story of the Eastern Front is harder to determine, but the Germans led in 1941–42, and the Soviets in 1944–45, neither gaining as much from intelligence as the Western Allies.

While it might seem paradoxical to include prisoners of war under the heading of 'fighting forces', being captured was a possible consequence of combat. Captured soldiers must be distinguished from *civilians* in occupied countries (and their mistreatment legally fell under the existing category of war crimes, rather than 'crimes against humanity'). Because the war was so long and global, an unprecedented number of POWs fell into enemy hands, and in a great variety of circumstances. Bob Moore provides a comprehensive discussion of the wide range of their treatment. The British and Americans, who initially had fewer prisoners and less demand for forced labour, handled POWs most humanely. The Germans conducted racially and ideologically based murder of certain categories of prisoner, certainly military 'commissars' and Jewish soldiers – and, arguably, ethnic Russians – as part of broader campaigns of mass murder and genocide. Japanese policy, especially toward Chinese prisoners, was murderous, for cultural and racial reasons. The Soviet treatment of German, Italian and Japanese prisoners of war was severe, especially lethal before the mid-war battles and longer-lasting; German, Italian and Japanese POWs were held for forced labour in the USSR until the early 1950s.

Treatment of POWs and attitudes toward guerrilla warfare might seem different matters, but they have similarities: both concern treatment of an 'enemy' population (captured soldiers, and civilians living in occupied regions, regardless of whether they resist the occupation). Ben H. Shepherd's chapter on guerrillas and counter-insurgency is impressive for its broad-ranging treatment, combining Europe and Asia. This chapter anticipates what nine chapters dealing with occupation and resistance will assess in Volume II, Part III. Shepherd handles the subject on a comparative basis, focusing on the military doctrine and practice of guerrillas and counter-insurgents. He emphasizes the inability of the Axis Powers to develop rational/political 'pacification' policies, as opposed simply to punitive ones. The Soviets were more successful at counter-insurgency than the Germans, but also had greater forces at their disposal. Overall, the military weight of the guerrilla movements was small, but its moral and political weight was considerable.

18

War planning

ELIOT A. COHEN

Strategic planning – defined here as the development of military plans, as opposed to the logistical or economic ones that are addressed in other chapters in this series – involves two activities.[1] The first is anticipating the requirements of war and preparing operations for its initial phases. This requires not just planning in the narrow sense of preparing campaigns, but the broader challenge of developing conceptions of future warfare – an act of imagination rather than calculation. The second task is intrawar planning, adjusting to the new circumstances that invariably develop, and drafting campaign plans to replace those rendered obsolete by events. During the tense peace of the 1930s, General Staffs speculated not only on the nature of future war, but on the initial moves that should take place. Following the initial clash of arms in the West in 1940, and the broadening of the Asian War in 1941–42, Axis, Allied and neutral powers all had to draw up new plans. And not just the principal protagonists either: neutral Switzerland, for example, which had a serious military before the war (a total of 700,000 reservists of all kinds) had to radically reshape its plans following the collapse of France in 1940, devising a desperate plan for a central redoubt in the Alps from which to fight a culminating battle against German invaders.[2]

In many respects, the planners of the Second World War wrestled with the problems that afflicted their predecessors a quarter of a century earlier, in the war of 1914–18. That conflict cemented some basic organizational forms, and clarified some – but far from all – of the challenges that planners faced in 1939–45. This is not to say that the participants in the Second World War met

---

1 I would like to acknowledge the assistance of Mr William Quinn in researching and revising this chapter.
2 This chapter's principal focus will be on the major powers. For more on the war planning of smaller powers, see Herman Amersfoort and Wim Klinkert (eds.), *Small Powers in the Age of the Total War, 1900–1940* (Leiden: Brill, 2011).

those challenges adequately (by definition, in a war with winners and losers, they did not): rather, the staffs understood the problems their predecessors had faced, and had rough, if inadequate solutions to them.

In the period from the American Civil War and the Germans wars of unification to the First World War, it became clear to all sophisticated military powers that they needed effective General Staffs to plan for and conduct large-scale conflict. The advent of armies numbering in the millions, sustained by rail-fed logistics, required no less. The last considerable European power that tried to fight a war without such careful planning, France in 1870, was, after a muddled mobilization and concentration on its borders, crushed by a much better managed German enemy.

Progress toward meeting this requirement was uneven across the major powers, each of which faced unique challenges in establishing an effective and efficient General Staff. Most of the military establishments tasked with centralizing war planning had been bastions of conservatism at the beginning of the nineteenth century, refusing to consider fundamental reform, while basking in stunning victories won by famed commanders like Napoleon at Austerlitz or Wellington at Waterloo. It is no accident that Prussia, an early innovator, was a second-rate power, forced to consider a new means of war after suffering a humiliating defeat at Jena in 1806, or that Britain, France, Russia and Italy did not seriously contemplate institutionalizing war planning until they had been dealt similar blows in the Crimea and elsewhere.[3] Once established, however, the General Staffs – particularly those in Continental Europe which were most likely to find themselves at war – produced detailed operational plans that they updated regularly in the years prior to the First World War; in France and Russia's cases, developing nearly twenty plans against Germany and Austria-Hungary alone.[4] The size of the staffs expanded accordingly, and grew further as positions on them grew in prestige.

The development of planning during the nineteenth century was hardly smooth, even though there was a clear trend toward it. The injection of the planning process into bureaucratic politics and civil-military relations created new problems for planners and policy-makers alike, who often left each other in the dark on the military and political implications of their respective intentions. The German General Staff never fully explained their plans to

---

3 Louise Richardson, 'Strategic and Military Planning, 1815–1856', in Talbot C. Imlay and Monica Duffy Toft (eds.), *The Fog of Peace and War Planning: Military and Strategic Planning Under Uncertainty* (New York: Routledge, 2006).

4 Holger H. Herwig, 'Conclusions', in Richard F. Hamilton and Holger H. Herwig (eds.), *War Planning 1914* (New York: Cambridge University Press, 2010), p. 228.

the Chancellors in the years prior to the war, while British generals were so removed from the debate over going to war in August 1914 that Field Marshal Sir John French called the British newspaper magnate, Lord George Riddell, and asked, 'Can you tell me, old chap, whether we are going to war? If so, are we going to put an army on the Continent, and, if we are, who is going to command it?'[5] The virtuosity of some of the products developed by General Staffs across the Continent was occasionally undercut by compartmentalization, the obsession with offensive as opposed to defensive operations, and a lack of coherent political direction.

Nonetheless, by 1939, few states laboured under the illusion (as both the United States and Great Britain had even in the years before the First World War) that a commanding general could take the field and pretty much leave headquarters to carry on without him. Rather, it was now understood that modern war planning required centrally organized staffs, located in the capital, with other departments of government, who would both plan a war and, in some measure, manage its conduct. Moreover, these staffs required high-level education at war colleges and specialized career tracks. While staff colleges had begun to appear in most developed countries in the nineteenth or very early twentieth centuries, after the First World War, military planners were given further opportunities for preparatory work. The United States, for example, created the Army Industrial College in 1924, for the purpose of preparing officers to play a role in economic mobilization, and encouraged close ties between the National War College and its planning staff in the War Department, stipulating that students would only work on war plans with practical significance to the General Staff.[6] The British created the Imperial Defence College in 1927 to consider problems of imperial defence on a global scale, and across three services. The Military Academy of the General Staff of the Soviet Union came into being in 1936, building on an already deep Russian tradition of military intellectualism.[7] Ironically, the Germans, who had pioneered the war college in the early nineteenth century, seem not to have revised or extended upward (say, to a joint military academy) their military educational system by 1939.

---

5 Lord Riddell, quoted in Richard F. Hamilton, 'War Planning: Obvious Needs, Not So Obvious Solutions', in Hamilton and Herwig (eds.), *War Planning 1914*, p. 12.
6 Henry G. Gole, *The Road to Rainbow: Army Planning for Global War, 1934–1940* (Annapolis, Md.: Naval Institute Press, 2003), p. 127.
7 Earle F. Ziemke, 'Soviet Net Assessment in the 1930s', in Williamson Murray and Allan R. Millett (eds.), *Calculations: Net Assessment and the Coming of World War II* (New York: The Free Press, 1992), p. 186.

The basic business of planning large-scale operations had consisted, before the First World War, chiefly of managing the complicated mobilization and logistics associated with calling up large numbers of reservists and moving them to the front lines by rail – or, in the case of navies, recalling smaller numbers of reservists and concentrating the fleet. Planners had also, notably, laid out the general directions in which armies would move, along with timetables for those movements, and had expectations of how these schemes of manoeuvre would bring victory. These plans were usually theatre-focused – that is, they dealt with fronts of up to several hundred miles, and in similar depths. The Schlieffen Plan that played such a disastrous role in launching the First World War was the apotheosis of this style of planning: 'the great symphony', as the head of the railroad section of the German General Staff called it, that 'could only be attempted once, and the conductor bungled it'.[8]

In the ordeal of the First World War, the limits of this approach to war became apparent. The great powers discovered that initial plans, however carefully drafted, would probably go awry; that General Staffs would not merely have to manage an ongoing conflict, but also to continue planning – and not merely improvising – during the course of a war, as well as before it. Even the most optimistic planners during the Second World War, the Germans and Japanese, understood that this war could easily turn into a long conflict. There was no real equivalent of the Schlieffen Plan in 1940–42, a plan predicated on a smashing victory won in a month or two, which would bring a global conflict to an end. Rather, the two aggressive powers hoped to knock out some key opponents, seizing impregnable positions at the outset, against which transcontinental enemies would batter themselves in vain. The approach was imperfect, since these fluid plans were formulated based on broad, and often unverified assumptions about adversaries' intentions, rather than on strategic intelligence. Even though all of the major powers collected intelligence on one another, the use of that intelligence to inform high-level policy-making was often inadequate, being hampered by politics, compartmentalization and an underdevelopment of the analytic as opposed to the collection functions of intelligence.[9] To the

8 Wilhelm Groener, quoted in Arden Bucholz, *Moltke, Schlieffen, and Prussian War Planning* (New York: Berg, 1991), p. 269.
9 Richard Overy, 'Strategic Intelligence and the Outbreak of the Second World War', *War in History* 5:4 (1998), 472 and *passim*.

extent that it filtered down to the level of strategic planning, it was often used to affirm optimistic, preconceived notions.[10]

This lesson was (and continues to be) difficult to learn, but the fact remains that most planners, commanders and political leaders spent the 1920s and 1930s profitably. They learned other lessons from the previous war as well: the need for systematic mobilization of manpower and industrial resources; the basic requirement for systematic collection, analysis and dissemination of operational intelligence, particularly that derived from signals intercepts; and the likely importance of subversive and economic warfare, waged not only in European imperial possessions, but in Europe itself. As other chapters in these volumes indicate, these were handled with differing degrees of success by the combatants.

There were, however, three broad problems of war planning that were not adequately resolved in the First World War, mastery of which would be critical to success in the Second World War. These problems, which stemmed partly from new technology, and partly from a change in the higher politics of war, were:

- the integration of two new instruments of military strength, air power and armour-led operations, which had not fully demonstrated their potency during the previous conflict and which were now deployed on a continental rather than a theatre scale;
- the closely related question of joint operations, in which two or more services had to engage in close and equal cooperation;
- the problem of Supreme Command, to include the relationship between military planners and civilian leadership, as well as with coalition allies.

Planning with the new instruments of war

Air power had played an important role in 1914–18, particularly for purposes of reconnaissance, but also close air support; and considerably more modestly for transport, and even long-range interdiction and bombing against deep targets. But all things considered, air power was in its earliest stages. By the late 1930s, however, its potential was much better understood, or at least more realistically imagined. Advocates of air power during the interwar

---

10 Donald Cameron Watt, 'British Intelligence and the Coming of the Second World War in Europe', in Ernest R. May (ed.), *Knowing One's Enemies: Intelligence Assessment Before the Two World Wars* (Princeton, NJ: Princeton University Press, 1984), pp. 251–2 and *passim*.

period had foreseen the possibility of attack on enemy industries and societies, and many believed that devastating blows could be thrown against an enemy's society without the need for combat between armed forces at all. Some, like the American General Billy Mitchell, foresaw as well the ways in which air power would prove indispensable, in some cases dominant, in naval warfare. Somewhat less well understood, but known nonetheless, was that air forces would make a major contribution to decisions in ground campaigns.[11]

In some countries – Germany and Britain most notably – independent air forces existed in 1939; in other countries (the United States, for instance), an independent land-based air force existed in all but name; in yet others, air forces were no more than adjuncts to a dominant service (the army in the Soviet Union, the army and navy separately in the case of Japan). Here was a major complication, because air forces engage in operational planning in ways very different from those of the other two branches of service – if, that is, they are allowed to do so. Air power's flexibility (no other form of force allows for such rapid concentration in space and time) and its peculiar requirements (above all, elaborate base, repair and maintenance infrastructure) create different needs as well as opportunities.

In the European theatre, the higher staffs of the British and German air forces stood out for having anticipated operational requirements in different fields. The Germans had mastered many of the organizational requirements for using air forces in support of ground operations. The Luftwaffe had arrived at this place less by design than by happenstance: the death of General Walther Wever, the pioneering Chief of Staff of the Luftwaffe, who died in an aeroplane crash in 1936. Wever had been an advocate of strategic bombing – the aggressive use of air power against enemy air forces and cities – much as was the case with bomber advocates in Britain and the United States. His replacement, Hans Jeschonnek, turned the Luftwaffe in the direction of support for ground operations. Moreover, crucial design decisions early on – including an infatuation with dive-bombing, and the preference for medium bombers like the Ju 88 – meant that Germany would not have the wherewithal to plan and conduct a large, sustained air offensive.[12] And as in many air forces at the time, the closeness of some air

---

11 Johnson Garner, 'Forgotten Progress: The Development of Close Air Support Doctrine Before World War II', *Air Power History* 46 (1999), 44–65.

12 Williamson Murray, *Luftwaffe* (Baltimore, Md.: The Nautical & Aviation Publishing Company of America, 1985), p. 15 and *passim*.

commanders to their army roots helps to explain this turn away from strategic bombing and to the support of ground operations as a doctrine. In any event, the German air force successfully planned the great air onslaughts on Norway, France, Belgium and Holland in 1940, and the assault on Russia in 1941. Each of these included a meticulously planned assault on the enemy's airfields, coupled with concentrated uses of air power in direct support of operations, like the crossing of the Meuse River in 1940, or the blitz against the Soviet air force in June 1941, which did a spectacular job, destroying 1,811 Russian aircraft for the loss of thirty-five Luftwaffe planes on the first day.[13]

The high command of the Royal Air Force had two countervailing planning successes behind it, both ultimately of greater importance. The first was anticipating the organizational requirements for the defence of the British Isles. By the late 1930s, the basic system for warning and command and control had been laid out, ready for the injection of a new technology, radar. No less important, the British were the first of the Western Allies to recognize the scale on which it would be necessary to build air forces. When war broke out, the Royal Air Force had but one overseas flying school, in Egypt. In September 1939, the first proposals for what became the Commonwealth Air Training Plan were made, and by December confirmed, with an initial goal of training 20,000 pilots and 30,000 other aircrew annually, throughout the empire.[14]

A somewhat similar pattern occurred in the Pacific. Japanese naval air forces did a brilliant job of anticipating the tactical needs for their attack on Pearl Harbor and other Allied installations in the Pacific. Their American counterparts, on the other hand, understood the importance of building vast air forces that would turn the tide. Even before the United States formally joined the war, in March 1941, it embarked on a 30,000-pilot training programme, and that was just the beginning.[15]

---

13 Horst Boog, 'The Conduct of Operations: The Luftwaffe', in *Germany and the Second World War*, vol. iv: *The Attack on the Soviet Union* (10 vols., Oxford: Clarendon Press, 1998), p. 764 and *passim*.

14 *Official History of New Zealand in the Second World War, 1939–1945* (Wellington, NZ: R. E. Owen, Government Printer, 1955), p. 50. For more on the eventual scope of the Commonwealth Air Training Plan, see John Terraine, *The Right of the Line: The Royal Air Force in the European War, 1939–1945* (London: Hodder & Stoughton, 1985), p. 258; and Peter Marshall, 'The British Commonwealth Air Training Plan', *Roundtable* 89 (2000), 267.

15 Wesley Frank Craven and James Lea Cate (eds.), *The Army Air Forces in World War II*, vol. vi: *Men and Planes* (University of Chicago Press, 1955), pp. 456–7 and *passim*.

The difference in these planning decisions and ensuing outcomes was not accidental: it reflected different conceptions of war. From the outset, the Anglo-Americans understood the impending conflict as a gruelling, attritional struggle in which the mobilization of resources and the development of forces to wage it were central issues. By contrast, the dominant culture of war in both Japan and Germany was one of decisive strokes administered by tactically competent forces. The results can be seen, for example, in the remorseless decline in Japanese fighter pilot competence compared with that of their American opponents. A system that produced outstanding pilots in the hundreds could not hope to compete with one that produced pretty good ones by the thousands. The issue, however, lay not only in the overall superiority of American resources, but rather in the planning decisions made by the Japanese military to do nothing to mitigate them.

The uses of air power were similarly a matter of choice. The United States and Great Britain bet most heavily on balanced forces, although only the United States could actually cover that bet, with vast fleets of heavy, medium and light bombers, fighters, ground support, maritime patrol and transport aircraft, as well as carrier-launched fighters, dive-bombers and torpedo bombers. The Soviet Union's leaders saw air power chiefly, and understandably, as an adjunct to the ground forces, and privileged fighters and ground attack aircraft over all other types. Japan's air forces were technically superior and tactically proficient when the war began, but the country was not prepared for the mass production of equipment or for the training of expert operators and organizations that war would require. One cause of this was a conception of war, taught in staff colleges and believed by the General Staffs, which ignored the power of attrition.

For all belligerents in the Second World War, planning for war also had to take into account the advent of the internal combustion engine. Even by the end of the First World War, it was clear that the age of movement by rail to depots, and then by foot or horse-drawn transport to a front, was coming to an end. By the 1930s, the problem of mechanization was obvious, having two components – the use of tanks, and the subtler question of the motorization of all land movement, to include infantry and all supplies.

There is no doubt that the Germans led all others in pioneering the conduct of armoured warfare, although Soviet military thought on the subject (and technological development) was on a par or even better.[16]

---

16 Mary Habeck, *Storm of Steel: The Development of Armor Doctrine in Germany and the Soviet Union, 1919–1939* (Ithaca, NY: Cornell University Press, 2003), p. xvii and *passim*.

Drawing in part on a careful reading of British achievements in the latter phases of the First World War, some Germans understood that a tank was something more than merely a machine that supported the infantry by destroying machine-gun nests. Even conservative figures like Chief of the General Staff Ludwig Beck, who was not a zealot for tank forces, tolerated the much more aggressive advocacy of armoured warfare from officers like Heinz Guderian.

The smashing victories of 1939–41, set against the backdrop of far more incremental operations in the First World War, shocked contemporaries and temporarily overthrew the European balance of power. However, historians still debate to what extent the German military consciously conceived a new way of war, involving the use of armoured spearheads launching deep penetrations and encirclements before the war.[17] Some have maintained that the basic concepts behind German operations were in the Michael offensive of 1918 and elsewhere, to which the lightning offensives against Poland in 1939, France in 1940 and the Soviet Union in 1941 bear more than a passing resemblance.[18]

They point out that the deep operations against Norway in 1940, and against Greece and Yugoslavia in 1941, which were not built around armoured divisions, exhibited similar features of speed, disregard for the advancing forces' flanks, delegation of decision-making authority down, and a relentless urgency in disabling an enemy's armed forces and government in a single stroke. Moreover, they note, Soviet doctrine had been no less forward-looking in the 1930s, but Stalin's massacre of his own generals, including the talented Mikhail Tukhachevskii, set back thinking about large-scale armoured operations.

All this is true enough, but misses the extent to which armoured warfare did involve radical breaks with the past, in terms of the depth of penetration of an enemy line, and what previous generations would have regarded as a reckless disregard of one's flanks. During the campaign of France in 1940, for

---

17 For an account that argues that the German military did not intentionally develop a new doctrine in the interwar period, see J. P. Harris, 'The Myth of Blitzkrieg', *War in History* 2 (1995), 335–52. For an account that argues for the gradual, but conscious emergence of a new doctrine of manoeuvre warfare during the interwar period, see Robert M. Citino, *The Path to Blitzkrieg: Doctrine and Training in the German Army, 1920–1939* (Boulder, Colo.: Lynne Rienner, 1999), p. 244 and *passim*.

18 Bruce I. Gudmunsson, *Stormtrooper Tactics: Innovation in the German Army, 1914–1918* (Westport, Conn.: Praeger, 1995), p. xii and *passim*; Citino, *The Path to Blitzkrieg*, pp. 16–18 and *passim*; Michael B. Barrett, *The Roots of Blitzkrieg: The 1916 Austro-German Campaign in Romania* (Bloomington: Indiana University Press, 2013), p. 310 and *passim*.

example, at one point, German lines of communication stretched 200 miles through enemy territory – at least an order of magnitude beyond what would have been tolerated in 1914–18. It involved, as well, evolving a style of command from the front for general officers that simply could not have worked before the advent of radios small enough to be packed into motor vehicles.

Although German military culture remained constant from 1918 to 1941 in its willingness to take risks, its aggressiveness and its expert exploitation of enemy tactical weaknesses or lapses, German organization had changed dramatically. The German planning triumph before the Second World War had much to do with the pre-war creation of the Panzer Division, an all-arms, balanced mechanized formation, built around the tank. Where the British struggled with tank units that had too many tanks and not enough support-ing arms, such as infantry, motorized or self-propelled artillery, and combat engineers, and where the French hit upon the idea of armoured divisions too late to do much good, the Germans built a pre-war organization ideally suited to their operational style. It did not matter that nine-tenths of their forces plodded on at the pace of horse-drawn carts (the British, oddly enough, had the only completely motorized army in Europe in 1940), the cutting edge was mechanized and expertly led.

Planning leads of this kind, however, do not last. The Allies, in their different ways, were hard at work on mastering the tools of armoured warfare (the Soviets, in particular, achieved extraordinary effects in the great offensives of 1944 and 1945). By its nature, the Germans' peacetime lead in conceptualizing armoured war, and creating organizations that could wage it, was bound to decay rapidly as learning replaced planning in a world at war.

Joint operations

Before the Second World War, the main form of joint operations consisted of amphibious operations, and only the British Empire had the need to conduct these on a large scale – and when it did so, at the Dardanelles in 1915, the result was a notable and bloody debacle. For the rest of the First World War, joint operations, properly speaking, consisted chiefly of raids and, to a limited extent, riverine operations by navies in support of land forces. Air forces were, at this juncture, merely arms of the ground and, to a modest degree, naval forces.

The Second World War was different: the coordination of air, sea and land forces was now an urgent task of strategic and operational planning for all the powers, albeit to different degrees. The Soviet Union, although it required naval forces to secure its northern flank, had in some ways the least pressing problem: the army dominated its three services. As we have noted, there was no independent air campaigning for the Soviets on the Eastern Front.

In all other countries, the situation was different, because strategic planning had in it a large element of inter-service politics. In the case of air forces, this usually involved an aspiration to deliver a decisive blow without the need for a costly land campaign. Such was the aspiration of the Luftwaffe, or at least its chief, Herman Göring, after the fall of France in 1940; but by then, the choices made in the late 1930s had crippled its ability to do more than give the British a good scare.

British and American air planners in the years before as well as during the war had been altogether more serious in their aspirations to win a war from the air, and the technologies they had developed – big four-engine bombers, above all – showed it. In the case of planning for war in maritime theatres, naval, air and land forces often had starkly different conceptions of how to conduct operations, where the main effort should take place and even, in some cases, who the main enemy was. In the case of Japan, for example, pre-war naval planners focused, understandably, primarily on the United States and, to a lesser extent, Southeast Asia and Great Britain, while army planners looked at China and the Soviet Union as their chief challenges.[19]

Mere coordination, it was soon discovered, could not answer the needs of modern warfare: Major General Short and Admiral Husband E. Kimmel had a regular golf date at Hawaii – but that did not save their commands from being in a fog of lack of mutual comprehension when the blow fell on 7 December 1941. Sooner or later, the major combatants saw the need to create ever more potent joint organizations to plan operations, which, in turn, would fall under a single, unified command. Indeed, the latter was, in some ways, the great innovation of the Second World War. Eisenhower in Europe, Nimitz and MacArthur in the Pacific, Wavell and his successors in the Middle East, and Mountbatten in Southeast Asia did not exercise dictatorial authority over the services under their commands, but they exercised powerful influence over the multi-service forces at their disposal.[20]

---

19 Atsushi Oi, 'The Japanese Navy in 1941', in Donald M. Goldstein and Katherine V. Dillon (eds.), *The Pacific War Papers: Japanese Documents of World War II* (Washington DC: Potomac Books, 2004), p. 14.
20 For a detailed account of how this system evolved in the USA, see Ray S. Cline, *Washington Command Post: The Operations Division* (Washington DC: Office of the Chief of Military History, 1951), p. 95.

Conceptions of war, and how to plan for war, are powerfully shaped by a commander's branch of service: an admiral, for whom losing half a dozen ships could be a disaster of war-changing proportions, is bound to have a different attitude toward attrition than a general in command of hundreds of thousands, for whom a steady stream of losses is merely a fact of life. Air generals believe, almost without exception, that the first job of air forces is to gain air superiority by defeating the enemy's air force, and then deliver consequential blows by massing on the enemy's vulnerable points, such as lines of communications or industry. Soldiers, by way of contrast, often view air power as a higher form of artillery, to be used to support a ground concept of manoeuvre. Conceptions of the significance of geography, the importance of mobilization of resources and priorities of effort – before and during the war – were all affected by service identity. At various junctures, the disputes were acute not merely in the conduct of operations, but in the selection of plans for them. The United States Navy and Army, for example, disagreed sharply over whether the war would have to conclude in an invasion of Japan rather than its blockade and bombardment in 1945.[21] Royal Air Force's Bomber Command was bitterly opposed to diversions from its attacks against German cities to go after what its commander, Arthur Harris, dismissed contemptuously as 'panacea targets'.[22]

The easiest, and most disastrous, solution to inter-service cooperation was found by the Japanese, whose navy and army simply fought the war in parallel, thereby minimizing the demands on joint planning. But the upshot of this was that although the initial campaigns launched by the Japanese in December 1941 and the early months of 1942 were stunningly successful, thereafter Japan failed to anticipate and coordinate the basic necessities of joint warfare. Thus the island chain so brilliantly seized in early 1942 (largely by the navy, with army landing units), was not fortified adequately (by the army, with navy logistical support) until late 1943, and never had the elaborate logistical build-up necessary to fight a war of attrition. In the Solomon Islands campaign of 1942, more Japanese died of malnutrition and disease than of American bullets and shells, in part because Japanese generals and admirals had not planned for an attritional struggle at the end of a long supply line. As a result, despite the heroic efforts of the Japanese navy to

21 Richard B. Frank, *Downfall: The End of the Imperial Japanese Empire* (New York: Penguin Books, 1999), pp. 146–8 and *passim*.
22 Arthur Harris, quoted in Richard Overy, *The Bombing War: Europe 1939–45* (London: Allen Lane, 2013), p. 298.

supply ground forces on Guadalcanal by pressing destroyers into service as transports, the garrison there was left languishing for want of supply. The Japanese admirals had not planned to build vast numbers of escorts to defend against submarines, to create construction units to build secure bases, to develop the organizations to coordinate the movement and protection of convoys or, indeed, to construct the fleets of transports and supply ships mandated by war across vast ocean spaces. The Americans and British quickly saw the need for these things, had anticipated some of them earlier and, in fact, had laid plans for them.

In one way, the United States made the Japanese solution of parallel efforts work, simply by having vast resources. The Army's conception of a Pacific strategy became a thrust along the southwestern island chain, from Australia, to Papua New Guinea, and northeasterly through the Philippines to the Japanese islands.[23] The Navy's interwar conception was a direct thrust across the Central Pacific, storming small islands to create advanced bases for blockade and bombardment. Both services got their wish, and the Navy even had its own land forces – a vastly expanded Marine Corps – to execute it.[24] In the European theatre too, American resources were great enough to allow the heavy bomber elements of the US Army Air Forces to pursue their strategy of precision daylight bombing, while turning over to the tactical air forces the task of supporting ground forces.

Still, this was a war in which the imperative of planning by tri-service committees became apparent, particularly in the case of the Anglo-Americans, who alone among the combatants had three largely independent services. Their success in so doing, however, required not only the creation of joint staffs under unified theatre commanders, but a degree of civilian intervention, guidance and, in some cases, control rarely seen in warfare to this point.

Supreme Command

In most cases, the requirements of strategic planning in the midst of war required reorganization as countries entered it. Thus in the spring of 1942, General George C. Marshall divided the Operations Division of the War Department General Staff into a theatre group (for each major arena of war),

---

23 Michael R. Matheny, *Carrying the War to the Enemy: American Operational Art to 1945* (Norman: University of Oklahoma Press, 2011), pp. 84–8.
24 Ibid., p. 153 and *passim*.

a logistics group, and a strategy and policy group, which handled long-range planning. His design reflected the imperatives of balancing current operations with long-term plans, and the need to separate planners from officers responsible for managing the day-to-day administration of the Army. 'OPD', the official historian writes, 'was in itself a virtually complete general staff'.[25] Other countries undertook similar overhauls in the transition from peace to war; none was fully ready for the demands of a truly global, multi-theatre conflict.

In most of the combatant nations of the Second World War, top commands that were, from a service point of view, unified in name, if not in practice, were established during the 1930s or shortly after war broke out. Hitler created the *Oberkommando der Wehrmacht* (OKW – the high command of the Wehrmacht) as early as 1938, although more in the context of a struggle for control of the army than as a well-considered measure for the conduct of war.[26] Nor was the OKW ever a proper joint body; the division of responsibilities between the OKW and the army high command (*Oberkommando des Heeres* – OKH) remained unclear to the very end.[27] Walter Warlimont, Deputy Chief of the Operations Staff at OKW recalled his initial impression when he joined the command in 1938:

> Taken as a whole all this could not but produce the extraordinary impression that the principal, if not the only, preoccupation of the OKW Operations Staff was to give patronizing acceptance to the plans which the Army General Staff had made... In comparison any question of unified command of the Wehrmacht as a whole in the strategic sense was pushed completely into the background but this was however probably unavoidable since the machinery for carrying out such a task was non-existent.[28]

Formal unity, in the German case, was a sham, the victim of Hitler's desire to consolidate control over the politically powerful army, without providing resources, staffing or supervision to make the new organ effective. It was, moreover, a reflection of the limited strategic utility of the German navy (save for the U-boat war), and the inability of the Luftwaffe to play an independent role after the initial campaigns of the war.

---

25 Cline, *Washington Command Post*, p. 95.
26 Geoffrey P. Megargee, *Inside Hitler's High Command* (Lawrence: University Press of Kansas, 2000), p. 44 and *passim*.
27 Ibid., p. 223.
28 Walter Warlimont, *Inside Hitler's Headquarters, 1939–1945* (New York: Praeger, 1964), p. 18.

Interestingly, the Soviet high command system only gelled after the German invasion during the summer of 1941, following the disasters of June and July. Stalin assumed the role of Supreme Commander-in-Chief, whose general headquarters (*Stavka*) existed chiefly to serve him. In August 1942, following more reverses and in a more dire set of circumstances, he appointed General Zhukhov as the first Deputy Commander-in-Chief and first Deputy Defence Minister – a merging of civilian and military roles and authority that seems to have been born of desperation. And in a move that echoed German practice in the First World War, Stalin sent key members of *Stavka*, including Zhukhov himself, to particularly critical fronts such as Stalingrad, there to plan and conduct the large-scale operations that he saw would be needed. But the catastrophes of the first phase of the war had much to do with Russia's failure to plan adequately for a German invasion – a failure attributable, at least in part, to a system in which terror ruled.

The American Joint Chiefs of Staff (JCS) only came into being in the first half of 1942, with a chairman (technically, Chief of Staff to the President, Admiral William Leahy) appointed to guide their deliberations. The predecessor organization, the Joint Army-Navy Board, had done some good preliminary work in the previous thirty years, but the advent of actual war made it clear that closer integration among the services was required. And even so, throughout the war, the members of the JCS believed, and with reason, that their British counterparts had them out-organized. The British Chiefs of Staff Committee had a strong joint planning staff who had been working together for years, with the habit of orderly drafting of estimates and options, and coordination with civilian authority through the British Cabinet system.

Indeed, despite all the hard-won experience of the First World War, a great deal of basic organizational design for planning had to be done at the outset of the Second World War. A regular routine of work, the fleshing out of planning staffs and the appointment of key personnel had not taken place before the war in many cases, and evolved during it. This reflected partly the growing complexity of large-scale military operations, but also the fact that strategic planning in this war was dominated by stronger civilian leaders than in the last war, where powerful civilians (Lloyd George and Clemenceau, most notably) came to the fore only at the end of the conflict, when the basic strategic pattern had been set. Here, the personalities of Mussolini, Hitler, Churchill, Stalin and Roosevelt – civilians each and every one – dominated, and they all had large strategic choices to make. Only in Japan was the military in charge, as it had been in Germany during the First World War, and even there, the deep divisions between the services created some manoeuvre space for the surviving civilian politicians.

Inevitably, the highest-level planning efforts of the major combatants therefore centred on the staffing of a powerful politician and his military subordinates. And it took time for those senior leaders, none of whom had ever run a war after all, to shape the systems that they wanted to support them in that effort.

The totalitarian leaders, despite their tyrannical and vicious natures, all had some strong civilian and military subordinates (Speer and Guderian, for example, in Germany; Zhukhov and Shaposhnikov in the Soviet Union). Hitler and Stalin were monsters, to be sure, but both brought aptitudes to war planning that deserve recognition. In the late 1930s, Hitler judged the temper of the Western powers correctly, and he provided the impetus and drive that culminated in the Wehrmacht's campaigns of the first two years of the war. But as a self-conceived artist, he could neither build nor operate an elite planning staff; nor could he tolerate around him subordinates, other than Speer, who could do so. Occasionally brilliant improvisation was his forte, but not his system.

Stalin's wilfulness and scorn for the bureaucracies that he had battered, brutalized and, in some cases, murdered led to the calamity of the summer of 1941. Yet once he recovered from his shock, he reshaped the high command into an organization that could not only react, but plan. In this respect, he was aided by the often under-appreciated military thinkers and planners of Russia's General Staff, as well as by outstanding figures such as Zhukhov.

Roosevelt and Churchill each had their weaknesses. Roosevelt, in particular, was less the man of system than his British partner – it was the President who hated note-takers and the orderly flow of memoranda, the Prime Minister who insisted on them. But both knew talent, hiring (and retaining) soldiers like George C. Marshall and Alan Brooke, who were the central figures making their respective planning staffs function.

In the case of the Anglo-Americans, moreover, the construction of a system for high-level planning required the creation of semi-permanent joint and coalition structures far surpassing anything created in previous wars. The formal establishment of the Combined Chiefs of Staff in early 1942, headquartered in Washington, with a strong British element headed by the former Chief of the Imperial General Staff, Sir John Dill, was one part of this. So, too, was a regular exchange of correspondence, not just between FDR and Churchill (enough to fill three fat volumes), but between staffs. There was grumbling from overworked colonels about a 'transatlantic essay

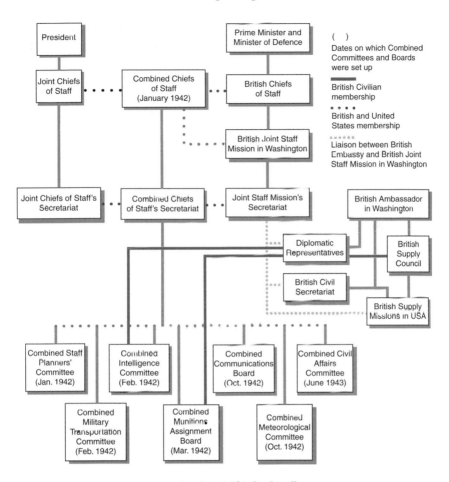

18.1 Combined Chiefs of Staff
From I. C. B Dear (ed.), *The Oxford Companion to the Second World War*
(Oxford University Press, 1995), p. 255.

contest', but the routinization of planning meant the coordination of the efforts of the British Empire and the United States in a manner unprecedented in military history.

This larger framework enabled the careful planning of the great enterprises which brought the Allies success, most notably the invasion of France in June 1944. It is remarkable, for example, that a Chief of Staff to the Supreme Allied Commander (COSSAC) was appointed in April 1943, with a supporting staff, well before an actual commander of the D-Day landing was appointed, and more than a year before the event itself.

An insightful novel by James Gould Cozzens, an aide to the commander of the USAAF, captures the temper of coalition planning brilliantly. One of his characters is appalled when he attends the Quebec Conference in August 1943. After an incisive sketch of the opposing sides, Cozzens writes:

> Their proceedings must often be less than sensible unless you understood the object of them. The object could not be simply to concert a wisest and best course. The object was to strike a bargain, a master bargain which was the congeries of a thousand small bargains wherein both high contracting parties had been trying, if possible, to get something for nothing; and if that were not possible, to give a little in order to gain a lot. Since, in each such arrangement, someone must come out on the short end, and since no subordinate could risk being the one, the chiefs must meet and agree.
>
> Agreement was ordinarily resisted by mutual misrepresentations, and obtained by a balance of disguised bribes and veiled threats. Plain honest people were often disgusted when they found out that high business was regularly done in these low ways. They were also indignant; because they knew a remedy for the shameful state of affairs. Let every man be just and generous, open and honorable, brave and wise. No higgling or overreaching would then be necessary.[29]

The strength of the Anglo-American system was that it concocted military plans in this mundane, plodding way, rather than by relying on the inspiration of the Führer or the intuitions of Generalissimo Stalin.

Indeed, herein lay the genius of the Anglo-American alliance: its institutionalization of strategic planning, and its conversion of the process into something like routine. The linked staffs, the constant transatlantic communications, and the fairly frequent meetings of senior leaders (thirteen alone involving Churchill and Roosevelt) created an alliance unparalleled in the history of warfare. As Churchill himself once observed, 'the history of all coalitions is a tale of the reciprocal complaints of allies' – but the system he and Roosevelt built managed sometimes sharply divergent views of where the Allies should direct their efforts.[30]

The Soviet Union's participation in coalitional planning was more difficult in most respects. Mutual suspicions that had lasted decades endured. On the big issues, and in particular that of an invasion of the Continent by Anglo-American forces in 1943, Stalin felt positively betrayed by his partners, who, for their part, accommodated him only because they realized that the Red

---

29 James Gould Cozzens, *Guard of Honor* (New York: Harcourt, Brace, 1948), pp. 394–5.
30 Winston S. Churchill, *Marlborough: His Life and Times,* vol. v: *1705–1708* (New York: Charles Scribner's Sons, 1936), p. 246.

Army was holding down the bulk of German forces. The conferences of the Allied Powers that involved Stalin in war planning – Tehran, Yalta and Potsdam – were each wary, tense and conflictual. Still, these were properly staffed events at which heads of state, supported by elaborate military staffs, met and came to conclusions.

The relationship among the Big Three was easier, however, in one critical respect: unlike the Anglo-Americans, the Soviets had rather little need or opportunity for intimate combined planning with their counterparts. The Soviet war was geographically distinct from that on the Western Front, and proceeded at its own pace. The one synchronized event, however, the near-simultaneous launching in June 1944 of the D-Day landings and the Soviets' BAGRATION offensive, which culminated in the destruction of the Germans' Army Group Centre, was of decisive importance in dealing the mortal blow to Germany.

One hallmark of Allied coalitional strategic planning was its remarkable acceptance of the limits of that enterprise. Again, it was Churchill who saw most clearly the limits of strategic foresight. While sailing to Washington in the weeks after Pearl Harbor for the first great wartime conference, code-named ARCADIA, he drafted a series of memoranda (ostensibly to his own Chiefs of Staff, actually addressed to President Roosevelt) that capture well pragmatic acceptance of the limits on foresight which informed the Anglo American effort. In them, he attempted to think through the massive problems with which he and the President would have to deal. He captured the heart of the problem in one paragraph:

> We must face here the usual clash between short-term and long-term projects. War is a constant struggle and must be waged from day to day. It is only with some difficulty and within limits that provision can be made for the future. Experience shows that forecasts are usually falsified and preparations always in arrear. Nevertheless, there must be a design and theme for bringing the war to a victorious end in a reasonable period. All the more is this necessary when under modern conditions no large-scale offensive operation can be launched without the preparation of elaborate technical apparatus.[31]

Churchill dug into the details when he thought appropriate, no doubt, but he bears a great deal of the credit, with Roosevelt, on the need for a 'design and

---

31 Memorandum to Chiefs of Staff Committee, 16 December 1941, in Warren F. Kimball (ed.), Churchill & Roosevelt: *The Complete Correspondence*, vol. 1: *Alliance Emerging* (Princeton, NJ: Princeton University Press, 1984), p. 303.

theme' for winning the war. And as Admiral William Leahy, Roosevelt's Chief of Staff, subsequently acknowledged, the Combined Chiefs of Staff 'were just artisans building definite patterns of strategy from the rough blueprints handed to us by our respective Commanders-in-Chief'.[32]

In a civil-military relations dynamic familiar in many wars, the civilian leaders, Churchill and Roosevelt, struggled to maintain flexibility, while military staffs, keenly aware of the limits posed by logistics, fought to convince their civilian masters that some choices precluded others. Often, the issue descended from the big questions (e.g. land in Europe in 1943 versus 1944, attack in southern France or just in Normandy) to seemingly minute matters of detail: how many Landing ship, tanks (LSTs) were available in the Mediterranean. But here, too, the distinctive genius of the Anglo-American alliance lay in its ability to discern that sometimes it is the minutiae, rather than the large conceptions, that are critical to successful war planning.

By and large, the Axis did not plan for coalition warfare at all. Although Japan, in particular, had a capable and well-respected ambassador in Berlin, his chief, unwitting function ended up being that of providing Anglo-American cryptanalysts with terrific insights into German planning through his regular transmissions to Tokyo. But Germany and Japan made no real effort to plan jointly. They might have, and to considerable effect. Had Japan gone to war with the Soviet Union in parallel with Germany in the summer of 1941, one has to wonder whether the USSR would have survived – Stalin's Siberian divisions, after all, helped defend Moscow as winter set in. Or Japan might have used its naval superiority in the spring of 1942 to wreak damage on the British position in the Persian Gulf, even as German forces were seizing the initiative in the Western Desert. Instead, the allies, though on cordial terms with one another, shared some bits of technology, a modest trade in strategic materials and little else. More to the point, they seem not to have coordinated the major strokes of 1941 – the German invasion of the Soviet Union and the Japanese attack on the United States and Great Britain – at all.

Nor did Germany do any better with its Italian partner: both Hitler and Mussolini ignored or, in some cases, actually misinformed their partners. The Germans were caught off-guard by Italian operations against Greece and Albania in 1939–41, which swiftly turned into a debacle from which the Italians had to be rescued. And as Italian forces were dealt one defeat after another by British and Imperial naval forces in the Mediterranean, and land

---

32 William D. Leahy, *I Was There* (New York: McGraw-Hill, 1950), p. 106.

forces in North and East Africa, that country soon ceased to be much of an independent actor at all. The plans for the Mediterranean war, after early 1941, were made in Berlin, not Rome, and not by negotiation, either.

The Allies also did a far better job of planning in conjunction with lesser allies. German allies like Hungary or Romania, or the Japanese-sponsored government in Manchukuo, had virtually no say in the planning of operations; the one sturdy minor ally, Finland, kept its distance from jointly planned campaigns, even when, as in the siege of Leningrad, a Finnish offensive might have doomed the second most important city in Russia. By contrast, a country like Australia had a much larger hand in shaping campaigns in its region, and Great Britain reluctantly acceded to Australia's insistence, after the disasters of early 1942, to concentrate its forces at home. Even a non-state actor, de Gaulle's Free French, ended up serving as more than mere shock troops for the Anglo-Americans, most notably in the early liberation of Paris in 1944. Again, the reduction of strategy to a certain amount of give and take – to something approaching normal politics – paid off in the long run.

Planning and victory

How important was war planning for the eventual outcome of the war? After all, many other elements count a great deal in war – quantities of troops and materiel, the quality of individual commanders and sheer luck. Moreover, as we have seen, forethought before the war often failed, and well-conceived plans went awry in the face of circumstance and the inherent unpredictability of conflict. In those circumstances, the ability to adapt – to react to sudden losses or newly visible opportunities – counted for as much as war planning.

In retrospect, the initial successes of the Germans and Japanese owed less to masterly planning than to the strength of their military organizations and tactical cultures, the excellence of their technology, and the sheer audacity of their operations. During the war, and for some time afterwards, their enemies thought that the operations of 1939–42 reflected deep, long-conceived plans for aggrandizement and aggression. In retrospect, historians have discovered, the great strokes, including the armoured thrust through the Ardennes in May 1940, the surprise attack at Pearl Harbor and the audacious lunge for Singapore via the jungles of Malaya, were concocted only months before they were implemented. These operations took advantage of the innate strengths of the Axis Powers, and were enabled by extraordinary personalities, to include, among military figures, Erich von Manstein (who devised the plan for the invasion of France) and Yamamoto Isoroku, whose authority allowed junior Japanese planners to come up with the Pearl Harbor plan. One must add that Hitler's remarkable willingness to take risks, his infatuation with modern military technology, and his affinity for bold field officers like Guderian and Rommel enabled them and others to act to their fullest potential.

The Allied powers, for their part, received one staggering surprise after another. Stalin's failure to plan for a German assault came very close to bringing about the utter defeat of the Soviet Union. But once the Soviets had recovered their equipoise, they outplanned their enemies again and again. At the level of grand operational planning – the organization of offensives on a continental scale – the Soviet conduct of the war in the East during 1944, in particular, is unmatched. The Soviet offensives launched against Army Group Centre from 22 June to 29 August 1944 (beginning with BAGRA-TION, the initial assault), like the equally methodically planned OVER-LORD, the invasion of Normandy, integrated armies numbering some 2.5 million soldiers, 45,000 artillery pieces, 6,000 tanks and assault guns, and 7,000 tactical aircraft against an opponent desperately short of all these things.[33] Similarly masterful planning characterized the great American Pacific offensives of that year. In all of these cases, the Allied successes benefited from the enormous superiority in materiel of more productive economies and larger populations, but other things as well. The adroit selection of targets, areas for assault or breakthrough, massive deception schemes, the integration of all arms and, no less important, the anticipation of the logistical requirements to sustain vast forces over long distances were all critical. Germany and Japan had less abundant resources, to be sure, but that made their failure adequately to calculate the logistical requirements for their plans all the more damaging. A case in point: on the eve of the invasion of Russia, which would lead to battles not of armies, but of army groups, the Chief of Staff of the German army was writing in his diary that 'The division as a self-contained operational unit becomes a dominant factor'.[34] He was thinking, in other words, three echelons too low for the war that awaited him. Nor had he or his colleagues – and not just Hitler – grasped the magnitude of the supply and logistical problem that awaited them, with

---

33 For a summary of these operations, see Karl-Heinz Frieser, Der Zusammenbruch der Heeresgruppe Mitte in Sommer 1944', in Das Deutsche Reich und der Zweite Weltkrieg, vol. VIII: Die Ostfront 1943/44 (Munich: Deutsche Verlags-Anstalt, 2007), pp. 526–603.

34 Franz Halder, The Halder War Diary, 1939–1942, ed. Charles Burdick and Hans-Adolf Jacobsen (Novato, Calif.: Presidio Press, 1988), 10 June 1941, p. 403.

the result that even as German troops rolled into Russia, production priorities were going to the German navy and air force.[35]

None of the combatants entered the war with a plan that carried through to the end: all were surprised, sometimes gravely so. The Germans and Japanese arguably did the worst job of planning, and paid the price. But students of the war should bear in mind that planning alone could only go so far. Had British nerve cracked in 1940, or Soviet will broken in 1941 or 1942; had the politicians not had the skill to build organizations without precedent in the history of coalition warfare, and to operate them under exceptional strain, the war might have had a different outcome. Without a Churchill, a Roosevelt or even a Stalin, it is entirely possible that the war's outcome might have been different, and the Allies' latent capacity for conceiving and then implementing vast enterprises would have been a matter for speculation, among historians born to a very different world than our own.

---

35 Hans Juergen Foerster, 'The Dynamics of Volksgemeinschaft: The Effectiveness of the German Military Establishment in the Second World War', in Williamson Murray and Allan R. Millet (eds.), *Military Effectiveness*, vol. III: *The Second World War* (Boston, Mass.: Allen & Unwin, 1988), pp. 194–6.

19

Armies, navies, air forces

The instruments of war

DENNIS SHOWALTER

The armed forces of the Second World War engaged each other in every corner of the globe, under every geographic, climatic and operational circumstance. They were created and sustained by every form of government and society, from the hyper-industrialized military establishment of the United States to the Ethiopian patriots who fought for their occupied country with spears as well as rifles. It is correspondingly impossible to acknowledge, much less incorporate, even representative examples from across the spectrum in a single chapter. This chapter proposes instead to present and evaluate thematically the fundamental values and structures shaping Second World War armed forces – their origins, their applications and their consequences – in the context of the combatants which defined the war's conduct. That category includes the armed forces engaged the longest, and those which made the largest general contributions to the war's conduct in terms of ideas, performance and technology, both directly and by sharing resources and information. Five met those criteria: Britain, the USA, the Soviet Union, Germany and Japan. Three more states, France, Italy and China, fought hard and costly wars, but for limited times and with limited external impact. The remaining military establishments were too small or too derivative to justify inclusion.

The chapter considers five central aspects of the Second World War armed forces. First is their addressing of war's fundamental shift of focus from mass to energy: the dominance of oil and electronics. Second comes armed forces' response to a dynamic of constant change: how best to keep at least abreast of the development curve. Third on the list comes purpose: the principles and intentions of armed forces composed essentially of citizens temporarily uniformed and disciplined. The fourth subject is control: who, in the final analysis, made policy and gave orders; who obeyed and to what degree. Last, as much a coda as a category, stands the question of how far institutions of war-making were willing to go in making war. Where – or if – did means become ends in themselves?

Energy and mass

The First World War was a war of mass, and mass was fundamentally based on lives. Whatever you did, from the Battles of the Frontiers to the Hundred Days, would cost a lot of them. The Second World War was also a war of mass – but mass now meant machines. Bombers over Germany, landing craft on Pacific beaches, T-34s in Russia or trucks everywhere, machines were as expendable as men had been a quarter-century earlier. And the machines were energy-dependent. Oil and electronics were the sinews of first-line military systems from 1939 to 1945. Oil and electronics enabled the Second World War's defining tropes. Tanks slicing across France in 1940 and again in 1944, as dazed prisoners shuffled in the other direction; the 'few' in their Spitfires and Hurricanes who saved the sum of things in the sky over Britain in 1940; the fleets that grappled across the Pacific without ever coming in sight of each other – these and their counterparts convey and sustain the high-tech realities of the Second World War.

Armed forces perceived the same reality: warfare's paradigm shift to an energy basis. Their responses, however, were structurally conditioned and situationally determined. Japan offers the clearest case study. In the interwar years, it was obvious that Japan could not match her most dangerous rivals when it came to energy – at least artificial energy. The armed forces coped in two ways. One was by emphasizing human 'energy': maximizing the quality of key technicians, from fighter pilots to warship lookouts. The other involved democratizing bushido: the code of honour and sacrifice associated with the aristocratic warriors of the samurai class was extended to every Japanese in uniform. Spirit power would match and transcend the forces of machinery and electricity.[1]

This emphasis on the human factor was extended to operational planning as well. Speed, shock and surprise were projected as neutralizing numbers and firepower. The best example is the still-unmatched economy-of-force campaign in the Pacific during the first six months after Pearl Harbor, when the same limited numbers of planes, troops and ships seemed to be every-where at once and conquered an empire on a shoestring.

---

1 Edward Drea, *Japan's Imperial Army: Its Rise and Fall, 1853–1945* (Lawrence: University Press of Kansas, 2009), pp. 125–62), is an excellent introduction to the subject.

Nazi Germany came almost as close, on a larger scale, and as much by accident as design. The principal conclusion German military thinkers derived from the 1914–18 experience was the limited effectiveness of an army on the pre-war model. Its immobility relative to its size meant it could only crush by sheer weight applied over an extended period of time – and Germany could count on having neither one of them. The tactical, doctrinal and institutional concepts developed in the Weimar Republic and refined after 1933 provided the prospect of decisive offensive operations, executed by specialized high-tech formations as the cutting edge of a main army energized by modernized transport and communications. The rapid and haphazard nature of German rearmament during the Nazi era, however, resulted in an 'army of layers', 90 per cent horse-drawn, with the tools enabled by oil and electricity concentrated in an elite – not in the racial sense of the Waffen-SS, or based on personnel selection like British and American airborne forces, but a functional elite based on learned skills. That elite overran Western Europe and the Balkans, destabilized the Middle East and brought Germany to the gates of Moscow – all by the winter of 1941.[2]

Yet the armed forces of Germany and Japan eventually encountered the same obstacle. Their respective cutting edges were irreparably dulled through overuse in what became a comprehensive attritional war on scales the Axis powers could not hope to match. From being an instrument of breakthrough and exploitation in 1940–41, by 1943 Germany's armoured force had devolved first into a force multiplier, then into tactical firewalls and fire brigades: emergency backups for muscle-powered formations that had developed into precisely the kind of low-average mass force that interwar German planners had sought to avoid, composed of anyone vaguely classifiable as 'German', armed with whatever could be made available. Increasingly overmatched and overextended against energy-driven enemies, the German combination proved capable enough of forcing a drawn-out endgame, but had no reasonable hope of regaining the initiative on any but local levels.[3]

Japan faced a similar problem. Its Pacific Ocean 'barrier and javelin' strategy cost in both the central and southern sectors losses in ships and aircraft that could not be replaced in terms of either quality or quantity. The land forces committed in China steadily demodernized in the context of a

---

2 The process is developed in Dennis Showalter, *Hitler's Panzers: The Lightning Attacks that Revolutionized Warfare* (New York: Berkeley, 2009), pp. 14–84.
3 The most detailed presentation of this fundamental transformation is *Das Deutsche Reich und der Zweite Weltkrieg*, vol. VIII: *Die Ostfront 1943/44* (Munich: Deutsche Verlags-Anstalt, 2007).

stagnant operational environment, combined with a toxic occupational climate that prioritized killing Chinese civilians over defeating Chinese soldiers.[4] Japan put more and more men in uniform between 1942 and 1945. It made less and less difference.

Both Japanese and German armed forces increasingly confronted energy with cultures of immolation. Neither ethos was fundamentally suicidal. What they shared was an emphasis on challenging and overcoming superior force with skill and character. Dying became not part of the soldier's contract, but central to it. Nazi Germany's version was individually heroic: tank killers like Michael Wittman and Ernst Barkmann; fighter *experten* on the lines of Adolf Galland or Erich Hartmann; such U-boat aces as Otto Kretschmer and Erich Topp. Japan's model tended toward the impersonal; one element of a national collective epitomized by the final anonymity of the Yasukuni Shrine.

General William Slim's familiar aphorism that all armies talk about fighting to the death, but only the Japanese actually did it was borne out everywhere in the Pacific and South Asian theatres in the war's final eighteen months. The extent, however, to which this was a reaction to particular operational circumstances, as opposed to being a consequence of Japan's general military culture, merits more attention than it has yet received.[5] In the Wehrmacht, particularly on the Eastern Front, willpower and ferocity compensated for increasingly overstretched technology. National Socialist ideology legitimated sacrifice. Its insistence that the German soldier was inherently superior to his enemies could be a barrier to despair. And at the last ditch, a Tiger's five-man crew, three infantrymen with an MG 42 or a schoolboy with a Panzerfaust could do a lot of damage before going under. The trope's enduring force is indicated – unintentionally – by the classic 1959 West German film *The Bridge*. The half-dozen teenagers meaninglessly sacrificed in the Third Reich's final days manage to chew up an American battle group in the process.

The USSR's armed forces followed a long-term path from mass toward energy. In 1931, Stalin had warned, 'we are fifty or a hundred years behind the advanced countries. We must make good this distance in ten years...or go

---

4 For this, see in particular the contributions to Mark Peattie, Edward Drea and Hans van de Ven (eds.), *The Battle for China: Essays on the Military History of the Sino-Japanese War of 1937–1945* (Stanford University Press, 2011).
5 A serviceable beginning is Kawano Hitoshi, 'A Comparative Study of Combat Organizations: Japanese and American during World War II' (PhD dissertation, Northwestern University, 1996).

under'. His demand was to make Russia 'a country of metal, a country of automobiles, a country of tractors' – and a country of tanks and aircraft.[6] With military spending privileged over civilian production and budget-balancing, the Red Army by 1938 had transformed itself from an infantry-based militia to, arguably, the world's most technologically progressive force, with a developed doctrine of deep penetration based on mechanized combined arms forces.

Stalin's fears of a military coup by a technocratic elite led, in the late 1930s, to the army's reconversion to an infantry-based force. The success of the Panzers in 1940 brought a reversal of that decision, and the recreation of large mechanized units. Training, command and equipment could not be so easily improvised. The same problems made a rapidly expanded air force, at best, marginally combat-ready in June 1941. The resulting near-catastrophe required the Red Army's fundamental reconstruction. This reconstruction, moreover, followed pre-purge principles The German-nurtured image of a heavy blunt military instrument depending on sheer bulk bears only a tangential relationship to the Red Army of 1944–45. The cutting edge of the final offensives against the Third Reich was mechanized. Though it was necessary to start at the bottom, tank brigades grew to corps size: two dozen of them. Eventually complemented by thirteen more infantry-heavy mechanized corps, they finished the war organized into five tank armies that taught the Germans brutal lessons in armoured exploitation. The tanks were supported by complete artillery divisions and entire artillery corps, and complemented by no fewer than a dozen air armies, whose equipment and tactics were focused on ground support. Logistics, maintenance and communications were basic by Western standards, but functioned effectively in context. And Red Army intelligence in the war's final years was successful in every aspect, from tactical deception to grand-strategic *maskirovka* (a term combining the meanings of the English words 'camouflage', 'deception' and 'security').[7]

The USSR's growing dependence on the products of energy as the war progressed reflected as well the fact that domestic production and Lend-Lease made it increasingly easier to replace materiel than men.[8] The Soviet system is

---

6 Joseph Stalin, *Works* (13 vols., Moscow: Foreign Languages Publishing House, 1952–55), vol. XII, p. 141, and vol. XIII, pp. 40–1.

7 This line of argument is best illustrated in the magisterial body of work by David Glantz, whose best overview remains the work co-authored with Jonathan M. House, *When Titans Clashed: How the Red Army Stopped Hitler* (Lawrence: University Press of Kansas, 1995).

8 See, generally, Mark Harrison, *Accounting for War: Soviet Production, Employment, and the Defence Burden, 1940–1945* (Cambridge University Press, 1996).

frequently described as being indifferent to human loss. A more accurate evaluation is that human beings were perceived instrumentally. Like everything else in the USSR, people were a means to an end. In a sense, they could even be mass-produced. The problem was that it took longer to qualify the product for military use. Eventually, priorities had to be established. While Russia mobilized over 500 rifle divisions by 1945, most fell well below even their relatively small authorized strength. The mechanized units, on the other hand, were kept close to full establishments of everyone and everything.

If one focuses on structure as opposed to scale, Britain surpassed even Russia in creating energy-based armed forces. This was a product of post-1918 civil electrification and motorization, and a consequence of public rejection of the concept of another bloody ground war on the Continent. British defence policy put the Royal Air Force at the head of the list, the Royal Navy a close second, and a future British Expeditionary Force at the bottom. Britain did not reject a continental commitment. It defined that commitment, however, in a context of high-tech force multipliers: a minimum of manpower and a maximum of machines and electronics.[9] The force Britain dispatched to the Continent in 1939 was fully motorized and mechanized: the only one of its kind in the world. But its initial strength was only four divisions – not exactly a diplomatic or operational balance-shifter, even when radar and the RAF are included.

Britain continued to emphasize energy in waging the Second World War. That reflected increasing overstretch of its human resources, male and female. Britain matched the USSR, and arguably surpassed it in the percentage of its population directly devoted to the war effort. It reflected as well the enduring spirit of 'Never again!' permeating Britain at all levels, from 10 Downing Street to the Anchor and Crown (*pace* Noel Coward). The new generation required and deserved careful handling and a comprehensive technological matrix. Firepower, logistics, communications, planning and medical care: these defined the 1939–45 'British way in warfare'.[10] The concept reached its apogee in Normandy, where tanks were sufficiently easier to replace than men; the practice developed of promptly reassigning crews from one knocked-out Sherman to another. While this application of

---

9 David French, *Raising Churchill's Army: The British Army and the War Against Germany, 1919–1945* (Oxford University Press, 2000). Harold R. Winton, *To Change an Army: General Sir John Burnett-Stuart and British Armored Doctrine, 1927–1938* (Lawrence: University Press of Kansas, 1988), remains useful for details.

10 John Buckley, *Monty's Men: The British Army and the Liberation of Europe* (New Haven, Conn.: Yale University Press, 2013).

human/mechanical interchangeability did not long survive the psychological realities of armoured combat, the Commonwealth juggernaut that eviscerated the Japanese in Burma during the war's final months is a case study in the combination of striking power and flexibility that energy-based war made possible, even at the far end of a fraying logistics system – given a creative commander like Bill Slim.

The Royal Navy's increasing and hard-won mastery of electronic war across the spectrum was decisive in its war against the U-boats. Sonar and radar, acoustic decoys and homing torpedoes – the list of gadgets and weapons is as long as the relationship between scientists and sailors is complex.[11] The definitive example of Britain's mass/energy balance, however, was the five-year campaign of RAF Bomber Command. Begun in part as the only way of striking Germany directly, it endured and flourished as an epitome of breaking the enemy at minimal cost in British lives and minimal risk of an all-or-nothing ground operation. Ironically, the bomber offensive resembles the Western Front of the First World War in that ultimate success seemed just ahead, yet always the means fell short of the ends. Only the optimism endured. Ironically, it became a case study in attrition. Forty-four per cent of Bomber Command's crews died in action – a percentage exceeded only by the German U-boat service. But on the other side of the coin, those 56,000 accreted over an entire war rather than a few specific days – like the 20,000 dead of 1 July 1916.

US armed forces struck the closest balance between mass and energy. The familiar images are all on one side of the scale, from bombers flowing endlessly off the lines at Willow Run to the colossal fleets of the Pacific War and the tanks standing nose to tail in the European theatre of operations. But not until well into 1942 did the Roosevelt administration develop the regulatory and administrative measures that moved the economy onto a war footing. Until 1943, the USA still produced almost a pre-war spectrum of civilian goods.

In the First World War, the nation's war effort had been rigidly and comprehensively controlled from the top. The second time around, time and again, private initiatives proved more productive than centralized fine-tuning, New Deal style. Secretary of War Henry Stimson put it bluntly and accurately: waging war in a capitalist economy was impossible unless business made money. Recognizing that meant slack persisted in the system – but it was slack the government increasingly understood to be an asset.

---

11 Stephen Budiansky, *Blackett's War: The Men Who Defeated the Nazi U-Boats and Brought Science to the Art of Warfare* (New York: Knopf, 2013).

In human terms, the USA made only marginal use of its women, and squandered a further 10 per cent of its resources by refusing to utilize its African American citizens in anything like their numbers or capacities. The USA maintained the most rigorous standards of all major combatants for induction into the armed forces. These factors eventually combined with the demands of the Navy, the Air Force and the factories to reduce an initial projection of 250 ground combat divisions to fewer than a hundred.[12]

Yet for all of these leaks and gaps, the USA waged a mass war at the sharp end. America put over 12 million men and women in uniform. It deployed and sustained significant forces across the world. The '90 division gamble' generated anxieties in the front line and at high levels in the war's final year – anxieties enhanced by a willingness of US generals to accept, at certain times for certain objectives, casualty rates that at times raised German eyebrows, to say nothing of British ones. But the gamble was justified by the same factor that was the critical multiplier of American mass: America's energy war. The USA created from scratch two entirely different military systems: one for Europe, one for the Pacific. Apart from jeeps and trucks, the USA manufactured enough first-category hardware to rearm France entirely and to supply over half of Britain's tank inventory in the D-Day campaign. American discards and rejects, the P-39 and the P-63, flew alongside the Shturmovik in the Red Air Force. The often-maligned Sherman was a welcome supplement to the T-34 among the *tankists*.

No less significant in terms of the 'mass' aspect of America's energy war was its sustainability. Whatever it took, wherever it took, by 1944 the USA was able to put more than enough on it – whether that meant replacing losses or reshaping landscapes. A joke current in the southwest Pacific had a local asked 'Who is the best jungle fighter?' He replied, 'The Japanese are very good in the jungle. The Australians are very good. But the Americans make the jungle disappear.' Sustainability involved as well the ability to mitigate the hardships of service in alien environments by providing a broad spectrum of physical amenities. Products of a society with high levels of consumerism, American servicemen saw timely delivery of mail and reasonable availability of chewing gum, cigarettes and cold beer as both indicators of support and evidence of a 'culture of competence' in both the armed forces and at the national level.[13] They responded positively. Americans in

---

12 Maury Klein, *A Call to Arms: Mobilizing America for World War II* (New York: Bloomsbury, 2013).
13 James J. Cooke, *Chewing Gum, Candy Bars, and Beer: The Army PX in World War II* (Columbia: University of Missouri Press, 2009).

uniform had their limitations. But the typical US serviceman met the physical and emotional challenges of a war that – by comparison to his British, Russian and German counterparts – was seldom directly his.[14]

The dynamics of change

The First World War was a comprehensively traumatizing experience for armed forces expected and required to play major roles in their government's policies. Even the Americans, engaged for a relatively brief time, and the Japanese, barely engaged at all, faced a contest between the experience of war and the hope of improving their performance next time. The Great War had been a war of accretion, with armies and fleets the cutting edge of a massive blade built from the entire material and moral resources of a state and its people. It had been a gridlocked war because of a drastic imbalance in the operational triangle of mobility, protection and firepower. Firepower was the obtuse angle, countered ultimately by weight of shells and number of bodies. The gridlock endured because the armed forces involved were unusually symmetrical; not since the mid-eighteenth century had like confronted like to such a degree across lines of combat. The result was mutual homogenization. Pre-war rivalries focused on details at the expense of thinking outside the box. Translated to the battlefield, this produced a war of nuances, of seeking small advantages that somehow might become decisive.

By 1918, the Allies had developed a form of semi-managed, semi-mobile battle, built around doctrinal, institutional and technological coherence among infantry, artillery, tanks and aircraft, partially powered by oil and partially coordinated by radio. Its attacks were able to lurch forward in a progress that grew steadier with practice, pushing back the enemy front without rupturing it, until the German generals demanded that the government sue for peace. Yet even in the war's final stages, technique and technology could not significantly reduce casualties. They could only improve the ratio of gains in a process of comprehensive attrition that left even the victors reeling with exhaustion. In professional hindsight, it seemed clear that victory had depended in good part on whose clock ran out first.[15]

---

14 But see Charles Glass, *The Deserters: A Hidden History of World War II* (New York: Penguin, 2013).
15 David Stevenson, *With Our Backs to the Wall: Victory and Defeat in 1918* (Cambridge, Mass.: Belknap Press of Harvard University Press, 2011).

Post-First World War armed forces thus confronted a fundamental question. How could they fight the next war so as to avoid not so much length as stalemate? America's response was most abstract. Its armed forces drew conclusions from their First World War experience in a theoretical context sufficiently extreme to be called a vacuum. Neither the Army nor Navy had a clear and present mission reflecting a clear and present danger. The Navy's focus was operational, on the Pacific and Japan. The Army's perspective was broader. It understood that modern war between industrialized nations inevitably tended toward stabilized fronts. Overcoming them required combined arms, able to emphasize firepower in an operation's initial stages, mobility in the later ones. Creating such a force in turn required comprehensive planning and national mobilization. Beginning in the 1920s, soldiers and businessmen cooperated in developing a number of mobilization plans based on broad, centralized administrative powers to mobilize and manage the nation's assets. Never directly implemented, these plans nevertheless provided experience in cooperation, facilitated personal contacts, and eased the transition to the next world war.[16]

The USSR comprehensively combined theory and institutions. The Soviet system's legitimating ideology of Marxism-Leninism defined war as a science. Its principles, systematically studied and properly applied, enabled anticipating the consequences of decisions, behaviours – even attitudes. A rising generation of technocrats sought to synergize mass and mechanization in order to vitalize and expand the Communist revolution. 'Shock armies', based on numbers and firepower, would rupture the front. 'Deep operations' by air supported, fully mechanized mobile groups would take the fight into the enemy's rear, demoralizing as well as destroying first the fighting forces, then their supporting systems, and eventually their political and social structures.[17]

The USA and the USSR processed experience in matrices of theory. Great Britain relied on hope. On the one hand, Britain after its First World War experience never seriously considered a return to the 'splendid isolation' of the previous century. The newly created Royal Air Force took the lead here. Its insistence on strategic bombing as potentially decisive morally and

---

16 Paul A. C. Koistinnen, *Planning War, Pursuing Peace: The Political Economy of American Warfare, 1920–1939* (Lawrence: University Press of Kansas, 1998).

17 Richard W. Harrison, *The Russian Way of War: Operational Art, 1907–1940* (Lawrence: University Press of Kansas, 2001); Sally W. Stoecker, *Forging Stalin's Army: Marshal Tukhachevsky and the Politics of Military Innovation* (Boulder, Colo.: Westview Press, 1998).

materially made it a logical instrument of power projection. But the training, the infrastructure, the technology and the doctrine of strategic bombardment developed slowly – so slowly that in August 1939 the Air Ministry described unrestricted air war as not in Britain's interests.[18] The interwar army developed a reasonably high level of consensus on modern warfare's nature and demands. But it was constrained to respond as well to an empire whose policing and control had little relevance to the internal combustion engine. A Royal Navy whipsawed by metastasizing institutional costs, and the restrictions imposed by interwar naval limitation treaties turned inward, de-emphasizing strategic considerations in favour of issues of tactics and ship design, and developing a spectrum of dubious answers.

German armed forces reacted to defeat in 1918 by building on a Prussian legacy of shock and awe. That meant challenging the Schlieffen-era concept of mass. Reconfiguring future war was also a function of necessity. The Weimar Republic could neither defend itself nor influence its neighbours with the armed forces allowed by the Versailles Treaty. The Reichswehr's response was to create an army able to fight outnumbered and win. It was not directly intended as a cadre for national mobilization. The intention was eventually to enlarge and enhance the existing force, enabling it to control operations by taking the initiative and forcing encounter battles where training and flexibility could compensate for numerical and material inferiority.[19] By the mid-1920s, the concept of using tanks not only in masses, but as part of a comprehensively motorized force was percolating in the literature, the service schools and the troop staffs. By the early 1930s, the postulate that quality enhanced by technology could overcome numbers was becoming the matrix of doctrine. The Nazi seizure of power would inaugurate a synergy of operational and ideological perspectives.

Among the interwar military powers, Japan was the most accepting of national aggrandizement by direct force – perhaps a consequence of its marginal involvement in the Great War. Of the world's navies, Japan's was by a solid margin the most hostile to the post-war limitation treaties, the least accepting of their provisions and paradigms.[20] The army maintained its commitment to the principle that a short, decisive war was both desirable

18 Richard Overy, *The Bombers and the Bombed: Allied Air War Over Europe, 1940–1945* (New York: Viking, 2013), p. 36.
19 James S. Corum, *The Roots of Blitzkrieg: Hans von Seeckt and German Military Reform* (Lawrence: University Press of Kansas, 2002).
20 John H. Maurer and Christopher Bell, *At the Crossroads between Peace and War: The London Naval Conference of 1930* (Annapolis, Md.: Naval Institute Press, 2013).

and an attainable way to achieve national military objectives. Both armed services, however, faced critical gaps between ends and means. Japan was unable to match its significant potential opponents, Russia, China and the USA, in any context of mass. Whether in the immediate post-war climate of budgetary retrenchment or the absolute and proportional increase in military expenditures undertaken in the 1930s, Japan's economy was unable to come near supporting full-spectrum technological modernization. The rift – better said, chasm – was bridged by acknowledging the fact. Aircraft designs were optimized for performance at the expense of survivability. Warships were configured to be individually superior to their counterparts in other navies. The army's light machine guns were fitted with bayonet attachments – a symbol of a national determination to seek decision at close quarters.

If victory in the Second World War had a common denominator of perspective, it was innovation. The USA and Britain, together and separately, came to set the pace – in good part because they had no choice. As late as the summer of 1940, Britain was barely surviving, hoping for assistance from a USA whose war industries were expanding from French and British orders, but whose ground and air forces were still in a risible state of becoming. The Navy had been increasing its size since 1938, and had a war-winning two-ocean fleet on its construction horizons.[21] Blueprints, however, do not fight. But by 1945, the armed forces of the Western Allies had gone through almost bewilderingly rapid incremental changes in terms of technology and doctrine. The Spitfire 1 of 1940 retained the familiar air frame in 1945 – but had little else beyond short range in common with the Spitfire xiv. The British Comet and the US Pershing tanks, though available only in small numbers toward the end of the war, resembled their 1940 predecessors only in basic outline. As for doctrine, the American learning curve was global in scope and steep in perspective. From Savo Island, Kasserine Pass and Schweinfurt, US Armed Forces seldom made the same mistake the same way a third time in succession. The British, especially in land war, were so concerned with adjusting to experience that they tended to prepare for the situation just past, as opposed to trying to leap ahead of the curve. That posed problems, from the Battle of the Atlantic to the killing fields of Caen – but not the kinds of problems caused by inanition.

German innovation differed from the Anglo-American model in being fundamental rather than incremental. To a degree arguably unique in the

---

21 John T. Kuehn, *Agents of Innovation: The General Board and the Design of the Fleet that Defeated the Japanese* (Annapolis, Md.: Naval Institute Press, 2008).

From the interwar German armed forces' perspective, national renewal ultimately depended on military regeneration of the army. That regeneration required national unity based on military service, military purpose and the militarization of German society. The form of government, in the view of Germany's military leaders, was not of central importance. While the Reichswehr refused to identify directly with the Weimar Republic, it was not a coup waiting to happen. That said, however, the Nazi seizure of power inaugurated more a synergy of operational and ideological perspectives than the rivalry often affirmed and presented by post-war historians. Such central principles as courage, comradeship and conformity were, from the beginning, central to both army and party. The coming of the war privileged the military's versions of them. And if men have never fought better in a worse cause than those who wore the swastika, there are worse explanations than the congruence of the Nazi twisted cross and the Wehrmacht's field grey.[25]

The ideology that Japan's armed forces institutionalized and facilitated was more fundamental than those of Germany and the USSR. Its heritage is traceable not to any samurai legacy, but to the Russo-Japanese War of 1904–5.[26] Government propaganda celebrating front-line sacrifices combined with popular rejection of Western cultural values generated ersatz samurai images that developed into an ethos encouraging fighting to the death and characterizing surrender as disgrace. An educational system that obsessively glorified national identity and martial values combined with an internal culture of brutality in the armed forces to nurture a sense of moral and racial superiority which, during the Second World War, was encouraged rather than restrained at all levels of policy and behaviour. But considered in context, the ideological dimension of Japan's armed forces contributed substantially to a war effort sustained well beyond rational calculation in any culture's context.

The armed forces of Great Britain are best understood as contributing attitudes rather than principles to the six-year conflict. Britain was sufficiently familiar with general war to support its 'way in warfare' as 'liberal

Socialism, 1919–1939 (Ithaca, NY: Cornell University Press, 2013); and the contributions to James Harris (ed.), *The Anatomy of Terror: Political Violence under Stalin* (Oxford University Press, 2013).

25 A good introduction to this complex subject is Wolfram Wette, *The Wehrmacht: History, Myth, Reality* (Cambridge, Mass.: Harvard University Press, 2006).

26 Naoko Shimazu, *Japanese Society at War: Death, Memory and the Russo-Japanese War* (Cambridge University Press, 2009).

militarism'.[27] Millions of men had served in uniform from 1914 to 1918. Millions of adults had experienced a society at war. Nor was the general revulsion to war as ultimate futility, widespread among interwar social and intellectual elites, a universal mindset. It was a particular form of human sacrifice, the trenches of France and Flanders, that was considered unacceptable and unrepeatable. In the Second World War, fundamentally civilian organizations like the ARP (Air Raid Precautions) and the Home Guard were vital to the British effort. Britain's mobilization of women combined comprehensiveness and visibility more than any other combatant's, including the Soviet Union. The British war's major defining experiences, Dunkirk, the Blitz, were held in common – at least in terms of national mythology.[28] More than any other major combatant, moreover, Britain's military fought a good percentage of its war from home. The RAF's major effort, the Combined Bomber Offensive, was British-based. Until mid-1944, a high proportion of the army was quartered in its own backyards, often in areas safer than the cities in the first line of a continuing German air offensive. The Royal Navy executed the Battle of the Atlantic, the Russian convoy campaign and its hunts for the *Bismarck* and the *Tirpitz* from familiar ports.

Great Britain, in short, had a homogenized war experience – one in which the armed forces were directly involved. David Low's cartoon of June 1940, captioned 'Very Well, Alone', with its steel-helmeted Tommy shaking a defiant fist, expresses a spirit, however it might fray around the edges, of the British fighting to a finish as one people, in uniform or not. The French, the Russians and the Yanks be damned! Britain and its people were in this together! And as the war progressed, becoming an endurance test rivalling and surpassing that of 1914–18, the armed forces became a focal point of a movement for Britain's post-war reconstruction. The men and women in uniform saw military service as a temporary stage in their lives, and a means to a better future – a better future, certainly, than the 'country fit for heroes' promised in 1918. The government provided increasingly detailed white papers; the armed forces sponsored increasingly comprehensive discussions. The result was an unexpectedly immediate and comprehensive commitment to post-war change.[29]

27 For this concept, see, particularly, David Edgerton, *Warfare State: Britain, 1920–1970* (Cambridge University Press, 2006)

28 David Reynolds, *The Long Shadow: The Legacies of the Great War in the Twentieth Century* (New York: W. W. Norton, 2014), pp. 253–8; Angus Calder, *The Myth of the Blitz* (London: Publico, 1991)

29 Jeremy Crang, *The British Army and the People's War* (Manchester University Press, 2000); and Roger Broad, *The Radical General: Sir Ronald Adam and Britain's New Model Army, 1941–46* (Stroud: Spellmount, 2013), pp. 121–71.

America's armed forces were the focal point of the distinctive US perception of the war as a job. As early as 1942, war correspondent Ernie Pyle noted that GIs in North Africa spoke of a mission in terms of 'I hear you've got a job', or 'What's this about a job?' Americans' collective indifference to high causes remained, however, the bane of the Office of War Information and of German POW interrogators alike. Germany had race and the USSR had the class struggle. The USA had the Four Freedoms – if anyone could remember what they were. The sense of the war as work may have owed something to the Depression, when work was a fundamental good. It may have been a way of 'normalizing' in a war that posed no credible, significant, direct risk to the USA proper. America's was a war fought across the globe, often in places as far away from the United States as it seemed possible to be. The logical question was, 'What are we doing here?' with expletives added to taste. The acceptable answer was 'Our jobs'. The acceptable subtext was 'Because that's the only way to get home'.[30]

Germans remained perceived as an abstract enemy. Japanese were seen as aliens with whom no meaningful contact was possible. Even American violence against civilians, from nuclear bombardment to rape, had a detached, almost impersonal quality compared to its German, Japanese and Soviet counterparts. But if the war was a job to be done, for American men and women in uniform it was a job to be completed. Unconditional surrender was not a government propaganda afterthought. The Armed Forces' prevailing ethos was not to demonize America's enemies, but to crush them: to make certain the job would never have to be repeated. Doing it right the first time was the American way of life; it became the American way of war.

Whether or not the Second World War was a total war remains a subject of discussion. What cannot be questioned is that it was a war to the finish. This is generally understood in terms of ideology, politics and propaganda. Nazi Germany's war aims and war methods were, from the beginning, devoid of principled restraint. The USSR saw itself as fighting not only for its own existence, not only for the survival of the global revolution, but to preserve the course of history itself. Franklin Roosevelt, the consummate pragmatist, defined America's war effort as morally based, and correspondingly unsusceptible of compromise. Even in the darkest days of 1940, Britain considered negotiation with Germany only as a last, desperate, above all temporary, resort. There is a certain irony in that Japan, the culture with the

---

30 'War as a job' is a recurrent theme in Gerald F. Linderman's seminal *The World within War: America's Combat Experience in World War II* (New York: Free Press, 1997).

most comprehensive ethic of 'no surrender', was the only one that accepted negotiation – with the Western powers at least – as the optional outcome of its war-making.[31]

Internally, when persuasion failed to impel participation, combatants turned to compulsions ranging from near-random mass executions in the Soviet Union, through Germany's Field Courts-Martial and Kin Liability Laws, to Japan's increasingly ubiquitous Kempeitai and America's internment of German-, Italian-and, above all, Japanese-Americans. Taken as a whole, however, duress and intimidation were touches of the whip. The Second World War's civilians, unlike their predecessors, continued to fear the enemy more than they hated their own governments.[32]

But neither governments nor civilians made or sustained war at the sharp end. The Second World War was fought to a finish because the 'successful' armed forces stood to a finish – and beyond, in the case of Germany and Japan.[33] This was in sharp contrast to the Great War of 1914–18. The Russian army began dissolving well before the Russian Revolution. Germany's war ended with a naval mutiny and a 'camouflaged strike' by the army. The Italian army came close to dissolution as a consequence of defeat in 1917; the Austro-Hungarians disintegrated a year later in the face of a final Allied offensive; the French army was approaching the end of its tether by the armistice. But the British in 1940 and the Russians in 1941 essentially held firm under strains arguably greater, and certainly more shocking than their First World War predecessors faced. By 1945, British infantrymen in Northwest Europe, Italy and Burma may have been concerned primarily with not being the last ones killed in a six-year war that seemed like forever – but they continued to cross their start-lines. Across the battle lines, the Wehrmacht was finally submerged, but never outfought. Japan mobilized over 10,000 aircraft, over 1,000 suicide boats, over sixty ground divisions, and over 30 million civilians for a final stand in the home islands.

Fear, hate and habit can keep soldiers fighting. Belief is an even more powerful imperative. The armed forces of the Second World War were essentially citizen institutions to a unique degree. Their Great War

---

31 Eri Hotta, *Countdown to Infamy: Japan 1941* (New York: Knopf, 2013), is excellent on the domestic dynamics of the decision for war.

32 Fearing one's government more than the enemy did remain an option. See Sven Keller, *Volksgeimschaft am Ende. Gesellschaft und Gewalt, 1944/45* (Munich: Oldenbourg, 2013).

33 The governments of France and Italy took their countries out of the war when their armed forces were still keeping the field – though arguably more or less. For France, in particular, see Martin S. Alexander, 'After Dunkirk: The French Army's Performance against Case Red', *War in History* 14 (2007), 219–64.

predecessors had retained far more of the traditional subject status than is generally recognized. To Russian and Austro-Hungarian soldiers, 'citizenship' prior to 1914 meant little more than police, taxes and conscription. By 1917, misery had been added to that short list. Even Britain, at the other end of the modernization spectrum, fought the war with an army heavily influenced by traditional class and caste values.

By 1939, and certainly by 1945, however, matters had changed fundamentally. After 1918, governments, often themselves direct creations of wartime disintegration, sought to add moral aspects to their consideration of the next time: to ensure what F. Scott Fitzgerald called 'a whole-souled emotional equipment'. The Second World War was in good part enabled by national psychological mobilizations that had in common a concept of stakeholding. Stakeholding was based as much on promise as delivery. It reflected conscious public affirmation of, and participation in, a system preferable to the alternatives – one that would, once the war ended, be realistically able and willing to provide not merely subsistence, but satisfaction to its members. For the armed forces in particular, the First World War had been an endurance test: something to be survived. The Second World War was predicated on a commitment to the future.

That commitment had two taproots: hope and faith. The fighting men and women of the Soviet Union were at the sharp end of a war for survival. It was obvious within six months that whatever was wrong with the Soviet system would not be fixed by a Nazi victory. Yet the USSR's front-line soldiers also increasingly believed that the state owed its people something. They hoped their sacrifices would bring about 'Communism with a human face': amelioration of agricultural collectivization and workplace discipline, more freedom of thought and speech, more decentralized decision-making.[34] British Labour's landslide in the general elections of July 1945 was also underwritten by hope. It represented less the result of a slow and steady rise to power than the consequence of an unexpected 'fair shares for all' tsunami, whose waves were tinged Army khaki, Royal Navy blue and RAF blue-grey.[35]

The future commitment of Nazi Germany's Wehrmacht, by contrast, was faith-based. Structurally, it was a paradox: best understood as a technocratic

---

34 Catherine Merridale, *Ivan's War: Life and Death in the Red Army, 1939–1945* (New York: Holt, 2006).
35 Steven Fielding, 'What Did "the People" Want? The Meaning of the 1945 General Election', *Historical Journal* 35 (1992), 623–39.

folk community, informed by faith in its cause and its leader. That faith grew more abstract as the war's prospects grew worse, but in the end it had to be crushed under tank treads and blasted by heavy bombs.[36] Japan's armed forces, too, depended on faith as a matrix of the future. In that case, it was faith in the imperial order, which embodied the order of the universe. As the war progressed, especially in the Pacific, faith eroded. This development reflected the deteriorating military situation, the deterioration of logistics systems and command effectiveness, and, to a surprising degree, the lack of substantive news as opposed to clearly uncredible propaganda. The latter two were widely processed as breaches of Japan's social contract: the imperial system regarded Japanese as stakeholders in a way its Nazi and Soviet counterparts did not. A correspondingly common response to disillusion was suicide, directly or 'by enemy action': death became an end in itself rather than a consequence of performing one's duty – which negated the original concept of bushido, and diminished operational effectiveness to a point where commanders inveighed against 'desperate self-destruction'.[37]

America's experience combined hope and faith. Among their major manifestations was the comprehensive voluntarism that underpinned the US war effort. Private initiatives synergized with executive authority to generate in individuals a powerful mixture of patriotism and self-interest. The US Navy was overwhelmingly volunteer throughout the war. USAAF air crews were self selected. Eleven of the ninety-five ground combat divisions (five Airborne and six Marine) were sustained essentially by volunteers. This volunteering must not be confused with free choice; but within the Selective Service matrix, white males of any social class had a spectrum of possibilities that even included the chance to attend college while in uniform. Doing good and doing well simultaneously: that too was part of the American way!

Organization: control and interaction

The armed forces of the Second World War were characterized by comprehensive civilianization. It began at the top. In 1914, the short-war illusion led

---

36 On this, see, esp., *Das Deutsche Reich und der Zweite Weltkrieg*, vol. x, pt. 1: *Der Zusammenbruch des Deutsche Reiches. Die militärische Niederwerfung der Wehrmacht* (Munich: Deutsche Verlags-Anstalt, 2008).

37 Allison B. Gilmore, *You Can't Fight Tanks with Bayonets: Psychological Warfare against the Japanese Army in the Southwest Pacific* (Lincoln: University of Nebraska Press, 1998), is a useful introduction to this overlooked subject. See, as a case study, Craig Collie and Hajime Marutani, *The Path of Infinite Sorrow: The Japanese on the Kokoda Track* (Crows Nest, NSW: Allen & Unwin, 2009).

governments to turn the war's conduct over to the soldiers. Between 1915 and 1917, politicians and generals grappled for control of a stagnating conflict. In France and Britain, the result was an uneasy compromise that outlasted the German solution of a de facto military dictatorship. In Russia and Austria-Hungary, the generals ran the show – largely by default – until the wheels came off. At the other end of the spectrum, Woodrow Wilson controlled America's war effort with an iron hand that frequently inhibited effectiveness.

In the later, greater conflict, Japan's armed forces came the closest to replicating the Great War pattern. The army and the navy devoted almost as much energy to fighting each other as the empire's enemies. But from the mid-1930s, their influence on state policy-making was decisive; their control of strategy and operations remained absolute until 1945; and the resulting catastrophe was no less spectacular than its 1914–18 predecessors.

Japan aside, civilian control during the Second World War followed three models. The most complex was the synergy that developed in Nazi Germany. Hitler may have insisted from the beginning that, as the Greatest Warlord of All Time, his was the only voice that counted. His surviving generals increasingly accepted the point as a way of transferring moral and professional responsibility. The result was near-complete congruence between the Führer and the Wehrmacht high command in the war's crucial years.[38] In the decisive Eastern theatre, from BARBAROSSA to CITADEL and well beyond, Hitler and his generals worked in a harmony not much less than that of the Allied high command in the Northwest Europe campaign. The tensions predictable among strong personalities developed toward open, fundamental conflict and dissent only in the war's final months – when it was far too late to make a difference in Hitler's war.

In the USSR, 'civilian' – that is to say, government and party – control over the armed forces had been strengthened by the purges of the 1930s. It was confirmed, however, only when Stalin recovered more quickly than his generals from the first weeks of disaster in the summer of 1941 – and when those generals proved unable to check the Nazi advance in military contexts. Stalin functioned as both the symbolic and the actual rallying point of the Soviet state. He mobilized the resources of an industrial base physically relocated beyond the Ural Mountains. He brokered the Lend-Lease that sustained the USSR's war effort in a spectrum of vital ways. He controlled

38 Geoffrey Megargee, *Inside Hitler's High Command* (Lawrence: University Press of Kansas, 2000).

the new generation of field commanders developed in the cauldron of the Eastern Front, fitting them into slots, playing them against each other – and never allowing them to forget the possible nine-gram consequence of failure.[39]

It is an open question whether Hitler or Stalin inspired more direct fear in their senior officers. What is known is that active military resistance was confined to the Third Reich – as much because after Stalingrad and Kursk, the reconfigured Soviet system was working well enough to keep its generals focused across the fighting line instead of behind it.

Civilian control in Britain and the USA was in good part indirect – if only because Churchill and Roosevelt had less drastic options for dealing with inadequate performance, military or civilian. FDR is generally and legitimately credited with directing America's war effort as opposed to managing it: integrating its complex elements with the same skill he had shown in peacetime at brokering and managing a New Deal that consisted of networks of lesser deals among parties and interest groups. While Roosevelt's preferences might have been for more of a controlling hand, 'Doctor Win-The-War' did most of the prescribing.[40]

Churchill, confronting fewer resources and a more fundamentally challenged status quo, regularly drove his military chiefs frantic with ideas usually ill-timed or impractical. He possessed, however, a corresponding sense of when to climb down – a sense that served him well in dealing with a parliament and a public opinion increasingly weary, increasingly fractious and increasingly concerned with post-war Britain's configuration.[41]

The Prime Minister's energy was also, fortunately, heavily engaged by the Anglo-American alliance. The Special Relationship required nurturing and management. In particular, Churchill and Roosevelt both understood that the balance among the 'core four' policy-makers, Churchill and Alan Brooke for the British, Roosevelt and Marshall for the Americans, could not be allowed to harden along national or professional lines. The result was a constant shifting of balances that kept both civilian war leaders more conscious generally of the uses of flexibility and conciliation than their respective

---

39 Geoffrey Roberts, *Stalin's Wars: From World War to Cold War, 1939–1953* (New Haven, Conn.: Yale University Press, 2006). See also Robert Gellately, *Stalin's Curse: Battling for Communism in War and Cold War* (New York: Knopf, 2013).

40 On Roosevelt and 'managed capitalism', see Richard P. Adelstein, 'The Nation as Economic Unit: Keynes, Roosevelt, and the Managerial Ideal', *Journal of American History* 78 (1991), 160–87.

41 Narrow front-runner in a strong field on this subject is Martin Gilbert, *Winston Churchill's War Leadership* (New York: Vintage, 2004).

temperaments warranted – and kept as well their respective war efforts running smoothly with limited lubrication.[42]

Civilianization had a second aspect: the synergizing of military and civilian systems in problem-solving contexts. Here, arguably more than anywhere else, the dichotomy between Allies and Axis was absolute. The British and the Americans developed what Paul Kennedy calls a 'culture of encouragement'. Their systems of production and management possessed effective feedback loops connecting top, middle and bottom. They stimulated initiative. They encouraged problem-solvers to address large issues without veering into dead ends. Above all, successful systems emphasized organization and supported those who could manage organizations. These 'middle people', whether in uniforms, lab coats or business suits, were the keys to the Western war effort.[43]

The USSR achieved something like the same results, though from radically different parameters. There is a question whether 'civilians', in the Anglo-American sense, even existed in the wartime Soviet Union. Unlimited loyalty and inexhaustible participation, part of the Soviet social contract since the revolution, were guaranteed by never-ending force and the absolute challenge of the Nazi invasion. Generals and aircraft designers were transferred directly from the Gulag to the battlefield and the drawing board – and gave distinguished service in both venues.

Germany and Japan, by contrast, kept their problem-solving militarized. Both military systems embodied the conviction that shoulder-straps conferred comprehensive brilliance in matters from logistics organization to weapons designing. Civilians were either marginalized or encysted. German aeronautical engineers, for example, spent over six years developing a long-range bomber whose four engines were mounted in two nacelles, and whose design incorporated a dive-bombing capacity. This aeronautical pushmi-pullyu was only one of the Third Reich's spectacular weapons-system failures. Wartime Japan developed wind-driven incendiary balloons to ignite American forests, and an ultimate anti-tank weapons system consisting of a soldier in a foxhole with a fused shell and a rock to set it off.

The civilianization of the Second World War's armed forces did not extend to their direct relations. Armies, navies and air forces are alpha

---

42 Andrew Roberts, *Masters and Commanders: How Four Titans Won the War in the West* (New York: Harper, 2008).
43 Paul M. Kennedy, *Engineers of Victory: The Problem-Solvers Who Turned the Tide in the Second World War* (New York: Random House, 2013). See generally and for the following, R. J. Overy's seminal *Why the Allies Won* (New York: W. W. Norton, 1995).

institutions, directed by alpha personalities. They exist in mutually exclusive operational environments. The result is an organic level of rivalry differing essentially – and exponentially – from those familiar in civilian institutions: board rooms, law offices, even academic departments. Three patterns of balance existed during the Second World War. In Germany and the USSR, armies were dominant. The Luftwaffe and the Kriegsmarine were nominally independent, but like lesser moons were irresistibly drawn into the land forces' orbit. The Soviet Union's air assets were divided between an army air force and a long-range bomber force directly under the high command, while during the war, the navy established most of its reputation in ground combat. In Britain, the Royal Navy remained the senior service throughout the war, with the RAF achieving eventual parity somewhat by default. The USA and Japan enjoyed – if the word is appropriate – an equal balance of forces: army and navy for Japan; in America, Army, Navy and a de facto air force which still bore the official title US *Army* Air Forces.

None of the wartime models emerged as clearly institutionally superior. What mattered was how well the participants were worked in, and how well they were held to task. And that, in turn, depended on their respective governments. Nazi Germany's ideologically based Hobbesian domestic policy pitted the services against each other to the point where, as early as 1939, competition for status and resources so overstrained the National Socialist system that war was its only alternative to chaos.[44] Japan's army and navy fought their wars in separate chimneys, behaving toward each other at times as if uncertain of who the real enemy was: essentially unaffected by a government dominated by the military factions.[45] In Britain and the USA, intra-service rivalry was in good part a customary matter, whose trails were sufficiently well worn to keep alpha-dog admirals and generals pulling in harness – given the existence of a strong arbitrator. Churchill and Roosevelt admirably fulfilled that function – not least because of long experience managing no less unlikely political coalitions.

The result was that the British and Americans, whether separately or as allies, developed a pattern ironically resembling the Communist principle of democratic centralism: unfettered discussion on a policy until a decision was announced, followed by unstinting cooperation. From Operation TORCH to

---

44 Wilhelm Deist, *The Wehrmacht and German Rearmament* (University of Toronto Press, 1981).
45 Mark Parillo, *The Loss of the Japanese Merchant Marine in World War II* (Annapolis, Md.: Naval Institute Press, 1993), is a hair-raising case study in an unlikely area.

the Philippines-Formosa controversy in the Pacific, it worked well enough to win the war – despite Admiral Halsey's alleged declaration during a frustrating period of the Guadalcanal campaign that he proposed to make athletic supporters the uniform of the day, and brand a star on everyone's backside to remind them that they were all fighting the same war. Josef Stalin's variant was no less successful. The Soviet system was structured to minimize intra-service, as opposed to personal, rivalry. But no one argued fundamentally with the Vozhd. Order – counter-order – disorder was conspicuously absent from the Soviet war effort after 1942.

'By any means necessary'

The Second World War was a total war in many aspects. Not least of these was the category of 'crimes and atrocities'. In the context of armed forces, these can be placed in three categories: those connected with combat and its aftermath, 'the filth of war'; those connected with particular military cultures; and those connected with general public policy.

In constructing a negative 'league table' of crimes directly committed by armed forces, Japan – perhaps surprisingly – heads the list. In terms of numbers, the Japanese military has been credited with anywhere from 3 million to 10 million victims. Methods included everything from vivisection to bayonet practice. Subjects were comprehensive: anyone from ostensibly 'liberated' Filipinos to uniformed enemies confronted in arms. Hot blood or cold; it made no difference. In November 1937, two lieutenants made national headlines with a contest over who would be first to kill a hundred Chinese with a sword. On 16 February 1942, twenty-two captured Australian nurses were machine-gunned – shot in the back as they walked into the surf of Banka Island. In China, 'baptism of blood' – bayoneting Chinese POWs – was a common training exercise for Japanese infantry replacements. Whatever wider explanations are offered for this typical behaviour, the best answer, incident by incident, is instrumentality: convenience. In China, for example, prisoners might be fed, shot or bayoneted, depending on the availability of food and ammunition – or the comfort zone of the Japanese involved. The result was a pattern of what might be called 'retail genocide', perpetrated by a military establishment meeting its own institutional standards.[46]

---

46 Toshiuki Tanaka, *Hidden Horrors: Japanese War Crimes in World War II* (Boulder, Colo.: Westview Press, 1996), is a path-breaking study.

This invites comparison to a German matrix of mass-murdering soldiers 'working towards the Führer'. Post-war German military narratives insisted for years on the Wehrmacht's 'clean shield': its status as a brave and honourable fighting force, even on the Eastern Front. The Waffen-SS claimed a similar status, insisting that it had nothing to do with the behaviour of rear-echelon, party-dominated elements. Atrocities there had been, but these were best understood as exceptions and excesses. In the past quarter-century, however, so much evidence has been presented demonstrating comprehensive, affirmative military compliance with the Third Reich's criminal policies that one sometimes wonders how the soldiers found time to fight a war.[47]

The armed forces' ordinary participation in the Third Reich's ordinary crimes was less a direct product of Nazification than a manifestation of a 'warrior spirit', based on boldness, decisiveness and hardness. That last was neither cruelty nor fanaticism. Nor was it a primary consequence of war's brutalizing effect. It is best understood as will focused by intelligence to accomplish a purpose. Compared to the Japanese counterpart, it had more of a conscious element – highlighted by the fundamental differences between Wehrmacht behaviour toward enemy combatants in the West and East. With the notable exception of French sub-Saharan African troops in 1940, one Russian front was enough.

This was a mindset particularly encouraged by National Socialism, even apart from the genocidal racism at the movement's core. It was also a mindset particularly enabling the brutal expediency that is an enduring aspect of war. Thomas Kuehne provocatively describes German soldiers as seeking the *Gemeinschaft*, the spiritual community described in such glowing terms by the Reich's intellectuals, romantics and politicians. Newcomers to the front, not only seeking but needing to belong in order to survive, sought and affirmed the collective's values. In order to be accepted as a man among men, soldiers were ultimately willing to participate in activities forbidden by religion, by law and even by the army itself.[48] This interpretation highlights the Nazi vision of Germany as a permanent war-making community. No return to civil society was projected. Germany's future reality was George

---

47 Hannes Heer and Klaus Naumann (eds.), *War of Extermination: The German Military in World War II* (New York: Berghahn 2004); and Alex J. Kay, Jeff Rutherford and David Stahel (eds.), *Nazi Policy on the Eastern Front, 1941: Total War, Genocide, and Rationalization* (Rochester, NY: University of Rochester Press, 2013), are comprehensive anthologies.

48 Thomas Kuehne, *Belonging and Genocide: Hitler's Community, 1918–1945* (New Haven, Conn.: Yale University Press, 2010).

Orwell's: boots eternally stamping on faces, in the eternal struggle of a community bound together by suffering – joy in enduring it; joy in inflicting it. And the Wehrmacht walked point.

From a Russian perspective, the Second World War was, in Stalin's words, 'a just and patriotic war of liberation'. However complex the conflict's origins, who had attacked whom on 21 June 1941 was not open to debate, any more than the USA could be accused of attacking the Japanese fleet at anchor on 6 December 1941. Since the Middle Ages at least, moreover, war in the Western world had developed a culture of accommodation, of not making things worse than they had to be. From the first days of BARBAROSSA, German behaviour at the front and behind the lines overtly denied such accommodation. Russian soldiers, for their part, were drawn from a society and a culture where suffering pain and inflicting it were the stuff of everyday. A quarter-century of Soviet rule refined, legitimated and institutionalized that mentality. But the war was an alienating experience as well. Once at the front, men remained there. Home leaves and local furloughs were chimeras. Mail delivery was haphazard. Memories faded into dreams. The Soviet soldiers' horizons and expectations shrank as the war moved forward.

In those contexts, the theme of self-defence was reinforced by the history of German barbarity. Familiar to every man and woman in the Red Army, it was reinforced at political meetings, through newspapers and radio broadcasts, nurtured by the encouragement to keep personal records of atrocities noted and repaid. For anyone seeking tangible evidence, Ukraine and Belorussia provided scenes of devastation inconceivable even to survivors of the great famines. The meme of vengeance metastasized as the Red Army crossed the Reich's borders. It was fuelled by rage at the Germans for attacking and despoiling a country in seeming defiance of their own immeasurably higher standard of living. It was fuelled by a sense of unfettered triumph, of power, foreign to the ordinary Soviet subject and correspondingly intoxicating. Mass rape was all the sweeter perpetrated in the presence of German men, unable to do anything beyond watch. The scope of victory was comprehensive. Civilian or soldier, German or forced labourer, made no essential difference. The rapes, the beatings, the killings, the deportations were a final, universal, direct manifestation of total war, Soviet style.[49]

America's combat atrocities in Europe were limited, episodic and disallowed. The Germans followed most of the conventional rules enough of

49 Merridale, *Ivan's War*; and Roger R. Reese, *Why Stalin's Soldiers Fought: The Red Army's Military Effectiveness in World War II* (Lawrence: University Press of Kansas, 2011).

the time that violations could be seen as exceptions, not justifying reprisals on any level. Even looting in conquered Germany was usually small-scale and involving Nazi artefacts. As for the Pacific War, the racist tropes of dehumanization and extermination are sufficiently associated with American behaviour that it is necessary as well as appropriate to note that comprehensive Japanese rejection of the 'culture of accommodation' mentioned above significantly limited their enemies' practical options at the sharp end. Operationally, Japanese neither broke nor withdrew under bombardment, when outflanked or overrun. They stood and died in fixed defences – almost 'suicide by enemy action'. The argument for the situational nature of America's conduct in the Pacific is further supported by wartime US policies emphasizing Japan's post-war reconstruction rather than its destruction – and by the behaviour of US servicemen in the immediate post-war occupation, when they took little and paid for most of it, from samurai swords to sex.[50]

Essentially the same points can be made for the British – with even fewer direct exceptions worth mentioning, beyond a brief and quickly suppressed exchange of POW shootings between Canadians and Waffen-SS in the weeks after D-Day. 'By any means necessary', however, has a much sharper point for both British and US Armed Forces when applied to the Combined Bomber Offensive. On the highest level, this was a matter of national policy, outside the scope of this chapter except for the observation that the CBO grew out of a thoroughly defensible mutual conclusion that it was war to the knife against a regime that recognized no limits. In terms of implementation, however, for both British and American air forces, strategic bombardment seemed the surest way to permanent institutional and doctrinal independence. The bomber commanders could not change state policy, but they were comfortable with it. Situational ambition combined with a desire to fulfil political objectives led the bomber forces, as mentioned, to overreach consistently. The nature of strategic-bomber combat also worked against detached analysis. The airmen's vulnerable humanity was all too exposed to the enemy's machines: Randall Jarrell's 'black flak and the nightmare fighters', with the pitiless searchlights added for night-flying RAF crews. The bomber offensive's moral ambiguity was a post-war construction by scholars and theologians.[51]

---

50 Dennis Showalter, 'War to the Knife: The US in the Pacific, 1942–45', *Proceedings of the NIDS International Forum on War History 2011: The Pacific War as Total War* (March 2012), 89–102.

51 Overy, *The Bombers and the Bombed*, pp. 107–230, is a balanced treatment. See also Tami Davis Biddle, *Rhetoric and Reality in Air Warfare: The Evolution of British and American Ideas about Strategic Bombing* (Princeton, NJ: Princeton University Press, 2002).

The same point can be made for the defining use of air power in the Second World War: the atomic bombing of Japan. By the second half of 1945, Japan still offered no significant indications of an interest in negotiation. The anticipated level of American casualties in the projected invasion remains a subject for debate. A meaningful indicator is the number of Purple Heart wound awards produced in anticipation – almost half a million. The war's end in Europe, and growing domestic pressure for peace and demobilization, further encouraged movement to the nuclear initiative. Operational planning already incorporated using poison gas and nerve gas against Japanese defences. In military circles particularly, the atomic bomb was considered just another weapon.[52] The decision to use the bomb may have been a final – or an initial – manifestation of total war. But it reflected, above all, the kind of war the world's armed forces had been moving toward since 1 September 1939.

52 Barton J. Bernstein, 'Roosevelt, Truman, and the Atomic Bomb: A Reinterpretation', *Political Science Quarterly* 90 (1975), 23–89; and Barton J. Bernstein, 'Truman and the A-Bomb: Targeting Noncombatants, Using the Bomb, and Defending the Decision', *Journal of Military History* 62 (1998), 547–70.

20

Filling the ranks

Conscription and personnel policies

SANDERS MARBLE

Conscription was universal among the major combatants in the Second World War, and not particularly controversial. Even in the Anglo-Saxon liberal democracies, with strong traditions of voluntary rather than compulsory service, the First World War had shown that volunteering was neither effective nor efficient for a mass industrial war. Britain and the USA, the largest holdouts from routine conscription in peacetime, adopted it before going to war in 1939 and 1941 respectively. Indeed, in the USA, adopting conscription in September 1940, just after France collapsed, proved less controversial than extending the law a year later when Germany seemed better contained. In contrast, some countries had traditionally, even positively, embraced conscription: France used it as a 'school of the republic' and Germany viewed the return to conscription in 1935 as an escape from one of the shackles of Versailles. In Japan, conscription had been associated with modernity when it was implemented in the late 1800s, and it was used to spread new ideas around the nation.[1] Certainly, a few years of military service might not have been what an individual wanted to do at that particular time in his life, but large armies were important for national defence, and there were larger themes that lauded service to the nation and kept it palatable. It was a mix of a passage into manhood and service to the nation, and it was tolerated because the military kept it tolerable.

Manpower is a very broad topic, affecting not only the military, but industry and society. Rüdiger Hachtmann's chapter in Volume III ('The war of the cities: industrial labouring forces') will examine industrial manpower topics in detail, and they will only be glossed here. I use 'manpower' in this chapter except when referring to females, because the overwhelming number of

---

1 Edward Drea, *Japan's Imperial Army: Its Rise and Fall, 1853–1945* (Lawrence: University Press of Kansas, 2009), ch. 2, discusses conscription and the modernization of Japan.

persons in the military in the Second World War were men. Women played important roles in the war efforts, but most of those efforts were not in the military and this chapter is about military personnel. Similarly, there are countries that will not be examined in detail here – for instance, China and France; in some cases, little source material was available, and in other cases, they closely mirrored the general trends.

Conscription was intended to efficiently obtain men for the mass military of industrial-era warfare. It usually did that, although politics could intervene and make a mockery of the training of those conscripts. Conscription also seemed to offer the best chance of balancing the manpower needs of both military and economy. (For instance, Britain chose to conscript older, less fit men and leave some younger men as key workers in the munitions industry.) Both volunteering and conscription in 1914 had wrought short-term havoc on munitions production, and as the First World War dragged on, the problems of sustaining a war economy and feeding the Moloch of battle had proved almost insoluble. While it might be optimistic to think in 1939 that planning use of manpower would solve all the problems involved, *not planning* (and thus repeating the problems of the First World War) was tantamount to giving the enemy a great advantage.

If the First World War had shown some problems with conscription and hinted at some solutions, other problems, especially administrative ones, were inevitable, and perhaps even insoluble. No country practised a full mobilization in the interwar period, which would have been both expensive and a military threat to neighbours, so problems inherent in the various systems remained untested. Peacetime conscription was also optimized for the pre-war plans rather than for what actually developed in the Second World War. In many cases, peacetime procedures had grown up which limited future wartime expansion. For instance, barracks and training areas were sized for the peacetime force, not any wartime expansion. Finally, there were beliefs that could go unchallenged in peacetime, but would prove problematic in wartime. For example, the peacetime exclusion of racial or ethnic minorities reduced the wartime manpower pool. No less problematic were medical ideas that mental breakdowns could be avoided by rigorous screening; these were untested in peacetime because of the lack of fighting.

Sustaining a long war would also challenge the conscription systems. The authorities sought to find more and more men. As they sought to be fair, to the men already in service, to those toiling in the economy, and to those in service but in no danger, they came into conflict with the politicians. Simply predicting the number of casualties, and how many would be infantry, tank crew, air crew or sailors, was well nigh impossible; without accurate casualty predictions, it was impossible to decide whether to form more units (and stockpile fewer replacements) or prepare for casualties. Every country faced higher infantry casualties than predicted and had to adjust, whether conscripting more men or moving men from other parts of the military into the infantry and rushing to make them into capable infantrymen before their lack of training led them to make mistakes.

In those countries that had peacetime conscription in the 1930s, the system was much the same: young men were called up around age twenty, given physical and mental tests for their aptitude, and many (but not all) of those who were eligible were conscripted for eighteen to thirty-six months of active service. Almost everywhere, divinity students and government employees were exempted, and many countries allowed university students (only perhaps 2 per cent of the population) ways out, on the grounds that they would be more valuable to the country doing something other than carrying a rifle. After serving their term, conscripts would then be in the reserves for roughly twenty years, although possibly liable for emergency home defence service until aged 60. The reserves were often graded by age, with younger men earmarked to fill out cadre combat units in wartime, while older reservists would be used in rear areas or for garrison duties, such as anti-aircraft or coast defence. (Some countries organized new home-defence militias during wartime, such as the British Home Guard and Canada's Veteran Home Guard of those over forty-five.) A number of countries had pre-military training in the 1930s, often organized through the ruling political party; this was intended as much to mould the young boys to ruling-party ideology as to strengthen their bodies and make them useful to the state. In this vein, Italy began rudimentary military training at the age of eight. In some countries, one military service administered conscription and typically used that advantage to obtain preferential access to manpower. The Imperial Japanese Navy had to seek volunteers, because the army had the lion's share of conscripts, while the German army tried to limit the access of the other services to high-quality recruits. In response, the Luftwaffe got some workers in aircraft factories classified as aircrew, not just as essential workers. Once the SS got control of the German replacement system in 1944, their share of recruits shot up to over 17 per cent.[2]

---

2 *Germany and the Second World War*, vol. v: *Organization and Mobilization of the German Sphere of Power* (10 vols., Oxford: Clarendon Press, 2003), pt. 2, p. 879. Jürgen Forster, 'The Dynamics of Volksgemeinschaft: The Effectiveness of the German Military

Peacetime conscription focused on producing a relatively stable number of young men of reasonable fitness and intellect who would train for a few years and then go into the reserves. Thus in peacetime, conscription was not about building forces for current use, but training men to fill out the forces if war ever occurred. For instance, it was expected that about half the personnel of French 'regular' divisions would be made up of reservists; first reserve divisions would have only a small regular cadre; and second reserve divisions would consist almost entirely of older reservists.

However, when war did come, the military needed to expand and do unpredictable things. There would be new units, new *types* of units and replacements. Technical specialists would also prove to be key bottlenecks – in short supply in the economy, increasingly necessary for modern warfare, and difficult to apportion among the various services, which could all make plausible cases about their needs. Countries such as Italy, with around one-third of draftees illiterate, and largely agricultural ones such as the USSR or Japan, had serious structural problems as warfare grew more technological. Italy lacked men with the technical background to be maintenance and logistics officers or NCOs. India also lacked literate men, and from February 1942, the British conscripted Indians at sixteen years for two years' education before military training; as a result, forming an armoured division in India took several years. Even Germany was short of specialists by 1942, which slowed the rebuilding of Panzer divisions.[3]

Fighting as part of a coalition or success in occupying other countries also affected manpower policies. For instance, Britain had proportionately more men both in industry and support roles within the military than the Dominions did, and certainly more than the British Empire as a whole. Much of this was necessity, as few parts of the empire had the industrial base to manufacture aircraft or enough men with technical skills. Thus there were things that only Britain itself could do in a reasonable amount of time. The American 'Lend-Lease' programme provided weapons from the 'arsenal of democracy' to many countries, which meant that a smaller proportion of Americans were fighting – and dying – than was the case with alliance partners of the USA. (In turn, Australia provided food and industrial support to American forces, and demobilized 20,000 men to support American forces.) Since the Soviets were

Establishment in the Second World War', in Allan Millett and Williamson Murray (eds.), *Military Effectiveness*, vol. iii: *The Second World War* (3 vols., Boston, Mass.: Unwin and Hyman, 1988), p. 189.

3 See Walter Dunn, *Second Front Now: 1943* (Tuscaloosa: University of Alabama Press, 1980), ch. 7, for problems rebuilding divisions in 1942.

receiving everything from raw materials to equipment such as trucks and radios, and weapons such as aircraft and tanks from the USA, they needed to produce less and could send more men into action. These situations were not necessarily unwelcome. The Free French did not want to form many support units; de Gaulle sought to form *combat* units from the finite manpower he had available (at least until Resistance members could be conscripted), hoping that this would maximize French impact in the coalition.[4] (He also judged that the French wanted to fight, not build roads or run laundries.) However, relying on another country had impacts: when the USA entered the war, it cut supplies to Britain and used the material for its own forces; in turn, this caused Britain to shift manpower from the armed forces and back into industry.

The Axis had less scope for sharing production. While output of the Third Reich rose until 1945, there was never enough for all German units, and the Germans had to keep obsolete weapons and also used captured weapons for their own second-line units. Nevertheless, they did provide some weapons to their European allies; they also formed three divisions with German cadres but 75,000 Croat troops.[5] The SS also fielded twenty-two divisions of mainly foreign troops. In general, Nazi ideology prevented extensive use of 'Eastern' troops (recruited from Soviet POWs) in actual combat.

During the war, manpower needs and shortages led to changes. Some changes involved broadening the labour pool (bringing workers in from outside), in order to release men for the military; others directly brought more and different personnel into the military. Armed forces also sought to manage available manpower efficiently. Politics interfered with all of these things.

Before looking at some of these themes, a brief chronological survey of British policy may shed light on how plans and events interacted within one country across the course of the whole war; it provides a useful example of the desirability and limitations of planning.[6] Britain took part in the European war from the beginning, and its experience shows the problems that developed over time; since it was on the winning side, it can be said that

---

4 Ronald Hood, 'Bitter Victory: French Military Effectiveness During the Second World War', in Millett and Murray (eds.), *Military Effectiveness*, vol. III, pp. 239–42.

5 See *Germany and the Second World War*, vol. V: pt. 2, pp. 198–229, for details on Axis production sharing, and p. 1058 for Croat units.

6 This section is drawn from Williamson Murray, 'British Military Effectiveness', in Millett and Murray (eds.), *Military Effectiveness*, vol. III; F. W. Perry, *Commonwealth Armies* (Manchester University Press, 1988), chs. 2 and 9; and David French, *Raising Churchill's Army* (Oxford University Press, 2000).

Britain's decisions (at least in aggregate) were correct. On 22 September 1939, only three weeks after Germany's invasion of Poland, the British Cabinet agreed a programme for fifty-five divisions; this balanced industrial production and manpower, although it left little slack. It also reflected a conscious effort on the part of the British government to avoid the hideous casualties of the First World War, by using aerial bombardment when possible and, when ground combat was unavoidable, substituting firepower and weapons (especially armour) for infantry manpower. This, in turn, required munitions workers and technical personnel rather than infantrymen, and is an example of how political decisions affected industry, military strategy, military operations and manpower decisions. The policy generally preserved morale among the infantry, but the fielding of fewer divisions affected alliance politics and diplomacy. Commonwealth, including Indian, divisions were included in the fifty-five-division total, and five divisions' worth of equipment would be provided.

The collapse of France (and British Expeditionary Force losses in personnel and equipment there) led to British reassessments of strategy and manpower resources. Troops were quickly needed for home defence, and a large number of poorly equipped infantry battalions were organized, which gradually were converted into armour or artillery units when equipment became available, or disbanded to provide replacements. US production of munitions freed some British workers for other uses. Various options for allocating manpower among the services were evaluated on paper, to see the effects on industry, but also to divine which industries were non-essential and to forecast the employment (military and industrial) of females. In 1941, military age limits had to be broadened to meet requirements, and by 1943, the strategic forecasts realized that 'income' of young men would not meet losses, and that from late 1944 the army would shrink. In 1943, Britain reached peak mobilization, with no more personnel available for the military or industry. Personnel could be moved around, but casualties would shrink the overall war effort. In November 1943, an ending date for the war was pencilled in, and it was accepted that the army would have to get men from the other services. The rotation scheme for men who had been overseas the longest (since 1937 for some regulars) was recognized as both necessary and a severe limitation on potential operations into Burma and against Japan. Over time, more and more men from the UK were in non-combat roles, partly because the Commonwealth and Imperial forces preferred to organize combat units and because they lacked men with the technical skills. By 1944, substantially more uniformed personnel were in rear areas than in combat, and even though over half the men in Normandy were combat troops, that was because they were close to the base areas established at home. Moreover, Britain would soon be forced start disbanding combat units to provide replacements for other units.

The manpower pool

Expanding the labour force was necessary in all the industrialized countries, so that national economies could increase military production at a time when males and females were being pulled from industry into the armed forces. The USA, for example, expanded its labour pool with retirees, women, African Americans and youths. Britain recruited workers from Eire. Employers routinely extended working hours. In mid-war, the Germans reached deeper, using concentration camp inmates, jail prisoners, corrective labour camp inmates and disabled ex-soldiers to replace other workers.[7] The USSR identified manpower as a strategic resource, and in 1941–42 tried to evacuate military-age males ahead of German advances. Despite these efforts, the Red Army needed more and more men. As it drove westward, the Red Army absorbed any adult males the Germans left behind, including partisans, as replacements, ultimately gathering almost 4 million men, roughly equivalent to 1944–45 losses.[8]

Labour pools were expanded by using foreign labour. In this light, Lend-Lease involved American workers effectively being foreign labour, while from the American perspective, the foreign troops using American weapons were replacing American workers who would otherwise have to be conscripted. The survival of the USSR allowed the USA to alter its plans, reducing the need to create combat forces, especially ground units, and to continue the emphasis on production of equipment – for example, heavy bombers.

The Germans took foreign labour to the extreme of slave labour, and the draconian round-ups in Western Europe probably boosted the Resistance there. The Germans also used foreign factories, both shutting down German non-munitions industry and importing consumer goods and having munitions produced abroad.[9] Without going into details about war economies, it is clear that their efficient or inefficient management affected the number of

---

7 *Germany and the Second World War*, vol. v, pt. 2, p. 996.
8 David Glantz, *Colossus Reborn: The Red Army at War, 1941–1943* (Lawrence: University Press of Kansas, 2005), pp. 541–4.
9 On foreign labour and German manpower, see *Germany and the Second World War*, vol. v, pt. 1, pp. 884–9, and vol. v, pt. 2, pp. 229–42, 960–81.

men available to the military. Fritz Todt and Albert Speer's rationalizations of industry were expected to release more than a quarter of the employees for military service.[10] Their effectiveness should thus be measured not just by munitions output, but by the number of men released to the Wehrmacht.

Women were used, both in the military and to take the place of conscripted male workers. Japan sent women and schoolboys to work in factories, then drafted the adult men who had been working there.[11] The Soviets did likewise; by 1944, 85 per cent of their overall workforce was made up of women and children.[12] In contrast to this enormous exploitation of women, the USA did not seek many female workers until mid-1942, and did not urge women into the workforce until 1943.[13] 'Rosie the Riveter' was a propaganda campaign to ease change, not a reflection of wartime reality. By 1944, 36 per cent of American women were in the workforce, and one-third of those had family responsibilities. This drove employers to offer crèches, so that women could bring preschool children to work. However, the USA did recruit 350,000 women into the military, some 70,000 of whom were nurses. The Soviets made the greatest use of women in combat, forming an aviation unit in early October 1941; by late March 1942, over 100,000 women had been conscripted into air defence units, and more than a million served.[14] Most were in rear areas, freeing men (even men who, on induction, had been rated physically fit only for rear-area duty) to fight, but some women were snipers or operated heavy infantry weapons. Britain imposed 'National Service' (not military service) on women in 1941, and conscripted them from early 1942. Germany's Military Service Law of 1935 declared, 'Every German is liable to military service', but Nazi ideology slowed their use of women. Censors' reports of soldiers' letters also showed that the German troops did not want women working (at least early in the war), and over 200,000 women left the workforce because of generous family allowances as part of military compensation.[15] The Germans did later increase the use of female workers (in 1943, requiring women aged seventeen to fifty to register for work), and hundreds of thousands entered or re-entered the workforce, helping production and freeing men to fight. Yet their morale and productivity were low, and many

10 Ibid., vol. v, pt. 1, p. 1074.
11 Alvin Coox, 'The Effectiveness of the Japanese Military Establishment in the Second World War', in Millett and Murray (eds.), *Military Effectiveness*, vol. III, pp. 7–11.
12 Earl Ziemke, 'Military Effectiveness in the Second World War', in Millett and Murray (eds.), *Military Effectiveness*, vol. III, p. 287.
13 Ibid., p. 288.
14 Glantz, *Colossus Reborn*, pp. 551–4.
15 *Germany and the Second World War*, vol. v, pt. 1, pp. 880–4.

replaced other women who had retired due to their age. Germany recruited relatively few women into military organizations: by 1944, around 300,000.[16]

Manpower for the armed forces

The rapid expansion in wartime and the drain of casualties led to reducing qualitative standards, both physical and mental. Standards were often dropped very early in wartime: Australia, for instance, cut standards in May/June 1940, less than a year into hostilities: age limits were broadened, more usefully at the lower end than at the upper, as most nineteen-year-olds had more military potential than forty-five-year-olds. (Australia even registered fourteen-year-olds, although the Germans and Soviets used even younger lads during their desperate days.) Some uses of lower-quality manpower, beyond the reserve systems, were anticipatory rather than reactive. In 1936, Britain formed the National Defence Corps, of veterans aged forty-five to fifty-five, and during the Sudeten crisis, a uniformed Auxiliary Territorial Service was formed of women.

The USA, for example, steadily reduced dental and vision requirements, and allowed most men suffering from venereal diseases to serve. Despite this, the USA had relatively strict standards, and over the period 1940–45, 5 million men failed the physical tests, of whom 1.5 million were rated unsuitable due to mental problems.[17] The USA raised the conscription age to forty-four in 1942, but by the end of the war had dropped it back to thirty-eight, as too few older men passed physical tests. Still, most US rejects (for physical or mental reasons) would not have been rejected by other countries.[18] Servicemen had better physical and mental abilities than the civilian average. US servicemen had more education than the general population, and even African Americans who served were more educated than the average of the white population.[19]

The Germans had to steadily cut physical standards. In late 1943, they formed units from deaf men and those with stomach troubles.[20] The 'stomach units' received special rations and extra medical support. The Germans also

16 See ibid., pt. 2, pp. 893, 907, 998 for women.
17 Allan Millett, 'The United States Armed Forces in the Second World War', in Millett and Murray (eds.), *Military Effectiveness*, vol. III, p. 52.
18 Allan Millett and Peter Maslowski, *For the Common Defense: A Military History of the United States* (2nd edn, New York: Free Press, 1994), p. 428.
19 George Q. Flynn, *The Draft, 1940–1973* (Lawrence: University Press of Kansas, 1993), p. 86.
20 Dunn, *Second Front Now*, p. 264.

drafted Alsatians and so-called *Volksliste* III from Poland. The latter were categorized as 'blood Germans' who had 'absorbed Polish ways', but they were considered so unreliable that they could not be promoted above lance corporal, and no more than one was allowed in any infantry squad.

Lowering recruiting standards had a counterpart: not discharging men who had been injured or wounded, but retaining them for some secondary duty. The Germans retained men who had suffered severe frostbite in Russia, stationing them on the Western Front, and formed security divisions from older men to police rear areas. Similarly, the US Army retained men for Limited Service who had useful skills even though they were not fit enough to recruit.

A response to dubious manpower quality was efforts to increase morale and even inculcate fanaticism. In 1940, Japan, which already relied on discipline and morale to compensate for lack of numbers and technology, began a 'national spirit mobilization campaign', as resources dwindled and manpower and morale had to be emphasized even more. In early 1941, a Code of Battlefield Conduct was issued, which stressed not being taken captive; and by May 1944, needing to distract the public from a series of defeats in the Pacific, the military and civilian suicides on Saipan featured in propaganda to the public.[21] The Germans tightened military discipline and executed tens of thousands for desertion, and also instituted National Socialist Leadership Officers to stiffen resistance.[22] The Nazis thought the *Volkssturm*, the national people's militia which they set up in the last months of the war, would have a harder ideological edge because it included large numbers of Hitler Youth members, individuals steeped from their formative years in Nazi ideology. In that light, far from being a desperation force of old men and young boys, it could be an ideologically tougher force than the Wehrmacht. Of course, from the start, Nazi and Japanese ideology assumed that numbers did not need to be equal, since racial/spiritual superiority would triumph; these indoctrination campaigns were not wholly new, only a change of emphasis. While the series of 'Why We Fight' movies in the USA was hardly an effort to drive men to fight to the death, it was intended to reduce apathy and encourage support for the war, especially among those who were not actually fighting. The Soviets certainly shot tens of thousands of their own soldiers – especially after Stalin's Order 227, 'Not one step back'. However, the Soviets switched from Communist Party propaganda to

---

21 Drea, *Japan's Imperial Army*, pp. 212, 232–4, 240.
22 David Yelton, '"Ein Volk Steht Auf": The Germany Volkssturm and Nazi Strategy, 1944–45', *Journal of Military History* **64** (2000), 1061–85.

Russian Nationalist propaganda – for instance, calling the conflict the Great Fatherland War – and eventually withdrew authority from political commissars, because the troops were considered to be well motivated by patriotic rather than political propaganda.

Colonial empires were tapped for military manpower, regardless of postwar political implications. Britain is the most notable, but the Free French also relied heavily on African troops, until D-Day brought renewed access to white Frenchmen. Despite significant cultural/racial hesitations, in 1944 45 military necessity caused Japan to begin conscripting Koreans and Taiwanese for combat service. Many countries without colonies recruited foreigners for combat service. Sometimes this was done through ideological appeals (as the Nazis tried); sometimes it was done through ethnic/Nationalistic appeals (as the Nazis tried with *Volksdeutsche*, their term for ethnic Germans living outside the Reich); sometimes it was done through compulsion (as the Germans resorted to with the *Volksdeutsche*, or as the Red Army did as it swept through Poland and the Balkans).[23] Without a colonial empire, the USA tapped a politically sensitive manpower pool by conscripting African Americans. African Americans knew that military service, especially in combat, would bring political advances. American whites were unsure if they wanted African Americans to have the opportunity to serve and thus raise their political power, or if it was better to conscript whites to die for African Americans. African Americans had a second-class education system and limited access to health care, and thus fewer African Americans would qualify for military service. However, the services did – often grudgingly – accept more African Americans and open more opportunities to them.[24]

Beyond purely military manpower, auxiliary forces were recruited or existing groups used as military auxiliaries. Red Cross societies played their role in several countries, and in the USA, groups such as the Boy Scouts conducted scrap drives and urged war bond sales, seeking to sustain morale and support for the war effort, if not directly helping the military. The Italians used their Ports Militia, Post and Telegraph Militia, Forests Militia and Roads Militia to help the military (e.g. with port security and road traffic control), and as the basis for some military specialities, such as military

---

23 On recruiting *Volksdeutsche*, see Valdis Lumans, 'Recruiting Volksdeutsche for the Waffen-SS: From Skimming the Cream to Scraping the Dregs', in Sanders Marble (ed.), *Scraping the Barrel: The Military Use of Sub-Standard Manpower, 1860–1960* (New York: Fordham University Press, 2012).

24 On the subject of US use of African American troops, see Ulysses Lee, *The Employment of Negro Troops* (Washington DC: US Government Printing Office, 1966).

censorship and field postal units.[25] A wide range of Nazi Party groups were used to supplement the armed forces, and non-party but non-military organizations such as the Reich Labour Service and the Organization Todt provided labour units. From December 1941, auxiliaries – ranging from schoolboys to women, workers (who would down tools during air raids) and even POWs – 'manned' many German anti-aircraft guns.[26] (The British also used the Home Guard and, from July 1941, women to operate anti-aircraft guns.) In the USSR, the People's Commissariat of Communications Routes handed its Special Corps of Railroad Forces to the Red Army, and the state-controlled civil air fleet was assigned to work with the Red Air Force. The NKVD (predecessor of the KGB) not only sustained its border guard units, but many NKVD men were used as cadres for Red Army units, and an entire army was formed from NKVD personnel.[27]

Men could be conscripted at gunpoint, but where they had no commitment to the cause they were serving, their performance was at best marginal. Chinese troops conscripted for Japan's puppet regime were unreliable, as was the Indian National Army the Japanese formed as a propaganda tool rather than a fighting unit.[28] The Germans recruited several thousand Russians per division as *Hilfswillige* (auxiliary volunteers). They served in rear areas on menial duties (in kitchens, as labour, driving wagons and trucks), thus freeing German men to fight, albeit Germans who previously had been considered physically suitable only for rear-area duties. They also half-overcame their ideological opposition to 'Easterners' as combat troops and recruited over a quarter-million *Osttruppen*, Eastern troops, from non-Russian ethnic groups. Most of these units served in rear areas for security/police duties. The Germans would never trust their Russian and Ukrainian units, further undermining the men's shaky motivation. Once one unit proved unreliable in front-line combat (for which it was ill-equipped), Hitler had many of the others sent to the Western Front, where they had even less motivation. After the Normandy invasion in 1944, the *Osttruppen* surrendered readily.[29]

---

25 US War Department, 'Order of Battle of the Italian Army July 1943' (Washington DC: n.p., 1943), pp. 45–7.
26 *Germany and the Second World War*, vol. v, pt. 2, p. 892.
27 Glantz, *Colossus Reborn*, pp. 157–77, 351–3.
28 Liu Shih-ming, 'Puppet Troops Revisited: A Case Study of the Northwestern Army During the Anti-Japanese War', *Journal of Modern Chinese History* 7 (2013), 87–107, gives an example of how little loyalty puppet troops had for the Japanese directly or the Wang Jingwei puppet regime.
29 See *Germany and the Second World War*, vol. v, pt. 2, pp. 1055–8 for an overview of *Osttruppen*.

The Germans discovered a small manpower pool among collaborators, who joined the SS rather than stay behind when their country was liberated; a mediocre SS division (34th, *Landstorm Nederland*) was one result. Perhaps the strangest recruiting pool was the Soviet use of political prisoners, almost a million of whom served, typically with 'blocking detachments' at their back, to prevent them from deserting either forward or backward.[30] The Germans also reclassified some 'undesirables' as fit to fight. Germans who had been in the French Foreign Legion were judged fit to fight for Hitler in March 1941, and in August 1942, both soldiers in prison and around 3,500 political prisoners were inducted into a penal division.[31] That month, the Wehrmacht was ordered to 'adjust the structure and organization of the army to the number of men available'; from that time, the steps to make men available became ever more frantic.

Allowing volunteers to pick their service and branch reduced the quality available for unpopular parts of the military – where they were often most needed. After the slaughter of infantry in the First World War, few men would volunteer for the infantry. Added to that was the glamour and employment prospects of technical fields such as aviation. Politically, it was hard to deny volunteers at least their preference for army, navy or air force, and conscripts, too, might wish to express a preference. This could result in insufficient volunteers and conscripts heading for the ground forces; Britain had less than 25 per cent of recruits opt for the army. In 1942, Canada, faced with disbanding units to move men where they were needed, was forced to start allotting volunteers by their aptitude and the military's needs, not the individual's preferences.[32]

Efficient allocation of manpower was sometimes facilitated by bringing an end to volunteering, although some organizations that prided themselves on a volunteer ethos, high morale and strict selection criteria found ways around this. The Waffen-SS formed a whole division from the Hitler Youth, while the US Marine Corps sent recruiters into high schools looking for seventeen-year-olds who could volunteer ahead of being conscripted.

Manpower management within the military

Many countries had trouble predicting when manpower would be more important in the factories than in the army; France demobilized many men

---

30 Glantz, *Colossus Reborn*, pp. 544–6.
31 *Germany and the Second World War*, vol. v, pt. 1, p. 989, and vol. v, pt. 2, p. 898.
32 Perry, *Commonwealth Armies*, pp. 143–4.

from the armed forces in 1939–40 to increase munitions production, which public opinion and the army found hard to understand. Italy mobilized in 1939; then, on 1 October 1940, Mussolini decided to demobilize half the army before, two weeks later, deciding to attack Greece. Rather than recall the trained men, reservists and untrained recruits were sent to war. Their combat performance was predictably wretched.[33] The Germans spent much of the year between the fall of France and the invasion of the Soviet Union debating which service to expand (and how), releasing older men and conscripting younger ones; training suffered, although more equipment was produced to fill gaps.[34]

Some manpower problems had no optimum solution. The Germans formed a large number of divisions, which allowed rotation of divisions, whether or not they had suffered heavy casualties. Historians have criticized them for this, as the system required larger numbers of specialists; each division needed a cadre of signalmen, bakers, postmen and other non-combatant specialists, as well as infantry. Forming more divisions needed more non-combatants than forming fewer divisions, and thus reduced the number of combat troops produced from a given number of men. The USA took the opposite tack, forming few divisions, but keeping them up to strength with individual replacements.[35] Not rotating divisions meant that an infantryman was under considerable psychological pressure: he would either be killed, wounded or survive the war, but he would never get a substantial period of rest out of the line. It also meant a decline in combat effectiveness, when replacements came to outnumber the well-trained and experienced veterans. If operations were continued too long, the inexperienced men suffered disproportionate casualties.[36] Lieutenant General Leslie McNair, Chief of US Army Ground Forces, predicted that forming too few divisions would mean they could not be rotated to rest. He also complained about internal policies that sent too few high-quality men to the infantry, but instead to supporting arms; this increased overall casualties, as less fit, less intelligent men were not the best suited for ground combat.[37] By 1944, 40 per

---

33 MacGregor Knox, *Hitler's Italian Allies: Royal Armed Forces, Fascist Regime, and the War of 1940–1943* (Cambridge University Press, 2000), pp. 79–80, 146–7.

34 *Germany and the Second World War*, vol. v, pt. 1, pp. 956–74.

35 Overall US policy, from the Army perspective, is given in *Biennial Reports of the Chief of Staff of the United States Army to the Secretary of War, 1 July 1939–30 June 1945* (repr., Washington DC: Center of Military History, 1996), pp. 196–201.

36 See Robert Rush, *Hell in Hürtgen Forest: The Ordeal and Triumph of an American Infantry Regiment* (Lawrence: University Press of Kansas, 2001), esp. chs. 5 and 13.

37 Millett, 'United States Armed Forces', p. 61.

cent of the enlisted men in ordinary infantry divisions were graded below-average for intelligence.[38] Meanwhile, what the army called 'overhead' and non-divisional units increased substantially during the war. In 1941, the US Army had 41 per cent of its men in combat divisions, but by 1945, only 23 per cent.[39] While divisions were not the only combat units, less than a third of the US Army was organized for ground combat, the core role of an army. On 30 June 1944, there were more enlisted men assigned to various functions in the USA (not counting replacements in training) than there were infantrymen in the European and Mediterranean theatres combined.

All countries shifted men between military services when strategic circumstances changed. In Germany, the Luftwaffe formed divisions for ground combat in late 1942, and the Kriegsmarine did so in 1944–45. The Soviets organized sailors from the Baltic, Black Sea and Pacific Fleets for ground combat. Armies over-expanded and had to contract, often investing manpower to address a current problem, but not able to predict that it would be solved through other means later. The British and Americans both formed many anti-aircraft units in 1940–42. By 1943, however, the Luftwaffe was so weakened that it was flying fewer and fewer offensive sorties, and the Allied AA units – and their men – were superfluous. Moreover, forming those AA units not only required enlisted men, but officers as well, and that in turn meant that officer-candidate programmes were too large, further diverting high-quality manpower.[40] It would not be until 1944–45 that the AA gunners were freed up for service as combat infantry; they were not well trained for infantry service and their morale was apparently not remarkable. In late 1944, the US Army 'combed out' (the standard term for selectively transferring men from rear areas to the front) fit men from the USA for the fighting fronts, closed some training units and installations (converting them into replacements or field units), and had the Army Air Forces (USAAF) transfer 65,000 men, while service units handed over 25,000 men, and Defence Commands (in areas such as the Caribbean) yielded 12,000 men. Even Army overseas theatres found 100,000 from their rear areas. Closing training areas had a cost: thirteen divisions never went through division-level manoeuvres and, as a result, deployed to combat less well trained.

---

38 Millett and Maslowski, *Common Defense*, p. 473.

39 Peter Mansoor, *The GI Offensive in Europe: The Triumph of American Infantry Divisions, 1941–1945* (Lawrence: University Press of Kansas, 1999), pp. 36–7.

40 John Brown, *Draftee Division: The 88th Infantry Division in World War II* (Novato, Calif.: Presidio, 1998), p. 15.

The USA made bold manpower predictions before entering the war, called the Victory Plan. While the gross totals of men in service were roughly right (around 12 million at peak in 1945), the allocations were mistaken. The USAAF was 15 per cent larger than predicted, while the Army ground forces were 200,000 men smaller – and much less efficient at producing combat divisions out of their manpower. Instead of the projected 215 divisions from 6.75 million men, it only produced 89, from around the same number. Service units, while useful, absorbed large quantities of men, and it also took many to produce the high standard of living the USA felt it needed to provide for GIs. However, shipping was also a limit on Army strength, because there was no sense having units that could not be deployed. During the war, the USA tried to use battlefield experience to predict how many replacements would be needed for future campaigns, but situations changed; while armoured units lost many men in the North African fighting, in Sicily and Italy losses were heavier among infantrymen, and the number of tank crewmen accumulated.

Units were also reorganized to save manpower. The British formed 'Lower Establishment' infantry divisions with less artillery and transport, but a full allotment of riflemen. Thus for a fixed number of troops, they maximized the number of combat troops. An expedient in 1941, they were later upgraded with equipment or disbanded, and the men were transferred to other units. From 1942, the Germans repeatedly reorganized divisions, cutting both rear and front-line strength. They allotted more and more automatic weapons, trying to substitute firepower for manpower. The reduction of support troops reduced flexibility – for example, a signals company simply could do less than a signals battalion; it might cope in a static sector, but not in mobile operations. Reducing the number of supply units saved manpower, but meant that divisions had trouble functioning far from rail lines. In mid-1943, the Germans decreed that support troops would be thirty-seven or older, with younger (presumably fitter) men sent into combat, even if they were technical specialists. When disbanding divisions to send manpower elsewhere, there was a tendency among all nations to preserve armoured units, which used less manpower, at the expense of infantry units.

Some units were formed of what the military authorities regarded as 'lower-quality men' to perform secondary missions. The British formed garrison battalions for internal security duties, for coastal defence and to hold fortresses. They also formed the Pioneer Corps, mainly for labour, and assigned to it older and younger men who were not suitable for combat units, and aliens (including enemy nationals) who could not be trusted with weapons, but who could be useful to the war effort. The Germans formed fortress and reserve divisions for occupation duty. The fortress divisions deterred raids and an early Western Allied invasion, while reserve divisions could both suppress Resistance activity and train individual replacements for other units.[41] The US Army mostly shunted African Americans into various labour units, until political pressure forced two African American divisions to be sent into action; the 92nd Division had a mediocre record in Italy, and the 93rd Division was deployed piecemeal in quiet parts of the Pacific theatre.[42] The US Marine Corps (USMC) tried to avoid taking any African Americans at all; when it had to accept African Americans, it formed them into Defence Battalions that had no operational purpose by the time they were fully trained. That was predictable, and possibly what the USMC intended when it organized the units.

Apparently sacrosanct institutions had to yield. Since casualties were not evenly spread, Britain found the vaunted 'regimental system' (that was supposed to engender esprit de corps and thus combat effectiveness among men who would serve their entire army career in one regiment) could not allot men where they would actually be needed.[43] Thus from July 1942, men were put in a General Service Corps for initial training and assessment, then sent to a branch of service to which they were reasonably suited.

Elite and special-purpose forces were formed and then, in many cases, not used as intended. The British 52nd (Lowland) Infantry Division was first trained for mountain operations and then to mount assault glider attacks. It never fulfilled these roles, and instead, it entered the line in the Dutch polders in 1944, a mountain division fighting below sea level. Italian 'assault divisions' never launched an amphibious attack. Instead, their time training was wasted. The British formed the widest variety of special-purpose units, including Chindits, Special Air Service, Special Boat Service, Commandos and paratroopers. While these units could be extremely effective in the right circumstances, those circumstances were rare. Sending specialist troops into ordinary ground combat not only wasted their training but frequently cost lives; as the special units were lightly equipped, they took heavy casualties when faced with tanks and artillery. Meanwhile, their presence could inhibit ordinary units from stepping up to challenging roles; General William Slim

---

41 See Dunn, *Second Front Now*, ch. 9 for reserve divisions, and ch. 16 for information on fortress divisions.
42 See Lee, *Employment of Negro Troops*, chs. 17–19.
43 See David French, *Military Identities: The Regimental System: The British Army, and the British People, c.1870–2000* (Oxford University Press, 2005).

complained that if a Royal Corps of Tree Climbers was formed, then nobody else would climb trees and would rely on the specialists. US paratroopers were more commonly used as elite infantry than as paratroopers, and German parachute divisions fought as ground infantry after April 1941. The Guards units of the Red Army were the exception to this rule: they were not special-purpose units, but units that had proved themselves highly effective in action. Awarded the 'Guards' honorific, they were then given newer and better equipment, accorded priority for rest and replacements, but also used where the fighting was fiercest.

Air forces also absorbed large numbers of intelligent and motivated young men, often using them in rear areas as ground crew, in airfield construction and maintenance units, in separate air force depots and the like, when they would have provided invaluable junior leaders in the ground forces. Britain had to borrow junior infantry officers from South Africa and Canada to take the place of its own men who had joined the Royal Air Force.

Political pressures

Democracies faced particular political pressures on conscription; these were grouped around competing concepts of fairness. While conscription was not particularly controversial in the abstract, or when it applied to young men with fewer community responsibilities; it was increasingly controversial when applied to older men, married men and fathers. An example of the confluence of these factors was when the USA had trouble justifying the drafting of 'pre-Pearl Harbor fathers' – that is, men who had children before the USA was at war. Why should these men, generally somewhat older and more established in the community, be drafted when younger men (who would, incidentally, be generally more fit and suitable for combat) received deferment based on their employment in the war economy? On the other hand, when the country needed military manpower to win the war, why should they be exempt simply because they had children before an arbitrary date? Should men be deferred for having dependants, especially since some wives left the workforce in order to become dependent on their husband's income and thus protect him from conscription?[44] In 1943, the USA had 15 million men deferred because they had dependants, while only 1.1 million were deferred because they were classed as key workers.

44 Flynn, *Draft*, pp. 54–6, 70–1.

To conscript the 'pre Pearl Harbor fathers', it was not enough to cite the military need for quality manpower; the US government had to produce a report from its Surgeon General that the pool of younger, physically and mentally qualified men had been exhausted. Moreover, it was noted that deferring fathers meant drafting teenagers, illiterates and over 200,000 VD sufferers; in any event, special training programmes were required to teach the illiterates.[45] American politicians were also concerned about sending eighteen-year-olds into combat, so the Army delayed that choice until November 1944, when heavier than predicted casualties in Europe forced them to do so.

The US military also faced internal problems about psychological standards. The services sought to avoid mental breakdowns by military personnel, and there was more than one reason for this. Obviously, it was desirable to have no weak spots in combat units. However, the policy was also affected by the American experience after the First World War, when roughly one-fifth of all veterans' hospital costs came from hospitalizing 50,000 veterans who had psychiatric problems. These two factors created a strong desire to screen all recruits for potential mental problems, and the Army set high standards, holding that 'a superior army cannot be moulded from inferior individuals'. Over the course of the war, 30 per cent of all Selective Service rejections were for psychiatric reasons, and the two-stage screening system meant that the overall rate was higher still (the Selective Service System had physicians screen men for physical and mental suitability, then the military performed another screening on those who passed). Ultimately, around 1.7 million men were rejected for military service for psychological reasons, although some of them were later accepted if they answered questions differently, had a different psychiatric examiner or standards had changed.

Yet screening failed. By the spring of 1943, just over a year into the war, there were 20,000 patients every month in psychiatric wards and there was a substantial problem with men breaking down in sustained combat. Screening failed mainly because there is no one cause of mental troubles related to military service. Some men could not adapt to the regimentation and loss of privacy, while others sank into depression from boring work in an unpleasant location, and still others broke down due to combat stresses. The US Army

---

45 Ibid., p. 72. In the pre-antibiotic era, venereal diseases often lasted for life. Some 5 per cent of the US males called up had syphilis, and more had gonorrhoea: see Robert Anderson and Charles Wiltse, *Physical Standards in World War II* (Washington DC: Office of the Surgeon General, 1967), pp. 27–30.

alone had around 500,000 men discharged for psychiatric reasons, and due to the stigma relating to psychiatric diagnoses, others were doubtless discharged under 'administrative' reasons. Meanwhile, studies on men who were rejected at one time, but accepted later, showed that most (82 per cent) served well in the military. This contrasted with a success rate of 94 per cent for men judged mentally acceptable the first time. Psychiatrists thus showed no ability to predict who would be complete failures or who would be remarkable successes. In 1944, with the manpower pool dwindling, the Army decided it could not keep standards so high, and ordered that men be accepted if the examiner thought they had a 'reasonable chance' of adapting. Of course, that was subjective, in the eye of the psychiatric examiner, and the Army provided a standard test (although without meaningful testing for scientific validity) so that men could be equitably assessed.

Politicians were also good at strong rhetoric, but weaker at taking action. For instance, US politicians talked of a policy of 'work or fight', but they never forced 'national' service. Instead, men faced only 'selective' service, and there was no compulsion at all for women. Even Selective Service was political – for instance, tobacco farmers were declared essential, while one Senator called military plans 'nonsense', because they contemplated conscripting farmers. But this political pressure kept Selective Service aligned with popular attitudes and managed to sustain broad support for the organization even among draft-age men that it sent to war.[46]

Democracies also faced problems keeping men in the military for long periods. Britain had begun a home-leave programme in 1943, for troops stationed overseas for long periods, but military necessity kept it small. More seriously, Australia and New Zealand had mobilized very large portions of their male population in the critical months when Japan was expanding southward. As the Japanese were beaten back, many men were returned to farms and factories. But by mid-1945, they were facing the question of contributing ground troops to an invasion of Japan. Both countries had sent ground troops to the Middle East in 1940, and some of those men had been away from home for five years. Should those men, experienced veterans and highly suitable for combat, be kept in service, or was it fairer to discharge them and conscript someone else who would be less suitable for ground combat? Canada brought long-service men home from November 1944, ostensibly only for leave, but the government admitted that only a few

---

46 Flynn, *Draft*, pp. 55–6, 67, 61.

specialists would be sent back overseas; the war ended before push came to shove. Finland had experienced a smaller-scale version of the same problem. After dramatic, if short, mobilization for the Winter War, it remobilized for the Continuation War alongside the Germans. However, that stretched for years and the Finns operated a de facto truce on much of their front and sent the men home on furlough, so that the economy did not collapse. Even so, the lack of agricultural labour meant that Finland needed to import food.

Racial or ethnic biases caused further problems, leading several countries to make poor use of qualified men, both in the military and the economy. Britain waited several years before recruiting from parts of India that were not considered to have 'martial races', and had language problems across the Indian Army. (Eventually, even Indian women were recruited, albeit not in large numbers.) Martial race thinking also led to delays in mobilizing troops from British West Africa, although there were also language problems and a shortage of men suitable to be NCOs. South Africa, unsurprisingly, had no pre-war plans to use black manpower. Instead, whites would be combat troops, non-whites could serve in support roles, and the black population was seen as labourers. Women were recruited for non-combat service, but white manpower was so exiguous that in 1944–45, black South Africans were recruited – but only for service in British anti-aircraft units in Italy, so as not to threaten Afrikaner values.

Canada conscripted for home defence, and while a 1942 referendum allowed conscripts to be sent overseas, the government delayed sending any outside North America until early 1945. Conscripts staying in Canada were disparaged as 'zombies', and a government-sponsored advertising campaign pressured them to volunteer for active service; this included a challenge to their manhood. New Zealand delayed conscripting Maoris, but ultimately did so, and sent them overseas. Britain did not apply conscription to Ulster, to avoid antagonizing Catholics (both there and in the Republic of Ireland, who would volunteer for the military and labour), and the USA delayed conscripting Japanese-Americans due to questions about their loyalty.

Inter-service politics also led to poor manpower decisions. In Germany, Herman Göring was politically powerful enough that when men were dislodged from his Luftwaffe, he insisted that they be formed into Luftwaffe Field Divisions rather than sent to the Army. Without adequate training for ground combat, they suffered heavy losses and performed poorly. Nazi political doctrines about women's role in society also contributed to low utilization of women in the military. The Soviets, generally ruthless about the sources of manpower, initially made little use of non-Slavic manpower, except for some mountain units formed in the Caucasus.[47] They also sent most minorities into rear-area units. There were some practical reasons, including language barriers, but in the crises of 1941–42, ways were found around these barriers, and non-Slavs were conscripted as thoroughly as Slavs. The USA had what was, on paper, a highly rational system that sent men judged fit for Limited Service to jobs that did not require men fit for General Service. However, unit commanders used both medical and administrative channels to discharge many of the men, expecting to get better-quality men as replacements. Over a million trained men were discharged, necessitating another million men to be conscripted and trained, and at one point in mid-1943, the US Army was discharging ninety-five men for every hundred it was conscripting.[48]

The US diverted tens of thousands of high-quality young men, who would have made excellent junior leaders in the military, into long-term programmes that trained them in engineering, science, medicine and other technical fields. While these men would have been useful in a war stretching beyond 1947, the programme was largely the product of effective lobbying by universities.[49] Called the Army Special Training Program, it had 150,000 men at the turn of 1943/44, but then was cut back by 80 per cent in the spring of 1944, as it was clear, first, that the war would be over before 1947, and second, that more and better-quality men were needed for ground combat units. Some of the men were sent into combat poorly trained. That not only vitiated their potential, it put them and their comrades at greater risk. The USA also allotted men who scored higher on aptitude tests to the Army Air Forces, based on the belief that air forces, being highly technical, had need for smarter men. Doubtless some positions required such men, but not to the extent that developed, which again robbed the ground combat units of highly qualified men who would have fought well. The British Commonwealth Air Training Plan (BCATP)/Empire Air Training Scheme also robbed the ground forces of high-quality men throughout the war, as nearly 200,000 men were trained as aircrew. The programme was only wound up in 1944,

---

47 David Glantz, *Stumbling Colossus: The Red Army on the Eve of World War* (Lawrence: University Press of Kansas, 1998), pp. 65–6, 98; Glantz, *Colossus Reborn*, pp. 547–8; David Glantz, 'Soviet Use of "Substandard" Manpower in the Red Army, 1941–1945', in Marble (ed.), *Scraping the Barrel*.

48 See Sanders Marble, 'Below the Bar: The US Army and Limited Service Manpower', in Marble (ed.), *Scraping the Barrel*; and Eli Ginzberg et al., *The Ineffective Soldier*, vol. 1: *The Lost Divisions: Lessons for Management and the Nation* (New York: Columbia University Press, 1959), pp. 75–8.

49 Flynn, *Draft*, p. 77.

although there had been a surplus of aircrew being trained for several years. The BCATP also absorbed capital and civilian labour that might have been employed in other aspects of the war effort.

No country found a permanent solution to manpower problems, not least because those problems were dynamic. Strategy, tactics and diplomacy played their roles, as did timing, politics and the needs of industry. It was difficult to predict, first of all, what forces (air, land or sea) would be needed several months in the future, let alone several years, and, second, how they would need to be equipped. The insurance needed to prevent such errors and cover more eventualities was larger forces. The peacetime system, where the military thought about its probable wartime needs, consulted with politicians and tried to influence industry, could only work haphazardly, since no society was Spartan, organized solely for war. Inevitably, the mistakes led to heavier casualties.

Railway

The railway was the foundational means of supply for the great land war in Europe. No other transportation system was capable of efficiently hauling such enormous tonnages of supplies, or large numbers of men, over long distances. One calculation is that a double-track railway line could haul an equivalent tonnage to 1,600 trucks.[4] Moreover, railway locomotives could carry considerably more fuel per tonnage than a truck, so could travel much further without needing to refuel. Also, railways could carry much heavier loads than trucks. This became particularly important as the war progressed and vital weapons systems, such as armoured fighting vehicles (AFV), became much heavier. In 1939, most AFVs were light vehicles. The German Mark II and III Panzers, which formed the majority of tanks that were used against France in 1940, weighed somewhere between eight and twenty tons, depending on model and construction year.[5] Even then, it was beneficial to move them by rail as far as possible to save wear and tear, especially on their tracks. Later in the war, with the advent of such famous AFVs as the Panzer V (Panther) and VI (Tiger), weights had more than doubled, to between forty-three and sixty tons per vehicle. This extra weight meant that these newer vehicles were even more prone to breakdowns for each mile spent on the road, and it was imperative that railways be used to get them as close to the battlefield as possible as part of their deployment.

Railways were therefore the crucial means of preparing for all major offensive and defensive operations, and it was their ability to be extended behind offensives that often determined the outcome of large-scale engagements. In particular, working railways allowed for the creation of large depots, which could be used to supply entire armies or even army groups. The closer these railhead depots were to the area of action, the fewer miles supplies had to travel by other means, and the quicker and more efficiently armed forces could be supported or rebuilt. Armed units that advanced relying on their own vehicles, even when their number was boosted above normal levels, had a predetermined sphere of action.

The railway had come to dominate military supply in the second half of the nineteenth and the first part of the twentieth century. During the American Civil War and the First World War, railways allowed mass armies

---

4 Martin van Creveld, *Supplying War: Logistics from Wallenstein to Patton* (Cambridge University Press, 2004), p. 143.
5 Peter Chamberlain and Hilary Doyle, *Encyclopedia of German Tanks of World War Two* (London: Cassell, 1999) pp 28–32, 58–62.

to be moved large distances in short times. German plans going into the First World War were dependent on using the country's excellent railway system to deploy the overwhelming mass of troops against France, and then, after that enemy had supposedly been defeated, moving a huge number of troops back east to confront the advancing Russians. Heading into the Second World War, the main European land powers, Germany, France and the USSR, all possessed relatively efficient rail systems and, crucially, systems that had been constructed to meet the supply needs of modern armies.[6]

All railway systems were made up of three main components. There were the tracks on which the trains moved, the rolling stock in which the supplies were carried, and the locomotives that were responsible for pulling the carriages on the track. The German railway network was one of the densest in the world. It allowed for the switch of the mass of the German Army twice in the first two years of the war. After the conquest of Poland, the Germans moved the vast majority of the army west by rail to prepare for the assault on France; and after the decision was made not to attempt an invasion of the United Kingdom, the army was moved hundreds of miles to the East to prepare for an invasion of the USSR.

The famous German Blitzkrieg success during the invasions of France, Belgium, Luxembourg and the Netherlands was partly dependent on their good fortune in capturing intact railway lines and getting supplies moving along them as soon as possible. On the first day of the attack into Luxembourg, 10 May 1940, Halder wrote approvingly in his diary that the entire railway system of the Duchy had been captured in working order, and the following day he noted that the system was now being used to haul supplies to the advancing Wehrmacht. However, much more important than this, a large percentage of the Belgian railway network would also soon fall into Germany's hands. By 15 May, the Germans had a working railway system that had reached the Belgian town of Bastogne (the city which would become famous during the Battle of the Bulge). If there was one great railway coup for the Germans during their rapid advance, it was the capture, almost entirely intact, of a railway line running from Germany to the large Belgian port of Antwerp – approximately 125 miles from the Ruhr, Germany's industrial heartland that sprawled near its western border. By 22 May,

6 For some interesting reflections on the importance of pre-war Soviet railway policy in allowing the USSR to survive the German invasions, see: E. A. Rees, *Stalinism and Soviet Rail Transport, 1928–1941* (Basingstoke: Palgrave Macmillan, 1995) pp. 209–10; Holland Hunter, *Soviet Transport Experience: Its Lessons for Other Countries* (Washington DC: Brookings Institution, 1968), p. 60.

significant volumes of supplies were reaching Antwerp for the German Armies which had already reached the English Channel.[7]

If capturing and utilizing railway lines during the conquest of France was important, the relative ease with which this occurred was usually not repeated.[8] For most of the great land campaigns in Europe after May 1940, the capture and utilization of railway systems was a far more complex task. Perhaps the greatest example of this was the German invasion of the USSR, which began in June 1941, Operation BARBAROSSA.

The German invasion, which failed to reach Moscow before grinding to a halt in December 1941, was really a series of shorter offensives broken up by unavoidable pauses, each lasting a number of weeks. These pauses were made necessary by the relatively long time that it took the Germans to exploit captured Soviet rail lines. The task undertaken by the Germans in moving a modern army into the Soviet Union was complicated by a wider Russian railway gauge than was standard practice in other European countries. Because of a decision made during the pre-revolutionary period, Russian rails were spaced five feet apart, while the German (and standard European) spacing was 4 feet 8.5 inches.

Making use of Russian railways was so important because much of the Wehrmacht was still far from being fully mechanized. Two distinct German armies took part in BARBAROSSA. There were twenty-six divisions, many of them part of the armoured spearheads that went into the attack with a relative oversupply of vehicles, which greatly increased their range of action. On the other hand, there were more than seventy divisions, almost all of them infantry, which to a large extent had to rely on horse-drawn transport or a motley collection of different captured vehicles, to get supplies.[9]

These latter units, in particular, needed access to railway-borne supplies to keep moving forward. The original German assumption going into the invasion, partly, it seems, based on their experience attacking France and Belgium, was that they would capture a large amount of Soviet rolling stock (as well as Soviet supplies). This, it was hoped, would allow the German

---

7 *Halder Diaries*, pp. 390, 393, 401, 412, 416.
8 It is interesting to see that in the German invasions of Yugoslavia and Greece in April 1941, the Wehrmacht was able to keep its supply lines relatively short by launching its attacks from the soil of its allies, most importantly Bulgaria. This meant that the units rarely went more than 150 miles from their start points. See *Germany and the Second World War*, vol. III: *The Mediterranean, South-east Europe and North Africa, 1939–1941* (10 vols., Oxford: Clarendon Press, 1995), pp. 500, 517.
9 *Germany and the Second World War*, vol. IV: *The Attack on the Soviet Union* (10 vols., Oxford: Clarendon Press, 1998), p. 220.

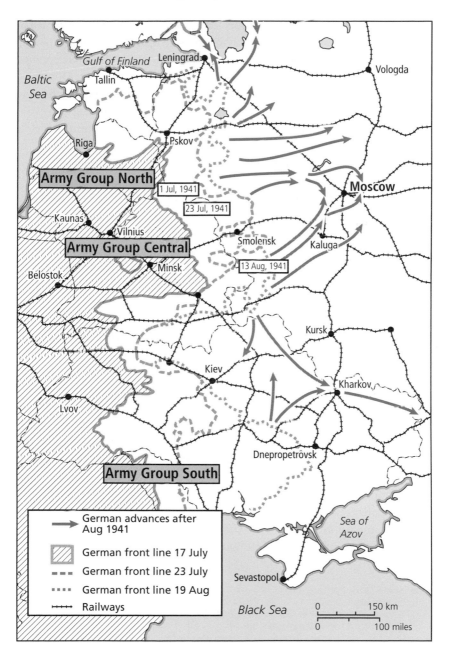

Baltic Sea

Gulf of Finland

Tallin

Leningrad

Vologda

Riga

Pskov

Army Group North

1 Jul, 1941

23 Jul, 1941

Moscow

Kaunas

Vilnius

Army Group Central

Smolensk

Kaluga

Belostok

Minsk

13 Aug, 1941

Kursk

Lvov

Kiev

Kharkov

Dnepropetrovsk

Army Group South

Sea of Azov

German advances after Aug 1941

German front line 17 July

German front line 23 July

German front line 19 Aug

Railways

Sevastopol

Black Sea

0   150 km

0   100 miles

21.1 German supply lines in Russia, 1941

army to establish large forward depots for its different army groups, which in turn would allow for only a short halt in offensive operations.[10] The intended depot locations were each between 150 and 200 miles from the launch points. Three depots for Army Groups North and Centre were at Dünaburg (Daugavpils), Minsk and Molodetschno (Molodechno).[11] Though both army groups reached the depot locations relatively quickly, getting adequate supplies down the railway lines proved to be considerably more difficult, especially for Army Group Centre.

Counter to German expectations, the Soviet Union, even during the chaos of the early days of BARBAROSSA, was able to pull back a great deal of its rolling stock and keep it out of German hands. In the first few weeks of fighting, the Germans were able to capture only 500 Russian locomotives, far fewer than anticipated.[12] This meant that the Germans were forced to reconstruct the captured lines and change the gauges to the European standard, so that their locomotives and cars could be used to bring supplies forward. This was instrumental in leading to the first halt in the German advance in mid-July.[13]

By concentrating their efforts on just a few major trunk lines, the Germans, through tremendous effort, were able to keep one major railhead not far behind each of their advancing army groups. For instance, they had reconstructed a railway line to Minsk by early July, and by the end of September had functional railway lines working as far east as Smolensk and Toropets.[14] However, the weight of supply that could be carried on these lines was considerably less than anticipated – leading to longer delays before the Germans could return to large-scale offensive operations.[15] A number of reasons contributed to this shortfall, including the different construction methods of Russian railroads when compared to German. Russian lines were laid on sandy soil and with less robust wooden ties, so could support a smaller load than standard German lines.

At first, the failure of the central trunk line to Minsk and Smolensk to carry enough tonnage became a cause of great concern to Halder. His diary is full

---

10 *Halder Diaries*, pp. 412, 416.
11 Ibid., p. 283.
12 Klaus Reinhardt, *Moscow – The Turning Point: The Failure of Hitler's Strategy in the Winter of 1941–1942* (Oxford: Berg, 1992), pp. 146–7.
13 David Stahel, *Operation Barbarossa and Germany's Defeat in the East* (Cambridge University Press, 2009), pp. 333–4.
14 For Minsk in July, see *Halder Diaries*, p. 994; for September, see Reinhardt, *Moscow*, p. 62.
15 Van Creveld, *Supplying War*, p. 160.

of worried references to the relatively small number of trains that were proceeding down this track. On 17 July, he complained that only two-thirds of the necessary numbers of trains were running to Army Group Centre.[16]

Later, there were major problems for Army Groups North and South. Halder mentioned the disappearance of whole ammunition trains, and it seems that throughout all of August 1941, offensive operations were strictly limited until the railway situation could be stabilized.[17] The four major reasons Halder gave for the railway supply problems were:

1. A shortage of captured Russian railroad stock, particularly locomotives.
2. A conflict between the demands of troops and the quartermasters. The troops wanted railway lines to be rebuilt as close to the front line as possible, but by rebuilding too quickly the lines were not as sturdy and could not handle as much freight as a solidly rebuilt line to a major depot.
3. The German army was simply not efficient at operating railways.
4. There were serious shortcomings in railway communications and signalling.[18]

Such railway shortcomings meant that after the initial stages of success, BARBAROSSA became a series of less comprehensive offensives that took in only part of the front lines. Army Group North, for instance, was never given enough support to take Leningrad and had to halt operations before reaching the city.[19] More famously, the controversial fact that the Germans had to decide between attacking toward Moscow or Ukraine in September 1941 was partly the result of the relatively slow pace of supplies heading down the railway lines into Russia, which meant that the operations had to be undertaken one after the other instead of simultaneously. In late November, Halder was complaining that the railheads were still too far behind the front lines.[20]

In the end, German inability to set up a fully functional railway system in 1941 was one of the major reasons that they were unable to reach Moscow before the onset of the bitterly cold Russian winter. By the start of December

16 *Halder Diaries*, p. 1052.
17 Ibid., pp. 1142, 1148, 1155, 1179–80.
18 Ibid., p. 1142. It does seem that throughout the campaign, the German army was considerably less efficient than the German national railway system with which it linked up. See Alfred C. Mierzejewski, *The Most Valuable Asset of the Reich: A History of the German National Railway* (Chapel Hill: University of North Carolina Press, 2000), pp. 98–9.
19 Van Creveld, *Supplying War*, p. 162.
20 *Halder Diaries*, p. 1314.

1941, the German-controlled railway system in Russia was still not efficient enough to deliver the quantities of supplies and replacements needed to keep the front-line units up to strength. This meant that in many cases the Germans had to choose between sending in new men to depleted units or sending fresh supplies – further delaying operations.[21] This delay, with the onset of the Russian winter, caused the final *coup de grâce* for German railway supply. Most German locomotives, designed for the still cold, but manageable Central European winters, had their cooling pipes on the outside of their frames. When faced with Russian winters, many of these pipes froze and then exploded, leaving large parts of the German armies without supplies for weeks.[22] The German armies that took part in the final assaults on Moscow were thus considerably weaker than their numerical strength indicated and were unable to fulfil their assignments. As an indication of the failure of the army to run its train network, in early 1942, all the rail lines in Russia up to the main army depots were passed over to civilian control, as the Reich Ministry of Transport was considered more competent to keep supplies moving.[23]

If it was a failure of the Germans to make use of the railways efficiently enough that aided Soviet survival in 1941, Soviet resilience and skill in this area played a crucial role in them pushing the Germans back.[24] By saving such a large percentage of their locomotives and rolling stock from the invaders in 1941, the USSR was able to keep its transport system functional. By 1943, which was before a great deal of Lend-Lease railway supplies had reached the USSR, the Soviets still had access to 85 per cent of the locomotives and 80 per cent of the rolling stock with which they had entered the war.[25] By ruthlessly suppressing any non-essential railway traffic, the Soviet Union was able to keep its far-flung armies supplied throughout 1942 and into 1943.[26] In 1943, after halting the Germans during the Battle of Kursk, the Soviets began the process of pushing the Germans back.

Again, as railways were a crucial aspect of these offensives, the Soviet breakthroughs of 1943 and 1944 (somewhat like those of the Germans in 1941) would proceed for 200–300 miles and then have to pause to allow railway communications to be rebuilt. The Germans did a thorough job of destroying

21 Ibid., p. 1334.
22 *Germany the Second World War*, vol. IV, pp. 1136–8.
23 Mierzejewski, *Most Valuable Asset*, pp. 101–2. See also *Halder Diaries*, p. 1380.
24 Hunter, *Soviet Transport Experience*, p. 60.
25 Holland Hunter, *Soviet Transportation Policy* (Cambridge, Mass.: Harvard University Press, 1957), p. 93.
26 Ernest Williams, *Freight Transportation in the Soviet Union, Including Comparisons with the United States* (Princeton, NJ: Princeton University Press, 1962), pp. 53–5.

railway lines that were about to fall into Soviet hands, so they had to be rebuilt almost in their entirety. In the second half of 1943 and the first half of 1944, the USSR rebuilt a remarkable 28,400 miles of track – by far the largest amount of railway work carried out by any major power in the war.[27] The Soviets also started requesting more and more railway equipment under Lend-Lease as the war went on. In the original Lend-Lease protocol, negotiated in the months immediately after BARBAROSSA began, no mention was made of the need for railway material.[28] During negotiations over the second protocol, in 1942, the Soviets started asking for large amounts of spare parts for railway operations, including railway wheels, axles and rails. However, they were still not in need of large amounts of new rolling stock. As the Red Army switched into offensive mode, however, the need for railway equipment became more intense. By the third protocol, the Soviets were requesting between 2,000 and 3,000 locomotives (though they received less than half this amount), and in the fourth protocol they asked for locomotives to the value of $6.3 million (and were given $3.3 million).[29]

These railway supplies were an important, but not decisive element in the Russian offensives.[30] If American locomotives were on the whole more reliable and better built than their Russian counterparts, the large majority of Soviet rail transport was carried on Soviet-built equipment. In the case of locomotives, the aid that the Soviets received under Lend-Lease between 1942 and 1944 was roughly equivalent to the aid that occupied France and Belgium provided for Germany.[31]

One of the final campaigns in which railways played a controlling role was the fighting in northern France in 1944. There were two competing railway events that helped to determine the outcome. The first was the potential ability of the Germans to use the excellent French rail network to resupply the Normandy coastal defences, once it was determined that the British and

---

27 Hunter, *Soviet Transportation Policy*, pp. 102–3.
28 For a published version of all the Lend-Lease protocols, see United States Department of State, *Soviet Supply Protocols* (Washington DC: US Government Printing Office, 1948).
29 US Department of State, *Soviet Supply Protocols*, pp. 61, 126.
30 Evan Mawdsley, *Thunder in the East: The Nazi-Soviet War, 1941–1945* (London: Bloomsbury, 2005), p. 46.
31 Between the start of 1942 and the end of 1944, France and Belgium constructed 659 locomotives that were sent to the Reich, which made 7 per cent of locomotive production in German-occupied Europe. See United States Strategic Bombing Survey (hereafter USSBS), European Report 200, exhibit 74. According to the US Department of State, *Soviet Supply Protocols*, the USSR would have received somewhat fewer than 1,000 locomotives from the USA during the same years.

Americans were landing there. Had the Germans been given unhindered access to the European rail network under their control in 1944, it is hard to see how the D-Day landings could have succeeded. As the British and Americans well knew, that would have allowed the Germans to concentrate more divisions in the Normandy area with a speed that the Allies could not have matched unloading by ship.[32] It was one of the decisive reasons that pushed the British and Americans into investing so many assets in one of the more effective air campaigns launched anywhere during the war: the spring 1944 plan to isolate potential French beachhead areas from the railway lines that ran to them. Before this campaign, the Germans had generally been able to move troops around the contiguous parts of their empire relatively efficiently. In July 1943, for example, when the decision was made to halt the Kursk offensives and redeploy forces to Italy in response to the Anglo-American invasion of Sicily, the vast majority of forces proceeded relatively unhindered. By November 1943, more than 36,000 railway cars of men and supplies had been sent into Italy by the Germans.[33]

However, in 1944 the Allies were determined to make it as difficult as possible for the Germans to utilize the French rail network. Over the complaints of both the main British and American strategic air force commanders, Arthur Harris and Carl Spaatz, but urged on by his most experienced air deputy, Arthur Tedder, Allied Supreme Commander Dwight Eisenhower ordered that all Anglo-American air assets make the destruction of rail transportation in France one of their highest priorities.[34] For the next few months, attacking railway lines, bridges and marshalling yards in France and Belgium received more dropped bomb tonnage by far than any other targeted system.[35]

The combined weight of these strategic attacks, added to attacks by Anglo-American tactical air power, ended up devastating the railway lines heading to the entire French northwest coast. The Germans eventually stopped using almost all the lines which went to the west and north of Paris.[36] In particular,

---

32 Phillips Payson O'Brien, *How the War Was Won: Air-Sea Power and Allied Victory in World War II* (Cambridge University Press, 2015).

33 Helmut Heiber and David M. Glantz (eds.), *Hitler and his Generals: Military Conferences, 1942–1945* (London: Greenhill, 2002), p. 296.

34 Wesley F. Craven and James L. Cate, *The Army Air Forces in World War II*, vol. III (University of Chicago Press, 1951), pp. 72–8. The order was given on 26 March 1944.

35 These figures come from 'Strategic Bombing of Axis Europe, January 1943–September 1944', AIR 40-1120, pp. 9–10, The National Archives, Kew, London (hereafter TNA).

36 Carl Spaatz papers, 1910–1981, Manuscript Division, Library of Congress, Washington DC, box 134, Milch interview, 23 May 1945, p. 4.

the campaign destroyed almost all of the major bridges over the Seine and Loire rivers. This meant that German divisions being sent to Normandy had to leave their trains and proceed by truck or foot to the battle area. It was quite a shock, particularly for units which had to be redeployed from the Eastern Front. To fight in this new environment, they not only had to have significantly augmented anti-aircraft weaponry, they often had to receive special training to move by road at night.[37]

The real effect of this campaign was revealed after the Allied landings began and the Germans attempted to send troops to Normandy. Twenty-two German divisions were ordered to the Normandy beaches in the two weeks after the Allies landed.[38] However, it took many weeks for them actually to get into action. One, the 276th Infantry Division, which was stationed in southern France, took more than thirty days to be assembled in the northern battle area.[39]

The destruction of French railway lines, yards and bridges also forced the Germans to keep their supply depots much further from the front than was the case on the Eastern Front. There, German AFVs and other supplies were often brought by rail to within ten to fifteen miles of their expected front destination.[40] At this time, because of a sustained attack on the railway systems in France, de-training of supplies often occurred far behind the front line.[41]

For Field Marshal Erwin Rommel, who was in charge of the German defence forces in Normandy, the crippling of the rail networks meant defeat. Just before he was himself badly wounded by Allied air power in July 1944, he wrote a report for Hitler which described the situation.

> The supply situation is so difficult, through the disruption of the railway network and the great danger of the major and minor roads up to 150 kilometers [90 miles] behind the front through the enemy air-force, that only what is most essential can be brought up and above all artillery and *werfer* [rocket launcher] ammunition must be spared everywhere to the utmost.

37 David C. Isby, *Fighting in Normandy: The German Army from D-Day to Villers-Bocage* (London: Greenhill, 2011), p. 207.

38 Henry Harley Arnold papers, 1903–1989, Manuscript Division, Library of Congress, Washington DC, reel 190, 'The Contribution of Airpower to the Defeat of Germany', appendix H: 'The Attack on Enemy Roads'. There is a superb chart and narrative in this appendix, describing the transport issues that confronted every German division that was sent to fight in Normandy.

39 Ibid.

40 USSBS, Keitel interview, 27 June 1945.

41 Carl Spaatz papers, box 134, Bayerlein interview, 19 May 1945.

These conditions are unlikely to improve in future, as the supply area is perpetually being decreased by enemy action and enemy air activity is likely to become still more effective by reason of their occupation of the many airfields in the bridgehead.[42]

If the destruction of French rail networks was of great aid in helping the Allies build up forces more effectively than the Germans in the Normandy area, it proved a great handicap to the British and Americans when they finally broke through German lines in late July. To begin with, the pace of the campaign was too rapid to allow the implementation of efficiently constructed rail supply of the advancing troops. The British and Americans had gone into D-Day imagining the campaign in France as a regular series of small advances that would allow for the construction of rail networks behind the front-line troops. Under the original plan, British and American troops would not cross the Seine for ninety days, though they would move steadily there from the beaches.[43] As it was, for more than fifty days after the initial landings, British and American advances went far slower than expected (which certainly helped their supply situation). However, in late July 1944, the German lines caved in after intense pressure; for the next few weeks, the Wehrmacht put up only limited resistance, as the Allies started moving across France at a completely unexpected rate and in an unanticipated direction (toward Le Mans), before reaching Paris – weeks ahead of schedule – on 24 August.

Like the Germans in their advances of 1940 and 1941, the Americans and British would have preferred to use captured or rebuilt railway lines to bring supplies as far as possible toward their fighting troops.[44] However, when they started pursuing the Germans through France, the Allies found the French railway network to be in chaos – not because of destruction meted out by retreating German forces, but instead by that inflicted their own bombs.[45]

The supply crisis began in earnest when Allied forces reached the town of Le Mans. There, the railway yard was discovered to have been almost completely

---

42 This is a British government translation of a captured copy of Rommel's report. It was released by the Air Ministry after the war. The copy consulted was in Templewood papers, Cambridge University Library, xiv:4/6.

43 L. F. Ellis, *Victory in the West*, vol. ii: *The Defeat of Germany* (London: HMSO, 1968), p. 2. See also Daniel Beaver, 'Deuce and a Half', in John A. Lynn (ed.), *Feeding Mars: Logistics in Western Warfare from the Middle Ages to the Present* (Boulder, Colo.: Westview, 1993), p. 264.

44 Roland G. Ruppenthal, *The European Theater of Operations: Logistical Support of the Armies*, vol. ii: *September 1944 – May 1945* (2 vols., Washington DC: US Government Printing Office, 1995 [1959]), p. 148.

45 Ibid., pp. 547–8.

destroyed by aerial bombardment, and repair efforts were relatively slow. Once the decision was made to cross the Seine and Loire rivers in August, it became almost impossible to use railway lines to get supplies to the advancing troops. So 18,000 personnel, of which 5,000 were captured German POWs, were put to work to try to reopen French rail links.[46] However, it was not until November that train lines were working well enough for the British and Americans to establish large depots near their forward troops in eastern France, Belgium and Holland.[47] Until then, the Allies, particularly the Americans who were advancing further from the coast than the British and Canadians, had to rely overwhelmingly on trucks to get supplies to their troops, and that meant that offensive operations ground to a halt in September.

Before leaving the railways, the war in the Asia/Pacific should be briefly mentioned. In this theatre, particularly the famous islands campaigns of the Central and Southwest Pacific, railways were unimportant for the supply of troops. The war in the Pacific, as opposed to that on the Asian mainland, ended up being dominated by shipping. However, the Japanese were keen on linking their mainland Asian empire by rail. Reports about this project started worrying those close to Franklin Roosevelt in late 1942.[48] Japanese railroads did play an important role, in particular for the Japanese army, which was trying to control China. Maintaining good railway communications was crucial for the Japanese to try to control their vast mainland empire with an army that was noticeably short in AFVs and other transport vehicles. In northern China and Manchuria, the Japanese position was aided by a relatively efficient rail network that operated well into 1945.[49] This situation led to one of the most unusual supply situations for a modern fighting force in the war – large armies providing for themselves. Other armies at different times were able to secure by force or purchase important supplies, particularly of food, from their local area of operations. The Germans when they went into Russia and the Russians when they went into Germany had little hesitation in stripping the conquered areas clean of food and other essentials to keep their forces moving. However, the Japanese armies in China and Manchuria took this to another level, not only getting food from their occupied territories, but creating an internal network of production for other

---

46 Ibid., pp. 547, 551. See also Ellis, *Victory in the West*, vol. II, p. 132.
47 Ellis, *Victory in the West*, vol. II, p. 136.
48 Harry Hopkins papers, FDR Presidential Library, Hyde Park, New York, 24 December 1942, intelligence appraisal of Japanese intentions.
49 Peter Duus (ed.), *The Japanese Empire, 1931–1945* (Princeton, NJ: Princeton University Press, 1996), p. 167.

important items, including uniforms and even ammunition. Because of this, which was made possible by their access to an efficient rail network, Japanese ground forces in China were only allocated 10 per cent of the normal supply tonnage that they could have expected.[50]

Trucks

The truck was the Second World War's most important tool for the exploitation of offensive actions. Unless an enemy's railway system was captured entirely intact and with a great deal of rolling stock, the truck was the best and most immediate way to bring supplies to advancing troops as they moved forward into enemy territory. However, this flexibility came at a cost. When compared to railways, trucks were less efficient, required considerably more manpower for the delivery of each ton of supplies, and needed greater support in terms of fuel and repair in order to fulfil their mission. This meant that an advance completely dependent upon trucks for its supply had a natural limit of operations of approximately 200 miles before new depots needed to be established.[51]

However, trucks had one crucial advantage over rail systems, which made them invaluable in any offensive action. They were not limited to pre-existing lines to deliver their product. Depending on the season and the road network in the region, trucks could, by using paved or dirt roads, reach advancing armoured spearheads that had strayed away from a major railway line. Also, they could move side by side with, or just behind, advancing spearheads, which meant that offensive operations could continue as long as they had supplies. As such, looking at the vehicle-lift capacity of an attacking force gave as good an indication of its possible area of advance as the number of AFVs it contained.

Trucks had shown their potential during the First World War, when all major powers, to a certain degree at least, started using them to replace horses in different situations. Far from being more expensive to run than a horse, a truck required less weight of fuel than a horse did fodder. For instance, a horse that could carry 200 lbs needed 20 lbs of fodder a day. To keep its horses fed, the British Army had to send a higher weight of fodder to its forces in France than it did ammunition.[52] In the interwar period, the

---

50 USSBS, Sato interview, 1 November 1945, pp. 1–3.
51 Van Creveld, *Supplying War*, p. 153.
52 John Norris, *World War II Trucks and Tanks* (London: History Press, 2012).

major powers all pushed to at least partly motorize their armed forces. The United States Army went the furthest down this road. In 1926, the Army decided that it needed to be completely motorized. However, even with a relatively small force, by 1939 it still had a way to go before being fully motorized.[53] This is when the designs were first put together for the great Allied workhorse of the war, the 2.5 ton ('deuce and a half') American truck, which would be found in every theatre of action. The Germans took considerably longer before they began standardizing their truck design. Before 1938, the Germans produced a bewildering array of vehicles of all types. Then, however, production was partially rationalized, and when the war started German trucks were divided into three main categories: light (carrying up to two tons), medium (carrying between two and four tons) and heavy (carrying more than four tons).[54]

However, when the war started, the German army was still a long way from being motorized. The standard German division in 1939 had 900 vehicles of all types, and 5,000 horses.[55] Most armies still relied on huge numbers of horses in lieu of internal combustion-engined vehicles. This was obviously a major drawback. One estimate was that, on average, an engined vehicle had at least four times the speed and eight times the range of horse-drawn transport.[56] Throughout the war, the demands for mobility placed on armies made trucks more and more valuable. and any opportunity to increase their numbers was eagerly taken. When the Italian government switched sides in 1943, and the Germans responded by occupying most of the country, Hitler spoke hopefully about confiscating 40,000 to 50,000 trucks from his erstwhile ally.[57] On the other hand, the British and Russians were asking for ever-increasing numbers of trucks from the Americans through Lend-Lease. In 1943, 26.7 per cent of all Lend-Lease deliveries were trucks, and in 1944, the percentage was an even higher 29.4 per cent.[58] This was a considerably higher percentage than any other category of deliveries.

The German army that went into France in 1940 chose, correctly, to concentrate its transport resources with its armoured spearheads, leaving the following infantry divisions to get by with a far larger percentage of

53 Beaver, 'Deuce and a Half', p. 259.
54 Jean-Denis Lepage, *German Military Vehicles of World War II* (Jefferson, NC: McFarland, 2007), p. 16.
55 Ibid., p. 17.
56 David M. Glantz, *Companion to Colossus Reborn: Key Documents and Statistics* (Lawrence: University Press of Kansas, 2005), p. 153.
57 Heiber and Glantz, *Hitler and his Generals*, p. 269.
58 H. Duncan Hall, *North American Supply* (London: HMSO, 1951), p. 431.

horse-driven vehicles. Each Panzer group which took part in the offensive through the Ardennes was given an additional vehicle lift of 4,800 tons, a very large sum by the standards of the time.[59] These extra vehicles were laden with supplies and gave the advancing German tanks greater range than that envisaged in pre-war thinking.

However, even with this oversupply, the German army had a small margin of error. In February 1940, Halder estimated that under expected wastage rates, the Germans might not be able to move forward after two months of operations, because of truck losses.[60] When the German attack started in May, he was constantly worried about the number of trucks in working order. He noted that the German army had quickly seized 1,000 trucks from the Dutch.[61] At another point, every truck in the Reich was put at the army's disposal. Because of these great efforts, and because the Germans were able to get the rail lines back into operation relatively efficiently and use air resupply selectively, France was conquered. However, such a success would be much more difficult when it came to the land invasion of the USSR.

On the one hand, the German Army that started BARBAROSSA had what seemed to be an impressive total of 600,000 vehicles of all types. However, this large number masked some major problems. It was a motley collection coming from many of Germany's conquered neighbours. At one count, there were 2,000 different vehicle types that needed to be serviced. The average German mobile division needed 300 tons of supply per day to operate. The total lift capacity of the German army going into BARBAROSSA was 10,000 tons a day. Therefore, after servicing the twenty-six mobile divisions, the amount left over for the slower infantry was very small indeed.[62]

Early in the campaign, it was clear that the strain of operating over the greater distances of Russia was extracting a much heavier toll on the German transportation corps than the fighting in France. By the second half of July, more than a quarter of the vehicles available were out of action in need of repair.[63] The primitive, mostly dirt Russian road network caused German tyres to wear out much more quickly than expected. Halder noted, rather

---

59 Karl-Heinz Frieser, *The Blitzkrieg Legend: The 1940 Campaign in the West* (Annapolis, Md.: Naval Institute Press, 2005), p. 107.
60 *Halder Diaries*, p. 222.
61 Ibid., p. 406.
62 The sources for this paragraph are *Germany the Second World War*, vol. IV, pp. 318, 1109, 1110; and Stahel, *Operation Barbarossa*, pp 129–30.
63 *Germany the Second World War*, vol. IV, pp. 1112–13.

pessimistically, in early August 1941 that 44,000 additional tyres had been allocated to the trucks supplying the army groups, but at present wastage rates they would all be used up in a month.[64]

However, the demands on German truck deliveries continued to rise. The daily use of ammunition was considerably higher during BARBAROSSA than had been the case during the fighting in Western Europe in 1940. By 16 August, the German army had already expended as much ammunition in Russia as it was originally assumed it would need during the entire campaign. While the Germans needed to supply their forces with more ammunition than expected, their trucks were being worn out by the stress of the campaign. For instance, after the decision was made to drive south toward Ukraine and not toward Moscow, the German army began this phase of the offensive with 22 per cent fewer trucks than they would have expected. When the final great drive toward Moscow began, the shortfall was approximately 50 per cent.[65]

At the same time, German truck production was woefully inadequate. To make up all the losses suffered in 1941, the Germans would have had to build 150,000 new vehicles of various sizes, while actual production was 39,000.[66] The extreme truck losses of 1941 were a main reason that the Germans had to have considerably more limited offensive aspirations in 1942 on the Eastern Front.[67] Truck production remained a general headache for the Germans for the rest of the war. Though the Reich would see impressive production for most major armament groups between 1942 and 1944, the situation for trucks lagged considerably behind. While Germany's overall indices of production (January 1942 equalling 100) averaged 142 in 1942, increasing to 222 for 1943, and 277 for 1944, the indices for trucks kept pace only for the first year. In 1942, truck production indices increased to 145, before falling considerably behind overall munitions production by reaching 174 for 1943, and a paltry 148 for 1944.[68] In numerical terms, the Germans, using both domestic production and that of its allies and conquests, built 81,276 trucks in all of 1942; 109,483 in 1943; and 89,069 in 1944.[69] Interestingly, the increase in production came mostly from companies outside of Germany, which in

---

64 *Halder Diaries*, p. 1148.
65 Ibid., pp. 1183, 1225, 1328.
66 *Germany the Second World War*, vol. iv, p. 1119. Total truck losses on the Eastern Front from June 1941 to January 1942 is given as 39,870 (see p. 1120).
67 Reinhardt, *Moscow*, p. 368.
68 USSBS, European Report 1, appendix table 106.
69 Ibid., appendix table 107.

the end made up three-eighths of all truck production after 1942.[70] The relative failure of the Germans to build trucks made them even more reliant on rail networks than their enemies, and hastened the German defeat on land.[71]

If the Germans experienced real truck shortages in 1941 and 1942, the Soviets did everything in their power to make sure that the same thing never happened to them. The main story of Lend-Lease in 1943 and 1944 was the massive transfer of trucks to the Red Army. It is interesting to see just how dramatically this change occurred. In the first Lend-Lease protocol of 1941, there was no mention of the need for trucks to be transferred to the USSR. However, the following year, trucks became by far the most numerous vehicles supplied, with the Soviets allocated 120,000, and in the third protocol they were allocated 132,000.[72] This enormous delivery of trucks to the Soviet Union became a top priority for Roosevelt and Harry Hopkins, both of whom were updated about its progress by General George Marshall, who assured them in the summer of 1942 that the Russians were receiving the maximum truck allocation possible.[73] In the end, the Russians received many more trucks under Lend-Lease than the Germans were able to build for themselves.

By the fourth protocol, the Soviets broadened their perspectives considerably. Almost all of the earlier deliveries had been the famous 2.5-ton (deuce and a half) Studebaker trucks. In 1944, they not only asked for a remarkable 157,814 trucks, they asked for a wide range of vehicles, from the monstrous five-ton trucks to dual use, land-water transports. Though they did not get every vehicle they wanted, in the end they were allocated 135,933 trucks of various kinds.[74]

These Lend-Lease supplies of trucks made the rapid and deep Soviet advances of 1943–45 possible. The Studebakers not only carried 50 per cent more tonnage, on average, than similar Soviet trucks, they were considerably more robust and could stay in operation much longer.[75] They were also far more numerous than Soviet-built models. Up to two-thirds of the trucks in

70 Ibid., p. 175.
71 War Office files, TNA, file 208-4340, Milch interview notes, 7 July 1945, p. 8.
72 US Department of State, *Soviet Supply Protocols*, pp. 20, 57.
73 George C. Marshall papers, George C. Marshall Research Library, Lexington Va., Marshall to Hopkins, 25 July 1942. At this time, the maximum per month was 4,000 trucks, though this number would soon skyrocket.
74 US Department of State, *Soviet Supply Protocols*, pp. 97–9.
75 Mawdsley, *Thunder in the East*, p. 199.

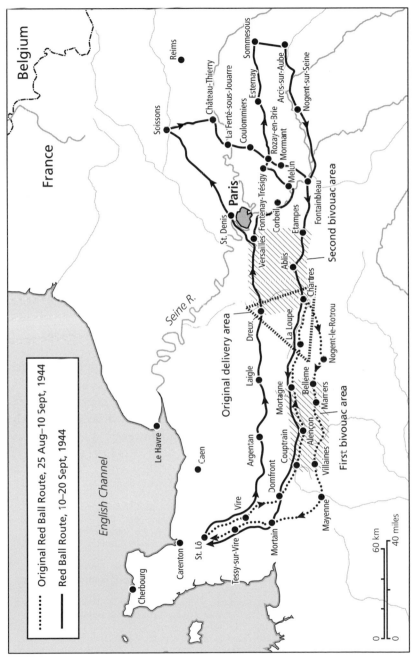

21.2 American supply system in Northwest Europe, 1944-45

the Russian army in the second half of the war were from Lend-Lease supplies, overwhelmingly Studebakers.[76]

If trucks were key to exploiting breakthroughs on the Eastern Front, it was in France, in 1944, that they were used in their most ambitious role – using motor transport in lieu of working rail lines to establish large depots and push offensives forward. As mentioned before, the aerial destruction of the French rail network meant that once Anglo-American troops crossed the Seine, they had no access to train-borne supplies.[77] A decision was made to mobilize a massive number of trucks to fill the gap. This mainly American effort started in late August 1944 and was nicknamed the Red Ball Express.[78]

The Red Ball Express showed, on the one hand, the great flexibility of truck supply, but at the same time highlighted its inefficiencies and natural limitations. The trucks involved did carry a large amount of supplies, but at a considerably higher cost in manpower and equipment than that which would have been used by a railway, even when they were allowed to carry more weight than their classes theoretically allowed.[79] The famous 2.5-ton trucks, the backbone of the supply effort, were authorized to carry up to five tons of supplies when operating in France.[80] The fact that two large American armies, the First and Third, could be supplied for a lengthy period of time without large depots built up through the use of rail supply was unprecedented.

The Red Ball Express operated on two parallel routes. Outbound trucks (those carrying supplies to the armies) travelled on a northern series of roads, leading from the Normandy depots to a forward supply point at Chartres. Trucks returning to Normandy to reload then travelled on a completely different one-way route that ran to the south. However, as the American

76 David M. Glantz and Jonathan House, *When Titans Clashed: How the Red Army Stopped Hitler* (Lawrence: University Press of Kansas, 1995), p. 150.
77 The supply problem was not so acute for British and Canadian troops. As they advanced to the north of the Americans along the French coast, their lines of advance were shorter and more contained, and they could receive some seaborne support. See L. F. Ellis, *Victory in the West*, vol. 1: *The Battle of Normandy* (London: HMSO, 1962), pp. 473–4.
78 The phrase 'Red Ball' had been used first to denote some express trains in America in the nineteenth century, and was then then used by some trucking companies after the First World War.
79 William F. Ross and Charles F. Romanus, *United States Army in World War II: The Quartermaster Corps: Operations in the War Against Germany* (Washington DC: US Government Printing Office, 1965), pp. 399–400.
80 Chester Wardlow, *United States Army in World War II: – The Transportation Corps: Responsibilities, Organization, and Operations* (Washington DC: US Government Printing Office, 1951), p. 91.

armies advanced westward, the distance that needed to be covered expanded by hundreds of miles. The need for supplies and more vehicles became so intense that Allied divisions newly arrived in France were often halted and stripped of all their equipment, so that it could be used to supply the advancing troops. Even then, the volume of materiel carried was not always sufficient; instead, the trucks were often sent as close to the front as possible to deliver their goods. When depots were established, the fast pace of the offensive meant that when they became functional they were already too far behind the front line.[81]

If there was one vital commodity being carried by the Red Ball Express, it was fuel. As the German army collapsed in France and began its headlong retreat, American usage of ammunition actually declined, compared to the period of intense fighting in Normandy. The great bulk of this fuel was loaded onto trucks in five-gallon containers called 'jerricans' or 'jerrycans'.[82] Though originally an Italian design, these containers received their nickname because American troops first came across them in North Africa and believed they were of German (jerry) design.

The amount of fuel needed by the advancing troops was enormous. In late July, after the US First and Third Armies broke through the German lines, their combined daily fuel needs were 600,000 gallons.[83] When they first crossed the Seine during the week beginning 20 August, the First and Third Armies jointly were using 800,000 gallons of fuel daily.[84] As they moved further into France, their targeted allocation of fuel was almost doubled to 1,500,000 gallons. These enormous fuel demands were further extended by the Red Ball Express itself, which required 300,000 gallons of fuel a day to operate.[85] However, such a large amount was impossible to deliver efficiently. The armies started operating with almost no fuel reserves, with their advances limited by whatever quantities of fuel they could get their hands on. At times, in a self-defeating move, the Third Army took the fuel the

81 Roland G. Ruppenthal, *The European Theater of Operations: Logistical Support of the Armies*, vol. 1: *May 1941 – September 1944* (2 vols., Washington DC: US Government Printing Office, 1995 [1953]), pp. 493–4.

82 David P. Colley, *The Road to Victory: The Untold Story of World War II's Red Ball Express* (Washington DC: Potomac, 2000), p. 151. There seems to be no set spelling for these containers. The US official histories use 'jerrican', so that is the spelling used in this chapter.

83 Pat Ware, *Red Ball Express: Supply Line from the D-Day Beaches* (London: Ian Allan, 2007), p. 58.

84 Ruppenthal, *European Theater*, vol. 1, p. 504.

85 Ware, *Red Ball Express*, p. 58.

Red Ball Express needed to function to keep its own advance going for another day.[86]

In the end, it was a lack of fuel that eventually brought the Allied advance to a halt, regardless of the great efforts of the Red Ball Express. By that time, most of France had been taken by the Allies, and a large portion of Belgium. However, further advances into Holland and Germany would have to wait until a pipeline, which was being worked on feverishly, could bring fuel closer to the front line, and an efficient rail system could be established.

The high wastage in trucks and supplies helped stopped the advance, and this shows how ultimately inefficient road resupply was in comparison to rail. For instance, millions of jerricans ended up littering the French country-side as troops tossed them aside, instead of sending them back to be reused. Going into the operation, the USA had approximately 12 million jerricans with which to carry fuel.[87] By October, 3.5 million were unaccounted for, reducing significantly the amount of fuel that could be delivered to the front lines. The trucks themselves suffered from the continual strain. By November, there were 15,000 broken American trucks in the European theatre.[88]

These truck deliveries also seemed to lead to a far greater loss of equipment and supplies than those by rail. During the height of the Red Ball Express, the US First Army was supposedly being sent 3,700 tons of supplies daily, but its own records indicate that it was receiving only 2,225. However, at least the First Army kept some kind of records. George Patton's Third Army, which was advancing the most rapidly, stopped keeping any records of its deliveries during the week of 27 August to 3 September.[89]

In the end, the truck had proved itself revolutionary to modern warfare – though in a limited sense. Supplies carried in trucks were what made possible the large Allied armoured breakthroughs, which are often seen as the most dramatic element of the war. However, without rail support, they could only press on for a few hundred miles before the strain became too much.

Aircraft

Using large numbers of aircraft in a supply role was one of the most innovative, if expensive and ultimately restricted, logistical developments

86 Ruppenthal, *European Theater*, vol. 1, p. 505.
87 Colley, *Road to Victory*, p. 153.
88 Ibid., p. 157.
89 Ruppenthal, *European Theater*, vol. 1, p. 492.

of the Second World War. The aircraft issue should be divided into two distinct areas; the use of aircraft to supply ground forces and the supply of air forces themselves. In the first case, the most important examples occurred when aircraft were used to supply land forces that were advancing rapidly or those that had been surrounded by the enemy and were thus unable to receive support from rail or road.

Using air supply was usually a much more expensive option because of the relatively small amount of tonnage that could be carried by plane when compared to rail and road. One C-47, the supply workhorse of the US Army Air Forces (USAAF), could carry approximately three tons of cargo, little more than the standard American truck. By way of comparison, the winding and relatively primitive Burma Road in 1942, before falling into Japanese hands, was still carrying about 13,000 tons of supplies a month to Chinese forces.[90] However, when this was cut off, air supplies into China, even with extreme effort, took until 1944 before they could reach 10,000 tons a month.[91] That being said, the delivery of small but vital amounts of supply by air could make a real difference. In 1940, when the German army first broke out of the Ardennes and began splitting the French and British armies into two, the Luftwaffe was able to deliver 400 tons of fuel to the advancing Panzer groups.[92] Almost every nation in the war did try air supply of ground forces at different times. Even the Japanese navy, which went into the war with no plans whatsoever to use aircraft to supply land forces, had to improvise a plan to fly in supplies to Japanese army units fighting in New Guinea.[93]

However, relying just on aircraft-delivered supplies was perilous, as the Germans would discover during the Battle of Stalingrad. When the German Sixth Army found itself completely surrounded by the Red Army on 23 November 1942, Hitler decided, on Göring's assurances, to leave the troops in place and supply them by air. Even though the Germans had one of the largest and most advanced air forces in the world at the time, this task was considerably beyond their abilities. During the seventy-two days of the Stalingrad airlift, the Germans were able to deliver just over 8,000 tons to the surrounded Sixth Army, a per day rate of 117 tons.[94] The German estimate

90 Franklin D. Roosevelt, Papers as President: The President's Secretary's File (PSF), 1933–1945, FDR Presidential Library, PSF 2, Arnold memorandum, 25 April 1942.
91 War Department Papers (US National Archives), Historical Files, RG 165, Boatner report of meeting with Roosevelt, 18 February 1944.
92 Frieser, *Blitzkrieg Legend*, p. 109.
93 USSBS, Ohmae interview, 6 December 1945, p. 9.
94 www.stalingrad.net/german-hq/the-stalingrad-airlift/airstat.html (accessed 20 October 2014).

was that the Sixth Army needed 300 tons per day, or 9,000 tons per month, to be adequately supplied. Interestingly, the Germans were able to fly in considerably more support to their armies in Tunisia at the same time. In early 1943, when Rommel's forces were actually being beefed up in a futile attempt to hold on in North Africa, the Luftwaffe started large regular supply flights, the average daily volume of which was 585 tons (five times the amount that was delivered into Stalingrad).[95] However, even this great effort only brought in one-quarter of the 60,000 tons of supplies Rommel needed every month.[96] When it came to land supply, air power was best used in certain short time periods – otherwise the strain on the delivery system could get too great.

One of the reasons for this comes from the second point to be discussed here, the supply of aircraft themselves – one of the most expensive and difficult tasks of the war for all the major powers. Making and arming aircraft was the single greatest economic task for four out of the five great powers in the war: Germany, Japan, the United Kingdom and the United States. The first three of these countries spent at least 50 per cent of their munitions building and arming aircraft – and the United States spent between 40 and 50 per cent. The Germans found that a large number of their aircraft broke down or were damaged in the ultimately futile attempt to get supplies to the surrounded Sixth Army. For the Allies in November 1943, when the Anglo-American armies in Italy were making slow progress up the peninsula, one-third of all the supplies in the region were being spent maintaining aircraft, which Winston Churchill argued was subverting the whole campaign.[97]

The best example of an extraordinarily expensive air operation, if one rarely discussed, is the attempt by the USAAF to bomb Japan from the Chinese mainland. Getting American supplies into China had been a major preoccupation of American grand strategists, including Franklin Roosevelt, from the moment the United States entered the war. The air campaign which was to be launched from China was close to the heart of General Arnold, the Chief of the USAAF. It was codenamed MATTERHORN; as eventually conceived, MATTERHORN was to involve the most expensive weapons system of the entire war, the B-29 'superbomber'. The development costs of

---

95 George F. Howe, *The United States Army in World War II – Northwest Africa: Seizing the Initiative in the West* (Washington DC: US Government Printing Office, 1993), p. 366.
96 Ibid., p. 365.
97 Air Ministry Papers, TNA, file 8-1146, Churchill to H. L. Ismay, 24 November 1943.

the B-29 exceeded those of the atomic bomb, but even after being built, the aircraft demanded constant supply and manpower allocation.[98]

In 1943, when the most ambitious plan for MATTERHORN was developed, Arnold hoped to use all the B-29s being built in operations from China, and their supply needs were staggering. He imagined operations starting in late 1944, with preparatory efforts taking place one year before. By October 1944, he wanted to have ten bombardment groups operational, a force that would double to twenty bombardment groups by May 1945. It would have taken one of the largest air forces in the world just to supply the B-29s. To start, in October 1944, Arnold planned to have 2,800 B-24s (far more than there were in the entire European theatre of operations) running supplies to the B-29s, and by May 1945, that figure would have reached 4,000. The infrastructure costs would have been enormous. Arnold expected that there would be 127 separate airfields in operation in China and India, 20 for the B-29 bombardment groups actually bombing Japan, and the remaining 107 to fly in supplies.[99]

Yet this airlift capacity would supply only 20,000 tons of supplies a month, just a small part of the enormous amount of support that the B-29s would need. Arnold also planned that the road into China from Burma would be reopened in 1944 and an oil pipeline would be constructed from India to China to supply fuel. This pipeline would provide 18,000 tons of fuel a month, while an additional 65,000 tons of supplies would be coming in by road in 1945.[100] Had this plan been put into place, it would dwarfed any other campaign of the war in cost. To put it into context, Arnold was planning on supplying his B-29s by early 1945 with 103,000 tons of supplies per month, eleven times what the Germans believed the Sixth Army needed in Stalingrad. As it was, MATTERHORN started, in a much reduced state, in June 1944. However, even a small version of MATTERHORN ended up consuming 70 per cent of the supplies that were getting into China at the time.[101]

---

98 The manpower needs of the B-29 were surprisingly large, and during the last year of the war materially reduced the number of American personnel that were available for the land war. See K. R. Greenfield (ed.), *Command Decisions* (Washington DC: US Government Printing Office, 2000), pp. 375, 379 (online at www.history.army.mil/books/70-7_15.htm – accessed 20 October 2014).

99 Records of the US Joint Chiefs of Staff (US National Archives), RG 218, Air Offensive from China, JCS meeting, 20 August 1943; includes Arnold memorandum, 'Air Plan for the Defeat of Japan', which has excerpts from the larger Committee of Operations Analysts report, pp. 13–14.

100 Ibid., p. 15.

101 Franklin D. Roosevelt, Papers as President, PSF 83, Arnold to Watson, 11 July 1944. At this time, the B-29s needed 8,000 tons a month to operate, but the highest monthly total of supplies that had made it to China was 15,000 tons.

Only after all the B-29s were shifted to the Marianas could a sensible and balanced supply system be integrated, based on much shorter shipping lines directly from the United States.

While MATTERHORN was an extreme example, the deployment and supply of aircraft in general was one of the most expensive, if least studied, undertakings of the war. In the end, this ended up destroying massive amounts of equipment, more than any specific battle. To begin with, as aircraft losses were constantly being made up, a significant percentage of aircraft in the world were on a constant cycle of redeployment or initial assignment. In 1943, approximately 22 per cent of American aircraft were in the process of deployment at any one time, and large numbers of these were lost due to accidents or weather.[102] As just one example, the USAAF lost 3,927 aircraft in inactive theatres between May and December 1942.[103]

During the war there was a major divergence between the proportion of losses suffered by the British and Americans in aircraft deployment, and those suffered by the Germans and Japanese. A number of factors contributed to this, but probably the most important were oil shortages that led to the Germans and Japanese decreasing pilot training hours. By 1944, the Germans and Japanese were both sending many of their aircraft on deployment with pilots who were simply not up to the task. They were deficient in flying in bad weather, in navigation and in takeoffs and landings. They could therefore damage or completely lose their aircraft (and their lives) in what should have been a routine flight. Also, they were often flying aircraft that were less robustly made, due to the pressures placed on the German and Japanese armaments industry because of the need to increase production. In 1944, the rush for production meant that substandard raw materials were used in some cases, and insufficient quality checks were enforced in others.[104]

Therefore, when the Germans reached their peak of production, in the summer of 1944, they were losing about 25 per cent of the aircraft they were building in the process of deployment to their operational units.[105] Japanese losses became even more catastrophic as the war went on. Earlier in the war, when Japanese pilot training was still excellent and fuel was relatively abundant, losses reaching deployment points varied between 5 and 10 per

---

[102] Ibid., Stratemeyer to FDR, 11 March 1943.
[103] Henry Harley Arnold papers, reel 121, 'Army Air Force Airplane Losses and Attrition Rates May–December 1942'.
[104] O'Brien, *How the War Was Won*.
[105] Carl Spaatz papers, box 135, Speer and Baumbach interview, 18 May 1945, p. 11. See also USSBS, Kaether interview, 24 April 1945, p. 1.

cent. Considering that Japanese pilots often had to make their initial deployment flights over the vast stretches of the Pacific Ocean, this figure was not surprising. However, by 1944, at least a quarter, and sometimes more than 50 per cent of aircraft sent on deployment were lost trying to reach their forward bases.[106]

Lost did not mean fully destroyed; it just meant inoperable when the aircraft reached its base – which points out another of the complex issues surrounding aircraft supply: the need for specialist technicians and supplies to keep aircraft in flying condition. Even aircraft in relatively quiet theatres needed constant maintenance. The USAAF, which kept its planes better supplied and maintained than any other power, lost a sobering 12,665 'plane months' in inactive theatres (North America, Latin America, etc.) between May and December 1942.[107] At the same time, it lost only a few more, 13,947 plane months, in active theatres such as North Africa and the Southwest Pacific.[108]

As the war went on, American maintenance actually improved significantly. In 1943, the USAAF accident rate fell below not only that of 1942, but also that achieved during the decade before the United States entered the war.[109] Also, maintaining and supplying aircraft required more specialized personnel than other forms of warfare. As the wastage rates for aircraft were so high, well-trained maintenance personnel became essential – otherwise the effective combat strengths of air units could dip far below their numerical strength. This became a particular problem for the Japanese from 1943, and for the Germans from 1944. As the Japanese defensive perimeter was pushed backward, the Japanese navy and army found themselves with many of their most efficient maintenance personnel stuck in forward bases that had been bypassed by the United States – for example, at Rabaul.[110] The Japanese navy even formed a special agency, the 101 *Kokusentai*, to try to reduce the heavy aircraft losses due to poor maintenance and support, but it was too little, too late.[111]

---

[106] USSBS, Kawabe interview, 26 November 1945, p. 3.
[107] Henry Harley Arnold papers, reel 121, 'Army Air Force Airplane Losses and Attrition Rates May–December 1942.' Plane months was a USAAF calculation which counted a plane in being that could not operate for a month at a time.
[108] The actual number of planes lost was 1,036 in active theatres and 471 in inactive theatres.
[109] Harry Hopkins papers, box 125, Lovett to Hopkins, 29 October 1943.
[110] War Department Papers, Historical Files, RG 165, Kenney to Arnold, September 1944. USSBS, Genda interview, 28 and 29 November 1945, p. 12.
[111] USSBS, Katsumata interview, 25 October 1945, p. 2.

Conclusion

By 1944, Allied forces were fighting under conditions which guaranteed them a regular flow of supply, while German and Japanese armies found themselves often with incomplete or fully broken supply lines. When it came to transport overland to armies, railway lines were usually the crucial factor, because only they allowed for the efficient establishment of large depots. This point is not always realized. While truck and aircraft resupply were more flexible, only railways could carry the heavy bulk of supplies needed for large modern armies. The more an army strayed from railway lines, the less efficient the supply process became, as both trucks and aircraft demanded a great amount of support to keep themselves in action.

That being said, air and truck resupply were more flexible, and at crucial times could be used to great effect. Trucks could continue offensive operation for somewhere between 200 and 300 miles from a railway line (though after that their effectiveness started to wane). They broadened the sphere of offensive activity and allowed for Blitzkrieg-type tactics. Aircraft could deliver supplies to spearhead forces, or those surrounded by the enemy. However, keeping up long-term air supply was such an expensive business that only the United States could have hoped to have done it for extended periods. In the end, of course, it was the ability of the Allies to integrate all three forms of supply discussed here – as well as the oceanic shipping lines – which allowed them to triumph so convincingly over Germany and Japan in the Second World War. It was the greatest test of modern warfare.

22

Intelligence

JOHN FERRIS

Until recently, much was hidden about the role of intelligence in the Second World War. Today, the evidence is strong, despite the destruction or withholding of records on Soviet, and particularly Japanese, intelligence. However, that evidence has not been assessed thoroughly by specialists, nor incorporated into broader accounts of the war. The story also is told uncritically, from the perspective of Allied sword against Axis shield, at the peak of the success of ULTRA. Actually, the intelligence war was a real competition, involving Axis successes and Allied failures. Axis intelligence services ranged from incompetent to good, mostly mediocre. Allied ones were poor to great, mostly good. Initially, however, the states superior in intelligence and material misused these advantages. American, British and Soviet forces often were too poor to exploit the advantages provided by intelligence, while failures of assessment exposed them to devastation from surprise attack. Before 1942, intelligence worked marginally in the Axis's favour, by multiplying the value of their large and good forces. From 1942, the balance of intelligence and power turned simultaneously and systematic- ally toward the Allies. Intelligence did little to cause Axis defeat, but much to shape how the Allies achieved victory.

Intelligence and war

Intelligence is the collection, collation and analysis of evidence to enable an effective and efficient use of scarce resources. Intelligence is not a form of power, but rather a means to guide its use. Intelligence does not win wars. It does help generals do so. It involves finding true and useful secrets while avoiding false notions, and forcing the opposite on the foe, through security and deception. Intelligence is collected through open and secret sources, each with power and limits. Open sources offer the most information, but are stymied by security procedures. Agents produce vast amounts of unreliable intelligence, and the rarest gems – key documents and inside commentary on their meaning; imagery provides accurate material, often in such quantities that a mass of trivialities masks what matters. From the fount of signals intelligence flows the richest streams of data, but usually these yield first-rate material on second-rate issues, while those on the greatest of matters are hard to tap. Sources matter not because they are secret or complex, but by providing accurate, relevant and timely information for action. A primitive source may equal a sophisticated one in value, an open source a secret one. Developments in open sources often revolutionize the information available for action, as occurred with radar in 1940. Sources rarely tell the whole truth and nothing else. Normally they offer masses of fragments, of uncertain accuracy or marginal relevance. They tell the truth partially and indirectly, by illustrating issues such as quartermasters' accounts or the views of second-rate figures, which illuminate greater matters.

The best intelligence is useless without efficient links between the organs which collect, evaluate and act upon it. Flaws are possible anywhere along the chain. When one link breaks, so will the whole. Accurate intelligence may not be collected or assessed properly. It may not reach a commander in time; he might be unable to use knowledge or mishandle the attempt. A good army with bad information can beat a bad army with good intelligence. At the Battles of Jutland and Midway, intelligence let two navies ambush an ambusher, but one alone won its battle. Fluke and friction so shaped both engagements that they could have gone either way, as in 1941 with the engagements that destroyed *Hood* and *Bismarck*. Knowledge affects war on land, air or sea in different ways, and also when mobile armies operate quickly over large spaces, rather than conducting long and slow campaigns of attrition. Where force-to-space ratios are low, flanks open, firepower far-reaching and precise, breakthrough easy and manoeuvre possible, espionage can contribute to epic victories – letting an attacker concentrate its strength against an enemy's weakness, or a defender focus its forces precisely where the foe plans to attack. In circumstances of high force-to-space ratios, of stickiness, equilibrium and attrition, intelligence provides a series of small advantages, which may wear down the enemy just slightly faster than otherwise might have happened. A mediocre intelligence service can affect a war of manoeuvre more than a good agency does a struggle of attrition. Two first-rate intelligence services may neutralize each other, while a mediocre espionage agency might guide its master to triumph over an incompetent.

Intelligence is one kind of input into many types of competition, ruled by power and comparative advantage, where small discrepancies in many fields between competitors have great consequences. The questions are, what actions does intelligence enable in any competition, and how can competitors use those chances? As intelligence affects every competition within any war in different ways, its overall effect can be measured only by adding its aggregate value in each case for one side, compared to that of the other. The normal result in each case, or all of them, is balance between both sides, or superiority without significance, but often intelligence is a winning factor. It might be a tiebreaker, the weight which determines the outcome of a match where all other factors are balanced. It can shape a competition asymmetrically, as by giving all defenders forewarning of assault against all attackers. It may multiply the effect of one force by 200 per cent, or divide another by 33 per cent. Intelligence might let you concentrate your strength against an enemy's weakness, or shelter your vulnerabilities from its power. In rare cases, usually through the working of an extraordinary source, intelligence strikes like lightning; you learn precisely what you need to know in order to act exactly as you want, as all the holes in the machine of war line up, suddenly and briefly. Such opportunities can be used only by throwing a thunderbolt, with force immediate and focused.

Intelligence before the war

The modern age of intelligence began in 1914, through developments in sources, organization and communication. Intelligence aided military forces, especially in operations, to unprecedented degrees. Collection and assessment agencies exploded in size. During 1913, for example, perhaps a hundred people in the world worked full-time in code-breaking or radio interception; by 1918, these numbers approached 10,000. Bureaucracy and technology enabled a transformation simultaneously in intelligence, power and war. The parts of intelligence changed, but more the whole, and its interaction with knowledge and strategy. Imagery and signals intelligence, joined to the General Staff system, telegraph and radio, produced powerful means to collect, assess and use intelligence. A tight cycle of command, control, communications and intelligence (C3I) emerged for *operations*, as it had done for *strategy* by the 1860s, when it had enabled the deployment of Union forces against Confederates, Prussians against Austrians and French, and British power across the globe.

No single source dominated intelligence in the 1914–18 war. Honours fell equally between observations by one's own troops, interrogation of prisoners and deserters, agents and communications intelligence; and traffic analysis (material acquired by monitoring the external features of signals systems, without reading the content of messages). By 1918, intelligence services used virtually every technique deployed between 1939 and 1945, including operational deception, controlled agents, and data-processing systems able to synthesize material from thousands of sources in real time and to guide immediate actions by forces or fire, as Britain did with blockade intelligence and defence against early German strategic bombers. Intelligence shaped every operation of all belligerents. The aggregate quality of intelligence in the First World War matched that in the Second World War, but in strategic terms, each side's successes cancelled each other out, while at the operational plane, intelligence was harder to use for dramatic results. Forces were too slow and clumsy to maximize the opportunities that intelligence enabled. The army best served by communications intelligence, that of Austria-Hungary, was too mediocre in overall quality to use it well. The greatest competition of the war, the Western Front, epitomized attrition. Nonetheless, in a war where power was measured by the ability to produce hundreds of thousands of soldiers and millions of tons of steel, intelligence mattered. It multiplied force more than in any previous conflict, as much as in any later one.[1]

Between 1939 and 1941, another great war spread across the world. Intelligence shaped that event, in general and particular ways. On the borders between war and peace, states receive confusing signals, which rivals manipulate. Net assessments – the integration of all sources of information about any competitor – involve many issues, where errors in your judgment of yourself matter as much as those you make about rivals, or they about you. You err by understanding a rival better than it does itself, if that difference in opinions drives actions you do not expect. Between 1936 and 1940, for example, British statesmen misunderstood Italian policy, because they estimated its power and interests better than Benito Mussolini did. He made mistakes, and so did they. During 1933–41, these problems were unusually great. Confusion and mistakes shaped the start of the war, while surprise attacks sucked neutral powers into it. The great powers possessed decent to excellent intelligence services, which often aided policy directly, as by showing Joseph Stalin during autumn 1941 that Japan would not attack the USSR. More generally, however, reason and information were bad guides for statesmen who interpreted power, interest, competition and competitors,

---

1 The best introduction is Jim Beach, *Haig's Intelligence* (Cambridge University Press, 2013).

and evidence on those matters very differently, in a reciprocal, multilateral and atomized system. Ideas and actions had paradoxical relations. Intentions were not affected, nor effects intended. Ideology, racism and ethnocentrism caused misinterpretations of capabilities and intentions in every capital. The belief that race and spirit made power, led German, Italian and Japanese statesmen to overrate themselves and underrate their foes. The latter misconstrued Axis actions because they interpreted intentions and capabilities through a materialist lens, whether liberal or Marxist-Leninist. They overrated German strength, because of its track record of quality in combat, and fables about its efficiency. Anglo-American statesmen understood Japanese power well, but underestimated the immediate capacity of its air power, and misconstrued its policy because of ethnocentrism: they assumed that Japanese leaders were cautious and rational, and must see their weakness compared to the United States. Neither assumption was correct.[2]

The effect of such errors is best measured by adding all of their elements. The extreme case, the greatest intelligence failure in history, produced an error of 10 million men, twice the size of the German army. During 1940–41, Soviet leaders thought Germany had twice the number of soldiers it really did, while Germans underrated Soviet strength in divisions by half.[3] This story had complex causes. Soviets overrated German strength because they misconstrued its incompetence in recruiting manpower, compared to their ruthlessness. Germans underrated Soviets for the opposite reason. They underestimated the quality of Soviet forces due to racism, but also due to overgeneralization from Russian failures in every war since 1904, while no other state ever has survived the damage inflicted on the USSR in 1941, let alone between 1941 and 1945.

Such problems distorted strategy less once war was under way, and reality trumped imagination. Ideology still shaped state aims, but leaders more accurately assessed comparative power and advantage, and correlated strategy and operations, and intelligence with actions. The Anglo-American alliance took a lead in these matters, with the USSR far behind, followed by Italy and Germany, with Japan lagging. The most powerful of states formulated and executed strategy in the most rational of fashions, and used intelligence best. Weaker ones did so less well, increasing the rate of their rout.

<hr/>

2 For analysis of these issues, and a discussion of the literature, see John Ferris, *Strategy and Intelligence: Selected Essays* (London: Routledge, 2005), pp. 99–137.

3 Roger Reese, *Stalin's Reluctant Soldiers: A Social History of the Red Army, 1925–1941* (Lawrence: University Press of Kansas, 1996), p 163; Geoffrey P. Megargee, *Inside Hitler's High Command* (Lawrence: University Press of Kansas, 2000), pp. 102–16.

Intelligence at war

Between 1939 and 1945, as during 1914–18, economic and demographic power shaped victory no less than did skill in operations. Until 1942, the two coalitions were comparable in economic terms, but the Axis Powers were superior in the conduct of operations, except against Britain in the air and at sea in European waters. From 1942, however, the Allies rapidly became stronger than their foes, and better in most military spheres. In this match, intelligence routinely served as force-multiplier and often as tiebreaker. It shaped the Second World War more than the First, because intelligence supported firepower which could kill and move, enabling more decisive actions, the effect was one-sided for a long time, and one side devoted far greater resources to the task. That outcome took years to emerge. It was manifested in many spheres. Decisions about strategy, at theatre level, or to allocate resources between them or to the construction of specific forces, were driven by ideology, perceptions, military rationality and information from open sources, not secret intelligence. Still, British intelligence did well in reconstructing Nazi economic power, and discerning its vulnerabilities, and even better in assessing technological developments in German weapons before they were deployed, in time to act.[4] Spies provided technological intelligence which boosted Soviet power after 1945.[5] The greatest impact of intelligence, however, lay in operations.

Every source mattered in this war, including prisoners, deserters, agents, captured documents and one's troops, but the leading sources combined technology and organization. During the Great War, limits to aircraft and cameras made imagery a source of tactical intelligence, focused on the trenches; so too aerial reconnaissance, though it provided some operational material. In the Second World War, aerial reconnaissance and imagery became major sources for operational and strategic intelligence, as one aircraft could provide reports on – or 10,000 images from – a location 1,000 miles away, in real time. A new source, radar, routinely acquired targets for

---

4 F. H. Hinsley et al. (eds.), *British Intelligence in the Second World War: Its Influence on Strategy and Operations* (4 vols., London: HMSO, 1984), vol. III, pt. 1, pp. 53–68, 329–458; R. V. Jones, *Most Secret War: British Scientific Intelligence, 1939–1945* (London: Hamish Hamilton, 1978). The evidence cited in Hinsley et al. is accurate, but their analysis is hampered because they accepted views about the German war economy which since have been exploded; cf. Adam Tooze, *The Wages of Destruction: The Making and the Breaking of the Nazi Economy* (London: Allen Lane, 2006).
5 Stephen T. Usdin, *Engineering Communism: How Two Americans Spied for Stalin and Founded the Soviet Silicon Valley* (New Haven, Conn.: Yale University Press, 2005).

strike warfare. Allied with traffic analysis, it transformed tactical combat at air and sea, and thus air power and sea power. During 1942–43, for example, centimetric radar and direction-finding overcame the greatest Allied naval weaknesses, by breaking the Axis superiority in night fighting which had underpinned the operations of the Japanese navy and German U-boat attacks on convoys.

Pre-eminent among these sources were the many forms of signals intelligence, especially ULTRA, the code word for high-grade Anglo-American communications intelligence against Germany, Italy and Japan. More than any other conflict in history, the Second World War was a communications intelligence war. By 1918, many states possessed signals intelligence bodies, which combined traffic analysis with cryptanalysis against systems with low, medium and high-grade security. After 1919, these bodies diverged. Some attacked only diplomatic telegrams on cable, others low-grade military traffic via radio, while developments in wireless and machine cryptography revolutionized the field. In 1939, the states which first reintegrated the components of signals intelligence and applied them to war had an edge; so, too, those which best did so, especially by mastering the revolutionary application of machines to cryptology.

The quality of intelligence services changed as they switched from competitions of power politics to those of war. The services of one state with decent capabilities, Japan, and of two leaders, Italy and the USSR, slipped because their strengths, like stealing codebooks from embassies, worked better in peace than war. The capabilities of three other powers surged, because they had better technology and emphasized the acquisition of intelligence through technical means, rather than spies. Germany took a quick lead with imagery and air reconnaissance, though Britain and then the United States rapidly passed it; no other country was in the race. Regarding radar, Britain held the lead, pulling the United States to its level, which the latter soon exceeded, the Germans hot on their heels. The story for signals intelligence and security was more complex. The signals security of the Imperial Japanese Navy (IJN) was poor, that of the army good. Both were weak in signals intelligence. The Soviets were poor on defence and attack, while the Italians were decent. In 1939, American military forces developed radio communications well, but were mediocre in signals intelligence and security, though the United States Navy (USN) made innovative use of data-processing machines against IJN cryptosystems. Britain initially suffered from technical misjudgements about signals and security because it underestimated the need for radio communications. Its code-breakers, while excellent, focused on cable and codebook. British signals security was mediocre, partly because of initial failures in the mechanization of cryptology, but it improved rapidly in both fields. During 1939, Germany led the powers in signals and security. Its military treated radio as a normal means to communicate, used flexibly and securely through the Enigma cipher machine, a good system which Germans handled badly. They focused on gathering signals intelligence from enemy radio nets, which meant they concentrated on easy cryptosystems and paid less attention to hard ones. These characteristics caused failure after 1941, but until then, Germany won the wireless war.

The turning point

In 1939–41, Axis intelligence stood at its peak – a high one, compared to previous history. Before the outbreak of the Pacific War, intelligence served Japan better than it did Britain or the United States, providing all the information needed to launch a surprise attack, while denying defenders the evidence necessary to avoid one. Through consuls, communications intelligence and spies, Japan grasped Anglo-American plans, expectations and deployed capabilities, while its enemies misconstrued Japanese aims and means. Japan maintained an edge in intelligence over China until 1945. German air and army intelligence supported Blitzkrieg well, by providing easily acquirable intelligence for immediate use in airstrike or ground and naval attack. Assisted by procedures of security and deception which masked intentions, they outweighed the performance of Britain and France in 1940, in all areas ranging from collection to assessment; they did so, too, against the Soviets during 1941–42. They matched British intelligence in the desert war. Erwin Rommel's great days as a general coincided precisely with those of his intelligence. When it declined, so did he, and other German generals. Axis commanders relied as heavily on intelligence as Allied ones – they just realized the fact, and nurtured the source, much less. In mobile operations, the interception of radio messages in plain language or low-grade systems multiplied German tactical skill against the British until 1942, the Americans in 1943, and the Soviets during 1944. Signals intelligence affected no aspect of the war more than it did German operations against Soviets. German air and naval agencies matched their Allied competitors until 1943. Above all, in 1941, good – if unsophisticated – deception, intelligence and security helped Germany to start a war with a surprise attack against the USSR, and Japan to do so against Britain and the United States. However, even more than usual in such cases, the main problem was intelligence failure by defenders, rather than success by attackers.[6] Each of these Axis strikes matched the effect of Allied ULTRA in Europe, or the Pacific. They enabled the Germans to destroy, at low cost, 50 per cent of the soldiers and 90 per cent of the tanks and aircraft which the USSR fielded in 1941; and the Japanese, 20 per cent of the warship tonnage of Britain and the United States. These strikes gave Germany and Japan valuable resources, a year of the strategic initiative and a boost to their slim chances for victory. As events proved, however, the Axis had greater intelligence failures in 1941 than did their enemies.

In 1939–41, intelligence was a low secondary strength for the Axis. From 1942, it became a high secondary strength for the Western Allies, and during 1943, a low but rising one for the USSR, as intelligence guided the big battalions. Measurement of the effect entails adding Allied rise to Axis decline. In particular, during 1939, Britain was mediocre in military signals intelligence and machine cryptology, but it knew what to do when it saw Poles bearing gifts – experience of the correct way to attack Enigma. Then the quality of its institutions enabled Britain to overcome error. Enigma and other high-grade German cryptosystems like *Geheimschreiber* combined communications and security well, though less so than their British and American counterparts, Typex and Sigaba, which remained unbroken.[7] Good machine systems sent messages with unprecedented ease, volume and security, and forced a new era of cryptanalysis, which moved from the craftsman's bench to the industrial age. Codebooks were attacked through analysis by language and logic, and machines by quantity handling. Mathematical analysis, chiselling the fractures of cryptosystems, reduced the number of ways to convert any letter into another, to a level which the brute force of data-processing machines could defeat. Britain led the world in the movement toward machine cryptanalysis, through its unique centralized system for the collection and analysis of intelligence, high coordination between soldiers and civilians, skill in data processing, and recognition of the value of knowledge in war.

By 1941, Britain organized its signals intelligence and imagery with unprecedented effect, enabling power in the collection and assessment of evidence, and the rapid and secure distribution of material to commanders. American

6 Barton Whaley, *Codeword Barbarossa* (Cambridge, Mass.: MIT Press, 1974); John Ferris, 'The Roots of Fortitude: The Evolution of British Deception in The Second World War', in Thomas Mahnken (ed.), *The Paradox of Intelligence: Essays in Memory of Michael Handel* (London: Frank Cass, 2003).
7 Cipher A. Devours and Louis Kruh, *Machine Cryptography and Modern Cryptanalysis* (Dedham, Mass.: Artech House, 1985); Ferris, *Strategy and Intelligence*, pp. 135–80.

intelligence followed these leads. The United States, Britain and the Commonwealth applied more brains and resources to intelligence than the Axis, because they had more of them, and greater respect for its value. British and American signals intelligence services expanded in numbers by 3,000 per cent between 1939 and 1945, and pursued new forms of organization and technique. The Italians and Japanese stagnated. The Germans were good, but their enemies were excellent. In 1940, German signals intelligence personnel outnumbered British, but the tide turned fast. At their peak, 30,000 Germans worked in signals intelligence, thrice the strength of every such organization on earth during 1918. The British and Americans had 35,000 each, with better cryptanalysts and mathematicians, including the founder of computing science, Alan Turing, and perhaps a hundred times the power of Germany in data-processing machines applied to cryptanalysis. One story shows how the wireless war was won. In October 1941, without notifying their superiors, the machine cryptanalysts at Bletchley Park, mid-level figures in British code-breaking, directly told Winston Churchill that unless they received top priority for data-processing machines and personnel, attack against Enigma must erode. Within hours, Churchill gave them that status, 'action this day'; within months, Bletchley had the world's greatest concentration of such devices.[8] Conversely, the Germany navy's B-Dienst (*Beobachtungsdienst*), the best cryptanalytical agency of the Third Reich, never owned any data-processing machines, but could only borrow time on them from other bureaus. The German code-breaking agencies which had such machines used them to attack low-grade Western systems, which sought to preserve the secrecy of traffic only for twenty-four hours.[9] In contrast, Allied ULTRA attacked the hardest shells, because they shielded the richest meat.

ULTRA and its enemies

In intelligence, the Western Allies multiplied each other's strengths. German and other Axis agencies divided them. They competed not only against the enemy, but against each other. They could not transfer best practices, nor pool their power, acquire the resources their rivals did, nor understand the need to do so. They failed to exploit the weaknesses in British cryptography during 1941, and then slid behind all their enemies. Only the weakest

8 Hinsley et al. (eds.), *British Intelligence in the Second World War*, vol. II (London: HMSO, 1981), pp. 655–8.
9 Ferris, *Strategy and Intelligence*, pp. 164–8.

Axis Powers, the non-Fascist ones, Hungary and Finland, cooperated in intelligence like Britain, the United States, Canada and Australia did.[10] The cooperation between the Western Allies in intelligence was imperfect, but better than anything ever known before.[11] They worked to expand the common pool, honed by cooperative competition in the pursuit of common tasks. British services worked better with American ones than German agencies (or, for that matter, the United States Army and Navy) did with each other. Cooperation with the USSR was low, because it rejected Western overtures.[12] The Western Allies developed unprecedented power in strategic sources of intelligence, where the Germans were poor. German imagery never provided strategic intelligence against the Western Allies. Its coverage of the USSR never passed the Urals and collapsed in 1943. German spies against Britain, the USSR and the United States were controlled by its enemies. The payoff was most particular in signals intelligence. The Germans failed to attack high-grade American or British cryptographic machines because the task was hard, resources scarce, and only massive and centralized cryptanalysis could break them. This, the divided German system could not provide. One German cryptanalyst called a unified system 'a monster organization'. Britons named it Bletchley Park.[13]

Nor did superiority with intelligence end at collection. For every belligerent, strategic assessments and decisions were made by rational bureaucracy joined to charismatic leadership. British and American leaders made errors in such areas, especially regarding Japan in 1941. At worst, they were as bad as anyone, but better on average and unmatched at their best. Thus intelligence often spurred Churchill toward odd proposals. These problems were mitigated because he had unique experience with the use of communications intelligence, including against dangerous foes in wartime, and because his military advisors were tough and smart; while great collection provided good evidence, which was processed through flexible and thorough analysis. Churchill had strong opinions, but could change them. He made his subordinates consider intelligence, and he used ULTRA as a spur to action. From 1942, Churchill was harnessed to an open and highest-common-denominator

---

10 Chief, Army Security Agency, *European Axis Signal Intelligence in World War II* (Washington DC: Army Security Agency, 1946), (www.nsa.gov/public_info/declass/european_axis_sigint.shtml – accessed 22 October 2014).

11 Bradley Smith, *The Ultra-Magic Deals and the Most Secret Special Relationship, 1940–1946* (Novato, Calif.: Presidio, 1993).

12 Bradley Smith, *Sharing Secrets with Stalin: How the Allies Exchanged Intelligence, 1941–1945* (Lawrence: University Press of Kansas, 1995).

13 Ferris, *Strategy and Intelligence*, pp. 164–5.

system of decision-making, which combined the best of British and American approaches, with Britain handling the collection and analysis of intelligence and its use in planning, and both states driving strategy and action. Anglo-American leaders treated intelligence as essential to action. They emphasized the source best suited to provide these gains, signals intelligence, and accepted the need for specialized assessment and a rational process of decision-making. Good consumers even of mediocre material, their fare often was excellent.

Stalin and Hitler used intelligence in ways poorly suited to war. Neither wished to hear contrary analyses from subordinates, merely echoes of their own opinions. Both wanted intelligence to provide just facts, which they filtered through ideology, personal preconceptions and the belief that their will created reality. Stalin and Hitler, overconfident micromanagers, created top-down systems where they tried to control all actions. They liked to use intelligence to guide a strong hand, in a political game they could rig, against competitors unable to strike back. These characteristics did not rule war. The dictators were poor to mediocre consumers of good intelligence, let alone the mixed bag they received. They dominated intelligence analysis and strategic decisions in their states, crippling the capabilities of their subordinates.

Few leaders ever took intelligence, especially on internal threats, so seriously as Stalin. He directed intelligence chiefs in detail, shaping questions, integrating reports into policy, acting on knowledge. Stalin used intelligence not as a staff to lead his subordinates, but as a knout to rule them. It became lies, made to meet Stalin's demands, which he used to construct a world of his own. Before Operation BARBAROSSA, Stalin told his military intelligence chief, Filipp Golikov, that any reports about a German attack on the USSR were false, the product of officers trapped by British deception. Despite the personal risk, Golikov did present reports of danger to Stalin. On 22 June 1941, in any case, the world bit back.[14]

Within Germany, collection and assessment were divided between institutions which did not cooperate much, and dominated by the Führer's faith in himself. He cared less about intelligence than Churchill or Stalin, and received worse material. He saw as much communications intelligence each day as Churchill did, but it was inferior in quality, about diplomacy rather than strategy. When he received material to match ULTRA, he never praised the product or strengthened the producers. Hitler made effective use of

---

14 David Murphy, *What Stalin Knew: The Enigma of Barbarossa* (New Haven, Conn.: Yale University Press, 2005).

communications intelligence when it was self-evident, addressed immediate concerns and he could judge its accuracy himself, as by pre-empting the Allied incursion into Norway of 1940, and Italy's defection in 1943. When he used intelligence after 1941, however, the sources mostly were weak, and controlled by his foes. So too, when possessing the initiative in operations, German fighting services used intelligence effectively, but less so when on the defensive, especially regarding strategic matters. Nor did Germans emphasize the improvement of intelligence, even when its quality was clearly eroding. They expected little, and increasingly got it. They underestimated the power of communications intelligence and overestimated that of spies. The more desperate the situation, the more Germans trusted agents controlled by enemies or forged by entrepreneurs who, like Karl-Heinz Krämer ('Josephine') in Sweden and the Klatt bureau in Bulgaria, made their material up, confusing all sides. Juan Pujol began as an entrepreneur, motivated by ideology, and ended as the greatest controlled agent in British deception, 'Garbo'.[15] German intelligence became a delivery system for disinformation to its leaders. Anglo-American leaders used intelligence better than those in other states, but their superiority lay in wanting the best, and pursuing it. Hitler and Stalin might have gained from an ULTRA: neither could have created one.

ULTRA was the greatest source of intelligence during this war, but never perfect. It took words straight from the enemy's mouth, but rarely were they straightforward. Its value differed with time and theatre. ULTRA became more successful and useful over time, but its history was replete with reversals of fortune. The Allies never read every important enemy message, or most of them. ULTRA was not the best source on everything; nor were technical achievements in cryptanalysis and battlefield success linked in a simple way. During the African campaign, ULTRA could have been most useful when it was technically most primitive rather than most mature, because of the conditions that governed operations. When ULTRA was most primitive, force-to-space ratios were low, as were both sides' strengths; hence victories with decisive consequences were possible. Intelligence helped Rommel to achieve some of them. By the time ULTRA became mature, from 1942, large and good armies were locked in prolonged and high-intensity struggles of

---

15 Thaddeus Holt, *The Deceivers: Allied Military Deception in the Second World War* (London: Weidenfeld & Nicolson, 2004), pp. 160–1; Robert W. Stephan, *Stalin's Secret War: Soviet Counterintelligence against the Nazis, 1941–1945* (Lawrence: University Press of Kansas, 2003), pp. 154–74; Vadim J. Birstein, *Smersh: Stalin's Secret Weapon: Soviet Military Counterintelligence in WW II* (Padstow: Biteback Publishing, 2011).

attrition on narrow fronts, comparable to those of the Great War, though more fluid. Even so, intelligence budged the balance of attrition toward the Allies. On the biggest of issues, enemy strength, deployments and intentions, the Allies were well-informed, while their enemies were not. The quality of Allied intelligence, and its superiority over the Axis, provided much certainty to Anglo-American assessment and planning, and let them use their forces with remarkable precision, against an enemy which increasingly was ignorant, uncertain and outgunned. When they held the initiative, the weaknesses in Axis intelligence were irrelevant, and their strengths in tactical collection counted. On the defensive, their strengths became irrelevant and their weaknesses a danger. As the power of the Third Reich declined, its chances for success hinged on deploying German elite forces to sectors the enemy would attack. There, supporting their weaker Axis allies, they hoped to stop enemy breakthroughs and force the Allies into costly and one-sided battles of attrition, thus moving toward strategic stalemate. This aim required Germany to guess where and when the enemy would attack; it did not do so. Instead, from Operation TORCH and El Alamein onward, Germans suffered a steady run of operational and strategic surprises at the hands of the Western Allies – and to a lesser extent at the hands of the Soviets after Stalingrad. German intelligence failed precisely when Nazi strategy most needed it to succeed. Given the material odds, however, Germany might have lost even had it possessed an ULTRA, and the Allies had not.

Intelligence and air power

Target acquisition for strike warfare involves attack by weapons against objects that their users cannot see, guided by command, control, communications and intelligence (C3I) systems which locate targets and guide fire. These technical and tactical matters drive power and strategy. When this phenomenon first emerged, between 1914 and 1918, C3I was stronger than the weapons it supported: artillery, with limited range, accuracy and power, attacking the hardest targets in the world, trenches and turrets, in exchanges against an enemy with equal capabilities. In strategic terms, this outcome sharpened the process of attrition by both sides at once. Twenty years on, revolutions occurred in operations and strike warfare, as forces exploited the opportunities enabled by C3I, guided by all sources, led by communications intelligence, traffic analysis and radar. Tactical and technological developments, manifested strike by strike, transformed the role of intelligence and air power for war, first aiding the Luftwaffe and then American and

Commonwealth forces.[16] In some cases, intelligence became target acquisition, and operations, strike warfare. Aircraft delivered distant and one-sided blows, of unprecedented weight and precision, reshaping the power of armies or navies, and the ways that they fought. Strike by aircraft and guns was central to land warfare, especially as practised by Anglo-American forces, through the quick and massive application of firepower, close support against soldiers and interdiction against soft and distant targets central to enemy power, like units on the move, logistics, communications and transport. At sea, the effect was revolutionary. Aircraft, based on ships and shore, became first-rate naval forces, gradually superseding guns and armour. To strike first might take a battle, and ambush or counter-ambush decide a campaign. Communications intelligence, backed by radar and traffic analysis, working through radio, aircraft, aircraft carriers and submarines, created new forms of maritime war, centred on distant and precise attack against soft targets – thin hulls or decks rather than armoured turrets.[17]

So, too, intelligence, allied to the emergence of electronic warfare, transformed strategic air war in an asymmetric fashion. The bomber could get through only at great cost. Traffic analysis and radar gave strategic air defence forewarning of assault and guided concentrations of force against all attackers, which fought blind. In the Battle of Britain, defenders smashed far larger numbers of attackers; so, too, over the skies of Germany, fighters contained bombers in a cost-effective fashion, until overwhelmed by air-superiority fighters.[18] Intelligence for strategic air offensives was harder to gather, and successful in only one case. Anglo-American forces integrated all forms of intelligence, especially imagery and communications intelligence, into command and bomb damage assessment for the Combined Bomber Offensive. By keeping a fair grip on the impact of raids, and the campaign, and the enemy's economy, intelligence boosted the effect and efficiency of complex operations, and moved the ratio of costs in strategic air warfare toward the attacker's favour during 1944–45.[19]

16 Brad Gladman, *Intelligence and Anglo-American Air Support in World War Two: The Western Desert and Tunisia, 1940–43* (Basingstoke: Palgrave, 2009).

17 Carl Boyd, *American Command of the Seas through Carriers, Codes and the Silent Service: World War II and Beyond* (Newport News, Va.: Mariners' Museum, 1995); Christopher A. Ford, with David Rosenberg, *The Admiral's Advantage: US Navy Operational Intelligence in World War II and the Cold War* (Annapolis, Md.: Naval Institute Press, 2005).

18 John Ferris and Evan Mawdsley, 'War in the West, 1939–1940: The Battle of Britain?', in the present volume; Donald Caldwell and Richard Muller, *The Luftwaffe over Germany: The Defence of the Reich* (London: Greenhill Books, 2007).

19 Robert Ehlers, *Targeting the Third Reich: Air Intelligence and the Allied Bombing Campaigns* (Lawrence: University Press of Kansas, 2009).

Intelligence in the West

The nearest-run intelligence competition of the war was fought on the Atlantic and Arctic Oceans and the Mediterranean and North Sea. These operations centred on raids, ambushes and counter-ambushes by flotillas, warships, submarines and aircraft. Britain was more exposed to attack than its enemies, and on the defensive, though the empire struck back on the Norwegian coast and in the central Mediterranean. Intelligence aided both sides simultaneously, in a one-sided struggle between navies. The Royal Navy outweighed its Italian and German enemies in strength, and also received American and Canadian aid. Intelligence was a tiebreaker in individual engagements, but across the board it aided both sides equally, which most helped the stronger navy.

Every British victory at sea stemmed to some degree from intelligence, sometimes because of fluke, as with the sinking of *Bismarck* in 1941, but mostly through system, as with the death of *Scharnhorst* in 1943, strikes on the Italian navy at Taranto and Cape Matapan during 1940–41, and ambushes of convoys in the Mediterranean Sea during 1941–43, and in the Norwegian Sea during 1944–45. These successes hastened Britain's aim to break its enemies, rapidly. Axis signals intelligence agencies, especially B-Dienst, won the wireless war for much of 1940–42, but not enough to win these campaigns as a whole. They backed aggressive German operations, sustained an Italian strategy of fleet in being, shaped the destruction of more British than Axis warships, and multiplied the power of U-boats. Yet at a strategic level, these successes were minor, even counterproductive. Pursuit of these objectives wrecked the German navy and smothered the Italian one, while Britain had battleships to burn. The entry cost to victory was high. Britain could take it. Simple sources of intelligence enabled Italian minelayers and frogmen to cripple the Royal Navy during late 1941, driving it from Malta, temporarily, so saving the Afrikakorps from strangulation. Neither the Luftwaffe nor the Italian *Regia Marina* exploited that victory. Within nine months, the RAF and Royal Navy, superior in force and intelligence, surged back to Malta, wielding a razor against Axis arteries. B-Dienst enabled Hitler to pre-empt an Allied attack on Norway in 1940. This action beat Allied strategy, but broke the German surface navy, which lost half its strength sunk and more crippled – heavier losses than those of Britain, which could better absorb them. Advance warning from communications intelligence, and tactical guidance from radar, traffic analysis and air reconnaissance, gave the Germans an edge against the Arctic convoys. Their force could hammer and occasionally halt the convoys, but these battles consumed what remained of the German surface navy, at disproportionate cost. Intelligence successes lured Germans into operational failures.

The same story marked the central instance of intelligence in European waters. Allied intelligence veterans thought their finest hour was the Battle of the Atlantic, as do many scholars. This claim has truth, but misses two points. German intelligence matched that of the Allies, while this campaign was won more by strategic, economic and administrative factors than by battles. The campaign never neared its strategic objectives, to sink so much shipping as to stall the Allies. It merely inflicted a cost-efficient, but minor drain on Allied resources. The U-boat was beaten by its technical limitations and by Allied power, while both ULTRA and B-Dienst played low, secondary roles, partly because each constrained the other. Until 1943, any attack on convoys by U-boats overwhelmed the few escorts and destroyed many merchant ships. U-boats could locate and ambush twice as many convoys when B-Dienst was effective and ULTRA was not than when the opposite held true. B-Dienst bolstered German attacks during the happy times of 1940 and 1942, when its victims were least adequately defended, first across the Atlantic Ocean, and then in the Caribbean Sea, the Gulf of Mexico and off the Eastern Seaboard of the United States. In 1941, ULTRA saved several million tons of shipping and their cargoes – a useful, although secondary gain – by enabling admirals to reroute convoys away from U-boats. In 1943, when so many submarines were at sea that evasion was impossible, and convoy battles unavoidable, ULTRA, radar and traffic analysis enabled growing Allied naval and air forces to counter-ambush U-boats and to wreck their campaign with ease and efficiency. Britain deliberately sailed convoys at U-boats, to make them fight, and die. That victory was inevitable, if at greater cost, once the Allies decided to achieve it, while escorts remained a costly necessity until the war's end. Under these Western waters, as on them, Britain won the war handily and speedily, because its sea power was greater, while ULTRA contained its competition. That was all it had to do. By the time ULTRA crushed its competitors, Axis navies already lay dead in the water.

These successes at sea enabled others on the Continent. Continual access to German operational and logistical traffic gave the Allies an excellent and certain grasp of enemy capabilities, perceptions and intentions, despite gaps, as about armoured strength in France before the invasion of Normandy. Knowledge let Western generals use their resources efficiently and effectively, better than any before. It sped the operations which drove the Axis from Africa, and then aided the success of Allied forces in the most complex and risky form of military operations. Allied amphibious operations hit the enemy like thunder at weak points and caught it by surprise, transforming the front, because German intelligence was incompetent and its command manipulated by British deception. When war began, Germany, with few agents in the British Empire, threw masses of untrained spies against its foe, hoping some would stick. Britain captured these agents and used them to pass masses of messages to German leaders, occasionally reaching Hitler, which were tailored to ease Allied attacks. Mastery over German intelligence and cryptosystems showed what the enemy expected and how it reacted to misdirection. Deception was the most precise and devastating form through which ULTRA damaged its enemy. Before the invasion of Sicily in 1943, and of Normandy in 1944, Britain deceived Hitler into thinking that the Allies would attack elsewhere. This success crippled the deployment of German forces before these invasions, ensuring that 33 per cent of their forces were in the wrong place – deception helped to keep many German formations from affecting the eighty-day Battle of Normandy. Intelligence and deception were fundamental to Allied success in those campaigns. Without these edges, the Germans might have deployed their forces in France or Italy so as to pin the Allies far longer in their beachheads, or else to force postponement of attacks. Once forces were ashore, however, that situation changed. Attrition could not be avoided in Europe. That war was dominated by a high-intensity clash between large and good armies on narrow fronts. In this struggle, intelligence aided the Allies, but not in a dramatic fashion. The rest was up to the men.

Intelligence on the Eastern Front

The effect of intelligence on the Eastern Front was constrained because tyrants who were military micromanagers, poor as strategists and consumers of information, dominated policy for both sides. Nowhere else in the war, or in history, was good intelligence used so badly, so often, as Hitler and Stalin raced each other to the bottom. This constraint most damaged Germany, which had superiority in intelligence to a greater degree and for a longer time, and more need for help. Preconception, and an idiosyncratic mode of military logic, drove Hitler's decisions. Intelligence was a tertiary factor, even when it matched ULTRA in quality. Hitler rarely mentioned signals intelligence as a source for his decisions on the Eastern Front, despite the high quality of the material available to him, though he often discussed human sources. His generals were better consumers of intelligence than he, many of them good ones. Hitler precluded the German superiority in intelligence from aiding theatre-level strategy or producing illumination through deduction drawn from fragments, the areas where ULTRA most aided his enemies, and also reduced its value in operations. This superiority was useful only where Hitler's generals had autonomy, essentially at the operational level, where it reinforced their greatest area of superiority over Soviet forces, in mobile warfare, most notably from June to November 1941, January to May 1942 and December 1942 to April 1943. Such autonomy was common for two years, however, and intelligence also aided planning for the first phase of campaigns in the summers of 1941 and 1942. Hitler's attitudes imposed an opportunity cost, but his direct mistakes with intelligence (as against strategy) do not seem to have caused any fundamental failures in operations which his generals would have avoided before May 1943; until then, Stalin hampered his commanders even more in all of these areas. Nor did Germany's flagging performance in the field afterward suggest that greater, or complete, freedom to act on knowledge would have done much to stall the inevitable, despite Hitler's incompetence when he dominated strategy and intelligence during 1944–45. On the Eastern Front, intelligence multiplied German force, which demonstrates just how inadequate the latter was to the task Hitler undertook.

The USSR led the world regarding intelligence in peacetime, but that strength had little value for war. More than any other power, spies gave it strategic intelligence, but against allies rather than enemies. After 1945, Eastern and Western propagandists claimed that commissars had mined war-winning intelligence across the world, especially Berlin. In fact, Soviet intelligence after the purges was amateurish, making errors which wrecked its networks during the 1940s. Many of its sources were walk-ins, not veterans.[20] The German ones, often courageous naïfs, provided good material, but perhaps no more nor better than that which American, Czechoslovak and especially Polish agencies received from the military opposition to Hitler, which Britain also integrated into strategy far better than the USSR did.[21] Even so, spies provided less intelligence on Germany than ULTRA.

20 The most accessible source is Oleg Mitrokhin and Christopher Andrew, *The Sword and the Shield: The Mitrokhin Archive and the Secret History of the KGB* (New York: Basic Books, 1999). Key documents are available in Russian: cf. Victor Gavrilov, *Voennaia razvedka informiruet: Dokumenty razvedupravleniia Krasnoii Armii, ianvar' 1939-iiun' 1941 g.* (Moscow: Mezhdunarodnyi fond 'Demokratiiā', 2008).

21 Allen Dulles, *From Hitler's Doorstep: The Wartime Intelligence Reports of Allen Dulles, 1942–1945* (University Park: Pennsylvania State University Press, 1999); Tessa Stirling, Daria Nale and Tadeucz Dubicki (eds.), *Intelligence Co-operation between Poland and Great Britain During World War II*, vol. 1: *The Report of the Anglo-Polish Historical*

The USSR largely ignored their reports. Spies among his allies did affect Soviet policy, especially by reinforcing Stalin's mistrust of them. Ironically, the British government (and his spies within it) gave him much valuable intelligence on Germany which the Soviets ignored, though it helped them before the Battle of Kursk.

In its main struggle of intelligence, at the operational sphere, the USSR began poor and became good, while its enemy declined from ability to mediocrity. Before Operation BARBAROSSA, both sides overestimated themselves and underestimated their enemy. Soviet intelligence was decent, but handicapped by Stalin's incompetence. German aerial reconnaissance, imagery and communications intelligence acquired crucial data across the western frontiers of the USSR. These successes were offset by errors of equal magnitude, which reinforced each other. Germans mastered the Soviet order of battle up to 500 miles behind its frontier, but were blind beyond. This failure, usually credited to the incompetence of German intelligence, actually stemmed from the power of Soviet security and the poverty of its technology. During the 1930s, the Soviet Union blocked any means to gather information in its territory, except from the radio traffic of its agencies. In 1939–41, precisely as the Red Army doubled in strength, signals intelligence, previously Britain's main source on the Soviet order of battle, and an excellent one, declined in accuracy. In 1941, Germany underestimated Soviet strength in divisions by 50 per cent, and Britain (with imperial intercept stations better positioned to take Russian traffic) did so by 25 per cent. Lack of wireless equipment in new divisions, radio silence and the Soviet use of low frequencies, hard to intercept from long distances, led foreign powers to miss much of the expansion of the Red Army and thus to underrate its size.[22] The Germans also grossly underestimated the quantity and quality of Soviet equipment, especially tanks, despite hints to the contrary. These errors marked a triumph of Soviet security, with a double edge. Security sapped the deterrent Stalin thought he had established; he knew his state was strong and assumed others did so. They did not. Though Hitler would have attacked had he known the real size of the Red Army, this underestimate affected that decision and, even more, the confusion of August 1941, as Germans realized that BARBAROSSA had failed and agonized over how to win.

Committee (2 vols., Portland, Oreg.: Valentine Mitchell, 2005); P. R. J. Winter, 'Penetrating Hitler's High Command: Anglo-Polish HUMINT, 1939–45', *War in History* 18 (2011), 85–108.

22 Ferris, *Strategy and Intelligence*, pp. 128–9.

Early operational successes sharpened German edges in intelligence. Soviet intelligence, communications and command dissolved. The collapse of Soviet air power and signals security unleashed German air reconnaissance and imagery. Nazi communications intelligence briefly soared as high as ULTRA would go later for the Western Allies, reading the highest levels of enciphered material by army groups, and even more below.[23] Routinely, Soviet commands signalled in plain language, while codebooks were captured, enabling competent Finnish and German code-breakers to reach places Bletchley could do only through genius and power. The Germans received great opportunities to pass agents behind enemy lines, though they muddled those chances, enabling the enemy to turn these sources into tools for deception.[24] During the first two years on the Eastern Front, German operations gained from excellent intelligence, better than that of the foe, precisely what its system needed to work well. This advantage explains some of its startling successes of that period, though given its other advantages, intelligence sped manoeuvres, rather than transformed power.

Despite this edge in intelligence, Germany was not winning the war. The blunting of this edge shaped the decline in German military success. The quality of German intelligence began a constant slide, as its Soviet equivalent rose, the slopes intersecting in June 1943. As the Germans less often overran Soviet headquarters, they captured fewer codebooks, which reduced their operational superiority and the key to their cryptanalysis, in a vicious circle. Soviet signals security broke Axis access to high-level communications by mid-1942, and slowly pressed it further down. Far more than against the Western Allies, German signals intelligence penetrated middle levels of

23 For the older literature, cf. Volker Detlef Heydorn, *Nachrichtennahaufklärung (Ost) und sowjetrussisches Heeresfunkwesen bis 1945* (Freiburg: Rombach Verlag, 1985), and Albert Praun, 'German Radio Intelligence', in John Mendelsohn (ed.), *Covert Warfare: Intelligence, Counterintelligence and Military Deception in the World War II Era*, vol. VI: *German Radio Intelligence and the Soldatsender* (18 vols., New York: Garland Press, 1989), pp. 1–128. My assessments rest on post-war Allied interrogations of German signals intelligence personnel, listing work against Soviet cryptosystems (Chief, Army Security Agency, *European Axis Signal Intelligence*) and German communications intelligence reports from the Eastern Front, 1941–44, in RG 457/72, US National Archives. One interrogation, DF-112, AS-14-TICOM, Survey of Russian Military Systems, 1 April 1948 (www.scribd.com/paspartoo/d/85583814-DF-112-Dettmann – accessed 22 October 2014), and accounts by Finnish code-breaker, Errki Pale, *Suomen Radiotiedustelu 1927–44*, ed. Reijo Ahtokari (Helsinki: Hakapaino, 1997), describe German and Finnish success against the highest of Soviet military cryptosystems, including the five-figure codebooks, during 1941–42. The standard accounts of operations on the Eastern Front have not incorporated this evidence.
24 Stephan, *Stalin's Secret War*; and Birstein, *Smersh*.

Soviet command, which controlled tens to hundreds of thousands of men, especially during battles, but often illuminating operational intentions in advance. By 1944, however, it withered merely into traffic analysis, vulnerable to Soviet security and deception. Meanwhile, Allied air power, east and especially west, eroded and then ended German air reconnaissance and imagery. Soviet security controlled all Nazi spies on the Eastern Front, who passed misleading reports which German intelligence trusted. With low force-to-space ratios, on a vast front against forces growing in size, firepower and mobility, increasingly Germany could not discover Soviet intentions or deployments. German commanders treated this decline as a condition, rather than as a problem to solve. Hitler was happy to rely on intuition, combined with reports from any source, like deserters. The head of German military assessment on the Eastern Front, General Reinhard Gehlen, simply accepted that signals intelligence could not penetrate enemy intentions, and believed he could do so through intuition, reconnaissance by ground and air (despite their obvious limits in range), and especially agents. He overstated spies as a source, and did not realize how far the enemy controlled German ones, and manipulated his views. Through Gehlen's trust in spies, and his superiors' trust in him, Soviet deception twisted German decisions.

Soviet attacks before Moscow in December 1941 and at Stalingrad in November 1942, its greatest achievements of that period, were among the few where it achieved superiority in intelligence and deception. That superiority stemmed less from its skill than from German error, especially the general disbelief that the USSR could absorb such losses and assemble such replacements, and from Hitler's particular incompetence. In December 1941, surprise was absolute because German incompetence was so great. Commanders denied that Russians could recover from such devastating losses, and intelligence mostly missed Red Army preparations for attack. In November 1942, the Germans predicted and stalled every attack across the front except those around Stalingrad, where they underestimated the quantity, and especially the quality and intentions, of Soviet forces. Hitler resisted any claims of lurking danger. Gehlen misinterpreted signals intelligence about order of battle, but not capabilities and intentions – the concentration of Soviet forces around the Stalingrad salient – as indicating just a minor offensive. He did this because he underestimated Soviet power, and doubted the Red Army could attack there as well as at all the other places where indications of assault were obvious. Conspiracy theorists suggest that Stalin deliberately sacrificed these other operations to aid that against Stalingrad. The truth is more mundane. German intelligence was competent and Soviet security and deception imperfect. Soviet commanders more thoroughly hid signs of attack before Stalingrad than elsewhere on the front, precisely because it was their main assault, involving the movement of great reinforcements in open terrain. In the classic manner, Soviet deception provided vague and erroneous indicators of every offensive except that around Stalingrad, which they hoped to hide through silence. Soviet intelligence was competent regarding the Axis order of battle, but underestimated German numbers at Stalingrad, and the quality of their forces across the front.

In neither December 1941 nor November 1942 did success with intelligence and deception guarantee victory. In most other cases before Kursk in 1943, the Soviets lost that struggle. Their signals intelligence and imagery were elementary, while those of the Germans remained good. The Soviet operation around Kharkov in May 1942 caught the Germans by surprise, and disrupted their strategy, yet failed disastrously. In July, the German attack in southern Russia instead of against Moscow took the Soviets by surprise and nearly caused another disaster, because their intelligence was poor and German deception effective. However, German intelligence and operations failed to stop Soviet forces from running away to fight another day, at a town called Stalingrad. Until March 1943, German attacks and counter-attacks usually surprised the Red Army. In the chaos of mobile operations, Soviet communications, intelligence and command collapsed, while the German ability to intercept messages between generals in low-grade codes or plain language multiplied their edges in generalship and manoeuvre, to devastating effect. Von Manstein's fabled successes of 1943 rested on good and superior intelligence, well used.

After Stalingrad, the Red Army painfully rose in intelligence, security and deception, as in all areas, each success multiplying the effect of the rest. Superiority in intelligence particularly reinforced skill in command. The deluge began at Kursk, where Soviet intelligence became good, and better than that of the Germans, who, for the first time, abandoned efforts to cover a summer offensive through surprise. Thereafter, Soviet air reconnaissance and imagery became competent, while human sources behind the front were outstanding. Signals intelligence became at least mediocre, outmatching that of the Germans. The loss of 8 million men by 1943 taught Stalin and his generals how to use intelligence, once they had the initiative, while Hitler, a poor consumer of evidence, increasingly controlled German operations under worsening circumstances. In order to win the intelligence struggle, the Red Army needed a good picture of enemy forces. It had an excellent one, because virtually all German divisions stood on the front, easily located.

Generally, Germany grasped enemy capabilities and intentions immediately on its front, but 90 per cent accuracy was a failing grade. It had to know the locations of all assault formations, aircraft and armour, deep in the rear, and track their deployments and intentions. The Germans underrated the quality and quantity of Soviet forces and the skill of its command, and failed to follow enemy movements to the front. Soviet deception hid precisely those matters. What the Russians call *maskirovka* (a term combining the meanings of the English words 'camouflage', 'deception' and 'security') rested on security, camouflage, misleading patterns of wireless signals and the spreading of rumours among Soviet troops, augmented by passing disinformation through controlled agents – by this stage, Germany's main source for strategic and operational intelligence. From summer 1943, Germany increasingly fell victim to enemy intelligence and deception, which found weaknesses in a Nazi force stretched out on a long line, and which meanwhile hid key Red Army redeployments from rear to front, and the timing and weight of Soviet attacks. Sometimes the Germans detected and exploited signs of attack, but mostly they did not.

During the last year of the war, intelligence and deception helped the Soviets against the Germans, as much as they did the Western Allies. Routinely, Soviet attacks struck German divisions with 1,000 per cent more forces than their defences were tailored to handle, and leveraged tactical breakthrough into operational triumph. Thus, before June 1944, German intelligence and commanders misread Soviet strategy and missed the redeployment of 400,000 men and 3,000 tanks into Belorussia, misjudging an attack that ate an army group and wrecked the front within weeks. Intelligence and deception helped to destroy more German forces on the Eastern Front than in Western Europe, but given the quantity and quality of forces on the fronts, it mattered less than ULTRA, and its impact was outweighed by German successes in those areas.

ULTRA in the Pacific

Across the Pacific, ULTRA of lesser quality than in Europe enabled greater operational triumphs, because conditions on the battlefield gave intelligence a more dramatic effect. Intelligence affected this war more than any other in history. Radio dominated communications for small forces scattered over millions of square miles. Prisoners and agents were less useful sources than usual; signals intelligence, radar, imagery and captured documents more so. In these disciplines, the Japanese were poor and their enemies good.

Japanese plans hinged on deception, knowledge, surprise and shaping enemy perceptions with precision. This approach worked when intelligence was good, as in December 1941, but not when it was poor and inferior to that of the foe – as from March 1942. Beyond the tactical realm, the main Japanese sources were Allied press communiqués and captured documents, followed by low-grade signals intelligence. Force-to-space ratios were low, most elements of either side rarely were in contact with the other, and their dispositions were masked. Rarely has possession of the initiative produced such power. Unexpected blows were hard to handle – weeks might be required to redeploy naval or air forces from one base to another; months to build the infrastructure necessary to maintain large forces in a new area or to move soldiers by sea or land. To destroy 20,000 men or 200 aeroplanes, capture one base or outmanoeuvre two divisions, transformed operations in New Guinea, a theatre the size of the Mediterranean. The opportunity to concentrate against the enemy's weakness, to catch it by surprise and to profit from knowledge of its intentions, were unusually large, especially for amphibious assaults. Failures in these areas were unusually expensive. ULTRA gave American power a razor, by showing how to execute lines of strategy, where to begin operations, how to force the enemy into error and prevent it from returning the favour. Poor signals security and intelligence, imagery and radar left Japan vulnerable to surprise, defeat in detail and loss of the crucial initiative.

Intelligence was fundamental to the battles between May and December 1942 which crippled the Imperial Japanese Navy and stemmed its tide. The USN in the Pacific was heavily outnumbered by a good enemy, but excellent intelligence and command let it concentrate its strength against fractions of Japan's fleet. Intelligence let bold American leaders use their forces to ambush Japanese fleets twice, in the Battles of Coral Sea and Midway, in one case scoring a tie and in the other a triumph – the exchange of four Japanese for one American carrier, after which the USN no longer was outnumbered. In both cases, the USN also shattered the enemy's strategy. Then, by the seizure of the island of Guadalcanal, intelligence enabled the Americans to make the Japanese fight, under disadvantageous circumstances, a prolonged struggle of attrition in the Solomon Islands, well-suited to the USN's strengths and Japanese weaknesses. This process culminated in a terrible campaign of maritime interdiction, where signals intelligence guided small forces of American aircraft and submarines precisely onto Japanese vessels over a large area. Throughout these campaigns, Japanese and American forces were evenly matched; intelligence was the tiebreaker.

One might have expected the significance of intelligence to wane in the Pacific after 1942, since American military superiority over Japan rapidly rose. That was not so. Intelligence gave little help to Allied operations on land in 1943. During 1944, however, it helped the United States to sidestep Japanese hopes to lure its enemy into a war of human attrition, and instead to shatter the outer perimeter of their defences in New Guinea and the Marshall Islands, and then the inner one in the Philippine Islands, luring what remained of Japanese naval and air forces to annihilation in the battles around Leyte Island in October 1944. The island-hopping strategy, which broke Japanese defences on the cheap, was possible only because intelligence showed how to strike where the enemy was weakest. From December 1944, however, the value of intelligence in the Pacific fell sharply for operations, though it remained influential for strategy. In particular, by revealing the strength of Japanese forces around the intended invasion sites in Kyushu, and the unwillingness of their government to surrender on Allied terms, intelligence drove the United States to use atomic bombs against Japan.

Conclusion

The United States won the Pacific War because of the quality of its forces and commanders and the scale of their resources, but intelligence let it win far more speedily and cheaply than could have happened otherwise. The same was true for the Allies in the Second World War as a whole, though to a lesser extent, varying by theatre and complicated by Axis successes, especially the great but overlooked ones against the USSR. There were many causes for Allied victory. To judge how any single factor shaped this outcome is hard, especially one like intelligence, which worked in such complex, often contradictory ways. Its effect is a matter for speculation, counterfactual logic and an attempt to winnow the effect of one cause from a complex process. The best-known effort is the 'conservative estimate' by F. H. Hinsley, a leading analyst at Bletchley Park during the war, and chief editor of the official history of British intelligence, that ULTRA saved the Allies three to four years of war and huge expenditures in lives and resources. His case focuses on the superiority of ULTRA to its German equivalent, its centrality to the Battle of the Atlantic, and of the latter to the war. One might reply that this case overestimates ULTRA's contribution to the U-boat campaign and of the latter to the war, and overlooks the Eastern Front. It also defines the value of Allied intelligence by adding its victories and ignoring its defeats – and also ignoring the enemy.[25] If one counted the results from all clashes between swords and shields between 1939 and 1945, conversely, one might conclude that victory in intelligence shaved a year and tens of thousands of Allied lives from the Pacific War, and months and hundreds of thousands of Allied soldiers from that in Europe. Did ULTRA hasten victory by months, or more? Did intelligence slay its thousands, or hundreds of thousands? The question, 'How many divisions had Bletchley Park?', cannot be answered definitively. It must be asked.

---

25 F. H. Hinsley, 'British Intelligence in the Second World War', in Christopher Andrew and Jeremy Noakes (eds.), *Intelligence and International Relations, 1900–1945* (University of Exeter Press, 1987), pp. 217–18.

23

Prisoners of war

BOB MOORE

The numbers of prisoners of war captured during the conflicts that make up the Second World War runs into millions, even if the military personnel that were interned at the end of hostilities are excluded. Taken together, they amount to in excess of 30 million men, and a small number of women who experienced surrender, captivity and, for the majority, eventual release and repatriation, although some would die in captivity. Thus being a prisoner of war was one of the most common military experiences, yet one to which, for obvious reasons, belligerent powers gave little or no prior consideration. In principle, the treatment of prisoners of war had been codified by a series of international treaties, including the Hague Conventions of 1899 and 1907, which culminated in the 1929 Geneva Convention. Taken together, this body of international law set out the guidelines for belligerent states to follow in their bilateral negotiations and handling of enemy prisoners. However, this relied on individual states ratifying these treaties and then abiding by their terms, something that was still imperfect when war came and which allowed belligerents to condone or even encourage breaches of humanitarian principles and, in some cases, inflict barbaric treatment on their captives.

Polish campaign

The first prisoners of war in Europe came with the German attack on Poland on 1 September. Both sides had ratified the Geneva Convention and it might have been expected that its terms would be upheld. However, from the very beginning, the nature of the warfare was framed by rules dictated from Berlin and reinforced by the regime's underlying ideology and propaganda, and by the predispositions of the Reich's soldiers. The last Polish forces surrendered on 6 October 1939, by which time the whole country had been overrun by German or Soviet forces. Estimates suggest that 700,000 Polish

serviccmen were taken prisoner by the Germans and 300,000 by the Russians.[1] During the five-week conflict, there were numerous accounts of
atrocities committed by German soldiers against their Polish counterparts,
with SS units widely thought to have been responsible for the murder of
military prisoners at Nisko, Rawa Mazowiecka and Ciepielów, but army
units were also implicated. German soldiers' testimonies suggest that they
felt they were responding to unwarranted Polish savagery rather than acting
as the instigators of a campaign of ethnic cleansing, and there is no means of
knowing if some of the German actions were in response to finding evidence
of Polish reprisals against prisoners or ethnic Germans.[2]

German treatment of Polish prisoners in captivity was governed by the
racial assumptions of the Nazi state and the economic necessities of the
regime. Labour shortages inside the Third Reich by 1939 were exacerbated by
Hitler's unwillingness to implement a total mobilization of the existing
workforce for the war economy. The subsequent invasion and occupation
of Poland effectively solved the immediate labour crisis, with 110,000 Polish
civilians and nearly 300,000 prisoners of war being used to gather the harvest.
Agriculture was the first priority, but the German instructions also permitted
their use in mining, railway maintenance, cable-laying and road construction.[3] Their conditions betrayed their lowly status in the Nazi's racial hierarchy. The agricultural and industrial labourers were underfed and
overworked; they were given 200 grams of bread and ersatz coffee each
day, with a ration of watery soup at noon. Any attempts by local populations
to alleviate their condition were severely punished. Those retained inside
prisoner-of-war camps fared no better. Until December 1939, they were
billeted in tents, sheds and sometimes in the open air, when temperatures
as low as -25 °C were recorded. Even when more adequately housed, their
treatment was reportedly much worse than that of the small numbers of
French and British prisoners then in German hands.[4]

Estimates on the total number of Polish prisoners of war actively
employed in the German economy by the summer of 1940 vary between
344,000 and 480,000. Further labour shortages in the Reich prompted further

---

1 *Germany and the Second World War*, vol. ii: *Germany's Initial Conquests in Europe* (10 vols.,
  Oxford: Clarendon Press, 1991), p. 124.
2 Charles W. Sydnor, Jr, *Soldiers of Destruction: The SS Death's Head Division, 1933–1945*
  (Princeton, NJ: Princeton University Press, 1977), p. 41. Ian Kershaw, *Hitler, 1936–1945:
  Nemesis* (London: Allen Lane, 2000), p. 240.
3 Polish Ministry of Information, *The German New Order in Poland* (London: Hutchinson,
  1942), pp. 117–18.
4 Ibid.

changes in the status of Polish prisoners of war. On 22 May 1940, the German general in charge of all prisoners, Hermann Reinecke, ordered the release of all Polish prisoners capable of working. Prisoners already employed in the Reich were to be converted to civilian status and sign labour contracts. This had important benefits for the German authorities, as they could now be used for a much wider range of tasks, untrammelled by the terms of the Geneva Convention, which restricted the use of prisoners to non-war work. Their transfer to civilian status also removed them from army control and placed them in the hands of the civil authorities and the security police. German figures indicate how this step rapidly changed the deployment of Polish prisoners. In January 1940, 95 per cent were employed in agriculture and only 5 per cent in industry. A year later, the respective figures were 52 per cent and 48 per cent.[5] This demobilization meant that the German army command effectively abrogated its responsibilities to its captured enemies and rendered the Poles subject to the civilian authorities within the Reich or to the power of Hans Frank in the General Government.

The Soviet invasion of Polish territory after 17 September 1939 led to the capture of around 230,000 Polish soldiers, later augmented by another 70,000 interned in the Baltic States. As there had been no formal declaration of war between Poland and the USSR, Moscow chose to treat captured Polish soldiers as counter-revolutionaries rather than as prisoners of war, and they were therefore handed over to the newly created Administration for the Affairs of Prisoners of War and Internees (GUPVI), a branch of the NKVD (predecessor of the KGB). Officers and men were segregated in camps established in the western USSR, with soldiers and NCOs put to work on road building and in heavy industry. The officers were mainly concentrated at Kozelsk and Starobielsk, where they were subjected to lengthy interrogations and propaganda campaigns. The failure to convert them and other members of the Polish intelligentsia to a pro-Soviet attitude led directly to an order, issued by Lavrentii Beria on 5 March 1940, for their execution and the mass murder of up to 22,000 victims in the forest of Katyn and at two other sites in the USSR during April and May of that year.[6]

---

5 Edward L. Homze, *Foreign Labor in Nazi Germany* (Princeton, NJ: Princeton University Press, 1967), pp. 23–5, 36–7.
6 See George Sanford, 'The Katyn Massacre and Polish-Soviet Relations', *Journal of Contemporary History* 41:1 (2006) 95–111; Paul Allen, *Katyń: Stalin's Massacre and the Triumph of Truth* (De Kalb, Ill.: 2010); Anna Cienciala, Natalia S. Lebedeva and Wojciech Materski (eds.), *Katyn: A Crime Without Punishment* (New Haven, Conn.: Yale University Press, 2008).

After the German attack on the Soviet Union and the conclusion of the Sikorski–Maisky agreements, which signalled the resumption of Polish-Soviet relations, General Władysław Anders was charged by the Polish Prime Minister-in-exile, Władysław Sikorski, with recruiting an army from among the former Polish soldiers in Soviet hands. In spite of having official sanction, Anders had difficulty persuading Gulag officials to hand over Polish inmates, and was also troubled by how few officers could be located in Soviet camps. Once established, the unit was kept in the USSR until March 1942, when food shortages prompted its evacuation through Iran and transfer to British command, where it became part of the Polish Second Corps that fought in the Italian campaigns.

Western Front

Although at war from 3 September 1939, Germany, Britain and France took few prisoners during the *drôle de guerre* (or Phoney War) of 1939–40. For both Britain and Germany, the majority of their captives were airmen and naval personnel, as well as merchant mariners, whom the Germans saw as military personnel, while the British did not. The number of French prisoners would increase hugely in May and June 1940, and a considerable number of British soldiers were captured during the fall of France. After that, relatively few prisoners were take on the Western Front by either the British or the Germans, until the defeat of Axis forces in North Africa in the winter of 1942–43.

Given the threat to the British Isles and the fear of a fifth column, German prisoners taken by the British before 1944 were considered too dangerous to be retained on the mainland and were thus transported to Canada. Christened as 'fur trappers' by their comrades, they were to spend several years in camps on the Canadian prairies. German prisoners from the Afrikakorps also had to be evacuated, and as Dominion territories in East and South Africa were unwilling to accommodate them, they also made the long journey via Suez and South Africa across the Atlantic to North America. Later joint operations with US forces led to responsibility for prisoners being divided on a 50:50 basis, irrespective of whose units had effected the captures; this resulted in some prisoners of the British being accommodated in camps in the United States.[7]

---

7 Louis E. Keefer, *Italian Prisoners of War in America, 1942–1946* (Westport, Conn.: Praeger, 1992), pp. 41, 44.

Britain and Germany, the major states actively at war in Western Europe from June 1940 to 1943, both complied with the demands of the Geneva convention, although reciprocity seems to have played a major part in dealing with issues at the margins. There were specific conflicts between London and Berlin. The so-called 'shackling crisis' was engendered by German claims that British forces had tied up prisoners during raids on the island of Sark and at Dieppe in 1942, in breach of the convention. This led to a tit-for-tat shackling of prisoners in camps by both sides, and became something of a battle of wills between Churchill and Hitler which lasted well into 1943. The result was a delay in proposed exchanges of the sick and wounded – negotiations that were further impeded by a German insistence on parity of numbers. The issue was resolved when large numbers of injured Germans were left in Allied hands after the Tunisian campaign, and Berlin in the meantime had become keen to free up hospital space occupied by British prisoners. The first exchanges finally took place in October 1943, with those selected being taken by ship to Gothenburg, Barcelona and Oran. These first two locations also saw a further exchange in 1944, and Switzerland was used in 1945. In all, this involved 4,249 British and Americans and 7,466 Germans.[8]

British fears that the Germans might depart from the terms of the Convention had begun with rumours of Hitler's *Kommandobefehl* of October 1942, which stipulated that captured raiding parties could be summarily liquidated, a fear heightened when the mass escape from Stalag Luft III (Sagan) on 24–25 March 1944 led to the execution of fifty recaptured escapees. By this stage, Gestapo and Security Police involvement in POW affairs had become clear, and was also apparent in Goebbels' campaign in the summer of 1944 to applaud and incite civilian reprisals against all downed Allied airmen as *Terrorflieger*. The Normandy landings of June 1944 necessitated the removal of German prisoners from the front line across the Channel, and this began a process that saw around 200,000 brought to camps in Britain before the war's end. Carefully guarded in the first instance, they were soon being screened and the less dangerous elements deployed as an auxiliary labour force, augmenting the now fixed supply of Italian prisoners working in agriculture.

Meanwhile, the situation with respect to French prisoners had been quite different. It has been estimated that after Marshal Pétain signed the armistice in June 1940 which brought France's war with Germany to an end, the Germans had 1.9 million NCOs and other ranks and 29,000 officers in captivity. Some had

8 Neville Wylie, *Barbed Wire Diplomacy: Britain, Germany and the Politics of Prisoners of War, 1939–1945* (Oxford University Press, 2010), p. 215.

been captured during the Phoney War or during hostilities in May and early June 1940, but the majority were formally surrendered by the armistice signed by the French state on 22 June. Approximately 1.6 million were interned and then taken to Germany. The discrepancy is accounted for by two factors. Large numbers of soldiers managed to escape from temporary camps inside France in the first weeks after the armistice and made their way home, and others were released by the Germans because they were from Alsace-Lorraine, which was to be reincorporated into the Reich. The detrimental side to this piece of German generosity was that these men could then be liable for service in the Wehrmacht.[9] There is no doubt that the acquisition of French POWs was a major bonus for the German domestic economy. Their usefulness as labour and as hostages, to ensure the future cooperation of Vichy France, made any rapid repatriation unlikely, especially when the expected defeat of Britain failed to materialize and end the war. Most of the French captives held in *Stammlager* (Stalags) were rapidly redeployed to sub-camps (Kommandos). These could be in small groups – as in rural areas – or in thousands – as in some urban environments, where masses of workers were required. Thus, for example, on 22 November 1940, Stalag XA (Schleswig) was reported to have a complement of 1,000 prisoners, of whom 500 were French; but the total administered by the camp was 51,800, including 30,000 Frenchmen.[10] Most French POW labour was deployed in the agricultural sector, and so successful was this process that by the spring of 1941, the Germans were able to send home and civilianize all but 80,000 of their Polish POWs. While useful on the land, the German war economy needed skilled industrial labour, and this led to the French POWs being used as bargaining counters with Vichy, to persuade the French to hand over industrial workers in exchange for the repatriation of prisoners – albeit on a 3:1 ratio. Later still, French prisoners were pressured into giving up their POW status to become civilian labourers, in exchange for promises of better conditions and periods of leave. Although some succumbed to German blandishments, the majority were unwilling to give up the protection of the Geneva Convention and remained in non-war work until their liberation in 1945.[11]

---

9 Yves Durand, 'Das Schicksal der französischen Kriegsgefangenen in deutschem Gewahrsam (1933–1945)', in Günther Bischof and Rüdiger Overmans (eds.), *Kriegsgefangenschaft im Zweiten Weltkrieg: Eine Vergleichende Perspektive* (Ternitz-Pottschach: Gerhard Höller, 1999), p. 71.
10 Homze, *Foreign Labor*, pp. 48–9.
11 Yves Durand, *La Captivité: Histoire des prisonniers de guerre français 1939–1945* (Paris: FNCGP, 1980), pp. 326–33.

The German treatment of the smaller nations overrun in 1940 varied. In Norway, the German invasion of 8 April overcame most Norwegian resistance, in spite of the Allied campaign around Narvik. However, the country's Sixth Division carried on the fight until 10 June, when it also surrendered. As a fellow 'Aryan' nation, it was decided that the Norwegians would be demobilized and sent home, leaving only a small number of officers in German captivity. A week after their country's surrender on 14 May 1940, the Dutch army still in the field, who were also considered racially 'Aryan' by the Germans, were ordered to report to the encampment they had occupied on 9 May for demobilization. Men who could prove they had a job to return to or could support themselves as self-employed were to be allowed home first, while the 20,000 taken prisoner during the five days of hostilities were returned home from Germany in early June 1940. The 14,400 career soldiers and officer cadets were also demobilized and returned to civilian life, having given an oath not to carry out any acts against German interests. Only sixty-nine refused to sign the undertaking and they, including their commander, General Winkelman, were (re-)interned in Germany as prisoners of war.[12] Berlin's attempts to re-intern the Dutch army in April 1943, in order to provide labour for the German war economy, led to widespread strikes and tens of thousands going into hiding.

The surrender of the Belgian armed forces took place on 28 May 1940, after nearly three weeks of fighting. Leopold III of the Belgians indicated that he would stay in the country as a 'prisoner of war' and that the soldiers should 'return to their homes and for the country to get to work again'. By this stage, large numbers of Belgian servicemen had already been captured and taken to Germany, but the surrender allowed perhaps as many as 65 per cent of the 600,000 men in the Belgian army simply to return home without any formal demobilization. Berlin's so-called *Flamenpolitik* (the favouring of Flemish interests in Belgium) resulted in 79,302 soldiers being repatriated. Nearly all were Flemish. This left a group of French-speaking Walloon Belgian servicemen, variously estimated at between 53,000 and 65,000 men, who remained in the Reich for the remainder of the war.[13] Apart from the Walloons, only officers and professional soldiers were kept in captivity, but even some of these were allowed home to carry out specific tasks, most

12 L. de Jong, *Het Koninkrijk der Nederlanden in de Tweede Wereldoorlog* (14 vols., 's-Gravenhage: Staatsuitgeverij, 1972), vol. IV, pp. 238, 240.
13 Jean-Léon Charles, *Les forces armées belges au cours de la deuxième guerre mondiale* (Brussels: La Renaissance du Livre, 1970), p. 262; Werner Warmbrunn, *The German Occupation of Belgium* (New York: Peter Lang, 1993), pp. 187–9.

notably to staff an organization to look after the welfare of demobilized soldiers and to augment the strength of a reformed Belgian gendarmerie.

The first large quantity of prisoners to fall into British hands were the Italians captured in North Africa toward the end of 1940. General Wavell's counter-attack in Egypt led to the complete destruction of more than nine divisions and the capture of 133,000 prisoners, and actions in Ethiopia and Italian Somaliland yielded a further 64,000 in early 1941. However, this overwhelming success brought its own problems, as Egypt was by no means politically secure, and finding food, guards and suitable accommodation for so many enemies, so close to a fluid war zone, could not be guaranteed. Various imperial territories were asked to help, and prisoners were sent to India, South Africa and Australia, while those in East Africa were taken south into Kenya. With the exception of the officers, all were soon being considered as an auxiliary labour force. For example, 90 per cent of the first 20,000 Italians sent to South Africa were prioritized for road building and agricultural work. As early as February 1941, eighteen prisoner-of-war labour companies were created to carry out battlefield salvage work in North Africa, and others were later used to augment manpower shortages in the Eighth Army.[14]

Initial British perceptions that most of the Italians were uncommitted to Fascism and pleased to be out of the war seem to have been borne out; so that in spite of security concerns, the import of Italian prisoners to the United Kingdom was being actively discussed early in 1941, to alleviate a grievous shortage of labour on the home front. The British imperial authorities looked to adhere to the spirit, if not the letter, of the Geneva Convention, and prisoners were generally employed only on non-war work – primarily agriculture, forestry and civil construction projects – although there were examples where expediency led to some blurring of distinctions. For example, Italians sent to the United Kingdom were used to help build some of the defences for the British naval base at Scapa Flow on Orkney.

The United States had its first large-scale captures during the Tunisian campaign. The need to keep combat troops supplied meant that Italian POWs were soon drafted in to augment existing French and Arab civilian workers in warehousing, transportation, road building and general labouring. The conclusion of the North African campaign led to the surrender of 252,415 German and Italian prisoners. Most of the Germans were shipped to the

14 Bob Moore and Kent Fedorowich, *The British Empire and its Italian Prisoners of War* (Basingstoke: Palgrave, 2003), pp. 19, 21, 24, 54.

United States, as part of the 50:50 agreement, but some 15,000 Italians and 5,000 Germans were also transferred into French hands, again ostensibly as a labour force, but in practice as insurance for any Free French prisoners taken by the Axis who might otherwise have been summarily executed as francs-tireurs.[15] This began a policy for both the US and the British Army, where the maximum number of Italians who were 'harmless to operations' would be retained to meet the labour needs associated with the build-up to the attack on the Italian peninsula.

Confusion over the status of Italians in captivity arose after their government's surrender on 8 September 1943. The Geneva Convention made no provision for a belligerent changing sides in a conflict, but the British and Americans were adamant that, whatever the future status of the prisoners, they should be regarded as a pool which Allied governments would continue to draw on in whatever way would best serve the manpower problem and the wider war effort. In Britain, shortages of camp accommodation and the need for greater flexibility in deployment meant that Italian prisoners were offered 'cooperator' status, which involved better pay, conditions and the chance of early repatriation, while remaining as prisoners. By the end of the war in Europe, 63 per cent of the 154,000 Italians in the United Kingdom had been persuaded to become cooperators, although a residual 40,000 or so steadfastly refused to succumb to the blandishments of their captors.[16] The Americans operated a similar policy, from October 1943, of mobilizing Italian captives into labour companies, and they were subsequently deployed across Tunisia and Algeria as Italian Service Units (ISU). Latterly, some 28,000 were also employed in supporting the invasion of southern France, and still later in the last stages of the campaign on the Italian mainland. Around 50,000 were transported to the United States in the spring and summer of 1943. Here, they probably enjoyed the best conditions of any experienced by their comrades in captivity; well-fed and employed in everything from cotton farming to ranching and forestry.

While Italy's transition from Axis power to co-belligerent in September 1943 had largely positive outcomes for the ideologically uncommitted Italians already in British or American captivity, the situation for the Italian forces still in the field was problematic in the extreme. The Italian army on the

---

15 George G. Lewis and John Mewha, *History of Prisoner of War Utilization by the United States Army, 1776–1945* (Honolulu, Haw.: University Press of the Pacific, 2002), p. 177.
16 Bob Moore and Kent Fedorowich, 'Allied Negotiations on Italian Co-belligerency and the Prisoner-of-War Question, 1943–45', *International History Review* 18 (1996), 28–47.

peninsula and in the Balkans had few options – instructed to stop fighting, but with no orders as to how to deal with their erstwhile German allies – and indecision was to result in some major tragedies. On Kefalonia, a force of 11,500 Italians had been 'reinforced' by 2,000 Germans in July 1943. At the armistice, the Italian commander received somewhat vague orders from his superiors to the effect that he should not confront the Germans unless threatened by them and should also not make common cause with the Allies or with the local Greek partisans. On 11 September, he was told to resist any German attempts to disarm his men, and their resistance lasted for around ten days before they ran out of ammunition. On orders issued from Berlin on the same day, most of the captured Italian officers involved were summarily executed as traitors, and a further order indicated that no prisoners were to be taken. The result was that around 5,000 men were executed, and a further 3,000 surviving prisoners died when the transport ships taking them into captivity struck mines in the Adriatic. On other Greek islands, officers were also shot in large numbers, and many ordinary soldiers also lost their lives when transported across waters dominated by Allied air and sea power. For example, some 13,000 Italians on the island of Rhodes suffered this fate out of a total strength of around 80,000.[17] The Wehrmacht disarmed around 1 million men in Italy, the Balkans and southern France. Berlin's response to the Italian collapse was brutal, but also pragmatic, taking over 600,000 former Italian servicemen as forced labourers to work in the Reich. Officially, the Italians were to be treated along the same lines as Western European prisoners of war, but in practice, the rations given to these men did not meet the basic provisions of the Geneva Convention. Sources suggest that 19,714 (3.5 per cent) of them died as a result of their internment – attributable to disease, industrial injuries, ill health and bombing.

Exceptions to the application of the Geneva Convention can also be seen in the inferior German and Italian treatment meted out to captured colonial prisoners in the West. During the fall of France, Senegalese and Moroccan troops were in much greater danger of summary execution than their white counterparts, and this differential treatment continued during captivity. Starvation and random executions were commonplace, and most black and North African soldiers were not sent to Germany, but kept in camps inside France. Here they continued to suffer from the most acute shortages of food,

---

17 Rüdiger Overmans, 'German Policy on Prisoners of War', *in Germany and the Second World War*, vol. IX: *German Wartime Society, 1939–1945* (10 vols., Oxford: Clarendon Press, 2014), pt. 2, pp. 832–3.

and from the vagaries of the climate, which led to many deaths. As the situation stabilized, they gained access to Red Cross parcels and a degree of protection from the Vichy Regime. Later still, some of the sick were released and a further 16,000 taken from camps and remobilized in Vichy-controlled North Africa. The relatively small number of non-white British imperial troops captured by Axis forces in North Africa suffered similar ill-treatment. Some 2,000 black South Africans were used as labourers on work not permitted by the Geneva Convention. Later they, and others, were distributed across German-occupied Europe, where their conditions varied enormously from one camp to another. African American soldiers also fell into German hands in the last stages of the war in Europe. They, too, were subject to summary executions at the front and harsh treatment in camps as the Third Reich collapsed. It has been argued that their plight would have been worse, but that reciprocity and German fears of being held to account overrode racial prejudices. For the most part, the Germans did not attempt to segregate Jews from among their Western prisoners and these men remained largely unmolested alongside their comrades. Only in the last stages of the Western campaign were captured US soldiers screened and approximately 300 Jews taken to forced labour camps.

Eastern Front

In the European theatre of war, it was the Eastern Front that generated by far the largest numbers of POWs. The brutal nature of the BARBAROSSA campaign and the four years of warfare that followed have been well documented, and there have been extensive debates about the origins and escalation of this 'war of annihilation'. There is no doubt that the German troops invading the Soviet Union had been ideologically primed to confront 'Bolshevik *Untermenschen*', and orders had been issued on the treatment of POWs before the campaign began, including Hitler's notorious *Kommissar-befehl*, which sanctioned the 'special treatment' of captured political commissars from the Red Army. More generally, the Germans were encouraged to see 'ordinary' Russians as culturally inferior and used to harsh conditions, but nonetheless capable of good work if properly led.

Although the Soviets had declared on 17 July 1941 that, on a reciprocal basis, they would abide by the earlier Geneva Conventions on the treatment of sick and wounded soldiers (1864 and 1906), and the Hague Conventions relating to the laws of war of 1899 and 1907, the German response was to reject these terms. Indeed, the reply framed by Hitler personally made great play of the appalling treatment supposedly meted out to German captives in Russian hands during the Great War, and this was widely disseminated to the front-line troops through the *Mitteilungen für die Truppen*, which also carried reports of atrocities carried out by Soviet forces against German POWs. This initial set of diplomatic exchanges set the tone for what followed. The Soviet Union dropped its declared adherence to the Hague Conventions and ceased using the intermediary and monitoring services of its protecting power, Sweden, and those of the International Committee of the Red Cross (ICRC). In addition, Stalin published Order No. 270 on 16 August 1941, which condemned Red Army officers who tore off their insignia and either surrendered or abandoned their posts as malicious deserters whose families were to be arrested. Likewise the families of ordinary soldiers who surrendered would be deprived of state welfare benefits and assistance. This was driven by a fear that Soviet troops being reasonably treated by their German captors would potentially reduce their will to fight to the death.[18] The attack on the families of potential deserters and those who surrendered was ostensibly designed to counteract any such sentiments in the most brutal manner possible. Later attempts by neutral intermediaries or the ICRC to ameliorate the situation were rendered useless in the face of top-level German intransigence. For example, the ICRC offer to provide food parcels and typhus injections for POWs on both sides was explicitly rejected by Hitler on the basis that it might encourage German soldiers to think they could survive imprisonment by the Soviets. Indeed, the German position did not change even after substantial numbers of their soldiers fell into Soviet hands after the defeat at Stalingrad. In sum, both Supreme Commanders had more or less written off any of their soldiers who fell into enemy hands on the Eastern Front.

The success of Operation BARBAROSSA meant that the Germans only lost 30,000 men to Soviet captivity while seizing around 3.35 million Russian prisoners in the first six months of the conflict. The *Oberkommando der Wehrmacht* (OKW – armed forces high command) POW Department had decreed on 16 June 1941 that although the USSR had not recognized the Geneva Convention, it would nonetheless be used as the basis for the treatment of its captured soldiers, but with certain exceptions. These included an exclusion from any contact with the outside world, a stricture that would include both the protecting power and ICRC. The directive made no mention of rations, accommodation or medical care, suggesting

---

18 Alfred Streim, *Die Behandlung sowjetischer Kriegsgefangenen im Fall Barbarossa* (Heidelberg: Müller Juristischer Verlag, 1981), pp. 203–7.

that the headline declaration was more for show and so heavily qualified as to make it largely meaningless. A further directive of 25 July 1941 – after the war had begun – insisted that German soldiers should treat properly obedient Russian POWs who were prepared to work, but that any insubordination was to be ruthlessly suppressed. In practice, the sheer speed of the Blitzkrieg meant that many complete Red Army units were captured *en masse*, but there was no shortage of indiscriminate killings at the front itself, and German soldiers were encouraged to treat all Russian soldiers found individually or in small groups behind the lines as partisans, and to execute them even if they surrendered. In spite of its existing machinery for dealing with POWs, the Wehrmacht proved unprepared to house and provision such large numbers of captives. Initial plans had been to accommodate the captives inside the Reich, but this instruction was rescinded by Hitler at the last minute and meant that prisoners would have to be held in camps within the theatre of operations on a more or less permanent basis.[19]

With officers and political commissars segregated out, no special provisions were made for the remaining hundreds of thousands of ordinary soldiers, who were often held in barbed-wire enclosures with little or no food and no sanitary arrangements. For example, some two weeks after the war began, a camp at Minsk designed for 30,000 men held some 100,000 POWs and a further 40,000 civilians. Prisoners were thus hardly able to move and compelled to relieve themselves where they stood. The small guard unit meant that discipline could only be maintained through the use of 'brutal force'.[20] Plans for huts were given a low priority, and earth-and-clay shelters were all that existed for the first months. Rations could have come from captured Red Army supplies and local harvests, but low priority was given to feeding POWs. Inside Soviet territory, local civilians were prepared to provide food for the prisoners, and some camp commanders allowed this to happen. Others forbade it and effectively allowed their charges to starve. This was bad enough during the autumn of 1941, and there were reports of prisoners digging into the ground to find roots and worms, and climbing trees to find green shoots, even though the guards would then shoot them. Cases of cannibalism were also punished by summary execution when perpetrators were identified.

As the temperatures dropped with the onset of winter, the mortality rates in these makeshift camps rocketed, with rates of 1 to 2.5 per cent per day.

---

19 Overmans, 'Die Kriegsgefangenenpolitik', p. 805.
20 Ibid., p. 807.

To compound this, POWs had often been stripped of their winter clothing, and especially their boots, to help stem deficiencies in Wehrmacht supplies caused by logistical problems and the severe weather conditions. Medical treatment for the wounded was restricted to Russian doctors using whatever equipment was available. Weakened by starvation and forced marches, those unable to march were usually summarily shot by their guards, and even previously fully fit prisoners had little resistance to the epidemics that raged through the transit camps. There were recorded instances of large camp populations being shot to prevent the spread of disease – for example at Stalag 359B – and POWs were also used in various forms of medical and firearms testing, not least in the testing of Zyklon B on 3 September 1941.

From the very beginning of the campaign, the German authorities had planned a screening of prisoners to identify two disparate elements; those who might be 'turned' and used for the German cause, and those who were inherently inimical to German interests; party leaders, intellectual and Jews. Jewish soldiers were habitually segregated from their comrades – as had been the case in the Polish campaign – and the numbers subjected to 'special treatment' (*Sonderbehandlung*) have been estimated at around 100,000. Officers were also removed from their men and committed to the SD (*Sicherheitsdienst* – Nazi Party security service) in rear areas. There was also differentiation between nationalities. Balts, ethnic Germans, Finns and Romanians were in principle released, as were Ukrainians and Belorussians before 13 November 1941. Muslim Caucasians were also afforded a high status. Whether there was a contemporary ideological or political rationale about these choices remains unclear, but the categorizations exactly mirror the ones employed during the German occupation of Russia during the First World War.

This mixture of ideology, logistical inefficiency and pragmatism took its toll and may have cost the lives of up to 2 million prisoners in the first six months, either in forward, transit or rear camps, or during forced marches or journeys in unheated goods trains. However, as with other theatres, these estimates take no account of soldiers who may have surrendered, but were then killed by their adversaries and never formally registered as captives. This initially cavalier attitude to the prisoners' survival underwent changes as the Wehrmacht and the wider German economy recognized its crippling manpower shortages. As early as July 1941, and in defiance of existing directives, the German field commanders began offering prisoners the chance to work for better rations as auxiliary troops (*Hilfswillige*, or *Hiwis*). This involved using them for road building, burying corpses, collecting booty and later clearing minefields. By the end of August, as many as 300,000 prisoners had been moved into Reich territory after Hitler had been persuaded to change his mind, and a further import of 660,000 was planned. They were intended for all manner of construction and agricultural work, but their poor physical condition and continued poor treatment both inside and outside the Reich led to further mass deaths, with the result that 'the vast majority' of the 3.3 million Russian POWs taken had lost their lives by March 1942.[21]

Elements within the high command were concerned by the cavalier disregard for the laws of war contemplated by the various directives from Hitler and the OKH/OKW (*Oberkommando des Heeres* – army high command/ *Oberkommando der Wehrmacht* – armed forces high command), if only because of the potentially damaging effect they might have on those Germans in Russian hands and on the conduct of the war itself. These concerns were initially dismissed in the interests of fighting an ideological war, but there were also more pragmatic objections. Targeting the commissars made it more likely that they would have their men fight to the death and thus increase German losses. A number of field commanders were clearly unhappy about the unruly behaviour of their men and issued orders in an attempt to stem the tide, but they were doubtless aware of the ideological driving force behind the 'war of annihilation', and their complaints therefore objected not to the killings per se, but because they pointed to a breakdown of military discipline. A final objection was that Russian POWs needed to be preserved to meet the grievous labour shortages in the war economy. Moreover, a successful occupation policy also demanded a cooperative Russian population – something that could be encouraged through better treatment of their countrymen in German hands. Even though Goebbels' Propaganda Ministry, General Reinhard Gehlen and some high-ranking officers could be found stressing the advantages of a more humane policy, this remained the exception rather than the rule.

Through the remainder of the conflict, the Germans continued to exploit their Red Army prisoners, and in a number of different ways. They were used as a camp-based labour force for industrial, construction and agricultural work, but often treated with little concern for their long-term welfare. The Germans lost up to 800,000 men killed or wounded in the first six months of Operation BARBAROSSA, and the shortfalls were made good by recruitment of POWs as *Hiwis*. Estimates suggest that the prisoners may

---

21 Ibid., p. 811.

have constituted up to 40 per cent of some support units by the end of 1941.[22] Later still, some were given armed roles. In spite of Hitler's intransigence, it seems that some military commanders would 'appropriate' captured Red Army personnel into their formations without ever declaring them as POWs or having them processed as such. In this way, unit strengths could be maintained in the face of mounting losses and an absence of ready replacements. The integration of these so-called Osttruppen into the Wehrmacht took on substantial proportions by the end of 1942, when there were estimated to be approximately 573,000 wearing German uniforms.[23] The many non-Russians represented here among these early 'recruits' should come as no great surprise. The animosity of the nationalities to Russian, let alone Soviet rule, was a matter of historical record, and, leaving aside the material advantages, many of these groups had a greater ideological and political motivation to escape the privations of captivity and assist the German war effort than their Russian counterparts. Even the total given for Russians here is probably somewhat misleading, as it includes large numbers of Ukrainians and Belorussians, many of whom had no love for Moscow or for Soviet Communism, but who had been drafted into the Soviet Army nonetheless.

Although not readily acknowledged in Berlin, this willingness of Soviet POWs to serve German interests – or rather to oppose Russian and Soviet hegemony – was soon being channelled into the formation of designated formations. By the end of 1941, the Wehrmacht had established a Cossack Division, albeit supplied by the SS, which saw active service but was largely used in anti-partisan operations. There were also Ukrainians who fought under German military command at Kharkov and Stalingrad, and a Turkistan Division established with around 50 per cent German soldiers and augmented by some Azerbaijanis. In addition, the SS itself established a Galician Division, composed largely of Ukrainians in April 1943. Although deployed on the Eastern Front, these formations were latterly transferred to other theatres of operations, with many ending the war in Italy or in Western Europe. However, much larger numbers of Osttruppen could be found scattered as smaller elements within Wehrmacht and SS formations. By the time of the D-Day invasion on 6 June 1944, the Wehrmacht had trained and stationed Osttruppen battalions largely away from the Eastern Front. There were nearly a hundred

22 Mark R. Elliott, *Pawns of Yalta: Soviet Refugees and America's Role in their Repatriation* (Urbana, Ill.: University of Illinois Press, 1982), p. 13.
23 Ibid., p. 15.

in France, and many more could be found in the Netherlands, Belgium and Norway. However, in Ukraine they were deployed against partisans and were also used as concentration camp guards. This blurring of origins, status and deployments makes any precise statistics about POWs in German service all but impossible. Figures between 1 million and 1.3 million have been widely used, but exact numbers remain elusive, the matter being complicated by the existence of deserters, militarized civilians and membership of paramilitary and partisan formations. The scale and scope of Soviet POW collusion with the Nazi invaders has often been equated with the creation of the *Russkaia Osvoboditel'naia Armiia* (Russian Liberation Army, ROA), under the leadership of General Andrei Vlasov, but in real terms the ROA was of only minor importance in the recruitment of prisoners to the German cause, and in contributing to the war effort. In practice, Vlasov was excluded from any overt military role until very late in the war; training of troops under his direct command only commenced in November 1944, and only one division ever became operational. The recruitment of Soviet POWs was therefore largely dependent on the selective policy of the Germans, the prisoners' anti-Russian and anti-Communist sentiments, and, perhaps overwhelmingly, on the 'wretchedness and brutality' of their incarceration.

The major debate on these prisoners has tended to crystallize around the numbers who died in German captivity and who was responsible. Given the chaos of the warfare and the complete destruction of the German armed forces in 1945, statistics are unreliable. The total number taken was probably between 5.35 and 5.7 million, and some 900,000 were still registered as POWs at the end of the war.[24] However, this ignores all those who escaped or were never formally registered, as well as those who were released into civilian labour or who took on other roles – as *Hiwis* or in armed formations fighting alongside the Axis. Given this uncertainty, it seems likely that between 50 and 60 per cent of the Red Army prisoners taken by the Germans failed to survive the war. Apportioning responsibility is complicated. It is undoubtedly true that the Commissar Order, the screening of prisoners for 'Communists' and the ideological commitment to a war of annihilation all played a role in POW mortality – and these were policies directly attributable to Hitler. Beyond this, the continuing high death rates were largely down to the conditions experienced by the prisoners, and responsibility for this lies with the Wehrmacht. Given that the Blitzkrieg against the USSR was meant to be

24 Overmans, 'Die Kriegsgefangenenpolitik', p. 820.

over in a matter of weeks, it cannot claim to have been unprepared for the numbers involved, although Hitler's ban on bringing the prisoners into the Reich undoubtedly had some disruptive effects. The idea that there was a deliberate policy of starvation has also been discredited, in spite of the 'General Plan for the East' having provisions for a reduction in the Soviet population. More likely is the fact that by the time the prisoners started dying in large numbers, the German army itself was also in crisis and would not be permitted to divert resources from either the home front or its own troops. Subsequently, prisoners were allowed to live only if they were deemed potentially useful as labour. A further explanation for the radical policies of the Third Reich comes from Hitler's concern that German soldiers should not think they could survive Soviet captivity – thus making them more likely to fight to the death. The ICRC was prevented from helping Soviet POWs – and this gave the USSR every reason to prohibit its access to Germans in Soviet hands. In this way, Hitler helped to create the very enemy he imagined and the one he wanted his troops to fear. However, none of this should exonerate either Hitler or his generals from responsibility for the deaths of approximately 2.5 million Soviet soldiers in captivity – one of the greatest crimes of the Second World War and surpassed only by the murder of the Jews.

Of the approximately 3,155,000 German soldiers recorded as captured by the Soviets, more than 360,000 were known to have died en route to camps or in captivity – an overall mortality rate of 13.9 per cent.[25] However, the chaotic nature of the fighting and poor organization of Soviet agencies in the early months of conflict and retreat led to further deaths – a situation that changed only with the mass captures after the Battle of Stalingrad. Changes of NKVD and Red Army personnel responsible for prisoners in early 1943 put greater emphasis on their economic and political value. Nevertheless, the survivors were put to work, and their contribution to the labour force was paramount and superseded any considerations about their material welfare or usefulness for political re-education. In spite of the fact that the majority of Germans taken prisoner by Soviet forces were captured in the last months of the war, the numbers of those missing after all repatriations had taken place was around 1.3 million, suggesting that actual losses were much higher than the official figures.[26]

---

25 Martin K. Sorge, *The Other Price of Hitler's War: German Military and Civilian Losses Resulting from World War II* (New York: Greenwood, 1986), p. 77.

26 For a detailed examination of this issue, see Klaus-Dieter Müller, Konstantin Nikisch-kin and Günther Wagenlehner (eds.), *Die Tragödie der Gefangenschaft in Deutschland und in der Sowjetunion, 1941–1956* (Köln/Weimar: Böhlau Verlag, 1998).

Far East and Pacific theatres

In one important respect, the story of prisoners of war in the Second World War begins with the Japanese incursions into China during and after 1937. This was the first occasion when Japanese forces had gone into action after the introduction of their revised 1936 Field Service Code, and represented the first test of a cultural and ideological shift in attitude toward military prisoners. In the Russo-Japanese War of 1904–5, and again during the First World War, the Japanese had been renowned for their consideration and good treatment of enemy prisoners. Much has been made of this change in attitude, although it seems clear that this was not just attributable to military regulations, but was also a result of shifts in wider cultural attitudes.[27] A directive from the Emperor on 5 August 1937 had explicitly removed Chinese prisoners from the protections afforded by the Hague Conventions, but even before this, in the days after the Marco Polo Bridge Incident of 8 July 1937, the Japanese public were being encouraged to support 'punishing the barbaric Chinese'. In the extensive military actions that followed, there are few references to the taking of prisoners by either side, although Japanese successes indicate that large numbers of Chinese soldiers must have fallen into their hands. The so-called 'Rape of Nanjing' at the end of the same year provides some evidence for the mindset and behaviour of the Japanese soldiers. After stiff Chinese resistance and heavy losses of their own men in the advance from Shanghai, the Japanese took control of the capital city on 13 December. Foreign and even some Japanese journalists recorded the indiscriminate killings of prisoners and civilians, including large numbers of surrendered Chinese troops. Orders received by individual units indicate that this policy had come directly from the Japanese high command.[28] A detachment commander of the 16th Division of the Shanghai Expeditionary Force, Major General Sasaki Touichi, subsequently blamed the mass killings on the inability of his officers to control their men, but formally ordered his soldiers not to take prisoners unless ordered to do so on 14 December. His superior, Lieutenant General Nakajima Kesago, noted that

> it is our policy not to take prisoners, so we decided to get them out of the way. But when it became a group of one thousand, five thousand, and finally

27 Philip Towle, *From Ally to Enemy: Anglo-Japanese Military Relations, 1900–1945* (Folkestone: Global Oriental, 2006), pp. 118–34.
28 Iris Chang, *The Rape of Nanking: The Forgotten Holocaust of World War II* (New York: Basic Books, 1997), pp. 40–6. See also Joshua A. Fogel (ed.), *The Nanjing Massacre in History and Historiography* (Berkeley: University of California Press, 2000).

ten thousand, we couldn't even disarm them all. [...] I later learned the Sasaki Detachment alone disposed of about fifteen thousand; the one company commander assigned to guard Taiping Gate disposed of about thirteen hundred.[29]

This brutal treatment of the Chinese continued throughout the conflict, and apart from cases of summary executions, there were also documented examples of prisoners being used as *marutas* (wood logs) by the infamous Japanese Unit 731, which specialized in chemical and biological experimentation.

This complete disregard for prisoners had both political and economic elements, but was undoubtedly grounded in cultural attitudes of military and racial superiority, attitudes that were to be repeated when the Japanese went to war against the Western colonial powers in Southeast Asia and the Pacific in December 1941. Their military successes led to the capture of large numbers of servicemen from the imperial European states. Britain saw the rapid capitulations of Hong Kong, Burma, Malaya and, especially, Singapore, the latter alone handing 16,000 British, 14,000 Australian and 32,000 Indian prisoners into Japanese hands, most of whom were initially accommodated in the British garrison at Changi.[30] In total, the first four months of hostilities produced some 320,000 captives. For pragmatic reasons, the vast majority of the indigenous soldiers were just demobilized, leaving around 140,000 Europeans, Americans and Indians. Japan had been a signatory and had honoured the terms of the Hague Conventions, but had not ratified the 1929 Geneva Convention. In negotiations at the outbreak of war, the Japanese government had stated that it would act in accordance with the Convention, except when its terms conflicted with existing state policies. This gave the military leadership, and individual camp commanders, extensive latitude to behave in any way they wished.[31] In practice, this meant that the conditions experiences by POWs could vary enormously from one camp to another. Escapes were rare and seldom successful, not least because of the terrain and the lack of potential sanctuaries for those on the run. Severe collective punishments were also enforced against those remaining in camps where escapes were attempted.

29 *Nanking Senshi Shiryoshu* (2 vols., Tokyo: Kaikosha, 1993), vol. 1, p. 220.
30 Robert Havers, 'The Changi POW Camp and the Burma–Thailand Railway', in Philip Towle, Margaret Kosuge and Yoichi Kibata (eds.), *Japanese Prisoners of War* (London: Hambledon and London, 2000), p. 20.
31 Hisakazu Fujita, 'POWs and International Law', in Towle et al. (eds.), *Japanese Prisoners*, pp. 99–100.

Prisoners captured during the campaign were also used as a source of labour and removed to work in Japan or in Japanese-occupied territories, and perhaps most famously on the Burma–Thailand railway project. At its height, this project employed 61,000 Australian, British and Dutch prisoners, of whom 12,000 succumbed to the brutality and appalling living conditions they experienced.[32] The same project also cost the lives of some 90,000 of the 270,000 *romusha* (forced civilian local labourers) working alongside them.[33] For the Australians in particular, those on the railway have become the leitmotif for remembrance of the war in general, and of Japanese war crimes and their compensation in particular. The United States also lost many men to Japanese captivity after the invasion of the Philippines. This was epitomized by the isolation and surrender of its forces on the Bataan Peninsula in April 1942, and the subsequent forced march of the surviving 78,000 soldiers and civilians, who were severely beaten and abused by their guards, leading to several thousand deaths.[34] The Indians were shipped to Sumatra and New Guinea, where some attempts were made to get them to join the Indian National Army, but limited success meant that they were soon all being used as slave labour, often under the most appalling conditions.[35]

This concentration on the Burma Railway and Bataan masks the captivity of many thousands of other Allied servicemen who were held elsewhere in occupied Southeast Asia, sometimes for the whole of the war. Their existence was living proof of Japanese superiority over the white races, and they would sometimes find themselves paraded before local populations to indicate the bankruptcy of colonial rule. This was also done with the increasing numbers of prisoners shipped to mainland Japan for further interrogation or as labour, where their propaganda value as captured enemies could also be exploited. Some lost their lives when transport ships were sunk, but those who survived were deployed in a wide range of tasks, and their conditions in captivity on the home islands were remarkably varied.

The disgrace associated with surrender meant that relatively few Japanese service personnel fell into Allied hands before the final stages of the conflict.

32 Clifford Kinvig, 'Allied POWs and the Burma–Thailand Railway', in Towle et al. (eds.), *Japanese Prisoners*, p. 40.

33 Gavan Daws, *Prisoners of the Japanese: POWs of World War II in the Pacific* (London: Robson, 1995), p. 223.

34 Kevin C. Murphy, '"Raw Individualists": American Soldiers on the Bataan Death March Reconsidered', *War and Society* 31 (2012), 42–63.

35 Gerry Douds, 'The Men Who Never Were: Indian POWs in the Second World War', *Journal of South Asia Studies* 27 (2004), 183–216.

For example, of the 22,000 Japanese troops involved in the defence of Iwo Jima, nearly all fought to the death and only 216 were taken prisoner. In a vain attempt to establish some reciprocal bargaining power, Britain and the United States attempted to maximize their haul of captives by including all the merchant seamen they could find, but the estimated 35,000 could not begin to match the numbers held by Tokyo. A proportion of the 800 prisoners held at the Featherston POW Camp in New Zealand rioted in February 1943 after refusing to work, and thirty-one were killed. More famously, the Cowra POW camp in Australia held 2,223 Japanese, including 544 merchant seamen in August 1944, and rumours of their movement to another camp led to an uprising and the escape of 359 inmates, ultimately resulting in the deaths of 231 captives and four guards.[36] The subsequent inquiry recorded that many of the men were killed by other prisoners or died by their own hands. Japanese prisoners in New Zealand were sent home at the end of December 1945, but the last transports from Australia did not take place until 1947. All inmates voiced concerns about how they might be treated when they returned home, having suffered the disgrace of being captured.

The involvement of the USSR in the war against Japan began only in July 1945, but in the few weeks of campaigning, the Soviets managed to capture around 20,000 prisoners. This was dwarfed by the number who were surrendered at the war's end. Estimates range from 560,000 to 760,000, and nearly all were subsequently designated as internees to disguise their military status, and used in the Soviet Union, Mongolia or Korea as labour. In excess of 50,000 died during the winter of 1945–46, and a small number were repatriated, but the following year saw more than 500,000 registered in camps run by the GUPVI. In the years between 1946 and 1950, all but those convicted of war crimes were released, and the last survivors of this group were returned home in December 1956.[37]

Post-war repatriation and rehabilitation

In the aftermath of the German unconditional surrender on 8 May 1945, US forces had in total more than 5 million German prisoners, and the British more than 2.4 million, with the official figure quoted for all the Western

---

36 Charlotte Carr-Gregg, *Japanese Prisoners in Revolt* (St Lucia: University of Queensland Press, 1978).
37 Ulrich Straus, *'The Anguish of Surrender': Japanese POWs of World War II* (Seattle: University of Washington Press, 2003); William Nimmo, *Behind a Curtain of Silence: Japanese in Soviet Custody, 1945–1956* (Westport, Conn.: Praeger, 1988).

Allies in June 1945 being a very precise 7,614,794.[38] Those taken captive in the last weeks of fighting and at the point of unconditional surrender were corralled wherever space could be found. These were often little more than barbed wire enclosures with no shelter, including the American 'Rhine Meadow' camps, which had no tents for the first few weeks of their existence – a situation made worse by poor weather conditions. Facing chronic food shortages, General Eisenhower ordered that these newly taken German prisoners be re-categorized as disarmed enemy forces, which would remove them from the stipulations of the Geneva Convention. The British undertook a similar exercise in rebranding their Germans as surrendered enemy personnel. The conditions experienced by these men in the first weeks of captivity were desperate, with food rations below starvation rates in many areas. Camp guards were also unsympathetic to their plight and prepared to take some revenge. New recruits who had not been involved in the fighting saw a chance to show what they could do, while older hands resented the unnecessary losses they had sustained in the last stages of the campaign, and all had been appalled by their witnessing of the concentration camps. There have been claims that anything up to 800,000 German soldiers were deliberately allowed to die in American captivity, but this theory does not stand close scrutiny, and a figure of around 56,000 (or about 1 per cent) seems more likely – extrapolated from the known death rates in certain camps.[39] While conditions for displaced persons and civilians outside the camps were little better, prisoner release was determined by the slow pace of de-Nazification, as the Allies combed their captives for Nazis and war criminals.

Although many of the German prisoners held in the United States were held back to help with the harvest before their repatriation began, at least 500,000 of their counterparts in Germany were drafted into Military Labor Service Units for reconstruction work inside the American Zone. Those in Britain, who numbered almost 200,000 in April 1945, and were augmented by a similar number in the following year, had a somewhat different experience. Many were subjected to de-Nazification and re-education programmes, including those who were shipped back from other parts of the empire, such

---

38 For an in-depth discussion of the numbers, see Rüdiger Overmans, 'German Historiography, the War Losses and Prisoners of War', in Günther Bischof and Stephen Ambrose (eds.), *Eisenhower and the German POWs: Facts Against Falsehood* (Baton Rouge: Louisiana State University Press, 1992), pp. 127–69.

39 The original claims were made in James Bacque, *Other Losses: An Investigation into the Mass Deaths of German Prisoners of War After World War II* (London: Macdonald, 1990), but the rejoinder can be found in the chapters of Bischof and Ambrose (eds.), *Eisenhower and the German POWs*.

as Canada and Australia. However, their usefulness as a labour force in the British domestic economy, coupled with difficulties of returning them to a shattered homeland, meant that final repatriation was delayed, and the last Germans did not leave British soil until November 1948, with 24,000 opting to stay in the country. This was in line with the decision taken by the Foreign Ministers of the four powers in April 1947 to release all prisoners by the end of 1948.

Some prisoners of the British and Americans had rather different experiences of the immediate post-war period, as they were transferred to other Allied Powers as reparations, to help with reconstruction work. Thus substantial numbers were given to the French, Belgian, Polish, Norwegian and Dutch governments for this purpose. French animosity toward the Germans had already been reflected in the poor treatment afforded earlier captives and those handed over by the British to the Free French in 1944, but this did not prevent a further 740,000 being transferred by the Americans. Many were transferred from the Rhine Meadow camps, where the men were already malnourished and sick, and this was used to excuse the higher levels of mortality among those transferred into French hands. In practice, conditions undoubtedly varied, but many experienced ill-treatment, or employment in dangerous conditions – for example, carrying out mine clearance on the Channel beaches with only minimal equipment. Toward the end of 1945, the French authorities admitted that more than 2,000 prisoners were being maimed or killed each month as a result of this work, but relative mortality figures from both the Netherlands and Norway were similarly high. Poland was given 50,000 captured Germans by the Soviet authorities, but this was linked to an agreement on coal exports and, as a result, most prisoners were employed in the mines, working long hours in harsh and often dangerous conditions. In spite of the international agreement, continuing labour shortages dictated that the last of them were not released until December 1950.

A further complication for the Western powers was the large numbers of non-Germans captured in the last stages of the war, wearing Wehrmacht and, in some cases, SS uniforms. These included many Soviet citizens and former Red Army soldiers. In principle, the Allies had agreed to send all such people back to their country of origin, and thus some former Soviet soldiers captured in Wehrmacht uniforms during the Normandy campaign were sent directly back by ship to the port of Archangel in the autumn of 1944. London and Washington were keen to continue this policy in order to ensure the safe return of their own soldiers in Germans hands who were likely to be liberated by the Soviets. However, this policy was compromised by increasing resistance by those designated for repatriation, who were aware of Stalin's well-publicized attitude toward Soviet soldiers who had become prisoners of war. Perhaps the most well-known case was of the Cossacks, some of whom committed suicide rather than be returned to the USSR.

Repatriations from the Soviet Union began after the war ended, but even in 1949, the Russians retained around 85,000 prisoners reclassified as 'war criminals', sentenced to long periods of incarceration and hard labour. These captives subsequently became political bargaining chips, with some limited releases when the East German government experienced some political difficulties in the summer of 1953, and definitively in 1955 as part of the agreement reached with West German Chancellor Konrad Adenauer to restore diplomatic relations between the two states.[40] The Italians captured on the Eastern Front also suffered heavy losses. A lack of accurate information meant that the Italians still believed there were more than 60,000 of their soldiers in Soviet hands at the end of the war, and were therefore shocked when only around 21,800 were repatriated, a total that included many Italians liberated from German captivity.[41] Figures in the 1990s revealed that some 64,500 prisoners had been taken into captivity alive, but the majority had succumbed to the severe conditions of their transfer and incarceration. In post-war Italy, their fate became part of a feud between the Communist Party and the Army General Staff. The former tried to blame the wartime generals (some of whom were still in post) for the defeat and the catastrophic loss of life, while the General Staff countered by accusing the Soviet Union of responsibility.

Conclusion

After the First World War and the testing of the provisions of the Hague Conventions, to which most belligerents were signatories, further attempts to protect prisoners of war were made in the new Geneva Convention of 1929. Its existence spoke to the increased diplomatic and political importance afforded to prisoners by governments now answerable to public scrutiny for the treatment of their soldiers in captivity. However, the Second World War

---

40 Rüdiger Overmans, *Soldaten hinter Stacheldraht. Deutsche Kriegsgefangene des Zweiten Weltkrieges* (Munich: Ullstein, 2002), p. 258; Andreas Hilger, *Deutsche Kriegsgefangene in der Sowjetunion, 1941–46 Kriegsgefangenenpolitik, Lageralltag, Erinnerung* (Essen: Klartext, 2000), p. 137.
41 Elena Agarossi and Victor Zaslavsky, *Stalin and Togliatti: Italy and the Origins of the Cold War* (Stanford University Press, 2011), p. 160.

demonstrated that international conventions could only work when belligerent states were prepared to recognize their terms and then abide by them.
On the Eastern Front in Europe and in the Pacific War, the decisions made
not to adhere to the conventions meant untold misery and often death for
the millions taken prisoner in these conflicts; but even in the Western
theatres of war, reciprocity seems to have played an equally important role
in determining the nature and conditions of captivity. Moreover, much of the
statistical data relates only to those servicemen who were formally registered
as prisoners, and not to the many thousands, and possibly millions, who were
killed in the act of surrender and who are numbered among the dead or still
regarded as missing in action. In sum, there was no single prisoner-of-war
experience in the Second World War, even among those from individual
units, captured at the same time and incarcerated by the same belligerent
power. All had different personal circumstances and all reacted differently to
the prospect of long-term imprisonment.

24

Guerrillas and counter-insurgency

BEN H. SHEPHERD

This chapter surveys military and operational aspects of the main guerrilla and counter-insurgency campaigns across Axis-occupied Europe and Asia. It emphasizes historical precedents, concepts of insurgency and counter-insurgency, and how far expectations for such warfare were met.

The guerrilla warfare examined here is not identical to the 'Resistance', which encompassed a broader spectrum of activity, *including* guerrilla warfare. Nor is it identical to Allied 'special' forces, such as the Chindits, who operated behind Axis lines. Guerrilla warfare has a rich theoretical basis, the contributors to which include T. E. Lawrence and Mao Zedong.[1] It developed particularly extensively after 1945.[2] Drawing on such theory, the chapter defines guerrillas as irregular fighters operating predominantly in large, armed groups, usually native to the region of operations, from a rural base that is difficult to access. They operate among a largely rural population who, though not directly involved in 'guerrilla' activities, are essential for supply and intelligence. Guerrilla activities during the Second World War typically included sabotaging occupiers' communications and supply, exacting reprisals against native 'collaborators', mounting attacks of varying scale upon Axis occupation personnel, and attempting to broaden support among the population. Guerrillas

---

1 T. E. Lawrence, *Seven Pillars of Wisdom* (Ware: Wordsworth, 1997); Mao Zedong, *Collected Writings*, vol. II: *Guerrilla Warfare* (El Paso, TX: El Paso Norte, 2009).

2 For a theoretical overview, see Azeem Ibrahim, 'Conceptualisation of Guerrilla Warfare', *Small Wars and Insurgencies* 15 (2004), 112–24. *Guerrilla* means 'small war', though of course not all small wars are guerrilla wars. Though guerrillas in Axis-occupied Europe are usually termed partisans, this chapter uses the term 'guerrilla' throughout (save for Yugoslav Partisans, for whom 'partisan' was the name of their movement). Given its breadth and its space limitations, the chapter necessarily omits certain amounts of detail and coverage of certain territories. See bibliographical essay, and related CHSSW chapters by Jay Taylor, Hans van de Ven and David Stone in Volume I; and by Paul H. Kratoska and Ken'ichi Goto, William I. Hitchcock, Gregor Kranjc, Jürgen Matthäus, Davide Rodogno, Nicholas Stargardt and Margharita Zanasi in Volume II.

during the Second World War, fighting as part of a wider global conflict, were often aided by the Allies and, in the case of Soviet guerrillas, supported directly from an adjacent unoccupied national hinterland. Guerrilla commanders often aspired to eventually extending their operations to urban areas or fighting their opponents in conventional battle.

Counter-insurgency is a term dating from after 1945, but it describes an already long-established practice. Its broad aim is to complete or maintain successful military occupation, and to contain or annihilate guerrillas in order to secure communications and occupation administration. During the Second World War, counter-insurgency also sought to secure occupied territory for economic exploitation, and to render it safe for transit of supplies to the front line. Counter-insurgency pursues its aims through various methods. One extreme can be termed 'terror' – use of often disproportionate violence to end or deter either guerrilla activity or potential support for guerrillas by the local population. But terror also risks alienating local populations and increasing their support for guerrillas. The other broad approach involves gaining support from local populations, a process known after 1945 as 'winning hearts and minds', by providing genuine security or more favourable conditions. Complementing any approach are tactical military measures for locating and destroying guerrilla groups. Because its practitioners generally command or serve in organized armies, counter-insurgency arguably possesses an even richer theoretical basis than guerrilla warfare.[3]

The racial, political and economic frameworks shaping occupation policy, the abrupt manner in which occupation was imposed following rapid military conquest, and occupation's increasingly oppressive and exploitative implementation all helped to create the conditions that engendered guerrilla movements during the Second World War. Guerrilla warfare and counter-insurgency were further shaped by protagonists' military strengths and weaknesses, ideological and military doctrine, Axis and Allied strategy, and the role of external Allied agencies, such as the Special Operations Executive (SOE). An occupied territory's topography, its social and cultural make-up, and conditions in the field further shaped such warfare.

How local populations behaved was shaped primarily by their calculations regarding their day-to-day survival, in the face of guerrillas who often pressurized

---

3 See, for instance, Manual FM 3-24, *Counter-Insurgency* (Washington DC: Headquarters, Department of the Army, 2006) (http://fas.org/irp/doddir/army/fm3-24fd.pdf – accessed 22 October 2014); Beatrice Heuser, 'The Cultural Revolution in Counter-Insurgency', *Journal of Strategic Studies* 30:1 (2007), 153–71.

them to provide supplies and recruits, and Axis forces inflicting reprisals. Counter-insurgency forces usually believed that terrorizing guerrillas and their local supporters was a justifiable response to a particularly 'underhand' form of warfare. Indeed, guerrillas during the Second World War regularly flouted key criteria of legal combatant status stipulated in the 1907 Hague Convention: they were not readily identifiable, did not carry arms openly, and, particularly in the occupied Soviet Union, often maltreated and murdered Axis prisoners and indigenous occupation officials.[4] Axis counter-insurgency was also brutalized by harsh military tradition and ideology.

Yet the pre-war counter-insurgencies of the future Axis partners did not eschew hearts and minds measures entirely. Such measures were practised increasingly, if inconsistently, by various counter-insurgency campaigns during the earlier decades of the twentieth century.[5] It was factors *during* the Second World War that caused the brutal counter-insurgency inclinations of the Axis partners to outweigh their more restrained ones.

Europe, summer 1940 to autumn 1941

In one sense, organized guerrilla warfare in Europe during the Second World War began with the British. Following the fall of France, the British sought to hit back at the Germans while replenishing their own strength, and formed the Special Operations Executive to help train and coordinate resistance and guerrilla warfare in occupied Europe. SOE initially sought to optimize the use of resistance through the 'detonator strategy': building, supplying and training vast numbers of fifth columnists, who would then take their cue from a relatively small British invasion force, which would 'detonate' revolt in strategically important areas.[6] The British were drawing on several precedents here. They believed that fifth columnists had aided German victory in the West in spring 1940, and were mindful of such recent guerrilla campaigns as those of the IRA in Ireland and the Communists in the Chinese Civil War.

---

4 Aubrey C. Dixon and Otto Heilbrunn, *Communist Guerrilla Warfare* (London: Allen & Unwin, 1954), p. 85; John Horne and Alan Kramer, *German Atrocities 1914: A History of Denial* (New Haven, Conn.: Yale University Press, 2001), pp. 444–5.
5 John Ellis, *From the Barrel of a Gun: A History of Guerrilla, Revolutionary and Counter-Insurgency Warfare, from the Romans to the Present* (London: Greenhill, 1995), pp. 125–51; Ian F. W. Beckett, *Modern Insurgencies and Counter-insurgencies: Guerrillas and their Opponents since 1750* (London: Routledge, 2001), pp. 36–51.
6 Evan Mawdsley, 'The Major Allied Powers and European Resistance', in Philip Cooke and Ben H. Shepherd (eds.), *The European Resistance in the Second World War* (Barnsley: Pen and Sword, 2013), pp. 14–17.

They could also draw on the guerrilla warfare experience of former Spanish Civil War volunteers.[7] More broadly, Britain had vast experience of insurgency from combating it across the empire. Finally, Britain had utilized foreign irregular forces in many past wars, such as Spanish guerrillas against Napoleon between 1808 and 1814, and Arab tribesmen against the Turks between 1916 and 1918.

Britain's limited means in 1940, and the implausibility of covertly raising and training such a huge force under the Germans' noses, rendered the detonator strategy nonsensical. In 1941, following the German invasion of the Soviet Union, British interest in the potential of irregular warfare was increased by awareness of how overstretched German occupation forces were becoming. But the nascent guerrilla movements which emerged that year, in the Soviet Union and Yugoslavia, would initially enjoy only limited success.

Both countries were abundant in terrain favouring guerrilla warfare, and in historical traditions of irregular resistance to foreign occupiers. Yet aspiring guerrilla leaders would have done well to consider historical precedents carefully. Russian *partizan* forces *had* harassed Napoleon Bonaparte's army during his invasion of Russia in 1812, but the Russian winter had played the greatest part in destroying it. Serb irregulars *had* harassed their Ottoman Turkish rulers in the years up to 1813, but had then overreached themselves and been defeated by an Ottoman counter-offensive. Nevertheless, for reasons particular to each country, 1941 saw anti-Axis guerrilla movements emerge in both of them.

Following the invasion and defeat of Yugoslavia in April 1941, the partition of the country saw the creation of a new Axis-affiliated Croat state. Mass murder and expulsion of ethnic Serbs by the state's governing party, the Fascist Ustaša, sparked an influx of refugees into Serbia, mounting Serb unrest and, from July 1941, a widespread Serb revolt against the Axis. On 3 July, with Germany's invasion of the Soviet Union a fortnight old, Stalin issued a general call for Communists across Europe to take up arms against fascism.[8] Accordingly, the Yugoslav Communists took the reins of the Serb revolt and began recruiting, around a core of Yugoslav veterans of the Spanish Civil War, for their Partisan movement. The already overstretched

---

7 See, for instance, Tom Wintringham, *New Ways of War* (London: Penguin, 1940).
8 Rundfunkrede Stalins vom 3.7.41. Reprinted in Wolfram Wette and Gerd R. Ueberschär (eds.), *Der deutsche Überfall auf die Sowjetunion 1941: Berichte, Analyse, Dokumente* (Frankfurt am Main: Fischer, 1991), pp. 273–5. Cited in Ben Shepherd, *War in the Wild East: The German Army and Soviet Partisans* (Cambridge, Mass.: Harvard University Press, 2004), p. 73.

Axis occupation forces, supplemented by Serbian auxiliaries and gendarmes, found their control slipping, particularly when Draža Mihailović's Serb Nationalist Chetnik guerrilla movement suspended its antagonism toward the Partisans and joined forces with them.

The German response to the revolt was the real start of large-scale organized counter-insurgency in occupied Europe. In September 1941, the Austrian-born Franz Boehme was appointed Plenipotentiary Commanding General in Serbia, and committed powerful, temporarily assigned forces to crushing the revolt. He invoked ruthless higher-level directives, including the stipulation that a hundred Serbs be shot for every German killed, and issued similar directives of his own. In particular, partly to set a terrorizing example to the population, he directed disproportionate reprisal shootings against Serbian Jews.[9]

Such measures partnered Nazi ideology with longer-established Austro-German conceptions of counter-insurgency. The German military viewed guerrilla warfare as the antithesis of the 'proper' waging of war: destroying enemy forces in a swift, decisive, conventional battle. Its attitude had been hardened by experience of francs-tireurs (French irregular forces) during the 1870–71 Franco-Prussian War, and in later conflicts in Europe and German colonies overseas. During the opening weeks of the First World War, for instance, German troops advancing through Belgium and northern France, and Austrian troops advancing into Serbia, reacted savagely to the slightest civilian resistance, real or imagined. During the war's closing stages and immediate aftermath, the experience of combating Bolshevik and Bolshevik-inspired insurgents gave the ruthlessness of Austro-German counter-insurgency a pronounced ideological flavour.

Yet there was no straightforward continuity between such examples and the even more ruthless Austro-German counter-insurgency of the Second World War. The Austrians' occupation of Serbia from 1916 onward, for instance, was less brutal than their treatment of Serb civilians in 1914. And in Ukraine in 1918, some German commanders operating against Bolshevik insurgents sought to undermine their opponents' popular support by restraining the conduct of their own troops toward civilians.[10]

9 Walter Manoschek, 'The Extermination of the Jews in Serbia', in Ulrich Herbert (ed.), *National Socialist Extermination Policies: Contemporary German Perspectives and Controversies* (Oxford: Berghahn, 2000), pp. 171–8.
10 Peter Lieb, 'Aufstandsbekämpfung im strategischen Dilemma: Die deutsche Besatzung in der Ukraine 1918', in Wolfram Dornik and Stefan Karner (eds.), *Die Besatzung der Ukraine 1918* (Graz: Ludwig Boltzmann-Institut, 2008), pp. 111–40. Cited in Ben

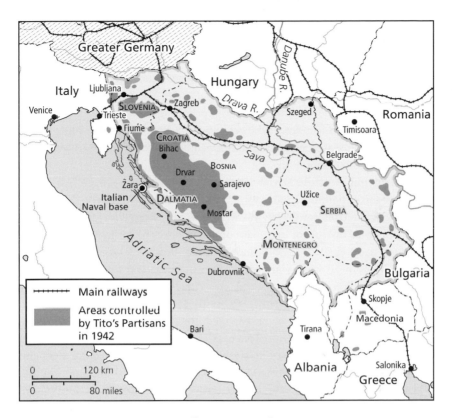

24.1 Guerrilla war in Yugoslavia, 1942

But in the freshly partitioned Yugoslavia in 1941, German counter-insurgency exuded not restraint, but ruthlessness. This was partly because of the particularly alarming situation. But it was also because ruthlessness chimed closely with Nazi ideological beliefs, beliefs that the military leadership widely shared and propagated among its troops. Boehme's directives displayed both Nazi ideological convictions and a then peculiarly Austrian animosity toward Serbs, founded on historical resentment dating back at least to 1914.[11]

German counter-measures alarmed the Chetniks, rupturing their already fragile alliance with the Partisans. The Partisans foolishly concentrated their

Shepherd, *Terror in the Balkans: German Armies and Partisan Warfare* (Cambridge, Mass.: Harvard University Press, 2012), p. 49.

11 For historical background to which, see Shepherd, *Terror in the Balkans*, chs. 1 and 2.

forces in a 'liberated zone' around Užice in western Serbia, rather than dispersing them in less accessible territory. This zone proved much less impenetrable than expected, and the Germans defeated the Partisans in conventional operations. The surviving Partisans, under Josep Broz ('Tito'), retreated into the mountains of the Croat state; the Mihailović Chetniks, fearing even more devastating German reprisals against the Serb population, were subdued into acquiescence. From 1942, Chetnik–Partisan antagonism grew increasingly violent, and Chetnik acquiescence to the Axis gradually developed into collaboration.

The beginnings of the Soviet guerrilla movement were even less propitious.[12] Stalin's regime initially disregarded the need to prepare the ground for effective guerrilla warfare in the Soviet Union's western regions. This was partly due to its distrust of irregular combatants, after Siberian and Ukrainian guerrillas had rebelled against authoritarian Bolshevik economic policies during the 1918–20 civil war. Moreover, before 1941, merely to suggest waging guerrilla war on Soviet soil was considered dangerously defeatist, doubting as it did the Red Army's ability to deter invaders at the border.

Stalin and his advisors soon changed their minds when the German invasion achieved alarming initial success and appeared to threaten the Soviet Union with annihilation. They now made a hasty attempt to ignite a general anti-Fascist revolt in the German rear, but it lacked any sound concept and was woefully unprepared. The first guerrilla commanders were local Communist officials, their rank and file mainly loyal officials and party members; virtually none had adequate military training or roots in the local countryside. Effective logistics and central control were lacking; so, too, was effective coordination, as the Red Army and the NKVD (predecessor of the KGB) secret police scrapped for influence. Efforts were also hindered by the less than effusive loyalty to the Soviet regime of rural populations in the newly occupied western borderlands; there, an initial wait-and-see attitude was adopted toward the invaders.

In fact, Wehrmacht security formations went into the Soviet Union subject to ruthless official guidelines, part of a corpus of what numerous historians have justifiably dubbed the 'criminal orders'.[13] These guidelines directed troops to use hostage-taking, reprisals and general harshness to terrorize

---

12 This chapter focuses on Soviet guerrillas, rather than on the less militarily important Nationalist guerrillas in Soviet regions. See the chapter by Nicholas Stargardt in Volume II ('Wartime occupation by Germany: food and sex').

13 See bibliographical essay.

occupied populations into subjugation. They were shaped by Nazi ideology, harsh counter-insurgency precedents, and the belief that the Wehrmacht's substandard, overstretched security units must exercise terror in order to compensate for their shortcomings. Jews, depicted in Wehrmacht propaganda as Bolshevism's puppet masters and instigators of any unrest in the German rear, were victimized in reprisals and in general from the start. On the other hand, many Wehrmacht commanders on the ground initially saw little sense in needlessly antagonizing the wider population, so far quiescent, and did not therefore implement ruthless higher-level guidelines as extensively as they might have done.

By late summer, however, German forces were increasingly unsettled by a guerrilla movement which, though insubstantial, was starting to land some blows on the occupiers' communications and supply. As it was, even substandard German troops were able, if often with difficulty, to suppress the even more substandard guerrilla groups they were facing. They received extensive support from SS *Einsatzgruppe* units, which roamed the rear areas, eliminating Communists, Jews and other sources of subversion, real or – more often – imagined. Partly in return for such assistance, high-level Wehrmacht commanders directed their units to tolerate and provide indirect support to the mushrooming mass murder of Jews by the *Einsatzgruppen* and other SS and police formations.[14] The rear areas now also contained hundreds of thousands of refugees and fugitive Red Army soldiers – people who, even if unarmed, might form nuclei of future guerrilla groups. Given the rising incidence of guerrilla attacks, the radicalizing intensity of the war in the East, and the ideological contempt towards Bolshevism and eastern Slavs which the German army shared at least partially with the SS, it comes as little surprise that the Germans increasingly directed their killing efforts against these groups also. As in Yugoslavia, then, it had taken circumstances *and* ideology to build on ruthless historical precedents and to brutalize German conduct.

The main reasons why guerrilla movements were so ineffective in 1941 were lack of preparation and, in the case of Yugoslavia, distrust and division. Both the Soviet and Yugoslav movements had sought to establish themselves in a chaotic and ill-conceived manner. They failed to meet essential criteria for effective guerrilla warfare, being insufficiently equipped, trained or supported. In Yugoslavia, they also lacked a suitable geographical

14 See chapter on 'Nazi Genocides' by Jürgen Matthäus in Volume ii.

base. Meeting these criteria did not guarantee a guerrilla movement's success, but not meeting them guaranteed its failure. Such, moreover, were the straitened circumstances of the two main Allied Powers, Britain and the Soviet Union, that they were unable to proffer significant help to guerrillas, let alone conduct an effective detonator strategy or a general anti-Fascist revolt. In these circumstances, European guerrilla movements could not withstand the pressure of often ferocious German counter-measures.

Yet though they had not achieved their ambitions, guerrilla movements in the Soviet Union and Yugoslavia had survived. In that sense, their failure was not complete; nor was the success of German counter-measures. From 1942 onward, both sides grew more cognizant of their limited means, and pursued more modest aims: guerrillas sought to build their strength and disrupt occupation, while the Axis increasingly sought to contain guerrilla movements rather than to suppress them altogether.

Europe, winter 1941/42 to spring 1943

Failure to defeat the Soviet Union in 1941, and growing Allied military and economic strength following the US entry into the war, precipitated important changes in Axis occupation policy. In particular, the Germans made increasingly concerted efforts to exploit occupied Europe in terms of labour, foodstuffs and other resources to feed their war economy's ever more desperate needs. Over time, the resulting deprivations and embitterment, above all over labour drafts and food seizures, buttressed support and recruitment for various types of resistance across Europe. So, too, from the end of the Battle of Stalingrad in February 1943, did a growing realization among occupied populations that the Axis was losing the war.

In the Soviet Union, saner heads within the German military and the German occupation administration, such as intelligence chief Colonel Reinhard Gehlen, hoped that imaginative political and economic initiatives would secure sufficient popular approval to at least contain any resurgent guerrilla movement. An example was the announcement, in February 1942, of the break-up of the widely despised Soviet collective farm system.[15] Yet the leadership of the Reich never accorded such initiatives sufficient support, and they were eclipsed by the Germans' increasingly voracious assault on the occupied Soviet Union's economic resources. The Germans' anti-guerrilla

---

15 Timothy P. Mulligan, *The Politics of Illusion and Empire: German Occupation Policy in the Soviet Union, 1942–1943* (New York: Praeger, 1988), pp. 93–105, 139.

effort employed large numbers of native auxiliaries, but these often enlisted out of economic desperation and possessed uneven military value at best.

Conversely, this period also saw the Soviet regime finally accord guerrillas more effective support and coordination. May 1942 saw a Central Partisan Headquarters established. New guerrilla groups were to include local activists and recruits, militia, NKVD commandos and special Red Army detachments. Stalin's September 1942 directive, 'On the Tasks of the Partisan Movement', stressed the importance of sabotage and subversion. The new approach also promoted the concept of 'all-people's war', in which guerrillas would seek to maximize popular support among the occupied population.[16] Meanwhile, the stabilization of the central and northern fronts, and increasing Soviet economic output, together boosted efforts to communicate with and supply the guerrillas. Belorussia, the occupied Soviet region hit hardest by German occupation, saw the largest increase in guerrilla sabotage and attacks on German and collaborationist personnel. Overstretched German-led security forces proved increasingly powerless to halt the increase. That said, their efforts to guard transport routes and economic installations were at least sufficient to prevent guerrillas from disrupting supply and administration to an extent that would have damaged the German war effort significantly.

Starting from a low base, and extensively dependent upon the quality of their leadership and the ease with which they could be logistically supported, some guerrilla units were more militarily effective than others. Furthermore, though some were more disciplined than others, many regularly plundered villages for supplies or coerced them for assistance more generally. One cause of such behaviour was higher-level sanction, founded on the belief that the lives and well-being of civilians were expendable in the pursuit of victory. Such an attitude, of course, contradicted the concept of 'all-people's war'. Outright collaborators were terrorized, but offered amnesty for defecting. The guerrillas undoubtedly reduced cooperation between local populations and the Germans, though exactly how far is unclear. But many guerrilla excesses, particularly the rape or murder of civilians, had less to do with calculating intimidation than with the riotous character of the more ill-disciplined groups.

The greatest peril to civilians in disputed areas was the German–guerrilla crossfire. Some German commanders advocated wooing the population

16 Kenneth Slepyan, *Stalin's Guerrillas: Soviet Partisans in World War II* (Lawrence: University Press of Kansas, 2006), pp. 40–59.

rather than terrorizing it. They employed various propaganda media, urged their troops to show restraint toward civilians, and sought to alleviate the worst effects of measures such as the labour draft.[17] On balance, however, brutality clearly outpaced moderation. From the second half of 1942, brutality was increasingly promoted and standardized by numerous directives emanating from Hitler and the military leadership, and by growing SS and Police control of counter-insurgency.

In Belorussia, above all, the Germans executed massive encircle-and-destroy operations (*Großunternehmen*) against purportedly pro-guerrilla areas. Civilians in the path of *Großunternehmen* faced indiscriminate killing or deportation, destruction of their villages and, particularly in 1943, plunder of their crops and livestock. Such destruction did not differentiate between guerrillas, civilians assisting them willingly or unwillingly, or civilians who happened to be in the way. It was also designed to deprive guerrillas of shelter and supply. Moreover, high body counts were used to suggest that *Großunternehmen* were succeeding. SS-led *Großunternehmen* were often used as cover for ideological aims: primarily slaughtering the remaining Jewish population, or reducing the Slavic population to levels conducive to future German colonization. But although *Großunternehmen* often temporarily disrupted guerrilla activity, they failed to destroy the guerrilla movement. The Germans usually lacked sufficient troops to secure the cordon or entrench security between operations, and the chaos the operations caused further fuelled popular resentment and, in turn, guerrilla support and recruitment.

In Yugoslavia, Tito's Partisans exploited the mountainous terrain of parts of the Fascist Croat state, and reconstituted their movement in eastern Bosnia.[18] They faced bitter rivals in the form of the Bosnian Chetniks, who comprised a sizeable amount of the Croat state's remaining ethnic Serb population. The latter, seeking to assert local Serb supremacy, often terrorized, expelled or slaughtered Croat and Muslim communities. By contrast, the Partisans appealed to all ethnic groups; Tito himself was a Croat. Moreover, as government control across much of the Croat state's hinterland dissolved, the Partisans' relatively disciplined behaviour and measured requisitioning benefited their support and recruitment. In autumn 1942, Tito, replicating the

---

17 Theo J. Schulte, *The German Army and Nazi Policies in Occupied Russia* (Oxford: Berg, 1989), pp. 150–79; Shepherd, *War in the Wild East*, ch. 5.

18 On Axis military performance against the Partisans, see Klaus Schmider, *Partisanenkrieg in Jugoslawien, 1941–1944* (Hamburg: Mittler, 2002), ch. 8. For an overview of Schmider's arguments, see Shepherd, *Terror in the Balkans*, pp. 236–42.

line of the Soviet 'all-people's movement', sought to broaden the Partisans' appeal by establishing a 'popular front' organization (AVNOJ), including non-Communist groups. This approach, not unlike the all-people's movement, was cynical; from late 1944, the Partisans increasingly employed terror to secure their post-war dominance. But it was useful in the short-term.

Tito also oversaw transformation of the Partisans' military organization; for instance, more effective troops were concentrated in especially well-equipped and well-trained elite detachments. Above all, Tito believed the Partisans must eventually transcend guerrilla warfare and face their opponents in conventional combat. Chetnik organization was amateurish by comparison; in March 1943, at the Battle of the Neretva, the Chetniks sided with the Axis against the Partisans, but the Partisans defeated them decisively.

But starting as it was from a low base, Partisan improvement was gradual, and interrupted by periodical Axis offensives. Though the Croat state was theoretically independent, it was actually occupied by German and Italian troops. To a great extent, German-led *Großunternehmen* here employed tactics similar to those employed in the Soviet Union, and with similar motives. Some German officers urged restraint; the commander of the 717th Infantry Division, for instance, argued that 'one must view the enemy as poorly-equipped troops, but not as bandits'.[19] But overall, *Großunternehmen* again killed non-combatants en masse while failing to destroy actual Partisan groups.

Some German tactics were more effective; for instance, newly constituted light divisions were better able to operate against Partisans by utilizing well-equipped but mobile troops in 'hunter groups' (*Jagdkommandos*). Yet in Yugoslavia, as in the Soviet Union, the Germans failed to consolidate such successes as they achieved with sustained pressure or sufficient troops on the ground between operations. By early 1943, partly for fear that the chaotic security situation might let in an Allied seaborne invasion, the Germans did employ more powerful forces of their own to the region, rather than rely on ineffective Croat and Italian troops. But these new forces were committed too late to prevent the Partisan movement from expanding. Germany and Italy also made ever-greater economic demands upon the Croat state, fuelling Partisan support and recruitment further.

Italian counter-insurgency possessed its own ruthless pedigree. From 1922, for instance, the new Italian Fascist regime intensified the racially permeated

---

19 Shepherd, *Terror in the Balkans*, p. 226.

ruthlessness of colonial counter-insurgency when its forces terrorized the rebellious Senussi in Libya. Shootings and public hangings, destruction of villages and livestock, and mass resettlement and incarceration were all employed. Italian counter-insurgency did not eschew moderation entirely; for instance, the Duke of Aosta, viceroy of the newly conquered Ethiopia from 1938, administered the country relatively humanely, employed reprisals selectively, and raised indigenous battalions to help combat guerrillas.[20] But in the Balkans during the Second World War, colonial-style ruthlessness, anti-Slavic racism and the Italians' sense of their own weakness together fuelled a counter-insurgency campaign that was harsh, cynical and ultimately self-defeating.

In the areas of the Croat state they occupied, the Italians relied heavily upon Bosnian Chetniks to keep the Partisans in check. But this policy gave Bosnian Chetniks licence to terrorize their ethnic 'enemies', further exacerbating inter-ethnic strife and causing civilians of all ethnicities to flock to the Partisans. The Italians themselves often destroyed purportedly pro-Partisan villages, and sometimes killed civilians en masse. Though they did not inflict body counts comparable to those of many *Grossunternehmen*, this tended to be due less to humanity than to lack of means. Higher-level directives encapsulated the harsh mentality; for instance, in March 1942, General Mario Roatta, Commander-in-Chief of the Second Army, issued a counter-insurgency directive designed to aid Italian colonization. It advocated mass internment and scorched-earth measures to clear areas of their Slavic populations.[21]

The period between winter 1941–42 and spring 1943, then, did not see European guerrilla movements start 'winning'; too many factors still constrained them. And divisions among Balkan guerrillas, together with logistical challenges, constrained efforts by SOE (and now also by its US counterpart, the Office of Strategic Services (OSS)) to support and coordinate

---

20 Angelo del Boca, *The Ethiopian War, 1935–1941* (University of Chicago Press, 1965), pp. 222, 247–9.
21 Davide Rodogno, *Fascism's European Empire: Italian Occupation During the Second World War* (Cambridge University Press, 2006), pp. 332–4, 343. Guerrilla warfare in Greece had much in common with its Yugoslav equivalent, in terms of historical precedents, causes (though, initially, famine played a large role in Greece's case), military limitations, political divisions, relations with the Allies, Axis counter-measures, and effects of the use of indigenous auxiliaries by the Axis. See chapters by Gregor Kranjc and Nicholas Stargardt in Volume II. See also Mark Mazower, *Inside Hitler's Greece: The Experience of Occupation, 1941–44* (New York: Yale University Press, 1992); Vangelis Tzoukas and Ben H. Shepherd, 'Greece', in Cooke and Shepherd (eds.), *European Resistance*.

guerrillas there.[22] But guerrilla groups were succeeding in consolidating themselves. They were becoming better equipped and trained, increasing their support, and making their presence felt by the occupiers.

Counter-insurgency terror, meanwhile, could only achieve so much when practised by overstretched forces against increasingly well-equipped, well-trained and well-supported guerrillas. Nor could it arrest growing popular resentment against increasingly rapacious occupation policies, or the perception that eventual Axis victory was increasingly unlikely. Indeed, in these circumstances, terror was becoming a counterproductive measure, guaranteed to alienate the population further. On the other hand, harder as it was becoming to contain guerrilla movements, Axis counter-insurgency forces were at least managing to slow their rate of growth. Nor were the core functions of occupation being dislocated by guerrilla activity to a degree that endangered the Axis war effort.

Europe, summer 1943 to spring 1944

Between summer 1943 and spring 1944, waning Axis military fortunes not only benefited guerrilla movements; they also caused guerrilla warfare to spread to new theatres. The period also saw guerrillas begin to assume an effective, if restricted, role as an adjunct to Allied conventional operations.

In the Soviet Union, the military shift against Germany following the end of the Battle of Stalingrad in February burgeoned in the months after the July Battle of Kursk. During that battle, moreover, guerrillas carried out extensive sabotage against German supplies and reinforcements – the first significant example of guerrillas working as an adjunct to conventional operations during the Second World War. This conception echoed the role of the Arab Revolt in Britain's campaign against the Turks during the First World War, and would be applied repeatedly over the next two years. Following Kursk, and the first of successive Soviet counter-offensives that would eventually see the Germans expelled from most of the Soviet Union a year later, Soviet guerrillas not only experienced further swelling in support and recruitment; they were also assigned new tasks. Stalin directed that, in addition to targeting German communications, guerrillas must protect local populations from the ravages

---

22 See, for instance, Michael McConville, *A Small War in the Balkans: British Military Involvement in Wartime Yugoslavia, 1941–1945* (London: Macmillan, 1986); Franklin Lindsay, *Beacons in the Night: With OSS and Tito's Partisans in Wartime Yugoslavia* (Stanford University Press, 1993).

of retreating German troops, and prevent the Germans from demolishing bridges and other transport installations helpful to the Red Army's advance. Guerrillas provided particularly important service on this latter score during the Red Army's crossing of the River Dnepr in autumn 1943.[23]

Only now did the Germans' conception of counter-insurgency in the Soviet Union start properly building on saner historical precedents, demonstrating an awareness of the counterproductive folly of their campaign's earlier brutality. For instance, a Wehrmacht high command directive of August 1943 instructed troops to treat captured guerrillas as prisoners of war rather than summarily shoot them.[24] But, not least because Germany was now losing the war anyway, such methods came too late to check the further growth in guerrilla numbers and activity.

And no such restraint informed German practice in Italy. July 1943 saw Italy begin defecting to the Allies, albeit not before the Germans occupied the country to head off an Allied advance north. There was an initial spontaneous wave of anti-German *Resistenza* across Italy, before the Germans, under Field Marshal Albert Kesselring, responded with savage reprisals. Kesselring, animated not just by brutal anti-guerrilla doctrine, but also by the aim of ensuring quiet conditions in a rear area so close to a battlefront, declared civilians collectively responsible for guerrilla attacks.[25] German counter-insurgency measures attained further ferocity through the Germans' feeling of betrayal by an erstwhile ally. There was also Italian-on-Italian violence. The Germans installed a puppet Fascist regime, the Italian Social Republic (RSI), in the north of the country. Its militias used counter-insurgency operations as cover to torture and execute 'traitors', irrespective of whether these were genuine anti-Fascists or merely ex-Fascists unenthusiastic about the RSI.

The Italian guerrilla movement (*partigiani*) had its genesis in the German invasion of September 1943, but its subsequent development was gradual. It initially comprised disparate groups fleeing persecution or forced labour. Their first concern was survival; only later did they acquire the strength, armament and leadership necessary to prosecute guerrilla warfare. Guerrillas came in different, sometimes antagonistic political shades; most numerous

---

23 Evan Mawdsley, *Thunder in the East: The Nazi-Soviet War, 1941–1945* (London: Bloomsbury, 2005), p. 236; Evan Mawdsley, 'Major Allied Powers', p. 24.

24 Hans Umbreit, 'Das unbewältigte Problem. Der Partisanenkrieg im Rücken der Ostfront', in Jürgen Förster (ed.), *Stalingrad: Ereignis, Wirkung, Symbol* (Zurich: Piper, 1992), p. 145. Cited in Shepherd, *War in the Wild East*, p. 140.

25 Massimo Storchi, 'Italy', in Cooke and Shepherd (eds.), *European Resistance*, pp. 127–8.

were the Communist Garibaldi brigades, especially prominent where Church influence was weakest.

Generally, however, antagonism among guerrilla groups was less destructive in Italy than in the Balkans. And the guerrillas' choice of environment and cultivation of popular support suggest that they had imbibed other lessons of effective guerrilla warfare. Their strongholds were largely in relatively inaccessible mountainous regions, such as the Apennines. They were proximate to peasant populations who were economically disadvantaged relative to the rest of the country, and therefore receptive to the reforms the guerrillas enacted in the areas they controlled. In order to avoid unleashing the Germans' full wrath upon the population, as well as to conserve their own strength, guerrillas usually made smaller-scale attacks. This particular contrast between Italian and Soviet guerrillas reflected, among other things, the different mentality of a guerrilla movement that was not the product of a ruthless Stalinist regime; indeed, though Italian guerrillas increasingly coordinated their efforts with the advancing Allies, they were not subject to rigid top-down direction. On the other hand, here, as elsewhere, the population was compelled, often resentfully, to keep guerrillas supplied, and had most to fear from Axis reprisals even for smaller scale guerrilla attacks. But by 1944, the scale of killing, destruction and plunder which German and RSI forces were inflicting was bringing guerrillas and peasants closer together.

Initially, the Allies were cautious about supporting Italian guerrillas. This was for various reasons, including Allied material limitations in a secondary theatre and concern about the Communists. Yet, by mid-1944, though they could have made more effort to utilize guerrilla-controlled areas as bridgeheads into Axis-controlled territory, the Allies increasingly saw guerrillas' value as an adjunct to conventional operations. Moreover, Allied air power was now well situated to make weaponry and equipment drops.

The disintegration of the original Italian Fascist regime and its armed forces also had important ramifications for guerrilla warfare in the Balkans. Here, copious amounts of Italian equipment and weaponry fell into Partisan hands. Moreover, though the Germans now took over the formerly Italian-occupied territories, they still relied upon indigenous forces to assume some of the counter-insurgency burden. In Yugoslavia, the task remained beyond Croat troops, and Bosnian Muslim units newly raised by the SS proved no lasting solution. The Germans, through *Großunternehmen* and mass reprisals, continued exercising a degree of terror that alienated the population even further. Then, during the second half of 1943, Britain, the main Allied power preoccupied with Balkan matters, shifted material support from Mihailović's ineffective Chetniks to Tito's Partisans.[26]

With their presence in Italy, moreover, the Allies were now well-placed to supply the Yugoslav Partisans by air. By early 1944, the Partisans in the Croat state were further burgeoning in strength, and German operations themselves were increasingly reactive, rather than shaped by any comprehensive conception of counter-insurgency. Nevertheless, claims that the Partisans tied down hundreds of thousands of German troops during 1943 and 1944 need qualifying: many such troops were stationed there mainly for fear of Allied landings, relatively few were stationed there long, and fewer still were of high quality. Nor, such were their residual combat limitations, could the Partisans fulfil their major aims of liberating Serbia and decisively defeating German forces in open combat.

Another new guerrilla theatre, albeit relatively subdued for the moment, was France. By September 1943, *maquis* groups comprised several thousand persons, mainly men, who had fled the German labour draft to live in socially egalitarian conditions in hilly, forested regions. The French police, on whom the Germans relied to administer the draft, frequently turned a blind eye to these groups. Though their direct participation in guerrilla warfare would come later, *maquisards*, too, exemplified how rapacious occupation policies boosted guerrilla membership, and how guerrillas could draw on broadly based support.

The period between summer 1943 and spring 1944, then, continued the overall trend toward guerrilla movements that enjoyed increased numbers, effectiveness, and support from both Allies and population. They also benefited from ever improving equipment and supply, not least courtesy of Allied air power. And divisions between guerrilla movements, though still present, no longer stymied guerrilla warfare's impact upon the occupiers.

Meanwhile, if some German counter-insurgency measures were insightful, they were also belated and piecemeal. Nor could they offset the brutality of German counter-insurgency. In particular, Italy's capitulation further stretched German security forces and, in doing so, further hardened their already brutal conduct. This in turn further alienated local populations. More generally, ever more exploitative occupation policies, and the growing likelihood of German defeat, undercut any remaining potential for German counter-insurgency to woo local populations with more considered methods.

---

26 For background to the surrounding controversy, see, for example, Simon Trew, *Britain, Mihailović, and the Chetniks, 1941–42* (London: St Martin's Press, 1997).

Nevertheless, beyond the Soviet Union and the Balkans, guerrilla movements were still in their infancy. And even in the Soviet Union and Balkans, although Axis efforts to contain guerrilla movements were waning, guerrilla movements' ongoing limitations continued to prevent them from making a more far-reaching impact.

Europe, summer 1944 to spring 1945

Summer 1944 saw guerrillas at their most numerous and active, expanding their role as adjuncts to conventional Allied offensives. Soviet guerrillas enjoyed the most success, extensively disrupting German supply and communications, and securing bridges and other transport installations, to help facilitate the massive offensive in Belorussia that brought the Red Army to the borders of the Reich. Yet the period to spring 1945 still exposed the residual shortcomings of guerrilla movements. It also demonstrated just how brutalized so much German conduct had become. The Italian setting provides examples of both.

Italian guerrilla membership had grown further by summer 1944, in reaction to the RSI's intensified press-ganging of civilians for labour in the Reich. Guerrillas were also coordinating their sabotage and intelligence-gathering efforts more effectively with the Allies. In early summer 1944, with Allied penetration of the Germans' Gustav Line south of Rome, guerrillas stepped up their attacks on Axis transport, communications and manpower. The Germans, under mounting pressure on the battlefront, were severely alarmed at this increase in rear-area unrest. Nevertheless, the guerrillas' membership surge caused shortages in equipment, food and weaponry, and by the end of the year they had failed to prevent German and RSI troops from overrunning all the *zone libre* the guerrillas had hitherto administered. The increasingly brutalized Axis forces inflicted reprisals that, especially in Tuscany, were more ferocious than ever. Over the winter, however, the guerrillas recovered sufficiently to play a sizeable role in the Allies' spring 1945 offensive. Among other things, they launched successful, if often violently contested, insurrections in several northern Italian towns and cities before the Allied armies reached them.[27]

In France, D-Day precipitated hundreds of sabotage operations, often supported and coordinated by SOE and OSS. Their impact varied, but their

---

27 Gustavo Corni, 'Italy', in Bob Moore (ed.), *Resistance in Western Europe* (Oxford: Berg, 2000), pp. 178–80; Storchi, 'Italy', pp. 128–9.

disruption to transport delayed many German units travelling toward the front, compelling them to take minor roads, where the *maquis* targeted them easily. But against the military value of these operations must be set the heavy loss of civilian life which the Germans then inflicted, in calculated reprisal or murderous frustration, at places like Vercors and Oradour. Moreover, when French guerrillas, untried in open combat, attempted to take on German troops in conventional clashes, they invariably came off worse. The Germans' brutal conduct toward civilians contrasted with their relatively measured reprisals during their earlier occupation of France. It was not just that some units involved, such as the SS *Das Reich* Division, were especially Nazified. Some, as was increasingly common among counter-insurgency units across what remained of German-occupied Europe, had imbibed a particularly harsh conception of counter-insurgency while fighting in the Soviet Union.[28]

Guerrillas' ongoing limitations were also visible in the Balkans. The Yugoslav Partisans, benefiting increasingly from Allied supply, converted themselves into a more conventional force. Yet it was not they, but the Red Army, that 'liberated' Belgrade in autumn 1944. In spring 1945, when Partisans fought conventionally against German and Fascist Croat lines west of Belgrade, they suffered heavy losses. But the shortcomings of guerrilla movements were most tragically apparent in East Central Europe.

The Polish resistance, mindful of the failure of nineteenth-century insurrections against Tsarist rule and fearful of German reprisals against the population, had hitherto largely restricted itself to activities such as intelligence gathering, while preparing for rural uprisings at the opportune moment. Ethically, this approach contrasted particularly with that of Soviet guerrillas; strategically, by waiting for the liberating army to arrive before rising up, it owed much to the detonator strategy. In late summer 1944, however, the Red Army's impending arrival prompted drastic, misconceived action. The main resistance group in Poland was the Polish Home Army (AK), the military wing of the government-in-exile in London. Its leaders believed that liberating the Polish capital was essential to strengthening the claim of the government-in-exile to post-war national leadership in the face of the imminent threat of Soviet domination.

But the omens were poor. In particular, the Western Allies were too far away to provide more than token assistance, and the Red Army halted short

---

28 Peter Lieb, 'Repercussions of Eastern Front Experiences on Anti-partisan Warfare in France, 1943–44', *Journal of Strategic Studies* 31 (2008), 797–823.

of Warsaw. It may have halted because it had outrun its supplies and faced German forces determined to defend the capital. Alternatively, it may have halted because Stalin wished to enable the Germans to annihilate the AK, thereby removing a potential obstacle to his aim of making Poland a Soviet satellite.[29]

Either way, the rising's failure was virtually guaranteed. Bereft of substantial Allied supply, the AK was also exposed in Warsaw's open spaces and committed to capturing heavily defended points, such as airfields and radio stations. The Germans defeated it with a devastating counter-attack, accompanied by bloodthirsty SS atrocities. In the battle's aftermath, they systematically destroyed what remained of Warsaw in order to prevent it from ever again becoming a centre of resistance. Such was the Nazi ideological view of the Poles that a hearts-and-minds type of response to Polish resistance was never a prospect. But German conduct of the Battle of Warsaw reflected a new level of harshness, fuelled by ruthless historical precedents, Nazi ideology and increasingly intractable conditions, but also by years of brutalizing fighting. The Germans did treat AK survivors as prisoners of war, though with an eye less to chivalry than to Germany's own impending defeat. They also viciously suppressed a major rising in Slovakia some weeks later.[30]

These events were a cruel reminder that, even by this stage, and for all their increased effectiveness, guerrillas could still only make a militarily meaningful impact under certain circumstances. Above all, their chances depended upon proper support and supply from the main Allied Powers, and upon acting in a clearly delineated role as an adjunct to conventional operations.

China, 1937–1945

Like the Germans and Italians, the Japanese were not inevitably predisposed to brutal counter-insurgency. For example, anti-bandit operations in Manchuria, annexed by Japan in 1931, often wooed local populations with 'peace preservation' measures, aimed at improving the quality of local officials, developing regional infrastructure and concentrating populations within protected villages.[31] But the Japanese lacked a viable concept of occupation

---

29 See, respectively, Mawdsley, 'Major Allied Powers', p. 28; Paul Latawski, 'Poland', in Cooke and Shepherd (eds.), *European Resistance*, p. 166.
30 Mawdsley, *Thunder in the East*, pp. 353–5.
31 Beckett, *Modern Insurgencies and Counter-Insurgencies*, p. 77.

for a long war; when they failed to defeat China swiftly following their 1937 invasion, they subjected the Chinese to organized plunder and barbaric cruelty in an ever more desperate effort to subdue them.

The invasion interrupted the civil war between the Nationalist Guomindang (GMD) and Chinese Communists (CCP), who now agreed an uneasy truce. China possesses an especially lengthy tradition of popular resistance to authority. It makes ideal guerrilla country, primarily through its size; this compelled the Japanese to defend strongpoints, and communication and supply lines, rather than seek to control the surrounding countryside. The primary guerrilla region during the period was the Japanese-occupied north.

GMD guerrilla operations did sometimes disrupt the Japanese considerably, particularly between late 1938 and early 1940. But by seeking actually to defend territory, GMD guerrillas exposed themselves to Japanese attack. Moreover, their often rowdy, marauding behaviour increasingly blighted local populations. GMD guerrilla warfare did not continue beyond 1943.[32] CCP guerrilla efforts were more sustained, but underwent a harsh learning process. Until spring 1940, operating from remote bases, they employed hit-and-run tactics, sniping at and occasionally attacking Japanese and collaborationist columns and strongpoints, and destroying roads. Primitive but effective communications, including signal fires, enabled the CCP to coordinate defence of villages. It cultivated popular support assiduously, raising local militias and organizing political and economic life in areas it controlled. Yet CCP guerrillas' numerical expansion diluted the quality and quantity of their arms and equipment.

In spring 1940, the Japanese, increasingly conscious of the CCP's threat to their control of northern China, intensified punitive operations against pro-CCP villages. From August to December, the CCP responded with an ambitious, conventional-style attack, the 'Hundred Regiments offensive', against significant points of Japanese control. But facing qualitatively superior Japanese troops, the CCP could not inflict lasting damage, and ferocious Japanese retaliation dealt it a severe blow. The Japanese targeted bases of guerrilla support and supply, killed civilians and destroyed villages indiscriminately, and flooded extensive areas. The Japanese military went to such lengths not just because of its alarm at CCP guerrilla operations, but also

---

32 See the chapters by Jay Taylor and Hans van de Ven in this volume. See also Hans van de Ven, *War and Nationalism in China, 1925–1945* (London: RoutledgeCurzon, 2003), pp. 283–6; Yang Kuisong, 'Nationalist and Communist Guerrilla Warfare in North China', in Mark Peattie, Edward Drea and Hans van de Ven (eds.), *The Battle for China: Essays on the Military History of the Sino-Japanese War of 1937–45* (Stanford University Press, 2011), pp. 308–27.

because of its anti-Chinese racism, frustration at its failure to defeat China rapidly, and contempt for a form of warfare that was anathema to its favoured doctrine – emulated from the Germans – of rapid offensive, encirclement and annihilation. In many ways, then, brutal Japanese counter-insurgency conformed to wider patterns not just of Japanese conduct in China, but also of Axis counter-insurgency.

Directed by Mao Zedong, the CCP returned to standard guerrilla tactics and rebuilt popular support and militia recruitment. It benefited from the fact that, between punitive operations, the Japanese lacked troops to control the interior and relied increasingly on substandard collaborationist personnel. Military demands elsewhere, in China or, from December 1941, against the Western Allies, thinned Japanese forces further. In these circumstances, the terror that Japanese counter-insurgency measures still periodically inflicted was more likely to increase CCP peasant support than undermine it. From early 1944, a replenished and expanded CCP guerrilla force increasingly aspired to fight the Japanese conventionally. That ambition, however, was rendered irrelevant by Japan's surrender in August 1945.

Like its European counterpart, CCP guerrilla warfare benefited from suitable geography, popular support fuelled by rapacious and oppressive occupation, and overstretched counter-insurgency forces employing increasingly counterproductive terror. The CCP's popular support, and the million-strong force it had amassed by 1945, would enable it both to triumph in the final round of the Chinese Civil War and to become a model for post-1945 insurgencies. In the context of the Second World War, however, CCP guerrilla warfare was just one of many ways in which China's vast geography and population subjected the Japanese to ever-increasing strain. The CCP's disastrous 1940 attempt at achieving more decisive results was supplanted by a conception of guerrilla warfare that recognized the forces constraining such warfare, as well as those facilitating it.

Southeast Asia, 1941–1945

Japanese military hard-headedness, racial disdain toward the occupied peoples and, above all, wartime economic pressure all rendered Japanese occupation of Southeast Asia increasingly ruthless and exploitative. Given also that much of Southeast Asia's terrain is heavily forested, hilly or mountainous, that several of its regions already possessed traditions of anti-colonial resistance, and that Japanese occupation forces were painfully overstretched, the potential for guerrilla warfare seemed clear.

But guerrilla warfare did not develop extensively. One obstacle was strategic: SOE and OSS provided little support for potential guerrilla movements in territories that were less strategically important to the Allies, such as Borneo and Sumatra. Other obstacles were political. Thailand, for instance, was officially independent of Japan. In Indochina, Allied hopes of utilizing sympathetic elements within the Japanese-supervised French colonial administration were dashed when the Japanese ruthlessly eliminated the administration in March 1945. In Malaya, a former British colony, the group best placed for guerrilla warfare was the Malayan Communist Party. In the event, the British backed the party; they were rewarded with anti-Japanese guerrilla activity during the war, but also a full-scale anti-British insurgency after it.

But the fact that much of their Southeast Asian territory was quiescent for much of the war meant that Japanese forces there generally lacked a clear concept of counter-insurgency. Their response to guerrillas could therefore be hesitant. Major General Orde Wingate commanded British long-range penetration units, not guerrillas, behind Japanese lines in Burma in 1943 and 1944, but he made the relevant observation that Japanese troops responded slowly and overly methodically to irregular warfare.[33] Yet Japanese counter-insurgency forces, including the ruthless Kempeitai military police, sometimes achieved considerable success. Exemplifying success and ruthlessness was their swift and ferociously punitive response to guerrilla attacks on Japanese police in Borneo in late 1943.[34]

Concern about Japanese retaliation, and the challenge to communications and supply posed by particularly inaccessible terrain, compelled caution in indigenous guerrillas and their Allied coordinators. Guerrilla movements were to be covertly built, trained and equipped, before being unleashed at an opportune moment to aid eventual Allied reconquest. This approach again alluded to the detonator strategy, and reflected awareness that guerrillas were most effective when supporting conventional operations.

One of the few Japanese-occupied territories with potential for guerrilla warfare was Burma.[35] Potential was strongest among the Kachin and Karen mountain peoples, despite particular difficulties in communicating with and

33 Simon Anglim, 'Orde Wingate, "Guerrilla" Warfare and Long-range Penetration, 1940–44', *Small Wars & Insurgencies* 17:3 (2006), 253.
34 Nicholas Tarling, *A Sudden Rampage: The Japanese Occupation of Southeast Asia, 1941–1945* (London: Hurst, 2001), p. 196.
35 On other such territories, particularly Malaya and the Philippines, see the chapter by Paul H. Kratoska and Ken'ichi Goto in Volume II; Paul H. Kratoska, *The Japanese Occupation of Malaya, 1941–1945: A Social and Economic History* (London: Hurst, 1998), pp. 289–96. See also bibliographical essay.

supplying them. Both had fiercely resisted British incursions during the nineteenth century. More recently, however, they had been advantaged by British policies, and now felt threatened by the Japanese-installed Burmese Nationalist government. From 1943, SOE organized guerrilla groups drawn from the two peoples to assist the British Fourteenth Army's eventual advance into Burma. For instance, the Karen, operating in particularly ideal guerrilla country, were well-situated to attack transport from Rangoon to Mandalay. The Kempeitai temporarily disrupted efforts in January 1944, arresting and torturing hundreds of Karen for aiding the British. But within a year, SOE was again coordinating its Karen groups effectively.[36] Early in 1945, they kept Fourteenth Army informed about Japanese dispositions, harried retreating Japanese troops, monitored their potential escape routes and called down air strikes against them.[37]

In many respects, guerrilla warfare in Southeast Asia faced similar challenges to its counterparts elsewhere. Its greatest impact came when it enjoyed similar advantages: a sufficiently inaccessible geographical base, overstretched occupation forces, popular embitterment at oppressive and exploitative occupation, effective Allied support, and a clearly defined role in coordination with conventional offensives.

Conclusion

Neither guerrilla warfare nor counter-insurgency determined the outcome of the Second World War. Not until 1944–45, operating in suitable terrain, and working as a properly resourced adjunct to conventional Allied forces, did guerrilla movements make a sizeable impact. And even then it was not decisive.

The limited achievements of guerrilla warfare during the Second World War contrast with numerous successful post-1945 guerrilla campaigns. But these campaigns enjoyed significant advantages over their forerunners. For instance, they benefited from technological changes to communications and weaponry. They were not conducted in the context of a global, total war; rather, they were often waged against a waning imperial power or a parliamentary democracy (or a nation possessing both characteristics), whose domestic population was disinclined to pay any price for victory.

---

36 Charles Cruickshank, *SoE in the Far East: The Official History* (Oxford University Press, 1986), pp. 166–70.
37 Ibid., pp. 186–90.

International legal constraints, Cold War tensions and increased scrutiny from the mass media all restricted a nation's freedom to prosecute unrestrained counter-insurgency. Comparing the performance of wartime and post-war guerrilla campaigns, then, is unfair.

If the military value of anti-Axis resistance was questionable, its moral and political value was considerable. Just by existing, resistance kept the spirit of freedom alive, and held out the promise that occupied peoples could help determine their future rather than wait passively to be liberated. However, this case can be made more strongly for lower-profile resistance, such as intelligence gathering and rescuing downed Allied pilots, than it can for guerrilla warfare. For set against the moral and political value of guerrilla warfare in Axis-occupied territory was the immense cost endured by the populations caught up in it. That cost could be higher still when guerrillas themselves terrorized civilians, or when they fought each other as much as, if not more than, they fought their occupiers.

Yet there is an argument, however qualified, for the moral and political value of guerrilla warfare, not least because some movements did seek to avoid antagonizing the occupiers unnecessarily and thereby limit civilian casualties. The case is strengthened further by the immense personal bravery of so many who were involved in guerrilla warfare. The importance of guerrilla warfare is further reflected in the prominent role of former guerrillas in immediate post-occupation politics and conflicts.[38] The guerrillas' main *military* value during the Second World War, meanwhile, lies in the fact that they did eventually provide worthwhile, if uneven, support for Allied conventional operations.

Such success, in turn, reflected not just the increasing strength of guerrilla movements, but also the increasing ineffectiveness of Axis counter-insurgency. Brutal historical precedent, racist ideology and mounting frustration fuelled an ever more counterproductive Axis predilection for terror. Some military measures, such as *Jagdkommandos*, did achieve results. But such results would have been more durable had they been combined less with increasing reliance on terror and more with hearts-and-minds measures. They would also have been more durable had the troops implementing them been of greater quality and quantity. Generally, any benefits that were accrued by attempts at such a combined approach were outweighed by the

<hr/>

38 See the chapters by William I. Hitchcock and Gregor Kranjc in Volume II.

increasingly alienating occupation policies the Axis implemented in response to ever more daunting wartime pressures.

Axis counter-insurgency *was* successful in that it prevented guerrilla movements from actually overthrowing the occupation. But had it been better-resourced and conducted with more insight from the outset, it would have contained guerrilla movements more effectively, and with less cost to and perhaps greater help from local populations. It might even have succeeded in suppressing guerrilla movements altogether. But the extent to which Axis forces were influenced by harsh ideology,[39] and the collective failure of the Axis to reconcile grandiose strategic aims with limited military and economic means, combined to preclude more effective counter-insurgency. For this combination guaranteed both ever more rapacious occupation policies and a campaign to safeguard them that was both over-stretched and brutally inclined. In those circumstances, achieving the necessary scale of rational, well-resourced and truly effective counter-insurgency was impossible.

---

39 Generally, the brutality of much Wehrmacht counter-insurgency doctrine and conduct notwithstanding, there remained a certain distinction between its degree of counter-insurgency brutality and that of the SS and Police.

Bibliographical essays

1 British military strategy
David French

The idea of the 'British way in warfare' was first developed by the journalist and strategist Sir Basil Liddell Hart, in his book *The British Way in Warfare* (London: Faber & Faber, 1932). The shortcomings of his thesis have been exposed by Michael Howard, 'The British Way in Warfare: A Reappraisal', in Michael Howard, *The Causes of War and Other Essays* (London: Temple, Smith, 1983), pp. 169–87. David French, *The British Way in Warfare, 1688–2000* (London: Allen & Unwin, 1990), reflects upon the realities of a British tradition of grand strategy over the last 300 years. The tradition of appeasement in British defence policy has been examined by Paul Kennedy, *The Realities Behind Diplomacy: Background Influences on British External Policy, 1865–1980* (London: Fontana, 1981).

The indispensable starting point for an analysis of British military strategy during the Second World War remains the official histories written by various hands: *Grand Strategy* (6 vols., London: HMSO, 1956–76). However, because they were published before the revelation that from 1940 onward British codebreakers were progressively able to read high-level German signals, they must be supplemented by the official histories of British intelligence, written by F. H. Hinsley et al. (eds.), *British Intelligence in the Second World War: Its Influence on Strategy and Operations* (4 vols., London: HMSO, 1979–90).

Pre-war military planning should be approached through N. H. Gibbs, *Grand Strategy. Vol. I: Rearmament Policy* (London: HMSO, 1976), supplemented by Brian Bond, *British Military Policy between the Wars* (Oxford: Clarendon Press, 1980); Malcolm Smith, *British Air Strategy between the Wars* (Oxford: Clarendon Press, 1984); and Stephen Roskill, *Naval Policy between the Wars. Vol. II: The Period of Reluctant Rearmament 1930–39* (London: Collins, 1984). Brief overviews of the three armed services during the war are provided by Corelli Barnett, *Engage the Enemy More Closely: The Royal Navy*

716

in the Second World War (London: Penguin, 2000); David French, *Raising Churchill's Army: The British Army and the War against Germany, 1918–45* (Oxford University Press, 2000); and John Terraine, *The Right of the Line: The Royal Air Force in the European War* (London: Hodder & Stoughton, 1985).

The development of military strategy from the outbreak of the war, through to the fall of France and the entry into the conflict of the USSR and the USA can be traced in Talbot Imlay, *Facing the Second World War: Strategy, Politics and Economics in Britain and France, 1938–1940* (Oxford University Press, 2003); David Stafford, 'The Detonator Concept: British Strategy, SOE and European Resistance after the Fall of France', *Journal of Contemporary History* 10:2 (1975), 185–217; Sheila Lawlor, *Churchill and the Politics of War, 1940–41* (Cambridge University Press, 1994); B. Farrell, 'Yes, Prime Minister: Barbarossa, Whipcord, and the Basis of British Grand Strategy, Autumn 1941', *Journal of Military History* 57 (1993), 599–625; and David Reynolds, 'Churchill and the British "Decision" to Fight On in 1940: Right Policy, Wrong Reasons', in Richard Langhorne (ed.), *Diplomacy and Intelligence During the Second World War: Essays in Honour of F. H. Hinsley* (Cambridge University Press 1985), pp. 147–67.

Churchill's role in the making of British policy has been examined by Geoffrey Best, *Churchill and War* (London: Hambledon and London, 2005); and Carlo d'Este, *Warlord: A Life of Winston Churchill at War, 1874–1945* (London: Harper Collins, 2008). Alex Danchev and Dan Todman (eds.), *War Diaries 1939–1945: Field Marshal Lord Alanbrooke* (London: Weidenfeld & Nicolson, 2001), provide fascinating insights into the daily problems faced by some of the key decision-makers who shaped British military strategy.

The literature on the Mediterranean strategy and OVERLORD is immense. Good starting points include Tuvia Ben-Moshe, 'Winston Churchill and the Second Front: A Reappraisal', *Journal of Modern History* 62 (1990), 503–38; the same author's *Churchill: Strategy and History* (Hemel Hempstead: Harvester Wheatsheaf, 1992); Alex Danchev, 'Waltzing with Winston', in P. Smith (ed.), *Government and the Armed Forces in Britain 1856–1990* (London: Hambledon and London, 1996), pp. 191–216; Michael Howard, *The Mediterranean Strategy in the Second World War* (Cambridge University Press, 1993); and Matthew Jones, *Britain, the United States and the Mediterranean War, 1942–1944* (London: St Martin's Press, 1996).

James Neidpath, *The Singapore Naval Base and the Defence of Britain's Eastern Empire, 1919–1941* (Oxford: Clarendon Press, 1981), Brian Farrell, *The Defence and Fall of Singapore 1940–1942* (Stroud, 2006), and C. Bell, 'The "Singapore Strategy" and the Deterrence of Japan: Winston Churchill, the Admiralty and the Dispatch of Force Z', *English Historical Review* 116 (2001), 604–34, have explored the rise and failure of the 'Singapore strategy'. The British war effort in the Far East thereafter can be followed in Louis Allen, *Burma: The Longest War 1941–45* (London: Phoenix, 2000), and Brian Bond and Kyoichi Tachikawa (eds.), *British and Japanese Military Leadership in the Far Eastern War 1941–1945* (London: Cass, 2004); and Russell Miller, *Uncle Bill: The Authorised Biography of Field Marshal Viscount Slim* (London: Weidenfeld & Nicolson, 2013).

2 China's long war with Japan
Jay Taylor

Writings by important participants in the long Sino-Japanese war can be found in numerous memoirs and other monographs. Probably the most important and largest single personal as well as archival source is *Jiang Jieshi er ji* (Chiang Kai-shek Diaries) (Stanford, Calif., Chiang Kai-shek Collection, Hoover Institution Archives, Stanford University, initial release to the public 2007). This massive collection, which of course provides only Chiang's views, covers his career from 1916 to 1972. Critically read and balanced, with a good range of contrary accounts, it is a key source for a new and more balanced understanding of the war's political and international dynamics, as well as Chiang's decisions before, during and after China's most traumatic war since the Mongol invasion.

Another valuable collection, consisting of twelve volumes, edited by Chiang's one-time secretary, Qin Xiaoyi, contains not just excerpts from the Chiang diaries, but also other selected Nationalist memos, radiograms, letters and speeches. Prepared by the GMD Historical Office, it may have left out embarrassing items, but it does not seem to have rewritten content – as seen, for example, by a detailed comparison of selections in Qin's work with the same passages in the actual, original diaries. Qin's series is titled *Zong tong Jiang gong da shi chang pian chu gao* (Preliminary Draft of President Chiang's Chronological Biography) (12 vols., Taipei: Chung Chang Cultural and Educational Foundation, various years).

A critical insider view of wartime events and of Chiang's entire leadership on the mainland was written by one of his warlord generals, Li Tsung-jen. Li wrote his autobiography – *The Memoirs of Lee Tsung-jen* (Boulder, Colo.: Westview, 1979) – with Tong Te-kong. Li and his Guangxi fellow warlord, Bai Chongxi, turned out to be among the best Chinese generals against the Japanese. Another important figure during Chiang's mainland years, Chen Lifu, also wrote an interesting and sometimes critical memoir: *The Storm Clouds Over China* (Stanford, Calif.: Hoover Institute Press, 1994).

Among the hundreds of other recollections by actors in the war in various military and civilian positions is Ray Huang, *Chiang Kai-shek and his Diary as a Historical Source* (Armonk, NY: M. E. Sharpe, 1996). Huang was a Nationalist army officer and has a unique feel for what Chiang Kai-shek was thinking.

For a first-hand review and analysis of economic and financial issues during the war, see two essential books by Arthur Young: *China and the Helping Hand, 1937–1945* (Cambridge, Mass.: Harvard University Press, 1963) and *China's Wartime Finance and Inflation* (Cambridge, Mass.: Harvard University Press, 1965). A more modern and comprehensive source is: William C. Kirby, Man-houng Lin, James Chin Shih and David A. Pietz (eds.), *State and Economy in Republican China: A Handbook for Scholars* (2 vols., Cambridge, Mass.: Harvard University Asia Center, 2001). A 2005 study by Martin L. Bian, *The Making of the State Enterprise System in Modern China* (Cambridge, Mass.: Harvard University Press), provides a detailed assessment of Chiang's efforts at modernization, including during the sharply austere war years.

For up-to-date surveys of the war that embrace key material available only in the past twenty years, see Mark Peattie, Edward J. Drea and Hans van de Ven (eds.), *The Battle for China* (Stanford University Press, 2011). Some of the chapters were originally papers produced for the Harvard University Conference on the Sino-Japanese War at Maui in 2011. They comprise a major piece of work. See, especially: Hans van de Ven and Edward J. Drea, 'Chronology of the Sino Japanese War' (pp. 7–26) and 'An Overview of Major Military Campaigns During the Sino-Japanese War' (pp. 27–47); Mark Peattie, 'The Dragon's Seed. Origins of the War' (pp. 48–78); Chiang Jui te, 'The Nationalist Army on the Eve of the War' (pp. 83–104); Yang Tianshi, 'Chiang Kai-shek and the Battles of Shanghai and Nanjing' (pp. 143–58); Hagiwara Mitsuru, 'The Japanese Air Campaigns in China, 1937–1945' (pp. 159–255); Zhang Baijia, 'China's Quest for Foreign Military Aid' (pp. 283–307); Yang Kuisong, 'Nationalist and Communist Guerrilla Warfare in North China' (pp. 308–27); Steven Mackinnon, 'The Defense of the Central Yangtze' (pp. 181–206); and Tomatsu Haruo, 'The Strategic Correlation Between the Sino-Japanese and Pacific Wars' (pp. 423–45).

Also outstanding is Rana Mitter's *Forgotten Ally: China's World War II, 1937–1945* (Boston, Mass.: Houghton Mifflin Harcourt, 2013) – an excellent and balanced account of the strange alliance in the historic fight for the future of Chinese civilization. Hans van de Ven's *War and Nationalism in China, 1925–1945* (London: Routledge, 2003) is a pioneer revisionist account of the Nationalist period and the entire war.

A large number of monographs published before the availability of the Chiang diaries and new post-Soviet era material from Chinese and Soviet archives still provide excellent studies on the entire war or specific issues or periods. Due to the absence of critical documents, however, some efforts miss the complexity of the Sino-American relationship. James C. Hsiung and Steven I. Levine (eds.), *China's Bitter Victory* (Armonk, NY: M. E. Sharpe, 1992) provides insightful papers on political and diplomatic issues. Lloyd E. Eastman, *The Nationalist Era in China, 1927–1949* (pbk edn, New York: Cambridge University Press, 1991), and Hsi-heng Ch'i, *Nationalist China at War: Military Defeat and Political Collapse* (Ann Arbor: University Michigan Press, 1982) are highly respected earlier works. For the dynamics of Japan's decision for a major, fairly short war in China, with limited goals, but which led to a costly eight-year conflict and, eventually, Pearl Harbor, see Akira Iriye, *The Origins of the Second World War in Asia and the Pacific* (London: Routledge, 1987). The fascinating subject of intelligence during the war in Asia is in Jerrold Schechter and Leona Schechter's *Sacred Secrets* (Washington DC: Brassey's, 2002), which reveals the important role of the famous Soviet spy, Richard Sorge, to Chiang's diplomacy.

For the key subject of Stalin's relations with the Nationalists and the Communists, see the ground-breaking book and articles by John W. Garver: *Chinese-Soviet Relations, 1937–1945* (New York: Oxford University Press, 1988), and 'Chiang Kai-shek's Quest for Soviet Entry into the Sino-Japanese War', *Political Science Quarterly* 102:2 (summer 1987), 295–316. Alexander Dallin and F. I. Firsov's *Dimitrov and Stalin, 1934–1943: Letters from the Soviet Archives* (New Haven, Conn.: Yale University Press, 2000), provides remarkable information on Soviet relations with and substantial aid provided to the CCP from 1927 to the early 1940s. The Comintern Archival Collection in the Russian State Archives of Social and Political History in Moscow also offers over a hundred valuable communications between the Comintern and the CCP's Central Committee in Shanghai.

Minguo dang an (Republican Archive), the journal of the Second National (Guomindang) Archive at Nanjing includes a fascinating variety of articles – for example, on correspondence between Chiang Kai-shek and Stalin, and Stalin and Voroshilov (the Soviet agent stationed at Yan'an), as well as H. H. Kong's talks with Hitler and Göring, and Nationalist General Chen Cheng's wartime recollections. Alexander Pantsov and Steven I. Levine's *Mao: The Real Story* (New York: Simon & Schuster, 2007), is a different and effective treatment of this dramatic and much assessed figure, drawing on additional rich, new material from the Soviet archives, including unique documents on Soviet aid to the Chinese Communists.

For interpretations of Nationalist–Communist rivalry, see Robert Kapp, 'The Kuomintang and Rural China in the War of Resistance, 1937–1945', in E. Gilbert Chan (ed.), *China at the Crossroads: Nationalists and Communists, 1927–1949* (Boulder, Colo.: Westview, 1980); and Chalmers Johnson, *Peasant Nationalism and Communist Power* (Stanford University Press, 1962). The latter argues that the Communist Party's radical economic ideology was not popular with the rural population of China and that it was nationalism, not ideology, which won the day for Mao Zedong. For a rebuttal to this thesis, see Donald G. Gillin, '"Peasant Nationalism" in the History of Chinese Communism', *Journal of Asian Studies* 23:2 (February 1964), 269–89.

The critical, standard American source on US relations with China during the war is the declassified Department of State and other US Government documents in the series, *Foreign Relations of the United States* (Washington DC: U.S. Government Printing Office, various years), http://history.state.gov/historicaldocuments (accessed 3 December 2014). The improbable Stilwell–Chiang imbroglio, which lasted until the last year of the war, is covered in depth by Charles F. Romanus and Riley Sunderland, who draw on voluminous US military archives in their three volumes on the *China, Burma, India Theater: Stilwell's Mission to China* (1953), *Stilwell's Command Problems* (1956) and *Time Runs Out in the CBI* (1959) (3 vols., Washington DC: US Army Center of Military History). Herbert Feis's *The China Tangle: The American Effort in China from Pearl Harbor to the Marshall Mission* (Princeton, NJ: Princeton University Press, 1953) is an early, but still very useful and insightful examination of the competing personalities, political currents and events driving the changing American policies regarding China's strategic role in the war.

Laura Tyson Li's *Madam Chiang Kai-shek* (New York: Atlantic Monthly Press, 2006) is the best, up-to-date account of Soong Mei-ling's role during the war. Theodore H. White (ed.), *The Stilwell Papers* (London: Macmillan, 1949), is, of course, a must-read for the Stilwell side of his conflict with Chiang. Likewise with the well-known study by Barbara Tuchman, *Sand Against the Wind: Stilwell and the American Experience in China* (London: Macmillan, 1971) – a view of the Stilwell–Chiang conflict based largely on the former's diaries and letters.

Also available is Jay Taylor's biography, *The Generalissimo: Chiang Kai-shek and the Struggle for Modern China* (Cambridge, Mass.: Harvard University Press, 2009).

3 French grand strategy and defence preparations
Martin S. Alexander

The literature on French interwar diplomacy, defence and the defeat of 1940 is vast. To explain this, the distinguished French international historian, Jean-Baptiste Duroselle, in his much-referenced book on French external policy from 1932–39, *La Décadence* (Paris: Imprimerie Nationale, 1979), invoked Montesquieu: big and important events have big explanations. French disappointment with the 1919 peace settlement was addressed by Herbert Tint in his *France since 1918* (London: Batsford, 1970); Jacques Néré's *The Foreign Policy of France from 1914 to 1945* (London: Routledge and Kegan Paul, 1975); and, most recently, in Zara Steiner's masterly *The Lights that Failed: European International History, 1919–1933* (Oxford University Press, 2005) and its sequel, *The Triumph of the Dark: European International History, 1933–1939* (Oxford University Press, 2011).

Interpretatively significant remains Philip C. F. Bankwitz's book, *Maxime Weygand and Civil-Military Relations in Modern France* (Cambridge, Mass.: Harvard University Press, 1967). This catalogued a profound rift between Third Republic political culture and a powerful conservative value system that warped the outlook of the senior French officer corps toward politicians and the regime. For many officers, according to this reading, defeat was not just inevitable, it was a release from intractable dilemmas. But perceptive studies of French interwar defence showed the perfectly logical emphasis on fortifications, including Vivian Rowe's *The Great Wall of France* (London: Putnam, 1959); P.-E. Tournoux's *Défense des Frontières: Haut Commandement-Gouvernement, 1919–1939* (Paris: Nouvelles Editions Latines, 1960); and Judith M. Hughes' *To the Maginot Line: The Politics of French Military Preparation in the 1920s* (Cambridge, Mass.: Harvard University Press, 1971).

Several scholars, mostly from Canada and the USA, sought to revise the 'decadence thesis' from the late 1970s onward. Robert J. Young argued in his book, *In Command of France: French Foreign Policy and Military Planning, 1933–1940* (Cambridge, Mass.: Harvard University Press, 1978), that French leaders enjoyed some success in fashioning rational, pragmatic policy responses to their interlocked conundrums: too few resources of their own after the exsanguination of 1914–18, too few allies, too many potential enemies. Developing these themes, Martin S. Alexander's *The Republic in Danger* (Cambridge University Press, 1993) emphasized the skilled politico-bureaucratic machinations of Weygand's successor as French army chief, General Gamelin, from 1935 to May 1940. Gamelin, in this view, cooperated with his Minister for National Defence and War, Edouard Daladier, preserved the fragile civil-military consensus, partly palliated the shortage of allies, and ensured that the French army – though not the air force, never under Gamelin's direct command – was sufficiently re-armed by 1939–40 to give Franco-British grand strategy a prospect of success. That strategy entailed stalemating any early Axis offensives; then securing victory by a naval blockade of Germany, mobilizing the combined Anglo-French empires, and drawing in more allies: Belgium and the Netherlands, the Scandinavians, Portugal and the USA.

The 1940 defeat prompted highly politicized accounts from 1945 onward – indeed, even sooner. These pitted Vichyite apologias against Resistance and Gaullist narratives. The former ascribed the disaster to defeatism, rooted in a long rise of individualistic, pacifist and irreligious sentiments – termed by Herbert Tint, *The Decline of French Patriotism, 1870–1940* (London: Weidenfeld & Nicolson, 1964). The counter-narratives drew on a patriotic conservatism in the case of Gaullists, and on a class-based and Communist Party dominated discourse of refusal to submit meckly to Nazism. Serious scholarly research lagged – partly because of high court trials in 1945–7, a parliamentary inquiry from 1945–51, and the polemics aroused by the merest mention of Pétain. But it was also because French government archives remained closed. Thus the best studies from *c.* 1950–75 came from Britons and North Americans – journalists and independent authors such as John Williams, *The Ides of May: The Defeat of France, May–June 1940* (London: Constable, 1968); William L. Shirer, *The Collapse of the Third Republic: An Inquiry into the Fall of France in 1940* (New York: Simon & Schuster, 1969); and Alistair Horne, *To Lose a Battle: France 1940* (London: Macmillan, 1969). Academics also contributed, most notably Philip M. H. Bell of the University of Liverpool, with *A Certain Eventuality: Great Britain and the Fall of France* (Farnborough: Saxon House, 1974); and John C. Cairns of the University of Toronto, with a portfolio of seminal articles, including 'Great Britain and the Fall of France: A Study in Allied Disunity', *Journal of Modern History* 27:4 (December 1955), 365–409, and 'Along the Road Back to France, 1940', *American Historical Review* 64:3 (April 1959), 583–603.

The opening of the official French archives permitted wider-ranging scholarly investigations after 1975. Notable works included Jeffery A. Gunsburg's detailed treatment, *Divided and Conquered: The French High Command and the Defeat of the West, 1940* (Westport, Conn.: Greenwood Press, 1979). Major books on the 1936–38 Popular Front left-centre government followed, from Julian Jackson, *Defending Democracy: The Popular Front in France, 1934–38* (Cambridge University Press, 1988); Nicole Jordan, *The Popular*

Front and Central Europe: The Dilemmas of French Impotence, 1918–1940 (Cambridge University Press, 1991), highly critical of Gamelin and French military passivity while Hitler annexed territories in East Central Europe; and Norman Ingram, with an authoritative analysis of interwar anti-militarism and conscientious objection, *The Politics of Dissent: Pacifism in France, 1919–1939* (Oxford: Clarendon Press, 1991).

Previously separate strands of work converged from the late 1990s, thanks to the constructive initiatives of a younger generation of French scholars, such as Maurice Vaisse and Robert Frank. They travelled, undertook research in German, Italian and Anglophone archives, and embraced opportunities to co-work with non-French scholars. This all added richer textures and fresh perspectives to the complexities of 1919–45. Two explorations were published of French interwar military tactics, training and organization: Robert A. Doughty, *The Seeds of Disaster: French Military Doctrine 1919–1939* (Hamden, Conn.: Archon Books, 1985); and Eugenia C. Kiesling, *Arming Against Hitler: France and the Limits of Military Planning* (Lawrence: University Press of Kansas, 1996). Next appeared innovative studies by two Canadians: Peter Jackson, *France and the Nazi Menace: Intelligence and Policy Making, 1933–1939* (Oxford University Press, 2000); and Talbot Imlay, with a multi-archival comparative look at pre-war Allied preparations, *Facing the Second World War: Strategy, Politics and Economics in Britain and France, 1938–1940* (Oxford University Press, 2003). According to Imlay, the Allies' attritional 'long game' was faltering the more the Phoney War dragged on – which caused Paul Reynaud, French Prime Minister after 21 March 1940, to lose faith that time was working for the Allies and encouraged him to gamble on offensives into Scandinavia, the Balkans and the Near East.

Beside these contested interpretations, attention to French imperial strategy – particularly around the Mediterranean – also revived. This was evident in the work of Christine Levisse-Touzé, *L'Afrique du Nord dans la guerre, 1939–1945* (Paris: Albin Michel, 1998); Reynolds M. Salerno, *Vital Crossroads: Mediterranean Origins of the Second World War, 1935–1940* (Ithaca, NY, and London: Cornell University Press, 2002); and Martin Thomas, *The French Empire between the Wars: Imperialism, Politics and Society* (Manchester University Press, 2005).

With operational 'bugles and bullets' history deeply unfashionable in French universities, re-evaluations of the 1940 campaign from the archives have been the province of non-French historians. Most notable are Robert A. Doughty, *The Breaking Point: Sedan and the Fall of France, 1940* (Hamden, Conn.: Archon Books, 1990); the writings of the Belgian scholar Jean

Vanwelkenhuyzen, founding director of the Centre for the Historical Study of the Second World War in Brussels, of which *1940: Pleins Feux sur un désastre* (Brussels: Racine, 1996) centres on the fight for the Low Countries and France; and Karl-Heinz Frieser with John T. Greenwood, *The Blitzkrieg Legend: The 1940 Campaign in the West* (Annapolis, Md.: Naval Institute Press, 2005). Bringing this work together accessibly for French readers is Maurice Vaïsse (ed.), *Ardennes 1940* (Paris: Henri Veyrier, 1991); and Maurice Vaïsse, *Mai-Juin 1940: Défaite française, victoire allemande sous l'oeil des historiens étrangers* (Paris: Editions Autrement, 2000). The Allied defeat of 1940, and its still disputed roots in interwar foreign and strategic planning, shifts in military doctrine and armaments policies, or in simple battlefield contingency, remains a big and important historical subject. Most assuredly, it is one on which more will be written.

4 German strategy, 1939–1945
Gerhard L. Weinberg

On the background of war and German plans, see Gerhard L. Weinberg, *Hitler's Foreign Policy 1933–1939: The Road to World War II* (New York: Enigma Books, 2005); and on the war itself and German decisions and choices in it, the same author's *A World at Arms: A Global History of World War II* (2nd edn, New York: Cambridge University Press, 2005), which includes both extensive notes and a bibliographical essay on pp. 921–44. Hitler's directives for the conduct of the war have been published in Walther Hubatsch (ed.), *Hitlers Weisungen für die Kriegführung 1939–1945* (Frankfurt am Main: Bernard and Graefe, 1962). A shorter English-language version is Hugh Trevor-Roper (ed.), *Hitler's War Directives* (London: Pan, 1966). Geoffrey Megargee's *Inside Hitler's High Command* (Lawrence: University Press of Kansas, 2000) is an excellent introduction to the realities of German military leadership during the war, while Mark Mazower provides a fine survey of the varieties and commonalities of German occupation policy in *Hitler's Empire: How the Nazis Ruled Europe* (New York: Penguin Press, 2008). The work of Michael Salewski, *Die deutsche Seekriegsleitung 1935–1945* (3 vols., Frankfurt am Main: Bernard & Graefe, 1970–73), remains of critical importance for the war at sea.

On the first stage of the war, Alexander B. Rossino's *Hitler Strikes Poland: Blitzkrieg, Ideology, and Atrocity* (Lawrence: University Press of Kansas, 2003), provides an excellent introduction; and Ernest R. May, in *Strange Victory: Hitler's Conquest of France* (New York: Hill and Wang, 2000), offers a new look at a critical subject. The Battle of Britain gets quite different treatment by Michael Korda, *With Wings Like Eagles: A History of the Battle of Britain* (New York: Harper Collins, 2009), and by Richard North, *The Many not the Few: The Stolen History of the Battle of Britain* (London: Continuum, 2012).

For the main fighting front of the war in 1941, there is now David Stahel's *Operation Barbarossa and Germany's Defeat in the East* (2009), *Kiev 1941* (2011), and *Operation Typhoon* (2013) (all Cambridge University Press); a volume on the later stages of the Battle of Moscow is to follow. An excellent survey of the whole campaign is David M. Glantz and Jonathan House, *When Titans Clashed: How the Red Army Stopped Hitler* (Lawrence: University Press of Kansas, 1995). Glantz has also published very detailed studies of specific battles on the Eastern Front and is in the process of finishing a three-volume account of the Battle of Stalingrad. Robert Citino has published a fine series of books on the German army in the Second World War: *The Path to Blitzkrieg: Doctrine and Training in the German Army* (Boulder, Colo.: Lynne Riener, 1999); and the following (all published Lawrence: University Press of Kansas): *The German Way of War: From the Thirty Years' War to the Third Reich* (2005), *Death of the Wehrmacht: The German Campaigns of 1942* (2007), and *The Wehrmacht Retreats: Fighting a Lost War, 1943* (2012). German decision-making is best analysed in Earl F. Ziemke and Magna E. Bauer, *Moscow to Stalingrad: Decision in the East* (Washington DC: Center of Military History, 1987); and Earl F. Ziemke, *Stalingrad to Berlin: The German Defeat in the East* (Washington DC: Government Printing Office, 1968).

On the strategic issues in the West after Germany's victory in 1940, there is Alan F. Wilt, *The Atlantic Wall 1941–1944: Hitler's Defenses for D-Day* (New York: Enigma Books, 2004); and on the German side of the D-Day invasion, one needs to turn to Dieter Ose, *Entscheidung im Westen 1944: Der Oberbefehlshaber West und die Abwehr der alliierten Invasion* (Stuttgart: Deutsche Verlags-Anstalt, 1982). For Germany's connection to the war in the Pacific, Johanna M. Meskill, *Hitler and Japan: The Hollow Alliance* (New York: Atherton, 1966), remains the best introduction. For the major issues in regard to the Southeast European theatre, North Africa, the Mediterranean and the fighting in Italy, as well as the final stage of the war in Western Europe, one should turn to the German official history very carefully produced by that country's Military History Research Office, under the German title *Das Deutsche Reich und der Zweite Weltkrieg* (Stuttgart: Deutsche Verlags-Anstalt, 1979–2008). This set has been published in English translation with the title *Germany and the Second World War* (10 vols., Oxford: Clarendon Press, 1990–). Up to 2014, all volumes have appeared in English apart from vols. VIII and x, which can be expected soon.

5 Mussolini's strategy, 1939–1943
John Gooch

For the reader with no Italian, coverage of Italy's war is patchy and generally unsatisfactory. Notable exceptions to this are MacGregor Knox, *Mussolini Unleashed 1939–1941* (Cambridge University Press, 1982); and H. James Burgwyn, *Mussolini Warlord: Failed Dreams of Empire 1940–1943* (New York: Enigma, 2012). The 'default source' for Italian high politics, Hugh Gibson (ed.), *The Ciano Diaries, 1939–1943* (Garden City, NY: Doubleday, 1946), should be used cautiously. There is useful coverage of Italian strategy and operations in *Germany and the Second World War*, vol. III: *The Mediterranean, South-east Europe, and North Africa, 1939–1941* (10 vols., Oxford: Clarendon Press, 1995); *Germany and the Second World War*, vol. VI: *The Global War* (10 vols., Oxford: Clarendon Press, 2001); Jack Greene and Alessandro Massignani, *Rommel's North African Campaign, September 1940–November 1942* (Conshohocken, Pa.: Combined Books, 1994); Martin Kitchen, *Rommel's Desert War* (Cambridge University Press, 2009). One volume of the excellent Italian official history of the North African campaign is available in translation: Mario Montanari, *The Three Battles of El Alamein (June–November 1942)* (Rome: Ufficio Storico dello Stato Maggiore dell'Esercito, 2007).

On the Greek campaign, Mario Cervi's now-dated *The Hollow Legions: Mussolini's Blunder in Greece, 1940–41* (New York: Doubleday, 1971) can be supplemented with Zacharias N. Tsirpanlis, 'The Italian view of the 1940–41 War', *Balkan Studies* 23 (1982), 27–79; James J. Sadkovich, 'The Italo-Greek War in Context: Italian Priorities and Axis Diplomacy', *Journal of Contemporary History* 28 (1993), 439–64; James J. Sadkovich, 'Anglo-American Bias and the Italo-Greek War of 1940–1941', *Journal of Military History* 54 (1994), 617–42. On Russia, there is for the moment only Hope Hamilton, *Sacrifice on the Steppe: The Italian Alpine Corps in the Stalingrad Campaign* (Havertown, Pa.: Casemate, 2011).

The relationship between strategy and the armed forces is surveyed by MacGregor Knox, 'The Italian Armed Forces, 1940–3', in Allan R. Millett and Williamson Murray (eds.), *Military Effectiveness*, vol. III: *The Second World War* (London: Allen & Unwin, 1988), pp. 136–79. On the Italian army, see MacGregor Knox, *Hitler's Italian Allies: Royal Armed Forces, Fascist Regime, and the War of 1940–1943* (Cambridge University Press, 2000). The Italian navy can be approached via Jack Greene and Alessandro Massignani, *The Naval War in the Mediterranean, 1940–1943* (London: Sarpedon, 1998), and James J. Sadkovich, *The Italian Navy in World War II* (Westport, Conn.: Greenwood, 1994). On the Italian air force, see Brian R. Sullivan, 'Downfall of the Regia

Aeronautica, 1933–1943', in Robin Higham and Stephen J. Harris (eds.), *Why Air Forces Fail* (Lexington: University Press of Kentucky, 2006), pp. 135–76. Finally, the relevant portion of Denis Mack Smith, *Mussolini's Roman Empire* (London: Penguin, 1979), although heavily reliant on Fascist memoirs and now somewhat aged, still repays reading.

6 Feigning grand strategy
Japan, 1937–1945
Alessio Patalano

Japanese historiography has pre-eminently approached the period 1937–45 as divided in two distinct phases, with the operations started in December 1941 separating them. This distinction has similarly informed the study of the Japanese war effort in English-language literature. In the early phases of the post-war period, a strong American professional interest in the period 1941–45 prompted the journal *Proceedings* of the US Naval Institute to seize the initiative by publishing a number of seminal articles. Former mid-ranking Japanese officers with direct experience in the main maritime campaigns in the Pacific penned the core of this literature, offering invaluable insight on their national experience, especially in regard to the navy's deficiencies in trade defence. These articles were eventually collected in a volume edited by David Evans, *The Japanese Navy in World War II: In the Words of Former Japanese Naval Officers* (Annapolis, Md.: Naval Institute Press, 1969).

These first short accounts by former officers were subsequently complemented by the memoirs of other prominent individuals, like Mitsuo Fuchida's *Midway: The Battle that Doomed Japan*, co-authored with Masatake Okumiya (London: Hutchinson, 1957). Fuchida's personal recollection of the battle became very influential, shaping the understanding of the Japanese perspective of the battle for several decades. In particular, he claimed that the Battle of Midway was lost because of a few minutes – when the American attacking force managed to catch the Japanese carriers with their decks full of planes ready to be launched. The appearance of *Shattered Sword: The Untold Story of the Battle of Midway* (Dulles, Va.: Potomac, 2005) by Jonathan Parshall and Anthony Tully represented the first challenge (in English) to Fuchida's account, suggesting that other factors – crucially among them, carrier doctrine – were behind the American victory.

Other books delivered powerful accounts of the war – rich in personal biographical references – that articulated the human experience behind the operational successes and the dramatic strategic failures of the Japanese navy. The most influential were Mochitsura Hashimoto's *Sunk: The Story of the*

Japanese Submarine Fleet, 1941–1945 (London: Cassell, 1954), dealing also with the sinking of the *Indianapolis*), and Masanori Ito's *The End of the Imperial Japanese Navy* (London: Weidenfeld & Nicolson, 1962). Ito was the leading pre-war newspaper correspondent and his book contained information based on hours of exclusive interviews with flag officers like Kurita Takeo, who spoke about his actions at the Leyte Gulf. On Ito's influence on post-war representations of the Imperial Japanese Navy, see Alessio Patalano, '"A Symbol of Tradition and Modernity": Itō Masanori and the Legacy of the Imperial Navy in the Early Post-war Rearmament Process', *Japanese Studies* 34:1 (2014), 61–82. Hiroyuki Agawa's portrayal of the navy's internal conflict and bureaucratic competition with the army through the experience of Admiral Yamamoto Isoroku in his *The Reluctant Admiral: Yamamoto and the Imperial Navy* (Tokyo: Kodansha, 1979), and Mitsuro Yoshida's *Requiem for Battleship Yamato* (London: Constable, 1999) proved equally influential.

The war fought from 1941 to 1945 remained pre-eminently a 'naval war', and the core literature focused on the origins and development of the confrontation between the Japanese and American navies in the maritime theatres of the Pacific. The first volume to offer a comprehensive narrative enriched by the study of Japanese documentations is Paul S. Dull's *A Battle History of the Imperial Japanese Navy, 1941–1945* (Cambridge: Patrick Stephens, 1978). This was followed in 1981 by Arthur Marder's *Old Friends, New Enemies: The Royal Navy and the Imperial Japanese Navy, Strategic Illusions, 1936–1941* (2 vols., Oxford: Clarendon, 1981, 1990) – a book that similarly drew on information on the Japanese navy obtained by Marder during his interactions with Minoru Nomura, one of Japan's leading military historians. In more recent years, Haruo Tohmatsu and H. P. Willmott's *A Gathering Darkness: The Coming of War to the Far East and the Pacific, 1921–1942* (London: Eurospan, 2004), Sadao Asada, *From Mahan to Pearl Harbor: The Imperial Japanese Navy and the United States* (Annapolis, Md.: Naval Institute Press, 2006), and the contributions by Tom Ishizu and Ken Kotani in Daniel Marston's edited volume, *The Pacific War Companion: From Pearl Harbor to Hiroshima* (Oxford: Osprey, 2005), all contributed to widening the understanding of the Japanese preparations and the strategic drivers underpinning the expansion of hostilities that took place in 1941. One volume that does not deal with the period after 1941, but it is by far the standard reference on the history of the Japanese navy is David C. Evans and Mark R. Peattie, *Kaigun: Strategy, Tactics, and Technology in the Imperial Japanese Navy* (Annapolis, Md.: Naval Institute Press, 1997).

Until recently, the literature that focused on the events before 1941 dealt pre-eminently with the operations conducted in China by the Imperial Army, with the exception of Mark Peattie's *Sunburst: The Rise of Japanese Naval Air Power, 1909–1941* (London: Chatham, 2001), which contained a first analysis of the impact of Japanese naval air operations in China on the development of the navy's air-power doctrine. A quarter of a century earlier, Mark Peattie authored a compelling narrative of the army's vision for Manchuria to become the engine of the Japanese Empire as leading army figure of the 1930s Kanji Ishiwara developed it, titled *Ishiwara Kanji and Japan's Confrontation with the West* (Princeton, NJ: Princeton University Press, 1975).

On the other hand, the key authors to uncover the full extent of Japanese military operations on the Asian continent were Alvin D. Coox and Edward Drea. As early as 1959, Coox defined the way Western scholarship studied the strategic outlook and operations conducted by the imperial army in the period after 1941, authoring together with Saburo Hayashi, *Kōgun: The Japanese Army in the Pacific* (Quantico, Va.: Marine Corps Association, 1959). He similarly contributed to the broader understanding of the military conflict with the essay 'The Pacific War', published in John Whitney Hall et al. (eds.), *Cambridge History of Japan* (6 vols., Cambridge University Press, 1991–), vol. VI, pp. 315–84. For the pre-1941 period, Coox's two studies, *The Anatomy of a Small War: The Soviet-Japanese Struggle for Changkufeng/Khashan, 1938* (London: Greenwood, 1977) and *Nomonhan: Japan against Russia, 1939* (2 vols., Stanford University Press, 1985), remain landmarks of strategic and operational analysis. Edward Drea's work on the imperial army's internal struggle to modernize, *In the Service of the Emperor: Essays on the Imperial Japanese Army* (Lincoln: University of Nebraska Press, 1998), and the more recent *Japan's Imperial Army: Its Rise and Fall, 1853–1945* (Lawrence: University Press of Kansas, 2009), complement Coox's ad hoc analysis. On the broader operations in China, in 2011, Mark Peattie, Edward J. Drea and Cambridge University China historian Hans van de Ven directed an international project, published with the title *The Battle for China: Essays on the Military History of the Sino-Japanese War of 1937–1945* (Stanford University Press, 2011), which included a number of essays breaking new ground on the impact of the China theatre on Japan's broader war efforts throughout the 1937–45 period.

The literature seeking to bring together army and navy strategic concerns and political dynamics during the period under examination remains limited. Nonetheless, a number of volumes of translated documents have been published in recent years, opening a window into the realm of Japanese concerns and priorities. These volumes include Donald M. Goldstein and Katherine V. Dillon (eds.), *The Pearl Harbor Papers: Inside the Japanese Plans* (Washington DC: Brassey's, 1993), and Akira Iriye, *Pearl Harbor and the*

Coming of the Pacific War: A Brief History with Documents and Essays (Boston, Mass.: Bedford/St. Martin's, 1999). Similarly, some important scholarship has been published throughout the past four decades that substantially contributed to an exploration of the structural, economic and domestic issues affecting Japanese policy-making in the 1930s and early 1940s. In 1987, Michael Barnhart fired the first salvos with his pioneering *Japan Prepares for Total War: The Search for Economic Security, 1919–1941* (Ithaca, NY: Cornell University Press, 1987); in more recent times, Herbert P. Bix, *Hirohito and the Making of Modern Japan* (London: Duckworth, 2001), and Richard B. Frank, *Downfall: The End of the Japanese Empire* (New York: Random House, 1999), added the relationship between the armed forces and the Emperor as an explanatory factor in Japan's military adventurism. Finally, in 2012, S. C. M. Paine's *The Wars for Asia, 1911 1949* (Cambridge University Press, 2012) represented the first attempt to offer a strategic overview of the conflicts that saw Japan involved both on continental Asia and in the maritime confines of the Pacific as components of the same picture, showing a new potential avenue of investigation for scholars interested in this period of history.

7 US grand strategy, 1939–1945
Thomas G. Mahnken

Several volumes provide an account of American grand strategy in the overall context of the Second World War, including Andrew Roberts, *The Storm of War: A New History of the Second World War* (New York: Harper-Collins, 2011), and Gerhard L. Weinberg, *A World at Arms: A Global History of World War II* (2nd edn, Cambridge University Press, 2005). Several other volumes emphasize the coalition dimension of the war. David Reynolds, Warren F. Kimball and A. O. Chubarian (eds.), *Allies at War: The Soviet, American, and British Experience, 1939–1945* (New York: St. Martin's, 1994) explores political, military, economic and technological cooperation between the United States, Great Britain and the Soviet Union. Warren F. Kimball, *Forged in War: Roosevelt, Churchill and the Second World War* (Chicago, Ill.: Ivan R. Dee, 1997) examines how the relationship between Roosevelt and Churchill shaped the war. Eric Larrabee, *Commander in Chief: Franklin Delano Roosevelt, His Lieutenants, and their War* (Annapolis, Md.: Naval Institute Press, 1987) focuses on Roosevelt's strategic leadership.

Several volumes published by the US Army Center of Military History cover American strategic planning for the Second World War, including Maurice Matloff and Edwin M. Snell, *The War Department: Strategic Planning for Coalition*

War, 1941–1942 (Washington DC: US Army Center of Military History, 1999), and Kent Roberts Greenfield (ed.), *Command Decisions* (Washington DC: Center of Military History, 1987). Books exploring the US military's role in shaping American strategy include Steven L. Rearden, *Council of War: A History of the Joint Chiefs of Staff, 1942–1991* (Washington DC: National Defense University Press, 2012), and Andrew Roberts, *Masters and Commanders: How Four Titans Won the War in the West, 1941–1945* (New York: Harper, 2009).

8 Soviet strategy
Bruce W. Menning and Jonathan House

On Soviet military-economic development during the interwar period, see David. R. Stone, *Hammer and Rifle: The Militarization of the Soviet Union, 1926–1933* (Lawrence: University Press of Kansas, 2000); Lennart Samuelson and V. V. Shlykov, *Plans for Stalin's War Machine: Tukhachevskii and Military-Economic Planning, 1925–1941* (Basingstoke: Palgrave, 2000); and James J. Schneider, *The Structure of Strategic Revolution: Total War and the Roots of the Soviet Warfare State* (Novato, Calif.: Presidio Press, 1994). For Soviet foreign and security policies in 1939–41, see Gabriel Gorodetsky, *Grand Delusion: Stalin and the German Invasion of Russia* (New Haven, Conn.: Yale University Press, 1999). Stalin's military background is discussed in Albert Seaton, *Stalin as Warlord* (London: Batsford, 1976).

Two overviews of Soviet military strategy are A. A. Kokoshin, *Soviet Strategic Thought, 1917–91* (Cambridge, Mass.: MIT Press, 1998); and David M. Glantz, *The Military Strategy of the Soviet Union: A History* (London and Portland, Oreg.: F. Cass, 1992). The best recent reassessment of Soviet strategy is Geoffrey Roberts, *Stalin's Wars: From World War to Cold War, 1939–1953* (New Haven, Conn.: Yale University Press, 2006). For Soviet wartime strategy, see Evan Mawdsley, *Thunder in the East: The Nazi-Soviet War, 1941–1945* (London: Hodder Arnold, 2005).

An excellent treatment of surprise at all levels remains R. A. Savushkin, 'In the Tracks of a Tragedy: On the 50th Anniversary of the Start of the Great Patriotic War', *Journal of Soviet Military Studies* 4:2 (1991), 213–51. A masterful insight into the concept of the strategic operational pause is Jacob W. Kipp, 'Barbarossa and the Crisis of Successive Operations: The Smolensk Engagements, July 10–August 7, 1941', *Soviet and Post Soviet Review* 19:1–3 (1992), 91–136. For background on the 'Icebreaker' controversy, see Evan Mawdsley, 'Crossing the Rubicon: Soviet Plans for Offensive War in 1940–41', *International History Review* 25:4 (2003), 818–65; and Teddy J. Uldricks,

'The Icebreaker Controversy: Did Stalin Plan to Attack Hitler?', *Slavic Review* 58:3, 626–43. Selected documents and commentary on 1941 appear in translation in Bruce W. Menning (ed.), 'At the Threshold of War: The Soviet High Command in 1941', *Russian Studies in History* 36:3 (1997–98).

On Lend-Lease, see Alexander Hill, *The Great Patriotic War of the Soviet Union, 1941–45* (London and New York: Routledge, 2009).

9 Campaigns in China, 1937–1945
Hans van de Ven

Little research was conducted on the China theatre until about a decade ago because it was considered that China had contributed little to the defeat of Japan, let alone Germany. Most historians believed that the roots of the Nationalists' defeat predated the war; hence it was considered historically insignificant. In the People's Republic of China, Maoist politics dictated that historians focus on the Communist revolution rather than Japanese aggression. The most significant early histories of China at war, centring on the US involvement, were grounded in these views. They included Barbara Tuchman, *Stilwell and the American Experience in China* (New York: Bantam Books, 1972); Theodore White (ed.), *The Stilwell Papers* (New York: William Sloane, 1948); Theodore White, *Thunder out of China* (New York: William Sloane, 1946); and C. F. Romanus and R. Sunderland's *Stilwell's Mission to China*, *Stilwell's Command Problems*, and *Stilwell's Mission to China* (all Washington DC: Office of the Chief of Military History, 1953, 1956, 1958).

In the late 1980s, after Deng Xiaoping began his reforms and Maoism lost its grip, People's Republic of China scholars of Chinese history initiated a radical reassessment of the Sino-Japanese War, including the wartime contribution of the Nationalists. Western historians also rethought the war, coming to see it as the most important turning point in China's modern history. Hans van de Ven, *War and Nationalism in China, 1925–1945* (London: Routledge, 2003) was an early example of this work. A more recent study that fuses political and military analysis is Rana Mitter, *China's War with Japan, 1937–1945: The Struggle for Survival* (London: Allen Lane, 2013). Mark Peattie, Edward Drea and Hans van de Ven (eds.), *The Battle for China: Essays on the Military History of the Sino-Japanese War of 1937–1945* (Stanford University Press, 2011) is the collective effort of Chinese, Japanese and Western historians to provide a detailed history of the most significant campaigns of the war.

The Sino-Japanese War is now a widely researched topic, with a range of studies analysing different aspects of this conflict. Joshua Howard has examined wartime industries in Nationalist areas in *Workers at War: Labor in China's Arsenals* (Palo Alto, Calif.: Stanford University Press, 2004). Morris Bian has shown in *The Making of the Chinese Industrial Workplace: State, Revolution, and Labor Management* (Cambridge University Press, 2002) that the state enterprise system of modern China originated in wartime China. New biographies of Chiang Kai-shek have been written by Jay Taylor (*The Generalissimo: Chiang Kaishek and the Struggle for Modern China* (Cambridge, Mass.: Harvard University Press, 2007)) and Jonathan Fenby (*Generalissimo: Chiang Kaishek and the China He Lost* (London: The Free Press, 2003)). Attention to the damage inflicted on China has stood central in Diana Lary, *The Chinese People at War: Suffering and Social Transformation, 1937–1945* (Cambridge University Press, 2010). Aaron William Moore has explored the soldiers' experience in *Writing War: Soldiers Record the Japanese Empire* (Cambridge, Mass.: Harvard University Press, 2013), while Stephen MacKinnon has analysed the Battle of Wuhan in *Wuhan, 1938: War, Refugees, and the Making of Modern China* (Berkeley: University of California Press, 2008). Peter Harmsen has provided a detailed description of the Battle of Shanghai in *Shanghai 1937: Stalingrad on the Yangtze* (Havertown, Pa.: Casemate Publishers, 2013). S. C. M. Paine, in *The Wars for Asia, 1911–1949* (Cambridge University Press, 2012), has argued that what began as a civil war became a regional war in 1937, and then part of a global war in 1941. This flowering of studies of wartime China is set to continue for some time.

History workers on the Communist front have become rather quiet. Early works, such as Chalmers Johnson, *Peasant Nationalism and Communist Power* (Stanford University Press, 1962) and Mark Selden, *The Yen'an Way* (Cambridge, Mass.: Harvard University Press, 1971) remain influential. Important work has been done on Communist base areas during the war, including by David Goodman in *Social and Political Change in Revolutionary China: The Taihang Base Area in the War of Resistance against Japan, 1937–1945* (Lanham, Md.: Rowman and Littlefield, 2000). Chen Yung-fa, *Making Revolution: The Communist Movement in Eastern and Central China, 1937–1945* (Berkeley: University of California Press, 1986), and Odoric Wou, *Mobilizing the Masses: Building Revolution in Henan* (Stanford University Press, 1994), have detailed how Communist cadres set about their task. Gregor Benton has drawn attention to the relatively forgotten Communist New 4th Army, which struggled against great odds in central China in *The New Fourth Army: Communist Resistance Along the Yangtze River* (Berkeley: University of California Press, 1999). Sherman Xiaogang Lai has analysed how the Communists established control over the strategically significant province of Shandong in *A Springboard to Victory: Shandong Province and Chinese Communist Military and*

Financial Strength, 1937–1945 (Leiden and Boston, Mass.: Brill, 2011). Chang Jung has provided a new assessment of Mao Zedong in *Mao: The Unknown Story* (London: Vintage, 2007). The history of the Chinese Communists and that of wartime China remain two separate subjects. New analytical models, a revival of scholarly interest in the Chinese Revolution and the opening of Communist archives will be required to integrate these two topics. There remains much work to be done.

10 The war in the West, 1939–1940
An unplanned Blitzkrieg
Karl-Heinz Freiser
Translated by Harvey L. Mendelsohn

This chapter is based primarily on the author's monograph, Karl-Heinz Frieser, *Blitzkrieg-Legende. Der Westfeldzug* 1940 (4th edn, Munich: Oldenbourg Verlag, 2012); English-language version: Karl-Heinz Frieser with John Greenwood, *The Blitzkrieg Legend. The 1940 Campaign in the West* (Annapolis, Md.: Naval Institute Press, 2005). For this monograph, more than 1,500 books and articles were consulted, but the most important materials were the primary and secondary sources. The author thoroughly studied the files in the German and French archives. Unfortunately, the documents in the German military archives proved to have large lacunae, since numerous files burned up in a bombardment during the war. By contacting veterans' associations, however, it was possible to obtain duplicates of many of the original documents. In addition, in the 1980s, the author conducted interviews with former German army officers who had participated in the campaign in the West.

From the abundant literature on the subject, a number of publications should be mentioned here. The series published by the Militärgeschichtliches Forschungsamt[1] in Potsdam, *Das Deutsche Reich und der Zweite Weltkrieg* (*Germany and the Second World War*), is, for the most part, already translated into English. The standard account of the war years 1939–1940 is vol. 11: *Germany's Initial Conquests in Europe* (10 vols., Oxford: Clarendon Press, 1991). For the British perspective, see the classic account by Alistair Horne, *To Lose a Battle: France 1940* (London: Macmillan, 1969). Among the American publications, see Robert Allan Doughty, *The Breaking Point: Sedan and the Fall of*

---

[1] In 2012, the Militärgeschichtliches Forschungsamt (Military History Research Office) was renamed the Zentrum für Militärgeschichte und Sozialwissenschaften der Bundeswehr (Centre for Military History and Social Sciences of the German Armed Forces).

France, 1940 (Hamden, Conn.: Archon Books, 1990). The author participated in a military history excursion through the Ardennes led by Doughty and, as a result, was inspired to write his own monograph on the subject. See also Ernest R. May, *Strange Victory: Hitler's Conquest of France* (New York: Hill and Wang, 2000). For the French perspective, see, above all, the classic Marc Bloch, *Strange Defeat: A Statement of Evidence Written in 1940* (New York: W. W. Norton, 1968). Detailed investigations can be found in Claude Paillat, *Le désastre de 1940. Dossiers secrets de la France contemporaine*, vol. I: *La répétion générale*; vol. II: *La guerre immobile. Avril 1939–10 mai 1940*; vol. III: *La guerre éclair. 10 mai–24 juin 1940* (3 vols., Paris: Robert Laffont, 1983, 1984, 1985).

Since the appearance of the monograph *Blitzkrieg-Legende*, nothing fundamentally new has been published regarding the campaign in the West, though the state of research has been advanced by the uncovering of more details – for example, concerning localized fighting. To be sure, there are publications which attempt to place the campaign in the West in a broader perspective and within a more comprehensive framework. This has been successfully done by Robert M. Citino, for example, in his *Blitzkrieg to Desert Storm: The Evolution of Operational Warfare* (Lawrence: University Press of Kansas, 2004).

11 The war in the West, 1939–1940
The Battle of Britain?
John Ferris and Evan Mawdsley

Published primary documents on German operational and strategic planning against Britain between May and September 1940 are in 'Fuehrer Conferences on Naval Affairs', *Brassey's Naval Annual* (1948), pp. 25–496 (available in German in Gerhard Wagner (ed.), *Lagevorträge der Oberbefehlshabers der Kriegsmarine vor Hitler, 1939–1945* (Munich: J. F. Lehman, 1972)); Franz Halder, *The Halder War Diary, 1939–1942*, ed. Charles Burdick and Hans-Adolf Jacobsen (London: Greenhill, 1988); a fuller version in *Kriegstagebuch: Tägliche Aufzeichnungen des Chefs des Generalstabes des Heeres, 1939–1942* (3 vols., Stuttgart: Kohlhammer, 1965); and Walter Warlimont, *Inside Hitler's Headquarters, 1939–45* (London: Weidenfeld & Nicolson, 1962).

Good accounts of SEELÖWE (which sometimes treat it more seriously than German decision-makers did) include Walter Ansel, *Hitler Confronts England* (Durham, NC: Duke University Press, 1960); Karl Klee, *Das Unternehmen Seelöwe: Die geplante deutche Landung in England 1940* (Göttingen: Musterschmidt, 1959); Peter Schenk, *The Invasion of England 1940: The Planning of Operation Sealion* (London: Conway, 1990); Hans Umbreit, 'Plans and

Preparations for a Landing in England', in *Germany and the Second World War*, vol. II: *Germany's Initial Conquests in Europe* (10 vols., Oxford: Clarendon Press, 1991), pp. 366–74; and Ronald Wheatley, *Operation Sea Lion: German Plans Made by the German High Command under Adolf Hitler for the Invasion of England, 1939–1942* (Oxford University Press, 1958).

Serious studies of Fighter Command and British air defence include Anthony J. Cumming, *The Royal Navy and The Battle of Britain* (Annapolis, Md.: Naval Institute Press, 2010); John Ferris, 'Achieving Air Ascendancy: Challenge and Response in British Strategic Air Defence, 1915–40', in Sebastian Cox and Peter Gray (eds.), *Air Power History: Turning Points from Kitty Hawk to Kosovo* (Portland, Oreg.: Frank Cass, 2002), pp. 21–50; T. C. G. James, *The Growth of Fighter Command, 1936–1940*, vol. I: *Air Defence of Great Britain*, ed. Sebastian Cox (London: Frank Cass, 2002); and David Zimmerman, *Britain's Shield: Radar and the Defeat of the Luftwaffe* (Stroud: Sutton Publishing, 2001). For the Royal Navy during this period, see Stephen W. Roskill, *The War at Sea* (3 vols., London: HMSO, 1954), vol. I, pp. 247–68. Good discussions of the Luftwaffe include Horst Boog, *Die deutsche Luftwaffenführung, 1935–1945: Führungsprobleme; Spitzengliederung; Generalstabsausbildung* (Stuttgart: Deutsche Verlags-Anstalt, 1982); and James S. Corum, *The Luftwaffe: Creating the Operational Air War, 1918–40* (Lawrence: University Press of Kansas, 1999).

Good accounts of the Battle of Britain are legion, including official histories such as Dennis Richards, *Royal Air Force*, vol. I: *The Fight at Odds* (London: HMSO, 1953); and Basil Collier, *The Defence of the United Kingdom* (London: HMSO, 1957). The most influential traditional account is Derek Wood and Derek Dempster, *The Narrow Margin: The Battle of Britain and the Rise of Airpower, 1930–1940* (London: Hutchinson, 1961). From the 1990s, scholars increasingly denied that the Battle of Britain had been near-run, and emphasized the power and preparations of Fighter Command. The best modern books are Stephen Bungay, *The Most Dangerous Enemy: A History of the Battle of Britain* (London: Aurum, 2000); Robin Higham, *Unflinching Zeal: The Air Battles over France and Britain, May–October 1940* (Annapolis, Md.: Naval Institute Press, 2012); and Richard Overy, *The Battle of Britain: Myths and Realities* (New York: W. W. Norton and Co., 2002). The best German account is Klaus A. Maier, 'The Battle of Britain', in *Germany and the Second World War*, vol. II: *Germany's Initial Conquests in Europe* (10 vols., Oxford: Clarendon Press, 1991), pp. 374–407. A key source on the battle, the Fighter Command Operational Diaries, are reproduced at www.raf.mod.uk/history/campaign_diaries.cfm (accessed 7 October 2014).

These events are prominent in the voluminous studies of Hitler and Churchill as warlords. For good accounts of Hitler's strategy during the summer of 1940, cf. Ian Kershaw, *Hitler 1936–1945: Nemesis* (London: Allen Lane, 2000), pp. 295–344; and the chapters in Part IX and Conclusion of *Germany and the Second World War*, vol. II: *Germany's Initial Conquests in Europe* (10 vols., Oxford: Clarendon Press, 1991), pp. 361–420. David Reynolds, *World War to Cold War: Churchill, Roosevelt and the International History of the 1940s* (Oxford University Press, 2008), analyses Churchill's strategy critically but sympathetically; while John Charmley, *Churchill: The End of Glory* (London: Hodder & Stoughton, 1993), offers the best, if unconvincing, argument that Churchill's decisions were wrong, and that Britain should have negotiated peace with Hitler. John Lukacs, *The Duel: 10 May–31 July 1940: The Eighty-Day Struggle between Churchill and Hitler* (New York: Ticknor & Fields, 1991), assesses this clash of strategies by combining individual and ideological perspectives.

12 Operations on the Eastern Front, 1941–1945
David R. Stone

At the close of the Second World War, Hitler's generals had every reason to get their own version of events on the Eastern Front on record, a project aided by the looming Cold War and Western militaries' desire to understand how the Soviets might be fought. The picture they gave, portraying the Red Army as a faceless mass, blaming war crimes on Hitler and the Nazi Party, but not the Wehrmacht itself, and Hitler himself as the source of all strategic blunders, proved remarkably resilient. The German generals, through their interviews with Allied interrogators and their post-war memoirs, enjoyed remarkable success in whitewashing their own responsibility, both for German war crimes and for defeat on the battlefield. In the Soviet Union, Stalin's stranglehold on history and his evident mismanagement of the war in its earliest stages likewise prevented an objective look at history. In subsequent decades, though, increasingly rich access to sources – additional memoirs, official histories, published documents and archival research – corrected many early misunderstandings and misrepresentations.

In the Soviet Union, the six-volume collective *Istoriia Velikoi Otechestvennoi voiny Sovetskogo Soiuza* (Moscow: Voenizdat, 1960–65) provided a wealth of operational detail, though it ignored Joseph Stalin, magnified then Soviet leader Nikita Khrushchev's accomplishments beyond all recognition, and neglected operations that did not reflect well on the Soviet Union. The subsequent twelve-volume *Istoriia vtoroi mirovoi voiny* (Moscow: Voenizdat,

1973–76), which broadened the focus from the Eastern Front to the Second World War as a whole, maintained the relentlessly pro-Soviet tone, but turned the now-purged Khrushchev into a non-entity. The mass of Soviet memoirs and secondary literature on the war tended to follow the same pattern: concrete and useful details on specific operational and tactical questions were matched by overall interpretations that followed in lockstep the political mandate of the time. More recently, the four-volume *Velikaia Otechestvennaia voina, 1941–1945* (Moscow: Nauka, 1998–99) continues the Soviet tradition of detailed operational narrative, but with much less overt political intervention in the account.

In the West, early histories of the Eastern Front relied heavily on the German generals. Two surveys which used the sources then available, thus unfortunately still looking predominantly at the German side of the war rather than the Soviet, are Alan Clark, *Barbarossa: The Russian-German Conflict 1941–1945* (New York: William Morrow, 1966); and Albert Seaton, *The Russo-German War, 1941–1945* (New York: Praeger, 1971). Earl F. Ziemke, in *Stalingrad to Berlin: The German Defeat in the East* (Washington DC: US Government Printing Office, 1968), and in collaboration with Magna E. Bauer, *Moscow to Stalingrad: Decision in the East* (Washington DC: Center of Military History, 1987), makes exhaustive use of German sources for a detailed and almost exclusively operational account. Recent overviews which are broader in their outlook are Richard Overy, *Russia's War* (London: Allen Lane, 1998); and Stephen G. Fritz, *Ostkrieg: Hitler's War of Extermination in the East* (Lexington: University of Kentucky Press, 2011). Both emphasize comprehensiveness and readability. German literature has produced remarkable pieces of analysis; in particular, the encyclopaedic, ten-volume *Das Deutsche Reich und der Zweite Weltkrieg*, a production of the historical section of the German *Bundeswehr* (post-war West German armed forces). English translations from Clarendon Press are ongoing and nearly complete. The best guide to German-language literature is Rolf-Dieter Müller and Gerd R. Ueberschär, *Hitler's War in the East, 1941–1945* (Oxford: Berghahn Books, 1997).

The biggest leap forward in using Soviet sources came with the work of John Erickson, who exhaustively mined Soviet memoirs and secondary literature. Integrating that material with Western sources, he produced two masterful volumes: *The Road to Stalingrad* (New York: Harper and Row, 1975) and *The Road to Berlin* (Boulder, Colo.: Westview, 1983). Emphasizing strategy and operations, and poorly supplied with maps, these books are intensely rewarding for the specialist, but hard-going for general readers. While there is a variety of popular histories of the Eastern Front, two user-friendly surveys do justice to the Soviet side of the war with full scholarly rigour. The best operational survey in one volume is David M. Glantz and Jonathan M. House, *When Titans Clashed: How the Red Army Stopped Hitler* (Lawrence: University Press of Kansas, 1995). This uses new Soviet sources, specifically the Red Army's own internal histories and self-evaluations, dating back to the war itself. Evan Mawdsley, *Thunder in the East* (London: Hodder Arnold, 2011), is less narrowly operational in its focus and incorporates the full range of recent Russian and Western scholarship.

There is a wealth of books and articles on specific operations on the Eastern Front, though it tends to be focused on the first two years of the war rather than the last. There is much more written on Stalingrad, for example, than on the destruction of Army Group Centre in 1944. In English, David Glantz and his sometime collaborator Jonathan House have written a series of massive studies of particular campaigns. They have gone further than almost all authors in using available Soviet sources. These sources, however, are often Red Army internal studies of its own operations, written during the war. A true mining of Soviet archival sources has not yet taken place, and will likely not take place until the Red Army's Second World War materials, still in possession of the Russian Ministry of Defence, are easily accessible to scholars.

13 The Mediterranean and North Africa, 1940–1944
Simon Ball

There are two recent one-volume histories of the conflict in the Mediterranean: Douglas Porch, *Hitler's Mediterranean Gamble: The North African and the Mediterranean Campaigns in World War II* (London: Weidenfeld & Nicolson, 2004); and Simon Ball, *The Bitter Sea: The Struggle for Mastery in the Mediterranean, 1935–1949* (London: Harper Press, 2009). The classic account of Mediterranean strategy remains Michael Howard, *The Mediterranean Strategy in the Second World War* (London: Weidenfeld & Nicolson, 1968). Its American counterpart is the study by Richard Leighton in Kent Roberts Greenfield (ed.), *Command Decisions* (Washington DC: Department of the Army, 1960). The American account has been updated in Mark Stoler, *Allies and Adversaries: The Joint Chiefs of Staff, the Grand Alliance and US Strategy in World War II* (Chapel Hill, NC: University of North Carolina Press, 2000). For readers with stamina, the war itself is best understood through the British official history: J. R. M. Butler et. al (eds.), *The Mediterranean and the Middle East* (6 vols., London: HMSO, 1954–87); supplemented by the official history of intelligence, F. H. Hinsley et al. (eds.), *British Intelligence in the Second World War:*

Its Influence on Strategy and Operations (5 vols., London: HMSO, 1979–90); and the official German ten-volume history of the war, *Germany and the Second World War*, especially vol. III: *The Mediterranean, South-east Europe and North Africa, 1939–1941* (10 vols., Oxford: Clarendon Press, 1995) and vol. VI: *The Global War, 1941–1943* (10 vols., Oxford: Clarendon Press, 2001). Anglophone historians have made a major contribution to the study of Italy in the Second World War: John Gooch, *Mussolini and his Generals: The Armed Forces and Fascist Foreign Policy, 1922–1940* (Cambridge University Press, 2007); MacGregor Knox, *Mussolini Unleashed, 1939–1941: Politics and Strategy in Fascist Italy's Last War* (Cambridge University Press, 1982); and James Sadkovich, *The Italian Navy in World War II* (Westport, Conn.: Greenwood Press, 1994). Above all, Mediterranean strategy can best be understood by reading the original papers of important policy-makers, many of which have been published: Martin Gilbert (ed.), *The Churchill War Papers, 1939–1941* (3 vols., New York: W. W. Norton, 1993–2001); Warren Kimball (ed.), *Churchill and Roosevelt: The Complete Correspondence* (3 vols., London: Collins, 1984); Alfred Chandler (ed.), *The Papers of Dwight David Eisenhower: The War Years* (5 vols., Baltimore, Md.: Johns Hopkins University Press, 1970); Alex Danchev and Dan Todman (eds.), *Field Marshal Lord Alanbrooke: War Diaries, 1939–1945* (London: Weidenfeld & Nicolson, 2001); Michael Simpson (ed.), *The Cunningham Papers* (2 vols., Aldershot: Naval Records Society, 1999 and 2006); Harold Macmillan, *War Diaries: The War in the Mediterranean, 1943–1945* (London: Macmillan, 1984); Hugh Trevor-Roper (ed.), *Hitler's War Directives, 1939–1945* (Edinburgh: Birlinn, 2004); The Admiralty, *Fuehrer Conferences on Naval Affairs,* (5 vols., London: Admiralty, 1947); Basil Liddell Hart (ed.), *The Rommel Papers* (London, 1953); Galeazzo Ciano, *Diary, 1937–1943* (London: Collins, 2002); the most interesting Axis autobiography is Albert Kesselring, *Memoirs* (London: William Kimber, 1953).

14 The war in the West, 1943–1945
Mary Kathryn Barbier

A wealth of books related to the war in West, 1943–45, exist. Two of the best overviews remain Williamson Murray and Allan R. Millett's *A War to Be Won: Fighting The Second World War* (Cambridge, Mass.: Belknap Press of Harvard University Press, 2000), and Gerhard L. Weinberg's *A World At Arms: A Global History of World War II* (Cambridge University Press, 1994). Although dated, Chester Willmott's *The Struggle for Europe* (New York: Harper and Brothers, 1952) remains a useful resource for historians, as does

Dwight Eisenhower's *Crusade in Europe* (Norwalk, Conn.: The Easton Press, 1948). More recent overviews that present new perspectives include *No Simple Victory: World War II in Europe, 1939–1945* by Norman Davies (New York: Penguin, 2006); Philip Bell's *Twelve Turning Points of the Second World War* (New Haven, Conn.: Yale University Press, 2012); and *Engineers of Victory: The Problem Solvers Who Turned the Tide in the Second World War* by Paul Kennedy (New York: Random House, 2013).

Two more recent publications provide new perspectives on the war in Europe. While both begin with the Normandy invasion, the authors conclude their narratives at different points. These monographs are Olivier Wieviorka's *Normandy: The Landings to the Liberation of Paris* (trans. M. B. DeBevoise, Cambridge, Mass.: Belknap Press of Harvard University Press, 2008), and Robin Neillands' *The Conquest of the Reich: D-Day to V-E Day* (New York University Press, 1995). Long romanticized, the Normandy invasion provides the subject for many historical assessments of the Second World War. Of particular note are *The Normandy Campaign 1944: Sixty Years On*, edited by John Buckley (London: Routledge, 2006); Carlo D'Este's *Decision in Normandy* (New York: Harper Perennial, 1991); John Keegan's *Six Armies in Normandy: From D-Day to the Liberation of Paris* (New York: Penguin, 1994); and *Fighting the Invasion: The German Army at D-Day*, edited by David C. Isby (London and Mechanicsburg, Pa.: Greenhill Books and Stackpole Books, 2000).

The best works related to the German military and the German perspective are those by Robert M. Citino: *Death of the Wehrmacht: The German Campaigns of 1942* (Lawrence: University Press of Kansas, 2007) and *The Wehrmacht Retreats: Fighting a Lost War, 1943* (Lawrence: University Press of Kansas, 2012). Niklas Zetterling provides detailed information about Wehrmacht organization and movements related to D-Day in *Normandy 1944: German Military Organization, Combat Power and Organizational Effectiveness* (Winnipeg, Man.: J. J. Fedorowicz Publishing, 2000). While Geoffrey Megargee, in *Inside Hitler's High Command* (Lawrence: University Press of Kansas, 2000), examines the Wehrmacht from the top, Bryan Mark Rigg investigates an unusual situation within the ranks in *Hitler's Jewish Soldiers: The Untold Story of Nazi Racial Laws and Men of Jewish Descent in the German Military* (Lawrence: University Press of Kansas, 2002).

Several monographs shift the focus to Allied boots on the ground. The American perspective is found in Michael D. Doubler's *Closing with the Enemy: How GIs Fought the War in Europe, 1944–1945* (Lawrence: University Press of Kansas, 1994), and Peter R. Mansoor's *The GI Offensive in Europe: The Triumph of American Infantry divisions, 1941–1945* (Lawrence: University Press of Kansas, 1999). John Buckley focuses on the British side in his most recent monograph, *Monty's Men: The British Army and the Liberation of Europe* (New Haven, Conn.: Yale University Press, 2013). An increasing number of books about the Allies' war effort in Europe focus on air offensives. In addition to Robert S. Ehlers, Jr's monograph, *Targeting the Third Reich: Air Intelligence and the Allied Bombing Campaigns*, which melds the air intelligence narrative with an assessment of bombing efforts, two other books deserve mention: Max Hastings' *Bomber Command* (New York: Dial Press, 1979), and *The Bombing War: Europe 1939–1945* by Richard Overy (London: Allen Lane, 2013). Overy expands the narrative in his latest book, *The Bombers and the Bombed: Allied Air War Over Europe, 1940–1945* (New York: Viking, 2014).

For those interested in deception and the Normandy invasion, a good starting point is Mary Kathryn Barbier's *D-Day Deception: Operation Fortitude and the Normandy Invasion* (Westport, Conn.: Praeger Security International, 2007). Two other works that add to the narrative are *Between Silk and Cyanide: A Codemaker's War, 1941–1945* by Leo Marks (New York: Free Press, 1998), and Thaddeus Holt's *The Deceivers: Allied Military Deception in the Second World War* (London: Weidenfeld & Nicolson, 1983).

Finally, Rick Atkinson's trilogy – *An Army at Dawn: The War in North Africa, 1942–1943* (New York: Henry Holt and Company, 2002), *The Day of Battle: The War in Sicily and Italy, 1943–1944* (New York: Henry Holt and Company, 2007), and *The Guns at Last Light: The War in Western Europe, 1944–1945* (New York: Henry Holt and Company, 2013) – updates older overviews of the war in the West, 1943–45.

15 The war in the Pacific, 1941–1945
John T. Kuehn

The best single-volume treatment for the Pacific War remains Ronald Spector's *Eagle Against the Sun* (New York: Vintage, 1985); and his *In the Ruins of Empire: The Japanese Surrender and the Battle for Postwar Asia* (New York: Random House, 2007) picks up where the first volume left off, following the turbulent years of insurgency and warfare in East Asia after the official conclusion of hostilities with Japan. H. P. Willmott's various books – *Empires in the Balance: Japanese and Allied Pacific Strategies to April 1942* (Annapolis, Md.: Naval Institute Press, 1982), *The Barrier and the Javelin* (Annapolis, Md.: Naval Institute Press, 1983) and, more recently, with Haruo Tohmatsu, *A Gathering Darkness: The Coming of War to the Far East and Pacific, 1921–1942* (Lanham, Md.: SR Books, 2004), all provide a good analysis of

Japanese and American strategic positions, choices and decision-making. David Rigby, *Allied Master Strategists: The Combined Chiefs of Staff* (Annapolis, Md.: Naval Institute Press, 2012), gives the perspective of the Allied Combined Chiefs of Staff; and Edward Drea's *Japan's Imperial Army: Its Rise and Fall, 1853–1945* (Lawrence: University Press of Kansas, 2009) and *In the Service of the Emperor: Essays on the Imperial Japanese Army* (Lincoln: University of Nebraska Press, 1998), provide both Imperial Army and Supreme Council for the Direction of the War perspectives.

The Pacific War stimulated a large official effort to chronicle strategy and operations. For the Japanese side, the War History series (*Senshi Sosho*) of over a hundred volumes was compiled in the 1960s and 1970s by the War History Office of the Japanese Ministry of Defence, and was made available for research in 1971. It is considered an essential resource for any scholar writing about the Pacific War. There is much knowledge to be gained about Japanese operations from US cryptographic operations that are now encompassed by a number of works, such as John Prados, *Combined Fleet Decoded: The Secret History of American Intelligence and the Japanese Navy in World War II* (Annapolis, Md.: Naval Institute Press, 1995); Edward J. Drea, *MacArthur's Ultra: Codebreaking and the War against Japan, 1942–1953* (Lawrence: University Press of Kansas, 1992); and, most recently, Elliot Carlson, *Joe Rochefort's War: The Odyssey of the Codebreaker Who Outwitted Yamamoto at Midway* (Annapolis, Md.: Naval Institute Press, 2011), about the key decryption unit in Pearl Harbor. There are also a number of excellent works on Japanese-American linguists, including James McNaughton's *Nisei Linguists: Japanese Americans in the Military Intelligence Service During World War II* (Washington DC: Department of the Army, Center of Military History, 2006), and Roger Dingman's *Deciphering the Rising Sun: Navy and Marine Corps Codebreakers, Translators, and Interpreters in the Pacific War* (Annapolis, Md.: Naval Institute Press, 2009).

On the American side, there is the excellent *The United States Army in World War II* series composed of fifty-five volumes, also known as the 'Greenbooks', which covers Army operations in detail, with an excellent volume, *Strategy and Command: The First Two Years* by Louis Morton (1962). For the Marine Corps, there is Frank O. Hough, Verle E. Ludwig and Henry I. Shaw, Jr et al., *History of US Marine Corps Operations in World War II* (5 vols., Washington DC: US Marine Corps, 1965).[1] For the aviation side, there are:

[1] This was released in digital format in 2000. The author owns the digital copy, which has no dates on any of the volumes. It is listed as Fleet Marine Force Reference Publication (FMFRP) 12-34.

Wesley Frank Craven and James Lea Cate (eds.), *The Army Air Forces in World War II* (7 vols., University of Chicago Press, 1950); Robert Sherrod, *History of Marine Corps Aviation in World War II* (Washington DC: Combat Forces Press, 1952); and Douglas Gillison, *Australia in the War of 1939–1945: Air* (4 vols., Canberra: Australian War Memorial, 1954–63).

For the US Navy, Admiral Earnest King's *US Navy at War, 1941–1945: Official Reports to the Secretary of the Navy* (Washington DC: United States Navy Department, 1946) remains a concise summary of strategy and operations; while Samuel Eliot Morison's semi-official *History of United States Naval Operations in World War II* (15 vols., Boston, Mass.: Little, Brown and Co., 1947–62) remains essential. For the Australian side, there is G. Hermon Gill, *Australia in the War of 1939–1945 – Navy* (2 vols., Canberra: Australian War Memorial, 1957, 1968). Although not an official history, the best recent source for major British naval operations is David Hobbs, *The British Pacific Fleet: The Royal Navy's Most Powerful Strike Force* (Annapolis, Md.: Naval Institute Press, 2011). The most recent source in English on pre-war Dutch naval policy is a monograph by Major Rene van den Berg, 'Patterns of Innovation: A Historical Case Study of Military Innovation in the Netherlands East Indies Navy from 1900 to 1942' (unpublished master's thesis, Army Command and General Staff College, Fort Leavenworth, Kan., 2013).

There are a number of excellent recent studies of the period between the wars. For the Washington Conference and the US Navy in the interwar period, see John T. Kuehn, *Agents of Innovation* (Annapolis, Md.: Naval Institute Press, 2008). For the deteriorating USA–Japan relationship, financial sanctions and eventual economic measures by the USA, see Edward S. Miller, *Bankrupting the Enemy: The US Financial Siege of Japan before Pearl Harbor* (Annapolis, Md.: Naval Institute Press, 2007); and for US Navy war planning, see Miller's earlier *War Plan ORANGE: The US Strategy to Defeat Japan, 1897–1945* (Annapolis, Md.: Naval Institute Press, 1991). For a look at military and naval innovation between the wars, see *Military Innovation in the Interwar Period*, edited by Williamson Murray and Allen Millett (Cambridge and New York: Cambridge University Press, 1996).

For the Japanese, the best treatment of the Imperial Navy's policies and bureaucratic politics is Sadao Asada, *From Mahan to Pearl Harbor: The Imperial Japanese Navy and the United States* (Annapolis, Md.: Naval Institute Press, 2006). For operations, planning and the fleet-building programme, see Mark R. Peattie and David C. Evans, *Kaigun: Strategy, Tactics, and Technology in the Imperial Japanese Navy, 1887–1941* (Annapolis, Md.: Naval Institute Press, 1997). For Japanese military policy and aggressions, see Michael A. Barnhart, *Japan*

Prepares for Total War: The Search for Economic Security, 1919–1941 (Ithaca, NY: Cornell University Press, 1987); and Mark R. Peattie, *Ishiwara Kanji and Japan's Confrontation with the West* (Princeton, NJ: Princeton University Press, 1975). Again, Edward Drea, *Japan's Imperial Army: Its Rise and Fall, 1853–1945* (Lawrence: University Press of Kansas, 2009) is essential to understand the Imperial Japanese Army's operations and policies for its entire history; see chapter 10 for a discussion of IJA operations in China prior to Pearl Harbor. For US strategy and aid vis-à-vis Nationalist China, see John D. Plating, *The Hump: America's Strategy for Keeping China in World War II* (College Station: Texas A&M University Press, 2011), as well as the dated but still useful *Stillwell and the American Experience in China, 1911–1945* by Barbara Tuchman (New York: Macmillan, 1970). For the ongoing East Asian War in China, see *The Battle for China: Essays on the Military History of the Sino-Japanese War of 1937–1945* (Stanford University Press, 2010), edited by Mark Peattie, Edward Drea and Hans van de Ven. For the Pacific War as a race war, see John Dower, *War Without Mercy: Race and Power in the Pacific War* (New York: Pantheon Books, 1986).

For preparation by the United States for war, see Glenn M. Williford, *Racing the Sunrise: Reinforcing America's Pacific Outposts* (Annapolis, Md.: Naval Institute Press, 2010). John Plating adds value for the steps taken in regard to supplying China with air power prior to Pearl Harbor in *The Hump: America's Strategy for Keeping China in World War II* (College Station, Texas A&M University Press, 2011). John Lundstrom's books, *The First South Pacific Campaign: Pacific Fleet Strategy, December 1941 – June 1942* (Annapolis, Md.: Naval Institute Press, 1976), and, most recently, *Black Shoe Carrier Admiral: Frank Jack Fletcher at Coral Sea Midway, and Guadalcanal* (Annapolis, Md.: Naval Institute Press, 2006), provide excellent context for 1941 and the first year of combat by the navy. For the Japanese naval air force prior to the war, see Mark Peattie, *Sunburst: The Rise of Japanese Naval Air Power, 1909–1941* (Annapolis, Md.: Naval Institute Press, 2001); and for a general account of the use of Japanese air power during the war, see the chapter by Osamu Tagaya, 'The Imperial Japanese Air Forces', in *Why Air Forces Fail*, edited by Robin Higham and Stephen Harris (Lexington: University Press of Kentucky, 2006). For the air war in general, there is Eric Bergerud's *Fire in the Sky* (Boulder, Colo.: Westview Press, 2000), which covers the air war in the south Pacific, and the more comprehensive, one-volume treatment by popular historian Barrett Tillman, *Whirlwind: The Air War Against Japan, 1942–1945* (New York: Simon & Schuster, 2010).

Debates over Pearl Harbor continue, with the standard narrative being Gordon Prange's *At Dawn We Slept* (1991). However, Prange's scholarship has been revised by Jonathan Parshall and J. Michael Wenger, 'Pearl Harbor's Overlooked Answer', *Naval History* 25:6 (December 2011); and, most recently, Alan D. Zimm, *Attack on Pearl Harbor: Strategy, Combat, Myths, Deceptions* (Philadelphia, Pa.: Casemate, 2011). All these historians heavily criticize Japanese naval strategy and Admiral Yamamoto, but Zimm is most effective in demonstrating that Yamamoto was after the American battleships and willing to sacrifice his carriers to get them.

A number of excellent works have come out recently on a variety of the Pacific War campaigns. Most useful for the pivotal Battle of Midway are Jonathan Parshall and Anthony Tully, *Shattered Sword: The Untold Story of the Battle of Midway* (Washington DC: Potomac Books, 2005), which provides the Japanese perspective of the battle. New analyses of the American side are provided by Craig Symonds in *The Battle of Midway* (Oxford and New York: Oxford University Press, 2011), and Thomas C. Hone (ed.), *The Battle of Midway: The Naval Institute Guide to the US Navy's Greatest Victory* (Annapolis, Md.: Naval Institute Press, 2013) For the authoritative account of Guadalcanal see Richard Frank, *Guadalcanal* (New York: Random House, 1990). Leyte Gulf, the last major fleet engagement in history has also been treated to recent revision and analysis in H. P. Willmott, *The Battle of Leyte Gulf: The Last Fleet Action* (Bloomington: Indiana University Press, 2005), as well as by Milan Vego from an operational-level perspective, in *The Battle for Leyte, 1944: Allied and Japanese Plans, Preparations, and Execution* (Annapolis, Md.: Naval Institute Press, 2006). For Okinawa, see Thomas M. Huber, *Japan's Battle of Okinawa: April–June 1945*, Leavenworth Paper no. 18 (Fort Leavenworth, Kan.: Combat Studies Institute, 1990), for the Japanese perspective and planning. Bill Sloan's *The Ultimate Battle: Okinawa 1945 – The Last Epic Struggle of World War II* (New York: Simon & Schuster, 2007) is a more recent comprehensive account, which includes both Allied and Japanese perspectives. For an excellent account of the kamikaze side of the campaign and ship losses, see Robin L. Rielly, *Kamikazes, Corsairs and Picket Ships: Okinawa, 1945* (Havertown, Pa.: Casemate, 2008).

The Pacific War also inspired classic military memoirs, but two works, one operational-strategic and one tactical, must be mentioned. Field Marshal Viscount Slim, *Defeat into Victory* (London: Cassell and Co. Ltd, 1956), about the Burma campaign, is among the greatest campaign works and commentaries on leadership existent. Eugene Sledge's profoundly disturbing *With the Old Breed* (Novato, Calif.: Presidio Press, 1981), about the First Marine Division at Peleliu and Okinawa, provides the gritty, horrifying perspective of war in the Pacific at the tactical level and below. On the Japanese side, a number of memoirs exist and many accounts were later published as articles in the United States Naval Institute *Proceedings* after the war. Among these, that of Admiral Raizo Tanaka (with the assistance of Roger Pineau), 'Japan's Losing Struggle for Guadalcanal', United States Naval Institute *Proceedings* 82:7 and 8 (July/August 1956), 687–99 (Part I) and 815–31 (Part II), is perhaps the best operational discussion, and Admiral Matome Ugaki's partially recovered diary, *Fading Victory: The Diary of Admiral Matome Ugaki, 1941–1945*, translated by Masataka Chihaya (Pittsburgh, Pa.: University of Pittsburgh Press, 1991), is a useful look into the mind of the man who served as Yamamoto's Chief of Staff and then architect of the Japanese Ketsu-Go (kamikaze) campaigns.

The end of the Pacific War remains shrouded in controversy, especially over the issue of the dropping of the atomic bombs and their relationship to the planned invasion, Operation DOWNFALL. The best discussion of the relationship of these factors can be found in D. M. Giangreco, *Hell to Pay: Operation Downfall and the Invasion of Japan, 1945–1947* (Annapolis, Md.: Naval Institute Press, 2009). Richard Frank's *Downfall: The End of the Imperial Japanese Empire* (London: Penguin, 2001) is also useful. The entire issue of the atomic bombs became politicized as the aftermath and implications of the use of atomic weapons became tied up in Cold War historiography. Gar Alperovitz's *Atomic Diplomacy: Hiroshima and Potsdam – The Use of the Atomic Bomb and the American Confrontation with Soviet Power* (New York: Simon & Schuster, 1965) has muddied the waters for several decades and continues to do so today, in arguing that Hiroshima and Nagasaki were the opening shots of the Cold War. For a fine review of the subsequent debates about the bomb and the end of the war, see Michael Kort, 'The Historiography of Hiroshima: The Rise and Fall of Revisionism', *New England Journal of History* 64:1 (fall 2007), 31–48. Finally, for the last act of the tragedy, the Soviet invasion that occurred simultaneously with the atomic bombs, see David M. Glantz, *The Soviet Strategic Offensive in Manchuria, 1954: August Storm* (London and Portland, Oreg.: Frank Cass, 2003); and Tsuyoshi Hasegawa, *Racing the Enemy: Stalin, Truman, and the Surrender of Japan* (Cambridge, Mass.: Belknap Press of Harvard University Press, 2006), which argues that President Harry Truman wanted to end the war prior to Soviet entry into the conflict.

16 The Atlantic war, 1939–1945
Marc Milner

The essential starting point for any look at the Atlantic and Arctic campaigns remains the official histories of the combatants. These include S. E. Morison's

History of United States Naval Operations in World War II, vols. 1 and x (Boston, Mass.: Little, Brown, 1947, 1962); three volumes of S. W. Roskill's *The War at Sea* (London: HMSO, 1954–61); F. H. Hinsley et al. (eds.), *British Intelligence in the Second World War: Its Influence on Strategy and Operations* (4 vols., London: HMSO, 1979–90); and D. Richards and H Saunders, *The Royal Air Force, 1939–1945* (London: HMSO, 1974). Recent Canadian official histories have drawn on extensive primary research and rebuilt the context of the Atlantic war: see W. A. B. Douglas et al., *The Official History of the Royal Canadian Air Force*, vol. 11: *The Creation of a National Air Force:* (University of Toronto Press, 1986); and W. A. B. Douglas, Roger Sarty, Michael Whitby et al., *No Higher Purpose: The Official History of the Royal Canadian Navy in the Second World War* (St Catharines, Ont.: Vanwell Publishing Ltd, 2002), vol. 11, pt. 1; and W. A. B. Douglas, Roger Sarty, Michael Whitby et al., *A Blue Water Navy: The Official History of the Royal Canadian Navy in the Second World War* (St Catharines, Ont.: Vanwell Publishing Ltd, 2007), vol. 11, pt. 2.

Some crucial staff histories on the Atlantic campaigns are now published. The most concise, if dated, account of the Russian convoys is *The Royal Navy and the Arctic Convoys: A Naval Staff History* (London: Routledge, 2007), with a superb preface by Malcolm Llewellyn-Jones. The larger issue of trade defence is covered in D. W. Waters, *Defeat of the Enemy Attack on Shipping* (Aldershot: Ashgate/Naval Records Society, 1997), edited by Eric Grove. And what passes for the 'official history' of the U-boat war, written by Günter Hessler for the British immediately after 1945, *The U-boat War in the Atlantic* (London: HMSO, 1989), is indispensable. Sadly, the best focused account of American anti-U-boat operations remains C. M. Sternhell and A. M. Thorndike, *Anti-submarine Warfare in World War II* (Washington DC: Office of the Chief of Naval Operations, 1946).

Unofficial compendia are invaluable. Among these are Arnold Hague's *The Allied Convoy System: Its Organization, Defence and Operation* (London: Chatham Publishing, 2000); J. Rohwer and G. Hummlechen's *Chronology of the War at Sea, 1939–1945* (Annapolis, Md.: Naval Institute Press, 1992); and Jurgen Rohwer, *Axis Submarine Success, 1939–1945* (Annapolis, Md.: Naval Institute Press, 1983). Clay Blair's massive two-volume *Hitler's U-Boat War: The Hunters, 1939–1942* (New York: Random House, 1997), is both history and compilation, with exhaustive detail and extensive appendices. Peter Elliot's *Allied Escort Ships of World War II* (London: Macdonald Janes, 1977) remains a standard reference for war-built classes, and a very useful supplement to a series of compendia on Second World War warships by H. T. Lenton, including his *German Warships of the Second World War* (New York: Arco,

1976). Eberhard Rossler's *The U-boat* (London: Arms and Armour Press, 1981) remains the standard work on U-boats. Of course, much of this material (especially information on U-boats), including lost or damaged merchant ships, is now readily available on the internet.

Civil and logistical official histories are also often neglected, but they have much to add, especially C. B. A. Behrens, *Merchant Shipping and the Demands of War* (London: HMSO and Longmans Green, 1955), part of the British civil series; and R. M. Leighton and R. W. Coakley's American official history, *Global Logistics and Strategy, 1940–1943* (Washington DC: Department of the Army, 1968). These speak to the limited and often fleeting impact of losses at sea compared to the larger administrative, production and allocation bottlenecks that plague a global total war. Martin Doughty's little book, *Merchant Shipping and War* (London: Royal Historical Society, 1982) highlights this point, especially the impact of the Blitz (rather than the U-boats) on British imports.

There are many monographs that deal with specific aspects of the Atlantic and Arctic campaigns. Patrick Abbazia's *Mr Roosevelt's Navy: The Private War of the US Atlantic Fleet, 1939–1942* (Annapolis, Md.: Naval Institute Press, 1975) on the USN's undeclared war in 1941 remains a classic. Marc Milner's *North Atlantic Run: The Royal Canadian Navy and the Battle for the Convoys* (University of Toronto Press, 1985) is the standard work on the RCN in the mid-ocean from 1941 to 1943. David Syrett's *The Defeat of the German U-boats: The Battle of the Atlantic* (Columbia: University of South Carolina Press, 1994), is the most detailed account of the use of ULTRA in the spring of 1943. Jurgen Rohwer's *Critical Convoy Battles of March 1943* (Annapolis, Md.: Naval Institute Press, 1977) dissects the crisis of March 1943, nicely complementing Martin Middlebrook's people-focused account of the same battles, *Convoy* (London: Allen Lane, 1976). Michael Gannon's *Operation Drumbeat: The Dramatic True Story of Germany's First U-boat Attacks Along the American Coast in World War II* (New York: Harper Collins, 1990) covers the opening phases of the attack along the US coast in 1942. *The Arctic Convoys, 1941–1945* by Richard Woodman (London: John Murray, 1984) is now the standard on that subject, while a glimpse into RN operations can be had through G. G. Connell's *Arctic Destroyers* (London: William Kimber, 1982), which tracks the 17th Destroyer Flotilla from PQ 8 to the end of the war.

Intelligence, especially ULTRA, has garnered a great deal of attention. David Kahn's *Seizing the Enigma: The Race to Break the German U-boat Codes, 1939–1943* (Boston, Mass.: Houghton, Mifflin, 1991) remains the best in that field. W. Jock Gardner's *Decoding History: The Battle of the Atlantic and Ultra* (London: MacMillan, 1999) does a nice job of marrying D. W. Water's holistic approach to the Atlantic war with the impact of ULTRA at certain critical phases. And David Syrett edited a useful reference on ULTRA for the Naval Records Society, *The Battle of the Atlantic and Signals Intelligence: U-Boat Tracking Papers, 1941–1947* (Aldershot: Ashgate/Naval Records Society, 2002).

Specific studies of convoys, incidents and ships abound. William T. Y'Blood's *Hunter Killer: US Escort Carriers in the Battle of the Atlantic* (Annapolis, Md.: Naval Institute Press, 1983) outlines American success at hunting U-boats in the final phases of the war. Kenneth Poolman's *Escort Carriers* (London: Ian Allen, 1972) tells the British tale of light carriers in the Atlantic and Arctic (without the benefit of the ULTRA revelation). Christopher Bell's *Churchill and Seapower* (Oxford University Press, 2013) has some excellent chapters on Churchill's attitude toward the Atlantic war, and provides a modern, scholarly insight beyond the standard fare in Captain S. W. Roskill, *Churchill and The Admirals* (London: William Collins and Sons, 1977). Curiously, it seems that no monograph has ever been published on the UK–Sierra Leone/West Africa convoys.

Memoir literature is now, of course, a finite resource. Some of the classics include Donald Macintyre's *U-boat Killer* (London: Weidenfeld & Nicolson, 1956); J. M. Waters' *Bloody Winter* (Princeton, NJ: Van Nostrand, 1967); Alan Easton's *50 North* (Toronto: Ryerson, 1966); Sir Peter Gretton's *Convoy Escort Commander* (London: Cassell, 1964); Denys A. Rayner, *Escort* (London: Kimber, 1953); Karl Dönitz, *Memoirs* (London: Weidenfeld & Nicolson, 1959); Erich Topp, *The Odyssey of a U-Boat Commander* (Westport, Conn.: Praeger, 1992); Herbert A. Werner, *Iron Coffins* (London: Barker, 1970). Biographies of key players in the Atlantic and Arctic campaigns are virtually non-existent, and those that exist are typically old and hagiographic, like Rear Admiral W. S. Chalmer's *Max Horton and the Western Approaches* (London: Hodder & Stoughton, 1954). The exception is Peter Padfield's *Dönitz* (New York: Harper and Row, 1984). Collections of reminiscences, such as Brian Lavery's *In Which They Served* (Annapolis, Md.: Naval Institute Press, 2008), Mac Johnston's *Corvettes Canada* (Toronto: McGraw-Hill Ryerson, 1994), and John T. Mason, Jr. (ed.), *The Atlantic War Remembered: An Oral History Collection* (Annapolis, Md.: Naval Institute Press, 1990), capture the flavour of the British, Canadian and American experience.

One-volume accounts of the Atlantic war are not numerous, but they serve as useful benchmarks for the state of the literature generally. Terry Hughes and John Costello's *The Battle of the Atlantic* (New York: Dial Press, 1977) reflects the stage of the art in the immediate post-ULTRA revelation years; while Dan Van der Vat's 1985 work, *The Atlantic Campaign: World War*

II's Greatest Struggle at Sea (Edgewood Cliffs, NJ: Prentice-Hall) captures more ULTRA and some of the emerging Canadian literature. Marc Milner's *Battle of the Atlantic* (Stroud: Tempus, 2003) strives to integrate the maturing consensus on ULTRA and the tremendous amount of work done by Canadian scholars on the Atlantic into a new narrative.

Despite the extensive, multinational nature of the literature on the Atlantic campaign, the subject remains one of the great underexplored subjects of the Second World War.

17 Anglo-American strategic bombing, 1940–1945
Tami Davis Biddle

Judgements on the British and American strategic air campaigns in the Second World War began to appear soon after the war ended, and the debate has never ceased. The literature is vast and shows no signs of abating. This is understandable, since writers are drawn to the controversial campaigns. An ongoing problem, however, is that many who write about the campaigns do not place them firmly in their historical context, and do not understand the profound tactical and operational complexities of long-range aerial bombing. The latter should not be surprising, since it requires no small investment of time to master the myriad factors affecting the employment of bombers and their effectiveness (or lack thereof) in war. While this brief essay cannot hope to be comprehensive, it will point to the books that may be most informative to researchers.

Both the British and the Americans undertook bombing surveys; the British had hoped for a joint survey, but the Americans declined. General Carl Spaatz of USSTAF (United States Strategic Air Forces) did not want the British effort to be merged, in the American mind, with the work of his own forces. Winston Churchill showed little interest in a bombing survey; indeed, he stalled when the Air Ministry asked for permission to begin, and then ensured that the effort by the British Bombing Survey Unit (BBSU) would be limited and its results circulated narrowly. More extensive background and analysis on the US Survey can be found in David MacIsaac, *Strategic Bombing in World War II* (New York: Garland, 1976); also Gian Peri Gentile, 'Advocacy or Assessment? The United States Strategic Bombing Survey of Germany and Japan', *Pacific Historical Review* 66:1 (February 1997). Both the British and American official historians comment helpfully on the surveys: Wesley Frank Craven and James Lea Cate (eds.), *The Army Air Forces in World War II*, vol. III: *Europe: Argument to VE Day, January 1944 to May 1945* (University of

Chicago Press, 1951), pp. 789–802; and Sir Charles Webster and Noble Frankland, *The Strategic Air Offensive Against Germany*, vol. IV: *Annexes and Appendices* (4 vols., London: HMSO, 1961), pp. 40–58. For further analysis, see Tami Davis Biddle, *Rhetoric and Reality in Air Warfare: The Evolution of British and American Ideas about Strategic Bombing, 1914–1945* (Princeton, NJ: Princeton University Press, 2002), pp. 270–86.

The RAF's Chief of Air Staff Sir Charles Portal understood the danger of allowing the Americans to control the story, and indeed his concerns were well-founded: the US survey downplayed and sometimes disparaged the British effort, shaping analysis and historiography to this day, and preventing Bomber Command's wide array of work to be fully recognized. On this dispute between Portal and Churchill, see Tami Davis Biddle, 'Winston Churchill and Sir Charles Portal: Their Wartime Relationship, 1940–1945', in Peter Gray and Sebastian Cox (eds.), *Air Power Leadership: Theory and Practice* (London: The Stationery Office, 2002), pp. 194–7.

This effect was countered, belatedly in the 1990s, by the publication of Sir Arthur Harris's 'Final Despatch' on the air campaign, and the 'Report of the British Bombing Survey Unit'. The RAF's chief historian, Sebastian Cox, added useful introductory material to both volumes: *Sir Arthur Harris: Despatch on War Operations* (London: Frank Cass, 1995); *The Strategic Air War Against Germany, 1939–1945: Report of the British Bombing Survey Unit* (London: Frank Cass, 1998). Because the BBSU report was heavily influenced by Tedder's principal advisor, Solly Zuckerman, it gave primary attention to the impact of the transportation plan; it assigned that plan responsibility for collapsing the German war economy in 1944–45. This view was reinforced by arguments made in several of the US reports, by the US official history, and by several subsequent studies – including a notable one by Alfred Mierzejewski that deepened the evidence base on which the argument rested: Alfred C. Mierzejewski, *The Collapse of the German War Economy, 1944–45* (Chapel Hill: University of North Carolina Press, 1988).

Adam Tooze's recent, masterful study of the Reich's war economy explains the impact of the 1943 Ruhr campaign on Germany, and the 1944–45 campaign's impact on the rail links and waterways running between the Ruhr and the rest of Germany: Adam Tooze, *The Wages of Destruction: The Making and Breaking of the Nazi Economy* (London: Allen Lane, 2006). By January 1945, coal shortages in the Mannheim region were resulting in production declines of 80 per cent in some industries.

The American analytical effort – which became the US Strategic Bombing Survey (USSBS) – was vast in scope (over 330 reports and annexes), and thus unwieldy. In light of this, the two documents read and cited most often were the 'Summary Reports' for the European and Pacific theatres. On 24 October 1945, USSBS Vice Chairman Henry Alexander read aloud to the press sections of the Overall and Summary Reports on the European war, which were compromise statements lacking analytical precision: 'Allied air power was decisive in the war in Western Europe'. This was a more qualified statement than it seemed, since it used 'air power' instead of 'strategic bombing', and 'Western Europe' instead of 'Europe'. It drew attention away from the more critical reports, including the main one on the Germany economy written by John Kenneth Galbraith, which pointed out that until 1944, the impact of bombing was limited. Similarly, the Summary Report on the Far Eastern theatre was more celebratory than readers of the individual reports might have anticipated. Many of the best reports of the USSBS indicated that industry could be resilient and adaptive, that civilians could endure and absorb far higher levels of bombing than had been anticipated before the war, and that the relationship between high pain levels and surrender was anything but straightforward. Air power advocates and post-war US Air Force histories were inclined to highlight USSBS data, focusing on Spaatz's preferred oil campaign of 1944–45.

Just three years after the war ended, American official historians – led by Wesley Frank Craven of New York University (later Princeton), and James Lea Cate of the University of Chicago – published the first volume of what would be a seven-volume history of the USAAF in the Second World War. Titled *The Army Air Forces in World War II*, it covered the use of air power in both the European and Pacific theatres, and included additional chapters on such topics as organization, recruitment, training, logistics, medicine, air-sea rescue and women in the Army Air Forces. In his foreword to a new imprint of the volumes in 1983, then Chief of the Office of Air Force History, Richard Kohn, explained that, like all history, the volumes reflected the prevailing sentiments of their time. They were constrained by classification of the Allied code-breaking effort (central to a comprehensive understanding of the oil campaign of 1944–45). But he observed that the volumes nonetheless met the highest professional standards of their day. The authors especially noted the value of sustained air supremacy. They credited transport and oil for key impacts in Europe, and, while highlighting the great effect of naval blockade and bomber-sown mines in the Pacific War, also gave credit to urban area bombing for significantly lowering Japanese industrial production and eroding civilian morale.

Several decades after the Craven and Cate volumes appeared, air force historian Richard G. Davis wrote and published two volumes so comprehensive and meticulous that they might be considered updates to the official history of the US strategic bombing campaign in Europe: *Carl A. Spaatz and the Air War in Europe* (Washington DC: Center for Air Force History, 1993), and *Bombing the European Axis Powers: A Historical Digest of the Combined Bomber Offensive, 1939–1945* (Maxwell Air Force Base, Ala.: Air University Press, 2006). In 1998, the US Air Force History Office published *Case Studies in Strategic Bombardment*, ed. R. Cargill Hall (Washington DC: Air Force History and Museums Program, 1998), which includes helpful chapters on the US and British strategic air offensive in the Second World War, and the US strategic air campaign in the Pacific. Richard Overy's chapter on the years leading up to 1939 covers a wide landscape with authority and wisdom.

The British official history of the bombing campaign, *The Strategic Air Offensive Against Germany, 1939–1945*, vols. I–III, plus appendices (vol. IV), finally appeared in 1961 (London: HMSO). The painstaking work that went into it paid off handsomely, as it is an example of official history at its finest. Deeply insightful, wise and a delight to read, the volumes are a testament to their able authors, the noted diplomatic historian Sir Charles Webster, and former RAF navigator Noble Frankland. Sadly, Webster died shortly after the volumes appeared. Frankland went on to a distinguished career that included leadership of Britain's Imperial War Museum. The volumes were controversial when they first appeared, since many interested parties, Harris included, had hoped they would be an uncritical defence of Bomber Command decisions. See Frankland, 'Some Thoughts about and Experience of Official Military History', *RAF Historical Society Journal* 17 (1997), 7–23; and Sebastian Cox, 'Setting the Historical Agenda: Webster and Frankland and the Debate over the Strategic Bombing Offensive Against Germany', in Jeffrey Grey (ed.), *The Last Word: Essays on Official History in the United States and British Commonwealth* (Westport, Conn.: Praeger, 2003), pp. 147–73. No writer who wishes to comment intelligently on the Combined Bomber Offensive can afford to ignore them.

For insights into the British home front under air attack, one should consult two other official volumes: *The Defence of the United Kingdom* (London: HMSO, 1957) by Basil Collier; and *Problems of Social Policy* (London: HMSO, 1950) by R. M. Titmuss. Years later, F. H. Hinsley was the principal editor of the official histories on British intelligence published by Cambridge University Press: *British Intelligence in the Second World War* (multiple volumes, beginning in 1979). Martin Middlebrook and Chris Everitt, *The Bomber Command War Diaries: An Operational Reference Book, 1939–1945* (New York: Viking, 1985) contains important detail and statistical material. Richard

Overy's 2013 volume, *The Bombing War, 1939–1945* (London: Allen Lane, 2013), is also a vital source on the German air offensive against Britain; it examines topics not often taken up, including the German bombing of Soviet cities, the Allied bombing of Italy and the Allied bombing of occupied territory in Europe.

The Canadian role in the Second World War air war, and in the strategic bombing campaign specifically, has long been under-appreciated. The Canadian official historians sought to correct that, and to offer their own considerable insights, in *The Official History of the Royal Canadian Air Force*, vol. III: *The Crucible of War, 1939–1945* (University of Toronto Press, 1994), by Brereton Greenhous, Stephen J. Harris, William C. Johnston and William G. P. Rawling. The German perspective has recently been brought to light in several volumes of the extensive and deeply researched German official history, *Germany and the Second World War*. Of particular importance are Hoorst Boog's chapters on the strategic air war in Europe, 1943–44, in volume VII: *The Strategic Air War in Europe and the War in the West and East Asia, 1943–1944/5* (10 vols., Oxford: Clarendon Press, 2006). But insights into various elements of the air war can be found throughout the volumes. For instance, one might wish to examine Ralf Blank, 'Wartime Daily Life and the Air War on the Home Front', in *Germany and the Second World War*, vol. IX: *German Wartime Society, 1939–1945* (10 vols., Oxford: Clarendon Press, 2008), pt. I, pp. 371–476.

Richard Overy's general history of the Second World War air war, *The Air War, 1939–1945* (New York: Stein and Day, 1981) remains essential. Overy continued to publish frequently on aspects of strategic bombing in the Second World War, and in his 1995 volume, *Why the Allies Won* (London: Jonathan Cape, 1995), he argued that 'the defeat of the German air force, the diversion of effort from the eastern front at a critical point in that struggle, the successful preliminaries to D-day, belie the view that bombing was a strategy of squandered effort. It is difficult to think of anything else the Allies might have done with their manpower and resources that could have achieved this much at such comparatively low cost'. But the final conclusion he draws in *The Bombing War, Europe 1939–1945* is harsher; he argues that resources devoted to Allied long-range bombing were largely misappropriated, and might have been more productively invested in such things as long-range fighters and precision weapons. 'Without so-called "smart" weapons, strategic bombing was a wasteful use of resources, since most bombs did not hit the intended target, even when that target was the size of a city centre' (p. 613). Earlier in the book, however, Overy acknowledges the myriad effects of bombing, including a vast diversion of German resources from the Eastern Front. The reader is left to interpret this apparent tension.

Max Hastings' critical and highly readable *Bomber Command,* published in 1979 (New York: Dial Press, 1979), re-energized the debate over strategic bombing that had commenced shortly after the war with Sir Gerald Dickens, *Bombing and Strategy: The Fallacy of Total War* (London: Sampson Low, 1946), and Marshall Andrews, *Disaster Through Air Power* (New York: Rinehart and Co., 1949), and continued with Anthony Verrier, *The Bomber Offensive* (London: Batsford, 1968). John Terraine's *The Right of the Line: The Royal Air Force in the European War, 1939-1945* (London: Hodder & Stoughton, 1985) offers a sweeping view, examining the many tactical, operational and strategic challenges that the entire RAF faced. Norman Longmate's *Bombers* (London: Hutchinson, 1988) and Denis Richards's *The Hardest Victory* (London: Hodder & Stoughton, 1994) are focused on Bomber Command alone. A more recent take is Roy Irons, *The Relentless Offensive: War and Bomber Command, 1939–1945* (Barnsley: Pen & Sword Books, 2009). Still useful as a general overview are Alan J. Levine, *The Strategic Bombing of Germany, 1940–1945* (New York: Praeger, 1992); and Robin Neillands, *The Bomber War* (London: John Murray, 2001). Important insights can be found in Horst Boog's edited volume, *The Conduct of the Air War in the Second World War: An International Comparison* (Oxford: Berg, 1992).

On ethics and the British air campaign, see Stephen Garrett, *Ethics and Air Power in World War II: The British Bombing of German Cities* (New York: St Martin's Press, 1993). Anthony Grayling's problematic *Among the Dead Cities: Was the Allied Bombing of Civilians in World War II a Necessity or a Crime?* (London: Bloomsbury, 2005) brought contested moral questions back to the surface. (A problem with many of the philosophical accounts is that their authors have an inadequate grasp of the technical and operational challenges involved in mid-twentieth-century aerial bombing.) Thoughtful insights into important questions can be found in Yuki Tanaka and Marilyn B. Young (eds.), *Bombing Civilians* (New York: The New Press, 2009). See also Michael Burleigh, *Moral Combat: A History of World War II* (New York: Harper, 2011). A useful starting place for the discussion remains Michael Walzer's *Just and Unjust Wars* (New York: Basic Books, 1977).

Shortly after the war, Sir Arthur Harris defended his command and his crews in his memoir, *Bomber Offensive* (London: Collins, 1947). Lord Tedder's *Air Power in War* (1948) and *With Prejudice: The War Memoirs of Marshal of the Royal Air Force Lord Tedder* (London: Cassell, 1966) remain essential; Sir Robert Saundby's *Air Bombardment* (New York: Harper, 1961) contains important personal insights. Key biographies include Denis Richards's *Portal of Hungerford* (London: Heinemann, 1977); Charles Messenger's *Harris and the Strategic Bombing Offensive* (London: Arms and Armour Press, 1984); Henry Probert's *Bomber Harris* (London: Greenhill Books, 2001); and Vincent Orange's *Tedder: Quietly in Command* (London: Frank Cass, 2004). Valuable accounts from British aircrew include Guy Gibson, *Enemy Coast Ahead* (London: Michael Joseph, 1946); Don Charlwood, *No Moon Tonight* (Manchester: Crécy, 2000 [1956]); Miles Tripp, *The Eighth Passenger* (London: Macmillan, 1969); and Leonard Cheshire, *Bomber Pilot* (New York: Harper Collins, 1975).

In the USA, criticism of the bombing campaign developed somewhat more slowly than in the UK. But important, deeply researched critiques emerged, including Ronald Schaffer's *Wings of Judgment* (New York: Oxford University Press, 1985); Michael Sherry's *The Rise of American Air Power* (New Haven, Conn.: Yale University Press, 1987); and Conrad Crane's more restrained *Bombs, Cities, and Civilians* (Lawrence: University Press of Kansas, 1993). On the Pacific campaign, one should also consult Kenneth Werrell, *Blankets of Fire* (Washington DC: Smithsonian Institution Scholarly Press, 1998). Important American biographies include (along with Davis's *Carl A. Spaatz*), Dik Daso's *Hap Arnold and the Evolution of American Air Power* (Washington DC: Smithsonian, 2003), and *Doolittle: Aerospace Visionary* (London: Brassey's, 2003). Personal memoirs by commanders include James Doolittle's *I Could Never Be So Lucky Again* (New York: Bantam, 1992); Haywood Hansell, *The Strategic Air War Against Germany and Japan* (Washington DC: Office of Air Force History, 1986); and Curtis LeMay and MacKinley Kantor, *Mission with LeMay* (New York: Doubleday, 1965). Notable US crew member memoirs include John Muirhead's *Those Who Fall* (New York: Random House, 1986); and Philip Ardery's *Bomber Pilot* (Lexington: University Press of Kentucky, 1978).

Important books focusing on the experience of bomber crews include John Nichol and Tony Rennell, *Tail-End Charlies*, on US and British crews (New York: Viking, 2004); and Donald Miller's *Masters of the Air* (New York: Simon & Schuster, 2006), which focuses on US crews. For a more academic treatment of crew morale and psychology, see Mark K. Wells, *Courage and Air Warfare* (London: Frank Cass, 1995). Martin Francis makes an initial attempt to locate the RAF inside British culture: *The Flyer* (Oxford University Press, 2008). Insightful memoirs by scientists working for Bomber Command include Solly Zuckerman's *From Apes to Warlords* (New York: Harper and Row, 1978); and Freeman Dyson's *Disturbing the Universe* (New York: Harper and Row, 1979).

For decades, writers have tried to capture what it was like for German citizens to experience the Anglo-American bombing campaign. Notable works include Hans Rumpf, *The Bombing of Germany* (New York: Holt, Rinehart and Winston, 1961); Earl R. Beck, *Under the Bombs* (Lexington: University of Kentucky Press, 1986); Olaf Groehler, *Bombenkrieg gegen Deutschland* (Berlin: Akademie Verlag, 1990); and Hermann Knell, *To Destroy a City* (Cambridge, Mass.: Da Capo, 2003). Jörg Arnold's *The Allied Air War and Urban Memory* (Cambridge University Press, 2011) covers the terrain from a cultural perspective. Richard Overy's *The Bombing War* devotes an informed chapter to the German home front. In 2002, Jorg Friedrich's highly provocative and uneven *Der Brand* (The Fire) gained great attention among a new generation of Germans, who were more openly critical of the Allied bombing of Germany than their parents had been (Munich: Ullstein Heyne List GmbH). The book was published in the USA by Columbia University Press: *The Fire: The Bombing of Germany, 1940–1945* (New York: 2006.)

Several authors have concentrated on particular campaigns or individual raids. Worthwhile examples include Martin Middlebrook's several volumes: *The Battle of Hamburg* (London: Allen Lane, 1980); *The Schweinfurt-Regensburg Mission* (London: Allen Lane, 1983); *The Berlin Raids* (London: Penguin, 1988); and *The Nuremberg Raid* (London: Allen Lane, 1973). See also Robert Mrazek, *To Kingdom Come* (New York: New American Library, 2012), about the American raid on Stuttgart in September 1943. The now notorious David Irving moved the February 1945 Dresden raid to the centre of the debate about strategic bombing in his 1963 book, *The Destruction of Dresden* (London: William Kimber). It was reprinted many times in subsequent years. More reliable accounts are Götz Bergander, *Dresden im Luftkrieg: Vorgeschicte – Zerstorung – Folgen* (Würzburg Verlagshaus, 1985); Frederick Taylor, *Dresden* (New York: HarperCollins, 2004); and Paul Addison and Jeremy Crang (eds.), *Firestorm: The Bombing of Dresden, 1945* (London: Pimlico, 2006).

Stephen McFarland drew the linkage between American bombing doctrine and technology in *America's Pursuit of Precision Bombing, 1910–1945* (Washington DC: Smithsonian, 1995). Also important is McFarland's account of the American attempt to gain air supremacy, *To Command the Sky* (Washington DC: Smithsonian, 1991). Tami Davis Biddle sought to comprehend the intellectual and organizational roots of the Anglo-American bomber campaign in *Rhetoric and Reality in Air Warfare* (Princeton, NJ: Princeton University Press, 2002). Interesting theoretical analyses of the bomber campaigns over Germany and Japan can be found in Robert Pape's *Bombing to Win* (Ithaca, NY: Cornell University Press, 1996). Some important specialized studies include Charles McArthur, *Operational Analysis in the US Army Eighth Air Force in World War II* (Providence, RI: American Mathematical Society, 1990); Edward Westermann, *Flak* (Lawrence: University Press of Kansas, 2005); Robert Ehlers, *Targeting the Third Reich* (Lawrence: University Press of Kansas, 2009); Randall Wakelam, *The Science of Bombing: Operational Research in Bomber Command* (Toronto University Press, 2009); John Stubbington, *Kept in the Dark* (Barnsley: Pen & Sword Aviation, 2010); and Alfred Price, *Battle Over the Reich* (New York: Scribners, 1973).

18 War planning
Eliot A. Cohen

War planning is, in most cases, a rather dreary subject, but only because historians have chosen to make it so, poking through sheaves of paper plans, and then, as it were, grading them on plausibility. A subtler and more difficult approach requires that the historian, so overwhelmingly benefited by hindsight, ask him or herself three questions: (1) how did these people understand the very activity of war itself, and what its future was likely to be? (2) what were the effects on their planning of political system and military culture? And (3) what could they have expected, and what is it unreasonable to have thought they should have expected?

To address some of these questions, the best place to start is still, after half a century or more, the official histories, such as the first couple of volumes of the British *Grand Strategy* series (in particular, volume I, to September 1939, by N. H. Gibbs, and volume II, September 1939-June 1941, by J. R. M. Butler); the United States Army's "green books," and in particular, Maurice Matloff and Edwin M. Snell's two volumes on *Strategic Planning for Coalition Warfare*; and the superb German official history, *Germany in the Second World War* (most, though not all of which has been translated). The *Foreign Relations of the United States* series (particularly its volumes on the Washington and Casablanca Conferences; the Cairo and Tehran Conferences; and the Washington and Quebec Conferences) also provides primary sources that shed light on the politics of planning between the Big Three and their subordinates throughout the war.

Biographies of key figures are necessary to understand the vagaries of planning in any of the countries: Geoffrey Roberts' 2012 biography of Georgy Zhukhov is particularly effective in bringing that soldier's role to the attention of an English speaking audience. Some collections of documents bring alive the planners' mentality, probably none better than Nobutaka Ike, ed., *Japan's Decision for War: Records of the 1941 Policy Conferences*. Indeed, fully to grasp the feel of planning, one needs to read these remarkably lively accounts of senior figures wrestling with the imponderables of impending war. Their collected correspondence is equally valuable, which is available in Warren F. Kimball's three volume set, *Churchill & Roosevelt: The Complete Correspondence*. And with all the caveats one must attach to memoirs, it would be foolish to ignore works such as Walter Warlimont's *Inside Hitler's Headquarters* or the now unexpurgated diaries of Alan Brooke, the general whom Churchill nearly drove mad with his prodding.

For balanced assessments of how the major powers approached war three anthologies repay a look. The first are the second and third volumes of *Military Effectiveness*, edited by Allan R. Millett and Williamson Murray, which deal with the interwar period and the Second World War, respectively. The same editors' *Calculations: Net Assessment and the Coming of World War II* is equally valuable. Finally, B. J. C. McKercher and Roch Legault, *Military Planning and the Origins of the Second World War in Europe*, though uneven, has some interesting passages.

19 Armies, navies, air forces
The instruments of war
Dennis Showalter

If this chapter were an independent exercise, practically every sentence would benefit from its own footnote. As part of a larger work, most of its specific points are developed and referenced in other contributions. Footnotes have therefore been restricted to a minimum and structured as guideposts: a basic reference or two, intended to point the way to more detailed source information. This bibliography follows a similar pattern. It is built around anthologies and similar collective works whose contents offer a more developed set of directions to specific subjects.

Heading that list are volumes II and III of *Military Effectiveness*. Edited in 1988 by Allan Millett and Williamson Murray, published in a new edition by Cambridge University Press in 2010, these volumes address the effectiveness of principal military systems during the interwar years and in the Second World War. The chapters' common structure, addressing political, strategic, operational and tactical effectiveness, facilitates comparison. *Challenge of Change*, edited by Harold R. Winton and David R. Mets (Lincoln: University of Nebraska Press, 2000), focuses on interwar innovation, again asking similar questions of the major systems. *Military Innovation in the Interwar Period*, again edited by Murray and Millett and published by Cambridge in 1996, addresses technological change at the oil-and-electricity level in six comparative contexts involving five systems. The contributions in *Time to Kill: The Soldier's Experience of War in the West 1939–1945*, edited by Paul Addison and Angus Calder (London: Pimlico, 1997), make up in thematic coverage of the Second World War's military experience what the collection sacrifices in terms of geography.

On a broader scale, the German Historical Institute sponsored a series of five volumes, addressing chronologically the subject of total war. The final two, *The Shadows of Total War: Europe, East Asia, and the United States, 1919–1939* (2003), and *A World at Total War: Global Conflict and the Politics of Destruction, 1937–1945* (2005), were edited respectively by Roger Chickering and Stig Foerster, and by Chickering, Foerster and Bernd Greiner, and published by Cambridge University Press. They contain a spectrum of essays addressing in various contexts the themes of change, purpose and control that inform the present chapter.

And in the absence of a Russian front counterpart to the previously cited anthologies, Rolf-Dieter Mueller and Gerd Ueberschar (eds.), *Hitler's War in the East: A Critical Assessment* (New York: Berghahn, 2009), remains a basic bibliographical reference for its subject in a traditional format: six thematic sections of references, each with an excellent introductory guide.

20 Filling the ranks
Conscription and personnel policies
Sanders Marble

Excellent starting points are the essays in Allan Millett and Williamson Murray (eds.), *Military Effectiveness*, vol. III: *The Second World War)* (Boston, Mass.: Unwin Hyman, 1988). Various countries have had widely different amounts written about them. On Japan, Edward Drea's *Japan's Imperial Army: Its Rise and Fall, 1853–1945* (Lawrence: University Press of Kansas, 2009), is more up-to-date than Meirion Harries and Susie Harries, *Soldiers of the Sun: The Rise and Fall of the Imperial Japanese Army* (New York: Random House, 1991), but both have excellent insights. On Italy, MacGregor Knox, *Hitler's Italian Allies: Royal Armed Forces, Fascist Regime, and the War of 1940–1943* (Cambridge University Press, 2000), is the best, but has relatively little on manpower. On the USSR, David Glantz's two-volume 'biography' of the Red Army (*Stumbling Colossus: The Red Army on the Eve of War* and *Colossus Reborn: The Red Army at War, 1941–43*, both Lawrence: University Press of Kansas, 1998 and 2005) should eventually be supplemented by a third volume, but will not be supplanted as a work on this subject for years to come. Walter S. Dunn, *Stalin's Keys to Victory: The Rebirth of the Red Army*

(Westport, Conn.: Praeger, 2006), is a fine, shorter work. On Germany, the best starting point for data and analysis is the official histories by the Military History Research Office, *Germany and the Second World War*, vol. v, pts. i and ii: *Organization and Mobilization of the German Sphere of Power: Wartime Administration, Economy, and Manpower Resources, 1939–1941* and *1942–1944/45* (10 vols., Oxford: Clarendon Press, 2000, 2003). For a deep focus on German female workers, see Eleanor Hancock, 'Employment in Wartime: The Experience of German Women during the Second World War', *War & Society* 12:2 (1994), 43–68. On the British Commonwealth, F. W. Perry, *The Commonwealth Armies: Manpower and Organization in Two World Wars* (Manchester University Press, 1988), is short for its breadth of scope, but packs in a great deal, while David French, *Raising Churchill's Army: The British Army and the War Against Germany, 1919–1945* (Oxford University Press, 2000), delves less specifically into manpower, but has much information and many insights. David French, *Military Identities: The Regimental System, the British Army, and the British People, c.1870–2000* (Oxford University Press, 2005), is the most thoughtful review of that facet of the British Army so far. On France, there is little on the Free French forces, but Eugenia Kiesling, *Arming Against Hitler: France and the Limits of Military Planning* (Lawrence: University Press of Kansas, 1996), is very good to 1940.

On the USA, the literature is relatively voluminous. George Flynn has made a career of studying the draft, and his *The Draft, 1940–1973* (Lawrence: University Press of Kansas, 1993) is the standard work. A series of modern studies of infantry divisions (including divisional histories) gives a narrow slice of the manpower question, but Peter Mansoor, *The GI Offensive in Europe: The Triumph of American Infantry Divisions, 1941–1945* (Lawrence: University Press of Kansas, 1999), is broadest. The army's seventy-eight-volume official history (all from Washington DC: Center of Military History) has many volumes that touch on manpower and strategy, but seven are largely devoted to manpower: *The Organization of Ground Combat Troops* (1947); *The Procurement and Training of Ground Combat Troops* (1948); *The Employment of Negro Troops* (1966); *The Women's Army Corps* (1954); *The Army and Industrial Manpower* (1959); *Chief of Staff: Prewar Plans and Preparations* (1950); and *The Army and Economic Mobilization* (1959). Unfortunately, the US Navy's histories are operational rather than organizational, and while the Army Air Forces were part of the Army during the Second World War, they separated in 1947, and neither service's official histories include much about manpower in the Army Air Forces.

One thematic volume with coverage of manpower in the Second World War is Sanders Marble (ed.), *Scraping the Barrel: The Military Use of Sub-Standard Manpower, 1860–1960* (New York: Fordham University Press, 2012).

21 Logistics by land and air
Phillips Payson O'Brien

Considering how crucial supply was during the Second World War, relatively little has been written about it – especially considering the amount that has been written about battles or generalship. Where supply has been included, the story is often patchy. There are some examples of narratives where issues of supply are discussed well. Williamson Murray and Allan Millett's *A War to be Won: Fighting the Second World War* (Cambridge Mass.: Harvard University Press, 2001) does integrate supply issues throughout. More recently, Thomas Zeiler's survey of the war, *Annihilation: A Global Military History of World War II* (Oxford University Press, 2012) also includes supply issues to good effect.

The best data to be found on the subject come from the various official histories, in particular the American and British ones, but also the state-sponsored German histories, published in English as the multi-volume series *Germany and the Second World War* (10 vols., Oxford: Clarendon Press, 1990–). Of all the national histories, the most lavish in terms of historical output, which reflects the scale of supply efforts during the war, was produced by the United States. For instance, it has produced separate volumes on such areas as the quartermaster corps and the transport corps: *The United States Army in World War II: The Quartermaster Corps – Operations in the War Against Japan* (Washington DC: US Government Printing Office, 1990), and *The United States Army in World War II: The Transportation Corps – Responsibilities, Organization, and Operations* (Washington DC: US Government Printing Office, 1999). American grand strategy and army supply, which had a tremendous impact on both the United States' allies and enemies, is discussed in Richard Leighton and Robert Coakley's two-volume effort, *The United States Army in World War II: Global Logistics and Strategy* (Washington DC: US Government Printing Office, 1989 and 1995). Most helpfully, these army histories are all available for free download at www.history.army.mil/html/bookshelves/collect/usaww2.html – accessed 20 October 2014). The United States Army Air Forces histories, edited by Wesley Craven and James Cate, and the United States Navy Histories, written by Samuel Eliot Morison, all make regular mention of logistics – if on a less developed level than those of the Army.

The British official histories also say a good deal about supply. The British histories of the Army campaigns in Northwest Europe in 1944 provide important data: L. F. Ellis, *Victory in the West*, vol. i: *The Battle of Normandy* (London: HMSO, 1962), and vol. ii: *The Defeat of Germany* (London: HMSO,

1968). If there is one area where they trump the US histories, it is in the amount of time spent analysing shipping – always a huge British consideration. There is even an entire volume, written by C. B. A. Behrens, entitled *Merchant Shipping and the Demands of War* (London: HMSO, 1955). *Germany and the Second World War*, vol. IV: *The Attack on the Soviet Union* (10 vols., Oxford: Clarendon Press, 1998), contains a great deal of information and comment about the supply issues that faced the Germans during BARBAROSSA. It discusses different crises in rail and road transportation as the German army plunged deeper and deeper into Russia, before failing at the gates of Moscow.

When it comes to specific works about supply and the war, there are important texts. Maybe the most widely cited is Martin van Creveld, *Supplying War: Logistics from Wallenstein to Patton* (Cambridge University Press, 2004). This is not a general history of supply in the Second World War, but provides three thought-provoking chapters – on BARBAROSSA, the war in North Africa, and the war in France in 1944. Other books on specific campaigns and armies do make mention of supply, sometimes briefly. When it comes to the German army other than BARBAROSSA, detailed discussion of supply issues can be scarce. Karl-Heinz Frieser, *The Blitzkrieg Legend: The 1940 Campaign in the West* (Annapolis, Md.: Naval Institute Press, 2012), makes a number of important points about supply and German success in the invasion of France and the Low Countries in 1940, yet there is almost certainly more to be written on the subject. The importance of logistics and the Russo-German war in the East is more widely discussed. Most of the key historians of the subject, from David Glantz, *Companion to Colossus Reborn* (Lawrence: University Press of Kansas, 2005) to Evan Mawdsley, *Thunder in the East: The Nazi Soviet War 1941–1945* (London: Bloomsbury, 2007) and David Stahel, *Operation Barbarossa and Germany's Defeat in the East* (Cambridge University Press, 2009), acknowledge the crucial role of supply in this theatre.

There has been more written about the Red Ball Express. The American official history by Roland G. Ruppenthal, *The European Theater of Operations: Logistical Support of the Armies* (2 vols., Washington DC: US Government Printing Office, 1995) is definitely the place to start reading. For an examination of the policies that led to the construction of the famous 'deuce and a half' truck, which provided much of the lift capacity of the effort, one should go to Daniel Beaver's chapter in John Lynn's study of historical military logistics, *Feeding Mars: Logistics in Western Warfare from the Middle Ages to the Present* (Boulder, Colo.: Westview Press, 1994) – which regrettably has only one chapter on the Second World War.

The war in the Pacific between the United States and Japan does receive discussion, usually to highlight the extraordinary differences between the lavish supply system of the Americans and the more modest efforts of the Japanese. For information on the successful American logistical operations in support of the large amphibious assaults of 1944 and 1945, one place to start is Worrall R. Carter's study, *Beans, Bullets and Black Oil: The Story of Fleet Logistics Afloat in the Pacific During World War II* (Washington DC: US Government Printing Office, 1953). Richard Frank's excellent book on the end of the war in the Pacific, *Downfall: The End of the Imperial Japanese Empire* (London: Penguin, 2001), also makes a number of important points about the collapse of Japan's supply system. Anyone wanting to read a short but interesting piece on the logistics of the air war could start with Robert P. Smith's chapter in Horst Boog's edited collection, *The Conduct of the Air War in the Second World War* (Oxford: Berg, 1992).

The issue of food supplies has also been covered in a number of works. One constant theme is that armies were relatively well provided for when compared to civilians, as long as transport systems were protected. William Moskoff, *The Bread of Affliction: The Food Supply in the USSR During World War II* (Cambridge University Press, 2002), deals with the imbalance in calorie allocation between soldiers and civilians. Lizzie Collingham, in *The Taste of War: World War II and the Battle of Food* (London: Allen Lane, 2011), has written an interesting survey of food for all the main powers during the war. She highlights the Japanese food crisis, which started in 1943 and saw even the army and navy suffering major cutbacks in calories consumed.

The histories of railroads can be useful for examining the supply situation on the Eastern Front, particularly for those looking for sources written in English. Alfred Mierzejewski's *The Most Valuable Asset: A History of the German National Railway* (Chapel Hill: University of North Carolina Press, 2000), is fascinating. In the 1950s and 1960s, Holland Hunter produced a number of works, *Soviet Transportation Policy* (Cambridge, Mass.: Harvard University Press, 1957), and *Soviet Transport Experience: Its Lessons for Other Countries* (Washington DC: Brookings Institution, 1968), describing how the USSR was able to withstand the German invasion of 1941 and then rebuild its rail network as it proceeded to push the Germans back after 1943. Ernest W. Williams, *Freight Transportation in the Soviet Union, Including Comparisons with the United States* (Princeton, NJ: Princeton University Press, 1962), and E. A. Rees, *Stalinism and Soviet Rail Transport, 1928–41* (Basingstoke: Palgrave Macmillan, 1995), are helpful on the general subject of Soviet transportation policy.

22 Intelligence
John Ferris

The literature on intelligence during the Second World War is unusually problematical. Much of it is popular in nature, though such works often are well-researched. Few fields are so bedevilled by fantasy and conspiracy theory. The literature has been shaped by the spasmodic release of documents, and the way historians slowly learned how to handle complex evidence and issues. Work has progressed in separate, almost watertight areas, divided by nationality and topic. Synoptic works, analysing how one source affected a campaign, or all of them affected decisions, or the competition between the services of warring nations, are rare. The best example is the multi-volume F. H. Hinsley et al. (eds.), *British Intelligence in the Second World War: Its Influence on Strategy and Operations* (3 vols., London: HMSO, 1981–88), vol. IV: *Security and Counter-Intelligence* (London: HMSO, 1990), and Michael Howard, vol. V: *Strategic Deception* (London: HMSO, 1990).

Much work focuses on specific sources. Stephen Budiansky, *Battle of Wits: The Complete Story of Codebreaking in World War II* (New York: Free Press, 2000), illuminates signals intelligence in broad terms; while Colin Burke, *Information and Secrecy: Vannevar Bush, Ultra and the Other Memex* (Metuchen, NJ: Scarecrow, 1994), Cipher A. Devours and Louis Kruh, *Machine Cryptography and Modern Cryptanalysis* (Dedham, Mass.: Artech House, 1985), John Ferris, *Strategy and Intelligence: Selected Essays* (London: Routledge, 2005), and R. A. Ratcliff, *Delusions of Intelligence: Enigma, Ultra and the End of Secure Ciphers* (Cambridge University Press, 2006), address key technical issues. A booming literature focuses on Bletchley Park, such as F. H. Hinsley and Alan Stripp, *Codebreakers: The Inside Story of Bletchley Park* (Oxford Paperbacks, 1993), and Ralph Erskine and Michael Smith (eds.), *The Bletchley Park Codebreakers* (Padstow: Biteback, 2011). Though imagery awaits a thorough analysis, Alfred Price, *Targeting the Reich: Allied Photographic Reconnaissance over Europe, 1939–1945* (London: Greenhill Books, 2003), Peter Mead, *The Eye in the Sky: History of Air Observation and Reconnaissance, 1785–1945* (London: HMSO, 1983), Constance Babington-Smith, *Evidence in Camera: The Story of Photographic Reconnaissance in the Second World War* (London: Chatto & Windus, 1958), and Robert Ehlers, *Targeting the Third Reich: Air Intelligence and the Allied Bombing Campaigns* (Lawrence: University Press of Kansas, 2009), outline Anglo-American experiences. A useful account of radar is Louis Brown, *A Radar History of World War Two: Technical and Military Imperatives* (Bristol: Institute of Physics Publishing, 1999).

For intelligence and Anglo-American land operations in Europe and Africa, the best accounts are Ralph Francis Bennett, *Ultra in the West: The Normandy Campaign, 1944–45* (New York: Scribner's, 1980), and *Ultra and Mediterranean Strategy, 1941–1945* (New York: Morrow, 1989); the relevant sections of F. H. Hinsley et al. (eds.), *British Intelligence in the Second World War: Its Influence on Strategy and Operations* (3 vols., London: HMSO, 1981–88); John Ferris, 'Intelligence and Overlord: A Snapshot from 6 June 1944', in John Buckley (ed.), *Overlord Sixty Years Later* (London: Routledge, 2006), pp. 185–214; and Kevin Jones, *Intelligence, Command and Military Operations: The Eighth Army Campaign in Italy, 1943–45* (London: Routledge, 2011). Many strong works focus on the role of deception, including Katherine Barbier, *D-Day Deception: Operation Fortitude and the Normandy Invasion* (Westport, Conn.: Praeger, 2007); Michael Handel, *Strategic and Operational Deception in the Second World War* (London: Frank Cass, 1987); Roger Hesketh, *Fortitude: The D-Day Deception Campaign* (New York: Overlook Hardcover, 2000); and Thaddeus Holt, *The Deceivers: Allied Military Deception in the Second World War* (London: Weidenfeld & Nicolson, 2004). The best studies of American intelligence are Bradley Smith, *The Shadow Warriors, OSS and the Origins of the CIA* (New York: Basic Books, 1983), and David Alvarez, *Secret Messages: Codebreaking and American Diplomacy, 1930–1945* (Lawrence: University Press of Kansas, 2000).

For intelligence and the war at sea in European waters and the Atlantic Ocean, cf. Alan Harris Bath, *Tracking the Axis Enemy: The Triumph of Anglo-American Naval Intelligence* (Lawrence: University Press of Kansas, 1998), W. J. R. Gardner, *Decoding History: The Battle of the Atlantic and Ultra* (Annapolis, Md.: Naval Institute Press, 2002), Jürgen Rohwer, *The Crucial Convoy Battles of March 1943* (Annapolis, Md.: Naval Institute Press, 1977), David Syrett, *The Defeat of the German U-Boats: The Battle of the Atlantic* (Columbia: University of South Carolina Press, 1994), and Christina Goulter, *A Forgotten Offensive: Royal Air Force Coastal Command's Anti-Shipping Campaign 1940–1945* (London: Frank Cass, 1995). For German intelligence, cf. Heinz Bonatz, *Seekrieg im Äther: Die Leistungen der Marin-Funkaufklärung, 1939–1945* (Herford: E. S. Mittler, 1981), and Jak P. Malmann-Shovell, *German Naval Codebreakers* (Annapolis, Md.: Naval Institute Press, 2003), though ample room remains for strong studies.

David Kahn, *Hitler's Spies: German Military Intelligence in World War Two* (London: Hodder & Stoughton, 1978), is the best work on German intelligence, augmented by Hans-Otto Behrendt, *Rommel's Intelligence in the Desert Campaign, 1941–1943* (London: Kimber, 1985), United States War Department General Staff, *German Military Intelligence, 1939–1945* (Frederick, Md.: University Publications of America, 1984), Albert Praun, 'German Radio Intelligence', in John Mendelsohn (ed.), *Covert Warfare: Intelligence, Counterintelligence and Military Deception in the World War II Era*, vol. vi: *German Radio Intelligence and the Soldatsender* (New York: Garland Press, 1989), pp. 1–128, and Chief, Army Security Agency, *European Axis Signal Intelligence in World War II* (Washington DC: Army Security Agency, 1946) (www.nsa.gov/public_info/declass/european_axis_sigint.shtml – accessed 22 October 2014). For German intelligence on the Eastern Front, cf. Magnus Pahl, *Fremde Heere Ost. Hitlers militärische Feindaufklärung* (Berlin: Christoph Links Verlag, 2013), David Thomas, 'Foreign Armies East and German Military Intelligence in Russia 1941–45', *Journal of Contemporary History* 22 (1987), 261–301, Volker Detlef Heydorn, *Nachrichtennahaufklärung (Ost) und sowjetrussisches Heeresfunkwesen bis 1945* (Freiburg: Rombach Verlag, 1985), and DF-112, AS-14-TICOM, 'Survey of Russian Military Systems', 1 April 1948 (www.scribd.com/paspartoo/d/85583814-DF-112-Dettmann – accessed 22 October 2014).

For Soviet military intelligence, cf. Vadim J. Birstein, *Smersh – Stalin's Secret Weapon: Soviet Military Counterintelligence in WW II* (Padstow: Biteback Publishing, 2011), David Glantz, *Soviet Military Deception in the Second World War* (London: Frank Cass, 1989), David Glantz, *Soviet Military Intelligence in War* (London: Frank Cass, 1990), and Robert W. Stephan, *Stalin's Secret War: Soviet Counterintelligence against the Nazis, 1941–1945* (Lawrence: University Press of Kansas, 2003). Barton Whaley, *Codeword Barbarossa* (Cambridge, Mass.: MIT Press, 1973), and David Murphy, *What Stalin Knew: The Enigma of Barbarossa* (New Haven, Conn.: Yale University Press, 2005), illuminate German deception and Soviet surprise in Operation BARBAROSSA.

Ken Kotani, *Japanese Intelligence During World War II* (London: Osprey, 2009), is the best study of that topic. For American intelligence and operations, cf. John Prados, *Combined Fleet Decoded: The Secret History of American Intelligence and the Japanese Navy in World War Two* (New York: Random House, 1995), Gordon W. Prange, with Donald M. Goldstein and Katherine V. Dillon, *At Dawn We Slept: The Untold Story of Pearl Harbor* (London: Penguin, 1991), Edward J. Drea, *MacArthur's ULTRA: Codebreaking and the War against Japan, 1942–1945* (Lawrence: University Press of Kansas, 1992), Ronald Spector (ed.), *Listening to the Enemy: Key Documents on the Role of Communications Intelligence in the War with Japan* (Wilmington, Del.: Scholarly Resources, 1988), and Jonathan Parshall and Anthony Tully, *Shattered Sword: The Untold Story of the Battle of Midway* (Dulles, Va.: Potomac Books, 2005).

23 Prisoners of war
Bob Moore

The historiography on prisoners of war has made great advances in the last twenty-five years. Immediately following the Second World War, literature on prisoners of war and their experiences was largely confined to memoirs and autobiographies, and these were heavily weighted toward stories of escape, evasion or privation. The military histories of the period made little or no mention of the capture and incarceration of enemy soldiers, and it was not until the late 1960s that the first, and to date the only comprehensive study of a captor power appeared. German policies toward prisoners, and the history of their prisoners in enemy hands, were examined in Erich Maschke (ed.), *Zur Geschichte der deutscher Kriegsgefangenen des Zweiten Weltkrieges* (15 vols., Bielefeld: Gieseking, 1962–74). While extremely informative in many respects, the volumes were based largely on German sources and the authors had no access to government documents of other captor powers. Social histories of British, French and US soldiers in German captivity all made use of interviews with those involved: David Rolf, *Prisoners of the Reich: Germany's Captives, 1939–1945* (London: Leo Cooper, 1988); Yves Durand, *La Captivité: Histoire des prisonniers de guerre français 1939–1945* (Paris: FNCPG, 1980); and David Foy, *For You the War Is Over: American Prisoners of War in Nazi Germany* (New York: Stein and Day, 1984). These were followed by works paying greater attention to the politics of captivity as more state papers became available. In this context, one can point to the studies by Vasilis Vourkoutiotis, *Prisoners of War and the German High Command: The British and American Experience* (Basingstoke: Palgrave Macmillan, 2003), Arieh Kochavi, *Confronting Captivity: Britain and the United States and their POWs in Nazi Germany* (Chapel Hill: University of North Carolina Press, 2005), and Neville Wylie, *Barbed Wire Diplomacy: Britain, Germany and the Politics of Prisoners of War* (Oxford University Press, 2010), whose books cover the relationship between Germany and the Western Powers; and to Bob Moore and Kent Fedorowich, *The British Empire and its Italian Prisoners of War, 1940–1947* (Basingstoke: Palgrave, 2003), who have examined British imperial policy toward captured Italians. Important social histories of captivity have also continued to appear, not least the crucial work by S. Paul MacKenzie, *The Colditz Myth: British and Commonwealth Prisoners of War in Nazi Germany* (Oxford University Press, 2004), which undermined the idea of British prisoners as inveterate escapees; and also studies on the effect of captivity on prisoners' families in France and Britain, by

Sarah Fishman, *We Will Wait: Wives of French Prisoners of War, 1940–1945* (New Haven, Conn.: Yale University Press, 1991), and Barbara Hately-Broad, *War and Welfare: British Prisoner of War Families, 1939–1945* (Manchester University Press, 2009), respectively.

Over the last twenty years, these major monographs have been augmented by numbers of important edited collections, which have brought together scholars working on different themes of captivity in different theatres of war, and in some cases also in different wars – for example, Bob Moore and Kent Fedorowich, *Prisoners of War and their Captors in World War II* (Oxford: Berg, 1996); Bob Moore and Barbara Hately-Broad, *Prisoners of War, Prisoners of Peace* (Oxford: Berg, 2005); Günther Bischof and Rüdiger Overmans (eds.), *Kriegsgefangenschaft im Zweiten Weltkrieg. Eine Vergleichende Perspektive* (Ternitz-Pottschach: G. Höller, 1999); Anne-Marie Pathé and Fabien Théofilakis (eds.), *La Captivité de Guerre au XXe Siècle* (Paris, 2012); and Sybille Scheipers (ed.), *Prisoners in War* (Oxford University Press, 2010).

Recent volumes show an increasing interest in the most under-represented aspect of military captivity during the Second World War, namely the millions taken prisoner on the Eastern Front. Although pioneered in the study by Christian Streit, *Keine Kameraden. Die Wehrmacht und die sowjetischer Kriegsgefangenen 1941–1945* (2nd edn, Bonn: J. H. W. Dietz, 1997), this was given greater weight by the politicized debate on Wehrmacht war crimes from the late 1980s onward, surveyed in Hamburger Institut für Sozialforschung, *Verbrechen der Wehrmacht: Dimensionen des Vernichtungskrieges 1941–1944: Ausstellungskatalog* (Hamburg: Hamburger Edition, 2002), and Hannes Heer und Klaus Naumann, *Vernichtungskrieg. Verbrechen der Wehrmacht 1941–1944* (Hamburg: Hamburger Edition, 1997), and further augmented by detailed studies on policy contained within the two parts of *Germany and the Second World War*, vol. IX: *German Wartime Society, 1939–1945* (10 vols., Oxford: Clarendon Press, 2008 and 2014), and *Das Deutsche Reich und der Zweiter Weltkrieg* (Munich: Deutsche Verlags-Anstalt, 2008), vol. X (which has yet to be published in English). There have also been many books devoted to individual camps, one of the more notable being the study by Barbara Stelzl-Marx, *Zwischen Fiktion und Zeitzeugenschaft. Amerikanische und sowjetische Kriegsgefangene im Stalag XVII B Krems-Gneixendorf* (Tübingen: Gunter Narr, 2000), where she compares the treatment of Russian and Western prisoners in the same camp. More recently still, studies that compare the experiences of prisoners of war with other captives within Nazi Germany or the Soviet Union are now beginning to appear, as are contributions from other disciplines – for example, from the field of archaeology. In this context, see, for example, the recent publications by Gilly Carr and Harold Mytum, *Prisoner of War: Archaeology, Memory and Heritage of 19th and 20th Century Mass Internment* (New York: Springer, 2013) and *Cultural Heritage of Prisoners of War: Creativity Behind Barbed Wire* (London: Routledge, 2012), and also Marianne Neerland Soleim (ed.), *Prisoners of War and Forced Labour: Histories of War and Occupation* (Newcastle upon Tyne: Cambridge Scholars, 2010).

Prisoners in the Far East have been less well-served by historians, although there are now many autobiographies and biographies of Western survivors. The first comprehensive surveys of captivity in this theatre came from Van Waterford, *Prisoners of the Japanese in World War Two: A Statistical Survey and Personal Narratives of POWs* (Jefferson, NC: McFarland, 1994), and Gavan Daws, *Prisoners of the Japanese* (London: Robson, 1995); and Brian MacArthur, *Surviving the Sword: Prisoners of the Japanese 1942–45* (London: Abacus, 2006), has used contemporary diaries and memoirs to paint a very vivid picture of life in Japanese captivity. Other academic scrutiny has usually been directed at specific national groups. For example, R. P. W. Havers, *Reassessing the Japanese Prisoner of War Experience: The Changi POW Camp, Singapore, 1942–5* (London: Routledge Curzon, 2003), examines the major POW Camp in Singapore; while Joan Beaumont, *Gull Force: Survival and Leadership in Captivity* (Sydney: Allen and Unwin Australia, 1988), and Hank Nelson, *P.O.W. Prisoners of War: Australians Under Nippon* (Crow's Nest, NSW: ABC Enterprises, 1990), have examined the Australians in captivity. Nathan M. Greenfield, *The Damned: The Canadians at the Battle of Hong Kong and the POW Experience, 1941–45* (Toronto: HarperCollins, 2010), and Bartlett E. Kerr, *Surrender and Survival: The Experience of American POWs in the Pacific, 1941–45* (New York: William Morrow, 1985), have chronicled the Canadian and American prisoners of the Japanese. The edited collection by Philip Towle, Margaret Kosuge and Yoichi Kibata, *Japanese Prisoners of War* (London: Hambledon and London, 2000), includes many relevant contributions on Western captivity, including ones from Japanese scholars. The changing Japanese perspective on prisoners of war has been expertly surveyed by Ikuhiko Hata, 'From Consideration to Contempt: The Changing Nature of Japanese Military and Popular Perceptions of Prisoners of War through the Ages', in Bob Moore and Kent Fedorowich, *Prisoners of War and their Captors in World War II* (Oxford: Berg, 1996), pp. 253–76, while Hirofumi Hayashi, 'Japanese Deserters and Prisoners of War in the Battle of Okinawa', and Yoshikuni Igarashi, 'Belated Homecomings: Japanese Prisoners of War in Siberia and their Return to postwar Japan', both in Bob Moore and Barbara Hately-Broad, *Prisoners of War, Prisoners of Peace* (Oxford: Berg, 2005), pp. 49–58 and 105–122, have provided welcome insights into Japanese prisoners in Okinawa and Siberia, respectively. Finally, there has been increasing interest in the wider assessment of Japanese war crimes, summarized by Yuki Tanaka, *Hidden Horrors: Japanese War Crimes in World War II* (Boulder, Colo.: Westview Press, 1996).

24 Guerrillas and counter-insurgency
Ben H. Shepherd

This is a selection of predominantly recent English-language works. Contextualizing surveys include Ian F. W. Beckett, *Modern Insurgencies and Counter-Insurgencies: Guerrillas and their Opponents since 1750* (London: Routledge, 2001); John Ellis, *From the Barrel of a Gun: A History of Guerrilla, Revolutionary and Counter-Insurgency Warfare, from the Romans to the Present* (London: Greenhill, 1995).

On the future Axis Powers' earlier counter-insurgencies, see Angelo del Boca, *The Ethiopian War, 1935–1941* (University of Chicago Press, 1965); Jonathan E. Gumz, *The Resurrection and Collapse of Empire in Habsburg Serbia, 1914–1918* (Cambridge University Press, 2009); John Horne and Alan Kramer, *German Atrocities 1914: A History of Denial* (New Haven, Conn.: Yale University Press, 2001); Isabel V. Hull, *Absolute Destruction: Military Culture and the Practice of War in Imperial Germany* (Ithaca, NY: Cornell University Press, 2006).

Edited works, providing introductory chapters on European partisan movements and Allied cooperation with them include Bob Moore (ed.), *Resistance in Western Europe* (Oxford: Berg, 2000); Ben H. Shepherd and Juliette Pattinson (eds.), *War in a Twilight World: Partisan and Anti-Partisan Warfare in Eastern Europe, 1939–45* (London: Palgrave, 2010); Philip Cooke and Ben H. Shepherd (eds.), *European Resistance in the Second World War* (Barnsley: Pen and Sword, 2013).

On Europe-wide counter-insurgency, see Philip W. Blood, *Hitler's Bandit Hunters: The SS and the Nazi Occupation of Europe* (Washington DC: Potomac, 2006); Mark Mazower, *Hitler's Empire: Nazi Rule in Occupied Europe* (London: Penguin, 2008); Davide Rodogno, *Fascism's European Empire: Italian Occupation During the Second World War* (Cambridge University Press, 2006). See also chapters by Wendy Lower (regarding Axis satellite counter-insurgency), Felix Roemer (German army 'criminal orders') and Jeff Rutherford (radicalization of German army occupation policies), in Alex J. Kay, Jeff Rutherford and David Stahel (eds.), *Nazi Policy on the*

Eastern Front, 1941: Total War, Genocide, and Radicalization (Rochester, NY: University of Rochester Press, 2012).

On guerrilla warfare across Japanese-occupied Asia, see Charles Cruickshank, *SOE in the Far East: The Official History* (Oxford University Press, 1986). On guerrilla warfare and counter-insurgency in China, see Yang Kuisong's chapter in Mark Peattie, Edward Drea and Hans van de Ven (eds.), *The Battle for China: Essays on the Military History of the Sino-Japanese War of 1937–45* (Stanford University Press, 2011). Worth consulting also are Mao biographies, such as Philip Short, *Mao: A Life* (London: John Murray, 2004). On the Japanese army, see Drea's chapter in Peattie et al., and Drea's *In the Service of the Emperor: Essays on the Imperial Japanese Army* (Lincoln: University of Nebraska Press, 1998).

For Southeast Asia, see Abu Talib Ahmad's chapter in Karl Hack and Tobias Rettig (eds.), *Colonial Armies in Southeast Asia* (London: Routledge, 2006); Paul H. Kratoska (ed.), *Southeast Asian Minorities in the Wartime Japanese Empire* (London: Routledge Curzon, 2002); Nicholas Tarling, *A Sudden Rampage: The Japanese Occupation of Southeast Asia, 1941–1945* (London: Hurst, 2001). On Allied long-range penetration, see Simon Anglim, 'Orde Wingate, "Guerrilla" Warfare and Long-Range Penetration, 1940–44', *Small Wars & Insurgencies*, 17 (2006), 241–62.

Index